Drama in English

FROM THE MIDDLE AGES TO THE EARLY TWENTIETH CENTURY

Drama in English

FROM THE MIDDLE AGES TO THE EARLY TWENTIETH CENTURY

AN ANTHOLOGY OF PLAYS WITH OLD SPELLING

EDITED BY
Christopher J. Wheatley

The Catholic University of America Press
Washington, D.C.

The paper used in this publication meets the minimum requirements of American National Standards for Information Science—Permanence of Paper for Printed Library Materials, ANSI Z39.48-1984.

∞

Cover art (clockwise from top right): William Hogarth's painting of John Gay's *The Beggar's Opera, Act 5*, 1728; illustration for an 1898 edition of *Volpone* by Aubrey Beardsley; John Dryden by John Michael Wright, 1668; Chester Mystery Play; John Millington Synge; mystery play, Flanders, 15th century; Anna-Lisa Ryding as "Joan of Arc" in *Saint Joan* by George Bernard Shaw, 1926; title page of *The Knight of the Burning Pestle* by Francis Beaumont, 1613; Sara Allgood as "Pegeen Mike" and J. M. Kerrigan as "Shawn Keogh" in J. M. Synge's play *The Playboy of the Western World*, 1911; Benjamin Jonson by Abraham van Blyenberch, 1617; frontispiece from edition of *Everyman* published by John Sklot, 1530; George Bernard Shaw, 1925.

Names: Wheatley, Christopher J., 1955– editor.
Title: Drama in English from the Middle Ages to the early twentieth century : an anthology of plays with old spelling / edited by Christopher J. Wheatley.
Description: Washington, D.C. : The Catholic University of America Press, 2016. | Includes bibliographical references and index.
Identifiers: LCCN 2015032401 | ISBN 9780813227870 (pbk. : alk. paper)
Subjects: LCSH: Drama—Collections.
Classification: LCC PN6111 .D76 2016 | DDC 808.82—dc23
LC record available at http://lccn.loc.gov/2015032401

seen with a grant from
Figure Foundation
to know a rainbow's begin

Contents

Acknowledgments

I owe thanks to many scholars who read my first versions of the texts and corrected and commented on them: Roland Berns (DARE at the University of Wisconsin–Madison), Kirk Combe (Denison University), William Demastes (Louisiana State University), Kevin Donovan (Middle Tennessee State University), Deborah Payne (American University), John Greene (University of Louisiana at Lafayette), and Jessica Munns (University of Denver). I also benefited from the wisdom of Barbara Cahalane and Tom Craughwell for help on annotations, and Thomas Stroik (University of Missouri–Kansas City) for advice on the introduction.

I especially owe gratitude to my generous and gifted colleagues at the Catholic University of America who also read many of these texts for me: Daniel Gibbons, Tobias Gregory, Glen Johnson, Lilla Kopar, Todd Lidh, Michael Mack, Taryn Okuma, Patrick Tuite, and Steve Wright.

As my notes indicate, I have relied heavily on the work of previous editors; any errors in the text were introduced by me. All notes and glosses are my own unless otherwise indicated.

Christopher J. Wheatley
WASHINGTON, D.C.

Introduction

This anthology was created for courses in the history of drama in English. Because such courses are the preserve of English and theater majors, and usually those students are required to take Shakespeare, no plays of Shakespeare are included. In any case, good editions of Shakespeare are widely available. When I began teaching the History of English Drama in 1989, my course texts for prior to the twentieth century were A. C. Cawley's *Everyman and Medieval Miracle Plays* (London: J. M. Dent & Sons, rev. 1977), R. C. Bald's *Six Elizabethan Plays* (Boston: Houghton Mifflin, 1963), John Harold Wilson's *Six Restoration Plays* (Boston: Houghton Mifflin, 1959), and Ricardo Quintana's *Eighteenth-Century Plays* (New York: The Modern Library, 1952); all of these texts are out of print. Large anthologies, such as *The Norton Anthology of Drama,* while doubtless useful for some courses, do not include enough examples of English drama to cover all of the significant periods in English drama; for instance, *The Norton Anthology of Drama* contains no medieval drama, no late sixteenth- or seventeenth-century comedy, no Restoration or eighteenth-century tragedy, and no nineteenth-century melodrama. In its selection it represents a sort of pseudo–comparative literature approach to drama, where it remains possible to talk about structure and characterization in the plays included in translation, while many of the aesthetic effects available in the original language must inevitably be lost. Volume One of the *Norton Anthology of English Literature* contains no Restoration or eighteenth-century tragedy, and only William Congreve's brilliant but unrepresentative *The Way of the World* to represent nonmusical Restoration and eighteenth century comedy.

Most of the plays in this anthology are available in electronic texts or PDF files online. They are, however, usually unedited or badly edited, or are sometimes simply a scanned text converted to a text file, the process of which invariably introduces numerous errors. When I attempted to teach using electronic texts, enormous amounts of time were spent explaining corruptions in the text. In any case, my students almost always printed the texts out, so there was no real cost savings in not ordering texts. The online texts also usually lack introductions, glosses, and notes. The notes and glosses in this anthology are based on my experience of what my students have needed to make sense of the plays. I have throughout annotated lightly and I have avoided "interpretive" notes; i.e., notes that implicitly argue for a particular reading of a play. Brief introductions to the four sections (Middle Ages, the late sixteenth and early seventeenth centuries, Restoration and eighteenth century, and nineteenth and early twentieth centuries) describe the theatrical practices of the period and their audiences. The introductions to the individual playwrights provide biographical and theatrical background.

The plays I have selected reflect their societies, illustrate the dramatic practice of their time, and represent a significant aesthetic achievement. Thus George Lillo's *The London Merchant* shows the eighteenth-century theater responding to the growing importance of the City of London, the economic engine of the expanding empire. By dramatizing the fall of an apprentice in prose, it introduces a new kind of tragedy. And the character Millwood rises above the conventional morality of the play with a searing indictment of her society's abuse of women. Boucicault's *The Shaughraun* is arguably not aesthetically admirable (although anyone who thinks it is easy to write a good melodrama should give it a try). But the play was popular, is a good example of the work of the most successful English-language dramatist of the nineteenth century, and is typical of the plays that the Abbey Theatre and both British and American realist drama were reacting against.

Further, I have chosen to provide not only an old-spelling edition of the plays, but one where the spelling, except in the case of character names, has not been made consistent throughout, and where accidentals such as capitalization and punctuation are, except in rare cases, unchanged. D. F. McKenzie has shown how capitalization and punctuation indicate meaning in texts in his analysis of how W. K. Wimsatt Jr. and M.C. Beardsley carelessly misrepresent Congreve in their use of an epigraph from *The Way of the World* for their famous essay "The Intentional Fallacy"; even aside from their misquotation of Congreve's prologue, their failure to include capitals and commas flatten both the seriousness and the irony of Congreve's verse.[1]

There are strong (and long-standing) arguments to be made for modernized spelling, particularly in student editions.[2] Yet spelling itself, whether by the author, scribe, or printer, represents a kind of creativity. Samuel Johnson in his preface to *The Dictionary of the English Language* (1755) writes disapprovingly,

> As language was at the beginning merely oral, all words of necessary or common use were spoken before they were written; and while they were unfixed by any visible signs, must have been spoken with great diversity, as we now observe those who cannot read to catch sounds imperfectly, and utter them negligently. When this wild and barbarous jargon was first reduced to an alphabet, every penman endeavoured to express, as he could, the sounds which he was accustomed to pronounce or to receive, and vitiated in writing such words as were already

1. *Bibliography and the Sociology of Texts* (Cambridge: Cambridge University Press, 1999), 18–23.

2. For the arguments for and against modernized spelling see John Russell Brown's "The Rationale of Old-Spelling Editions of the Plays of Shakespeare and His Contemporaries," *Studies in Bibliography* 13 (1960): 54–68, and Arthur Brown's "The Rationale of Old-Spelling Editions of the Plays of Shakespeare and His Contemporaries: A Rejoinder," *Studies in Bibliography* 13 (1960): 69–76. For an overview of what textual critics, writers, and printers have thought about spelling and punctuation—insofar as they bothered to think about spelling and punctuation at all—see James Thorpe's *Principles of Textual Criticism* (San Marino, Calif.: The Huntington Library, 1972), 134–170.

vitiated in speech. The powers of the letters, when they were applied to a new language, must have been vague and unsettled, and therefore different hands would exhibit the same sound by different combinations.[3]

While Johnson's purpose in his dictionary is prescriptive, to "fix" and correct the language, he recognizes its dynamic nature. Dialect pronunciations are reflected in differing orthography: the spelling of words in the York cycle's *The Crucifixion* and the Brome manuscript's *Abraham and Isaac* indicates the geographical, and consequently linguistic, distance between the two communities at a time when travel was difficult. And the use of the word "powers" here suggests the almost magical character of the transference of spoken language to the printed page: when Prospero renounces "this rough magic" he must "drown [his] book" (act 5, scene 1). Using the spelling of the period gets us closer to the author's conception of his work, and the spell he thereby performs upon the reader.

The etymology of English words is often indicated by their spelling, and the extensive borrowing of the English language is apparent through the retained "foreign" spelling of naturalized words.[4] The spelling of English began to be standardized in the fifteenth century by the law clerks in chancery, and the London dialect became the most prestigious.[5] But wide variations in spelling persisted. A sixteenth-century playwright (or printer) might spell the word "mistress" in the form we now use, but might in the same text spell it "mistris" or "mistresse"—and nobody had trouble understanding what they meant. As Andrew Jackson is supposed to have said, "It's a damn poor mind that can think of only one way to spell a word!" And playwrights had options on how to pronounce a word to fit their meter. A word like "composed" could be pronounced as three syllables or two, and in the latter case it might be printed "compos'd" to indicate that it should be spoken with two syllables.

Preserving the old spelling also aids in tracking the history of the language. The "l" in "should" and "would" (Middle English "sholde" and "wolde") was pronounced in the fifteenth century, but by the late seventeenth century the words are frequently printed "wou'd" and "shou'd" to indicate the changed pronunciation where the "l" is silent. "Could" (Middle English "coude") never had a pronounced "l" but the letter was added in orthography by analogy with "would" and "should"; in the Restoration it was sometimes printed "cou'd" to indicate it should be pronounced without an "l" that was never in the word to begin with.[6] The Old English word "acsian" became the Middle English "aks" or "axe" or "ax" until eventually becoming "ask" around the seventeenth century. Dialect speakers of English (such as some New Yorkers) who "aks" a question are actually using a historically attested form and are entitled to more linguistic tolerance than they usually get.[7]

Undoubtedly, the old spelling and nonmodern punctuation slow the process of read-

3. Samuel Johnson, *A Dictionary of the English Language* (1979; repr., London: Times Books).

4. Albert C. Baugh, *A History of the English Language*, 2nd ed. (London: Routledge & Kegan Paul, 1959), 13.

5. David Burnley, *The History of the English Language, a Sourcebook*, 2nd ed. (Harlow, England: Longman, 2000), 212–213.

6. I am indebted to Steve Wright and Brian Lee for this example of the relationship between spelling and changing pronunciation.

7. I am indebted to Thomas Stroik for this example of dialect diversity.

ing. The act of reading develops what Jerome J. McGann calls "radial inertia," as the reader must abstract themselves from the act of reading itself to consider what the text conveys in an unfamiliar orthography.[8] But this is a beneficial consequence of old-spelling editions. These plays were produced by authors who are not our contemporaries, and their works represent different social and economic contexts. Ultimately I side with William Proctor Williams and Craig S. Abbot who write,

> One assumes that regularized and modernized editions are intended for the classroom or for that largely mythical figure, the general reader. However, little evidence has ever been brought forward to prove that the general reader will be more inclined to read Sir Thomas Wyatt or Michael Drayton or Fulke Greville if he or she is given a modernized edition. The general reader's inclination to read these authors will bring with it a willingness, if not desire, to read them as they wrote.[9]

If nothing else, this old-spelling edition may convince the students that spelling and punctuation became important only fairly recently, and the fact that Shakespeare signed his name in multiple ways does not mean that he was semi-literate and could not have written his plays.[10] Students *can* read medieval and early modern English—and learn to do so routinely in Chaucer courses all over the United States—and *do* gain a sense of satisfaction when doing so.

8. See *The Textual Condition* (Princeton: Princeton University Press, 1991), particularly 118–122. McGann contrasts radial reading with linear reading, as in reading a Harlequin romance, where the product is intended to eliminate difficulties and consequently reflection in the experience of understanding the text.

9. *An Introduction to Bibliographical or Textual Studies,* 4th ed. (New York: The Modern Language Association, 2009), 104–105.

10. The notion that Shakespeare could not have written Shakespeare because of his supposed inability to spell has even worked its way down to young adult fiction. See James Shapiro's discussion of Elise Broach's *Shakespeare's Secret* in his brilliant analysis of the "authorship question" in *Contested Will: Who Wrote Shakespeare?* (New York: Simon & Schuster, 2010), 6.

Drama in English

FROM THE MIDDLE AGES TO THE EARLY TWENTIETH CENTURY

PART 1

Drama

OF THE MIDDLE AGES

THE ENGLISH DRAMA that survives from the Middle Ages is almost exclusively on religious subjects, written in the vernacular, and with the addition of humor and folk elements. There are individual plays, such as *Abraham and Isaac*, in this collection, but also four great cycles are preserved: York, Wakefield/Towneley, Chester, and N. town, the latter so called because it is not associated with a particular location for performance. These plays depict biblical history from the Creation to the Last Judgment. Records suggest that at least some of the actors were paid, and the surviving regulations for productions indicate that the towns and guilds required competence in performance. Performance of the cycles could extend from dawn to dark, and over several days. For the cycle plays, guilds which regulated the crafts and trades (or "masteries") bore responsibility for each play and provided the cast, costumes, and "pageant," the large and ornate wagon on which the play was performed. But performance also extended from the pageant to the street, and some individual plays were probably performed in whatever space was available. A few words spoken by a character would reveal to the audience the location of any particular speech or play. The anonymous authors were possibly clerics, because numerous plays indicate a knowledge of religious sources written in Latin. From the early fourteenth century to the cessation of cycle dramas in the reign of Elizabeth I, the plays were mostly associated with the Feast of Corpus Christi. Morality plays, unlike the cycle plays, were complete in themselves and taught a lesson through allegorical characters. The cycle and morality plays were known by Christopher Marlowe and William Shakespeare and clearly influenced the drama of the late sixteenth and early seventeenth centuries.

The *Noah's Flood* in this collection is from the Chester cycle. In its current form it is the product of the sixteenth century, and probably the most recent of the great cycle texts although the first mentions of the Chester cycle are from 1421 and 1422. By that point the Chester companies were already performing the plays and this date should not be taken as when the cycle began. The cycles are usually referred to as *The Corpus Christi Play,* which in its subject matter extends from the Creation to Doomsday. Individual sections are referred to as pageants, after the pageant wagons on which they were performed (at least at York and Chester). The wagons moved through five stations in Chester, with each wagon performing a single pageant repeatedly. The play was not performed every year, and pageant wagons were stored for future use. By 1521 the Chester cycle was referred to as "The Whitsun [Pentecost] Play" and was performed on Monday, Tuesday, and Wednesday of Whitsun Week. Divided thus in three parts, the pageants dramatized the actions of God the Father on the first day, the incarnation of God the Son on the second day, and the coming of the Holy Spirit on the third day. The pageant is written in tail rhyme which is the form of the "Chester stanza" throughout the cycle: typically aaabaaab or aaabcccb with four stresses to the *a* or *c* lines and three stresses to the *b* lines.

The audience of the play would have been used to homilies where Old Testament texts were explained as operating on four levels. First, the story of Noah is literally true, a historical event. Second, the event allegorically represents the life of Christ; thus Noah is a "type" or prefiguration of Christ, saving humanity from its sins. Third, the event has a moral lesson; people must obey God, no matter how difficult the command (such as building a ship in the desert). Finally, the *anagogical* or *tropological* level of the text refers to the salvation of Church as a whole; the ark is the Church, the only vessel through which man can be saved.

Noah's Flood

Noah's Flood is of particular interest both for its stage directions and the treatment of Noah's shrewish wife who is saved despite herself. She represents the combination of biblical narratives with popular traditions, and her relationship with Noah is not unlike that of Judy and Punch in puppet shows.

The Chester Pageant of *Noah's Flood*

GOD	NOAH'S WIFE
NOAH	SHEM'S WIFE
SHEM	HAM'S WIFE
HAM	JAPHETH'S WIFE
JAPHETH	GOSSIPS

pagina tertia. De Deluvio Noe[1]

The waterleaders and drawers in dye.° — Dee (a river)

(Et primo in aliquo supremo loco sive in nubibus, si fieri poterit, loquatur Deus ad Noe extra Archam existentem cum tota familia sua.)[2]

GOD. I God that all the world hath wrought,
heaven and earth, and all of nought,
I see my people, in deede and thought
are sett fowle in sinne.

My text is that established by The Early English Text Society from the notes of Dr. Hermann Deimling (1892; repr., London: Oxford University Press, 1968), 48–63; his text is from James Miller's 1607 copy. I also consulted A. C. Cawley's *Everyman and Medieval Miracle Plays* particularly for my notes. In the headings of speeches I have changed the Latin headings to the English name; thus, "Deus" is changed to "God" and "Noe" to "Noah" etc.

1. "The Thirde Pageante of Noyes Fludd" (from the Early English Text Society edition's notes).

2. "And firste in some high place—or in the clowdes, if it may bee—God speaketh unto Noe standinge without the arke with all his familye" (from the Early English Text Society's notes).

My ghost shall not lenge in man
that through fleshlie-likinge is my fone,
but till VI° skore yeares be gone — six
to looke if they will blynne.° — stop
Manne that I made will I distroy,
beast, worme, and fowle to flie;
for on earthe they doe mee nye,
the folke that are theron.
hit harmes me so hartefullie,
the malyce now that can multeply,
that sore it greueth mee Inwardlie
that ever I made manne.
therfore Noah, my servant free,
that righteous man art as I see,
a shipp sone thou shalt make the
of trees drye and lighte.
Little chambers therein thou make
and bynding slich° also thou take, — pitch
with-in and -out thou ne slake° — slacken
to anoynte it through all thy mighte.
300 Cubytes yt shall be long,
and 50 of breadeth, to mak it stronge,
of height 50: the mete° thou fonge,° — measure; find
thus measure it about.
One wyndow worch through thy wytte,
One cubyte of length and breadeth make it,
upon the side a dore shall sit
for to come in and out.
Eating places thou make also,
three roofed chambers, [on a row];[3]
for with water I thinke to flow
man that I can make.
Destroyed all the world shalbe,
save thou; thy wife, thy sonnes three,
and all there wives also with thee
shall saved be for thy sake.
NOAH. A! lord I thanke the lowd and still° — always
that to me art in such will,
and spares me and my house to spill,
as now I sothlie fynde.
Thy bydding, lord, I shall fulfill,
nor never more the greeve ne gryll,° — offend
that suche grace hath sent me till
among all mankinde.

3. The Early English Text Society has "one or two"; the emendation is from Cawley.

have done, yow men and women all!
helpe for ought that may befall
to worke this shipp, chamber and hall,
as God hath bydden vs doe.
SHEM. Father, I am already bowne:° prepared
anne axe I have, by my crowne,
as sharpe as any in all this towne
for to goe there to.
HAM. I haue an hatchet wonder-kene
to byte well, as may be seene,
a better grownden, as I weene,° think
is not in all this towne.
JAPHETH. And I can well make a pyn,
and with this hammer knocke yt in;
goe and worche without more dynne,
and I am ready bowne.
NOAH'S WIFE. And wee shall bring tymber to,
for wee mon nothing els doe;
women be weake to vnderfoe
any great travayle.° labor
SHEM'S WIFE. Here is a good hackstock;° chopping-block
on this yow maye hew and knock.
shall non be Idle in this flock,
ne now may no man fayle.
HAM'S WIFE. and I will goe gather sliche,
the ship for to cleane[4] and piche.
anoynted yt muste bee with stiche,
board, tree,° and pyn. mast
JAPHETH'S WIFE. And I will gather chippes here
to make a fire for yow in feere,
and for to dight° your dynner, prepare
against yow come in.

(Tunc faciunt signa, quasi laborarent cum diversis Instrumentia)[5]

NOAH. Now in the name of God I will begin
to make the shippe that we shall In,
that we be ready for to swym
at the cominge of the flood
These bordes I joyne here together,
to kepe vs safe from the wedder,
that wee may row both hither and thider,
and safe be from this floode.
of this tree will I make the mast

4. Cawley has "caulk."
5. "Then they make signs as if they were working with different tools" (Cawley).

tyde with gables that will last,
with a sayle-yarde for each blast,
and each thinge in ther kinde.
With topcastle and bewsprytt,
bothe coardes and ropes I haue all meete,
to sayle forthe at the next weete;
this shipp is at an ende.

(Tunc Noe Iterum cum tota familia faciunt signa laborandi cum diversis Instrumentis.)[6]

Wife, in this Castle wee shall be keped,
my childer and thou, I wold, in leaped.
NOAH'S WIFE. In faith, Noah, I had as lief thou sleppit;
for all thy frankish fare,[7]
I will not doe after thy red.° — instructions
NOAH. Good wife, doe now as I the bydd.
NOAH'S WIFE. By Christ! not or I see more neede,
though thou stand all the day and stare.
NOAH. Lord, that women be crabbed aye,
and never are meke, that dare I saye.
this is well sene by me to daye,
In witnes of yow each one.
Good wife, let be all this beere° — clamor
that thou makes in this place here;
for all they wene thou arte master,
and soe thou art by St. John.
GOD. Noah, take thou thy meanye,° — household
and in the shippe hye that yee bee;
for non so righteous man to me
is now on earth lyvinge.
of cleane beastes with thee thou take
seaven and seaven, or° then thou slake; — before
hee and shee, make° to make,° — mate
by lyve° in that thou bringe; — be lively
of beastes uncleane two and two,
male and female, without moe;
of cleane fowles seaven alsoe,
the hee and shee together;
of fowles uncleane twayne and no more,
as I of beastes said before;
that shalbe saved throughe my lore,
against I send this wedder.
Of all meates that must be eaten

6. "The Noah with all his family again make signs of working with different tools" (Cawley).
7. Frenchified, and hence courtly, behavior.

into the ship loke there be getten;
for that no way may be foryeten,
and doe all this bydeene,° at once
to sustayne man and beastes therein,
aye till the water cease and blyn.
this world is filled full of synne,
and that is now well sene.
Seaven dayes be yet coming,
you shall haue space them into bringe.
after that is my lyking
mankinde for to nye.° annoy
40 dayes and 40 nightes
rayne shall fall for there vnrightes,
and that I haue made through mightes
now think I to distroye.

NOAH. Lord, at your byddinge I am bayne,° ready
sith non other grace will gayne,
hit will I fulfill fayne,° willingly
for gratious I thee fynde.
A 100 wynters and 20
this shipp making taried haue I,
if through amendment any mercye
wolde fall vnto mankinde.
Haue done, you men and women all!
hye you lest this water fall,
that each beast were in his stall,
and into the ship broughte.
Of cleane beastes seaven shalbe,
of vncleane two, this God bade me;
this floode is nye, well may we see,
therfore tary you noughte.

(Tunc Noe introibit archam, et familia sua dabit et recitabit omnia animalia depicta in cartis et, postquam vnusquisque suam locutus est partem, ibit in archam, vxore Noe excepta, et animalia depicta cum verbis concordare debent, et sic incipiet primus filius.)[8]

SHEM. Syr, here are lyons, libardes in,
horses, mares, oxen, and swyne,
geates, calves, sheepe, and kine
here sytten thou may see.

HAM. Camels, asses men may fynde,
bucke, doe, harte and hynde,

8. "Then noye shall goe into the arke with all his family, his wief except, and the arke muste bee borded rounde aboute, and one the bordes all the beastes and fowles hereafter receaved [rehearsed] muste bee painted, that thes wordes may agree with the pictures" (Early English Text Society's notes).

and beastes of all manner kinde
here bene, as thinkes mee.
JAPHETH. Take here cattes and doggs to,
Otter, fox, fulmart° also,   skunk
hares hopping gaylie can goe
have cowle° here for to eate.   cabbage
NOAH'S WIFE. And here are Beares, wolfes sett,
Apes, owles, marmoset,
weesells, squirrels, and firret;
here they eaten their meate.
SHEM'S WIFE. Yet more beastes are in this howse:
here cattis maken it full crowse,°   crouse (lively)
here a rotten, here a mowse,
they stand nye together.
HAM'S WIFE. And here are fowles, les and more:
hearnes, cranes, and byttour,
swans, peacockes, and them before
meate for this wedder.
JAPHETH'S WIFE. Here are cockes, kites, crowes,
rookes, ravens, many rowes,
duckes, curlewes, who euer knowes,
eache one in his kinde?
and here are doves, diggs,° drakes,   ducks
redshankes runninge through the lakes;
and each fowle that ledden° makes   song
in this shipp men may finde.
NOAH. Wife, come in! Why standes thou here?
thou art ever froward, that dare I sweare.
come in, on gods half![9] tyme yt were,   for God's
for feare lest that we drowne.   sake!
NOAH'S WIFE. Yea, Sir, set vp your sayle
and rowe forth with evill heale!°   luck
for without any fayle,
I will not out of this towne.
But I haue my gossips everichon,
one foote further I will not gone;
they shall not drowne, by St. John,
and I may save there lyfe.
they loved me full well, by christ;
but thou wilt let them in thy chist,
els rowe forth, Noah, whether thou list,
and get thee a newe wife.
NOAH. Shem, sonne, loe, thy mother is wraw.°   wrathful
for sooth such another I do not know.

9. "for God's sake" (Cawley).

SHEM. Father, I shall fett her in, I trow,
without any fayle.
Mother, my father after thee send,
and bydds the into yonder ship wend.
loke vp and se the wynde,
for we be readye to sayle.
NOAH'S WIFE. Sonne, goe again to him and say:
I will not come therein to daye.
NOAH. Come in, wife, in 20 devills waye,
or els stand there without.
HAM. shall wee all fet her in?
NOAH. yea, sonnes, in Christs blessinge and myne,
I would, yow hyde yow betyme,
for of this flood I am in doubte.
THE GOOD GOSSIPS. The flood comes in, full fleetinge faste,
on every side it spredeth full fare;
for feare of drowning I am agast,
good gossip, let us draw neare.
and let vs drinke or we depart,
for often tymes wee have done soe;
for at a draught thou drinkes a quarte,
and so will I doe, or I goe.[10]
JAPHETH. Mother, we praye you altogether
—or we are here your owne childer—
come into the ship for feare of the wedder,
for his° love that you boughte. (i.e., Jesus)
NOAH'S WIFE. That will I not for all your call,
but I haue my gossoppes all.
SHEM. In feith, mother, yet you shall,
whether you will or not.

(tunc ibit.)[11]

NOAH. Welcome, wife, into this boate.
NOAH'S WIFE. And haue thou that for thy mote!

(Et dat alapam vita.)[12]

NOAH. A! ha! mary, this is hote;
it is good to be still.
a! children, me thinkes my boate remeves,
our tarying here hugely me greves.
Over the lande the water spredes,
God doe as hee will.

10. The Early English Text Society edition lists among the variants another four lines to the speech of the Gossips: "here is a pottell full of malmesy good and stronge, / it will reioye both hart and tong; / though noy [Noah] thinke vs neuer so long / yet wee will drinke alyke."

11. "Then she shall go" (Cawley).

12. She gives a lively slap.

[*Then the singe, and Noe shall speake agayne.*][13]

Ah! great God that art soe good!
that worchis not thie will is wood.° mad
now all this world is on a flood,
as I see well in sighte.
This window I will shut anon,
And into my chamber will I gone
till this water, soe greate one,
be slaked throughe thy mighte.

(Tunc Noe claudet fenestram Archæ et per modicum spatium infra tectum cantent psalmum "Save mee o God" *et aperiens fenestram et respiciens.)*[14]

Now forty dayes are fullie gone.
send a raven I will anone
if ought-where earth, tree, or stone
be drye in any place.
And if this foule come not againe,
it is a signe, soth to sayne,
that drye it is on a hill or playne,
and god hath done some grace.

(Tunc dimittet corvum et capiens columbam in manibus dicat.)[15]

Ah! lord, wherever this raven be
somewhere is drye, well I see;
but yet a dove, by my lewtye,° faith
after I will sende.
Thou wilt turne againe to me[16]
for of all fowles that may flye,
thou art most meke and hend.° gentle

(Tunc emittet columbam et erit in nave alia columba ferens olivam in ore, quam dimittet ex malo per funem in manus Noe, et postes dicat Noe.)[17]

Ah! lord, blessed be thou aye,
that me hast comfort thus to-day;
by this sight I may well saye

13. This stage direction is among the variants listed in the Early English Text Society edition.

14. "Then Noye shall shutt the windowe of the arke, and for a littell space within bord he shalbe silent, and afterwardes opening the windowe and looking round about, saying" (note in Early English Text Society edition). During the space indicated Psalm 69 ("Save me O God for the waters have come up to my neck") may have been sung.

15. "Then he shall send forth a raven, and taking a dove in his hand let him say" (Cawley).

16. The Early English Text Society edition indicates a missing line between this and the next.

17. "Then he shall send forth a dove; and there shall be in the ship another dove bearing an olive branch in his mouth, which Noah shall let down from the mast by a cord in his hand, and afterwards let Noah say" (Cawley).

this flood beginnes to cease.
My sweete dove to me brought hase
a branch of olyve from some place,
this betokeneth God has done vs some grace,
and is a signe of peace.
Ah! lord, honoured most thou be,
all earthe dryes now, I see,
but yet tyll thou commaunde me,
hence I will not hye.
All this water is awaye,
therfore as sone as I maye
Sacryfice I shall doe in faye
to thee devoutly.
GOD. Noah, take thy wife anone
and thy children every one;
out of thy shippe thou shalt gone,
and they all with thee.
Beastes and all that can flie
out anone they shall hye,
on earth to grow and multeplye.
I will that yt be soe.
NOAH. Lord, I thanke the through thy mighte,
thy bidding shall be done in height,° haste
and as fast as I may dighte
I will doe the honoure,
And to thee offer sacrifice;
therfore comes in all wise,
for of these beastes that bene hise,
offer I will this stower.

(Tunc egrediens archam cum tota familia sua accipiet animalia sua et volucres et offeret ea et mactabit.)[18]

Lord, God in maiestye
that such grace hast graunted me,
where all was lorne, save to be,
therfore nowe I am bowne,
My wife, my Childer, and my meanye
with sacrifice to honoure thee
with beastes, fowles, as thou may see,
I offer here right sone.
GOD. Noah, to me thou arte full able,° obedient
and thy sacrifice acceptable;
for I have fownd thee trew and stable,

18. "Then going out of the Ark with all his family he shall take his animals and birds and offer them in sacrifice" (Cawley).

on thee now muste I myn.° be mindful
warry earth will I no more
for mans synne that greves me sore;
for of youth man full yore
has byn enclyned to syne.
you shall now grow and multeply,
and earth againe to edefye.° build up
each beast and fowle that may flie,
shall be afrayd of you.
And fishe in sea, that may flytte
shall susteyne yow, I yow behite,° promise
to eate of them yow ne lett,
that cleane bene you may knowe.
Thereas you have eaten before
grasses and rootes sith you were bore,
of cleane beastes now, les and more,
I geve you leave to eate,
Safe bloode and flesh bothe in feare
of wrong dead carren that is here,
eates not of that in no manere;
for that aye you shall let.
Manslaughter also you shall flee,
for that is not pleasant to me.
that shedes bloode, he or shee,
ought-where amongst mankinde,
that blood foule sheede shalbe
and vengeance have, that men shall se;
therfore beware now all yee,
you fall not in that synne.
a forwarde° now with thie I make, covenant
and all thy seede for thy sake
of suche vengeance for to slake,
for now I haue my will.
Here I behet the a heaste
that man, woman, fowle, ne beaste
with water, while the worlde shall last,
I will no more spill.
My Bowe betwene you and me
in the firmament shall bee,
by verey token that you may see
that such vengeance shall cease.
That man ne woman shall never more
be wasted by water as is before,
but for syn that greveth me sore,
therfore this vengeance was.
Where cloudes in the welkin° bene, sky

that ilke° bowe shall be sene — same
In tokeninge that my wrath and tene° — anger
shall never this wroken° be. — wreaked
The stringe is turned toward you
and toward me is bent the bowe
that such wedder shall never showe;
and this behett I thee.
my blessing now I geue the here
to thee, Noah, my servant dere,
for vengeance shall no more appeare;
and now fare well, my darling deere.

Finis pagina Tertiæ.

Abraham and Isaac

The Brome manuscript play of *Abraham and Isaac* certainly looks like a pageant from a cycle (and, indeed, a large part of the Chester pageant of Abraham and Isaac may be derived from the Brome play). But there is no evidence that the text, from a mid- to late fifteenth-century commonplace book from the manor of Brome in Suffolk, was performed in a cycle.

The play may, therefore, be intended for solitary performance, which was one of the striking characteristics of the thriving East Anglia theatrical milieu, where performances of individual plays were relatively common. East Anglia was both rural and prosperous because of the wool trade. Individual towns and parishes would put on festivals involving feasts, games, and plays, as a way to raise money. The parish or town could hire a "property player" who would arrange production of a piece (including such details as costumes), and he might bring in players from elsewhere to act.

If the Brome play was intended for such an event, it would explain the pathos emphasized in the character Isaac. The lamb that substitutes for Isaac at the sacrifice still represents Jesus, and Abraham is typologically a priest. But the cycle plays do not repeatedly reference Isaac's mother and how much she will mourn over the death of her son. In the Brome *Abraham and Isaac,* the typological is subordinated to the theatrical. Written in a variety of rhyme schemes and meters, the play revolves around the reactions of Abraham and Isaac to God's command and seeks to evoke an emotional response from an audience.

The text is that established by John Matthews Manly (New York: Ginn and Company, 1897), 41–57. My notes and glosses are indebted to A. C. Cawley's *Everyman and Medieval Miracle Plays* (New York: E. P. Dutton, 1959).

Abraham and Isaac 15

The Brome Play Of Abraham And Isaac

CHARACTERS

GOD ABRAHAM

ANGELL YSAAC

DOCTOR

ABRAHAM. Fader of Heuyn Omnipotent,
With all my hart to the I call;
Thow hast ȝoffe°[1] me both lond and rent,° given; revenue
And my lyvelod thow hast me sent;
I thanke the heyly euer-more of all.
Fyrst off the erth thou madyst Adam,
And Eue also to be hys wyffe;
All other creatures of them too cam;
And now thow hast grant to me, Abraham,
Her in thys lond to lede my lyffe.
In my age thou hast grantyd me thys,
That thys ȝowng chyld wyth me schall wone;° dwell
I love no-thyng so myche, I-wysse,° indeed
Excepe thin owyne selffe, der Fader of blysse,
As Ysaac her, my owyne swete sone
I haue dyuerse chyldryn moo,
The wych I love not halffe so wyll;
Thys fayer swet chyld, he scһereys° me soo, cheers
In euery place wer that I goo,
That noo dessece° her may I fell. disease
And therfor, Fadyr of Heuyn, I the prey,
For hys helth and also for hys grace;
Now, Lord, kepe hym both nygth and day
That neuer dessese nor noo fray
Cume to my chyld in noo place.
Now cum on, Ysaac, my owyne swet chyld;
Goo we hom and take owre rest.
YSAAC. Abraham, myne owyne fader so myld,
To folowe ȝow I am full prest,° ready
Bothe erly and late.
ABRAHAM. Cume on, swete chyld, I love the best
Off all the chyldryn that euer I be-gat.

1. The sound value of the Middle English character *yogh* can be either [j] or [g] depending on the phonological environment.

16 Abraham and Isaac

[*God speaks above*]

GOD. Myn angell, fast hey the thy wey,
And onto medyll-erth anon thou goo;
Abrams hart now wyll I asay,° test
Wether that he be stedfast or noo.
Sey I commaw[n]dyd hym for to take
Ysaac, hys ȝowng sonne, that he love so wyll,
And wyth hys blood sacryfyce he make,
Yffe ony off my freynchepe he wyll ffell.
Schow hym the wey on-to the hylle
Wer that hys sacryffyce schall be;
I schall a-say now hys good wyll,
Whether he lovyths better hys chyld or me.
All men schall take exampyll be hym
My commawmentes how they schall kepe.

[*The angel begins to descend*]

ABRAHAM. Now, Fader of Heuyn, that formyd all thyng,
My preyeres I make to the a-ȝeyn,° again
For thys day my tender offryng
Here mvst I ȝeve to the, certeyn.
A! Lord God, all-myty Kyng,
Wat maner best woll make the most fayn?° glad
Yff I had ther-of very knoyng,
Yt schuld be don with all my mayne° force
Full sone anone.
To don thy plesyng on an hyll,
Verely yt ys my wyll,
Dere Fader, God in trinyte.
THE ANGELL. Abraham, Abraham, wyll thou rest!
Owr Lord comandyth the for to take
Ysaac, thy ȝowng sone that thow lovyst best,
And with hys blod sacryfyce that thow make.
In-to the Lond of V[i]syon thow goo,[2]
And offer thy chyld on-to thy Lord;
I schall the lede and schow all-soo.
Vnto Goddes hest,° Abraham, a-cord, command
And folow me vp-on thys grene.
ABRAHAM. Wolle-com to me be my Lordes sond,° messenger
And hys hest I wyll not with-stond;
ȝyt Ysaac, my ȝowng sonne in° lond, on
A full dere chyld to me haue byn.
I had lever,° yf God had be plesyd rather
For to a for-bore° all the good that I haue, done without

2. "The land of vision" is derived from the Vulgate's mistranslation of "the land of Moriah" (Genesis 22:2).

Than Ysaac my sone schuld a be desessyd,° harmed
So God in Heuyn my sowll mot saue!
I lovyd neuer thyng soo mych in erde,° earth
And now I mvst the chyld goo kyll.
A! Lord God, my conseons ys stronly steryd,
And ȝyt my dere Lord, I am sore a-ferd
To groche° ony thyng aȝens ȝowr wyll. grudge
I love my chyld as my lyffe,
But ȝyt I love my God myche more,
For thow my hart woold make ony stryffe,
ȝyt wyll I not spare for chyld nor wyffe,
But don after my Lordes lore.° instruction
Thow I love my sonne neuer so wyll,
ȝyt smythe of hys hed sone I schall.
A! Fader of Heuyn, to the I knell,
An hard dethe my son schall fell
For to honor the, Lord, with-all.

THE ANGELL. Abraham, Abraham, thys ys wyll seyd,
And all thys comamentes loke that thou kepe;
But in thy hart be no-thyng dysmayd.

ABRAHAM. Nay, nay, for-soth, I hold me wyll pleysd,
To plesse my God to the best that I haue.
For thow my hart be heuely sett
To see the blood of my owyn dere sone,
ȝyt for all thys I wyll not lett,° delay
But Ysaac, my son, I wyll goo fett,
And cum asse fast as euer we can.
Now, Ysaac, my owyne son dere,
Wer art thow, chyld? Speke to me.

YSAAC. My fayer swet fader, I am here,
And make my preyrys to the Trenyte.

ABRAHAM. Rysse vp, my chyld, and fast cum heder,
My gentyll barn° that art so wysse, child
For we to, chyld, must goo to-geder,
And on-to my Lord make sacryffyce.

YSAAC. I am full redy, my fader, loo!
ȝevyn at ȝowr handes I stand rygth here,
And wat-so-euer ȝe byd me doo,
Yt schall be don with glad chere,
Full wyll and fyne.

ABRAHAM. A! Ysaac, my owyn son soo dere,
Godes blyssyng I ȝyffe the, and myn.
Hold thys fagot vpon thi bake,
And her my-sellfe fyre schall bryng.

YSAAC. Fader, all thys her wyll I packe;
I am full fayn to do ȝowr bedyng.

ABRAHAM. A! Lord of Heuyn, my handes I wryng,

Thys chyldes wordes all to-wond my harte.
Now, Ysaac son, goo we owr wey
Onto ȝon mownte, wyth all owr mayn.° — strength
YSAAC. Go we, my dere fader, as fast as I may;
To folow ȝow I am full fayn,
All-thow I be slendyr.

ABRAHAM. A! Lord, my hart brekyth on tweyn,
Thys chyldes wordes, they be so tender.

[*They arrive at the mount*]

A! Ysaac, son, a-non ley yt down,
No lenger vp-on thi backe yt hold;
For I mvst make redy bon° — preparation
To honowr my Lord God as I schuld.
YSAAC. Loo, my dere fader, wer yt ys!
To cher ȝow all-wey I draw me ner;
But, fader, I mervell sore of thys,
Wy that ȝe make thys heuy chere;
And also, fader, euer-more dred I:
Wer ys ȝowr qweke° best° that ȝe schuld kyll? — quick (living); beast
Both fyer and wood we haue redy,
But queke best haue we non on this hyll.
A qwyke best, I wot wyll, must be ded,
Ȝowr sacryfyce for to make.
ABRAHAM. Dred the nowyth, my chyld, I the red,° — advise
Owr Lord wyll send me on-to thys sted° — place
Summ maner a best for to take,
Throw hys swet sond.
YSAAC. Ȝa, fader, but my hart begynnyth to quake,
To se that scharpe sword in ȝowr hond.
Wy bere ȝe ȝowr sword drawyn soo?
Off ȝowre conwnauns° I haue mych wonder. — countenance
ABRAHAM. A! Fader of Heuyn, so I am woo!
Thys chyld her brekyth my harte on-sonder.
YSAAC. Tell me, my dere fader, or that ȝe ses,° — cease
Bere ȝe ȝowr sword draw[yn] for me?
ABRAHAM. A! Ysaac, swet son, pes! pes!
For i-wys thow breke my harte on° thre. — in
YSAAC. Now trewly, sum-wat, fader, ȝe thynke
That ȝe morne thus more and more.
ABRAHAM. A! Lord of Heuyn, thy grace let synke,° — fall
For my hart was neuer halffe so sore.
YSAAC. I preye ȝow, fader, that ȝe wyll let me that wyt,[3]
Wyther schall I haue ony harme or noo?

3. Give me that knowledge.

ABRAHAM. I-wys, swet son, I may not tell the ʒyt,
My hart ys now soo full of woo.
YSAAC. Dere fader, I prey ʒow, hyd yt not fro me,
But sum of ʒowr thowt that ʒe tell me.[4]
ABRAHAM. A! Ysaac, Ysaac! I must kyll the.
YSAAC. Kyll me, fader? alasse! wat haue I don?
Yff I haue trespassyd a-ʒens ʒow owt,° aught
With a ʒard° ʒe may make me full myld; stick
And wyth ʒowr scharp sword kyll me nogth,
For i-wys, fader, I am but a chyld.
ABRAHAM. I am full sory, son, thy blood for to spyll,
But truly, my chyld, I may not chese.
YSAAC. Now I wold to God my moder were her on this hyll!
Sche woold knele for me on both hyr kneys
To save my lyffe.
And sythyn that my moder ys not here,
I prey ʒow, fader, schonge° ʒowr chere,° change; expression
And kyll me not wyth ʒowyr knyffe.
ABRAHAM. For-sothe, son, but ʒyf° I the kyll, unless
I schuld greve God rygth sore, I drede;
Yt ys hys commawment and also hys wyll
That I schuld do thys same dede.
He commawndyd me, son, for serteyn,
To make my sacryfyce wyth thy blood.
YSAAC. And ys yt Goddes wyll that I schuld be slayn?
ABRAHAM. ʒa, truly, Ysaac, my son soo good,
And ther-for my handes I wryng.
YSAAC. Now, fader, aʒens my Lordes wyll
I wyll neuer groche,° lowd nor styll; complain
He mygth a sent me a better desteny
Yf yt had a be hys plecer.
ABRAHAM. For-sothe, son, but yf Y ded this dede,
Grevosly dysplessyd owr Lord wyll be.
YSAAC. Nay, nay, fader, God for-bede
That euer ʒe schuld greve hym for me.
ʒe haue other chyldryn, on or too,
The wyche ʒe schuld love wyll be kynd;° by nature
I prey ʒow, fader; make ʒe no woo,
For, be I onys ded and fro ʒow goo,
I schall be sone owt of ʒowre mynd.
Ther-for doo owre Lordes byddyng,
And wan I am ded, than prey for me;
But, good fader, tell ʒe my moder no-thyng,
Say that I am in a-nother cuntre dwellyng.

4. But tell me that part of your thought (that you are hiding from me).

ABRAHAM. A! Ysaac, Ysaac, blyssyd mot thow be!
My hart be-gynnyth stronly to rysse,
To see the blood off thy blyssyd body.
YSAAC. Fadyr, syn yt may be noo other wysse,
Let yt passe ouer as wyll as I.
But, fader, or I goo on-to my deth,
I prey ȝow blysse me wyth ȝowre hand.
ABRAHAM. Now, Ysaac, wyth all my breth,
My blyssyng I ȝeve the vpon thys lond,
And Godes also ther-to, i-wys.
Ysaac, Ysaac, sone, vp thow stond,
Thy fayer swete mowthe at I may kys.
YSAAC. Now, for-wyll, my owyne fader so fyn,
And grete wyll my moder in erde.
But I prey ȝow, fader, to hyd my eyne,
That I se not the stroke of ȝowr scharpe swerd,
That my fleysse schall defyle.
ABRAHAM. Sone, thy wordes make me to wepe full sore;
Now, my dere son Ysaac, speke no more.
YSAAC. A! my owyne dere fader, were-fore?
We schall speke to-gedyr her but a wylle.
And sythyn that I must nedysse° be ded, of necessity
ȝyt, my dere fader, to ȝow I prey,
Smythe but fewe strokes at my hed,
And make an end as sone as ȝe may,
And tery not to longe.
ABRAHAM. Thy meke wordes, chyld, make me afray;
So "welawey!" may be my songe,
Excepe alonly Godes wyll.
A! Ysaac, my owyn swete chyld,
ȝyt kysse me a-ȝen vpon thys hyll!
In all thys war[l]d ys non soo myld.
YSAAC. Now truly, fader, all thys teryyng
Yt doth my hart but harme;
I prey ȝow, fader, make an enddyng.
ABRAHAM. Cume vp, swet son, on-to my arme.
I must bynd thy handes too
All-thow thow be neuer soo myld.
YSAAC. A, mercy, fader! Wy schuld ȝe do soo?
ABRAHAM. That thow schuldyst not let,° my chyld. hinder
YSAAC. Nay, i-wysse, fader, I wyll not let ȝow;
Do on for me ȝowre wyll,
And on the purpos that ȝe haue set ȝow,
For Godes love kepe yt forthe styll.
I am full sory thys day to dey,
But ȝyt I kepe° not my God to greve; wish

Do on ȝowr lyst° for me hardly, will
My fayer swete fader, I ȝeffe ȝow leve.
But, fader, I prey ȝow euer-more,
Tell ȝe my moder no dell;° deal (part)
Yffe sche wost° yt, sche wold wepe full sore, knew
For i-wysse, fader, sche lovyt me full wylle;
Goddes blyssyng mot sche haue!
Now for-wyll, my moder so swete,
We too be leke no mor to mete.
ABRAHAM. A! Ysaac, Ysaac! son, thou makyst me to gret,° cry
And with thy wordes thow dystempurst° me. upsets
YSAAC. I-wysse, swete fader, I am sory to greve ȝow,
I cry ȝow mercy of that I haue donne,
And of all trespasse that euer I ded meve ȝow;
Now, dere fader, forȝyffe me that I haue donne.
God of Heuyn be with me!
ABRAHAM. A! dere chyld, lefe of thy monys;° moans
In all thy lyffe thow grevyd me neuer onys;
Now blyssyd be thow, body and bonys,
That euer thow were bred and born!
Thow hast be to me chyld full good.
But i-wysse, chyld, thow I morne neuer so fast,
ȝyt must I nedes here at the last
In thys place sched all thy blood.
Ther-for, my dere son, here schall thou lye,
On-to my warke I must me stede,° start
I-wysse I had as leve my-selffe to dey—
Yffe God wyll be plecyd wyth my dede—
And myn owyn body for to offer.
YSAAC. A! mercy, fader, morne ȝe no more,
ȝowr wepyng make my hart sore
As my owyn deth that I schall suffer.
ȝowre kerche,° fader, abowt my eyn ȝe wynd! handkerchief
ABRAHAM. So I schall, my swettest chyld in erde.
YSAAC. Now ȝyt, good fader, haue thys in mynd,
And smyth me not oftyn wyth ȝowr scharp swerd,
But hastely that yt be sped.

Here Abraham leyd a cloth on Ysaaces face, thus seyyng:

ABRAHAM. Now, fore-wyll, my chyld, so full of grace.
YSAAC. A! fader, fader, torne downgward my face,
For of ȝowre scharpe sword I am euer a-dred.
ABRAHAM. To don thys dede I am full sory,
But, Lord, thyn hest I wyll not with-stond.
YSAAC. A! Fader of Heuyn, to the I crye,
Lord, reseyve me in-to thy hand!
ABRAHAM. Loo! now ys the tyme cum, certeyn,

That my sword in hys necke schall bite.
A! Lord, my hart reysyth ther-ageyn,
I may not fynd yt in my harte to smygth,—
My hart wyll not now ther-too.
ȝyt fayn I woold warke my Lordes wyll;
But thys ȝowng innosent lygth so styll,
I may not fynd yt in my hart hym to kyll.
O! Fader of Heuyn! what schall I doo?

YSAAC. A! mercy, fader, wy tery ȝe so,
And let me ley thus longe on this hethe?
Now I wold to God the stroke were doo.
Fader, I prey ȝow hartely, schorte me of my woo,
And let me not loke thus after my degth.

ABRAHAM. Now, hart, wy wolddyst not thow breke on thre?
ȝyt schall th[o]u not make me to my God on-myld.° *disobedient*
I wyll no lenger let° for the, *delay*
For that my God a-grevyd wold be;
Now hoold tha stroke, my owyn dere chyld.

Her Abraham draw hys stroke and the angell toke the sword in hys hond soddenly.

THE ANGELL. I am an angell, thow mayist se blythe,° *gladly*
That fro heuyn to the ys senth.
Owr Lord thanke the an C sythe° *a hundred times*
For the kepyng of hys commawment.
He knowyt thi wyll and also thy harte,
That thow dredyst hym above all thyng;
And sum of thy hevynes for to departe
A fayr ram ȝynder I gan brynge;
He standyth teyed, loo! a-mong the breres.° *briars*
Now, Abraham, a-mend thy mood,
For Ysaac, thy ȝowng son that her ys,
Thys day schall not sched hys blood;
Goo, make thy sacryfece wyth ȝon rame.
Now for-wyll, blyssyd Abraham,
For on-to heuyn I goo now hom;
The wey ys full gayn.° *straight*
Take up thy son soo free.

[*Exit.*]

ABRAHAM. A! Lord, I thanke the of thy gret grace,
Now am I yeyed° on dyuers° wysse; *eased; many*
A-rysse vp, Ysaac, my dere sunne, a-rysse;
A-rysse vp, swete chyld, and cum to me.

YSAAC. A! mercy, fader, wy smygth ȝe nowt?
A, smygth on, fader, onys wyth ȝowre knyffe!

ABRAHAM. Pesse, my swet son, and take no thowt,
For owr Lord of Heuyn hath grant thi lyffe,
Be hys angell now,
That thou schalt not dey this day, sunne, truly.
YSAAC. A! fader, full glad than wer I,
I-wys, fader, I sey i-wys,
Yf thys tall wer trew!
ABRAHAM. An hundyrd tymys, my son fayer of hew,
For joy thi mowth now wyll I kys.
YSAAC. A! my dere fader, Abraham,
Wyll not God be wroth that we do thus?
ABRAHAM. Noo, noo! har[de]ly, my swyt son,
For ȝyn same rame he hath us sent
Hether down to vs.
Ȝyn best schall dey here in thi sted,
In the worthschup of owr Lord a-lon;
Goo, fet hym hethyr, my chyld, in-ded.
YSAAC. Fader, I wyll goo hent° hym be the hed, — take
And bryng ȝon best with me a-non.

[*Isaac catches the ram.*]

A! scheppe, scheppe, blyssyd mot thou be
That euer thow were sent down heder!
Thow schall thys day dey for me,
In the worthschup of the Holy Trynyte.
Now cum fast and goo we to-geder
To my fader in heuyn.
Thow thou be neuer so jentyll and good,
Ȝyt had I leuer thow schedyst thi blood,
I-wysse, scheppe, than I.
Loo! fader, I haue browt here full smerte° — quickly
Thys jentyll scheppe, and hym to ȝow I ȝyffe:
But, Lord God, I thank the with all my hart,
For I am glad that I schall leve,
And kys onys my dere moder.
ABRAHAM. Now be rygth myry, my swete chyld,
For thys qwyke best that ys so myld,
Here I schall present be-fore all othere.
YSAAC. And I wyll fast be-gynne to blowe;
Thys fyer schall brene a full good spyd.
But, fader, wyll I stowppe downe lowe,[5]
Ȝe wyll not kyll me with ȝowr sword, I trowe?
ABRAHAM. Noo, har[de]ly, swet son, haue no dred,
My mornyng° ys past. — mourning

5. If I should stoop.

YSAAC. ȝa! but I woold that sword wer in a gled,° — fire
For i-wys, fader, yt make me full yll a-gast.° — frightened

Here Abraham mad hys offryng, knelyng and seyyng thus:

ABRAHAM. Now, Lord God of Heuen, in Trynyte,
All-myty God Omnipotent,
My offeryng I make in the worchope of the,
And with thys qweke best I the present.
Lord, reseyve thow myn intent,
As [thow] art God and grownd of owr grace.
GOD. Abraham, Abraham, wyll mot thow sped,
And Ysaac, thi ȝowng son the by!
Trvly, Abraham, for thys dede
I schall mvltyplye ȝowres botheres sede
As thyke as sterres be in the skye,
Bothe more and lesse;
And as thyke as gravell in the see,
So thyke mvltyplyed ȝowr sede schall be;
Thys grant I ȝow for ȝowr goodnesse.
Off ȝow schall cume frowte° gret [won]° — fruit; quantity
And euer be in blysse with-owt ȝynd,° — end
For ȝe drede me as God a-lon
And kepe my commawmentes eueryschon,° — everyone
My blyssyng I ȝeffe, wer-so-euer ȝe wend.
ABRAHAM. Loo! Ysaac, my son, how thynke ȝe
Be thys warke that we haue wrogth?
Full glad and blythe we may be,
Aȝens the wyll of God that we grucched nott,
Vp-on thys fayer hetth.
YSAAC. A! fader, I thanke owr Lord euery dell,° — entirely
That my wyt servyd me so wyll
For to drede God more than my detth.
ABRAHAM. Why! dere-wordy son, wer thow a-dred?
Hardely, chyld, tell me thy lore.
YSAAC. ȝa! be my feyth, fader, now haue I red,° — thought
I wos neuer soo afrayd be-fore
As I haue byn at ȝyn hyll.
But, be my feyth, fader, I swere
I wyll neuer-more cume there
But yt be a-ȝens my wyll.
ABRAHAM. ȝa! cum on with me, my owyn swet sonn,
And hom-ward fast now let vs goon.
YSAAC. Be my feyth, fader, ther-to I grant,
I had neuer so good wyll to gon hom,
And to speke with my dere moder.
ABRAHAM. A! Lord of Heuyn, I thanke the,
For now may I led hom with me

Ysaac, my ʒownge son so fre,—
The gentyllest chyld a-bove all other,
Thys may I wyll a-voee.
Now goo we forthe, my blyssyd son.
YSAAC. I grant, fader, and let vs gon,
For be my trowthe, wer I at home
I wold neuer gon owt vnder that forme.
I pray God ʒeffe vs grace euer-mo,
And all thow that we be holdyng° to. — obliged

[*Exeunt. Enter Doctor*]

DOCTOR. Lo! sovereyns and sorys, now haue we schowyd,
Thys solom story to gret and smale;
It ys good lernyng to lernd and lewyd,° — unlearned
And the wysest of vs all,
Wyth-owtyn ony berryng.° — clamor
For thys story schoyt ʒowe [her]
How we schuld kepe to owr po[we]re° — ability
Goddes commawments wyth-owt grochyng.
Trowe ʒe, sores,° and God sent an angell — sirs
And commawndyd ʒow ʒowre chyld to slayn,
Be ʒowr trowthe ys ther ony of ʒow
That eyther wold groche or stryve ther-ageyn?
How thyngke ʒe now, sorys, ther-by?
I trow ther be iij or iiij° or moo. — three or four
And thys women that wepe so sorowfully
Whan that hyr chyldryn dey them froo,
As nater woll, and kynd,—
Yt ys but folly, I may wyll awooe,
To groche a-ʒens God or to greve ʒow,
For ʒe schall neuer se hym myschevyd, wyll I know,
Be lond nor watyr, haue thys in mynd;
And groche not a-ʒens owr Lord God
In welthe or woo, wether° that he ʒow send, — whichever
Thow ʒe be neuer so hard be-stad;
For whan he wyll, he may yt a-mend
Hys comawmentes trevly yf ʒe kepe with goo[d] hart,
As thys story hath now schowyd ʒow befor[n]e,
And feytheffully serve hym qwyll° ʒe be qvart,° — while; healthy
That ʒe may plece God bothe euyn and morne.
Now Jesu, that weryt the crown of thorne,
Bryng vs all to heuyn-blysse!

Finis.

The Second Shepherds Play

The Second Shepherds Play is part of the late fifteenth-century Towneley cycle, after the name of the family that owned the manuscript. A Catholic family, their manor was in North Lancashire, but some references in the plays are to places close to Wakefield. There is some scholarly debate whether Wakefield ever had a cycle, but *The Second Shepherds Play* almost certainly was performed there. However, a number of the plays are clearly derived from the York cycle. From the physical manuscript it is clear that the Towneley cycle is meant for reading; it is an expensive anthology highly and elaborately decorated and compiled from various sources, rather than a playbook for performance.

The Second Shepherds Play (so called because the Towneley manuscript also contains another shepherds play) is normally ascribed to the Wakefield Master, usually regarded as the author of at least six of the pageants in the Towneley cycle. Written in a bob-and-wheel stanza, the pageant eschews the sort of stage directions that would indicate it was played on a pageant wagon. The only essential set elements are some sort of structure indicating the house of Mak and Gyll, which could double as the stable for Mary and the infant Jesus, and a crib for the stolen sheep and the son of God. But whether or not the text is a play script, it is intensely dramatic and is frequently performed today.

The verbal gusto and structural freedom of his work is significantly different from the work of other cycle playwrights: for example, in the parallel structure of the stolen sheep and the lamb of God. In essence, the pageant answers the question of why the Messiah would be announced to three shepherds. The first answer is that they need one: they are burdened by the harsh weather, an oppressive upper class (and its servants), henpecked by their wives, and, in the case of Daw, mistreated even by the other shepherds, his employers. Despite this, even when disappointed and deceived by the initially successful

The text is that established by A. C. Cawley in *The Wakefield Pageants in the Towneley Cycle* (Manchester: Manchester University Press, 1958), 43–63. I have throughout changed the Latin designation of the characters to their English names.

disguise of their stolen sheep by Mak and Gyll, they reproach themselves for lack of charity toward the sheep-child, and when after returning to remedy their fault discover the fraud, act charitably toward Mak by tossing him in a blanket when his crime is a capital offense. In short, they also deserve a savior who can give them the eternal charity they have shown on a small scale.

The Wakefield Second Shepherds' Play

Incipit Alia eorundum[1]

Primus Pastor (COLL)	*Angelus*
Secundus Pastor (GYB)	*Maria*
Tercius Pastor (DAW)	*Christ-child*
Mak	
Uxor eius° (GYLL) his wife	

COLL. Lord, what these weders ar cold! And I am yll
happyd;° — covered
I am nere hande dold,° so long haue I nappyd; — numb
My legys thay fold, my fyngers ar chappyd,
It is not as I wold, for I am al lappyd
In sorow.
In stormes and tempest,
Now in the eest, now in the west,
Wo is hym has neuer rest
Myd day nor morow!

Bot we sely° husbandys that walkys on the moore, — poor
In fayth we are nere handys outt of the doore.
No wonder as it standys, if we be poore,
For the tylthe° of oure landys lyys falow as the floore, — arable land
As ye ken.
We ar so hamyd,° — hamstrung
Fortaxed° and ramyd, — overtaxed
We ar mayde handtamyd,
With° thyse gentlery-men. — by

Thus thay refe° vs oure rest, oure Lady theym wary!° — rob, curse
These men that ar lord fest,[2] thay cause the ploghe tary.

1. "Another of the same"; that is, another Shepherds Play. The pageant is not so much the second in a sequence, as an alternative dramatic treatment of the shepherds.
2. Bound to their lord.

That men say is for the best, we fynde it contrary;
Thus ar husbandys oppress, in ponte to myscary,° perish
On lyfe.
Thus hold thay vs hunder,
Thus thay bryng vs in blonder;
It were greatte wonder
And euer shuld we thryfe.

For may he gett a paynt slefe or a broche now-on-dayes,[3]
Wo is hym that hym grefe or onys agane says!
Dar noman hym reprefe, what mastry he mays,[4]
And yit may noman lefe° oone word that he says— believe
No letter.
He can make purveance,° requisitions
With boste and bragance,
And all is thrugh mantenance
Of men that are gretter.

Ther shall com a swane as prowde as a po;° peacock
He must borow my wane,° my ploghe also, wagon
Then I am full fane to graunt or° he go. ere
Thus lyf we in payne, anger, and wo,
By nyght and day;
He must haue if he langyd,° desired
If° I shuld forgang° it; even if; forgo
I were better be hangyd
Then oones say hym nay.

It dos me good as I walk thus by myn oone,° self
Of this warld, for to talk in maner of mone.
To my shepe wyll I stalk and herkyn anone,
Ther abyde on a balk,[5] or sytt on a stone
Full soyne.
For I trowe, perdé,° by God
Trew men if thay be,
We gett more compané
Or it be noyne.° noon

GYB. Bensté° and dominus, what may this bemeyne? bless us
Why fares this warld thus? Oft haue we not sene.
Lord, thyse weders ar spytus,° and the wyndys full kene. cruel
And the frostys so hydus° thay water myn eeyne— hideous
No ly.

3. The livery of a lord.
4. Whatever authority he claims.
5. "a strip of rough grassland dividing two plowed portions of a common field" (Cawley).

Now in dry, now in wete,
Now in snaw, now in slete,
When my shone freys to my fete,
It is not all esy.

Bot as far as I ken, or yit as I go,
We sely° wedmen° dre° mekyll wo; poor; husbands;
We haue sorow then and then; it fallys oft so. suffer
Sely Copyle, oure hen, both to and fro
She kakyls;
Bot begyn she to crok,
To groyne or to clok,
Wo is hym is oure cok,
For he is in the shakyls.

These men that ar wed haue not all thare wyll,
When they ar full hard sted,° thay sygh full styll; beset
God wayte° thay ar led full hard and full yll; knows
In bowere° nor in bed thay say noght thertyll, a woman's bed-
This tyde. chamber
My parte° haue I fun,° share; found
I know my lesson.
Wo is hym that is bun,° bound (in
For he must abyde. wedlock)

Bot now late in oure lyfys—a meruell to me,
That I thynk my hart ryfys° sich wonders to see; breaks
What that destany dryfys° it shuld so be— drives
Som men wyll have two wyfys, and som men thre
In store;
Som ar wo that has any.
Bot so far can° I: know
Wo is hym that has many,
For he felys sore.

Bot, yong men, of wowyng, for god that you boght,
Be well war of wedyng, and thynk in youre thoght:
"Had-I-wyst°" is a thyng that seruys of noght. known
Mekyll° styll mowrnyng has wedyng home broght, mickle (much)
And grefys,
With many a sharp showre,
For thou may cach in an owre
That shall sow the fulle sowre° sour
As long as thou lyffys.

For, as euer rede I pystyll,° I haue oone to my fere° Epistle; mate
As sharp as thystyll, as rugh as a brere;

She is browyd lyke a brystyll, with a sowre-loten°
  chere;°   looking; expression
Had she oones wett hyr whystyll, she couth syng full clere
Hyr Paternoster.
She is as greatt as a whall,
She has a galon of gall:
By hym° that dyed for vs all,   Jesus
I wald I had ryn to I had lost hir!

COLL. God looke ouer the raw! Full defly ye stand.
GYB. Yee, the dewill in thi maw,° so tariand.°   stomach; tarried
  Sagh thou awre of Daw?
COLL. Yee, on a ley-land°   fallow field
  Hard° I hym blaw.° He commys here at hand,   heard; blow
  Not far.
  Stand styll.
GYB. Qwhy?
COLL. For he commys, hope° I.   think
GYB. He wyll make° vs both a ly   tell
  Bot° if we be war.   unless

DAW. Crystys crosse me spede° and sant Nycholas!   aid
  Ther of had I nede; it is wars then it was.
  Whoso couthe take hede and lett the warld pas,
  It is euer in drede and brekyll° as glas,   brittle
  And slythys.°   slides away
  This warld fowre° neuer so,   fared
  With meruels mo and mo—
  Now in weyll,° now in wo,   good fortune
  And all thyng wrythys.°   changes

  Was neuer syn Noe floode sich floodys seyn,
  Wyndys and ranys so rude, and stormes so keyn—
  Som stamerd, som stod in dowte, as I weyn.
  Now god turne all to good! I say as I mene,
  For ponder:
  These floodys so thay drowne,
  Both in feyldys and in towne,
  And berys all downe;
  And that is a wonder.

  We that walk on the nyghtys, oure catell to kepe,
  We se sodan syghtys when othere men slepe.
  Yit me thynk my hart lyghtys; I se shrewys° pepe.   rogues
  Ye ar two all-wyghtys°—I wyll gyf my shepe   monsters
  A turne.
  Bot full yll haue I ment;

As I walk on this bent,° — open field
I may lyghtly repent,
My toes if I spurne.° — stub

A, sir, God you saue and master myne!
A drynk fayn wold I haue, and somwhat to dyne.
COLL. Crystys curs, my knaue, thou art a ledyr hyne!° — lazy servant
GYB. What! the boy lyst rave! Abyde vnto syne;° — later
We haue mayde it.° — (a meal)
Yll thryft on thy pate!
Though the shrew cam late,
Yit is he in state
To dyne—if he had it.
DAW. Sich seruandys° as I that swettys and swynkys,° — servants; toil
Etys oure brede full dry, and that me forthynkys.° — displeases
We ar oft weytt and wery when master-men wynkys;° — sleeps
Yit commys full lately both dyners and drynkys.
Bot nately° — thoroughly
Both oure dame and oure syre,
When we haue ryn in the myre,
Thay can nyp at oure hyre,
And pay vs full lately.

Bot here my trouth, master: for the fayr that ye make,
I shall do therafter—wyrk as I take;
I shall do a lytyll, sir, and emang° euer lake,° — in between; play
For yit lay my soper neuer on my stomake
In feyldys.
Wherto shuld I threpe?° — haggle
With my staf can I lepe;
And men say 'lyght chepe
letherly for-yeldys.'[6]

COLL. Thou were an yll lad to ryde on wowyng
With a man that had bot lytyll of spendyng.
GYB. Peasse, boy, I bad. No more iangling° — chattering
Or I shall make the full rad° by the heuen's kyng! — very quickly
With thy gawdys;° — tricks
Wher ar oure shepe, boy?—we skorne.
DAW. Sir, this same day at morne
I thaym left in the corne,
When thay rang lawdys.° — Lauds (prayers at daybreak)

Thay haue pasture good, thay can not go wrong.

6. "A cheap bargain pays badly" (Cawley).

COLL. That is right. By the roode,° thyse nyghtys ar long! cross
Yit I wold, or we yode,° oone gaf vs a song. went
GYB. So I thoght as I stode, to myrth° vs emong. entertain
DAW. I grauntt.
COLL. Lett me syng the tenory.
GYB. And I the tryble so hye.
DAW. Then the meyne fallys to me;
Lett se how ye chauntt.

Tunc intrat Mak in clamide se super togam vestitus[7]

MAK. Now, Lord, for thy naymes vij,° that made both moyn and starnes seven
Well mo then I can neuen,° thi will, Lorde, of me tharnys;° name; lacks
I am all vneuen; that moves oft my harnes.° brains
Now Wold god I were in heuen, for there wepe no barnes° children
So styll.° constantly
COLL. Who is that pypys so poore?
MAK. Wold, god ye wyst how I foore!° fare
Lo, a man that walkys on the moore,
And has not all his wyll!

GYB. Mak, where has thou gon? Tell vs tythyng.° news
DAW. Is he commen? then ylkon° take hede to his thyng. everyone

[*Et accipit clamidem ab ipso.*][8]

MAK. What! ich be a yoman,[9] I tell you, of the king,
The self and the some sond° from a greatt lordyng, messenger
And sich.
Fy on you! Goyth hence
Out of my presence!
I must haue reuerence.
Why, who be ich?

COLL. Why make ye it so qwaynt?[10] Mak, ye do wrang.
GYB. Bot, Mak, lyst ye saynt? I trow that ye lang.[11]
DAW. I trow the shrew can paynt,° the dewyll myght hym hang! represent falsely
MAK. Ich shall make complaynt, and make you all to thwang° be flogged

7. "Then enters Mak with a cloak covering his tunic" (Cawley).
8. "He takes Mak's cloak from him" (Cawley).
9. Here, an officer in a noble household (later a freeman owning his own land).
10. Why do you act so proud?
11. Do you desire to play the saint? I believe you long to.

At a worde,
And tell euyn how ye doth.
COLL. Bot, Mak, is that sothe?
Now take outt that Sothren tothe,[12]
And sett in a torde!

GYB. Mak, the dewill in youre ee! A stroke wold I
leyne° you. — give
DAW. Mak, know ye not me? By god I couthe teyn° you. — hurt
MAK. God looke you all thre! Me thoght I had sene you.
Ye ar a fare compané.
COLL. Can ye now mene° you? — remember
GYB. Shrew, pepe!
Thus late as thou goys,
What wyll men suppos?
And thou has an yll noys° — reputation
Of stelyng of shepe.

MAK. And I am trew as steyll, all men waytt;° — know
Bot a sekenes I feyll that haldys me full haytt:° — hot
My belly farys not weyll; it is out of astate.° — condition
DAW. Seldom lyys the dewyll dede by the gate.
MAK. Therfor
Full sore am I and yll,
If I stande stone-styll.
I ete not an nedyll° — morsel
Thys moneth and more.

COLL. How farys thi wyff? By thi hoode, how farys she?
MAK. Lyys walteryng°—by the roode—by the fyere, lo! — sprawling
And a howse full of brude.° She drynkys well, to; — children
Yll spede othere good that she wyll do!
Bot sho
Etys as fast as she can,
And ilk° yere that commys to man — every
She bryngys furth a lakan°— — baby
And, som yeres, two.

Bot were I now more gracyus° and rychere befar, — prosperous
I were eten outt of howse and of harbar.° — home
Yit is she a fowll dowse° if ye com nar; — wench
Ther is none that trowse° nor knowys a war, — believes
Then ken I.

12. Mak has been attempting an accent consistent with his claim to be a servant of the king and a great lord.

Now wyll ye se what I profer?—
To gyf all in my cofer
To-morne at next to offer
Hyr hed-maspenny.[13]

GYB. I wote so forwakyd° is none in this shyre; — exhausted
I wold slepe, if° I takyd les to my hyere. — even if
DAW. I am cold, and nakyd, and wold haue a fyere.
COLL. I am wery, forrakyd,° and run in the myre— — worn out with walking
Wake thou!
GYB. Nay, I wyll lyg downe by,
For I must slepe, truly.
DAW. As good a mans son was I
As any of you.

Bot, Mak, com heder! Betwene shall thou lyg downe.
MAK. Then myght I lett you bedene of that ye wold rowne,
No drede.[14]
Fro my top to my too,
Manus tuas commendo,
Poncio Pilato,[15]
Cryst crosse me spede!

[*Tunc surgit, pastoribus dormientibus, et dicit:*][16]

Now were tyme for a man that lakkys what he wold
To stalk preuely than vnto a fold,
And neemly° to wyrk than, and be not to bold, — nimbly
For he might aby° the bargan, if it were told — rue
At the endyng.
Now were tyme for to reyll;° — move quickly
Bot he nedys good counsell
That fayn wold fare weyll,
And has bot lytyll spendyng.

Bot abowte you a serkyll, as rownde as a moyn,
To I haue done that I wyll, tyll that it be noyn,
That ye lyg stone-styll to that I haue doyne;
And I shall say thertyll of good wordys a foyne:° — few
"On hight
Ouer youre heydys my hand I lyft.
Outt go youre een! Fordo° your syght!" — lose
Bot yit I must make better shyft,
And it be right.

13. Mak would give all his money for a mass for her soul.
14. "Then I might keep you from whispering what you want, no doubt" (Cawley).
15. I commend your hands to Pontius Pilate (mangled scripture).
16. Then he rises from among the sleeping shepherds, and says.

Lord! what thay slepe hard! That may ye all here.
Was I neuer a shepard, bot now wyll I lere.° — learn
If the flok be skard, yit shall I nyp nere,
How! drawes hederward! Now mendys oure chere
From sorow[.]
A fatt shepe I dar say,
A good flese, dar I lay.
Eft-whyte° when I may, — repay
Bot this will I borow.

[*Mak steals off*]

How, Gyll, art thou In? Gett vs some lyght.
GYLL. Who makys sich dyn this tyme of the nyght?
I am sett for to spyn; I hope not I myght
Ryse° a penny to wyn, I shrew° them on hight! — earn; curse
So farys
A huswyff that has bene
To be rasyd thus betwene.° — continually
Here may no note° be sene° — work; get done
For sich small charys.° — chores

MAK. Good wyff, open the hek!° Seys thou not what I bryng? — door
GYLL. I may thole the dray the snek.[17] A, com in, my swetyng!
MAK. Yee, thou thar not rek° of my long standyng. — care about
GYLL. By the nakyd nek art thou lyke for to hyng.
MAK. Do way!
I am worthy my mete,
For in a strate° can I get — tight pinch
More then thay that swynke° and swette — labor
All the long day.

Thus it fell to my lott, Gyll, I had sich grace.
GYLL. It were a fowll blott to be hanged for the case.
MAK. I haue skapyd, Ielott,[18] oft as hard a glase.° — blow
GYLL. "Bot so long goys the pott to the water," men says,
"At last
Comys it home broken."
MAK. Well knowe I the token,° — proverb
Bot let it neuer be spoken!
Bot com and help fast.
I wold he were slayn; I lyst well ete:
This twelmothe was I not so fayn of oone shepe-mete.
GYLL. Com thay or° he be slayn, and here the shepe blete— — before

17. "I will let you draw the latch" (Cawley).
18. An affectionate diminutive of Gyll.

MAK. Then myght I be tane. That were a cold swette!
Go spar
The gaytt-doore.
GYLL. Yis, Mak,
For and thay com at thy bak—
MAK. Then myght I by,° for° all the pak, — get; from
The dewill of the war.° — worse

GYLL. A good bowrde° haue I spied syn thou can none: — jest
Here shall we hym hyde, to thay be gone,
In my credyll. Abyde! lett me alone,
And I shall lyg besyde in chylbed, and grone.
MAK. Thou red,° — get ready
And, I shall say thou was lyght° — delivered
Of a knaue-childe this nyght.
GYLL. Now well is me day bright,
That euer was I bred![19]

This is a good gyse° and a far cast;° — method; cunning trick
Yit a woman avyse helpys at the last.
I wote neuer who spyse, agane° go thou fast. — back
MAK. Bot° I com or thay ryse, els blawes a cold blast! — unless
I wyll go slepe.
Yit slepys all this meneye;° — company
And I shall go stalk preuely,
As it had neuer bene I
That caryed thare shepe.

COLL. *Resurrex a mortruus!* Haue hald, my hand.
Iudas carnas dominus![20] I may not well stand;
My foytt slepys, by Iesus, and I water fastand.° — totter fasting
I thoght that we layd vs full nere Yngland.
GYB. A, ye!
Lord! what I haue slept weyll!
As fresh as an eyll,
As lyght I me feyll
As leyfe on a tre.

DAW. Benste° be herein! so me qwakys, — blessing
My hart is outt of skyn, whatso° it makys.° — whatever; causes
Who makys all this dyn? So my browes blakys,° — blackens
To the dowore wyll I wyn.° Harke, felows, wakys! — go
We were fowre—
Se ye awre of Mak now?

19. "I'm happy when I think of the bright day when I was born" (Cawley).
20. Garbled Latin from the Creed, in the first phrase apparently meaning "rise from the dead"; the second phrase perhaps means "Judas, lord of the flesh."

COLL. We were vp or thou.
GYB. Man, I gyf god avowe,° *swear to God*
Yit yede° he nawre.° *gone; nowhere*

DAW. Me thoght he was lapt in a wolfe skyn.
COLL. So are many hapt now, namely within.
DAW. When we had long napt me thoght with a gyn° *snare*
A fatt shepe he trapt; bot he mayde no dyn.
GYB. Be styll!
Thi dreme makys the woode;° *mad*
It is bot fantom, by the roode.
COLL. Now God turne all to good,
If it be his wyll.

GYB. Ryse, Mak, for shame! Thou lygys right lang.
MAK. Now Crystys holy name be vs emang!
What is this? For sant Iame, I may not well gang!° *walk*
I trow I be the same. A! my nek has lygen wrang
Enoghe;
Mekill thank! syn yister-euen,
Now by Sant Stevyn,
I was flayd° with a swevyn°— *tormented; dream*
My hart out of sloghe!° *skin*

I thoght Gyll began to crok and trauell° full sad, *labor*
Wel-ner at the fyrst cok, of a yong lad,
For to mend° oure flok. Then be I neuer glad. *add to*
I haue tow on my rok more then euer I had.[21]
A, my heede!
A house full of yong tharmes,° *bellies*
The dewill knok outt thare harnes!° *brains*
Wo is hym has many barnes,
And therto lytyll brede.

I must go home, by youre lefe, to Gyll, as I thoght.
I pray you looke my slefe, that I steyll noght;
I am loth you to grefe, or from you take oght.
DAW. Go furth, yll myght thou chefe!° Now wold I we soght, *achieve*
This morne,
That we had all oure store.
COLL. Bot I will go before, let vs mete.
GYB. Whore?
DAW. At the crokyd thorne.

[*The Shepherds Exit.*]

21. "I have more tow on my distaff (i.e., more trouble in store) than ever I had" (Cawley).

MAK. Vndo this doore! Who is here? How long shall I stand?
GYLL. Who makys sich a bere?° Now walk in the Wenyand.[22]   clamor
MAK. A, Gyll, what chere? It is I, Mak, youre husbande.
GYLL. Then may we se here the dewill in a bande,°   noose
Syr Gyle;°   Guile
Lo, he commys with a lote°   noise
As he were holden in the throte.
I may not syt at my note,°   work
A handlang° while.

MAK. Wyll ye here what fare she makys to gett hir a glose,°   excuse
And dos noght bot lakys° and clowse° hir toose.   play; claws
GYLL. Why, who wanders, who wakys? Who commys, who gose?
Who brewys, who bakys? What makys me thus hose?
And than,
It is rewthe° to beholde—   pity
Now in hote, now in colde,
Full wofull is the householde
That wantys a woman.

Bot what ende has thou mayde with the hyrdys,° Mak?   shepherds
MAK. The last worde that thay sayde when I turnyd my bak,
Thay wold looke that thay hade thare shepe, all the pak.
I hope thay wyll nott be well payde when thay thare shepe lak,
Perdé!°   by God
Bot howso the gam gose,
To me thay wyll suppose,
And make a fowll noyse,
And cry outt apon me.

Bot thou must do as thou hyght.°   promised

GYLL. I accorde me thertyll;
I shall swedyll hym right in my credyll;
If it were a gretter slyght,° yit couthe I help tyll.   trick
I wyll lyg downe stright. Com hap° me.   cover
MAK. I wyll.
GYLL. Behynde!
Com Coll and his maroo,°   mates
Thay will nyp vs full naroo.
MAK. Bot I may cry 'out, haroo!'
The shepe if thay fynde.

GYLL. Harken ay when thay call; thay will com onone.
Com and make redy all, and syng by thyn oone;
Syng 'lullay' thou shall, for I must grone,

22. The Wenyand is the waning moon and was regarded as an ill omen.

And cry outt by the wall on Mary and Iohn,
For sore.
Syng 'lullay' on fast
when thou heris at the last;
And bot° I play a fals cast,° — unless; trick
Trust me no more.

[*Enter Shepherds.*]

DAW. A, Coll, goode morne! Why slepys thou nott?
COLL. Alas, that euer was I borne! We haue a fowll blott—
A fat wedir[23] haue we lorne.
DAW. Mary, Godys forbott!
GYB. Who shuld do vs that skorne? That were a fowll spott.

COLL. Som shrewe.° — rascal
I haue soght with my dogys
All Horbery[24] shrogys,° — thickets
And of xv° hogys° — fifteen; young sheep
Fond I bot oone ewe.

DAW. Now trow° me, if ye will—by Sant Thomas of Kent, — trust
Ayther Mak or Gyll was at that assent.
COLL. Peasse, man, be still! I sagh when he went.
Thou sklanders hym yll; thou aght to repent,
Goode spede.
GYB. Now as euer myght I the,° — thrive
If I shuld euyn here de,
I wold say it were he,
That dyd that same dede.

DAW. Go we theder, I rede,° and ryn on oure feete. — advise
Shall I neuer ete brede, the sothe° to I wytt.° — truth; know
COLL. Nor drynk in my heede with hym tyll I mete.
GYB. I wyll rest in no stede° tyll that I hym grete, — place
My brothere.
Oone I will hight:° — promise
Tyll I se hym in sight
Shall I neuer slepe one nyght
Ther I do anothere.

DAW. Will ye here how thay hak? Oure syre° lyst croyne.° — gentleman; croon
COLL. Hard I neuer none crak so clere out of toyne.[25]
Call on hym.
GYB. Mak! Undo youre doore soyne!

23. A wether is a neutered ram.
24. A village near Wakefield.
25. "Crak" is to make a loud noise; the lines indicate Mak is snoring loudly.

MAK. Who is that spak, as it were noyne,
On loft?° — aloud
Who is that I say?
DAW. Goode felowse, were it day.
MAK. As far as ye may,
Good,° spekys soft, — good men

Ouer a seke woman's heede that is at mayllease;° — distress
I had leuer be dede or she had any dyseasse.
GYLL. Go to anothere stede! I may not well qweasse;° — breathe
Ich fote that ye trede goys thorow my nese
So hee.
COLL. Tell vs, Mak, if ye may,
How fare ye, I say?
MAK. Bot ar ye in this towne to-day?
Now how fare ye?

Ye haue ryn in the myre, and ar weytt yit;
I shall make you a fyre, if ye will syt.
A nores wold I hyre. Thynk ye on yit?
Well qwytt is my hyre[26]—my dreme this is itt—
A seson.
I haue barnes, if ye knew,
Well mo then enewe;
Bot we must drynk as we brew,
And that is bot reson.

I wold ye dynyd or ye yode.° Me thynk that ye swette. — go
GYB. Nay, nawther mendys oure mode drynke nor mette.
MAK. Why, sir, alys° you oght bot goode? — ails
DAW. Yee, oure shepe þat we gett,° — tend
Ar stollyn as thay yode. Oure los is grette.
MAK. Syrs, drynkys!
Had I bene thore,
Som shuld haue boght° it full sore. — paid for
COLL. Mary, som men trowes° that ye wore, — believe
And that vs forthynkys.° — displeases

GYB. Mak, som men trowys that it shuld be ye.
DAW. Ayther ye or youre spouse, so say we.
MAK. Now if ye haue suspowse to Gill or to me,
Com and rype° oure howse, and then may ye se — ransack
Who had hir.
If I any shepe fott,° — fetched
Aythor cow or stott°— — heifer

26. My wages are paid.

And Gyll, my wyfe, rose nott
Here syn she lade hir—

As I am true and lele,° to God here I pray   honest
That this be the fyrst mele that I shall ete this day.
COLL. Mak, as haue I ceyll,° avyse the, I say: happiness
"He lernyd tymely to steyll that couth not say nay."
GYLL. I swelt!°   faint
Outt, thefys, fro my wonys!°   house
Ye com to rob vs for the nonys.
MAK. Here ye not how she gronys?
Youre hartys shuld melt.

GYLL. Outt,° thefys, fro my barne! Negh° hym not thor.   away; near
MAK. Wyst ye how she had farne,° youre hartys wold be sore.   labored
Ye do wrang, I you warne, that thus commys before
To a woman that has farne—bot I say no more.
GYLL. A, my medyll!
I pray to God so mylde,
If euer I you begyld,
That I ete this chylde
That lygys in this credyll.

MAK. Peasse, woman, for Godys payn, and cry not so!
Thou spyllys thy brane, and makys me full wo.

GYB. I trow oure shepe be slayn. What finde ye two?
DAW. All wyrk we in vayn; as well may we go.
Bot hatters!°   darn it
I can fynde no flesh,
Hard nor nesh,°   soft
Salt nor fresh,
Bot two tome° platers.   empty

Whik° catell bot this, tame nor wylde,   living
None, as haue I blys, as lowde° as he smylde.°   strongly; smelled
GYLL. No, so God me blys, and gyf me ioy of my chylde!
COLL. We haue merkyd amys; I hold vs begyld.
GYB. Syr, don.°   completely
Syr—oure lady hym saue!—
Is youre chyld a knaue?°   boy
MAK. Any lord myght hym haue,
This chyld, to his son.

When he wakyns he kyppys,° that ioy is to se.   snatches
DAW. In good tyme to hys hyppys, and in celé![27]

27. "A good and happy future to him" (Cawley).

Bot who was his gossyppys° so sone redé? — godparents
MAK. So fare fall thare lyppys!
COLL. Hark now, a le.° — lie

MAK. So God thaym thank,
Parkyn, and Gybon Waller, I say,
And gentill Iohn Horne, in good fay—
He made all the garray,° — commotion
With the greatt shank.° — leg(s)

GYB. Mak, freyndys will we be, for we ar all oone.
MAK. We? Now I hald for me, for mendys° gett I none. — amends
Fare well all thre! All glad were ye gone.

[*exeunt* shepherds.][28]

DAW. Fare wordys may ther be, bot luf is ther none þis yere.
COLL. Gaf ye the chyld, any thyng?
GYB. I trow not oone farthyng.
DAW. Fast agane will I flyng,
Abyde ye me there.

[*The Shepherds return to Mak's house.*]

Mak, take it to no grefe, if I com to thi barne.
MAK. Nay, thou dos me greatt reprefe, and fowll has thou farne.° — behaved
DAW. The child will it not grefe, that lytyll day starne.
Mak, with youre leyfe, let me gyf youre barne,
Bot vj° pence. — six
MAK. Nay, do way! he slepys.
DAW. Me thynk he pepys.
MAK. When he wakyns he wepys.
I pray you go hence!

DAW. Gyf me lefe hym to kys, and lyft vp the clowtt.° — cloth
What the dewill is this? He has a long snowte!
COLL. He is merkyd amys. We wate ill abowte.
GYB. Ill spon weft,° iwys, ay commys foull owte. — weaving
Ay, so!
He is lyke to oure shepe!
DAW. How, Gyb, may I pepe?
COLL. I trow, kynde° will crepe — nature
where it may not go.° — walk
GYB. This was a qwantt gawde° and a far-cast.° — scheme; cunning trick
It was a hee frawde.

28. Cawley's edition has the shepherds exiting after Daw's next line. In that case, Daw's line is commentary on Mak's anger. In my view, the line makes more sense as a commentary on the suspicion of the shepherds, and Coll and Gyb's next lines indicate agreement that they have been ungenerous.

DAW. Yee, syrs, wast.
Lett bren° this bawde, and bynd hir fast. burn
A fals skawde hang at the last;
So shall thou.
Wyll ye se how thay swedyll
His foure feytt in the medyll?
Sagh I neuer in a credyll
A hornyd lad or now.

MAK. Peasse byd I. What, lett be youre fare!° uproar
I am he that hym gatt, and yond woman hym bare.
COLL. What dewill shall he hatt,° Mak? Lo, God, Makys ayre.° be named; heir
GYB. Lett be all that! Now God gyf hym care,
I sagh.
GYLL. A pratty child is he
As syttys on a waman's kne;
A dyllydowne,° perdé, darling
To gar a man laghe.

DAW. I know hym by the eere marke; that is a good tokyn.
MAK. I tell you, syrs, hark! hys noyse was brokyn.
Sythen° told me a clerk that he was forspokyn.° since; bewitched
COLL. This is a fals wark; I wold fayn be wrokyn:° avenged
Gett wepyn!
GYLL. He was takyn with° an elfe, by
I saw it myself;
When the clok stroke twelf
Was he forshapyn.° transformed

GYB. Ye two ar well feft sam in a stede.[29]
COLL. Syn thay manteyn thare theft, let do thaym to dede.
MAK. If I trespas eft,° gyrd of my heede. again
With you will I be left.[30]

DAW. Syrs, do my reede.
For this trespas,
We will nawther ban° ne flyte,° curse; quarrel
Fyght nor chyte,° chide
Bot haue done as tyte,° immediately
And cast hym in canvas.

[*After tossing Mak in a blanket, the Shepherds leave.*]

[COLL]. Lord, what I am sore, in poynt for to bryst.° burst
In fayth, I may no more; therfor wyll I ryst.

29. "You two are well endowed together in one place" (Cawley).
30. I throw myself on your mercy.

GYB. As a shepe of vij° skore, he weyd in my fyst. seven
For to slepe aywhore me thynk that I lyst.
DAW. Now I pray you,
Lyg downe on this grene.
COLL. On these thefys yit I mene.° think
DAW. Wherto shuld ye tene?° vex
Do, as I say you.

Angelus cantat "Gloria in excelsis"; postea dicat:[31]

ANGEL. Ryse, hyrd-men heynd,° for now is he borne gentle
That shall take fro the feynd that Adam had lorne:
That warloo to sheynd,° this nyght is he borne. destroy
God is made youre freynd now at this morne,
He behestys.° promises
At Bedlem go se
Ther lygys that fre° noble one
In a cryb full poorely,
Betwyx two bestys.

COLL. This was a qwant stevyn° that euer yit I hard. elegant voice
It is a meruell to neuyn,° thus to be skard. tell of
GYB. Of Godys son of heuyn he spak vpward.
All the wod on a leuyn° me thoght that he gard lightning
Appere.
DAW. He spake of a barne
In Bedlem, I you warne.
COLL. That betokyns yond starne;
Let vs seke hym there.

GYB. Say, what was his song? Hard ye not how he crakyd° it, sang
Thre brefes to a long?
DAW. Yee, Mary, he hakt° it: trilled
Was no crochett wrong, nor nothyng that lakt it.
COLL. For to syng vs emong, right as he knakt° it, sang
I can.
GYB. Let se how ye croyne!
Can ye bark at the mone?
DAW. Hold youre tonges! haue done!
COLL. Hark after, than.

GYB. To Bedlem he bad that we shuld gang;
I am full fard that we tary to lang.
DAW. Be mery and not sad—of myrth is oure sang!
Euerlastyng glad° to mede° may we fang,° joy; reward; get
Withoutt noyse.

31. "The Angel sings 'Glory to God in the highest'; afterwards let him say" (Cawley).

COLL. Hy we theder forthy;° therefore
If we be wete and wery,
To that chyld and that lady;
We haue it not to lose.° forget

GYB. We fynde by the prophecy—let be youre dyn!—
Of Dauid and Isay mo then I myn—
Thay prophecyed by clergy°—that in a vyrgyn learning
Shuld he lyght and ly, to slokyn° oure syn, slacken
And slake° it, relieve
Oure kynde from wo;
For Isay sayd so,
Ecce virgo
Concipiet[32] a chylde that is nakyd.

DAW. Full glad may we be, and abyde that day
That lufly to se, that all myghtys may.[33]
Lord, well were me for ones and for ay,
Myght I knele on my kne, som word for to say
To that chylde.
Bot the angell sayd
In a cryb wos he layde;
He was poorly arayd
Both mener° and mylde. meek

COLL. Patryarkes that has bene, and prophetys beforne,
Thay desyryd to haue sene this chylde that is borne.
Thay ar gone full clene; that haue thay lorne.
We shall se hym, I weyn or it be morne,
To tokyn.° as a sign
When I se hym and fele,
Then wote I full weyll
It is true as steyll
That prophetys haue spokyn:

To so poore as we ar that he wold appere,
Fyrst fynd, and declare by his messyngere.
GYB. Go we now, let vs fare, the place is vs nere.
DAW. I am redy and yare;° go we in fere° eager, together
To that bright.
Lord, if thi wylles be—
We ar lewde° all thre— simple
Thou grauntt vs somkyns gle
To comforth thi wight.[34]

32. Behold, a virgin shall conceive.
33. That is almighty.
34. "Grant us some joyful way of comforting thy child" (Cawley).

COLL. Hayll, comly and clene!° Hayll, yong child! pure
Hayll, maker, as I meyne, of a madyn so mylde!
Thou has waryd,° I weyne, the warlo so wylde: cursed
The fals gyler of teyn,° now goys he begylde. malice
Lo, he merys,° is merry
Lo, he laghys, my swetyng!
A wel fare° metyng! very fine
I haue holden my hetyng:° promise
Haue a bob of cherys.

GYB. Hayll, sufferan sauyoure! for thou has vs soght!
Hayll, frely° foyde[35] and floure that all thyng has wroght! noble
Hayll, full of fauoure that made all of noght!
Hayll! I kneyll and I cowre. A byrd haue I broght
To my barne.
Hayll, lytyll tyne mop!° moppet
Of oure crede thou art crop;° head
I wold drynk on thy cop,
Lytyll day starne.

DAW. Hayll, derlyng dere, full of Godhede!
I pray the be nere when that I haue nede.
Hayll! swete is thy chere! my hart wold blede
To se the sytt here in so poore wede,° clothing
With no pennys.
Hayll! put furth thy dall!° hand
I bryng the bot a ball:
Haue and play the withall,
And go to the tenys.° tennis (a royal sport)

MARY. The fader of heuen, God omnypotent,
That sett° all on seuen, his son has he sent. made
My name couth he neuen,° and lyght° or° he went. name; alighted; before
I conceyuyd hym full euen thrugh myght, as he ment,
And now is he borne.
He kepe you fro wo!
I shall pray hym so.
Tell furth as ye go,
And myn° on this morne. remember

COLL. Farewell, lady, so fare to beholde,
With thy childe on thi kne!
GYB. Bot he lygys full cold.
Lord, well is me! Now we go, thou behold.

35. Fode (foyde) can mean both food and child.

DAW. Forsothe allredy it semys to be told
Full oft.
COLL. What grace we haue fun!
GYB. Com furth; now ar we won!° — redeemed
DAW. To syng ar we bun—
Let take on loft.° — loudly

Explicit pagina Pastorum[36]

36. End of the Shepherds pageant.

The Crucifixion

The York pageant of *The Crucifixion* is part of a cycle of fifty separate pageants, more perhaps than could be performed in a day, even though the performers needed to be ready to begin at 4:30 a.m. by city ordinance and may have run until midnight, and daylight in York around Corpus Christi (which can fall anywhere between May 23 and June 24 depending on the date of Easter) lasts around seventeen hours. Guilds paid for the cycle with a tax called "pageant silver" and were responsible for the wagons, their storage, costumes, and the quality of their own section of the cycle, subject to inspection by players under the direction of the city council. The pageants were performed at twelve stations, but given the nature of the city's streets and squares, no more than a few hundred people could watch each pageant at a time. The cycle depicted the world from Creation to the Last Judgment, with emphasis on the Nativity and the Passion of Christ. The first mention of the pageant is 1376, and the last documented performance was in 1569.

The Crucifixion pageant is sometimes ascribed to a playwright called The York Realist, who modern scholars increasingly doubt was a single playwright. Nevertheless, some of the plays in the York cycle share an alliterating twelve-line stanza, rhyming abababababcdcd with four stresses in the *a* and *b* lines, and three in the *c* and *d* lines. Colloquial speech and realistic details also characterize these plays. Stichomythia occurs as the soldiers struggle to attach Jesus to a cross where the holes have been misbored (the pageant was produced by the Painters and Pinners, the latter being the maker of wooden "nails"). Ultimately, they must stretch the victim to fit the cross. They then have enormous difficulty in lifting the cross. The pageant wagons were large, with a stage perhaps as much as four feet above ground level. This means that for much of *The Crucifixion* and for most of the crowd who did not have seats in favorably situated houses or in the front rows of standing spectators, Jesus is not visible for half of the

The text is that established by Richard Beadle in *The York Plays* (Washington, D.C.: Edward Arnold, 1982), 315–323. I have changed the Latin "Miles" to "Soldier" throughout. I am also indebted to A. C. Cawley's notes in *Everyman and Medieval Miracle Plays.*

performance. Thus, the soldiers' inability to perform the crucifixion efficiently takes on the character of a Three Stooges routine because the crowd cannot see the body tormented by the soldiers' actions. Not until Jesus and the cross are slammed into the mortise built into the pageant does the audience remember that they have laughed their way through the crucifixion. Thus Jesus' cry from the cross, "What they work, wot they nought," comments on the action on a number of levels. The soldiers do not know who they are crucifying any more than they know how to do the job well. Inept, quarrelsome, and brutal, they are nevertheless saved because Jesus asks it of the Father. And the audience, complicit in the crucifixion both through their sins and their behavior through the performance, can hope they will be saved through the same agent.

The York Pinners' Pageant of *The Crucifixion*

JESUS — SOLDIER 3
SOLDIER 1 — SOLDIER 4
SOLDIER 2

SOLDIER 1. Sir knyghtis, take heede hydir in hye,
This dede on dergh we may noght drawe.[1]
3ee wootte youreselffe als wele as I
Howe lordis and leders of owre lawe
Has geven dome° þat þis[2] doote° schall dye. — judgment; fool
SOLDIER 2. Sir, alle þare counsaile wele we knawe.
Sen we are comen to Caluarie
Latte ilke° man helpe nowe as hym awe.° — each; ought
SOLDIER 3. We are alle redy, loo,
Þat forward° to fulfille. — agreement
SOLDIER 4. Late here howe we schall doo,
And go we tyte° þertille. — quickly

SOLDIER 1. It may no3t helpe her for to hone° — delay
If we schall any worshippe° wynne. — honor
SOLDIER 2. He muste be dede nedelyngis° by none. — by necessity
SOLDIER 3. Þanne is goode tyme that we begynne.
SOLDIER 4. Late dynge° hym doune, than is he done — knock
He schall nought dere° vs with his dynne. — harm
SOLDIER 1. He schall be sette° and lerned° sone, — set down; taught
With care° to hym and all his kynne. — sorrow
SOLDIER 2. Þe foulest dede° of all — death
Shalle he dye for his dedis.

1. We cannot delay this deed much longer.
2. "Þ" is the medieval character *thorn* which has the value of "th" both voiced and unvoiced. "3" represent the medieval character *yogh*; its sound value can be either [j] or [g] depending on the phonological environment.

SOLDIER 3. That menes crosse° hym we schall. *crucify*
SOLDIER 4. Behalde, so right he redis.° *advises*

SOLDIER 1. Thanne to þis werke vs muste take heede,
So þat oure wirkyng be noght wronge.
SOLDIER 2. None othir noote° to neven° is nede, *business; mention*
But latte vs haste hym for to hange.
SOLDIER 3. And I haue gone for gere goode speede,
Bothe hammeres and nayles large and lange.
SOLDIER 4. Þanne may we boldely do this dede.
Commes on, late kille this traitoure strange.° *strong*
SOLDIER 1. Faire myght ȝe falle in feere[3]
Þat has wrought on this wise.° *in this manner*
SOLDIER 2. Vs nedis nought for to lere° *learn*
Suche faitoures° to chastise. *deceivers*

SOLDIER 3. Sen ilke a thyng es right arrayed,
The wiselier nowe wirke may we.
SOLDIER 4. Þe crosse on grounde is goodely graied° *made ready*
And boorede even as it awith° to be. *ought*
SOLDIER 1. Lokis þat þe ladde on lenghe be layde
And made be þane° vnto þis tree. *fastened*
SOLDIER 2. For alle his fare° he schalle be flaied, *behavior*
That one assaie° sone schalle ye see. *tried (put to the test)*
SOLDIER 3. Come forthe þou cursed knave,
Thy comforte sone schall kele.° *grow cold*
SOLDIER 4. Thyne hyre° here schall þou haue. *reward*
SOLDIER 1. Walkes oon-now wirke we wele.

JESUS. Almyghty God, my fadir free,° *noble*
Late þis materes be made° in mynde: *remembered*
Þou badde þat I schulde buxsome° be *obedient*
For Adam plyght for to be pyned.
Here to dede° I obblisshe° me *death, pledge*
Fro þat synne for to saue mankynde,
And soueraynely° beseke I þe *above all*
That þai for me may fauoure fynde.
And fro þe fende° þame fende,° *fiend; defend*
So þat þer saules be saffe
In welthe° withouten ende— *happiness*
I kepe° nought ellis to craue.° *have; request*

SOLDIER 1. We[!] herke sir knyghtis, for Mahoundis° bloode, *Mahomet's*
Of Adam-kynde° is all his þoght. *mankind*

3. "Good luck to you all" (Cawley).

SOLDIER 2. Þe warlowe waxis werre þan woode,°	mad
Þis doulfull dede ne dredith he noght.
SOLDIER 3. Þou schulde haue mynde, with mayne and moode,[4]
Of wikkid werkis þat þou haste wrought.
SOLDIER 4. I hope þat he hadde bene as goode
Haue sesed of sawes° þat he vppe-sought.°	sayings; made up
SOLDIER 1. Thoo sawes schall rewe hym sore
For all his saunteryng° sone.	babbling
SOLDIER 2. Ille spede þame þat hym spare
Tille he to dede be done.

SOLDIER 3. Haue done belyue° boy, and make þe boune,°	at once; prepared
And bende þi bakke vnto þis tree.
SOLDIER 4. Byhalde, hymselffe has laide hym doune
In lenghe and breede as he schulde bee.
SOLDIER 1. This traitoure here teynted° of treasoune,	convicted
Gose faste and fetter hym þan ȝe thre;
And sen he claymeth kyngdome with croune,
Even as a kyng here hange schall hee.
SOLDIER 2. Nowe, certis, I schall noȝt fyne°	stop
Or° his right hande be feste.	until
SOLDIER 3. Þe lefte hande thanne is myne—
Late see who beres hym beste.

SOLDIER 4. Hys lymmys° on lenghe þan schalle I lede,	limbs
And even vnto þe bore° þame bringe.	hole
SOLDIER 1. Vnto his heede I schall take hede,
And with myne hande helpe hym to hyng.
SOLDIER 2. Nowe sen we foure schall do þis dede
And medill with þis vnthrifty° thyng,	unprofitable
Late no man spare for speciall speede
Tille that we haue made endyng.
SOLDIER 3. Þis forward may not faile;
Nowe are we right arraiede.°	in proper position
SOLDIER 4. This boy here in oure baile°	charge
Shall bide full bittir brayde.°	torment

SOLDIER 1. Sir knyghtis, saie, howe wirke we nowe?
SOLDIER 2. Ȝis, certis, I hope I holde þis hande,
And to þe boore I haue it brought
Full boxumly withouten bande.°	rope
SOLDIER 1. Strike on þan harde, for hym° the boght.°	Jesus; redeemed
SOLDIER 2. Ȝis, here is a stubbe° will stiffely stande,	spike
Though bones and senous it schall be soght—
This werke is wele, I will warande.°	swear

4. You should remember, with strength and (sad) emotion.

SOLDIER 1. Saie sir, howe do we þore?° there
Þis bargayne° may not blynne.° work; stop
SOLDIER 3. It failis a foote and more,
Þe senous are so gone ynne.° shrunken

SOLDIER 4. I hope° þat marke amisse be bored. think
SOLDIER 2. Þan muste he bide in bittir bale.° torment
SOLDIER 3. In faith, it was ouere-skantely scored,° drilled
Þat makis it fouly for to faile.
SOLDIER 1. Why carpe ȝe so? Faste on a corde
And tugge hym to, by toppe and taile.
SOLDIER 3. Ȝa, thou comaundis lightly as a lorde;
Come helpe to haale, with ille haile.° a curse
SOLDIER 1. Nowe certis that schall I doo—
Full snelly° as a snayle quickly
SOLDIER 3. And I schall tacche° hym too, fasten
Full nemely° with a nayle. nimbly

Þis werke will holde, þat dar I heete,° promise
For nowe are feste° faste both his hende. fixed
SOLDIER 4. Go we all foure þanne to his feete,
So schall oure space° be spedely° spende. time; well
SOLDIER 2. Latte see what bourde° his bale myght beete,° jest; lessen
Tharto my bakke nowe wolde I bende.
SOLDIER 4. Owe, þis werke is all vnmeete—
This boring muste all be amende.
SOLDIER 1. A, pees man, for Mahounde,
Latte no man wotte° þat wondir, know
A roope schall rugge° hym doune yank
Yf all his synnous go asoundre.

SOLDIER 2. Þat corde full kyndely° can I knytte, thoroughly
Þe comforte of this karle° to kele. churl
SOLDIER 1. Feste on þanne faste° þat all be fytte, firmly
It is no force° howe felle° he feele. matter; cruelly
SOLDIER 2. Lugge on ȝe both a litill ȝitt.
SOLDIER 3. I schalle nought sese, as I haue seele.° happiness
SOLDIER 4. And I schall fonde° hym for to hitte. try
SOLDIER 2. Owe, haylle!° haul
SOLDIER 4. Hoo nowe, I halde it wele.
SOLDIER 1. Haue done, dryue in þat nayle,
So þat no faute be foune.
SOLDIER 4. Þis wirkyng wolde noȝt faile
Yf foure bullis here were boune.

SOLDIER 1. Ther cordis haue evill encressed his paynes,
Or° he wer tille þe booryngis brought. before

SOLDIER 2. Ȝaa, assoundir are bothe synnous and veynis
On ilke° a side, so haue we soughte.° each; seen
SOLDIER 3. Nowe all his gaudis° nothyng hym gaynes, tricks
His sauntering° schall with bale be bought. babbling
SOLDIER 4. I wille goo saie to oure soueraynes
Of all þis werkis howe we haue wrought.
SOLDIER 1. Nay sirs, anothir thyng
Fallis firste to youe and me,
Þei badde we schulde hym hyng
On heghte þat men myght see.

SOLDIER 2. We woote° wele so ther wordes wore, know
But sir, þat dede will do vs dere.° cause us distress
SOLDIER 1. It may not mende for to moote° more, argue
Þis harlotte° muste be hanged here. scoundrel
SOLDIER 2. The mortaise is made fitte þerfore.
SOLDIER 3. Feste on youre fyngeres þan, in feere.° altogether
SOLDIER 4. I wene it wolle neuere come þore-
We foure rayse it noȝt right to-yere.
SOLDIER 1. Say man, whi carpis þou soo?
Thy liftyng was but light.
SOLDIER 2. He menes ther muste be moo
To heve hym vppe on hight.

SOLDIER 3. Now certis, I hope it schall noght nede
To calle to vs more companye.
Methynke we foure schulde do þis dede
And bere hym to ȝoone hille on high.
SOLDIER 1. It muste be done, withouten drede.° doubt
No more, but loke ȝe be redy,
And þis parte schalle I lifte and leede;
On lenghe he schalle no lenger lie.
Therfore nowe makis you boune,° ready
Late bere hym to yoone hill.
SOLDIER 4. Thanne will I bere here doune,
And tente° his tase° vntill. attend; toes

SOLDIER 2. We twoo schall see tille aythir side,
For ellis this werke wille wrie all wrang.
SOLDIER 3. We are redy.
SOLDIER 4. Gode sirs, abide,
And late me first his fete vp fang.° take
SOLDIER 2. Why tente ȝe so to tales þis tyde?
SOLDIER 1. Lifte vppe!
SOLDIER 4. Latte see!
SOLDIER 2. Owe, lifte alang.
SOLDIER 3. Fro all þis harme he schulde hym hyde
And he war God.

SOLDIER 4. Þe deuill hym hang!
SOLDIER 1. For-grete harme haue I hente,° suffered
My schuldir is in soundre.° disjointed
SOLDIER 2. And sertis I am nere schente,° exhausted
So lange haue I borne vndir.

SOLDIER 3. This crosse and I in twoo muste twynne,° part
Ellis brekis my bakke in sondre° sone. assunder
SOLDIER 4. Laye downe agayne and leue youre dynne,
Þis dede for vs will neuere be done.
SOLDIER 1. Assaie sirs, latte se yf any gynne° machine
May helpe hym vppe withouten hone,° delay
For here schulde wight° men worschippe wynne, brave
And noght with gaudis° al day to gone. jests
SOLDIER 2. More wighter men þan we
Full fewe I hope ȝe fynde.
SOLDIER 3. Þis bargayne will noght bee,
For certis me wantis wynde.° breath

SOLDIER 4. So wille° of werke neuere we wore— unable
I hope° þis carle° some cautellis° caste. think; churl; tricks
SOLDIER 2. My bourdeyne satte me wondir soore,
Vnto þe hill I myght noght laste.
SOLDIER 1. Lifte vppe, and sone he schall be þore,
Therfore feste on youre fyngeres faste.
SOLDIER 3. Owe, lifte!
SOLDIER 1. We, loo!
SOLDIER 4. A litill more.
SOLDIER 2. Holde þanne!
SOLDIER 1. Howe nowe?
SOLDIER 2. Þe werste is paste.

SOLDIER 3. He weyes a wikkid weght.
SOLDIER 2. So may we all foure saie,
Or he was heued on heght
And raysed in þis array.

SOLDIER 4. He made vs stande as any stones,
So boustous° was he for to bere. bulky
SOLDIER 1. Nowe raise hym nemely° for þe nonys nimbly
And sette hym be þis mortas heere,
And latte hym falle in alle at ones,
For certis þat payne schall haue no pere.
SOLDIER 3. Heue vppe!
SOLDIER 4. Latte doune, so all his bones
Are asoundre nowe on sides seere.° everywhere
SOLDIER 1. Þis fallyng was more felle
Þan all the harmes he hadde.

Nowe may a man wele telle
Þe leste lith° of þis ladde. — limb

SOLDIER 3. Methynkith þis crosse will noght abide
Ne stande stille in þis morteyse ȝitt.
SOLDIER 4. Att þe firste tyme was it made ouere-wyde;
Þat makis it wave, þou may wele witte.
SOLDIER 1. Itt schall be sette on ilke a side
So that it schall no forther flitte.° — wobble
Goode wegges schall we take þis tyde
And feste þe foote, þanne is all fitte.
SOLDIER 2. Here are wegges arraied
For þat, both grete and smale.
SOLDIER 3. Where are oure hameres laide
Þat we schulde wirke withall?

SOLDIER 4. We haue them here euen atte oure hande.
SOLDIER 2. Gyffe me þis wegge, I schall it in dryue.
SOLDIER 4. Here is anodir ȝitt ordande.° — ready
SOLDIER 3. Do take it me hidir belyue.° — quickly
SOLDIER 1. Laye on þanne faste.
SOLDIER 3. Ȝis, I warrande.
I thryng þame same,[5] so motte I thryve.
Nowe will þis crosse full stabely stande,
All-yf he raue° þei will noght ryve.° — writhes; come apart
SOLDIER 1. Say sir, howe likis you nowe,
Þis werke þat we haue wrought?
SOLDIER 4. We praye youe sais vs howe
Ȝe fele, or faynte ȝe ought.

JESUS. Al men þat walkis by waye or strete,
Takes tente ȝe schalle no trauayle tyne.° — suffering waste
Byholdes myn heede, myn handis, and my feete,
And fully feele nowe, or ȝe fyne,° — go away
Yf any mournyng may be meete,° — equal
Or myscheue mesured vnto myne.
My fadir, þat alle bales° may bete,° — ills; better
Forgiffis þes men that dois me pyne.
What þei wirke wotte thai noght;
Therfore, my fadir, I craue,
Latte neuere þer synnys be sought,° — examined
But see þer saules to saue.

SOLDIER 1. We, harke, he jangelis° like a jay. — chatters
SOLDIER 2. Methynke he patris° like a py.° — patters; magpie

5. "press them together" (Cawley).

SOLDIER 3. He has ben doand° all þis day,   doing so
And made grete meuyng of mercy.
SOLDIER 4. Es þis þe same þat gune° vs say   did
That he was Goddis sone almyghty?
SOLDIER 1. Therfore he felis full felle affraye,°   terror
And demyd° þis day for to dye.   judged
SOLDIER 2. Vath, *qui destruis templum!*[6]
SOLDIER 3. His sawes° wer so, certayne.   sayings
SOLDIER 4. And sirs, he saide to some
He myght rayse it agayne.

SOLDIER 1. To mustir þat he hadde no myght,
For all the kautelles° þat he couthe kaste.   spells
All-yf° he wer in worde so wight,°   even if; brave
For all his force nowe he is feste.
Als Pilate demed is done and dight,°   performed
Therfore I rede þat we go reste.
SOLDIER 2. Þis race° mon be rehersed° right,   action; reported
Thurgh° þe worlde both este and weste.   through
SOLDIER 3. 3aa, late hym hynge here stille
And make mowes° on þe mone.°   grimaces; moon
SOLDIER 4. Þanne may we wende at wille.
SOLDIER 1. Nay goode sirs, noght so sone,

For certis vs nedis anodir note:°   task
Þis kirtill° wolde I of you craue.   robe
SOLDIER 2. Nay, nay sir, we will loke be lotte
Whilke of vs foure fallis it to haue.
SOLDIER 3. I rede° we drawe cutte for þis coote-   advise
Loo, se howe sone—alle sidis to saue.[7]
SOLDIER 4. The schorte cutte schall wynne, þat wele 3e woote,
Whedir itt falle to knyght or knave.
SOLDIER 1. Felowes, 3e thar noght flyte,°   argue
For þis mantell is myne.
SOLDIER 2. Goo we þanne hense tyte,°   quickly
Þis trauayle° here we tyne°[.][8]   labor; waste

6. "Ah, thou that destroyest the temple" (Cawley), misquoted from John 2:19.
7. To protect everyone's interests.
8. The soldier's comment explains the movement of the wagon to the next station.

Everyman

Everyman was probably written in the late fifteenth century although it was first published in London in the early sixteenth century. A morality play, the title character is called to judgment for his life, sees the emptiness of earthly relationships and wealth, is instructed in the path of a holy life, and achieves salvation. The staging illustrates the intended universality as no structures or costumes are specified, and thus dramatically speaking the character is not of a specific place or time. The play is closely related to a Flemish play, *Elkerlyc,* printed in 1495. Whichever play was written first, their similarities show that both are a product of Catholic Europe. While faith in the saving power of God's grace is essential to salvation, the work of grace is expressed through the good works of charity and the performance of the seven sacraments. There is no predestination: God has made all people potentially elect. Mary is invoked to intercede with Christ for sinful man. And the priesthood has powers beyond that of the angels in that it can turn bread and wine into the body and blood of Christ.

The time of the play's composition is, however, indicated by the dialogue about the religious tensions wracking Europe. Priests who sell sacraments and whose children sit by other men's fires are singled out for criticism, and while this is common in literature of the late middle ages, dissatisfaction with the clergy may have been a factor in the Protestant Reformation. The play's intended audience is urban. The parable of the talents informs the play in that Everyman is repeatedly reminded that his life (and his property) are lent to him, not his own possession. But the recurring metaphor of the account book appeals to an audience involved in trade and balancing assets and liabilities both in business and religion. London was already the commercial center of the kingdom, and *Everyman* speaks to an audience distinct from either the aristocracy or the agrarian audience of, for instance, *The Second Shepherds Play.*

The text is that established by A. C. Cawley's *Everyman and Medieval Miracle Plays* (Manchester: Manchester University Press, 1961), 1–28. I have eliminated the headings that announce the entrance of a character. I have also standardized the spellings of characters' names throughout; for example, "Strength" can appear either with that spelling or as "Strengthe" in the text, and I have used the former throughout.

The Moral Play of *Everyman*

Here begynneth a treatyse how the hye Fader of heuen sendeth Dethe to somon euery creature to come and gyue a counte of theyr lyues in this world / and is in maner of a morall playe.

GOD
MESSENGER
DEATH
EVERYMAN
FELLOWSHIP
KINDRED
COUSIN
GOODS
KNOWLEDGE
CONFESSION
BEAUTY
STRENGTH
DISCRETION
FIVE-WITS
ANGEL
DOCTOR
GOOD DEEDS

MESSENGER. I pray you all gyue your audyence,[1]
And here this mater with reuerence,
By fygure° a morall play: form
The Sommonynge of Everyman called it is,
That of our lyues and endynge shewes
How transytory we be all day.°   always
This mater is wonders precyous,
But the entent of it is more gracyous,
And swete to bere awaye.
The story sayth: Man, in the begynnynge
Loke well, and take good heed to the endynge,
Be you neuer so gay!
Ye thynke synne in the begynnynge full swete,
Whiche in the ende causeth the soule to wepe,
Whan the body lyeth in claye.
Here shall you se how Felawshyp and Iolyte,°   cheerfulness
Bothe / Strengthe / Pleasure / and Beaute,
Wyll fade from the as floure° in Maye;   flower
For ye shall here how our Heuen Kynge
Calleth Eueryman to a general rekonynge.
Gyue° audyence, and here what he doth say.   give
GOD. I perceyue, here in my maieste,
How that all creatures be to me vnkynde,
Lyuynge without drede in worldly prosperyte.
Of ghostly° syght the people be so blynde,   spiritual
Drowned in synne, they know me not for theyr God.
In worldely ryches is all theyr mynde;

1. Grant us your attention.

They fere not my rightwysnes,° the sharp rod. — righteousness
My lawe that I shewed, whan I for them dyed,
They forgete clene / and shedynge of my blode rede.
I hanged bytwene two theues, it can not be denyed;
To gete them lyfe I suffred to be deed;
I heled theyr fete[2] / with thornes hurt was my heed:
I coude do no more than I dyde, truely;
And nowe I se the people do clene° for-sake me. — entirely
They vse the seuen deedly synnes dampnable,
As pryde, coueytyse,° wrath, and lechery — avarice
Now in the worlde be made commendable;
And thus they leue of aungelles the heauenly company.
Euery man lyueth so after his owne pleasure,
And yet of theyr lyfe they be nothynge sure.
I se the more that I them forbere
The worse they be fro yere to yere.
All that lyueth appayreth° faste; — is impaired
Therfore I wyll, in all the haste,
Haue a reckenynge of euery mannes persone;
For, and° I leue the people thus alone — if
In theyr lyfe and wycked tempestes,
Veryly they will become moche worse than beestes,
For now one wolde by enuy another vp ete;
Charyte they all do clene forgete.
I hoped well that euery man
In my glory sholde make his mansyon,
And therto I had them all electe;
But now I se, lyke traytours deiecte,[3]
They thanke me not for the pleasure that I to them ment,
Nor yet for theyr beynge that I them haue lent.
I profered the people grete multytude of mercy,
And fewe there be that asketh it hertly.° — heartily
They be so combred with worldly ryches,
That nedes on them I must do iustyce,
On euery man lyuynge without fere.
Where arte thou, Deth, thou myghty messengere?

DETHE. Almyghty God, I am here at your wyll,
Your commaundement to fulfyll.

GOD. Go thou to Eueryman
And shewe hym, in my name,
A pylgrymage he must on hym take,
Whiche he in no wyse may escape;

2. Jesus washed the feet of his disciples, which symbolized the healing power of his ministry.
3. 1) cast away; 2) debased in character.

And that he brynge with hym a sure rekenynge
Without delay or ony taryenge.
DETHE. Lorde, I wyll in the worlde go renne ouer-all,
And cruelly out-serche° bothe grete and small.   search out
Euery man wyll I beset that lyueth beestly
Out of Goddes lawes, and dredeth not foly.
He that loueth rychesse I wyll stryke with my darte,
His syght to blynde, and fro heuen to departe—
Excepte that almes° be his good frende—   charitable acts
In hell for to dwell, world without ende.
Loo, yonder I se Eueryman walkynge.
Full lyttel he thynketh on my comynge;
His mynde is on flesshely lustes and his treasure,
And grete payne it shall cause hym to endure
Before the Lorde, Heuen Kynge.
Everyman, stand styll! Whyder arte thou goynge
Thus gayly? / Hast thou thy Maker forgete?
EUERYMAN. Why askest thou?
Woldest thou wete?°   know
DETHE. Ye, syr. I wyll shewe you:
In grete hast I am sende to the
Fro God out of his mageste.
EUERYMAN. What, sente to me?
DETHE. Ye, certaynly.
Thoughe thou haue forgete hym here,
He thynketh on thee in the heuenly spere,
As, or° we departe, thou shalt knowe.   before
EUERYMAN. What desyreth God of me?
DETHE. That shall I shewe the:
A rekenynge he wyll nedes haue
Without ony lenger respyte.
EUERYMAN. To gyue a rekenynge longer layser° I craue!   leisure
This blynde° mater troubleth my wytte.   obscure
DETHE. On the thou must take a longe iourney;
Therfore thy boke of counte with the thou brynge,
For tourne agayne thou can not by no waye.
And loke thou be sure of thy rekenynge,
For before God thou shalte answere, and shewe
Thy many badde dedes and good but a fewe;
How thou hast spente thy lyfe, and in what wyse,
Before the chefe Lorde of paradyse.
Haue ado that thou were in that waye,
For, wete thou well, thou shalte make none attournay.[4]

4. No one may act in Everyman's place to represent him.

EUERYMAN. Full vnredy I am suche reckenynge to gyue.
I knowe the not. What messenger arte thou?
DETHE. I am Dethe that no man dredeth—
For euery man I rest°—and no man spareth; arrest
For it is Goddes commaundement
That all to me sholde be obedyent.
EUERYMAN. O Deth, thou comest when I had the leest in mynde!
In thy power it lyeth me to save;
Yet of my good wyl I gyue the, yf ye wyl be kynde—
Ye, a thousande pounde shalte thou haue—
And dyfferre this mater tyll another daye.
DETHE. Eueryman, it may not be by no waye.
I set not by golde, syluer, nor rychesse,
Ne by pope / emperour / kynge / duke, ne prynces;
For, and I wolde receyue giftes grete,
All the worlde I myght gete;
But my custome is clene contrary.
I gyue the no respyte. Come hens,° and not tary! hence
EUERYMAN. Alas, shall I haue no lenger respyte?
I may saye Deth gyueth no warnynge!
To thynk on the, it maketh my herte seke,
For all vnredy is my boke of reckenyng.
But xii.° yere and I myght haue a-bydynge,[5] twelve
My countynge-boke I wolde make so clere
That my rekenynge I sholde not nede to fere.
Wherfore, Deth, I pray the, for Goddes mercy,
Spare me tyll I be prouyded of remedy.
DETHE. The auayleth not[6] to crye, wepe, and praye;
But hast the lyghtly that thou were gone the iourneye,
And preue° thy frendes yf thou can. try
For, wete thou well, the tyde abydeth no man,
And in the worlde eche lyuynge creature
For Adams synne must dye of nature.
EUERYMAN. Dethe, yf I sholde this pylgrymage take,
And my rekynynge suerly° make, surely
Shewe me, for saynt charyte,
Sholde I not come agayn shortly?
DETHE. No, Eueryman; and thou be ones there,
Thou mayst neuer more come here,
Trust me veryly.
EUERYMAN. O gracyous God in the hye sete celestyall,
Haue mercy on me in this moost nede!

5. If I could have a delay of twelve years.
6. It gains you nothing.

Shall I haue no company fro this vale terrestryal
Of myne acqueyntaunce, that way me to lede?
DETHE. Ye, yf ony be so hardy
That wolde go with the and bere the company.
Hye the that thou were gone to Goddes magnyfycence,
Thy rekenynge to gyue before his presence.
What, wenest° thou thy lyue is gyuen the, *believe*
And thy worldely gooddes also?
EUERYMAN. I had wende so, veryle.
DETHE. Nay, nay; it was but lende the;
For as soone as thou arte go,
Another a whyle shall haue it, and then go ther-fro,
Euen as thou hast done.
Eueryman, thou arte made!° Thou hast thou wyts fyue, *mad*
And here on erthe wyll not amende thy lyue;
For sodeynly I do come.
EUERYMAN. O wretched caytyfe, wheder shall I flee,
That I myght scape this endless sorowe?
Now, gentyll Deth, spare me tyll to-morowe,
That I may amende me
With good aduysement.
DETHE. Naye, therto I wyll not consent,
Nor no man wyll I respyte,
But to the herte sodeynly I shall smyte
Without ony aduysement.° *warning*
And now out of thy syght I wyll me hy.
Se thou make the redy shortely,
For thou mayst saye this is the daye
That no man lyuynge may scape a-way.
EUERYMAN. Alas, I may well wepe with syghes depe!
Now haue I no maner of company
To helpe me in my iourney, and me to kepe;
And also my wrytynge° is full vnredy. *accounts*
How shall I do now for to exscuse me?
I wolde to God I had neuer be gete!° *been begotten*
To my soule a full grete profyte it had be,
For now I fere paynes huge and grete.
The tyme passeth. Lorde, helpe, that all wrought!
For though I mourne, it auayleth nought.
The day passeth and is almost ago;
I wote not well what for to do.
To whome were I best my complaynt to make?
What and I to Felawshyp thereof spake,
And shewed hym of this sodeyne chaunce?
For in hym is all myne affyaunce;° *trust*
We haue in the worlde so many a daye
Be good frendes in sporte and playe.

I see hym yonder, certaynely.
I trust that he wyll bere me company;
Therefore to hym wyll I speke to ese my sorowe.
Well mette, good Felawshyp, and good morowe!

FELAWSHIP. Eueryman, good morowe, by this daye!
Syr, why lokest thou so pyteously?
If ony thynge be a-mysse, I praye the me saye,
That I may helpe to remedy.

EUERYMAN. Ye, good Felawshyp, ye,
I am in greate ieoparde.

FELAWSHIP. My true frende, shewe to me your mynde.
I wyll not forsake the to my lyues ende,
In the waye of good company.

EUERYMAN. That was well spoken, and louyngly.

FELAWSHIP. Syr, I must nedes knowe your heuynesse;
I have pyte to se you in ony dystresse.
If ony haue you wronged, ye shall reuenged be,
Thoughe I on the grounde be slayne for the,
Though that I knowe before° that I sholde die. beforehand

EUERYMAN. Veryly, Felawshyp, gramercy.° great thanks

FELAWSHIP. Tusshe! by thy thankes I set not a strawe.
Shewe me your grefe, and saye no more.

EUERYMAN. If I my herte sholde to you breke,
And than you to tourne your mynde fro me,
And wolde not me comforte whan ye here me speke,
Than sholde I ten tymes soryer be.

FELAWSHIP. Syr, I saye as I wyll do in dede.

EUERYMAN. Than be you a good frende at nede!
I haue founde you true here-before.

FELAWSHIP. And so ye shall euermore;
For, in fayth, and thou go to hell,
I wyll not forsake the by the waye.

EUERYMAN. Ye speke lyke a good frende; I byleue you well.
I shall deserue it, and I maye.

FELAWSHIP. I speke of no deseruynge, by this daye!
For he that wyll saye, and nothynge do,
Is not worthy with good company to go;
Therfore shewe me the grefe of your mynde,
As to your frende moost louynge and kynde.

EUERYMAN. I shall shewe you how it is:
Commaunded I am to go on a iournaye,
A longe waye harde and daungerous,
And gyue a strayte counte, without delaye,
Before the hye Iuge, Adonay.° God (from Hebrew)
Wherfore, I pray you, bere me company,
As ye haue promysed, in this iournaye.

FELAWSHIP. That is mater in dede! Promyse is duty;

But, and I sholde take suche a vyage on me,
I knowe it well, it sholde be to my payne:
Also it maketh me aferde, certayne.
But let vs take counsell here as well we can,
For your wordes wolde fere a stronge man.
EUERYMAN. Why, ye sayd, yf I had nede,
Ye wolde me neuer forsake, quycke ne deed,[7]
Thoughe it were to hell, truely.
FELAWSHIP. So I sayd, certaynely,
But suche pleasures be set a-syde, the sothe to saye;
And also, yf we toke suche a iournaye,
Whan sholde we agayne come?
EUERYMAN. Naye, neuer agayne tyll the daye of dome.° judgment
FELAWSHIP. In fayth, than wyll not I come there!
Who hath you these tydynges brought?
EUERYMAN. In dede; Deth was with me here.
FELAWSHIP. Now, by God that all hathe brought,
If Deth were the messenger,
For no man that is lyuynge to-daye
I wyll not go that lothe° iournaye— loathsome
Not for the fader that bygate me!
EUERYMAN. Ye promysed other wyse, parde° by God
FELAWSHIP. I wote well I sayd so truely;
And yet, yf thou wylte ete, & drynke & make good chere,
Or haunt to women the lusty company,[8]
I wolde not forsake you whyle the daye is clere,
Trust me veryly!
EUERYMAN. Ye, therto ye wolde be redy!
To go to myrth, solas,° and playe entertainment
Your mynde wyll soner apply,
Than to bere me company in my longe iournaye.
FELAWSHIP. Now, in good fayth, I wyll not that waye;
But and thou wyll murder, or ony man kyll,
In that I wyll helpe the with a good wyll.
EUERYMAN. O, that is a symple aduyce° in dede. foolish advice
Gentyll felawe, helpe me in my necessyte!
We have loued longe, and now I nede:
And now, gentyll Felawshyp, remembre me.
FELAWSHIP. Wheder ye have loued me or no,
By Saynt Iohan,° I wyll not with the go! John
EUERYMAN. Yet I pray the, take the labour & do so moche for me
To brynge me forwarde, for saynt charyte,
And comforte me tyll I come without the towne.

7. Living or dead.
8. "or frequent the pleasant company of women" (Cawley).

FELAWSHIP. Nay, and thou wolde gyue me a newe gowne,
I wyll not a fote with the go;
But, and you had taryed, I wolde not haue lefte the so.
And as now God spede the in thy iournaye,
For from the I wyll departe as fast as I maye.
EUERYMAN. Wheder a-waye, Felawshyp? Wyll thou forsake me?
FELAWSHIP. Ye, by my faye! To God I be-take° the. commend
EUERYMAN. Farewell, good Felawshyp! for the my herte is sore.
A-dewe for euer! I shall se the no more.
FELAWSHIP. In fayth, Eueryman, fare well now at the endynge!
For you I wyll remembre that partynge is mournyng.
EUERYMAN. A-lacke, shall we thus departe in dede—
A, Lady, helpe!—without ony more comforte?
Lo, Felawshyp forsaketh me in my moost nede.
For helpe in this worlde wheder shall I resorte?
Felawship here-before with me wolde merry make,
And now lyttell sorowe for me dooth he take.
It is sayd, "In prosperyte men frendes may fynde,
Whiche in aduersyte be fully vnkynde."
Now wheder for socoure shall I flee,
Syth that Felawshyp hath forsaken me?
To my kynnesmen I wyll truely,
Prayenge them to helpe me in my necessyte.
I byleue that they wyll do so,
For kynde° will crepe where it may not go. kinship
I wyll go saye,° for yonder I se them. assay (test, try)
Where be ye now, my frendes and kynnesmen?
KYNREDE. Here be we now at your commaundement.
Cosyn, I praye you shewe vs your entent
In ony wyse, and not spare.
COSYN. Ye, Eueryman, and to vs declare
If ye be dysposed to go ony-whyder;° anywhere
For, wete you well, we wyll lyue and dye to-gyder.
KYNREDE. In welth and wo we will wyth you holde,
For ouer his kynne a man may be bolde.
EUERYMAN. Gramercy, my frendes and kynnesmen kynde.
Now shall I shewe you the grefe of my mynde.
I was commaunded by a messenger,
That is a hye kynges chefe offycer.
He bad me go on a pylgrymage, to my payne,
And I knowe well I shall neuer come agayne.
Also I must gyue a rekenynge strayte,
For I haue a grete enemy, that hath me in wayte,
Whiche entendeth me for to hynder.
KYNREDE. What a counte is that whiche ye must render?
That wolde I knowe.

EUERYMAN. Of all my workes I must shewe
How I have lyued and my dayes spent;
Also of yll dedes, that I have vsed° [done]
In my tyme, syth lyfe was me lent;
And of all vertues that I haue refused.
Therefore, I praye you, go thyder with me
To helpe to make myn accounte, for saynt charyte.[9]
COSYN. What, to go thyder? Is that the mater?
Nay, Eueryman, I had leuer° fast brede and water [rather]
All this fyue yere and more.
EUERYMAN. Alas, that euer I was bore!° [born]
For now shall I neuer be mery,
If that you forsake me.
KYNREDE. A, syr, what, ye be a mery man!
Take good herte to you, and make no mone.
But one thynge I warne you, by Saynt Anne—
As for me, ye shall go alone.
EUERYMAN. My Cosyn, wyll you not with me go?
COSYN. No, by our Lady! I haue the crampe in my to.
Trust not to me; for, so God me spede,
I wyll deceyue you in your moost nede.
KYNREDE. It auayleth not vs to tyse.° [entice]
Ye shall haue my mayde with all my herte;
She loueth to go to feestes, there to be nyse,° [finicky]
And to daunce, and a-brode to sterte.
I wyll gyue her leue to helpe you in that iourney,
If that you and she may a-gree.
EUERYMAN. Now shewe me the very effecte of your mynde:
Wyll you go with me, or abyde be-hynde?
KYNREDE. Abyde behynde? / Ye, that wyll I, and I maye!
Therfore farewell tyll another daye.
EUERYMAN. How sholde I be mery or gladde?
For fayre promyses men to me make,
But whan I have moost nede, they me forsake.
I am deceyued; that maketh me sadde.
COSYN. Cosyn Eueryman, farewell now,
For veryly I wyll not go with you.
Also of myne owne an vnredy rekenynge
I haue to accounte; therfore I make taryenge.
Now God kepe the, for now I go.
EUERYMAN. A, Iesus, is all come here-to?[10]
Lo, fayre wordes maketh fooles fayne;[11]

9. "Saint" was frequently prefixed to various common nouns, especially charity, cross, spirit, and trinity (Oxford English Dictionary).
10. Has everything come to this?
11. Fools feign to make fair words.

They promyse, and nothynge wyll do, certayne.
My kynnesmen promysed me faythfully
For to a-byde with me stedfastly,
And now fast a-waye do they flee.
Euen so Felawshyp promysed me.
What frende were best me of to prouyde?
I lose my tyme here longer to abyde.
Yet in my mnde a thynge there is:
All my lyfe I haue loued ryches;
If that my Good° now helpe me myght, Goods
He wolde make my herte full lyght.
I wyll speke to hym in this dystresse.
Where arte thou, my Gooddes and ryches?
GOODES. Who calleth me? Eueryman? / What, hast thou haste?
I lye here in corners, trussed and pyled so hye,
And in chestes I am locked so fast,
Also sacked in bagges. Thou mayst se with thyn eye,
I cannot styre;° in packes, lowe I lye. stir
What wolde ye haue? Lyghtly me saye.
EUERYMAN. Come hyder, Good, in al the hast thou may,
For of counseyll I must desyre the.
GOODES. Syr, & ye in the worlde haue sorowe or aduersyte,
That can I helpe you to remedy shortly.
EUERYMAN. It is another dysease that greueth me;
In this worlde it is not, I tell the so.
I am sent for another way to go,
To gyue a strayte counte generall
Before the hyest Iupyter of all.
And all my lyfe I haue had ioye & pleasure in the,
Therfore, I pray the, go with me;
For, parauenture,° thou mayst before God Almyghty peradventure
My rekenynge helpe to clene and puryfye,
For it is sayd euer amonge
That "money maketh all ryght that is wronge."
GOODES. Nay, Eueryman, I synge an other songe.
I folowe no man in suche vyages;
For, and I wente with the,
Thou sholdest fare moche the worse for me.
For bycause on me thou dyd set thy mynde,
Thy rekenynge I haue made blotted and blynde,
That thyne accounte thou cannot make truly—
And that hast thou for the loue of me.
EUERYMAN. That wolde greue me full sore,
Whan I sholde come to that ferefull answere.[12]
Vp, let vs go thyder to-gyder.

12. i.e., answer for his life to God.

GOODES. Nay, not so! I am to brytell, I may not endure.
I wyll folowe no man one fote, be ye sure.
EUERYMAN. Alas, I haue the loued, and had grete pleasure
All my lyfe-dayes on good and treasure.
GOODES. That is to thy dampnacyon, without lesynge,° release
For my loue is contrary to the loue euerlastynge.
But yf thou had me loued moderately durynge,
As to the poore gyue parte of me,
Than sholdest thou not in this dolour be,
Nor in this grete sorowe and care.
EUERYMAN. Lo, now was I deceyued or° I was ware! before
And all I may wyte° my spendynge of time. blame
GOODES. What, wenest° thou that I am thyne? think
EUERYMAN. I had went so.
GOODES. Naye, Eueryman, I saye no.
As for a whyle I was lente the;
A season thou hast had me in prosperyte.
My condycyon is mannes soul to kyll;
If I saue one, a thousande I do spyll.
Wenest thou that I wyll folowe the?
Nay, fro this worlde not, veryle.
EUERYMAN. I had wende otherwyse.
GOODES. Therfore to thy soule Good is a thefe;
For whan thou arte deed, this is my gyse°— practice
Another to deceyue in the same wyse.
As I haue done the, and all to his soules reprefe.° reproof
EUERYMAN. O false Good, cursed thou be,
Thou traytour to God, that hast deceyued me
And caught me in thy snare!
GOODES. Mary, thou brought thy selfe in care,
Whereof I am glad.
I must nedes laugh; I cannot be sad.
EUERYMAN. A, Good, thou hast had longe my hertely loue;
I gaue the that whiche sholde be the Lordes aboue.
But wylte thou not go with me in dede?
I praye the trouth to say.
GOODES. No, so God me spede!
Therfore fare well, and haue good daye.
EUERYMAN. O, to whome shall I make my mone
For to go with me in that heuy° iournaye? heavy
Fyrst Felawshyp sayd he wolde with me gone;
His wordes were very pleasaunt and gaye,
But afterwarde he lefte me alone.
Than spake I to my kynnesmen all in dyspayre,
And also they gaue me wordes fayre;
They lacked no fayre spekynge,

But all forsake me in the endynge.
Than wente I to my Goodes that I loued best,
In hope to haue comforte; but there had I leest,
For my Goodes sharpely dyd me tell
That he bryngeth many to hell.
Than of my selfe I was ashamed,
And so I am worthy to be blamed;
Thus may I well my selfe hate.
Of whome shall now counseyll take?
I thynke that I shall neuer spede
Tyll that I go to my Good-Dede.
But, alas, she is so weke
That she can nother go nor speke;
Yet I wyll venter on her now.
My Good-Dedes, where be you?

GOOD DEDES. Here I lye, colde in the grounde.
Thy synnes hath me sore bounde,
That I can not stere.

EUERYMAN. O, Good Dedes, I stande in fere!
I must you pray of counseyll,
For helpe now sholde° come ryght well. — would

GOOD DEDES. Eueryman, I haue vnderstandyng
That ye be somonde, a counte to make
Before Myssyas,° of Iherusalem kynge; — Messiah
And you do by me, that iournay with you wyll I take.

EUERYMAN. Therfore I come to you my moone to make.
I praye you, that ye wyll go with me.

GOOD DEDES. I wolde full fayne, but I can not stande, veryly.

EUERYMAN. Why, is there ony thynge on you fall?° — fallen

GOOD DEDES. Ye, syr, I may thanke you of all.
If ye had parfytely chered° me, — encouraged
Your boke of counte now full redy had be.
Loke, the bokes of your workes and dedes eke° — also
Ase how they lye vnder the fete,
To your soules heuynes.

EUERYMAN. Our Lorde Iesus, helpe me!
For one letter here I can not se.

GOOD DEDES. There is a blynd rekyninge in tyme of dystres.[13]

EUERYMAN. Good-Dedes, I praye you, helpe me in this nede,
Or elles I am for euer dampned in dede;
Therfore helpe me to make rekenynge
Before the Redemer of all thynge,
That Kynge is, and was, and euer shall.

13. At this time of distress, the account of Everyman's Good Deeds is hard to read.

GOOD DEDES. Eueryman, I am sory of your fall,
And fayne wolde I helpe you, and I were able.
EUERYMAN. Good Dedes, you counseyll I pray you gyue me.
GOOD DEDES. That shall I do, veryly.
Thoughe that on my fete I may not go,
I haue a syster, that shall with you also,
Called Knowlege, whiche shall you abyde,
To helpe you make that dredefull rekenynge.
KNOWLEGE. Eueryman, I wyll go with the and be thy gyde,
In thy moost nede to go by thy syde.
EUERYMAN. In good condycyon I am now in euery thynge,
And am hole content with this good thynge,
Thanked be God my creature.° creator
GOOD DEDES. And whan she hath brought you there
Where thou shalte hele the of thy smarte,° pain
Than go you with your rekyninge & your Good Dedes togyder,
For to make you ioyfull at herte
Before the Blessyd Trynyte.
EUERYMAN. My Good Dedes, gramercy!
I am well content, certaynly,
With your wordes swete.
KNOWLEGE. Now we go togyder louyngly
To Confessyon, that clensynge ryuere.° river
EUERYMAN. For ioy I wepe; I wolde we were there!
But, I pray you, gyue me cognycyon
Where dwelleth that holy man, Confessyon.
KNOWLEGE. In the hous of saluacyon;
We shall fynde hym in that place,
That shall vs comforte, by Goddes grace.
Lo, this is Confessyon. Knele downe & aske mercy,
For he is in good conceyte° with God Almyghty. esteem
EUERYMAN. O gloryous fountayne, that all vnclennes doth claryfy,
Wasshe fro me the spottes of vyce vnclene,
That on me no synne may be sene.
I come with Knowlege for my redempcyon,
Redempte° with herte° and full contrycyon; redeemed; hearty
For I am commaunded a pylgrymage to take,
And grete accountes before God to make.
Now, I praye you, Shryfte° mother of saluacyon, Confession
Helpe my good Dedes for my pyteous exclamacyon.
CONFESSYON. I knowe your sorowe well, Eueryman.
Bycause with Knowlege ye come to me,
I wyll you comforte as well as I can.
And a precyous iewel I wyll gyue the,
Called penaunce, voyder° of aduersyte; expeller
Therwith shall your body chastysed be,

With abstynence & perseueraunce in Goddes seruyture.° service
Here shall you receyue that scourge of me,
Whiche is penaunce stronge that ye must endure,
To remembre thy Sauyour was scourged for the
With sharp scourges, and suffred it pacyently;
So must thou or thou scape[14] that paynful pylgrymage.
Knowlege, kepe hym in this vyage,
And by that tyme Good Dedes wyll be with the.
But in ony wyse, be seker of mercy,
For your tyme draweth fast; and ye wyll saued be,
Aske God mercy, and he wyll graunte truly.
Whan with the scourge of penaunce man doth hym bynde,
The oyle of forgyuenes than shall he fynde.
EUERYMAN. Thanked be God for his gracyous werke!
For now I wyll my penaunce begyn.
This hath reioysed and lyghted my herte,
Though the knottes be paynful and harde, within.
KNOWLEGE. Eueryman, loke your penaunce that ye fulfyll,
What payne that euer it to you be;
And Knowlege shall gyue you counseyll at wyll
How your accounte ye shall make clerely.
EUERYMAN. O eternall God / O heuenly fygure,
O way of ryghtwysenes / O goodly vysyon,
Whiche dyscended downe in a vyrgyn pure
Because he wolde euery man redeme,
Whiche Adam forfayted by his dysobedyence:
O blessyd God-heed, electe and hye deuyne,
Forgyue me my greuous offence!
Here I crye the mercy in this presence.
O ghostly treasure, O raunsomer and redemer,
Of all the worlde hope and conduyter,° guide
Myrrour of ioye, and foundatour° of mercy, founder
Whiche ellumyneth heuen and erth therby,
Here my clamorous complaynt, though it late be,
Receyue my prayers vnworthy in this heuy° lyfe! heavy
Though I be, a synner moost abhomynable,
Yet let my name be wryten in Moyses° table. Moses'
O Mary, praye to the Maker of all thynge,
Me for to helpe at my endynge;
And saue me fro the power of my enemy,
For Deth assayleth me strongly.
And, Lady, that I may by meane of thy prayer
Of your Sones glory to be partynere,
By the meanes of his passyon, I it craue;

14. Before thou can escape.

I beseche you, helpe my soule to saue.
Knowlege, gyue me the scourge of penaunce;
My flesshe therwith shall gyue acqueyntaunce.
I wyll now begyn, yf God gyue me grace.
KNOWLEGE. Eueryman, God gyue you tyme and space!
Thus I bequeth you in the handes of our Sauyour;
Now may you make your rekenyge sure.
EUERYMAN. In the name of the Holy Trynyte,
My body sore punysshed shall be:
Take this, body, for the synne of the flesshe!
Also° thou delytest to go gay and fresshe, in addition
And in the way of dampnacyon thou dyd me brynge;
Therfore suffre now strokes of punysshynge.
Now of penaunce I wyll wade the water clere,
To saue me from purgatory, that sharpe fyre.
GOOD DEDES. I thanke God, now I can walke and go,
And am delyuered of my sykenesse and wo.
Therfore with Eueryman I wyll go, and not spare;
His good workes I will helpe hym to declare.
KNOWLEGE. Now, Eueryman, be mery and glad!
Your Good Dedes cometh now; ye may not be sad.
Now is your Good Dedes hole and sounde,
Goynge vpryght vpon the grounde.
EUERYMAN. My herte is lyght, and shal be euermore;
Now wyll I smyte faster than I dyde before.
GOOD DEDES. Eueryman, pylgryme, my specyall frende,
Blessyd be thou without ende!
For the is preparate the eternall glory.
Ye haue me made hole and sounde,
Therfore I wyll byde by the in every stound.° trial
EUERYMAN. Welcome, my Good Dedes! Now I here thy voyce
I wepe for very swetenes of loue.
KNOWLEGE. Be no more sad, but euer reioyce;
God seeth thy lyuynge in his trone aboue.
Put on this garment to thy behoue,° advantage
Whiche is wette with your teres,
Or elles before God you may it mysse,
Whan you to your iourneys ende come shall.
EUERYMAN. Gentyll Knowlege, what do ye it call?
KNOWLEGE. It is a garment of sorowe;
Fro payne it wyll you borowe.° take from
Contrycyon it is,
That getteth forgyuenes;
He pleaseth God passynge well.
GOOD DEDES. Eueryman, wyll you wear it for your hele?
EUERYMAN. Now blessyd by Iesu, Maryes sone,

From now haue I on true contrycyon;
And lette vs go now without taryenge.
Good Dedes, haue we clere our rekenynge?
GOOD DEDES. Ye, in dede, I haue it here.
EUERYMAN. Than I trust we nede not fere.
Now, frendes, let vs not parte in twayne.
KNOWLEGE. Nay, Eueryman, that wyll we not, certayne.
GOOD DEDES. Yet must thou lede with the
Thre persones of grete myght.
EUERYMAN. Who sholde they be?
GOOD DEDES. Dyscrecyon and Strength they hyght,° — are called
And thy Beaute may not abyde behynde.
KNOWLEGE. Also ye must call to mynde
Your Fyue Wyttes as for your counseylours.
GOOD DEDES. You must haue them redy at all houres.
EUERYMAN. Howe shall I gette them hyder?
KNOWLEGE. You must call them all togeyder,
And they wyll here you in-contynent.° — immediately
EUERYMAN. My frendes, come hyder and be present
Dyscrecyon, Strengthe, my Fyue Wyttes, and Beaute.
BEAUTE. Here at you wyll we be all redy.
What wyll ye that we sholde do?
GOOD DEDES. That ye wolde with Eueryman go,
And helpe hym in his pylgrymage.
Aduyse° you / wyll ye with him or not in that vyage? — consider
STRENGTH. We wyll brynge hym all thyder,
To his helpe and comforte / ye may byleue me.
DYSCRECION. So wyll we go with hym all togyder.
EUERYMAN. Almyghty God, loued may thou be!
I gyue the laude° that I have hyder brought — praise
Strength, Dyscrecyon, Beaute, & V. Wyttes. Lacke I nought;
And my Good Dedes, with Knowlege clere,
All be in company at my wyll here.
I desyre no more to my besynes.
STRENGTH. And I, Strength, wyll by you stande in dystres,
Though thou wolde in batayle fyght on the grounde.
V. WYTTES. And though it were thrugh the worlde rounde,
We wyll not departe for swete nor soure.
BEAUTE. No more wyll I vnto dethes houre,
What so euer thereof befall.
DYSCRECION. Eueryman, aduyse you fyrst of all;
Go with a good aduysement and delyberacyon.
We all gyue you vertuous monycyon° — prediction
That all shall be well.
EUERYMAN. My frendes, harken what I wyll tell:
I praye God rewarde you in his heuenly spere.

Now herken, all that be here,
For I wyll make my testament
Here before you all present.
In alms / halfe my good I wyll gyue with my handes twayne
In the way of charyte with good entent,
And the other halfe styll shall remayne
In queth°, to be retourned there it ought to be. bequest
This I do in despyte of the fende of hell,
To go quyte out of his perell
Euer after and this daye.
KNOWLEGE. Eueryman, herken what I saye:
Go to Presthode, I you aduyse,
And receyue of hym in ony wyse
The holy sacrament and oyntement togyder.
Then shortly se ye tourne agayne hyder;
We wyll all abyde you here.
V. WYTTES. Ye, Eueryman, hye° you that ye redy were. hurry
There is no Emperour, Kynge, Duke, ne Baron,
That of God hath commycyon,
As hath the leest priest in the worlde beynge;
For of the blessyd sacramentes pure and benygne
He bereth the keyes, and thereof hath the cure
For mannes redempcyon—it is euer sure—
Whiche God for our soules medycyne
Gaue vs out of his herte with grete pyne.
Here in this transytory lyfe, for the and me,
The blessyd sacramentes vii.° there be: seven
Baptym, confyrmacyon, with preesthode good,
And the sacrament of Goddes precyous flesshe & blod,
Maryage, the holy extreme vnccyon, and penaunce.
Gracyous sacramentes of hye deuynyte.
EUERYMAN. Fayne wolde I receyue that holy body,
And mekely to my ghostly fader I wyll go.
V. WYTTES. Eueryman, that is the best that ye can do.
God wyll you to saluacyon brynge,
For preesthode excedeth all other thynge:
To vs holy scrypture they do teche,
And conuerteth man fro synne, heuen to reche;
God hath to them more power gyuen
Than to ony aungell that is in heuen.
With v.° wordes he may consecrate, five
Goddes body in flesshe and blode to make,[15]
And handeleth his Maker bytwene his handes.
The preest byndeth and vnbyndeth all bandes,

15. In the Latin mass, "Hoc est enim corpus meum": For this is my body.

Bothe in erthe and in heuen;
Thou mynystres all the sacramentes seuen;
Though we kysse thy fete, thou were worthy.
Thou arte surgyon that cureth synne deedly;
No remedy we fynde vnder God
But all onely preesthode.[16]
Eueryman, God gave preest that dygnyte,
And setteth them in his stede° amonge vs to be; place
Thus be they aboue aungelles in degree.
KNOWLEGE. If preestes be good, it is so, suerly.
But whan Iesu hanged on the crosse with grete smarte,
There he gaue out of his blessyd herte
The seuen sacramentes in grete tourment;
He solde them not to vs, that Lorde omnypotent.
Therfore Saynt Peter the apostell dothe saye
That Iesus curse hath all they
Whiche God theyr Sauyour do by or sell,
Or they for ony money do take or tell.
Synfull preestes gyueth the synners example bad:
Theyr chyldren sytteth by other mennes fires, I have harde;
And some haunteth° womens company frequently seek
With vnclean lyfe, as lustes of lechery.
These be with synn made blynde.
V. WYTTES. I trust to God no suche may we fynd;
Therfore let vs preesthode honour,
And folowe theyr doctryne for our soules socoure.° succor (aid)
We be theyr shepe, and they shepeherdes be
By whome we all be kepte in suerte.
Peas! for yonder I se Eueryman come,
Whiche hath made true satysfaccyon.
GOOD DEDES. Me thynke it is he in dede.
EUERYMAN. Now Iesu be our alder spede![17]
I have receyued the sacrament for my redemp[cy]on,[18]
And than myne extreme vnccyon.
Blessyd be all they that counseyled me to take it!
And now, frendes, let vs go with-out longer respyte.
I thanke God that ye have taryed so longe.
Now set eche of you on this rodde° your honde, rood (cross)
And shortely folowe me.
I go before there I wolde be. God be our gyde!
STRENGTH. Eueryman, we wyll not fro you go,
Tyll ye haue done this vyage longe.

16. Except from the priesthood alone.
17. "be the helper of you all" (Cawley).
18. "redempycon" in Cawley.

DYSCRECION. I, Discrecyon, wyll byde by you also.
KNOWLEGE. And though this pylgrymage be neuer so stronge,° hard
I wyll neuer parte you fro.
STRENGTH. Eueryman, I wyll be as sure by the
As euer I dyde by Iudas Machabee.[19]
EUERYMAN. Alas, I am so faynt I may not stande;
My lymmes vnder me doth folde.
Frendes, let vs not tourn agayn to this lande,
Not for all the worldes golde;
For into this caue must I crepe
And tourne to the erth, and there to slepe.
BEAUTE. What, into this graue? Alas!
EUERYMAN. Ye, there shall you consume more, and lesse.
BEAUTE. And what, sholde I smoder here?
EUERYMAN. Ye, by my fayth, and never more appere.
In this worlde lyue no more we shall,
But in heuen before the hyest Lorde of all.
BEAUTE. I crosse out all this. / Adewe, by Saynt Iohan!
I take° my tappe° in my lappe and am gone. doff, cap
EUERYMAN. What, Beaute, whyder wyll ye?
BEAUTE. Peas! I am defe. I loke not behynde me,
Not & thou woldest gyue me all the golde in thy chest.
EUERYMAN. Alas, wherto may I truste?
Beaute gothe fast awaye from me.
She promysed with me to lyue and dye.
STRENGTH. Eueryman, I wyll the also forsake and denye;
Thy game lyketh me not at all.
EUERYMAN. Why, than, ye wyll forsake me all?
Swete Strength, tary a lytell space.
STRENGTH. Nay, syr, by the rode° of grace! cross
I wyll hye me from the fast,
Though thou wepe to thy herte to-brast.° break
EUERYMAN. Ye wolde euer byde by me, ye sayd.
STRENGTH. Ye, I haue you ferre ynoughe conueyede.
Ye be olde ynoughe, I vnderstande,
Your pylgrymage to take on hande.
I repent me that I hyder came.
EUERYMAN. Strength, you to dysplease I am to blame.
Wyll ye breke promyse that is dette?
STRENGTH. In fayth, I care not.
Thou arte but a foole to complayne;
You spende your speche and wast your brayne.
Go thryst the in to the grounde.

19. Judas Machabee was leader of the Jews in their revolt against Syria in 168 BC, as recounted in the Books of the Maccabees.

EUERYMAN. I had wende surer I sholde you have founde.[20]
He that trustest in his Strength,
She hym deceyueth at the length.
Bothe Strength and Beaute forsaketh me;
Yet they promysed me fayre and louyngly.
DYSCRECION. Eueryman, I wyll after Strength be gone.
As for me I wyll leue you alone.
EUERYMAN. Why, Dyscrecyon, wyll ye forsake me?
DYSCRECION. Ye, in fayth, I wyll go fro the,
For whan Strength goth before
I folowe after euer more.
EUERYMAN. Yet, I pray the, for the loue of the Trynyte,
Loke in my graue ones pyteously.
DYSCRECION. Nay, so nye wyll I not come.
Fare well, euerychone!
EUERYMAN. O, all thynge fayleth, saue God alone—
Beaute, Strength, and Dyscrecyion;
For when Deth bloweth his blast,
They all renne fro me full fast.
V. WYTTES. Eueryman, my leue now of the I take.
I wyll folowe the other, for here I the forsake.
EUERYMAN. Alas, than may I wayle and wepe,
For I toke you for my best frende.
V. WYTTES. I wyll no lenger the kepe.
Now fare well, and there an ende.
EUERYMAN. O Iesu, helpe! All hath forsaken me.
GOOD DEDES. Nay, Eueryman, I wyll byde with the.
I wyll not forsake the in dede;
Thou shalte fynde me a good frend at nede.
EUERYMAN. Gramercy, Good Dedes! Now may I true frendes see;
They haue forsaken me, euerychone;
I loued them better than my Good Dedes alone.
Knowlege, wyll ye forsake me also?
KNOWLEGE. Yea, Eueryman, whan ye to Deth shall go;
But not yet, for no maner of daunger.
EUERYMAN. Gramercy, Knowlege, with all me herte
KNOWLEGE. Nay, yet I wyll not from hens departe
Tyll I se where ye shall be-come.
EUERYMAN. Me thynke, alas, that I must be gone
To make my rekyninge and my dettes paye,
For I se my tyme is nye spent awaye.
Take example, all ye that this do hear or se,
How they that I loued best do forsake me,
Excepte my Good Dedes that bydeth truely.

20. I had thought you would be more reliable.

GOOD DEDES. All erthly thynges is but vanyte:
Beaute, Strength / and Dyscrecyon, do man forsake,
Folysshe frendes and kynnesmen that fayre spake—
All fleeth saue Good Dedes, and that am I.
EUERYMAN. Haue mercy on me, God moost myghty.
And stande by me, thou moder & mayde, holy Mary!
GOOD DEDES. Fere not; I wyll speke for the.
EUERYMAN. Here I crye God mercy.
GOOD DEDES. Shorte our ende and mynysshe our payne;[21]
Let vs go and neuer come agayne.
EUERYMAN. In to thy handes, Lorde, my soul I commende;
Receyue it, Lorde, that it be not lost.
As thou me boughtest,° so me defende, [redeemed]
And saue me from the fendes boost,° [fiend's boast]
That I may appere with that blessyd hoost
That shall be saued at the day of dome.° [judgment]
In manus tuas, of myghtes moost
For euer, *commendo spiritum meum.*[22]
KNOWLEGE. Now hath he suffred that we all shall endure;
The Good Dedes shall make all sure.
Now hath he made endynge;
Me thynketh that I hear aungelles synge,
And make grete ioy and melody
Where Euerymannes soule receyued shall be.
THE AUNGELL. Come, excellente elect spouse, to Iesu!
Here aboue thou shalte go
Bycause of thy synguler vertue.
Now thy soule is taken the body fro,
Thy rekenynge is crystall-clere.
Now shalte thou into the heauenly spere,
Vnto the whiche all ye shall come
That lyueth well before the daye of dome.
DOCTOUR. This morall men may haue in mynde.
Ye herers, take it of worth, olde and yonge,
And forsake Pryde, for he deceyueth you in the ende;
And remembre Beaute, V. Wyttes, Strength, & Dyscrecyon,
They all at the last do Eueryman forsake,
Saue his Good Dedes there dothe he take.
But be-ware, for and they be small,
Before God he hath no helpe at all:
None excuse may be there for Eueryman.
Alas, how shall he do than?
For, after dethe, amendes may no man make,

21. Make our end quick and diminish our pain.
22. Into your hands I commend my spirit.

For than mercy and pyte do him forsake.
If his rekynynge be not clere whan he doth come,
God wyll saye, '*ite, maledicti, in ignem aeternum*'.[23]
And he that hath his accounte hole and sounde,
Hye in heuen he shall be crounde.
Vnto whiche place God brynge vs all thyder,
That we may lyue body and soule togyder.
Thereto helpe the Trynyte!
Amen, saye ye, for saynt charyte.

FINIS.

Thus endeth this morall play of Eueryman.
Imprynted at London in Poules
chyrche yarde by me
Iohan Skot.

23. Go, accursed, into everlasting fire.

PART 2

Drama

OF THE LATE SIXTEENTH AND EARLY SEVENTEENTH CENTURIES

THE LONDON STAGE FROM 1567 (when the first theater specifically meant as a dramatic performance space was built) to the closing of all the theaters by Parliament in 1642 was a commercial theater. Actors (all men and boys) were paid professionals and some were "sharers" in their companies; that is, they received a percentage of the profits. Playwrights, too, were paid by the companies for their scripts, although it was a dicey way to make a living. The audience was urban and diverse, since the price of theater attendance ranged from the inexpensive standing area in public theaters to expensive boxes in the private theaters. Plays would also be performed at court by royal command. The theaters tended to be outside the City of London to avoid the authority of the City's officers, such as the lord mayor. The most expensive aspect of any production was the costumes. Plays were normally performed in the afternoon (starting around 2 p.m.) under natural light in the public theaters and illuminated by candles in the private theaters. Fire in the theaters was a hazard. A large number of genres developed for the audiences of the late sixteenth and early seventeenth centuries: city comedies, tragi-comedies, revenge tragedies, and historical plays were just some of the possibilities staged for enthusiastic crowds. Comedies could be written in either prose or verse, and blank verse was the language of tragedy.

The Shoemaker's Holiday

As is the case with many of the playwrights of the late sixteenth and early seventeenth centuries, little is known of Thomas Dekker's early life. He was apparently born in the early 1570s and may be the Thomas Dekker who was buried in Clerkenwell in 1632. His name may indicate Dutch descent. Some of his plays indicate familiarity with Latin and European texts, but translations of non-English works were not difficult to find, so one can draw no conclusions from this about his level of education. Starting in 1598, he is listed in the account book of Phillip Henslowe as an author and co-author of plays for Henslowe's Admiral's Men. Dekker illustrates the popular and to some extent ephemeral nature of the plays: only twenty plays survive of the nearly sixty with which his name is associated. Many of his plays were written in collaboration with others: Ben Jonson, John Webster, and John Ford are only the most recognizable of the playwrights with whom he worked. Attacked by Jonson in *Poetaster,* Dekker retaliated in *Satiromastix* (both 1601). But by 1603, Dekker and Jonson were collaborators on a royal pageant. He was imprisoned for debt in 1598 and 1599, and from 1613 to 1619. Playwrights received payment (often in advance) for a script, but once the play was sold to the theater company there were no subsequent royalties. Shakespeare's value to his company was as a playwright, but he made his money as a sharer for which he was eligible as an actor in the company. Dekker wrote rapidly: not only plays, but pamphlets about the criminal life of London. It was a precarious existence, and not a career to which anyone from a higher station in life would have been attracted. The title page of *THE SHOMAKERS Holiday OR, The Gentle Craft* proudly announces it was performed for the

The text is based on that established by Fredson Bowers (Cambridge: Cambridge University Press, 1953), 18–89. Also consulted, R. C. Bald's *Six Elizabethan Plays* (Boston: Houghton Mifflin, 1963), 71–130, and Anthony Parr's edition for the New Mermaid series (London: A & C Black, 1990). I have standardized names ("Rafe" for "Raph," "Maior" for "Mayor," etc., for the spelling used most commonly in the text), although I have not standardized other spellings, which can vary from one sentence to the next ("cozen" for "cosin," for example). I have also italicized foreign phrases or speeches (although not Firke's pidgin Dutch).

"Queen on New-years day by the Lord Admiral's Servants"—but the author's name is not listed.

In short, Dekker was a professional writer of popular entertainment for any audience able to pay for admission to the theater. It does not follow from this that his work lacked complexity. *The Shoemaker's Holiday* dramatizes a hierarchical society with social rank mirrored in the play's language: the Earl of Lincolne speaks in blank verse while the shoemakers speak in prose. Moreover, each rank is loyal to its own. Not only does Lincolne not want his cousin to marry the lord mayor's daughter (the mayor is a grocer), but neither Otley nor Simon think it appropriate for Rose to marry Lacie on the grounds that the nobility are unthrifty and generally useless in that they lack a trade. Advantages are conveyed by rank. Lacie can disregard his command in France to pursue Rose and be forgiven by the king since he was not acting out of an ignoble motive (cowardice). The shoemaker Rafe, on the other hand, though newly married, cannot be released from his enlistment.

Still, the play embodies a possibility of social mobility. Rose does marry Lacie with the blessing of the king, and thus the wealthy alderman Otley and the earl become kin through marriage. Simon Eyre can rise to be lord mayor of London through the sudden wealth brought by trade (and openings created among the aldermen through the plague). Virtue is not exclusive to any class; Rafe and Jane are faithful lovers. And the play ends with a joyful Feast of Fools, as on the same day Simon feasts both the apprentices and the king. Social order is not rejected, but a harmonious society is maintained through the portrayal of a London where class is not destiny, and comic reversals lead to general reconciliation of opponents.

The Shoemaker's Holiday: A pleasant Comedie of the Gentle Craft

DRAMATIS PERSONAE

KING OF ENGLAND
EARL OF LINCOLNE *(Sir Hugh Lacy)*
EARL OF CORNWALL
ROGER LACIE, *nephew to Lincoln, afterwards disguised as Hans Meulter*
ASKEW, *cousin to Lacie*
SIR ROGER OTLEY, *Lord Maior of London*
MASTER SCOTT, *friend to Otley*
Hammon, *a city gentleman*
WARNER, *cousin to Hammon*
SIMON EYRE, *shoemaker and afterwards Lord Maior*
HODGE (ALSO CALLED RODGER), *foreman to Eyre*
FIRKE, *journeyman to Eyre*
RAFE DAMPORT, *journeyman to Eyre*
LOUELL, *servant to the king*
DODGER, *parasite to Lincoln*
DUTCH SKIPPER
BOY, *apprentice to Eyre*

BOY, *servant to Otley*
MARGERY, *wife to Eyre*
ROSE, *daughter to Otley*
IANE (JANE), *wife to Rafe Damport*
SIBIL, *maid to Rose*
NOBLEMEN, SOLDIERS, HUNTSMEN, SHOEMAKERS, APPRENTICES, SERVANTS

[ACT I, SCENE I]

Enter Lord Maior, Lincolne.

LINCOLNE. My Lord Maior, you haue sundrie times
Feasted my selfe, and many Courtiers more,
Seldome, or neuer can we be so kind,
To make requitall of your courtesie:
But leauing this, I heare my cousin *Lacie*
Is much affected to your daughter *Rose.*
LORD MAIOR. True my good Lord, and she loues him so wel,
That I mislike her boldnesse in the chase.
LINCOLNE. Why, my lord Maior, think you it then a shame,
To ioyne a *Lacie* with an *Otleys* name?
L. MAIOR. Too meane is my poore girle for his high birth,
Poore Cittizens must not with Courtiers wed,
Who will in silkes, and gay apparrell spend
More in one yeare than I am worth, by farre,
Therefore your honour neede not doubt my girle.
LINCOLNE. Take heede my Lord, aduise you what you do,
A verier vnthrift liues not in the world,
Then is my cosen, for Ile tel you what,
Tis now almost a yeare since he requested
To trauell countries for experience,
I furnisht him with coyne, billes of exchange,
Letters of credite, men to waite on him,
Solicited my friends in *Italie*
Well to respect him: but to see the end:
Scant had he iourneied through halfe *Germanie,*
But all his coyne was spent, his men cast off,
His billes imbezeld, ° and my iolly coze, — cashed in
Asham'd to shew his bankerupt presence here,
Became a Shoomaker in *Wittenberg,*[1]
A goodly science° for a gentleman — trained skill
Of such discent: now iudge the rest by this.
Suppose your daughter haue a thousand pound,

1. German city on the Elbe, closely associated with the Protestant Reformation.

He did consume me more in one halfe yeare,
And make him heyre to all the wealth you haue,
One twelue moneth's rioting wil waste it all,
Then seeke (my Lord) some honest Cittizen
To wed your daughter to.

L. MAIOR. I thank your Lordship,
[*Aside.*] Wel Foxe, I vnderstand your subtiltie,
As for your nephew, let your lordships eie
But watch his actions, and you neede not feare,
For I haue sent my daughter farre enough,
And yet your cosen *Rowland* might do well
Now he hath learn'd an occupation,
[*Aside.*] And yet I scorn to call him son-in-law.

LINCOLNE. I but I haue a better trade for him,
I thanke his grace he hath appointed him,
Chiefe colonell of all those companies
Mustred in *London* and the shires about,
To serue his highnesse in those warres of *France:*
See where he comes:

Enter Louell, Lacie, *and* Askew

Louell, what news with you?

LOUELL. My Lord of *Lincolne,* 'tis his highnesse will,
That presently your cosen ship for *France*
With all his powers, he would not for a million,
But they should land at *Deepe*° within foure daies. — Dieppe

LINCOLNE. Goe certifie his grace, it shall be done:

Exit Lovell.

Now cosen *Lacie,* in what forwardnesse
Are all your companies?

LACIE. All wel prepar'd,
The men of *Hertfordshire* lie at Mile end,
Suffolke, and *Essex,* traine in Tuttle° fields, — Tothill
The *Londoners,* and those of *Middlesex,*
All gallantly prepar'd in Finsbury,
With frolicke spirits long for their parting hower.° — hour

L. MAIOR. They haue their imprest,° coates, and furniture,° — pay; equipment
And if it please your cosen *Lacie* come
To the Guild Hall, he shall receiue his pay,
And twentie pounds besides my bretheren
Will freely giue him, to approue° our loues — demonstrate
We beare vnto my lord, your vncle here.

LACIE. I thanke your honour.

LINCOLNE. Thankes my good Lord Maior.

L. MAIOR. At the Guild Hal we will expect your comming.

Exit.

LINCOLNE. To approue your loues to me? no, subtiltie:
Nephew, that twentie pound he doth bestow
For ioy to rid you from his daughter *Rose:*
But cosens both, now here are none but friends,
I would not haue you cast an amorous eie
Vpon so meane a project, as the loue
Of a gay wanton painted cittizen,
I know this churle, euen in the height of scorne,
Doth hate the mixture of his bloud with thine,
I pray thee do thou so, Remember, coze,
What honourable fortunes wayt on thee,
Increase the kings loue, which so brightly shines,
And gilds thy hopes, I haue no heire but thee:
And yet not thee, if with a wayward spirit
Thou start from the true byas of my loue.
LACIE. My Lord, I will (for honor (not desire
Of land or liuings) or to be your heire)
So guide my actions in pursuit of *France,*
As shall adde glorie to the *Lacies* name.
LINCOLNE. Coze, for those words heres thirtie Portugues[2]
And Nephew *Askew,* there's a few for you,
Faire Honour, in her loftiest eminence
Staies in *France* for you, till you fetch her thence,
Then Nephewes, clap swift wings on your dissignes,
Be gone, be gone, make haste to the Guild Hall,
There presently Ile meete you, do not stay:
Where honour becons, shame attends delay.

Exit.

ASKEW. How gladly would your vncle haue you gone?
LACIE. True coze, but Ile ore-reach his policies,
I haue some serious businesse for three dayes,
Which nothing but my presence can dispatch,
You therefore cosen with the companies,
Shall haste to *Douer,* there Ile meete with you,
Or, if I stay past my prefixed time,
Away for *France,* weele meet in *Normandie*[.]
The twentie pounds my Lord Maior giues to me
You shall receiue, and these ten portugues,
Part of mine vncle's thirtie, gentle coze,
Haue care to our great charge, I know, your wisedom
Hath tride it selfe in higher consequence.
ASKEW. Coze, al my selfe am yours, yet haue this care,
To lodge in *London* with al secrecie,
Our vncle *Lincolne* hath (besides his owne)

2. Large gold coins from Portugal.

Many a iealous eie, that in your face
Stares onely to watch meanes for your disgrace.

LACIE. Stay, cosen, who be these?

Enter Simon Eyre, *his* Wife, Hodge, Firk, Iane,
and Rafe *with a peece*° musket

EYRE. Leaue whining, leaue whining, away with this whimpring, this pewling, these blubbering teares, and these wet eies! Ile get thy husband discharg'd, I warrant thee, sweete *Iane:* go to!

HODGE. Master, here be the captaines.

EYRE. Peace *Hodge,* husht ye knaue, husht.

FIRKE. Here be the caualiers, and the coronels, maister.

EYRE. Peace *Firke,* peace my fine *Firke,* Stand by with your pishery pasherie, away, I am a man of the best presence, Ile speake to them, and they were Popes: gentlemen, captaines, colonels, commanders: braue men, braue leaders, may it please you to giue me audience, I am *Simon Eyre,* the mad Shoomaker of Towerstreete, this wench with the mealy mouth that will neuer tire, is my wife, I can tel you, heres *Hodge* my man, and my foreman, heres *Firke,* my fine firking iourneyman, and this is blubbered *Iane,* al we come to be suters for this honest *Rafe,* keepe him at home, and as I am a true shoomaker, and a gentleman of the Gentle Craft, buy spurs your self, and Ile find ye bootes these seuen yeeres.

WIFE. Seuen yeares, husband?

EYRE. Peace Midriffe, peace, I know what I do, peace.

FIRKE. Truly master cormorant, you shal do God good seruice to let *Rafe* and his wife stay together, shees a yong new married woman, if you take her husband away from her a night, you vndoo her, she may beg in the daytime, for hees as good a workman at a pricke and an awle, as any is in our trade.

IANE. O let him stay, else I shall be vndone.

FIRKE. I truly, she shal be laid atone side like a paire of old shooes else, and be occupied for no vse.

LACIE. Truly my friends, it lies not in my power,
The *Londoners* are prest,[3] paide, and set forth
By the Lord Maior, I cannot change a man.

HODGE. Why, then you were as good be a corporall, as a colonel, if you cannot discharge one good fellow; and I tell you true, I thinke you doe more than you can answere, to presse a man within a yeare and a day of his marriage.

EYRE. Wel said melancholy *Hodge,* gramercy my fine foreman.

WIFE. Truly gentlemen, it were il done, for such as you, to stand so

3. Put into military service.

stiffely against a poore young wife: considering her case, she is new married, but let that passe: I pray deale not roughly with her, her husband is a yong man, and but newly entred, but let that passe.

EYRE. Away with your pisherie pasherie, your pols and your edipolls,[4] peace, Midriffe, silence, Cisly Bumtrincket, let your head speake.

FIRKE. Yea and the hornes too, master.

EYRE. Tawsoone,° [too soon] my fine *Firk*, tawsoone, peace scoundrels: see you this man, Captaines? you will not release him, wel let him go, hee's a proper shot, let him vanish, peace *Iane*, drie vp thy teares, theile make his powder dankish, take him braue men, *Hector* of *Troy* was an hackney° [cab horse] to him, *Hercules* and *Termagant*[5] scoundrelles, Prince *Arthurs* Round table, by the Lord of Ludgate, nere fed such a tall,° [brave] such a dapper swordsman, by the life of *Pharo*, a braue resolute swordman: peace *Iane*, I say no more, mad knaues.

FIRKE. See, see *Hodge*, how my maister raues in commendation of *Rafe*.

HODGE. *Rafe*, thart a gull° [fool] by this hand, an thou goest not.

ASKEW. I am glad (good Master *Eyre*) it is my hap
To meete so resolute a souldiour.
Trust me, for your report, and loue to him,
A common slight regard shall not respect him.

LACIE. Is thy name *Rafe*?

RAFE. Yes, sir.

LACIE. Giue me thy hand,
Thou shalt not want, as I am a gentleman:
Woman, be patient, God (no doubt) wil send
Thy husband safe againe, but he must go,
His countries quarrel sayes, it shall be so.

HODGE. Thart a gull, by my stirrop,[6] if thou dost not goe, I wil not haue thee strike thy gimblet° [tool for boring holes] into these weake vessels, pricke thine enemies *Rafe*.

Enter Dodger.

DODGER. My lord, your vncle on the Tower hill,
Stayes with the lord Maior and the Aldermen,
And doth request you with al speede you may
To hasten thither.

ASKEW. Cosin, let vs go.

LACIE. *Dodger*, runne you before, tel them we come.

Exit Dodger.

4. "pols" is a nonsense word, "edipolls" means "foolish chatter."
5. In Bald, the line reads, "A supposed Mohammedan deity, boisterous and boastful."
6. Cobbler's vise.

This *Dodger* is mine vncles parasite,
The arrantst varlet that e're breathd on earth,
He sets more discord in a noble house
By one daies broching of his pickethanke tales,[7]
Than can be salu'd° againe in twenty yeares, healed
And he (I feare) shall go with vs to *France,*
To prie into our actions.

ASKEW. Therefore, coze,
It shall behooue you to be circumspect.

LACIE. Feare not good cosen: *Rafe,* hie to your colours.° regiment's flag

[*Exit* Lacie *and* Askew.]

RAFE. I must, because there's no remedie,
But gentle maister and my louing dame,
As you haue alwaies beene a friend to me,
So in mine absence thinke vpon my wife.

IANE. Alas my *Rafe.*

WIFE. She cannot speake for weeping.

EYRE. Peace you crackt groates,° you mustard tokens,[8] disquiet not the braue souldier, goe thy waies *Rafe.* coins worth 4d.

IANE. I, I, you bid him go, what shal I do when he is gone?

FIRKE. Why be doing with me, or my felow *Hodge,* be not idle.

EYRE. Let me see thy hand *Iane,* this fine hand, this white hand, these prettie fingers must spin, must card, must worke, worke you bombast cotton-candle-queane; worke for your liuing, with a pox to you: hold thee *Rafe,* heres fiue sixpences for thee, fight for the honour of the *Gentle Craft,* for the gentlemen Shoomakers, the courageous Cordwainers, the flower of saint *Martins,* the mad knaues of Bedlem, Fleetstreete, Towerstreete and white Chapell,[9] cracke me the crownes of the French knaues; a poxe on them, cracke them, fight, by the lord of Ludgate, fight my fine boy.

FIRKE. Here *Rafe,* here's three two pences, two carry into *France,* the third shal wash our soules at parting (for sorrow is drie) for my sake, firke the *Basa mon cues.*[10]

HODGE. *Rafe,* I am heauy at parting; but heres a shilling for thee, God send thee to cramme thy slops with French crownes, and thy enemies bellies with bullets.

RAFE. I thanke you maister, and I thanke you all:
Now, gentle wife, my louing louely *Iane,*
Rich men at parting, giue their wiues rich gifts,
Iewels and rings, to grace their lilie hands,

7. Tales told to elicit thanks.
8. Informal currency used by shopkeepers.
9. Bedlam, Fleetstreet, Towerstreet, and White Chapel are neighborhoods in the City of London.
10. From the French *baisez mon cul,* or "kiss my ass."

Thou know'st our trade makes rings for womens heeles:
Here take this paire of shooes cut out by *Hodge,*
Sticht by my fellow *Firke,* seam'd by my selfe,
Made vp and pinckt,° with letters for thy name, ornamented
Weare them my deere *Iane,* for thy husbands sake,
And euerie morning, when thou pull'st them on,
Remember me, and pray for my returne,
Make much of them, for I haue made them so,
That I can know them from a thousand mo.

Sound drumme, enter Lord Maior, Lincolne, Lacie, Askew, Dodger, *and souldiers. They passe over the stage,* Rafe *falles in amongest them,* Firke *and the rest cry farewel, etc. and so Exeunt.*

[ACT I, SCENE II]

Enter Rose *alone making a Garland.*

ROSE. Here sit thou downe vpon this flowry banke,
And make a garland for thy *Lacies* head,
These pinkes, these roses, and these violets,
These blushing gilliflowers, these marigoldes,
The faire embrodery of his coronet,
Carry not halfe such beauty in their cheekes,
As the sweete countanaunce of my Lacie doth.
O my most vnkinde father! O my starres!
Why lowrde you so at my nativity,
To make me loue, yet liue robd of my loue?
Here as a theefe am I imprisoned
(For my dear Lacies sake) within those walles,
Which by my fathers cost were builded vp
For better purposes: Here must I languish
For him that doth as much lament (I know)
Mine absence, as for him I pine in woe.

Enter Sibil.

SIBIL. Good morrow yong Mistres, I am sure you make that garland for me, against I shall be Lady of the Haruest.

ROSE. *Sibil,* what news at *London?*

SIBIL. None but good: my lord Maior your father, and maister *Philpot* your vncle, and maister *Scot* your coosin, and mistris *Frigbottom* by Doctors Commons, doe all (by my troth) send you most hearty commendations.

ROSE. Did *Lacie* send kind greetings to his loue?

SIBIL. O yes, out of cry, by my troth, I scant knew him, here a wore a scarffe, and here a scarfe, here a bunch of feathers, and here precious stones and iewells, and a paire of garters: O monstrous!

like one of our yellow silke curtains, at home here in Old-ford house, here in maister *Bellymounts* chamber. I stoode at our doore in Cornehill, lookt at him, he at me indeed, spake to him, but he not to me, not a word, marry gup,° thought I, with a wanion,° he passt by me as prowde, marry foh, are you growne humorous,° thought I? and so shut the doore, and in I came.

go up / vengeance / moody

ROSE. O *Sibil,* how dost thou my *Lacie* wrong?
My *Rowland* is as gentle as a lambe,
No doue was euer halfe so milde as he.

SIBIL. Milde? yea, as a bushel of stampt crabs, he lookt vpon me as sowre as veriuice:° goe thy wayes thought I, thou maist be much in my gaskins,° but nothing in my neatherstocks:° this is your fault mistris, to loue him that loues not you, he thinkes scorne to do as he's done to, but if I were as you, Ide cry, go by *Ieronimo,* go by,[11] Ide set mine olde debts against my new driblets, And the hares foot against the goose giblets, For if euer I sigh, when sleepe I shoulde take, Pray God I may lose my mayden-head when I wake.

sour juice / breeches; / stockings

ROSE. Will my loue leave me then, and go to *France?*

SIBIL. I knowe not that, but I am sure I see him stalke before the souldiers, by my troth, he is a propper man, but he is proper that proper doth, let him goe snicke-vp° yong mistris.

hang

ROSE. Get thee to *London,* and learne perfectly,
Whether my *Lacie* go to *France,* or no:
Do this, and I will giue thee for thy paines,
My cambricke apron, and my romish gloues,
My purple stockings, and a stomacher.[12]
Say, wilt thou do this *Sibil* for my sake?

SIBIL. Will I quoth a? at whose suite? by my troth yes, Ile go, a cambricke apron, gloues, a paire of purple stockings, and a stomacher, Ile sweat in purple mistris for you, [I]le take any thing that comes a Gods name, O rich, a Cambricke apron; Faith, then have at vp tailes all,[13] Ile go, Iiggy, Ioggy to *London,* and be here in a trice, young mistris.

Exit.

ROSE. Do so good Sibil, meane time wretched I
Will sit and sigh for his lost companie.

Exit.

11. From Thomas Kyd's *The Spanish Tragedy,* act 3, scene 12, line 31.

12. A decorated panel that fills in the front of a woman's gown or bodice.

13. In the seventeenth century, "Up Tails All" was a popular song about ducks dabbling for food. Here Sibil seems to mean for these rewards she will cheerfully go dig for information.

[ACT I, SCENE III]

Enter Rowland Lacie *like a Dutch Shooe-maker.*

LACIE. How many shapes haue gods and Kings deuisde,
Thereby to compasse their desired loues!
It is no shame for *Rowland Lacie* then,
To clothe his cunning with the Gentle Craft,
That thus disguisde, I may vnknowne possesse,
The onely happie presence of my *Rose:*
For her haue I forsooke my charge in *France,*
Incurd the Kings displeasure, and stir'd vp
Rough hatred in mine vncle *Lincolnes* brest:
O loue, how powerfull art thou, that canst change
High birth to basenesse, and a noble mind,
To the meane semblance of a shooemaker?
But thus it must be: for her cruell father,
Hating the single vnion of our soules,
Has secretly conueyd my *Rose* from *London,*
To barre me of her presence, but I trust,
Fortune and this disguise will furder me
Once more to view her beautie, gaine her sight.
Here in Towerstreete, with *Eyre* the shooe-maker,
Meane I a while to worke, I know the trade,
I learn't it when I was in *Wittenberge:*
Then cheere thy hoping sprites, be not dismaide,
Thou canst not want, do fortune what she can,
The Gentle Craft is liuing for a man.

Exit.

[ACT I, SCENE IV]

Enter Eyre *making himselfe readie.*° — getting dressed

EYRE. Where be these boyes, these girles, these drabes, these scoundrels, they wallow in the fat brewisse° of my bountie, and licke vp the crumbs of my table, yet will not rise to see my walkes cleansed: come out, you powder-beef°-queanes, what *Nan,* what *Madge-mumble-crust,* come out you fatte Midriff-swag-belly whores, and sweepe me these kennels,° that the noysome stench offende not the noses of my neighbours: what *Firke* I say, what *Hodge?* open my shop windowes, what *Firke* I say.

brewisse: broth
powder-beef: corned beef
kennels: gutter

Enter Firke.

FIRKE. O master, ist you that speake bandog[14] and bedlam this morning, I was in a dreame, and muzed what madde man was got into the streete so earlie, haue you drunke this morning that your throate is so cleere?

EYRE. Ah well saide *Firke,* well said *Firke,* to worke my fine knaue, to worke, wash thy face, and thou't be more blest.

FIRKE. Let them wash my face that will eate it, good maister send for a sowce wife,° if youle haue my face cleaner. pickled pork seller

Enter Hodge.

EYRE. Away, slouen, auaunt, scoundrell, good morrow, *Hodge,* good morrow, my fine foreman.

HODGE. O maister, good morrow; yare an earlie stirrer, heeres a faire morning, good morrow *Firke,* I could haue slept this howre, heeres a braue day towards.

EYRE. Oh haste to worke my fine foreman, haste to worke.

FIRKE. Maister I am drie as dust, to heare my fellow *Roger* talke of faire weather, let vs pray for good leather, and let clownes and plowboyes, and those that worke in the fieldes, pray for braue dayes, wee worke in a drie shop, what care I if it raine?

Enter Eyres Wife.

EYRE. How now dame *Margery,* can you see to rise? Trip and go, call vp the drabs your maides.

WIFE. See to rise? I hope tis time inough, tis earlie inough for any woman to be seene abroad, I maruaile how manie wiues in Tower-street are vp so soon? Gods me, tis not noone, heres a yawling.° howling

EYRE. Peace *Margery,* peace, wheres *Cisly Bumtrinket,* your maide? She has a priuie fault, she fartes in her sleepe, call the quean vp, if my men want shooethread, [I]le swinge her in a stirrop.

FIRKE. Yet thats but a drie beating, heres still a signe of drought.

Enter Lacie *singing.*

LACIE. *Der was een bore van Gelderland*
Frolick si byen,
He was als dronck he cold nyet stand,
Vpsolce se byen,
Tap eens de canneken,
Drincke schone mannekin.[15]

FIRKE. Maister, for my life yonders a brother of the Gentle Craft, if he beare not Saint *Hughes* bones,° Ile forfeit my bones, hees shoemaker's tools

14. "Fiercely (like a watch dog)" (Bald).

15. "There was a farmer of Gelderland, / Jolly they be; / He was so drunke he could not stand, / Tipsy (?) they be. / Tap once with the can, / Drink, pretty little man" (Bald).

some vplandish workman, hire him good master, that I may learne some gibble, gabble, twill make vs worke the faster.

EYRE. Peace, *Firke,* a hard world, let him passe, let him vanish, we have iourneymen enow, peace, my fine *Firke.*

WIFE. Nay, nay, y'are best follow your mans councell, you shal see what will come on't: We haue not men enow, but we must entertaine euerie butter-boxe:[16] but let that passe.

HODGE. Dame, fore God if my maister follow your counsell, heele consume little beefe, he shal be glad of men an hee can catch them.

FIRKE. I that he shall.

HODGE. Fore God a proper man, and I warrant a fine workman: maister farewell, dame adew,° if such a man as he cannot find worke, *Hodge* is not for you. adieu

Offer[s] to goe.

EYRE. Stay my fine *Hodge.*

FIRKE. Faith, and your foreman goe, dame you must take a iourney to seeke a new iourneyman, if *Roger* remoue, *Firke* followes, if saint *Hughs* bones shall not be set a worke, I may pricke mine awle in the wals, and goe play: fare ye wel master, God buy dame.

EYRE. Tarrie my fine *Hodge,* my briske foreman, stay *Firke,* peace pudding broath, by the lord of Ludgate I loue my men as my life, peace you gallimafrie,[17] Hodge if he want work Ile hire him, one of you to him, stay, he comes to vs.

LACIE. *Goeden dach meester, ende v vro oak.*[18]

FIRKE. Nayls° if I should speake after him without drinking, I shuld choke, and you frind Oake, are you of the Gentle Craft? God's nails (an oath)

LACIE. *Yaw, yaw, Ik bin den skomaker.*

FIRKE. Den skomaker quoth a, and heark you skomaker, haue you all your tooles, a good rubbing pinne, a good stopper, a good dresser, your foure sorts of awles, and your two balles of waxe, your paring knife, your hand and thumb-leathers, and good saint *Hughs* bones to smooth vp your worke[?]

LACIE. *Yaw yaw be niet vorveard, Ik hab all de dingen, voour mack skoes groot and cleane.*[19]

FIRKE. Ha ha good maister hire him, heele make me laugh so that I shal worke more in mirth, then I can in earnest.

EYRE. Heare ye friend, haue ye any skill in the mistery of Cordwainers?

16. The Dutch proverbially ate enormous quantities of butter.

17. "gallimaufry". originally meaning stew, but also an unorganized collection of things, here the wife's opinions.

18. "Good day, master, and you too, Lady" (Bald).

19. "Yes, yes, don't be afraid. I have all the things for making shoes great and small" (Bald).

LACIE. *Ik weet niet wat yow seg ich verstaw you niet.*[20]

FIRKE. Why thus man Ich verste v niet, quoth a.[21]

LACIE. *Yaw, yaw, yaw, ick can dat wel doen.*

FIRKE. Yaw, yaw, he speakes yawing like a Iacke daw, that gapes to be fed with cheese curdes, O heele giue a villanous pul at a Can of double Beere, but Hodge and I haue the vantage, we must drinke first, because wee are the eldest iourneymen.

EYRE. What is thy name?

LACIE. *Hans, Hans, Meulter.*

EYRE. Giue me thy hand, th'art welcome, *Hodge* entertaine him, *Firke* bid him welcome, come *Hans,* runne wife, bid your maids, your Trullibubs,[22] make readie my fine mens breakefasts: to him *Hodge.*

HODGE. *Hans,* th'art welcome, vse thyselfe friendly, for we are good fellowes, if not thou shalt be fought with, wert thou bigger than a Giant.

FIRKE. Yea and drunke with, wert thou *Gargantua,* my maister keepes no cowards, I tel thee: hoe, boy, bring him an heele-block, heers a new iourneyman.

Enter boy.

LACIE. *O ich wersto you, Ich moet een halue dossen Cans betaelen:* here boy *nempt dis skilling, tap eens freelicke.*[23]

Exit boy.

EYRE. Quicke snipper snapper, away: *Firke,* scowre thy throate, thou shalt wash it with Castilian licuor, come, my last of the fiues,

Enter boy.

give me a Can, haue to thee *Hans,* here *Hodge,* here *Firke,* drinke you mad Greeks, and worke like true Troians, and pray for *Simon Eyre,* the Shoomaker: here *Hans,* and th'art welcome.

FIRKE. Lo dame you would haue lost a good fellow that wil teach vs to laugh, this beere cam hopping in wel.

WIFE. *Simon* it is almost seuen.

EYRE. Is't so dame clapper dudgeon, is't seuen a clocke, and my mens breakfast not readie? trip and goe you sowst cunger,[24] away, come, you madde Hiperboreans, follow me, *Hodge,* follow me *Hans,* come after my fine *Firke,* to worke, to worke a while, and then to breakfast.

20. "I don't know what you say, I don't understand you" (Bald).

21. The implication is that Firke imitates the actions of a shoemaker here.

22. A butcher's term for the entrails of animals, also anything trifling.

23. "O, I understand you, I must pay for a half dozen cans; here, boy, take this shilling; draw (from the cask) freely" (Bald).

24. i.e., soused (pickled) conger eel.

FIRKE. Soft, yaw, yaw, good *Hans,* though my master have no more wit, but to call you afore mee, I am not so foolish to go behind you, I being the elder iourneyman.

Exeunt.

[ACT II, SCENE I]

Hollowing within. Enter Warner, *and* Master Hammon, *like hunters.*

HAMMON. Cosen, beate euery brake, the game's not farre,
This way with winged feete he fled from death,
Whilst the pursuing hounds senting his steps,
Find out his high way to destruction:
Besides, the millers boy told me euen now,
He saw him take soile,° and he hallowed him — refuge
Affirming him to have been so embost° — foaming at the mouth
That long he could not hold.
WARNER. If it be so,
Tis best we trace these meddowes by Old Ford.

A noise of hunters within, enter a boy.

HAMMON. How now, boy, wheres the deere? speak, saw'st thou him?
BOY. O, yea I saw him leape through a hedge, and then ouer a ditch, then at my Lord Maiors pale,° over he skipt me, and in he went me, and holla the hunters cride, and there boy there boy, but there he is, a mine honestie. — fence
HAMMON. Boy God amercy, cosen, let's away,
I hope we shal find better sport to day.

Exeunt.

[ACT II, SCENE II]

Hunting within, enter Rose, *and* Sibil.

ROSE. Why *Sibil* wilt thou proue a forrester?
SIBIL. Vpon some no, forrester, go by: no faith mistris, the deere came running into the barne through the orchard, and ouer the pale, I wot wel, I lookt as pale as a new cheese to see him, but whip saies goodman *Pinne-close,* vp with his flaile, and our *Nicke* with a prong, and downe he fel, and they vpon him, and I vpon them, by my troth we had such sport, and in the end we ended him, his throate we cut, flead him, vnhorn'd him, and my lord Maior shal eat of him anon when he comes.

Hornes sound within.

ROSE. Heark heark, the hunters come, y'are best take heed:
Theyle haue a saying to you for this deede.

Enter Hammon, Warner, huntsmen, *and* boy

HAMMON. God saue you faire ladies.
SIBIL. Ladies! O gross!° stupid
WARNER. Came not a bucke this way?
ROSE. No, but two Does.
HAMMON. And which way went they? faith weel hunt at those.
SIBIL. At those? vpon some no: when, can you tell?
WARNER. Vpon some, I.
SIBIL. Good Lord!
WARNER. Wounds° then farewell. God's wounds
HAMMON. Boy, which way went he?
BOY. This way sir he ranne.
HAMMON. This way he ranne indeede, faire mistris *Rose,*
Our game was lately in your orchard seene.
WARNER. Can you aduise, which way he tooke his flight?
SIBIL. Followe your nose, his hornes will guide you right.
WARNER. Thart a mad wench.
SIBIL. O rich!
ROSE. Trust me, not I.
It is not like that the wild forrest deere,
Would come so neare to places of resort,
You are deceiu'd, he fled some other way.
WARNER. Which way, my sugar-candie, can you shew?
SIBIL. Come vp good honnisops,[25] vpon some, no.
ROSE. Why doe you stay, and not pursue your game?
SIBIL. Ile hold my life their hunting nags be lame.
HAMMON. A deere, more deere is found within this place.
ROSE. But not the deere (sir) which you had in chace.
HAMMON. I chac'd the deere, but this deere chaceth me.
ROSE. The strangest hunting that euer I see.
But wheres your parke?

She offers to goe away.

HAMMON. Tis here: O stay.
ROSE. Impale[26] me, and then I will not stray.
WARNER. They wrangle wench, we are more kind then they.
SIBIL. What kind of hart is that (deere hart) you seeke?
WARNER. A hart, deare heart.
SIBIL. Who euer saw the like?
ROSE. To loose your heart, is't possible you can?

25. Honey-sops (bread soaked in honey).
26. Fence me in, with obvious pun on impale.

HAMMON. My heart is lost.
ROSE. Alacke good gentleman.
HAMMON. This poore lost hart would I wish you might find.
ROSE. You by such lucke might proue your hart a hind.
HAMMON. Why Lucke had hornes, so haue I heard some say.
ROSE. Now God and't be his wil send Luck into your way.

Enter Lord Maior, *and servants*

L. MAIOR. What maister *Hammon,* welcome to old Ford.
SIBIL. Gods pittikins,° hands off sir, heers my Lord. — pity (diminutive form)
L. MAIOR. I heare you had ill lucke, and lost your game.
HAMMON. Tis true, my lord.
L. MAIOR. I am sorie for the same.
What gentleman is this?
HAMMON. My brother in law.
L. MAIOR. Y'are welcome both, sith Fortune offers you
Into my hands, you shal not part from hence,
Vntil you haue refresht your wearied limmes:
Go Sibil couer the boord, you shal be guest
To no good cheare, but euen a hunters feast.
HAMMON. I thanke your Lordship: cosen, on my life,
For our lost venison, I shal find a wife.

Exeunt [all but Maior].

L. MAIOR. In gentlemen, Ile not be absent long.
This *Hammon* is a proper gentleman,
A citizen by birth, fairely allide,
How fit an husband were he for my girle?
Wel, I will in, and do the best I can,
To match my daughter to this gentleman.

Exit.

[ACT II, SCENE III]

Enter Lacie [*as* Hans], Skipper, Hodge, *and* Firke.

SKIPPER. *Ick sal yow wat seggen* Hans, *dis skip dat comen from* Candy *is al wol, by gots sacrament, van sugar, ciuet, almonds, cambrick, end alle dingen towsand towsand ding, nempt it* Hans, *nempt it vor v meester, daer be de bils van laden, your meester* Simon Eyre *sal hae good copen, wat seggen yow* Hans?[27]

27. I'll tell you what, Hans, this ship that comes from Crete is all full, by God's sacrament, with sugar, civet, almonds, cambric, and all things, a thousand thousand things; buy it, Hans, buy it for your master, there be the bills of laden, your master Simon Eyre shall have a good bargain: what say you, Hans?

FIRKE. Wat seggen de reggen de copen, slopen, laugh *Hodge* laugh.

LACIE. *Mine lieuer broder* Firke, *bringt meester* Eyre *tot det signe vn swannekin; daer sal yow finde dis skipper end me, wat seggen yow, broder* Firke? *doot it* Hodge, *come skipper.*[28]

Exeunt.

FIRKE. Bring him quoth you, heers no knauery, to bring my master to buy a ship worth, the lading of two or three hundred thousand pounds, alas thats nothing, a trifle, a ba[u]ble, Hodge.

HODGE. The truth is Firke, that the marchant owner of the ship dares not shew his head, and therefore this skipper that deales for him, for the loue he bears to *Hans,* offers my master *Eyre* a bargaine in the commodities, he shal haue a reasonable day of payment, he may sel the wares by that time, and be an huge gainer himselfe.

FIRKE. Yea, but can my fellow *Hans* lend my master twentie porpentines as an earnest pennie[?]

HODGE. Portegues thou wouldst say, here they be *Firke,* heark, they gingle in my pocket like saint *Mary Oueries*[29] bels.

Enter Eyre and his Wife *[and a boy]*.

FIRKE. Mum, here comes my dame and my maister, sheele scold on my life, for loytering this Monday, but al's one, let them al say what they can, Monday's our holiday.

WIFE. You sing sir sauce, but I beshrew your heart,
I feare for this your singing we shal smart.

FIRKE. Smart for me dame, why dame, why?

HODGE. Maister I hope yowle not suffer my dame to take downe your iourneymen.

FIRKE. If she take me downe, Ile take her vp, yea and take her downe too, a button-hole lower.[30]

EYRE. Peace *Firke,* not I *Hodge,* by the life of *Pharao,* by the Lord of Ludgate, by this beard, euery haire whereof I valew at a kings ransome, shee shal not meddle with you, peace you bumbast-cotton-candle Quean, away queene of Clubs, quarrel not with me and my men, with me and my fine *Firke,* Ile firk you, if you do.

WIFE. Yea, yea man, you may vse me as you please: but let that passe.

EYRE. Let it passe, let it vanish away: peace, am I not *Simon Eyre?* are not these my braue men? braue shoomakers, all gentlemen of the gentle craft? prince am I none, yet am I noblie borne,

28. My dear brother Firke, bring Master Eyre to the sign of the Swan [a tavern]; there shall you find this skipper and me. What say you, brother Firke? Do it, Hodge.

29. A church "over" the Thames from the City of London.

30. Rebuke her, but with sexual pun.

as beeing the sole sonne of a Shoomaker, away rubbish, vanish, melt like kitchin stuffe.

WIFE. Yea, yea, tis well; I must be cald rubbish, kitchinstuffe, for a sort° of knaves.

group

FIRKE. Nay dame, you shall not weepe and waile in woe for me: master Ile stay no longer, here's an vennentorie of my shop tooles: adue master, *Hodge* farewel.

HODGE. Nay stay *Firke,* thou shalt not go alone.

WIFE. I pray let them goe, there be mo maides than mawkin, more men than *Hodge,* and more fooles than *Firke.*

FIRKE. Fooles? nailes if I tarry nowe, I would my guts might be turn'd to shoo-thread.

HODGE. And if I stay, I pray God I may be turnd to a Turke, and set in Finsbury° for boyes to shoot at: come *Firke.*

location of archery fields

EYRE. Stay my fine knaues, you armes of my trade, you pillars of my profession. What, shal a tittle tattles words make you forsake *Simon Eyre?* auaunt kitchinstuffe, rip° you brown bread tannikin,° out of my sight, moue me not, haue not I tane you from selling tripes in Eastcheape, and set you in my shop, and made you haile fellowe with *Simon Eyre* the shoomaker? and now do you deale thus with my Iourneymen? Looke you powder beefe queane, on the face of *Hodge,* heers a face for a lord.

get out

diminutive of Anne

FIRKE. And heers a face for any Lady in Christendome.

EYRE. Rip you chitterling auaunt boy, bid the tapster of the Bores head fil me a doozen Cannes of beere for my iourneymen.

FIRKE. A doozen Cans? O braue, *Hodge* now Ile stay.

EYRE. [*Aside.*] And the knaue fils any more than two, he payes for them. [*Exit boy. Aloud*] a doozen Cans of beere for my iourneymen. [*enter boy with two cans and exit*] heare, you mad Mesopotamians, wash your liuers with this liquor, where be the odde ten? no more *Madge,* no more, wel saide, drinke and to work: what worke dost thou *Hodge?* what work?

HODGE. I am a making a paire of shooes for my Lord Maiors daughter, mistresse *Rose.*

FIRKE. And I a paire of shooes for *Sibil* my Lords maid. I deale with her.

EYRE. *Sibil?* fie, defile not thy fine workemanly fingers with the feete of Kitchinstuffe, and basting ladles, Ladies of the Court, fine Ladies, my lads, commit their feete to our apparelling, put grosse worke to *Hans:* yarke° and seame, yarke and seame.

stitch

FIRKE. For yarking and seaming let me alone, and I come toot.

HODGE. Wel maister, al this is from the bias, do you remember the ship my fellow *Hans* told you of? the Skipper and he are both drinking at the swan, here be the Portigues to give earnest, if you go through with it, you can not choose but be a Lord at least.

FIRKE. Nay dame, if my master proue not a Lord, and you a Ladie, hang me.

WIFE. Yea like inough, if you may loiter and tipple° thus.

drink

FIRKE. Tipple dame? no, we haue beene bargaining with Skellum° Skanderbag° can you Dutch spreaken for a ship of silke Cipresse, laden with sugar Candie.

rascal; Albanian hero

Enter the boy with a veluet coate, and an Aldermans gowne, Eyre *puts them on.*

EYRE. Peace Firke, silence tittle tattle: *Hodge,* Ile go through with it, heers a seale ring, and I haue sent for a garded° gown and a damask Casock, see where it comes, looke here *Maggy,* help me *Firke,* apparrel me *Hodge,* silke and satten you mad Philistines, silk and satten.

braided

FIRKE. Ha, ha, my maister wil be as proud as a dogge in a dublet, al in beaten° damaske and veluet.

embroidered

EYRE. Softly° *Firke,* for rearing of the nap, and wearing thread-bare my garments: how dost thou like mee *Firke?* how do I looke, my fine *Hodge?*

carefully

HODGE. Why now you looke like your self, master, I warrant you, ther's few in the city but wil give you the wal,[31] and come vpon you with the right worshipful.

FIRKE. Nailes my master lookes like a thred-bare cloake new turn'd and drest: Lord, Lord, to see what good raiment doth? dame, dame, are you not enamoured?

EYRE. How saist thou *Maggy,* am I not brisk? am I not fine?

WIFE. Fine? by my troth, sweet hart, very fine: by my troth I neuer likte thee so wel in my life sweete heart. But let that passe, I warrant there be many women in the citie haue not such handsome husbands, but only for their apparell, but let that passe too.

Enter [Lacie *as*] Hans *and* Skipper.

LACIE. *Godden day mester, Dis be de skipper dat heb de skip van marchandice, de commodity ben good, nempt it, master, nempt it.*

EYRE. Godamercy *Hans,* welcome skipper, where lies this ship of marchandise?

SKIPPER. *De skip ben in reuere:° dor be van Sugar, Cyuet, almonds, Cambricke, and a towsand, towsand tings, gotz sacrament, nempt it mester, ye sal heb good copen.*

river

FIRKE. To him maister, O sweete maister, O sweet wares, prunes, almons, sugar-candy, carrat roots, turnups, O brave fatting meate, let not a man buye a nutmeg but your selfe.

EYRE. Peace *Firke,* Come Skipper, Ile go aboarde with you, *Hans* haue you made him drinke?

SKIPPER. *Yaw, yaw, ic heb veale gedrunck.*[32]

31. Defer to Eyre by letting him walk close to the wall of buildings, away from the dirty street.
32. Yes, yes, I have drunk well.

EYRE. Come *Hans* follow me: Skipper, thou shalt haue my countenance in the Cittie.

Exeunt.

FIRKE. Yaw heb veale ge drunck, quoth a: they may well be called butter-boxes, when they drinke fat veale, and thick beare too: but come dame, I hope you'le chide vs no more.

WIFE. No faith *Firke,* no perdy *Hodge,* I do feele honour creepe vpon me, and which is more, a certaine rising in my flesh, but let that passe.

FIRKE. Rising in your flesh do you feele say you? I you may be with childe, but why should not my maister feele a rising in his flesh, hauing a gowne and a gold ring on, but you are such a shrew, youl'e soone pull him downe.

WIFE. Ha, ha, prethee peace, thou mak'st my worshippe laugh, but let that passe: come Ile go in, *Hodge* prethee goe before me, *Firke* follow me.

FIRKE. *Firke* doth follow, *Hodge* passe out in state.

Exeunt.

[ACT II, SCENE IV]

Enter Lincolne *and* Dodger.

LINCOLNE. How now good Dodger, whats the newes in *France?*
DODGER. My lord, upon the eighteene day of May
The French and English were preparde to fight;
Each side with eager furie gaue the signe
Of a most hot encounter, fiue long howres
Both armies fought together: at the length
The lot of victorie fel on our sides,
Twelue thousand of the Frenchmen that day dide,
Foure thousand English, and no man of name,
But Captain *Hyam* and young *Ardington.*
LINCOLNE. Two gallant Gentlemen, I knew them well.
But *Dodger,* prethee tell me in this fight
How did my cozen *Lacie* beare himselfe?
DODGER. My lord, your cosen *Lacie* was not there.
LINCOLNE. Not there?
DODGER. No, my good lord.
LINCOLNE. Sure thou mistakest,
I saw him shipt, and a thousand eies beside
Were witnesses of the farewels which he gaue,
When I, with weeping eies, bid him adew:
Dodger take heede.
DODGER. My lord, I am aduis'd

That what I spake is true: to proue it so,
His cosen *Askew* that supplide his place,
Sent me for him from *France,* that secretly
He might conuey himselfe thither.

LINCOLNE. Ist euen so.
Dares he so carelessely venture his life
Vpon the indignation of a King?
Has he despis'd my loue, and spurn'd those fauours
Which I with prodigal hand powr'd on his head?
He shall repent his rashness with his soule,
Since of my loue he makes no estimate,
Ile make him wish he had not knowne my hate.
Thou hast no other newes?

DODGER. None else, my Lord.

LINCOLNE. None worse I know thou hast: procure the king
To crowne his giddie browes with ample honors,
Send him cheefe Colonell, and all my hope
Thus to be dasht? but tis in vain to grieue,
One euill cannot a worse releeue:
Vpon my life, I have found out his plot,
That old dog Loue that fawnd vpon him so,
Loue to that puling° girle, his faire cheek't *Rose,* whining
The Lord Maiors daughter, hath distracted him,
And in the fire of that loues lunacie,
Hath he burnt vp himselfe, consum'd his credite,
Lost the kings loue, yea and I feare, his life,
Onely to get a wanton to his wife:
Dodger, it is so.

DODGER. I feare so, my good Lord.

LINCOLNE. It is so, nay, sure it cannot be,
I am at my wits end. *Dodger—*

DODGER. Yea, my Lord.

LINCOLNE. Thou art acquainted with my Nephewes haunts,
Spend this gold for thy paines, goe seeke him out,
Watch at my Lord Maiors (there if he liue)
Dodger, thou shalt be sure to meete with him:
Prethee be diligent. *Lacie* thy name
Liu'd once in honour, now dead in shame.
Be circumspect.

Exit.

DODGER. I warrant you my Lord.

Exit.

[ACT III, SCENE I]

Enter Lord Maior, *and master* Scott.

L. MAIOR. Good maister *Scott,* I haue beene bolde with you,
To be a witnesse to a wedding knot,
Betwixt young maister *Hammon* and my daughter,
O stand aside, see where the louers come.

Enter Hammon, *and* Rose

ROSE. Can it be possible you loue me so?
No, no, within those eie-bals I espie,
Apparent likelihoods of flattery,
Pray now, let go my hand.
HAMMON. Sweete mistris *Rose,*
Misconstrue not my words, nor misconceiue
Of my affection, whose deuoted soule
Sweares that I loue thee dearer then my heart.
ROSE. As deare as your owne heart? I iudge it right.
Men loue their hearts best when th'are out of sight.
HAMMON. I loue you, by this hand.
ROSE. Yet hands off now:
If flesh be fraile, how weake and frail's your vowe?
HAMMON. Then by my life I sweare.
ROSE. Then do not brawle,
One quarrell looseth wife and life and all,
Is not your meaning thus?
HAMMON. In faith you iest.
ROSE. Loue loues to sport, therfore leaue loue y'are best.
L. MAIOR. What? square° they maister *Scott?* quarrel
SCOTT. Sir, never doubt,
Louers are quickly in, and quickly out.
HAMMON. Sweet *Rose,* be not so strange in fansying me,
Nay, neuer turne aside, shunne not my sight,
I am not grown so fond,° to fond° my loue foolish; bestow
On any that shall quit it with disdaine,
If you wil loue me, so, if not, farewell.
L. MAIOR. Why how now, louers, are you both agreede?
HAMMON. Yes faith my Lord.
L. MAIOR. Tis well, giue me your hand.
Giue me yours daughter. How now, both pull backe,
What meanes this, girle?
ROSE. I meane to liue a maid.
HAMMON. [*Aside.*] But not to die one, pawse ere that be said.
L. MAIOR. Wil you still crosse me? still be obstinate?
HAMMON. Nay chide her not my Lord for doing well,

If she can liue an happie virgins life,
Tis farre more blessed then to be a wife.[33]
ROSE. Say sir I cannot, I haue made a vow,
Who euer be my husband, tis not you.
L. MAIOR. Your tongue is quicke, but Master *Hammon* know,
I bade you welcome to another end.
HAMMON. What, would you haue me pule, and pine, and pray,
With louely lady mistris of my heart,
Pardon your seruant, and the rimer play,
Rayling on *Cupid* and his tyrants dart,
Or shal I vndertake some martiall spoile,
Wearing your gloue at turney, and at tilt,
And tel how many gallants I vnhorst
Sweete, wil this pleasure you?
ROSE. Yea, when wilt begin?
What, louerimes man? fie on that deadly sinne.
L. MAIOR. If you wil haue her, Ile make her agree.
HAMMON. Enforced loue is worse than hate to me,
[*Aside.*] There is a wench keepes shop in the old change,
To her wil I, it is not wealth I seeke,
I haue enough, and wil preferre her loue
Before the world: [*Aloud.*] My good lord *Maior* adew,
Old loue for me, I haue no lucke with new.

Exit.

L. MAIOR. Now mammet° you haue wel behau'd your selfe, doll
But you shal curse your coynes if I liue,
Whose within there? see you conuay your mistris
Straight to th'old Forde, Ile keepe you straight enough.
Fore God I would haue sworne the pulling girle,
Would willingly accepted *Hammon*'s loue,
But banish him, my thoughts, go minion in[.]

Exit Rose.

Now tel me master *Scott* would you haue thought,
That master *Simon Eyre* the shoomaker,
Had beene of wealth to buy such marchandize?
SCOTT. Twas wel my Lord, your honour, and my selfe,
Grew partners with him, for your bils of lading
Shew that *Eyres* gaines in one commoditie
Rise at the least to ful three thousand pound,
Besides like gaine in other marchandize.
L. MAIOR. Wel he shal spend some of his thousands now
For I haue sent for him to the Guild Hal,

33. *The Shoemaker's Holiday* was performed for Queen Elizabeth, and hence the compliment to virginity.

Enter Eyre

See, where he comes: good morrow master *Eyre.*
EYRE. Poore *Simon Eyre,* my Lord, your shoomaker.
L. MAIOR. Wel wel, it likes your selfe to terme you so.

Enter Dodger

Now master *Dodger,* whats the news with you?
DODGER. Ide gladly speake in priuate to your honour.
L. MAIOR. You shal, you shal: master *Eyre* and master *Scott,*
I haue some businesse with this gentleman,
I pray let me intreate you to walke before
To the Guild hal, Ile follow presently,
Master *Eyre,* I hope ere noone to call you Shiriffe.[34]
EYRE. I would not care (my Lord) if you might cal me king of *Spaine,* come master *Scott.*

[*Exeunt* Eyre and Scott.]

L. MAIOR. Now maister *Dodger,* whats the newes you bring?
DODGER. The Earle of *Lincolne* by me greets your lordship
And earnestly requests you (if you can)
Informe him where his Nephew *Lacie* keepes.
L. MAIOR. Is not his Nephew *Lacie* now in *France?*
DODGER. No I assure your lordship, but disguisde
Lurkes here in *London.*
L. MAIOR. *London?* ist euen so?
It may be, but vpon my faith and soule,
I know not where he liues, or whether he liues,
So tel my Lord of *Lincolne,* lurch° in *London?* lurk
Well master *Dodger,* you perhaps may start° him, flush
Be but the meanes to rid him into *France,*
Ile giue you a dozen angels for your paines,
So much I loue his honour, hate his Nephew.
And, prethee so informe thy lord from me.
DODGER. I take my leaue.
L. MAIOR. Farewell good master *Dodger.*
Lacie in *London?* I dare pawne my life,
My daughter knowes thereof, and for that cause,
Denide young master *Hammon* in his loue,
Wel I am glad I sent her to old Forde,
Gods lord tis late to Guild Hall I must hie,
I know my brethren stay my company.

Exit.

34. Second highest office in the city of London, and usually a stepping stone to the mayoralty, the sheriff was responsible for collecting revenue and keeping order in the city.

[ACT III, SCENE II]

Enter Firke, Eyres wife, [Lacie *as*] Hans, *and* Roger

WIFE. Thou goest too fast for me *Roger.* O *Firke.*

FIRKE. I forsooth.

WIFE. I pray thee runne (doe you heare) runne to Guild Hall, and learne if my husband, master *Eyre* wil take that worshipfull vocation of master Shiriffe vpon him, hie thee, good *Firke.*

FIRKE. Take it? well I goe, an he should not take it, *Firke* sweares to forsweare him, yes forsooth I goe to Guild Hall.

WIFE. Nay when? thou art too compendious, and tedious.

FIRKE. O rare, your excellence is full of eloquence, how like a new cart wheele my dame speakes, [*aside*] and she lookes like an old musty ale-bottle going to scalding.

WIFE. Nay when? thou wilt make me melancholy.

FIRKE. God forbid your worship should fall into that humour; I runne.

Exit.

WIFE. Let me see now *Roger* and *Hans.*

HODGE. I forsooth dame (mistris I should say) but the old terme so stickes to the roofe of my mouth, I can hardly lick it off.

WIFE. Even what thou wilt good *Roger,* dame is a faire name for any honest christian, but let that passe, how dost thou *Hans?*

HANS. *Mee tanck you, vro.*° mistress

WIFE. Well *Hans* and *Roger* you see God hath blest your master, and perdie° if euer he comes to be master Shiriffe of *London* (as we are al mortal) you shal see I will haue some odde thing or other in a corner for you: I will not be your backe friend, but let that passe, *Hans* pray thee tie my shoee. by God

HANS. *Yaw ic sal*° *vro.* will

WIFE. *Roger,* thou knowst the length of my foote, as it is none of the biggest, so I thanke God it is handsome enough, prethee let me haue a paire of shooes made, cork, good Roger, woodden heele too.

HODGE. You shall.

WIFE. Art thou acquainted with neuer a fardingale-maker,[35] nor a French-hoode maker? I must enlarge my bumme, ha ha, how shall I looke in a hoode I wonder? perdie odly I thinke.

HODGE. [*Aside.*] As a cat out of a pillory.[36] [*to her*] verie wel I warrant you mistresse.

35. Hooped underskirt–maker.

36. The French hood was a close fitting hood; the wife's face surrounded by the hood will look like a cat's face between the wooden blocks of the pillory, a form of punishment where a person's head and hands were pinioned for a length of time in public.

WIFE. Indeede all flesh is grasse, and *Roger,* canst thou tell where I may buye a good haire?

HODGE. Yes forsooth, at the poulterer's[37] in Gracious Street.

WIFE. Thou art an vngracious wag, perdy, I meane a false haire for my periwig.

HODGE. Why mistris, the next time I cut my beard, you shall haue the shauings of it; but they are all true haires.

WIFE. It is verie hot, I must get me a fan or else a maske.

HODGE. [*Aside.*] So you had neede, to hide your wrinkld face.

WIFE. Fie vpon it, how costly this world's calling is, perdy, but that it is one of the wonderfull works of God, I would not deale with it: Is not *Firke* come yet? *Hans,* bee not so sad, let it passe and vanish, as my husbands worshippe saies.

HANS. *Ick bin vrolicke, lot see yow soo.*[38]

HODGE. Mistris, wil you drinke° a pipe of Tobacco? smoke

WIFE. O fie vppon it *Roger,* perdy, these filthie Tobacco pipes are the most idle slauering bables that euer I felt: out vppon it, God blesse vs, men looke not like men that vse them.

Enter Rafe *being lame.*

HODGE. What fellow *Rafe?* Mistres looke here, *Ianes* husband: why how now, lame? *Hans* make much of him, hees a brother of our trade, a good workeman, and a tall° souldier. brave

HANS. You be welcome broder.

WIFE. Pardie I knew him not, how dost thou good *Rafe?* I am glad to see thee wel.

RAFE. I would to God you saw me dame as wel,
As when I went from *London* into *France.*

WIFE. Trust mee I am sorie *Rafe* to see thee impotent, Lord how the warres haue made him Sunburnt: The left leg is not wel: t'was a faire gift of God the infirmitie tooke not hold a litle higher, considering thou camest from *France:*[39] but let that passe.

RAFE. I am glad to see you wel, and I reioyce
To heare that God hath blest my master so
Since my departure.

WIFE. Yea truly *Rafe,* I thanke my maker: but let that passe.

HODGE. And sirra *Rafe,* what newes, what newes in *France?*

RAFE. Tel mee good *Roger* first, what newes in *England?*
How does my Iane? when didst thou see my wife?
Where liues my poore heart? sheel be poore indeed,
Now I want limbs to get whereon to feed.

HODGE. Limbs? hast thou not hands man? thou shalt neuer see a

37. Where hares were sold.
38. I am cheerful, let's see you so.
39. With a pun on venereal disease.

shoomaker want bread, though he haue but three fingers on a hand.

RAFE. Yet all this while I heare not of my *Iane.*

WIFE. O *Rafe* your wife, perdie we knowe not whats become of her: she was here a while, and because she was married grewe more stately than became her, I checkt her, and so forth, away she flung, neuer returned, nor saide bih nor bah: and *Rafe* you knowe ka me, ka thee.[40] And so as I tell ye. *Roger* is not *Firke* come yet?

HODGE. No forsooth.

WIFE. And so indeede we heard not of her, but I heare shee liues in *London:* but let that passe. If she had wanted, shee might haue opened her case to me or my husband, or to any of my men, I am sure theres not any of them perdie, but would haue done her good to his power. *Hans* looke if *Firke* be come.

LACIE. *Yaw ic sal vro.*

Exit.

WIFE. And so as I saide: but *Rafe,* why dost thou weepe? thou knowest that naked wee came out of our mothers wombe, and naked we must returne, and therefore thanke God for al things.

HODGE. No faith *Iane* is a straunger heere, but *Rafe* pull vp a good heart, I knowe thou hast one, thy wife man, is in *London,* one tolde mee hee sawe her a while agoe verie braue and neate, weele ferret her out, and *London* holde her.

WIFE. Alas, poore soule, hees ouercome with sorrowe, he does but as I doe, weepe for the losse of any good thing: but *Rafe,* get thee in, call for some meate and drinke, thou shalt find me worshipful towards thee.

RAFE. I thanke you dame, since I want lims and lands,
Ile to God, my good friends, and to these my hands.

Enter [Lacie *as*] Hans, *and* Firke *running.*

FIRKE: Runne good *Hans,* O *Hodge,* O mistres, *Hodge* heaue vp thine eares, mistresse smugge° vp your lookes, on with your best apparell, my maister is chosen, my master is called, nay, condemn'd[41] by the crie of the countrie to be shiriffe of the Citie, for this famous yeare nowe to come, and time now being: a great many men in blacke gownes were asked for their voyces, and their hands, and my master had al their fists about his eares presently, and they cried I, I,
I, I, and so I came away,
Wherefore without all other grieue
I doe salute you, mistresse shrieue,

smarten

40. If you do me a favor, I'll do you another.
41. Malapropism for confirmed.

HANS. *Yaw, my mester is de groot man, de shrieue.*

HODGE. Did not I tell, you mistris? nowe I may boldly say, good morrow to your worship.

WIFE. Good morrow good *Roger,* I thanke you my good people all. *Firke,* hold vp thy hand, heer's a three-peny peece for thy tidings.

FIRKE. 'Tis but three halfe pence, I thinke: yes, tis three pence, I smel the rose.[42]

HODGE. But mistresse, be rulde by me, and doe not speake so pulingly.

FIRKE. Tis her worship speakes so, and not she, no faith, mistresse, speake mee in the olde key, too it *Firke,* there, good *Firke,* plie your businesse *Hodge, Hodge,* with a full mouth: Ile fill your bellies with good cheare till they crie twang.

Enter Simon Eyre *wearing a gold chaine.*

HANS. *See, myn lieuer° broder, heer compt my meester.* dear

WIFE. Welcome home maister shrieue; I pray God continue you in health and wealth.

EYRE. See here my Maggy, a chaine, a gold chaine for *Simon Eyre,* I shal make thee a Lady, heer's a French hood for thee, on with it, on with it, on with it, dresse thy browes with this flap of a shoulder of mutton, to make thee looke louely: where be my fine men? *Roger,* Ile make ouer my shop and tooles to thee: *Firke,* thou shalt be the foreman: *Hans,* thou shalt haue an hundred for twentie, bee as mad knaues as your maister *Sim Eyre* hath bin, and you shall liue to be Sheriues of *London:* how dost thou like me *Margerie?* Prince am I none, yet am I princely borne, *Firke, Hodge,* and *Hans.*

ALL 3. I forsooth, what saies your worship [Master][43] Sherife?

EYRE. Worship and honour you Babilonion knaues, for the Gentle Craft: but I forgot my selfe, I am bidden by my Lord Maior to dinner to Old Foord, hees gone before, I must after: come *Madge,* on with your trinkets: nowe my true Troians, my fine *Firke,* my dapper *Hodge,* my honest *Hans,* some deuice, some odde crotchets, some morris, or such like, for the honour of the gentlemen shooemakers, meete me at Old Foord, you know my minde: Come Madge, away. Shut up the shop, knaves, and make holiday.

Exeunt.

FIRKE. O rare, O braue, come *Hodge,* follow me *Hans,* Weele be with them for a morris daunce.

Exeunt.

42. An emblem of the Tudors that appeared on coins.
43. "mistriss" in Bowers.

[ACT III, SCENE III]

Enter Lord Maior, Eyre, his wife in a French hood, [Rose,] Sibil, and other Servants

L. MAIOR. Trust mee you are as welcome to old Foord
As I my selfe.

WIFE. Truely I thanke your Lordship.

L. MAIOR. Would our bad cheere were worth the thanks you giue.

EYRE. Good cheere my Lord Maior, fine cheere, a fine house, fine walles, all fine and neat.

L. MAIOR. Now by my troth Ile tel thee maister *Eyre*,
It does me good and al my bretheren,
That such a madcap fellow as thy selfe
Is entred into our societie.

WIFE. I but my Lord, hee must learne nowe to putte on grauitie.

EYRE. Peace *Maggy*, a fig for grauitie, When I go to Guildhal in my scarlet gowne, Ile look as demurely as a saint, and speake as grauely as a Iustice of peace, but now I am here at old Foord, at my good Lord Maiors house, let it go by, vanish *Maggy*, Ile be merrie, away with flip flap, these fooleries, these gulleries: what hunnie? prince am I none, yet am I princly borne: what sayes my Lord Maior?

L. MAIOR. Ha, ha, ha, I had rather then a thousand pounds, I had an heart but halfe so light as yours.

EYRE. Why what should I do My Lord? a pound of care paies not a dram of debt: hum, lets be merry whiles we are yong; olde age, sacke and sugar will steal vpon us, ere we be aware.

THE FIRST THREE-MANS SONG.[44]

O the month of Maie, the merrie month of Maie,
So frolicke, so gay, and so greene, so greene, so greene:
O and then did I, vnto my true loue say:
Sweete Peg, thou shalt be my Summers Queene.

Now the Nightingale, the prettie Nightingale,
The sweetest singer in all the forrests quier:
Intreats thee, sweete Peggie, to heare thy true loues tale,
Loe, yonder she sitteth, her breast against a brier.

But O I spie the Cuckoo, the Cuckoo, the Cuckoo,
See where she sitteth, come away, my ioy:
Come away, I prithee, I do not like the Cuckoo
Should sing where my Peggie and I kisse and toy.

44. Bald's edition places the First Three-mans Song here, although I am using Bowers' edition for the song itself.

O the month of Maie, the merrie month of Maie,
So frolike, so gay, and so greene, so greene, so greene:
And then did I, vnto my true loue say,
Sweete Peg, thou shalt be my Summers Queene.

L. MAIOR. Its wel done: mistris *Eyre,* pray giue good counsell to my daughter.

WIFE. I hope mistris *Rose* will haue the grace to take nothing thats bad.

L. MAIOR. Pray God she do, for ifaith, mistris *Eyre,*
I would bestow vpon that peeuish girle
A thousand Marks[45] more than I meane to giue her,
Vpon condition sheed be rulde by me.
The Ape still crosseth me: there came of late,
A proper Gentleman of faire reuenewes,
Whom gladly I would call sonne in law:
But my fine cockney would have none of him.
You'le proue a cockscombe for it ere you die,
A courtier, or no man must please your eie.

EYRE. Be rulde sweete *Rose,* th'art ripe for a man: marrie not with a boy, that has no more haire on his face than thou hast on thy cheekes: a courtier, wash, go by, stand not vppon pisherie pasherie: those silken fellowes are but painted Images, outsides, outsides *Rose,* their inner linings are torne: no my fine mouse, marry me with a Gentleman Grocer like my Lord Maior, your Father, a Grocer is a sweete trade, Plums, Plums: had I a sonne or Daughter should marrieout of the generation and bloud of the shoe-makers, he should packe: what, the Gentle trade is a liuing for a man through Europe, through the world.

A noyse within of a Taber and a Pipe.

L. MAIOR. What noyse is this?

EYRE. O my lord Maior, a crue of good fellowes that for loue to your honour, are come hither with a morrisdance, come in, my Mesopotamians, cheerely.

Enter Hodge, [Lacie *as*] Hans, Rafe, Firke, *and other shooe-makers, in a morris: after a little dauncing the* Lord Maior *speakes.*

L. MAIOR. Maister *Eyre,* are all these shoe-makers?

EYRE. Al Cordwainers my good Lord Maior.

ROSE. [*Aside.*] How like my *Lacie* lookes yond shooe maker.

LACIE. [*Aside.*] O that I durst but speake vnto my loue!

L. MAIOR. *Sibil,* go fetch some wine to make these drinke, You are al welcome.

45. Worth two-thirds of a pound.

ALL. We thanke your Lordship.

Rose *takes a cup of wine and goes to* Hans.

ROSE. For his sake whose faire shape thou representst,
Good friend I drinke to thee.
LACIE. *Ic be dancke, good frister.*° maid
WIFE. I see mistris *Rose* you do not want iudgment; you haue drunke to the properest man I keepe.
FIRKE. Here bee some haue done their parts to be as proper as he.
L. MAIOR. Wel, vrgent busines cals me back to *London:*
Good fellowes, first go in and taste our cheare,
And to make merrie as you homeward go,
Spend these two angels in beere at *Stratford Boe.*[46]
EYRE. To these two (my madde lads) *Sim Eyre* adds another, then cheerely, *Firke,* tickle it *Hans,* and al for the honour of shoemakers.

All goe dauncing out.

L. MAIOR. Come maister *Eyre,* lets have your companie.

Exeunt.

ROSE. *Sibil* What shal I do?
SIBIL. Why whats the matter?
ROSE. That *Hans* the shoemaker is my love *Lacie,*
Disguisde in that attire to find me out,
How should I find the meanes to speake with him?
SIBIL. What mistris, neuer feare; I dare venter my maidenhead to nothing, and thats great oddes, that *Hans* the Dutchman when we come to *London,* shal not onely see and speake with you, but in spight of al your Fathers pollicies, steale you away and marrie you, will not this please you?
ROSE. Do this, and euer be assured of my loue.
SIBIL. Away then and follow your father to *London,* lest your absence cause him to suspect something:
To morrow, if my counsel be obayde,
Ile binde you prentise to the gentle trade.

[*Exeunt.*]

46. Stratford Bow, "a small village outside London, whose tavern was a regular stopping point on the road into the city" (Parr).

[ACT III, SCENE IV]

Enter Iane *in a Semsters shop working, and* Hammon *muffled at another doore, he stands aloofe.*

HAMMON. Yonders the shop, and there my faire loue sits,
Shees faire and louely, but she is not mine,
O would she were, thrise haue I courted her,
Thrise hath my hand beene moistned with her hand,
Whilst my poore famisht eies do feed on that
Which made them famish: I am infortunate,
I still loue one, yet nobody loues me,
I muse in other men what women see,
That I so want? fine mistris *Rose* was coy,
And this too curious,° oh no, she is chaste, [particular]
And for she thinkes me wanton, she denies
To cheare my cold heart with her sunnie eies:
How prettily she workes, oh pretty hand!
Oh happie worke, it doth me good to stand
Vnseene to see her, thus I oft have stood,
In frostie euenings, a light burning by her,
Enduring biting cold, only to eie her,
One onely looke hath seem'd as rich to me
As a kings crowne, such is loues lunacie.
Muffeled Ile passe along, and by that trie
Whether she know me.
IANE. Sir, what ist you buy?
What ist you lacke sir? callico, or lawne,° [linen]
Fine cambricke shirts, or bands,° what will you buy? [collars]
HAMMON. [*Aside.*] That which thou wilt not sell, faith yet Ile trie:
How do you sell this handkercher?
IANE. Good cheape.
HAMMON. And how these ruffes?
IANE. Cheape too.
HAMMON. And how this band?
IANE. Cheape too.
HAMMON. All cheape, how sell you then this hand?
IANE. My handes are not to be solde.
HAMMON. To be giuen then:
Nay, faith, I come to buy.
IANE. But none knowes when.
HAMMON. Good sweete, leave work a little while, lets play.
IANE. I cannot liue by keeping holliday.
HAMMON. Ile pay you for the time which shall be lost.
IANE. With me you shall not be at so much cost.
HAMMON. Look how you wound this cloth, so you wound me.

IANE. It may be so.
HAMMON. Tis so.
IANE. What remedie?
HAMMON. Nay faith you are too coy.
IANE. Let goe my hand.
HAMMON. I will do any task at your command,
I would let goe this beautie, were I not
Inioind to disobey you by a power
That controlles kings: I love you.
IANE. So, now part.
HAMMON. With hands I may, but neuer with my heart.
In faith I loue you.
IANE. I beleeue you doe.
HAMMON. Shall a true loue in me breede hate in you?
IANE. I hate you not.
HAMMON. Then you must loue.
IANE. I do.
What are you better now? I loue not you.
HAMMON. All this I hope is but a womans fray,
That means, come to me, when she cries, away:
In earnest mistris I do not iest,
A true chaste loue hath entred in my brest,
I loue you dearley as I loue my life,
I loue you as a husband loues a wife.
That, and no other loue my loue requires,
Thy wealth I know is little, my desires
Thirst not for gold, sweete beauteous Iane whats mine,
Shall (if thou make my selfe thine) all be thine,
Say, iudge, what is thy sentence, life, or death?
Mercie or crueltie lies in thy breath.
IANE. Good sir, I do beleeue you love me well:
For tis a seely° conquest, seely pride   insignificant
For one like you (I meane a gentleman)
To boast, that by his loue tricks he hath brought,
Such and such women to his amorous lure:
I thinke you do not so, yet many doe,
And make it euen a very trade to wooe,
I could be coy, as many women be,
Feede you with sunne-shine smiles, and wanton lookes,
But I detest witchcraft, say that I
Doe constantly beleeue you constant haue--
HAMMON. Why dost thou not beleeue me?
IANE. I beleeue you,
But yet good sir, because I will not greeue you,
With hopes to taste fruite, which will neuer fall,
In simple truth this is the summe of all,

My husband liues, at least, I hope he liues,
Prest was he to these bitter warres in *France,*
Bitter they are to me by wanting° him, lacking
I haue but one heart, and that hearts his due,
How can I then bestow the same on you?
Whilst he liues, his I liue, be it nere so poore,
And rather be his wife, then a kings whore.
HAMMON. Chaste and deare woman, I will not abuse thee,
Although it cost my life, if thou refuse me,
Thy husband prest for *France,* what was his name?
IANE. *Rafe Damport.*
HAMMON. *Damport,* heres a letter sent
From *France* to me, from a deare friend of mine,
A gentleman of place, here he doth write,
Their names that haue bin slaine in euery fight.
IANE. I hope deaths scroll containes not my loues name.
HAMMON. Cannot you read?
IANE. I can.
HAMMON. Peruse the same,
To my remembrance such a name I read
Amongst the rest: see here.
IANE. Aye me, hees dead:
Hees dead, if this be true my deare hearts slaine
HAMMON. Haue patience, deare loue.
IANE. Hence, hence.
HAMMON. Nay sweete *Iane,*
Make not poore sorrow prowd with these rich teares,
I mourne thy husbands death, because thou mournst.
IANE. That bil is forgde, tis signde by forgerie.
HAMMON. Ile bring thee letters sent besides to many
Carrying the like report: *Iane* tis too true,
Come, weepe not: mourning though it rise from loue
Helpes not the mourned, yet hurtes them that mourne.
IANE. For God's sake, leave me.
HAMMON. Whither dost thou turne?
Forget the deade, loue them that are aliue,
His loue is faded, trie how mine wil thriue.
IANE. Tis now no time for me to thinke on loue.
HAMMON. Tis now best time for you to thinke on loue,
Because your loue liues not.
IANE. Thogh he be dead,
My loue to him shal not be buried:
For Gods sake leaue me to my selfe alone.
HAMMON. Twould kil my soule to leaue thee drownd in mone:
Answere me to my sute, and I am gone,
Say to me, yea, or no.

IANE. No.
HAMMON. Then farewell,
One farewel will not serue, I come again,
Come drie these wet cheekes, tel me faith sweete *Iane,*
Yea, or no, once more.
IANE. Once more I say no,
Once more be gone I pray, else wil I goe.
HAMMON. Nay then I wil grow rude, by this white hand
Until you change that colde no, here ile stand,
Til by your hard heart—
IANE. Nay, for Gods loue peace,
My sorrowes by your presence more increase,
Not that you thus are present, but al griefe
Desires to be alone, therefore in briefe
Thus much I say, and saying bid adew,
If euer I wed man, it shall be you.
HAMMON. Oh blessed voyce, deare *Iane* Ile vrge no more,
Thy breath hath made me rich.
IANE. Death makes me poor.

Exeunt.

[ACT IV, SCENE I]

Enter Hodge *at his shop boord,* Rafe, Firke, [Lacie *as*] Hans, *and a boy at work.*

ALL. Hey downe, a downe, downe derie.

HODGE. Well said my hearts, plie your worke to day, we loytred yesterday, to it pell mel, that we may liue to be Lord Maiors, or Aldermen at least.

FIRKE. Hey downe a downe derie.

HODGE. Well said yfaith, how saist thou *Hans,* doth not *Firke* tickle it?

LACIE. *Yaw mester.*

FIRKE. Not so neither, my organe pipe squeaks this morning, for want of licoring: hey downe a downe derie! [listen]

LACIE. *Forware Firke, tow best vn iolly yongster, hort° I mester ic bid yo cut me vn pair vampie*[47] *vor mester Ieffres bootes.*

HODGE. Thou shalt *Hans.*

FIRKE. Master.

HODGE. How now, boy?

FIRKE. Pray, now you are in the cutting vaine, cut mee out a paire of counterfeits, or else my worke will not passe currant, hey downe a downe.

47. Vamps, "the front end of the upper shoe" (Parr).

HODGE. Tell me sirs, are my coosin mistris *Priscillas* shooes done?

FIRKE. Your coosin? no maister, one of your auntes, hang her, let them alone.

RAFE. I am in hand with them, she gaue charge that none but I should doe them for her.

FIRKE. Thou do for her? then twill be a lame doing, and that she loues not: *Rafe,* thou mightst haue sent her to me, in faith I would haue yearkt and firkt your *Priscilla,* hey downe a downe derry, this geere will not holde.

HODGE. How saist thou *Firke?* were we not merry at old Ford?

FIRKE. How merry? why our buttockes went Iiggy ioggy like a quagmyre: wel sir *Roger Oatmeale,* if I thought all meale of that nature, I would eate nothing but bagpuddings.[48]

RAFE. Of all good fortunes, my fellow *Hans* had the best.

FIRKE. Tis true, because mistris *Rose* dranke to him.

HODGE. Wel, wel, worke apace, They say, seuen of the aldermen be dead, or very sicke.

FIRKE. I care not, Ile be none.

RAFE. No, nor I, but then my maister *Eyre* will come quickly to be Lord Mayor.

Enter Sibil

FIRKE. Whoop, yonder comes *Sibil.*

HODGE. *Sibil,* welcome yfaith; and how dost thou madde wench?

FIRKE. *Sib* whoore, welcome to *London.*

SIBIL. Godamercy sweete *Firke:* good Lord *Hodge,* what a delitious shop you haue got, you tickle it yfaith.

RAFE. Godamercy *Sibil* for our good cheere at old Ford.

SIBIL. That you shal haue *Rafe.*

FIRKE. Nay by the masse, we hadde tickling cheere *Sibil,* and how the plague dost thou and mistris *Rose,* and my Lord Mayor? I put the women in first.

SIBIL. Wel Godamercy: but Gods me, I forget my self, wheres *Hans* the Fleming?

FIRKE. Hearke butter-boxe, nowe you must yelp out some spreken.

LACIE. *Vat begaie you, Vat vod you, Frister?*

SIBIL. Marrie you must come to my yong mistris, to pull on her shooes you made last.

LACIE. *Vare ben your edle fro,*° *vare ben your mistris?* (noble lady)

SIBIL. Marrie here at our *London* house in Cornewalle.

FIRKE. Will no bodie serue her turne but *Hans?*

SIBIL. No sir, come *Hans,* I stand vpon needles.

HODGE. Why then *Sibil,* take heede of pricking.

SIBIL. For that let me alone, I haue a tricke in my budget,° come *Hans.* (wallet)

48. An English style of steamed puddings (or desserts) cooked in a bag.

LACIE. *Yaw, yaw, ic sall meete yo gane.*

HODGE. Go *Hans,* make haste againe: come, who lacks worke?

Exit Lacie *and* Sibil.

FIRKE. I maister, for I lacke my breakfast, tis munching time, and past.

HODGE. Ist so? why then leaue worke *Rafe,* to breakfast, boy looke to the tooles, come *Rafe,* come *Firke.*

Exeunt.

[ACT IV, SCENE II]

Enter a Seruingman.

SERU. Let me see now, the signe of the last[49] in Towerstreet; mas° yonders the house: what haw, whoes within?

"mass" (mild oath)

Enter Rafe.

RAFE. Who calles there, what want you sir?

SERU. Marrie I would haue a paire of shooes made for a Gentlewoman against to morrow morning, what can you do them?

RAFE. Yes sir, you shall haue them, but what lengths her foote?

SERU. Why you must make them in all parts like this shoe, but at any hand faile not to do them, for the Gentlewoman is to be married very early in the morning.

RAFE. How, by this shoe must it be made? by this, are you sure sir by this?

SERU. How, by this am I sure, by this? art thou in thy wits? I tell thee I must have a paire of shooes, dost thou marke me? a paire of shooes, two shooes, made by this verie shoe, this same shoe, against to morrow morning by foure a clock, dost vnderstand me, canst thou do't?

RAFE. Yes sir, yes, I, I, I can do't, by this shoe, you say: I should knowe this shoe, yes sir, yes, by this shoe, I can do't, foure a clocke, well, whither shall I bring them?

SERU. To the signe of the golden ball in Watlingstreete, enquire for one maister *Hammon* a gentleman, my maister.

RAFE. Yea sir, by this shoe, you say.

SERU. I say maister Hammon at the golden ball, hee's the Bridegroome, and those shooes are for his bride.

RAFE. They shal be done by this shoe. wel, well, Maister *Hammon* at the golden shoe, I would say, the golden Ball, verie well, verie well, but I pray you sir where must maister *Hammon* be married?

49. Holding device shaped like a human foot. Since most people could not read, an artisan indicated his shop with a sign showing an object associated with his trade.

SERU. At Saint *Faiths* Church vnder *Paules:* but whats that to thee? prethee dispatch those shooes, and so farewel.

Exit.

RAFE. By this shoe said he, how am I amasde
At this strange accident? vpon my life,
This was the verie shoe I gaue my wife
When I was prest for *France,* since when alas,
I neuer could heare of her: It is the same,
And *Hammons* bride no other but my *Iane.*

Enter *Firke.*

FIRKE. Snailes° *Raph,* thou hast lost thy part of three pots, a countrieman of mine gaue me to breakfast. God's nails

RAFE. I care not, I haue found a better thing.

FIRKE. A thing? away, is it a mans thing, or a womans thing?

RAFE. *Firke,* dost thou know this shooe?

FIRKE. No by my troth, neither doth that know me[.] I haue no acquaintance with it, tis a meere stranger to me.

RAFE. Why then I do, this shooe I durst be sworne
Once couered the instep of my *Iane:*
This is her size, her breadth, thus trod my loue,
These true loue knots I prickt, I hold my life,
By this old shooe I shall finde out my wife.

FIRKE. Ha ha old shoo, that wert new, how a murren° came this ague fit of foolishnes vpon thee? plague

RAFE. Thus *Firke,* euen now here came a seruingman,
By this shooe would he have a new paire made
Against to morrow morning for his mistris,
Thats to be married to a Gentleman,
And why may not this be my sweete *Iane?*

FIRKE. And why maist not thou be my sweete Asse? ha, ha.

RAFE. Wel, laugh, and spare not: But the truth is this.
Against to morrow morning Ile prouide
A lustie crue of honest shoomakers,
To watch the going of the bride to church,
If she proue *Iane,* Ile take her in despite,
From *Hammon* and the diuel, were he by,
If it be not my *Iane,* what remedy?
Hereof I am sure, I shall liue till I die,
Although I neuer with a woman lie.

Exit.

FIRKE. Thou lie with a woman to builde nothing but Cripplegates![50] Well, God sends fooles fortune, and it may be he may light vpon

50. One of the gates of the City, frequented, as the name indicates, by crippled beggars.

his matrimony by such a deuice, for wedding and hanging goes by destiny.

Exit.

[ACT IV, SCENE III]

Enter [Lacie *as*] Hans, *and* Rose *arme in arme.*

LACIE. How happie am I by embracing thee,
Oh I did feare such crosse mishaps did raigne,
That I should neuer see my *Rose* againe.
ROSE. Sweet Lacie, since faire Oportunitie
Offers her selfe to furder our escape,
Let not too ouer-fond esteem of me
Hinder that happie hower, inuent the meanes,
And *Rose* will follow thee through all the world.
LACIE. Oh how I surfeit with excesse of ioy,
Made happie by thy rich perfection,
But since thou paist sweete intrest to my hopes,
Redoubling loue on loue, let me once more,
Like to a bold facde debter craue of thee,
This night to steale abroade, and at *Eyres* house,
Who now by death of certaine Aldermen,
Is Maior of *London,* and my master once,
Meete thou thy *Lacie,* where in spite of change,
Your fathers anger, and mine vncles hate,
Our happie nuptialls will we consummate.

Enter Sibil.

SIBIL. Oh God, what will you doe mistris? shift for your selfe, your father is at hand, hees comming, hees coming, master *Lacie* hide your selfe in my mistris, for Gods sake, shift for your selues!

LACIE. Your father come, sweete *Rose,* what shall I doe?
Where shall I hide me? how shall I escape?
ROSE. A man, and want wit in extremitie,
Come, come, be *Hans* still, play the shoomaker,
Pull on my shoe.

Enter [former] Lord Maior

LACIE. Mas, and thats well remembred.
SIBIL. Here comes your father.

LACIE. *Forware metresse, tis vn good skow, it sal vel dute, or ye sal neit betallen.*° pay for it

ROSE. Oh God it pincheth me, what wil you do?
LACIE. [*Aside.*] Your fathers presence pincheth, not the shoo.

L. MAIOR. Well done, fit my daughter well, and shee shall please thee well.

LACIE. *Yaw, yaw, ick weit dat well, forware, 'tis un good skoo,*
'tis gi mait van neits leither, se euer mine here.[51]

Enter a prentice.

L. MAIOR. I do beleeue it, whats the newes with you?
PRENTICE. Please you, the Earle of *Lincolne* at the gate
Is newly lighted, and would speake with you.
L. MAIOR. The Earle of *Lincolne* come to speak with me?
Well, well, I know his errand: daughter *Rose,*
Send hence your shoomaker, dispatch, haue done:
Sib, make things handsome: sir boy follow me.

Exit [Lord Maior, Sibil, *and prentice*].

LACIE. Mine vncle come, oh what may this portend?
Sweete *Rose,* this of our loue threatens an end.
ROSE. Be not dismaid at this: what ere befall,
Rose is thine owne, to witnes I speake truth,
Where thou appoints the place Ile meete with thee,
I will not fixe a day to follow thee,
But presently steale hence, do not replie.
Loue which gaue strength to beare my fathers hate,
Shall now adde wings to further our escape.

Exeunt.

[ACT IV, SCENE IV]

Enter [former] Lord Maior, *and* LINCOLNE.

L. MAIOR. Beleeue me, on my credite I speak truth,
Since first your nephew *Lacie* went to *France,*
I haue not seene him. It seemd strange to me,
When *Dodger* told me that he staide behinde,
Neglecting the hie charge the king imposed.
LINCOLNE. Trust me (sir *Roger Otley*) I did thinke
Your counsell had giuen head to this attempt,
Drawne to it by the loue he beares your child.
Here I did hope to find him in your house;
But now I see mine error, and confesse
My iudgment wrongd you by conceiuing so.
L. MAIOR. Lodge in my house, say you? trust me my Lord,
I loue your Nephew *Lacie* too too dearely
So much to wrong his honor, and he hath done so,
That first gaue him aduise to stay from *France.*
To witnesse I speake truth, I let you know,

51. Yes, yes, I know that well, indeed it is a good shoe, it is made of cow's leather, just look, my lord.

How carefull I haue beene to keepe my daughter
Free from all conference, or speech of him,
Not that I skorne your Nephew, but in loue
I beare your honour, lest your noble bloud,
Should by my meane worth be dishonoured.

LINCOLNE. [*Aside.*] How far the churles tongue wanders from his hart[.]
Well, well sir Roger Otley I beleeve you,
With more than many thankes for the kind loue,
So much you seeme to beare me: but my Lord,
Let me request your helpe to seeke my Nephew,
Whom if I find, Ile straight embarke for *France,*
So shal your *Rose* be free, my thoughts at rest,
And much care die which now lies in my brest.

Enter Sibil.

SIBIL. Oh Lord, help for Gods sake, my mistris; oh my yong mistris.

L. MAIOR. Where is thy mistris? whats become of her?

SIBIL. Shees gone, shees fled.

L. MAIOR. Gone? whither is she fled?

SIBIL. I know not forsooth, shes fled out of doores with *Hans* the shoomaker, I saw them scud, scud, scud, apace, apace.

L. MAIOR. Which way? what *Iohn,* where be my men? which way?

SIBIL. I know not, an it please your worship.

L. MAIOR. Fled with a shoomaker, can this be true?

SIBIL. Oh Lord sir, as true as Gods in Heauen.

LINCOLNE. Her loue turnd shoomaker? I am glad of this.

L. MAIOR. A fleming butter boxe, a shoomaker,
Will she forget her birth? requite my care
With such ingratitude? Skornd she yong *Hammon,*
To love a honnikin,° a needie knaue? — despised fellow
Wel let her flie, Ile not flie after her,
Let her starue, if she wil, shees none of mine.

LINCOLNE. Be not so cruel, sir.

Enter Firke *with shooes.*

SIBIL. I am glad shees scapt.

L. MAIOR. Ile not account of her as of my child:
Was there no better obiect for her eies,
But a foul drunken lubber, swill bellie,
A shoomaker, thats braue.° — excellent (said sarcastically)

FIRKE. Yea forsooth, tis a very braue shooe, and as fit as a pudding.

L. MAIOR. How now, what knaue is this, from whence commest thou?

FIRKE. No knaue sir, I am *Firke* the shoomaker, lusty *Rogers* cheefe lustie iourneyman, and I come hither to take vp the prettie legge of sweete mistris Rose, and thus hoping your worshippe is in as good health as I was at the making hereof, I bid you farewell, yours *Firke.*

L. MAIOR. Stay stay sir knaue.

LINCOLNE. Come hither, shoomaker.

FIRKE. Tis happie the knaue is put before the shoomaker, or else I would not haue vouchsafed to come backe to you, I am moued, for I stirre.

L. MAIOR. My Lorde, this villaine calles vs knaues by craft.

FIRKE. Then tis by the Gentle Craft, and to cal one knaue gently, is no harme: sit your worship merie: *Sib* your yong mistris, Ile so bob° them, now my Maister *Eyre* is Lorde Maior of *London.* — deceive

L. MAIOR. Tell me sirra, whoes man are you?

FIRKE. I am glad to see your worship so merrie, [*pointing to* Sibil] I haue no maw to this geere, no stomacke as yet to a red peticote.

LINCOLNE. He means not sir to wooe you to his maid,
But onely doth demand whose man you are.

FIRKE. I sing now to the tune of Rogero, *Roger* my felow is now my master.

LINCOLNE. Sirra, knowst thou one *Hans* a shoomaker?

FIRKE. *Hans* shoomaker, oh yes, stay, yes, I haue him, I tel you what, I speake it in secret, mistris *Rose,* and he are by this time: no not so, but shortly are to come ouer one another with Can you dance the shaking of the sheetes? it is that *Hans* [*Aside.*] Ile so gull these diggers.[52]

L. MAIOR. Know'st thou then where he is?

FIRKE. Yes, forsooth, yea marry.

LINCOLNE. Canst thou, in sadnesse?° — seriousness

FIRKE. No forsooth, no, marrie.

L. MAIOR. Tell me, good honest fellow, where he is,
And thou shalt see what Ile bestow of thee.

FIRKE. Honest fellow, no sir, not so sir, my profession is the Gentle Craft, I care not for seeing, I loue feeling, let me feele it here, *aurium tenus,*° ten peeces of gold, *genuum tenus,*° ten pieces of silver, and then *Firke* is your man in a new paire of strechers.°[53] — up to the ears; up to the knees; quibbles

L. MAIOR. Here is an angel, part of thy reward,
Which I will giue thee, tell me where he is.

FIRKE. No point: shal I betray my brother? no, shal I prove *Iudas* to *Hans?* no, shall I crie treason to my corporation? no, I shall be firkt and yerkt then, but giue me your angell, your angell shal tell you.

LINCOLNE. Doe so good fellow, tis no hurt to thee.

FIRKE. Send simpering *Sib* away.

52. "diggers" in the sense that Otley and Lincolne are digging for information.
53. Bald's edition has "in a new paire of strechers" as an aside.

L. MAIOR. Huswife,° get you in. hussy

Exit Sibil.

FIRKE. Pitchers have eares, and maides haue wide mouthes: but for *Hans Prauns,* vpon my word, to morrow morning, he and young mistris *Rose* goe to this geere,° they shall be married together, by this rush, or else tourne Firke to a firkin of butter, to tanne leather withal. business

L. MAIOR. But art thou sure of this?

FIRKE. Am I sure that *Paules* steeple is a handfull higher than *London* stone? or that the pissing conduit leakes nothing but pure mother Bunch?[54] am I sure I am lustie *Firke*, Gods nailes do you thinke I am so base to gull you?

LINCOLNE. Where are they married? dost thou know the church?

FIRKE. I neuer goe to church, but I know the name of it, it is a swearing church,[55] stay a while, 'tis: I by the mas, no, no, tis I by my troth, no nor that, tis I by my faith, that that, tis I by my *Faithes* Church vnder *Paules* crosse, There they shall be knit like a paire of stockings in matrimonie, there theile be in conie.° well in

LINCOLNE. Vpon my life, my Nephew *Lacie* walkes
In the disguise of this Dutch shoomaker.

FIRKE. Yes forsooth.

LINCOLNE. Doth he not honest fellow?

FIRKE. No forsooth, I thinke *Hans* is no bodie but *Hans,* no spirite.

L. MAIOR. My mind misgiues me now tis so, indeede.

LINCOLNE. My cosen speakes the language, knowes the trade.

L. MAIOR. Let me request your companie my Lord,
Your honourable presence may, no doubt,
Refraine their head-strong rashnesse, when my selfe
Going alone perchance may be oreborne,
Shall I request this fauour?

LINCOLNE. This, or what else.

FIRKE. Then you must rise betimes, for they meane to fal to their hey passe, and repasse,° pindy pandy, which hand will you haue, very earely. magician's spiel

L. MAIOR. My care shal euery way equal their haste,
This night accept your lodging in my house,
The earlier shal we stir, and at Saint *Faithes*
Preuent this giddy hare-braind nuptiall,
This trafficke of hot loue shal yeeld cold gaines,
They ban our loues, and weele forbid their baines.[56]

Exit.

54. Strong ale, from the establishment of a woman who also supposedly ran a brothel.

55. i.e., a church whose name could be used in an oath, as in "Faith. . . ."

56. The public announcement of an intent to marry was made to allow objections to be placed; as a father, the mayor has the right to forbid his daughter's marriage.

LINCOLNE. At Saint *Faithes* Church thou saist?
FIRKE. Yes, by their troth.
LINCOLNE. Be secret on thy life.

Exit.

FIRKE. Yes, when I kisse your wife, ha, ha, heres no craft in the Gentle Craft, I came hither of purpose with shooes to sir *Rogers* worship, whilst *Rose* his daughter be coniecatcht° by *Hans:* soft nowe, these two gulles will be at Saint *Faithes* Church to morrow morning, to take master Bridegroome, and mistris Bride napping, and they in the meane time shal chop vp the matter at the Sauoy:[57] but the best sport is, sir *Roger Otley* wil find my felow, lame *Rafes* wife going to marry a gentleman, and then heele stop her in steede of his daughter; oh braue, there wil be fine tickling sport: soft now, what haue I to doe? oh I know; now a messe of shoomakers meate at the wooll sack° in Ivie Lane, to cozen my gentleman of lame Rafes wife, thats true,

won by a trick

the name of a tavern

Alacke, alacke
Girles, holde out tacke,
For now smockes for this iumbling
Shall goe to wracke.

Exit.

[ACT V, SCENE I]

Enter Eyre, *his* Wife, [Lacie *as*] Hans, *and* Rose.

EYRE. This is the morning then, stay, my bully, my honest *Hans,* is it not?

LACIE. This is the morning that must make vs two
Happy, or miserable, therefore, if you—

EYRE. Away with these iffes and ands *Hans,* and these *et caeteras,* by mine honour, *Rowland Lacie* none but the king shall wrong thee: come, feare nothing, am not I *Sim Eyre?* Is not *Sim Eyre* Lord mayor of *London?* feare nothing *Rose,* let them al say what they can, dainty come thou to me: laughest thou?

WIFE. Good my lord, stand her friend in what thing you may.

EYRE. Why my sweete Lady *Madgy,* thincke you *Simon Eyre* can forget his fine dutch Iourneyman? No vah. Fie I scorne it, it shall neuer be cast in my teeth, that I was vnthankeful. Lady *Madgy,* thou hadst never couered thy Saracens head with this french flappe, nor loaden thy bumme with this farthingale, tis trash, trumpery, vanity, *Simon Eyre* had neuer walkte in a redde petti-

57. The chapel of a charity hospital outside city jurisdiction, and hence useful for marriages that lacked family approval.

coate, nor wore a chaine of golde, but for my fine Iourneymans portigues, and shall I leaue him? No: Prince am I none, yet beare a princely minde.

LACIE. My Lorde, tis time for vs to part from hence.

EYRE. Lady *Madgy,* lady *Madgy,* take two or three of my pie-crust eaters, my buffe-ierkin varlets, that doe walke in blacke gownes at *Simon Eyres* heeles, take them good lady *Madgy,* trippe and goe, my browne Queene of Perriwigs, with my delicate *Rose,* and my iolly *Rowland* to the Sauoy, see them linckte, countenaunce the marriage, and when it is done, cling, cling together, you Hamborow° [Hamburg] Turtle Doues, Ile beare you out, come to *Simon Eyre,* come, dwell with me *Hans,* thou shalt eate mincde pies and marchpane. *Rose,* away cricket, trippe and goe my Lady *Madgy* to the Sauoy, *Hans,* wed, and to bed, kisse, and away, go, vanish.

WIFE. Farewel my lord.

ROSE. Make haste sweete loue.

WIFE. Sheede faine the deede were done.

LACIE. Come my sweete *Rose,* faster than Deere weele runne.

They goe out.

EYRE. Goe, vanish, vanish, auaunt I say: by the lorde of Ludgate, its a madde life to be a lorde Mayor; its a stirring life, a fine life, a velvet life, a carefull life. Well *Simon Eyre,* yet set a good face on it, in the honour of sainct *Hugh.* Soft, the king this day comes to dine with me, to see my new buildings, his maiesty is welcome, he shal haue good cheere, delicate cheere, princely cheere. This day my felow prentises of *London* come to dine with me too, they shall have fine cheere, gentlemanlike cheere. I promised the mad Cappidosians, when we all serued at the Conduit together, that if euer I came to be Mayor of *London,* I woould feast them al, and Ile doot, Ile doot, by the life of *Pharaoh,* by this beard, *Sim Eyre* will be no flincher. Besides, I have procurd, that vpon euery Shrove-tuesday, at the sound of the pancake bell: my fine dapper Assyrian lads, shall clap vp their shop windows, and away, this is the day, and this day they shall doot, they shall doot: Boyes, that day are you free, let masters care, And prentises shall pray for *Simon Eyre.*

Exit.

[ACT V, SCENE II]

Enter Hodge, Firke, Rafe, *and five or sixe shoomakers, all with cudgels, or such weapons.*

HODGE. Come *Rafe,* stand to it *Firke:* my masters, as we are the braue bloods of the shooemakers, heires apparant to Saint

Hugh, and perpetual benefactors to all good fellowes, thou shalt haue no wrong: were *Hammon* a king of spades, he should not delue in thy close without thy sufferaunce: but tell me *Rafe,* art thou sure tis thy wife?

RAFE. Am I sure this is *Firke?* This morning, when I strokte on her shooes, I lookte vpon her, and she vpon me, and sighed, askte me if euer I knew one *Rafe.* Yes sayde I: for his sake saide she (teares standing in her eyes) and for thou art somewhat like him, spend this peece of golde: I tooke it: my lame leg, and my trauel beyond sea made me vnknown, all is one for that, I know shees mine.

FIRKE. Did she giue thee this gold? O glorious glittering gold; shees thine owne, tis thy wife, and she loues thee, for Ile stand toot, theres no woman will giue golde to any man, but she thinkes better of him than she thinkes of them shee giues siluer to: and for *Hammon,* neither *Hammon* nor Hangman shall wrong thee in *London:* Is not our olde maister *Eyre* lord Mayor? Speake my hearts.

ALL. Yes, and *Hammon* shall know it to his cost.

Enter Hammon, *his men,* Iane, *and others.*

HODGE. Peace my bullies, yonder they come.

RAFE. Stand toot, my hearts, *Firke,* let me speak first.

HODGE. No *Rafe,* let me: *Hammon,* whither away so earely?

HAMMON. Vnmannerly rude slaue, whats that to thee?

FIRKE. To him sir? yes sir, and to me, and others: good morow *Iane,* how doost thou? good Lord, how the world is changed with you, God be thanked.

HAMMON. Villaines, handes off, howe dare you touch my loue?

ALL. Villaines? downe with them, cry clubs for prentises.

HODGE. Hold, my hearts: touch her *Hammon?* Yea and more than that, weele carry her away with vs. My maisters and gentlemen, neuer draw your bird spittes, shooemakers are steele to the backe, men euery inch of them, all spirite.

ALL OF HAMMONS SIDE. Wel, and what of all this?

HODGE. Ile shew you: *Iane,* dost thou know this man? tis *Rafe* I can tell thee: nay, tis he in faith, though he be lamde by the warres, yet looke not strange, but run to him, fold him about the necke and kisse him.

IANE. Liues then my husband? oh God let me go,
Let me embrace my *Rafe.*

HAMMON. What meanes my *Iane?*

IANE. Nay, what meant you to tell me, he was slaine?

HAMMON. Pardon me deare loue for being misled.
[*To* Rafe.] Twas rumord here in *London* thou wert dead.

FIRKE. Thou seest he liues: Lasse, goe packe home with him: now maister *Hammon,* wheres your mistris your wife?

SERU. Swounds maister, fight for her, will you thus lose her?
ALL. Downe with that creature, clubs, downe with him.
HODGE. Hold, hold.
HAMMON. Hold foole, sirs he shal do no wrong.
Wil my *Iane* leaue me thus, and break her faith?
FIRKE. Yea sir, she must sir, she shal sir, what then? mend it.
HODGE. Hearke fellow *Rafe,* folowe my counsel, set the wench in the midst, and let her chuse her man, and let her be his woman.
IANE. Whom should I choose? whom should my thoughts affect,
But him whom Heauen hath made to be my loue?
Thou art my husband, and these humble weedes,
Makes thee more beautiful than all his wealth,
Therefore I wil but put off his attire,
Returning it into the owners hand,
And after euer be thy constant wife.
HODGE. Not a ragge *Iane,* the law's on our side, he that sowes in another mans ground forfets his haruest, get thee home *Rafe,* follow him *Iane,* he shall not haue so much as a buske point° (corset lace) from thee.
FIRKE. Stand to that *Rafe,* the appurtenances are thine owne, *Hammon,* looke not at her.
SERU. O swounds no.
FIRKE. Blew coate be quiet, weele giue you a new liuerie[58] else, weele make Shroue Tuesday Saint *Georges* Day for you: looke not *Hammon,* leare not, Ile firke you, for thy head now, one glance, one sheepes eie, any thing at her, touch not a ragge, least I and my brethren beat you to clowtes.° (rags)
SERU. Come master *Hammon,* theres no striuing here.
HAMMON. Good fellowes, heare me speake: and, honest *Rafe,*
Whom I have iniured most by louing *Iane,*
Marke what I offer thee: here in faire gold
Is twentie pound, Ile giue it for thy *Iane,*
If this content thee not, thou shalt haue more.
HODGE. Sell not thy wife *Rafe,* make her not a whore.
HAMMON. Say, wilt thou freely cease thy claime in her
And let her be my wife?
ALL. No, do not *Rafe.*
RAFE. Sirra *Hammon, Hammon,* dost thou thinke a Shooe-maker is so base, to bee a bawde to his owne wife for commoditie, take thy golde, choake with it, were I not lame, I would make thee eate thy words.
FIRKE. A shoomaker sell his flesh and bloud, oh indignitie!
HODGE. Sirra, take vp your pelfe,[59] and be packing.

58. i.e., a new servant's uniform, possibly in this case because the blue coat will be stained with the red of the servant's blood.

59. Money or other objects of wealth, but with the connotation of ill-gotten gain.

HAMMON. I will not touch one pennie, but in liew
Of that great wrong I offered thy *Iane,*
To *Iane* and thee I giue that twentie pound,
Since I haue faild of her, during my life
I vow no woman else shall be my wife:
Farewell good fellowes of the Gentle trade,
Your mornings mirth my mourning day hath made.

Exeunt.

FIRKE. [To *seruant going out*] Touch the gold, creature if you dare, ya're best be trudging: here *Iane* take thou it, now lets home, my hearts.

HODGE. Stay, who comes here? *Iane,* on againe with thy maske.

Enter Lincolne, [*former*] Lord Maior *and servants.*

LINCOLNE. Yonders the lying varlet mockt vs so.
L. MAIOR. Come hither sirra.
FIRKE. I sir, I am sirra, you meane me, do you not?
LINCOLNE. Where is my Nephew married?
FIRKE. Is he married? God give him ioy, I am glad of it: they haue a faire day, and the signe is in a good planet, *Mars in Venus.*

L. MAIOR. Villaine, thou toldst me that my daughter *Rose,*
This morning should be married at Saint *Faithes,*
We haue watcht there these three houres at the least,
Yet see we no such thing.
FIRKE. Truly, I am sorie for't, a Bride's a prettie thing.
HODGE. Come to the purpose, yonder's the Bride and Bridegroome you looke for I hope: Though you be Lordes, you are not to barre, by your authoritie, men from women, are you?

L. MAIOR. See see my daughters maskt.
LINCOLNE. True, and my Nephew,
To hide his guilt, counterfeits him lame.
FIRKE. Yea truely god helpe the poore couple, they are lame and blind.

L. MAIOR. Ile ease her blindnes.
LINCOLNE. Ile his lameness cure.
FIRKE. Lie downe sirs, and laugh, my felow *Rafe* is taken for *Rowland Lacie,* and *Iane* for mistris damaske *Rose,* this is all my knavery.

L. MAIOR. What, haue I found you, minion?
LINCOLNE. O base wretch,
Nay hide thy face, the horror of thy guilt,
Can hardly be washt off: where are thy powers?
What battels haue you made? O yes, I see
Thou foughtst with Shame, and Shame hath conquerd thee.
This lameness will not serue.
L. MAIOR. Vnmaske your selfe.

LINCOLNE. Leade home your daughter.
L. MAIOR. Take your Nephew hence.
RAFE. Hence, swounds, what meane you? are you mad? I hope you cannot inforce my wife from me, wheres *Hammon?*
L. MAIOR. Your wife?
LINCOLNE. What Hammon?
RAFE. Yea my wife and therfore the prowdest of you that laies hands on her first, Ile lay my crutch crosse his pate.° head
FIRKE. To him lame *Rafe,* here's braue sport.
RAFE. *Rose* call you her? why her name is *Iane,* [*unmasking* Iane.] looke here else, do you know her now?
LINCOLNE. Is this your daughter?
L. MAIOR. No, nor this your nephew:
My Lord of *Lincolne,* we are both abusde
By this base craftie varlet.
FIRKE. Yea forsooth no varlet, forsooth no base, forsooth I am but meane,[60] no craftie neither, but of the Gentle Craft.
L. MAIOR. Where is my daughter *Rose?* where is my child?
LINCOLNE. Where is my nephew *Lacie* married?
FIRKE. Why here is good lacde mutton as I promist you.
LINCOLNE. Villaine, Ile haue thee punisht for this wrong.
FIRKE. Punish the iornyman villaine, but not the iorneyman shoomaker.

Enter Dodger.

DODGER. My Lord I come to bring vnwelcome newes,
Your Nephew *Lacie,* and your daughter *Rose,*
Earely this morning wedded at the Sauoy,
None being present but the Ladie Mairesse:
Besides I learnt among the officers,
The Lord Maior vowes to stand in their defence,
Gainst any that shal seeke to crosse the match.
LINCOLNE. Dares *Eyre* the shoomaker vphold the deede?
FIRKE. Yes sir, shoomakers dare stand in a womans quarrel I warrant you, as deepe as another, and deeper too.
DODGER. Besides, his grace, to day dines with the Maior;
Who on his knees humbly intends to fall,
And beg a pardon for your Nephewes fault.
LINCOLNE. But Ile preuent him: come sir *Roger Otley,*
The king will doe vs iustice in this cause,
How ere their hands haue made them man and wife,
I will disioyne the match, or loose my life.

Exeunt.

60. To be taken in two senses: 1) of lower station; 2) the mean, or middle part, in a song requiring three voices; that is, Firke is not the "base."

FIRKE. Adue monsieur *Dodger,* farewel fooles, ha ha, Oh, if they had staide I would haue so lambde them with floutes,° O heart, my codpeece point is readie to flie in peeces euery time I thinke vpon mistris *Rose,* but let that passe, as my Ladie Mairesse saies.

insults

HODGE. This matter is answerd:° come *Rafe,* home with thy wife, come, my fine shoomakers, lets to our masters the new lord Maior and there swagger this shroue Tuesday, ile promise you wine enough, for Madge keepes the seller.

resolved

ALL. O rare! *Madge* is a good wench.

FIRKE. And Ile promise you meate enough, for simpring *Susan* keepes the larder, Ile leade you to victuals my braue souldiers, follow your captaine, O braue, hearke, hearke.

Bell ringes.

ALL. The Pancake bell rings, the pancake bel, tri-lill, my hearts.

FIRKE. Oh braue, oh sweete bell, O delicate pancakes, open the doores my hearts, and shut vp the windowes, keepe in the house, let out the pancakes: oh rare my heartes, lets march together for the honor of Saint *Hugh* to the great new hall in Gratious streete corner, which our Maister the newe lord Maior hath built.

RAFE. O the crew of good fellows that will dine at my lord Maiors cost to day!

HODGE. By the lord, my lord Maior is a most braue man, how shal prentises be bound to pray for him, and the honour of the gentlemen shoomakers? lets feede and be fat with my lordes bountye.

FIRKE. O musical bel stil! O *Hodge,* O my brethren! theres cheere for the heauens, venson pasties walke vp and down piping hote, like sergeants, beefe and brewesse comes marching in drie fattes,° fritters and pancakes comes trowling in in wheele barrowes; hennes and orenges hopping in porters baskets, colloppes and egges in scuttles,[61] and tartes and custardes comes quauering in in malt shouels.

barrels

Enter more prentises.

ALL. Whoop, looke here, looke here.

HODGE. How now, madde laddes, whither away so fast?

1 PRENTISE. Whither, Why, to the great new hall, know you not why? The lorde Maior hath bidden all the prentises in *London* to breakfast this morning.

ALL. Oh braue shoomaker, oh braue lord of incomprehensible good fellowship, whoo, heark you, the pancake bell rings.

Cast vp cups.

61. A shallow, open basket for carrying food.

FIRKE. Nay more, may hearts, euery Shrouetuesday is our yeere of Iubile: and when the pancake bel rings, we are as free as my lord Maior, we may shut vp our shops, and make holiday: Ile haue it calld, Saint *Hughes* Holiday.

ALL. Agreed, agreed, Saint *Hughes Holiday.*

HODGE. And this shal continue for euer.

ALL. Oh braue! come come my hearts, away, away.

FIRKE. O eternall credite to vs of the gentle Craft! march faire my hearts, oh rare.

Exeunt.

[ACT V, SCENE III]

Enter King and *his traine ouer the stage.*

KING. Is our lord Maior of *London* such a gallant?

NOBLE-MAN. One of the merriest madcaps in your land,
Your Grace will thinke, when you behold the man,
Hees rather a wilde ruffin than a Maior:
Yet thus much Ile ensure your majestie,
In al his actions that concerne his state,
He is as serious, prouident, and wise,
As full of gravitie amongst the graue,
As any maior hath beene these many yeares.

KING. I am with child, till I behold this huffe cap,[62]
But all my doubt is, when we come in presence,
His madnesse wil be dasht cleane out of countenance.

NOBLE-MAN. It may be so, my Liege.

KING. Which to preuent,
Let some one giue him notice, tis our pleasure,
That he put on his woonted merriment:
Set forward.

ALL. On afore.

Exeunt.

[ACT V, SCENE IV]

Enter Eyre, Hodge, Firk, Ralph, *and other shoemakers, all with napkins on their shoulders*

EYRE. Come my fine *Hodge,* my iolly gentlemen shooemakers, soft, where be these Caniballes, these varlets my officers, let them al walke and waite vpon my brethren, for my meaning is, that

62. Blusterer or swaggerer, from a kind of strong ale.

none but shoomakers, none but the liuery of my Company shall in their sattin hoodes wait vppon the trencher° of my soueraigne.

wooden plate

FIRKE. O my lord, it will be rare.

EYRE. No more *Firke,* come liuely, let your fellowe prentises want no cheere, let wine be plentiful as beere, and beere as water, hang these penny pinching fathers, that cramme wealth in innocent lamb skinnes, rip knaues, auaunt, looke to my guests!

HODGE. My Lord, we are at our wits end for roome, those hundred tables will not feast the fourth part of them.

EYRE. Then couer me those hundred tables againe, and againe, til all my iolly prentises be feasted: auoyde *Hodge,* runne *Rafe,* friske about my nimble *Firke,* carowse me fadome° healths to the honor of the shoomakers: do they drink liuely *Hodge?* do they tickle it *Firke?*

fathom

FIRKE. Tickle it? some of them haue taken their licuor standing so long, that they can stand no longer: but for meate, they would eate it and they had it.

EYRE. Want they meate? wheres this swag-belly, this greasie kitchinstuffe cooke, call the varlet to me: Want meat! *Firke, Hodge,* lame *Rafe,* runne my tall men, beleaguer the shambles,° beggar al East-Cheape, serue me whole oxen in chargers, and let sheepe whine vpon the tables like pigges for want of good felowes to eate them. Want meate! vanish, *Firke,* auaunt *Hodge.*

butcher shops

HODGE. Your lordship mistakes my man Firke, he means, their bellies want meate, not the boords; for they haue drunk so much, they can eate nothing.

Enter [Lacie *in the attire of*] Hans, Rose, *and* Wife.

WIFE. Where is my Lord[?]

EYRE. How now Lady *Madgy*[?]

WIFE. The kings most excelent maiesty is new come, hee sends me for thy honor: one of his most worshipful Peeres, bade me tel thou must be mery, and so forth: but let that passe.

EYRE. Is my Soueraigne come? vanish my tall shoomakers, my nimble brethren, looke to my guests, the prentises: yet stay a little, how now *Hans,* how lookes my little *Rose?*

LACIE. Let me request you to remember me,
I know your honour easily may obtaine,
Free pardon of the king for me and *Rose,*
And reconcile me to my vncles grace.

EYRE. Haue done my good *Hans,* my honest iorneyman, looke cheerely, Ile fall vpon both my knees till they be as hard as horne, but Ile get thy pardon.

WIFE. Good my Lord haue a care what you speake to his grace.

EYRE. Away, you Islington whitepot,° hence you happerarse,° you

a kind of custard; ass like a hopper

barly pudding° ful of magots, you broyld carbonado,° auaunt, auaunt, auoide, Mephostophilus: shall *Sim Eyre* learne to speake of° you Lady *Madgie?* vanish mother Miniuer cap,° vanish, goe, trip and goe, meddle with your partlets° and your pishery pasherie, your flewes° and your whirligigs, go, rub, out of mine alley: *Sim Eyre* knowes how to speake to a Pope, to Sultan *Soliman,* to *Tamburlaine* and he were here: and shal I melt? shal I droope before my Soueraigne? no, come my Lady *Madgie,* follow me *Hans,* about your businesse my frolicke free-booters:° *Firke,* friske about, and about, and about, for the honour of mad *Simon Eyre,* Lord Maior of *London.*

sausage, grilled meat
from; fur-trimmed cap;
collars; flaps
pirates

FIRKE. Hey for the honour of the shoemakers.

Exeunt.

[ACT V, SCENE V].

A long flourish or two: enter King, *Nobles,* Eyre, *his* wife, Lacie, Rose: Lacie *and* Rose *kneele.*

KING. Well *Lacie,* though the fact was verie foule,
Of your reuolting from our kingly loue,
And your owne duetie, yet we pardon you,
Rise both, and, mistris *Lacie,* thanke my Lord Maior
For your yong bridegroome here.

EYRE. So my deere liege, *Sim Eyre* and my brethren, the gentlemen shoomakers shal set your sweete maiesties image, cheeke by iowle by Saint *Hugh,* for this honour you haue done poore *Simon Eyre.* I beseech your grace, pardon my rude behauiour, I am a handicraftsman, yet my heart is without craft, I would be sory at my soule, that my boldnesse should offend my king.

KING. Nay, I pray thee good lord Maior, be euen as mery
As if thou wert among thy shoomakers,
It does me good to see thee in this humour.

EYRE. Saist thou me so my sweete *Dioclesian?*[63] then hump, Prince am I none, yet am I princely borne, by the Lord of Ludgate my Liege, Ile be as merrie as a pie.°

magpie

KING. Tel me infaith mad *Eyre,* how old thou art.

EYRE. My Liege a verie boy, a stripling, a younker, you see not a white haire on my head, not a gray in this beard, euerie haire I assure thy maiestie that stickes in this beard, *Sim Eyre* values at the king of *Babilons* ransome, *Tamar Chams*[64] beard was a rub-

63. Diocletian (emperor AD 284–305) was a notable reformer who brought relative peace and stability to the Roman Empire.

64. Subject of a two-part play (now lost) originally performed in 1592 but revived by Henslowe's Admiral's Men in 1596.

bing brush toot: yet Ile shaue it off, and stuffe tennis balls with it, to please my bully king.

KING. But all this while I do not know your age.

EYRE. My liege, I am sixe and fiftie yeare olde, yet I can crie humpe, with a sound heart for the honour of Saint *Hugh:* marke this old wench, my king, I dauncde the shaking of the sheetes with her sixe and thirtie yeares agoe, and yet I hope to get two or three yong Lord Maiors ere I die: I am lustie still, *Sim Eyre* still: care, and colde lodging brings white haires. My sweete Maiestie, let care vanish, cast it vppon thy Nobles, it will make thee looke always young like *Apollo,* and crye humphe:
Prince am I none, yet am I princely borne.

KING. Ha ha:
Saye *Cornewall,* didst thou euer see his like?

NOBLE-MAN. Not I, my lorde.

Enter Lincolne, *and [former]* Lord Maior.

KING. *Lincolne,* what newes with you?

LINCOLN. My gracious Lord, haue care vnto your selfe,
For there are traytors here.

ALL. Traytors, where? who?

EYRE. Traitors in my house? God forbid, where be my officers? Ile spend my soule ere my king feel harme.

KING. Where is the traytor, *Lincolne?*

LINCOLNE. Here he stands.

KING. *Cornewall,* lay hold on *Lacie: Lincolne,* speake:
What canst thou lay vnto thy Nephewes charge?

LINCOLNE. This my deere liege: your grace to doe me honour,
Heapt on the head of this degenerate boy,
Desertlesse fauours, you made choise of him,
To be commander ouer powers in *France.*
But he—

KING. Good Lincolne prythee pawse a while,
Euen in thine eies I reade what thou wouldst speake,
I know how *Lacie* did neglect our loue,
Ranne himselfe deepely (in the highest degree)
Into vile treason

LINCOLNE. Is he not a traytor?

KING. Lincolne, he was: now haue we pardned him,
Twas not a base want of true valors fire,
That held him out of *France,* but loues desire.

LINCOLNE. I will not bear his shame upon my back.

KING. Nor shalt thou *Lincolne,* I forgiue you both.

LINCOLNE. Then (good my liege) forbid the boy to wed
One, whose meane birth will much disgrace his bed.

KING. Are they not married?

LINCOLNE. No my Liege.
BOTH. We are.
KING. Shall I diuorce them then? O be it farre,
That any hand on earth should dare vntie,
The sacred knot, knit by Gods maiestie,
I would not for my crowne disioyn their hands,
That are conioynd in holy nuptiall bands,
How saist thou *Lacie?* wouldst thou loose thy *Rose?*
LACIE. Not for all *Indias* wealth, my soueraigne.
KING. But *Rose* I am sure her *Lacie* would foregoe.
ROSE. If *Rose* were askt that question, sheed say, no.
KING. You heare them *Lincolne.*
LINCOLNE. Yea my liege, I do.
KING. Yet canst thou find ith° heart to part these two? in thy
Who seeks, besides you, to diuorce these louers?
L. MAIOR. I do (my gracious Lord) I am her father.
KING. Sir *Roger Otley,* our last Maior I thinke?
NOBLE-MAN. The same, my liege.
KING. Would you offend Loues lawes?
Wel, you shal haue your wills, you sue to me,
To prohibite the match: Soft, let me see,
You both are married, *Lacie,* art thou not?
LACIE. I am, dread Soueraigne.
KING. Then vpon thy life,
I charge thee, not to call this woman wife.
L. MAIOR. I thanke your grace.
ROSE. O my most gratious Lord! *Kneele[s].*
KING. Nay *Rose,* neuer wooe me, I tel you true,
Although as yet I am a batchellor,
Yet I beleeve I shal not marry you.
ROSE. Can you diuide the body from the soule,
Yet make the body liue?
KING. Yea, so profound?
I cannot *Rose,* but you I must diuide:
Faire maide, this bridegroome cannot be your bride.
Are you pleasde *Lincolne? Oteley,* are you pleasde?
BOTH. Yes my Lord.
KING. Then must my heart be easde;
For credit me, my conscience liues in paine,
Till these whom I deuorcde be ioynd againe:
Lacie, giue me thy hand, *Rose,* lend me thine.
Be what you would be: kisse now: so, thats fine,
At night (louers) to bed: now let me see,
Which of you all mislikes this harmony.
L. MAIOR. Wil you then take from me my child perforce?
KING. Why tell me *Oteley,* shines not *Lacies* name,

As bright in the worldes eye as the gay beames
Of any citizen?
LINCOLNE. Yea but, my gratious Lord,
I do mislike the match farre more than he,
Her bloud is too too base.
KING. *Lincolne,* no more,
Dost thou not know, that loue respects no bloud?
Cares not for difference of birth, or state,
The maide is yong, wel borne, faire, vertuous,
A worthy bride for any gentleman:
Besides, your nephew for her sake did stoope
To bare necessitie: and as I heare,
Forgetting honors, and all courtly pleasures,
To gaine her loue, became a shooemaker.
As for the honor which he lost in *France,*
Thus I redeeme it: *Lacie,* kneele thee downe,
Arise sir *Rowland Lacie:* tell me now,
Tell me in earnest Oteley, canst thou chide,
Seeing thy *Rose* a ladie and a bryde?
L. MAIOR. I am content with what your grace hath done.
LINCOLNE. And I my liege, since theres no remedie.
KING. Come on then, al shake hands, Ile haue you friends;
Where there is much loue, all discord ends,
What sayes my mad Lord Maior to all this loue?
EYRE. O my liege, this honour you haue done to my fine iourney-man here, *Rowland Lacie,* and all these fauours which you haue showne to me this daye in my poore house, will make *Simon Eyre* liue longer by one dozen of warme summers more than he should.
KING. Nay, my mad Lord Maior (that shall be thy name)
If any grace of mine can length thy life,
One honour more Ile doe thee: that new building,
Which at thy cost in Cornehill is erected,
Shall take a name from vs, weele have it cald
The Leaden hall, because in digging it
You found the lead that couereth the same.
EYRE. I thanke your Maiestie.
WIFE. Gold blesse your grace.
KING. *Lincolne,* a word with you.

Enter Hodge, Firke, Ralph, *and more shoomakers.*

EYRE. How now my mad knaues? Peace, speake softly, yonder is the king.
KING. With the olde troupe which there we keepe in pay,
We wil incorporate a new supply:
Before one summer more passe ore my head,

France shall repent *England* was iniured.
What are all those?

LACIE. All shoomakers, my Liege,
Sometime my fellowes, in their companies
I livde as merry as an emperor.

KING. My mad lord Mayor, are all these shoomakers?

EYRE. All Shooemakers, my Liege, all gentleman of the Gentle Craft, true Troians, couragious Cordwainers, they all kneele to the shrine of holy saint *Hugh.*

ALL SHOOMAKERS. God saue your maiesty.

KING. Mad *Simon,* would they anything with vs?

EYRE. Mum mad knaues, not a word, Ile doot, I warrant you. They are all beggars, my Liege, all for themselues: and I for them all, on both my knees do intreate, that for the honor of poore *Simon Eyre,* and the good of his brethren these mad knaues, your Grace would vouchsafe some priuilege to my new Leden hall, that it may be lawfull for vs to buy and sell leather there two dayes a weeke.

KING. Mad *Sim,* I grant your suite, you shall haue patent
To hold two market dayes in Leden hall,
Mondayes and Fridayes, those shal be the times:
Will this content you?

ALL. Iesus blesse your Grace.

EYRE. In the name of these my poorebrethren shoomakers, I most humbly thanke your Grace. But before I rise, seeing you are in the Giuing vaine, and we in the Begging, graunt *Sim Eyre* one boone more.

KING. What is it my Lord Maior?

EYRE. Vouchsafe to taste of a poore banquet that standes sweetely waiting for your sweete presence.

KING. I shall vndo thee *Eyre,* only with feasts,
Already haue I beene too troublesome,
Say, haue I not?

EYRE. O my deere king, *Sim Eyre* was taken vnawares vpon a day of shrouing which I promist long ago to the prentises of *London:*
For andt please your Highnes, in time past
I bare the water tankerd,[65] and my coate
Sits not a whit the worse vpon my backe:
And then vpon a morning, some mad boyes,
It was Shrouetuesday euene as tis now,
gaue me my breakefast, and I swore then by the stopple of my tankerd, if euer I came to be Lord Maior of *London,* I would feast al the prentises. This day (my liege) I did it, and the slaues

65. Simon was an apprentice.

had an hundred tables fiue times couered, they are gone home and vanisht:
Yet adde more honour to the Gentle Trade,
Taste of *Eyres* banquet, *Simon's* happie made.

KING. *Eyre,* I wil taste of thy banquet, and wil say,
I haue not met more pleasure on a day,
Friends of the Gentle Craft, thankes to you al,
Thanke, my kind Ladie Mairesse for our cheere,
Come Lordes, a while lets reuel it at home,
When all our sports, and banquetings are done,
Warres must right wrongs which Frenchmen haue begun.

Exeunt.

Finis.

The Jew of Malta

Christopher Marlowe—the name as it usually appears in contemporary references, although his signature was "Cristofer Marley"—is somewhat unusual among his contemporaries because of the amount of detail we have on his life as a consequence of his academic and criminal records: this has invited speculation which, while plausible, cannot be confirmed. Born in 1564 (the same year as Shakespeare), he was the son of a Canterbury shoemaker, but received a scholarship to the King's School in Canterbury. He then received a Parker scholarship to Corpus Christi College, Cambridge. This scholarship required the candidate to express an intention to take holy orders, but Marlowe was never ordained. At Cambridge, Marlowe began his literary career writing the exquisite pastoral lyric "The Passionate Shepherd to His Love" and a play, *Dido, Queen of Carthage,* and translating Ovid's *Amores.*

In 1584 Marlowe took his AB. In 1587 he applied for his MA. Records show that he had been absent from Cambridge so often that he did not meet the residency requirement, and when he was at Cambridge he spent money in the buttery more freely than his means would seem to allow. He was granted his degree at the request of the Privy Council because, according to the council, while Marlowe was away he had done the queen "good service," nor had he permanently intended to join the Catholic seminary at Rheims. This has led many to the conclusion that he had spied for the government on Catholics abroad.

His dramatic breakthrough was *Tamburlaine the Great,* produced in 1587 and printed with Part Two of *Tamburlaine* in 1590. All of Marlowe's other plays were published posthumously, unsurprisingly since no one regarded popular drama as terribly important, and the author was paid for the play by the company acting it, and received no further income from it. *Dr. Faustus* probably follows *Tamburlaine* and exists in two texts, quartos from 1604 and 1616. Sometime during these years, Marlowe also wrote the brief play *The Massacre*

The text is based on Roma Gill's *The Complete Works of Christopher Marlowe,* vol. IV (Oxford: The Clarendon Press, 1995), 2–88. I have, in places, altered the punctuation and have standardized the spelling of names (i.e., "Barabas" throughout, "Abigall" throughout, etc).

of Paris. *The Jew of Malta* was performed in 1592 and entered in the Stationer's Register in 1594, although the earliest printed text is from 1633. *Edward the Second* was acted around 1592 and entered in the Stationer's Register in 1593 after Marlowe's death. Marlowe also wrote the long narrative poem *Hero and Leander*, published posthumously in 1598.

Marlowe was frequently in trouble with the law. In 1589 he was charged with murder and sent to Newgate, but acquitted two weeks later. In 1592 Marlowe was involved in a street fight in which a man was killed, although Marlowe was ultimately not prosecuted. Also in 1592 he was charged with counterfeiting in the Netherlands and expelled from the country. In 1593 a complex series of events involving an anonymous anti-Protestant refugee poster, written in blank verse and signed "Tamburlaine," led to the rooms of the playwright Thomas Kyd being searched, and a treatise was found that the authorities found heretical. Under torture, Kyd claimed that the treatise belonged to Marlowe. A warrant for Marlowe was issued by the Privy Council, and he presented himself to the council on May 20 and was ordered to attend them daily until further notice. On May 30, 1593, Marlowe was at a house in Deptford with three men, Ingram Frizer, Robert Poley, and Nicholas Skeres, all of whom had been employed by Sir Francis Walsingham or Thomas Walsingham, the former of whom was Elizabeth's head of espionage. In a dispute over the reckoning, Marlowe was stabbed over the right eye by Frizer, who was subsequently pardoned after a jury found he had acted in self-defense.

Enormous amounts of speculation surround Marlowe's death, sexuality, and religious beliefs, or lack thereof. But his real importance was what Ben Jonson called "Marlowe's mighty line," a stately, powerful blank verse that for the most part determined the poetic form of English serious drama for several hundred years, and Marlowe's ambitious, villainous protagonists, who are defined by their will to power. Inevitably, his protagonists are punished for their crimes, but at the same time their enemies seem equally culpable and less vital. In *The Jew of Malta*, only Abigall is sympathetic; like Shakespeare's Shylock, Barabas does not claim that he is as good as the Christians, only that they are every bit as bad as he—just not as good at it.

The Jew of Malta

DRAMATIS PERSONAE

MACHEVIL, *Prologue*
BARABAS, *the Jew of Malta*
ABIGALL, *the Jew's daughter*
ITHIMORE, *the Jew's slave*
GOVERNOR (FERNEZE), *of Malta*
DON LODOWICKE, *the Governor's Son*
DON MATHIAS, *friend to Don Lodowicke*
MATER (KATHERIN), *mother to Mathias*
SELIM CALYMATH, *son to the Grand Signior of Turkey*
BASSO (CALLAPINE), *to Calymath*
MARTIN DEL BOSCO, *the Spanish Vice-Admiral*
1 FRYAR (JACOMO)
2 FRYAR (BERNADINE)
ABBASE
PILIA-BORZA°, pickpocket
CURTEZANE
Two Merchants
Three Jews
Knights, Bassoes, Officers, Nun, Slaves, Messenger, Carpenters.

[PROLOGUE.]

[*Enter.*] Machevil.[1]

Albeit the world thinke *Machevill* is dead,
Yet was his soule but flowne beyond the *Alpes,*
And now the *Guize* is dead,[2] is come from *France*
To view this Land, and frolicke with his friends.
To some perhaps my name is odious,
But such as love me, gard me from their tongues,
And let them know that I am *Machevill,*
And weigh not men, and therefore not mens words:
Admir'd I am of those that hate me most.

1. Niccolò Machiavelli (1449–1527) was the author of *The Prince* (first printed in 1532). Manuscripts of the work were in England by around 1540; the work was officially banned in England in 1559, and the first printed translation in English was not published until 1640. Especially to those who had not read him, he came to be seen as the archetype of the "cunning or duplicitious statesman" (Oxford English Dictionary).

2. Henry I, Duke of Guise (1550–88), was the founder of the Catholic League in France and was associated with the St. Bartholomew's Day Massacre of French Protestants in 1572. He was assassinated by Henry III, king of France, when he challenged royal authority.

Though some speake openly against my bookes,
Yet will they reade me and thereby attaine
To *Peters* chayre: And when they cast me off,
Are poyson'd by my climing followers.
I count religion but a childish Toy,
And hold there is no sinne but Ignorance.
Birds of the aire will tell of murders past;
I am asham'd to heare such fooleries:
Many will talke of Title to a Crowne.
What right had *Caesar* to the Empery?
Might first made Kings, and Lawes were then most sure
When like the *Dracos* they were writ in blood.[3]
Hence comes it, that a strong built Citadell
Commands much more then letters can import:
Which maxime had but *Phaleris* observ'd,
H'had never bellowed in a brasen Bull[4]
Of great ones envy: o'th poore petty wites,
Let me be envy'd and not pittied!
But whither am I bound, I come not, I,
To reade a lecture here in *Britanie*,
But to present the Tragedy of a Jew,
Who smiles to see how full his bags are cramb'd
Which mony was not got without my meanes.
I crave but this, Grace him as he deserves,
And let him not be entertain'd the worse
Because he favours me.

[*Exit.*]

ACTUS PRIMUS [SCAENA 1].

Enter Barabas *in his Counting-house, with heaps of gold before him.*

BARABAS. So that of thus much that returne was made:
And of the third part of the Persian ships
There was the venture summ'd and satisfied.
As for those Samnites, and the men of *Uzz*,
That bought my Spanish Oyles, and Wines of *Greece*,
Here have I purst their paltry silverlings.° chief Hebrew coin
Fye; what a trouble tis to count this trash.

3. Draco (c. seventh-century BC) created a written code of law administered by courts: an advance on blood feud, the code was so harsh that the adjective "draconian" is derived from it.

4. Phalaris was a Sicilian tyrant from c. 570–554 BC: supposedly he roasted his enemies in a brass bull so he could hear their screams, and was himself roasted when he fell. In Pindar's *First Pythian Ode*, he is the scorn and detestation of mankind.

Well fare the Arabians, who so richly pay,
The things they traffique for with wedge of gold,
Whereof a man may easily in a day
Tell° that which may maintaine him all his life. — count
The needy groome that never fingered groat,
Would make a miracle of thus much coyne:
But he whose steele-bard coffers are cramb'd full,
And all his life time hath bin tired,
Wearying his fingers ends with telling it,
Would in his age be loath to labour so,
And for a pound to sweate himself to death:
Give me the Merchants of the Indian Mynes,
That trade in mettall of the purest mould;
The wealthy Moore, that in the Easterne rockes
Without controule can picke his riches up,
And in his house heape pearle like pibble-stones,
Receive them free, and sell them by the weight;
Bags of fiery Opals, Saphires, Amatists,
Jacints,[5] hard Topas, grasse-greene Emeraulds,
Beauteous Rubyes, sparkling Diamonds,
And seildsene° costly stones of so great price, — seldom seen
As one of them, indifferently rated,
And of a Carrect° of this quantity, — carat
May serve in perill of calamity
To ransome great Kings from captivity.
This is the ware wherein consists my wealth:
And thus me thinkes should men of judgement frame
Their meanes of traffique from the vulgar trade,
And as their wealth increaseth, so inclose
Infinite riches in a little room.
But now how stands the wind?
Into what corner peeres my Halcions bill?
Ha, to the east? yes: See how stand the Vanes?
East and by-South: why then I hope my ships
I sent for *Egypt* and the bordering Iles
Are gotten up by *Nilus* winding bankes:
Mine Argosie from *Alexandria*,
Loaden with Spice and Silks, now under saile,
Are smoothly gliding down by *Candie*° shoare — Crete
To *Malta*, through our *Mediterranean* sea.
But who comes heare?

5. Among the ancients a blue stone, by Marlowe's time it could be a garnet or a topaz.

Enter a MERCHANT.

How now?
I MERCHANT. Barabas,
Thy ships are safe, riding in Malta Rhode:
And all the Merchants with ther Merchandize
Are safe arriv'd, and have sent me to know
Whether your selfe will come and custome° them. pay customs duty
BARABAS. The ships are safe thou saist, and richly fraught[?]
I MERCHANT. They are.
BARABAS. Why, then goe bid them come ashore,
And bring with them their bils of entry:
I hope our credit in the Custome-house
Will serve as well as I were present there.
Goe send 'um threescore Camels, thirty Mules,
And twenty Waggons to bring up the ware.
But art thou master in a ship of mine,
And is thy credit not enough for that?
I MERCHANT. The very Custome barely comes to more
Than many Merchants of the towne are worth,
And therefore farre exceeds my credit, Sir.
BARABAS. Goe tell 'em the Jew of Malta sent thee, man:
Tush, who amongst 'em knowes not *Barabas?*
I MERCHANT. I goe.
BARABAS. So then, there's somewhat come.
Sirra, which of my ships art thou Master of?
I MERCHANT. Of the *Speranza,* Sir.
BARABAS. And sawst thou not
Mine Argosie at *Alexandria?*
Thou couldst not come from *Egypt,* or by *Caire*
But at the entry there into the sea,
Where *Nilus* payes his tribute to the maine,
Thou needs must saile by *Alexandria.*
I MERCHANT. I neither saw them nor inquir'd of them.
But this we heard some of our sea-men say:
They wondred how you durst with so much wealth
Trust such a crazed Vessell, and so farre.
BARABAS. Tush, they are wise; I know her and her strength:
But goe, goe thou thy wayes, discharge thy Ship,
And bid my Factor bring his loading° in. ship's manifest

[*Exit* I Merchant.]

And yet I wonder at this Argosie.

Enter a Second Merchant.

2 MERCHANT. Thine Argosie from *Alexandria,*
Know *Barabas* doth ride in *Malta* Rhode,

Laden with riches, and exceeding store
Of Persian silkes, of gold, and Orient perle[.]
BARABAS. How chance you came not with those other ships
That sail'd by *Egypt?*
2 MERCHANT. Sir we saw 'em not.
BARABAS. Belike they coasted round by *Candie* shoare
About their Oyles, or other businesses.
But 'twas ill done of you to come so farre
Without the ayd or conduct of their ships.
2 MERCHANT. Sir, we were wafted by a Spanish fleet
That never left us till within a league,
That had the Gallies of the Turke in chase.
BARABAS. Oh, they were going up to *Sicily*: well, goe
And bid the Merchants and my men dispatch
And come ashore, and see the fraught discharg'd.
2 MERCHANT. I goe.

Exit.

BARABAS. Thus trowles[6] our fortune in by land and Sea,
And thus are wee on every side inriched:
These are the Blessings promis'd to the Jewes,
And herein was old *Abrams* happinesse.
What more may heaven doe for earthly men
Than thus to powre out plenty in their laps,
Ripping the bowels of the earth for them,
Making the Seas their servant, and the winds
To drive their substance with successefull blasts?
Who hateth me but for my happinesse?
Or who is honour'd now but for his wealth?
Rather had I a Jew be hated thus,
Than pittied in a Christian poverty:
For I can see no fruits in all their faith,
But malice, falshood, and excessive pride,
Which me thinkes fits not their profession.
Happily some haplesse man hath conscience,
And for his conscience lives in beggery.
They say we are a scatter'd nation:
I cannot tell, but we have scrambled up
More wealth by farre than those that brag of faith.
There's *Kirriah Jairim,* the great Jew of *Greece,*
Obed in *Bairseth, Nones* in *Portugall,*
My selfe in *Malta,* some in *Italy,*
Many in France, and wealthy every one:
I, wealthier farre than any Christian.

6. Comes in routinely or repetitively.

I must confesse we come not to be Kings:
That's not our fault: Alas, our number's few,
And Crownes come either by succession
Or urg'd by force; and nothing violent,
Oft have I heard tell, can be permanent.
Give us a peacefull rule, make Christians Kings,
That thirst so much for Principality.
I have no charge, nor many children,
But one sole Daughter, whom I hold as deare
As *Agamemnon* did his *Iphigen:*[7]
And all I have is hers. But who comes here?

Enter three Jewes.

1 JEW. Tush, tell not me, 'twas done of policie.
2 JEW. Come therefore let us goe to *Barabas;*
For he can counsell best in these affaires;
And here he comes.
BARABAS. Why how now Countrymen?
Why flocke you thus to me in multitudes?
What accident's betided to the Jewes?
1 JEW. A Fleet of warlike Gallyes, *Barabas,*
Are come from *Turkey,* and lye in our Rhode:
And they this day sit in the Counsell-house
To entertaine them and their Embassie.
BARABAS. Why, let 'em come, so they come not to warre;
Or let 'em warre, so we be conquerors:
[*Aside*] Nay, let 'em combat, conquer, and kill all,
So they spare me, my daughter, and my wealth.
1 JEW. Were it for confirmation of a League,
They would not come in warlike manner thus.
2 JEW. I feare their comming will afflict us all.
BARABAS. Fond° men, what dreame you of their multitudes? foolish
What need they treat of peace that are in league?
The Turkes and those of *Malta* are in league.
Tut, tut, there is some other matter in't.
1 JEW. Why, *Barabas,* they come for peace or warre.
BARABAS. Happily for neither, but to passe along
Towards *Venice* by the *Adriatick* Sea;
With whom they have attempted many times,
But never could effect their Stratagem.
3 JEW. And very wisely sayd, it may be so.
2 JEW. But there's a meeting in the Senate house,
And all the Jewes in *Malta* must be there.

7. In some Greek stories, the Grecian fleet was embayed by the winds at Aulis because of an insult Agammemnon had given Artemis; to allow the fleet to continue, he sacrificed his daughter.

BARABAS. Umh; all the Jewes in *Malta* must be there?
I, like enough, why then, let every man
Provide him, and be there for fashion-sake.
If anything shall there concerne our state,
Assure your selves I'le looke unto *(aside)* my selfe.
I JEW. I know you will; well brethren let us goe.
2 JEW. Let's take our leaves; Farewell good *Barabas.*

[*Exeunt* Jewes.]

BARABAS. Doe so; Farewell *Zaareth,* farewell *Temainte.*
And *Barabas* now search this secret out.
Summon thy sences, call thy wits together:
These silly men mistake the matter cleane.
Long to the Turke did *Malta* contribute;
Which Tribute all in policie, I fear,
The Turkes have let increase to such a summe,
As all the wealth of *Malta* cannot pay;
And now by that advantage thinkes, belike,
To seize upon the Towne: I, that he seekes.
How ere the world goe, I'le make sure for one,
And seeke in time to intercept the worst,
Warily garding that which I ha got.
Ego mihimet sum semper proximus.[8]
Why let 'em enter, let 'em take the Towne.

[*Exit.*]

[*SCAENA* 2.]

Enter Governor of Malta, Knights [*and* Officers], met by Bassoes of the Turke; Calymath.

GOVERNOR. Now Bassoes, what demand you at our hands?
BASSO. Know Knights of *Malta,* that we came from *Rhodes,*
From *Cyprus, Candy,* and those other Iles
That lye betwixt the *Mediterranean* seas.
GOVERNOR. What's *Cyprus, Candy,* and those other Iles
To us, or *Malta?* What at our hands demand ye?
CALYMATH. The ten yeares tribute that remaines unpaid.
GOVERNOR. Alas, my Lord, the summe is overgreat,
I hope your Highnesse will consider us.
CALYMATH. I wish, grave Governour t'were in my power
To favour you, but 'tis my fathers cause,
Wherein I may not, nay I dare not dally.
GOVERNOR. Then give us leave, great *Selim-Calymath.*

8. A proverbial expression: I am always nearest to myself (or, every man for himself).

CALYMATH. Stand all aside, and let the Knights determine,
And send to keepe our Gallies under-saile,
For happily we shall not tarry here:
Now Governour how are you resolv'd?
GOVERNOR. Thus: Since your hard conditions are such
That you will needs have ten yeares tribute past,
We may have time to make collection
Amongst the Inhabitants of *Malta* for't.
BASSO. That's more than is in our Commission.
CALYMATH. What *Callapine* a little courtesie.
Let's know their time, perhaps it is not long;
And 'tis more Kingly to obtaine by peace
Then to enforce conditions by constraint.
What respit ask you Governour?
GOVERNOR. But a month.
CALYMATH. We grant a month, but see you keep your promise.
Now launch our Gallies backe again to Sea,
Where wee'll attend the respit you have tane,° taken
And for the mony send our messenger.
Farewell, great Governour, and brave Knights of *Malta*.

Exeunt [Turkes].

GOVERNOR. And all good fortune wait on *Calymath*.
Goe one and call those Jewes of *Malta* hither:
Were they not summon'd to appeare today?
OFFICER. They were, my Lord; and here they come.

Enter Barabas *and three* Jewes.

I KNIGHT. Have you determin'd what to say to them?
GOVERNOR. Yes; give me leave, and Hebrews now come neare.
From the Emperour of *Turkey* is arriv'd
Great *Selim-Calymath*, his Highnesse sonne,
To levie of us ten yeares tribute past,
Now then, here know that it concerneth us[.]
BARABAS. Then, good my Lord, to keepe your quiet still,
Your Lordship shall doe well to let them have it.
GOVERNOR. Soft *Barabas*, there's more longs too't than so.
To what this ten yeares tribute will amount
That we have cast,° but cannot compasse it calculated
By reason of the warres, that robb'd our store;
And therefore are we to request your ayd.
BARABAS. Alas, my Lord, we are no souldiers:
And what's our aid against so great a Prince?
I KNIGHT. Tut, Jew, we know thou art no souldier;
Thou art a Merchant and a moneyed man,
And 'tis thy mony, *Barabas*, we seeke.
BARABAS. How, my Lord? My mony?

GOVERNOR. Thine and the rest;
For, to be short, amongst you 'tmust be had.
I JEW. Alas, my Lord, the most of us are poore!
GOVERNOR. Then let the rich increase your portions[.]
BARABAS. Are strangers° with your tribute to be tax'd? noncitizens
2 KNIGHT. Have strangers leave with us to get their wealth?
Then let them with us contribute.
BARABAS. How, equally?
GOVERNOR. No, Jew, like infidels;
For through our sufferance of your hatefull lives,
Who stand accursed in the sight of heaven,
These taxes and afflictions are befal'ne,° befallen us
And therefore thus we are determined;
Reade there the Articles of our decrees.
READER. First, the tribute mony of the Turkes shall all be levyed amongst the Jewes, and each of them to pay one halfe of his estate.
BARABAS. How, halfe his estate? I hope you meane not mine.
GOVERNOR. Read on.
READER. Secondly, hee that denies to pay, shal straight become a Christian.
BARABAS. How a Christian? Hum, what's here to doe?
READER. Lastly, he that denies this, shall absolutely lose al he has.
ALL THREE JEWS. Oh, my lord, we will give halfe.
BARABAS. Oh earth-mettall'd villaines, and no Hebrews born!
And will you basely thus submit your selves
To leave your goods to their arbitrament?
GOVERNOR. Why Barabas wilt thou be christned?
BARABAS. No, Governour, I will be no convertite.
GOVERNOR. Then pay thy halfe.
BARABAS. Why know you what you doe by this device?
Halfe of my substance is a Cities wealth.
Governour, it was not got so easily;
Nor will I part so slightly therewithall.
GOVERNOR. Sir, halfe is the penalty of our decree,
Either pay that, or we will seize on all.
BARABAS. *Corpo di Dio;*[9] stay: you shall have halfe,
Let me be us'd but as my brethren are.
GOVERNOR. No, Jew, thou hast denied the Articles,
And now it cannot be recall'd.

[*Exeunt* Officers.]

BARABAS. Will you then steale my goods?
Is theft the ground of your Religion?

9. By God's body.

GOVERNOR. No, Jew, we take particularly thine
To save the ruine of a multitude:
And better one want for a common good,
Than many perish for a private man:
Yet *Barabas* we will not banish thee,
But here in *Malta,* where thou gotst thy wealth,
Live still; and, if thou canst, get more.
BARABAS. Christians; what, or how can I multiply?
Of nought is nothing made.
I KNIGHT. From nought at first thou camst to little welth,
From little unto more, from more to most,
If your first curse fall heavy on thy head,
And make thee poore and scorn'd of all the world,
'Tis not our fault, but thy inherent sinne.
BARABAS. What, bring you Scripture to confirm your wrongs?
Preach me not out of my possessions.
Some Jewes are wicked, [*Aside*] as all Christians are:
But say the Tribe that I descended of
Were all in generall cast away for sinne,
Shall I be tryed for their transgression?
The man that dealeth righteously shall live:
And which of you can charge me otherwise?
GOVERNOR. Out wretched *Barabas,* sham'st thou not
To justifie thy selfe, as if we knew not
Thy profession? If thou rely upon thy righteousnesse,
Be patient, and thy riches will increase.
Excesse of wealth is cause of covetousnesse:
And covetousnesse, oh 'tis a monstrous sinne.
BARABAS. I, but theft is worse: tush, take not from me then,
For that is theft; and if you rob me thus,
I must be forc'd to steale and compasse more.
I KNIGHT. Grave Governor, list not to his exclames:
Convert his mansion to a Nunnery,
His house will harbour many holy Nuns.

Enter Officers.

GOVERNOR. It shall be so: now Officers, have you done?
OFFICER. I, my Lord, we have seiz'd upon the goods
And wares of *Barabas,* which being valued,
Amount to more than all the wealth in *Malta.*
And of the other we have seized halfe.
GOVERNOR. Then wee'll take order[10] for the residue.
BARABAS. Well then my Lord, say, are you satisfied?
You have my goods, my mony, and my wealth,

10. "Measure or steps taken for the accomplishment of a purpose" (Oxford English Dictionary).

My ships, my store, and all that I enjoy'd;
And having all, you can request no more;
Unlesse your unrelenting flinty hearts
Suppresse all pitty in your stony breasts,
And now shall move you to bereave my life.
GOVERNOR. No, *Barabas,* to staine our hands with blood
Is farre from us and our profession.
BARABAS. Why I esteeme the injury farre lesse,
To take the lives of miserable men
Than be the causers of their misery.
You have my wealth the labour of my life,
The comfort of mine age, my childrens hope,
And therefore ne'er distinguish of the wrong.
GOVERNOR. Content thee, *Barabas,* thou hast nought but right.
BARABAS. Your extreme right does me exceeding wrong:
But take it to you, i'th'devil's name.
GOVERNOR. Come, let us in and gather of these goods
The mony for this tribute of the Turke.
I KNIGHT. 'Tis necessary that be look'd unto:
For if we breake our day, we breake the league,
And that will prove but simple° policie. foolish

Exeunt.
[*Manent* Barabas *and the three* Jewes.]

BARABAS. I, policie? that's their profession,
And not simplicity, as they suggest.
The plagues of *Egypt* and the curse of heaven,
Earths barrennesse, and all mens hatred
Inflict upon them, thou great *Primus Motor.*[11]
And here upon my knees, striking the earth,
I banne° their souls to everlasting paines, curse
And extreme tortures of the fiery deepe,
That thus have dealt with me in my distresse.
I JEW. Oh yet be patient, gentle *Barabas.*
BARABAS. Oh silly brethren, borne to see this day!
Why stand you thus unmov'd with my laments?
Why weepe you not to thinke upon my wrongs?
Why pine not I, and dye in this distresse?
I JEW. Why, *Barabas,* as hardly can we brooke
The cruell handling of our selves in this:
Thou seest they have taken halfe our goods.
BARABAS. Why did you yeeld to their extortion?
You were a multitude, and I but one,
And of me onely have they taken all.

11. "First Mover": the Aristotelian conception of God.

1 JEW. Yet brother *Barabas* remember *Job.*
BARABAS. What tell you me of *Job?* I wot° his wealth [know]
Was written thus: he had seven thousand sheepe,
Three thousand Camels, and two hundred yoake
Of labouring Oxen, and five hundred
Shee Asses: But for every one of those,
Had they been valued at indifferent rate,[12]
I had at home, and in mine Argosie
And other ships that came from *Egypt* last,
As much as would have bought his beasts and him,
And yet have kept enough to live upon;
So that not he, but I may curse the day,
Thy fatall birth-day, forlorne *Barabas,*
And henceforth wish for an eternall night,
That clouds of darknesse may inclose my flesh,
And hide these extreme sorrowes from mine eyes:
For onely I have toyl'd to inherit here
The months of vanity and losse of time,
And painefull nights have bin appointed me.
2 JEW. Good *Barabas* be patient.
BARABAS. I, I
Pray leave me in my patience. You that
Were ne're possest of wealth are pleas'd with want.
But give him liberty at least to mourne,
That in a field amidst his enemies,
Doth see his souldiers slaine, himselfe disarm'd,
And knowes no meanes of his recoverie:
I, let me sorrow for this sudden chance,
'Tis in the trouble of my spirit I speake;
Great injuries are not so soone forgot.
1 JEW. Come, let us leave him in his ireful mood,
Our words will but increase his ecstasie.° [frenzy]
2 JEW. On, then: But trust me 'tis a misery
To see a man in such affliction:
Farewell *Barabas.*

Exeunt

BARABAS. I, fare you well.
See the simplicitie of these base slaves,
Who for the villaines have no wit themselves,
Thinke me to be a senselesse lumpe of clay
That will with every water wash to dirt:
No, *Barabas* is borne to better chance,
And fram'd of finer mould then common men

12. Fairly, by one without an interest in the outcome of a transaction.

That measure nought but by the present time.
A reaching thought will search his deepest wits,
And cast° with cunning for the time to come: forecast
For evils are apt to happen every day.
But whither wends my beauteous *Abigall?*

Enter Abigall, *the Jewes daughter.*

Oh what has made my lovely daughter sad?
What? woman, moane not for a little losse:
Thy father has enough in store for thee.
ABIGALL. Not for my selfe, but aged *Barabas:*
Father, for thee lamenteth *Abigall:*
But I will learne to leave these fruitlesse teares.
And urg'd thereto with my afflictions,
With fierce exclaimes run to the Senate-house,
And in the Senate reprehend them all,
And rend their hearts with tearing of my haire,
Till they reduce the wrongs done to my father.
BARABAS. No, *Abigall,* things past recovery
Are hardly cur'd with exclamations.
Be silent, Daughter. Sufferance breeds ease,
And time may yeeld us an occasion
Which on the sudden cannot serve the turne.
Besides, my girle, thinke me not all so fond
As negligently to foregoe so much
Without provision for thyselfe and me.
Ten thousand Portagues,° besides great Perles,   gold Portuguese coins
Rich costly Jewels, and Stones infinite,
Fearing the worst of this before it fell,
I closely hid.
ABIGALL. Where father?
BARABAS. In my house my girle.
ABIGALL. Then shall they ne're be seene of *Barabas:*
For they have seiz'd upon thy house and wares.
BARABAS. But they will give me leave once more, I trow,
To go into my house.
ABIGALL. That may they not:
For there I left the Governour placing Nunnes,
Displacing me; and of thy house they meane
To make a Nunnery, where none but their owne sect
Must enter in; men generally barr'd.
BARABAS. My gold, my gold, and all my wealth is gone.
You partiall heavens, have I deserv'd this plague?
What, will you thus oppose me, lucklesse Starres,
To make me desperate in my poverty?
And knowing me impatient in distresse

Thinke me so mad as I will hang my selfe,
That I may vanish ore the earth in ayre,
And leave no memory that e're I was[?]
No, I will live; nor loath I this my life:
And since you leave me in the Ocean thus
To sinke or swim, and put me to my shifts,
I'le rouse my senses, and awake my selfe.
Daughter, I have it: thou perceiv'st the plight
Wherein these Christians have oppressed me:
Be rul'd by me, for in extremitie
We ought to make barre of no policie.[13]

ABIGALL. Father, what e're it be to injure them
That have so manifestly wronged us,
What will not *Abigall* attempt?

BARABAS. Why so;
Then thus, thou toldst me they have turn'd my house
Into a Nunnery, and some nuns are there.

ABIGALL. I did.

BARABAS. Then, *Abigall,* there must my girle
Intreate the Abbasse to be entertain'd.

ABIGALL. How, as a Nunne?

BARABAS. I, Daughter, for Religion
Hides many mischiefes from suspition.

ABIGALL. I, but father they will suspect me there.

BARABAS. Let 'em suspect, but be thou so precise
As they may thinke it done of Holinesse.
Intreat 'em faire, and give them friendly speech,
And seeme to them as if thy sinnes were great,
Till thou hast gotten to be entertain'd.

ABIGALL. Thus father shall I much dissemble.

BARABAS. Tush, as good dissemble that thou never mean'st
As first meane truth and then dissemble it,
A counterfet profession is better
Then unseene hypocrisie.

ABIGALL. Well father, say I be entertain'd,
What then shall follow?

BARABAS. This shall follow then;
There have I hid, close underneath the plancke
That runs along the upper chamber floore,
The gold and Jewels which I kept for thee.
But here they come; Be cunning *Abigall.*

ABIGALL. Then father goe with me.

BARABAS. No, *Abigall,* in this
It is not necessary I be seene,

13. Eliminate no options (for revenge).

For I will seeme offended with thee for't.
Be close,° my girle, for this must fetch my gold. secret

Enter two Fryars *and two* Nuns.

1 FRYAR. Sisters,we now are almost at the new made Nunnery.
ABBASSE. The better; for we love not to be seene:
'Tis thirtie winters long since some of us
Did stray so farre amongst the multitude.
1 FRYAR. But, Madam, this house
And waters of this new made Nunnery
Will much delight you.
ABBASSE. It may be so: but who comes here?
ABIGALL. Grave Abbasse, and you happy Virgins guide,
Pitty the state of a distressed maid.
ABBASSE. What art thou, daughter?
ABIGALL. The hopelesse daughter of a haplesse *Jew,*
The *Jew* of *Malta,* wretched *Barabas;*
Sometimes the owner of a goodly house,
Which they have now turn'd to a Nunnery.
ABBASSE. Well, daughter, say, what is thy suit with us?
ABIGALL. Fearing the afflictions which my father feeles,
Proceed from sinne, or want of faith in us,
I'de passe away my life in penitence,
And be a Novice in your Nunnery,
To make attonement for my labouring soule.
1 FRYAR. No doubt, brother, but this proceedeth of the spirit.
2 FRYAR. I, and of a moving spirit too, brother, but come,
Let us intreat she may be entertain'd.
ABBASSE. Well, daughter, we admit you for a Nun.
ABIGALL. First let me as a Novice learne to frame
My solitary life to your streight lawes,
And let me lodge where I was wont to lye.
I doe not doubt, by your divine precepts
And mine owne industry, but to profit much.
BARABAS. *(Aside)* As much I hope as all I hid is worth.
ABBASSE. Come daughter, follow us.
BARABAS. Why how now *Abigall,*
What makst thou amongst these hateful Christians?
1 FRYAR. Hinder her not, thou man of little faith,
For she has mortified her selfe.
BARABAS. How, mortified!
1 FRYAR. And is admitted to the Sister-hood.
BARABAS. Child of perdition, and thy fathers shame,
What wilt thou doe among these hatefull fiends?
I charge thee on my blessing that thou leave
These divels and their damned heresie.

ABIGALL. Father give me—
BARABAS. Nay backe, *Abigall,*

Whispers to her.

And thinke upon the Jewels and the gold,
The boord is marked thus † that covers it.

[*Makes sign.*]

Away accursed, from thy fathers sight.
I FRYAR. *Barabas,* although thou art in mis-beleefe,
And wilt not see thine own afflictions,
Yet let thy daughter be no longer blinde.
BARABAS. Blind, Fryar, I wrecke not thy perswasions.
[*Aside, makes sign.*] The boord is marked thus † that covers it,
For I had rather dye, than see her thus.
Wilt thou forsake me too in my distresse,
Seduced Daughter, *(Aside to her)* Goe forget not.
Becomes it Jewes to be so credulous?
(Aside to her) To morrow early Il'e be at the doore.
No come not at me, if thou wilt be damn'd,
Forget me, see me not; and so be gone.
Farewell, *(Aside to her)* remember to morrow morning.
Out, out, thou wretch.

[*Exeunt,* different ways.]

[*SCAENA* 3.]

Enter Mathias.

MATHIAS. Whose this?
Faire Abigall, the rich Jewes daughter
Become a nun, Her fathers sudden fall
Has humbled her and brought her downe to this.
Tut, she were fitter for a tale of love
Then to be tired out with Orisons:° prayers
And better would she farre become a bed
Embraced in a friendly lovers armes,
Then rise at midnight to a solemne mass.

Enter Lodowicke.

LODOWICKE. Why how now Don *Mathias,* in a dump?
MATHIAS. Believe me, noble *Lodowicke,* I have seene
The strangest sight, in my opinion,
That ever I beheld.
LODOWICKE. What wast I prethe?
MATHIAS. A faire young maid, scarce fourteene years of age,
The sweetest flower in *Citherea's*° field, Venus

Cropped from the pleasures of the fruitfull earth,
And strangely metamorphis'd Nun.
LODOWICKE. But say, What was she?
MATHIAS. Why, the rich Jewes daughter.
LODOWICKE. What *Barabas,* whose goods were lately seiz'd?
Is she so faire?
MATHIAS. And matchlesse beautifull;
As had you seene her 'twould have mov'd your heart,
Though countermur'd° with walls of brasse, to love — doubly walled
Or, at the least, to pitty.
LODOWICKE. And if she be so faire as you report,
'Twere time well spent to goe and visit her:
How say you, Shall we?
MATHIAS. I must and will, Sir, there's no remedy.
LODOWICKE. *(Aside.)* And so will I too, or it shall goe hard.
Farewell *Mathias.*
MATHIAS. Farewell *Lodowicke.*

Exeunt.

ACTUS SECUNDUS [*SCAENA I*].

Enter Barabas *with a light.*

BARABAS. Thus, like the sad presaging raven that tolls
The sicke mans passeport° in her hollow beake, — discharge
And in the shadow of the silent night
Doth shake contagion from her sable wings;
Vex'd and tormented runnes poore *Barabas*
With fatall curses towards these Christians.
The incertaine pleasures of swift-footed time
Have tane their flight, and left me in despaire;
And of my former riches rests no more
But bare remembrance; like a souldiers skarre,
That has no further comfort for his maime.
Oh thou that with a fiery piller led'st
The sonnes of *Israel* through the dismall shades,
Light *Abrahams* off-spring; and direct the hand
Of *Abigall* this night; or let the day
Turne to eternall darknesse after this:
No sleepe can fasten on my watchfull eyes,
Nor quiet enter my distemper'd thoughts,
Till I have answer of my *Abigall.*

Enter Abigall *above.*

ABIGALL. Now have I happily espy'd a time
To search the plancke my father did appoint;

And here, behold (unseene) where I have found
The gold, the perles, and Jewels, which he hid.
BARABAS. Now I remember those old womens words,
Who in my wealth, wud tell me winters tales,
And speake of spirits and ghosts that glide by night
About the place where Treasure hath bin hid:
And now me thinkes that I am one of those:
For whilst I live, here lives my soules sole hope,
And when I dye, here shall my spirit walk.
ABIGALL. Now that my fathers fortune were so good
As but to be about this happy place;
'Tis not so happy: Yet when we parted last,
He said he wud attend me in the morne.
Then, gentle sleepe, where e're his bodie rests,
Give charge to *Morpheus*[14] that he may dreame
A golden dreame, and of the sudden walke,
Come, and receive the Treasure I have found.
BARABAS. *Bien para todos mi ganada no es.*[15]
As good goe on, as sit so sadly thus.
But stay, what starre shines yonder in the east?
The Loadstarre of my life, if Abigall.
Who's there?
ABIGALL. Who's that?
BARABAS. Peace, Abigall, 'tis I.
ABIGALL. Then father here receive thy happinesse.
BARABAS. Hast thou't?
ABIGALL. Here.

(Throwes down bags.)

Hast thou't? There's more, and more, and more.
BARABAS. O my girle,
My gold, my fortune, my felicity;
Strength to my soule, death to mine enemy;
Welcome the first beginner of my blisse:
Oh Abigall, Abigall, that I had thee here too,
Then my desires were fully satisfied,
But I will practise thy enlargement thence:
Oh girle, oh gold, oh beauty, oh my blisse!

hugs his bags.

ABIGALL. Father, it draweth towards midnight now,
And 'bout this time the Nuns begin to wake;
To shun suspition, therefore, let us part.

14. One of the sons of Somnus, god of sleep.
15. My gain is not good for everybody.

BARABAS. Farewell my joy, and by my fingers take
A kiss from him that sends it from his soule.

[*Exit* Abigall.]

Now *Phoebus* ope the eye-lids of the day,
And for the Raven wake the morning Larke,
That I may hover with her in the Ayre;
Singing ore these, as she does ore her young.
Hermoso Placer, de los Dineros.[16]

Exit.

[*SCAENA* 2.]

Enter Governor, Martin Del Bosco, *the* Knights [*and* Officers].

GOVERNOR. Now Captaine tell us whither thou art bound?
Whence is thy ship that anchors in our Rhoad?
And why thou cam'st ashore without our leave?
BOSCO. Governor of *Malta,* hither am I bound;
My ship, *the flying Dragon,* is of *Spaine,*
And so am I, *Delbosco* is my name;
Vizadmirall unto the Catholike King.
I KNIGHT. 'Tis true, my lord, therefore intreat him well.
BOSCO. Our fraught is Grecians, Turks, and Africk Moores.
For late upon the coast of *Corsica,*
Because we vail'd not° to the Turkish Fleet, lowered sails
Their creeping Gallyes had us in the chase:
But suddenly the wind began to rise,
And then we luft, and tackt, and fought at ease:
Some have we fir'd, and many have we sunke;
But one amongst the rest became our prize:
The Captains slaine, the rest remain our slaves,
Of whom we would make sale in *Malta* here.
GOVERNOR. *Martin del Bosco,* I have heard of thee;
Welcome to *Malta,* and to all of us;
But to admit a sale of these thy Turkes
We may not, nay we dare not give consent
By reason of a Tributary league.
I KNIGHT. *Delbosco,* as thou lovest and honour'st us,
Perswade our Governor against the Turke;
This truce we have is but in hope of gold,
And with that summe he craves might we wage warre.
BOSCO. Will Knights of *Malta* be in league with Turkes,
And buy it basely too for summes of gold?
My Lord, Remember that, to *Europ's* shame,
The Christian Ile of *Rhodes,* from whence you came,

16. Beautiful pleasure of money.

Was lately lost, and you were stated here
To be at deadly enmity with Turkes.
GOVERNOR. Captaine we know it, but our force is small.
BOSCO. What is the summe that *Calymath* requires?
GOVERNOR. A hundred thousand Crownes.
BOSCO. My Lord and King hath title to this Isle,
And he meanes quickly to expell them hence;
Therefore be rul'd by me, and keepe the gold:
I'le write unto his Majesty for ayd,
And not depart until I see you free.
GOVERNOR. On this condition shall thy Turkes be sold.
Goe Officers, and set them straight in shew.

[*Exeunt* Officers.]

Bosco, thou shalt be *Malta's* Generall;
We and our warlike Knights will follow thee
Against these barbarous mis-beleeving Turkes.
BOSCO. So shall you imitate those you succeed:
For when their hideous force environ'd *Rhodes,*
Small though the number was that kept the Towne,
They fought it out, and not a man surviv'd
To bring the haplesse newes to Christendome.
GOVERNOR. So will we fight it out; come let's away:
Proud-daring *Calymath,* instead of gold,
We'll send thee bullets wrapt in smoake and fire:
Claime tribute where thou wilt, we are resolv'd,
Honor is bought with bloud and not with gold.

Exeunt.

[*SCAENA* 3.]

Enter Officers *with* Slaves.

1 OFFICER. This is the Market-place; here let 'em stand:
Feare not their sale, for they'll be quickly bought.
2 OFFICER. Every ones price is written on his backe,
And so much must they yeeld, or not be sold.

Enter Barabas.

1 OFFICER. Here comes the Jew, had not his goods bin seiz'd,
Hee'de give us present mony for them all.
BARABAS. In spite of these swine-eating Christians,
(Unchosen Nation, never circumciz'd;
Such as poore villaines, were ne're thought upon
Till *Titus* and *Vespasian* conquer'd us.)[17]

17. Vespasin and his son Titus destroyed Jerusalem in AD 70.

Am I become as wealthy as I was:
They hop'd my daughter would ha bin a Nun;
But she's at home, and I have bought a house
As great and faire as is the Governors;
And there, in spite of *Malta,* will I dwell:
Having *Fernezes* hand, whose heart I'le have;
I, and his sonnes too, or it shall goe hard.
I am not of the tribe of *Levy,* I,
That can so soone forget an injury.
We Jewes can fawne like Spaniels when we please;
And when we grin, we bite, yet are our lookes
As innocent and harmelesse as a Lambes.
I learn'd in *Florence* how to kisse my hand,
Heave up my shoulders when they call me dogge,
And ducke as low as any bare-foot Fryar,
Hoping to see them starve upon a stall,
Or else be gather'd for in our Synagogue;
That when the offering-Bason comes to me,
Even for charity I may spit intoo't.
Here comes Don *Lodowicke* the Governors sonne,
One that I love for his good fathers sake.

Enter Lodowicke.

LODOWICKE. I heare the wealthy Jew walked this way;
I'le seeke him out, and so insinuate,
That I may have a sight of *Abigall;*
For Don *Mathias* tels me she is faire.
BARABAS. *(Aside)* Now will I shew my selfe to have more of the
Serpent than the Dove;[18] that is, more knave than foole.
LODOWICKE. Yond walks the Jew, now for faire *Abigall.*
BARABAS. *(Aside)* I, I, no doubt but shee's at your command.
LODOWICKE. *Barabas,* thou know'st I am the Governors sonne.
BARABAS. *(Aside)* I wud you were his father too, Sir, thats al
the harm I wish you: the slave looks like a hogs
cheek new sindg'd.
LODOWICKE. Whither walk'st thou *Barabas?*
BARABAS. No further: 'tis a custome held with us,
That when we speake with Gentiles like to you
We turne into the Ayre to purge our selves:
For unto us the Promise doth belong.
LODOWICKE. Well, *Barabas,* canst helpe me to a Diamond?
BARABAS. Oh, Sir, your father had my Diamonds.
Yet have I one left that will serve your turne:
(aside) I meane my daughter:—but, ere he shall have her

18. Matthew 10:16.

I'le sacrifice her on a pile of wood.
I ha the poyson of the City for him,
And the white leprosie.
LODOWICKE. What sparkle does it give without a foile?
BARABAS. The Diamond that I talk of, ne'r was foil'd:
(aside) But, when he touches it, it will be foild:
Lord *Lodowicke,* it sparkles bright and faire.
LODOWICKE. Is't square or pointed, pray you let me know.
BARABAS. Pointed it is, good Sir,—*(aside)* but not for you.
LODOWICKE. I like it much the better.
BARABAS. So doe I too.
LODOWICKE. How showes it by night?
BARABAS. Outshines *Cinthia's*° rayes. the moon
(aside) You'le like it better farre a nights than dayes.
LODOWICKE. And what's the price?
BARABAS. *(Aside)* Your life and if you have it.—Oh my Lord
We will not jarre about the price; come to my house
And I will giv't your honour—*(aside)* with a vengeance.
LODOWICKE. No, *Barabas,* I will deserve it first.
BARABAS. Good Sir, your father has deserv'd it at my hands,
Who, of meere charity and Christian ruth,° pity
To bring me to religious purity,
And as it were in Catechising sort,
To make me mindfull of my mortall sinnes,
Against my will, and whether I would or no,
Seiz'd all I had, and thrust me out a doores,
And made my house a place for Nuns most chast.
LODOWICKE. No doubt your soule shall reape the fruit of it.
BARABAS. I, but, my Lord, the harvest is farre off:
And yet I know the prayers of those Nuns
And holy Fryars, having mony for their paines,
Are wondrous; *(aside)* and indeed doe no man good:
And seeing they are not idle, but still doing,
'Tis likely they in time may reape some fruit,
I meane in fulnesse of perfection.
LODOWICKE. Good *Barabas* glance not at our holy Nuns.
BARABAS. No, but I do it through a burning zeale,
(Aside) Hoping ere long to set the house a fire;
For though they doe a while increase and multiply,
I'le have a saying to that Nunnery.
As for the Diamond, Sir, I told you of,
Come home and there's no price shall make us part,
Even for your Honourable fathers sake.
(Aside) It shall goe hard but I will see your death,
But now I must be gone to buy a slave.
LODOWICKE. And, *Barabas,* I'le beare thee company.

BARABAS. Come then, here's the market place; whats the
price of this slave, 200 Crowns? Do the Turkes weigh so much?
I OFFICER. Sir, that's his price.
BARABAS. What, can he steale that you demand so much?
Belike he has some new tricke for a purse;
And if he has, he is worth three hundred plats.
So that, being bought, the Town-seale might be got
To keepe him for his lifetime from the gallowes.
The Sessions day is criticall to theeves,
And few or none scape but by being purg'd.
LODOWICKE. Ratest thou this Moore but at two hundred plats?
I OFFICER. No more, my Lord.
BARABAS. Why should this Turke be dearer than that Moore?
I OFFICER. Because he is young and has more qualities.
BARABAS. What, hast the Philosophers stone? and thou
hast, breake my head with it, I'le forgive thee.
SLAVE. No, Sir, I can cut and shave.
BARABAS. Let me see, sirra, are you not an old shaver?
SLAVE. Alas, Sir, I am a very youth.
BARABAS. A youth? I'le buy you and marry you to Lady Vanity,
if you doe well.
SLAVE. I will serve you, Sir.
BARABAS. Some wicked trick or other. It may be, under
colour of shaving, thou'lt cut my throat for my goods.
Tell me, hast thou thy health well?
SLAVE. I, passing well.
BARABAS. So much the worse. I must have one that's sickly,
and be but for sparing vittles: 'tis not a stone of
beef a day will maintaine you in these chops; let me
see one that's somewhat leaner.
I OFFICER. Here's a leaner, how like you him?
BARABAS. Where wast thou borne?
ITHIMORE. In *Trace;* brought up in *Arabia.*
BARABAS. So much the better, thou art for my turne,
An hundred Crownes, I'le have him; there's the coyne.
I OFFICER. Then marke him, Sir, and take him hence.
BARABAS. I, marke him, you were best, *(aside)* for this is he
That by my helpe shall doe much villainie.
My Lord, farewell: Come Sirra you are mine.
As for the diamond, it shall be yours;
I pray, Sir, be no stranger at my house,
All that I have shall be at your command.

[*Exit* Lodowicke.]
Enter Mathias, Mater.

MATHIAS. What makes the Jew and *Lodowicke* so private?
I feare me tis about fair *Abigall.*
BARABAS. *(Aside)* Yonder comes Don *Mathias,* let us stay;
He loves my daughter, and she holds him deare:
But I have sworne to frustrate both their hopes,
And be revenged upon the—Governor.
MATER. This Moore is comeliest, is he not? speake son.
MATHIAS. No, this is the better, mother, view this well.
BARABAS. Seeme not to know me here before your mother
Lest she mistrust the match that is in hand:
When you have brought her home, come to my house;
Thinke of me as thy father; Sonne farewell.
MATHIAS. But wherefore talked Don *Lodowicke* with you?
BARABAS. Tush man, we talk'd of Diamonds, not of *Abigall.*
MATER. Tell me, *Mathias,* is not that the Jew?
BARABAS. As for the Comment on the *Machabees*[19]
I have it, Sir, and 'tis at your command.
MATHIAS. Yes, Madam, and my talke with him was but
About the borrowing of a booke or two.
MATER. Converse not with him, he is cast off from heaven.
Thou hast thy Crownes, fellow, come, lets away.
MATHIAS. Sirra, Jew, remember the booke.
BARABAS. Marry, will I, sir.

Exeunt Mater *and* Mathias.

I OFFICER. Come, I have made a reasonable market, let's away.

Exeunt Officers *and* Slaves.

BARABAS. Now let me know thy name, and therewithall
Thy birth, condition, and profession.
ITHIMORE. Faith, Sir, my birth is but meane, my name's
Ithimore, my profession what you please.
BARABAS. Hast thou no Trade? then listen to my words,
And I will teach thee that shall sticke by thee:
First, be thou voyd of these affections,
Compassion, love, vaine hope, and hartlesse feare,
Be mov'd at nothing, see thou pitty none,
But to thy selfe smile when the Christians moane.
ITHIMORE. Oh brave, master, I worship your nose for this.
BARABAS. As for my selfe, I walke abroad a nights
And kill sicke people groaning under walls:
Sometimes I goe about and poyson wells;
And now, and then, to Cherish Christian theeves,
I am content to lose some of my Crownes;

19. Narrations of Jewish liberation in the second century BC.

That I may, walking in my Gallery,
See 'em goe pinion'd along by my doore.
Being young I studied Physicke, and began
To practise first upon the Italian;
There I enrich'd the Priests with burials,
And alwayes kept the Sexton's armes in ure° practice
With digging graves and ringing dead mens knels:
And after that was I an Engineere,
And in the warres 'twixt *France* and *Germanie,*
Under pretence of helping *Charles* the fifth,
Slew friend and enemy with my stratagems.
Then after that was I an Usurer,
And with extorting, cozening, forfeiting,
And tricks belonging unto Brokery,
I fill'd the Jailes with Bankrouts in a yeare,
And with young Orphans planted Hospitals,
And every Moone made some or other mad,
And now and then one hang himselfe for griefe,
Pinning upon his breast a long great Scrowle
How I with interest tormented him.
But marke how I am blest for plaguing them,
I have as much coyne as will buy the Towne.
But tell me now, How hast thou spent thy time?

ITHIMORE. Faith, Master,
In setting Christian villages on fire,
Chaining of Eunuches, binding gally-slaves.
One time I was an Hostler at an Inne,
And in the night time secretly would steale
To travellers Chambers, and there cut their throats:
Once at *Jerusalem,* where the pilgrims kneel'd,
I strowed powder on the Marble stones
And therewithall their knees would ranckle, so
That I have laugh'd agood to see the cripples
Goe limping home to Christendome on stilts.

BARABAS. Why, this is something: make account of me
As of thy fellow; we are villaines both:
Both circumcized, we hate Christians both:
Be true and secret; thou shalt want no gold.
But stand aside, here comes Don *Lodowicke.*

Enter Lodowicke.

LODOWICKE. Oh, *Barabas,* well met; where is the Diamond
You told me of?

BARABAS. I have it for you, Sir; Please you walke in with me:
What, ho, *Abigall;* open the doore I say.

Enter Abigall.

ABIGALL. In good time, father, here are letters come
From *Ormus*,° and the Post stayes here within. Hormuz
BARABAS. Give me the letters, daughter, doe you heare?
Entertaine *Lodowicke* the Governors sonne
With all the courtesie you can affoord;
Provided that you keepe your Maiden-head.
(Aside) Use him as if he were a Philistine.
Dissemble, sweare, protest, vow love to him,
He is not of the seed of *Abraham*.
I am a little busie, Sir, pray, pardon me
Abigall, bid him welcome for my sake.
ABIGALL. For your sake and his own he's welcome hither.
BARABAS. Daughter, a word more; *(aside)* kisse him, speake him faire,
And like a cunning Jew so cast about,
That ye be both made sure e're you come out.
ABIGALL. Oh father, Don *Mathias* is my love.
BARABAS. I know it: yet I say make love to him;
Doe, it is requisite it should be so.
Nay on my life, it is my Factors° hand. mercantile agent
But goe you in, I'le thinke upon the account[.]

[*Exeunt* Lodowicke *and* Abigall.]

The account is made, for *Lodowicke* dyes.
My Factor sends me word a Merchant's fled
That owes me for a hundred Tun of Wine:
I weigh it thus much; I have wealth enough.
For now by this has he kissed *Abigall;*
And she vowes love to him, and hee to her.
As sure as heaven rain'd MANNA for the Jewes,
So sure shall he and Don *Mathias* dye:
His father was my chiefest enemie.
Whither goes Don *Mathias?* stay a while.

Enter Mathias.

MATHIAS. Whither but to my faire love *Abigall?*
BARABAS. Thou know'st, and heaven can witnesse it is true,
That I intend my daughter shall be thine.
MATHIAS. I, *Barabas*, or else thou wrong'st me much.
BARABAS. Oh, heaven forbid I should have such a thought.
Pardon me though I weepe; the Governors sonne
Will, whether I will or no, have *Abigall:*
He sends her letters, bracelets, jewels, rings.
MATHIAS. Does she receive them?
BARABAS. Shee? No, *Mathias*, no, but sends them backe,
And, when he comes, she lockes her selfe up fast;
Yet through the key-hole will he talke to her,

While she runs to the window looking out
When you should come and hale him from the doore.
MATHIAS. Oh treacherous *Lodowicke!*
BARABAS. Even now, as I came home, he slipt me in,
And I am sure he is with *Abigall.*
MATHIAS. I'le rouze him thence.
BARABAS. Not for all *Malta,* therefore sheathe your sword;
If you love me, no quarrels in my house;
But steale you in, and seeme to see him not;
I'le give him such a warning e're he goes
As he shall have small hopes of *Abigall.*
Away, for here they come.

Enter Lodowicke, Abigall.

MATHIAS. What, hand in hand, I cannot suffer this.
BARABAS. *Mathias,* as thou lov'st me, not a word.
MATHIAS. Well, let it passe, another time shall serve.

Exit.

LODOWICKE. *Barabas,* is not that the widowes sonne?
BARABAS. I, and take heed, for he hath sworne your death.
LODOWICKE. My death? what is the base born peasant mad?
BARABAS. No, no, but happily he stands in feare
Of that which you, I thinke, ne're dreame upon,
My daughter here, a paltry silly girle.
LODOWICKE. Why loves she Don *Mathias?*
BARABAS. Doth she not with her smiling answer you?
ABIGALL. *(Aside)* He has my heart, I smile against my will.
LODOWICKE. *Barabas,* thou know'st I have lov'd thy daughter long.
BARABAS. And so has she done you, even from a child.
LODOWICKE. And now I can no longer hold my minde.
BARABAS. Nor I the affection that I beare to you.
LODOWICKE. This is thy Diamond, tell me, shall I have it?
BARABAS. Win it, and weare it, it is yet unsoyl'd.
Oh but I know your Lordship wud disdaine
To marry with the daughter of a Jew:
And yet I'le give her many a golden crosse
With Christian posies round about the ring.
LODOWICKE. 'Tis not thy wealth, but her that I esteeme,
Yet crave I thy consent.
BARABAS. And mine you have; yet let me talke to her;
(Aside) This offspring of *Cain,* this Jebusite[20]
That never tasted of the Passeover,
Nor e're shall see the land of *Canaan,*

20. Inhabitant of Jerusalem prior to the Jews, and hence not one of the chosen people.

Nor our *Messias* that is yet to come,
This gentle Maggot, *Lodowicke* I meane,
Must be deluded: let him have thy hand,
But keep thy heart till Don *Mathias* comes.

ABIGALL. What Shall I be betroth'd to *Lodowicke?*

BARABAS. It's no sinne to deceive a Christian;
For they themselves hold it a principle,
Faith is not to be held with Heretickes;
But all are Heretics that are not Jewes.
This followes well, and therefore daughter feare not.
I have intreated her, and she will grant.

LODOWICKE. Then gentle *Abigall* plight thy faith to me.

ABIGALL. *(Aside)* I cannot chuse, seeing my father bids:
Nothing but death shall part my love and me.

LODOWICKE. Now have I that for which my soule hath long'd.

BARABAS. *(Aside)* So have not I, but yet I hope I shall.

ABIGALL. Oh wretched *Abigall,* what hast thou done?

LODOWICKE. Why on the sudden is your colour chang'd?

ABIGALL. I know not, but farewell, I must be gone.

BARABAS. Stay her, but let her not speake one word more.

LODOWICKE. Mute a the sudden; here's a sudden change.

BARABAS. Oh muse not at it, 'tis the Hebrewes guize,
That maidens new betroth'd should weepe a while:
Trouble her not, sweet *Lodowicke,* depart:
Shee is thy wife, and thou shalt be mine heire.

LODOWICKE. Oh, is't the custome, then I am resolv'd:
But rather let the brightsome heavens be dim,
And Natures beauty choake with stifeling clouds,
Then my fair *Abigall* should frowne on me.
There comes the villaine, now I'le be revenged.

Enter Mathias.

BARABAS. Be quiet *Lodowicke,* it is enough
That I have made thee sure to *Abigall.*

LODOWICKE. Well, let him goe.

Exit.

BARABAS. Well, but for me, as you went in at dores
You had bin stab'd, but not a word on't now;
Here must no speeches passe, nor swords be drawne.

MATHIAS. Suffer me, *Barabas,* but to follow him.

BARABAS. No; so shall I, if any hurt be done,
Be made an accessary of your deeds;
Revenge it on him when you meet him next.

MATHIAS. For this I'le have his heart.

BARABAS. Doe so; loe here I give thee *Abigall.*

MATHIAS. What greater gift can poore *Mathias* have?

Shall *Lodowicke* rob me of so faire a love?
My life is not so deare as *Abigall.*
BARABAS. My heart misgives me that to crosse your love,
Hee's with your mother, therefore, after him.
MATHIAS. What, is he gone unto my mother?
BARABAS. Nay, if you will, stay till she comes her selfe.
MATHIAS. I cannot stay; for, if my mother come,
She'll dye with griefe.

Exit.

ABIGALL. I cannot take my leave of him for teares.
Father, why have you thus incenst them both?
BARABAS. What's that to thee?
ABIGALL. I'le make 'em friends againe.
BARABAS. You'll make 'em friends?
Are there not Jewes enow in *Malta,*
But thou must dote upon a Christian?
ABIGALL. I will have Don *Mathias,* he is my love.
BARABAS. Yes, you shall have him: Goe put her in.
ITHIMORE. I, I'le put her in.

Exit Abigall.

BARABAS. Now tell me, *Ithimore,* how lik'st thou this?
ITHIMORE. Faith Master, I thinke by this
You purchase both their lives; is it not so?
BARABAS. True, and it shall be cunningly perform'd.
ITHIMORE. Oh, master, that I might have a hand in this.
BARABAS. I, so thou shalt, 'tis thou must doe the deed:
Take this and beare it to *Mathias* streight,
And tell him that it comes from *Lodowicke.*
ITHIMORE. 'Tis poyson'd, is it not?
BARABAS. No, no, and yet it might be done that way:
It is a challenge feign'd from *Lodowicke.*
ITHIMORE. Feare not, I'le so set his heart a fire,
That he shall verily thinke it comes from him.
BARABAS. I cannot choose but like thy readinesse:
Yet be not rash, but doe it cunningly.
ITHIMORE. As I behave my selfe in this, employ me hereafter.

Exit Ithimore.

BARABAS. Away then.
So, now will I goe in *to Lodowicke,*
And like a cunning spirit feigne some lye
Till I have set 'em both at enmitie.

Exit.

ACTUS TERTIUS [SCAENA I.]

Enter a Curtezane.

CURTEZANE. Since this Towne was besieg'd, my gaine growes cold.
The time has bin, that but for one bare night
A hundred Ducets have bin freely given:
But now against my will I must be chast.
And yet I know my beauty doth not faile.
From *Venice* Merchants, and from *Padua*
Were wont to come rare witted Gentlemen,
Schollers I meane, learned and liberall;
And now, save *Pilia-borza,* comes there none,
And he is very seldome from my house;
And here he comes.

Enter Pilia-Borza.

PILIA-BORZA. Hold thee, wench, there's something for thee to spend.
CURTEZANE. 'Tis silver; I disdaine it.
PILIA-BORZA. I, but the Jew has gold,
And I will have it or it shall goe hard.
CURTEZANE. Tell me, how cam'st thou by this?
PILIA-BORZA. Faith, walking the backe lanes through the Gardens I chanc'd to cast my eye up to the Jewes counting-house, where I saw some bags of mony, and in the night I clamber'd up with my hooks, and, as I was taking my choyce, I heard a rumbling in the house; so I tooke onely this, and runne my way: but heres the Jews man.

Enter Ithimore.

CURTEZANE. Hide the bagge.
PILIA-BORZA. Looke not towards him, lets away. Zoons, what a looking thou keep'st, thou'lt betraye's anon.

Exeunt.

ITHIMORE. O the sweetest face that ever I beheld! I know
she is a Curtezane by her attire: now would I give a
hundred of the Jewes crownes that I had such a Concubine.
Well, I have deliver'd the challenge in such sort,
as meet they will and fighting dye; brave sport.

Exit

[*SCAENA* 2.]

Enter Mathias.

MATHIAS. This is the place, now *Abigall* shall see
Whether Mathias holds her deare or no.

Enter Lodowicke *reading.*

LODOWICKE. What, dares the villain write in such base terms?
MATHIAS. I did it, and revenge it, if thou dar'st.

Fight: Enter Barabas *above.*

BARABAS. Oh, bravely fought, And yet they thrust not home.
Now *Lodowicke,* now *Mathias,* so;

[*Both fall.*]

So now they have shew'd themselves to be tall° fellowes. brave
[VOICES *within*] Part 'em, part 'em.
BARABAS. I, part 'em now they are dead. Farewell, farewell.

Exit.
Enter Governor, Mater [*and* Attendants].

GOVERNOR. What sight is this? my *Lodowicke* slaine!
These armes of mine shall be thy Sepulchre.
MATER. Who is this? my sonne *Mathias* slaine!
GOVERNOR. Oh *Lodowicke!* hadst thou perish'd by the Turke,
Wretched *Ferneze* might have veng'd thy death.
MATER. Thy sonne slew mine, and I'le revenge his death.
GOVERNOR. Looke, *Katherin,* looke, thy sonne gave mine these wounds.
MATER. O leave to grieve me, I am griev'd enough.
GOVERNOR. Oh, that my sighs could turne to lively breath;
And these my teares to blood, that he might live.
MATER. Who made them enemies?
GOVERNOR. I know not, and that grieves me most of all.
MATER. My sonne lov'd thine.
FERNEZE. And so did *Lodowicke* him.
MATER. Lend me that weapon that did kill my sonne,
And it shall murder me.
GOVERNOR. Nay Madam, stay, that weapon was my son's,
And on that rather should *Ferneze* die.
MATER. Hold, let's inquire the causers of their deaths,
That we may venge their blood upon their heads.
GOVERNOR. Then take them up, and let them be interr'd
Within one sacred monument of stone;
Upon which Altar I will offer up
My daily sacrifice of sighes and teares,

And with my prayers pierce impartiall heavens,
Till they reveal the causers of our smarts,
Which forc'd their hands divide united hearts:
Come, *Katherin,* our losses equall are,
Then of true griefe let us take equall share.

Exeunt.

[*SCAENA* 3.]

Enter *Ithimore.*

ITHIMORE. Why was there ever seene such villainy,
So neatly plotted, and so well perform'd?
Both held in hand, and flatly both beguil'd?

Enter Abigall.

ABIGALL. Why how now, *Ithimore,* why laugh'st thou so?
ITHIMORE. Oh, mistresse, ha ha ha.
ABIGALL. Why what ayl'st thou?
ITHIMORE. Oh, my master!
ABIGALL. Ha.
ITHIMORE. Oh Mistris! I have the bravest, gravest, secret, subtil bottle-nos'd knave to my Master, that ever Gentleman had.
ABIGALL. Say, knave, why rail'st upon my father thus?
ITHIMORE. Oh, my master has the bravest policy.
ABIGALL. Wherein?
ITHIMORE. Why, know you not?
ABIGALL. Why no.
ITHIMORE. Know you not of *Mathias* and Don *Lodowickes* disaster?
ABIGALL. No, what was it?
ITHIMORE. Why the devil invented a challenge, my Master writ it, and I carried it, first to *Lodowicke,* and *imprimis*[21] to *Mathias.*
And then they met, and as the story sayes,
In dolefull wise they ended both their dayes.
ABIGALL. And was my father furtherer of their deaths?
ITHIMORE. Am I *Ithimore?*
ABIGALL. Yes.
ITHIMORE. So sure did your father write, and I cary the challenge.
ABIGALL. Well, *Ithimore,* let me request thee this:
Goe to the new made Nunnery, and inquire
For any of the Fryars of Saint *Jaques,*
And say, I pray them come and speake with me.
ITHIMORE. I pray, mistris, will you answer me to one question?
ABIGALL. Well, sirra, what is't?

21. First of all (a malapropism).

ITHIMORE. A very feeling one; Have not the Nuns fine sport
with the Fryars now and then?
ABIGALL. Go to, sirra sauce, is this your question? get ye gone!
ITHIMORE. I will, forsooth, Mistris.

Exit.

ABIGALL. Hard-hearted Father, unkind *Barabas,*
Was this the pursuit of thy policie?
To make me shew them favour severally,
That by my favour they should both be slaine?
Admit thou lov'dst not *Lodowicke* for his sire,
Yet Don *Mathias* ne're offended thee:
But thou wert set upon extreme revenge,
Because the Pryor dispossesset thee once,
And couldst not venge it, but upon his sonne,
Nor on his sonne, but by *Mathias* meanes;
Nor on *Mathias,* but by murdering me.
But I perceive there is no love on earth,
Pitty in Jewes, nor piety in Turkes.
But here comes cursed *Ithimore* with the Fryar.

Enter Ithimore, I Fryar.

I FRYAR. *Virgo, salve.*° — greetings, maiden
ITHIMORE. When ducke you?
ABIGALL. Welcome grave Fryar: Ithimore begon,

Exit [Ithimore].

Know, holy Sir, I am bold to solicite thee.
I FRYAR. Wherein?
ABIGALL. To get me be admitted for a Nun.
I FRYAR. Why *Abigall* it is not yet long since
That I did labour thy admition,
And then thou didst not like that holy life.
ABIGALL. Then were my thoughts so fraile and unconfirm'd
As I was chain'd to follies of the world:
But now experience, purchased with griefe,
Has made me see the difference of things.
My sinful soule, alas, hath pac'd too long
The fatall Labyrinth of misbeleefe,
Farre from the Sonne that gives eternall life.
I FRYAR. Who taught thee this?
ABIGALL. The Abbasse of the house,
Whose zealous admonition I embrace:
Oh, therefore, *Jacomo,* let me be one,
Although unworthy, of that Sister-hood.
I FRYAR. *Abigall* I will, but see thou change no more,
For that will be most heavy to thy soule.

ABIGALL. That was my father's fault.
I FRYAR. Thy father's, how?
ABIGALL. Nay, you shall pardon me: *(aside)* oh *Barabas,*
Though thou deservest hardly at my hands,
Yet never shall these lips bewray thy life.
I FRYAR. Come, shall we goe?
ABIGALL. My duty waits on you.

Exeunt.

[*SCAENA 4.*]

Enter Barabas *reading a letter.*

BARABAS. What, *Abigall* become a Nunne again?
False, and unkinde; What, hast thou lost thy father?
And all unknowne, and unconstrain'd of me,
And thou againe got to the Nunnery?
Now here she writes, and wils me to repent.
Repentance? *Spurca:*° what pretendeth this? filth
I feare she knowes ('tis so) of my device
In Don *Mathias* and *Lodovicoes* deaths:
If so, 'tis time that it be seene into:
For she that varies from me in beleefe
Gives great presumption that she loves me not;
Or loving, doth dislike of something done:
But who comes here?

[*Enter* Ithimore.]

Oh *Ithimore,* come neere;
Come neere my love, come neere thy masters life,
My trusty servant, nay, my second selfe;
For I have now no hope but even° in thee; except
And on that hope my happinesse is built:
When sawst thou *Abigall?*
ITHIMORE. To day.
BARABAS. With whom?
ITHIMORE. A Fryar.
BARABAS. A Fryar! false villaine, he hath done the deed.
ITHIMORE. How, Sir?
BARABAS. Why made mine *Abigall* a Nunne.
ITHIMORE. That's no lye, for she sent me for him.
BARABAS. Oh unhappy day,
False, credulous, inconstant *Abigall!*
But let 'em goe: And *Ithimore,* from hence
Ne're shall she grieve me more with her disgrace,
Ne're shall she live to inherit ought of mine,
Be blest of me, nor come within my gates,

But perish underneath my bitter curse
Like *Cain* by *Adam,* for his brother's death.
ITHIMORE. Oh master.
BARABAS. Ithimore, intreat not for her, I am mov'd,
And she is hatefull to my soule and me:
And least° thou yeeld to this that I intreat, lest
I cannot thinke but that thou hat'st my life.
ITHIMORE. Who I, master? Why, I'le run to some rocke
And throw my selfe headlong into the sea;
Why, I'le doe any thing for your sweet sake.
BARABAS. Oh trusty *Ithimore;* no servant, but my friend;
I here adopt thee for mine onely heire
All that I have is thine when I am dead,
And whilst I live use halfe; Spend as my selfe;
Here, take my keyes, I'le give 'em thee anon:
Goe buy thee garments: But thou shalt not want:
Onely know this, that thus thou art to doe:
But first goe fetch me in the pot of Rice
That for our supper stands upon the fire.
ITHIMORE. I hold° my head my master's hungry. I goe Sir. wager

Exit.

BARABAS. Thus every villaine ambles after wealth,
Although he ne're be richer then in hope:
But, hush't!

Enter Ithimore *with the pot.*

ITHIMORE. Here 'tis, Master.
BARABAS. Well said, *Ithimore;*
What hast thou brought the Ladle with thee too?
ITHIMORE. Yes, Sir, The proverb saies, he that eats with the devil had need of a long spoone, I have brought you a Ladle.
BARABAS. Very well, *Ithimore,* then now be secret;
And for thy sake, whom I so dearely love,
Now shalt thou see the death of *Abigall,*
That thou mayst freely live to be my heire.
ITHIMORE. Why, master, wil you poison her with a messe of rice porredge? That wil preserve life, make her round and plump, and batten more then you are aware.
BARABAS. I but *Ithimore* seest thou this?
It is a precious powder that I bought
Of an Italian in *Ancona* once,
Whose operation is to binde, infect,
And poyson deeply: yet not appeare
In forty houres after it is tane.
ITHIMORE. How master?

BARABAS. Thus *Ithimore:*
This Even° they use in *Malta* here ('tis call'd — evening
Saint *Jaques* Even) and then I say they use
To send their almes unto the Nunneries:
Among the rest beare this, and set it there;
There's a darke entry where they take it in,
Where they must neither see the messenger,
Nor make enquiry who hath sent it them.
ITHIMORE. How so?
BARABAS. Belike there is some Ceremony in't.
There *Ithimore* must thou goe place this pot:
Stay, let me spice it first.
ITHIMORE. Pray doe, and let me help you Master.
Pray, let me taste first.
BARABAS. Prethe doe: What saist thou now?
ITHIMORE. Troth Master I'm loth such a pot of pottage
should be spoyled.
BARABAS. Peace, *Ithimore,* 'tis better so than spar'd.
Assure thy selfe thou shalt have broth by the eye.[22]
My purse, my Coffer, and my selfe is thine.
ITHIMORE. Well, Master, I goe.
BARABAS. Stay, First let me stirre it *Ithimore.*
As fatall be it to her as the draught
Of which great *Alexander* drunke, and dyed:
And with her let it worke like *Borgias* wine,
Whereof his sire, the Pope, was poyson'd.[23]
In few, the blood of *Hydra, Lerna's* bane;[24]
The jouyce of Hebon,° and *Cocitus* breath,[25] — yew
And all the poysons of the Stygian poole
Breake from the fiery kingdome: and in this
Vomit your venome, and invenom her
That like a fiend hath left her father thus.
ITHIMORE. What a blessing has he given't? was ever pot
of rice porredge so sauc't? what shall I doe with it?
BARABAS. Oh my sweet *Ithimore* goe set it downe
And come againe as soone as thou hast done,
For I have other businesse for thee.
ITHIMORE. Heres a drench to poyson a whole stable of
Flanders mares: I'le carry't to the Nuns with a powder.

22. The Oxford English Dictionary cites this example of the phrase "by the eye" and conjectures it means "in unlimited quantity."

23. Alexander VI was rumored to have been poisoned by his son Cesare with the Borgia's special arsenic drink, cantarella.

24. Lerna was the region in Greece associated with the Hydra, slain by Hercules.

25. Cocytus, one of the rivers of Hades.

BARABAS. And the horse pestilence to boot; away.
ITHIMORE. I am gone.
Pay me my wages for my worke is done.

Exit.

BARABAS. I'le pay thee with a vengeance *Ithimore.*

Exit.

[*SCAENA* 5.]

Enter Governor, Bosco, Knights, Basso.

GOVERNOR. Welcome, great Bashaw, how fares *Calymath,*
What wind drives you thus into Malta rhode?
BASSO. The wind that bloweth all the world besides,
Desire of gold.
GOVERNOR. Desire of gold, great Sir?
That's to be gotten in the Western *Inde:*
In *Malta* are no golden Minerals.
BASSO. To you of *Malta* thus saith *Calymath:*
The time you tooke for respite, is at hand,
For the performance of your promise past;
And for the Tribute-mony I am sent.
GOVERNOR. Bashaw, in briefe, shalt have no tribute here,
Nor shall the Heathens live upon our spoyle:
First will we race° the City wals our selves, — raze
Lay waste the Iland, hew the Temples downe,
And, shipping off our goods to *Sicily,*
Open an entrance for the wastfull sea,
Whose billowes beating the resistlesse bankes,
Shall overflow it with their refluence.
BASSO. Well, Governor, since thou hast broke the league
By flat denyall of the promis'd Tribute,
Talke not of racing downe your City wals,
You shall not need trouble your selves so farre,
For *Selim-Calymath* shall come himselfe,
And with brasse-bullets batter downe your Towers,
And turne proud *Malta* to a wildernesse
For these intolerable wrongs of yours;
And so farewell.

[*Exit.*]

GOVERNOR. Farewell:
And now, you men of *Malta* looke about,
And let's provide to welcome *Calymath;*
Close your Port-cullise, charge your Basiliskes,° — cannon

And as you profitably take up Armes,
So now couragiously encounter them;
For by this Answer, broken is the league,
And nought is to be look'd for now but warres,
And nought to us more welcome is then warres.

Exeunt.

[SCAENA 6.]

Enter two Fryars.

1 FRYAR. Oh brother, brother, all the Nuns are sicke,
And Physicke will not helpe them; they must dye.
2 FRYAR. The Abbasse sent for me to be confessed:
Oh what a sad confession will there be?
1 FRYAR. And so did faire *Maria* send for me:
I'le to her lodging; hereabouts she lyes.

Exit.

Enter Abigall.

2 FRYAR. What, all dead save onely *Abigall?*
ABIGALL. And I shall dye too, for I feele death comming.
Where is the Fryar that converst with me?
2 FRYAR. Oh he is gone to see the other Nuns.
ABIGALL. I sent for him, but seeing you are come,
Be you my ghostly father;° and first know, confessor
That in this house I liv'd religiously,
Chast, and devout, much sorrowing for my sinnes.
But, e're I came—
2 FRYAR. What then?
ABIGALL. I did offend high heaven so grievously,
As I am almost desperate for my sinnes:
And one offence torments me more than all.
You knew *Mathias* and Don *Lodowicke?*
2 FRYAR. Yes, what of them?
ABIGALL. My father did contract me to 'em both:
First to Don *Lodowicke*, him I never lov'd;
Mathias was the man that I held deare,
And for his sake did I become a Nunne.
2 FRYAR. So say how was their end?
ABIGALL. Both, jealous of my love, envied each other:
And by my father's practice, which is there

[*Gives paper.*]

Set downe at large, the Gallants were both slaine.
2 FRYAR. Oh monstrous villainy[.]

ABIGALL. To worke my peace, this I confesse to thee;
Reveale it not, for then my father dyes.
2 FRYAR. Know that confession must not be reveal'd,
The Canon Law forbids it, and the Priest
That makes it knowne, being degraded first,
Shall be condemn'd, and then sent to the fire.
ABIGALL. So I have heard; pray therefore keepe it close.
Death seizeth on my heart. Ah, gentle Fryar
Convert my father that he may be sav'd,
And witnesse that I dye a Christian.

[*Dies.*]

2 FRYAR. I, and a Virgin too, that grieves me most:
But I must to the Jew, and exclaime on him,
And make him stand in feare of me.

Enter I Fryar.

I FRYAR. Oh brother, all the Nuns are dead, let's bury them.
2 FRYAR. First helpe to bury this, then goe with me
And helpe me to exclaime against the Jew.
I FRYAR. Why? what has he done?
2 FRYAR. A thing that makes me tremble to unfold.
I FRYAR. What has he crucified a child?
2 FRYAR. No, but a worse thing: 'twas told me in shrift,° — confession
Thou know'st 'tis death and if it be reveal'd.
Come, lets away.

Exeunt.

ACTUS QUARTUS [*SCAENA I*].

Enter Barabas, Ithimore. *Bells within.*

BARABAS. There is no musicke to a Christians knell:
How sweet the Bels ring, now the Nuns are dead
That sound at other times like Tinkers pans?
I was afraid the poyson had not wrought,
Or though it wrought, it would have done no good,
For every yeare they swell, and yet they live;
Now all are dead, not one remaines alive.
ITHIMORE. That's brave, Master, but think you it will not be known?
BARABAS. How can it, if we two be secret?
ITHIMORE. For my part feare you not.
BARABAS. I'de cut thy throat if I did.
ITHIMORE. And reason too;
But here's a royall Monastry hard by;

Good master let me poyson all the Monks.
BARABAS. Thou shalt not need, for now the Nuns are dead,
They'll dye with griefe.
ITHIMORE. Doe you not sorrow for your daughters death?
BARABAS. No, but I grieve because she liv'd so long,
An Hebrew borne, and would become a Christian.
Cazzo,° diabolo! penis

Enter the two Fryars.

ITHIMORE. Look, look, Master. Here come two religious caterpillars.
BARABAS. I smelt 'em e're they came.
ITHIMORE. God-a-mercy nose; come, let's begone.
2 FRYAR. Stay wicked Jew; repent, I say, and stay[.]
1 FRYAR. Thou hast offended, therefore must be damn'd.
BARABAS. I feare they know we sent the poyson'd broth.
ITHIMORE. And so doe I, master; therefore speak 'em faire.
2 FRYAR. *Barabas,* thou hast—
1 FRYAR. I, that thou hast—
BARABAS. True, I have mony, What though I have?
2 FRYAR. Thou art a—
1 FRYAR. I, that thou art a—
BARABAS. What needs all this? I know I am a Jew.
2 FRYAR. Thy daughter—
1 FRYAR. I, thy daughter—
BARABAS. Oh speake not of her; then I dye with griefe.
2 FRYAR. Remember that—
1 FRYAR. I, remember that—
BARABAS. I must needs say that I have beene a great usurer.
2 FRYAR. Thou hast committed—
BARABAS. Fornication? But that was in another Country:
And besides, the Wench is dead.
2 FRYAR. I, but *Barabas* remember *Mathias* and Don *Lodowicke.*
BARABAS. Why, what of them?
2 FRYAR. I will not say that by a forged challenge they met.
BARABAS. [*Aside.*] She has confest, and we are both undone;
My bosome inmates,[26] but I must dissemble.
Oh holy Fryars, the burthen of my sinnes
Lye heavy on my soule; then pray you tell me
Is't not too late now to turne Christian?
I have been zealous in the Jewish faith,
Hart harted to the poore, a covetous wretch,
That would for Lucars sake have sold my soule.
A hundred for a hundred° I have tane; 100% interest
And now for store of wealth may I compare
With all the Jewes in *Malta;* But what is wealth?

26. "inmates" in Gill's text.

I am a Jew, and therefore am I lost.
Would penance serve for this my sinne,
I could afford to whip my selfe to death.
ITHIMORE. And so could I, but penance will not serve.
BARABAS. To fast, to pray, and wear a shirt of haire,
And on my knees creepe to *Jerusalem.*
Cellers of Wine, and Sollers° full of Wheat, lofts
Ware-houses stuft with spices and with drugs,
Whole Chests of Gold, in Bullione, and in Coyne,
Besides I know not how much weight in Pearle
Orient and round, have I within my house;
At *Alexandria,* Merchandise unsold:
But yesterday two ships went from this Towne,
Their voyage will be worth ten thousand Crownes.
In *Florence, Venice, Antwerpe, London, Civill,*
Frankeford, Lubecke, Mosco, and where not,
Have I debts owing; and in most of these,
Great summes of mony lying in the bancho;
All this I'le give to some religious house
So I may be baptiz'd and live therein.
1 FRYAR. Oh good *Barabas* come to our house.
2 FRYAR. Oh no, good *Barabas* come to our house.
And *Barabas,* you know—
BARABAS. I know that I have highly sinn'd,
You shall convert me, You shall have all my wealth.
1 FRYAR. Oh *Barabas,* their Lawes are strict.
BARABAS. I know they are, and I will be with you.
2 FRYAR. They weare no shirts, and they goe bare-foot too.
BARABAS. Then 'tis not for me; and I am resolv'd
You shall confesse me, and have all my goods.
1 FRYAR. Good *Barabas* come to me.
BARABAS. You see I answer him, and yet he stayes;
Rid him away, and goe you home with me.
2 FRYAR. I'le be with you tonight.
BARABAS. Come to my house at one a clocke this night.
1 FRYAR. You heare your answer, and you may be gone.
2 FRYAR. Why goe get you away.
1 FRYAR. I will not goe for thee.
2 FRYAR. No, then I'le make thee, rogue.
1 FRYAR. How, dost call me rogue?

Fight.

ITHIMORE. Part 'em, master, part 'em.
BARABAS. This is meere frailty, brethren, be content.
Fryar *Barnardine,* goe you with *Ithimore.*
(Aside) You know my mind, let [me] alone with him.

Exeunt [Ithimore and 2 Fryar].

I FRYAR. Why does he goe to thy house, let him begone.
BARABAS. I'le give him something and so stop his mouth.
I never heard of any man but he
Malign'd the order of the Jacobines:° (Dominican Black Friars)
But doe you thinke that I beleeve his words?
Why Brother you converted *Abigall;*
And I am bound in charitie to requite it,
And so I will, oh *Jacomo,* faile not but come.
I FRYAR. But *Barabas* who shall be your godfathers,
For presently you shall be shriv'd.° (absolved in confession)
BARABAS. Marry the Turke shall be one of my godfathers,
But not a word to any of your Convent.
I FRYAR. I warrant thee, *Barabas.*

Exit.

BARABAS. So, now the feare is past, and I am safe:
For he that shriv'd her is within my house,
What if I murder'd him e're *Jacomo* comes?
Now I have such a plot for both their lives,
As never Jew nor Christian knew the like:
One turn'd my daughter, therefore he shall dye;
The other knowes enough to have my life,
Therefore 'tis requisite he should not live.
But are not both these wise men to suppose
That I will leave my house, my goods, and all,
To fast and be well whipt; I'le none of that.
Now Fryar *Barnardine* I come to you,
I'le feast you, lodge you, give you faire words,
And after that, I and my trusty Turke—
No more, but so: it must and shall be done.

Enter Ithimore.

Ithimore, tell me, is the Fryar asleepe?
ITHIMORE. Yes; and I know not what the reason is,
Doe what I can he will not strip himselfe,
Nor goe to bed, but sleepes in his owne clothes;
I feare me he mistrusts what we intend.
BARABAS. No, 'tis an order which the Fryars use:
Yet, if he knew our meanings, could he scape?
ITHIMORE. No, none can heare him, cry he ne're so loud.
BARABAS. Why true, therefore did I place him there:
The other Chambers open towards the street.
ITHIMORE. You loyter, master, wherefore stay we thus?
Oh how I long to see him shake his heeles.

[2 Fryar *is revealed.*]

BARABAS. Come on, sirra, off with your girdle, make a hansom noose;
Fryar awake.
2 FRYAR. What doe you meane to strangle me?
ITHIMORE. Yes, 'cause you use° to confesse. practice
BARABAS. Blame not us but the proverb, Confes and be hang'd. confession
Pull hard.
2 FRYAR. What will you have my life?
BARABAS. Pull hard, I say, you would have had my goods.
ITHIMORE. I, and our lives too, Therefore pull amaine.

[2 Fryar *falls.*]

'Tis neatly done, Sir, here's no print at all.
BARABAS. Then is it as it should be, take him up.
ITHIMORE. Nay, Master, be rul'd by me a little; so, let him leane
upon his staffe; excellent, he stands as if he were begging of Bacon.
BARABAS. Who would not thinke but that this Fryar liv'd?
What time a night is't now, sweet *Ithimore?*
ITHIMORE. Towards one.
BARABAS. Then will not *Jacomo* be long from hence.

[*Exeunt.*]
Enter I Fryar.

I FRYAR. This is the houre wherein I shall proceed;
Oh happy houre, wherein I shall convert
An Infidell, and bring his gold into our treasury.
But soft, is not this *Bernardine?* it is;
And understanding I should come this way,
Stands here a purpose, meaning me some wrong,
And intercept my going to the Jew.
Bernardine;
Wilt thou not speake? thou think'st I see thee not;
Away, I'de wish thee, and let me goe by:
No, wilt thou not? nay, then I'le force my way;
And see, a staffe stands ready for the purpose:
As thou lik'st that, stop me another time.

Strikes him, he fals.
Enter Barabas [*and* Ithimore].

BARABAS. Why how now *Jacomo,* what hast thou done?
I FRYAR. Why stricken him that would have stroke at me.
BARABAS. Who is it, *Bernardine?* now out alas, he is slaine.
ITHIMORE. I, Master, he's slain; look how his brains drop
out on's nose.
I FRYAR. Good sirs I have don't,° but no body knows done it
it but you two, I may escape.
BARABAS. So might my man and I hang with you for company.
ITHIMORE. No, let us beare him to the Magistrates.

I FRYAR. Good *Barabas* let me goe.
BARABAS. No, pardon me, the Law must have his course.
I must be forc'd to give in evidence
That being importun'd by this *Bernardine*
To be a Christian, I shut him out,
And there he sate: Now I, to keepe my word,
And give my goods and substance to your house,
Was up thus early; with intent to goe
Unto your Friery because you staid.° [were late]
ITHIMORE. Fie upon 'em, Master, will you turne Christian, when holy friars turne devils and murder one another[?]
BARABAS. No, for this example I'le remaine a Jew:
Heaven blesse me; what, a Fryar a murderer?
When shall you see a Jew commit the like?
ITHIMORE. Why, a Turke could ha done no more.
BARABAS. Tomorrow is the Sessions; you shall to it.
Come *Ithimore,* let's helpe to take him hence.
I FRYAR. Villaines, I am a sacred person, touch me not.
BARABAS. The Law shall touch you, we'll but lead you, we:
'Las I could weepe at your calamity.
Take in the staffe too, for that must be showne:
Law wils that each particular be knowne.

Exeunt.

[*SCAENA* 2.]

Enter Curtezane, *and* Pilia-Borza.

CURTEZANE. *Pilia-borza,* didst thou meet with *Ithimore?*
PILIA-BORZA. I did.
CURTEZANE. And didst thou deliver my letter?
PILIA-BORZA. I did.
CURTEZANE. And what think'st thou? Will he come?
PILIA-BORZA. I think so, and yet I cannot tell, for, at the reading of the letter he look'd like a man of another world.
CURTEZANE. Why so?
PILIA-BORZA. That such a base slave as he should be saluted by such a tall man as I am, from such a beautiful dame as you.
CURTEZANE. And what said he?
PILIA-BORZA. Not a wise word, only gave me a nod, as who should say, Is it even so; And so I left him, being driven to a *Non-plus*° at the critical aspect of my terrible countenance. [bewilderment]
CURTEZANE. And where didst meet him?
PILIA-BORZA. Upon mine owne free-hold, within fortie foot of the

gallowes, conning his neck-verse,[27] I take it, looking of A Fryars Execution, whom I saluted with an old hempen proverb, *Hodie tibi, cras mihi,*[28] and so I left him to the mercy of the hangman: but the Exercise being done, see where he comes.

Enter Ithimore.

ITHIMORE. I never knew a man take his death so patiently as this Fryar; He was ready to leape off e're the halter was about his necke; And when the Hangman had put on
his hempen Tippet,° he made such haste to his prayers, priestly stole
as if hee had had another Cure° to serve; well, goe parish
whither he will, I'le be none of his followers in haste: And now I thinke on't, going to the execution,
a fellow met me with a muschatoes° like a Ravens wing, moustache
and a Dagger with a hilt like a warming-pan, and he gave me a letter from one Madam *Bellamira,* saluting me in such sort as if he had meant to make cleane my Boots with his lips; the effect was, that I should come to her house; I wonder what the reason is; it may be she sees more in me than I can find in my selfe; for she writes further, that she loves me ever since she saw me, and who would not requite such love? here's her house, and here she comes, and now would I were gone, I am not worthy to looke upon her.

PILIA-BORZA. This is the Gentleman you writ to.

ITHIMORE. Gentleman, he flouts me, what gentry can be in a poore Turke of ten pence? I'le be gone.

CURTEZANE. Is't not a sweet fac'd youth, *Pilia?*

ITHIMORE. Again, sweet youth; did not you, Sir, bring the sweet youth a letter?

PILIA-BORZA. I did Sir, and from this Gentlewoman, who as my selfe, and the rest of the family, stand or fall at your service.

CURTEZANE. Though womans modesty should hale me backe, I can withold no longer; welcome sweet love.

ITHIMORE. [*Aside.*] Now am I cleane, or rather fouly out of the way.

CURTEZANE. Whither so soone?

ITHIMORE. [*Aside.*] I'le goe steale some mony from my Master to make me hansome. Pray pardon me; I must go see a ship discharg'd.

CURTEZANE. Canst thou be so unkind to leave me thus?

PILIA-BORZA. And ye did but know how she loves you, Sir.

ITHIMORE. Nay, I care not how much she loves me; sweet *Allamira,* would I had my Masters wealth for thy sake.

27. According to Gill, "The ability to read, in Latin, the first verse of Ps. 51 entitled a criminal to plead 'benefit of clergy' and escape the gallows."

28. You today, me tomorrow.

PILIA-BORZA. And you can have it, Sir, and if you please.
ITHIMORE. If 'twere above ground I could, and would have it;
but hee hides and buries it up as Partridges doe their egges,
under the earth.
PILIA-BORZA. And is't not possible to find it out?
ITHIMORE. By no meanes possible.
CURTEZANE. [*Aside.*] What shall we do with this base villaine then?
PILIA-BORZA. [*Aside.*] Let me alone, doe but you speake him fair:
But you know some secrets of the Jew, which, if they were reveal'd,
would doe him harme.
ITHIMORE. I, and such as—Goe to, no more, I'le make him
send me half he has, and glad he scapes so too. Pen
and Inke: I'le write unto him, we'le have mony strait.
PILIA-BORZA. Send for a hundred Crownes at least.
ITHIMORE. *(He Writes)* Ten hundred thousand crownes—Master
Barabas.
PILIA-BORZA. Write not so submissively, but threatning him.
ITHIMORE. Sirra *Barabas,* send me a hundred crownes.
PILIA-BORZA. Put in two hundred at least.
ITHIMORE. I charge thee send me three hundred by this
bearer, and this shall be your warrant; if you do not, no more, but so.
PILIA-BORZA. Tell him you will confesse.
ITHIMORE. Otherwise I'le confess all; vanish and returne
in a twinkle.
PILIA-BORZA. Let me alone, I'le use him in his kinde.

[*Exit.*]

ITHIMORE. Hang him Jew.
CURTEZANE. Now, gentle *Ithimore,* lye in my lap.
Where are my Maids? provide a running Banquet;
Send to the Merchant, bid him bring me silkes,
Shall *Ithimore* my love goe in such rags?
ITHIMORE. And bid the Jeweller come hither too.
CURTEZANE. I have no husband, sweet, I'le marry thee.
ITHIMORE. Content, but we will leave this paltry land,
And saile from hence to *Greece,* to lovely *Greece,*
I'le be thy *Jason,* thou my golden Fleece;[29]
Where painted Carpets o're the meads are hurl'd,
And *Bacchus* vineyards over-spread the world:
Where woods and forests goe in goodly greene,

29. Jason achieved the tasks to claim the Golden Fleece from King Aeetes with the aid of Medea, the king's daughter. Subsequently he becomes bethrothed to Creusa, the daughter of the king of Corinth, Creon. Enraged, Medea creates a dress in which Creusa is burned to death. Creon dies trying to save Creusa, and Medea also murders the two sons she has had with Jason and escapes safely. Jason dies alone and unhappy.

I'le be *Adonis,* thou shalt be Loves Queene.[30]
The Meads, the Orchards, and the Primrose lanes,
Instead of Sedge and Reed, beare Sugar Canes:
Thou in those Groves, by *Dis*[31] above,
Shalt live with me, and be my love.

CURTEZANE. Whither will I not go with gentle *Ithimore?*

Enter Pilia-Borza.

ITHIMORE. How now? hast thou the gold?

PILIA-BORZA. Yes.

ITHIMORE. But came it freely, did the cow give down her milk freely?

PILIA-BORZA. At reading of the letter, he star'd and stamp'd, and turnd aside, I tooke him by the beard, and look'd upon him thus; told him he were best to send it, then he hug'd and imbrac'd me.

ITHIMORE. Rather for feare then love.

PILIA-BORZA. Then, like a Jew he laugh'd and jeer'd, and told me he lov'd me for your sake, and said what a faithfull servant you had bin.

ITHIMORE. The more villaine he to keep me thus: here's goodly 'parell, is there not?

PILIA-BORZA. To conclude, he gave me ten crownes.

ITHIMORE. But ten? I'le not leave him worth a gray groat, give me a Reame of paper, we'll have a kingdome of gold for't.

PILIA-BORZA. Write for five hundred Crownes.

ITHIMORE. Sirra Jew, as you love your life, send me five hundred crowns and give the Bearer one hundred. Tell him I must hav't.

PILIA-BORZA. I warrant your worship shall hav't.

ITHIMORE. And, if he aske why I demand so much, tell him, I scorne to write a line under a hundred crownes.

PILIA-BORZA. You'd make a rich Poet, Sir. I am gone.

Exit.

ITHIMORE. Take thou the mony, spend it for my sake.

CURTEZANE. 'Tis not thy mony, but thy selfe I weigh:
Thus *Bellamira* esteemes of gold;

[*Throws it aside.*]

But thus of thee.—*Kisse him.*

ITHIMORE. That kisse againe; She runs division of my lips.
What an eye she casts on me? It twinckles like a Starre.

30. Venus falls in love with Adonis and urges him to hunt no more. He is killed by a wild boar.
31. God of the underworld (Pluto).

CURTEZANE. Come my deare love, let's in and sleepe together.
ITHIMORE. Oh that ten thousand nights were put in one,
That wee might sleepe seven yeeres together
Afore we wake.
CURTEZANE. Come, Amorous wag, first banquet, and then sleepe.

[*Exeunt.*]

[*SCAENA* 3.]

Enter Barabas *reading a letter.*

BARABAS. *Barabas* send me three hundred Crownes.
Plaine *Barabas:* oh that wicked Curtezane!
He was not wont to call me *Barabas.*
Or else I will confesse: I, there it goes:
But, if I get him, *Coupe de Gorge*[32] for that.
He sent a shaggy totter'd, staring slave,
That when he speakes, drawes out his grisly beard
And winds it twice or thrice about his eare;
Whose face has bin a grind-stone for mens swords,
His hands are hackt, some fingers cut quite off;
Who when he speakes, grunts like a hog, and looks
Like one that is imploy'd in Catzerie,[33]
And crosbiting; such a Rogue
As is the husband to a hundred whores:
And I by him must send three hundred crownes.
Well, my hope is, he will not stay there still;
And, when he comes: Oh that he were but here!

Enter Pilia-Borza.

PILIA-BORZA. Jew, I must ha more gold.
BARABAS. Why wantst thou any of thy tale?° bill, account
PILIA-BORZA. No; but three hundred will not serve his turne.
BARABAS. Not serve his turne, Sir?
PILIA-BORZA. No Sir; and therefore I must have five hundred more.
BARABAS. I'le rather—
PILIA-BORZA. Oh good words, Sir, and send it you were best;
see, there's his letter.
BARABAS. Might he not as well come as send; pray bid him
come and fetch it, what hee writes for you, ye shall have streight.

32. I'll cut his throat.

33. This is apparently a neologism. If the Oxford English Dictionary is right that the word derives from "cazzo," then its suggested definition of "cheating, trickery" seems unlikely, especially since "crosbiting" in the next line also means that. More likely, Barabas means that Pilia-Borza is involved in the business of the penis, that is, he is a pimp or pander.

PILIA-BORZA. I, and the rest too, or else—
BARABAS. I must make this villaine away; please you
dine with me, Sir, *(aside)* and you shall be most hartily
poyson'd.
PILIA-BORZA. No god-a-mercy, shall I have these crownes?
BARABAS. I cannot doe it, I have lost my keyes.
PILIA-BORZA. Oh, if that be all, I can picke ope your locks.
BARABAS. Or climbe up to my Counting-house window: you
know my meaning?
PILIA-BORZA. I know enough, and therefore talke not to me of
your counting-house, the gold, or know Jew it is in
my power to hang thee.
BARABAS. [*Aside.*] I am betraid.
'Tis not five hundred Crownes that I esteeme,
I am not mov'd at that: this angers me,
That he who knowes I love him as my self
Should write in this imperious vaine[.] Why Sir,
You know I have no childe, and unto whom
Should I leave all but unto *Ithimore?*
PILIA-BORZA. Here's many words but no crownes; the crownes.
BARABAS. Commend me to him, Sir, most humbly,
And unto your good mistres as unknowne.
PILIA-BORZA. Speake, shall I have 'um, Sir?
BARABAS. Sir, here they are.
[*Aside*] Oh that I should part with so much gold!
Here take 'em, fellow, with as good a will—
—[*Aside*] As I would see thee hang'd:
oh, love stops my breath:
Never lov'd man servant as I doe *Ithimore.*
PILIA-BORZA. I know it, Sir.
BARABAS. Pray when, Sir, shall I see you at my house?
PILIA-BORZA. Soone enough to your cost, Sir. Fare you well.

Exit.

BARABAS. Nay to thine owne cost, villaine, if thou com'st.
Was ever Jew tormented as I am?
To have a shag-rag knave to come demand
Three hundred Crownes, and then five hundred Crownes!
Well, I must seeke a meanes to rid 'em all,
And presently: for in his villany
He will tell all he knowes and I shall dye for't.
I have it.
I will in some disguize goe see the slave,
And how the villaine revels with my gold.

Exit.

[*SCAENA 4.*]

Enter Curtezane, Ithimore, Pilia-Borza.

CURTEZANE. I'le pledge thee, love, and therefore drinke it off.
ITHIMORE. Saist thou me so? Have at it; and doe you heare?

[*Whispers to her.*]

CURTEZANE. Goe to, it shall be so.
ITHIMORE. Of that condition I wil drink it up; here's to thee.
CURTEZANE. Nay, I'le have all or none.
ITHIMORE. There, if thou lovs't me doe not leave a drop.
CURTEZANE. Love thee, fill me three glasses.
ITHIMORE. Three and fifty dozen, I'le pledge thee.
PILIA-BORZA. Knavely spoke and like a Knight at Armes.
ITHIMORE. Hey, *Rivo Castiliano,*° a man's a man. — river of Castille
CURTEZANE. Now to the Jew.
ITHIMORE. Ha to the Jew, and send me mony you were best.
PILIA-BORZA. What wudst thou doe if he should send thee none?
ITHIMORE. Doe nothing; but I know what I know, He's a murderer.
CURTEZANE. I had not thought he had been so brave a man.
ITHIMORE. You knew *Mathias* and the Governors son, he and I kild 'em both, and yet never touch'd 'em.
PILIA-BORZA. Oh, bravely done.
ITHIMORE. I carried the broth that poyson'd the Nuns, and he and I snickle hand too fast,[34] strangled a Fryar.
CURTEZANE. You two alone?
ITHIMORE. We two, and 'twas never knowne, nor never shall be for me.
PILIA-BORZA. [*Aside.*] This shall with me unto the Governor.
CURTEZANE. [*Aside.*] And fit it should: but first let's ha more gold:
Come gentle *Ithimore,* lie in my lap.
ITHIMORE. Love me little, love me long, let musicke rumble,
Whilst I in thy incony° lap doe tumble. — delicate

Enter Barabas *with a Lute, disguis'd.*

CURTEZANE. A French Musician, come let's heare your skill[.]
BARABAS. Must tuna my Lute for sound, twang, twang, first.
ITHIMORE. Wilt drinke French-man, Here's to thee with a— pox on this drunken hick-up!
BARABAS. Gramercy Mounsier.
CURTEZANE. Prethe, *Pilia-borza,* bid the Fidler give me the posey in his hat there.
PILIA-BORZA. Sirra, you must give my mistris your posey.

34. Probably a corrupt passage. A snickle is a noose; perhaps the passage means "a noose fast in our hands."

BARABAS. *A voustre commandement Madam.*[35]
CURTEZANE. How sweet, my *Ithimore*, the flowers smell.
ITHIMORE. Like thy breath, sweet-hart, no violet like 'em.
PILIA-BORZA. Foh, me thinkes they stinke like a Holly-Hoke.
BARABAS. [*Aside.*] So, now I am reveng'd upon 'em all. The scent thereof was death, I poyson'd it.
ITHIMORE. Play, Fidler, or I'le cut your cats guts° into chitterlins. lute strings
BARABAS. Pardona moy, be no in tune yet; so now, now all be in.
ITHIMORE. Give him a crowne, and fill me out more wine.
PILIA-BORZA. There's two crownes for thee, play.
BARABAS. [*Aside.*] How liberally the villain gives me mine own gold.
PILIA-BORZA. Me thinke he fingers very well.
BARABAS. [*Aside.*] So did you when you stole my gold.
PILIA-BORZA. How swift he runnes.
BARABAS. [*Aside.*] You run swifter when you threw my gold out of my Window.
CURTEZANE. Musician, hast been in *Malta* long?
BARABAS. Two, three, foure month Madam.
ITHIMORE. Dost not know a Jew, one *Barabas?*
BARABAS. Very mush, Mounsier, you no be his man?
PILIA-BORZA. His man?
ITHIMORE. I scorne the Peasant, tell him so.
BARABAS. [*Aside.*] He knowes it already.
ITHIMORE. 'Tis a strange thing of that Jew, he lives upon pickled Grasshoppers, and sauc'd Mushrumbs.
BARABAS. [*Aside.*] What a slave's this? The Governour feeds not as I doe.
ITHIMORE. He never put on cleane shirt since he was circumcis'd.
BARABAS. [*Aside.*] Oh rascall! I change my selfe twice a day.
ITHIMORE. The Hat he weares, *Judas* left under the Elder when he hang'd himselfe.
BARABAS. [*Aside.*] 'Twas sent me for a present from the great *Cham.*[36]
PILIA-BORZA. A nasty slave he is; whither now, Fidler?
BARABAS. Pardona moy, Mounsier, me be no well.

Exit.

PILIA-BORZA. Farewell, Fidler: One letter more to the Jew.
CURTEZANE. Prethe sweet love, one more, and write it sharp.
ITHIMORE. No, I'le send by word of mouth now; bid him deliver thee a thousand Crownes, by the same token, that the Nuns lov'd Rice, that Fryar *Bernardine* slept in his owne clothes, any of 'em will doe it.

35. At your command, madam.
36. Or "Khan," the term for an important ruler of a Mongol or Turkish tribe.

PILIA-BORZA. Let me alone to urge it now I know the meaning.
ITHIMORE. The meaning has a meaning; come lets in:
To undoe a Jew is charity, and not sinne.

Exeunt.

ACTUS QUINTUS [SCAENA I].

Enter Governor, Knights, Martin del Bosco [and Officers].

GOVERNOR. Now, Gentlemen, betake you to your Armes,
And see that *Malta* be well fortifi'd;
And it behoves you to be resolute;
For *Calymath* having hover'd here so long,
Will winne the Towne, or dye before the wals.
I KNIGHT. And dye he shall, for we will never yeeld.

Enter Curtezane, Pilia-Borza.

CURTEZANE. Oh bring us to the Governor.
GOVERNOR. Away with her, She is a Curtezane.
CURTEZANE. What e're I am, yet Governor heare me speake;
I bring thee newes by whom thy sonne was slaine:
Mathias did it not, it was the Jew.
PILIA-BORZA. Who, besides the slaughter of these Gentlemen, poyson'd his owne daughter and the Nuns, strangled a Fryar, and I know not what Mischiefe beside.
GOVERNOR. Had we but proofe of this.
CURTEZANE. Strong proofe, my Lord, His man's now at my lodging that was his Agent, he'll confesse it all.
GOVERNOR. Goe fetch him straight.

[*Exeunt* Officers.]

I alwayes fear'd that Jew.

Enter Barabas, Ithimore [*with* Officers].

BARABAS. I'le go alone, dogs, do not hale me thus.
ITHIMORE. Nor me neither, I cannot out-run you, constable, oh my belly.
BARABAS. [*Aside.*] One dram of powder more had made all sure. What a damn'd slave was I!
GOVERNOR. Make fires, heat irons, let the racke be fetch'd.
I KNIGHT. Nay stay, my Lord, 'tmay be he will confesse.
BARABAS. Confesse; what meane you, Lords, who should confesse?
GOVERNOR. Thou and thy Turk; 'twas you that slew my son.
ITHIMORE. Gilty, my Lord, I confesse; your sonne and *Mathias* were both contracted unto *Abigall,* he forg'd a counterfeit challenge.

BARABAS. Who carried that challenge?
ITHIMORE. I carried it, I confesse, but who writ it?
Marry, even he that strangled *Bernardine,* poyson'd the Nuns,
and his owne daughter.
GOVERNOR. Away with him, his sight is death to me.
BARABAS. For what? you men of *Malta,* heare me speake;
She is a Curtezane and he a theefe,
And he my bondman, let me have law,
For none of this can prejudice my life[.]
GOVERNOR. Once more, away with him; you shall have law.
BARABAS. Devils doe your worst, I'le live in spite of you.
As these have spoke, so be it to their soules:
[*Aside.*] I hope the poyson'd flowers will worke anon.

[*Exeunt* Barabas, Ithimore, Curtezane, Pilia-Borza, Officers].
Enter Mater.

MATER. Was my *Mathias* murder'd by the Jew?
Ferneze, 'twas thy sonne that murder'd him.
GOVERNOR. Be patient, gentle Madam, it was he,
He forged the daring challenge made them fight.
MATER. Where is the Jew, Where is that murderer?
GOVERNOR. In prison till the Law has passed on him.

Enter Officer.

OFFICER. My Lord, the Curtezane and her man are dead;
So is the Turke, and *Barabas* the Jew.
GOVERNOR. Dead?
OFFICER. Dead, my Lord, and here they bring his body.

[*Enter* Officers *carrying* Barabas *as dead.*]

BOSCO. This sudden death of his is very strange.
GOVERNOR. Wonder not at it, Sir, the heavens are just:
Their deaths were like their lives, then think not of 'em;
Since they are dead, let them be buried.
For the Jewes body, throw that o're the wals
To be a prey for Vultures and wild beasts.
So, now away and fortifie the Towne.

Exeunt [*Manet* Barabas].

BARABAS. What, all alone? well fare, sleepy drinke.
I'le be reveng'd on this accursed Towne;
For by my meanes *Calymath* shall enter in.
I'le helpe to slay their children and their wives,
To fire the Churches, pull their houses downe,
Take my goods too, and seize upon my lands:
I hope to see the Governour a slave,
And, rowing in a Gally, whippt to death.

Enter Calymath, Bassoes, Turkes.

CALYMATH. Whom have we there, A spy?
BARABAS. Yes, my good Lord, one that can spy a place
Where you may enter, and surprise the Towne:
My name is *Barabas;* I am a Jew.
CALYMATH. Art thou that Jew whose goods we heard were sold
For Tribute-mony?
BARABAS. The very same, my Lord:
And since that time they have hir'd a slave, my man,
To accuse me of a thousand villainies:
I was imprison'd, but escap'd their hands.
CALYMATH. Didst breake prison?
BARABAS. No, no:
I dranke of Poppy and cold mandrake juyce;
And being asleepe, belike they thought me dead,
And threw me o're the wals: so, or how else,
The Jew is here and rests at your command.
CALYMATH. 'Twas bravely done: but tell me, *Barabas,*
Canst thou, as thou reportest, make *Malta* ours?
BARABAS. Feare not, my Lord, for here against the Sluice,
The rocke is hollow, and of purpose digg'd,
To make a passage for the running streames
And common channels of the City.
Now, whilst you give assault unto the wals,
I'le lead five hundred souldiers through the Vault,
And rise with them i'th' middle of the Towne,
Open the gates for you to enter in,
And by this means the City is your owne.
CALYMATH. If this be true, I'le make thee Governor.
BARABAS. And if it be not true, then let me dye.
CALYMATH. Thou'st doom'd thy selfe, assault it presently.

Exeunt.

[*SCAENA* 2.]

Alarmes. Enter [Calymath *and*] Turkes and Barabas, Governor, *and* Knights *prisoners.*

CALYMATH. Now vaile your pride, you captive Christians,
And kneele for mercy to your conquering foe:
Now where's the hope you had of haughty *Spaine?*
Ferneze, speake, Had it not beene much better
To have kept thy promise then be thus surpris'd?
GOVERNOR. What should I say, we are captives, and must yeeld.
CALYMATH. I, villains, you must yeeld, and under Turkish yokes
Shall groaning beare the burthen of our ire;

And *Barabas,* as erst we promis'd thee,
For thy desert we make thee Governor,
Use them at thy discretion.

BARABAS. Thanks, my Lord.

GOVERNOR. Oh fatall day, to fall into the hands
Of such a Traitor and unhallowed Jew!
What greater misery could heaven inflict?

CALYMATH. 'Tis our command: and *Barabas,* we give
To guard thy person, these our Janizaries:[37]
Intreate them well, as we have used thee.
And now, brave Bashawes, come, wee'll walke about
The ruin'd Towne, and see the wracke we made:
Farewell brave Jew, farewell, great Barabas.

Exeunt [Calymath *and* Turkes.]

BARABAS. May all good fortune follow *Calymath,*
And now, as entrance to our safety,
To prison with the Governour and these
Captives, his consorts and confederates.

GOVERNOR. Oh villaine, Heaven will be reveng'd on thee.

BARABAS. Away! No more! let him not trouble me.

Exeunt [Governor *and* Knights].

Thus hast thou gotten, by thy policie,
No simple place, no small authority,
I now am Governour of *Malta;* true,
But *Malta* hates me, and, in hating me
My life's in danger, and what boots it thee,
Poore *Barabas,* to be the Governour,
When as thy life shall be at their command?
No, *Barabas,* this must be look'd into;
And since by wrong thou got'st Authority,
Maintaine it bravely by firme policy;
At least unprofitably lose it not:
For he that liveth in Authority,
And neither gets him friends, nor fils his bags,
Lives like the Asse that *Aesope* speaketh of,
That labours with a load of bread and wine
And leaves it off to snap on Thistle tops:
But *Barabas* will be more circumspect.
Begin betimes, Occasion's bald behind,[38]
Slip not thine opportunity, for feare too late

37. Balkan Christians raised from boyhood in the sultan's household, they formed the household guards of Turkish rulers.

38. Conventionally, Occasion (or opportunity) has a long forelock of hair and is bald behind, and thus must be grasped immediately when it presents itself.

Thou seek'st for much, but canst not compasse it.
Within here.

Enter Governor *with a* Guard.

GOVERNOR. My Lord?
BARABAS. I, lord, Thus slaves will learne.
Now Governor—stand by there, wait within;

[*Exit* Guard.]

This is the reason that I sent for thee;
Thou seest thy life and *Malta's* happinesse,
Are at my Arbitrament; and *Barabas*
At his discretion may dispose of both:
Now tell me, Governor, and plainely too,
What think'st thou shall become of it and thee?
GOVERNOR. This; *Barabas,* since things are in thy power,
I see no reason but of *Malta's* wracke,
Nor hope of thee but extreme cruelty;
Nor feare I death, nor will I flatter thee.
BARABAS. Governor, good words, be not so furious;
'Tis not thy life which can availe me ought;
Yet you doe live, and live for me you shall:
And as for *Malta's* ruine, thinke you not
'Twere slender policy for *Barabas*
To dispossesse himselfe of such a place?
For sith, as once you said, within this Ile
In *Malta* here, that I have got my goods,
And in this city still have had successe,
And now at length am growne your Governor,
Your selves shall see it shall not be forgot:
For as a friend not knowne, but in distresse,
I'le reare up *Malta* now remedilesse.
GOVERNOR. Will *Barabas* recover *Malta's* losse?
Will *Barabas* be good to Christians?
BARABAS. What wilt thou give me, Governor, to procure
A dissolution of the slavish Bands
Wherein the Turke hath yoak'd your land and you?
What will you give me if I render you
The life of *Calymath,* surprise his men,
And in an out-house of the City shut
His souldiers, till I have consum'd 'em all with fire?
What will you give him that procureth this?
GOVERNOR. Doe but bring this to passe which thou pretendest,
Deale truly with us as thou intimatest,
And I will send amongst the Citizens
And by my letters privately procure

Great summes of mony for thy recompense:
Nay more, doe this, and live thou Governor still.
BARABAS. Nay, doe thou this, *Ferneze,* and be free;
Governor, I enlarge thee, live with me.
Goe walke about the City, see thy friends:
Tush, send not letters to 'em, goe thy selfe,
And let me see what mony thou canst make;
Here is my hand that I'le set *Malta* free:
And thus we cast it: To a solemne feast
I will invite young *Selim-Calymath,*
Where be thou present onely to performe
One stratagem that I'le impart to thee,
Wherein no danger shall betide thy life,
And I will warrant *Malta* free for ever.
GOVERNOR. Here is my hand, beleeve me, *Barabas,*
I will be there, and doe as thou desirest;
When is the time?
BARABAS. Governor, presently.
For *Callymath,* when he hath view'd the Towne,
Will take his leave and saile toward *Ottoman.*
GOVERNOR. Then will I, *Barabas,* about this coyne,
And bring it with me to thee in the evening.
BARABAS. Doe so, but faile not; now farewell, *Ferneze:*

[*Exit* Governor.]

And thus farre roundly goes the businesse:
Thus, loving neither, will I live with both,
Making a profit of my policie;
And he from whom my most advantage comes,
Shall be my friend.
This is the life we Jewes are us'd to lead;
And reason too, for Christians doe the like:
Well, now about effecting this device:
First to surprise great *Selims* souldiers,
And then to make provision for the feast,
That at one instant all things may be done,
My policie detests prevention:
To what event my secret purpose drives
I know; and they shall witnesse with their lives.

Exit.

[*SCAENA* 3].

Enter Calymath, Bassoes.

CALYMATH. Thus have we view'd the City, seene the sacke,
And caus'd the ruines to be new-repair'd,
Two lofty Turrets that command the Towne,
Which with our Bombards' shot and Basiliske,
We rent in sunder at our entry:
And now I see the Scituation,
And how secure this conquer'd I'land stands
Inviron'd with the *Mediterranean* Sea,
Strong countermur'd with other petty Iles;
And toward *Calabria* back'd by Sicily,
Where Siracusian Dionisius[39] reigned,
I wonder how it could be conquer'd thus?

Enter a Messenger.

MESSENGER. From *Barabas, Malta's* Governor, I bring
A message unto mighty *Calymath;*
Hearing his Soveraigne was bound for Sea,
To saile to *Turkey,* to great *Ottoman,*
He humbly would intreat your majesty
To come and see his homely Citadell,
And banquet with him e're thou leav'st the Ile.
CALYMATH. To banquet with him in his Citadell,
I feare me, Messenger, to feast my traine
Within a Towne of warre so lately pillag'd
Will be too costly and too troublesome:
Yet would I gladly visit *Barabas,*
For well has *Barabas* deserv'd of us.
MESSENGER. *Selim,* for that, thus saith the Governor,
That he hath in store a Pearle so big,
So precious, and withall so orient,
As, be it valued but indifferently,
The price thereof will serve to entertaine
Selim and all his souldiers for a month;
Therefore he humbly would intreat your Highnesse
Not to depart till he has feasted you.
CALYMATH. I cannot feast my men in *Malta* wals,
Except he place his Tables in the streets.
MESSENGER. Know, *Selim,* that there is a monastery
Which standeth as an out-house to the Towne;
There will he banquet them, but thee at home,
With all thy Bashawes and brave followers.

39. Dionysios I, tyrant of Syracuse in Sicily (432–367 BC).

CALYMATH. Well, tell the Governor we grant his suit,
Wee'll in this Summer Evening feast with him.
MESSENGER. I shall, my Lord.

Exit.

CALYMATH. And now bold Bashawes, let us to our Tents,
And meditate how we may grace us best
To solemnize our Governors great feast.

Exeunt.

[*SCAENA 4.*]

Enter Governor, Knights, Del-Bosco.

GOVERNOR. In this, my Countrimen, be rul'd by me.
Have speciall care that no man sally forth
Till you shall heare a Culverin° discharg'd — small-bore cannon
By him that beares the Linstocke,° kindled thus; — a match used to light cannon
Then issue out and come to rescue me,
For happily I shall be in distresse,
Or you released of this servitude.
I KNIGHT. Rather than thus to live as Turkish thrals,
What will we not adventure?
GOVERNOR. On, then; begone.
KNIGHTS. Farewell grave Governor.

Exeunt.

[*SCAENA 5.*]

Enter [Barabas] *with a Hammer, above, very busie,* [and Carpenters].

BARABAS. How stand the cords? How hang these hinges, fast?° — securely
Are all the Cranes and Pulleyes sure?
CARPENTER. All fast.
BARABAS. Leave nothing loose, all leveld to my mind.
Why now I see that you have Art indeed.
There, Carpenters, divide that gold amongst you.
Goe swill in bowles of Sacke and Muscadine:
Downe to the Celler, taste of all my wines.
CARPENTER. We shall, my Lord, and thanke you[.]

Exeunt.

BARABAS. And if you like them, drinke your fill—and dye:
For so I live, perish may all the world.

Now *Selim-Calymath* returne me word
That thou wilt come, and I am satisfied.

Enter Messenger.

Now sirra, what, will he come?
MESSENGER. He will; and has commanded all his men
To come ashore, and march through *Malta* streets,
That thou maist feast them in thy Citadell.

[*Exit* Messenger.]

BARABAS. Then now are all things as my wish wud have 'em,
There wanteth nothing but the Governors pelfe,
And see, he brings it:

Enter Governor.

Now Governor, the summe.
GOVERNOR. With free consent a hundred thousand pounds.
BARABAS. Pounds saist thou, Governor, wel, since it is no more
I'le satisfie my selfe with that; nay, keepe it still,
For if I keepe not promise, trust not me.
And Governour, now partake my policy:
First for his Army they are sent before,
Enter'd the Monastery, and underneath
In severall places are field-pieces pitch'd,
Bombards, whole Barrels full of Gunpowder,
That on the sudden shall dissever it,
And batter all the stones about their eares,
Whence none can possibly escape alive:
Now, as for *Calymath* and his consorts,
Here have I made a dainty Gallery,
The floore whereof, this Cable being cut,
Doth fall asunder, so that it doth sinke
Into a deepe pit past recovery.
Here, hold that knife, and when thou seest he comes
And with his Bashawes shall be blithely set,
A warning-peece shall be shot off from the Tower,
To give thee knowledge when to cut the cord,
And fire the house; say, will not this be brave?
GOVERNOR. Oh excellent! here, hold thee, *Barabas*,
I trust thy word, take what I promis'd thee.
BARABAS. No, Governor, I'le satisfie thee first,
Thou shalt not live in doubt of any thing.
Stand close, for here they come:

[Governor *retires.*]

why, is not this
A kingly kinde of trade, to purchase Townes

By treachery, and sell 'em by deceit?
Now tell me, worldlings, underneath the sunne,
If greater falshood ever has bin done?

Enter Calymath *and* Bassoes.

CALYMATH. Come, my Companion-Bashawes, see I pray
How busie *Barabas* is there above
To entertaine us in his Gallery;
Let us salute him, Save thee, *Barabas.*
BARABAS. Welcome, great *Calymath.*
GOVERNOR. How the slave jeeres at him[.]
BARABAS. Will't please thee, mighty *Selim-Calymath,*
To ascend our homely stayres?
CALYMATH. I, *Barabas,*
Come Bashawes, attend.
GOVERNOR. [*Comes forward.*] Stay, *Calymath;*
For I will shew thee greater courtesie
Then *Barabas* would have affoorded thee.
1 KNIGHT. Sound a charge there.

A charge [within], the cable cut. A Cauldron discovered [*and* Barabas *falls into it*]. [*Enter* Del Bosco *and* Knights.]

CALYMATH. How now! what means this?
BARABAS. Helpe, helpe me, Christians, helpe.
GOVERNOR. See *Calymath,* This was devis'd for thee.
CALYMATH. Treason, treason, Bashawes flye.
GOVERNOR. No, *Selim,* doe not flye:
See his end first, and flye then if thou canst[.]
BARABAS. Oh helpe me, *Selim,* helpe me, Christians,
Governour, why stand you all so pitilesse?
GOVERNOR. Should I in pitty of thy plaints or thee,
Accursed *Barabas;* base Jew, relent:
No, thus I'le see thy treachery repaid,
But wish thou hadst behav'd thee otherwise.
BARABAS. You will not helpe me then?
GOVERNOR. No, villaine, no.
BARABAS. And villaines, know you cannot helpe me now.
Then *Barabas* breathe forth thy latest fate,
And in the fury of thy torments, strive
To end thy life with resolution:
Know, Governor, 'twas I that slewe thy sonne;
I fram'd the challenge that did make them meet:
Know, *Calymath,* I aym'd thy overthrow,
And had I but escap'd this stratagem,
I would have brought confusion on you all,
Damn'd Christian dogges, and Turkish Infidels;
But no[w] begins the extremity of heat

To pinch me with intolerable pangs:
Dye life! flye soule, tongue curse thy fill and dye.

[*Dies.*]

CALYMATH. Tell me, you Christians, what doth this portend?
GOVERNOR. This traine he laid to have intrap'd thy life;
Now *Selim* note the unhallowed deeds of Jewes:
Thus he determin'd to have handled thee,
But I have rather chose to save thy life.
CALYMATH. Was this the banquet he prepar'd for us?
Let's hence, lest further mischiefe be pretended.
GOVERNOR. Nay, *Selim,* stay, for, since we have thee here,
We will not let thee part so suddenly:
Besides, if we should let thee goe, all's one,
For with thy Gallyes couldst thou not get hence,
Without fresh men to rigge and furnish them.
CALYMATH. Tush, Governor, take thou no care for that,
My men are all aboord,
And doe attend my comming there by this.
GOVERNOR. Why, heard'st thou not the trumpet sound a charge?
CALYMATH. Yes, what of that?
GOVERNOR. Why then the house was fir'd,
Blowne up and all thy souldiers massacred.
CALYMATH. Oh, monstrous treason!
GOVERNOR. A Jewes courtesie:
For he that did by treason worke our fall,
By treason hath delivered thee to us:
Know therefore, till thy father hath made good
The ruines done to *Malta* and to us,
Thou canst not part: for *Malta* shall be freed,
Or *Selim* ne're return to Ottoman.
CALYMATH. Nay rather, Christians, let me goe to *Turkey,*
In person there to mediate your peace;
To keepe me here will nought advantage you.
GOVERNOR. Content thee, *Calymath,* here thou must stay,
And live in *Malta* prisoner; for come all the world
To rescue thee, so will we guard us now,
As sooner shall they drinke the Ocean dry,
Than conquer *Malta,* or endanger us.
So march away, and let due praise be given
Neither to Fate nor Fortune, but to Heaven.

[*Exeunt.*]

FINIS

Volpone

Ben Jonson was born in 1572, the son of a minister who died before Jonson's birth. He attended Westminster School where William Camden, a noted antiquary, was an usher, and with whom Jonson remained friends until Camden's death. There he received a grammar school education with an emphasis on the classics, an education some have seen as too much in evidence in Jonson's tragedies. Jonson worked as a bricklayer (his stepfather's trade) and served as a soldier in the Netherlands, where he killed a man in single combat, according to William Drummond, whose record of his conversations with Jonson are an important source for Jonson's critical opinions.

In 1597 Jonson appeared in Henslowe's diaries as an actor for the Admiral's Men.[1] The lost play Jonson wrote with Thomas Nashe that year, *The Isle of Dogs,* was Jonson's first recorded trouble with the authorities: he was imprisoned in Marshalsea Prison and the play was suppressed. In 1598, Jonson killed an actor Gabriel Spenser in a duel; he escaped hanging by pleading "benefit of clergy"—he had to read and translate a biblical passage in Latin—and suffered the loss of his property and burning on the thumb. Jonson became involved in the "War of the Theatres," attacking John Marston and Thomas Dekker; Dekker in particular responded effectively, but both playwrights subsequently collaborated with him. Jonson, Marston, and George Chapman collaborated on a play *Eastward Ho* in 1605, which James I's Scottish court regarded as insulting to Scots, and all three were briefly imprisoned.

Jonson then began to write the comic masterpieces still frequently produced today: *Volpone* (1606), *Epicoene* (1609), *The Alchemist* (1610), and *Bartholomew Fair* (1614). Meanwhile, he was writing some of the finest poetry in the English language. "To Penshurst" is both a superb Horatian ode and an important example of a poem about a great house. "The Carey-Morrison Ode" is one of the finest

The text is that established by J. L. Halio (Berkeley: University of California Press, 1968), 18–133. Also consulted, Richard Harp's *Ben Jonson's Plays and Masques,* 2nd ed. (New York: Norton, 2001).

1. Philip Henslowe's diaries are a record of the expenses of the Admiral's Men.

Pindaric odes in English and a powerful elegy. He also became the preeminent author of masques for the court. In 1616 Jonson was awarded a pension of 100 marks a year and published his *Works,* which included his plays. This was a bold statement on Jonson's part and was greeted with some derision because Jonson was asserting his plays were worthy of being regarded as literature at a time when plays were considered popular entertainment. The erstwhile bricklayer had royal patronage, was honored by the universities, and revered by younger poets such as Robert Herrick and John Suckling; he was the first English dramatist to be recognized in his own lifetime as a major literary figure. He died in 1637 and is buried in Westminster Abbey.

Chapman was the first author of "humours comedy," but Jonson is the playwright most associated with the genre. In psychological theory of the period, the four bodily fluids (blood, phlegm, black bile, and yellow bile) need to be in balance; a superfluity of any leads to physical and mental illness. For instance, a healthy amount of blood leads to an enthusiastic personality and one is sanguine. An excess of black bile can render one melancholic. In Jonson's plays, the theory of humours is more of a metaphor than a theory of behavior; a humour is an irrational ruling passion or obsession. When characters allow a humour to dominate it becomes a vice. In *Volpone,* the gentry are consumed with avarice and destroyed by it. The subplot of Sir Politique Would-bee shows a knight who wishes to be thought an intimate of statesmen and invites his own humiliation. Venice, as in Shakespeare's plays, stands in for London, and Jonson is satirizing the social vices of his era.

But the energy and wit of Volpone and Mosca make them appealing. They play off classical motifs *(hic et ubique, carpe diem)* in exuberant blank verse, and only their own lack of self-restraint destroys them. Their final punishments are harsh—the galleys and prison amount to a slow death sentence—but necessary because of the ease with which they have previously overthrown social order and the inability of society to cope with their combination of ability and greed.

Volpone

THE PERSONS OF THE COMŒDYE

VOLPONE,[2] *a Magnifico*° gentleman
MOSCA, *his Parasite*
VOLTORE, *an Advocate*
CORBACCIO, *an olde Gentleman*
CORVINO, *a Marchant*
AVOCATORI, *four Magistrates*
NOTARIO, *the Register*
NANO, *a Dwarfe*
CASTRONE, *an Eunuch*
GREGE° the mob
POLITIQUE WOULD-BE, *a Knight*
PEREGRINE, *a Gentleman-travailer*
BONARIO, *a yong Gentleman*
FINE MADAM WOULD-BE, *the Knight's wife*
CELIA, *the Merchants wife*
COMMANDADORI, *Officers*
MERCATORI, *three Merchants*
ANDROGYNO, *a Hermaphrodite*
SERVITORE, *a servant*
TWO WOMEN

The Scene

Venice

THE ARGUMENT

V *olpone,* childlesse, rich, faines sick, despaires,
O ffers his state to hopes of severall heyres,
L ies languishing; His *Parasite* receaves
P resents of all, assures, deludes: Then weaves
O ther crosse-plots, which ope' themselves, are told.
N ew tricks for safety'are sought; They thrive: When, bold,
E ach tempt's th'other againe, and all are sold.

2. The names of the leading characters are charactonyms, i.e., names that describe their essential attributes–Volpone: the fox; Mosca: the fly; Voltore: the vulture; Corbaccio: the raven; Corvino: the crow; Bonario: good-natured; Celia: heavenly; Politique: devious or subtle; Peregrine: a falcon, but also a pilgrim.

THE PROLOGUE

Now, luck God send us, and a little wit
Will serve, to make our PLAY hit;
(According to the palates of the season)
Here is ri'me, not emptie of reason:
This we were bid to credit, from our Poët,
Whose true scope, if you would knowe it,
In all his Poëmes, *still, hath beene this measure,*
To mixe profit, with your pleasure;
And not as some (whose throates their envie fayling)
Crie hoarcely, All he writes, is rayling:
And, when his PLAYES *come forth, thinke they can flout them,*
With saying, He was a yeare about them.
To these there needes no Lye, *but this his creature,*
Which was, two months since, no feature;
And, though he dares give them five lives to mend it,
'tis knowne, five weekes fully pen'd it:
From his owne hand, without a Co-adjutor,
Novice, Jorney-man, *or* Tutor.
Yes, this much I can give you, as a token
Of his Playes *worth, No egges are broken;*
Nor quaking Custards with feirce teeth affrighted,
Wherewith your route are so delighted;
Nor hales he in a Gull, *old ends reciting,*
To stop gappes in his loose writing;
With such a deale of monstrous, and forc'd action:
As might make Bethlem° *a faction:* — London madhouse
Nor made he his Play, *for jests, stolne from each Table,*
But makes jests, to fit his Fable.
And, so presents quick Comœdy, *refined,*
As best Criticks *have designed,*
The Lawes *of Time, Place, Person he observeth,*
From no needefull Rule *he swerveth.*[3]
All gall, and coppresse,° from his inke, he drayneth, — vitriol
Onelie, a little salt remaineth;
Wherewith, he'll rub your cheekes, till (red with laughter)
They shall looke fresh, a weeke after.

3. Dramatic rules partially derived from Aristotle, sometimes called the unities. The unity of time limited the time of a play to 24 hours. The unity of place limited the action to a single location. The unity of character restricted a character's actions and dialogue to those appropriate to his station and the genre of the play.

ACT I

SCENE I

Volpone, Mosca.

VOLPONE. Good morning to the Day;[4] and, next, my Gold:
Open the shrine, that I may see my *Saint.*
Hayle the worlds soule, and mine. More glad then is
The teeming earth, to see the longd-for *Sunne,*
Peepe through the hornes of the *Cœlestiall Ram,*[5]
Am I, to view thy splendor, darkening his:
That lying here, amongst my hoordes,
Shew'st like a flame, by night; or like the Day
Strooke out of *Chaos,* when all darknes fled
Unto the center. O thou Sonne of *Sol,*° the sun
(But brighter then they father) let me kisse,
With adoration, thee, and every relique
Of sacred treasure, in this blessed roome.
Well did wise *Poets,* by thy glorious name,
Title that age, which they would have the best;
Thou being the best of things: and far transcending
All stile of joy, in children, parents, friends,
Or any other waking dreame on earth.
Thy lookes when they to *Venus* did ascribe,
They should have giv'n her twenty thousand *Cupids;*
Such are thy beauties, and our loves. Deare *Saint,*
Riches, the dombe God, that giv'st all men tongues;
That canst doe naught, and yet mak'st men doe all things;
The price of soules; even hell, with thee to boote,
Is made worth heaven. Thou art vertue, fame,
Honor, and all things else. Who can get thee
He shall be noble, valiant, honest, wise,—
MOSCA. And what he will Sir. Riches are in fortune
A greater good, then wisedome is in nature.
VOLPONE. True, my beloved *Mosca.* Yet, I glory
More in the cunning purchase of my wealth,
Then in the glad possession; since I gaine
No common way: I use no trade, no venter;
I wound no earth with plow-shares; fat no beasts
To feede the shambles;° have no mills for iron, butcher shops
Oyle, corne, or men, to grinde 'hem into poulder;° powder
I blow no subtill glasse; expose no shipps
To threatnings of the furrow-faced sea;

4. Volpone's opening speech is an aubade, or dawn song; the aubade is normally sung to one's beloved as in Romeo's aubade to Juliet.

5. Indicating March 21, the beginning of spring. See *The Canterbury Tales* lines 5–8.

I turne no moneys, in the publike banke;
Nor usure private.
MOSCA. No Sir, nor devoure
Soft prodigalls. You shall ha' some will swallow
A melting heire, as glibly, as your *Dutch*
Will pills of butter, and nêre purge for't;
Teare forth the fathers of poore families
Out of their beds, and coffin them, alive,
In some kinde, clasping prison, where their bones
May be forth-coming, when the flesh is rotten:
But your sweet nature doth abhorre these courses;
You loath, the widdowes, or the orphans teares
Should washe your pavements; or their pityous cries
Ring in your roofes: and beate the ayre, for vengeance.
VOLPONE. Right, *Mosca,* I do loath it.
MOSCA. And besides, Sir,
You are not like a thresher, that doth stand
With a huge flaile, watching a heape of corne,
And, hungry, dares not taste the smallest graine,
But feedes on mallowes, and such bitter herbes;
Nor like the merchant, who hath fill'd his vaults
With *Romagnía,*° rich *Candian*° wines, [region of Greece; Crete]
Yet drinkes the lees of *Lombards*° vineger: [region of Italy]
You will not lie in straw, whilst mothes, and wormes
Feed on your sumptuous hangings, and soft bedds.
You know the use of riches, and dare give, now,
From that bright heape, to mee, your poore observer,
Or to your *Dwarfe,* or your *Hermaphrodite,*
Your *Eunuch,* or what other houshold-trifle
Your pleasure allowes maint'nance.
VOLPONE. Hold thee, *Mosca,*
Take of my hand; thou strik'st on truth, in all:
And they are envious, terme thee *Parasite.*
Call forth my *Dwarfe,* my *Eunuch,* and my *Foole,*
And let 'hem make me sport.

[*Exit* Mosca.]

What should I do
But cocker° up my *Genius,* and live free [indulge]
To all delights, my fortune calls me to?
I have no wife, no parent, childe, allye,
To give my substance to; but whom I make,
Must be my heyre: and this makes men observe me.
This drawes newe clients, dayly, to my house,
Women, and men, of every sexe, and age,
That bring me presents, send me plate, coyne, jewels,
With hope, that when I die, (which they expect

Each greedy minute) it shall then returne,
Ten-fold, upon them; whil'st some, covetous
Above the rest, seeke to engrosse° me, whole, buy
And counter-worke, the one, unto the other,
Contend in gifts, as they would seeme, in love:
All which I suffer, playing with their hopes,
And am content to coyne 'hem into profit,
And look upon their kindnesse, and take more,
And looke on that; still bearing them in hand,
Letting the cherry knock against their lips,
And, drawe it, by their mouths, and back againe. How now!

SCENE II

NANO. ANDROGYNO. CASTRONE
VOLPONE. MOSCA.

NANO. *Now roome, for fresh Gamsters, who do will you to know,*
They do bring you neither Play, nor University *Show;*
And therefore do intreat you, that whatsoever they reherse,
May not fare a whit the worse, for the false pase of the verse.
If you wonder at this, you will wonder more, ere we passe,
For know, here is inclos'd the Soule of Pithagoras,
That Jugler divine, as hereafter shall follow;
Which Soule (fast, and loose, Sir) came first from Apollo,
And was breath'd in Æthalides, Mercurius *his sonne,*
Where it had the gift to remember all that ever was done.
From thence it fled forth, and made quicke transmigration
To goldy-lockt Euphorbus, *who was kill'd, in good fashion,*
At the seege of old Troy, *by the cuckold of* Sparta.
Hermotimus *was next (I finde it, in my* Chartâ)
To whom it did passe, where no sooner it was missing,
But with one Pirrhus, *of* Delos, *it learn'd to go a fishing:*
And thence, did it enter the Sophist *of* Greece.
From Pithagore, *she went into a beautifull peece,*
Hight° Aspasia, *the Meretrix;° and the next tosse of her* named; prostitute
Was, againe, of a Whore, *she became a* Philosopher,
Crates *the* Cynicke: *(as it selfe doth relate it)*
Since, Kings, Knights, *and* Beggars, Knaves, Lords *and* Fooles *gat it,*
Besides, Oxe, and Asse, Cammel, Mule, Goat, and Brock,° badger
In all which it hath spoke, as in the Coblers *Cock.*[6]
But I come not here, to discourse of that matter,
Or his One, Two, *or* Three, or his great Oath, by Quarter,
His Musicks, *his* Trigon, *his golden Thigh,*
Or his telling how Elements *shift: but I*

6. A dialogue by the Greek satirist Lucian.

Would aske, how of late, thou hast suffered translation,
And shifted thy coat, in these dayes of Reformation?
ANDROGYNO. *Like one of the Reformed,*° a Foole, *as you see,* Protestant
Counting all old Doctrine heresie.
NANO. *But not on thine owne forbid meates hast thou venter'd?*
ANDROGYNO. *On fish, when first, a* Carthusian *I enter'd.*[7]
NANO. *Why, then thy dogmaticall Silence hath left thee?*
ANDROGYNO. *Of that an obstreporous* Lawyer *bereft mee.*
NANO *O wonderfull change! when* Sir Lawyer *forsooke thee,*
For Pithagore's *sake, what body then tooke thee?*
ANDROGYNO. *A good dull Moyle.*° mule
NANO. *And how? by that meanes,*
Thou wert brought to allow of the eating of Beanes?
ANDROGYNO. *Yes.*
NANO. *But, from the Moyle, into whom did'st thou passe?*
ANDROGYNO. *Into a very strange Beast, by some* Writers *cal'd an Asse;*
By others, a precise, pure, illuminate Brother,
Of those that devoure flesh, and sometimes one an other:
And will drop you forth a libell, *or a sanctified lie,*
Betwixt every spooneful of a Nativity *Pie.*
NANO. *Now quit thee, for Heaven, of that profane nation;*
And gently, report thy next transmigration.
ANDROGYNO. *To the same that I am.*
NANO. *A Creature of delight!*
And (what is more then a Foole) *an* Hermaphrodite?
Now 'pray thee, sweete Soule, in all thy variation,
Which Body wouldst thou choose, to take up thy station?
ANDROGYNO. *Troth, this I am in, even here would I tarry.*
NANO. *'Cause here, the delight of each Sexe thou canst varie?*
ANDROGYNO. *Alas, those pleasures be stale, and forsaken;*
No, tis your Foole, *wherewith I am taken,*
The onely one Creature, that I can call blessed:
For all other formes I have prov'd most distressed.
NANO. *Spoke true, as thou wert in* Pithagoras *still.*
This learned opinion we celebrate will,
Fellow Eunuch *(as behooves us) with all our wit, and arte,*
To dignifie that, whereof our selves are so great, and special a part.
VOLPONE. Now very, very pretty: *Mosca,* this
Was thy invention?
MOSCA. If it please my Patron,
Not else.
VOLPONE. It doth good *Mosca.*
MOSCA. Then it was Sir.

7. As a monk he eats fish, forbidden by Pythagoras, who also forbade the eating of beans. Also, Carthusians take a vow of silence, which when his spirit inhabits a lawyer he breaks.

[NANO *and* CASTRONE *sing.*]

SONG

Fooles, they are the onely Nation
Worth mens envy, or admiration;
Free from care, or sorrow-taking,
Selves, and others merry making:
All they speake, or do, is sterling.
Your Foole, *he is your great mans darling,*
And your Ladies sport, and pleasure;
Tongue, and Bable are his treasure.
Eene his face begetteth laughter,
And he speakes truth, free from slaughter;
He's the grace of every feast,
And, sometimes, the cheefest guest:
Hath his trencher, and his stoole,
When Wit waites upon the Foole:
O, who would not bee
Hee, hee, hee.

One knocks without.

VOLPONE. Who's that? away, looke *Mosca.*
MOSCA. *Foole,* be gon,

[*Exeunt* NANO, CASTRONE, ANDROGYNO.]

'Tis Signior *Voltore,* the Advocate,
I know him, by his knock.
VOLPONE. Fetch me my gowne,
My furres, and night-caps; say, my couch is changing:
And let him intertaine himselfe, a while,
Within i'th' gallery.

[*Exit* MOSCA.]

Now, now, my clients
Beginne their visitation; *Vulture, Kite,*
Raven, and *gor-Crowe,* all my birds of prey,
That thinke me turning carcasse, now they come:
I am not for 'hem yet. How now? the newes?

[*Enter* MOSCA.]

MOSCA. A peece of plate, Sir.
VOLPONE. Of what bignesse?
MOSCA. Huge,
Massie, and antique, with your name inscrib'd,
And armes ingraven.
VOLPONE. Good, and not a *Foxe*
Stretch'd on the earth, with fine delusive sleights,
Mocking a gaping *Crow?* ha, *Mosca?*

MOSCA. Sharpe, Sir.
VOLPONE. Give me my furres. Why dost thou laugh so, man?
MOSCA. I cannot choose, Sir, when I apprehend
What thoughts he has (within) now, as he walks:
That this might be the last gift, he should give;
That this would fetch you; if you died to day,
And gave him all, what he should be to morrow;
What large returne would come out of all his venters;
How he should worship'd bee, and reverenc'd;
Ride, with his furres, and foote-cloths;[8] waited on
By heards of *Fooles,* and clients; have cleare way
Made for his moyle, as letter'd as himselfe;
Be cald the great, and learned *Advocate:*
And then concludes, there's nought impossible.
VOLPONE. Yes, to be learned, *Mosca.*
MOSCA. O no: rich
Implies it. Hood an asse, with reverend purple,
So you can hide his two ambitious eares,
And, he shall passe for a *cathedrall Doctor.*
VOLPONE. My caps, my caps, good *Mosca,* fetch him in.
MOSCA. Stay, Sir, your ointment for your eyes.
VOLPONE. That's true;
Dispatch, dispatch: I long to have possession
Of my newe present.
MOSCA. That, and thousands more,
I hope, to see you lord of.
VOLPONE. Thankes, kind *Mosca.*
MOSCA. And that, when I am lost in blended dust,
And hundreds such, as I am, in succession—
VOLPONE. Nay, that were too much, *Mosca.*
MOSCA. You shall live,
Still, to delude these *Harpyies.*
VOLPONE. Loving *Mosca,*
'Tis well, my pillow now, and let him enter.

[*Exit* Mosca.]

Now, my fain'd *Cough,* my *Phthisick,*° and my *Goute,* — throat or lung disease
My *Apoplexie, Palsie,* and *Catarrhe,*° — mucus discharge
Helpe, with your forced functions, this my posture,
Wherein, this three yeare, I have milk'd their hopes.
He comes, I heare him (uh, uh, uh, uh) ô

8. Decorative tapestries on a horse.

SCENE III

MOSCA. VOLTORE. VOLPONE.

MOSCA. You still are, what you were, Sir. Onely you
(Of all the rest) are he, commands his love:
And you do wisely to preserve it, thus,
With early visitation, and kinde notes
Of your good meaning to him, which, I know,
Cannot but come most gratefull. *Patron,* Sir.
Here's Signior *Voltore* is come—
VOLPONE. What say you?
MOSCA. Sir, Signior *Voltore* is come, this morning,
To visit you.
VOLPONE. I thanke him.
MOSCA. And hath brought
A peece of antique plate, bought of St. *Marke,*
With which he here presents you.
VOLPONE. He is welcome.
Pray him, to come more often.
MOSCA. Yes.
VOLTORE. What saies he?
MOSCA. He thankes you, and desires you see him often.
VOLPONE. *Mosca.*
MOSCA. My Patron?
VOLPONE. Bring him neare, where is he?
I long to feele his hand.
MOSCA. The plate is here Sir.
VOLTORE. How fare you Sir?
VOLPONE. I thanke you, Signior *Voltore.*
Where is the plate? mine eyes are bad.
VOLTORE. I'm sorry,
To see you still thus weake.
MOSCA. [*Aside.*] That hee is not weaker.
VOLPONE. You are too munificent.
VOLTORE. No Sir, would to heaven,
I could as well give health to you, as that plate.
VOLPONE. You give Sir, what you can. I thanke you. Your love
Hath tast in this, and shall not be unanswer'd.
I pray you see me often.
VOLTORE. Yes, I shall Sir.
VOLPONE. Be not far from mee.
MOSCA. Do you observe that Sir?
VOLPONE. Hearken unto mee, still. It will concerne you.
MOSCA. You are a happy man Sir, know your good.
VOLPONE. I cannot now last long.
MOSCA. You are his heyre Sir.

VOLTORE. Am I?
VOLPONE. I feele mee going, (uh, uh, uh, uh.)
I am sayling to my port, (uh, uh, uh, uh?)
And I am glad, I am so neere my haven.
MOSCA. Alas, kinde gentleman, well, we must all go.
VOLTORE. But, *Mosca.*
MOSCA. Age will conquer.
VOLTORE. 'Pray thee heare mee.
Am I inscrib'd his heire, for certaine?
MOSCA. Are you?
I do beseech you Sir, you will vouchsafe
To write me, i' your family. All my hopes,
Depend upon your worship; I am lost,
Except the rising Sunne do shine on me.
VOLTORE. It shall both shine, and warme thee, *Mosca.*
MOSCA. Sir.
I am a man, that have not done your love
All the worst offices, here I weare your keys,
See all your coffers, and your caskets lockt,
Keepe the poore inventorie of your jewels,
Your plate, and moneyes, am your Steward Sir,
Husband your goods here.
VOLTORE. But am I sole heyre?
MOSCA. Without a partner Sir, confirmde this morning;
The waxe is warme yet, and the inke scarse dry
Upon the parchment.
VOLTORE. Happy, happy mee!
By what good chance, sweete *Mosca?*
MOSCA. Your desert Sir;
I know no second cause.
VOLTORE. Thy modesty
Is loath to know it; well, we shall requite it.
MOSCA. He ever lik'd your course Sir, that first tooke him.
I, oft, have heard him say, how he admir'd
Men of your large profession, that could speake
To every cause, and things mere° contraries, pure
Till they were hoarse againe, yet all bee *Law;*
That, with most quicke agility, could turne,
And returne; make knots, and undoe them;
Give forked councell; take provoking gold
On eyther hand, and put it up: These men,
He knewe, would thrive, with their humility.
And (for his part) he thought, he should be blest
To have his heyre of such a suffering spirit,
So wise, so grave, of so perplex'd a tongue,
And loud withall, that would not wag, nor scarce

Lie still, without a fee; when every word
Your worship but lets fall, is a *Cecchine.*° gold coin
Who's that? One knockes, I would not have you seene Sir.
And yet—pretend you came, and went in hast;
Ile fashion an excuse. And, gentle Sir,
When you do come to swim, in golden lard,
Up to the armes, in honey, that your chin
Is borne up stiffe, with fatnesse of the flood,
Thinke on your vassall; but remember mee:
I ha' not beene your worst of clients.

VOLTORE *Mosca*—

MOSCA. When will you have your inventory brought, Sir,
Or see a coppy of the Will? Anone,
Ile bring 'hem to you Sir. Away, be gon,
Put business i' your face.

[*Exit* Voltore.]

VOLPONE. Excellent *Mosca!*
Come hither, let me kisse thee.

MOSCA. Keepe you still Sir.
Here is *Corbaccio.*

VOLPONE. Set the plate away,
The Vulture's gone, and the old Raven's come.

SCENE IV

MOSCA. CORBACCIO. VOLPONE.

MOSCA. Betake you, to your silence, and your sleepe:
Stand there, and multiply. Now, shall we see
A wretch, who is (indeed) more impotent,
Then this can fayne to bee; yet hopes to hop
Over his grave. Signior *Corbaccio,*
Yo'are very welcome, Sir.

CORBACCIO. How do's your Patron?

MOSCA. Troth as he did, Sir, no amends.

CORBACCIO. What? mendes hee?

MOSCA. No, Sir: he is rather worse.

CORBACCIO. That's well. Where is hee?

MOSCA. Upon his couch Sir, newly fall'n a sleepe.

CORBACCIO. Do's hee sleepe well?

MOSCA. No winke, Sir, all this night.
Nor yesterday, but slumbers.

CORBACCIO. Good. He should take
Some counsell of *Physitians:* I have brought him
An *Opiate* here, from mine owne *Doctor*—

MOSCA. He will not heare of drugs.

CORBACCIO. Why? I my selfe
Stood by, while 'twas made; saw all th'ingredients:
And know, it cannot but most gently worke.
My life for his, 'tis but to make him sleepe.
VOLPONE. I, his last sleepe, if he would take it.
MOSCA. Sir.
He ha's no faith in Physick.
CORBACCIO. 'Say you? 'say you?
MOSCA. He has no faith in Physick: He do's thinke
Most of your *Doctors* are the greatest danger,
And worse disease, t'escape. I often have
Heard him protest, that your *Physitian*
Should never be his heyre.
CORBACCIO. Not I his heyre?
MOSCA. Not your *Physitian,* Sir.
CORBACCIO. O, no, no, no,
I do not meane it.
MOSCA. No Sir, nor their fees
He cannot brooke: He sayes, they flea a man,
Before they kill him.
CORBACCIO. Right, I doe conceive you.
MOSCA. And then, they doe it by experiment;
For which the *Law* not onely doth absolve 'hem,
But gives them great reward: And, he is loath
To hire his death, so.
CORBACCIO. It is true, they kill,
With as much licence, as a Judge.
MOSCA. Nay more;
For he but kills, Sir, where the *Law* condemnes,
And these can kill him, too.
CORBACCIO. I, or mee:
Or any man. How do's his *Apoplexe?*
Is that strong on him, still?
MOSCA. Most violent.
His speech is broken, and his eyes are set,
His face drawne longer, then t'was wont—
CORBACCIO. How? how?
Stronger, then he was wont?
MOSCA. No, Sir: his face
Drawne longer, then t'was wont.
CORBACCIO. O, good.
MOSCA. His mouth
Is ever gaping, and his eye-lids hang.
CORBACCIO. Good.
MOSCA. A freezing numnesse stiffens all his joynts,
And makes the colour of his flesh like lead.

CORBACCIO. 'Tis good.
MOSCA. His pulse beats slow, and dull.
CORBACCIO. Good *symptomes,* still.
MOSCA. And, from his braine—
CORBACCIO. Ha? how? not from his braine?
MOSCA. Yes, Sir, and from his braine—
CORBACCIO. I conceive you, good.
MOSCA. Flowes a cold sweat, with a continuall rhewme,
Forth the resolved° corners of his eyes. — relaxed
CORBACCIO. Is't possible? yet I am better, ha!
MOSCA. O, Sir tis past the *Scotomy;*° he, now, — dizziness
Hath lost his feeling, and hath left to snort:
You hardly can perceive him, that he breaths.
CORBACCIO. Excellent, excellent, sure I shall outlast him:
This makes me yong againe, a score of yeares.
MOSCA. I was a comming for you, Sir.
CORBACCIO. Has he made his Wil?
What has he giv'n me?
MOSCA. No, Sir.
CORBACCIO. Nothing? ha?
MOSCA. He has not made his Will, Sir.
CORBACCIO. Oh, oh, oh.
But what did *Voltore,* the Lawyer, here?
MOSCA. He smelt a carcasse Sir, when he but heard
My maister was about his Testament;
As I did urge him to it, for your good—
CORBACCIO. He came unto him, did he? I thought so.
MOSCA. Yes, and presented him this peece of plate.
CORBACCIO. To be his heire?
MOSCA. I do not know Sir.
CORBACCIO. True,
I know it too.
MOSCA. By your owne scale, Sir.
CORBACCIO. Well,
I shall prevent him, yet. See *Mosca,* looke,
Here, I have brought a bag of bright *Cecchines,*
Will quite weigh downe his plate.
MOSCA. Yea marry, Sir,
This is true Physick, this your *sacred Medicine,*
No talke of *Opiates,* to this great *Elixir.*
CORBACCIO. 'Tis *Aurum palpabile,*° if not *potabile.*° — gold touchable; drinkable
MOSCA. It shall be minister'd to him, in his boule?
CORBACCIO. I, doe, doe, doe.
MOSCA. Most blessed *Cordiall,*
This will recover him.
CORBACCIO. Yes, doe, doe, doe.

MOSCA. I thinke, it were not best, Sir.
CORBACCIO. What?
MOSCA. To recover him.
CORBACCIO. O, no, no, no; by no meanes.
MOSCA. Why, Sir, this
Will worke some strange effect, if he but feele it.
CORBACCIO. Tis true, therefore forbeare; Ile take my venter:
Give mee't againe.
MOSCA. At no hand, pardon mee;
You shall not doe yourselfe that wrong Sir. I
Will so advise you, you shall have it all.
CORBACCIO. How?
MOSCA. All Sir, 'tis your right, your own; no man
Can claime a part: 'tis yours, with a rivall,
Decre'd by destiny.
CORBACCIO. How? how, good *Mosca?*
MOSCA. Ile tell you Sir. This fit he shall recover—
CORBACCIO. I do conceive you.
MOSCA. And, of first advantage
Of his gain'd sense, will I re-importune him
Unto the making of his Testament:
And shew him this.
CORBACCIO. Good, good.
MOSCA. 'Tis better yet,
If you will heare, Sir.
CORBACCIO. Yes, with all my heart.
MOSCA. Now, would I councell you, make home with speed;
There, frame a Will; whereto you shall inscribe
My maister your soul heyre.
CORBACCIO. And disinherit
My sonne?
MOSCA. O Sir, the better: for that colour
Shall make it much more taking.
CORBACCIO. O, but colour?
MOSCA. This Will Sir, you shall send it unto me.
Now, when I come to inforce (as I will do)
Your cares, your watchings, and your many prayers,
Your more then many gifts, your this dayes present,
And, last, produce your Will; where (without thought,
Or least regard, unto your proper issue,
A sonne so brave, and highly meriting)
The streame of your diverted love hath throwne you
Upon my maister, and made him your heyre:
He cannot be so stupide, or stone dead,
But, out of conscience, and mere gratitude—
CORBACCIO. He must pronounce me, his?

MOSCA. 'Tis true.
CORBACCIO. This plot
Did I thinke on before.
MOSCA. I do beleeve it.
CORBACCIO. Do you not beleeve it?
MOSCA. Yes Sir.
CORBACCIO. Mine own project.
MOSCA. Which when he hath done, Sir—
CORBACCIO. Publish'd me his heire?
MOSCA. And you so certaine, to survive him—
CORBACCIO. I.
MOSCA. Beeing so lusty a man—
CORBACCIO. 'Tis true.
MOSCA. Yes Sir.
CORBACCIO. I thought on that too. See, how he should be
The very organ, to expresse my thoughts!
MOSCA. You have not onely done your selfe a good—
CORBACCIO. But multiplied it on my sonne?
MOSCA. 'Tis right, Sir.
CORBACCIO. Still, my invention.
MOSCA. 'Lasse Sir, heaven knowes,
It hath beene all my study, all my care,
(I 'eene grow grey withall) how to worke things—
CORBACCIO. I do conceive, sweet *Mosca.*
MOSCA. You are he,
For whom I labour, here.
CORBACCIO. I, doe, doe, doe:
Ile straight about it.
MOSCA Rooke[9] go with you, Raven.
CORBACCIO. I know thee honest.
MOSCA. You do lie, Sir.
CORBACCIO. And—
MOSCA. Your knowledge is no better then your eares, Sir.
CORBACCIO. I do not doubt, to be a father to thee.
MOSCA. Nor I, to gull my brother of his blessing.
CORBACCIO. I may ha'my youth restor'd to mee, why not?
MOSCA. Your worship is a precious asse.
CORBACCIO. What sai'st thou?
MOSCA. I do desire your worship, to make hast, Sir.
CORBACCIO. 'Tis done, 'tis done, I go.

[*Exit* CORBACCIO.]

VOLPONE. O, I shall burst;
Let out my sides, let out my sides—

9. 1) crow; 2) cheat.

MOSCA. Containe
Your fluxe of laughter, Sir; you know, this hope
Is such a baite, it covers any hooke.
VOLPONE. O, but thy working, and thy placing it!
I cannot hold; good rascall, let me kisse thee:
I never knew thee, in so rare a humour.
MOSCA. Alas Sir, I but do, as I am taught;
Follow your grave instruction; give 'hem words;
Powre oyle in their eares: and send them hence.
VOLPONE. 'Tis true, 'tis true. What a rare punishment
Is avarice, to it selfe?
MOSCA. I, with our helpe, Sir.
VOLPONE. So many cares, so many maladies,
So many feares attending on old age,
Yea, death so often call'd on, as no wish
Can be more frequent with 'hem, their limbes faint,
Their sense dull, their seeing, hearing, going
All dead before them; yea, their very teeth,
Their instruments of eating, failing them:
Yet this is reckon'd life! Nay, here was one,
Is now gone home, that wishes to live longer!
Feeles not his gout, nor palsy, faines himselfe
Yonger, by scores of yeares, flatters his age,
With confident belying it, hopes he may
With charmes, like *Æson,*[10] have his youth restor'd,
And with these thoughts so battens,° as if *Fate* grows fat
Would be as easily cheated on, as he,
And all turnes ayre!

Another knocks.

Who's that, there, now? a third?
MOSCA. Close, to your couch againe: I heare his voice.
It is *Corvino,* our spruce merchant.
VOLPONE. Dead.
MOSCA. Another bout, Sir, with your eyes. Who's there?

SCENE V

MOSCA. CORVINO. VOLPONE.

MOSCA. Signior *Corvino!* come most wisht for! O,
How happy were you, if you knew it, now!
CORVINO. Why? what? wherein?
MOSCA. The tardie houre is come, Sir.

10. Father of Jason of the Argonauts, restored to life by Medea.

CORVINO. He is not dead?
MOSCA. Not dead, Sir, but as good;
He knowes no man.
CORVINO. How shall I do then?
MOSCA. Why Sir?
CORVINO. I have brought him, here, a Pearle.
MOSCA. Perhaps, he has
So much remembrance left, as to know you, Sir;
He still calls on you, nothing but your name
Is in his mouth: Is your Pearle orient,° Sir? lustrous
CORVINO. *Venice*° was never owner of the like. i.e., the doge
VOLPONE. Signior *Corvino.*
MOSCA. Hearke.
VOLPONE. Signior *Corvino.*
MOSCA. 'He calls you, step and give it him. H'is here, Sir,
And he has brought you a rich Pearle.
CORVINO. How doe you Sir?
Tell him, it doubles the twelfe *Caract.*
MOSCA. Sir,
He cannot understand, his hearing's gone;
And yet it comforts him, to see you—
CORVINO. Say,
I have a Diamant for him, too.
MOSCA. Best shew't Sir,
Put it into his hand; 'tis onely there
He apprehends: He has his feeling, yet.
See, how he graspes it!
CORVINO. 'Lasse, good gentleman!
How pittiful the sight is!
MOSCA. Tut, forget sir.
The weeping of an heyre should still be laughter,
Under a visor.
CORVINO. Why? am I his heyre?
MOSCA. Sir, I am sworne, I may not shew the Will,
Till he be dead: But, here has beene *Corbaccio,*
Here has beene *Voltore,* here were others too,
I cannot nomber 'hem, they were so many,
All gaping here for legacyes; but I,
Taking the vantage of his naming you,
(Signior *Corvino,* Signior *Corvino,*) tooke
Paper, and pen, and ynke, and there I ask'd him,
Whom he would have his heyre? *Corvino:* Who
Should be executor? *Corvino:* And,
To any question he was silent too,
I still interpreted the noddes, he made,
(Through weakenesse) for consent: and sent home th'others,

Nothing bequeath'd them, but to crie, and curse.
CORVINO. [*They embrace.*] O, my deare *Mosca.* Do's he not perceive us?
MOSCA. No more then a blinde harper. He knowes no man,
No face of friend, nor name of any servant,
Who 'twas that fed him last, or gave him drinke:
Not those, he hath begotten, or brought up
Can he remember.
CORVINO. Has he children?
MOSCA. Bastards,
Some dozen, or more, that he begot on beggars,
Gipseys, and *Jewes,* and *Black-moores,* when he was drunke.
Knew you not that Sir? 'Tis the common fable.
The *Dwarfe,* the *Foole,* the *Eunuch* are all his;
H'is the true father of his familie,° household
In all, save mee: but he has giv'n 'hem nothing.
CORVINO. That's well, that's well. Art sure he does not heare us?
MOSCA. Sure Sir? why looke you, credit your owne sense.
[*To* VOLPONE.] The *Poxe* approch, and adde to your diseases,
If it would sende you hence the sooner, Sir.
For, your incontinence, it hath deserv'd it
Throughly, and throughly, and the *Plague* to boot.
(You may come neere, Sir.) Would you would once close
Those filthy eyes of yours, that flowe with slime,
Like two frog-pits; and those same hanging cheekes,
Cover'd with hide, in steede of skinne: (nay, helpe, Sir)
That looke like frozen dish-clouts, set on end.
CORVINO. Or, like an old smoak'd wall, on which the raine
Ran downe in streakes.
MOSCA. Excellent, Sir, speake out;
You may be lowder yet: A Culvering° small cannon
Discharged in his eare, would hardly bore it.
CORVINO. His nose is like a common sewre, still running.
MOSCA. 'Tis good: and, what his mouth?
CORVINO. A very draught.° cesspool
MOSCA. O stop it up—
CORVINO. By no meanes.
MOSCA. 'Pray you let mee.
Faith, I could stifle him, rarely, with a pillow,
As well, as any woman, that should keepe him.
CORVINO. Do as you will, but Ile be gone.
MOSCA. Be so;
It is your presence makes him last so long.
CORVINO. I pray you, use no violence.
MOSCA. No, Sir? why?
Why should you be thus scrupulous? 'pray you, Sir.
CORVINO. Nay, at your discretion.

MOSCA. Well, good Sir, be gone.
CORVINO. I will not trouble him now, to take my Pearle?
MOSCA. Puh, nor your Diamant. What a needelesse care
Is this afflicts you? Is not all, here, yours?
Am not I here? whom you have made? your creature?
That owe my beeing to you?
CORVINO. Gratefull *Mosca:*
Thou art my friend, my fellow, my companion,
My partner, and shalt share in all my fortunes.
MOSCA. Excepting one.
CORVINO. What's that?
MOSCA. Your gallant wife, Sir.

[*Exit* CORVINO.]

Now, is he gone; we had no other meanes,
To shoote him hence, but this.
VOLPONE. My divine *Mosca!*
Thous hast to day out-gone thy selfe.

Another knock.

Who's there?
I will be troubled with no more. Prepare
Me musicke, dances, banquets, all delights;
The *Turke* is not more sensual, in his pleasures,
Then will *Volpone.*

[*Exit* MOSCA.]

Let me see, a Pearle?
A Diamant? Plate? *Cecchines?* good mornings purchase;
Why, this is better then rob *Churches,* yet:
Or fat, by eating (once a mon'th) a man.

[*Re-enter* MOSCA.]

Who is't?
MOSCA. The beauteous Lady *Would-bee,* Sir,
Wife, to the *English* Knight, Sir *Politique Would-bee,*
(This is the stile, Sir, is directed mee)
Hath sent to know, how you have slept to night,
And if you would be visited.
VOLPONE. Not, now.
Some three houres, hence—
MOSCA. I told the *Squire,* so much.
VOLPONE. When I am high with mirth, and wine; then, then.
'Fore heaven, I wonder at the desperate valure
Of the bold *English,* that they dare let loose
Their wives, to all encounters!
MOSCA. Sir, this Knight

Had not his name for nothing, he is *politique,*
And knowes, how ere his wife affect strange ayres,
She hath not yet the face, to be dishonest.
But, had she Signior *Corvino's* wives face—
VOLPONE. Has she so rare a face?
MOSCA. O Sir, the wonder,
The blazing Starre of *Italy;* a wench
O' the first yeare, a beauty, ripe, as harvest!
Whose skinne is whiter then a *Swan,* all over!
Then *silver, snow,* or *lillies!* a soft lip,
Would tempt you to eternity of kissing!
And flesh, that melteth, in the touch, to bloud!
Bright as your gold, and lovely, as your gold!
VOLPONE. Why had not I knowne this, before?
MOSCA. Alas, Sir.
My selfe, but yesterday, discover'd it.
VOLPONE. How might I see her?
MOSCA. O, not possible;
She's kept as warily, as is your gold:
Never do's come abroad, never takes ayre,
But at a windore. All her lookes are sweet,
As the first grapes, or cherries; and are watch'd
As neare, as they are.
VOLPONE. I must see her—
MOSCA. Sir.
There is a guard, of ten spies thick, upon her;
All his whole houshold: each of which is set
Upon his fellow, and have all their charge,
When he goes out, when he comes in, examin'd.
VOLPONE. I will go see her, though but at her windore.
MOSCA. In some disguise, then?
VOLPONE. That is true, I must
Maintaine mine owne shape, still, the same: wee'll thinke.

[*Exeunt.*]

ACT II

SCENE I

POLITIQUE WOULD-BEE. PEREGRINE.

POLITIQUE. Sir, to a wise man, All the world's his soile,
It is not *Italy,* nor *France,* nor *Europe,*
That must bound me, if my *Fates* call me forth.
Yet, I protest, it is no salt° desire — frivolous
Of seeing *Countries,* shifting a *Religion,*

Nor any dis-affection to the *State*
Where I was bred, (and, unto which I owe
My dearest plots) hath brought me out; much lesse,
That idle, antique, stale, grey-headed project
Of knowing mens mindes, and manners, with *Ulisses:*
But, a peculiar humour of my wives,
Layd for this height° of *Venice,* to observe, latitude
To quote, to learne the language, and so forth—
I hope you travell, Sir, with license?
PEREGRINE. Yes.
POLITIQUE. I dare the safelier converse—How long, Sir,
Since you left *England?*
PEREGRINE. Seaven weekes.
POLITIQUE. So lately!
You ha' not beene with my Lord *Ambassador?*
PEREGRINE. Not yet, Sir.
POLITIQUE. 'Pray you, what newes, Sir, vents our climate?
I heard, last night, a most strange thing reported
By some of my Lords followers, and I long
To heare, how't will be seconded!
PEREGRINE. What was't, Sir.
POLITIQUE. Marry, Sir, of a Raven, that should build
In a ship royall of the *Kings.*
PEREGRINE. This fellow
Do's he gull me, trow?° or is gull'd? your name, Sir? do you think
POLITIQUE. My name is *Politique Would-bee.*
PEREGRINE. O, that speaks him.
A Knight, Sir?
POLITIQUE. A poore Knight, Sir.
PEREGRINE. Your Lady
Lies here, in *Venice,* for intelligence
Of tires,° and fashions, and behaviour, clothes or headresses
Among the Curtizans? the fine *Lady Would-be?*
POLITIQUE. Yes, Sir, the spider, and the bee, oft times,
Suck from one flower.
PEREGRINE. Good Sir *Politique!*
I crie you mercy; I have heard much of you:
'Tis true, Sir, of your Raven.
POLITIQUE. On your knowledge?
PEREGRINE. Yes, and your Lions whelping, in the *Tower.*
POLITIQUE. Another whelpe?
PEREGRINE. Another, Sir.
POLITIQUE. Now heaven!
What prodigies be these? The Fires at *Berwike!*[11]

11. In January of 1605, the northern lights were seen as apparitions of two armies fighting over Berwicke.

And the new *Starre!*[12] these things concurring, strange!
And full of *omen!* Saw you those *Meteors?*
PEREGRINE. I did Sir.
POLITIQUE. Fearefull! Pray you Sir, confirme me,
Were there three Porcpisces seene, above the *Bridge,*
As they give out?[13]
PEREGRINE. Sixe, and a Sturgeon, Sir.
POLITIQUE. I am astonish'd.
PEREGRINE. Nay Sir, be not so;
Ile tell you a greater prodigie, then these—
POLITIQUE. What should these things portend?
PEREGRINE. The very day
(Let me be sure) that I put forth from *London,*
There was a Whale discover'd, in the river,
As high as *Woollwich,* that had waited there
(Few know how many mon'ths) for the subversion
Of the *Stode*-Fleete.[14]
POLITIQUE. Is't possible? Beleeve it,
'Twas either sent from *Spaine,* or the *Arch-Duke,*[15]
Spinola's[16] Whale, upon my life, my credit;
Will they not leave these projects? Worthy Sir,
Some other newes.
PEREGRINE. Faith, *Stone,* the Foole, is dead;
And they do lack a taverne-Foole, extremely.
POLITIQUE. Is *Mass' Stone* dead?
PEREGRINE. H'is dead Sir, why? I hope
You thought him not immortall? O this Knight
(Were he well well knowne) would be a precious thing
To fit our *English* Stage: He that should write
But such a fellow, should be thought to faine
Extremely, if not maliciously.
POLITIQUE. *Stone* dead?
PEREGRINE. Dead. Lord! how deepely Sir you apprehend it?
He was no kinsman to you?
POLITIQUE. That I know of.
Well! that same fellow was an unknowne° Foole. undiscovered
PEREGRINE. And you knew him, it seemes?
POLITIQUE. I did so, Sir,
I knew him one of the most dangerous heads
Living within the *State,* and so I held him.
PEREGRINE. Indeed Sir?

12. Discovered by Kepler in 1604.
13. A porpoise was captured above London Bridge in 1606, and a whale was seen in the Thames about eight miles below the bridge a few days later.
14. Stade, a port northwest of Hamburg.
15. Albert, ruler of the Spanish Netherlands.
16. Ambrosio Spinola, Spanish general.

POLITIQUE. While he liv'd, in action.
He has receiv'd weekely intelligence,
Upon my knowledge, out of the *Low Countries,*
(For all parts of the world) in cabages;
And those dispens'd, againe, to'*Ambassadors,*
In oranges, musk-melons, apricocks,
Limons, pome-citrons,° and such like: sometimes, limes
In *Colchester*-oysters, and your *Selsey*-cockles.
PEREGRINE. You make me wonder!
POLITIQUE. Sir, upon my knowledge.
Nay, I have observ'd him, at your publique Ordinary,° eating house
Take his advertisement,° from a *Traveller* message
(A conceald *States*-man) in a trencher of meate;
And, instantly, before the meale was done,
Convay an answer in a tooth-pick.
PEREGRINE. Strange!
How could this be, Sir?
POLITIQUE. Why, the meate was cut
So like his character,° and so layd, as he code
Must easily read the cipher.
PEREGRINE. I have heard
He could not read, Sir.
POLITIQUE. So, 'twas given out,
(In pollitie,) by those that did imploy him:
But he could read, and had your *languages,*
And to't, as sound a noddle—
PEREGRINE. I have heard, Sir
That your *Babiouns* were spies; and that they were
A kinde of subtle Nation, neare to *China.*
POLITIQUE. I, I, your *Mamuluchi.*[17] Faith, they had
Their hand in a *French* plot, or two; but they
Were so extremely given to women, as
They made discovery of all: Yet I
Had my *advises*° here (on wensday last) dispatches
From one of their owne coat, they were return'd,
Made their relations (as the fashion is)
And now stand faire, for fresh imployment.
PEREGRINE. 'Hart!
This Sir *Poll:* will be ignorant of nothing.
It seemes Sir, you know all?
POLITIQUE. Not all Sir. But,
I have some generall notions; I do love
To note, and to observe: Though I live out,
Free from the active torrent, yet I'ld marke

17. Circassian slaves who seized the throne of Egypt and controlled it from the thirteenth to nineteenth centuries.

The currents, and the passage of things,
For mine owne private use; and knowe the ebbes,
And flowes of *State.*
PEREGRINE. Beleeve it, Sir, I hold
My selfe, in no small tie, unto my fortunes,
For casting mee thus luckely, upon you;
Whose knowledge (if your bounty equall it)
May do me great assistance, in instruction
For my behaviour, and my bearing, which
Is yet so rude,° and raw— uninstructed
POLITIQUE. Why? came you forth
Empty of rules, for travayle?
PEREGRINE. Faith, I had
Some common ones, from out that vulgar *Grammar,*
Which hee, that cri'd° *Italian* to mee, taught mee. taught
POLITIQUE. Why, this it is, that spoiles all our brave bloods,
Trusting our hopefull *gentry* unto *Pedants,*
Fellowes of out-side, and mere barke. You seeme
To be a gentleman, of ingenuous race—
I not professe it, but my fate hath beene
To be, where I have beene consulted with,
In this high kinde, touching some great mens sonnes,
Persons of bloud, and honour—
PEREGRINE. Who be these, Sir?

SCENE II

MOSCA. POLITIQUE. PEREGRINE.
VOLPONE. NANO. GREGE.

MOSCA. Under that windore, there't must be. The same.
POLITIQUE. Fellowes, to mount a banke! Did your instructer
In the deare° *Tongues,* never discourse to you esteemed
Of the *Italian Montebankes?*
PEREGRINE. Yes, Sir.
POLITIQUE. Why,
Here you shall see one.
PEREGRINE. They are *Quack-salvers,*
Fellowes, that live by venting oyles, and drugs?
POLITIQUE. Was that the character hee gave you of them?
PEREGRINE. As I remember.
POLITIQUE. Pittie his ignorance.
They are the onely-knowing men of *Europe,*
Great, generall *Schollers,* excellent *Phisitians,*
Most admir'd *States-men,* profest *Favorites,*
And cabinet-*Councellors,* to the greatest *Princes:*
The onely *Languag'd*-men, of all the world.
PEREGRINE. And I have heard, they are most lewd impostors;

Made all of termes, and shreds; no lesse beliers
Of great-mens favors, then their owne vile med'cines;
Which they will utter, upon montrous othes:
Selling that drug, for two pence, ere they part,
Which they have valew'd at twelve *Crownes,* before.

POLITIQUE. Sir, calumnies are answer'd best with silence;
Your selfe shall judge. Who is it mounts, my friends?

MOSCA. *Scoto* of *Mantua,* Sir.

POLITIQUE. Is't hee? nay, then
Ile proudly promise, Sir, you shall behold
Another man, then has beene phant'sied, to you.
I wonder, yet, that hee should mount his banke
Here, in this nooke, that has been wont t'appeare
In face of the *Piazza!* Here, he comes.

VOLPONE. Mount *Zany.*

GREGE. Follow, follow, follow, follow, follow.

POLITIQUE. See how the people follow him! hee's a man
May write 10000. *Crownes,* in Banke, here. Note,
Marke but his gesture; I do use to observe
The state hee keepes, in getting up!

PEREGRINE. 'Tis worth it, Sir.

VOLPONE. *Most noble Gentlemen and my worthy Patrons, it may seeme strange, that I, your* Scoto Mantuano, *who was ever wont to fixe my Banke in face of the publike* Piazza, *neare the shelter of the* portico, *to the* Procuratia, *should, now (after eight months absence, from this illustrious Citty of* Venice) *humbly retire my selfe, into an obscure nooke of the* Piazza.

POLITIQUE. Did not I, now, object the same?

PEREGRINE. Peace, Sir.

VOLPONE. *Let me tel you: I am not (as your* Lombard *Proverbe sayth) cold on my feete, or content to part with my commodities at a cheaper rate, then I am accustomed; looke not for it. Nor, that the calumnious reports of that impudent detractor, and shame to our profession,* (Alessandro Buttone, *I meane) who gave out, in publike, I was condemn'd a* 'Sforzato° [against my will] *to the Galleys, for poysoning the Cardinall* Bemboo's—*Cooke, hath at all attached, much lesse dejected mee. No, no, worthie Gentlemen:* (to tell you true) *I cannot indure, to see the rable of these grand* Ciarlitani,° [charlatans] *that spread their clokes on the pavement, as if they meant to do feates of activitie, and then come in, lamely, with their mouldy tales out of* Boccacio, *like stale* Tabarine[18] *the Fabulist: some of them discoursing their travells, and of their tedious captivity in the* Turkes *Galleyes, when indeed (were the truth knowne) they were the* Christians *Galleyes, where very*

18. Italian comedian.

temperately, they eate bread, and drunke water, as a wholesome pennance (enjoyn'd them by their Confessors) *for base pilferies.*

POLITIQUE. Note but his bearing, and contempt of these.

VOLPONE. *These turdy-facy-nasty-patie°-lousie-farticall rogues, with one poore groats-worth of unprepar'd* antimony,° *finely wrapt up in severall* 'Scartoccios,° *are able, very well, to kill their twenty a weeke, and play; yet these meagre sterv'd spirits, who have halfe stopt the organs of their mindes with earthy oppilations,° want not their favourers among your shrivel'd, sallad-eating* Artizans, *who are overjoy'd, that they may have their halfeperth of Physick, though it purge 'hem into another world, makes no matter.*

clever (derogatory); an emetic; envelopes; obstructions

POLITIQUE. Excellent! ha you heard better *Language,* Sir?

VOLPONE. *Well, let 'hem go. And Gentlemen, honourable Gentlemen, know, that for this time, our Banque, being thus remov'd from the clamours of the* Canaglia,° *shall be the* Scene *of pleasure, and delight: For I have nothing to sell, little or nothing to sell.*

rabble

POLITIQUE. I told you, Sir; his ende.

PEREGRINE. You did so, Sir.

VOLPONE. *I protest, I, and my sixe servants, are not able to make of this pretious liquor, so fast, as it is fetch'd away from my lodging, by Gentlemen of your Citty; Strangers of the* Terra-ferma;[19] *worshipful Merchants; I, and Senators too: who, ever since my arrivall, have detained mee to their uses, by their splendidous liberalities. And worthily. For what avayles your rich man to have his* magazines° *stuft with* Moscadelli, *or the purest grape, when his* Physitians *prescribe him (on paine of death) to drinke nothing but water, cocted with* Anise-seeds? *O health! health! the blessing of the rich, the riches of the poore! who can buy thee at to deare a rate, since there is no enjoying this world, without thee? Be not then so sparing of your purses, honorable Gentlemen, as to abridge the naturall course of life—*

storehouses

PEREGRINE. You see his ende?

POLITIQUE. I, is't not good?

VOLPONE. *For, when a* humide Fluxe, *or* Catarrhe, *by the mutability of ayre, falls from your head, into an arme, or shoulder, or any other part; take you a* Duckat, *or* Cecchine *of gold, and applie to the place affected: see, what good effect it can worke. No, no, 'tis this blessed* Unguento, *this rare Extraction, that hath onely power to disperse all malignant humors, that proceede, either of hot, cold, moist, or windy causes—*

PEREGRINE. I would he had put in dry to.

POLITIQUE. 'Pray you, observe.

19. People from the mainland of Italy.

VOLPONE. *To fortifie the most indigest, and crude stomacke, I, were it of one, that (through extreame weaknesse) vomited bloud, applying onely a warme napkin to the place, after the* unction, *and* fricace.° *For the* Vertigine, *in the head, putting but a drop into your nostrills, likewise, behind the eares; a most soveraigne, and approoved remedy. The* Mall-caduco,° Crampes, Convulsions, Paralysies, Epilepsies, Tremor-cordia, retired-Nerves, *ill* vapours of the Spleene, Stoppings of the Liver, *the* Stone, *the* Strangury,° Hernia ventosa, Iliaca passio; *stops a* Disenteria, *immediatly; easeth the* torsion of the small guts: *and cures* Melancolia hypocondriaca, *being taken and applied, according to my* printed Receipt. *For, this* [*Pointing to his bill and glasse.*] *is the* Physitian, *this the medicine; this councells, this cures; this gives the direction, this works the effect: and (in summe) both together may be term'd an abstract of the* theorick, *and* practick *in the* Æsculapian *Art. 'Twill cost you eight* Crownes. *And,* Zan Fritada, *'pray thee sing a verse,* extempore, *in honour of it.*

massage

epilepsy

painful urination

POLITIQUE. How do you like him, Sir?

PEREGRINE. Most strangely, I!

POLITIQUE. Is not his language rare?

PEREGRINE. But *Alchimy,*
I never heard the like: or *Broughtons* bookes.[20]

[NANO *sings.*]

SONG

Had old Hippocrates, *or* Galen,
(That to their bookes put med'cines all in)
But knowne this secret, they had never
(Of which they will bee guilty ever)
Beene murderers of so much paper,
Or wasted many a hurtlesse taper:
No Indian *drug had ere beene famed,*
Tabacco, Sassafras *not named;*
Ne yet, of Guacum° *one small stick, Sir,* — a tree resin
Nor Raymund Lullies[21] *greate* Elixir,
Ne, had beene knowne the danish Gonswart,[22]
Or, Paracelsus,[23] *with his long sword.*

PEREGRINE. All this, yet, will not do, eight *Crownes* is high.

VOLPONE. *No more; Gentlemen, if I had but time to discourse to you the miraculous effects of this my oyle, surnamed* oglio del

20. Hugh Broughton, rabbinical scholar.

21. Thirteenth-century Spanish mystic.

22. J. L. Halio suggests Johan Wessel (1420–89), a theologian from Gansfort, Westphalia, may be meant here.

23. Sixteenth-century German doctor and alchemist. His sword had a long, hollow handle in which he kept his "quintessences."

Scoto, *with the count-lesse Catalogue of those I have cured of th'aforesayd, and many more diseases, the Pattents and Privileges of all the* Princes, *and the Common-wealthes of* Christendome, *or but the depositions of those that appear'd on my part, before the* Signiary *of the* Sanitâ,[24] *and most learned* Colledge *of* Physitians; *where I was authorized, upon notice taken of the admirable vertues of my medicaments, and mine owne excellency, in matters of rare, and unknowne secrets, not onely to disperse them publiquely in this famous Citty, but in all the Territories, that happely joy under the government of the most pious and magnificant* States *of* Italy. *But may some other gallant fellow say, O, there be divers, that make profession to have as good, and as experimental receipts, as yours: Indeed, very many have assay'd, like Apes, in imitation of that, which is really, and essentially in mee, to make of this oyle; bestow'd great cost in furnaces, stilles, alembekes, continuall fires, and preparation of the* ingredients, *as indeede there goes to it sixe hundred severall Simples,°* [single herbs] *beside, some quantity of humane fat, for their conglutination,°* [cohesion] *which we buy of the* Anatomistes. *But, when these* Practitioners *come to the last decoction, blow, blow, puff, puff, and all flies in* fumo: *ha, ha, ha. Poore wretches! I rather pitty their folly, and indiscretion, then their losse of time, and money; for those may be recover'd by industry: but to be a Foole borne is a disease incurable. For my selfe, I alwaies from my youth have indeavor'd to get the rarest secrets, and booke°* [record] *them; eyther in exchange, or for money; I spared nor cost, nor labour, where any thing was to be learned. And Gentlemen, honourable Gentlemen, I will undertake (by vertue of* Chymicall *Art) out of the honourable hat, that covers your head, to extract the foure* Elements; *that is to say, the* Fire, Ayre, Water, *and* Earth, *and returne you your felt, without burne, or staine. For, whil'st others have beene at the* balloo,° [ball game] *I have beene at my booke: and am now past the craggy pathes of study, and come to the flowrie plaines of honour, and reputation.*

POLITIQUE. I do assure you, Sir, that is his ayme.

VOLPONE. *But, to our price.*

PEREGRINE. And that withall, Sir *Poll.*

VOLPONE. *You all know (honourable Gentlemen) I never valew'd this* ampulla, *or viall, at lesse then eight* Crownes, *but for this time, I am content, to be depriv'd of it for sixe; sixe* Crownes *is the price; and lesse, in curtesie, I know you cannot offer mee; take it, or leave it, howsoever, both it, and I am at your service. I aske you not, as the valew of the thing, for then I should demand of you a thousand* Crownes, *as the* Cardinalls Montalto, Fernese, *the great* Duke *of* Tuscany, *my Gossip,°* [sponsor] *with divers other* Princes *have given*

24. Board of medical examiners in Venice.

me; but I despise money: only to shew my affection to you, honorable Gentlemen, and your illustrous State *here, I have neglected the messages of these* Princes, *mine owne offices, fram'd my journey hither, onely to present you with the fruicts of my travells. Tune your voyces once more, to the touch of your instruments, and give the honorable assembly some delightfull recreation.*

PEREGRINE. What monstrous, and most painefull circumstance
Is here, to get some three, or foure *Gazets?*°
Some three-pence, i'th whole, for that 'twill come too.

small coin

[NANO *sings.*]

SONG

You that would last long, list to my song,
Make no more coyle, but buy of this oyle.
Would you ever be faire? and yong?
Stout of teeth? and strong of tongue?
Tart of palat? quick of eare?
Sharpe of sight? of nostrill cleare?
Moist of hand? and light of foot?
(Or I will come neerer to't)
Would you live free from all diseases?
Do the act, your mistress pleases;
Yet fright all aches from your bones[25]
Here's a med'cine, for the nones.

VOLPONE. *Well, I am in a humor (at this time) to make a present of the small quantity my coffer containes: to the rich, in courtesie, and to the poore, for Gods sake. Wherefore, nowe marke; I ask'd you sixe* Crownes; *and sixe* Crownes, *at other times, you have payd mee; you shall not give mee sixe* Crownes, *nor five, nor foure, nor three, nor two, nor one; nor halfe a* Duckat; no, nor a Muccingo:° *six* pence *it will cost you, or sixe hundred* pound—*expect no lower price, for by the banner of my front, I will not bate a* bagatine,° *that I will have, onely, a pledge of your loves, to carry something from amongst you, to shew, I am not contemn'd by you. Therefore, now, tosse your handkerchiefes, chearefully, chearefully; and bee advertised, that the first* heroique *spirit, that deignes to grace mee, with a handkerchiefe, I will give it a little remembrance of something, besides, shall please it better, then if I had presented it with a double* Pistolet.°

coin worth nine pennies
very small coin
Spanish gold coin

PEREGRINE. Will you be the *heroique* Sparke, Sir *Pol?*

CELIA *at the windo' throwes downe her handkerchiefe.*

O see! the windore has prevented you.

25. i.e., prevent venereal disease.

VOLPONE. *Lady, I kisse your bounty; and for this timely grace, you have done your poore* Scoto of Mantua, *I will returne you, over and above my oyle, a secret, of that high, and inestimable nature, shall make you for ever enamour'd on that minute, wherein your eye first descended on so meane, yet not altogether to be despis'd an object. Here is a Poulder,° conceal'd in this paper, of which, if I* [powder] *should speake to the worth, nine thousand* volumes *were but as one* page, *that* page *as a* line, *as a* word; *so short is this* Pilgrimage of man *(which some call Life) to the expressing of it: would I reflect on the price? why, the whole* World *were but as an* Empire, *that* Empire *as a* Province, *that* Province *as a* Banke, *that* Banke *as a* private Purse, *to the purchase of it. I will, onely, tell you; it is the Poulder, that made* Venus a Goddesse (*given her by* Apollo) *that kept her perpetually, yong, clear'd her wrincles, firm'd her gummes, fill'd her skinne, colour'd her hayre; from her, deriv'd to* Helen, *and at the Sack of* Troy *(unfortunately) lost: Till now, in this our age, it was as happily recover'd by a studious* Antiquary, *out of some ruines of* Asia, *who sent a moyetie of it, to the* Court of France (*but much sophisticated*°) *wherewith the Ladyes there, now, colour their* [adulterated] *hayre. The rest (at this present) remaines with mee; extracted, to a* Quintessence: *so that, where ever it but touches, in youth it perpetually preserves, in age restores the complexion; seats your teeth, did they dance like* Virginall *jacks, firme as a wall; makes them white, as Ivory, that were black, as—*

SCENE III

CORVINO. POLITIQUE. PEREGRINE.

CORVINO. Bloud of the devill, and my shame! come downe, here;
Come downe: No house but mine to make your *Scene?*

He beates away the mountebanke, etc.

Signior Flaminio, will you downe, Sir? downe?
What is my wife your *Franciscina?*[26] Sir?
No windores on the whole *Piazza,* here,
To make your properties, but mine? but mine?
Hart! ere to morrow, I shall be new christen'd,
And cald the *Pantalone di Besogniosi,*[27]
About the towne.

[*Exit* CORVINO.]

PEREGRINE. What would this meane, Sir *Poll?*

26. Flamino was a popular Italian comic actor of the period; Fransicina is the character of the serving girl from the *commedia dell' arte.*

27. Pantaloon of the Paupers; the Pantaloon is another character from the *commedia dell' arte,* the old man with a younger wife, and, therefore, in danger of being cuckolded.

POLITIQUE. Some trick of *State,* beleeve it. I will home.
PEREGRINE. It may be some designe on you.
POLITIQUE. I knowe not.
Ile stand upon my guard.
PEREGRINE. 'Tis your best, Sir.
POLITIQUE. This three weekes, all my *advises,* all my letters
They have beene intercepted.
PEREGRINE. Indeed, Sir?
Best have a care.
POLITIQUE. Nay so I will.

[*Exit* Politique.]

PEREGRINE. This Knight,
I may not loose him, for my mirth, till night.

[*Exit.*]

SCENE IV

VOLPONE. MOSCA.

VOLPONE. O I am wounded.
MOSCA. Where, Sir.
VOLPONE. Not without;
Those blowes were nothing: I could beare them ever.
But angry *Cupid,* boulting from her eyes,
Hath shot himselfe into me, like a flame;
Where, now, he flings about his burning heat,
As in a furnace, some ambitious fire,
Whose vent is stopt. The fight is all within mee.
I cannot live, except thou helpe me, *Mosca;*
My liver melts, and I, without the hope
Of some soft ayre, from her refreshing breath,
Am but a heape of cinders.
MOSCA. 'Lasse, good Sir,
Would you had never seene her.
VOLPONE. Nay, would thou
Had'st never told me of her.
MOSCA. Sir 'tis true;
I do confesse, I was unfortunate,
And you unhappy: but I'am bound in conscience,
No lesse then duety, to effect my best
To your release of torment, and I will, Sir.
VOLPONE. Deare *Mosca,* shall I hope?
MOSCA. Sir, more then deare,
I will not bidd you to dispaire of ought,
Within a humane compasse.

VOLPONE. O, there spoke
My better *Angell. Mosca,* take my keyes,
Gold, plate, and jewells, all's at thy devotion;
Employ them, how thou wilt; nay, coyne me, too:
So thou, in this, but crowne my longings. *Mosca?*
MOSCA. Use but your patience.
VOLPONE. So I have.
MOSCA. I doubt not
To bring successe to your desires.
VOLPONE. Nay, then,
I not repent me of my late disguise.
MOSCA. If you can horne him, Sir, you neede not.
VOLPONE. True:
Besides, I never meant him for my heyre.
Is not the colour of my beard, and eye-browes,
To make me knowne?
MOSCA. No jot.
VOLPONE. I did it well.
MOSCA. So well, would I could follow you in mine,
With halfe the happinesse; and, yet, I would
Escape your *Epilogue.*
VOLPONE. But, were they gull'd
With a beleefe, that I was *Scoto.*
MOSCA. Sir,
Scoto himselfe could hardly have distinguish'd;
I have not time to flatter you, wee'll part:
And, as I prosper, so applaud my art.

[*Exeunt.*]

SCENE V

CORVINO. CELIA.

CORVINO. Death of mine honour, with the citties *Foole?*
A jugling, tooth-drawing, prating *Montebanke?*
And, at a publique windore? where whil'st hee,
With his strain'd action, and his dole of faces,
To his *drug-Lecture* drawes your itching eares,
A crewe of old, un-mari'd, noted lechers,
Stood leering up, like *Satyres;* and you smile,
Most graciously? and fanne your favours forth,
To give your hote *Spectators* satisfaction?
What; was your *Mountebanke* their call? their whistle?
Or were you'enamour'd on his copper rings?
His saffron jewell, with the toade-stone in't?
Or his imbroydred sute, with the cope-stitch,

Made of a herse-cloath? or his old tilt-feather?
Or his starch'd beard? well; you shall have him, yes.
He shall come home, and minister unto you
The *fricace,* for the *Mother.* Or, let me see,
I thinke, you'had rather mount? would you not mount?
And so, you may be seene, downe to th' foote.
Get you a citterne, *Lady Vanity,*
And be a *Dealer,* with the *Vertuous Man;*[28]
Make one: Ile but protest my selfe a cuckold,
And save your dowry. I am a *Dutchman,* I;
For, if you thought me an *Italian,*
You would be damn'd, ere you did this, you Whore:
Thou'ldst tremble, to imagine, that the murder
Of father, mother, brother, all thy race,
Should follow, as the subject of my justice.

CELIA. Good Sir, have patience.

CORVINO. What couldst thou propose
Lesse to thy selfe, then, in this heate of wrath,
And stung with my dishonour, I should strike
This steele into thee, with as many stabs,
As thou wert gaz'd upon with goatish eyes?

CELIA. Alas Sir, be appeas'd; I could not thinke
My beeing at the windore should more, now,
Move your impatience, then at other times.

CORVINO. No? not to seeke, and entertaine a *parlee;*° conversation
With a knowne knave? before a multitude?
You were an *Actor,* with your handkerchiefe;
Which he, most sweetly, kist in the receipt,
And might (no doubt) returne it, with a letter,
And point the place, where you might meete: your sisters,
Your mothers, or your aunts might serve the turne.

CELIA. Why, deare Sir, when do I make these excuses?
Or ever stirre, abroad, but to the *Church?*
And that, so seldome—

CORVINO. Well, it shall be lesse;
And thy restraint, before, was liberty,
To what I now decree: And therefore, marke mee.
First, I will have this baudy light damn'd up;
And, till't be done, some two, or three yards of,° off
Ile chalke a line: ore which, if thou but (chance
To) set thy desp'rate foote; more hell, more horror,
More wilde, remorcelesse rage shall seize on thee,
Then on a *Conjurer,* that had heed-lesse left,
His *Circles* saftie, ere his *Devill* was layd.

28. Characters out of the morality plays.

Then, here's a lock, which I will hang upon thee;
And, now I thinke on't, I will keepe thee back-wards;
Thy lodging shall be back-wards; and no pleasure,
That thou shalt know, but back-wards: Nay, since you force
My honest nature, know, it is your owne
Being to open, makes me use you thus.
Since you will not containe your subtill nostrills
In a sweete roome, but, they must snuffe the ayre
Of ranke, and sweaty passengers—

Knocke within.

One knocks.
Away, and be not seene, paine of thy life;
Not looke toward the windore: if thou dost—
(Nay stay, heare this) let me not prosper, Whore,
But I will make thee an *Anatomy,*
Dissect thee mine owne selfe, and read a *lecture*
Upon thee, to the citty, and in publique.
Away. Who's there?

[*Exit* CELIA. *Enter* SERVITORE.]

SERVITORE. 'Tis Signior *Mosca,* Sir.

SCENE VI

CORVINO. MOSCA.

CORVINO. Let him come in, his master's dead.

[*Exit* SERVITORE.]

There's yet
Some good, to helpe the bad. My *Mosca,* welcome;
I gesse your newes.
MOSCA. I feare, you cannot, Sir.
CORVINO. Is't not his death?
MOSCA. Rather, the contrary.
CORVINO. Not his recovery?
MOSCA. Yes, Sir
CORVINO. I am curst,
I am bewitch'd, my crosses meete to vexe mee.
How? how? how? how?
MOSCA. Why, Sir, with *Scoto's* oyle;
Corbaccio, and *Voltore* brought of it,
Whilst I was busy in an inner roome—
CORVINO. Death! that damn'd *Mountebanke;* but, for the *Law,*
Now, I could kill the raskall: 't cannot bee,
His oyle should have that vertue. Ha' not I

Knowne him a common rogue, come fidling in
To th'*Osteria*,° with a tumbling whore, tavern
And, when he ha's done al his forc'd tricks, beene glad
Of a poore spoonefull of dead wine, with flies in't?
It cannot bee. All his *ingredients*
Are a sheepes gall, a rosted bitches marrow,
Some fewe sod earewigs, pounded caterpillers,
A little capons grease, and fasting spitle:
I know 'hem, to a *dram*.

MOSCA. I know not, Sir,
But some on't, there, they pour'd into his eares,
Some in his nostrills, and recover'd him;
Applying but the *fricace*.

CORVINO. Pox o' that *fricace*.

MOSCA. And since, to seeme the more officious,
And flatt'ring of his health, there, they have had
(At extreme fees) the *Colledge* of *Physitians*
Consulting on him, how they might restore him;
Where, one would have a *cataplasme* of spices,[29]
Another a flead *Ape* clapt to his breast,
A third would ha'it a *Dog*, a fourth an *oyle*
With wild *Catts* skinnes: At last, they all resolv'd
That to preserve him, was no other means,
But some young woman must be streight sought out,
Lusty, and full of juice, to sleepe by him;
And, to this service (most unhappily,
And most unwillingly) am I now imploy'd,
Which, here, I thought to pre-acquaint you with,
For your advise, since it concernes you most,
Because, I would not do that thing might crosse
Your ends, on whome I have my whole dependance, Sir:
Yet, if I do it not, they may delate° inform against
My slacknesse to my Patron, worke me out
Of his opinion; and there, all your hopes,
Venters, or whatsoever, are all frustrate.
I do but tell you, Sir. Besides, they are all
Now striving, who shall first present him. Therefore—
I could intreate you, breefly, conclude some-what:
Prevent 'hem if you can.

CORVINO. Death to my hopes!
This is my villainous fortune! best to hire
Some common Curtezan?

MOSCA. I, I thought on that, Sir.
But they are all so subtle, full of art,

29. A bandage infused with spices placed on a sore.

And age againe, doting, and flexible,
So as—I cannot tell—we may perchance
Light on a queane,° may cheate us all. prostitute
CORVINO. 'Tis true.
MOSCA. No, no: it must be one, that has no tricks, Sir,
Some simple thing, a creature, made unto it;
Some wench you may command. Ha'you no kinswoman?
Gods so—Thinke, thinke, thinke, thinke, thinke, thinke, thinke, Sir.
One o' the *Doctors* offer'd, there, his daughter.
CORVINO. How!
MOSCA. Yes, Signior *Lupo,* the *Physitian.*
CORVINO. His daughter?
MOSCA. And a virgin, Sir. Why? Alasse
He knowes the state of's body, what it is;
That naught can warme his bloud, Sir, but a *fever;*
Nor any incantation raise his spirit:
A long forgetfullnesse hath seiz'd that part.
Besides, Sir, who shall know it? some one, or two.
CORVINO. I pray thee give mee leave: If any man
But I, had had this luck—The thing, in't selfe,
I know, is nothing—Wherefore should not I
As well command my bloud, and my affections,
As this dull *Doctor?* In the point of honor,
The cases are all one, of wife, and daughter.
MOSCA. I heare him coming.
CORVINO. She shall doo't: Tis done.
Slight, if this *Doctor,* that is not engag'd,
Unlesse't bee for his councell (which is nothing)
Offer his daughter, what should I, that am
So deepely in? I will prevent him, wretch!
Covetous wretch! *Mosca,* I have determin'd.
MOSCA. How, Sir?
CORVINO. Wee'll make all sure. The party, you wot° of, know
Shall be mine owne wife, *Mosca.*
MOSCA. Sir. The thing,
(But that I would not seeme to councell you)
I should have motion'd to you, at the first:
And, make your count, you have cut all their throtes.
Why! Tis directly taking a possession!
And, in his next fit, we may let him go.
'Tis but to pul the pillow, from his head,
And he is thratled: 't had beene done, before,
But for your scrupulous doubts.
CORVINO. I, a plague on't.
My conscience fooles my wit. Well, Ile be briefe,
And, so be thou, least they should be before us:

Go home, prepare him, tell him, with what zeale,
And willingness, I do it; sweare it was,
Of the first hearing, (as thou mayst do, truly)
Mine owne free motion.

MOSCA. Sir, I warrant you,
Ile so possesse him with it, that the rest
Of his sterv'd clients shall be banisht, all;
And onely you receiv'd. But come not, Sir,
Untill I send, for I have something, else
To ripen, for your good (you must not know't).

CORVINO. But do not you forget to send, now.

MOSCA. Feare not.

[*Exit* MOSCA.]

SCENE VII

CORVINO. CELIA.

CORVINO. Where are you, wife? my *Celia?* wife? what, blubbering?
Come, drye those teares. I thinke, thou thought'st mee in earnest?
Ha? by this light, I talk'd so but to trie thee.
Me thinkes, the lightnesse of the occasion
Should ha' confirm'd thee. Come, I am not jealous.

CELIA. No?

CORVINO. Faith, I am not, I, nor never was:
It is a poore, unprofitable humor.
Do not I know, if women have a will,
They'll doo 'gainst all the watches, o' the world?
And that the feircest spies, are tam'd with gold?
Tut, I am confident in thee thou shalt see't:
And see, Ile give thee cause too, to beleeve it.
Come, kisse mee. Go, and make thee ready straight,
In all thy best attire, thy choicest jewells,
Put 'hem all on, and, with 'hem, thy best lookes:
We are invited to a solemne feast,
At old *Volpone's,* where it shall appeare
How far I'am free, from jealousie, or feare.

[*Exeunt.*]

ACT III

SCENE I

MOSCA.

MOSCA. I feare, I shall begin to grow in love
With my deare selfe, and my most prosp'rous parts,
They do so spring, and burgeon; I can feele
A whimsey i' my bloud: (I know not how)
Successe hath made me wanton. I could skip
Out of my skinne, now, like a subtill snake,
I am so limber. O! Your *Parasite*
Is a most pretious thing, dropt from above,
Not bred 'mongst clods, and clot-poules, here on earth.
I muse, the *Mysterie*° was not made a *Science,*   craft
It is so liberally profest! Almost,
All the wise world is little else, in nature,
But *Parasites,* or *Sub-parasites.* And, yet,
I meane not those, that have your bare *Towne-art,*
To know, who's fit to feede 'hem; have no house,
No family, no care, and therefore mould
Tales for mens eares, to baite° that sense; or get   please
Kitchin-invention, and some stale receipts
To please the belly, and the groine; nor those,
With their *Court*-dog-trickes, that can fawne, and fleere,
Make their revenue out of legges,° and faces,   bows
Eccho my-*Lord,* and lick away a moath:
But your fine, elegant rascall, that can rise,
And stoope (almost together) like an arrow;
Shoote through the aire, as nimbly as a starre;
Turne short, as doth a swallow; and be here,
And there, and here, and yonder, all at once;
Present to any humour, all occasion;
And change a visor, swifter, then a thought.
This is the creature, had the art borne with him;
Toyles not to learne it, but doth practise it
Out of most excellent nature. And such sparkes,
Are the true *Parasites,* others but their *Zani's.*°   montebank's assistant

SCENE II

MOSCA. BONARIO.

MOSCA. Who's this? *Bonario?* old *Corbaccio's* sonne?
The person I was bound to seeke. Fayre Sir,
You are happ'ly met.
BONARIO. That cannot be, by thee.

MOSCA. Why Sir?
BONARIO. Nay 'pray thee know thy way, and leave me;
I would be loath to inter-change discourse,
With such a mate, as thou art.
MOSCA. Curteous Sir.
Scorne not my poverty.
BONARIO. Not I, by heaven,
But thou shalt give mee leave to hate thy basenesse.
MOSCA. Basenesse?
BONARIO. I. Answer me, Is not thy sloth
Sufficient argument? thy flattery?
Thy means of feeding?
MOSCA. Heaven, be good to me.
These imputations are too common, Sir,
And eas'ly stuck on vertue, when shee's poore;
You are unequall to me, and how ere
Your sentence may be righteous, yet you are not,
That ere you know me, thus, proceed in censure:
St. *Marke* beare witnesse 'gainst you, 'tis inhumane.
BONARIO. What? do's he weepe? the signe is soft, and good;
I do repent mee, that I was so harsh.
MOSCA. 'Tis true, that sway'd, by strong necessity,
I am enforc'd to eate my carefull bread
With to much obsequy; 'tis true, beside,
That I am faine to spin mine owne poore rayment,
Out of mere observance, being not borne,
To a free fortune: but that I have done
Base offices, in rending friends asunder,
Dividing families, betraying councells,
Whispering false lies, or mining men with prayses,
Train'd their credulitie with perjuries,
Corrupted chastity, or am in love
With mine owne tender ease, but would not rather
Prove the most rugged, and laborious course,
That might redeeme, my present estimation;
Let me here perish, in all hope of goodnesse.
BONARIO. This cannot be a personated passion.
I was too blame, so to mistake thy nature;
'Pray thee forgive mee: and speake out thy bus'nesse.
MOSCA. Sir, it concernes you; and though I may seeme,
At first, to make a maine offence, in manners,
And in my gratitude, unto my maister,
Yet, for the pure love, which I beare all right,
And hatred of the wrong, I must reveale it.
This very houre, your father is in purpose
To disinherit you—
BONARIO. How?

MOSCA. And thrust you forth,
As a mere stranger to his bloud; tis true, Sir:
The worke no way ingageth mee, but, as
I claime an interest in the generall state
Of goodnesse, and true vertue, which I heare
T'abound in you: and, for which mere respect,
Without a second ayme, Sir, I have done it.
BONARIO. This tale hath lost thee much of the late trust,
Thou hadst with me; it is impossible:
I know not how to lend it any thought,
My father should be so unnaturall.
MOSCA. It is a confidence, that well becomes
Your piety; and form'd (no doubt) it is,
From your owne simple innocence: which makes
Your wrong more monstrous, and abhor'd. But, Sir,
I now, will tell you more. This very minute,
It is, or will be doing: And, if you
Shall be but pleas'd to goe with me, Ile bring you,
(I dare not say where you shall see, but) where
Your eare shall be a witnesse of the deed;
Heare your selfe written *Bastard;* and profest
The common issue of the earth.
BONARIO. I'm maz'd.
MOSCA. Sir, if I do it not, draw your just sword,
And score your vengeance, on my front, and face;
Marke me your villayne: You have too much wrong,
And I do suffer for you, Sir. My heart
Weepes bloud, in anguish—
BONARIO. Lead. I follow thee.

[*Exeunt.*]

SCENE III

VOLPONE. NANO. ANDROGYNO. CASTRONE.

VOLPONE. *Mosca* stayes long, me thinkes. Bring forth your Sports
And helpe, to make the wretched time more sweete.
NANO. Dwarfe, Foole, and Eunuch, *well mett here wee be.*
A question it were now, whether of us three,
Being, all, the knowne delicates, of a rich man,
In pleasing him, claime the precedency can.
CASTRONE. *I Claime for my selfe.*
ANDROGYNO. *And so doth the* Foole.
NANO. *Tis foolish indeed: let me set you both to schoole.*
First, for your Dwarfe, *hee's little, and witty,*
And every thing, as it is little, is pritty;

Else, why do men say to a creature (of my shape)
So soone as they see him, it's a pritty little Ape?
And, why a pritty Ape? but for pleasing imitation
Of greater mens action, in a ridiculous fashion.
Beside, this feat body of mine doth not crave
Halfe the meat, drinke, and cloth, one of your bulkes will have.
Admit, your Fooles *face be the Mother of laughter,*
Yet, for his braine, it must alwaies come after:
And, though that do feede him, it's a pittiful case,
His body is beholding to such a bad face.

[One *knocks.*]

VOLPONE. Who's there? my couch. Away, looke *Nano,* see:
Give mee my cappes, first—go, enquire.

[*Exeunt* NANO, ANDROGYNO, CASTRONE.]

Now, *Cupid*
Send it be *Mosca,* and with faire returne.

[*Re-enter* NANO.]

NANO. It is the beauteous *Madam*—
VOLPONE. *Would-bee?* is it?
NANO. The same.
VOLPONE. Now, torment on me; squire her in:
For she will enter, or dwell here for ever.
Nay, quickly, that my fit were past. I feare

[*Exit* NANO.]

A second hell too, that my loathing this
Will quite expell my appetite to the other:
Would she were taking, now, her tedious leave.
Lord, how it threateS mee, what I am to suffer.

SCENE IV

LADY [POLITIQUE WOULD-BEE]. VOLPONE. NANO.

LADY. I thanke you, Good Sir. 'Pray you signifie
Unto your Patron, I am here. This band
Shewes not my neck inough (I trouble you, Sir,
Let me request you, bid one of my women
Come hether to me).

[*Exit* NANO.]

In good faith, I'am drest
Most favorably, to day, it is no matter,
'Tis well inough.

[*Re-enter* NANO *with* FIRST WOMAN.]

Looke, see, these petulant things,
How they have done this!

VOLPONE. I do feele the *Fever*
Entring, in at mine eares; O, for a charme,
To fright it hence.

LADY. Come nearer: Is this curle
In his right place? or this? why is this higher
Then all the rest? you ha' not wash'd your eies, yet?
Or do they not stand even 'i your head?
Where's your fellow? call her.

[*Exit* FIRST WOMAN.]

NANO. Now, *St. Marke*
Deliver us: anone, she'll beate her women,
Because her nose is red.

[*Enter* FIRST *and* SECOND *Woman.*]

LADY. I pray you, view
This tire,° forsooth; are all things apt, or no? headress

FIRST WOMAN. One haire a little, here, sticks out, forsooth.

LADY. Do's't so forsooth? and where was your deare sight
When it did so, forsooth? what now? bird-eyed?° sharp-sighted
And you, too? 'pray you both approach, and mend it.
Now (by that light) I muse, yo'are not asham'd.
I, that have preach'd these things, so oft, unto you,
Read you the principles, argu'd all the grounds,
Disputed every fitnesse, every grace,
Call'd you to councell of so frequent dressings—

NANO. (More carefully, then of your fame, or honor.)

LADY. Made you acquainted, what an ample dowry
The knowledge of these things would be unto you,
Able, alone, to get you *Noble* husbands
At your returne: And you, thus, to neglect it?
Besides, you seeing what a curious° *Nation* particular
Th'*Italians* are, what will they say of mee?
The *English Lady* cannot dresse her selfe;
Here's a fine imputation, to our Country:
Well, goe your waies, and stay, i' the next roome.
This *fucus*° was to course too, it's no matter. makeup
Good Sir, you'll give 'hem entertaynment?

[*Exeunt* NANO, FIRST *and* SECOND WOMAN.]

VOLPONE. The storme comes toward me.

LADY. How do's my *Volpone.*

VOLPONE. Troubled with noyse, I cannot sleepe; I dreamt,
That a strange *Fury* entred, now, my house,

And, with the dreadfull tempest of her breath,
Did cleave my roofe asunder.
LADY. Beleeve me, and I
Had the most fearefull dreame, could I remember't—
VOLPONE. Out on my fate; I ha' giv'n her the occasion
How to torment mee: shee will tell me hers.
LADY. Me thought, the *golden Mediocrity*° mean
Polite, and delicate—
VOLPONE. O, if you do love mee,
No more; I sweate, and suffer, at the mention
Of any dreame: feele, how I tremble yet.
LADY. Alasse, good soule! the Passion of the heart.
Seede-pearle were good now, boild with *sirrope of Apples,*
Tincture of Gold, and *Corral, Citron-pills,*
Your *Elicampane* roote, *Mirobalanes*—
VOLPONE. Ay me, I have tâne a grasse-hopper by the wing.
LADY. *Burnt silke,* and *Amber,* you have *Muscadell*
Good i' the house—
VOLPONE. You will not drinke, and part?
LADY. No, feare not that. I doubt, wee shall not get
Some *English saffron* (halfe a *dram* would serve)
Your sixteene *Cloves,* a little *Muske,* dri'd *Mintes,*
Buglosse,[30] and *barley-meale*—
VOLPONE. Shee's in againe,
Before I fayn'd diseases, now I have one.
LADY. And these appli'd, with a right scarlet-cloth—
VOLPONE. Another floud of words! a very torrent!
LADY. Shall I, Sir, make you a *Poultise?*
VOLPONE. No, no, no;
I am very well: you neede prescribe no more.
LADY. I have, a little, studied *Physick;* but, now,
I'am all for *Musique:* save, i' the forenoones,
An houre, or two, for *Paynting.* I would have
A *Lady,* indeed, t'have all, *Letters,* and *Artes,*
Be able to discourse, to write, to paynt,
But principall (as *Plato* holds) your *Musique*
(And, so do's wise *Pithagoras,* I take it)
Is your true rapture; when there is concent
In face, in voice, and clothes: and is, indeed,
Our sexes chiefest ornament.
VOLPONE. The *Poët,*
As old in time, as *Plato,* and as knowing,
Say's that your highest female grace is *Silence.*[31]

30. Used for a number of plants with "hairy" leaves, but here probably Viper's Bugloss, which, among other medicinal uses, was thought to be an aphrodisiac.

31. Sophocles in *Ajax.*

LADY. Which o' your *Poëts? Petrarch?* or *Tasso?* or *Dante?*
Guerrini? Ariosto? Aretine?
Cieco di Hadria? I have read them all.
VOLPONE. Is everything a cause, to my distruction?
LADY. I thinke, I ha' two or three of 'hem, about mee.
VOLPONE. The sunne, the sea will sooner, both, stand still,
Then her æternall tongue; nothing can scape it.
LADY. Here's *Pastor Fido*—[32]
VOLPONE. Professe obstinate silence,
That's, now, my safest.
LADY. All our *English Writers,*
I meane such, as are happy in th'*Italian,*
Will deigne to steale our of this *Author,* mainely;
Almost as much, as from *Montagnié;*
He has so moderne, and facile a veine,
Fitting the time, and catching the *Court*-eare.
Your *Petrarch* is more passionate, yet he,
In dayes of *Sonetting,* trusted 'hem, with much:
Dante is hard, and fewe can understand him.
But, for a desperate wit, there's *Aretine;*
Onely, his *pictures* are a little obscene—
You marke mee not?
VOLPONE. Alasse, my mind's perturb'd.
LADY. Why, in such cases, we must cure our selves,
Make use of our *Philosophie*—
VOLPONE. O'ay mee.
LADY. And, as we finde our passions do rebell,
Encounter 'hem with reason; or divert 'hem,
By giving scope unto some other humour
Of lesser danger: As, in *politique* bodyes,
There's nothing, more, doth overwhelme the judgment,
And clouds the understanding, then too much
Setling, and fixing, and (as't were) subsiding
Upon one object. For the incorporating
Of these same outward things, into that part,
Which we call *mentall,* leaves some certaine *fæces,*
That stop the *organs,* and, as *Plato* sayes,
Assassinates our knowledge.
VOLPONE. Now, the spirit
Of patience helpe me.
LADY. Come, in faith, I must
Visit you more, a dayes; and make you well:
Laugh, and be lusty.
VOLPONE. My good *Angell* save mee.

32. *The Faithful Shepherd,* pastoral drama by Battista Guarini.

LADY. There was but one sole man, in all the world,
With whom I ere could sympathize; and hee
Would lie you often, three, foure, houres together,
To heare me speake: and be (sometime) so rap't,
As he would answer me, quite from the purpose.
Like you, and you are like him, just. Ile discourse
(And't be but onely, Sir, to bring you a sleepe)
How we did spend our time, and loves, together
For some sixe yeares.
VOLPONE. Oh, oh, oh, oh, oh, oh.
LADY. For we were *Coætanei,*° and brought up— of an age
VOLPONE. Some power, some fate, some fortune rescue mee.

SCENE V

MOSCA. LADY. VOLPONE.

MOSCA. God save you, *Madam.*
LADY. Good Sir.
VOLPONE. *Mosca?* welcome,
Welcome to my redemption.
MOSCA. Why, sir?
VOLPONE. Oh,
Rid me of this my torture, quickly, there;
My *Madam,* with the everlasting voyce:
The Bells, in time of pestilence, nêre made
Like noyse, or were in perpetuall motion;
The Cock-pit comes not neare it. All my house,
But now, steam'd like a bath, with her thicke breath.
A *Lawyer* could not have beene heard; nor scarse
Another woman: such a hayle of words
She has let fall. For hells sake, ridd her hence.
MOSCA. Has she presented?
VOLPONE. O, I do not care,
I'le take her absence, upon any price,
With any losse.
MOSCA. *Madam.*
LADY. I ha' brought your Patron
A toy, a cap here, of mine owne worke—
MOSCA. 'Tis well,
I had forgot to tell you, I saw your Knight,
Where you'ld little thinke it—
LADY. Where?
MOSCA. Marry,
Where yet, if you make hast you may apprehend him,
Rowing upon the water in a *gondole,*
With the most cunning Curtizan, of *Venice.*

LADY. Is't true?

MOSCA. Pursue 'hem, and beleeve your eyes:
Leave mee, to make your gift.

[*Exit.* LADY.]

I knew, 'twould take.

For lightly, they, that use themselves most licence,
Are still most jealous.

VOLPONE. *Mosca,* hearty thanks,
For the quick fiction, and delivery of mee.
Nor, to my hopes, what saist thou?

[*Re-enter* Lady.]

LADY. But do you heare, Sir?

VOLPONE. Againe; I feare a *paroxisme.*

LADY. Which way
Row'd they together?

MOSCA. Toward the *Rialto.*

LADY. I pray you, lend me your *Dwarfe.*

MOSCA. I pray you, take him—

[*Exit* LADY.]

Your hopes, Sir, are like happy blossomes, fayre,
And promise timely fruict, if you will stay
But the maturing; keepe you, at your couch,
Corbaccio will arrive straight, with the Will:
When he is gone, Ile tell you more.

[*Exit* MOSCA.]

VOLPONE. My bloud,
My spirits are return'd; I am alive:
And like your wanton gam'ster, at *Primero,*
Whose thoughts had whisper'd to him, *not go lesse,*
Me thinkes I lie, and drawe—for an encounter.[33]

[*Withdraws to his couch.*]

SCENE VI

MOSCA. BONARIO.

MOSCA. Sir, here conceald, you may here all. But 'pray you
Have patience, Sir;

33. Primero, the predecessor of poker, allowed players to bluff through betting.

One knockes.

the same's your father, knocks:
I am compeld, to leave you.

BONARIO. Do so. Yet,

[*Exit* MOSCA.]

Cannot my thought imagine this a truth.

SCENE VII

MOSCA. CORVINO. CELIA. BONARIO. VOLPONE.

MOSCA. Death on me! you are come to soone, what meant you?
Did not I say, I would send?

CORVINO. Yes, but I feard
You might forget it, and they prevent us.

MOSCA. Prevent? did ere man hast so, for his hornes?
A *Courtier* would not ply it so, for a place.
Well, now there's no helping it, stay here;
Ile presently returne.

CORVINO. Where are you, *Celia?*
You know not, wherefore I have brought you hether?

CELIA. Not well, except you told mee.

CORVINO. Now, I will:
Hearke hether.

MOSCA. [*To* BONARIO.] Sir, your father hath sent word,
It will be halfe an houre, ere he come;
And therefore, if you please to walke, the while,
Into that gallery—at the upper end,
There are some bookes, to entertaine the time:
And Ile take care, no man shall come unto you, Sir.

BONARIO. Yes, I will stay there; I do doubt this fellow.

[*Exit* BONARIO.]

MOSCA. There, he is farre inough; he can heare nothing:
And, for his father, I can keepe him of.

[*Withdraws to* VOLPONE.]

CORVINO. Nay, now, there is no starting back; and therefore,
Resolve upon it: I have so decree'd.
It must be done. Now, would I move't, afore,
Because I would avoyd all shifts, and tricks,
That might deny mee.

CELIA. Sir, let me beseech you
Affect not these strange trialls; if you doubt
My chastity, why lock me up, for ever:
Make me the heyre of darknesse. Let me live,

Where I may please your feares, if not your trust.
CORVINO. Beleeve it, I have no such humor, I.
All that I speake, I meane; yet I am not mad:
Not horne-mad, see you? Go too, shew your selfe
Obedient, and a wife.
CELIA. O heaven!
CORVINO. I say it,
Do so.
CELIA. Was this the traine?° trap
CORVINO. I'have told you reasons;
What the *Phisitians* have set downe; how much,
It may concerne mee; what my ingagements are;
My meanes; and the necessity of those meanes,
For my recovery: wherefore, if you bee
Loyall, and mine, be wonne, respect my venture.
CELIA. Before your honour?
CORVINO. Honour? tut, a breath;
There's no such thing, in nature: a mere terme
Invented to awe fooles. What is my gold
The worse, for touching? clothes, for being look'd on?
Why, this's no more. And old, decrepit wretch,
That ha's no sense, no sinewe; takes his meate
With others fingers; onely knows to gape,
When you do scald his gummes; a voice; a shadow;
And what can this man hurt you?
CELIA. Lord! what spirit
Is this hath entred him?
CORVINO. And, for your fame,
That's such a *Jigge;*° as if I would go tell it, joke
Crie it, on the *Piazza!* who shall know it?
But hee, that cannot speake it; and this fellow,
Whose lippes are i' my pocket: save your selfe,
If you'll proclame't, you may. I know no other,
Should come to knowe it.
CELIA. Are heaven, and *Saints* then nothing?
Will they be blind, or stupide?
CORVINO. How?
CELIA. Good Sir,
Be jealous still, æmulate them; and thinke
What hate they burne with, toward every sinne.
CORVINO. I graunt you; if I thought it were a sinne,
I would not urge you. Should I offer this
To some young *Frenchman,* or hot *Tuscane* bloud,
That had read *Aretine,* conn'd all his *printes,*
Knew every quirke within lusts *Laborinth,*
And were profest *Critique,* in lechery;

And I would looke upon 'him, and applaud him,
This were a sinne: but here, tis contrary,
A pious worke, mere charity, for Physick,
And honest politie, to assure mine owne.
CELIA. O heaven, canst thou suffer such a change?
VOLPONE. Thou art mine honor, *Mosca,* and my pride,
My joy, my tickling, my delight: go, bring 'hem.
MOSCA. Please you drawe neare, Sir.
CORVINO. Come on, what—
You will not be rebellious? By that light—
MOSCA. Sir, Signior *Corvino,* here, is come to see you.
VOLPONE. Oh.
MOSCA. And, hearing of the consultation had,
So lately, for your health, is come to offer,
Or rather, Sir, to prostitute—
CORVINO. Thankes, sweete *Mosca.*
MOSCA. Freely, un-ask'd, or un-intreated—
CORVINO. Well.
MOSCA. (As the true, fervent insurance of his love)
His owne most faire, and proper wife; the beauty,
Onely of price, in *Venice*—
CORVINO. 'Tis well urg'd.
MOSCA. To bee your comfortresse, and to preserve you.
VOLPONE. Alasse, I'am past already. 'Pray you, thanke 'him,
For his good care, and promptnesse. But for that,
'Tis a vain labour, eene to fight, 'gainst heaven;
Applying fire to a stone: (uh, uh, uh, uh.)
Making a dead leafe grow againe. I take
His wishes gently, though; and, you may tell him,
What I'have done for'him: Mary, my state is hopelesse.
Will him, to pray for mee; and t'use his fortune,
With reverence, when he comes to't.
MOSCA. Do you heare, Sir?
Go to him, with your wife.
CORVINO. Heart of my father!
Wilt thou persist thus? Come. I pray thee, come.
Thou seest 'tis nothing: *Celia.* By this hand,
I shall grow violent. Come, do't, I say.
CELIA. Sir, kill mee, rather: I will take downe poyson,
Eate burning coales, do any thing—
CORVINO. Be damn'd.
(Heart) I will drag thee hence, home, by the haire;
Cry thee a strumpet, through the streetes; rip up
Thy mouth, unto thine eares; and slit thy nose,
Like a raw rotchet°—Do not tempt mee, come, a kind of fish
Yeld, I am loth—(Death) I will buy some slave,

Whom I will kill, and binde thee to him, alive;
And, at my windore, hang you forth: devising
Some monstrous crime, which I, in CAPITAL letters,
Will eate into thy flesh, with *Aqua-fortis,*° acid
And burning cor'sives, on this stubborne brest.
Now, by the bloud, thou hast incens'd, Ile doo't.
CELIA. Sir, what you please, you may, I am your *Martyr.*
CORVINO. Bee not thus obstinate, I ha' not deserv'd it:
Thinke, who it is, intreats you. 'Pray thee, sweete;
(Good 'faith) thou shalt have jewells, gownes, attires,
What thou wilt thinke, and aske—Do, but, goe kisse him.
Or touch him, but. For my sake. At my sute.
This once. No? Not? I shall remember this.
Will you disgrace mee, thus? Do'you thirst my'undoing.
MOSCA. Nay, gentle Lady, bee advis'd.
CORVINO. No, no.
She has watch'd her time. God's precious—this is skirvy;
'Tis very skirvie: And you are—
MOSCA. Nay, good, Sir.
CORVINO. An errant *Locust,* by heaven, a *Locust.* Whore,
Crocodile, that hast thy teares prepar'd,
Expecting, how thou'lt bid hem flow.
MOSCA. Nay, 'pray you, Sir,
Shee will consider.
CELIA. Would my life would serve
To satisfie—
CORVINO. (S'death) if she would but speake to him,
And save my reputation, 'twere somewhat;
But, spightfully to affect my utter ruine—
MOSCA. I, now you'have put your fortune, in her hands.
Why i'faith, it is her modesty, I must quiet her;
If you were absent, shee would be more comming;
I know it: and dare undertake for her.
What woman can, before her husband? 'pray you,
Let us departe, and leave her, here.
CORVINO. Sweete *Celia,*
Thou mayst redeeme all, yet; Ile say no more:
If not esteeme your selfe as lost,—Nay, stay there.

[*Exeunt* MOSCA, CORVINO.]

CELIA. O *God,* and his good *Angells!* whether, whether
Is shame fled humane brests? that, with such ease,
Men dare put of your honors, and their owne?
Is that, which ever was a cause of life,
Now plac'd beneath the basest circumstance?
And modesty an exile made, for money?

VOLPONE. I, in *Corvino,* and such earth-fed mindes,

He leapes off from his couch.

That never tasted the true heav'n of love.
Assure thee, *Celia,* he that would sell thee,
Onely for hope of gaine, and that uncertaine,
He would have sold his part of *Paradise*
For ready money, had he met a Cope-man.° dealer
Why art thou maz'd, to see mee thus reviv'd?
Rather, applaud thy beauties miracle;
'Tis thy great worke: that hath, not now alone,
But sundry times, 'rays'd mee, in severall shapes,
And, but this morning, like a *Mountebanke,*
To see thee at thy windore. I, before
I would have left my practise, for thy love,
In varying figures, I would have contended
With the blew *Proteus,* or the *horned Floud.*[34]
Now, art thou welcome.

CELIA. Sir.

VOLPONE. Nay, flie mee not;
Nor, let thy false imagination
That I was bedrid, make thee thinke, I am so:
Thou shalt not find it. I am, now, as fresh,
As hot, as high, and, in as *Joviall* plight,
As when (in that so celebrated *Scene,*
At recitation of our *Comœdie,*
For entertayment of the great *Valoys*[35])
I acted young *Antinous;*[36] and attracted
The eyes, and eares of all the *Ladies,* present,
T'admire each gracefull gesture, note, and footing.

SONG

Come, my Celia, *let us prove,*
While wee can, the sports of love;
Time will not be ours, for ever,
He, at length, our good will sever;
Spend not then his guiftes, in vaine.
Sunnes, that set, may rise againe:
But if, once, we loose this light,
'Tis with us perpetuall night.

34. Proteus, the shape-changing god, is called blue in Virgil's *Georgics,* book IV. "The horned flood" could indicate either Oceanus, whom Jonson describes as "horned" in *The Masque of Blacknesse,* or Achelious, who changes shapes in his fight with Hercules in Ovid's *Metamorphoses,* book IX.

35. King Henry III of France, who visited Venice in 1574.

36. Either the favorite of the Emperor Hadrian who drowned in the river Nile or the suitor of Penelope in the *Odyssey.*

Why should wee deferre our joyes?
Fame, and rumor are but toyes.
Cannot wee delude the eyes
Of a few poore houshold-spies?
Or his easier eares beguile,
Thus remooved, by our wile?
Tis no sinne, loves fruicts to steale;
But the sweete thefts to reveale:
To be taken, to be seene,
These have crimes accounted beene.

CELIA. Some *serene*° blast me, or dire lightning strike — toxic mist
This my offending face.
VOLPONE. Why droopes my *Celia?*
Thou hast, in place of a base husband, found
A worthy lover: use thy fortune well,
With secrecy, and pleasure. See, behold,
What thou are *Queene* of; not in expectation,
As I feede others: but possess'd, and crown'd.
See, here, a rope of pearle; and each, more *orient*
Then that the brave *Ægiptian Queene* carrous'd:
Dissolve, and drinke 'hem. See, a Carbuncle,° — ruby
May put out both the eyes of our St. *Marke;*
A Diamant, would have bought *Lollia Paulina,*[37]
When she came in, like star-light, hid with jewells,
That were the spoyles of *Provinces;* take these,
And weare, and loose 'hem: Yet, remaines an Eare-ring
To purchase them againe, and this whole *State.*
A Gem, but worth a private patrimony,
Is nothing: we will eate such at a meale.
The heads of parrots, tongues of nightingalles,
The braynes of peacocks, and of estriches
Shall be our foode: and, could we get the phœnix,
(Though *Nature* lost her kind) she were our dish.
CELIA. Good Sir, these things might move a minde affected
With such delightes; but I, whose innocence
Is all I can thinke wealthy, or worth th'enjoying,
And, which once lost, I have nought to loose beyond it,
Cannot be taken with these sensuall baytes:
If you have conscience—
VOLPONE. 'Tis the Beggars vertue,
If thou hast wisdome, heare me *Celia.*

37. According to Halio, in Pliny's *Natural History* Pliny writes that Cleopatra dissolved an expensive pearl in vinegar and drank it to impress Marc Antony. Also in Pliny, Lollia Paulina wears jewels worth several provinces at a banquet (IX, LVII).

Thy bathes shall be the juyce of *July*-flowers,
Spirit of roses, and of violets,
The milke of unicornes, and panthers breath
Gather'd in bagges, and mixt with *Cretan* wines.
Our drinke shal be prepared gold, and amber;
Which we will take, untill my roofe whirle round
With the *vertigo:* and my *Dwarfe* shall dance,
My *Eunuch* sing, my *Foole* make up the *antique.*° — performance
Whil'st, we, in changed shapes, act *Ovids* tales,
Thou, like *Europa* now, and I like *Jove,*
Then I like *Mars,* and thou like *Erycine,*° — Venus
So, of the rest, till we have quite run through
And weary'd all the *fables* of the *Gods.*
Then will I have thee, in more moderne formes,
Attired like some sprightly Dame of *France,*
Brave *Tuscan* Lady, or proud *Spanish* Beautie;
Sometimes, unto the *Persian Sophies* Wife;
Or the *grand-Signiors* Mistresse; and, for change,
To one of our most arte-full Curtezans,
Or some quick *Negro,* or cold *Russian;*
And I will meete thee, in as many shapes:
Where we may, so, trans-fuse our wandring soules,
Out at our lippes, and score up summes of pleasure,
That the curious shall not know
How to tell them, as they flow;
And the envious, when they find
What there number is, be pind.° — upset

CELIA. If you have eares, that will be pierc'd—or eyes,
That can be open'd—a heart may be touch'd—
Or any part, that yet sounds *man,* about you—
If you have touch of holy *Saints*—or *Heaven*—
Do mee the grace, to let me scape—if not,
Be bountifull, and kill mee—you do knowe,
I am a creature, hether ill betrayd,
By one, whose shame I would forget it were—
If you will daigne mee neither of these graces,
Yet feede your wrath, Sir, rather then your lust—
(It is a vice, comes nearer manlinesse—)
And punish that unhappy crime of nature,
Which you miscall my beauty—Flea my face,
Or poison it, with oyntments, for seducing
Your bloud to this rebellion—Rub these hands,
With what may cause an eating leprosie,
E'ene to my bones, and marrow—Any thing,
That may dis-favour mee, save in my honour—
And I will kneele to you, 'pray for you, pay downe

A thousand howrely vowes, Sir, for your health—
Report, and thinke you vertuous—
VOLPONE. Thinke me cold,
Frosen, and impotent, and so report me?
That I had *Nestor's hernia,*[38] thou wouldst thinke.
I do degenerate, and abuse my *Nation,*
To play with opportunity, thus long:
I should have done the act, and then have parlee'd.
Yeeld, or Ile force thee.
CELIA. O, just God.
VOLPONE. In vaine—
BONARIO. Forbeare, foule ravisher, libidinous swine,

He leapes out from where Mosca had plac'd him.

Free the forc'd lady, or thou dy'st, Impostor.
But that I am loath to snatch thy punishment
Out of the hand of *Justice,* thou shouldst, yet,
Be made the timely sacrifice of vengeance,
Before this *Altar,* and this drosse, they *Idoll.*
Lady, lets quit the place, it is the den
Of villainy; feare nought, you have a guard:
And he, ere long, shall meete his just reward.

[*Exuent* BONARIO *and* CELIA.]

VOLPONE. Fall on mee, roofe, and bury mee in ruine,
Become my grave, that wert my shelter. O,
I am un-masqu'd, un-spirited, un-done,
Betray'd to beggary, to infamy—

SCENE VIII

MOSCA. VOLPONE.

MOSCA. Where shall I runne, most wretched shame of men,
To beate out my un-luckie braines?
VOLPONE. Here, here.
What? dost thou bleede?
MOSCA. O, that his well-driv'n sword
Has beene so curteous, to have cleft me downe,
Unto the navill; ere I liv'd to see
My life, my hopes, my spirits, my Patron, all
Thus desperately engaged, by my error.
VOLPONE. Woe, on thy fortune.
MOSCA. And my follies, Sir.

38. From Juvenal's sixth satire.

VOLPONE. Th'hast made mee miserable.
MOSCA. And my selfe, Sir.
Who would have thought, he would have harken'd so?
VOLPONE. What shall wee doe?
MOSCA. I know not, if my heart
Could expiate the mischance, Il'd pluck it out.
Will you be pleas'd to hang mee? or cut my throate?
And ile requite you, Sir. Let's die like *Romanes,*
Since wee have liv'd, like *Grecians.*

[*They knock without.*]

VOLPONE. Hearke, who's there?
I heare some footing, Officers, the *Saffi,*
Come to apprehend us! I do feele the brand
Hissing, already, at my fore-head: now,
Mine eares are boring.
MOSCA. To our couch, Sir, you
Make that place good, how ever. Guilty men
Suspect, what they deserve still. Signior *Corbaccio!*

SCENE IX

CORBACCIO. MOSCA. VOLTORE. VOLPONE.

CORBACCIO. Why! how now? *Mosca!*
MOSCA. O, undone, amaz'd, Sir.
Your sonne (I know not, by what accident)
Acquainted with your purpose, to my Patron,
Touching your Will, and making him your heire;
Entred our house with violence, his sword drawne,
Sought for you, call'd you wretch, unnaturall,
Vow'd he would kill you.
CORBACCIO. Mee?
MOSCA. Yes, and my Patron.
CORBACCIO. This act, shall disinherit him, indeed:
Here is the Will.
MOSCA. 'Tis well, Sir.
CORBACCIO. Right, and well.
Be you as carefull, now, for me.
MOSCA. My life, Sir,
Is not more tenderd, I am onely yours.
CORBACCIO. How do's he? will hee die shortly, think'st thou?
MOSCA. I feare
He'll out-last *May.*
CORBACCIO. To day?
MOSCA. No, last-out *May,* Sir.
CORBACCIO. Couldst thou not gi'him a *dram?*

MOSCA. O by no meanes, Sir.
CORBACCIO. Nay, Ile not bid you.
VOLTORE. This's a knave, I see.
MOSCA. How, Signior *Voltore!* did he heare mee?
VOLTORE. *Parasite.*
MOSCA. Who's that? O, Sir, most timely welcome—
VOLTORE. Scarse,
To the discovery of your tricks, I feare.
You are his, onely? and mine, also? are you not?
MOSCA. Who? I, Sir?
VOLTORE. You, Sir. What devise is this
About a Will?
MOSCA. A plot for you, Sir.
VOLTORE. Come,
Put not your foyst's upon me, I shall sent 'hem.
MOSCA. Did you not heare it?
VOLTORE. Yes, I heare, *Corbaccio*
Hath made your Patron, there, his heire.
MOSCA. 'Tis true,
By my devise, drawne to it by my plot,
With hope—
VOLTORE. Your Patron should reciprocate?
And, you have promis'd?
MOSCA. For your good, I did, Sir.
Nay more, I told his sonne, brought, hid him here,
Where he might heare his father passe the deed;
Being perswaded to it, by this thought, Sir,
That the unnaturallnesse, first, of the act,
And then, his fathers oft disclayming in him,
Which I did meane t'helpe on, would sure enrage him
To do some violence upon his parent,
On which the *Law* should take sufficient hold,
And you be stated in a double hope:
Truth be my comfort, and my conscience,
My onely ayme was, to dig you a fortune
Out of these two, old rotten Sepulchers—
VOLTORE. I cry thee mercy *Mosca.*
MOSCA. Worth your patience,
And your great merit, Sir. And, see the change!
VOLTORE. Why? what successe?
MOSCA. Most happlesse! you must helpe, Sir.
Whilst wee expected th'old Raven, in comes
Corvino's wife, sent hether, by her husband—
VOLTORE. What, with a present?
MOSCA. No, Sir, on visitation;
(Ile tell you how, anone) and, staying long,

The youth, hee growes impatient, rushes forth,
Seizeth the lady, wound's mee, makes her sweare
(Or he would murder her, that was his vow)
T'affirme my Patron would have done her rape:
Which how unlike it is, you see! and, hence,
With that pretext, hee's gone t'accuse his father;
Defame my Patron; defeate you—

VOLTORE. Where's her husband?
Let him bee sent for, streight

MOSCA. Sir, Ile go fetch him.

VOLTORE. Bring him, to the *Scrutineo.*° court

MOSCA. Sir, I will.

VOLTORE. This must be stopt.

MOSCA. O, you do nobly, Sir.
Alasse, twas labor'd all, Sir, for your good;
Nor was there want of councell, in the plot:
But fortune can, at any time, ore throw
The projects of a hundred learned *Clearkes,* Sir.

CORBACCIO. What's that?

VOLTORE. Wilt please you, Sir, to go along?

[*Exeunt* VOLTORE, CORBACCIO.]

MOSCA. Patron, go in, and pray for our successe.

VOLPONE. Need makes devotion: Heaven your labor blesse.

[*Exeunt.*]

ACT IV

SCENE I

POLITIQUE. PEREGRINE.

POLITIQUE. I told you, Sir, it was a plot: you see
What observation is. You mention'd mee,
For some instructions: I will tell you, Sir,
(Since we are met, here, in this *height of Venice*)
Some few perticulars, I have set downe,
Onely, for this *meridian,* fit to be knowne
Of your crude Travailer, and they are these.
I will not touch, Sir, at your *phrase,* or clothes,
For they are old.

PEREGRINE. Sir, I have better.

POLITIQUE. Pardon,
I meant, as they are *Theames.*

PEREGRINE. O, Sir, proceed:
Ile slander you no more of wit, good Sir.

POLITIQUE. First, for your *garbe,* it must be grave, and serious,
Very reserv'd, and lock't; not tell a secret,
On any termes, not to your father; scarse
A *fable,* but with caution; make sure choise
Both of your company, and discourse; beware,
You never speake a truth—
PEREGRINE. How?
POLITIQUE. Not to *strangers,*
For those be they, you must converse with, most;
Others I would not know, Sir, but, at distance,
So as I still might be a saver, in 'hem:
You shall have tricks, else, past upon you, hourely.
And then, for your *Religion,* professe none;
But wonder, at the diversity of all;
And, for your part, protest, were there no other
But simply the *Lawes,* o'th' *Land,* you could content you:
Nic: Machiavell, and *Monsieur Bodine,* both,
Were of this mind.[39] Then, you must learne the use,
And handling of your silver forke, at meales;
The mettall of your glasse—These are maine matters,
With your *Italian,* and to know the hower,
When you must eat your *melons,* and your *figges.*
PEREGRINE. Is that a point of *State,* too?
POLITIQUE. Here it is,
For your *Venetian,* if hee see a man
Preposterous, in the least, he has him straight;
Hee has: hee strippes him. Ile acquaint you, Sir.
I now have liv'd here ('Tis some fourteene monthes):
Within the first weeke, of my landing here,
All tooke me for a Citizen of *Venice:*
I knew the formes, so well—
PEREGRINE. And nothing else.
POLITIQUE. I had read *Contarene,*[40] tooke mee a house,
Dealt with my *Jewes,* to furnish it with moveables—
Well, if I could but finde one man—one man,
To mine owne heart, whome I durst trust—I would—
PEREGRINE. What? what, Sir?
POLITIQUE. Make him rich; make him a fortune:
He should not thinke, againe. I would command it.
PEREGINE. As how?
POLITIQUE. With certaine projects, that I have;
Which, I may not discover.

39. Niccolò Machiavelli (1469–1527) was popularly assumed to be irreligious; Jean Bodin (1530–96), a French philosopher, advocated religious toleration.

40. Cardinal Gasparo Contarini (1483–1542), author of *The Commonwealth and Government of Venice,* translated into English in 1599.

PEREGRINE. If I had
But one to wager with, I would lay odds, now,
Hee tells me, instantly.
POLITIQUE. One is, (and that
I care not greatly, who knowes) to serve the *State*
Of *Venice*, with red herrings, for three yeares,
And at a certaine rate, from *Roterdam*,
Where I have correspondence. There's a letter
Sent me from one o'th' *States*,° and to that purpose; States-General in Holland
He cannot write his name, but that's his *marke*.
PEREGRINE. He is a Chaundler?
POLITIQUE. No, a Cheesemonger.
There are some other two, with whome I treate
About the same negotiation;
And—I will undertake it: For, tis thus,
Ile do't with ease, I'have cast it all. Your hoigh° hoy (small ship)
Carries but three men in her, and a boy;
And she shall make me three returnes a yeare:
So, if there come but one of three, I save,
If two, I can defalke.° But, this is now, reduce expenditures
If my mayne project faile.
PEREGRINE. Then, you have others?
POLITIQUE. I should be loath to draw the subtill ayre
Of such a place, without my thousand aymes.
Ile not dissemble, Sir, where ere I come,
I love to be considerative; and, 'tis true,
I have, at my free houres, thought upon
Some certaine *Goods*, unto the *State* of *Venice*,
Which I do call my Cautions: and, Sir, which
I meane (in hope of pension) to propound
To the great *Councell*, then unto the *Forty*,
So to the *Ten*. My meanes are made already—
PEREGRINE. By whome?
POLITIQUE. Sir, one, that though his place b'obscure,
Yet, he can sway, and they will heare him. H'is
A *Commandadore*.
PEREGRINE. What, a common *sergeant?*
POLITIQUE. Sir, such, as they are, put it in their mouthes,
What they should say, sometimes: as well as greater.
I thinke I have my *notes*, to shew you—
PEREGRINE. Good, Sir.
POLITIQUE. But, you shall sweare unto mee, on your gentry,
Not to anticipate—
PEREGRINE. I, Sir?
POLITIQUE. Nor reveale
A circumstance—My paper is not with mee.

PEREGRINE. O, but you can remember, Sir.
POLITIQUE. My first is
Concerning Tinder-boxes. You must know,
No family is, here, without it's boxe;
Now Sir, it being so portable a thing,
Put case, that you, or I were ill affected
Unto the *State:* Sir, with it, in our pockets,
Might I not go into the *Arsenale?*[41]
Or you? come out againe? and none the wiser?
PEREGRINE. Except your selfe, Sir.
POLITIQUE. Go too, then. I, therefore,
Advertise to the *State,* how fit it were,
That none, but such as were knowne *Patriots,*
Sound lovers of their country, should be sufferd
T'enjoy them in their houses: And, even those,
Seald, at some office, and at such a bignesse,
As might not lurke in pockets.
PEREGRINE. Admirable!
POLITIQUE. My next is, how t'enquire, and be resolv'd,
By present demonstration, whether a Ship,
Newly arrived from *Soria,*° or from Syria
Any suspected part of all the *Levant,*
Be guilty of the *Plague:* And, where they use,
To lie out forty, fifty dayes, sometimes,
About the *Lazaretto,* for their triall;
Ile save that charge, and losse unto the merchant,
And, in an houre, cleare the doubt.
PEREGRINE. Indeede, Sir?
POLITIQUE. Or—I will loose my labour.
PEREGRINE. 'My faith, that's much.
POLITIQUE. Nay, Sir, conceive me. 'Twill cost mee, in onions,
Some thirty *Liv'res*°— small French gold coins
PEREGRINE. Which is one pound *sterling.*
POLITIQUE. Beside my water-workes: For this I do, Sir.
First, I bring in your ship, 'twixt two brickwalles;
(But those the *State* shall venter) on the one
I straine me a fayre tarre-paulin; and, in that,
I stick my onions, cut in halfes: the other
Is full of loope holes, out at which, I thrust
The noses of my bellowes; and, those bellowes
I keepe, with water-workes, in a perpetuall motion,
(Which is the easi'st matter of a hundred.)
Now, Sir, your onion, which doth naturally

41. State-owned military and ship-building complex, the core of Venetian power.

Attract th'infection, and your bellowes, blowing
The aire upon him, will shew (instantly)
By his chang'd colour, if there be contagion;
Or else, remaine as faire, as at the first:
Now 'tis knowne, tis nothing.
PEREGRINE. You are right, Sir.
POLITIQUE. I would, I had my note.
PEREGRINE. 'Faith, so would I:
But, you ha' done well, for once, Sir.
POLITIQUE. Were I false,
Or would be made so, I could shew you reasons,
How I could sell this *State,* now, to the *Turke;*
Spight of their *Galleys,* or their—
PEREGRINE. Pray you, Sir *Poll.*
POLITIQUE. I have 'hem not, about mee.
PEREGRINE. That I fear'd.
They'are there, Sir?
POLITIQUE. No. This is my *Diary,*
Wherein I note my actions of the day.
PEREGRINE. 'Pray you, let's see, Sir. What is here? *Notandum,*
A Rat had gnawne my spur-lethers; notwithstanding,
I put on new, and did go forth: but, first,
I threw three beanes over the threshold. *Item,*
I went, and brought two tooth-pickes, whereof one
I burst, immediatly, in a discourse
With a *dutch* Merchant, 'bout *Ragion del stato.*° — reason(s) of state
From him, I went, and payd a *moccinigo,*° — small Venetian coin
For peecing° my silke stockings; by the way, — mending
I cheapend° sprats: and at *St. Markes,* I urin'd. — bargained for
'Faith, these are politique notes!
POLITIQUE. Sir, I do slippe
No action of my life, thus, but I quote it.
PEREGRINE. Beleeve me, it is wise!
POLITIQUE. Nay, Sir, read forth.

SCENE II

LADY (WOULD-BEE). NANO. WOMEN. POLITIQUE. PEREGRINE.

LADY. Where should this loose Knight be, trow? sure, h'is hous'd.
NANO. Why, then he's fast.
LADY. I, he plaies both, with me:
I pray you, stay. This heate will do more harme
To my complexion, then his heart is worth;
(I do not care to hinder, but to take him)
How it comes of!
FIRST WOMAN. My maister's, yonder.

LADY. Where?
FIRST WOMAN. With a yong Gentleman.
LADY. That same's the party,
In mans apparell. 'Pray you, Sir, jog my Knight:
I will be tender to his reputation,
How ever he demerit.
POLITIQUE. My Lady!
PEREGRINE. Where?
POLITIQUE. 'Tis shee indeed, Sir, you shall know her. She is,
Were she not mine, a *Lady* of that merite,
For fashion, and behaviour; and, for beauty
I durst compare—
PEREGRINE. It seemes, you are not jealous,
That dare commend her.
POLITIQUE. Nay, and for discourse—
PEREGRINE. Beeing your wife, shee cannot misse that.
POLITIQUE. Madame,
Here is a Gentleman, 'pray you, use him, fayrely,
He seemes a youth, but he is—
LADY. None?
POLITIQUE. Yes, one
Has put his face, as soone, into the world—
LADY. You meane, as early? but to day?
POLITIQUE. How's this?
LADY. Why in this habit, Sir, you apprehend mee.
Well *Mr. Would-bee,* this doth not become you;
I had thought, the odour, Sir, of your good name,
Had beene more precious to you; that you would not
Have done this dire massacre, on your honour;
One of your gravitie, and ranke, besides:
But, *Knights,* I see, care little for the oath
They make to *Ladies;* chiefely, their owne *Ladies.*
POLITIQUE. Now by my Spurres (the *Symbole* of my *Knighthood*)[—]
PEREGRINE. (Lord! how his brayne is humbled, for an oath.)
POLITIQUE. I reach° you not. understand
LADY. Right, Sir, your *politie*
May beare it through, thus. Sir, a word with you.
I would be loath, to contest, publikely,
With any Gentlewóman; or to seeme
Froward, or violent (as the *Courtier* sayes)
It comes to neare rusticity, in a *Lady,*
Which I would shun, by all meanes: and, how ever
I may deserve from Mr. *Would-bee,* yet,
T'have one fayre Gentlewóman, thus, be made
Th' unkind instrument, to wrong another,
And one she knowes not; I, and to persever:

In my poore judgment, is not warranted
From being a *solecisme* in our sexe,
If not in manners.

PEREGRINE. How is this!

POLITIQUE. Sweete Madame,
Come nearer to your ayme.

LADY. Mary, and will, Sir.
Since you provoke me, with your impudence,
And laughter of your light land-*Syren,* here,
Your *Sporus,*[42] your *Hermaphrodite*—

PEREGRINE. What's here?
Poëtique fury, and *Historique* stormes?

POLITIQUE. The Gentleman, beleeve it, is of worth,
And of our *Nation.*

LADY. I, your *white-Friars nation?*[43]
Come, I blush for you, *Mr. Would-bee,* I;
And am asham'd, you should ha' no more forehead.° shame
Then, thus, to be the Patron, or *Saint George*
To a lewd harlot, a base *fricatrice,*° whore
A female devill, in a male out-side.

POLITIQUE. Nay,
And you be such a one! I must bid, *adieu*
To your delights. The case appeares too liquide.

[*Exit* POLITIQUE.]

LADY. I, you may carry't cleare, with your *State*-face;
But, for your *Carnivale Concupiscence,*
Who here is fled, for liberty of conscience,
From furious persecution of the *Marshall,*
Her will I disc'ple.

PEREGRINE. This is fine, i' faith!
And do you use this, often? is this part
Of your wits exercise, 'gainst you have occasion?
Madam—

LADY. Go to, Sir.

PEREGRINE. Do you heare mee, *Lady?*
Why, if your *Knight* have set you to begge shirts,
Or to invite me home, you might have done it
A nearer way, by farre.

LADY. This cannot worke you,
Out of my snare.

PEREGRINE. Why? am I in it, then?
Indeede, your husband told mee, you were fayre,

42. Castrated lover of Nero, whom he dressed in female clothes and with whom he went through a wedding ceremony.

43. London neighborhood frequented by prostitutes.

And so you are; onely, your nose enclines
(That side, that's next the Sunne) to the *Queene-apple.*
LADY. This cannot be indur'd, by any patience.

SCENE III

MOSCA. LADY (WOULD-BEE). PEREGRINE. (NANO. WOMEN.)

MOSCA. What's the matter, Madame?
LADY. If the *Senate*
Right not my quest, in this; I will protest 'hem,
To all the world, no *Aristocracye.*
MOSCA. What is the injurie, Lady?
LADY. Why, the callet,° strumpet
You told mee of, here I have tâne disguis'd.
MOSCA. Who? this? What meanes your Ladiship? The creature
I mention'd to you, is apprehended, now,
Before the *Senate,* you shall see her—
LADY. Where?
MOSCA. Ile bring you to her. This yong Gentleman
I saw him land, this morning, at the *Port.*
LADY. Is't possible! how has my judgment wander'd?
Sir, I must, blushing, say to you, I have err'd:
And plead your pardon.
PEREGRINE. What! more changes, yet?
LADY. I hope, yo'ha' not the malice to remember
A Gentlewómans passion. If you stay,
In *Venice,* here, please you to use mee, Sir—
MOSCA. Will you goe, Madam?
LADY. 'Pray you, Sir, use mee. In faith,
The more you use mee the more I shall conceive,
You have forgot our quarrell.

[*Exeunt* LADY, MOSCA, NANO, WOMEN.]

PEREGRINE. This is rare!
Sir *Politique Would-bee?* No, Sir *Politique* Baud.
To bring me, thus, acquainted with his wife!
Well, wise Sir *Pol:* since you have practis'd, thus,
Upon my freshman-ship, Ile trie your salt-head,
What proofe it is against a counter-plot.

[*Exit.*]

SCENE IV

VOLTORE. CORBACCIO. CORVINO. MOSCA.

VOLTORE. Well, now you know the carriage of the businesse,
Your constancy is all, that is requir'd
Unto the safety of it.
MOSCA. Is the *lie*
Safely convai'd amongst us? Is that sure?
Knowes every man his burden?
CORVINO. Yes
MOSCA. Then shrinke not.
CORVINO. But, knowes the Advocate the truth?
MOSCA. O, Sir
By no meanes. I devis'd a formall tale,
That salv'd your reputation. But, be valiant, Sir.
CORVINO. I feare no one, but him; that, this his pleading
Should make him stand for a co-heire—
MOSCA. Co-halter,
Hang him: wee will but use his tongue, his noise,
As we do *Croakers,* here.
CORVINO. I, what shall he do?
MOSCA. When we ha' done, you meane?
CORVINO. Yes.
MOSCA. Why, wee'll thinke,
Sell him for *Mummia,*[44] hee's halfe dust already.
[*To* VOLTORE.] Do not you smile, to see this *Buffalo*
How he do's sport it with his head?—[*Aside.*] I should
If all were well, and past. [*To* CORBACCIO.] Sir, onely you
Are hee, that shall enjoy the crop of all,
And these not know for whom they toile.
CORBACCIO. I, peace.
MOSCA. [*To* CORVINO.] But you shall eat it. [*Aside.*] Much. [*To* VOLTORE.]
Worshipful Sir,
Mercury sit upon your thundring tongue,
Or the *French Hercules,*[45] and make your language
As conquering as his club, to beate along,
(As with a tempest) flat, our adversaries;
But, much more, yours, Sir.
VOLTORE. Here they come, ha' done.
MOSCA. I have another witnesse, if you neede, Sir
I can produce.

44. A medicine supposedly derived from embalmed bodies.
45. According to Harp, "Both Mercur, Roman god of thieves, and the French Hercules were patrons of eloquence; the latter is specifically discussed by the classical burlesque-writer, Lucian."

VOLTORE. Who is it?
MOSCA. Sir, I have her.

SCENE V

FOUR AVOCATORI. BONARIO. CELIA. VOLTORE. CORBACCIO. CORVINO. MOSCA. NOTARIO. COMMANDADORI.

FIRST AVOCATORE. The like of this the *Senate* never heard of.
SECOND AVOCATORE. 'Twil come most strange to them, when we report it.
FOURTH AVOCATORE. The Gentlewóman has beene ever held
Of un-reproved name.
THIRD AVOCATORE. So has the youth.
FOURTH AVOCATORE. The more unnaturall part that of his father.
SECOND AVOCATORE. More, of the husband.
FIRST AVOCATORE. I not know to give
His act a name, it is so monstrous!
FOURTH AVOCATORE. But the Impostor, he is a thing created
T'exceed example!
FIRST AVOCATORE. And all after times!
SECOND AVOCATORE. I never heard a true voluptuary
Discrib'd, but him.
THIRD AVOCATORE. Appeare yet those were cited?
NOTARIO. All, but the old Magnifico, *Volpone.*
FIRST AVOCATORE. Why is not hee here?
MOSCA. Please your *Father-hoods,*
Here is his Advocate. Himselfe's, so weake,
So feeble—
FOURTH AVOCATORE. What are you?
BONARIO. His *Parasite,*
His Knave, his Pandar—I beseech the *Court,*
He may be forc'd to come, that your grave eies
May beare strong witnesse of his strange impostures.
VOLTORE. Upon my faith, and credit, with your vertues,
Hee is not able to endure the ayre.
SECOND AVOCATORE. Bring him, howe ever.
THIRD AVOCATORE. We will see him.
FOURTH AVOCATORE. Fetch him.

[*Exeunt* COMANDADORI.]

VOLTORE. Your *Father-hoodes* fit pleasures be obey'd,
But sure, the sight will rather moove your pittyes,
Then indignation; may it please the *Court,*
In the meane time, hee may be heard in me.
I know this *Place* most voide of prejudice,
And therefore crave it, since we have no reason
To feare our truth should hurt our cause.

THIRD AVOCATORE. Speake free.
VOLTORE. Then know, most honor'd *Fathers,* I must now
Discover, to your strangely'abused eares,
The most prodigious, and most frontless piece
Of solid impudence, and trechery,
That ever vicious Nature yet brought forth
To shame the *State* of *Venice.* This lewd woman
(That wants no artificiall lookes, or teares,
To helpe the visor,° she has now put on) — mask
Hath long beene knowne a close° adulteresse, — secret
To that lascivious youth there, not suspected,
I say, but knowne; and taken, in the act,
With him; and by this man, the easie husband,
Pardon'd: whose timelesse° bounty makes him, now, — badly timed
Stand here, the most unhappy, innocent person,
That ever mans owne vertue made accus'd.
For these, not knowing how to owe a gift
Of that deare grace, but with their shame; being plac'd
So'above all powers of their gratitude,
Began to hate the benefit; and, in place
Of thankes, devise t'extirpe the memory
Of such an act: wherein, I pray your *Father-hoods,*
To observe the malice, yea, the rage of creatures
Discover'd in their evils; and what heart
Such take, even, from their crimes. But that, anone,
Will more appeare. This Gentleman, the father,
Hearing of this foule fact, with many others,
That dayly strooke at his too-tender eares,
And, griev'd in nothing more, then that he could not
Preserve himselfe a parent (his sonnes ills
Growing to this strange floud) at last decreed
To dis-inherit him.
FIRST AVOCATORE. These be strange turnes!
SECOND AVOCATORE. The yong mans fame was ever faire, and honest.
VOLTORE. So much more full of danger in his vice,
That can beguile so, under shade of vertue.
But as I said (my honour'd *Sires*) his father
Having this setled purpose, (by what meanes
To him betray'd, we know not) and this day
Appointed for the deed, that Parricide,
(I cannot stile him better) by confederacy
Preparing this his Paramour, to bee there,
Entred *Volpone's* house (who was the man
Your *Father-hoods* must understand, design'd
For the inheritance) there, sought his father;
But, with what purpose sought he him, my *Sires?*

(I tremble to pronounce it, that a sonne
Unto a father, and to such a father
Should have so foule, felonious intent)
It was, to murder him. When, being prevented
By his more happy absence, what then did hee?
Not check his wicked thoughts; no, now new deedes:
(Mischiefe doth ever ende, where it begins)
An act of horror, *Fathers!* he drag'd forth
The aged Gentleman, that had there lien, bed-rid,
Three yeares, and more, out off his innocent couch,
Naked, upon the floore, there left him; wounded
His servant in the face; and, with this strumpet
The stale° to his for'gd practise, who was glad   decoy
To be so active, (I shall here desire
Your *Father-hoods* to note but my collections,
As most remarkable) thought, at once to stop
His fathers ends; discredit his free choise,
In the old Gentleman; redeeme themselves,
By laying infamy, upon this man
To whome, with blushing, they should owe their lives.

FIRST AVOCATORE. What proofes have you of this?

BONARIO. Most honour'd *Fathers,*
I humbly crave, there be no credite given
To this mans mercenary tongue.

SECOND AVOCATORE. Forbeare.

BONARIO. His soule moves in his fee.

THIRD AVOCATORE. O, Sir.

BONARIO. This fellow,
For six *sols*° more, would pleade against his *Maker.*   threepence

FIRST AVOCATORE. You do forget your selfe.

VOLTORE. Nay, nay, grave *Fathers,*
Let him have scope; can any man imagine
That hee will spare'his accuser, that would not
Have spar'd his parent?

FIRST AVOCATORE. Well, produce your proofes.

CELIA. I would, I could forget, I were a creature.

VOLTORE. Signior *Corbaccio.*

FOURTH AVOCATORE. What is hee?

VOLTORE. The father.

SECOND AVOCATORE. Has he had an oath?

NOTARIO. Yes.

CORBACCIO. What must I doe now?

NOTARIO. Your testimony's crav'd.

CORBACCIO. Speake to the knave?
Ile ha' my mouth, first, stopt with earth; my heart
Abhors his knowledge: I disclaime in him.

FIRST AVOCATORE. But, for what cause?
CORBACCIO. The mere portent of nature.
Hee is an utter stranger to my loynes.
BONARIO. Have they made you to this?
CORBACCIO. I will not heare thee,
Monster of men, swine, goate, wolfe, Parricide,
Speake not, thou viper.
BONARIO. Sir, I will sit downe,
And rather wish my innocence should suffer,
Then I resist the authority of a father.
VOLTORE. Signior *Corvino.*
SECOND AVOCATORE. This is strange!
FIRST AVOCATORE. Who's this?
NOTARIO. The husband.
FOURTH AVOCATORE. Is he sworne?
NOTARIO. Hee is.
THIRD AVOCATORE. Speake then.
CORVINO. This woman (please your *Father-hoods*) is a whore,
Of most hot exercise, more then a partrich,
Upon record—
FIRST AVOCATORE. No more.
CORVINO. Neighes, like a gennet.
NOTARIO. Preserve the honour of the *Court.*
CORVINO. I shall,
And modesty of your most reverend eares.
And, yet, I hope that I may say, these eyes
Have seene her glew'd unto that peece of Cedar;
That fine well-timber'd gallant: and that, here,
The letters may be read, through the horne,
That make the story perfect.[46]
MOSCA. Excellent, Sir.
CORVINO. There is no harme in this, now, is there?
MOSCA. None.
CORVINO. Or if I said, I hop'd that she were onward
To her damnation, if there be a hell
Greater then whore, and woman; a good *Christian*
May make the doubt.
THIRD AVOCATORE. His griefe hath made him frantique.
FIRST AVOCATORE. Remove him, hence.

She swownes.

SECOND AVOCATORE. Looke to the woman.

46. Children learned to read with a "horn-book"; a book where the letters of the alphabet were printed and covered with a thin sheet of horn. The signs Corvino indicates here are the horns of a cuckold.

CORVINO. Rare!
Prettily fain'd! againe!
FOURTH AVOCATORE. Stand from about her.
FIRST AVOCATORE. Give her the ayre.
THIRD AVOCATORE. What can you say?
MOSCA. My wound
(May't please your wisdomes) speakes for mee, receiv'd
In ayde of my good Patron, when he mist
His sought for father, when that well-taught dame
Had her *Que*° given her, to crie out a rape. — cue
BONARIO. O, Most lay'd° impudence! *Fathers*— — carefully planned
THIRD AVOCATORE. Sir, be silent,
You had your hearing free, so must they theirs.
SECOND AVOCATORE. I do begin to doubt th'impostures, here.
FOURTH AVOCATORE. This woman, has too many moodes.
VOLTORE. Grave *Fathers*,
She is a creature, of a most profest,
And prostituted lewdnesse.
CORVINO. Most impetuous,
Unsatisfied, grave *Fathers*.
VOLTORE. May her faynings
Not take your wisdomes: but, this day, she bayted° — enticed
A stranger, a grave Knight, with her loose eyes,
And more lascivious kisses. This man saw 'hem
Together, on the water, in a *Gondola*.
MOSCA. Here is the Lady herselfe, that saw hem too,
Without; who, then, had in the open streetes
Pursew'd them, but for saving her Knights honour.
FIRST AVOCATORE. Produce that Lady.
SECOND AVOCATORE. Let her come.
FOURTH AVOCATORE. These things
They strike, with wonder!
THIRD AVOCATORE. I am turn'd a stone!

SCENE VI

MOSCA. LADY (POLITIQUE WOULD BEE). AVOCATORI. etc.

MOSCA. Bee resolute, Madam.
LADY. I, this same is shee.
Out, thou *Chameleon* harlot; now, thine eyes
Vie teares with the *Hyæna*: darst thou looke
Upon my wronged face? I crie your pardons.
I feare, I have (forgettingly) transgrest
Against the dignity of the *Court*—
SECOND AVOCATORE. No, Madame.
LADY. And beene exorbitant—

FOURTH AVOCATORE. You have not, Lady.
SECOND AVOCATORE. These proofes are strong.
LADY. Surely, I had no purpose,
To scandalize your *Honors,* or my sexes.
THIRD AVOCATORE. We doe beleeve it.
LADY. Surely, you may beleeve it.
SECOND AVOCATORE. Madame, wee doe.
LADY. Indeede, you may; my breeding
Is not so course—
FOURTH AVOCATORE. We know it.
LADY. To offend
With pertinacy—
THIRD AVOCATORE. Lady.
LADY. Such a presence;
No, surely.
FIRST AVOCATORE. Wee well thinke it.
LADY. You may thinke it.
FIRST AVOCATORE. Let her o'recome. What witnesses have you,
To make good your report?
BONARIO. Our consciences.
CELIA. And heaven, that never fayles the innocent.
FOURTH AVOCATORE. These are no testimonies.
BONARIO. Not, in your *Courts,*
Where multitude, and clamour, overcomes.
FIRST AVOCATORE. Nay, then you do waxe insolent.

VOLPONE *is brought in, as impotent.*

VOLTORE. Here, here,
The testimony comes, that will convince,
And put to utter dumbnesse, their bold tongues.
See here, grave *Fathers,* here's the Ravisher,
The Rider on mens wives, the great Impostor,
The grand Voluptuary: Do you not thinke,
These limbes should affect *Venery?* or these eyes
Covet a concubine? 'Pray you, marke these hands,
Are they not fit to stroke a Ladies brests?
Perhaps, he doth dissemble.
BONARIO. So he do's.
VOLTORE. Would you ha'him tortur'd.
BONARIO. I would have him prov'd.
VOLTORE. Best trie him, then, with goades, or burning Irons;
Put him to the *strapado;* I have heard,
The Rack hath cur'd the *goute;* faith, give it him,
And helpe him of a malady, bee courteous:
Ile undertake, before these honor'd *Fathers,*
He shall have, yet, as many left diseases,

As she has knowne adulterers, or thou strumpets.
O, my most equall° *Hearers,* if these deedes, just
Acts, of this bold, and most exorbitant straine,
May passe with suffrance; what one Cittizen,
But owes the forfeit of his life, yea fame,
To him that dares traduce him? Which of you
Are safe, my honord *Fathers?* I would aske
(With leave of your grave *Father-hoods*) if their plot
Have any face, or colour like to truth?
Or if, unto the dullest nostrill, here,
It smell not ranke, and most abhorred slaunder?
I crave your care of this good Gentleman,
Whose life is much indanger'd, by their *fable;*
And, as for them, I will conclude with this,
That vicious persons when they'are hot, and flesh'd
In impious acts, their constancy abounds:
Damn'd deedes are done with greatest confidence.

FIRST AVOCATORE. Take 'hem to custody, and sever them.
SECOND AVOCATORE. 'Tis pitty, two such prodigies should live.

[*Exeunt* COMMANDODORI *with* BONARIO *and* CELIA.]

FIRST AVOCATORE. Let the old Gentleman be return'd, with care;
I'am sory, our credulity wrong'd him.

[*Exeunt* COMMANDADORI *with* VOLPONE.]

FOURTH AVOCATORE. These are two creatures!
THIRD AVOCATORE. I have an earthquake in me!
SECOND AVOCATORE. Their shame (even in their cradles) fled their faces.
FOURTH AVOCATARE. You'have done a worthy service to the *State,* Sir,
In their discovery.
FIRST AVOCATORE. You shall heare, ere night,
What punishment the *Court* decrees upon 'hem.
VOLTORE. Wee thanke your *Father-hoods.*

[*Exeunt* AVOCATORI *and* NOTARIO.]

How like you it?
MOSCA. Rare.
I'ld ha' your tongue, Sir, tipt with gold, for this;
I'd ha' you be the heyre to the whole Citty;
The earth I'ld have want men, ere you want living:
They'are bound t'erect your *Statue,* in St. *Markes.*
Signior *Corvino,* I would have you goe,
And shew your selfe, that you have conquer'd.
CORVINO. Yes.
MOSCA. It was much better, that you should professe
Your selfe a cuckold, thus; then that the other
Should have beene prov'd.

CORVINO. Nay, I consider'd that;
Now it is her fault.
MOSCA. Then, it had beene yours.
CORVINO. True, I do doubt this Advocate, Still.
MOSCA. I'faith,
You neede not, I dare ease you of that care.
CORVINO. I trust thee, *Mosca.*
MOSCA. As your owne soule, Sir.

[*Exit* CORVINO.]

CORBACCIO. *Mosca.*
MOSCA. Now for your businesse, Sir.
CORBACCIO. How, ha' you busines?
MOSCA. Yes, yours, Sir.
CORBACCIO. O, none else?
MOSCA. None else, not I.
CORBACCIO. Be carefull, then.
MOSCA. Rest you, with both your eies, Sir.
CORBACCIO. Dispatch it.
MOSCA. Instantly.
CORBACCIO. And looke, that all,
What-ever, bee put in, jewells, plate, moneyes,
House-holdstuffe, bedding, curtines.
MOSCA. Curtine-rings, Sir.
Onely, the Advocates fee must be deducted.
CORBACCIO. Ile pay him, now: you'll be too prodigall.
MOSCA. Sir, I must tender it.
CORBACCIO. Two *Cecchines* is well?
MOSCA. No, sixe, Sir.
CORBACCIO. 'Tis too much.
MOSCA. He talk'd a great while,
You must consider that, Sir.
Well, there's three—
MOSCA. Ile give it him.
CORBACCIO. Doe so, and there's for thee.

[*Exit.*]

MOSCA. Bountifull bones! What horride strange offence
Did he commit 'gainst nature, in his youth,
Worthy this age? You see, Sir, how I worke
Unto your ends; take you not notice.
VOLTORE. No,
Ile leave you.

[*Exit* VOLTORE.]

MOSCA. All, is yours; the Devill, and all,
Good Advocate. Madame, I'le bring you home.

LADY. No, Ile go see your Patron.
MOSCA. That you shall not:
Ile tell you, why. My purpose is, to urge
My Patron to reforme his Will; and, for
The zeale, you'have shew'n to day, whereas before
You were but third, or fourth, you shall be now
Put in the first; which would appeare as beg'd
If you be present. Therefore—
LADY. You shall sway mee.

[*Exeunt.*]

ACT V

SCENE I

VOLPONE. Well, I am here; and all this brunt is past:
I nêre was in dislike with my disguise,
Till this fled moment; here, 'twas good, in private,
But, in your publike, *Cave,*° whil'st I breath. beware (Latin)
'Fore God, my left legge 'gan to have the crampe;
And I apprênded, straight, some power had strooke mee
With a dead *Palsey:* Well, I must be merry,
And shake it off. A many of these feares
Would put mee into some villainous disease,
Should they come thick upon mee: Ile prevent 'hem.
Give mee a boule of lusty wine, to fright
This humor from my heart; (Hum, hum, hum)

He drinkes.

'Tis almost gone, already: I shall conquer.
Any devise, now, of rare, ingenious knavery,
That would possesse mee with a violent laughter,
Would make mee up, againe: So, so, so, so.

Drinkes againe.

This heate is life; 'tis blood, by this time: *Mosca!*

SCENE II

MOSCA. VOLPONE.

MOSCA. How now, Sir? do's the day looke cleare againe?
Are we recoverd? and wrought out of error,
Into our way? to see our path, before us?
Is our trade free, once more?
VOLPONE. Exquisite *Mosca!*
MOSCA. Was it not carry'd learnedly?

VOLPONE. And stoutly.
Good wits are greatest in extremities.
MOSCA. It were a folly, beyond thought, to trust
Any grand act unto a cowardly spirit:
You are not taken with it, enough, mee thinkes?
VOLPONE. O, more, then if I had enjoy'd the wench:
The pleasure of all wóman-kind's not like it.
MOSCA. Why, now you speake, Sir. We must, here be fixt;
Here, we must rest; this is our maister-peice;
We cannot thinke, to goe beyond this.
VOLPONE. True.
Thou'hast playd thy prise, my precious *Mosca.*
MOSCA. Nay Sir,
To gull the *Courts*—
VOLPONE. And, quite divert the torrent,
Upon the innocent.
MOSCA. Yes, and to make
So rare a *Musique,* out of *Discordes*—
VOLPONE. Right.
That, yet, to mee's the strangest! how th'hast borne it!
That these (being so divided 'mongst them selves)
Should not sent some-what, or in mee, or thee,
Or doubt their owne side.
MOSCA. True. They will not see't;
Too much light blinds 'hem, I thinke: each of 'hem
Is so possest, and stuft with his owne hopes,
That any thing, unto the contrary,
Never so true, or never so apparent,
Never so palpable, they will resist it—
VOLPONE. Like a temptation of the Devill.
MOSCA. Right Sir.
Merchants may talke of trade, and your great Signiors
Of land, that yeelds well; but if *Italy*
Have any glebe, more fruictfull, then these fellowes,
I am deceiv'd. Did not your Advocate rare?
VOLPONE. O, *my most honor'd* Fathers, *my grave* Fathers,
Under correction of your Father-hoods,
What face of truth is, here? If these strange deedes
May passe, most honour'd Fathers—I had much a doe
To forbeare laughing.
MOSCA. 'T seem'd to mee, you sweate, Sir.
VOLPONE. In troth, I did, a little.
MOSCA. But confesse, Sir,
Were you not daunted?
VOLPONE. In good faith, I was
A little in a mist; but not dejected:
Never, but still my selfe.

MOSCA. I thinke it, Sir.
Now (so truth helpe mee) I must needes say this, Sir,
And, out of conscience; for your Advocate:
He'has taken paynes, in faith, Sir, and deserv'd,
In my poore judgment, I speake it, under favour,
Not to contrary you, Sir, very richly—
Well—to be cosend.
VOLPONE. 'Troth, and I thinke so too,
By that I heard him, in the latter ende.
MOSCA. O, but before, Sir; had you heard him, first,
Draw it to certaine heads, then aggravate,
Then use his vehement figures—I look'd stil,
When he would shift a shirt; and, doing this
Out of pure love, no hope of gaine—
VOLPONE. 'Tis right.
I cannot answer him, *Mosca,* as I would,
Not yet; but, for thy sake, at thy intreaty,
I will beginne, even now, to vexe 'hem all:
This very instant.
MOSCA. Good, Sir.
VOLPONE. Call the *Dwarfe,*
And *Eunuch,* forth.
MOSCA. *Castrone, Nano.*

[*Enter* NANO *and* CASTRONE.]

NANO. Here.
VOLPONE. Shall we have a *Jig,* now?
MOSCA. What you please, Sir.
VOLPONE. Goe,
Streight, give out, about the streetes, you two,
That I am dead; doe it, with constancy,
Sadly, do you heare? impute it to the griefe
Of this late slander.

[*Exeunt* NANO *and* CASTRONE.]

MOSCA. What doe you meane, Sir?
VOLPONE. O,
I shall have, instantly, my *Vulture, Crow,*
Raven, come flying hither (on the newes)
To peck for carrion, my shee-*Wolfe,* and all,
Greedy, and full of expectation—
MOSCA. And then, to have it ravish'd from their mouths?
VOLPONE. 'Tis true, I will ha' thee put on a gowne,
And take upon thee, as thou wert mine heire;
Shew 'hem a Will. Open that chest, and reach
Forth one of those, that has the *Blankes.* Ile straight
Put in thy name.

MOSCA. It will be rare, Sir.
VOLPONE. I,
When they e'ene gape, and finde themselves deluded—
MOSCA. Yes.
VOLPONE. And, thou use them skirvily. Dispatch,
Get on thy gowne.
MOSCA. But, what, Sir, if they aske
After the body?
VOLPONE. Say, it was corrupted.
MOSCA. Ile say, it stunke, Sir; and was faine t'have it
Coffin'd up instantly, and sent away.
VOLPONE. Any thing, what thou wilt. Hold, heres my Will.
Get thee a cap, a count'booke, pen and inke,
Papers afore thee; sit, as thou wert taking
An inventory of parcells: Ile get up,
Behind the curtine, on a stoole, and hearken;
Sometime, peepe over; see, how they do looke;
With what degrees, their bloud doth leave their faces;
O, 'twill afford me a rare meale of laughter.
MOSCA. Your Advocate will turne starke dull, upon it.
VOLPONE. It will take of his *Oratories* edge.
MOSCA. But your *Clarissimo,* old round-backe, hee
Will crumpe° you, like a hog-louse, with the touch. curl up
VOLPONE. And what *Corvino?*
MOSCA. O, Sir, looke for him,
To morrow morning, with a rope, and a dagger,
To visite all the streetes; he must runne madd.
My Lady too, that came into the *Court,*
To beare false witnesse, for your Worship.
VOLPONE. Yes,
And kist mee 'fore the *Fathers;* when my face
Flow'd all with oyles.
MOSCA. And sweate—Sir. Why, your gold
Is such another med'cine, it dries up
All those offensive savors! It transformes
The most deformed, and restores 'hem lovely,
As't were the strange *poëticall Girdle.*[47] *JOVE*
Could not invent, t'himselfe, a shroud more subtle,
To passe *Acrisius* guardes.[48] It is the thing
Makes all the world her grace, her youth, her beauty.
VOLPONE. I thinke, she loves me.
MOSCA. Who? the Lady, Sir?
Shee's jealous of you.

47. Aphrodite possessed a girdle that inspired passion: cf. *Iliad,* book 14.

48. Father of Danae, who locked his daughter up in a tower, and whom Zeus visited in the form of a shower of gold.

VOLPONE. Do'st thou say so?
MOSCA. Hearke,
There's some, already.
VOLPONE. Looke.
MOSCA. It is the *Vulture:*
He has the quickest sent.
VOLPONE. Ile to my place,
Thou, to thy posture.
MOSCA. I am set.
VOLPONE. But, *Mosca,*
Play the Artificer now, torture 'hem, rarely.

SCENE III

VOLTORE. MOSCA. CORBACCIO.
CORVINO. LADY [WOULD-BEE].
VOLPONE.

VOLTORE. How now, my *Mosca?*
MOSCA. *Turkie Carpets, nine—*
VOLTORE. Taking an inventory? that is well.
MOSCA. *Two Sutes of bedding, Tissew—*
VOLTORE. Where's the *Will?*
Let me read that, the while.
CORBACCIO. So, set me downe:
And, get you home.
VOLTORE. Is he come, now, to trouble us?
MOSCA. *Of Cloth of gold, two more—*
CORBACCIO. Is it done, *Mosca?*
MOSCA. *Of severall vellets,*° *eight—* velvets
VOLTORE. I like his care.
CORBACCIO. Dost thou not heare?
CORVINO. Ha, is th'houre come, *Mosca?*
VOLPONE. I, now, they muster.

VOLPONE *peepes from behinde a traverse.*

CORVINO. What do's the Advocate, here?
Or this *Corbaccio?*
CORBACCIO. What doe these here?
LADY. *Mosca?*
Is his thred spunne?
MOSCA. *Eight Chests of Linnen—*
VOLPONE. O,
My fine *Dame would-bee,* too!
CORVINO. *Mosca,* the Will,
That I may shew it these, and rid 'hem hence.

MOSCA. *Six Chests of Diaper, foure of Damaske*[49]—There.
CORBACCIO. Is that the Will?
MOSCA. *Downe-Beds, and Boulsters*—
VOLPONE. Rare!
Bee busie still. Now, they begin to flutter:
They never thinke of me. Looke, see, see, see!
How their swift eies runne over the long *deed*,
Unto the *Name*, and to the *Legacies*,
What is bequeath'd them, there—
MOSCA. *Ten Sutes of Hangings*°— tapestries
VOLPONE. I i' their garters, *Mosca*. Now, their hopes
Are at the gaspe.
VOLTORE. *Mosca* the heire?
CORBACCIO. What's that?
VOLPONE. My Advocate is dumbe. Looke to my Merchant,
Hee has heard of some strange storme, a ship is lost:
He faintes. My Lady will swoune. Old Glazen-eies,
Hé hath not reach'd his dispaire, yet.
CORBACCIO. All these
Are out of hope, I'am sure the man.
CORVINO. But, *Mosca*—
MOSCA. *Two Cabinets.*
CORVINO. Is this in earnest?
MOSCA. *One*
Of Ebony—
CORVINO. Or, do you but delude mee?
MOSCA. *The other, Mother of Pearle*—I am very busie.
Good faith, it is a fortune throwne upon me—
Item, one Salt of Agat—not my seeking.
LADY. Do you heare, Sir?
MOSCA. *A perfum'd Boxe*—'pray you forbeare,
You see I am troubled—*made of an Onyx*—
LADY. How!
MOSCA. To morrow, or next day, I shall be at leasure,
To talke with you all.
CORVINO. Is this my large hopes issue?
LADY. Sir, I must have a fayrer answere.
MOSCA. Madame?
Mary, and shall: 'pray you, fairely quit my house.
Nay, raise no tempest with your lookes; but hearke you:
Remember, what your Ladyship offerd mee,
To put you in, an heire; go to, thinke on't.
And what you said, eene your best *Madames* did
For maintaynance, and why not you? Inough.

49. Expensive fabrics with patterns in the weave.

Go home, and use the poore Sir *Poll.* your Knight, well;
For feare I tell some riddles: Go, be melancholique.

[*Exit* Lady.]

VOLPONE. O, my fine Devill!
CORVINO. *Mosca,* 'pray you a word.
MOSCA. Lord! will not you take your dispatch hence, yet?
Me thinkes (of all) you should have beene th'example.
Why should you stay, here? with what thought? what promise?
Heare you; do you not know, I know you an asse?
And, that you would, most faine, have beene a wittol,° — willing cuckold
If fortune would have let you? that you are
A declar'd cuckold, on good termes? This Pearle,
You'll say, was yours? right. This Diamant?
Ile not deny't, but thanke you. Much here, else?
It may be so. Why, thinke that these good workes
May helpe to hide your bad: Ile not betray you,
Although you be but extraordinary,
And have it onely in title, it sufficeth.
Go home; be melancholique, too: or mad.

[*Exit* CORVINO.]

VOLPONE. Rare *Mosca!* how his villainy becomes him.
VOLTORE. Certaine, he doth delude all these, for mee.
CORBACCIO. *Mosca* the heire?
VOLPONE. O, his fowre eies have found it.
CORBACCIO. I'am cosen'd, cheated, by a *Parasite*-slave;
Harlot, t'hast gul'd mee.
MOSCA. Yes, Sir. Stop your mouth,
Or I shall draw the only tooth, is left.
Are not you he, that filthy covetous wretch,
With the three legges, that, here, in hopes of prey,
Have, any time this three yeare, snuft about,
With your most grov'ling nose; and would have hir'd
Mee, to the pois'ning of my Patron? Sir?
Are not you he, that have, to day, in *Court,*
Profess'd the dis-inheriting of your sonne?
Perjur'd your selfe? goe home, and die, and stinke;
If you but croake a sillable, all comes out:
Away, and call your porters, go, go stinke.

[*Exit* CORBACCIO.]

VOLPONE. Excellent varlet!
VOLTORE. Now, my faithfull *Mosca,*
I finde thy constancie.
MOSCA. Sir?
VOLTORE. Sincere.

MOSCA. *A Table*
Of Porphiry—I mar'le, you'll be thus troublesome.
VOLTORE. Nay, leave off now, they are gone.
MOSCA. Why? who are you?
What? who did send for you? O 'crie you mercy,
Reverend Sir: good faith, I am griev'd for you,
That any chance of mine should thus defeate
Your (I must needs say) most deserving travailes:
But, I protest, Sir, it was cast upon me,
And I could, almost, wish to be without it,
But, that the will o'th' dead must be observ'd.
Mary, my joy is, that you need it not,
You have a gift, Sir, (thanke your education)
Will never let you want, while there are men,
And malice, to breed causes. Would I had
But halfe the like, for all my fortune, Sir.
If I have any sutes (as I do hope,
Things being so easie, and direct, I shall not)
I will make bold with your obstreporous aide,
(Conceive me) for your fee, Sir. In meane time,
You, that have so much law, I know ha'the conscience,
Not to be covetous of what is mine.
Good Sir, I thanke you, for my plate; 'twill helpe
To set up a yong man. Good faith, you looke
As you were costive;° best goe home, and purge, Sir. constipated

[*Exit* VOLTORE.]

VOLPONE. Bid him, eate lettuce well: my witty *mischiefe,*
Let me embrace thee. O, that I could now
Transforme thee to a *Venus*—*Mosca,* goe
Streight, take my habite of *Clarissimo,*
And walke the streets; bee seene, torment 'hem more:
Wee must pursew, as well as plot. Who would
Have lost this feast?
MOSCA. I doubt, it will loose them.
VOLPONE. O, my recovery shall recover all.
That I could now but thinke on some disguise,
To meete 'hem in: and aske 'hem questions.
How I would vexe 'hem still, at every turne?
MOSCA. Sir, I can fit you.
VOLPONE. Canst thou?
MOSCA. Yes. I knowe
One o'the *Commandadori,* Sir, so like you,
Him will I streight make drunke, and bring you his habite.
VOLPONE. A rare disguise, and answering thy braine!
O, I will be a sharpe disease unto 'hem.

MOSCA. Sir, you must looke for curses—
VOLPONE. 'Till they burst;
The FOXE fares ever best, when he is curst.

[*Exeunt.*]

SCENE IV

PEREGRINE. THREE MERCATORI.

PEREGRINE. Am I inough disguis'd?
FIRST MERCATORE. I warrant you.
PEREGRINE. All my ambition is to fright him, onely.
SECOND MERCATORE. If you could ship him away, twere excellent.
THIRD MERCATORE. To *Zant,*° or to *Alepo?* Zakynthos
PEREGRINE. Yes, and have's
Adventures put i'th' *Booke of voyages,*[50]
And his guld story registred, for truth?
Well, Gentlemen, when I am in, a while,
And that you thinke us warme in our discourse,
Know your approaches.
FIRST MERCATORE. Trust it, to our care.

[*Exeunt* MERCATORI, *enter* WOMAN].

PEREGRINE. 'Save you faire Lady. Is Sir *Poll.* within?
WOMAN. I do not know, Sir.
PEREGRINE. 'Pray you, say unto him,
Here is a merchant, upon earnest businesse,
Desires to speake with him.
WOMAN. I will see, Sir.
PEREGRINE. 'Pray you.

[*Exit* WOMAN.]

I see the Family° is all female, here. household

[*Re-enter* WOMAN.]

WOMAN. Hee sai's, Sir, hee has waighty affaires of *State,*
That now require him whole;° some other time, entirely
You may possesse him.
PEREGRINE. Pray you, say againe,
If those require him whole; these will exact° him, require
Whereof I bring him tidings. [*Exit* WOMAN.] What might bee
His grave affaire of *State,* now? how, to make

50. Richard Hakluyt published books about the discoveries of English navigators in 1582, 1598, and 1600.

Bolognian sauseges, here, in *Venice,* sparing
One o'th' *Ingredients.*

[*Re-enter* WOMAN.]

WOMAN. Sir, he sai's, he knowes
By your word *tidings,* that you are no *States-man,*
And therefore, wills you stay.
PEREGRINE. Sweet, 'pray you returne him,
I have not read so many *Proclamations,*
And studied them, for words, as hee has done—

[*Enter* POLITIQUE.]

But, here he deignes to come.

[*Exit* WOMAN.]

POLITIQUE. Sir! I must crave
Your courteous pardon. There hath chanc'd (to day)
Unkinde disaster, 'twixt my Lady, and mee:
And I was penning my *Apologie*
To give her satisfaction, as you came, now.
PEREGRINE. Sir, I am greiv'd, I bring you worse disaster;
The Gentlemen, you met at th'*Port* to day,
That told you, he was newly arriv'd—
POLITIQUE. I, was
A fugitive-*Punke?*° whore
PEREGRINE. No, Sir, a Spie, set on you,
And, hee has made relation to the *Senate,*
That you profest to him, to have a plot,
To sell the *State* of *Venice,* to the *Turke.*
POLITIQUE. O' mee.
PEREGRINE. For which, warrants are sign'd by this time,
To apprehend you, and to search your study,
For papers—
POLITIQUE. Alasse, Sir, I have none, but *notes,*
Drawne out of *Play-bookes*—
PEREGRINE. All the better, Sir.
POLITIQUE. And some *Essayes.* What shall I doe?
PEREGRINE. Sir. Best
Convay your selfe into a Sugar-Chest;
Or, if you could lie round, a Frayle° were rare: fruit basket
And I could send you, aboard.
POLITIQUE. Sir, I but talk'd so,
For discourse sake, merely.

They knocke within.

PEREGRINE. Hearke, they are there.
POLITIQUE. I am a wretch, a wretch.

PEREGRINE. What, will you doe Sir?
Ha you nere a Curren-Butt to leape into?
They'll put you to the Rack, you must be sodaine.
POLITIQUE. Sir, I have an ingine°— device

[*They call without.*]

THIRD MERCATORE. Sir *Politique Would-be/*
SECOND MERCATORE. Where is hee?
POLITIQUE. That I have thought upon, before time.
PEREGRINE. What is it?
POLITIQUE. I shall nêre indure the torture.
Mary, it is, Sir, of a *Tortoyse*-shell,
Apted, for these extremities: 'Pray you Sir, helpe mee.
Here, I'have a place, Sir, to put back my leggs,
Please you to lay it on, Sir, with this cap,
And my black gloves, Ile lie, Sir, like a *Tortoyse,*
Till they are gone.
PEREGRINE. And, call you this an ingine?
POLITIQUE. Mine owne devise—Good Sir, bid my wives women
To burne my papers.

[*Exit* PEREGRINE.]
They rush in.

FIRST MERCATORE. Where's hee hid?
THIRD MERCATORE. We must,
And will, sure, finde him.
SECOND MERCATORE. Which is his study.

[*Re-enter* PEREGRINE.]

FIRST MERCATORE. What
Are you, Sir?
PEREGRINE. I'm a merchant, that came here
To looke upon this *Tortoyse.*
THIRD MERCATORE. Howe?
FIRST MERCATORE. *St. Marke!*
What Beast is this?
PEREGRINE. It is a fish.
SECOND MERCATORE. Come out, here.
PEREGRINE. Nay, you may strike him, Sir, and tread upon him.
Hee'll beare a cart.
FIRST MERCATORE. What, to runne over him.
PEREGRINE. Yes.
THIRD MERCATORE. Letts jumpe, upon him.
SECOND MERCATORE. Can hee not goe?
PEREGRINE. He creepes, Sir.
FIRST MERCATORE. Letts see him creepe.
PEREGRINE. No, good Sir, you will hurt him.

SECOND MERCATORE. (Heart) Ile see him creepe; or prick his gutts.
THIRD MERCATORE. Come out here.
PEREGRINE. 'Pray you, Sir, (creepe a little.)
FIRST MERCATORE. Forth.
SECOND MERCATORE. Yet furder.
PEREGRINE. Good Sir, (creepe).
SECOND MERCATORE. Wee'll see his leggs.

They pull of the shell and discover him.

THIRD MERCATORE. Gods'so hee has garters!
FIRST MERCATORE. I, and gloves!
SECOND MERCATORE. Is this
Your fearefull *Tortoyse?*
PEREGRINE. Now, Sir *Poll.* Wee are even;
For your next project, I shall bee prepar'd:
I am sory, for the funerall of your notes, Sir.
FIRST MERCATORE. 'Twere a rare motion,° to be seene in *Fleete-street!* — puppet-show
SECOND MERCATORE. I, i' the *Terme.*[51]
FIRST MERCATORE. Or *Smithfield,* in the *Faire.*
THIRD MERCATORE. Me thinkes, tis but a melancholique sight!
PEREGRINE. Farewell, most *politique Tortoyse.*

[*Exeunt* PEREGRINE *and* MERCATORI, *re-enter* WOMAN.]

POLITIQUE. Where's my Lady?
Knowes she of this?
WOMAN. I knowe not, Sir.
POLITIQUE. Enquire.

[*Exit* WOMAN.]

O, I shall be the *fable* of all the feasts;
The freight of the *Gazetti;*° ship-boies tale; — newsletters
And, which is worse, even talke for Ordinaries.° — taverns

[*Re-enter* WOMAN.]

WOMAN. My Lady's come most melancholique, home,
And say's, Sir, she will straight to sea, for *Physick.*
POLITIQUE. And I, to shunne, this *place,* and *clime* for ever;
Creeping, with house, on back: and thinke it well,
To shrink my poore head, in my *politique* shell.

[*Exeunt.*]

51. The period when the law courts were in session.

SCENE V

VOLPONE. MOSCA.

The first, in the habit of a Commandadore: the other, of a Clarissimo.

VOLPONE. Am I then like him?
MOSCA. O, Sir, you are hee:
No man can sever you.
VOLPONE. Good.
MOSCA. But, what am I?
VOLPONE. 'Fore heav'n, a brave *Clarissimo,* thou becom'st it!
Pitty, thou wert not borne one.
MOSCA. If I hold
My made one, 'twill be well.
VOLPONE. Ile goe, and see
What newes, first, at the *Court.*
MOSCA. Do so.

[*Exit* VOLPONE.]

My FOXE
Is out on his hole, and, ere he shall re-enter,
Ile make him languish, in his borrow'd case,
Except he come to composition, with mee:
Androgyno, Castrone, Nano.

[*Enter* ANDROGYNO, CASTRONE, NANO.]

ALL. Here.
MOSCA. Go, recreate your selves, abroad; go, sport:

[*Exeunt.*]

So, now I have the keies, and am possest.
Since hee will, needes, be dead, afore his time,
Ile burie him, or gaine by him; I'am his heyre:
And so will keepe me, till he share at least.
To cosen him of all, were but a cheat
Well plac'd; no man would construe it a sinne:
Let his sport pay for't, this is call'd the FOXE-trap.

[*Exit.*]

SCENE VI

CORBACCIO. CORVINO. VOLPONE.

CORBACCIO. They say, the *Court* is set.
CORVINO. We must mainteine
Our first tale good, for both our reputations.
CORBACCIO. Why? mine's no tale: my sonne would, there, have kild me.

CORVINO. That's true, I had forgot. Mine is, I am sure.
But, for your Will, Sir.
CORBACCIO. I, Ile come upon him,
For that, hereafter; now his Patron's dead.
VOLPONE. Signior *Corvino!* and *Corbaccio!* Sir,
Much joy unto you.
CORVINO. Of what?
VOLPONE. The sodaine good,
Dropt downe upon you—
CORBACCIO. Where?
VOLPONE. (And, none knowes how)
From old *Volpone,* Sir.
CORBACCIO. Out, errant Knave.
VOLPONE. Let not your too much wealth, Sir, make you furious.
CORBACCIO. Away, thou varlet.
VOLPONE. Why Sir?
CORBACCIO. Do'st thou mock me?
VOLPONE. You mock the world, Sir, did you not change Wills?
CORBACCIO. Out, harlot.
VOLPONE. O! belike you are the man,
Signior *Corvino?* 'faith, you carry it well;
You grow not mad withall: I love your spirit.
You are not over-leavend, with your fortune.
You should ha' some would swell, now, like a wine-fat,
With such an *Autumne*°—Did he gi' you all, Sir? harvest
CORVINO. Avoid, you Rascall.
VOLPONE. 'Troth, your wife has shew'ne
Her selfe a very woman; but, you are well,
You need not care, you have a good estate,
To beare it out Sir: better, by this chance.
Except *Corbaccio* have a share?
CORVINO. Hence varlet.
VOLPONE. You will not be a'knowne, Sir: why, 'tis wise,
Thus doe all Gam'sters, at all games, dissemble;
No man will seeme to winne: here, comes my *Vulture,*

[*Exeunt* CORBACCIO, CORVINO.]

Heaving his beake up i' the ayre, and snuffing.

SCENE VII

VOLTORE. VOLPONE.

VOLTORE. Out-stript thus, by a *Parasite?* a slave?
Would run on errands? and make legs, for crums?
Well, what Ile do—
VOLPONE. The *Court* stayes for your worship.

I eêne rejoyce, Sir, at your worships happinesse,
And, that it fell into so learned hands,
That understands the fingering.
VOLTORE. What do you meane?
VOLPONE. I meane to be a sutor to your worship,
For the small tenement, out of reparations;
That, at the end of your long row of houses,
By the *Piscaria:*° It was, in *Volpone's* time, fish market
Your predecessor, êre he grew diseas'd,
A handsome, pretty, custom'd, baudy-house,
As any was in *Venice* (none disprais'd)
But fell with him. His body, and that house
Decay'd, together.
VOLTORE. Come, Sir, leave your prating.
VOLPONE. Why, if your worship give me but your hand,
That I may ha'the refusall; I have done.
'Tis a meere toy, to you, Sir; candle rents:
As your learn'd worship knowes—
VOLTORE. What doe I know?
VOLPONE. Mary, no end of your wealth, Sir, God decrease it.
VOLTORE. Mistaking knave! what, mockst thou my mis-fortune.

[*Exit.*]

VOLPONE. His blessing on your heart, Sir, would 'twere more.
Now, to my first, againe; at the next corner.

SCENE VIII

CORBACCIO. CORVINO. [MOSCA *passant.*]
VOLPONE.

CORBACCIO. See, in our habite! see the impudent varlet!
CORVINO. That I could shoote mine eyes at him, like gun-stones.
VOLPONE. But, is this true, Sir, of the *Parasite?*
CORBACCIO. Againe, t'afflict us? Monster!
VOLPONE. In good faith, Sir,
I'am hartily greev'd, a beard of your grave length
Should be so over-reach'd. I never brook'd
That *Parasites* hayre, mee thought his nose should cosen,
There still was somewhat, in his looke, did promise
The bane of a *Clarissimo.*
CORBACCIO. Knave—
VOLPONE. Mee thinkes,
Yet you, that are so traded i' the world,
A witty merchant, the fine bird, *Corvino,*
That have such morall *Emblemes* on your name,
Should not have sung your shame; and dropt your cheese:
To let the FOXE laugh at your emptinesse.

CORVINO. Sirrah, you thinke, the priviledge of the place,
And your red saucy cap, that seemes (to mee)
Nayl'd to your jolt-head, with those two *Cecchines,*
Can warrant your abuses; come you, hither:
You shall perceive, Sir, I dare beate you. Approch.
VOLPONE. No hast, Sir, I do know your valure, well:
Since you durst publish what you are, Sir.
CORVINO. Tarry,
I'ld speake, with you.
VOLPONE. Sir, Sir, another time—
CORVINO. Nay, now.
VOLPONE. O God, Sir! I were a wise man,
Would stand the fury of a distracted cuckold.

MOSCA *walkes by 'hem.*

CORBACCIO. What! come againe?
VOLPONE. Upon 'hem, *Mosca;* save mee.
CORBACCIO. The ayre's infected, where he breathes.
CORVINO. Lets flye him.

[*Exeunt* CORBACCIO. CORVINO.]

VOLPONE. Excellent *Basiliske!* Turne upon the *Vulture.*

SCENE IX

VOLTORE. MOSCA. VOLPONE.

VOLTORE. Well, flesh-flie, it is *Sommer* with you, now;
Your *Winter* will come on.
MOSCA. Good Advocate,
'Pray thee, not rayle, nor threaten out of place, thus;
Thoult make a *solœcisme* (as Madam sayes).
Get you a biggen,[52] more: your brayne breakes loose.
VOLTORE. Well, Sir.
VOLPONE. Would you ha' me beate the insolent slave?
Throwe durt, uppon his first good cloathes?
VOLTORE. This same
Is, doubtlesse, some *Familiar!*
VOLPONE. Sir, the *Court,*
In troth, stayes for you. I am madd, a Mule,
That never read *Justinian,* should get up,
And ride an Advocate. Had you no quirk,
To avoide gullage, Sir, by such a creature?
I hope, you do but jest; he has not done't:
This's but confederacy, to blinde the rest.
You are the heyre?

52. Cap worn by lawyers.

VOLTORE. A strange, officious,
Trouble-some knave! thou dost torment mee.
VOLPONE. I know—
It cannot bee, Sir, that you should be cosen'd;
'Tis not within the wit of man, to do it:
You are so wise, so prudent—And, 'tis fit,
That wealth, and wisdome still, should go together—

[*Exeunt.*]

SCENE X

FOUR AVOCATORI. NOTARIO. COMMANDADORI.
BONARIO. CELIA. CORBACCIO. CORVINO.
VOLTORE. VOLPONE.

FIRST AVOCATORE. Are all the parties, here?
NOTARIO. All, but the Advocate.
SECOND AVOCATORE. And, here he comes.
FIRST AVOCATORE. Then bring 'hem
forth, to sentence.
VOLTORE. O, my most honourd *Fathers*, let your mercy
Once winne upon your justice, to forgive—
I am distracted—
VOLPONE. (What will he do, now?)
VOLTORE. O,
I know not which t'addresse my selfe to, first,
Whether your *Father-hoods*, or these innocents—
CORVINO. (Will hee betray himselfe?)
VOLTORE. Whome, equally,
I have abus'd, out of most covetous endes—
CORVINO. (The man is mad!
CORBACCIO. What's that?
CORVINO. Hee is possest.)
VOLTORE. For which, now strooke in conscience, here I prostrate
My selfe, at your offended feete, for pardon.
FIRST, SECOND AVOCATORE. Arise.
CELIA. O heav'n, how just thou art!
VOLPONE. I'am caught.
I' myne owne noose—
CORVINO. Be constant, Sir, nought now
Can helpe, but impudence.
FIRST AVOCATORE. Speake forward.
COMMANDADORE. Silence.
VOLTORE. It is not passion in mee. reverend *Fathers*,
But onely conscience, conscience, my good *Sires*,
That makes me, now, tell trueth. That *Parasite*,
That Knave hath beene the instrument of all—

SECOND AVOCATORE. Where is the Knave? fetch him.
VOLPONE. I go

[*Exit.*]

CORVINO. Grave *Fathers,*
This man's distracted, he confest it, now;
For, hoping to bee old *Volpone's* heyre,
Who now is dead—
THIRD AVOCATORE. How?
SECOND AVOCATORE. Is *Volpone* dead?
CORVINO. Dead since, grave *Fathers*—
BONARIO. O, sure vengeance!
FIRST AVOCATORE. Stay,—
Then, he was no deceiver?
VOLTORE. O, no, none:
The *Parasite,* grave *Fathers*—
CORVINO. He do's speake
Out of mere envie, 'cause the servant's made
The thing, he gap't for; please your *Father-hoods,*
This is the truth: though, Ile not justifie
The other, but he may bee somewhat faulty.
VOLTORE. I, to your hopes, as well as mine, *Corvino:*
But Ile use modesty. 'Pleaseth your wisedomes
To viewe these certaine notes, and but conferre them;
As I hope favour, they shall speake cleare truth.
CORVINO. The Devill ha's entred him.
BONARIO. Or bides in you.
FOURTH AVOCATORE. We have done ill, by a publike Officer,
To send for him, if he be heire.
SECOND AVOCATORE. For whome?
FOURTH AVOCATORE. Him, that they call the *Parasite*
THIRD AVOCATORE. 'Tis true;
He is a man, of great estate, now left.
FOURTH AVOCATORE. Goe you, and learne his name; and say, the *Court*
Intreates his presence, here: but, to the clearing
Of some few doubts.

[*Exit* NOTARIO.]

SECOND AVOCATORE. The same's a *labyrinth!*
FIRST AVOCATORE. Stand you unto your first report?
CORVINO. My state,
My life, my fame—
BONARIO. (Where is't)
CORVINO. Are at the stake.
FIRST AVOCATORE. Is yours so too?
CORBACCIO. The Advocate's a knave:
And has a forked tongue—

SECOND AVOCATORE. Speake to the point.
CORBACCIO. So is the *Parasite,* too.
FIRST AVOCATORE. This is confusion.
VOLTORE. I do beseech your *Father-hoods,* read but those.
CORVINO. And credit nothing, the false spirit hath writ:
It cannot be (my *Sires*) but he is possest.

[*The scene closes.*]

SCENE XI

VOLPONE.

VOLPONE. To make a snare, for mine owne neck! and run
My head into it, wilfully! with laughter!
When I had newly scap't, was free, and cleare!
Out of mere wantonesse! ô, the dull Devill
Was in this braine of mine, when I devis'd it;
And *Mosca* gave it second: Hé must now
Helpe to seare up this veyne, or we bleed dead.

[*Enter* NANO, ANDROGYNO, CASTRONE.]

How now! who let you loose? whether go you, now?
What? to buy Ginger-bread? or to drowne Kitlings?
NANO. Sir, Maister *Mosca* call'd us out of dores,
And bid us all go play, and tooke the keyes.
ANDROGYNO. Yes.
VOLPONE. Did Maister *Mosca* take the keyes? who, so!
I am farder, in. These are my fine conceipts!
I must be merry, with a mischiefe to me!
What a vile wretch was I, that could not beare
My fortune, soberly? I must ha' my *Crotchets!*° whims
And my *Conundrums!* well, go you, and seeke him:
His meaning may be truer, then my feare.
Bid him he, streight, come to me, to the *Court;*
Thether will I; and, if't be possible,
Un-screw my Advocate, upon new hopes:
When I provok'd him, then I lost my selfe.

[*Exeunt.*]

SCENE XII

AVOCATORI, etc.

FIRST AVOCATORE. These things can nêre be reconcil'd. He, here,
Professeth, that the Gentleman was wrong'd;
And that the Gentlewóman was brought thether,
Forc'd by her husband: and there left.

VOLTORE. Most true.
CELIA. How ready is heav'n to those, that pray.
FIRST AVOCATORE. Bút, that
Volpone would have ravish'd her, he holds
Utterly false; knowing his impotence.
CORVINO. Grave *Fathers,* he is possest; againe, I say
Possest: nay, if there be *possession,*
And *obsession,* he has both.
THIRD AVOCATORE. Here comes our Officer.

[*Enter* VOLPONE.]

VOLPONE. The *Parasite* will streight be here, grave *Fathers.*
FOURTH AVOCATORE. You might invent some other name, Sir varlet.
THIRD AVOCATORE. Did not the *Notarie* meet him?
VOLPONE. Not, that I know.
FOURTH AVOCATORE. His comming will cleare all.
SECOND AVOCATORE. Yet it is misty.
VOLTORE. May't please your *Father-hoods*—

VOLPONE *whispers the* ADVOCATE.

VOLPONE. Sir, the *Parasite*
Will'd me to tell you, that his Maister lives;
That you are still the man; your hopes the same;
And this was, onely a jest—
VOLTORE. How?
VOLPONE. Sir, to trie
If you were firme, and how you stood affected.
VOLTORE. Art' sure he lives?
VOLPONE. Do I live, Sir?
VOLTORE. O me!
I was too violent.
VOLPONE. Sir, you may redeeme it,
They said, you were possest; fall downe, and seeme so:
Ile helpe to make it good. God blesse the man!

VOLTORE *falls.*

(Stop your wind hard, and swell): See, see, see, see!
He vomits crooked pinnes! his eyes are set,
Like a dead hares, hung in a poulters shop!
His mouth's running away! Do you see, Signior?
Now, 'tis in his belly!
CORVINO. I, the Devill!
VOLPONE. Now, in his throate.
CORVINO. I, I perceive it plaine.
VOLPONE. 'Twill out, 'twill out; stand cleere. See, where it flyes!
In shape of a blew toad, with a battes wings!
Do not you see, it, Sir?

CORBACCIO. What? I thinke I doe.
CORVINO. 'Tis too manifest.
VOLPONE. Looke! he comes t'himselfe!
VOLTORE. Where am I?
VOLPONE. Take good heart, the worst is past, Sir.
You are dis-possest.
FIRST AVOCATORE. What accident is this?
SECOND AVOCATORE. Sodaine, and full of wonder!
THIRD AVOCATORE. If hee were
Possest, as it appeares, all this is nothing.
CORVINO. He has beene, often, subject to these fitts.
FIRST AVOCATORE. Shew him that writing, do you know it, Sir?
VOLPONE. Deny it, Sir, forsweare it, know it not.
VOLTORE. Yes, I do know it well, it is my hand:
But all, that it containes, is false.
BONARIO. O practise!
SECOND AVOCATORE. What maze is this!
FIRST AVOCATORE. Is hee not guilty, then,
Whome you, there, name the *Parasite?*
VOLTORE. Grave *Fathers,*
No more then, his good Patron, old *Volpone.*
FOURTH AVOCATORE. Why, hee is dead?
VOLTORE. O no, my honor'd *Fathers,*
Hee lives—
FIRST AVOCATORE. How! lives?
VOLTORE. Lives.
SECOND AVOCATORE. This is subtler, yet!
THIRD AVOCATORE. You sayd, hee was dead?
VOLTORE. Never.
THIRD AVOCATORE. You sayd so?
CORVINO. I heard so.
FOURTH AVOCATORE. Here comes the Gentleman, make him way.
THIRD AVOCATORE. A stoole.

[*Enter* MOSCA.]

FOURTH AVOCATORE. A proper man! and, were *Volpone* dead,
A fit matche for my daughter.
THIRD AVOCATORE. Give him way.
VOLPONE. *Mosca,* I was almost lost, the Advocate
Had betrayd all; but, now, it is recover'd:
Al's on the henge° againe—say, I am living. hinge
MOSCA. What busie knave is this! Most reverend *Fathers,*
I sooner, had attended your grave pleasures,
But that my order, for the funerall
Of my deare Patron did require me—
VOLPONE. *(Mosca!)*

MOSCA. Whome I intend to bury, like a Gentleman—
VOLPONE. I, quick,° and cosen me of all. living
SECOND AVOCATORE. Still stranger!
More intricate!
FIRST AVOCATORE. And come about, againe!
FOURTH AVOCATORE. It is a match, my daughter is bestow'd.
MOSCA. (Will you gi' mee halfe?
VOLPONE. First, Ile bee hang'd
MOSCA. I know,
Your voice is good, cry not so low'd.)
FIRST AVOCATORE. Demand
The Advocate, Sir, did not you affirme,
Volpone was alive?
VOLPONE. Yes, and he is;
This Gent'man told me so. (Thou shalt have halfe.)
MOSCA. Whose drunkard is this same? speake some, that knows him:
I never saw his face. (I cannot now
Afford it you so cheape.
VOLPONE. No?)
FIRST AVOCATORE. What say you?
VOLTORE. The Officer told mee.
VOLPONE. I did, grave *Fathers,*
And will maintayne, he lives, with mine owne life.
And that this creature told me. (I was borne,
With all good starres my enemies.)
MOSCA. Most grave *Fathers,*
If such an insolence, as this, must passe
Upon me, I am silent: 'Twas not this,
For which you sent, I hope.
SECOND AVOCATORE. Take him, away.
VOLPONE. *(Mosca.)*
THIRD AVOCATORE. Let him be whipt.
VOLPONE. (Wilt thou betray mee?
Cosen me?)
THIRD AVOCATORE. And taught, to beare himselfe
Toward a person of his ranke.
FOURTH AVOCATORE. Away.
MOSCA. I humbly thanke your *Father hoods.*
VOLPONE. Soft, soft: whipt?
And loose all that I have? If I confesse,
It cannot bee much more.
FOURTH AVOCATORE. Sir, are you married?
VOLPONE. They'll bee ally'd, anone; I must be resolute:
The FOXE shall, here, uncase.

He puts off his disguise.

MOSCA. (Patron.)

VOLPONE. Nay, now,
My ruines shall not come alone; your match
Ile hinder sure: my substance shall not glew you,
Nor screw you, into a Family.
MOSCA. (Why, Patron!)
VOLPONE. I am *Volpone,* and this is my Knave;
This, his owne Knave; this avarices Foole;
This, a *Chimæra* of Wittall, Foole, and Knave;
And, reverend *Fathers,* since we all can hope
Nought, but a sentence, let's not now dispaire it.
You heare mee breife.
CORVINO. May it please your *Father-hoods*—
COMMANDADORE. Silence.
FIRST AVOCATORE. The knot is now undone, by miracle!
SECOND AVOCATORE. Nothing can be more cleare.
THIRD AVOCATORE. Or, can more prove
These innocent.
FIRST AVOCATORE. Give 'hem their liberty.
BONARIO. Heaven could not, long, let such grosse crimes be hid.
SECOND AVOCATORE. If this be held the high way, to get riches,
May I be poore.
THIRD AVOCATORE. This's not the gaine, but torment.
FIRST AVOCATORE. These possese wealth, as sick men possesse *Fevers,*
Which, trulyer, may be sayd to possesse them.
SECOND AVOCATORE. Disrobe that *Parasite.*
CORVINO *and* MOSCA. Most honor'd *Fathers*—
FIRST AVOCATORE. Can you plead ought to stay the course of Justice?
If you can, speake.
CORVINO *and* VOLTORE. We beg favor.
CELIA. And mercy.
FIRST AVOCATORE. You hurt your innocence, suing for the guilty.
Stand forth; and, first, the *Parasite.* You appeare
T'have beene the chiefest minister, if not plotter,
In all these leud° impostures; and now, lastly, base
Have, with your impudence, abus'd the *Court,*
And habite of a Gentleman of *Venice,*
Being a fellow of no birth or bloud:
For which, our sentence is, first thou be whipt;
Then live perpetuall prisoner in our *Gallies.*
VOLTORE. I thanke you, for him.
MOSCA. Bane to thy wolvish nature.
FIRST AVOCATORE. Deliver him to the *Saffi.*° bailiffs

[COMMANDADORI *take* MOSCA *out.*]

By bloud, and ranke a Gentleman, canst not fall
Under like censure. But our judgement on thee
Is, that thy substance all be, straight, confiscate

To the *Hospitall,* of the *Incurabili:*
And, since the most was gotten by imposture,
By fayning *lame, gout, palsey* and such diseases,
Thou art to lie in prison, crampt with irons,
Till thou bee'st sick, and lame indeed. Remove him.
VOLPONE. This is call'd mortifying of a FOXE.

[COMMANDADORI *take* VOLPONE *out.*]

FIRST AVOCATORE. Thou, *Voltore,* to take away the scandale
Thou hast giv'n all worthy men, of thy profession,
Art banish'd from their *Fellowship,* and our *State.*
Corbaccio, bring him neare. We here possesse
Thy sonne, of all thy'estate; and confine thee
To the *Monastery* of *San Spirito:*
Where, since thou knew'st not how to live well here,
Thou shalt be learn'd to die well.
CORBACCIO. Ha! what said he?
COMMANDADORE. You shall know anone, Sir.
FIRST AVOCATORE. Thou *Corvino,* shalt
Be straight imbarqu'd from thine owne house, and row'd
Round about *Venice,* through the *grand Canale,*
Wearing a cap, with fayre, long Asses eares,
In steed of hornes: and so, to mount (a paper
Pin'd on thy brest) to the *Berlino*°— [pillory]
CORVINO. Yes,
And, have mine eyes beat out with stinking fish,
Brus'd fruit, and rotten egges—'Tis well. I'm glad,
I shall not see my shame, yet.
FIRST AVOCATORE. And to expiate
Thy wrongs done to thy wife, thou art to send her
Home, to her father, with her dowrie trebled:
And these are all your Judgements—
ALL. (Honour'd *Fathers,*)
FIRST AVOCATORE. Which may not be revok'd. Now, you begin
When crimes are done, and past, and to be punish'd,
To thinke what your crimes are; away, with them.
Let all, that see these vices thus rewarded,
Take heart, and love to study 'hem. Mischiefes feed
Like beasts, till they be fat, and then they bleed.

[*Exeunt.*]

[EPILOGUE]

VOLPONE.

The seasoning of a *Play,* is the applause.
Now, though the *Foxe* be punish'd by the lawes,
He, yet, doth hope there is no suffring due,
For any face, which he hath done 'gainst you;
If there be, censure him: here he, doubtfull, stands.
If not, fare *Jovially,* and clap your hands.

THE END.

The Duchess of Malfy

John Webster is one of the many playwrights of the Elizabethan and Jacobean period about whom we know little. His parents were married in 1577, which provides a starting point to guess when he was born. His father, also John, was a coachmaker, a capital-intensive business, so was probably well off for an artisan, and his mother, Elizabeth, was the daughter of a blacksmith. Both father and son were members of the Merchant Taylors' Company, one the twelve livery companies of the City of London. Originally a tailors' association, by this time it had expanded to become a social and philanthropic body and was the governing body of the Merchant Taylors' School, which the playwright had the right to attend. He subsequently probably had legal training; a John Webster was admitted to the Middle Temple from the New Inn in 1598. This may have been his introduction to theatrical circles, for John Marston was also a member. By 1602 Webster was collaborating on plays with numerous others, the most important of whom were Thomas Dekker, Thomas Heywood, and Thomas Middleton. Many of the plays no longer exist. In 1606 Webster married Sara Peniall and they had a son named John and apparently other children. He is important for the two tragedies he composed mostly alone: *The Duchess of Malfy* and *The White Devil* (1612). He continued to collaborate with others at least into the 1620s and was dead by 1634.

The Duchess of Malfy was performed around 1613 and first printed in 1623 in an expanded version that included scenes that were not in the stage productions because of length. In 1608 The King's Men had bought Blackfriars, and the play was performed both in the "private" theater there and in the public theater of the Globe. The existence of the boys' companies meant there were teenagers and young men who had grown up in the theater, able to portray con-

The text is based on that established by F. L. Lucas (New York: Oxford University Press, 1937), 37–124. I have standardized spelling (i.e., "Cardinal" for "Cardinall" throughout). Also consulted are R. C. Bald's *Six Elizabethan Plays* (Boston: Houghton Miflin Company, 1963), 299–387, and Russell A. Fraser and Norman Rabkin's *Drama of the English Renaissance: II The Stuart Period* (New York: Macmillan, 1976), 475–515.

vincingly difficult women's roles such as the title character. The play is based on events in Italy that took place between 1508 and 1513.

The play is dark in theme, setting, and action, and frequently written in a blank verse so rough it is difficult to determine when the poetic line begins or ends. Indeed, the plot at crucial moments depends on characters unable to see in the dark. The corruption of Catholic Italy was a byword in Protestant England, but even so, the madness of Ferdinand is an example of the increasingly morbid tone of Jacobean drama. Very nearly metaphysical wit informs the play's conceits, especially in the speeches of Bosola. The duchess, however, is the center of the play. She marries beneath her, and against the wishes of two very dangerous brothers. Nevertheless, her punishment is so disproportionate to her tragic mistake that it is impossible to see her as deserving her fate, which includes the murder of most of her family. Her tragic stature comes from the heroic assertion in the face of her murderers that whatever torments they subject her to, she is Duchess of Malfy still.

The Duchess of Malfy

DRAMATIS PERSONAE

BOSOLA
FERDINAND
CARDINAL, his brother
ANTONIO
DELIO
FOROBOSCO
MALATESTE
The Marquesse of PESCARA
SILVIO
CASTRUCHIO
RODERIGO
GRISOLAN
The DUCHESSE
The CARDINALS Mis (Julia)
The DOCTOR
CARIOLA
COURT OFFICERS
[Old Lady.]
Three young Children
Two Pilgrimes
[Ladies, Executioners, and Atendants.]
The Several Madmen

ACTUS PRIMUS. SCENA PRIMA.

[Amalfi. The Palace of the Duchess.]
[Enter Antonio and Delio.]

DELIO. You are wel-come to your country (deere *Antonio*)
You have bin long in *France*, and you returne
A very formall French-man, in your habit.
How doe you like the French court?
ANTONIO. I admire it—
In seeking to reduce both State, and People
To a fix'd Order, their juditious King

Begins at home: Quits first his Royall Pallace
Of flattring Sicophants, of dissolute,
And infamous persons—which he sweetely termes
His Masters Master-peece (the worke of Heaven)
Considring duely, that a Princes Court
Is like a common Fountaine, whence should flow
Pure silver-droppes in generall: But if 't chance
Some curs'd example poyson 't neere the head,
Death, and diseases through the whole land spread.
And what is't makes this blessed government,
But a most provident Councell, who dare freely
Informe him the corruption of the times?
Though some oth'Court hold it presumption
To instruct Princes what they ought to doe,
It is a noble duety to informe them
What they ought to fore-see: Here comes *Bosola*

[*Enter Bosola.*]

The onely Court-Gall: yet I observe his rayling
Is not for simple love of Piety:
Indeede he rayls at those things which he wants,
Would be as lecherous, covetous, or proud,
Bloody, or envious, as any man,
If he had meanes to be so: Here's the Cardinal.

[*Enter Cardinal.*]

BOSOLA. I doe haunt you still.

CARDINAL. So.

BOSOLA. I have done you better service than to be slighted thus: miserable age, where onely the reward of doing well, is the doing of it!

CARDINAL. You inforce your merrit too much.

BOSOLA. I fell into the Gallies[1] in your service, where, for two yeares together, I wore two Towells in stead of a shirt, with a knot on the shoulder, after the fashion of a Romaine Mantle: Slighted thus? I will thrive some way: black-birds fatten best in hard weather: why not I, in these dogge dayes?

CARDINAL. Would you could become honest—

BOSOLA. With all your divinity, do but direct me the way to it—I have knowne many travell farre for it, and yet return as arrant knaves, as they went forth; because they carried themselves alwayes along with them[.] [*Exit Cardinal*] Are you gone? Some fellowes (they say) are possessed with the divell, but this great fellow, were able to possesse the greatest Divell, and make him worse.

1. For (unspecified) crimes done by Bosola in the service of the cardinal, he was sentenced to rowing in a galley, a harsh punishment and an anachronism for the historical period of the play.

ANTONIO. He hath denied thee some suit?

BOSOLA. He, and his brother, are like Plum-trees (that grow crooked over standing-pooles) they are rich, and ore-laden with Fruite, but none but Crowes, Pyes,° and Catter-pillers feede on them: Could I be one of their flattring Panders, I would hang on their eares like a horse-leech, till I were full, and then droppe off: I pray leave me. Who would relie upon these miserable dependances, in expectation to be advanc'd to-morrow? what creature ever fed worse, than hoping *Tantalus?*[2] nor ever died any man more fearefully, than he that hop'd for a pardon: There are rewards for hawkes, and dogges, when they have done us service; but for a Souldier, that hazards his Limbes in a battaile, nothing but a kind of Geometry, is his last Supportation.

magpies

DELIO. Geometry?

BOSOLA. I, to hang in a faire paire of slings, take his latter-swinge in the world, upon an honorable pare of Crowtches, from hospitall to hospitall—fare ye well Sir. And yet do not you scorne us, for places in the Court, are but like beds in the hospitall, where this mans head lies at that mans foote, and so lower and lower.

[*Exit.*]

DELIO. I knew this fellow seaven yeares in the Gallies,
For a notorious murther, and 'twas thought
The Cardinal suborn'd it: he was releas'd
By the French Generall (*Gaston de Foux*[3])
When he recover'd *Naples.*

ANTONIO. 'Tis great pity
He should be thus neglected—I have heard
He's very valiant: This foule mellancholly
Will poyson all his goodnesse, for (i 'le tell you)
If too immoderate sleepe be truly sayd
To be an inward rust unto the soule;
It then doth follow want of action
Breeds all blacke mal-contents, and their close rearing
(Like mothes in cloath) doe hurt for want of wearing.

[*Enter Silvio, Castruchio, Roderigo, & Grisolan.*]

DELIO. The Presence 'gins to fill, you promis'd me
To make me the partaker of the natures
Of some of your great Courtiers.

2. Tantalus sacrificed his son to the gods and tried to feed him to them. His punishment was to stand in a pool of water below a fruit tree. When he tried to reach the fruit, it drew out of reach. When he tried to drink the water, it receded. Pools of water and trees are recurring images in the play.

3. Gaston de Foix (1489–1512) defeated Spanish and papal forces at Ravenna in 1512; he had nothing to do with the capture of Naples in 1501.

ANTONIO. The Lord Cardinal's
And other strangers', that are now in Court?—
I shall: here comes the great *Calabrian* Duke.

[*Enter Ferdinand.*]

FERDINAND. Who tooke the Ring oftenest?[4]

SILVIO. *Antonio Bologna* (my Lord.)

FERDINAND. Our Sister Duchesse' great Master of her household? Give him the Jewel: when shall we leave this sportive-action, and fall to action indeed?

CASTRUCHIO. Me thinkes (my Lord) you should not desire to go to war, in person.

FERDINAND. Now for some gravity: why (my Lord?)

CASTRUCHIO. It is fitting a Souldier arise to be a Prince, but not necessary a Prince descend to be a Captaine.

FERDINAND. Noe?

CASTRUCHIO. No, (my Lord) he were far better do it by a Deputy.

FERDINAND. Why should he not as well sleepe, or eate, by a Deputy? This might take idle, offensive, and base office from him, whereas the other deprives him of honour.

CASTRUCHIO. Beleeve my experience: that Realme is never long in quiet, where the Ruler, is a Souldier.

FERDINAND. Thou toldst me thy wife could not endure fighting.

CASTRUCHIO. True (my Lord.)

FERDINAND. And of a jest, she broke of a Captaine she met, full of wounds: I have forgot it.

CASTRUCHIO. She told him (my Lord) he was a pittifull fellow, to lie, like the Children of *Ismael,* all in Tents.[5]

FERDINAND. Why, there's a wit were able to undo all the Chyrurgeons o' the City, for although Gallants should quarrell, and had drawne their weapons, and were ready to goe to it; yet her perswasions would make them put up.

CASTRUCHIO. That she would (my Lord)—How doe you like my Spanish Gennit?° saddle horse

RODERIGO. He is all fire.

FERDINAND. I am of *Pliney's* opinion, I thinke he was begot by the wind, he runs, as if he were ballass'd with Quick-silver.

SILVIO. True, my lord, he reels from the tilt often.

RODERIGO. *Grisolan.* Ha, ha, ha.

FERDINAND. Why do you laugh? Me thinks you that are Courtiers should be my touch-wood, take fire, when I give fire; that is, laugh when I laugh, were the subject never so wity—

4. Horsemen would ride with lances at a ring suspended from a string.
5. A pun on the ordinary sense of tents and on an alternate meaning of "rolls of lint."

CASTRUCHIO. True (my Lord) I my selfe have heard a very good jest, and have scorn'd to seeme to have so silly a wit, as to understand it.
FERDINAND. But I can laugh at your Foole (my Lord.)
CASTRUCHIO. He cannot speake (you know) but he makes faces, my lady cannot abide him.
FERDINAND. No?
CASTRUCHIO. Nor endure to be in merry Company: for she saies too much laughing, and too much Company, fils her too full of the wrinckle.
FERDINAND. I would then have a Mathematicall Instrument made for her face, that she might not laugh out of compasse: I shall shortly visit you at *Millaine* (Lord *Silvio.*)
SILVIO. Your Grace shall arrive most wel-come.
FERDINAND. You are a good Horse-man *(Antonio)* you have excellent Riders in *France*—what do you thinke of good horsemanship?
ANTONIO. Noblely (my Lord)—as out of the Grecian-horse issued many famous Princes: So, out of brave Horse-man-ship, arise the first Sparkes of growing resolution, that raise the minde to noble action.
FERDINAND. You have be-spoake it worthely.
SILVIO. Your brother, the Lord Cardinal, and sister Duchesse.

[*Enter Cardinal, Duchess, Cariola, & Julia*].

CARDINAL. Are the Gallies come about?
GRISOLAN. They are, my lord.
FERDINAND. Here's the Lord *Silvio,* is come to take his leave.
DELIO. Now (Sir) your promise: what's that Cardinal?
I meane his temper? they say he's a brave fellow,
Will play his five thousand crownes, at Tennis, Daunce,
Court Ladies, and one that hath fought single Combats.
ANTONIO. Some such flashes superficially hang on him, for forme:
but observe his inward Character: he is a mellancholly Churchman:
The Spring in his face, is nothing but the Ingendring of Toades:
where he is jealious of any man, he laies worse plots for them,
then ever was impos'd on *Hercules:* for he strewes in his way
Flatterers, Panders, Intelligencers, Athiests, and a thousand such
politicall Monsters: he should have been Pope: but in stead of
comming to it by the primitive decencie of the church, he did
bestow bribes, so largely, and so impudently, as if he would have
carried it away without heavens knowledge. Some good he hath done[—]
DELIO. You have given too much of him: what's his brother?
ANTONIO. The Duke there? a most perverse, and turbulent Nature—
What appeares in him mirth, is meerely outside,
If he laugh hartely, it is to laugh
All honesty out of fashion.
DELIO. Twins?

ANTONIO. In quality.
He speakes with others Tongues, and heares men's suites,
With others Eares: will seeme to sleepe o' the bench
Onely to intrap offenders, in their answeres;
Doombes men to death, by information,
Rewards, by heare-say.
DELIO. Then the Law to him
Is like a fowle blacke cob-web, to a Spider—
He makes it his dwelling, and a prison
To entangle those shall feede him.
ANTONIO. Most true:
He nev'r paies debts, unlesse they be shrewd turnes,° injuries
And those he will confesse that he doth owe.
Last: for his brother, there, (the Cardinal)
They that doe flatter him most, say Oracles
Hang at his lippes: and verely I beleeve them:
For the Divell speakes in them.
But for their sister, (the right noble Duchesse)
You never fix'd your eye on three faire Meddalls,
Cast in one figure, of so different temper:
For her discourse, it is so full of Rapture,
You onely will begin, then to be sorry
When she doth end her speech: and wish (in wonder)
She held it lesse vaine-glory, to talke much,
Then your pennance, to heare her: whilst she speakes,
She throwes upon a man so sweet a looke,
That it were able to raise one to a Galliard
That lay in a dead palsey; and to doate
On that sweete countenance: but in that looke,
There speaketh so divine a continence,
As cuts off all lascivious, and vaine hope.
Her dayes are practis'd in such noble vertue,
That sure her nights (nay more, her very Sleepes)
Are more in Heaven, than other Ladies Shrifts.° confessions
Let all sweet ladies break their flattering glasses,
And dress themselves in her.
DELIO. Fie, *Antonio*,
You play the wire-drawer with her commendations.
ANTONIO. I'll case the picture up: only thus much—
All her particular worth growes to this somme:
She staines the time past: lights the time to come—
CARIOLA. You must attend my lady in the gallery,
Some half an hour hence.
ANTONIO. I shall.

[*Exeunt Antonio & Delio.*]

FERDINAND. Sister, I have a suit to you.
DUCHESSE. To me, sir?
FERDINAND. A gentleman here, *Daniel de Bosola:*
One that was in the Gallies.
DUCHESSE. Yes, I know him.
FERDINAND. A worthy fellow h'is: pray, let me entreat for
The provisorship of your horse.
DUCHESSE. Your knowledge of him
Commends him, and prefers him.
FERDINAND. Call him hither.

[*Exit Servant.*]

Wee [are] now upon parting: Good Lord *Silvio*
Do us commend to all our noble friends
At the Leaguer.° camp
SILVIO. Sir, I shall.
DUCHESSE. You are for *Millaine?*
SILVIO. I am.
DUCHESSE. Bring the caroches.° We'll bring you down carriages
To the haven.

[*Exeunt, except Cardinal & Ferdinand*].

CARDINAL. Be sure you entertaine that *Bosola*
For your Intelligence: I would not be seene in't.
And therefore many times I have slighted him,
When he did court our furtherance: as this Morning.
FERDINAND. *Antonio,* the great Master of her houshold
Had been farre fitter[.]
CARDINAL. You are deceiv'd in him,
His Nature is too honest for such businesse,
He comes: I'll leave you.

[*Exit. Enter Bosola.*]

BOSOLA. I was lur'd to you.
FERDINAND. My brother here (the Cardinal) could never
Abide you.
BOSOLA. Never since he was in my debt.
FERDINAND. May be some oblique character in your face,
Made him suspect you?
BOSOLA. Doth he study phisiognomie?
There's no more credit to be given to th'face,
Then to a sicke mans uryn, which some call
The Physitians whore, because she cozens him:
He did suspect me wrongfully.
FERDINAND. For that
You must give great men leave to take their times:
Distrust, doth cause us seldome be deceiv'd;

You see, the oft shaking of the Cedar-Tree
Fastens it more at roote.

BOSOLA. Yet, take heed:
For to suspect a friend unworthely
Instructs him the next way to suspect you,
And prompts him to deceive you.

FERDINAND. There's gold.

BOSOLA. So:
What followes? (Never raind such showres as these
Without thunderbolts i'the taile of them;) whose throat must I cut?

FERDINAND. Your inclination to shed blood rides post
Before my occasion to use you: I give you that
To live i'the Court, here: and observe the Duchesse,
To note all the particulars of her haviour:
What suitors doe sollicite her for marriage
And whom she best affects: she's a young widowe,
I would not have her marry againe.

BOSOLA. No, sir?

FERDINAND. Doe not you aske the reason; but be satisfied,
I say I would not.

BOSOLA. It seemes you would create me
One of your familiars.

FERDINAND. Familiar? what's that?

BOSOLA. Why, a very quaint invisible Divell, in flesh:
An intelligencer.

FERDINAND. Such a kind of thriving thing
I would wish thee: and ere long, thou maist arrive
At a higher place by 't.

BOSOLA. Take your Divels,
Which Hell calls Angels:[6] these curs'd gifts would make
You a corrupter, me an impudent traitor,
And should I take these, they'll'd take me [to] Hell.

FERDINAND. Sir, I'll take nothing from you, that I have given:
There is a place, that I procur'd for you
This morning: (the Provisor-ship o'the horse)—
Have you heard on't?

BOSOLA. No.

FERDINAND. 'Tis yours, is't not worth thankes?

BOSOLA. I would have you curse your selfe now, that your bounty
(Which makes men truly noble) eer should make me
A villaine: oh, that to avoid ingratitude
For the good deed you have done me, I must doe
All the ill man can invent: Thus the Divell

6. A coin with a design of St. Michael killing a dragon on it.

Candies all sinnes o'er: and what Heaven termes vild,
That names he complementall.
FERDINAND. Be your selfe:
Keepe your old garbe of melencholly: 'twill expresse
You envy those that stand above your reach,
Yet strive not to come neere'em: This will gaine
Accesse, to private lodgings, where your selfe
May (like a pollitique dormouse—
BOSOLA. As I have seene some,
Feed in a Lords dish, halfe asleepe, not seeming
To listen to any talke: and yet these Rogues
Have cut his throat in a dreame: whats my place?
The Provisor-ship o'th horse? say, then, my corruption
Grew out of horse-doong: I am your creature.
FERDINAND. Away!
BOSOLA. Let good men, for good deeds, covet good fame,
Since place, and riches oft are bribes of shame—
Sometimes the Divell doth preach.

Exit Bosola.
[*Enter Duchesse, Cardinal, & Cariola.*]

CARDINAL. We are to part from you: and your owne discretion
Must now be your director.
FERDINAND. You are a Widowe:
You know already what man is: and therefore
Let not youth . . . high promotion, eloquence—
CARDINAL. No,
Nor anything without the addition, *Honor,*
Sway your high blood.
FERDINAND. Marry? they are most luxurious
Will wed twice.
CARDINAL. O, fie!
FERDINAND. Their livers are more spotted
Than *Labans* sheepe.[7]
DUCHESSE. Diamonds are of most value
They say, that have past through most Jewellers hands.
FERDINAND. Whores, by that rule, are precious:
DUCHESSE. Will you heare me?
I'll never marry[.]
CARDINAL. So most Widowes say:
But commonly that motion lasts no longer
Then the turning of an houreglasse—the funeral Sermon
And it, end both together.
FERDINAND. Now heare me:
You live in a ranke pasture here, i'the Court—

7. Genesis 30:31–42.

There is a kind of honney-dew, that's deadly:
'Twill poison your fame: looke to't: be not cunning:
For they whose faces doe belye their hearts,
Are Witches, ere they arrive at twenty yeeres,
I, and give the divell sucke.

DUCHESSE. This is terrible good councell[.]

FERDINAND. Hypocrisie is woven of a fine small thred,
Subtler than *Vulcans* Engine:[8] yet, (beleve't)
Your darkest actions: nay, your privat'st thoughts,
Will come to light.

CARDINAL. You may flatter your selfe,
And take your owne choice: privately be married
Under the Eaves of night . . .

FERDINAND. Think't the best voyage
That ere you made; like the irregular Crab,
Which, though't goes backward, thinks that it goes right,
Because it goes its owne way: but observe;
Such weddings, may more properly be said
To be executed, then celibrated.

CARDINAL. The marriage night
Is the entrance into some prison.

FERDINAND. And those joyes,
Those lustfull pleasures, are like heavy sleepes
Which doe fore-run mans mischiefe.

CARDINAL. Fare you well.
Wisdome begins at the end: remember it.

[*Exit.*]

DUCHESSE. I thinke this speech betweene you both was studied,
It came so roundly off.

FERDINAND. You are my sister,
This was my Fathers poyniard:° doe you see, dagger
I'll'd be loth to see't looke rusty, 'cause 'twas his:
I would have you give ore these chargeable Revels;
A Visor, and a Masque are whispering-roomes
That were nev'r built for goodnesse: fare ye well:
And woemen like that part, which (like the Lamprey)
Hath nev'r a bone in't.

DUCHESSE. Fye Sir!

FERDINAND. Nay,
I meane the Tongue: varietie of Courtship;
What cannot a neate knave with a smooth tale,
Make a woman beleeve? farewell, lusty Widowe.

[*Exit.*]

8. The fine mesh within which Vulcan caught his wife, Venus, copulating with Mars.

DUCHESSE. Shall this move me? If all my royall kindred
Lay in my way unto this marriage
I'll'd make them my low foote-steps: And even now,
Even in this hate (as men in some great battailes
By apprehending danger, have atchiev'd
Almost impossible actions: I have heard soldiers say so),
So I, through frights, and threatnings, will assay
This dangerous venture: Let old wives report
I wincked and chose a husband: *Cariola,*
To thy knowne secricy I have given up
More than my life, my fame[.]
CARIOLA. Both shall be safe:
For I'll conceale this secret from the world
As warily as those that trade in poyson,
Keepe poyson from their children.
DUCHESSE. Thy protestation
Is ingenious and hearty: I beleeve it.
Is *Antonio* come?
CARIOLA. He attends you.
DUCHESSE. Good deare soul,
Leave me: but place thy selfe behind the Arras,° tapestry
Where thou maist over-heare us: wish me good speed
For I am going into a wildernesse,
Where I shall find nor path, nor friendly clewe
To be my guide—

[*Cariola withdraws behind the arras. The Duchesse draws the traverse revealing Antonio.*]

I sent for you, Sit downe:
Take Pen and Incke, and write: are you ready?
ANTONIO. Yes.
DUCHESSE. What did I say?
ANTONIO. That I should write some-what.
DUCHESSE. Oh, I remember:
After these triumphs, and this large expence
It's fit (like thrifty husbands) we enquire
What's laid up for to-morrow[.]
ANTONIO. So please your beauteous Excellence.
DUCHESSE. Beauteous?
Indeed, I thank you: I look yong for your sake.
You have tane my cares upon you.
ANTONIO. I'll fetch your grace
The particulars of your revinew, and expence.
DUCHESSE. Oh, you are
An upright treasurer: but you mistooke,
For when I said I meant to make enquiry,

What's layd up for to-morrow: I did meane
What's layd up yonder for me.

ANTONIO. Where?

DUCHESSE. In Heaven,
I am making my will, (as 'tis fit Princes should,
In perfect memory) and I pray Sir, tell me
Were not one better make it smiling, thus?
Then in deepe groanes, and terrible ghastly lookes,
As if the guifts we parted with, procur'd
That violent distraction?

ANTONIO. Oh, much better.

DUCHESSE. If I had a husband now, this care were quit:
But I intend to make you Over-seer;
What good deede, shall we first remember? say.

ANTONIO. Begin with that first good deed began i'th'world,
After mans creation, the Sacrament of marriage—
I'ld have you first provide for a good husband,
Give him all.

DUCHESSE. All?

ANTONIO. Yes, your excellent selfe.

DUCHESSE. In a winding sheete?

ANTONIO. In a cople.

DUCHESSE. *Saint Winifred,*[9] that were a strange will.

ANTONIO. 'Twere stranger if there were no will in you
To marry againe.

DUCHESSE. What doe you think of marriage?

ANTONIO. I take't, as those that deny Purgatory,
It locally containes, or heaven, or hell,
There's no third place in't.

DUCHESSE. How do you affect it?

ANTONIO. My banishment, feeding my mellancholly,
Would often reason thus.

DUCHESSE. Pray, let's hear it.

ANTONIO. Say a man never marry, nor have children,
What takes that from him? onely the bare name
Of being a father, or the weake delight
To see the little wanton ride a cocke-horse
Upon a painted sticke, or heare him chatter
Like a taught Starling.

DUCHESSE. Fye, fie, what's all this?
One of your eyes is blood-shot, use my ring to't,
They say 'tis very soveraigne, 'twas my wedding- Ring,

9. A seventh-century saint, she refused the advances of a chieftain, who struck off her head. Her head was restored by St. Bruno, and she became a nun.

And I did vow never to part with it,
But to my second husband.

ANTONIO. You have parted with it now.

DUCHESSE. Yes, to helpe your eye-sight.

ANTONIO. You have made me starke blind.

DUCHESSE. How?

ANTONIO. There is a sawcy, and ambitious divell
Is dauncing in this circle.

DUCHESSE. Remove him.

ANTONIO. How?

DUCHESSE. There needs small conjuration, when your finger
May doe it: thus, is it fit?

ANTONIO. What sayd you?

he kneeles

DUCHESSE. Sir,
This goodly roofe of yours, is too low built,
I cannot stand upright in't, nor discourse,
Without I raise it higher: raise your selfe,
Or if you please, my hand to helpe you: so.

ANTONIO. Ambition (Madam) is a great mans madnes,
That is not kept in chaines, and close-pent-roomes,
But in faire lightsome lodgings, and is girt
With the wild noyce of pratling visitants,
Which makes it lunatique, beyond all cure—
Conceive not, I am so stupid, but I ayme
Whereto your favours tend: But he's a foole
That (being a-cold) would thrust his hands i'th'fire
To warme them.

DUCHESSE. So, now the ground's broake,
You may discover what a wealthy Mine,
I make you lord of.

ANTONIO. O my unworthinesse.

DUCHESSE. You were ill to sell your selfe,
This darkning of your worth, is not like that
Which trades-men use i'th'City—their false lightes
Are to rid bad wares off: and I must tell you
If you will know where breathes a compleat man,
(I speake it without flattery) turne your eyes,
And progresse through your selfe.

ANTONIO. Were there nor heaven, nor hell,
I should be honest: I have long serv'd vertue,
And nev'r tane wages of her.

DUCHESSE. Now she paies it—
The misery of us, that are borne great!—
We are forc'd to woo, because none dare woo us:

And as a Tyrant doubles with his words,
And fearefully equivocates: so we
Are forc'd to expresse our violent passions
In ridles, and in dreames, and leave the path
Of simple vertue, which was never made
To seeme the thing it is not: Goe, go brag
You have left me heartlesse—mine is in your bosome,
I hope 'twill multiply love there: You doe tremble:
Make not your heart so dead a peece of flesh
To feare, more then to love me: Sir, be confident,
What is't distracts you? (This is flesh, and blood, (Sir,)
'Tis not the figure cut in Allablaster
Kneeles at my husband's tombe[)]. Awake, awake, (man)
I do here put off all vaine ceremony,
And onely doe appeare to you a yong widow
That claimes you for her husband, and like a widow,
I use but halfe a blush in't.

ANTONIO. Truth speake for me,
I will remaine the constant Sanctuary
Of your good name.

DUCHESSE. I thanke you (gentle love)
And 'cause you shall not come to me in debt,
(Being now my Steward) here upon your lippes
I signe your *Quietus est:*[10] This you should have beg'd now,
I have seene children oft eate sweete-meates thus,
As fearefull to devoure them too soone.

ANTONIO. But for your Brothers?

DUCHESSE. Do not thinke of them,
All discord without this circumference,

[*she puts her arms about him.*]

Is onely to be pittied, and not fear'd:
Yet, should they know it, time will easily
Scatter the tempest.

ANTONIO. These words should be mine,
And all the parts you have spoke, if some part of it
Would not have savour'd flattery.

DUCHESSE. Kneele.

[*Cariola shows herself.*]

ANTONIO. Hah?

DUCHESSE. Be not amaz'd, this woman's of my Councell,
I have heard Lawyers say, a contract in a Chamber,
(Per verba presenti)[11] is absolute marriage:

10. Acquittal of his obligations (his debts are paid).
11. By words referring to the present time.

Blesse (Heaven) this sacred Gordian,[12] which let violence
Never untwine.
ANTONIO. And may our sweet affections, (like the Sphears)
Be still in motion.
DUCHESSE. Quickning, and make
The like soft Musique.
ANTONIO. That we may imitate the loving Palmes
(Best Embleme of a peacefull marriage)
That nev'r bore fruite devided.
DUCHESSE. What can the Church force more?
ANTONIO. That Fortune may not know an accident
Either of joy, or sorrow, to devide
Our fixed wishes.
DUCHESSE. How can the church build faster?
We now are man, and wife, and 'tis the Church
That must but eccho this: Maid, stand apart,
I now am blinde.
ANTONIO. What's your conceit in this?
DUCHESSE. I would have you leade your Fortune by the hand,
Unto your marriage-bed:
(You speake in me this, for we now are one)
We'll onely lie, and talke together, and plot
T'appease my humorous kindred; and if you please,
(Like the old tale, in *Alexander* and *Lodowicke*)[13]
Lay a naked sword betweene us, keepe us chast:
Oh, let me shrowd my blushes in your bosome,
Since 'tis the treasury of all my secrets.

[*Exeunt Duchess and Antonio.*]

CARIOLA. Whether the spirit of greatnes, or of woman
Raigne most in her, I know not, but it shewes
A fearefull madnes. I owe her much of pitty.

[*Exit.*]

ACTUS II. SCENA I.

[*Enter Bosola & Castruchio.*]

BOSOLA. You say you would faine be taken—for an eminent
Courtier?
CASTRUCHIO. 'Tis the very maine of my ambition.

12. Referring to the Gordian knot, which, since he could not untie it, Alexander cut with a sword.
13. Lodowicke marries the princess of Hungary in Alexander's place, and to keep from wronging his friend, lays a sword between the princess and himself in bed.

BOSOLA. Let me see, you have a reasonable good face for't already, and your night-cap° expresses your eares sufficient largely—I would have you learne to twirle the strings of your band° with a good grace; and in a set speech (at th'end of every sentence,) to hum, three, or foure times, or blow your nose (till it smart againe,) to recover your memory—when you come to be a president in criminall causes, if you smile upon a prisoner, hang him, but if you frowne upon him, and threaten him, let him be sure to scape the Gallowes.

lawyer's coif

collar

CASTRUCHIO. I would be a very merrie president—

BOSOLA. Do not sup a nights, 'twill beget you an admirable wit.

CASTRUCHIO. Rather it would make me have a good stomake to quarrel, for they say, your roaring-boyes eate meate seldome, and that makes them so valiant: but how shall I know whether the people take me for an eminent fellow?

BOSOLA. I will teach a tricke to know it—give out you lie a-dying, and if you heare the common people curse you, be sure you are taken for one of the prime night-caps—

[*Enter Old Lady.*]

You come from painting now?

OLD LADY. From what?

BOSOLA. Why, from your scurvy face-physicke—to behold thee not painted enclines somewhat neere a miracle: These . . . in thy face here, were deepe rutts and foule sloughes the last progresse:[14] There was a Lady in *France,* that, having had the small pockes, flead the skinne off her face, to make it more levell; and whereas before she look'd like a Nutmeg-grater, after she resembled an abortive hedge-hog.

OLD LADY. Do you call this painting?

BOSOLA. No, no, but I call [it] carreening[15] of an old morphew'd[16] Lady, to make her disembogue° againe—There's rough-cast° phrase to your plastique.°

put to sea

plaster; modelling

OLD LADY. It seemes you are well acquainted with my clossett?

BOSOLA. One would suspect it for a shop of witch-craft, to finde in it the fat of Serpents; spawne of Snakes, Jewes spittle, and their young children's ordures—and all these for the face: I would sooner eate a dead pigeon, taken from the soles of the feete of one sicke of the plague, then kisse one of you fasting: here are two of you, whose sin of your youth is the very patrimony of the Physition, makes him renew his foote-cloth[17] with the Spring, and change his high-priz'd curtezan with the fall of the leafe: I do wonder you doe

14. A royal tour of the provinces was a sufficiently important event to be used as a convenient marker of time.

15. Beaching a ship to scrape its hull.

16. A skin eruption.

17. Hangings on a horse or mule that indicate a physician.

not loathe your selves—observe my meditation now:
What thing is in this outward forme of man
To be belov'd? We account it ominous,
If Nature doe produce a Colt, or Lambe,
A Fawne, or Goate, in any limbe resembling
A Man; and flye from't as a prodegy.
Man stands amaz'd to see his deformity,
In any other Creature but himselfe.
But in our owne flesh, though we beare diseases
Which have their true names onely tane from beasts,
As the most ulcerous Woolfe, and swinish Meazeall;
Though we are eaten up of lice, and wormes,
And though continually we beare about us
A rotten and dead body, we delight
To hide it in rich tissew—all our feare,
(Nay all our terrour) is, least our Phisition
Should put us in the ground, to be made sweete.
Your wife's gone to *Rome:* you two cople, and get you to the wells at Lucca to recover your aches. I have other work on foot.

[*Exeunt Castruchio & Old Lady.*]

I observe our Duchesse
Is sicke a dayes, she puykes, her stomacke seethes,
The fins of her eie-lids looke most teeming blew,
She waines i'th'cheeke, and waxes fat i'th'flanke;
And (contrary to our *Italian* fashion,)
Weares a loose-bodied Gowne—there's somewhat in't,
I have a tricke, may chance discover it
(A pretty one)—I have bought some Apricocks,
The first our Spring yeelds.

[*Enter Delio & Antonio.*]

DELIO. And so long since married? You amaze me.
ANTONIO. Let me seale your lipps for ever,
For did I thinke, that any thing but th'ayre
Could carry these words from you, I should wish
You had no breath at all. [*To Bosola*] Now, sir, in your contemplation? You are studying to become a great wise fellow.
BOSOLA. Oh Sir, the opinion of wisedome is a foule tettor, that runs all over a mans body: if simplicity direct us to have no evill, it directs us to a happy being: For the subtlest folly proceeds from the subtlest wisedome: Let me be simply honest.
ANTONIO. I do understand your in-side.
BOSOLA. Do you so?
ANTONIO. Because you would not seeme to appeare to th'world
Puff'd up with your preferment: You continue
This out-of-fashion mellancholly—leave it, leave it.

BOSOLA. Give me leave to be honest in any phrase, in any complement whatsoever—shall I confesse my selfe to you? I looke no higher than I can reach: they are the gods, that must ride on winged horses, a Lawyers mule of a slow pace will both suit my disposition, and businesse: For (marke me) when a mans mind rides faster than his horse can gallop, they quickly both tyre.

ANTONIO. You would looke up to Heaven, but I thinke
The Divell, that rules i'th'aire, stands in your light.

BOSOLA. Oh (Sir) you are Lord of the ascendant, chiefe man with the Duchesse, a Duke was your cosen German, remov'd: Say you were lineally descended from King *Pippin,*[18] or he himselfe, what of this? search the heads of the greatest rivers in the World, you shall finde them but bubbles of water: Some would thinke the soules of Princes were brought forth by some more weighty cause, then those of meaner persons—they are deceiv'd, there's the same hand to them: The like passions sway them, the same reason, that makes a Vicar goe to Law for a tithe-pig, and undoe his neighbours, makes them spoile a whole Province, and batter downe goodly Cities, with the Cannon.

[*Enter Duchesse & Ladies.*]

DUCHESSE. Your arme *Antonio,* do I not grow fat?
I am exceeding short-winded: *Bosola,*
I would have you (Sir) provide for me a Littor,
Such a one, as the Duchesse of *Florence* roade in.

BOSOLA. The duchesse us'd one, when she was great with childe.

DUCHESSE. I thinke she did: come hether, mend my ruffe—
Here, when? thou art such a tedious Lady; and
Thy breath smells of Lymmon pils, would thou hadst done—
Shall I sound° under thy fingers? I am [swoon]
So troubled with the mother!

BOSOLA. I fear too much.

DUCHESSE. I have heard you say, that the French Courtiers
Weare their hats on fore the King.

ANTONIO. I have seene it.

DUCHESSE. In the Presence?

ANTONIO. Yes.

DUCHESSE. Why should not we bring up that fashion?
'Tis ceremony more than duty that consists
In the remooving of a peece of felt:
Be you the example to the rest o'th'court,
Put on your hat first.

ANTONIO. You must pardon me:
I have seene, in colder countries then in *France,*

18. King of France AD 752–68 and father of Charlemagne.

Nobles stand bare to th'Prince; and the distinction
Methought show'd reverently.
BOSOLA. I have a present for your Grace.
DUCHESSE. For me sir?
BOSOLA. Apricocks (Madam.)
DUCHESSE. O sir, where are they?
I have heard of none to yeare.
BOSOLA. [*aside*] Good; her colour rises.
DUCHESSE. Indeed I thanke you: they are wondrous faire ones:
What an unskilfull fellow is our Gardiner!
We shall have none this moneth.
BOSOLA. Will not your Grace pare them?
DUCHESSE. No, they tast of muske (me thinkes) indeed they doe[.]
BOSOLA. I know not: yet I wish your Grace had parde 'em.
DUCHESSE. Why?
BOSOLA. I forget to tell you the knave Gardner,
(Onely to raise his profit by them the sooner)
Did ripen them in horse-doung.
DUCHESSE. O you jest:
You shall judge: pray, tast one.
ANTONIO. Indeed, madam,
I do not love the fruit.
DUCHESSE. Sir, you are loath
To rob us of our dainties: 'tis a delicate fruit,
They say they are restorative?
BOSOLA. 'Tis a pretty Art:
This grafting.
DUCHESSE. 'Tis so: a bettering of nature.
BOSOLA. To make a pippin grow upon a crab,
A dampson on a black-thorne: [*aside*] How greedily she eats them!
A whirlewinde strike off these bawd-farthingalls,
For, but for that, and the loose-bodied gowne,
I should have discover'd apparently
The young spring-hall° cutting a caper in her belly. stripling
DUCHESSE. I thanke you *(Bosola:)* they were right good ones,
If they doe not make me sicke.
ANTONIO. How now Madame?
DUCHESSE. This green fruit . . . and my stomake are not friends—
How they swell me!
BOSOLA. [*aside*] Nay, you are too much swell'd already.
DUCHESSE. Oh, I am in an extreame cold sweat.
BOSOLA. I am very sorry[.]

[*Exit.*]

DUCHESSE. Lights to my chamber: O, good *Antonio,*
I feare I am undone.

Exit Duchesse

DELIO. Lights there, lights!
ANTONIO. O my most trusty *Delio,* we are lost:
I feare she's falne in labour: and ther's left
No time for her remove.
DELIO. Have you prepar'd
Those Ladies to attend her? and procur'd
That politique safe conveyance for the Mid-wife
Your Duchesse plotted?
ANTONIO. I have[.]
DELIO. Make use then of this forc'd occasion:
Give out that *Bosola* hath poyson'd her,
With these Apricocks: that will give some colour
For her keeping close.
ANTONIO. Fye, fie, the Physitians
Will then flocke to her.
DELIO. For that you may pretend
She'll use some prepar'd Antidote of her owne,
Least the Physitians should repoyson her.
ANTONIO. I am lost in amazement: I know not what to think on't.

Exeunt.

ACTUS II. SCENA II.

[*Enter Bosola & old Lady.*]

BOSOLA. [*aside*] So, so: ther's no question but her techiness and most vulturous eating of the Apricocks, are apparant signes of breeding—[*to the old Lady*] now?

OLD LADY. I am in hast (Sir.)

BOSOLA. There was a young wayting-woman, had a monstrous desire to see the Glasse-house.° glass factory

OLD LADY. Nay, pray let me goe[.]

BOSOLA. And it was onely to know what strange instrument it was, should swell up a glasse to the fashion of a womans belly.

OLD LADY. I will heare no more of the Glasse-house—you are still abusing woemen?

BOSOLA. Who—I? no, onely (by the way now and then) mention your fraileties. The Orrenge tree bears ripe and greene fruit, and blossoms all together: And some of you give entertainment for pure love: but more, for more precious reward. The lusty Spring smels well: but drooping Autumne tasts well: If we have the same golden showres that rained in the time of *Jupiter* the Thunderer: you have the same *Danaes* still, to hold up their laps to receive them: Didst thou never study the *Mathematiques?*

OLD LADY. What's that (Sir?)

BOSOLA. Why, to know the trick how to make a many lines meete in one center: Goe, goe; give your foster-daughters good councell: tell them, that the Divell takes delight to hang at a womans girdle, like a false rusty watch, that she cannot discerne how the time passes.

[*Exit Old Lady. Enter Antonio, Delio, Roderigo & Grisolan.*]

ANTONIO. Shut up the Court gates.
RODERIGO. Why sir? what's the danger?
ANTONIO. Shut up the Posternes presently: and call
All the Officers o'th' Court.
GRISOLAN. I shall instantly.

[*Exit.*]

ANTONIO. Who keepes the key o'th' Parke-gate?
RODERIGO. *Forobosco.*
ANTONIO. Let him bring't presently.

[*Re-enter Grisolan with Servants.*]

FIRST SERVANT. Oh, gentleman o'th'Court, the fowlest treason.
BOSOLA. [*aside*] If that these Apricocks should be poysond, now;
Without my knowledge!
FIRST SERVANT. There was taken even now a Switzer[19] in the Duchesse Bed-chamber.
SECOND SERVANT. A Switzer?
FIRST SERVANT. With a Pistoll in his great cod-piece.
BOSOLA. Ha, ha, ha.
FIRST SERVANT. The cod-piece was the case for't.
SECOND SERVANT. There was a cunning traitor: who would have search'd his cod-piece?
FIRST SERVANT. True, if he had kept out of the Ladies chambers: and all the mowldes of his buttons, were leaden bullets.
SECOND SERVANT. O wicked Caniball: a fire-lock in's cod-piece?
FIRST SERVANT. 'Twas a French plot, upon my life.
SECOND SERVANT. To see what the Divell can doe!
ANTONIO. All the officers here?
FIRST SERVANT. We are[.]
ANTONIO. Gentlemen,
We have lost much Plate you know; and but this evening
Jewels, to the value of foure thousand Duckets,
Are missing in the Duchesse Cabinet—
Are the Gates shut?
FIRST SERVANT. Yes.
ANTONIO. 'Tis the Duchesse pleasure
Each Officer be lock'd into his chamber

19. Swiss mercenaries were used by the popes starting in the fifteenth century.

Till the Sun-rysing: and to send the keyes
Of all their chests, and of their outward doores
Into her bed-chamber: She is very sicke.

RODERIGO. At her pleasure.

ANTONIO. She intreates you take't not ill: The Innocent
Shall be the more approv'd by it.

BOSOLA. Gentlemen o'th' Wood-yard, where's your Switzer now?

FIRST SERVANT. By this hand, 'twas credibly reported by one
o'th' Black-guard.° kitchen workers

[*Exeunt except Antonio & Delio.*]

DELIO. How fares it with the Duchesse?

ANTONIO. She's expos'd
Unto the worst of torture, paine, and feare;

DELIO. Speake to her all happy comfort.

ANTONIO. How I do play the foole with mine own danger!
You are this night (deere friend) to post to Rome,
My life lies in your service.

DELIO. Doe not doubt me—

ANTONIO. Oh, 'Tis farre from me: and yet feare presents me
Somewhat that looks like danger.

DELIO. Believe it,
'Tis but the shadow of your feare, no more:
How superstitiously we mind our evils!
The throwing downe salt, or crossing of a Hare;
Bleeding at nose, the stumbling of a horse:
Or singing of a Criket, are of powre
To daunt whole man in us: Sir, fare you well:
I wish you all the joyes of a bless'd Father;
And (for my faith) lay this unto your brest,
Old friends (like old swords) still are trusted best.

[*Exit.*]

[*Enter Cariola with a child.*]

CARIOLA. Sir, you are the happy father of a sonne
Your wife commends him to you.

ANTONIO. Blessed comfort:
For heaven-sake, tend her well: I'll presently
Go set a figure for's Nativitie.[20]

Exeunt.

20. Have his horoscope cast.

ACTUS II, SCENA III.

[*Enter Bosola, with a dark lanthorn.*]

BOSOLA. Sure I did heare a woman shreike: list, hah!
And the sound came (if I receivd it right)
From the Duchesse lodgings: ther's some stratagem
In the confyning all our Courtiers
To their severall wards: I must have part of it,
My Intelligence will freize else: List againe—
It may be 'twas the mellencholly bird,
(Best friend of silence, and of solitarines)
The Oowle, that schreamd so: hah? *Antonio?*

[*Enter Antonio with a candle, his sword drawn.*]

ANTONIO. I heard some noyse: who's there? what art thou? speake.
BOSOLA. *Antonio?* put not your face; nor body
To such a forc'd expression of feare—
I am *Bosola;* your friend.
ANTONIO. *Bosola?* (This Moale do's undermine me) heard you not
A noyce even noe?
BOSOLA. From whence?
ANTONIO. From the *Duchesse* lodging.
BOSOLA. Not I: did you?
ANTONIO. I did, or else I dream'd.
BOSOLA. Let's walke towards it.
ANTONIO. No: it may be, 'twas
But the rising of the winde[.]
BOSOLA. Very likely:
Me thinkes 'tis very cold, and yet you sweat.
You looke wildly.
ANTONIO. I have bin setting a figure
For the Duchesse Jewells[.]
BOSOLA. Ah: and how falls your question?
Doe you find it radicall?[21]
ANTONIO. What's that to you?
'Tis rather to be question'd what designe
(When all men were commanded to their lodgings)
Makes you a night-walker.
BOSOLA. In sooth I'll tell you:
Now all the Court's asleepe, I thought the Divell
Had least to doe here, I come to say my prayers,
And if it doe offend you I doe so,
You are a fine Courtier.

21. A technical term from astrology meaning "fit to be judged."

ANTONIO. [*aside*] This fellow will undoe me;
You gave the Duchesse Apricocks to-day,
Pray heaven they were not poysond?
BOSOLA. Poysond? a spanish figge[22]
For the imputation.
ANTONIO. Traitors are ever confident,
Till they are discover'd: There were Jewels stolne too—
In my conceit, none are to be suspected
More than your selfe.
BOSOLA. You are a false steward.
ANTONIO. Saucy slave! I'll pull thee up by the rootes[.]
BOSOLA. May be the ruyne will crush you to peeces.
ANTONIO. You are an impudent snake indeed (sir)—
Are you scarce warme, and doe you shew your sting?
You Libell well (sir.)
BOSOLA. No (sir,) copy it out:
And I will set my hand to't.
ANTONIO. [*aside*] My nose bleedes:
One that were superstitious, would count
This ominous: when it meerely comes by chance.
Two letters, that are wrought here, for my name
Are drown'd in blood:
Meere accedent: [*to Bosola*] for you (sir) I'll take order:
I'th the morne you shall be safe: [*aside*] 'tis that must colour
Her lying-in: sir, [*to Bosola*] this doore you passe not:
I doe not hold it fit, that you come neere
The Duchesse lodgings, till you have quit your selfe;
[*aside*] *The Great are like the Base; nay, they are the same,*
When they seeke shamefull waies, to avoid shame.

[*Exit.*]

BOSOLA. *Antonio* here about, did drop a Paper—
Some of your helpe (falce-friend)°—oh, here it is: (his dark lantern)
What's here? a childes Nativitie calculated!

The Duchesse was deliver'd of a Sonne, 'tweene the houres twelve, and one, in the night: Anno Dom: 1504. *(that's this yeere)* decimo nono Decembris, *(that's this night) taken according to the Meridian of Malfy (that's our Duchesse: happy discovery!). The Lord of the first house, being combust in the ascendant, signifies short life: and* Mars *being in a human signe, joyn'd to the taile of the Dragon, in the eighth house, doth threaten a violent death;* Caetera non scrutantur.[23]

22. A gesture of contempt made by placing the thumb between the first and second fingers.
23. The rest are not investigated.

Why, now 'tis most apparent: This precise fellow
Is the Duchesse Bawde: I have it to my wish:
This is a parcell of Intelligency
Our Courtiers were cas'de-up for[.] It needes must follow,
That I must be committed, on pretence
Of poysoning her: which I'll endure, and laugh at:
If one could find the father now! but that
Time will discover: Old *Castruchio*
I'th morning posts to Rome; by him I'll send
A Letter, that shall make her brothers Galls° bile (rancor)
Ore-flowe their Livours—this was a thrifty way.
Though Lust doe masque in ne'er so strange disguise,
She's oft found witty, but is never wise.

[*Exit.*]

ACTUS II. SCENA IIII.

[*Enter Cardinal and Julia.*]

CARDINAL. Sit: thou art my best of wishes—pre-thee, tell me
What tricke didst thou invent to come to Rome,
Without thy husband?
JULIA. Why, (my Lord) I told him
I came to visit an old Anchorite° hermit
Heare, for devotion.
CARDINAL. Thou art a witty false one:
I meane to him.
JULIA. You have prevail'd with me
Beyond my strongest thoughts: I would not now
Find you inconstant.
CARDINAL. Doe not put thy selfe
To such a voluntary torture: which proceedes
Out of your owne guilt.
JULIA. How (my Lord?)
CARDINAL. You feare
My constancy, because you have approov'd
Those giddy and wild turnings in your selfe.
JULIA. Did you ere find them?
CARDINAL. Sooth generally for woemen,
A man might strive to make glasse male-able,
Ere he should make them fixed.
JULIA. So, (my Lord)!—
CARDINAL. We had need goe borrow that fantastique glasse
Invented by *Galileo* the Florentine,[24]

24. An anachronism, since Galileo devised a telescope for his own use in 1609, although the Dutchman Hans Lippershey had one by 1608.

To view another spacious world i'th'Moone,
And looke to find a constant woman there.
JULIA. This is very well (my Lord.)
CARDINAL. Why do you weepe?
Are teares your justification? the selfe-same teares
Will fall into your husbands bosome, (Lady)
With a loud protestation, that you love him
Above the world: Come, I'll love you wisely,
That's jealously; since I am very certaine
You cannot make me cuckould.
JULIA. I'll go home
To my husband.
CARDINAL. You may thanke me, (Lady)
I have taken you off your mellancholly pearch,
Boare you upon my fist, and shew'd you game,
And let you flie at it: I pray thee kisse me—
When thou wast with thy husband, thou wast watch'd
Like a tame Ellephant: (still you are to thank me)
Thou hadst onely kisses from him, and high feeding,
But what delight was that? 'twas just like one
That hath a little fingring on the Lute,
Yet cannot tune it: (still you are to thanke me.)
JULIA. You told me of a piteous wound i'th'heart,
And a sicke livour, when you woed me first,
And spake like one in physicke.
CARDINAL. Who's that?

[*Enter Servant.*]

Rest firme, for my affection to thee,
Lightning mooves slow to't.
SERVANT. Madam, a gentleman
That's comes post from *Malfy,* desires to see you.
CARDINAL. Let him enter, I'll with-draw.

Exit.

SERVANT. He sayes,
Your husband (old *Castruchio*) is come to *Rome,*
Most pittifully tyr'd with riding post.

[*Exit. Enter Delio.*]

JULIA. *Signior Delio?* 'tis one of my old Suitors.
DELIO. I was bold to come and see you.
JULIA. Sir, (you) are wel-come.
DELIO. Do you lie here?
JULIA. Sure, your owne experience
Will satisfy you no—our Romane Prelates
Do not keepe lodging, for Ladies.

DELIO. Very well:
I have brought you no comendations from your husband,
For I know none by him.
JULIA. I heare he's come to *Rome?*
DELIO. I never knew man, and beast, of a horse and a knight,
So weary of each other—if he had had a good backe,
He would have undertooke to have borne his horse,
His breech was so pittifully sore.
JULIA. Your laughter
Is my pitty.
DELIO. Lady, I know not whether
You want mony, but I have brought you some.
JULIA. From my husband?
DELIO. No, from mine owne allowance.
JULIA. I must heare the condition, ere I be bound to take it.
DELIO. Looke on't, 'tis gold: hath it not a fine colour?
JULIA. I have a Bird more beautifull.
DELIO. Try the sound on't.
JULIA. A Lute-string far exceedes it,
It hath no smell, like Cassia, or Cyvit,
Nor is it phisicall, though some fond° Doctors — foolish
Perswade us seethe't in Cullises—I'le tell you,
This is a Creature bred by—

[*Enter Servant.*]

SERVANT. Your husband's come,
Hath deliver'd a letter to the Duke of *Calabria,*
That, to my thinking, hath put him out of his wits.

[*Exit.*]

JULIA. Sir, you heare,
Pray let me know your busines, and your suite,
As briefely as can be.
DELIO. With good speed, I would wish you
(At such time as you are non-resident
With your husband) my mistris.
JULIA. Sir, I'le go aske my husband if I shall,
And straight returne your answere.

Exit.

DELIO. Very fine—
Is this her wit, or honesty, that speakes thus?
I heard one say the Duke was highly mov'd
With a letter sent from *Malfy:* I doe feare
Antonio is betray'd: how fearefully
Shewes his ambition now, (unfortunate Fortune)!—

"They passe through whirle-pooles, and deepe woes do shun,
Who the event weigh, ere the action's done.

Exit

ACTUS II, SCENA V

[*Enter*] *Cardinal, and Ferdinand, with a letter.*

FERDINAND. I have this night dig'd up a man-drake.[25]
CARDINAL. Say you?
FERDINAND. And I am growne mad with't.
CARDINAL. What's the prodegy?
FERDINAND. Read there—a sister dampn'd°—she's loose i'th'hilts; damned
Growne a notorious Strumpet.
CARDINAL. Speake lower.
FERDINAND. Lower?
Rogues do not whisper't now, but seeke to publish't,
(As servants do the bounty of their Lords)
Aloud; and with a covetous searching eye,
To marke who note them: Oh confusion sease her,
She hath had most cunning baudes to serve her turne,
And more secure conveyances for lust,
Than Townes of garrison, for Service.
CARDINAL. Is't possible?
Can this be certaine?
FERDINAND. Rhubarbe, oh, for rhubarbe
To purge this choller—here's the cursed day
To prompt my memory, and here'it shall sticke
Till of her bleeding heart, I make a spunge
To wipe it out.
CARDINAL. Why doe you make your selfe
So wild a Tempest?
FERDINAND. Would I could be one,
That I might tosse her pallace 'bout her eares,
Roote up her goodly forrests, blast her meades,
And lay her generall territory as wast,
As she hath done her honors.
CARDINAL. Shall our blood,
(The royall blood of *Arragon,* and *Castile*)
Be thus attaincted?
FERDINAND. Apply desperate physicke—
We must not now use Balsamum, but fire,
The smarting cupping-glasse, for that's the meane

25. When the mandrake was pulled up, the shrieking of its roots supposedly drove people mad.

To purge infected blood, (such blood as hers:)[26]
(There is a kind of pitty in mine eie,
I'll give it to my hand-kercher; and now 'tis here,
I'll bequeath this to her Bastard.
CARDINAL. What to do?
FERDINAND. Why, to make soft lint for his mother's wounds,
When I have hewed her to peeces.
CARDINAL. Curs'd creature—
Unequall nature, to place womens hearts
So farre upon the left-side!
FERDINAND. Foolish men,
That ere will trust their honour in a Barke[27]
Made of so slight, weake bull-rush, as is woman,
Apt every minnit to sinke it!
CARDINAL. Thus Ignorance, when it hath purchas'd honour,
It cannot weild it.
FERDINAND. Me thinkes I see her laughing,
Excellent *Hyenna*—talke to me somewhat, quickly,
Or my imagination will carry me
To see her, in the shamefull act of sinne.
CARDINAL. With whom?
FERDINAND. Happily, with some strong-thigh'd Bargeman;
Or one o'th'wood-yard, that can quoit the sledge,
Or tosse the barre, or else some lovely Squire
That carries coles up, to her privy lodgings.
CARDINAL. You flie beyond your reason.
FERDINAND. Goe to (Mistris.)
'Tis not your whores milke, that shall quench my wild-fire,
But your whores blood.
CARDINAL. How idlely shewes this rage!—which carries you,
As men convai'd by witches, through the ayre,
On violent whirle-winds—this intemperate noyce,
Fitly resembles deafe-mens shrill discourse,
Who talke aloud, thinking all other men
To have their imperfection.
FERDINAND. Have not you
My palsey?
CARDINAL. Yes—I can be angry
Without this rupture—there is not in nature
A thing, that makes man so deform'd, so beastly,
As doth intemperate anger: chide your selfe—
You have divers men, who never yet exprest

26. A heated glass was applied to skin; as the glass cooled it sucked up the skin, and, if the skin had been lanced, blood.

27. A square-rigged ship of three or more masts.

Their strong desire of rest, but by unrest,
By vexing of themselves: Come, put your selfe
In tune.

FERDINAND. So—I will onely study to seeme
The thing I am not: I could kill her now,
In you, or in my selfe, for I do thinke
It is some sinne in us, Heaven doth revenge
By her.

CARDINAL. Are you starke mad?

FERDINAND. I would have their bodies
Burn't in a coale-pit, with the ventage stop'd,
That their curs'd smoake might not ascend to Heaven:
Or dippe the sheetes they lie in, in pitch or sulphure,
Wrap them in't, and then light them like a match:
Or else to boile their Bastard to a cullise,
And give't his lecherous father, to renew
The sinne of his backe.

CARDINAL. I'll leave you.

FERDINAND. Nay, I have done.
I am confident, had I bin damn'd in hell,
And should have heard of this, it would have put me
Into a cold sweat: In, in, I'll go sleepe—
Till I know who leapes my sister, i'll not stirre:
That knowne, i'll finde Scorpions to string my whips,
And fix her in a generall ecclipse.

Exeunt.

ACTUS III, SCENA I

[*Enter Antonio and Delio.*]

ANTONIO. Our noble friend (my most beloved *Delio*)
Oh, you have bin a stranger long at Court,
Came you along with the Lord *Ferdinand?*

DELIO. I did Sir, and how faires your noble *Duchesse?*

ANTONIO. Right fortunately well: She's an excellent
Feeder of pedegrees: since you last saw her,
She hath had two children more, a son and daughter.

DELIO. Me thinkes 'twas yester-day: Let me but wincke,
And not behold your face, which to mine eye
Is somewhat leaner, verily I should dreame
It were within this halfe houre.

ANTONIO. You have not bin in Law, (friend *Delio*)
Nor in prison, nor a Suitor at the Court,
Nor beg'd the reversion of some great mans place,

Nor troubled with an old wife, which doth make
Your time so insensibly hasten.

DELIO. Pray Sir tell me,
Hath not this newes arriv'd yet to the eare
Of the lord *Cardinal?*

ANTONIO. I feare it hath,
The Lord *Ferdinand,* (that's newly come to Court,)
Doth beare himselfe right dangerously.

DELIO. Pray why?

ANTONIO. He is so quiet, that he seemes to sleepe
The tempest out (as Dormise do in Winter)—
Those houses, that are haunted, are most still,
Till the divell be up.

DELIO. What say the common people?

ANTONIO. The common-rable, do directly say
She is a Strumpet.

DELIO. And your graver heades,
(Which would be politique) what censure they?

ANTONIO. They do observe I grow to infinite purchase
The leaft-hand way, and all suppose the Duchesse
Would amend it, if she could. For, say they,
Great princes, though they grudge their Officers
Should have such large, and unconfined meanes
To get wealth under them, will not complaine
Least thereby they should make them odious.
Unto the people—for other obligation
Of love, or marriage, betweene her and me,
They never dreame of.

[*Enter Ferdinand, Duchesse, & Bosola.*]

DELIO. The Lord *Ferdinand*
Is going to bed.

FERDINAND. I'll instantly to bed,
For I am weary: I am to be-speake
A husband for you.

DUCHESSE. For me (Sir?)—pray who is't?

FERDINAND. The great Count *Malateste.*

DUCHESSE. Fie upon him,
A Count! he's a meere sticke of sugar-candy,
(You may looke quite through him)—when I choose
A husband, I will marry for your honour.

FERDINAND. You shall do well in't: How is't (worthy *Antonio?*)

DUCHESSE. But (Sir) I am to have private conference with you,
About a scandalous report, is spread
Touching mine honour.

FERDINAND. Let me be ever deafe to't:

One of Pasquils paper-bullets,[28] court-calumney,
A pestilent ayre, which Princes pallaces
Are seldome purg'd of: Yet say that it were true,
I powre it in your bosome, my fix'd love
Would strongly excuse, extenuate, nay, deny
Faults, were they apparent in you: Goe be safe
In your owne innocency.
DUCHESSE. [*aside*] O bless'd comfort—
This deadly aire is purg'd.

Exeunt, [*except Ferdinand & Bosola*].

FERDINAND. Her guilt treads on
Hot-burning cultures:° Now *Bosola,* cutting edge of a plow
How thrives our intelligence?
BOSOLA. (Sir) uncertainly—
'Tis rumour'd she hath had three bastards, but
By whom, we may go read i'th'Starres.
FERDINAND. Why some
Hold opinion all things are written there.
BOSOLA. Yes, if we could find Spectacles to read them—
I do suspect, there hath bin some Sorcery
Us'd on the Duchesse.
FERDINAND. Sorcery?—to what purpose?
BOSOLA. To make her doate on some desertles fellow,
She shames to acknowledge.
FERDINAND. Can your faith give way
To thinke there's powre in potions, or in Charmes,
To make us love, whether we will or no?
BOSOLA. Most certainly.
FERDINAND. Away, these are meere gulleries, horred things
Invented by some cheating mounte-banckes
To abuse us: Do you thinke that hearbes, or charmes
Can force the will? Some trialls have bin made
In this foolish practice; but the ingredients
Were lenative° poysons, such as are of force slow
To make the patient mad; and straight the witch
Sweares (by equivocation) they are in love.
The witch-craft lies in her rancke blood: this night
I will force confession from her: You told me
You had got (within these two dayes) a false key
Into her Bed-chamber.
BOSOLA. I have.
FERDINAND. As I would wish.
BOSOLA. What do you intend to doe?

28. A statue in Rome upon which students affixed satirical remarks.

FERDINAND. Can you ghesse?
BOSOLA. No.
FERDINAND. Doe not aske then:
He that can compasse me, and know my drifts,
May say he hath put a girdle 'bout the world,
And sounded all her quick-sands.
BOSOLA. I doe not
Thinke so.
FERDINAND. What doe you thinke then, pray?
BOSOLA. That you
Are your own Chronicle too much: and grosly
Flatter your selfe.
FERDINAND. Give me thy hand, I thanke thee:
I never gave Pention but to flatterers,
Till I entertained thee: farewell,
That Friend a Great mans ruine strongly checks,
Who railes into his beliefe, all his defects.

Exeunt.

ACTUS III, SCENA II.

[*The Bed-chamber of the Duchesse.*]
[*Enter Duchesse, Antonio, & Cariola.*]

DUCHESSE. Bring me the Casket hither, and the Glasse;
You get no lodging here, to-night (my Lord.)
ANTONIO. Indeed, I must perswade one[.]
DUCHESSE. Very good!
I hope in time 'twill grow into a custome,
That Noblemen shall come with cap, and knee,
To purchase a nights lodging of their wives.
ANTONIO. I must lye here.
DUCHESSE. Must? you are a Lord of Misse-rule.[29]
ANTONIO. Indeed, my Rule is onely in the night.
DUCHESSE. To what use will you put me?—
ANTONIO. Wee'll sleepe together[.]
DUCHESSE. Alas, what pleasure can two Lovers find in sleep?
CARIOLA. My lord, I lye with her often: and I know
She'll much disquiet you.
ANTONIO. See, you are complain'd of.
CARIOLA. For she's the sprawlingst bedfellow.
ANTONIO. I shall like her the better for that.
CARIOLA. Sir, shall I aske you a question?

29. A person appointed to rule over festivities at Christmas.

ANTONIO. I pray thee *Cariola.*
CARIOLA. Wherefore still, when you lie with my Lady
Doe you rise so early?
ANTONIO. Labouring men
Count the Clocke oftnest *Cariola,*
Are glad when their task's ended.
DUCHESSE. I'll stop your mouth.

[*kisses him.*]

ANTONIO. Nay, that's but one, *Venus* had two soft Doves
To draw her Chariot: I must have another:

[*kisses her.*]

When wilt thou marry, *Cariola?*
CARIOLA. Never (my Lord.)
ANTONIO. O fie upon this single life: forgoe it:
We read how *Daphne,* for her peevish flight
Became a fruitlesse Bay-tree: *Sirinx* turn'd
To the pale empty Reede: *Anaxarete*
Was frozen into Marble:[30] whereas those
Which married, or prov'd kind unto their friends
Were, by a gracious influence, transhap'd
Into the Oliffe, Pomgranet, mulberry:
Became flowres, precious stones, or eminent Starres.
CARIOLA. This is a vaine Poetry: but I pray you tell me,
If there were propos'd me, Wisdome, Riches, and Beauty,
In three severall young men, which should I choose?
ANTONIO. 'Tis a hard question: This was *Paris'* case,
And he was blind in't, and there was a great cause:
For how was't possible he could judge right,
Having three amorous Goddesses in view,
And they starcke naked?[31] 'twas a Motion
Were able to be-night the apprehention
Of the seveerest Counsellor of Europe.
Now I looke on both your faces, so well form'd,
It puts me in mind of a question, I would aske.
CARIOLA. What is't?
ANTONIO. I doe wonder why hard-favour'd Ladies,
For the most part, keepe worse-favour'd waieting women,
To attend them, and cannot endure faire-ones.

30. Daphne, fleeing Apollo, was transformed into the laurel tree. Sirius, fleeing Pan, became hollow reeds, which Pan used as pipes. Anaxarete refused the shepherd Iphis; when she was unmoved by his suicide, Aphrodite turned her into marble.

31. Athena, Hera, and Aphrodite contested for an apple to be awarded to the fairest of the goddesses. Paris was chosen as judge and offered bribes of wisdom, wealth, and beauty. He chose Aphrodite, who helped him win Helen, the event that began the Trojan War.

DUCHESSE. Oh, that's soone answer'd.
Did you ever in your life know an ill Painter
Desire to have his dwelling next door to the shop
Of an excellent Picture-maker? 'twould disgrace
His face-making, and undoe him: I pre-thee
When were we so merry? my haire tangles.
ANTONIO. Pray-thee *(Cariola)* let's steale forth the roome,
And let her talke to her selfe: I have divers times
Serv'd her the like—when she hath chafde extreamely.
I love to see her angry: Softly, *Cariola.*

Exeunt [*Antonio & Cariola*].

DUCHESSE. Doth not the colour of my haire 'gin to change?
When I waxe gray, I shall have all the Court
Powder their haire, with Arras, to be like me.
You have cause to love me, I entred you into my heart
Before you would vouchsafe to call for the keyes.

[*Enter Ferdinand unseen.*]

We shall one day have my brothers take you napping:
Me thinkes his Presence (being now in Court)
Should make you keepe your owne Bed: but you'll say
Love mixt with feare, is sweetest: I'll assure you
You shall get no more children till my brothers
Consent to be your Ghossips:° Have you lost your tongue? godparents

[*She turns and sees Ferdinand holding a poniard.*]

'Tis welcome:
For know whether I am doomb'd to live, or die,
I can doe both like a Prince.
FERDINAND. Die then, quickle:

Ferdinand gives her ponyard.

Vertue, where art thou hid? what hideous thing
Is it, that doth ecclipze thee?
DUCHESSE. Pray sir heare me[.]
FERDINAND. Or is it true, thou art but a bare name,
And no essentiall thing?
DUCHESSE. Sir!
FERDINAND. Doe not speake.
DUCHESSE. No sir:
I will plant my soule in mine eares, to heare you.
FERDINAND. Oh most imperfect light of humaine reason,
That mak'st us so unhappy, to foresee
What we can least prevent: Pursue thy wishes:
And glory in them: there's in shame no comfort
But to be past all bounds, and sence of shame.

DUCHESSE. I pray sir, heare me: I am married—
FERDINAND. So!
DUCHESSE. Happily, not to your liking: but for that
Alas: your sheeres do come untimely now
To clip the birds wings that's already flown:
Will you see my Husband?
FERDINAND. Yes, if I could change
Eyes with a Basilisque.[32]
DUCHESSE. Sure, you came hither
By his confederacy.
FERDINAND. The howling of a Wolfe
Is musicke to thee (schrech-Owle) pre'thee, peace:
What ere thou art, that hast enjoy'd my sister,
(For I am sure thou hearst me) for thine owne sake
Let me not know thee: I came hither, prepar'd
To worke thy discovery: yet am now perswaded
It would beget such violent effects
As would dampne us both: I would not for ten Millions
I had beheld thee: therefore use all meanes
I never may have knowledge of thy name;
Enjoy thy lust still, and a wretched life,
On that condition: And for thee (vilde woman,)
If thou doe wish thy Leacher may grow old
In thy Embracements, I would have thee build
Such a roome for him, as our Anchorites
To holier use enhabite: Let not the Sunne
Shine on him, till he's dead: let Dogs, and Monkeys
Onely converse with him, and such dombe things
To whom Nature denies use to sound his name.
Doe not keepe a Paraqueto, lest she learne it;
If thou doe love him, cut out thine owne tongue
Least it bewray him.
DUCHESSE. Why might not I marry?
I have not gone about, in this, to create
Any new world, or custome.
FERDINAND. Thou art undone:
And thou hast ta'ne that massiy sheete of lead
That hid thy husbands bones, and foulded it
About my heart.
DUCHESSE. Mine bleedes for't.
FERDINAND. Thine? thy heart?
What should I nam't, unlesse a hollow bullet[33]
Fill'd with unquenchable wild-fire?

32. Mythical creature whose gaze turned men into stone.
33. A cannonball filled with powder.

DUCHESSE. You are, in this
Too strict: and were you not my Princely brother
I would say too wilfull: My reputation
Is safe.
FERDINAND. Dost thou know what reputation is?
I'll tell thee—to small purpose, since th'instruction
Comes now too late:
Upon a time Reputation, Love, and Death,
Would travell ore the world: and it was concluded
That they should part, and take three severall wayes:
Death told them, they should find him in great Battailes:
Or Cities plagu'd with plagues: Love gives them councell
To enquire for him 'mongst unambitious shepheards,
Where dowries were not talk'd of: and sometimes
'Mongst quiet kindred, that had nothing left
By their dead Parents: stay (quoth Reputation)
Doe not forsake me: for it is my nature
If once I part from any man I meete,
I am never found againe: And so, for you:
You have shooke hands with Reputation,
And made him invisible: So fare you well.
I will never see you more.
DUCHESSE. Why should onely I,
Of all the other Princes of the World
Be cas'de-up, like a holy Relique? I have youth,
And a little beautie.
FERDINAND. So you have some Virgins
That are witches: I will never see thee more.

Exit.
Enter Antonio with a Pistoll, [*& Cariola.*]

DUCHESSE. You saw this apparition?
ANTONIO. Yes: we are
Betraid; how came he hither? I should turne
This, to thee, for that.
CARIOLA. Pray sir doe: and when
That you have cleft my heart, you shall read there
Mine innocence[.]
DUCHESSE. That Gallery gave him entrance.
ANTONIO. I would this terrible thing would come againe,
That (standing on my guard) I might relate
My warrantable love: [*she shows the poniard.*] ha, what meanes this?
DUCHESSE. He left this with me.
ANTONIO. And it seemes, did wish
You would use it on your selfe?
DUCHESSE. His Action seem'd
To intend so much.

ANTONIO. This hath a handle to't,
As well as a point—turne it towards him, and
So fasten the keene edge, in his rancke gall:

[Knocking within.]

How now? who knocks? more Earthquakes?
DUCHESSE. I stand
As if a Myne beneath my feete, were ready
To be blowne up.
CARIOLA. 'Tis *Bosola.*
DUCHESSE. Away!—
O misery, me thinkes unjust actions
Should weare these masques, and curtaines; and not we:
You must instantly part hence: I have fashion'd it already.

Ex[it]. Ant[onio]. [Enter Bosola.]

BOSOLA. The Duke your brother is ta'ne up in a whirlewind—
Hath tooke horse, and's rid poast to Rome.
DUCHESSE. So late?
BOSOLA. He told me, (as he mounted into th'saddle,)
You were undone.
DUCHESSE. Indeed, I am very neere it.
BOSOLA. What's the matter?
DUCHESSE. *Antonio,* the master of our house-hold
Hath dealt so falsely with me, in's accounts:
My brother stood engag'd with me for money
Ta'ne up of certaine Neapolitane Jewes,
And *Antonio* lets the Bonds be forfeyt.
BOSOLA. Strange: [*aside*] this is cunning:
DUCHESSE. And hereupon
My brothers Bills at Naples are protested
Against: call up our Officers.
BOSOLA. I shall.

Exit. [Enter Antonio.]

DUCHESSE. The place that you must flye to, is *Ancona*—
Hire a house there. I'll send after you
My Treasure, and my Jewells: our weake safetie
Runnes upon engenous wheeles:° short sillables, — intricate machinery
Must stand for periods:° I must now accuse you — long sentences
Of such a fained crime as *Tasso* calls
Magnanima Mensogna:[34] a Noble Lie,
'Cause it must shield our honors: harke, they are comming.

34. A pious fraud, from *Jerusalem Delivered,* book 2, where Sophronia lies in an attempt to protect other Christians by taking the blame for a stolen image of the Virgin Mary.

[*Enter Bosola & Officers.*]

ANTONIO. Will your grace heare me?
DUCHESSE. I have got well by you: you have yeelded me
A million of losse; I am like to inherit
The peoples curses for your Stewardship:
You had the tricke, in Audit time to be sicke,
Till I had sign'd your *Quietus;* and that cur'de you
Without helpe of a Doctor. Gentlemen,
I would have this man be an example to you all:
So shall you hold my favour: I pray let him;
For h'as done that (alas) you would not thinke of,
And (because I intend to be rid of him)
I meane not to publish: use your fortune else-where.
ANTONIO. I am strongely arm'd to brooke my over-throw,
As commonly men beare with a hard yeere:
I will not blame the cause on't; but doe thinke
The necessitie of my malevolent starre
Procures this, not her humour: O the inconstant,
And rotten ground of service, you may see:
'Tis ev'n like him, that in a winter night
Takes a long slumber, ore a dying fire;
A-loth to part from't: yet parts thence as cold,
As when he first sat downe.
DUCHESSE. We doe confiscate
(Towards the satisfying of your accounts)
All that you have.
ANTONIO. I am all yours: and 'tis very fit
All mine should be so.
DUCHESSE. So, sir; you have your Passe.
ANTONIO. You may see (Gentlemen) what 'tis to serve
A Prince with body, and soule.

Exit.

BOSOLA. Heere's an example for extortion; what moysture is drawne out of the Sea, when fowle weather comes, powres down, and runnes into the Sea againe.
DUCHESSE. I would know what are your opinions
Of this *Antonio.*
2 OFFICER. He could not abide to see a Pigges head gaping—
I thought your Grace would find him a Jew[.]
3 OFFICER. I would you had bin his Officer, for your owne sake.
4 OFFICER. You would have had more money.
1 OFFICER. He stop'd his eares with blacke wooll: and (to those came to him for money) said he was thicke of hearing.
2 OFFICER. Some said he was an hermaphrodite, for he could not abide a woman.

4 OFFICER. How scurvy prowd he would looke, when the
Treasury was full: Well, let him goe[.]
1 OFFICER. Yes, and the chippings of the Buttrey fly after him,
to scowre his gold Chaine.
DUCHESSE. Leave us. *Exeunt* [*Officers.*] What do you think of these?
BOSOLA. That these are Rogues; that in's prosperitie.
But to have waited on his fortune, could have wish'd
His dirty Stirrop rivited through their noses:
And follow'd after's Mule, like a Beare in a Ring.
Would have prostituted their daughters, to his Lust:
Made their first-borne Intelligencers: thought none happy
But such as were borne under his bles'd Plannet
And wore his Livory: and doe these Lyce drop off now?
Well, never looke to have the like againe;
He hath left a sort of flattring rogues behind him,
Their doombe must follow: Princes pay flatterers,
In their owne money: Flatterers dissemble their vices,
And they dissemble their lies, that's Justice:
Alas, poore gentleman!—
DUCHESSE. Poore! he hath amply fill'd his cofers.
BOSOLA. Sure he was too honest: *Pluto* the god of riches,
When he's sent (by *Jupiter*) to any man
He goes limping, to signifie that wealth
That comes on god's name, comes slowly, but when he's sent
On the divells arrand, he rides poast, and comes in by scuttles.[35]
Let me shew you what a most unvalu'd jewell,
You have (in a wanton humour) throwne away,
To blesse the man shall find him: He was an excellent
Courtier, and most faithfull, a souldier that thought it
As beastly to know his owne value too little,
As devillish to acknowledge it too much,
Both his vertue, and forme, deserv'd a farre better fortune:
His discourse rather delighted to judge it selfe, then shew it selfe.
His breast was fill'd with all perfection,
And yet it seem'd a private whispering-roome
It made so little noyse of't.
DUCHESSE. But he was basely descended.
BOSOLA. Will you make your selfe a mercinary herald,
Rather to examine mens pedegrees than vertues?
You shall want him,
For know an honest states-man to a Prince,
Is like a Cedar, planted by a spring,
The Spring bathes the trees roote, the gratefull tree
Rewards it with his shadow: you have not done so—

35. 1) with quick steps; 2) in baskets.

I would sooner swim to the *Bernoothes* on
Two Politisians rotten bladders, tide
Together with an Intelligencers hart-string
Than depend on so changeable a Princes favour.
Fare-thee-well *(Antonio)* since the mallice of the world
Would needes downe with thee, it cannot be sayd yet
That any ill happened unto thee, considering thy fall
Was accompanied with vertue.

DUCHESSE. Oh, you render me excellent Musicke.
BOSOLA. Say you?
DUCHESSE. This good one that you speake of, is my husband.
BOSOLA. Do I not dreame? can this ambitious age
Have so much goodness in't, as to prefer
A man, meerely for worth: without these shadowes
Of wealth and painted honors? possible?
DUCHESSE. I have had three children by him.
BOSOLA. Fortunate Lady,
For you have made your private nuptiall bed
The humble, and faire Seminary of peace,
No question but: many an unbenefic'd Scholler
Shall pray for you, for this deed, and rejoyce
That some preferment in the world can yet
Arise from merit. The virgins of your land
(That have no dowries) shall hope your example
Will raise them to rich husbands: Should you want
Souldiers, 'twould make the very *Turkes* and *Moores*
Turne Christians, and serve you for this act.
Last, the neglected Poets of your time,
In honour of this trophee of a man,
Rais'd by that curious engine, (your white hand)
Shall thanke you, in your grave, for't; and make that
More reverend than all the Cabinets[36]
Of living Princes: For *Antonio*—
His fame shall likewise flow from many a pen,
When Heralds shall want coates, to sell to men.[37]
DUCHESSE. As I taste comfort, in this friendly speech,
So would I finde concealement.
BOSOLA. O the secret of my Prince,
Which I will weare on th'in-side of my heart.
DUCHESSE. You shall take charge of all my coyne and jewels,
And follow him, for he retires himselfe
To *Ancona*.

36. Collections of rare objects.

37. One method of raising money was to sell honors. The implication here is that heralds will claim Antonio is an ancestor of someone with a newly bought coat of arms.

BOSOLA. So.
DUCHESSE. Whither, within few days,
I mean to follow thee.
BOSOLA. Let me think:
I would wish your Grace, to faigne a Pilgrimage
To our Lady of *Loretto,*[38] (scarce seaven leagues
From faire *Ancona*)—so may you depart
Your Country, with more honour, and your flight
Will seeme a Princely progresse, retaining
Your usuall traine about you.
DUCHESSE. Sir, your direction
Shall lead me by the hand.
CARIOLA. In my opinion,
She were better progresse to the bathes at *Leuca,*
Or go visit the *Spaw*
In *Germany,* for (if you will beleeve me)
I do not like this jesting with religion,
This faigned Pilgrimage.
DUCHESSE. Thou art a superstitious foole,
Prepare us instantly for our departure:
Past sorrowes, let us moderately lament them,
For those to come, seeke wisely, to prevent them.

Exit [*Duchesse with Cariola*].

BOSOLA. A Polititian is the divells quilted anvell,
He fashions all sinnes on him, and the blowes
Are never heard—he may worke in a Ladies Chamber,
(As here for proofe)—what rests, but I reveale
All to my Lord? oh, this base quality
Of Intelligencer! why, every Quality i'th'world
Preferres but gaine, or commendation:
Now for this act, I am certaine to be rais'd,
And men that paint weedes, (to the life) are prais'd.

Exit.

ACTUS III, SCENA III

[*Enter*] *Cardinal, Ferdinand, Malateste, Pescara, Silvio, Delio.*

CARDINAL. Must we turne Souldier then?
MALATESTE. The emperor,
Hearing your worth that way, (ere you attain'd

38. Site of the Holy House of Mary at Nazareth, miraculously brought there, after a stop in Dalmatia, when threatened by the Turks.

This reverend garment,) joynes you in commission
With the right fortunate souldier the Marquis of *Pescara,*
And the famous *Lanoy.*
CARDINAL. He that had the honour
Of taking the *French* King Prisoner?
MALATESTE. The same—
Here's a plot drawne, for a new Fortification,
At *Naples.*
FERDINAND. This great Count *Malateste,* I perceive,
Hath got employment?
DELIO. No employment (my Lord)—
A marginall note in the muster-booke, that he is
A voluntary Lord.
FERDINAND. He's no Souldier?
DELIO. He has worne gun-powder, in's hollow tooth for the
tooth-ache.
SILVIO. He comes to the leaguer, with a full intent,
To eate fresh beefe, and garlicke, meanes to stay
Till the sent be gon, and straight returne to Court.
DELIO. He hath read all the late service
As the City Chronicle relates it,
And keepes two [Painters] going, only to expresse
Battailes in modell.
SILVIO. Then he'l fight by the booke.
DELIO. By the Almanacke, I thinke,
To choose good dayes, and shun the Criticall.
That's his mistris' skarfe.
SILVIO. Yes, he protests
He would do much for that taffita—
DELIO. I thinke he would run away from a battaile
To save it from taking prisoner.
SILVIO. He is horribly afraid,
Gun-powder will spoile the perfume on't—
DELIO. I saw a Dutch-man breake his pate once
For calling him pot-gun[39]—he made his head
Have a boare in't, like a musket.
SILVIO. I would he had made a touch-hole to't.
He is indeede a guarded sumpter-cloath,° (ornamental saddle blanket)
Onely for the remoove of the Court.

[*Enter Bosola.*]

PESCARA. *Bosola* arriv'd? what should be the businesse?
Some falling-out amongst the Cardinalls.
These factions amongst great men, they are like

39. Pop gun, a person full of hot air.

Foxes—when their heads are devided
They carry fire in their tailes,[40] and all the Country
About them, goes to wracke for't.

SILVIO. What's that *Bosola?*

DELIO. I knew him in *Padua,* a fantasticall scholler, like such, who studdy to know how many knots was in *Hercules* club, of what colour *Achilles* beard was, or whether *Hector* were not troubled with the tooth-ach—He hath studdied himselfe halfe bleare-ei'd, to know the true semitry of *Caesars* nose by a shooing-horn, and this he did to gaine the name of a speculative man.

PESCARA. Marke Prince *Ferdinand,*
A very *Salamander* lives in's eye,
To mocke the eager violence of fire.

SILVIO. That Cardinal hath made more bad faces with his oppression then ever *Michael Angelo* made good ones, he lifts up's nose, like a fowle Por-pisse before a storme—

PESCARA. The Lord *Ferdinand* laughes.

DELIO. Like a deadly Cannon,
That lightens ere it smoakes.

PESCARA. These are your true pangues of death,
The pangues of life, that struggle with great statesmen—

DELIO. In such a deformed silence, witches whisper their charmes.

CARDINAL. Doth she make religion her riding hood
To keep her from the sun, and tempest?

FERDINAND. That: that damnes her: Me thinkes her fault, and beauty
Blended together, shew like leprosie—
The whiter, the fowler: I make it a question
Whether her beggerly brats were ever christned.

CARDINAL. I will instantly sollicite the state of *Ancona*
To have them banish'd.

FERDINAND. You are for *Loretto?*
I shall not be at your Ceremony: fare you well,
Write to the Duke of Malfy, my yong Nephew,
She had by her first husband, and acquaint him
With's mothers honesty.

BOSOLA. I will.

FERDINAND. *Antonio!*
A slave, that onely smell'd of yncke and coumpters,
And nev'r in's life, look'd like a Gentleman,
But in the audit-time—go, go presently,
Draw me out an hundreth and fifty of our horse,
And meete me at the fort-bridge.

Exeunt.

40. Judges 15:4.

ACTUS III, SCENA IIII.

[*Enter*] *Two Pilgrimes to the Shrine of our Lady of* Loretto.

1 PILGRIM. I have not seene a goodlier Shrine than this,
Yet I have visited many.
2 PILGRIM. The Cardinal of *Arragon*
Is, this day, to resigne his Cardinals hat,
His sister Duchesse likewise is arriv'd
To pay her vow of Pilgrimage—I expect
A noble Ceremony.
1 PILGRIM. No question:—They come.

Here the ceremony of the Cardinal's enstalment, in the habit of a Souldier: perform'd in delivering up his Crosse, Hat, Robes, and Ring, at the Shrine; and investing him with Sword, Helmet, Shield, and Spurs: then Antonio, *the* Duchesse, *and their Children (having presented themselves at the Shrine) are (by a forme of Banishment in dumbe-shew, expressed towards them by the Cardinal, and the State of* Ancona*) banished: During all which Ceremony, this Ditty is sung (to very sollemne Musique) by divers Church-men; and then Exeunt.*

Armes, and Honors decke thy story,
To thy Fames eternall glory,
Adverse Fortune ever flie-thee,
No disastrous fate come nigh-thee.

The Author disclaimes this Ditty to be his.

I alone will sing thy praises,
Whom to honour vertue raises;
And thy study, that divine-is,
Bent to Marshiall discipline-is:
Lay aside all those robes lie by thee,
Crown thy arts, with armes: they'll beautifie thee.

O worthy of worthiest name, adorn'd in this manner,
Lead bravely thy forces on, under wars warlike banner:
O mayst thou prove fortunate, in all Marshial courses,
Guide thou still, by skill, in artes, and forces:
Victory attend thee nigh, whilst fame sings loud thy powres,
Triumphant conquest crowne thy head, and blessings powre downe showres.

1 PILGRIM. Here's a strange turne of state—who would have thought
So great a Lady, would have match'd her selfe
Unto so meane a person? yet the Cardinal
Beares himselfe much too cruell.
2 PILGRIM. They are banish'd.

1 PILGRIM. But I would aske what power hath this state
Of *Ancona,* to determine of a free Prince?
2 PILGRIM. They are a free state sir, and her brother shew'd
How that the Pope fore-hearing of her loosenesse,
Hath seaz'd into th'protection of the Church
The Dukedome, which she held as dowager.
1 PILGRIM. But by what justice?
2 PILGRIM. Sure, I thinke by none,
Only her brothers instigation.
1 PILGRIM. What was it, with such violence he tooke
Off from her finger?
2 PILGRIM. 'Twas her wedding-ring,
Which he vow'd shortly he would sacrifice
To his revenge.
1 PILGRIM. Alasse *Antonio,*
If that a man be thrust into a well,
No matter who sets hand to't, his owne weight
Will bring him sooner to th'bottome: Come, let's hence.
Fortune makes this conclusion generall,
All things do helpe th'unhappy man to fall.

Exeunt.

ACTUS III, SCENA V.

[*Enter*] *Antonio, Duchesse. Children, Cariola, Servants.*

DUCHESSE. Banish'd *Ancona!*
ANTONIO. Yes, you see what powre
Lightens in great mens breath.
DUCHESSE. Is all our traine
Shrunke to this poore remainder?
ANTONIO. These poore men,
(Which have got little in your service) vow
To take your fortune: but your wiser buntings
Now they are fledg'd, are gon.
DUCHESSE. They have done wisely—
This puts me in minde of death, Physitians thus,
With their hands full of money, use to give ore
Their Patients.
ANTONIO. Right the fashion of the world—
From decaide fortunes, every flatterer shrinkes,
Men cease to build, where the foundation sinkes.
DUCHESSE. I had a very strange dreame to-night.
ANTONIO. What was't?
DUCHESSE. Me thought I wore my Coronet of State,

And on a sudaine all the Diamonds
Were chang'd to Pearles.
ANTONIO. My Interpretation
Is, you'll weepe shortly, for to me, the pearles
Doe signifie your teares[.]
DUCHESSE. The Birds, that live i'th field
On the wilde benefit of Nature, live
Happier than we; for they may choose their Mates,
And carroll their sweet pleasures to the Spring[.]

[*Enter Bosola with a letter.*]

BOSOLA. You are happily ore-ta'ne.
DUCHESSE. From my brother?
BOSOLA. Yes, from the Lord *Ferdinand* . . . your brother
All love, and safetie—
DUCHESSE. Thou do'st blanch mischiefe—
Wouldst make it white: See, see; like to calme weather
At Sea, before a tempest, false hearts speak faire
To those they intend most mischief.

Reads A Letter.

Send Antonio *to me; I want his head in a business:*
A politicke equivocation—
He doth not want your councell, but your head;
That is, he cannot sleepe till you be dead.
And here's annother Pitfall, that's strew'd ore
With Roses: marke it, 'tis a cunning one.
I stand ingaged for your husband, for severall debts at Naples: *let not that trouble him, I had rather have his heart, then his mony.*
And I beleeve so too.
BOSOLA. What doe you beleeve?
DUCHESSE. That he so much distrusts my husbands love,
He will by no meanes beleeve his heart is with him
Untill he see it: the Divell is not cunning enough
To circumvent us in Ridles.
BOSOLA. Will you reject that noble, and free league
Of amitie, and love which I present you?
DUCHESSE. Their league is like that of some politick Kings
Onely to make themselves of strength, and powre
To be our after-ruine: tell them so[.]
BOSOLA. And what from you?
ANTONIO. Thus tell him: I will not come.
BOSOLA. And what of this?
ANTONIO. My brothers have dispers'd
Blood-hounds abroad; which till I heare are muzell'd,
No truce, though hatch'd with nere such politick skill

Is safe, that hangs upon our enemies will.
I'll not come at them.
BOSOLA. This proclaimes your breeding.
Every small thing drawes a base mind to feare:
As the Adamant draws yron: fare you well sir,
You shall shortly heare from's.

Exit.

DUCHESSE. I suspect some Ambush:
Therefore by all my love . . . I doe conjure you
To take your eldest sonne, and flye towards *Millaine;*
Let us not venture all this poore remainder
In one unlucky bottom.
ANTONIO. You councell safely:
Best of my life, farewell: Since we must part,
Heaven hath a hand in't; but no otherwise,
Than as some curious Artist takes in sunder
A Clocke, or Watch, when it is out of frame
To bring't in better order.
DUCHESSE. I know not which is best,
To see you dead, or part with you: Farewell Boy.
Thou art happy, that thou hast not understanding
To know thy misery: For all our wit
And reading, brings us to a truer sence
Of sorrow: In the eternall Church, Sir,
I doe hope we shall not part thus.
ANTONIO. Oh, be of comfort,
Make Patience a noble fortitude:
And thinke not how unkindly we are us'de:
Man (like to *Cassia*) is prov'd best, being bruiz'd.
DUCHESSE. Must I like to a slave-borne Russian,
Account it praise to suffer tyranny?
And yet (O Heaven) thy heavy hand is in't.
I have seene my litle boy oft scourge his top,
And compar'd my selfe to't: naught made me ere
Go right, but Heavens scourge-sticke.
ANTONIO. Doe not weepe:
Heaven fashion'd us of nothing: and we strive,
To bring our selves to nothing: farewell *Cariola,*
And thy sweet armefull: if I doe never see thee more,
Be a good Mother to your litle ones,
And save them from the Tiger: fare you well.
DUCHESSE. Let me looke upon you once more: for that speech
Came from a dying father: your kisse is colder
Then that I have seene an holy Anchorite
Give to a dead mans skull.

ANTONIO. My heart is turnde to a heavy lumpe of lead,
With which I sound my danger: fare you well.

Exit, [*with son.*]

DUCHESSE. My Laurell is all withered.
CARIOLA. Looke (Madam) what a troope of armed men
Make toward us.

Enter Bosola [masked] *with a Guard*

DUCHESSE. O, they are very welcome:
When Fortunes wheele is over-charg'd with Princes,
The waight makes it move swift. I would have my ruine
Be sudden: I am your adventure, am I not?
BOSOLA. You are, you must see your husband no more—
DUCHESSE. What Divell art thou, that counterfeits heavens thunder?
BOSOLA. Is that terrible? I would have you tell me whether
Is that note worse, that frights the silly birds
Out of the corne; or that which doth allure them
To the nets? you have hearkned to the last too much.
DUCHESSE. O misery: like to a rusty ore-charg'd Cannon,
Shall I never flye in peeces? come: to what Prison?
BOSOLA. To none[.]
DUCHESSE. Whither then?
BOSOLA. To your Pallace.
DUCHESSE. I have heard
That *Charons* boate serves to convay all ore
The dismal Lake, but brings none backe againe.
BOSOLA. Your brothers meane you safety, and pitie.
DUCHESSE. Pitie!
With such a pitie men preserve alive
Pheasants, and Quailes, when they are not fat enough
To be eaten.
BOSOLA. These are your children?
DUCHESSE. Yes.
BOSOLA. Can they pratle?
DUCHESSE. No:
But I intend, since they were borne accurs'd;
Cursses shall be their first language.
BOSOLA. Fye (Madam)
Forget this base, low-fellow
DUCHESSE. Were I a man:
I'll'd beat that counterfeit face, into thy other—
BOSOLA. One of no Birth.
DUCHESSE. Say that he was born meane . . .
Man is most happy, when's owne actions
Be arguments, and examples of his Vertue.
BOSOLA. A barren, beggerly vertue.

DUCHESSE. I pre-thee who is greatest, can you tell?
Sad tales befit my woe: I'll tell you one.
A Salmon, as she swam unto the Sea,
Met with a Dog-fish; who encounters her
With this rough language: why art thou so bold
To mixe thy selfe with our high state of floods
Being no eminent Courtier, but one
That for the calmest, and fresh time o'th' yeere
Do'st live in shallow Rivers, rank'st thy selfe
With silly Smylts, and Shrympes? and darest thou
Passe by our Dog-ship, without reverence?
O (Quoth the Salmon) sister, be at peace:
Thank *Jupiter,* we both have pass'd the Net—
Our value never can be truely knowne,
Till in the Fishers basket we be showne:
I'th' Market then my price may be the higher,
Even when I am neerest to the Cooke, and fire.
So, to Great men, the Morrall may be stretched.
Men oft are valu'd high, when th'are most wretched.
But come: whither you please: I am arm'd 'gainst misery:
Bent to all swaies of the Oppressors will.
There's no deepe Valley, but neere some great Hill.

Exeunt.

ACTUS IIII, SCENA I.

[*Enter Ferdinand & Bosola.*]

FERDINAND. How doth our sister Duchess beare her selfe
In her imprisonment?
BOSOLA. Nobly: I'll describe her:
She's sad as one long us'd to't: and she seemes
Rather to welcome the end of misery
Then shun it: a behaviour so noble,
As gives a majestie to adversitie:
You may discerne the shape of lovelinesse
More perfect, in her teares, than in her smiles;
She will muse foure houres together: and her silence,
(Me thinkes) expresseth more, then if she spake.
FERDINAND. Her mellancholly seemes to be fortifide
With a strange disdaine.
BOSOLA. 'Tis so: and this restraint
(Like English Mastiffes, that grow feirce with tying)
Makes her too passionately apprehend
Those pleasures she's kept from.

FERDINAND. Curse upon her!
I will no longer study in the booke
Of anothers heart: informe her what I told you.

Exit.
[*Enter Duchesse & Attendants.*]

BOSOLA. All comfort to your grace[.]
DUCHESSE. I will have none:
Pray thee, why do'st thou wrap thy poysond Pilles
In Gold, and Sugar?
BOSOLA. Your elder brother the Lord *Ferdinand*
Is come to visite you: and sends you word,
'Cause once he rashly made a solemne vowe
Never to see you more; he comes i'th' night:
And prayes you (gently) neither Torch, nor Taper
Shine in your Chamber: he will kisse your hand:
And reconcile himselfe: but for his vowe,
He dares not see you[.]
DUCHESSE. At his pleasure:
Take hence the lights: he's come.

[*Exeunt Servants with light; enter Ferdinand.*]

FERDINAND. Where are you?
DUCHESSE. Here sir.
FERDINAND. This darkenes suites you well.
DUCHESSE. I would aske you pardon.
FERDINAND. You have it;
For I account it the honorabl'st revenge
Where I may kill, to pardon: where are your Cubbs?
DUCHESSE. Whom!
FERDINAND. Call them your children;
For though our nationall law distinguish Bastards
From true legitimate issue: compassionate nature
Makes them all equall.
DUCHESSE. Doe you visit me for this?
You violate a Sacrament o'th' Church
Shall make you howle in hell for't.
FERDINAND. It had bin well,
Could you have liv'd thus alwayes: for indeed
You were too much i'th' light: But no more—
I come to seale my peace with you: here's a hand, *gives her a*
To which you have vow'd much love: the Ring upon't *dead mans hand.*
You gave.
DUCHESSE. I affectionately kisse it:
FERDINAND. Pray doe: and bury the print of it in your heart:
I will leave this Ring with you, for a Love-token:
And the hand, as sure as the ring: and doe not doubt

But you shall have the heart too: when you need a friend,
Send it to him, that ow'de it: you shall see
Whether he can ayd you.

DUCHESSE. You are very cold.
I feare you are not well after your travell:
Hah? lights: oh horrible!

FERDINAND. Let her have lights enough.

Exit. [*Re-enter Servants with lights.*]

DUCHESSE. What witch-craft doth he practise, that he hath left
A dead-man's hand here?———*Here is discover'd, (behind a Travers;) the artificial figures of* Antonio, *and his children; appearing as if they were dead.*

BOSOLA. Looke you: here's the peece, from which 'twas ta'ne;
He doth present you this sad spectacle,
That, now you know directly they are dead,
Hereafter you may (wisely) cease to grieve
For that which cannot be recovered.

DUCHESSE. There is not betweene heaven, and earth one wish
I stay for after this: it wastes me more,
Then were't my picture, fashion'd out of wax,
Stucke with a magicall needle, and then buried
In some fowle dung-hill: and yond's an excellent property
For a tyrant, which I would account mercy—

BOSOLA. What's that?

DUCHESSE. If they would bind me to that liveles trunke,
And let me freeze to death.

BOSOLA. Come, you must live.

DUCHESSE. That's the greatest torture soules feele in hell,
In hell: that they must live, and cannot die:
Portia,[41] I'll new kindle thy Coales againe,
And revive the rare, and almost dead example
Of a loving wife.

BOSOLA. O fye: despaire? remember
You are a Christian.

DUCHESSE. The Church enjoynes fasting:
I'll starve my selfe to death.

BOSOLA. Leave this vaine sorrow;
Things being at the worst, begin to mend: the Bee
When he hath shot his sting into your hand
May then play with your eye-lyd.

DUCHESSE. Good comfortable fellow,
Perswade a wretch that's broke upon the wheele
To have all his bones new set: entreate him live,
To be executed againe: Who must despatch me?

41. Portia, Brutus's wife, killed herself by choking on hot coals.

I account this world a tedious Theatre,
For I doe play a part in't 'gainst my will.
BOSOLA. Come, be of comfort, I will save your life.
DUCHESSE. Indeed I have not leysure to tend so small a busines.
BOSOLA. Now, by my life, I pitty you.
DUCHESSE. Thou art a foole then,
To wast thy pitty on a thing so wretch'd
As cannot pitty itself: I am full of daggers:
Puffe: let me blow these vipers from me.

[*she turns suddenly to a Servant.*]

What are you?
SERVANT. One that wishes you long life.
DUCHESSE. I would thou wert hang'd for the horrible curse
Thou hast given me: I shall shortly grow one
Of the miracles of pitty: I'll goe pray:
No, I'll go curse.
BOSOLA. Oh fye!
DUCHESSE. I could curse the Starres.
BOSOLA. Oh fearefull!
DUCHESSE. And those three smyling seasons of the yeere
Into a Russian winter: nay the world
To its first Chaos.
BOSOLA. Looke you, the Starres shine still:
DUCHESSE. Oh, but you must remember, my curse hath a great way to goe:
Plagues, (that make lanes through largest families)
Consume them!
BOSOLA. Fye Lady!
DUCHESSE. Let them like tyrants,
Never be remembred, but for the ill they have done:
Let all the zealous prayers of mortefied
Church-men forget them—
BOSOLA. O uncharitable!
DUCHESSE. Let heaven, a little while, cease crowning Martirs,
To punish them:
Goe, howle them this: and say, I long to bleed—
It is some mercy when men kill with speed.

Exit, [*with Servants: re-enter Ferdinand.*]

FERDINAND. Excellent; as I would wish: she's plagu'd in Art.
These presentations are but fram'd in wax
By the curious Master in that Qualitie,
Vincentio Lauriola,[42] and she takes them
For true substantiall Bodies.

42. No positive identification exists for Lauriola.

BOSOLA. Why doe you do this?
FERDINAND. To bring her to despaire.
BOSOLA. 'Faith, end here:
And go no farther in your cruelty—
Send her a penetentiall garment, to put on,
Next to her delicate skinne, and furnish her
With beads and prayer bookes.
FERDINAND. Damne her, that body of hers,
While that my blood ran pure in't, was more worth
Then that which thou wouldst comfort, (call'd a soule)—
I will send her masques of common Curtizans,
Have her meate serv'd up by baudes, and ruffians,
And ('cause she'll needes be mad) I am resolv'd
To move forth the common Hospitall
All the mad-folke, and place them neere her lodging:
There let them practise together, sing, and daunce,
And act their gambols to the full o'th'moone:
If she can sleepe the better for it, let her,
Your worke is almost ended.
BOSOLA. Must I see her againe?
FERDINAND. Yes.
BOSOLA. Never.
FERDINAND. You must.
BOSOLA. Never in mine owne shape,
That's forfeited, by my intelligence,
And this last cruell lie: when you send me next,
The business shalbe comfort.
FERDINAND. Very likely!—
Thy pity is nothing of kin to thee: *Antonio*
Lurkes about *Millaine,* thou shalt shortly thither,
To feede a fire, as great as my revenge,
Which nev'r will slacke, till it hath spent his fuell—
Intemperate agues make Physitians cruell.

Exeunt.

ACTUS IIII, SCENA II.

[*Enter Duchesse & Cariola.*]

DUCHESSE. What hideous noyse was that?
CARIOLA. 'Tis the wild consort
Of Mad-men (Lady) which your Tyrant brother
Hath plac'd about your lodging: This tyranny,
I thinke was never practis'd till this howre.
DUCHESSE. Indeed I thanke him: nothing but noyce, and folly
Can keepe me in my right wits, whereas reason

And silence, make me starke mad: Sit downe,
Discourse to me some dismall Tragedy.
CARIOLA. O 'twill encrease your mellancholly.
DUCHESSE. Thou art deceiv'd,
To heare of greater griefe, would lessen mine—
This is a prison?
CARIOLA. Yes, but you shall live
To shake this durance off.
DUCHESSE. Thou art a foole,
The Robin red-brest, and the Nightingale,
Never live long in cages.
CARIOLA. Pray drie your eyes.
What thinke you of, Madam?
DUCHESSE. Of nothing:
When I muse thus, I sleepe.
CARIOLA. Like a mad-man, with your eyes open?
DUCHESSE. Do'st thou thinke we shall know one another,
In th'other world?
CARIOLA. Yes, out of question.
DUCHESSE. O that it were possible we might
But hold some two dayes conference with the dead,
From them, I should learne somewhat, I am sure
I never shall know here: I'll tell thee a miracle—
I am not mad yet, to my cause of sorrow.
Th'heaven ore my head, seemes made of molten brasse,
The earth of flaming sulphure, yet I am not mad:
I am acquainted with sad misery,
As the tan'd galley-slave is with his Oare,
Necessity makes me suffer constantly,
And custome makes it easie—Who do I looke like now?
CARIOLA. Like to your picture in the gallery,
A deale of life in shew, but none in practise:
Or rather like some reverend monument
Whose ruines are even pittied.
DUCHESSE. Very proper:
And Fortune seemes onely to have her eie-sight,
To behold my Tragedy:

[*Enter Servant.*]

How now,
What noyce is that?
SERVANT. I am come to tell you,
Your brother hath entended you some sport:
A great Physitian, when the Pope was sicke
Of a deepe mellancholly, presented him
With severall sorts of mad-men, which wilde object
(Being full of change, and sport,) forc'd him to laugh,

And so th'impost-hume° broke: the selfe same cure, ulcer
The Duke intends on you.
DUCHESSE. Let them come in.
SERVANT. There's a mad Lawyer, and a secular Priest,[43]
A Doctor that hath forfeited his wits
By jealousie: an Astrologian,
That in his workes, sayd such a day o'th'moneth
Should be the day of doome; and, fayling of't,
Ran mad: an English Taylor, crais'd i'th'braine,
With the studdy of new fashions: a gentleman usher
Quite beside himselfe, with care to keepe in minde,
The number of his Ladies salutations,
Or "how do you", she employ'd him in each morning:
A Farmer too, (an excellent knave in graine)[44]
Mad, 'cause he was hindred transportation,° export
And let one Broaker° (that's mad) loose to these, pawnbroker
You'ld thinke the divell were among them.
DUCHESSE. Sit, *Cariola:* let them loose when you please,
For I am chain'd to endure all your tyranny.

[*Enter Madmen.*]

Here (by a Mad-man) this song is sung, to a dismall kind of Musique.

O let us howle, some heavy note,
some deadly-dogged howle,
Sounding, as from the threatning throat,
of beastes, and fatall fowle.
As Ravens, Schrich-owles, Bulls, and Beares,
We'll bell, and bawle our parts,
Till yerk-some noyce have cloy'd your eares,
and corasiv'd° your hearts. corroded
At last when as our quire wants breath,
our bodies being blest,
We'll sing, like Swans, to welcome death,
and die in love and rest.

1 MAD-MAN. Doomes-day not come yet? I'll draw it neerer by a
perspective, or make a glasse,° that shall set all the world telescope
on fire upon an instant: I cannot sleepe, my pillow is stuff't with a
littour of Porcupines.
2 MAD-MAN. Hell is a meere glasse-house, where the divells
are continually blowing up womens soules, on hollow yrons,
and the fire never goes out.

43. Members of the secular clergy, unlike the "regular" clergy, were not under the rule of an order, such as the Benedictines, and lived among the laity.

44. A pun on "in grain": 1) a trader in grain; 2) a knave to the very grain of his being.

3 MAD-MAN. I will lie with every woman in my parish the tenth night: I will tithe them over, like hay-cockes.

4 MAD-MAN. Shall my Pothecary out-go me, because I am a cuck-old? I have found out his roguery: he makes allom out of his wives urin, and sells it to Puritaines, that have sore throates with over-strayning.

1 MAD-MAN. I have skill in Harroldry.

2 MAD-MAN. Hast?

1 MAD-MAN. You do give for your crest a wood-cockes head, with the Braines pickt out on't, you are a very ancient Gentleman.

3 MAD-MAN. Greeke is turn'd Turke, we are onely to be sav'd by the Helvetian translation.[45]

1 MAD-MAN. Come on Sir, I will lay the law to you.

2 MAD-MAN. Oh, rather lay a corazive—the law will eate to the bone.

3 MAD-MAN. He that drinkes but to satisfie nature is damn'd.

4 MAD-MAN. If I had my glasse here, I would shew a sight should make all the women here call me mad Doctor.

1 MAD-MAN. What's he, a rope-maker?

2 MAD-MAN. No, no, no, a snufling knave, that, while he shewes the tombes, will have his hand in a wenches placket.[46]

3 MAD-MAN. Woe to the Caroach, that brought home my wife from the Masque, at three a clocke in the morning, it had a large Feather-bed in it.

4 MAD-MAN. I have paired the divells nayles forty times, roasted them in Ravens egges, and cur'd agues with them.

3 MAD-MAN. Get me three hundred milch bats, to make possets, to procure sleepe.

4 MAD-MAN. All the Colledge may throw their caps at me,[47] I have made a Soape-boyler costive,° it was my master-peece:— constipated

Here the Daunce, consisting of 8. Mad-men, with musicke answerable thereunto, after which, Bosola (like an old man) enters.

DUCHESSE. Is he mad too?

SERVANT. Pray question him: I'll leave you.

[*Exeunt Servant & Madmen.*]

BOSOLA. I am come to make thy tombe.

DUCHESSE. Hah, my tombe?
Thou speak'st, as if I lay upon my death bed,
Gasping for breath: dost thou perceive me sicke?

BOSOLA. Yes, and the more dangerously, since thy sicknesse is insensible.

DUCHESSE. Thou art not mad, sure, do'st know me?

45 The Geneva Bible, banned in England until 1576 because of its seditious character, and subsequently called by James I the worst translation available.

46. 1) pocket; 2) a slit in a skirt; 3) petticoat.

47. Give up in despair.

BOSOLA. Yes.

DUCHESSE. Who am I?

BOSOLA. Thou art a box of worme-seede, at best, but a salvatory° of greene° mummey: what's this flesh? a little cruded° milke, phantasticall puffe-paste: our bodies are weaker then those paper prisons boyes use to keep flies in: more contemptible: since ours is to preserve earth-wormes: didst thou ever see a Larke in a cage? such is the soule in the body: this world is like her little turfe of grasse, and the Heaven ore our heades, like her looking glasse, onely gives us a miserable knowledge of the small compasse of our prison.

[salvatory°: ointment box; greene°: undried; cruded°: curdled]

DUCHESSE. Am not I, thy Duchesse?

BOSOLA. Thou art some great woman sure, for riot begins to sit on thy fore-head (clad in gray haires) twenty yeares sooner, then on a merry milkemaydes. Thou sleep'st worse, then if a mouse should be forc'd to take up her lodging in a cats eare: a little infant, that breedes its teeth, should it lie with thee, would crie out, as if thou wert the more unquiet bed-fellow.

DUCHESSE. I am Duchesse of *Malfy* still.

BOSOLA. That makes thy sleepe so broken:
Glories (like glowe-wormes) afarre off, shine bright,
But look'd to neere, have neither heate, nor light.

DUCHESSE. Thou art very plaine.

BOSOLA. My trade is to flatter the dead, not the living—I am a tombe-maker.

DUCHESSE. And thou com'st to make my tombe?

BOSOLA. Yes.

DUCHESSE. Let me be a little merry—of what stuffe wilt thou make it?

BOSOLA. Nay, resolve me first, of what fashion?

DUCHESSE. Why, do we grow phantasticall on our death-bed? Do we affect fashion in the grave?

BOSOLA. Most ambitiously: Princes images on their tombes do not lie, as they were wont, seeming to pray up to heaven: but with their hands under their cheekes, (as if they died of the tooth-ache)—they are not carved with their eies fix'd upon the starres; but as their mindes were wholy bent upon the world, the self-same way they seem to turne their faces.

DUCHESSE. Let me know fully therefore the effect
Of this thy dismall preparation,
This talke, fit for a charnell?

BOSOLA. Now, I shall—

[Enter Executioners] with a Coffin, Cords, and a Bell.

Here is a present from your Princely brothers,
And may it arrive wel-come, for it brings
Last benefit, last sorrow.

DUCHESSE. Let me see it—

I have so much obedience, in my blood,
I wish it in their veines, to do them good.
BOSOLA. This is your last presence Chamber.
CARIOLA. O my sweete lady.
DUCHESSE. Peace, it affrights not me.
BOSOLA. I am the common Bell-man
That usually is sent to condemn'd persons
The night before they suffer[.]
DUCHESSE. Even now thou said'st,
Thou wast a tombe-maker?
BOSOLA. 'Twas to bring you
By degrees to mortification: Listen.
Hearke, now everything is still—
The Schritch-Owle and the whistler shrill,
Call upon our Dame, aloud,
And bid her quickly don her shrowd:
Much you had of Land and rent,
Your length in clay's now competent.
A long war disturb'd your minde,
Here your perfect peace is sign'd—
Of what is't fooles make such vaine keeping?
Sin their conception, their birth, weeping:
Their life, a generall mist of error,
Their death, a hideous storme of terror—
Strew your haire, with powders sweete:
Don cleane linnen, bathe your feete,
And (the foule feend more to checke)
A crucifix let blesse your necke,
'Tis now full tide, 'tweene night, and day,
End your groane, and come away.
CARIOLA. Hence villaines, tyrants, murderers: alas!
What will you do with my Lady? call for helpe.
DUCHESSE. To whom, to our next neighbours? they are mad-folkes.
BOSOLA. Remoove that noyse.
DUCHESSE. Far[e]well *Cariola.*
In my last will, I have not much to give—
A many hungry guests have fed upon me,
Thine will be a poore reversion.
CARIOLA. I will die with her.
DUCHESSE. I pray-thee looke thou giv'st my little boy
Some sirrop, for his cold, and let the girle
Say her prayers, ere she sleepe. Now what you please,
What death? [*Cariola is forced off.*]
BOSOLA. Strangling, here are your Executioners.
DUCHESSE. I forgive them:

The apoplexie, cathar,° or cough o'th'loongs, *inflammation of the lungs*
Would do as much as they do.
BOSOLA. Doth not death fright you?
DUCHESSE. Who would be afraid on't?
Knowing to meete such excellent company
In th'other world?
BOSOLA. Yet, me thinkes,
The manner of your death should much afflict you,
This cord should terrifie you?
DUCHESSE. Not a whit—
What would it pleasure me, to have my throate cut
With diamonds? or to be smothered
With Cassia? or to be shot to death, with pearles?
I know death hath ten thousand severall doores
For men, to take their *Exits:* and 'tis found
They go on such strange geometricall hinges,
You may open them both wayes: any way, (for heaven sake)
So I were out of your whispering: Tell my brothers,
That I perceive death, (now I am well awake)
Best guift is, they can give, or I can take—
I would faine put off my last womans-fault,
I'ld not be tedious to you.
EXECUTIONER. We are ready.
DUCHESSE. Dispose my breath, how please you, but my body
Bestow upon my women, will you?
FIRST EXECUTIONER. Yes.
DUCHESSE. Pull, and pull strongly, for your able strength,
Must pull downe heaven upon me:
Yet stay, heaven gates are not so highly arch'd
As Princes pallaces—they that enter there
Must go upon their knees: Come violent death,

[*She kneels*].

Serve for *Mandragora,*[48] to make me sleepe;
Go tell my brothers, when I am laid out,
They then may feede in quiet.

They strangle her.

BOSOLA. Where's the waiting woman?
Fetch her: some other strangle the children:
Look you, there sleeps your mistris. [*Re-enter Executioner with Cariola.*]
CARIOLA. Oh you are damn'd
Perpetually for this: My turne is next,
Is't not so ordered?

48. Mandrake is related to nightshade; its roots can be used as poisons.

BOSOLA. Yes, and I am glad
You are so well prepar'd for't.
CARIOLA. You are deceiv'd Sir,
I am not prepar'd for't, I will not die,
I will first come to my answere; and know
How I have offended.
BOSOLA. Come, dispatch her:
You kept her counsell, now you shall keepe ours.
CARIOLA. I will not die, I must not, I am contracted
To a young Gentle-man.
EXECUTIONER. Here's your wedding Ring.
CARIOLA. Let me but speake with the Duke: I'll discover
Treason to his person.
BOSOLA. Delayes: throttle-her.
EXECUTIONER. She bites: and scratches[.]
CARIOLA. If you kill me now
I am damn'd: I have not bin at Confession
This two yeeres.
BOSOLA. When!
CARIOLA. I am quicke with child.
BOSOLA. Why then,
Your credit's saved: beare her into th'next roome:

[*They strangle her, and bear her away. Enter Ferdinand.*]

Let these lie still.
FERDINAND. Is she dead?
BOSOLA. Shee is what
You'll'd have her: But here begin your pity— *Shewes the children strangled.*
Alas, how have these offended?
FERDINAND. The death
Of young Wolffes, is never to be pittied.
BOSOLA. Fix your eye here.
FERDINAND. Constantly.
BOSOLA. Doe you not weepe?
Other sinnes onely speake; Murther shreikes out:
The Element of water moistens the Earth,
But blood flies upwards, and bedewes the Heavens.
FERDINAND. Cover her face: Mine eyes dazzell: she di'd yong.
BOSOLA. I thinke not so: her infelicitie
Seem'd to have yeeres too many.
FERDINAND. She, and I were Twinnes:
And should I die this instant, I had liv'd
Her Time to a Mynute.
BOSOLA. It seemes she was borne first:
You have bloodely approv'd the auncient truth,
That kindred commonly doe worse agree
Then remote strangers.

FERDINAND.[49] Let me see her face
Againe; Why didst thou not pitty her? what
An excellent honest man might'st thou have bin
If thou hadst borne her to some Sanctuary!
Or (bold in a good cause) oppos'd thy selfe
With thy advanced sword above thy head,
Betweene her Innocence, and my Revenge!
I bad thee, when I was distracted of my wits,
Goe kill my dearest friend, and thou hast don't.
For let me but examine well the cause;
What was the meanenes of her match to me?
Onely I must confesse, I had a hope
(Had she continu'd widow) to have gain'd
An infinite masse of Treasure by her death:
And that was the mayne cause; her Marriage—
That drew a streame of gall quite through my heart;
For thee, (as we observe in Tragedies
That a good Actor many times is curss'd
For playing a villaines part) I hate thee for't:
And (for my sake) say, thou hast done much ill, well.

BOSOLA. Let me quicken your memory: for I perceive
You are falling into ingratitude: I challenge
The reward due to my service.

FERDINAND. I'll tell thee.
What I'll give thee—

BOSOLA. Doe[.]

FERDINAND. I'll give thee a pardon
For this murther.

BOSOLA. Hah?

FERDINAND. Yes: and 'tis
The largest bounty I can studie to doe thee.
By what authority did'st thou execute
This bloody sentence?

BOSOLA. By yours—

FERDINAND. Mine? was I her Judge?
Did any ceremoniall forme of Law,
Doombe her to not-Being? did a compleat Jury
Deliver her conviction up i'th Court?
Where shalt thou find this judgment registerd
Unlesse in hell? See: like a bloody foole
Th'hast forfeyted thy life, and thou shalt die for't.

BOSOLA. The Office of Justice is perverted quite
When one Thiefe hangs another: who shall dare
To reveal this?

49. My lineation here differs from that of Lucas.

FERDINAND. Oh, I'll tell thee:
The Wolfe shall finde her Grave, and scrape it up:
Not to devoure the corpes, but to discover
The horrid murther.
BOSOLA. You; not I, shall quake for't.
FERDINAND. Leave me[.]
BOSOLA. I will first receive my Pention.
FERDINAND. You are a villaine[.]
BOSOLA. When your Ingratitude
Is Judge, I am so.
FERDINAND. O horror!
That not the feare of him, which bindes the divels
Can prescribe man obedience.
Never looke upon me more.
BOSOLA. Why fare thee well:
Your brother, and your selfe are worthy men;
You have a paire of hearts, are hollow Graves,
Rotten, and rotting others: and your vengeance,
(Like two chain'd bullets) still goes arme in arme—
You may be Brothers: for treason, like the plague,
Doth take much in a blood: I stand like one
That long hath ta'ne a sweet, and golden dreame.
I am angry with my selfe, now that I wake.
FERDINAND. Get thee into some unknowne part o'th' world
That I may never see thee.
BOSOLA. Let me know
Wherefore I should be thus neglected? sir,
I serv'd your tyranny: and rather strove,
To satisfie your selfe, then all the world;
And though I loath'd the evill, yet I lov'd
You that did councell it: and rather sought
To appeare a true servant, then an honest man.
FERDINAND. I'll goe hunt the Badger, by Owle-light:
'Tis a deed of darkeness.

Exit.

BOSOLA. He's much distracted: Off my painted honour!—
While with vaine hopes, our faculties we tyre,
We seeme to sweate in yce, and freeze in fire;
What would I doe, were this to doe againe?
I would not change my peace of conscience
For all the wealth of Europe: She stirres; here's life:
Returne (faire soule) from darkenes, and lead mine
Out of this sencible hell: She's warme, she breathes:
Upon thy pale lips I will melt my heart
To store them with fresh colour: who's there?
Some cordiall drinke! Alas! I dare not call:

So, pitty would destroy pitty: her Eye opes,
And heaven in it seemes to ope, (that late was shut)
To take me up to mercy.

DUCHESSE. *Antonio.*

BOSOLA. Yes (Madam) he is living,
The dead bodies you saw, were but faign'd statues;
He's reconcil'd to your brothers: the Pope hath wrought
The attonement.

DUCHESSE. Mercy!

she dies.

BOSOLA. Oh, she's gone againe: there the cords of life broake:
Oh sacred Innocence, that sweetely sleepes
On Turtles° feathers: whilst a guilty conscience turtledoves
Is a blacke Register wherein is writ
All our good deedes, and bad: a Perspective
That showes us hell; that we cannot be suffer'd
To doe good when we have a mind to it!
This is manly sorrow:
These teares, I am very certaine, never grew
In my Mothers Milke. My estate is suncke
Below the degree of feare: where were[50]
These penitent fountaines, while she was living?
Oh, they were frozen up: here is a sight
As direfull to my soule, as is the sword
Unto a wretch hath slaine his father: Come,
I'll beare thee hence,
And execute thy last will; that's deliver
Thy body to the reverend dispose
Of some good women: that the cruell tyrant
Shall not deny me: Then, I'll post to *Millaine,*
Where somewhat I will speedily enact
Worth my dejection.

Exit.

ACTUS V, SCENA I

[*Enter Antonio & Delio.*]

ANTONIO. What thinke you of my hope of reconcilement
To the *Arragonian* brethren?

DELIO. I misdoubt it,
For though they have sent their letters of safe conduct
For your repaire to *Millaine,* they appeare

50. Lineation change from Lucas.

But Nets to entrap you: The Marquis of *Pescara*
Under whom you hold certaine land in Cheit,° escheat[51]
Much 'gainst his noble nature, hath been mov'd
To ceize those lands, and some of his dependants
Are at this instant, making it their suit
To be invested in your Revenewes.
I cannot thinke, they meane well to your life,
That doe deprive you of your meanes of life,
Your living.
ANTONIO. You are still an heretique
To any safety, I can shape my selfe.
DELIO. Here comes the Marquis: I will make my selfe
Petitioner for some part of your land,
To know whither it is flying.
ANTONIO. I pray doe.

[*Enter Pescara.*]

DELIO. Sir, I have a suit to you.
PESCARA. To me?
DELIO. An easie one:
There is the Cittadell of Saint *Bennet,*° Benedict
With some demeasnes, of late in the possession
Of *Antonio Bologna*—please you bestow them on me?
PESCARA. You are my friend: But this is such a suit,
Nor fit for me to give, nor you to take.
DELIO. No sir?
PESCARA. I will give you ample reason for't,
Soone in private: Here's the Cardinalls Mistris.

[*Enter Julia.*]

JULIA. My Lord, I am growne your poore Petitioner,
And should be an ill beggar, had I not
A Great mans letter here, (the Cardinalls)
To Court you in my favour.

[*gives letter.*]

PESCARA. He entreates for you
The Cittadell of Saint Bennet, that belong'd
To the banish'd *Bologna.*
JULIA. Yes.
PESCARA. I could not have thought of a friend I could
Rather pleasure with it: 'tis yours[.]
JULIA. Sir, I thanke you:
And he shall know how doubly I am engag'd

51. Land subject to reversion to the holder (here, the marquis) upon the death of the tenant without heir or the tenant's commission of a felony.

Both in your guift, and speedinesse of giving,
Which makes your graunt, the greater.

Exit.

ANTONIO. [*aside*] How they fortify
Themselves with my ruine!
DELIO. Sir: I am
Little bound to you.
PESCARA. Why?
DELIO. Because you denide this suit, to me, and gav't
To such a creature.
PESCARA. Doe you know what it was?
It was *Antonios* land: not forfeyted
By course of lawe; but ravish'd from his throate
By the Cardinals entreaty: it were not fit
I should bestow so maine a peece of wrong
Upon my friend: 'tis a gratification
Onely due to a Strumpet: for it is injustice;
Shall I sprinckle the pure blood of Innocents
To make those followers, I call my friends
Looke ruddier upon me? I am glad
This land, (ta'ne from the owner by such wrong)
Returnes againe unto so fowle an use,
As Salary for his Lust. Learne (good *Delio*)
To aske noble things of me, and you shall find
I'll be a noble giver.
DELIO. You instruct me well[.]
ANTONIO. [*aside*] Why, here's a man, now, would fright impudence
From sawciest Beggers.
PESCARA. Prince *Ferdinand's* come to *Millaine*
Sicke (as they give out) of an Apoplexie:
But some say, 'tis a frenzie; I am going
To visite him.

Exit.

ANTONIO. 'Tis a noble old fellow[.]
DELIO. What course doe you meane to take, *Antonio?*
ANTONIO. This night, I meane to venture all my fortune
(Which is no more than a poore lingring life)
To the Cardinals worst of mallice: I have got
Private access to his chamber: and intend
To visit him, about the mid of night.
(As once his brother did our noble Duchesse.)
It may be that the sudden apprehension
Of danger (for I'll goe in mine owne shape)
When he shall see it fraight° with love, and dutie, fraught
May draw the poyson out of him, and worke

A friendly reconcilement; if it faile . . .
Yet, it shall rid me of this infamous calling,
For better fall once, then be ever falling.
DELIO. I'll second you in all danger: and (how ere)
My life keepes rancke with yours.
ANTONIO. You are still my lov'd, and best friend.

Exeunt.

ACTUS V, SCENA II.

[*Enter Pescara and Doctor.*]

PESCARA. Now doctor; may I visit your Patient?
DOCTOR. If 't please your Lordship: but he's instantly
To take the ayre here in the Gallery,
By my direction.
PESCARA. Pray-thee, what's his disease?
DOCTOR. A very pestilent disease (my Lord)
They call *Licanthropia.*
PESCARA. What 's that?
I need a dictionary to't.
DOCTOR. I'll tell you:
In those that are possess'd with't there ore-flowes
Such mellancholy humour, they imagine
Themselves to be transformed into Woolves,
Steale forth to Church-yards in the dead of night,
And dig dead bodies up: as two nights since
One met the Duke, 'bout midnight in a lane
Behind Saint *Markes* Church, with the leg of a man
Upon his shoulder; and he howl'd fearefully:
Said he was a Woolffe: onely the difference
Was, a Woolffes skinne was hairy on the out-side,
His on the In-side: bad them take their swords,
Rip up his flesh, and trie: straight I was sent for,
And, having ministerd to him, found his Grace
Very well recover'd
PESCARA. I am glad on't.
DOCTOR. Yet not without some feare
Of a relaps: If he grow to his fit againe,
I'll goe a nearer way to worke with him
Then ever *Paracelsus*[52] dream'd of: If
They'll give me leave, I'll buffet his madnesse out of him.
Stand aside. he comes.

52. Paracelsus (1493–1541), a physician and alchemist.

[*Enter Ferdinand, Malateste, Cardinal & Bosola.*]

FERDINAND. Leave me.

MALATESTE. Why doth your Lordship love this solitarines?

FERDINAND. Eagles commonly fly alone: They are Crowes, Dawes, and Sterlings that flocke together: Looke, what's that followes me?

MALATESTE. Nothing (my Lord).

FERDINAND. Yes.

MALATESTE. 'Tis your shadow.

FERDINAND. Stay it, let it not haunt me.

MALATESTE. Impossible; if you move, and the Sun shine.

FERDINAND. I will throtle it.

[*Throws himself on the ground.*]

MALATESTE. Oh, my Lord: you are angry with nothing.

FERDINAND. You are a foole: How is't possible I should catch my shadow, unless I fall upon't? When I goe to Hell, I meane to carry a bribe: for looke you good guifts ever-more make way, for the worst persons.

PESCARA. Rise, good my Lord.

FERDINAND. I am studying the Art of Patience.

PESCARA. 'Tis a noble Vertue[.]

FERDINAND. To drive six Snailes before me, from this towne to *Mosco;* neither use Goad, nor Whip to them, but let them take their owne time: (the patientst man i'th' world match me for an experiment) and I'll crawle after like a sheepe-biter.[53]

CARDINAL. Force him up.

FERDINAND. Use me well, you were best: What I have don, I have don: I'll confesse nothing.

DOCTOR. Now let me come to him: Are you mad (my Lord?) Are you out of your Princely wits?

FERDINAND. What's he?

PESCARA. Your doctor.

FERDINAND. Let me have his beard saw'd off, and his eye-browes filed more civil.

DOCTOR. I must do mad trickes with him, for that's the only way on't. I have brought your grace a Salamander's skin, to keepe you from sun-burning.

FERDINAND. I have cruell sore eyes.

DOCTOR. The white of a Cockatrixes-egge[54] is present remedy.

FERDINAND. Let it be a new-layd one, you were best: Hide me from him: Phisitians are like Kings, They brooke no contradiction.

DOCTOR. Now he begins to feare me, now let me alone with him.

53. Literally self-explanatory, figuratively a thief.

54. The cockatrice is a mythical serpent born from an egg laid by a cock and able to kill with its glance.

CARDINAL. How now, put off your gowne?[55]

DOCTOR. Let me have some forty urinalls fill'd with Rose-water: He, and I'll go pelt one another with them—now he begins to feare me: Can you fetch a friske, sir? Let him go, let him go, upon my perrill: I finde by his eye, he stands in awe of me, I'll make him—as tame as a Dormouse.

FERDINAND. Can you fetch your friskes, sir? I will stamp him into a Cullice:° Flea off his skin, to cover one of the Anatomies,° this rogue hath set i'th' cold yonder, in Barber-Chyrurgeons hall: Hence, hence, you are all of you, like beasts for sacrifice,

medicinal broth
skeletons

[*Throws the doctor down & beats him*]

there's nothing left of you, but tongue, and belly, flattery and lechery.

[Exit.]

PESCARA. Doctor, he did not feare you throughly.
DOCTOR. True, I was somewhat too forward.
BOSOLA. Mercy upon me, what a fatall judgment
Hath falne upon this *Ferdinand!*
PESCARA. Knowes your grace
What accident hath brought unto the Prince
This strange distraction?
CARDINAL. [*aside*] I must faigne somewhat: Thus they say it grew.
You have heard it rumor'd, for these many yeares,
None of our family dies, but there is seene
The shape of an old woman, which is given
By tradition, to us, to have bin murther'd
By her Nephewes, for her riches: Such a figure
One night (as the Prince sat up late at's booke)
Appear'd to him—when crying out for helpe,
The gentlemen of's chamber, found his grace
All on a cold sweate, alter'd much in face
And language: since which apparition,
He hath growne worse, and worse, and I much feare
He cannot live.
BOSOLA. Sir, I would speake with you.
PESCARA. We'll leave your grace,
Wishing to the sicke Prince, our noble Lord,
All health of minde, and body.
CARDINAL. You are most welcome.

[*Exeunt. Manent Cardinal and Bosola.*]

55. The 1708 quarto has the stage direction "puts off his four cloaks, one after another." Some editors include this on the grounds that it is quite possibly a traditional bit of business.

Are you come? so: [*aside*] this fellow must not know
By any meanes I had intelligence
In our Duchesse death: for (though I counsell'd it,)
The full of all th'ingagement seem'd to grow
From *Ferdinand:* [*to Bosola*] Now sir, how fares our sister?
I do not thinke but sorrow makes her looke
Like to an oft-di'd garment: She shall now
Tast comfort from me: why do you looke so wildely?
Oh, the fortune of your master here, the Prince
Dejects you—but be you of happy comfort:
If you'll do one thing for me I'll entreate,
Though he had a cold tombe-stone ore his bones,
[I'll] make you what you would be.

BOSOLA. Any thing—
Give it me in a breath, and let me flie to't:
They that thinke long, small expedition win,
For musing much o'th'end, cannot begin.

[*Enter Julia.*]

JULIA. Sir, will you come in to Supper?

CARDINAL. I am busie, leave me.

JULIA. [*aside*] What an excellent shape hath that fellow!

Exit.

CARDINAL. 'Tis thus: *Antonio* lurkes here in *Millaine,*
Enquire him out, and kill him: while he lives,
Our sister cannot marry, and I have thought
Of an excellent match for her: do this, and stile me
Thy advancement.

BOSOLA. But by what meanes shall I find him out?

CARDINAL. There is a gentleman, call'd *Delio*
Here in the Campe, that hath bin long approv'd
His loyall friend: Set eie upon that fellow,
Follow him to Mass—may be *Antonio,*
Although he do account religion
But a Schoole-name, for fashion of the world,
May accompany him—or else go enquire out
Delio's Confessor, and see if you can bribe
Him to reveale it: there are a thousand wayes
A man might find to trace him: As to know,
What fellowes haunt the Jewes, for taking up
Great summes of money, for sure he's in want,
Or else to go to th'Picture-makers, and learne
Who bought her Picture lately—some of these
Happily may take—

BOSOLA. Well, I'll not freeze i'th'businesse,

I would see that wretched thing, *Antonio*
Above all sightes i'th'world.
CARDINAL. Do, and be happy.

Exit.

BOSOLA. This fellow doth breed Bazalisques in's eies,
He's nothing else, but murder: yet he seemes
Not to have notice of the Duchesse death:
'Tis his cunning: I must follow his example,
There cannot be a surer way to trace,
Than that of an old Fox.

[*Enter Julia, pointing a pistol at him.*]

JULIA. So, sir, you are well met.
BOSOLA. How now?
JULIA. Nay, the doores are fast enough:
Now, Sir, I will make you confesse your treachery.
BOSOLA. Treachery?
JULIA. Yes, confesse to me
Which of my women 'twas you hyr'd, to put
Love-powder into my drinke?
BOSOLA. Love-powder?
JULIA. Yes, when I was at *Malfy*—
Why should I fall in love with such a face else?
I have already suffer'd for thee so much paine,
The onely remedy to do me good,
Is to kill my longing.
BOSOLA. Sure your Pistoll holds
Nothing but perfumes, or kissing comfits:
Excellent lady,
You have a pritty way on't to discover
Your longing: Come, come, I'll disarme you,
And arme you thus—yet this is wondrous strange.
JULIA. Compare thy forme, and my eyes together,
You'll find my love no such great miracle:
Now you'll say,
I am wanton: This nice modesty, in Ladies
Is but a troublesome familiar,
That haunts them.
BOSOLA. Know you me, I am a blunt souldier.
JULIA. The better,
Sure, there wants fire, where there are no lively sparkes
Of roughnes.
BOSOLA. And I want complement.
JULIA. Why, ignorance
In court-ship cannot make you do amisse,
If you have a heart to do well.

BOSOLA. You are very faire.
JULIA. Nay, if you lay beauty to my charge,
I must plead unguilty.
BOSOLA. Your bright eyes
Carry a Quiver of darts in them, sharper
Than Sun-beames.
JULIA. You will mar me with commendation,
Put your selfe to the charge of courting me,
Whereas now I woo you.
BOSOLA. [*aside*] I have it, I will worke upon this Creature—
Let us grow most amorously familiar:
If the great Cardinal now should see me thus,
Would he not count me a villaine?
JULIA. No, he might count me a wanton,
Not lay a scruple of offence on you:
For if I see, and steale a Diamond,
The fault is not i'th'stone, but in me the thiefe,
That purloines it: I am sudaine with you—
We that are great women of pleasure, use to cut off
These uncertaine wishes, and unquiet longings,
And in an instant joyne the sweete delight
And the pritty excuse together: had you bin in'th'streete,
Under my chamber-window, even there
I should have courted you.
BOSOLA. Oh, you are an excellent Lady.
JULIA. Bid me do somewhat for you presently,
To expresse I love you.
BOSOLA. I will, and if you love me,
Fail not to effect it:
The Cardinal is growne wondrous mellancholly,
Demand the cause, let him not put you off,
With faign'd excuse, discover the maine ground on't.
JULIA. Why would you know this?
BOSOLA. I have depended on him,
And I heare that he is falne in some disgrace
With the Emperour—if he be, like the mice
That forsake falling houses, I would shift
To other dependance.
JULIA. You shall not neede
Follow the warres, I'll be your maintenance.
BOSOLA. And I your loyall servant, but I cannot
Leave my calling.
JULIA. Not leave an Ungratefull
Generall, for the love of a sweete Lady?
You are like some, cannot sleepe in feather-beds,
But must have blockes for their pillowes.

BOSOLA. Will you do this?
JULIA. Cunningly.
BOSOLA. To-morrow I'll expect th'intelligence.
JULIA. To-morrow! get you into my Cabinet
You shall have it with you: do not delay me,
No more than I do you: I am like one
That is condemn'd: I have my pardon promis'd.
But I would see it seal'd: Go, get you in,
You shall see me winde my tongue about his heart,
Like a skeine of silke.

[*Exit Bosola, into her cabinet. Enter Cardinal.*]

CARDINAL. Where are you?

[*Enter Servants.*]

SERVANTS. Here.
CARDINAL. Let none, upon your lives, have conference
With the Prince *Ferdinand*, unless I know it:
[*aside*] In this distraction he may reveale

[*Exeunt Servants.*]

The murther.
Yond's my lingring consumption:
I am weary of her; and by any meanes
Would be quit off.
JULIA. How now, my Lord? What ailes you?
CARDINAL. Nothing.
JULIA. Oh, you are much alterd:
Come, I must be your Secretary, and remove
This lead from off your bosome, what's the matter?
CARDINAL. I may not tell you.
JULIA. Are you so farre in love with sorrow,
You cannot part with part of it? or thinke you
I cannot love your grace, when you are sad,
As well as merry? or do you suspect
I, that have a bin a secret to your heart,
These many winters, cannot be the same
Unto your tongue?
CARDINAL. Satisfie thy longing,
The onely way to make thee keepe my councell,
Is not to tell thee.
JULIA. Tell your eccho this,
Or flatterers, that (like ecchoes) still report
What they heare (though most imperfect), and not me:
For, if that you be true unto your selfe,
I'll know.
CARDINAL. Will you racke me?

JULIA. No, judgement shall
Draw it from you: it is an equall fault,
To tell ones secrets, unto all, or none.
CARDINAL. The first argues folly.
JULIA. But the last tyranny.
CARDINAL. Very well; why, imagine I have committed
Some secret deed, which I desire the world
May never heare of.
JULIA. Therefore may not I know it?
You have conceal'd for me, as great a sinne
As adultery: Sir, never was occasion
For perfect triall of my constancy
Till now: Sir, I beseech you.
CARDINAL. You'll repent it.
JULIA. Never.
CARDINAL. It hurries thee to ruine: I'll not tell thee—
Be well advis'd, and thinke what danger 'tis
To receive a Princes secrets: they that do,
Had neede have their breasts hoop'd with adamant
To containe them: I pray thee, yet be satisfi'd,
Examine thine owne frailety, 'tis more easie
To tie knots, then unloose them: 'tis a secret
That (like a lingring poyson) may chance lie
Spread in thy vaines, and kill thee seaven yeare hence.
JULIA. Now you dally with me.
CARDINAL. No more—thou shalt know it.
By my appointment, the great Duchesse of *Malfy*,
And two of her yong children, foure nights since
Were strangled.
JULIA. Oh heaven! (sir) what have you done?
CARDINAL. How now? how setles this? thinke you your bosome
Will be a grave, darke and obscure enough
For such a secret?
JULIA. You have undone your selfe (sir.)
CARDINAL. Why?
JULIA. It lies not in me to conceale it.
CARDINAL. No?
Come, I will sweare you to't upon this booke.
JULIA. Most religiously.
CARDINAL. Kisse it.
Now you shall never utter it, thy curiosity
Hath undone thee: thou'rt poyson'd with that booke—
Because I knew thou couldst not keepe my councell,
I have bound thee to't by death.

[*Enter Bosola.*]

BOSOLA. For pitty sake, hold.

CARDINAL. Ha, *Bosola?*

JULIA. I forgive you
This equall peece of Justice you have done:
For I betraid your councell to that fellow,
He over-heard it; that was the cause I said
It lay not in me, to conceale it.

BOSOLA. O foolish woman,
Couldst thou not have poyson'd him?

JULIA. 'Tis weaknesse,
Too much to thinke what should have binn done—I go,
I know not whither.

[*Dies.*]

CARDINAL. Wherefore com'st thou hither?

BOSOLA. That I might finde a great man, (like your selfe,)
Not out of his wits (as the Lord *Ferdinand*)
To remember my service.

CARDINAL. I'll have thee hew'd in peeces.

BOSOLA. Make not your selfe such a promise of that life
Which is not yours, to dispose of.

CARDINAL. Who plac'd thee here?

BOSOLA. Her lust, as she intended.

CARDINAL. Very well,
Now you know me for your fellow murderer.

BOSOLA. And wherefore should you lay faire marble colours,
Upon your rotten purposes to me?
Unlesse you imitate some that do plot great Treasons,
And when they have done, go hide themselves i'th'graves
Of those were Actors in't?

CARDINAL. No more, there is
A fortune attends thee.

BOSOLA. Shall I go sue to Fortune any longer?
'Tis the fooles Pilgrimage.

CARDINAL. I have honors in store for thee.

BOSOLA. There are many wayes that conduct to seeming
Honor, and some of them very durty ones.

CARDINAL. Throw to the divell
Thy mellancholly—the fire burnes well,
What neede we keepe a-stirring of't, and make
A greater smoother? thou wilt kill *Antonio?*

BOSOLA. Yes.

CARDINAL. Take up that body.

BOSOLA. I think I shall
Shortly grow the common Biere, for Church-yards?

CARDINAL. I will allow thee some dozen of attendants,
To aide thee in the murther.

BOSOLA. Oh, by no meanes—Phisitians that apply horse-leiches to any rancke swelling, use to cut off their tailes, that the blood may run through them the faster: Let me have no traine, when I goe to shed blood, least it make me have a greater, when I ride to the Gallowes.

CARDINAL. Come to me after midnight, to helpe to remove
That body to her owne Lodging: I'll give out
She dide o'th' Plague; 'Twill breed the lesse enquiry
After her death.

BOSOLA. Where's *Castruchio,* her husband?

CARDINAL. He's rode to *Naples* to take possession
Of *Antonio's* Cittadell.

BOSOLA. Beleeve me, you have done a very happy turne.

CARDINAL. Faile not to come: there is the Master-key
Of our Lodgings: and by that you may conceive
What trust I plant in you.

BOSOLA. You shall find me ready.

Exit [*Cardinal*].

Oh poore *Antonio,* though nothing be so needfull
To thy estate, as pitty, Yet I finde
Nothing so dangerous: I must looke to my footing;
In such slippery yce-pavements, men had neede
To be frost-nayld well: they may breake their neckes else.
The precedent's here afore me: how this man
Beares up in blood!—seems fearless!—why, 'tis well:
Securitie some men call the Suburbs of Hell,
Onely a dead wall betweene. Well (good *Antonio*)
I'll seeke thee out; and all my care shall be
To put thee into safety from the reach
Of these most cruell biters, that have got
Some of thy blood already. It may be,
I'll joyne with thee, in a most just revenge.
The weakest Arme is strong enough, that strikes
With the sword of Justice: Still me thinkes the Duchesse
Haunts me: there, there! . . . 'tis nothing but my mellancholy.
O Penitence, let me truely tast thy Cup,
That throwes men downe, only to raise them up.

Exit.

ACTUS V, SCENA III.

[*Enter Antonio & Delio. There is an Eccho, (from the Duchesse Grave.)*]

DELIO. Yond's the Cardinal's window: This fortification
Grew from the ruines of an auncient Abbey:

And to yond side o'th' river, lies a wall,
(Peece of a Cloyster) which in my opinion
Gives the best Eccho that you ever heard;
So hollow, and so dismall, and withall
So plaine in the destinction of our words,
That many have supposde it is a Spirit
That answers.

ANTONIO. I doe love these auncient ruynes:
We never tread upon them, but we set
Our foote upon some reverend History.
And questionles, here in this open Court
(Which now lies naked to the injuries
Of stormy weather) some men lye Enterr'd
Lov'd the Church so well, and gave so largely to't,
They thought it should have canopide their Bones
Till Doombes-day: But all things have their end:
Churches, and Citties (which have diseases like to men)
Must have like death that we have.

ECCHO. Like death that we have.

DELIO. Now the *Eccho* hath caught you[.]

ANTONIO. It groan'd (me thought) and gave
A very deadly Accent?

ECCHO. *Deadly Accent.*

DELIO. I told you 'twas a pretty one: you may make it
A Huntes-man, or a Faulconer, a Musitian,
Or a Thing of Sorrow.

ECCHO. *A Thing of Sorrow.*

ANTONIO. I sure: that suites it best.

ECCHO. *That suites it best.*

ANTONIO. 'Tis very like my wifes voyce.

ECCHO. *I, wifes-voyce.*

DELIO. Come: let's walke farther from't:
I would not have you go to th' *Cardinals* to-night:
Doe not.

ECCHO. *Doe not.*

DELIO. Wisdome doth not more moderate wasting Sorrow
Then time: take time for't: be mindfull of thy safety.

ECCHO. *Be mindfull of thy safety.*

ANTONIO. Necessitie compells me:
Make scruteny through the passages
Of your owne life; you'll find it impossible
To flye your fate.

ECCHO. *O flye your fate.*

DELIO. Harke: the dead stones seeme to have pitty on you
And give you good counsell.

ANTONIO. *Eccho,* I will not talk with thee;
For thou art a dead Thing.

ECCHO. *Thou art a dead Thing.*
ANTONIO. My Duchesse is asleepe now,
And her litle-Ones, I hope sweetly: oh Heaven
Shall I never see her more?
ECCHO. *Never see her more*[.]
ANTONIO. I mark'd not one repetition of the Eccho
But that: and on the sudden, a cleare light
Presented me a face folded in sorrow.
DELIO. Your fancy; meerely.
ANTONIO. Come: I'll be out of this Ague;
For to live thus, is not indeed to live:
It is a mockery, and abuse of life—
I will not henceforth save my selfe by halves,
Loose all, or nothing.
DELIO. Your owne vertue save you!
I'll fetch your eldest sonne; and second you:
It may be that the sight of his owne blood
Spred in so sweet a figure, may beget
The more compassion.
[ANTONIO.] How ever, fare you well:
Though in our miseries, Fortune have a part,
Yet, in our noble suffrings she hath none—
Contempt of paine, that we may call our owne.

Exeunt.

ACTUS V, SCENA IIII.

[*Enter Cardinal, Pescara, Malateste, Roderigo, and Grisolan.*]

CARDINAL. You shall not watch to-night by the sicke Prince,
His Grace is very well recover'd.
MALATESTE. Good my lord suffer us.
CARDINAL. Oh, by no meanes:—
The noyce, and change of object in his eye,
Doth more distract him: I pray, all to bed,
And though you heare him in his violent fit,
Do not rise, I intreat you.
PESCARA. So, sir; we shall not—
CARDINAL. Nay, I must have you promise
Upon your honors, for I was enjoyn'd to't
By himselfe; and he seem'd to urge it sencibly.
PESCARA. Let our honors bind this trifle.
CARDINAL. Nor any of your followers.
MALATESTE. Neither.
CARDINAL. It may be, to make triall of your promise,
When he's asleepe, my selfe will rise, and faigne

Some of his mad trickes, and crie out for helpe,
And faigne my selfe in danger.
MALATESTE. If your throate were cutting,
I'll'd not come at you, now I have protested against it.
CARDINAL. Why, I thanke you.

[*withdraws a little.*]

GRISOLAN. 'Twas a foule storm to-night.
RODERIGO. The Lord *Ferdinand's* chamber shooke like an Ozier.° willow
MALATESTE. 'Twas nothing but pure kindnesse in the Divell,
To rocke his owne child.

Exeunt, [*except Cardinal.*]

CARDINAL. The reason why I would not suffer these
About my brother, is, because at midnight
I may with better privacy, convay
Julias body to her owne Lodging: O, my Conscience!
I would pray now: but the Divell takes away my heart
For having any confidence in Praier.
About this houre, I appointed *Bosola*
To fetch the body: when he hath serv'd my turne,
He dies.

Exit. [*Enter Bosola.*]

BOSOLA. Hah? 'twas the Cardinals voyce: I heard him name,
Bosola, and my death: listen, I heare ones footing.

Enter Ferdinand.

FERDINAND. Strangling is a very quiet death.
BOSOLA. Nay then I see, I must stand upon my Guard.
FERDINAND. What say' to that? whisper, softly: doe you agree to't?
So—it must be done i'th' darke: the Cardinal would not for a
thousand pounds, the Doctor should see it.

Exit.

BOSOLA. My death is plotted; here's the consequence of murther.
We value not desert, nor Christian breath,
When we know blacke deedes must be cur'de with death.

[*Enter Antonio & Servant.*]

SERVANT. Here stay Sir, and be confident, I pray:
I'll fetch you a darke Lanthorn.

Exit.

ANTONIO. Could I take him at his prayers,
There were hope of pardon
BOSOLA. Fall right, my sword:

[*Strikes him.*]

I'll not give thee so much leysure, as to pray.

ANTONIO. Oh, I am gone: Thou hast ended a long suit,
In a mynut.
BOSOLA. What art thou?
ANTONIO. A most wretched thing,
That onely have thy benefit in death,
To appeare my selfe.

[*Re-enter Servant with light.*]

SERVANT. Where are you Sir?
ANTONIO. Very neere my home: *Bosola?*
SERVANT. Oh misfortune!
BOSOLA. Smother thy pitty, thou art dead else: *Antonio?*
The man I would have sav'de 'bove mine owne life!
We are meerely the Starres tennys-balls (strooke, and banded
Which way please them)—oh good *Antonio,*
I'll whisper one thing in thy dying eare,
Shall make thy heart breake quickly: Thy faire Duchesse
And two sweet Children . . .
ANTONIO. Their very names
Kindle a litle life in me.
BOSOLA. Are murderd!
ANTONIO. Some men have wish'd to die,
At the hearing of sad tydings: I am glad
That I shall do't in sadnes: I would not now
Wish my wounds balm'de nor heal'd: for I have no use
To put my life to: In all our Quest of Greatnes . . .
(Like wanton Boyes, whose pastime is their care)
We follow after bubbles, blowne in th'ayre.
Pleasure of life, what is't? onely the good houres
Of an Ague: meerely a preparative to rest,
To endure vexation: I doe not aske
The processe of my death: only commend me
To *Delio.*
BOSOLA. Breake heart!
ANTONIO. And let my Sonne, flie the Courts of Princes.

[*Dies.*]

BOSOLA. Thou seem'st to have lov'd *Antonio?*
SERVANT. I brought him hether,
To have reconcil'd him to the Cardinal.
BOSOLA. I doe not aske thee that:
Take him up, if thou tender thine owne life,
And beare him, where the Lady *Julia*
Was wont to lodge: Oh, my fate moves swift.
I have this Cardinal in the forge already,
Now I'll bring him to th'hammer: (O direfull misprision:)
I will not Imitate things glorious,

No more than base: I'll be mine own example.
On, on: and looke thou represent, for silence,
The thing thou bear'st.

Exeunt.

ACTUS V, SCENA V.

[*Enter*] *Cardinal (with a Booke).*

CARDINAL. I am puzzll'd in a question about hell:
He saies, in hell, there's one materiall fire,
And yet it shall not burne all men alike.
Lay him by: How tedious is a guilty conscience!
When I looke into the Fish-ponds, in my Garden,
Me thinkes I see a thing, arm'd with a Rake
That seemes to strike at me:

[*Enter Bosola & Servant bearing Antonio's body.*]

Now? art thou come?
Thou look'st ghastly:
There sits in thy face, some great determination,
Mix'd with some feare.
BOSOLA. Thus it lightens into Action:
I am come to kill thee.
CARDINAL. Hah? helpe! our Guard!
BOSOLA. Thou art deceiv'd: they are out of thy howling.
CARDINAL. Hold: and I will faithfully devide
Revenewes with thee.
BOSOLA. Thy prayers, and proffers
Are both unseasonable.
CARDINAL. Raise the Watch:
we are betraid.
BOSOLA. I have confinde your flight:
I'll suffer your retreyt to *Julias* Chamber,
But no further.
CARDINAL. Helpe: we are betraid!

[*Enter Malateste, Roderigo, Pescara, Grisolan, above.*]

MALATESTE. Listen[.]
CARDINAL. My Dukedome, for rescew!
RODERIGO. Fye upon his counterfeyting!
MALATESTE. Why, 'tis not the Cardinal.
RODERIGO. Yes, yes, 'tis he[.]
But, I'll see him hang'd, ere I'll goe down to him.
CARDINAL. Here's a plot upon me, I am assaulted: I am lost,
Unlesse some rescew.

GRISOLAN. He doth this pretty well:
But it will not serve; to laugh me out of mine honour!
CARDINAL. The sword's at my throat[.]
RODERIGO. You would not bawle so lowd then.
MALATESTE. Come, come: let's goe to bed: he told us this much aforehand.
PESCARA. He wish'd you should not come at him: but, beleeve't,
The accent of the voyce sounds not in jest.
I'll downe to him, howsoever, and with engines
Force ope the doores.

[*Exit above.*]

RODERIGO. Let's follow him aloofe,
And note how the Cardinal will laugh at him.

[*Exeunt above.*]

BOSOLA. There's for you first:
'Cause you shall not unbarracade the doore
To let in rescew.

[*He kills the Servant.*]

CARDINAL. What cause hast thou to pursue my life?
BOSOLA. Looke there[.]
CARDINAL. *Antonio?*
BOSOLA. Slaine by my hand unwittingly:
Pray, and be sudden: when thou killd'st thy sister,
Thou tookst from Justice her most equall ballance,
And left her naught but her sword.
CARDINAL. O mercy!
BOSOLA. Now it seemes thy Greatnes was onely outward:
For thou fall'st faster of thy selfe, than calamitie
Can drive thee: I'll not wast longer time: There.

[*Wounds him.*]

CARDINAL. Thou hast hurt me[.]
BOSOLA. Againe[.]
CARDINAL. Shall I die like a Levoret° young hare
Without any resistance? helpe, helpe, helpe:
I am slaine.

[*Enter Ferdinand.*]

FERDINAND. Th'allarum? give me a fresh horse:
Rally the vaunt-guard: or the day is lost:
Yeeld, yeeld: I give you the honour of Armes,
Shake my Sword over you—will you yielde?
CARDINAL. Helpe me, I am your brother.
FERDINAND. The divell?

My brother fight upon the adverse party?
There flies your ransom.

He wounds the Cardinal, and (in the scuffle) gives Bosola his death-wound.

CARDINAL. Oh Justice:
I suffer now, for what hath former bin:
Sorrow is held the eldest child of sin.

FERDINAND. Now you're brave fellowes: *Caesars* Fortune was harder than *Pompeys: Caesar* died in the armes of prosperity, *Pompey* at the feete of disgrace: you both died in the field—the paine's nothing: paine many times is taken away with the apprehension of greater, (as the tooth-ache with the sight of a Barbor, that comes to pull it out) there's Philosophy for you.

BOSOLA. Now my revenge is perfect: sinke (thou maine cause
Of my undoing)—the last part of my life,
Hath done me best service.

[*He kills Ferdinand.*]

FERDINAND. Give me some wet hay, I am broken-winded—
I do account this world but a dog-kennell:
I will vault credit, and affect high pleasures,
Beyond death.

BOSOLA. He seemes to come to himselfe,
Now he's so neere the bottom.

FERDINAND. My sister, oh! my sister, there's the cause on't.
Whether we fall by ambition, blood, or lust,
Like Diamonds, we are cut with our owne dust.

[*Dies.*]

CARDINAL. Thou hast thy payment too.

BOSOLA. Yes, I hold my weary soule in my teeth,
'Tis ready to part from me: I do glory
That thou, which stood'st like a huge Piramid
Begun upon a large, and ample base,
Shalt end in a little point, a kind of nothing.

[*Enter Pescara, Malateste, Roderigo & Grisolan.*]

PESCARA. How now (my Lord?)

MALATESTE. Oh sad disastre!

RODERIGO. How comes this?

BOSOLA. Revenge, for the Duchesse of Malfy, murdered
By th'*Aragonian* brethren: for *Antonio*,
Slaine by this hand: for lustfull *Julia*,
Poyson'd by this man: and lastly, for my selfe,
(That was an Actor in the maine of all,
Much 'gainst mine owne good nature, yet i'th'end
Neglected.)

PESCARA. How now (my Lord?)

CARDINAL. Looke to my brother:

He gave us these large wounds, as we were strugling
Here i'th' rushes: And now, I pray, let me
Be layd by, and never thought of.

[*Dies.*]

PESCARA. How fatally (it seemes) he did withstand
His owne rescew!
MALATESTE. Thou wretched thing of blood,
How came *Antonio* by his death?
BOSOLA. In a mist: I know not how,
Such a mistake, as I have often seene
In a play: Oh, I am gone—
We are onely like dead wals, or vaulted graves,
That ruin'd, yieldes no eccho: Fare you well—
It may be paine: but no harme to me to die,
In so good a quarrell: Oh this gloomy world,
In what a shadow, or deepe pit of darknesse,
Doth (womanish, and fearefull) mankind live!
Let worthy mindes nere stagger in distrust
To suffer death, or shame, for what is just—
Mine is another voyage.

[*Dies.*]

PESCARA. The noble *Delio,* as I came to th'Pallace,
Told me of *Antonio's* being here, and shew'd me
A pritty gentleman his sonne and heire.

[*Enter Delio with Antonio's Son.*]

MALATESTE. Oh Sir, you come too late.
DELIO. I heard so, and
Was arm'd for't ere I came: Let us make noble use
Of this great ruine; and joyne all our force
To establish this yong hopefull Gentleman
In's mothers right. These wretched eminent things
Leave no more fame behind 'em, than should one
Fall in a frost, and leave his print in snow—
As soone as the sun shines, it ever melts,
Both forme, and matter: I have ever thought
Nature doth nothing so great, for great men,
As when she's pleas'd to make them Lords of truth:
Integrity of life, is fames best friend,
Which noblely (beyond Death) shall crowne the end.

Exeunt.

FINIS

The Knight of the Burning Pestle

Francis Beaumont was unusual among Elizabethan and Jacobean playwrights in that he was a gentleman, the son of a judge; he shares this distinction with John Fletcher, the son of a bishop, with whom he collaborated on perhaps seven to nine plays (there is some debate over the exact number). Beaumont was born in 1584 in Leicestershire, the third son in the family, attended Oxford (although he did not take a degree), and studied law at the Inner Temple (although he did not practice it). He is most known for his collaborations with Fletcher such as *Philaster* (1609) and *A King and No King* (1611), called tragicomedies, according to Fletcher, because characters are brought near to death but do not die. Around 1613 Beaumont married a country heiress and ceased to write for the theater. He died in 1616 and was buried in Westminster Abbey.

The Knight of the Burning Pestle was first performed at Blackfriars Theatre, built on what had been the grounds of a Dominican monastery. The theater was home to one of the boys' companies; the Chapel Children were recruited as choristers but were acting in plays by the late 1570s. Admission was six pence, and hence the audience would probably have been more affluent than was common at theaters such as the Globe and the Rose. It was also roofed. The company was noted for producing satires and plays of unusual sexual frankness, often perverse.

The Knight of the Burning Pestle satirizes a London citizen and his wife who have money to spend and no taste. Citizens were members of City guilds, craftsmen and merchants who with their growing economic clout constituted a vague threat to the established order. A part of the humor of the play comes from children spouting endless puns (including the title) on venereal disease and its symptoms. The

My text is based on that established by Fredson Bowers for *The Dramatic Works in the Beaumont and Fletcher Canon*, vol. 1 (Cambridge: Cambridge University Press, 1966), 10–87; also consulted is R. C. Bald's *Six Elizabethan Plays* (Boston: Houghton Miflin, 1963). I have standardized the character names ("Rafe" for "Ralph" and "Raph," "Humphrey" for "Humfery," etc.).

play reveals details about the experience of attending a play; the wife complains about the gentlemen in the audience smoking and sends her husband out for beer. There is much singing and between each act there is dancing.

The play is also a brilliant metatheatrical piece, commenting on its own artificiality. Jasper's absurd and nearly disastrous decision to test Luce in the forest, for instance, is not unlike the sort of thing that would happen in one of Beaumont and Fletcher's tragicomedies. Nevertheless, good humor reconciles not only the characters in the "play" about the love of Jasper and Luce, but the characters of the citizen and his wife with the Blackfriars audience. Unsuccessful when first performed, it has been repeatedly revived ever since and is the ancestor of numerous metatheatrical pieces such as the Duke of Buckingham and Robert Howard's *The Rehearsal* and Henry Fielding's *The Author's Farce.*

The famous Historie of the Knight of the burning Pestle

The Speakers Names.

THE PROLOGUE.

THEN A CITIZEN [George].

THE CITTIZENS WIFE [Nell], AND.

RAFE [RALPH] HER MAN, SITTING BELOW AMIDST THE SPECTATORS.

A RICH MARCHANT [VENTUREWELL]

JASPER, HIS APPRENTICE

MASTER HUMPHREY, A FRIEND TO THE MARCHANT.

LUCE, THE MARCHANTS DAUGHTER.

MISTRESSE MERRI-THOUGHT, JASPERS MOTHER.

MICHAEL, A SECOND SONNE OF MISTRESSE MERRI-THOUGHT.

OLD MASTER MERRY-THOUGHT [CHARLES].

[TIM] A SQUIRE
[GEORGE] A DWARFE } [APPRENTICES]

A TAPSTER.

A BOY THAT DANCETH AND SINGETH.

AN HOST.

A BARBER.

[THREE CAPTIVE] KNIGHTS.

[CAPTIVE WOMAN.]

A SERGEANT.

SOULDIERS.

[BOYS.]

WILLIAM HAMMERTON, A PEWTERER.

GEORGE GREEN-GOOSE, POULTERER.

POMPIONA, DAUGHTER TO THE KIND OF MOLDAVIA.

Enter Prologue. [*Gentlemen seated on stage.*]

[INDUCTION]

From all that's neere the Court, from all that's great
Within the compasse of the Citty-wals,
We now have brought our Sceane.

Enter Citizen [from audience below].

CITIZEN. Hold your peace good-man boy.

PROLOGUE. What do you meane sir?

CITIZEN. That you have no good meaning: this seven yeares there hath beene playes at this house, I have observed it, you have still° girds at Citizens; and now you call your play, *The London Marchant.* Downe with your Title, boy, downe with your Title.

still°: always

PROLOGUE. Are you a member of the noble Citty?

CITIZEN. I am.

PROLOGUE. And a Free-man?

CITIZEN. Yea, and a Grocer.

PROLOGUE. So Grocer, then by your sweet favour, we intend no abuse to the Citty.

CITIZEN. No sir, yes sir, if you were not resolv'd to play the Jacks,° what need you study for new subjects, purposely to abuse your betters? why could not you be contented, as well as others, with the legend of *Whittington,*[1] or the life and death of sir *Thomas Gresham?* with the building of the Royall Exchange?[2] or the story of Queene Elenor, with the rearing of London Bridge upon woolsackes?[3]

Jacks°: knaves

PROLOGUE. You seeme to bee an understanding[4] man: what would you have us do sir?

CITIZEN. Why, present something notably in honour of the Commons of the citty.

PROLOGUE. Why what doe you say to the life and death of fat *Drake,* or the repairing of Fleet-privies?[5]

CITIZEN. I do not like that, but I will have a Citizen, and hee shall be of my owne trade.

1. Richard Whittington was a wealthy lord mayor of London; the legend, however, is that he rose to be a wealthy merchant and lord mayor from poverty. This was the title of a play entered on the Stationer's Register in 1604.

2. Sir Thomas Gresham was a wealthy merchant, lord mayor, and financial adviser to several Tudor monarchs. He founded the Royal Exchange in 1565. Thomas Heyward's *If You Know Not Me, You Know Nobody, the Second Part* (1606) includes this episode.

3. There are several legends of bridges (notably that at Wadebridge) being built upon woolsacks after an angelic vision. According to Pliny, a temple built upon coal and woolsacks on slippery ground protected against the foundations slipping.

4. 1) knowledgeable; 2) a groundling (with pun on "under-standing").

5. Invented play titles.

PROLOGUE. Oh you should have told us your minde a moneth since, our play is ready to begin now.

CITIZEN. 'Tis all one for that, I will have a Grocer, and he shall do admirable things.

PROLOGUE. What will you have him do?

CITIZEN. Marry, I will have him—

WIFE. Husband, husband.

Wife *below.*

RAFE. Peace mistresse.

Rafe *below*

WIFE. Hold thy peace *Rafe,* I know what I do, I warrant tee. Husband, husband.

CITIZEN. What sayest thou cunny?°

cony (rabbit, used affectionately)

WIFE. Let him kill a Lyon with a pestle husband, let him kill a Lyon with a pestle.

CITIZEN. So he shall, Il'e have him kill a Lyon with a pestle.

WIFE. Husband, shall I come up husband?

CITIZEN. I cunny. *Rafe* helpe your mistresse this way: pray gentlemen, make her a little roome, I pray you sir lend me your hand to helpe up my wife: I thanke you sir. So.

[Wife *comes on the Stage.*]

WIFE. By your leave Gentlemen all, Im'e something troublesome, Im'e a stranger here, I was nere at one of these playes as they say, before; but I should have seene *Jane Shore*[6] once, and my husband hath promised me any time this Twelvemoneth, to carry me to The *Bold Beauchams,*[7] but in truth he did not, I pray you beare with me.

CITIZEN. Boy, let my wife and I have a cupple stooles, and then begin, and let the Grocer do rare things.

PROLOGUE. But sir, we have never a boy to play him, every one hath a part already.

WIFE. Husband, husband, for Gods sake let *Rafe* play him, beshrew mee if I do not thinke hee will goe beyond them all.

CITIZEN. Well remembred wife, come up *Rafe:* Il'e tell you Gentlemen, let them but lend him a suit of reparrell, and necessaries, and by Gad, if any of them all blow winde in the taile on him, Il'e be hang'd.

[Rafe *comes up on the stage.*]

WIFE. I pray you youth let him have a suit of reparrell, Il'e be sworne Gentlemen, my husband tels you true, hee will act you some-times at our house, that all the neighbours cry out on him:

6. Mistress of Edward IV, and a character in Heyward's *Edward IV.*

7. Probably a lost play about the fourteenth-century British hero, the Bold (Thomas) Beauchamps, who supposedly in 1346 with a squire and six archers defeated one hundred men.

hee will fetch you up a couraging part so in the garret, that we are all as feard I warrant you, that we quake againe: wee'l feare our children with him if they bee never so un-ruly, do but cry, *Rafe comes, Rafe comes* to them, and they'l be as quyet as Lambes. Hold up thy head *Rafe,* shew the Gentlemen what thou canst doe, speak a huffing° part, I warrant you the Gentlemen will accept of it. swaggering

CITIZEN. Do *Rafe,* do.

RAFE. By heaven me thinkes it were an easie leap
To plucke bright honour from the pale-fac'd Moone,
Or dive into the bottome of the sea,
Where never fathame line touch't any ground,
And plucke up drowned honor from the lake of hell.[8]

CITIZEN. How say you Gentlemen, is it not as I told you?

WIFE. Nay Gentlemen, hee hath playd before, my husband sayes, *Musidorus*[9] before the Wardens of our Company.

CITIZEN. I, and hee should have played *Jeronimo*[10] with a Shooemaker for a wager.

PROLOGUE. He shall have a suit of apparell if he will go in.

CITIZEN. In Rafe, in Rafe, and set out the Grocery in their kinde, if thou lov'st me.

[*Exit* Rafe.]

WIFE. I warrant our Rafe will looke finely when hee's dresst.

PROLOGUE. But what will you have it cal'd?

CITIZEN. *The Grocers Honour.*

PROLOGUE. Me thinks *The Knight of the burning Pestle* were better.

WIFE. Il'e be sworn husband, that's as good a name as can be.

CITIZEN. Let it be so, begin, begin, my wife and I wil sit downe.

PROLOGUE. I pray you do.

CITIZEN. What stately musicke have you? you have shawmes?° oboes

PROLOGUE. Shawmes? no.

CITIZEN. No? Im'e a thiefe if my minde did not give me so. *Rafe* playes a stately part, and he must needs have shawmes: Il'e be at the charge of them my selfe, rather than wee'l be without them.

PROLOGUE. So you are like to be.

CITIZEN. Why and so I will be: ther's two shillings, let's have the waits of South-wark,[11] they are as rare fellowes as any are in *England;* and that will fetch them all or'e the water with a vengeance, as if they were mad.

PROLOGUE. You shall have them: Will you sit downe then?

CITIZEN. I come wife.

8. Slightly misquoted from a speech by Hotspur in *1 Henry IV,* act 1, scene 3.
9. *Mucedorus,* a popular play by an unknown author, first printed in 1598.
10. Protagonist in Thomas Kyd's *The Spanish Tragedy* (c. 1589).
11. A band of professional musicians who played on civic occasions.

WIFE. Sit you merry all Gentlemen, Im'e bold to sit amongst you for my ease.

PROLOGUE. From all that's neere the Court, from all that's great,
Within the compasse of the Citty-walles,
We now have brought our Sceane: flye farre from hence
All private taxes,° immodest phrases, aspersions
What ere may but shew like vicious:
For wicked mirth never true pleasure brings,
But honest minds are pleas'd with honest things.
Thus much for that we do: but for *Rafes* part you must answere for your selfe.

[*Exit.*]

CITIZEN. Take you no care for *Rafe,* hee'l discharge himselfe I warrant you.
I faith Gentlemen, Il'e give my word for *Rafe.*

Enter Marchant, *and* Jasper *his Prentice.*

[I.]

MARCHANT. Sirrah, Il'e make you know you are my Prentice,
And whom my charitable love redeem'd
Even from the fall of fortune, gave thee heate
And growth, to be what now thou art, new cast thee,
Adding the trust of all I have, at home,
In forren Staples,° or upon the Sea, trading posts
To thy direction, ti'de the good opinions
Both of my selfe and friends to thy endeavours,
So faire were thy beginnings; But with these,
As I remember, you had never charge,
To love your Maisters daughter, and even then,
When I had found a wealthy husband for her,
I take it, sir, you had not; but, how ever,
Il'e break the necke of that commission,
And make you know you are but a Merchants factor.

JASPER. Sir, I do liberally confesse I am yours,
Bound, both by love and duty, to your service;
In which, my labour hath bene all my profit;
I have not lost in bargaine, nor delighted
To weare your honest gaines upon my backe,
Nor have I given a pencion to my bloud,° indulged my appetites
Or lavishly in play consum'd your stocke.
These, and the miseries that do attend them,
I dare, with innocence, proclaime are strangers
To all my temperate actions; for your daughter,
If there be any love, to my deservings,

Borne by her vertuous selfe, I cannot stop it!
Nor, am I able to refraine her wishes.
She's private to her selfe and best of knowledge,
Whom she'le make so happy as to sigh for.
Besides, I cannot thinke you meane to match her,
Unto a felow of so lame a presence,
One that hath little left of *Nature* in him.

MARCHANT. 'Tis very well, sir, I can tell your wisedome
How all this shall bee cur'd.

JASPER. Your care becomes you.

MARCHANT. And thus it must be sir, I heere discharge you
My house and service, take your liberty,
And when I want a sonne I'le send for you.

Exit.

JASPER. These be the faire rewards of them that love.
O you that live in freedome never prove
The travell of a mind led by desire.

Enter Luce.

LUCE. Why, how now, friend, struck with my fathers thunder?

JASPER. Strucke, and strucke dead unlesse the remedy
Be full of speede and vertue; I am now,
What I expected long, no more your fathers.

LUCE. But mine.

JASPER. But yours, and onely yours I am,
That's all I have to keepe me from the Statute,[12]
You dare be constant still?

LUCE. O feare me not,
In this I dare be better than a woman.
Nor shall his anger, nor his offers move me,
Were they both equall to a Princes power.

JASPER. You know my rivall?

LUCE. Yes, and love him deerly
Even as I love an ague, or foule weather,
I prethee *Jasper* feare him not.

JASPER. O no,
I do not meane to do him so much kindnesse;
But to our owne desires, you know the plot
We both agreed on.

LUCE. Yes, and will performe
My part exactly.

JASPER. I desire no more,
Fare-well, and keepe my heart, 'tis yours.

12. Probably a reference to the Poor Law of 1597, which put boys without work under the authority of church wardens.

LUCE. I take it,
He must do miracles makes me forsake it.

Exeunt.

CITIZEN. Fye upon am little infidels, what a matters here now? well, I'le be hang'd for a halfe-penny, if there be not some abomination knavery in this Play, well, let 'em looke toot, *Rafe* must come, and if there be any tricks a-brewing,—

[*Enter* Boy.]

WIFE. Let 'em brew and bake too husband, a Gods name, *Rafe* will find all out I warrant you, an they were older than they are. I pray, my pretty youth is Rafe ready[?]

BOY. He will be presently.

WIFE. Now, I pray you make my commendations unto him, and withall carry him this sticke of Licoras, tell him his Mistresse sent it him, and bid him bite a peece, 'twill open his pipes the better, say.

[*Exit* Boy.]
Enter Marchant, *and Maister* Humphrey.

MARCHANT. Come sir, shee's yours, upon my faith she's yours,
You have my hand, for other idle lets° hindrances
Betweene your hopes and her, thus, with a wind
They are scattered and no more: my wanton Prentice,
That like a bladder, blew himselfe with love,
I have let out, and sent him to discover
New Maisters yet unknowne.

HUMPHREY. I thanke you sir,
Indeed I thanke you sir, and ere I stir
It shall bee knowne, how ever you do deeme,
I am of gentle bloud and gentle seeme.

MARCHANT. O sir, I know it certaine.

HUMPHREY. Sir my friend,
Although, as Writers say, all things have end,
And that we call a pudding, hath his two,
O let it not seeme strange I pray to you,
If in this bloudy simile, I put
My love, more endlesse, than fraile things or gut.

WIFE. Husband, I prethee sweete lambe tell me one thing, but tell mee truly: stay youths I beseech you, till I question my husband.

CITIZEN. What is it mouse?

WIFE. Sirrah, didst thou ever see a prettier child? how it behaves it selfe, I warrant yee, and speakes, and lookes, and pearts up the head? I pray you brother, with your favor, were you never none of Maister *Monkesters*[13] schollars?

13. Richard Mulcaster, headmaster of St. Paul's School from 1596 to 1608.

CITIZEN. Chicken, I prethee heartely containe thy selfe, the childer are pretty childer, but when *Rafe* comes, Lambe—

WIFE. I when *Rafe* comes conny; well my youth, you may proceed.

MARCHANT. Wel sir, you know my love, and rest, I hope,
Assur'd of my consent, get but my daughters,
And wed her when you please; you must be bold,
And clap in close unto her, come, I know
You have language good enough to win a wench.

WIFE. A whoreson tyrant, has been an old stringer° in's daies I warrant him. — rake

HUMPHREY. I take your gentle offer and withall
Yeeld love againe for love reciprocall.

MARCHANT. What *Luce,* within there.

Enter Luce.

LUCE. Cal'd you sir?

MARCHANT. I did.
Give entertainement to this Gentleman
And see you bee not froward:° to her sir, — contrary
My presence will but bee an eye-soare to you.

Exit.

HUMPHREY. Faire Mistresse *Luce,* how do you, are you well?
Give me your hand and then I pray you tell,
How doth your little sister, and your brother?
And whether you love me or any other.

LUCE. Sir, these are quickely answered.

HUMPHREY. So they are,
Where women are not cruel: but how farre
Is it now distant from the place we are in,
Unto that blessed place your father's warren.° — enclosed land for breeding game

LUCE. What makes you thinke of that sir?

HUMPHREY. Even that face.
For stealing Rabbets whilome° in that place, — once
God *Cupid,* or the Keeper, I know not whether,
Unto my cost and charges brought you thither,
And there began—

LUCE. Your game sir.

HUMPHREY. Let no game,
Or any thing that tendeth to the same,
Bee ever more remembred, thou faire killer
For whom I sate me downe and brake my Tiller.° — crossbow

WIFE. There's a kind Gentleman, I warrant you, when will you do as much for me *George?*

LUCE. Beshrew me sir, I am sorry for your losses,

But as the proverb saies, I cannot cry,
I would you had not seene me.
HUMPHREY. So would I.
Unlesse you had more maw° to do me good. appetite
LUCE. Why, cannot this strange passion be withstood?
Send for a Constable, and raise the Towne.
HUMPHREY. O no, my valiant love will batter downe
Millions of Constables, and put to flight,
Even that great watch of Mid-summer day at night.
LUCE. Beshrew me sir, 'twere good I yeelded then,
Weake women cannot hope, where valiant men
Have no resistance.
HUMPHREY. Yeeld then, I am full
Of pitty, though I say it, and can pull
Out of my pocket, thus, a paire of gloves,
Looke *Lucy,* looke, the dogs tooth, nor the Doves
Are not so white as these; and sweete they bee,
And whipt about with silke, as you may see.
If you desire the price, sute from your eie
A beame to this place, and you shall espie
F. S. which is to say, my sweetest hony,
They cost me three and two pence, or no mony.
LUCE. Well sir, I take them kindly, and I thanke you,
What would you more?
HUMPHREY. Nothing.
LUCE. Why then fare-well.
HUMPHREY. Nor so, nor so, for Lady I must tell,
Before we part, for what we met together,
God grant me time, and patience, and faire weather.
LUCE. Speake and declare your minde in termes so briefe.
HUMPHREY. I shall, then, first and formost for reliefe
I call to you, if that you can affoord it.
I care not at what price, for on my word, it
Shall be repaid againe, although it cost me
More than I'le speake of now, for love hath tost me,
In furious blanket like a Tennis ball,
And now I rise aloft, and now I fall.
LUCE. Alas good Gentleman, alas the day.
HUMPHREY. I thanke you hartely, and as I say,
Thus do I still continue without rest,
I'th' morning like a man, at night a beast,
Roaring and bellowing myne owne disquiet,
That much I feare, forsaking of my diet,
Will bring me presently to that quandary,
I shall bid all adiew.

LUCE. Now by Saint *Mary*
That were great pitty.
HUMPHREY. So it were beshrew me,
Then ease me lusty° Luce, and pity shew me. merry
LUCE. Why sir, you know my will is nothing worth
Without my fathers grant, get his consent,
And then you may with assurance try me.
HUMPHREY. The Worshipfull your sire will not deny me,
For I have askt him, and he hath repli'd,
Sweete Maister *Humphrey, Luce* shall be thy Bride.
LUCE. Sweete Maister *Humphrey* then I am content.
HUMPHREY. And so am I intruth.
LUCE. Yet take me with you,
There is another clause must be annext,
And this it is, I swore, and will performe it;
No man shall ever joy me as his wife
But he that stole me hence. If you dare venter,
I am yours; you need not feare, my father loves you;
If not, farewell for ever.
HUMPHREY. Stay nimph, staie
I have a double Gelding coulored bay,
Sprung by his father from Barbarian kind,
Another for my selfe, though somewhat blind,
Yet true as trusty tree.
LUCE. I am satisfied,
And so I give my hand, our course must lie
Through *Waltham* Forrest, where I have a friend
Will entertaine us, so fare-well sir *Humphrey,*
And thinke upon your businesse.

Exit Luce.

HUMPHREY. Though I die,
I am resolv'd to venter life and lim,
For one so yong, so faire, so kind, so trim.

Exit Humphrey.

WIFE. By my faith and troth *George*, and as I am vertuous, it is e'ne the kindest yong man that ever trod on shooe leather. Well, go thy waies, if thou hast her not, 'tis not thy fault 'faith.
CITIZEN. I prethee mouse be patient. a shall have her, or i'le make some of 'em smoake for't.
WIFE. That's my good lambe *George*, fie, this stinking Tobacco kils men, would there were none in *England:* now I pray Gentlemen, what good does this stinking Tobacco do you? nothing, I warrant you; make chimnies a your faces: o husband, husband, now, now, there's *Rafe*, there's *Rafe.*

Enter Rafe *like a Grocer in's shop, with two Prentices* [Tim and George] *Reading Palmerin of England.*[14]

CITIZEN. Peace foole, let *Rafe* alone, harke you *Rafe;* doe not straine your selfe too much at the first, peace, begin *Rafe.*

RAFE. *Then* Palmerin *and* Trineus, *snatching their Launces from their Dwarfes, and clasping their Helmets gallopt amaine after the Gyant, and* Palmerin *having gotten a sight of him, came posting amaine, saying: Stay trayterous thiefe, for thou maist not so carry away her, that is worth the greatest Lord in the world, and, with these words gave him a blow on the shoulder, that he stroake him besides his Elephant, And* Trineus *comming to the Knight that had* Agricola *behind him, set him soone besides his horse, with his necke broken in the fall, so that the Princesse getting out of the thronge, betweene joy and griefe said; all happy Knight, the mirror of all such as follow Armes, now may I bee well assured of the love thou bearest me.* I wonder why the Kings doe not raise an army of foureteene or fifteene hundred thousand men, as big as the Army that the Prince of *Portigo* brought against *Rosicler,* and destroy these Giants, they do much hurt to wandering Damsels, that go in quest of their Knights.

WIFE. Faith husband and *Rafe* saies true, for they say the King of *Portugall* cannot sit at his meate, but the Giants and the Ettins° will come and snatch it from him.

giants

CITIZEN. Hold thy tongue, on *Rafe.*

RAFE. And certainely those Knights are much to be commended, who neglecting their possessions, wander with a Squire and a Dwarfe through the Desarts to relieve poore Ladies.

WIFE. I by my faith are they *Rafe,* let 'em say what they will, they are indeed, our Knights neglect their possessions well enough, but they do not the rest.

RAFE. There are no such courteous and faire well spoken Knights in this age, they will call one the sonne of a whore, that *Palmerin* of England, would have called faire sir; and one that *Rosicler* would have cal'd right beauteous Damsell they will call damn'd bitch.

WIFE. I'le be sworne will they *Rafe,* they have cal'd mee so an hundred times about a scurvy pipe of Tobacco.

RAFE. But what brave spirit could be content to sit in his shop with a flappet° of wood and a blew apron before him, selling *Methridatum*° and *Dragons water*° to visited houses, that might pursue feats of Armes, and, through his noble atchievements procure such a famous history to be written of his heroicke prowesse.

fly swatter
antidote to poison; plague medicine

14. One of the romances of knightly adventures popular at the time.

CITIZEN. Well said *Rafe,* some more of those words *Rafe.*

WIFE. They go finely by my troth.

RAFE. Why should not I then pursue this course, both for the credit of my selfe and our Company, for amongst all the worthy bookes of Atchievements I doe not call to minde that I yet read of a Grocer Errant. I will be the said Knight: have you heard of any that hath wandred unfurnished of his Squire and Dwarfe? My elder Prentice *Tim* shall be my trusty Squire, and little *George* my dwarfe. Hence my blew Aprone, yet in remembrance of my former Trade, upon my shield shall be portraide, a burning Pestle, and I will be cal'd the *Knight of the burning Pestle.*

WIFE. Nay, I dare sweare thou wilt not forget thy old Trade, thou wert ever meeke.

RAFE. *Tim.*

TIM. Anon.

RAFE. My beloved Squire, and *George* my Dwarfe, I charge you that from hence-forth you never call me by any other name, but the *Right Courteous and Valiant Knight of the burning Pestle,* and that you never call any female by the name of a woman or wench, but faire Ladie, if she have her desires, if not distressed Damsell; that you call all Forrests and Heaths Desarts, and all horses Palfries.

WIFE. This is very fine, faith, do the Gentlemen like *Rafe,* thinke you, husband?

CITIZEN. I, I warrant thee, the Plaiers would give all the shooes in their shop for him.

RAFE. My beloved Squire *Tim,* stand out, admit this were a Desart, and over it a Knight errant pricking, and I should bid you inquire of his intents, what would you say?

TIM. Sir, my Maister sent me, to know whether you are riding?

RAFE. No, thus; faire sir, the *Right Courteous and Valiant Knight of the burning Pestle,* commanded me to enquire, upon what adventure you are bound, whether to relieve some distressed Damsels, or otherwise.

CITIZEN. Whoresonne blocke-head cannot remember.

WIFE. I'faith, and Rafe told him on't before, all the Gentlemen heard him, did he not Gentlemen, did not Rafe tel him on't?

GEORGE. *Right courteous and valiant Knight of the burning Pestle,* here is a distressed Damsell, to have a halfe pennyworth of pepper.

WIFE. That's a good boy, see, the little boy can hit it, by my troth it's a fine child.

RAFE. Relieve her with all courteous language, now shut up shoppe, no more my Prentice, but my trusty Squire and Dwarfe, I must bespeake my shield and arming-pestle.

[*Exeunt* Tim *and* George.]

CITIZEN. Go thy waies *Rafe,* as Im'e a true man, thou art the best on 'em all.

WIFE. *Rafe, Rafe.*

RAFE. What say you, mistresse?

WIFE. I pre'thee, come againe quickly sweet *Rafe.*

RAFE. By and by.

Exit Rafe.

Enter Jasper *and his mother mistresse* Merri-thought.

MISTRESSE MERRI-THOUGHT. Give thee my blessing? No, Il'e ner'e give thee my blessing, Il'e see thee hang'd first; it shall ner'e bee said I gave thee my blessing, th'art thy fathers owne sonne, of the right bloud of the *Merri-thoughts,* I may curse the time that er'e I knew thy father, he hath spent all his owne, and mine too, and when I tell him of it, he laughes and dances, and sings, and cryes, *A merry heart lives long-a.* And thou art a wast-thrift, and art run away from thy maister, that lov'd thee well, and art come to me, and I have laid up a little for my yonger sonne *Michael,* and thou think'st to bezell that, but thou shalt never be able to do it.

Enter Michael.

Come hither *Michael,* come *Michael,* downe on thy knees, thou shalt have my blessing.

MICHAEL. I pray you mother pray to God to blesse me.

MISTRESSE MERRI-THOUGHT. God blesse thee: but *Jasper* shal never have my blessing, he shall be hang'd first, shall hee not *Michael?* how saist thou?

MICHAEL. Yes forsooth mother, and grace of God.

MISTRESSE MERRI-THOUGHT. That's a good boy.

WIFE. I faith it's a fine-spoken child.

JASPER. Mother, though you forget a parents love
I must preserve the duty of a child.
I ran not from my maister, nor returne
To have your stocke maintaine my Idlenesse.

WIFE. Ungracious childe I warrant him, harke how hee chops logicke with his mother: thou hadst best tell her she lyes; do, tell her she lyes.

CITIZEN. If hee were my sonne, I would hang him up by the heeles, and flea him, and salt him, whoore-sonne halter-sacke.

JASPER. My comming onely is to begge your love,
Which I must ever, though I never gaine it,
And, howsoever you esteeme of me,
There is no drop of bloud hid in these veines,
But, I remember well belongs to you
That brought me forth, and would be glad for you
To rip them all againe, and let it out.

MISTRESSE MERRI-THOUGHT. I faith I had sorrow enough for thee (God knowes) but Il'e hamper thee well enough: get thee in thou vagabond, get thee in, and learne of thy brother *Michael.*

[*Exeunt* Jasper *and* Michael.]

OLD MERRI-THOUGHT *(within).*

Nose, nose, jolly red nose,
And who gave thee this jolly red nose?

MISTRESSE MERRI-THOUGHT. Harke, my husband hee's singing and hoiting,° and Im'e faine to carke° and care, and all little enough. Husband, *Charles, Charles Merri-thought.* [reveling; care]

Enter old Merri-thought.

OLD MERRI-THOUGHT.

Nutmegs and Ginger, Cinnamon and Cloves,
And they gave me this jolly red Nose.

MISTRESSE MERRI-THOUGHT. If you would consider your state, you would have little list to sing, I-wisse.

OLD MERRI-THOUGHT. It should never bee considered while it were an estate, if I thought it would spoyle my singing.

MISTRESSE MERRI-THOUGHT. But how wilt thou do *Charles,* thou art an old man, and thou canst not worke, and thou hast not fortie shillings left, and thou eatest good meat, and drinkest good drinke, and laughest?

OLD MERRI-THOUGHT. And will do.

MISTRESSE MERRI-THOUGHT. But how wilt thou come by it *Charles?*

OLD MERRI-THOUGHT. How? why, how have I done hitherto this forty yeares? I never came into my dining roome, but at eleven and six a clocke, I found excellent meat and drink a'th table, my clothes were never worne out, but next morning a Taylor brought me a new suit; and without question it will be so ever: use makes perfectnesse. If all should faile, it is but a little straining my selfe extraordinary, and laugh my selfe to death.

WIFE. It's a foolish old man this: is not he *George?*

CITIZEN. Yes Cunny.

WIFE. Give me a peny i'th purse while I live *George.*

CITIZEN. I by Ladie cunnie, hold thee there.

MISTRESSE MERRI-THOUGHT. Well *Charles,* you promis'd to provide for *Jasper,* and I have laid up for *Michael,* I pray you, pay *Jasper* his portion, hee's come home, and hee shall not consume *Michaels* stocke: he saies his maister turnd him away, but I promise you truly, I thinke he ran away.

WIFE. No indeed mistresse *Merri-thought,* though he bee a notable gallowes, yet Il'e assure you his maister did turne him away, even in this place 'twas, I'faith, within this halfe hour, about his daughter, my husband was by.

CITIZEN. Hang him rougue, he serv'd him well enough: love his maisters daughter! by my troth Cunnie if there were a thousand boies, thou wouldst spoile them all with taking their parts, let his mother alone with him.

WIFE. I *George,* but yet truth is truth.

OLD MERRI-THOUGHT. Where is *Jasper,* hee's welcome how ever, call him in, hee shall have his portion, is he merry?

MISTRESSE MERRI-THOUGHT. I foule chive him,[15] he is too merrie. *Jasper, Michael.*

Enter Jasper *and* Michael.

OLD MERRI-THOUGHT. Welcome *Jasper,* though thou runst away, welcome, God blesse thee: 'tis thy mothers minde thou should'st receive thy portion; thou hast beene abroad, and I hope hast learn'd experience enough to governe it, thou art of sufficient yeares, hold thy hand: one, two, three, foure, five, sixe, seven, eight, nine, there's ten shillings for thee, thrust thy selfe into the world with that, and take some setled course, if fortune crosse thee, thou hast a retiring place, come home to me, I have twentie shillings left. Bee a good husband, that is, weare ordinary clothes, eate the best meate, and drinke the best drinke, bee merrie, and give to the poore, and, beleeve me, thou hast no end of thy goods.

JASPER. Long may you live free from all thought of ill,
And long have cause to be thus merry still.
But father?

OLD MERRI-THOUGHT. No more words *Jasper,* get thee gone, thou hast my blessing, thy fathers spirit upon thee. Farewell *Jasper,*

But yet or ere you part (oh cruell!)
Kisse me, kisse me sweeting, mine own deere jewell:

So, now begone; no words.

Exit Jasper.

MISTRESSE MERRI-THOUGHT. So *Michael,* now get thee gone too.

MICHAEL. Yes forsooth mother, but Il'e have my fathers blessing first.

MISTRESSE MERRI-THOUGHT. No *Michael,* 'tis no matter for his blessing, thou hast my blessing, begone; Il'e fetch my money and jewels, and follow thee: Il'e stay no longer with him, I warrant thee, truly Charles Il'e begone too.

15. Ill luck to him.

OLD MERRI-THOUGHT. What, you will not?

MISTRESSE MERRI-THOUGHT. Yes indeed will I.

OLD MERRI-THOUGHT.

> *Hey ho, fare-well, Nan,*
> *Il'e never trust wench more againe, if I can.*

MISTRESSE MERRI-THOUGHT. You shall not thinke (when all your owne is gone) to spend that I have beene scraping up for *Michael.*

OLD MERRI-THOUGHT. Farewell good wife, I expect it not; all I have to doe in this world, is to bee merry: which I shall, if the ground be not taken from me: and. if it be,

> *When earth and seas from me are reft,*
> *The skyes aloft for me are left.*

Exeunt.

Boy *danceth.* *Musicke. Finis Actus Primi.*

[I. INTERLUDE]

WIFE. Il'e be sworne hee's a merry old Gentleman for all that.
Harke, harke husband, harke, fiddles, fiddles; now surely they go
finely. They say, 'tis present death for these fidlers to tune their
Rebeckes° before the great Turkes grace, is't not, three-stringed
George? But looke, looke, here's a youth dances: now good youth instrument
do a turne a'th toe, sweet heart, I'faith, Ile have *Rafe* come and do
some of his Gambols; hee'l ride the wild mare° Gentlemen, see-saw
'twould do your hearts good to see him. I thanke you kinde youth,
pray bid *Rafe* come.

CITIZEN. Peace Cunnie. Sirrah, you scurvie boy, bid the plaiers send *Rafe,* or by Gods—an they do not, Ill'e teare some of their periwigs beside their heads: this is all Riffe Raffe.

{Exit Boy.
Enter Marchant *and* Humphrey.

[II.]

MARCHANT. And how faith? how goes it now son *Humphrey?*

HUMPHREY. Right worshipfull, and my beloved friend
And father deere, this matters at an end.

MARCHANT. 'Tis well, it should be so,
Im'e glad the girle is found so tractable.

HUMPHREY. Nay she must whirle
From hence, (and you must winke: for so I say,
The storie tels,) to morrow before day.

WIFE. *George,* do'st thou thinke in thy conscience now 'twil be a match? tell me but what thou thinkst sweet rogue, thou seest the poore Gentleman (deere heart) how it labours and throbs I warrant you, to be at rest: Il'e goe move the father for't.

CITIZEN. No, no, I pre'thee sit still, hony-suckle, thoul't spoile all. If he deny him, Il'e bring halfe a dozen good fellows my selfe, and in the shutting of an evening knock't up, and ther's an end.

WIFE. Il'e busse thee for that, i'faith boy; well *George,* well, you have beene a wag in your daies I warrant you: but God forgive you, and I do with all my heart.

MARCHANT. How was it sonne? you told me that to morrow
Before day breake, you must convey her hence.

HUMPHREY. I must, I must, and thus it is agreed,
Your daughter rides upon a browne-bay steed,
I on a sorrell, which I bought of *Brian,*
The honest Host of the red roaring Lion
In *Waltham* situate: Then if you may,
Consent in seemely sort, lest, by delay,
The fatall sisters come and do the office,
And then you'l sing another song.

MARCHANT. Alasse
Why should you be thus full of griefe to me?
That do as willing as your selfe agree
To any thing, so it be good and faire,
Then steale her when you will, if such a pleasure
Content you both, Il'e sleepe and never see it,
To make your joyes more full, but tell me why
You may not here performe your marriage?

WIFE. Gods blessing a thy soule old man, i'faith thou art loath to part true hearts, I see, a has her *George,* and I'me as glad on't, well, go thy waies *Humphrey,* for a faire spoken man, I beleeve thou hast not thy fellow within the wals of *London,* an I should say the Suburbes too, I should not lie, why dost not rejoyce with me *George?*

CITIZEN. If I could but see *Rafe* againe, I were as merry as mine Host i'faith.

HUMPHREY. The cause you seeme to aske, I thus declare,
Helpe me ô Muses nine, your daughter sweare
A foolish oath, and more it was the pitty,
Yet no one but my selfe within this Citty,
Shall dare to say so, but a bold defiance
Shall meete him, were he of the noble Science.° fencing
And yet she sweare, and yet why did she sweare?
Truely I cannot tell unlesse it were
For her owne ease, for, sure, sometimes an oath,
Being sworne thereafter is like cordiall broth.

And this it was shee swore, never to marry
But such a one, whose mighty arme could carry
(As meaning me, for I am such a one)
Her bodily away, through sticke and stone,
Till both of us arrive, at her request,
Some ten miles off, in the wilde *Waltham* Forrest.

MARCHANT. If this be all, you shall not need to feare
Any deniall in your love, proceed,
Il'e neither follow, nor repent the deed.

HUMPHREY. Good-night, twenty good-nights, and twenty more,
And twenty more good-nights, that makes three-score.

Exeunt.

Enter mistresse Merri-thought [*with jewel casket and purse of money*], *and her son* Michael.

MISTRESSE MERRI-THOUGHT. Come Michael, art thou not weary boy?

MICHAEL. No for-sooth mother not I.

MISTRESSE MERRI-THOUGHT. Where be we now child?

MICHAEL. Indeed for-sooth mother I cannot tell, unlesse we be at Mile-End, is not all of the world Mile-End, Mother?

MISTRESSE MERRI-THOUGHT. No *Michael,* not all the world boy, but I can assure thee, *Michael,* Mile-End is a goodly matter, there has bene a pitch-field my child between the naughty *Spaniels* and the *English-men,* and the *Spaniels* ran away Michael, and the *English-men* followed, my neighbour *Coxstone* was there, boy, and kil'd them all with a birding peece.

MICHAEL. Mother forsooth

MISTRESSE MERRI-THOUGHT. What says my white boy?° (favorite)

MICHAEL. Shall not my father go with us too?

MISTRESSE MERRI-THOUGHT. No *Michael,* let thy father go snicke-up,° (hang) he shall never come between a paire of sheets with me againe, while he lives, let him stay at home and sing for his supper boy, come child, sit downe, and Il'e shew my boy fine knacks indeed, look here *Michael,* here's a Ring, and here's a Bruch, and here's a Bracelet, and here's two Rings more, and here's mony and gold bi'th eie° (in crowds) my boy.

MICHAEL. Shall I have all this mother?

MISTRESSE MERRI-THOUGHT. I *Michael* thou shalt have all *Michael.*

CITIZEN. How lik'st thou this, wench?

WIFE. I cannot tell, I would have *Rafe, George;* I'le see no more else indeed-law, and I pray you let the youths understand so much by word of mouth, for, I tell you truely, I'me afraid a my boy, come, come *George,* let's be merry and wise, the child's a father-lesse child, and say they should put him into a streight paire of Gaskins, 'twere worse than knot-grasse, he would never grow after it.

Enter Rafe, [Tim *as*] *Squire, and* [George *as*] *Dwarfe.*

CITIZEN. Here's *Rafe,* here's *Rafe.*

WIFE. How do you do *Rafe?* you are welcome *Rafe,* as I may say, it's a good boy, hold up thy head, and be not afraid, we are thy friends *Rafe,* the Gentlemen will praise thee *Rafe,* if thou plaist thy part with audacity, begin *Rafe* a Gods name.

RAFE. My trusty Squire unlace my Helme, give mee my hat, where are we, or what Desart may this be?

GEORGE. Mirrour of Knight-hood, this is, as I take it, the perrilous *Waltham* downe, in whose bottome stands the inchanted Valley.

MISTRESSE MERRI-THOUGHT. O *Michael,* we are betrai'd, we are betraid, here be Gyants, flie boy, flie boy, flie.

Exeunt mother and Michael [*dropping purse and casket*].

RAFE. Lace on my helme againe: what noise is this?
A gentle Ladie flying the imbrace
Of some uncurteous knight? I will releive her.
Go squire, and say, the Knight, that weares this pestle,
In honour of all Ladies, sweares revenge
Upon that recreant coward that pursues her.
Go comfort her, and that same gentle squire
That beares her companie.

TIM. I go brave Knight.

[*Exit.*]

RAFE. My trustie Dwarfe and friend, reach me my shield,
And hold it while I sweare: First by my knight-hood,
Then by the soule of *Amadis de Gaule,*
My famous Ancestor, then by my sword,
The beauteous *Brionella* girt about me,
By this bright burning pestle, of mine honour
The living Trophie, and by all respect
Due to distressed Damsels, here I vow
Never to end the quest of this faire Lady
And that forsaken squire, till by my valour
I gaine their liberty.

GEORGE. Heaven blesse the Knight
That thus relieves poore errant Gentlewomen.

Exeunt.

WIFE. I marrie *Rafe,* this has some savour in't, I would see the proudest of them all offer to carrie his bookes after him. But *George,* I will not have him go away so soone, I shall bee sicke if he go away, that I shall; call *Rafe* againe *George,* call *Rafe* againe, I pre'thee sweet heart let him come fight before me, and let's ha some drums, and some trumpets, and let him kill all that comes neere him, and thou lov'st me *George.*

CITIZEN. Peace a little, bird, hee shall kill them all an they were twentie more on 'em then there are.

Enter Jasper.

JASPER. Now Fortune, if thou bee'st not onely ill,
Shew me thy better face, and bring about
Thy desperate wheele, that I may clime at length
And stand, this is our place of meeting,
If love have any constancie. Oh age!
Where onely wealthy men are counted happie:
How shall I please thee? how deserve thy smiles?
When I am onely rich in misery?
My fathers blessing, and this little coine
Is my inheritance, a strong revenew;
From earth thou art, and to the earth I give thee,
There grow and multiply, whilst fresher aire,
Breeds me a fresher fortune: how, illusion!

Spies the casket.

What, hath the Divell coin'd himselfe before me?
'Tis mettle good, it rings well, I am waking,
And taking too I hope, now Gods deere blessing
Upon his heart that left it here, 'tis mine,
These pearles, I take it, were not left for swine.

Exit.

WIFE. I do not like that this unthrifty youth should embecill away the money, the poore Gentlewoman his mother will have a heavy heart for it, God knowes.
CITIZEN. And reason good, sweet heart.
WIFE. But let him go, I'le tell *Rafe* a tale in's eare shall fetch him againe with a Wanion I warrant him, if hee bee above ground, and besides *George,* heere are a number of sufficient Gentlemen can witnesse, and my selfe, and your selfe, and the Musitians, if we be cal'd in question, But here comes Rafe, George; thou shalt hear him speake, as he were an Emperall.

Enter Rafe *and* [George *as*] *Dwarfe.*

RAFE. Comes not sir Squire againe?
GEORGE. Right courteous Knight,
Your Squire doth come and with him comes the Lady,
For and the Squire of Damsels, as I take it.

Enter mistresse Merri-thought *and* Michael, *and* [Tim *as*] *Squire.*

RAFE. Madam if any service or devoire° — task
Of a poore errant Knight may right your wrongs,
Command it, I am prest to give you succour,
For to that holy end I beare my Armour.

MISTRESSE MERRI-THOUGHT. Alas sir, I am a poore Gentlewoman, and I have lost my monie in this forrest.

RAFE. Desart, you would say Lady, and not lost
Whilst I have sword and launce: dry up your teares
Which ill befits the beauty of that face,
And tell the storie, if I may request it,
Of your disasterous fortune.

MISTRESSE MERRI-THOUGHT. Out alas, I left a thousand pound, a thousand pound, e'ne all the monie I had laid up for this youth, upon the sight of your Maistership, you lookt so grim, and as I may say it, saving your presence, more like a Giant than a mortall man.

RAFE. I am as you are, Ladie, so are they
All mortall, but why weepes this gentle Squire[?]

MISTRESSE MERRI-THOUGHT. Has hee not cause to weepe doe you thinke, when he hath lost his inheritance?

RAFE. Yong hope of valour, weepe not, I am here
That will confound thy foe and paie it deere
Upon his coward head, that dares denie,
Distressed Squires and Ladies equitie.
I have but one horse, on which shall ride
This Ladie faire behind me, and before
This courteous Squire, fortune will give us more
Upon our next adventure; fairelie speed
Beside us Squire and Dwarfe to do us need.

Exeunt.

CITIZEN. Did not I tell you *Nel* what your man would doe? by the faith of my bodie wench, for cleane action and good deliverie they may all cast their caps at him.

WIFE. And so they may i'faith, for I dare speake it boldly, the twelve Companies[16] of *London* cannot match him, timber for timber, well *George*, an hee be not inveigled by some of these paltrie Plaiers, I ha much marvell, but George wee ha done our parts if the boy have any grace to be thankefull.

CITIZEN. Yes, I warrant thee, duckling.

Enter Humphrey and Luce.

HUMPHREY. Good Mistresse *Luce,* however I in fault am
For your lame horse; you're welcome unto *Waltham.*
But which way now to go, or what to saie
I know not truely till it be broad daie.

LUCE. O feare not Maister Humphrey, I am guide
For this place good enough.

16. The livery companies were the descendants of the medieval guilds and controlled entry into the trades.

HUMPHREY. Then up and ride,
Or, if it please you walke for your repose,
Or sit, or if you will go plucke a rose:
Either of which shall be indifferent,
To your good friend and *Humphrey,* whose consent
Is so entangled ever to your will,
As the poore harmlesse horse is to the Mill.
LUCE. Faith and you say the word, we'le e'ne sit downe
And take a nap.
HUMPHREY. 'Tis better in the Towne,
Where we may nap together, for beleeve me
To sleepe without a snatch° would mickle° grieve me. snack; very much
LUCE. You're merrie Maister *Humphrey.*
HUMPHREY. So I am,
And have been ever merrie from my Dam.
LUCE. Your nurce had the lesse labour.
HUMPHREY. Faith it may bee,
Unlesse it were by chance I did beray° me. befoul

Enter Jasper.

JASPER. *Luce,* deere friend *Luce.*
LUCE. Heere *Jasper.*
JASPER. You are mine.
HUMPHREY. If it be so, my friend, you use me fine,
What do you thinke I am?
JASPER. An arrant noddy.
HUMPHREY. A word of obloquie,° now by Gods bodie, abuse
I'le tell thy maister for I know thee well.
JASPER. Nay, an you be so forward for to tell,
Take that, and that, and tell him sir I gave it,

[*Beats him.*]

And saie I paid you well.
HUMPHREY. O sir I have it,
And do confesse the paiement, praie be quiet.
JASPER. Go, get you to your night-cap and the diet,
To cure your beaten bones
LUCE. Alas poore *Humphrey*
Get thee some wholsome broth with sage and comfrie:
A little oile of Roses and a feather,
To noint thy backe withall.
HUMPHREY. When I came hether
Would I had gone to *Paris* with *John Dorrie.*[17]

17. Traditional children's song: "As it fell on a holy-day, / And vpon an holy-tide-a, / Iohn Dory bought him an ambling nag, / To Paris for to ride-a."

LUCE. Fare-well my pretty Nump, I am verie sorrie
I cannot beare thee companie.
HUMPHREY. Fare-well,
The Divels Dam was ne're so bang'd in hell.

Exeunt [Luce *and* Jasper].
Manet Humphrey.

WIFE. This young *Jasper* will prove me another Things, a my conscience an he may be suffered; *George,* dost not see, *George* how a swaggers, and flies at the very heads a fokes, as he were a Dragon; well if I do not do his lesson for wronging the poore Gentleman, I am no true woman, his friends that brought him up might have been better occupied, I wis, then ha taught him these fegaries, hee's e'ne in the high-way to the gallows, God blesse him.

CITIZEN. You're too bitter conny; the young man may do wel enough for all this.

WIFE. Come hither Maister *Humphrey,* has hee hurt you? now beshrew his fingers for't, here sweet heart, here's some greene ginger for thee, now beshrew my heart but a has pepper-nel in's head, as big as a pullets egge, alas sweete lamb, how thy Tempels beate; take the peace on him sweete heart, take the peace on him.

Enter a Boy.

CITIZEN. No, no, you talke like a foolish woman, I'le ha *Rafe* fight with him, and swing him up welfavourdlie, sirrah boie come hither, let *Rafe* come in and fight with *Jasper.*

WIFE. I, and beate him well, he's an unhappy boy.

BOY. Sir, you must pardon us, the plot of our Plaie lies contrarie, and 'twill hazard the spoiling of our Plaie.

CITIZEN. Plot mee no plots, I'le ha *Rafe* come out, I'le make your house too hot for you else.

BOY. Why sir he shall, but if anie thing fall out of order, the Gentlemen must pardon us.

CITIZEN. Go your waies good-man boie, I'le hold him a pennie he shall have his bellie-full of fighting now.

[*Exit* Boy.]

Ho heere comes Rafe, no more.

Enter Rafe, *mistress* Merri-thought, Michael, [Tim *as*] *Squire, and* [George *as Dwarfe.*

RAFE. What Knight is that Squire, aske him if he keep
The passage, bound by love of Ladie faire,
Or else but prickant.° riding by
HUMPHREY. Sir I am no Knight,
But a poore Gentleman, that this same night,
Had stolne from me, on yonder Greene,
My lovelie wife, and suffered (to be seene

Yet extant on my shoulders) such a greeting,
That whilst I live, I shall thinke of that meeting.
WIFE. I *Rafe* hee beate him unmercifully, *Rafe,* an thou spar'st
him *Rafe,* I would thou wert hang'd.
CITIZEN. No more, wife no more.
RAFE. Where is the caitife° wretch hath done this deed. base
Lady your pardon, that I may proceed
Upon the quest of this injurious Knight.
And thou faire Squire, repute me not the worse,
In leaving the great venture of the purse,
And the rich casket till some better leasure.

Enter Jasper *and* Luce.

HUMPHREY. Here comes the Broker hath purloin'd my treasure.
RAFE. Go, Squire, and tell him I am here,
An Errant Knight at Armes, to crave delivery
Of that faire Lady to her owne Knights armes.
If he deny, bid him take choice of ground,
And so defye him.
TIM. From the Knight that beares
The Golden Pestle, I defie thee Knight,
Unlesse thou make fair restitution,
Of that bright Lady.
JASPER. Tell the Knight that sent thee
Hee is an Asse, and I will keepe the wench
And knocke his Head-peece.
RAFE. Knight, thou art but dead,
If thou recall not thy uncurteous tearmes.
WIFE. Breake's pate *Rafe,* breake's pate *Rafe,* soundly.
JASPER. Come Knight, I am ready for you, now your Pestel

Snatches away his Pestle.

Shall try what temper, sir, your Morters off:
With that he stood upright in his stirrops,
And gave the Knight of the Calve-skinne such a knocke,

[*Knocks* Rafe *down.*]

That he forsooke his horse, and downe he fell,
And then he leaped upon him and plucking of his Helmet—
HUMPHREY. Nay, an my noble Knight be downe so soone,
Though I can scarcely go, I needs must runne.

Exeunt Humphrey *and* Rafe.

WIFE. Runne Rafe, runne Rafe, runne for thy life boy, *Iasper*
comes, *Jasper* comes.
JASPER. Come Luce, we must have other Armes for you,
Humphrey and *Golden Pestle* both adiew.

Exeunt.

WIFE. Sure the divell, God blesse us, is in this Springald;° youngster why *George,* didst ever see such a fire-drake, I am afraid my boie's mis-carried; if he be, though hee were Maister Merri-thoughts sonne a thousand times, if there bee any Law in England, I'le make some of them smart for't.

CITIZEN. No, no, I have found out the matter, sweete-heart, *Jasper* is inchanted, as sure as we are heere, he is inchanted, he could no more have stood in *Rafe's* hands, then I can in my Lord Maiors, I'le have a ring to discover all inchantments, and *Rafe* shall beate him yet: be no more vext for it shall be so.

Enter Rafe, [Tim *as*] *Squire,* [George *as*] *Dwarfe, mistress* Merri-thought *and* Michael.

WIFE. O husband heere's *Rafe* againe, stay *Rafe* let mee speake with thee, how dost thou *Rafe?* art thou not shrodly° badly hurt? the foule great Lungeis° lout laid unmercifully on thee, there's some suger-candy for thee, proceed, thou shalt have another bout with him.

CITIZEN. If Rafe had him at the Fencing-schoole, if hee did not make a puppy of him, and drive him up and downe the schoole he should nere come in my shop more.

MISTRESSE MERRI-THOUGHT. Truely Maister Knight of the *Burning Pestle* I am weary.

MICHAEL. Indeed law mother and I am very hungry.

RAFE. Take comfort gentle Dame, and you faire Squire,
For in this Desart there must needs be plac't,
Many strong Castles, held by curteous Knights,
And till I bring you safe to one of those,
I sweare by this my Order nere to leave you.

WIFE. Well said *Rafe; George, Rafe* was ever comfortable, was he not?

CITIZEN. Yes Ducke.

WIFE. I shall nere forget him, when wee had lost our child, you know it was straid almost, alone, to *Puddle-wharfe* and the Criers were abroad for it, and there it had drown'd itselfe but for a Sculler, *Rafe* was the most comfortablest to me: peace Mistresse, saies he, let it go, I'le get you another as good, did he not *George?* did he not say so?

CITIZEN. Yes indeed did he mouse.

GEORGE. I would we had a messe of Pottage, and a pot of drinke Squire, and were going to bed.

TIM. Why we are at *Waltham* Townes end, and that's the *Bell* Inne.

GEORGE. Take courage valiant Knight, Damsel, and Squire,
I have discovered, not a stones cast off,
An ancient Castle held by the old Knight

Of the most holy order of the *Bell,*
Who gives to all Knights errant entertaine:
There plenty is of food, and all prepar'd,
By the white hands of his owne Lady deere.
He hath three Squires that welcome all his Guests.
The first hight° *Chamberlino,* who will see   called
Our beds prepar'd, and bring us snowy sheetes,
Where never foote-man stretched his butter'd Hams.
The second hight *Tapstero,* who will see
Our pots full filled and no froth therein.
The third, a gentle Squire *Ostlero* hight,
Who will our Palfries slicke with wisps of straw,
And in the Maunger put them Oates enough,
And never grease their teeth with candle snuffe.

WIFE. That same Dwarfe's a pretty boy, but the Squire's a groutnole.°   blockhead

RAFE. Knocke at the Gates my Squire with stately launce.

Enter Tapster.

TAPSTER. Who's there, you're welcome Gentlemen, will you see a roome?

GEORGE. Right curteous and valiant Knight of the *burning Pestle,*
This is the Squire *Tapstero.*

RAFE. Faire Squire *Tapstero,* I a wandring Knight,
Hight of the *burning Pestle,* in the quest
Of this faire Ladies Casket, and wrought purse,
Loosing my selfe in this vast Wildernesse
Am to this Castle well by fortune brought,
Where hearing of the goodly entertaine°   reception
Your Knight of holy Order of the *Bell*
Gives to all Damsels, and all errant Knights,
I thought to knocke, and now am bold to enter.

TAPSTER. An't please you see a chamber, you are very welcome.

Exeunt.

WIFE. *George* I would have something done, and I cannot tell what it is.

CITIZEN. What is it *Nel?*

WIFE. Why George, shall Rafe beate nobody againe? prethee sweete-heart let him.

CITIZEN. So he shall Nel, and if I joyne with him, wee'le knocke them all.

Enter Humphrey *and* Marchant.

WIFE. O George here's maister *Humphrey* againe now, that lost Mistresse *Luce,* and Mistresse *Lucies* father. Maister *Humphrey* will do some-bodies errant I warrant him.

HUMPHREY. Father, it's true, in armes I nere shall claspe her,
For shee is stolne away by your man *Jasper.*
WIFE. I thought he would tell him.
MARCHANT. Unhappy that I am, to loose my child,
Now I beginne to thinke on *Jaspers* words,
Who oft hath urg'd to me thy foolishnesse,
Why didst thou let her go? thou lovst her not,
That wouldst bring home thy life, and not bring her.
HUMPHREY. Father forgive me, shall I tell you true,
Looke on my shoulders they are black and blew.
Whilst too and fro faire *Luce* and I were winding,
Hee came and basted me with a hedge binding.° cane
MARCHANT. Get men and horses straight, we will be there
Within this houre, you know the place againe?
HUMPHREY. I know the place, where he my loines did swaddle,
I'le get six horses, and to each a saddle.
MARCHANT. Meane time I'le go talke with *Jaspers* father.

Exeunt.

WIFE. *George,* what wilt thou laye with mee now, that Maister *Humphrey* has not Mistresse *Luce* yet, speake *George,* what wilt thou laie with me?
CITIZEN. No *Nel,* I warrant thee *Jasper* is at *Puckeridge* with her, by this.
WIFE. Nay *George,* you must consider Mistresse *Lucies* feete are tender, and besides, 'tis darke, and I promise you truely, I doe not see how hee should get out of *Waltham* forrest with her yet.
CITIZEN. Nay Cunny, what wilt thou laie with me that *Rafe* has her not yet.
WIFE. I will not lay against *Rafe* hunny, because I have not spoken with him, but looke *George,* peace, heere comes the merry old Gentleman againe.

Enter old Merri-thought.

OLD MERRI-THOUGHT.

When it was growne to darke midnight,
And all were fast asleepe,
In came Margarets *grimely Ghost,*
And stood at Williams *feet.*

I have mony, and meate and drinke before hand, till to morrow at noone, why should I be sad? mee thinkes I have halfe a dozen Joviall spirits within mee.

I am three merry men, and three merry men[.]

To what end should any man be sad in this world? give me a man that when hee goes to hanging cries,

troule° the black bowle to mee[.] pass around

and a woeman that will sing a catch in her Travell.° I have seene a man come by my dore, with a serious face, in a blacke cloake, without a hat-band, carrying his head as if hee lookt for pinnes in the streete; I have lookt out of my window halfe a yeare after, and have spide that mans head upon London-bridge: 'tis vile, never trust a Tailor that does not sing at his worke, his mind is of nothing but filching.

labor

WIFE. Marke this *George,* 'tis worth noting: *Godfrey* my Tailor, you know, never sings, and hee had fourteene yards to make this Gowne, and I'le be sworne Mistresse *Penistone* the Drapers wife had one made with twelve.

OLD MERRI-THOUGHT.

'Tis mirth that fils the veines with bloud,
More then wine, or sleepe, or food.
Let each man keep his heart at ease,
No man dies of that disease.
He that would his body keepe
From diseases, must not weepe,
But who ever laughes and sings,
Never he his body brings
Into fevers, gouts, or rhumes,
Or lingringly his lungs consumes:
Or meets with aches in the bone,
Or Catharhes,° or griping stone:
But contented lives for aye,
The more he laughes, the more he may.

mucus discharge

WIFE. Looke George, how saist thou by this George? is't not a fine old man? Now Gods blessing a'thy sweet lips. When wilt thou be so merry George? Faith thou art the frowningst little thing when thou art angry, in a Countrey.

Enter Marchant.

CITIZEN. Peace Coney, thou shalt see him taken downe too I warrant thee; here's *Luces* father come now.

OLD MERRI-THOUGHT.

As you came from Walsingham,
From that holy land,
There met you not with my tru-love
By the way as you came?

MARCHANT. Oh Maister *Merri-thought!* my daughter's gone.
This mirth becomes you not, my daughter's gone.

OLD MERRI-THOUGHT.

Why an if she be, what care I?
Or let her come, or go, or tarry.

MARCHANT. Mocke not my misery, it is your sonne,
Whom I have made my owne, when all forsooke him,
Has stolne my onely joy, my childe away.

OLD MERRI-THOUGHT.

He set her on a milk-white steed,
And himselfe upon a gray,
He never turn'd his face againe,
But he bore her quite away.

MARCHANT. Unworthy of the kindnesse I have shewn
To thee, and thine: too late I well perceive
Thou art consenting to my daughters losse.

OLD MERRI-THOUGHT. Your daughter, what a stur's here wi' yer daughter? Let her goe, thinke no more on her, but sing lowd. If both my sons were on the gallows, I would sing,

Downe, down, downe: *they fall*
Downe, and arise they never shall.

MARCHANT. Oh, might I behold her once againe,
And she once more embrace her aged sire.

OLD MERRI-THOUGHT. Fie, how scurvily this goes: and she once more imbrace her aged sire? you'l make a dogge on her, will yee? she cares much for her aged sire I warrant you.

She cares not for her daddy, nor
Shee cares not for her mammie,
For she is, she is, she is, she is
My Lord of Low-gaves *Lassie.*

MARCHANT. For this thy scorne, I will pursue that sonne
Of thine to death.

OLD MERRI-THOUGHT. Do, and when you ha kild him,

Give him flowers i'now Palmer: give him flowers i'now,
Give him red, and white, and blew, greene, and yellow.

MARCHANT. Il'e fetch my daughter.

OLD MERRI-THOUGHT. Il'e heare no more a your daughter, it spoyles my mirth.

MARCHANT. I say, Il'e fetch my daughter.

OLD MERRI-THOUGHT.

Was never man for Ladies sake,
Downe, downe,
Tormented as I poore Sir Guy!
De derry downe,
For Lucies *sake, that Lady bright,*
Downe, downe,
As ever men beheld with eye!
De derry downe.

MARCHANT. Il'e be reveng'd, by Heaven.

Exeunt.
Musicke. Finis Actus secundi.

[2. INTERLUDE]

WIFE. How do'st thou like this *George?*

CITIZEN. Why this is well coney: but if *Rafe* were hot° once, thou shouldst see more. (angry)

WIFE. The Fidlers go againe husband.

CITIZEN. I *Nell,* but this is scurvy musicke: I gave the whoreson gallowes money, and I thinke hee has not got mee the waits of South-warke, if I heare 'em not anan, Il'e twinge him by the eares. You Musicians, play *Baloo.*

WIFE. No good *George,* lets ha *Lachrimæ.*

CITIZEN. Why this is it cony.

WIFE. It's all the better *George:* now sweet lambe, what story is that painted upon the cloth? the Confutation of Saint *Paul?*

CITIZEN. No lambe, that's *Rafe* and *Lucrece.*

WIFE. *Rafe* and *Lucrece?* which *Rafe?* our *Rafe?*

CITIZEN. No mouse, that was a Tartarian.[18]

WIFE. A Tartarian? well, I'wood the fidlers had done, that wee might see our *Rafe* again.

Enter Jasper and *Luce.*

[III.]

JASPER. Come my deere deere, though we have lost our way,
We have not lost our selves: are you not weary
With this nights wandring, broken from your rest?
And frighted with the terrour that attends
The darknesse of this wilde un-peopled place?

LUCE. No, my best friend, I cannot either feare,
Or entertaine a weary thought, whilst you
(The end of all my full desires) stand by me.
Let them that loose their hopes, and live to languish
Amongst the number of forsaken lovers,
Tell the long weary steps, and number time,
Start at a shadow, and shrinke up their bloud,
Whilst I (possesset with all content and quiet)
Thus take my prettie love, and thus imbrace him.

18. A whole series of malapropisms are exchanged in the interlude: confutation = conversion; Rafe and Lucrece = the rape of Lucrece; Tartarian = Tarquin.

JASPER. You have caught me *Luce,* so fast, that whilst I live,
I shall become your faithfull prisoner,
And weare these chaines for ever. Come sit downe,
And rest your body, too too delicate
For these disturbances; so, will you sleep?
Come, do not be more able than you are,
I know you are not skilfull in these watches:
For women are no souldiers; be not nice,
But take it, sleepe I say.
LUCE. I cannot sleepe,
Indeed I cannot friend.
JASPER. Why, then, wee'l sing,
And try how that will worke upon our sences.
LUCE. Il'e sing, or say, or any thing but sleepe.
JASPER. Come little Mer-maid, rob me of my heart
With that inchanting voyce.
LUCE. You mocke me *Jasper.*
JASPER. *Tell me (dearest) what is love?*
LUCE. *'Tis a lightning from above,*
'Tis an arrow, 'tis a fire,
'Tis a boy, they call desire.
'Tis a smile
Doth beguile
JASPER. *The poore hearts of men that prove.*
Tell me more, are women true?
LUCE. *Some love change, and so do you.*
JASPER. *Are they faire, and never kind?*
LUCE. *Yes, when men turne with the winde.*
JASPER. *Are they froward?*
LUCE. *Ever toward*
Those that love, to love a new.
JASPER. Dissemble it no more, I see the God
Of heavy sleepe, lay on his heavy mace
Upon your eye-lids.
LUCE. I am very heavy.
JASPER. Sleep, sleep, and quiet rest crowne thy sweet thoughts:
Keepe from her faire bloud, distempers, startings,
Horrors, and fearefull shapes: let all her dreames
Be joyes, and chast delights, imbraces, wishes,
And such new pleasures, as the ravisht soule
Gives to the sences. So, my charmes have tooke.
Keepe her, you powers divine, whilst I contemplate
Upon the wealth and beauty of her minde.
She is onely faire, and constant: onely kinde,
And onely to thee *Jasper.* Oh my joyes!
Whither will you transport me? let not fulnesse

Of my poore buried hopes, come up together,
And over-charge my spirits: I am weake.
Some say (how ever ill) the sea and women
Are governd by the Moone, both ebbe and flow,
Both full of changes: yet to them that know,
And truly judge, these but opinions are,
And heresies, to bring on pleasing warre
Betweene our tempers, that without these were
Both void of after-love and present feare,
Which are the best of *Cupid.* Oh thou child!
Bred from despaire, I dare not entertaine thee,
Having a love without the faults of women,
And greater in her perfect goods than men:
Which to make good, and please my selfe the stronger,
Though certainely I am certaine of her love,
Il'e try her, that the world and memory
May sing to after times her constancie.
Luce, Luce, awake.

LUCE. Why do you fright me, friend,
With those distempered lookes? what makes your sword
Drawne in your hand? who hath offended you?
I pre'thee Jasper sleepe, thou art wilde with watching.

JASPER. Come make your way to heaven, and bid the world
(With all the villanies that sticke upon it)
Fare-well; you'r for another life.

LUCE. Oh *Jasper!*
How have my tender yeares committed evill,
(Especially against the man I love)
Thus to be cropt untimely?

JASPER. Foolish girle,
Canst thou imagine I could love his daughter,
That flung me from my fortune into nothing?
Discharged me his service, shut the doores
Upon my poverty, and scornd my prayers,
Sending me, like a boat without a mast,
To sinke or swim? Come, by this hand, you dye,
I must have life and bloud to satisfie
Your fathers wrongs.

WIFE. Away *George,* away, raise the watch at *Ludgate,* and bring a Mittimus[19] from the Justice for this desperate villaine. Now I charge you Gentlemen, see the Kings peace kept. O my heart what a varlet's this to offer man-slaughter upon the harmelesse Gentlewoman?

CITIZEN. I warrant thee (sweet heart) wee'l have him hampered.

19. A warrant committing one to prison.

LUCE. Oh *Jasper!* be not cruell,
If thou wilt kill me, smile and do it quickly,
And let not many deaths appeare before me.
I am a woman made of feare and love,
A weake, weake woman, kill not with thy eyes,
They shoot me through and through. Strike I am ready,
And dying stil I love thee.

Enter Marchant, Humphrey, *and his men.*

MARCHANT. Where abouts?
JASPER. No more of this, now to my selfe againe.
HUMPHREY. There, there he stands with sword, like martial knight
Drawne in his hand, therefore beware the fight
You that be wise: for, were I good sir *Bevis,*
I would not stay his comming, by your leaves.
MARCHANT. Sirrah, restore my daughter.
JASPER. Sirrah, no.
MARCHANT. Upon him then.
WIFE. So, downe with him, downe with him, downe with him: cut him i'the leg boies, cut him i'the leg.
MARCHANT. Come your waies Minion, Il'e provide a Cage
For you, your growne so tame. Horse her away.
HUMPHREY. Truly Ime glad your forces have the day.

Exeunt [Luce, Humphrey, Marchant *and men*].

Manet Jasper.

JASPER. They are gone, and I am hurt, my love is lost,
Never to get againe. Oh me unhappy!
Bleed, bleed and dye, I cannot: Oh, my folly!
Thou hast betraid me. Hope, where art thou fled?
Tell me if thou bee'st any where remaining,
Shall I but see my love againe? Oh no!
She will not daine to looke upon her butcher,
Nor is it fit she should; yet I must venter.
Oh chance, or fortune, or what ere thou art,
That men adore for powerfull, heare my cry,
And let me loving, live; or loosing, die.
WIFE. Is a gone *George?*
CITIZEN. I conie.
WIFE. Marie and let him goe (sweet heart,) by the faith a my body a has put me into such a fright, that I tremble (as they say) as 'twere an Aspine leafe: looke a my little finger *George,* how it shakes: now i'truth every member of my body is the worse for't.
CITIZEN. Come, hugge in mine armes sweet mouse, hee shall not fright thee any more: alas mine owne deere heart, how it quivers.

Enter Mistress Merri-thought, Rafe, Michael, [Tim *as*] *Squire,* [George *as*] *Dwarfe,* Host, *and a* Tapster.

WIFE. O *Rafe,* how dost thou *Rafe?* how hast thou slept to night?
has the knight us'd thee well?
CITIZEN. Peace Nell, let *Rafe* alone.
TAPSTER. Maister, the reckoning is not paid.
RAFE. Right curteous knight, who for the orders sake
Which thou hast tane, hang'st out the holy bell,
As I this flaming pestle beare about,
We render thankes to your puissant selfe,
Your beauteous Lady, and your gentle Squires,
For thus refreshing of our wearied limbes,
Stiffned with hard atchievements in wilde desert.
TAPSTER. Sir, there is twelve shillings to pay.
RAFE. Thou merry Squire *Tapstero,* thankes to thee
For comforting our soules with double Jug,° strong ale
And if adventrous fortune pricke thee forth,
Thou *Joviall* Squire, to follow feats of armes,
Take heed thou tender every Ladies cause,
Every true Knight, and every damsell faire;
But spill the bloud of treacherous Sarazens,
And false inchanters, that with magicke spels,
Have done to death full many a noble Knight.
HOST. Thou valiant Knight of the *burning Pestle,* give eare to me, there is twelve shillings to pay, and, as I am a true Knight, I will not bate° a penny. deduct
WIFE. *George,* I pray thee tell me, must *Rafe* pay twelve shillings now?
CITIZEN. No *Nell,* no, nothing but the old Knight is merrie with *Rafe.*
WIFE. O is't nothing else? *Rafe* will be as merry as he.
RAFE. Sir Knight, this mirth of yours becomes you well,
But to requite this liberall curtesie,
If any of your Squires will follow armes,
Hee shall receive from my heroicke hand
A Knight-hood, by the vertue of this Pestle.
HOST. Faire Knight I thank you for your noble offer,
Therefore gentle Knight,
Twelve shillings you must pay, or I must cap° you. arrest
WIFE. Looke *George,* did not I tell thee as much, the Knight of the *Bel* is in earnest, *Rafe* shall not bee beholding to him, give him his money *George,* and let him go snick up.
CITIZEN. Cap *Rafe?* no, Hold your hand, sir Knight of the *Bel,* theres your mony, have you any thing to say to *Rafe* now? Cap *Rafe?*
WIFE. I would you should know it, *Rafe* has friends that will not

suffer him to be capt for ten times so much, and ten times to the end of that, now take thy course Rafe.

MISTRESSE MERRI-THOUGHT. Come *Michael,* thou and I will go home to thy father, he hath enough left to keep us a day or two, and we'le set fellows abrod to cry our Purse and our Casket; Shal we *Michael?*

MICHAEL. I, I pray Mother, intruth my feete are full of chilblaines with travelling.

WIFE. Faith and those chilblanes are a foule trouble, Mistresse *Merri-thought* when your youth comes home, let him rub all the soles of his feete, and his heeles, and his ancles, with a mouse skinne, or, if none of your people can catch a mouse, when hee goes to bed, let him rowle his feete in the warme embers, and I warrant you hee shall be well, and you may make him put his fingers betweene his toes and smell to them, it's very soveraigne for his head if he be costive.° constipated

MISTRESSE MERRI-THOUGHT. Maister Knight of the *burning Pestle,* my son *Michael* and I, bid you farewel, I thanke your Worship heartily for your kindnesse.

RAFE. Fare-well faire Lady and your tender Squire,
If, pricking through these Desarts, I do heare
Of any traiterous Knight, who through his guile,
Hath light upon your Casket and your Purse,
I will despoile him of them and restore them.

MISTRESSE MERRI-THOUGHT. I thanke your Worship.

Exit with Michael.

RAFE. Dwarfe beare my shield, Squire, elevate my lance,
And now fare-well you Knight of holy *Bell.*

CITIZEN. I, I *Rafe,* all is paid.

RAFE. But yet before I go, speake worthy Knight,
If ought you do of sad adventures know,
Where errant Knight may through his prowesse winne,
Eternall fame and free some gentle soules,
From endlesse bonds of steele and lingring paine.

HOST. Sirrah go to *Nicke* the *Barbor,* and bid him prepare himselfe, as I told you before, quickely.

TAPSTER. I am gone sir.

Exit Tapster.

HOST. Sir Knight, this wildernesse affoordeth none
But the great venter, where full many a Knight
Hath tride his prowesse and come off with shame,
And where I would not have you loose your life,
Against no man, but furious fiend of hell.

RAFE. Speake on sir Knight, tell what he is, and where,
For heere I vow, upon my blazing badge,

Never to blaze a day in quietnesse;
But bread and water will I onely eate,
And the greene hearbe and rocke shall be my couch,
Till I have queld that man, or beast, or fiend,
That workes such damage to all Errant Knights.
HOST. Not far from hence, neere to a craggy cliffe,
At the North end of this distressed Towne,
There doth stand a lowly house
Ruggedly builded, and in it a Cave,
In which an ougly Gyant now doth won,
Ycleped *Barbaroso:* in his hand
He shakes a naked lance of purest steele,
With sleeves turn'd up; and him before he weares,
A motley garment, to preserve his cloaths
From bloud of those Knights which he massacres,
And Ladies Gent: without his dore doth hang
A copper bason, on a prickant° speare: upright
At which, no sooner gentle Knights can knocke,
But the shrill sound, fierce *Barbaroso* heares,
And rushing forth, brings in the errant Knight,
And sets him downe in an inchanted chaire.
Then with an Engine which he hath prepar'd,
With forty teeth, he clawes his courtly crowne,
Next makes him winke, and underneath his chinne,
Hee plants a brazen peece of mighty bord,° circumference
And knocks his bullets° round about his cheeks, soap pellets
Whilst with his fingers, and an instrument
With which he snaps his haire off, he doth fill
The wretches eares with a most hideous noise.
Thus every Knight Adventurer he doth trim,
And now no creature dares encounter him.
RAFE. In Gods name, I will fight with him; kinde sir,
Go but before me to this dismall Cave,
Where this huge Gyant *Barbaroso* dwels,
And by that vertue that brave *Rosicleere,*[20]
That damned brood of ougly Gyants slew,
And *Palmerin Frannarco*[21] overthrew:
I doubt not but to curbe this Traitor foule,
And to the Divell send his guilty soule.
HOST. Brave sprighted° Knight, thus far I will performe spirited
This your request, I'le bring you within sight
Of this most lothsome place, inhabited

20. Knight in the romance *The Mirrour of Princely Deeds and Knighthood,* originally Spanish, but translated into English by the end of the sixteenth century.

21. A giant killed in the Spanish romance *Palmerin d'Oliva* (1525), translated into English in 1588.

By a more loathsome man: but dare not stay,
For his maine force swoopes all he sees away.

RAFE. Saint *George* set on before, march Squire and page.

Exeunt.

WIFE. *George,* dost thinke *Rafe* will confound the Gyant?

CITIZEN. I hold my cap to a farthing he does: why *Nel* I saw him wrastle with the great Dutch-man and hurle him.

WIFE. Faith and that Dutch-man was a goodly man, if all things were answerable to his bignesse, and yet they say there was a Scotsh-man higher than hee, and that they two and a Knight met, and saw one another for nothing, but of all the sights that ever were in *London,* since I was married, mee thinkes the little child that was so faire growne about the members was the prettiest, that, and the *Hermaphrodite.*

CITIZEN. Nay by your leave *Nel, Ninivy* was better.

WIFE. *Ninivie,* O that was the story of *Jone* and the Wall, was it not *George?*[22]

CITIZEN. Yes lam.

Enter mistresse Merri-thought.

WIFE. Looke George, heere comes Mistresse *Merri-thought* againe, and I would have *Rafe* come and fight with the Giant, I tell you true, I long to see't.

CITIZEN. Good Mistresse *Merri-thought* be gone, I pray you for my sake, I pray you forbeare a little, you shall have audience presently, I have a little businesse.

WIFE. Mistresse *Merri-thought* if it please you to refraine your passion a little, til Rafe have dispatcht the Giant out of the way, we shal think our selves much bound to you, I thank you, good Mistresse *Merri-thought.*

Exit mistresse Merri-thought.
Enter a Boy.

CITIZEN. Boy, come hither, send away *Rafe* and this whoresonne Giant quickely.

BOY. In good faith, sir we cannot, you'le utterly spoile our Play, and make it to be hist, and it cost money, you will not suffer us to go on with our plot, I pray Gentlemen rule him.

CITIZEN. Let him come now and despatch this, and I'le trouble you no more.

BOY. Will you give me your hand of that?

WIFE. Give him thy hand *George,* do, and I'le kiss him, I warrant thee, the youth meanes plainely.

BOY. I'le send him to you presently.

22. A puppet show about the biblical story of Jonah.

WIFE. I thanke you little youth, [*Exit* Boy] feth, the child hath a sweete breath *George*, but I think it bee troubled with the wormes, *Carduus benedictus*[23] and Mares milke were the onely thing in the world for't.

Enter Rafe, Host, [Tim *as*] *Squire, and* [George *as*] *Dwarfe.*

WIFE. O *Rafe's* here *George*, God send thee good lucke *Rafe.*
HOST. Puissant knight yonder his Mansion is,
Lo where the speare and Copper Bason are,
Behold that string on which hangs many a tooth,
Drawne from the gentle jaw of wandring Knights,
I dare not stay to sound, hee will appeare.

Exit Host.

RAFE. Oh, faint not heart, *Susan* my Lady deere,
The Coblers Maid in Milke-streete, for whose sake,
I take these Armes, O let the thought of thee,
Carry thy Knight through all adventerous deeds,
And in the honor of thy beauteous selfe,
May I destroy this monster *Barbaroso.*
Knocke Squire upon the Bason till it breake
With the shrill stroakes, or till the Giant speake.

Enter Barbor.

WIFE. O *George*, the Giant, the Giant, now *Rafe* for thy life.
BARBER. What fond° unknowing wight is this? that dares — foolish
So rudely knocke at *Barbarossa's* Cell,
Where no man comes but leaves his fleece behind?
RAFE. I, traitorous Caitiffe, who am sent by fate
To punish all the sad enormities
Thou hast committed against Ladies Gent° — high-born
And errant Knights: traitor to God and men,
Prepare thy selfe, this is the dismall houre
Appointed for thee, to give strickt account
Of all thy beastly treacherous villanies.
BARBER. Foole-hardy Knight, full soone thou shalt aby° — pay for

He takes downe his pole.

This fond reproach, thy body will I bang,
And loe upon that string thy teeth shall hang:
Prepare thy selfe, for dead soone shalt thou bee.
RAFE. Saint *George* for me.
BARBER. *Gargantua* for me.

They fight.

23. Thistle used as a medicinal herb.

WIFE. To him *Rafe,* to him, hold up the Giant, set out thy leg before *Rafe.*

CITIZEN. Falsifie a blow *Rafe,* falsifie a blow, the Giant lies open on the left side.

WIFE. Beare't off, beare't of still; there boy, O *Rafe's* almost downe, *Rafe's* almost downe.

RAFE. *Susan* inspire me, now have up againe.

WIFE. Up, up, up, up, up, so *Rafe,* downe with him, downe with him, *Rafe.*

CITIZEN. Fetch him ore the hip boy.

WIFE. There boy, kill, kill, kill, kill, kill, *Rafe.*

CITIZEN. No *Rafe* get all out of him first.

[Rafe *gets him down.*]

RAFE. Presumptuous man, see to what desperate end
Thy treachery hath brought thee, the just Gods,
Who never prosper those that do despise them,
For all the villanies which thou hast done
To Knights and Ladies, now have paid thee home
By my stiffe arme, a Knight adventurous,
But say vile wretch, before I send thy soule
To sad *Avernus* whether it must go,
What captives holdst thou in thy sable cave.

BARBER. Go in, and free them all, thou hast the day.

RAFE. Go Squire and Dwarfe, search in this dreadfull Cave
And free the wretched prisoners from their bonds.

Exeunt [Tim *as*] *Squire and* [George *as*] *Dwarfe.*

BARBER. I crave for mercy, as thou art a Knight,
And scornst to spill the bloud of those that beg.

RAFE. Thou showdst no mercy, nor shalt thou have any,
Prepare thy selfe for thou shalt surely die.

Enter [Tim *as*] *Squire leading one winking, with a Bason under his chin.*

TIM. Behold brave Knight heere is one prisoner,
Whom this wilde man hath used as you see.

WIFE. This is the first wise word I heard the Squire speake.

RAFE. Speake what thou art, and how thou hast bene us'd,
That I may give him condigne punishment.

1. KNIGHT. I am a Knight that tooke my journey post
North-ward from *London,* and in curteous wise,
This Giant train'd me to his loathsome den,
Under pretence of killing of the itch,
And all my body with a powder strew'd,
That smarts and stings, and cut away my beard,
And my curl'd lockes wherein were ribands ti'de,
And with a water washt my tender eyes,

(Whilst up and down about me still he skipt,)
Whose vertue is, that till my eyes be wip't
With a dry cloath, for this my foule disgrace,
I shall not dare to looke a dog i'th' face.

WIFE. Alas poore Knight, relieve him Rafe, releive poore Knights whilst you live.

RAFE. My trusty Squire convey him to the Towne,
Where he may find releife, adiew faire Knight.

Exit Knight.
Enter [George *as*] *Dwarfe leading one with a patch ore his Nose.*

GEORGE. Puisant Knight of the *burning Pestle* hight,
See heere another wretch, whom this foule beast
Hath scorcht and scor'd in this inhumaine wise.

RAFE. Speake me thy name, and eke thy place of birth,
And what hath bene thy usage in this Cave.

2. KNIGHT. I am a Knight, Sir *Pocke-hole* is my name,
And by my birth I am a *Londoner*
Free by my Coppy, but my Ancestors
Were *French-men* all, and riding hard this way,
Upon a trotting horse, my bones did ake,
And I faint Knight to ease my weary limbes,
Light at this Cave, when straight this furious fiend,
With sharpest instrument of purest steele,
Did cut the gristle of my Nose away,
And in the place this velvet plaister stands,
Relieve me, gentle Knight, out of his hands.

WIFE. Good Rafe releive Sir *Pocke-hole* and send him away, for, intruth, his breath stinkes.

RAFE. Convey him straight after the other Knight,
Sir *Pocke-hole* fare you well.

2. KNIGHT. Kinde sir good-night.

Exit.
Cryes within.

3. KNIGHT. Deliver us.

WOMAN. Deliver us.

WIFE. Hearke *George*, what a woefull cry there is, I thinke some woman lies in there.

3. KNIGHT. Deliver us.

WOMAN. Deliver us.

RAFE. What gastly noise is this? speake *Barbaroso*,
Or by this blasing steele thy head goes off.

BARBER. Prisoners of mine whom I in diet keepe.
Send lower downe into the Cave,
And in a Tub that's heated smoaking hot,
There may they finde them and deliver them.

RAFE. Run Squire and Dwarfe, deliver them with speed.

Exeunt Squire *and* Dwarfe.

WIFE. But will not Rafe kill this giant, surely I am afeard if hee let him go he will do as much hurt, as ever he did.
CITIZEN. Not so mouse neither, if hee could convert him.
WIFE. I *George* if hee could convert him, but a Giant is not so soone converted as one of us ordinary people: there's a pretty tale of a Witch, that had the divels marke about her, God blesse us, that had a Giant to her sonne, that was cal'd *Lob-lie-by-the-fire,* didst never here it *George?*

Enter [Tim *as*] *Squire leading a man with a glasse of Lotion in his hand, and* [George *as*] *the Dwarfe leading a Woman, with diet-bread*[24] *and drinke.*

CITIZEN. Peace *Nel,* heere comes the prisoners.
GEORGE. Here be these pined wretches, manfull Knight,
That for this sixe weekes have not seene a wight.
RAFE. Deliver what you are, and how you came
To this sad Cave, and what your usage was?
3. KNIGHT. I am an Errant Knight that followed Armes,
With speare and shield, and in my tender yeares
I stricken was with *Cupids* fiery shaft,
And fell in love with this my Lady deere,
And stole her from her friends in Turne-bull-streete,
And bore her up and downe from Towne to Towne,
Where we did eate and drinke and Musicke heare,
Till at the length, at this unhappy Towne
Wee did arrive, and comming to this Cave
This beast us caught and put us in a Tub,
Where we this two months sweate, and should have done
Another moneth if you had not reliev'd us.[25]
WOMAN. This bread and water hath our diet bene,
Together with a rib cut from a necke
Of burned Mutton, hard hath been our fare,
Release us from this ougly Giants snare.
3. KNIGHT. This hath bene all the food we have receiv'd,
But onely twice a day for novelty,
He gave a spoonefull of this hearty broth,

Puls out a sirringe[26]

To each of us, through this same slender quill.

24. Special bread prepared for invalids (Oxford English Dictionary).
25. A treatment for venereal disease was to place the sufferer in a box where a fire vaporized mercury; in theory the mercury entered through the open pores caused by the heat.
26. The syringe replaced the medieval clyster as a means of giving enemas in the sixteenth and seventeenth centuries.

RAFE. From this infernall monster you shall go,
That useth Knights and gentle Ladies so,
Convey them hence.

Exeunt man and woman.

CITIZEN. Cony, I can tell thee the Gentlemen like *Rafe.*

WIFE. I *George,* I see it well inough. Gentlemen I thanke you all heartily for gracing my man *Rafe,* and I promise you you shall see him oftner.

BARBER. Mercy great knight, I do recant my ill,
And henceforth never gentle bloud will spill.

RAFE. I give thee mercy, but yet shalt thou sweare
Upon my burning pestle, to performe
Thy promise utterd.

BARBER. I sweare and kisse.

RAFE. Depart then, and amend.
Come squire and dwarfe, the Sunne growes towards his set,
And we have many more adventures yet.

Exeunt.

CITIZEN. Now Rafe is in this humour, I know hee would ha beaten all the boyes in the house, if they had beene set on him.

WIFE. I *George,* but it is well as it is, I warrant you the Gentlemen do consider what it is to overthrow a gyant: but looke *George,* heere comes mistresse *Merri-thought* and her sonne *Michael;* now you are welcome mistresse *Merri-thought,* now *Rafe* has done, you may go on.

Enter mistresse Merri-thought *and* Michael.

MISTRESSE MERRI-THOUGHT. *Micke* my boy?

MICHAEL. I forsooth mother.

MISTRESSE MERRI-THOUGHT. Be merry *Micke* we are at home now; where I warrant you, you shall finde the house flung out at the windowes: Harke, hey dogges, hey, this is the old world, I'faith with my husband; if I get in among 'em, Ile play em such a lesson, that they shall have little list to come scraping hither, againe. Why maister *Merri-thought,* husband, *Charles Merri-thought.*

OLD MERRI-THOUGHT *(within).*

If you will sing and daunce, and laugh,
And hollow, and laugh againe,
And then cry there boyes, there: why then
One, two, three, and foure,
We shall be merry within this houre.

MISTRESSE MERRI-THOUGHT. Why *Charles,* doe you not know your owne naturall wife? I say, open the doore, and turne me out those mangy companions; 'tis more than time that they were fellow and fellow like with you: you are a Gentleman *Charles,* and an old man, and father of two children; and I my selfe (though I say it) by my mothers side, Neece to a worshipfull Gentleman, and a Conductor, he has beene three times in his Majesties service at *Chester,* and is now the fourth time, God blesse him, and his charge, upon his journey.

OLD MERRI-THOUGHT. [*within*].

Go from my window, love, goe;
Go from my window my deere,
The winde and the raine
Will drive you backe againe,
You cannot be lodged heere.

Harke you Mistresse *Merri-thought,* you that walke upon adventures, and forsake your husband, because hee sings with never a peny in his purse; What, shall I thinke my selfe the worse? Faith no, Ile be merry. You come not heere, heer's none but lads of mettle, lives of a hundred yeares, and upwards, care never drunke their bloude, nor want made 'em warble,

Hey-ho, my heart is heavy.

MISTRESSE MERRI-THOUGHT. Why Maister *Merri-thought,* what am I that you should laugh me to scorne thus abruptly? am I not your fellow-feeler (as we may say) in all our miseries? your comforter in health and sicknesse? have I not brought you Children? are they not like you *Charles?* looke upon thine owne Image, hard-hearted man; and yet for all this—

OLD MERRI-THOUGHT *(within).*

Begone, begone, my Juggy, my puggy,
Begone, my love, my deere.
The weather is warme,
'Twill do thee no harme,
Thou canst not be lodged heere.

Be merry boyes, some light musicke, and more wine.

WIFE. He's not in earnest, I hope *George,* is he?

CITIZEN. What if he be, sweet heart?

WIFE. Marie if hee be *George,* Ile make bold to tell him hee's an Ingrant° old man, to use his bed-fellow so scurvily. ungrateful

CITIZEN. What, how does he use her hunny?

WIFE. Marie come up sir sauce-box, I thinke you'l take his part, will you not? Lord how hot you have growne: you are a fine man an' you had a fine dogge, it becomes you sweetly.

CITIZEN. Nay pre'thee *Nell* chide not: for as I am an honest man, and a true Christian Grocer, I doe not like his doings.

WIFE. I cry you mercie then *George;* you know we are all fraile, and full of infirmities. Dee heare Maister *Merri-thought,* may I crave a word with you?

OLD MERRI-THOUGHT *(within).* Strike up lively lads.

WIFE. I had not thought in truth, Maister *Merri-thought,* that a man of your age and discretion (as I may say) being a Gentleman, and therefore knowne by your gentle conditions, could have used so little respect to the weaknesse of his wife: for your wife is your owne flesh, the staffe of your age, your yoke-fellow, with whose helpe you draw through the mire of this transitory world: Nay, she's your owne ribbe. And againe—

OLD MERRI-THOUGHT *(within).*

I came not hither for thee to teach,
I have no pulpit for thee to preach,
I would thou hadst kist me under the breech,
As thou art a Lady gay.

WIFE. Marie with a vengeance. I am hartely sorry for the poor gentlewoman: but if I were thy wife, I'faith gray-beard, I'faith—

CITIZEN. I pre'thee, sweet hunny-suckle, be content.

WIFE. Give me such words that am a gentlewoman borne, hang him hoary rascall. Get me some drinke George, I am almost molten with fretting: now beshrew his knaves heart for it.

[*Exit* Citizen.]

OLD MERRI-THOUGHT [*within*]. Play me a light *Lavalto:* come, bee frolicke, fill the good fellowes wine.

MISTRESSE MERRI-THOUGHT. Why Maister *Merri-thought,* are you disposed to make me wait here: you'l open, I hope, Il'e fetch them that shall open else.

OLD MERRI-THOUGHT [*within*]. Good woman if you wil sing Il'e give you something, if not—

You are no love for me Margret,
I am no love for you.

Come aloft Boyes, aloft.

MISTRESSE MERRI-THOUGHT. Now a Churles fart in your teeth sir: Come *Micke,* wee'l not trouble him, a shall not ding us i'th teeth with his bread and his broth: that he shall not: come boy, Il'e provide for thee, I warrant thee: wee'l goe to maister *Venterwels* the Merchant, Il'e get his letter to mine Host of the *Bell* in *Waltham,* there Il'e place thee with the Tapster; will not that doe well for thee *Micke?* and let me alone for that old Cuckoldly knave your father, Il'e use him in his kinde, I warrant yee.

[*Exeunt.*]

Finis Actus tertii. *Musicke.*

[3. INTERLUDE]

[*Re-enter* Citizen.]

WIFE. Come *George,* wher's the beere?

CITIZEN. Here love.

WIFE. This old fornicating fellow wil not out of my mind yet; Gentlemen, Il'e begin to you all, and I desire more of your acquaintance, with all my heart. Fill the Gentlemen some beere *George.*

Boy *daunceth.*

Looke *George,* the little boy's come againe, mee thinkes he lookes something like the prince of *Orange* in his long stocking, if hee had a little harnesse° [armor] about his necke. *George* I will have him dance *Fading; Fading* is a fine Jigge Il'e assure you Gentlemen: begin brother, now a capers sweet heart, now a turne a'th toe, and then tumble: cannot you tumble youth?

BOY. No indeed forsooth.

WIFE. Nor eate fire?

BOY. Neither.

WIFE. Why then I thanke you heartily, there's two pence to buy you points[27] withal.

Enter Jasper *and* Boy.

[IV.]

JASPER [*gives letter*]. There, boy, deliver this: but do it well.
Hast thou provided me foure lusty fellowes?
Able to carry me? and art thou perfect
In all thy businesse?

BOY. Sir, you need not feare,
I have my lesson here, and cannot misse it:
The men are ready for you, and what else
Pertaines to this imployment.

JASPER [*gives money*]. There my boy,
Take it, but buy no land.

BOY. Faith sir 'twere rare
To see so yong a purchaser: I flye,
And on my wings carry your destinie.

Exit.

27. Laces used for tying up hosiery or breeches.

JASPER. Go, and be happy. Now my latest hope
Forsake me not, but fling thy Anchor out,
And let it hold: stand fixt thou rolling stone,
Till I enjoy my deerest: heare me all
You powers that rule in men cœlestial.

Exit.

WIFE. Go thy wayes, thou art as crooked a sprigge as ever grew in *London;* I warrant him hee'l come to some naughty end or other: for his lookes say no lesse: Besides, his father (you know *George*) is none of the best, you heard him take me up like a flirt Gill,° strumpet and sing baudy songs upon me: but Ifaith, if I live *George*—

CITIZEN. Let me alone sweet-heart, I have a tricke in my head shall lodge him in the Arches[28] for one yeare, and make him sing *Peccavi,*° I have sinned er'e I leave him, and yet hee shall never know who hurt him neither.

WIFE. Do my good *George,* do.

CITIZEN. What shall we have *Rafe* do now boy?

BOY. You shall have what you will sir.

CITIZEN. Why so sir, go and fetch me him then, and let the Sophy of *Persia* come and christen him a childe.

BOY. Beleeve me sir, that will not doe so well, 'tis stale, it has beene had before at the red Bull.[29]

WIFE. *George* let *Rafe* travell over great hils, and let him be very weary, and come to the King of *Cracovia's* house, covered with black velvet, and there let the Kings daughter stand in her window all in beaten gold, combing her golden locks with a combe of Ivory, and let her spy *Rafe,* and fall in love with him, and come down to him, and carry him into her fathers house, and then let *Rafe* talke with her.

CITIZEN. Well said *Nell,* it shal be so: boy let's ha't done quickly.

BOY. Sir, if you will imagine all this to be done already, you shall heare them talke together: but wee cannot present a house covered with blacke velvet, and a Lady in beaten gold.

CITIZEN. Sir boy, lets ha't as you can then.

BOY. Besides it will shew ill-favouredly to have a Grocers prentice to court a kings daughter.

CITIZEN. Will it so sir? you are well read in Histories: I pray you what was sir *Dagonet?* was not he prentice to a Grocer in *London?* read the play of *The Foure Prentices of London,*[30] where they tosse their pikes so: I pray you, fetch him in sir, fetch him in.

BOY. It shall be done, it is not our fault gentlemen.

Exit.

28. "Ecclesiastical court which had jurisdiction in marital cases" (Bald).
29. Theater built in 1604.
30. A play by Thomas Heywood, c. 1594.

WIFE. Now we shall see fine doings I warrant tee *George.* O here they come; how pretily the King of *Cracovia's* daughter is drest.

Enter Rafe *and the Lady* [Pompiona], [Tim *as*] *Squire and* [George *as*] *Dwarfe.*

CITIZEN. I *Nell,* it is the fashion of that country, I warrant tee.

LADY. Welcome sir Knight unto my fathers Court,
King of *Moldavia,* unto me *Pompiona,*
His daughter deere: but sure you do not like
Your entertainment, that will stay with us
No longer but a night.

RAFE. Damsell right faire,
I am on many sad adventures bound,
That call me forth into the wildernesse;
Besides, my horses backe is something gal'd,
Which will inforce me ride a sober pace.
But many thankes (faire Lady) be to you,
For using errant Knight with curtesie.

LADY. But say (brave knight) what is your name and birth?

RAFE. My name is Rafe, I am an Englishman,
As true as steele, a hearty Englishman,
And prentice to a Grocer in the strond,
By deed Indent, of which I have one part:° copy
But fortune calling me to follow Armes,
On me this only order I did take,
Of Burning pestle, which in all mens eyes,
I beare, confounding Ladies enemies.

LADY. Oft have I heard of your brave country-men,
And fertill soyle, and store of holesome food:
My father oft will tell me of a drinke
In *England* found, and *Nipitato*° cal'd, strong ale
Which driveth all the sorrow from your hearts.

RAFE. Lady 'tis true, you need not lay your lips
To better *Nipitato* then there is.

LADY. And of a wild-fowle he will often speake,
Which poudred° beefe and mustard called is: salted
For there have beene great warres 'twixt us and you,
But truly *Rafe,* it was not long of me.
Tell me then *Rafe,* could you contented be,
To weare a Ladies favour in your shield?

RAFE. I am a knight of religious order,
And will not weare a favour of a Ladies
That trusts in Antichrist, and false traditions.

CITIZEN. Well sayd *Rafe,* convert her if thou canst.

RAFE. Besides, I have a Lady of my owne
In merry *England,* for whose vertuous sake
I tooke these Armes, and *Susan* is her name,

A Coblers maid in Milke-street, whom I vow
Nere to forsake, whilst life and Pestle last.
LADY. Happy that Cobling dame, who ere she be,
That for her owne (deere *Rafe*) hath gotten thee.
Unhappy I, that nere shall see the day
To see thee more, that bearst my heart away.
RAFE. Lady fare-well, I needs must take my leave.
LADY. Hard-hearted *Rafe,* that Ladies dost deceive.
CITIZEN. Harke thee Rafe, there's money for thee; give something in the King of *Cracovia's* house, be not beholding to him.
RAFE. Lady before I go, I must remember
Your fathers Officers, who truth to tell,
Have beene about me very diligent.
Hold up thy snowy hand thou princely maid,
There's twelve pence for your fathers Chamberlaine,
And another shilling for his Cooke,
For, by my troth the Goose was rosted well.
And twelve-pence for your fathers horse-keeper,
For nointing my horse backe; and for his butter
There is another shilling. To the maid
That wash't my boot-hose, there's an English groat;
And two pence to the boy that wip't my boots:
And last, faire Lady, there is for your selfe
Three pence to buy you pins at *Bumbo* faire.
LADY. Full many thankes, and I will keepe them safe
Till all the heads be off, for thy sake *Rafe.*
RAFE. Advance my Squire and Dwarfe, I cannot stay.
LADY. Thou kilst my heart in parting thus away.

Exeunt.

WIFE. I commend Rafe yet that hee will not stoope to a *Cracovian,* there's properer women in *London* then any are there I-wis. But here comes Maister *Humphrey* and his love againe now *George.*
CITIZEN. I cony, peace.

Enter Marchant, Humphrey, Luce *and a* Boy.

MARCHANT. Go get you up, I will not be intreated
And gossip mine, Il'e keepe you sure hereafter
From gadding out againe with boyes and unthrifts,
Come, they are womens teares, I know your fashion.
Go sirrah, locke her in, and keepe the key
Safe as you love your life.

Exeunt Luce and *Boy.*

Now my sonne *Humphrey,*
You may both rest assured of my love
In this, and reape your owne desire.

HUMPHREY. I see this love you speake of, through your daughter,
Although the hole be little; and hereafter
Will yeeld the like in all I may, or can,
Fitting a Christian, and a gentleman.
MARCHANT. I do beleeve you (my good sonne) and thanke you:
For 'twere an impudence to thinke you flattered.
HUMPHREY. It were indeed, but shall I tell you why,
I have beene beaten twice about the lye.
MARCHANT. Well son, no more of complement, my daughter
Is yours againe; appoint the time, and take her,
We'le have no stealing for it, I my selfe
And some few of our friends will see you married.
HUMPHREY. I would you would i'faith, for be it knowne
I ever was afraid to lie alone.
MARCHANT. Some three daies hence then.
HUMPHREY. Three daies, let me see,
'Tis some-what of the most,[31] yet I agree,
Because I meane against the appointed day,
To visit all my friends in new array.

Enter Servant.

SERVANT. Sir, there's a Gentlewoman without would speake with your Worship.
MARCHANT. What is shee?
SERVANT. Sir I askt her not.
MARCHANT. Bid her come in.

Enter mistresse Merri-thought *and* Michael.

MISTRESSE MERRI-THOUGHT. Peace be to your Worship, I come as a poore Suter to you sir, in the behalfe of this child.
MARCHANT. Are you not wife to *Merri-thought?*
MISTRESSE MERRI-THOUGHT. Yes truly, would I had nere seene his eies, he has undone me and himselfe and his children, and there he lives at home, and sings, and hoights, and Revels among his drunken companions, but, I warrant you, where to get a peny to put bread in his mouth, he knowes not: and therefore if it like your Worship, I would entreate your letter, to the honest Host of the *Bel* in *Waltham,* that I may place my child under the protection of his Tapster, in some setled course of life.
MARCHANT. I'me glad the heavens have heard my prayers: thy husband
When I was ripe in sorrows laught at me;
Thy sonne like an unthankefull wretch, I having
Redeem'd him from his fall and made him mine,
To shew his love againe, first stole my daughter,

31. A long time to wait.

Then wrong'd this Gentleman, and last of all,
Gave me that griefe, had almost brought me downe
Unto my grave, had not a stronger hand
Releiv'd my sorrowes; go, and weepe, as I did
And be unpittied, for I heere professe
An everlasting hate to all thy name.

MISTRESSE MERRI-THOUGHT. Will you so sir, how say you by that? come *Micke,* let him keepe his winde to coole his Porrage, we'le go to thy Nurces Micke, shee knits silke stockings boy, and we'le knit too boy, and bee beholding to none of them all.

Exeunt Michael *and mother.*
Enter a Boy *with a letter.*

BOY. Sir, I take it you are the Maister of this house.
MARCHANT. How then boy?
BOY. Then to your selfe sir comes this letter.
MARCHANT. From whom my pretty Boy?
BOY. From him that was your servant, but no more
Shall that name ever be, for hee is dead,
Griefe of your purchas'd anger broke his heart,
I saw him die, and from his hand receiv'd
This paper, with a charge to bring it hither,
Reade it, and satisfie your selfe in all.

MARCHANT [*reads*]. *Sir, that I have wronged your love, I must confesse, in which I have purchast to my selfe, besides myne owne undoing, the ill opinion of my friends; let not your anger, good sir, outlive me, but suffer mee to rest in peace with your forgivenesse; let my body (if a dying man may so much prevaile with you) bee brought to your daughter, that shee may truely know my hote flames are now buried, and, withall, receive a testimony of the zeale I bore her vertue: fare-well for ever, and be ever happy.* Jasper.

Gods hand is great in this, I do forgive him,
Yet I am glad he's quiet, where I hope
He will not bite againe: boy bring the body
And let him have his will, if that be all.
BOY. 'Tis here without sir.
MARCHANT. So sir, if you please
You may conduct it in, I do not feare it.
HUMPHREY. Il'e be your Usher boy, for, though I say it,
He ow'd me something once, and well did pay it.

Exeunt.
Enter Luce *alone.*

LUCE. If there be any punishment inflicted
Upon the miserable, more then yet I feele,
Let it together ceaze me, and at once

Presse downe my soule, I cannot beare the paine
Of these delaying tortures: thou that art
The end of all, and the sweete rest of all;
Come, come ô death, bring me to thy peace,
And blot out all the memory I nourish
Both of my father and my cruell friend.
O wretched maide still living to be wretched,
To be a say° to fortune in her changes, assay (experiment)
And grow to number times and woes together,
How happy had I bene, if being borne
My grave had bene my cradle?

Enter Servant.

SERVANT. By your leave
Yong Mistresse, here's a boy hath brought a coffin,
What a would say I know not, but your father
Charg'd me to give you notice, here they come.

[*Exit.*]
Enter two [Carrier *and* Boy] *bearing a Coffin,* Jasper *in it.*

LUCE. For me I hope 'tis come, and 'tis most welcome.
BOY. Faire Mistresse let me not adde greater griefe
To that great store you have already; *Jasper*
That whilst he liv'd was yours, now dead,
And here enclos'd, commanded me to bring
His body hither, and to crave a teare
From those faire eyes, though he deserv'd not pitty,
To decke his funerall, for so he bid me
Tell her for whom he di'de.
LUCE. He shall have many:
Good friends depart a little, whilst I take
My leave of this dead man, that once I lov'd:

Exeunt Coffin Carrier *and* Boy.

Hold, yet a little, life and then I give thee
To thy first heavenly being; O my friend!
Hast thou deceiv'd me thus, and got before me?
I shall not long bee after, but beleeve me,
Thou wert too cruell *Jasper* gainst thy selfe,
In punishing the fault, I could have pardoned,
With so untimely death; thou didst not wrong me,
But ever wert most kind, most true, most loving;
And I the most unkind, most false, most cruell.
Didst thou but aske a teare? Il'e give thee all,
Even all my eies can powre downe, all my sighs
And all my selfe, before thou goest from me.
These are but sparing rites: But if thy soule

Be yet about this place, and can behold
And see what I prepare to deck thee with,
It shall go up, borne on the wings of peace
And satisfied: first will I sing thy dirge,
Then kisse thy pale lips, and then die my selfe,
And fill one Coffin and one grave together.

SONG.
Come, you whose loves are dead,
And whiles I sing
Weepe and wring
Every hand, and every head
Bind with Cipres and sad Ewe,
Ribands blacke, and candles blew,
For him that was of men most true.
Come with heavy moaning,
And on his grave
Let him have
Sacrifice of sighes and groaning,
Let him have faire flowers enow,
White and purple, greene and yellow,
For him that was of men most true.

Thou sable cloth, sad cover of my joies
I lift thee up, and thus I meete with death.
JASPER. And thus you meete the living.
LUCE. Save me Heaven.
JASPER. Nay, do not flie me faire, I am no spirit,
Looke better on me, do you know me yet?
LUCE. O thou deere shadow of my friend.
JASPER. Deere substance,
I sweare I am no shadow, feele my hand,
It is the same it was, I am your *Jasper,*
Your *Jasper* that's yet living, and yet loving,
Pardon my rash attempt, my foolish proofe
I put in practise of your constancy,
For sooner should my sword have drunke my bloud,
And set my soule at liberty, then drawne
The least drop from that body; for which boldnesse
Doome me to any thing: if death I take it,
And willingly.
LUCE. This death I'le give you for it,

[*Kiss.*]

So, now I am satisfied: you are no spirit,
But my owne truest, truest, truest friend,
Why doe you come thus to mee[?]

JASPER. First to see you,
Then to convey you hence.

LUCE. It cannot bee,
For I am lockt up here, and watcht at all howers,
That 'tis impossible for me to scape.

JASPER. Nothing more possible, within this coffin
Do you convey your selfe, let me alone,
I have the wits of twenty men about me,
Onely I crave the shelter of your Closet
A little, and then feare me not; creepe in
That they may presently convey you hence:
Feare nothing, deerest love, Il'e be your second,
Lie close, so, all goes well yet; Boy.

[*Enter* Boy *and* Coffin Carrier.]

BOY. At hand sir.

JASPER. Convey away the Coffin, and be wary.

BOY. 'Tis done already.

JASPER. Now must I go conjure.

Exit.
Enter Marchant.

MARCHANT. Boy, Boy.

BOY. Your servant sir.

MARCHANT. Do me this kindnesse Boy, hold here's a crowne: Before thou bury the body of this fellow, carry it to his old merie father, and salute him from mee, and bid him sing, he hath cause.

BOY. I will sir.

MARCHANT. And then bring me word what tune he is in, and have another crowne: but do it truely. I have fitted him a bargaine, now, will vex him.

BOY. God blesse your Worships health sir.

MARCHANT. Fare-well, boy.

Exeunt.
Enter Maister Merri-thought.

WIFE. Ah old Merri-thought, art thou there againe, let's here some of thy songs.

OLD MERRI-THOUGHT.

Who can sing a merrier noate,
Then he that cannot change a groat?

Not a *Denier* left, and yet my heart leapes; I do wonder yet, as old as I am, that any man will follow a Trade, or serve, that may sing and laugh, and walke the streetes: my wife and both my sonnes are I know not where, I have nothing left, nor know I how to come by meate to supper, yet am I merry still; for I know I shall finde it upon the Table at sixe a clocke, therefore hang Thought.

I would not be a Serving-man to carry the cloke-bag still,
Nor would I be a Fawleconer the greedy Hawlkes to fill.
But I would be in a good house, and have a good Maister too.
But I would eat and drink of the best, and no work would I do.

This it is that keepes life and soule together, mirth, this is the Philosophers stone that they write so much on, that keepes a man ever yong.

Enter a Boy.

BOY. Sir, they say they know all your mony is gone, and they will trust you for no more drinke.

OLD MERRI-THOUGHT. Will they not? let am choose, the best is I have mirth at home, and neede not send abroad for that, let them keepe their drinke to themselves.

For Jillian of Berry *shee dwels on a Hill,*
And shee hath good Beere and Ale to sell.
And of good fellowes she thinks no ill,
And thether will we go now, now, now,
And thether will we go now.
And when you have made a little stay,
You need not aske what is to pay,
But kisse your Hostesse and go your way,
And thither, &c.

Enter another Boy.

2. BOY. Sir, I can get no bread for supper.

OLD MERRI-THOUGHT. Hang bread and supper, let's preserve our mirth, and we shall never feele hunger, I'le warrant you, let's have a Catch, boy follow me, come.

Ho, ho, no body at home,
Meate, nor drinke, nor money ha we none,
Fill the pot Eedy,
Never more need I.

So boies enough, follow mee, let's change our place and we shall laugh afresh.

Exeunt.

Finis Act. 4.

[4. INTERLUDE]

WIFE. Let him goe *George,* a shall not have any countenance from us, nor a good word from any i'th'Company, if I may strike stroke in't.

CITIZEN. No more a shannot love; but *Nel* I will have *Rafe* doe a very notable matter now, to the eternall honour and glory of all *Grocers,* sirrah you there boy, can none of you heare?

BOY. Sir, your pleasure.

CITIZEN. Let *Rafe* come out on May-day in the morning and speake upon a Conduit° with all his Scarfes about him, and his fethers and his rings and his knacks.°

fountain
knickknacks

BOY. Why sir you do not thinke of our plot, what will become of that then?

CITIZEN. Why sir, I care not what become on't, I'le have him come out, or I'le fetch him out my selfe, I'le have something done in honor of the Citty, besides, he hath bene long enough upon Adventures, bring him out quickely, or if I come in amongst you—

BOY. Well sir hee shall come out, but if our play miscarry, sir you are like to pay for't.

CITIZEN. Bring him away then.

Exit Boy.

WIFE. This will be brave i'faith, George shall not he dance the morrice too for the credit of the Strand[?]

CITIZEN. No sweete heart it will bee too much for the boy, ô there he is *Nel,* hee's reasonable well in reparell, but hee has not rings enough.

Enter *Rafe.*

RAFE. *London,* to thee I do present the merry Month of May,
Let each true Subject be content to heare me what I say:
For from the top of Conduit head, as plainely may appeare,
I will both tell my name to you and wherefore I came heere.
My name is *Rafe,* by due discent, though not ignoble I,
Yet far inferior to the Flocke of gratious Grocery.
And by the Common-councell, of my fellowes in the Strand,
With guilded Staffe, and crossed Skarfe, the May-lord here I stand.
Rejoyce, ô English hearts, rejoyce, rejoyce ô Lovers deere,
Rejoyce ô Citty, Towne, and Country, rejoyce eke every Shire;
For now the fragrant Flowers do spring and sprout in seemely sort,
The little Birds do sit and sing, the Lambes do make fine sport.
And now the Burchen Tree doth bud that maks the Schoole boy cry,
The Morrice rings while Hobby-horse doth foote it feateously:° nimbly
The Lords and Ladies now abroad for their disport and play,
Do kisse sometimes upon the Grasse, and sometimes in the Hey.
Now Butter with a leafe of Sage is good to Purge the bloud,
Fly *Venus* and Phlebotomy° for they are neither good. bleeding
Now little fish on tender stone, beginne to cast their bellies,
And sluggish snails, that erst were mute, do creep out of their shelies.
The rumbling Rivers now do warme for little boies to padle,
The sturdy Steede, now goes to grasse, and up they hang his saddle.
The heavy Hart, the bellowing Bucke, the Rascal and the Pricket,

Are now among the Yeomans Pease, and leave the fearefull thicket.
And be like them, ô you, I say, of this same noble Towne,
And lift aloft your velvet heads, and slipping off your gowne:
With bels on legs, and napkins cleane unto your shoulders tied,
With Scarfes and Garters as you please, and Hey for our Town cri'd.
March out and shew your willing minds by twenty and by twenty
To Hogsdon or to Newington, where Ale and Cakes are plenty:
And let it nere be said, for shame, that we the youths of *London*,
Lay thrumming of our Caps at home, and left our custome undone.
Up then, I say, both yong and old, both man and maide a Maying,
With Drums and Guns that bounce alowd, and mery Taber playing.
Which to prolong, God save our king, and send his Country peace,
And roote out Treason from the Land, and so, my friends, I cease.

Enter Marchant, *solus.*

[V.]

MARCHANT. I will have no great store of company at the wedding, a cupple of neighbours and their wives, and wee will have a Capon in stewed broth, with marrow, and a good peece of beefe, stucke with rose-mary.

Enter Jasper, his face *mealed.*° — floured

JASPER. Forbeare thy paines fond man, it is too late.
MARCHANT. Heaven blesse me: *Jasper?*
JASPER. I, I am his Ghost
Whom thou hast injur'd for his constant love:
Fond worldly wretch, who dost not understand
In death that true hearts cannot parted be.
First know thy daughter is quite borne away,
On wings of Angels, through the liquid aire,
To farre out of thy reach, and never more
Shalt thou behold her face: but shee and I
Will in another world enjoy our loves,
Where neither fathers anger, povertie,
Nor any crosse that troubles earthly men
Shall make us sever our united hearts.
And never shalt thou sit, or be alone
In any place, but I will visit thee
With gastly lookes, and put into thy minde
The great offences which thou didst to me.
When thou art at thy Table with thy friends
Merry in heart, and fild with swelling wine,
Il'e come in midst of all thy pride and mirth,
Invisible to all men but thy selfe,
And whisper such a sad tale in thine eare,

Shall make thee let the Cuppe fall from thy hand,
And stand as mute and pale as Death it selfe.

MARCHANT. Forgive me *Jasper;* Oh! what might I doe?
Tell me, to satisfie thy trobled Ghost?

JASPER. There is no meanes, too late thou thinkst of this.

MARCHANT. But tell me what were best for me to doe?

JASPER. Repent thy deede, and satisfie my father,
And beat fond *Humphrey* out of thy dores.

Exit Jasper.
Enter Humphrey.

WIFE. Looke George, his very Ghost would have folkes beaten.

HUMPHREY. Father, my bride is gone, faire mistresse *Luce,*
My soule's the fount of vengeance, mischiefes sluce.

MARCHANT. Hence foole out of my sight, with thy fond passion
Thou hast undone me.

[*Beats him.*]

HUMPHREY. Hold my father deere,
For Luce thy daughters sake, that had no peere.

MARCHANT. Thy father, foole? there's some blows more, begone.
Jasper, I hope thy Ghost bee well appeased,
To see thy will performd, now will I go
To satisfie thy father for thy wrongs.

Exit.

HUMPHREY. What shall I doe? I have beene beaten twice,
And mistresse *Luce* is gone! helpe me device:
Since my true-love is gone, I nevermore,
Whilst I do live, upon the sky will pore;
But in the darke will weare out my shooe-soles
In passion, in Saint *Faiths* Church under *Paules.*

Exit.

WIFE. *George* call *Rafe* hither, if you love me call *Rafe* hither, I have the bravest thing for him to do *George;* pre'thee call him quickly.

CITIZEN. *Rafe,* why *Rafe* boy.

Enter Rafe.

RAFE. Heere sir.

CITIZEN. Come hither *Rafe,* come to thy mistresse, boy.

WIFE. *Rafe* I would have thee call all the youthes together in battle-ray, with drums, and guns, and flags, and march to Mile-End in pompous fashion, and there exhort your Souldiers to be merry and wise, and to keepe their beards from burning *Rafe,* and then skirmish, and let your flagges flye, and cry kill, kill, kill: my husband shall lend you his Jerkin, *Rafe,* and there's a scarfe; for the rest, the house shall furnish you, and wee'l pay for't: doe it bravely *Rafe,* and thinke before whom you performe, and what person you represent.

RAFE. I warrant you mistresse if I do it not for the honour of the Citty, and the credit of my maister, let me never hope for freedome.

WIFE. 'Tis well spoken Ifaith; go thy wayes, thou art a sparke indeed.

CITIZEN. *Rafe, Rafe,* double your files bravely *Rafe.*

RAFE. I warrant you sir.

Exit Rafe.

CITIZEN. Let him looke narrowly to his service, I shall take him else, I was there my selfe a pike-man once, in the hottest of the day,[32] wench; had my feather shot sheere away, the fringe of my pike burnt off with powder, my pate broken with a scouring-sticke, and yet, I thanke God, I am heere.

Drums within.

WIFE. Harke *George* the drums.

CITIZEN. Ran, tan, tan, tan; ran, tan: O wench, an thou hadst but seene little *Ned* of Algate, drum *Ned,* how hee made it rore againe, and layd on like a tyrant: and then stroke softly till the ward[33] came up, and then thundred againe, and together we go: sa, sa, sa, bounce quoth the guns: courage my hearts, quoth the Captaines: Saint *George,* quoth the pike-men; and withall here they lay, and there they lay: And yet for all this I am heere wench.

WIFE. Be thankfull for it *George,* for indeed 'tis wonderfull.

Enter Rafe *and his company with Drummes and colours.*

RAFE. March faire my hearts, Lieuetenant beate the reare up: Ancient,[34] let your colours flye; but have a great care of the Butchers hookes at white-Chapell, they have beene the death of many a faire Ancient. Open your files that I may take a view both of your persons and munition: Sergeant call a muster.

SERGEANT. A stand, William Hammerton peuterer.

HAMMERTON. Here Captaine.

RAFE. A Corslet and a spanish pike; 'tis well, can you shake it with a terror?

HAMMERTON. I hope so Captaine.

RAFE. Charge upon me, 'tis with the weakest: put more strength *William Hammerton,* more strength: as you were againe. Proceed Sergeant.

SERGEANT. *George Greene-goose,* Poulterer[.]

GREEN-GOOSE. Heere.

32. In the heat of battle at its height.
33. Company of guards.
34. The ancient (or ensign) was a junior officer who carried the regiment's flag.

RAFE. Let me see your peece neighbour *Greene-goose,* when was she shot in?

GREEN-GOOSE. And like you maister Captaine, I made a shot even now, partly to scoure her, and partly for audacity.

RAFE. It should seeme so certainely, for her breath is yet inflamed: besides, there is a maine fault in the touch-hole, it runnes, and stinketh; and I tell you moreover, and beleeve it: Ten such touch-holes would breed the pox in the Army. Get you a feather, neighbour, get you a feather, sweet oyle, and paper, and your peece may do well enough yet. Where's your powder?

GREEN-GOOSE. Heere.

RAFE. What in a paper? as I am a Souldier, and a Gentleman, it craves a Martiall Court: you ought to dye for't. Where's your horne? answere me to that.

GREEN-GOOSE. An't like you sir, I was oblivious.

RAFE. It likes me not you should bee so; 'tis a shame for you, and a scandall to all our neighbours, beeing a man of worth and estimation, to leave your horne behinde you: I am afraid 'twill breed example. But let me tell you no more on't; stand, till I view you all. What's become o'th nose of your flaske?

1. SOULDIER. Indeed law Captaine, 'twas blowne away with powder.

RAFE. Put on a new one at the Cities charge. Wheres the stone of this peece?

2. SOULDIER. The Drummer tooke it out to light Tobacco.

RAFE. 'Tis a fault my friend, put it in againe: You want a Nose, and you a Stone; Sergeant, take a note on't, for I meane to stoppe it in the pay. Remove and march, soft and faire Gentlemen, soft and faire: double your files, as you were, faces about. Now you with the sodden face, keepe in there: looke to your match sirrah, it will be in your fellowes flaske anone. So, make a crescent now, advance your pikes, stand and give eare. Gentlemen, Countrey-men, Friends, and my fellow-Souldiers, I have brought you this day from the Shops of Security, and the Counters of Content, to measure out in these furious fields, Honour by the ell; and prowesse by the pound: Let it not, ô let it not, I say, bee told hereafter, the noble issue of this Citie fainted: but beare your selves in this faire action, like men, valiant men, and freemen; Feare not the face of the enemy, nor the noise of the guns: for beleeve me brethren, the rude rumbling of a Brewers Carre is farre more terrible, of which you have a daily experience: Neither let the stinke of powder offend you, since a more valiant stinke is nightly with you. To a resolved minde, his home is every where: I speake not this to take away the hope of your returne; for you shall see (I do not doubt it) and that very shortly, your loving wives againe, and your sweet children, whose care doth beare you company in baskets. Remember then whose cause you have in hand, and like a sort of true-borne Scavingers, scoure me this famous Realme of enemies. I have no more to say but this:

Stand to your tacklings lads, and shew to the world you can as well brandish a sword, as shake an apron. Saint *George* and on, my hearts.

OMNES. *Saint George, Saint George.*

Exeunt

WIFE. 'Twas well done *Rafe,* Il'e send thee a cold Capon a field, and a bottle of March-beere; and it may be, come my selfe to see thee.

CITIZEN. *Nell,* the boy has deceived me much, I did not thinke it had been in him: he has performed such a matter wench, that if I live, next yeare Il'e have him Captaine of the Gally-foist,[35] or Il'e want my will.

Enter old Merri-thought.

OLD MERRI-THOUGHT. Yet I thanke God, I breake not a rinkle more than I had. Not a stoope boyes? Care live with Cats, I defie thee, my heart is as sound as an Oke; and though I want drinke to wet my whistle, I can sing:

Come no more there boyes, come no more there:
For we shall never whilst we live, come any more there.

Enter a Boy *with a Coffin.*

BOY. God save you sir.

OLD MERRI-THOUGHT. It's a brave boy: canst thou sing?

BOY. Yes sir, I can sing, but 'tis not so necessary at this time.

OLD MERRI-THOUGHT.

Sing wee, and chaunt it,
Whilst love doth grant it.

BOY. Sir, sir, if you knew what I have brought you, you would have little list° to sing. desire

OLD MERRI-THOUGHT.

O the Minion round,
Full long I have thee sought,
And now I have thee found,
And what hast thou here brought?

BOY. A Coffin sir, and your dead son *Jasper* in it.

OLD MERRI-THOUGHT. Dead?

Why fare-well he:
Thou wast a bonny boy, and I did love thee.

Enter Jasper.

JASPER. Then, I pray you sir do so still.

35. Official barge used in processions of the lord mayor of the City of London.

OLD MERRI-THOUGHT. *Jaspers* ghost?

Thou art welcome from Stygian lake so soone,
Declare to mee what wondrous things in Pluto's *court are done.*

JASPER. By my troth sir, I nere came there, tis too hot for me sir.

OLD MERRI-THOUGHT. A merry ghost, a very merry ghost.

And where is your true-love? ô where is yours?

JASPER. Marie looke you sir.

Heaves up the Coffin.

OLD MERRI-THOUGHT. Ah ha! Art thou good at that Ifaith?

With hey trixie terlery-whiskin,
The world it runnes on wheeles,
When the young mans—[36]
Up goes the maidens heeles.

Mistresse Merri-thought, *and* Michael *within.*

MISTRESSE MERRI-THOUGHT. What Maister *Merri-thought,* will you not let's in? what do you thinke shall become of us?

OLD MERRI-THOUGHT. What voyce is that that calleth at our doore?

MISTRESSE MERRI-THOUGHT. You know me well enough, I am sure I have not beene such a stranger to you.

OLD MERRI-THOUGHT.

And some they whistled, and some they sung,
Hey downe, downe:
And some did lowdly say,
Ever as the Lord Barnets *horne blew,*
Away, Musgrave, away.

MISTRESSE MERRI-THOUGHT. You will not have us starve here, will you, Maister *Merri-thought?*

JASPER. Nay good sir be perswaded, she is my mother: if her offences have been great against you, let your owne love remember she is yours, and so forgive her.

LUCE. Good Maister *Merri-thought* let mee entreat you, I will not be denied.

MISTRESSE MERRI-THOUGHT. Why Maister *Merri-thought,* will you be a vext thing still?

OLD MERRI-THOUGHT. Woman I take you to my love againe, but you shall sing before you enter: therefore despatch your song, and so come in.

MISTRESSE MERRI-THOUGHT. Well, you must have your will when al's done. *Micke* what song canst thou sing boy?

36. A rhyme word is missing here (indicated by the dash), probably a vulgar expression.

MICHAEL. I can sing none forsooth, but a Ladies daughter of *Paris* properly.

MISTRESSE MERRI-THOUGHT [and MICHAEL].

It was a Ladies daughter, &c.

OLD MERRI-THOUGHT. Come, you'r welcome home againe.

If such danger be in playing,
And jest must to earnest turne,
You shall go no more a maying.

MARCHANT *(within).* Are you within sir, Maister *Merri-thought?*

JASPER. It is my maisters voyce, good sir go hold him in talke whilst we convey our selves into Some inward roome.

[*Exit with Luce.*]

OLD MERRI-THOUGHT. What are you? are you merry? you must bee very merry, if you enter.

MARCHANT. I am sir.

OLD MERRI-THOUGHT. Sing then.

MARCHANT. Nay good sir open to me.

OLD MERRI-THOUGHT. Sing, I say, or by the merry heart you come not in.

MARCHANT. Well sir, Il'e sing.

Fortune, my Foe, &c.

OLD MERRI-THOUGHT. You are welcome sir, you are welcome, you see your entertainment, pray you bee merry.

MARCHANT. Oh Maister *Merri-thought,* I am come to aske you
Forgivenesse for the wrongs I offered you,
And your most vertuous sonne, they're infinite,
Yet my contrition shall be more than they.
I do confesse my hardnesse broke his heart,
For which, just heaven hath given me punishment
More than my age can carry; his wandring spirit
Not yet at rest, pursues me every where,
Crying, I'le haunt thee for thy cruelty.
My daughter, she is gone, I know not how,
Taken invisible, and whether living,
Or in the grave, 'tis yet uncertaine to me.
O Maister *Merri-thought,* these are the weights,
Will sinke me to my grave, forgive me sir.

OLD MERRI-THOUGHT. Why sir, I do forgive you, and be merry,
And if the wag, in's life time plaid the knave,
Can you forgive him too?

MARCHANT. Withall my heart sir.

OLD MERRI-THOUGHT. Speake it againe, and hartely.

MARCHANT. I do sir,
Now by my soule I do.

OLD MERRI-THOUGHT.

With that came out his Paramoure,
Shee was as white as the Lillie flower,
Hey troule trollie lollie.

Enter Luce *and* Jasper.

With that came out her owne dear Knight,
He was as true as ever did fight. &c.

Sir, if you will forgive 'ham, clap their hands together, there's no more to be said i'th' matter.

MARCHANT. I do, I do.

CITIZEN. I do not like this, peace boies, heare me one of you, every bodies part is come to an end but *Rafes,* and hee's left out.

BOY. 'Tis long of your selfe sir, wee have nothing to doe with his part.

CITIZEN. *Rafe* come away, make on him as you have done of the rest, boies; come.

WIFE. Now good husband let him come out and die.

CITIZEN. He shall *Nel, Rafe* come away quickely and die boy.

BOY. 'Twill be very unfit he should die sir, upon no occasion, and in a Comedy too.

CITIZEN. Take you no care of that sir boy, is not his part at an end, thinke you, when he's dead? come away *Rafe.*

Enter Rafe, *with a forked arrow through his head.*

RAFE. When I was mortall, this my costive corps
Did lap up Figs and Raisons in the Strand,
Where sitting I espi'd a lovely Dame,
Whose Maister wrought with Lingell° and with All, — waxed thread
And underground he vampied° many a boote, — patched
Straight did her love pricke forth me, tender sprig,
To follow feats of Armes in warlike wise,
Through *Waltham* Desert, where I did performe
Many atchievements, and did lay on ground
Huge *Barbaroso* that insulting Giant,
And all his Captives soone set at liberty.
Then honour prickt me from my native soile,
Into *Moldavia,* where I gain'd the love
Of *Pompiana* his beloved daughter:
But yet prov'd constant to the blacke thum'd maide
Susan, and skorn'd *Pompianaes* love:
Yet liberall I was and gave her pinnes,
And money for her fathers Officers.
I then returned home, and thrust my selfe
In action, and by all men chosen was
Lord of the May, where I did flourish it,

With Skarfes and Rings, and Posie in my hand:
After this action, I preferred was,
And chosen Citty Captaine at Mile-End,
With hat and feather and with leading staffe,
And train'd my men and brought them all off cleere,
Save one man that berai'd him° with the noise. beshit himself
But all these things I *Rafe* did undertake,
Onely for my beloved *Susans* sake.
Then comming home, and sitting in my Shop
With Apron blew, Death came unto my Stall
To cheapen° *Aqua-vitæ,* but ere I bargain for
Could take the bottle downe, and fill a taste,
Death caught a pound of Pepper in his hand,
And sprinkled all my face and body ore,
And in an instant vanished away.

CITIZEN. 'Tis a pretty fiction, i'faith.

RAFE. Then tooke I up my Bow and Shaft in hand,
And walkt into *Moore-fields* to coole my selfe,
But there grim cruell death met me againe,
And shot this forked arrow through my head,
And now I faint, therefore be warn'd by me,
My fellowes every one of forked heads.
Fare-well all you good boies in merry *London,*
Nere shall we more upon Shrove-tuesday meete
And plucke downe houses of iniquitie.
My paine increaseth, I shall never more
Hold open, whilst another pumpes both legs,
Nor daube a Satten gowne with rotten eggs:
Set up a stake, ô never more I shall,
I die, flie, flie my soule to *Grocers* Hall. Oh, oh, oh, &c.

WIFE. Well said *Rafe,* doe your obeysance to the Gentlemen and go your waies, well said *Rafe.*

Exit Rafe.

OLD MERRI-THOUGHT. Me thinkes all we, thus kindly and unexpectedly reconciled should not depart without a song.

MARCHANT. A good motion.

OLD MERRI-THOUGHT. Strike up then.

SONG.
Better Musicke nere was knowne,
Than a quire of hearts in one.
Let each other that hath beene,
Troubled with the gall or spleene:
Learne of us to keepe his brow,
Smooth and plaine as ours are now.
Sing, though before the houre of dying,

He shall rise, and then be crying.
Hey ho, 'tis nought but mirth,
That keepes the body from the earth.

Exeunt Omnes.

CITIZEN. Come *Nel,* shall we go, the Plaies done.

WIFE. Nay by my faith *George,* I have more manners than so, I'le speake to these Gentlemen first: I thanke you all Gentlemen, for your patience and countenance to *Rafe,* a poore fatherlesse child, and if I might see you at my house, it should go hard, but I would have a pottle of wine and a pipe of Tobacco for you, for truely I hope you do like the youth, but I would bee glad to know the truth: I referre it to your owne discretions, whether you will applaud him or no, for I will winke, and whilst you shall do what you will, I thanke you with all my heart, God give you good night; come *George.*

FINIS.

PART 3

Drama

OF THE RESTORATION AND EARLY EIGHTEENTH CENTURY

WHEN CHARLES II was restored to the throne of England in 1660, he granted patents to two theatrical companies, the King's Company and the Duke's Company. These companies performed indoors and since ticket prices were more expensive than earlier in the century, the audience was somewhat more upper class, although prologues indicate that plenty of servants, apprentices, and members of the City of London were also in attendance. Unlike the earlier English theater, members of the nobility, gentry, and women took to writing drama. French drama had some influence on genres, as did the plays of John Fletcher, William Shakespeare, and Ben Jonson. With a smaller audience, theatrical competition was intense until 1682, when the King's Company went out of business and the United Company was formed. Among the theatrical innovations were the introduction of women on stage and elaborate scenery. The appeal of great stars such as Elizabeth Barry, Thomas Betterton, and Anne Bracegirdle became as important as the play script in attracting audiences to the theater. But when John Gay's *The Beggar's Opera* ignited audience interest in attending the theater, Gay and Henry Fielding produced a series of plays to satirize the administration of Sir Robert Walpole. In 1737, Walpole proceeded to pass the Licensing Act, which introduced a censorship that largely defanged English theater until the end of the nineteenth century.

All for Love

John Dryden's works not only illustrate but helped to shape the political and religious debates of seventeenth-century England. He was born in 1631, the eldest of fourteen children of landowning gentry in Aldwincle, Northamptonshire. His family came from Puritan stock and were supporters of Parliament against Stuart absolutism. Yet Dryden went to Westminster School as a King's Scholar. The headmaster there, Richard Busby, taught a rigorous classical curriculum, and was a Royalist and an Anglican traditionalist. At Trinity College, Cambridge, Dryden studied in an environment much more sympathetic to Puritanism and parliamentary supremacy. Dryden took his BA in 1654 (and was awarded an honorary MA in 1668). Dryden attended the funeral of Oliver Cromwell in 1658 and published that year *Heroique Stanzas* in praise of Cromwell.

Nevertheless, Dryden became the premier Stuart poet. In 1663 he married Elizabeth Howard, the daughter of an earl and from a branch of one of the oldest and most important families in England. *Annus Mirabilis,* in 1667, praises Charles II's actions during the Great Fire of London in 1666, and James, Duke of York's, victory over a Dutch fleet in the same year. In 1668 he was named poet laureate and in 1670 historiographer royal, receiving a stipend from the crown for these posts.

Despite this income and that of a small estate, Dryden made most of his money writing for the theater, for many years on contract for the King's Company, and churning out a steady stream of heroic plays, tragedies, and comedies. He also participated in a number of literary controversies, arguing with his brother-in-law, Sir Robert Howard, over whether serious drama should be written in heroic couplets or blank verse, and with Thomas Shadwell over the relative merits of wit and judgment in comedy; the latter was the target of *MacFlecknoe* (probably written in 1676) although, according to Shadwell, Dryden denied having written the work when

The text is that established in *The Works of John Dryden,* vol. XIII, ed. Maximillian E. Novak, Allan Roper, George R. Guffey, and Vinton A. Dearing (Berkeley: University of California Press, 1985), 20–111.

Shadwell confronted him, and Dryden wrote a prologue for Shadwell's *A True Widow* in 1679. Dryden and heroic drama were the subject of satire in Howard's and the Duke of Buckingham's play *The Rehearsal* (1671). In 1679 Dryden was savagely beaten in Rose Alley; the attack is sometimes ascribed (with very little evidence) to men hired by John Wilmot, the Earl of Rochester, who had both denigrated Dryden and praised Shadwell, and whom Dryden had criticized. Dryden wrote a number of works in support of Charles II in the conflicts over the king's prerogative with Parliament, most importantly in *Absalom and Achitophel* (1681), one of the best political poems in the language.

Dryden's *Religio Laici* (1682) defended Anglicanism against the extremes of Puritanism and Catholicism, but when the Catholic James II became king in 1685, Dryden converted to Catholicism and in 1687 wrote *The Hind and the Panther*, a defense of Catholicism. The revolution of 1688 placed William III, a firm Protestant, on the throne. Dryden refused to take the oath of allegiance and was replaced as poet laureate by Shadwell. Dryden continued to write plays and turned out a number of translations; his translation of *The Aeneid* (1697) remained the standard English version for at least two centuries. He died in 1700 and was buried in Westminster Abbey. His last great work, *The Secular Masque* (1700), looked back on the seventeenth century and its struggles and commented, "'Tis well an old age is out, and time to ring in a new."

Dryden is a seminal figure in the rise of English literary nationalism. In his dialogue *Of Dramatick Poesie* (1668) he argues the radical claims that modern drama is better than classical drama and that English drama is better than French. He also establishes what the canon of English drama will be, and at the top are Jonson and Shakespeare. *All for Love* (1678) is written "in Imitation of *Shakespeare's* Stile"; Shakespeare, according to Dryden, is the preeminent poet of the passions. Almost apologetically, Dryden defends in his introduction his use of the French conventions of "decorum" (characters speaking in a manner appropriate to their role in the plays), and the unities of time, place, and action. He says these are not really necessary to English drama, but the use of the latter emphasizes an important facet of Restoration tragedy. Shakespeare's *Antony and Cleopatra* has a cast of nearly three dozen and takes place in many locations over many years; the play shows the choices Antony makes that lead to his destruction. Dryden's play takes place on the last day of Antony and Cleopatra's lives; all the significant choices have already been made, and the audience is invited to feel their tempestuous emotions. The play is also notable for its polarities inviting comparison between Rome and Egypt: the Roman virtue of Ventidius versus the scheming of Egyptian eunuch Alexas, the cold virtue of Octavia versus the impulsive sensuality of Cleopatra, and the cold calculation of Octavius (frequently discussed although not present in the play) versus the passionate and fiery Antony. Rome conquers Egypt, but at the same time the subtitle of the play suggests the world is well lost for such a transcendent passion.

All for Love: or, the World Well Lost.

PROLOGUE

to Antony and Cleopatra.

WHAT Flocks of Critiques hover here today,
As Vultures wait on Armies for their Prey,
All gaping for the Carcass of a Play!
With Croaking Notes they bode some dire event;
And follow dying Poets by the scent.
Ours gives himself for gone; y'have watch'd your time!
He fights this day unarm'd; without his Rhyme;[1]
And brings a Tale which often has been told;
As sad as Dido's;[2] *and almost as old.*
His Heroe, whom you Wits his Bully *call,*
Bates° *of his mettle, and scarce rants at all:* — diminishes
He's somewhat lewd; but a well-meaning mind;
Weeps much; fights little; but is wond'rous kind:
In short, a Pattern, and Companion fit,
For all the keeping Tonyes[3] *of the Pit.*
I cou'd name more; A Wife, and Mistress too;
Both (to be plain) too good for most of you:
The Wife well-natur'd, and the Mistress true.
        Now, Poets, if your fame has been his care;
Allow him all the candour you can spare.
A brave Man scorns to quarrel once a day;
Like Hectors,° *in at every petty fray.* — bullies
Let those find fault whose Wit's so very small,
They've need to show that they can think at all:
Errours like Straws upon the surface flow;
He who would search for Pearls must dive below.
Fops may have leave to level all they can;
As Pigmies wou'd be glad to lopp a Man.
Half-Wits are Fleas; so little and so light;
We scarce cou'd know they live, but that they bite.
But, as the Rich, when tir'd with daily Feasts,
For change, become their next poor Tenants Ghests;
Drink hearty Draughts of Ale, from plain brown Bowls,

1. Up to *Aureng-Zebe* (1676) Dryden had championed rhymed "heroic" couplets over blank verse as the most appropriate language for serious drama on the grounds that drama was an imitation of nature heightened.

2. Founder of Carthage who commits suicide when deserted by Aeneas in Virgil's *Aeneid.*

3. Someone who keeps a mistress, but also with a pun on Antony.

And snatch the homely Rasher from the Coals:
So you, retiring from much better Cheer,
For once, may venture to do penance here.
And since that plenteous Autumn now is past,
Whose Grapes and Peaches have Indulg'd your taste,
Take in good part from our poor Poets boord,
Such rivell'd Fruits as Winter can afford.

PERSONS REPRESENTED.

MARC ANTONY,
VENTIDIUS, his General,
DOLLABELLA, his Friend,
ALEXAS, the Queens Eunuch,
SERAPION, Priest of *Isis,*
Another Priest [Myris],
Servants to *Antony.*
CLEOPATRA, Queen of *Ægypt,*
OCTAVIA, *Antony's* Wife,
CHARMION, IRAS, } *Cleopatra's* Maids.
Antony's TWO LITTLE DAUGHTERS.

Scene *Alexandria.*

ACT I. SCENE I.

Scene, the Temple of Isis.
Enter Serapion, Myris, *Priests of* Isis.

SERAPION. Portents, and Prodigies, are grown so frequent,
That they have lost their Name. Our fruitful *Nile*
Flow'd ere the wonted Season, with a Torrent
So unexpected, and so wondrous fierce,
That the wild Deluge overtook the haste
Ev'n of the Hinds that watch'd it: Men and Beasts
Were borne above the tops of Trees, that grew
On th' utmost Margin of the Water-mark.
Then, with so swift an Ebb, that Floud drove backward,
It slipt from underneath the Scaly Herd:
Here monstrous *Phocæ*° panted on the Shore; seals
Forsaken *Dolphins* there, with their broad tails,
Lay lashing the departing Waves: Hard by 'em,
Sea-Horses° floundring in the slimy mud, hippopotami

Toss'd up their heads, and dash'd the ooze about 'em.

Enter Alexas *behind them.*

MYRIS. Avert these Omens, Heav'n.
SERAPION. Last night, between the hours of Twelve and One,
In a lone Isle o'th' Temple while I walk'd,
A Whirl-wind rose, that, with a violent blast,
Shook all the Dome: the Doors around me clapt,
The Iron Wicket, that defends the Vault,
Where the long Race of *Ptolemies* is lay'd,
Burst open, and disclos'd the mighty dead.
From out each Monument, in order plac'd,
An Armed Ghost start up: the Boy-King[4] last
Rear'd his inglorious head. A peal of groans
Then follow'd, and a lamentable voice
Cri'd, Ægypt *is no more.* My blood ran back,
My shaking knees against each other knock'd;
On the cold pavement down I fell intranc'd,
And so unfinish'd left the horrid Scene.
ALEXAS *showing himself.* And, Dream'd you this? or, Did invent the Story,
To frighten our *Ægyptian* Boys withal,
And train 'em up, betimes, in fear of Priesthood?
SERAPION. My Lord, I saw you not,
Nor meant my words should reach your ears; but what
I utter'd was most true.
ALEXAS. A foolish Dream,
Bred from the fumes of indigested Feasts,
And holy Luxury.° — overindulgence
SERAPION. I know my duty:
This goes no further.
ALEXAS. 'Tis not fit it should.
Nor would the times now bear it, were it true.
All Southern, from yon hills, the *Roman* Camp
Hangs o'er us black and threatning, like a Storm
Just breaking on our heads.
SERAPION. Our faint *Ægyptians* pray for *Antony;*
But in their Servile hearts they own *Octavius.*
MYRIS. Why then does *Antony* dream out his hours,
And tempts not Fortune for a noble Day,
Which might redeem, what *Actium*[5] lost?
ALEXAS. He thinks 'tis past recovery.
SERAPION. Yet the Foe
Seems not to press the Siege.

4. Ptolemy XIV, Cleopatra's half-brother and second husband; she was suspected of poisoning him.
5. Battle where Octavius defeated Antony in 31 BC.

ALEXAS. O, there's the wonder.
Mæcenas and *Agrippa,*[6] who can most
With Cæsar, are his Foes. His Wife *Octavia,*
Driv'n from his House, solicits her revenge;
And *Dollabella,* who was once his Friend,
Upon some private grudge, now seeks his ruine:
Yet still War seems on either side to sleep.
SERAPION. 'Tis strange that *Antony,* for some dayes past,
Has not beheld the face of *Cleopatra;*
But here, in *Isis* Temple, lives retir'd,
And makes his heart a prey to black despair.
ALEXAS. 'Tis true; and we much fear he hopes by absence
To cure his mind of Love.
SERAPION. If he be vanquish'd,
Or make his peace, *Ægypt* is doom'd to be
A *Roman* Province; and our plenteous Harvests
Must then redeem the scarceness° of their Soil. poorness
While *Antony* stood firm, our *Alexandria*
Rival'd proud *Rome* (Dominions other Seat)
And Fortune striding, like a vast *Colossus,*
Cou'd fix an equal foot of Empire here.
ALEXAS. Had I my wish, these Tyrants of all Nature
Who Lord it o'er Mankind, should perish, perish,
Each by the others Sword; but, since our will
Is lamely followed by our power, we must
Depend on one; with him to rise or fall.
SERAPION. How stands the Queen affected?
ALEXAS. O, she dotes,
She dotes, *Serapion,* on this vanquish'd Man,
And winds herself about his mighty ruins;
Whom would she yet forsake, yet yield him up,
This hunted prey, to his pursuers hands,
She might preserve us all; but 'tis in vain—
This changes my designs, this blasts my Counsels,
And makes me use all means to keep him here,
Whom I could wish divided from her Arms
Far as the Earth's deep Center. Well, you know
The state of things; no more of your ill Omens
And black Prognostics; labour to confirm
The peoples hearts.

Enter Ventidius, *talking aside with a Gentleman of* Antony's.

SERAPION. These *Romans* will o'rehear us.
But, Who's that Stranger? By his Warlike port,

6. Gauis Maecenas arranged the marriage of Antony and Octavia. Agrippa commanded Octavius's forces at Actium.

His fierce demeanor, and erected look,
He's of no vulgar note.

ALEXAS. O 'tis *Ventidius*,[7]
Our Emp'rors great Lieutenant in the East,
Who first show'd *Rome* that *Parthia* could be conquer'd.
When *Antony* return'd from *Syria* last,
He left this Man to guard the *Roman* Frontiers.

SERAPION. You seem to know him well.

ALEXAS. Too well. I saw him at *Cilicia*° first, Turkey
When *Cleopatra* there met *Antony:*
A mortal foe he was to us, and *Ægypt.*
But, let me witness to the worth I hate,
A braver *Roman* never drew a Sword:
Firm to his Prince; but, as a friend, not slave.
He ne'r was of his pleasures; but presides
O're all his cooler hours, and morning counsels:
In short, the plainness, fierceness, rugged virtue
Of an old true-stampt *Roman* lives in him.
His coming bodes I know not what of ill
To our affairs. Withdraw, to mark him better;
And I'll acquaint you why I sought you here,
And what's our present work.

[*They withdraw to a corner of the Stage; and* Ventidius, *with the other, comes forward to the front.*

VENTIDIUS. Not see him, say you?
I say, I must, and will.

1 GENTLEMAN. He has commanded,
On pain of death, none should approach his presence.

VENTIDIUS. I bring him news will raise his drooping Spirits,
Give him new life.

1 GENTLEMAN. He sees not *Cleopatra.*

VENTIDIUS. Would he had never seen her.

1 GENTLEMAN. He eats not, drinks not, sleeps not, has no use
Of any thing, but thought; or, if he talks,
'Tis to himself, and then 'tis perfect raving:
Then he defies the World, and bids it pass;
Sometimes he gnawes his Lip, and Curses loud
The boy *Octavius;* then he draws his mouth
Into a scornful smile, and cries, *Take all,*
The World's not worth my care.

VENTIDIUS. Just, just his nature.
Virtues his path; but sometimes 'tis too narrow
For his vast Soul; and then he starts out wide,

7. Ventidius defeated the Parthians in 39–38 BC, but he was dead by the time of this play and is Dryden's addition.

And bounds into a Vice, that bears him far
From his first course, and plunges him in ills:
But, when his danger makes him find his fault,
Quick to observe, and full of sharp remorse,
He censures eagerly his own misdeeds,
Judging himself with malice to himself,
And not forgiving what as Man he did,
Because his other parts are more than Man.
He must not thus be lost.

[Alexas *and the Priests come forward.*

ALEXAS. You have your full Instructions, now advance;
Proclaim your Orders loudly.
SERAPION. *Romans, Ægyptians,* hear the Queen's Command.
Thus *Cleopatra* bids, Let Labor cease,
To Pomp and Triumphs give this happy day,
That gave the World a Lord: 'tis *Antony's.*
Live, *Antony;* and *Cleopatra* live.
Be this the general voice sent up to Heav'n,
And every publick place repeat this eccho.
VENTIDIUS. Fine pageantry!
SERAPION. Set out before your doors
The Images of all your sleeping Fathers,
With Laurels crown'd; with Laurels wreathe your posts,
And strow with Flow'rs the Pavement; Let the Priests
Do present Sacrifice; pour out the Wine,
And call the Gods to joyn with you in gladness.
VENTIDIUS. Curse on the tongue that bids this general joy.
Can they be friends of *Antony,* who Revel
When *Antony's* in danger? Hide, for shame,
You *Romans,* your Great grandsires Images,
For fear their Souls should animate their Marbles,
To blush at their degenerate Progeny.
ALEXAS. A love, which knows no bounds, to *Antony,*
Would mark the Day with honors; when all Heav'n
Labor'd for him, when each propitious Star
Stood wakeful in his Orb, to watch that hour,
And shed his better influence. Her own Birth-day
Our Queen neglected, like a vulgar Fate,
That pass'd obscurely by.
VENTIDIUS. Would it had slept,
Divided far from his; till some remote
And future Age had call'd it out, to ruin
Some other Prince, not him.
ALEXAS. Your Emperor,
Tho grown unkind, would be more gentle, than
T' upbraid my Queen, for loving him too well.

VENTIDIUS. Does the mute Sacrifice upbraid the Priest?
He knows him not his Executioner.
O, she has deck'd his ruin with her love,
Led him in golden bands to gaudy slaughter,
And made perdition pleasing: She has left him
The blank of what he was;
I tell thee, Eunuch, she has quite unman'd him:
Can any *Roman* see, and know him now,
Thus alter'd from the Lord of half Mankind,
Unbent, unsinew'd, made a Womans Toy,
Shrunk from the vast extent of all his honors,
And crampt within a corner of the World?
O, *Antony!*
Thou bravest Soldier, and thou best of Friends!
Bounteous as Nature; next to Nature's God!
Could'st thou but make new Worlds, so wouldst thou give 'em,
As bounty were thy being: Rough in Battel,
As the first *Romans,* when they went to War;
Yet, after Victory, more pitiful° — full of pity
Than all their Praying Virgins left at home!

ALEXAS. Would you could add, to those more shining Virtues,
His truth to her who loves him.

VENTIDIUS. Would I could not.
But, Wherefore waste I precious hours with thee?
Thou art her darling mischief, her chief Engin,
Antony's other Fate. Go, tell thy Queen,
Ventidius is arriv'd, to end her Charms.
Let your *Ægyptian* Timbrels play alone;
Nor mix Effeminate Sounds with *Roman* Trumpets.
You dare not fight for *Antony;* go Pray
And keep your Cowards-Holy-day in Temples.

[*Exeunt* ALEXAS, SERAPION.
Enter second Gentleman of M. ANTONY.

2 GENTLEMAN. The Emperor approaches, and commands,
On pain of Death, that none presume to stay.

1 GENTLEMAN. I dare not disobey him.

[*Going out with the other.*

VENTIDIUS. Well, I dare.
But I'll observe him first unseen, and find
Which way his humour drives: The rest I'll venture.

[*Withdraws.*
Enter ANTONY, *walking with a disturb'd Motion, before he speaks.*

ANTONY. They tell me, 'tis my Birth-day, and I'll keep it
With double pomp of sadness.

'Tis what the day deserves, which gave me breath.
Why was I rais'd the Meteor of the World,
Hung in the Skies, and blazing as I travel'd,
Till all my fires were spent; and then cast downward
To be trod out by Cæsar?

VENTIDIUS. *aside.* On my Soul,
'Tis mournful, wondrous mournful!

ANTONY. Count thy gains.
Now, *Antony,* Wouldst thou be born for this?
Glutton of Fortune, thy devouring youth
Has starv'd thy wanting Age.

VENTIDIUS. How sorrow shakes him!

[*Aside.*

So, now the Tempest tears him up by th' Roots,
And on the ground extends the noble ruin.

ANTONY. *having thrown himself down.*
Lye there, thou shadow of an Emperor;
The place thou pressest on thy Mother Earth
Is all thy Empire now: now it contains thee;
Some few days hence, and then twill be too large,
When thou'rt contracted in thy narrow Urn,
Shrunk to a few cold Ashes; then *Octavia,*
(For *Cleopatra* will not live to see it),
Octavia then will have thee all her own,
And bear thee in her Widow'd hand to *Cæsar;*
Cæsar will weep, the Crocodile will weep,
To see his Rival of the Universe
Lye still and peaceful there. I'll think no more on't.
Give me some Musick: look that it be sad:
I'll soothe my Melancholy, till I swell,
And burst myself with sighing—

[*Soft Musick.*

'Tis somewhat to my humor. Stay, I fancy
I'm now turn'd wild, a Commoner of Nature;
Of all forsaken, and forsaking all;
Live in a shady Forrest's Sylvan Scene,
Stretch'd at my length beneath some blasted Oke;
I lean my head upon the Mossy Bark,
And look just of a piece, as I grew from it:
My uncomb'd Locks, matted like Mistletoe,
Hang o're my hoary Face; a murm'ring Brook
Runs at my foot.

VENTIDIUS. Methinks I fancy
My self there too.

ANTONY. The Herd come jumping by me,
And fearless, quench their thirst, while I look on,
And take me for their fellow-Citizen.
More of this Image, more; it lulls my thoughts.

[*Soft Musick again.*

VENTIDIUS. I must disturb him; I can hold no longer.

[*Stands before him.*

ANTONY. *starting up.* Art thou *Ventidius?*
VENTIDIUS. Are you *Antony?*
I'm liker what I was, than you to him
I left you last.
ANTONY. I'm angry.
VENTIDIUS. So am I.
ANTONY. I would be private: leave me.
VENTIDIUS. Sir, I love you,
And therefore will not leave you.
ANTONY. Will not leave me?
Where have you learnt that Answer? Who am I?
VENTIDIUS. My Emperor; the Man I love next Heav'n:
If I said more, I think 'twere scarce a Sin;
Y'are all that's good, and god-like.
ANTONY. All that's wretched.
You will not leave me then?
VENTIDIUS. 'Twas too presuming
To say I would not; but I dare not leave you:
And, 'tis unkind in you to chide me hence
So soon, when I so far have come to see you.
ANTONY. Now thou hast seen me, art thou satisfy'd?
For, if a Friend, thou hast beheld enough;
And, if a Foe, too much.
VENTIDIUS. *weeping.* Look, Emperor, this is no common Deaw,
I have not wept this Forty years; but now
My mother comes afresh into my eyes;
I cannot help her softness.
ANTONY. By Heav'n, he weeps, poor good old Man, he weeps!
The big round drops course one another down
The furrows of his cheeks. Stop 'em, *Ventidius,*
Or I shall blush to death: they set my shame,
That caused 'em, full before me.
VENTIDIUS. I'll do my best.
ANTONY. Sure there's contagion in the tears of Friends:
See, I have caught it too. Believe me, 'tis not
For my own griefs, but thine—Nay, father.
VENTIDIUS. Emperor.

ANTONY. Emperor! Why, that's the style of Victory,
The Conqu'ring Soldier, red with unfelt wounds,
Salutes his General so: but never more
Shall that sound reach my ears.
VENTIDIUS. I warrant you.
ANTONY. *Actium, Actium!*[8] Oh—
VENTIDIUS. It sits too near you.
ANTONY. Here, here it lies; a lump of Lead by day,
And, in my short distracted, nightly slumbers,
The Hag that rides my Dreams—
VENTIDIUS. Out with it; give it vent.
ANTONY. Urge not my shame.
I lost a Battel.
VENTIDIUS. So has *Julius* done.
ANTONY. Thou favour'st me, and speak'st not half thou think'st;
For *Julius* fought it out, and lost it fairly:
But *Antony*—
VENTIDIUS. Nay, stop not.
ANTONY. *Antony,*
(Well, thou wilt have it) like a coward, fled,
Fled while his Soldiers fought; fled first, *Ventidius.*
Thou long'st to curse me, and I give thee leave.
I know thou cam'st prepar'd to rail.
VENTIDIUS. I did.
ANTONY. I'll help thee.—I have been a Man, *Ventidius.*
VENTIDIUS. Yes, and a brave one; but—
ANTONY. I know thy meaning.
But, I have lost my Reason, have disgrac'd
The name of Soldier, with inglorious ease.
In the full Vintage of my flowing honors,
Sate still, and saw it prest by other hands.
Fortune came smiling to my youth, and woo'd it,
And purple greatness met my ripen'd years.
When first I came to Empire, I was born
On Tides of People, crouding to my Triumphs;
The wish of Nations, and the willing World
Receiv'd me as its pledge of future peace;
I was so great, so happy, so belov'd,
Fate could not ruine me; till I took pains,
And work'd against my Fortune, chid her from me,
And turn'd her loose; yet still she came again.
My careless dayes, and my luxurious nights,
At length have weary'd her, and now she's gone,
Gone, gone, divorc'd for ever. Help me, Soldier,

8. At Actium in 31 BC, Antony followed Cleopatra away from the battle.

To curse this Mad-man, this industrious Fool,
Who labour'd to be wretched: pr'ythee, curse me.

VENTIDIUS. No.

ANTONY. Why?

VENTIDIUS. You are too sensible already
Of what y'have done, too conscious of your failings,
And, like a Scorpion, whipt by others first
To fury, sting your self in mad revenge.
I would bring Balm, and pour it in your wounds,
Cure your distemper'd mind, and heal your fortunes.

ANTONY. I know thou would'st.

VENTIDIUS. I will.

ANTONY. Ha, ha, ha, ha.

VENTIDIUS. You laugh.

ANTONY. I do, to see officious love
Give Cordials to the dead.

VENTIDIUS. You would be lost then?

ANTONY. I am.

VENTIDIUS. I say, you are not. Try your fortune.

ANTONY. I have, to th' utmost. Dost thou think me desperate,
Without just cause? No, when I found all lost
Beyond repair, I hid me from the World,
And learnt to scorn it here; which now I do
So heartily, I think it is not worth
The cost of keeping.

VENTIDIUS. Cæsar thinks not so:
He'l thank you for the gift he could not take.
You would be kill'd like *Tully,*[9] would you? do,
Hold out your Throat to *Cæsar,* and dye tamely.

ANTONY. No, I can kill my self; and so resolve.

VENTIDIUS. I can dy with you too, when time shall serve;
But Fortune calls upon us now to live,
To fight, to Conquer.

ANTONY. Sure thou Dream'st, *Ventidius.*

VENTIDIUS. No; 'tis you Dream; you sleep away your hours
In desperate sloth, miscall'd *Phylosophy.*
Up, up, for Honor's sake; twelve Legions wait you,
And long to call you Chief: by painful journeys
I led 'em, patient, both of heat and hunger,
Down from the *Parthian* Marches, to the *Nile.*
'Twill do you good to see their Sun-burnt faces,
Their skar'd cheeks, and chopt° hands; there's virtue in 'em, chapped
They'l sell those mangled limbs at dearer rates
Than yon trim Bands can buy.

9. Cicero was killed by the orders of the triumvirate of Antony, Octavius, and Lepidus in 43 BC; when the soldiers captured his litter, rather than fight, he bent his head to receive the blow.

ANTONY. Where left you them?
VENTIDIUS. I said, in lower *Syria.*
ANTONY. Bring 'em hither;
There may be life in these.
VENTIDIUS. They will not come.
ANTONY. Why did'st thou mock my hopes with promis'd aids
To double my despair? They'r mutinous.
VENTIDIUS. Most firm and loyal.
ANTONY. Yet they will not march
To succor me. O trifler!
VENTIDIUS. They petition
You would make haste to head 'em.
ANTONY. I'm besieg'd.
VENTIDIUS. There's but one way shut up: How came I hither?
ANTONY. I will not stir.
VENTIDIUS. They would perhaps desire
A better reason.
ANTONY. I have never used° accustomed
My Souldiers to demand a reason of
My actions. Why did they refuse to March?
VENTIDIUS. They said they would not fight for *Cleopatra.*
ANTONY. What was't they said?
VENTIDIUS. They said, they would not fight for *Cleopatra.*
Why should they fight indeed, to make her Conquer,
And make you more a Slave? to gain you Kingdoms,
Which, for a kiss, at your next midnight Feast,
You'l sell to her? Then she new-names her Jewels,
And calls this Diamond such or such a Tax,
Each Pendant in her ear shall be a Province.
ANTONY. *Ventidius,* I allow your Tongue free licence
On all my other faults; but, on your life,
No word of *Cleopatra:* She deserves
More World's than I can lose.
VENTIDIUS. Behold, you Pow'rs,
To whom you have intrusted Humankind;
See *Europe, Africk, Asia,* put in ballance,
And all weigh'd down by one light worthless Woman!
I think the gods are *Antony's,* and give,
Like Prodigals, this neather World away,
To none but wastful hands.
ANTONY. You grow presumptuous.
VENTIDIUS. I take the priviledge of plain love to speak.
ANTONY. Plain love! plain arrogance, plain insolence.
Thy Men are Cowards; thou, an envious Traitor;
Who, under seeming honesty, hast vented
The burden of thy rank o'reflowing Gall.

O that thou wert my equal; great in Arms
As the first *Cæsar* was, that I might kill thee
Without a Stain to Honor!

VENTIDIUS. You may kill me;
You have done more already, call'd me Traitor.

ANTONY. Art thou not one?

VENTIDIUS. For showing you your self,
Which none else durst have done? but had I been
That name, which I disdain to speak again,
I needed not have sought your abject fortunes,
Come to partake your fate, to dye with you.
What hindred me t' have led my Conqu'ring Eagles
To fill *Octavius's* Bands? I could have been
A Traitor then, a glorious happy Traitor,
And not have been so call'd.

ANTONY. Forgive me, Soldier:
I've been too passionate.

VENTIDIUS. You thought me false;
Thought my old age betray'd you: kill me, Sir;
Pray kill me; yet you need not, your unkindness
Has left your Sword no work.

ANTONY. I did not think so;
I said it in my rage: pr'ythee forgive me:
Why did'st thou tempt my anger, by discovery
Of what I would not hear?

VENTIDIUS. No Prince but you,
Could merit that sincerity I us'd,
Nor durst another Man have ventur'd it;
But you, ere Love misled your wandring eyes,
Were sure the chief and best of Human Race,
Fram'd in the very pride and boast of Nature,
So perfect, that the gods who form'd you wonder'd
At their own skill, and cry'd *A lucky hit*
Has mended our design. Their envy hindred,
Else you had been immortal, and a pattern,
When Heav'n would work for ostentation sake,
To copy out again.

ANTONY. But *Cleopatra*—
Go on; for I can bear it now.

VENTIDIUS. No more.

ANTONY. Thou dar'st not trust my Passion; but thou may'st:
Thou only lov'st; the rest have flatter'd me.

VENTIDIUS. Heav'n's blessing on your heart, for that kind word.
May I believe you love me? speak again.

ANTONY. Indeed I do. Speak this, and this, and this.

[*Hugging him.*

Thy praises were unjust; but, I'll deserve 'em,
And yet mend all. Do with me what thou wilt;
Lead me to victory, thou know'st the way.
VENTIDIUS. And, Will you leave this—
ANTONY. Pr'ythee, do not curse her,
And I will leave her; though, Heav'n knows, I love
Beyond Life, Conquest, Empire; all, but Honor:
But I will leave her.
VENTIDIUS. That's my Royal Master;
And, Shall we fight?
ANTONY. I warrant thee, old Soldier,
Thou shalt behold me once again in Iron,
And at the head of our old Troops, that beat
The *Parthians,*[10] cry alloud, *Come follow me.*
VENTIDIUS. O now I hear my Emperor! in that word
Octavius fell. Gods, let me see that day,
And, if I have ten years behind, take all;
I'll thank you for th' exchange.
ANTONY. Oh *Cleopatra!*
VENTIDIUS. Again?
ANTONY. I've done: in that last sigh, she went.
Cæsar shall know what 'tis to force a Lover,
From all he holds most dear.
VENTIDIUS. Methinks you breath
Another Soul: Your looks are more Divine;
You speak a Heroe, and you move a God.
ANTONY. O, thou hast fir'd me; my Soul's up in Arms,
And Mans each part about me: once again,
That noble eagerness of fight has seiz'd me;
That eagerness, with which I darted upward
To *Cassius's* Camp: In vain the steepy Hill,
Oppos'd my way; in vain a War of Speares
Sung round my head; and planted on my shield:
I won the Trenches, while my formost Men
Lag'd on the Plain below.
VENTIDIUS. Ye Gods, ye Gods,
For such another hour.
ANTONY. Come on, My Soldier!
Our hearts and armes are still the same: I long
Once more to meet our foes; that Thou and I,
Like Time and Death, marching before our Troops,
May taste fate to 'em; Mowe 'em out a passage,

10. The Parthians were a Middle Eastern nation with numerous victories over the Romans. Ventidius was sent to fight them by Antony and starting in 39 BC won a series of victories over them.

And, entring where the foremost Squadrons yield,
Begin the noble Harvest of the Field.

[*Exeunt.*

ACT II. SCENE I

Enter Cleopatra, Iras, *and* Alexas.

CLEOPATRA. What shall I do, or whither shall I turn?
Ventidius has o'rcome, and he will go.
ALEXAS. He goes to fight for you.
CLEOPATRA. Then he wou'd see me, ere he went to fight:
Flatter me not: if once he goes, he's lost:
And all my hopes destroy'd.
ALEXAS. Does this weak passion
Become a Mighty Queen?
CLEOPATRA. I am no Queen:
Is this to be a Queen, to be besieg'd
By yon insulting *Roman;* and to wait
Each hour the Victor's Chain? These ills are small;
For *Antony* is lost, and I can mourn
For nothing else but him. Now come, *Octavius,*
I have no more to lose; prepare thy Bands;
I'm fit to be a Captive: *Antony*
Has taught my mind the fortune of a Slave.
IRAS. Call Reason to assist you.
CLEOPATRA. I have none,
And none would have: my Love's a noble madness,
Which shows the cause deserv'd it. Moderate sorrow
Fits vulgar Love; and for a vulgar Man:
But I have lov'd with such transcendent passion,
I soard, at first, quite out of Reasons view,
And now am lost above it—No, I'm proud
'Tis thus: Would *Antony* could see me now;
Think you be would not sigh? though he must leave me,
Sure he would sigh; for he is noble-natur'd,
And bears a tender heart: I know him well.
Ah, no, I know him not; I knew him once,
But now 'tis past.
IRAS. Let it be past with you.
Forget him, Madam.
CLEOPATRA. Never, never, *Iras.*
He once was mine; and once, though now 'tis gone,
Leaves a faint Image of possession still.
ALEXAS. Think him unconstant, cruel, and ungrateful.

CLEOPATRA. I cannot: If I could, those thoughts were vain;
Faithless, ungrateful, cruel, though he be,
I still must love him.

Enter *Charmion.*

Now, what news my *Charmion?*
Will he be kind? and, Will he not forsake me?
Am I to live, or dye? nay, Do I live?
Or am I dead? for, when he gave his answer,
Fate took the word, and then I liv'd or dy'd.
CHARMION. I found him, Madam—
CLEOPATRA. A long Speech preparing?
If thou bring'st comfort, hast, and give it me;
For never was more need.
IRAS. I know he loves you.
CLEOPATRA. Had he been kind, her eyes had told me so,
Before her tongue could speak it: now she studies,
To soften what he said. But give me death,
Just as he sent it, *Charmion,* undisguis'd,
And in the words he spoke.
CHARMION. I found him then
Incompass'd round, I think, with Iron Statues;
So mute, so motionless his Soldiers stood,
While awfully he cast his eyes about,
And ev'ry Leaders hopes or fears survey'd:
Methought he look'd resolv'd, and yet not pleas'd.
When he beheld me struggling in the croud,
He blush'd, and bade, make way.
ALEXAS. There's comfort yet.
CHARMION. *Ventidius* fixt his eyes upon my passage,
Severely, as he meant to frown me back,
And sullenly gave place: I told my message,
Just as you gave it, broken and disorder'd;
I numbred in it all your sighs and tears:
And while I mov'd your pitiful request,
That you but only beg'd a last farewel,
He fetch'd an inward groan, and ev'ry time
I nam'd you, sigh'd, as if his heart were breaking,
But, shun'd my eyes, and guiltily look'd down;
He seem'd not now that awful *Antony*
Who shook an Arm'd Assembly with his Nod,
But making show as he would rub his eyes,
Disguis'd and blotted out a falling tear.
CLEOPATRA. Did he then weep? and, was I worth a tear?
If what thou hast to say be not as pleasing,
Tell me no more, but let me dye contented.

CHARMION. He bid me say, He knew himself so well,
He could deny you nothing, if he saw you;
And therefore—
CLEOPATRA. Thou would'st say, he wou'd not see me?
CHARMION. And therefore beg'd you not to use a power,
Which he could ill resist; yet he should ever
Respect you, as he ought.
CLEOPATRA. Is that a word
For *Antony* to use to *Cleopatra?*
O that faint word, *Respect!* how I disdain it!
Disdain my self, for loving after it!
He should have kept that word for cold *Octavia.*
Respect is for a Wife: Am I that thing,
That dull insipid lump, without desires,
And without pow'r to give 'em?
ALEXAS. You misjudge;
You see through Love, and that deludes your sight;
As, what is strait, seems crooked through the Water:
But I, who bear my reason undisturb'd,
Can see this *Antony,* this dreaded Man,
A fearful slave, who fain would run away,
And shuns his Master's eyes: If you pursue him,
My life on't, he still drags a chain along,
That needs must clog his flight.
CLEOPATRA. Could I believe thee!—
ALEXAS. By ev'ry circumstance I know he Loves.
True, he's hard prest, by Intrest and by Honor;
Yet he but doubts, and parlyes, and casts out
Many a long look for succor.
CLEOPATRA. He sends word,
He fears to see my face.
ALEXAS. And would you more?
He shows his weakness who declines the Combat;
And you must urge your fortune. Could he speak
More plainly? To my ears, the Message sounds
Come to my rescue, Cleopatra, *come;*
Come, free me from Ventidius; *from my Tyrant:*
See me, and give me a pretence to leave him.
I hear his Trumpets. This way he must pass.
Please you, retire a while; I'll work him first,
That he may bend more easie.
CLEOPATRA. You shall rule me;
But all, I fear, in vain.

[*Exit with* Charmion and Iras.

ALEXAS. I fear so too;

Though I conceal'd my thoughts, to make her bold:
But, 'tis our utmost means, and Fate befriend it.

[*Withdraws.*

Enter Lictors *with* Fasces;[11] *one bearing the Eagle: then*

Enter Antony *with* Ventidius, *follow'd by other Commanders.*

ANTONY. Octavius is the Minion of blind Chance,
But holds from Virtue nothing.
VENTIDIUS. Has he courage?
ANTONY. But just enough to season him from Coward.
O, 'tis the coldest youth[12] upon a Charge,
The most deliberate fighter! if he ventures
(As in *Illyria* once, they say, he did,
To storm a Town) 'tis when he cannot chuse,
When all the World have fixt their eyes upon him;
And then he lives on that for seven years after.
But, at a close revenge he never fails.
VENTIDIUS. I heard, you challeng'd him.
ANTONY. I did, *Ventidius.*
What think'st thou was his answer? 'twas, so tame,—
He said, he had more wayes than one to dye;
I had not.
VENTIDIUS. Poor!
ANTONY. He has more wayes than one;
But he would chuse 'em all before that one.
VENTIDIUS. He first would choose an Ague, or a Fever.
ANTONY. No: it must be an Ague, not a Fever;
He has not warmth enough to dye by that.
VENTIDIUS. Or old Age, and a Bed.
ANTONY. I, there's his choice.
He would live, like a Lamp, to the last wink,
And crawl upon the utmost verge of life:
O *Hercules!* Why should a Man like this,
Who dares not trust his fate for one great action,
Be all the care of Heav'n? Why should he Lord it
O're Fourscore thousand Men, of whom, each one
Is braver than himself?
VENTIDIUS. You conquer'd for him:
Philippi knows it; there you shar'd with him
That Empire, which your Sword made all your own.
ANTONY. Fool that I was, upon my Eagles Wings
I bore this Wren, till I was tir'd with soaring,
And now he mounts above me.[13]

11. A bundle of rods and an axe carried by attendants as a symbol of the authority of a dignitary.
12. At the time of the play, Octavius is 33 and Antony is 53.
13. At Philippi, in 42 BC Brutus overran the camp of Octavius, and Antony's troops won the battle.

Good Heav'ns, Is this, is this the Man who braves me?
Who bids my age make way? drives me before him,
To the World's ridge, and sweeps me off like rubbish?

VENTIDIUS. Sir, we lose time; the Troops are mounted all.

ANTONY. Then give the word to March:
I long to leave this Prison of a Town,
To joyn thy Legions; and, in open Field,
Once more to show my face. Lead, my Deliverer.

Enter Alexas.

ALEXAS. Great emperor,
In mighty Arms renown'd above Mankind,
But, in soft pity to th' opprest, a God:
This message sends the mournful *Cleopatra*
To her departing Lord.

VENTIDIUS. Smooth Sycophant!

ALEXAS. A thousand wishes, and ten thousand Prayers,
Millions of blessings wait you to the Wars,
Millions of sighs and tears she sends you too,
And would have sent
As many dear embraces to your Arms,
As many parting kisses to your Lips;
But those, she fears, have weary'd you already.

VENTIDIUS. *aside.* False Crocodyle!

ALEXAS. And yet she begs not now, you would not leave her,
That were a wish too mighty for her hopes,
Too presuming
For her low Fortune, and your ebbing love,
That were a wish for her more prosp'rous dayes,
Her blooming beauty, and your growing kindness.

ANTONY. *aside.* Well, I must Man it out.—What would the Queen?

ALEXAS. First, to these noble Warriors, who attend,
Your daring courage in the Chase of Fame,
(Too daring, and too dang'rous for her quiet)
She humbly recommends all she holds dear,
All her own cares and fears, the care of you.

VENTIDIUS. Yes, witness *Actium*.

ANTONY. Let him speak, *Ventidius*.

ALEXAS. You, when his matchless valor bears him forward,
With ardor too Heroick, on his foes,
Fall down, as she would do, before his feet;
Lye in his way, and stop the paths of Death:
Tell him, this God is not invulnerable,
That absent *Cleopatra* bleeds in him;
And, that you may remember her Petition,
She begs you wear these Trifles, as a pawn,
Which, at your wisht return, she will redeem

[*Gives Jewels to the Commanders.*

With all the Wealth of *Ægypt.*
This, to the great *Ventidius* she presents,
Whom she can never count her Enemy,
Because he loves her Lord.

VENTIDIUS. Tell her I'll none on't;
I'm not asham'd of honest Poverty:
Not all the Diamonds of the East can bribe
Ventidius from his faith. I hope to see
These, and the rest of all her sparkling store,
Where they shall more deservingly be plac'd.

ANTONY. And who must wear 'em then?

VENTIDIUS. The wrong'd *Octavia.*

ANTONY. You might have spar'd that word.

VENTIDIUS. And he that Bribe.

ANTONY. But have I no remembrance?

ALEXAS. Yes, a dear one:
Your slave, the Queen—

ANTONY. My Mistress.

ALEXAS. Then your Mistress,
Your Mistress would, she sayes, have sent her Soul,
But that you had long since; she humbly begs
This Ruby bracelet, set with bleeding hearts,
(The emblems of her own) may bind your Arme.

[*Presenting a Bracelet.*

VENTIDIUS. Now, my best Lord, in Honor's name, I ask you,
For Manhood's sake, and for your own dear safety,
Touch not these poyson'd gifts,
Infected by the sender, touch 'em not,
Miriads of blewest Plagues lye underneath 'em,
And more than Aconite° has dipt the Silk. wolfsbane (poison)

ANTONIO. Nay, now you grow too Cynical, *Ventidius.*
A Lady's favors may be worn with honor.
What, to refuse her Bracelet! On my Soul,
When I lye pensive in my Tent alone,
'Twill pass the wakeful hours of Winter nights,
To tell these pretty Beads upon my arm,
To count for every one a soft embrace,
A melting kiss at such and such a time;
And now and then the fury of her love.
When—And what harm's in this?

ALEXAS. None, none my Lord,
But what's to her, that now 'tis past for ever.

ANTONY. *going to tye it.* We Soldiers are so awkward—help me tye it.

ALEXAS. In faith, my Lord, we Courtiers too are aukward

In these affairs: so are all Men indeed;
Ev'n I, who am not one. But shall I speak?
ANTONY. Yes, freely.
ALEXAS. Then, my Lord, fair hands alone
Are fit to tye it; she, who sent it, can.
VENTIDIUS. Hell, Death; this Eunuch Pandar ruins you.
You will not see her?

[ALEXAS *whispers an Attendant, who goes out.*

ANTONY. But to take my leave.
VENTIDIUS. Then I have washed an *Æthiope.* Y'are undone;
Y'are in the Toils;° y'are taken; y'are destroy'd: [nets used in hunting]
Her eyes do *Cæsar's* work.
ANTONY. You fear too soon.
I'm constant to my self: I know my strength;
And yet she shall not think me Barbarous, neither;
Born in the depths of *Africk:* I am a *Roman,*
Bred in the Rules of soft humanity.
A guest, and kindly us'd, should bid farewel.
VENTIDIUS. You do not know
How weak you are to her, how much an Infant,
You are not proof against a smile, or glance;
A sigh will quite disarm you.
ANTONY. See, she comes!
Now you shall find your error. Gods, I thank you:
I form'd the danger greater than it was,
And now 'tis near, 'tis lessen'd.
VENTIDIUS. Mark the end yet.

Enter Cleopatra, Charmion, *and* Iras.

ANTONY. Well, Madam, we are met.
CLEOPATRA. Is this a Meeting?
Then, we must part?
ANTONY. We must.
CLEOPATRA. Who sayes we must?
ANTONY. Our own hard fates.
CLEOPATRA. We make those Fates our selves.
ANTONY. Yes, we have made 'em; we have lov'd each other,
Into our mutual ruin.
CLEOPATRA. The Gods have seen my Joys with envious eyes;
I have no friends in Heav'n, and all the World,
(As 'twere the bus'ness of Mankind to part us)
Is arm'd against my Love: ev'n you your self
Joyn with the rest; you, you are arm'd against me.
ANTONY. I will be justify'd in all I do
To late Posterity, and therefore hear me.
If I mix a lye

With any truth, reproach me freely with it;
Else, favor me with silence.
CLEOPATRA. You command me,
And I am dumb.
VENTIDIUS. *aside.* I like this well: he shows Authority.
ANTONY. That I derive my ruin
From you alone—
CLEOPATRA. O Heav'ns! I ruin you!
ANTONY. You promis'd me your silence, and you break it
Ere I have scarce begun.
CLEOPATRA. Well, I obey you.
ANTONY. When I beheld you first, it was in *Ægypt,*
Ere *Cæsar* saw your Eyes; you gave me love,
And were too young to know it; that I setled
Your Father in his Throne, was for your sake:
I left th' acknowledgment for time to ripen.
Cæsar stept in, and, with a greedy hand
Pluck'd the green fruit, ere the first blush of red,
Yet cleaving to the bough. He was my Lord,
And was, beside, too great for me to rival,
But, I deserv'd you first, though he enjoy'd you.
When, after, I beheld you in *Cilicia,*
An enemy to *Rome,* I pardon'd you.
CLEOPATRA. I clear'd my self—
ANTONY. Again you break your Promise.
I lov'd you still, and took your weak excuses,
Took you into my bosome, stain'd by *Cæsar,*
And not half mine: I went to *Ægypt* with you,
And hid me from the bus'ness of the World,
Shut out inquiring Nations from my sight,
To give whole years to you.
VENTIDIUS. Yes, to your shame be't spoken.

[*Aside.*

ANTONY. How I lov'd
Witness ye Dayes and Nights, and all ye hours,
That Danc'd away with Down upon your Feet,
As all your bus'ness were to count my passion.
One day past by, and nothing saw but Love;
Another came, and still 'twas only Love:
The Suns were weary'd out with looking on,
And I untyr'd with loving.
I saw you ev'ry day, and all the day;
And ev'ry day was still but as the first:
So eager was I still to see you more.
VENTIDIUS. 'Tis all too true.

ANTONY. *Fulvia,* my Wife, grew jealous,
As she indeed had reason; rais'd a War
In *Italy,* to call me back.
VENTIDIUS. But yet
You went not.
ANTONY. While within your arms I lay,
The World fell mouldring from my hands each hour,
And left me scarce a grasp (I thank your love for't.)
VENTIDIUS. Well push'd: that last was home.
CLEOPATRA. Yet may I speak?
ANTONY. If I have urg'd a falshood, yes; else, not.
Your silence says, I have not. *Fulvia* dy'd;
(Pardon, you gods, with my unkindness dy'd.)
To set the World at Peace, I took *Octavia,*
This *Cæsar's* Sister; in her pride of youth
And flow'r of Beauty did I wed that Lady,
Whom blushing I must praise, because I left her.
You call'd; my Love obey'd the fatal summons:
This rais'd the *Roman* Arms; the Cause was yours.
I would have fought by Land, where I was stronger;
You hindred it: yet, when I fought at Sea,
Forsook me fighting; and (Oh stain to Honor!
Oh lasting shame!) I knew not that I fled;
But fled to follow you.
VENTIDIUS. What haste she made to hoist her purple Sails!
And, to appear magnificent in flight,
Drew half our strength away.
ANTONIO. All this you caus'd.
And, Would you multiply more ruins on me?
This honest Man, my best, my only friend,
Has gather'd up the Shipwreck of my Fortunes;
Twelve Legions I have left, my last recruits,
And you have watch'd the news, and bring your eyes
To seize them too. If you have ought to answer,
Now speak, you have free leave.
ALEXAS. *aside.* She stands confounded:
Despair is in her eyes.
VENTIDIUS. Now lay a Sigh i'th' way to stop his passage:
Prepare a Tear, and bid it for his Legions;
'Tis like they shall be sold.
CLEOPATRA. How shall I plead my cause, when you, my Judge
Already have condemn'd me? Shall I bring
The Love you bore me for my Advocate?
That now is turn'd against me, that destroys me;
For, love once past, is, at the best, forgotten;
But oftner sours to hate: 'twill please my Lord

To ruine me, and therefore I'll be guilty.
But, could I once have thought it would have pleas'd you,
That you would pry, with narrow searching eyes
Into my faults, severe to my destruction,
And watching all advantages with care,
That serve to make me wretched? Speak, my Lord,
For I end here. Though I deserved this usage,
Was it like you to give it?

ANTONY. O you wrong me,
To think I sought this parting, or desir'd
To accuse you more than what will clear my self,
And justifie this breach.

CLEOPATRA. Thus low I thank you.
And, since my innocence will not offend,
I shall not blush to own it.

VENTIDIUS. After this
I think she'll blush at nothing.

CLEOPATRA. You seemed griev'd,
(And therein you are kind) that *Cæsar* first
Enjoy'd my love, though you deserv'd it better:
I grieve for that, my Lord, much more than you;
For, had I first been yours, it would have sav'd
My second choice: I never had been his,
And ne'r had been but yours. But *Cæsar* first,
You say, possess'd my love. Not so, my Lord:
He first possess'd my Person; you my Love:
Cæsar loved me; but I lov'd *Antony.*
If I endur'd him after, 'twas because
I judg'd it due to the first name of Men;
And, half constrain'd, I gave, as to a Tyrant,
What he would take by force.

VENTIDIUS. O Syren! Syren!
Yet grant that all the love, she boasts were true,
Has she not ruin'd you? I still urge that,
The fatal consequence.

CLEOPATRA. The consequence indeed,
For I dare challenge him, my greatest foe,
To say it was design'd: 'tis true, I lov'd you,
And kept you far from an uneasie Wife,
(Such *Fulvia* was.)
Yes, but he'll say, you left *Octavia* for me;—
And, Can you blame me to receive that love,
Which quitted such desert, for worthless me?
How often have I wish'd some other *Cæsar,*
Great as the first, and as the second young,
Would court my Love, to be refus'd for you!

VENTIDIUS. Words, words; but *Actium,* Sir, remember *Actium.*

CLEOPATRA. Ev'n there, I dare his malice. True, I Counsel'd
To fight at Sea; but, I betray'd you not.
I fled; but not to th'Enemy. 'Twas fear;
Would I had been a Man, not to have fear'd,
For none would then have envy'd me your friendship,
Who envy me your Love.
ANTONY. We're both unhappy:
If nothing else, yet our ill fortune parts us.
Speak; Would you have me perish, by my stay?
CLEOPATRA. If as a friend you ask my Judgment, go;
If as a Lover, stay. If you must perish:
'Tis a hard word; but stay.
VENTIDIUS. See now th' effects of her so boasted love!
She strives to drag you down to ruine with her:
But, could she scape without you, oh how soon
Would she let go her hold, and haste to shore,
And never look behind!
CLEOPATRA. Then judge my love by this.

[*Giving* Antony *a Writing.*

Could I have borne
A life or death, a happiness or woe
From yours divided, this had giv'n me means.
ANTONY. By *Hercules,* the Writing of *Octavius!*
I know it well; 'tis that Proscribing hand,
Young as it was, that led the way to mine,
And left me but the second place in Murder.—
See, see, *Ventidius!* here he offers *Ægypt,*
And joyns all *Syria* to it, as a present,
So, in requital, she forsake my fortunes,
And joyn her Arms with his.
CLEOPATRA. And yet you leave me!
You leave me, *Antony;* and, yet I love you.
Indeed I do: I have refus'd a Kingdom,
That's a Trifle:
For I could part with life; with any thing,
But onely you. O let me die but with you!
Is that a hard request?
ANTONY. Next living with you,
'Tis all that Heav'n can give.
ALEXAS. *aside.* He melts; We conquer.
CLEOPATRA. No: you shall go: your Int'rest calls you hence;
Yes, your dear int'rest pulls too strong, for these
Weak Armes to hold you here.—

[*Takes his hand.*

Go; leave me, Soldier;
(For you're no more a Lover:) leave me dying:
Push me all pale and panting, from your bosome,
And, when your March begins, let one run after,
Breathless almost for Joy, and cry, *She's dead!*
The Souldiers shout; you then perhaps may sigh,
And muster all your *Roman* gravity:
Ventidius chides; and strait your Brow cleares up,
As I had never been.

ANTONY. Gods, 'tis too much; too much for Man to bear!

CLEOPATRA. What is't for me then,
A weak forsaken Woman? and a Lover?—
Here let me breathe my last: envy me not
This minute in your Armes: I'll dye apace:
As fast as ere I can; and end your trouble.

ANTONY. Dye! Rather let me perish: looss'nd Nature
Leap from its hinges, sink the props of Heav'n,
And fall the Skyes to crush the neather World.
My Eyes, my Soul; my all!—

[*Embraces her.*

VENTIDIUS. And what's this Toy,
In ballance with your fortune, Honor, Fame?

ANTONY. What is't, *Ventidius?* it out-weighs 'em all;
Why, we have more than conquer'd *Cæsar* now:
My Queen's not only Innocent, but Loves me.
This, this is she who drags me down to ruin!
But, could she scape without me, with what haste
Would she let slip her hold, and make to shore,
And never look behind!
Down on thy knees, Blasphemer as thou art,
And ask forgiveness of wrong'd Innocence.

VENTIDIUS. I'll rather dye, than take it. Will you go?

ANTONY. Go! Whither? Go from all that's excellent!
Faith, Honor, Virtue, all good things forbid,
That I should go from her, who sets my love
Above the price of Kingdoms. Give, you Gods,
Give to your Boy, your *Cæsar,*
This Rattle of a Globe to play withal,
This Gu-gau° World, and put him cheaply off: geegaw
I'll not be pleased with less than *Cleopatra.*

CLEOPATRA. She's wholly yours. My heart's so full of joy,
That I shall do some wild extravagance
Of Love, in publick; and the foolish World,
Which knows not tenderness, will think me Mad.

VENTIDIUS. O Women! Women! Women! all the gods

Have not such pow'r of doing good to Man,
As you of doing harm.

[*Exit.*

ANTONY. Our men are Arm'd.
Unbar the Gate that looks to *Cæsar's* Camp;
I would revenge the Treachery he meant me:
And long security makes Conquest easie.
I'm eager to return before I go;
For, all the pleasures I have known, beat thick
On my remembrance: How I long for night!
That both the sweets of mutual love may try,
And once Triumph o're *Cæsar* ere we dye.

[*Exeunt.*

ACT III. SCENE I.

At one door, Enter Cleopatra, Charmion, Iras, *and* Alexas, *a Train of* Ægyptians: *at the other,* Antony *and* Romans.

The entrance on both sides is prepar'd by Musick; the Trumpets first sounding on Antony's *part: then answer'd by Timbrels, &c. on* Cleopatra's.

Charmion *and* Iras *hold a Laurel Wreath betwixt them. A Dance of* Ægyptians. *After the Ceremony,* Cleopatra *Crowns* Antony.

ANTONY. I thought how those white arms would fold me in,
And strain me close, and melt me into love;
So pleas'd with that sweet Image, I sprung forwards,
And added all my strength to every blow.
CLEOPATRA. Come to me, come, my Soldier, to my Arms.
You've been too long away from my embraces;
But, when I have you fast, and all my own,
With broken murmurs, and with amorous sighs,
I'll say, you were unkind, and punish you,
And mark you red with many an eager kiss.
ANTONY. My Brighter *Venus!*
CLEOPATRA. O my greater *Mars!*
ANTONY. Thou joinst us well, my Love!
Suppose me come from the *Phlegræan* plains,[14]
Where gasping Gyants lay, cleft by my Sword:
And Mountain tops par'd off each other blow,
To bury those I slew: receive me, goddess:
Let *Cæsar* spread his subtile Nets, like *Vulcan,*
In thy embraces I would be beheld

14. Mythical site of the victory of Hercules and the gods over the giants.

By Heav'n and Earth at once:
And make their envy what they meant their sport.
Let those who took us blush; I would love on,
With awful State, regardless of their frowns,
As their superior gods.
There's no satiety of Love in thee;
Enjoy'd, thou still art new; perpetual Spring
Is in thy armes; the ripen'd fruit but falls,
And blossoms rise to fill its empty place;
And I grow rich by giving.

Enter VENTIDIUS, *and stands apart.*

ALEXAS. O, now the danger's past, your General comes.
He joyns not in your joys, nor minds your Triumphs;
But, with contracted brows, looks frowning on,
As envying your Success.
ANTONY. Now, on my Soul, he loves me; truly loves me;
He never flatter'd me in any vice,
But awes me with his virtue: even this minute,
Methinks he has a right of chiding me.
Lead to the Temple: I'll avoid his presence;
It checks too strong upon me.

[*Exeunt the rest.*
[*As* Antony *is going,* Ventidius *pulls him by the Robe.*

VENTIDIUS. Emperor.
ANTONY. *looking back.* 'Tis the old argument; I pr'ythee, spare me.
VENTIDIUS. But this one hearing, Emperor.
ANTONY. Let go
My Robe; or, by my Father *Hercules*—
VENTIDIUS. By Hercules his Father, that's yet greater,
I bring you somewhat you would wish to know.
ANTONY. Thou see'st we are observ'd; attend me here,
And I'll return.

[*Exit.*

VENTIDIUS. I am waining in his favor, yet I love him;
I love this Man, who runs to meet his ruine;
And, sure the gods, like me, are fond of him:
His Virtues lye so mingled with his Crimes,
As would confound their choice to punish one,
And not reward the other.

Enter Antony.

ANTONY. We can conquer, you see, without your aid.
We have dislodg'd their Troops,
They look on us at distance, and, like Curs

Scap'd from the Lion's paws, they bay far off,
And lick their wounds, and faintly threaten War.
Five thousand *Romans,* with their faces upward,
Lye breathless on the Plain.
VENTIDIUS. 'Tis well: and he
Who lost 'em, could have spar'd Ten thousand more.
Yet if, by this advantage, you could gain
An easier Peace, while *Cæsar* doubts the Chance
Of Arms!—
ANTONY. O think not on't, *Ventidius;*
The Boy pursues my ruin, he'll no peace:
His malice is considerate in advantage;
O, he's the coolest Murderer, so stanch,
He kills, and keeps his temper.
VENTIDIUS. Have you no friend
In all his Army, who has power to move him?
Mæcenas, or *Agrippa* might do much.
ANTONY. They're both too deep in *Cæsar's* interests.
We'll work it out by dint of Sword, or perish.
VENTIDIUS. Fain I would find some other.
ANTONY. Thank thy love.
Some four or five such Victories as this
Will save thy further pains.
VENTIDIUS. Expect no more; *Cæsar* is on his Guard:
I know, Sir, you have conquer'd against ods;
But still you draw Supplies from one poor Town,
And of *Ægyptians:* he has all the World,
And, at his back, Nations come pouring in,
To fill the gaps you make. Pray think again.
ANTONY. Why dost thou drive me from my self, to search
For Foreign aids? to hunt my memory,
And range all o're a waste and barren place
To find a Friend? The wretched have no Friends—
Yet I had one, the bravest youth of *Rome,*
Whom *Cæsar* loves beyond the love of Women;
He could resolve his mind, as Fire does Wax,
From that hard rugged Image, melt him down,
And mould him in what softer form he pleas'd.
VENTIDIUS. Him would I see; that man of all the world:
Just such a one we want.
ANTONY. He lov'd me too,
I was his Soul; he liv'd not but in me:
We were so clos'd within each other's brests,
The rivets were not found that join'd us first.
That does not reach us yet: we were so mixt,
As meeting streams, both to our selves were lost;

We were one mass; we could not give or take,
But from the same; for he was I, I he.

VENTIDIUS. *aside.* He moves as I would wish him.

ANTONY. After this,
I need not tell his name: 'twas *Dollabella.*

VENTIDIUS. He's now in *Cæsar's* Camp.

ANTONY. No matter where,
Since he's no longer mine. He took unkindly,
That I forbade him *Cleopatra's* sight;
Because I fear'd he lov'd her: he confest
He had a warmth, which, for my sake, he stifled;
For 'twere impossible that two, so one,
Should not have lov'd the same. When he departed,
He took no leave; and that confirm'd my thoughts.

VENTIDIUS. It argues that he lov'd you more than her,
Else he had staid; but he perceiv'd you jealous,
And would not grieve his friend: I know he loves you.

ANTONY. I should have seen him then ere now.

VENTIDIUS. Perhaps
He has thus long been lab'ring for your peace.

ANTONY. Would he were here.

VENTIDIUS. Would you believe he lov'd you?
I read your answer in your eyes; you would.
Not to conceal it longer, he has sent
A Messenger from *Cæsar's* Camp, with Letters.

ANTONY. Let him appear.

VENTIDIUS. I'll bring him instantly.

[*Exit* Ventidius, *and re-enters immediately with* Dollabella.

ANTONY. 'Tis he himself, himself, by holy Friendship!

[*Runs to embrace him.*

Art thou return'd at last, my better half?
Come, give me all my self. Let me not live,
If the young Bridegroom, longing for his night,
Was ever half so fond.

DOLLABELLA. I must be silent; for my soul is busie
About a nobler work: she's new come home,
Like a long-absent man, and wanders o'er
Each room, a stranger to her own, to look
If all be safe.

ANTONY. Thou hast what's left of me.
For I am now so sunk from what I was,
Thou find'st me at my lowest water-mark.
The Rivers that ran in, and rais'd my fortunes,
Are all dry'd up, or take another course:
What I have left is from my native Spring;

I've still a heart that swells, in scorn of fate,
And lifts me to my banks.
DOLLABELLA. Still you are Lord of all the World to me.
ANTONY. Why, then I yet am so; for thou art all.
If I had any joy when thou wert absent,
I grudg'd it to my self; methought I robb'd
Thee of thy part. But, Oh my *Dollabella!*
Thou hast beheld me other than I am.
Hast thou not seen my morning Chambers fill'd
With Scepter'd Slaves, who waited to salute me:
With Eastern Monarchs, who forgot the Sun,
To worship my uprising? Menial Kings
Ran coursing up and down my Palace-yard,
Stood silent in my presence, watch'd my eyes,
And, at my least command, all started out,
Like Racers to the Goal.
DOLLABELLA. Slaves to your fortune.
ANTONY. Fortune is *Cæsar's* now; and what am I?
VENTIDIUS. What you have made your self; I will not flatter.
ANTONY. Is this friendly done?
DOLLABELLA. Yes, when his end is so, I must join with him;
Indeed I must, and yet you must not chide;
Why am I else your friend?
ANTONY. Take heed, young man,
How thou upbraid'st my love: The Queen has eyes,
And thou too hast a Soul. Canst thou remember
When, swell'd with hatred, thou beheld'st her first,
As accessary to thy Brothers death?
DOLLABELLA. Spare my remembrance; 'twas a guilty day,
And still the blush hangs here.
ANTONY. To clear her self,
For sending him no aid, she came from *Ægypt.*
Her Gally down the Silver *Cydnus* row'd,
The Tackling Silk, the Streamers wav'd with Gold,
The gentle Winds were lodg'd in Purple sails:
Her Nymphs, like *Nereids,* round her Couch were plac'd;
Where she, another Sea-born *Venus,* lay.
DOLLABELLA. No more: I would not hear it.
ANTONY. O, you must!
She lay, and leant her cheek upon her hand,
And cast a look so languishingly sweet,
As if, secure of all beholders hearts,
Neglecting, she could take 'em: Boys, like *Cupids,*
Stood fanning, with their painted wings, the winds
That plaid about her face: but if she smil'd,
A darting glory seem'd to blaze abroad:
That mens desiring eyes were never weary'd;

But hung upon the object: to soft Flutes
The Silver Oars kept time; and while they plaid,
The hearing gave new pleasure to the sight;
And both to thought: 'twas Heav'n, or somewhat more;
For she so charm'd all hearts, that gazing crowds
Stood panting on the shore, and wanted breath
To give their welcome voice.
Then, *Dollabella,* where was then thy Soul?
Was not thy fury quite disarm'd with wonder?
Didst thou not shrink behind me from those eyes
And whisper in my ear, *Oh tell her not*
That I accus'd her with my Brothers death?

DOLLABELLA. And should my weakness be a plea for yours?
Mine was an age when love might be excus'd,
When kindly warmth, and when my springing youth
Made it a debt to Nature. Yours—

VENTIDIUS. Speak boldly.
Yours, he would say, in your declining age,
When no more heat was left but what you forc'd,
When all the sap was needful for the Trunk,
When it went down, then you constrain'd the course,
And robb'd from Nature, to supply desire;
In you (I would not use so harsh a word)
But 'tis but plain dotage.

ANTONY. Ha!

DOLLABELLA. 'Twas urg'd too home.
But yet the loss was private that I made;
'Twas but my self I lost: I lost no Legions;
I had no World to lose, no peoples love.

ANTONY. This from a friend?

DOLLABELLA. Yes, *Antony,* a true one;
A friend so tender, that each word I speak
Stabs my own heart, before it reach your ear.
O, judge me not less kind, because I chide:
To *Cæsar* I excuse you.

ANTONY. O ye Gods!
Have I then liv'd to be excus'd to *Cæsar?*

DOLLABELLA. As to your equal.

ANTONY. Well, he's but my equal:
While I wear this,° he never shall be more. (i.e., his sword)

DOLLABELLA. I bring Conditions from him.

ANTONY. Are they Noble?
Methinks thou shouldst not bring 'em else; yet he
Is full of deep dissembling; knows no Honour,
Divided from his Int'rest. Fate mistook him;
For Nature meant him for an Usurer:
He's fit indeed to buy, not conquer Kingdoms.

VENTIDIUS. Then, granting this,
What pow'r was theirs who wrought so hard a temper
To honourable Terms?
ANTONY. It was my *Dollabella,* or some God.
DOLLABELLA. Nor I; nor yet *Mæcenas,* nor *Agrippa:*
They were your Enemies; and I a Friend
Too weak alone; yet 'twas a *Roman's* deed.
ANTONY. 'Twas like a *Roman* done: show me that man
Who has preserv'd my life, my love, my honour;
Let me but see his face.
VENTIDIUS. That task is mine,
And, Heav'n, thou know'st how pleasing.

[*Exit* VENTIDIUS.

DOLLABELLA. You'll remember
To whom you stand oblig'd?
ANTONY. When I forget it,
Be thou unkind, and that's my greatest curse.
My Queen shall thank him too.
DOLLABELLA. I fear she will not.
ANTONY. But she shall do't: the Queen, my *Dollabella!*
Hast thou not still some grudgings of thy Fever?
DOLLABELLA. I would not see her lost.
ANTONY. When I forsake her,
Leave me, my better Stars; for she has truth
Beyond her beauty. *Cæsar* tempted her,
At no less price than Kingdoms, to betray me;
But she resisted all: and yet thou chid'st me
For loving her too well. Could I do so?
DOLLABELLA. Yes; there's my reason.

Re-enter Ventidius, *with* Octavia, *leading* Antony's *two little Daughters.*

ANTONY. Where?—Octavia there!

(Starting back.)

VENTIDIUS. What, is she poyson to you? a Disease?
Look on her, view her well; and those she brings:
Are they all strangers to your eyes? has Nature
No secret call, no whisper they are yours?
DOLLABELLA. For shame, my Lord, if not for love, receive 'em
With kinder eyes. If you confess a man,
Meet 'em, embrace 'em, bid 'em welcome to you.
Your arms should open, ev'n without your knowledge,
To clasp 'em in; your feet should turn to wings,
To bear you to 'em; and your eyes dart out,
And aim a kiss ere you could reach the lips.
ANTONY. I stood amaz'd to think how they came hither.

VENTIDIUS. I sent for 'em; I brought 'em in unknown
To *Cleopatra*'s Guards.
DOLLABELLA. Yet are you cold?
OCTAVIA. Thus long I have attended for my welcome;
Which, as a stranger, sure I might expect.
Who am I?
ANTONY. *Cæsar*'s sister.
OCTAVIA. That's unkind!
Had I been nothing more than *Cæsar*'s Sister,
Know, I had still remained in *Cæsar*'s camp;
But your *Octavia,* your much injur'd Wife,
Tho' banish'd from your Bed, driv'n from your House,
In spite of *Cæsar*'s Sister, still is yours.
'Tis true, I have a heart disdains your coldness,
And prompts me not to seek what you should offer;
But a Wife's Virtue still surmounts that pride:
I come to claim you as my own; to show
My duty first, to ask, nay beg, your kindness:
Your hand, my Lord; 'tis mine, and I will have it.

[*Taking his hand.*

VENTIDIUS. Do, take it, thou deserv'st it.
DOLLABELLA. On my Soul,
And so she does: she's neither too submissive,
Nor yet too haughty; but so just a mean,
Shows, as it ought, a Wife and *Roman* too.
ANTONY. I fear, *Octavia,* you have begg'd my life.
OCTAVIA. Begg'd it, my Lord?
ANTONY. Yes, begg'd it, my Ambassadress,
Poorly and basely begg'd it of your Brother.
OCTAVIA. Poorly and basely I could never beg;
Nor could my Brother grant.
ANTONY. Shall I, who, to my kneeling Slave, could say,
Rise up, and be a King; shall I fall down
And cry, *Forgive me,* Cæsar? shall I set
A Man, my Equal, in the place of *Jove,*
As he could give me being? No; that word,
Forgive, would choke me up,
And die upon my tongue.
DOLLABELLA. You shall not need it.
ANTONY. I will not need it. Come, you've all betray'd me:
My Friend too! To receive some vile conditions.
My Wife has bought me, with her prayers and tears;
And now I must become her branded Slave.
In every peevish mood, she will upbraid
The life she gave: if I but look awry,
She cries *I'll tell my Brother.*

OCTAVIA. My hard fortune
Subjects me still to your unkind mistakes.
But the Conditions I have brought are such
You need not blush to take: I love your Honour,
Because 'tis mine; it never shall be said,
Octavia's Husband was her Brother's Slave.
Sir, you are free; free, ev'n from her you loath;
For, tho' my Brother bargains for your love,
Makes me the price and cement of your peace,
I have a Soul like yours; I cannot take
Your love as alms, nor beg what I deserve.
I'll tell my Brother we are reconcil'd;
He shall draw back his Troops, and you shall march
To rule the East: I may be dropt at *Athens;*
No matter where, I never will complain,
But only keep the barren Name of Wife,
And rid you of the trouble.
VENTIDIUS. Was ever such a strife of sullen Honour!
Both scorn to be oblig'd.
DOLLABELLA. O, she has touched him in the tender'st part;
See how he reddens with despight and shame
To be out-done in Generosity!
VENTIDIUS. See how he winks! how he dries up a tear,
That fain would fall!
ANTONY. *Octavia,* I have heard you, and must praise
The greatness of your Soul;
But cannot yield to what you have propos'd:
For I can ne'er be conquer'd but by love;
And you do all for duty. You would free me,
And would be dropt at *Athens;* was't not so?
OCTAVIA. It was, my Lord.
ANTONY. Then I must be oblig'd
To one who loves me not, who, to her self,
May call me thankless and ungrateful Man:
I'll not endure it, no.
VENTIDIUS. *aside.* I'm glad it pinches there.
OCTAVIA. Would you triumph o'er poor *Octavia*'s Virtue?
That pride was all I had to bear me up;
That you might think you ow'd me for your life,
And ow'd it to my duty, not my love.
I have been injur'd, and my haughty Soul
Could brook but ill the Man who slights my Bed.
ANTONY. Therefore you love me not.
OCTAVIA. Therefore, my Lord,
I should not love you.
ANTONY. Therefore you wou'd leave me?

OCTAVIA. And therefore I should leave you—if I could.
DOLLABELLA. Her Souls too great, after such injuries,
To say she loves; and yet she lets you see it.
Her modesty and silence plead her cause.
ANTONY. O, *Dollabella,* which way shall I turn?
I find a secret yielding in my Soul;
But *Cleopatra,* who would die with me,
Must she be left? Pity pleads for *Octavia;*
But does it not plead more for *Cleopatra?*
VENTIDIUS. Justice and Pity both plead for *Octavia;*
For *Cleopatra,* neither.
One would be ruin'd with you; but she first
Had ruin'd you: the other, you have ruin'd,
And yet she would preserve you.
In every thing their merits are unequal.
ANTONY. O, my distracted Soul!
OCTAVIA. Sweet Heav'n compose it.
Come, come, my Lord, if I can pardon you,
Methinks you should accept it. Look on these;
Are they not yours? Or stand they thus neglected
As they are mine? Go to him, Children, go;
Kneel to him, take him by the hand, speak to him;
For you may speak, and he may own you too,
Without a blush; and so he cannot all
His Children: go, I say, and pull him to me,
And pull him to your selves, from that bad Woman.
You, *Agrippina,* hang upon his arms;
And you, *Antonia,* clasp about his waste:
If he will shake you off, if he will dash you
Against the Pavement, you must bear it, Children;
For you are mine, and I was born to suffer.

[*Here the Children go to him,* &c.

VENTIDIUS. Was ever sight so moving! Emperor!
DOLLABELLA. Friend!
OCTAVIA. Husband!
BOTH CHILDREN. Father!
ANTONY. I am vanquish'd: take me,
Octavia; take me, Children; share me all.

(Embracing them.)

I've been a thriftless Debtor to your loves,
And run out much, in riot, from your stock;
But all shall be amended.
OCTAVIA. O blest hour!
DOLLABELLA. O happy change!

VENTIDIUS. My joy stops at my tongue;
But it has found two chanels here for one,
And bubbles out above.
ANTONY. *to Octavia.* This is thy Triumph; lead me where thou wilt;
Ev'n to thy Brothers Camp.
OCTAVIA. All there are yours.

Enter ALEXAS *hastily.*

ALEXAS. The Queen, my Mistress, sir, and yours—
ANTONY. 'Tis past.
Octavia, you shall stay this night: To morrow,
Cæsar and we are one.

[*Exit leading* Octavia; Dollabella, *and the Children follow.*

VENTIDIUS. There's news for you; run, my officious Eunuch,
Be sure to be the first; haste forward:
Haste, my dear Eunuch, haste.

[*Exit.*

ALEXAS. This downright fighting Fool, this thick-scull'd Hero,
This blunt unthinking Instrument of death,
With plain dull Virtue, has out-gone my Wit:
Pleasure forsook my early'st Infancy,
The luxury of others robb'd my Cradle,
And ravish'd thence the promise of a Man:
Cast out from Nature, disinherited
Of what her meanest Children claim by kind;
Yet, greatness kept me from contempt: that's gone.
Had *Cleopatra* follow'd my advice,
Then he had been betray'd who now forsakes.
She dies for love; but she has known its joys:
Gods, is this just, that I, who know no joys,
Must die, because she loves?

Enter Cleopatra, Charmion, Iras, *Train.*

Oh, Madam, I have seen what blasts my eyes!
Octavia's here!
CLEOPATRA. Peace with that Raven's note.
I know it too; and now am in
The pangs of death.
ALEXAS. You are no more a Queen;
Ægypt is lost.
CLEOPATRA. What tell'st thou me of *Ægypt?*
My Life, my Soul is lost! *Octavia* has him!
O fatal name to *Cleopatra*'s love!
My kisses, my embraces now are hers;
While I—But thou hast seen my Rival; speak,

Does she deserve this blessing? Is she fair,
Bright as a Goddess? and is all perfection
Confin'd to her? It is. Poor I was made
Of that course matter which, when she was finish'd,
The Gods threw by, for rubbish.

ALEXAS. She's indeed a very Miracle.

CLEOPATRA. Death to my hopes, a Miracle!

ALEXAS. *bowing.* A Miracle;
I mean of Goodness; for in Beauty, Madam,
You make all wonders cease.

CLEOPATRA. I was too rash:
Take this in part of recompense. But, Oh,

[*Giving a Ring.*

I fear thou flatter'st me.

CHARMION. She comes! she's here!

IRAS. Flie, Madam, *Cæsar*'s Sister!

CLEOPATRA. Were she the Sister of the Thund'rer *Jove,*
And bore her Brothers Lightning in her eyes,
Thus would I face my Rival.

[*Meets* Octavia *with* Ventidius. Octavia *bears up to her. Their Trains come up on either side.*

OCTAVIA. I need not ask if you are *Cleopatra,*
Your haughty carriage—

CLEOPATRA. Shows I am a Queen:
Nor need I ask you, who you are.

OCTAVIA. A *Roman:*
A name, that makes, and can unmake a queen.

CLEOPATRA. Your Lord, the Man who serves me, is a *Roman.*

OCTAVIA. He was a *Roman,* till he lost that name,
To be a Slave in *Ægypt;* but I come
To free him thence.

CLEOPATRA. Peace, peace, my Lover's *Juno.*
When he grew weary of that Houshold-Clog,
He chose my easier bonds.

OCTAVIA. I wonder not.
Your bonds are easie; you have long been practis'd
In that lascivious art: he's not the first
For whom you spread your snares: let *Cæsar* witness.

CLEOPATRA. I lov'd not *Cæsar;* 'twas but gratitude
I paid his love: The worst your malice can,
Is but to say the greatest of Mankind
Has been my Slave. The next, but far above him,
In my esteem, is he whom Law calls yours,
But whom his love made mine.

OCTAVIA. *coming up close to her.* I would view nearer

That face, which has so long usurp'd my right,
To find th' inevitable charms, that catch
Mankind so sure, that ruin'd my dear Lord.
CLEOPATRA. O, you do well to search; for had you known
But half these charms, you had not lost his heart.
OCTAVIA. Far be their knowledge from a *Roman* Lady,
Far from a modest Wife. Shame of our Sex,
Dost thou not blush, to own those black endearments
That make sin pleasing?
CLEOPATRA. You may blush, who want 'em.
If bounteous Nature, if indulgent Heav'n
Have giv'n me charms to please the bravest Man;
Should I not thank 'em? should I be asham'd,
And not be proud? I am, that he has lov'd me;
And, when I love not him, Heav'n change this Face
For one like that.
OCTAVIA. Thou lov'st him not so well.
CLEOPATRA. I love him better, and deserve him more.
OCTAVIA. You do not; cannot: you have been his ruine.
Who made him cheap at *Rome*, but *Cleopatra?*
Who made him scorn'd abroad, but *Cleopatra?*
At *Actium,* who betray'd him? *Cleopatra.*
Who made his Children Orphans, and poor me
A wretched Widow? only *Cleopatra.*
CLEOPATRA. Yet she who loves him best is *Cleopatra.*
If you have suffer'd, I have suffer'd more.
You bear the specious Title of a Wife,
To gild your Cause, and draw the pitying World
To favour it: the World contemns poor me;
For I have lost my Honour, lost my Fame,
And stain'd the glory of my Royal House,
And all to bear the branded Name of Mistress.
There wants but life, and that too I would lose
For him I love.
OCTAVIA. Be't so then; take thy wish.

[*Exit cum suis.*° with associates

CLEOPATRA. And 'tis my wish,
Now he is lost for whom alone I liv'd.
My sight grows dim, and every object dances,
And swims before me, in the maze of death.
My spirits, while they were oppos'd, kept up,
They could not sink beneath a Rivals scorn:
But now she's gone, they faint.
ALEXAS. Mine have had leisure
To recollect their strength, and furnish counsel,
To ruine her; who else must ruine you.

CLEOPATRA. Vain Promiser!
Lead me, my *Charmion;* nay, your hand too, *Iras:*
My grief has weight enough to sink you both.
Conduct me to some solitary Chamber,
And draw the Curtains round;
Then leave me to my self, to take alone
My fill of grief:
There I till death will his unkindness weep;
As harmless Infants moan themselves asleep.

[*Exeunt.*

ACT IV. SCENE I.

Enter Antony, Dollabella.

DOLLABELLA. Why would you shift it from your self, on me?
Can you not tell her, you must part?
ANTONY. I cannot.
I could pull out an eye, and bid it go,
And t'other should not weep. Oh, *Dollabella,*
How many deaths are in this word *Depart!*
I dare not trust my tongue to tell her so:
One look of hers would thaw me into tears
And I should melt till I were lost agen.
DOLLABELLA. Then let *Ventidius;*
He's rough by nature.
ANTONY. Oh, he'll speak too harshly;
He'll kill her with the news: Thou, only thou.
DOLLABELLA. Nature has cast me in so soft a mould,
That but to hear a story feign'd for pleasure
Of some sad Lovers death, moistens my eyes,
And robs me of my Manhood.—I should speak
So faintly; with such fear to grieve her heart,
She'd not believe it earnest.
ANTONY. Therefore, therefore
Thou only, thou art fit: think thy self me,
And when thou speak'st (but let it first be long)
Take off the edge from every sharper sound,
And let our parting be as gently made,
As other Loves begin: Wilt thou do this?
DOLLABELLA. What you have said, so sinks into my Soul,
That, if I must speak, I shall speak just so.
ANTONY. I leave you then to your sad task: Farewel.
I sent her word to meet you.

(Goes to the door, and comes back.)

I forgot;
Let her be told, I'll make her peace with mine:
Her Crown and Dignity shall be preserv'd,
If I have pow'r with *Cæsar.*—O, be sure
To think on that.

DOLLABELLA. Fear not, I will remember.

[Antony goes again to the door, and comes back.

ANTONY. And tell her, too, how much I was constrain'd;
I did not this, but with extreamest force:
Desire her not to hate my memory,
For I still cherish hers;—insist on that.

DOLLABELLA. Trust me, I'll not forget it.

ANTONY. Then that's all.

(Goes out, and returns again.)

Wilt thou forgive my fondness° this once more? — foolishness
Tell her, tho' we shall never meet again,
If I should hear she took another Love,
The news would break my heart.—Now I must go;
For every time I have return'd, I feel
My Soul more tender; and my next command
Would be to bid her stay, and ruine both.

[Exit.

DOLLABELLA. Men are but Children of a larger growth,
Our appetites as apt to change as theirs,
And full as craving too, and full as vain;
And yet the Soul, shut up in her dark room,
Viewing so clear abroad, at home sees nothing;
But, like a Mole in Earth, busie and blind,
Works all her folly up, and casts it outward
To the Worlds open view: thus I discover'd,
And blam'd the love of ruin'd *Antony;*
Yet wish that I were he, to be so ruin'd.

Enter Ventidius *above.*

VENTIDIUS. Alone? and talking to himself? concern'd too?
Perhaps my ghess is right; he lov'd her once,
And may pursue it still.

DOLLABELLA. O Friendship! Friendship!
Ill canst thou answer this; and Reason, worse:
Unfaithful in th' attempt; hopeless to win;
And, if I win, undone: mere madness all.
And yet th' occasion's fair. What injury,
To him, to wear the Robe which he throws by?

VENTIDIUS. None, none at all. This happens as I wish,
To ruine her yet more with *Antony.*

Enter Cleopatra, *talking with* Alexas; Charmion, Iras *on the other side.*

DOLLABELLA. She comes! What charms have sorrow on that face!
Sorrow seems pleas'd to dwell with so much sweetness;
Yet, now and then, a melancholy smile
Breaks loose, like Lightning, in a Winter's night,
And shows a moments day.
VENTIDIUS. If she should love him too! Her Eunuch there!
That *Porcpisce*[15] bodes ill weather. Draw, draw nearer,
Sweet Devil, that I may hear.
ALEXAS. Believe me; try

[Dollabella *goes over to* Charmion *and* Iras; *seems to talk with them.*

To make him jealous; jealousie is like
A polisht Glass held to the lips when life's in doubt:
If there be breath, 'twill catch the damp and show it.
CLEOPATRA. I grant you jealousie's a proof of love,
But 'tis a weak and unavailing Med'cine;
It puts out the disease, and makes it show,
But has no pow'r to cure.
ALEXAS. 'Tis your last remedy, and strongest too:
And then this *Dollabella,* who so fit
To practise on? He's handsom, valiant, young,
And looks as he were laid for Nature's bait
To catch weak Womens eyes.
He stands already more than half suspected
Of loving you: the least kind word, or glance,
You give this Youth, will kindle him with love:
Then, like a burning Vessel set adrift,
You'll send him down amain before the wind,
To fire the heart of jealous *Antony.*
CLEOPATRA. Can I do this? Ah, no; my love's so true,
That I can neither hide it where it is,
Nor show it where it is not. Nature meant me
A Wife, a silly harmless household Dove,
Fond without art; and kind without deceit;
But Fortune, that has made a Mistress of me,
Has thrust me out to the wide World, unfurnish'd
Of falshood to be happy.
ALEXAS. Force yourself.
Th' event will be, your Lover will return
Doubly desirous to possess the good
Which once he fear'd to lose.

15. Porpoises and dolphins conventionally presaged bad weather.

CLEOPATRA. I must attempt it;
But Oh with what regret!

[*Exit* Alexas. (*She comes up to* DOLLABELLA.)

VENTIDIUS. So, now the Scene draws near; they're in my reach.
CLEOPATRA. *to Dollabella.* Discoursing with my Women! might not I
Share in your entertainment?
CHARMION. You have been
The Subject of it, Madam.
CLEOPATRA. How; and how?
IRAS. Such praises of your beauty!
CLEOPATRA. Meer Poetry.
Your *Roman* Wits, your *Gallus* and *Tibullus,*
Have taught you this from *Citheris* and *Delia.*[16]
DOLLABELLA. Those *Roman* wits have never been in *Ægypt,*
Citheris and *Delia* else had been unsung:
I, who have seen—had I been born a Poet,
Should chuse a nobler name.
CLEOPATRA. You flatter me.
But, 'tis your Nation's vice: all of your Country
Are flatterers, and all false. Your Friend's like you.
I'm sure he sent you not to speak these words.
DOLLABELLA. No, Madam; yet he sent me—
CLEOPATRA. Well, he sent you—
DOLLABELLA. Of a less pleasing errand.
CLEOPATRA. How less pleasing?
Less to your self, or me?
DOLLABELLA. Madam, to both;
For you must mourn, and I must grieve to cause it.
CLEOPATRA. You, *Charmion,* and your Fellow, stand at distance.
(Aside.) Hold up, my Spirits.—Well, now your mournful matter;
For I'm prepar'd, perhaps can ghess it too.
DOLLABELLA. I wish you would; for 'tis a thankless office
To tell ill news: And I, of all your Sex,
Most fear displeasing you.
CLEOPATRA. Of all your Sex,
I soonest could forgive you, if you should.
VENTIDIUS. Most delicate advances! Woman! Woman!
Dear damn'd, inconstant Sex!
CLEOPATRA. In the first place,
I am to be forsaken; is't not so?
DOLLABELLA. I wish I could not answer to that question.

16. Gaius Cornelius Gallus (69–26 BC) and Albius Tibullus (c. 48–19 BC) wrote love poetry to Cytheris, a courtesan, and Delia, a faithless mistress, respectively. The former are lost. Cytheris was also a mistress of Antony.

CLEOPATRA. Then pass it o'er, because it troubles you:
I should have been more griev'd another time.
Next, I'm to lose my Kingdom.—Farewel, *Ægypt.*
Yet, is there any more?
DOLLABELLA. Madam, I fear
Your too deep sense of grief has turn'd your reason.
CLEOPATRA. No, no, I'm not run mad; I can bear Fortune:
And Love may be expell'd by other Love,
As Poysons are by Poysons.
DOLLABELLA. You o'erjoy me, Madam,
To find your griefs so moderately borne.
You've heard the worst; all are not false, like him.
CLEOPATRA. No; Heav'n forbid they should.
DOLLABELLA. Some men are constant.
CLEOPATRA. And constancy deserves reward, that's certain.
DOLLABELLA. Deserves it not; but give it leave to hope.
VENTIDIUS. I'll swear, thou hast my leave. I have enough:
But how to manage this! Well, I'll consider.

[*Exit.*

DOLLABELLA. I came prepar'd,
To tell you heavy news; news, which I thought,
Would fright the blood from your pale cheeks to hear:
But you have met it with a cheerfulness
That makes my task more easie; and my tongue,
Which on anothers message was employ'd,
Would gladly speak its own.
CLEOPATRA. Hold, *Dollabella.*
First tell me, were you chosen by my Lord?
Or sought you this employment?
DOLLABELLA. He pick'd me out; and, as his bosom friend,
He charg'd me with his words.
CLEOPATRA. The message then
I know was tender, and each accent smooth,
To mollifie that rugged word *Depart.*
DOLLABELLA. Oh, you mistake: he chose the harshest words,
With fiery eyes, and with contracted brows,
He coyn'd his face in the severest stamp:
And fury, shook his Fabrick like an Earthquake;
He heav'd for vent, and burst like bellowing *Ætna,*
In sounds scarce humane, *Hence, away for ever:*
Let her begone, the blot of my renown,
And bane of all my hopes:

[*All the time of this speech, Cleopatra seems more and more concern'd, till she sinks quite down.*

Let her be driv'n as far as men can think,
From Mans commerce: She'll poyson to the Center.
CLEOPATRA. Oh, I can bear no more!
DOLLABELLA. Help, help! Oh Wretch! Oh cursed, cursed Wretch!
What have I done!
CHARMION. Help, chafe her Temples, *Iras.*
IRAS. Bend, bend her forward quickly.
CHARMION. Heav'n be prais'd,
She comes again.
CLEOPATRA. Oh, let him not approach me.
Why have you brought me back to this loath'd Being,
Th' abode of Falshood, violated Vows,
And injur'd Love? For pity, let me go;
For, if there be a place of long repose,
I'm sure I want it. My disdainful Lord
Can never break that quiet; nor awake
The sleeping Soul, with hollowing in my Tomb
Such words as fright her hence. Unkind, unkind.
DOLLABELLA. Believe me, 'tis against my self I speak;
That sure desires belief. I injur'd him:
My Friend ne'er spoke those words. Oh, had you seen
How often he came back, and every time
With something more obliging and more kind,
To add to what he said; what dear Farewels;
How almost vanquisht by his love he parted,
And lean'd to what unwillingly he left:
I, Traitor as I was, for love of you,
(But what can you not do, who made me false!)
I forg'd that lye; for whose forgiveness kneels
This self-accus'd, self-punish'd Criminal
CLEOPATRA. With how much ease believe we what we wish!
Rise, *Dollabella;* if you have been guilty,
I have contributed, and too much love
Has made me guilty too.
Th' advance of kindness, which I made, was feign'd,
To call back fleeting love by jealousie;
But 'twould not last. Oh, rather let me lose
Than so ignobly trifle with his heart.
DOLLABELLA. I find your breast fenc'd round from humane reach,
Transparent as a Rock of solid Crystal;
Seen through, but never pierc'd. My Friend, my Friend!
What endless treasure hast thou thrown away,
And scatter'd, like an Infant, in the Ocean,
Vain sums of Wealth, which none can gather thence.
CLEOPATRA. Could you not beg
An hours admittance to his private ear?

Like one who wanders through long barren Wilds,
And yet foreknows no hospitable Inn
Is near to succour hunger,
Eats his fill, before his painful march:
So would I feed a while my famish'd eyes
Before we part; for I have far to go,
If death be far, and never must return.

Enter Ventidius, *with* Octavia, *behind.*

VENTIDIUS. From hence you may discover—Oh, sweet, sweet!
Would you indeed? the pretty hand in earnest?
DOLLABELLA. *takes her hand.* I will, for this reward.—Draw it not back.
'Tis all I e'er will beg.
VENTIDIUS. They turn upon us.
OCTAVIA. What quick eyes has guilt!
VENTIDIUS. Seem not to have observ'd 'em, and go on.

They come forward.

DOLLABELLA. Saw you the Emperor, *Ventidius?*
VENTIDIUS. No.
I sought him; but I heard that he was private,
None with him, but *Hipparchus* his freedman.
DOLLABELLA. Know you his bus'ness?
VENTIDIUS. Giving him Instructions,
And Letters, to his Brother *Cæsar.*
DOLLABELLA. Well,
He must be found.

[*Exeunt* Dollabella *and* Cleopatra.

OCTAVIA. Most glorious impudence!
VENTIDIUS. She look'd methought
As she would say, *Take your old man,* Octavia;
Thank you, I'm better here. Well, but what use
Make we of this discovery?
OCTAVIA. Let it die.
VENTIDIUS. I pity *Dollabella;* but she's dangerous:
Her eyes have pow'r beyond *Thessalian* Charms
To draw the Moon from Heav'n; for Eloquence,
The Sea-green Syrens taught her voice their flatt'ry;
And, while she speaks, Night steals upon the Day,
Unmark'd of those that hear: Then she's so charming,
Age buds at sight of her, and swells to youth:
The holy Priests gaze on her when she smiles;
And with heav'd hands forgetting gravity,
They bless her wanton eyes: Even I who hate her,
With a malignant joy behold such beauty;
And, while I curse, desire it. *Antony*

Must needs have some remains of passion still,
Which may ferment into a worse relapse,
If now not fully cur'd. I know, this minute,
With *Cæsar* he's endeavouring her peace.

OCTAVIA. You have prevail'd:—but for a further purpose

(Walks off.)

I'll prove how he will relish this discovery.
What, make a Strumpet's peace! it swells my heart:
It must not, sha' not be.

VENTIDIUS. His Guards appear.
Let me begin, and you shall second me.

Enter ANTONY.

ANTONY. *Octavia,* I was looking you, my love:
What, are your Letters ready? I have giv'n
My last Instructions.

OCTAVIA. Mine, my Lord, are written.

ANTONY. *Ventidius!*

[*Drawing him aside.*

VENTIDIUS. My Lord?

ANTONY. A word in private.
When saw you *Dollabella?*

VENTIDIUS. Now, my Lord,
He parted hence; and *Cleopatra* with him.

ANTONY. Speak softly. 'Twas by my command he went,
To bear my last farewel.

VENTIDIUS. *aloud.* It look'd indeed
Like your farewel.

ANTONY. More softly.—My farewel?
What secret meaning have you in those words
Of my Farewel? He did it by my Order.

VENTIDIUS. *aloud.* Then he obey'd your Order. I suppose
You bid him do it with all gentleness,
All kindness, and all—love.

ANTONY. How she mourn'd, the poor forsaken Creature!

VENTIDIUS. She took it as she ought; she bore your parting
As she did *Cæsar*'s, as she would anothers,
Were a new Love to come.

ANTONY. *aloud.* Thou dost belye her;
Most basely, and maliciously belye her.

VENTIDIUS. I thought not to displease you; I have done.

OCTAVIA. *coming up.* You seemed disturb'd, my Lord.

ANTONY. A very trifle.
Retire, my Love.

VENTIDIUS. It was indeed a trifle.
He sent—

ANTONY. *angrily.* No more. Look how thou disobey'st me;
Thy life shall answer it.
OCTAVIA. Then 'tis no trifle.
VENTIDIUS. *to Octavia.* 'Tis less; a very nothing: you too saw it,
As well as I, and therefore 'tis no secret.
ANTONY. She saw it!
VENTIDIUS. Yes: she saw young *Dollabella*—
ANTONY. Young *Dollabella!*
VENTIDIUS. Young, I think him young.
And handsom too; and so do others think him.
But what of that? He went by your command,
Indeed 'tis probable, with some kind message;
For she receiv'd it graciously; she smil'd:
And then he grew familiar with her hand,
Squeez'd it, and worry'd it with ravenous kisses;
She blush'd, and sigh'd, and smil'd, and blush'd again;
At last she took occasion to talk softly,
And brought her cheek up close, and lean'd on his:
At which, he whisper'd kisses back on hers;
And then she cry'd aloud, That constancy
Should be rewarded.
OCTAVIA. This I saw and heard.
ANTONY. What Woman was it, whom you heard and saw
So playful with my Friend! Not *Cleopatra?*
VENTIDIUS. Even she, my Lord!
ANTONY. My *Cleopatra?*
VENTIDIUS. Your *Cleopatra;*
Dollabella's *Cleopatra:*
Every Man's *Cleopatra.*
ANTONY. Thou ly'st.
VENTIDIUS. I do not lye, my Lord.
Is this so strange? Should Mistresses be left,
And not provide against a time of change?
You know she's not much us'd to lonely nights.
ANTONY. I'll think no more on't.
I know 'tis false, and see the plot betwixt you.
You needed not have gone this way, *Octavia.*
What harms it you that *Cleopatra*'s just?
She's mine no more. I see; and I forgive:
Urge it no further, Love.
OCTAVIA. Are you concern'd,
That she's found false?
ANTONY. I should be, were it so;
For, tho' 'tis past, I would not that the World
Should tax my former choice: That I lov'd one
Of so light note; but I forgive you both.

VENTIDIUS. What has my age deserv'd, that you should think
I would abuse your ears with perjury?
If Heav'n be true, she's false.
ANTONY. Though Heav'n and Earth
Should witness it, I'll not believe her tainted.
VENTIDIUS. I'll bring you, then, a Witness
From Hell to prove her so. Nay, go not back;

[*Seeing* ALEXAS *just entring, and starting back.*

For stay you must and shall.
ALEXAS. What means my Lord?
VENTIDIUS. To make you do what most you hate; speak truth.
You are of *Cleopatra*'s private Counsel
Of her Bed-Counsel, her lascivious hours;
Are conscious of each nightly change she makes,
And watch her, as *Chaldeans* do the Moon,
Can tell what Signs she passes through, what day.
ALEXAS. My noble Lord.
VENTIDIUS. My most Illustrious Pandar,
No fine set Speech, no Cadence, no turn'd Periods,
But a plain home-spun Truth, is what I ask:
I did, my self, o'erhear your Queen make love
To *Dollabella*. Speak; for I will know,
By your confession, what more passed betwixt 'em;
How near the bus'ness draws to your employment;
And when the happy hour.
ANTONY. Speak truth, *Alexas,* whether it offend
Or please *Ventidius,* care not: justifie
Thy injur'd Queen from malice: dare his worst.
OCTAVIA. *aside.* See, how he gives him courage! how he fears
To find her false! and shuts his eyes to truth,
Willing to be misled!
ALEXAS. As far as love may plead for Woman's frailty,
Urg'd by desert and greatness of the Lover;
So far (Divine *Octavia!*) may my Queen
Stand ev'n excus'd to you, for loving him,
Who is your Lord: so far, from brave *Ventidius,*
May her past actions hope a fair report.
ANTONY. 'Tis well, and truly spoken: mark, *Ventidius.*
ALEXAS. To you, most Noble Emperor, her strong passion
Stands not excus'd, but wholly justifi'd.
Her Beauty's charms alone, without her Crown,
From *Ind*° and *Meroe*° drew the distant Vows — India; an island in the upper Nile
Of sighing Kings; and at her feet were laid
The Scepters of the Earth, expos'd on heaps,
To choose where she would Reign:

She thought a *Roman* only could deserve her;
And, of all *Romans,* only *Antony.*
And, to be less than Wife to you, disdain'd
Their lawful passion.

ANTONY. 'Tis but truth.

ALEXAS. And yet, tho love, and your unmatch'd desert,
Have drawn her from the due regard of Honor,
At last, Heav'n open'd her unwilling eyes
To see the wrongs she offer'd fair *Octavia,*
Whose holy Bed she lawlesly usurpt;
The sad effects of this improsperous War,
Confirm'd those pious thoughts.

VENTIDIUS. *aside.* O, wheel you there?
Observe him now; the Man begins to mend,
And talk substantial reason. Fear not, Eunuch,
The Emperor has giv'n thee leave to speak.

ALEXAS. Else had I never dar'd t' offend his ears
With what the last necessity has urg'd
On my forsaken Mistress; yet I must not
Presume to say, her heart is wholly alter'd.

ANTONY. No, dare not for thy life, I charge thee dare not
Pronounce that fatal word.

OCTAVIA. *aside.* Must I bear this? good Heav'n, afford me patience.

VENTIDIUS. On, sweet Eunuch; my dear half man, proceed.

ALEXAS. Yet *Dollabella*
Has lov'd her long: he, next my God-like Lord,
Deserves her best; and should she meet his passion,
Rejected, as she is, by him she lov'd—

ANTONY. Hence, from my sight; for I can bear no more:
Let Furies drag thee quick to Hell; let all
The longer damn'd have rest; each torturing hand
Do thou employ, till *Cleopatra* comes,
Then joyn thou too, and help to torture her.

[*Exit* Alexas, *thrust out by* Antony.

OCTAVIA. 'Tis not well,
Indeed, my Lord, 'tis much unkind to me,
To show this passion, this extream concernment,
For an abandon'd, faithless Prostitute.

ANTONY. *Octavia,* leave me; I am much disorder'd.
Leave me, I say.

OCTAVIA. My Lord?

ANTONY. I bid you leave me.

VENTIDIUS. Obey him, Madam: best withdraw a while,
And see how this will work.

OCTAVIA. Wherein have I offended you, my Lord,
That I am bid to leave you? Am I false,

Or infamous? Am I a *Cleopatra?*
Were I she,
Base as she is, you would not bid me leave you;
But hang upon my neck, take slight excuses,
And fawn upon my falshood.

ANTONY. 'Tis too much.
Too much, *Octavia;* I am prest with sorrows
Too heavy to be born; and you add more:
I would retire, and recollect what's left
Of Man within, to aid me.

OCTAVIA. You would mourn
In private, for your Love, who has betray'd you;
You did but half return to me: your kindness
Linger'd behind with her. I hear, my Lord,
You make Conditions for her,
And would include her Treaty. Wondrous proofs
Of love to me!

ANTONY. Are you my Friend, *Ventidius?*
Or are you turn'd a *Dollabella* too,
And let this Fury loose?

VENTIDIUS. Oh, be advis'd,
Sweet Madam, and retire.

OCTAVIA. Yes, I will go; but never to return.
You shall no more be haunted with this Fury.
My Lord, my Lord, love will not always last,
When urg'd with long unkindness and disdain;
Take her again, whom you prefer to me;
She stays but to be call'd. Poor cozen'd Man!
Let a feign'd parting give her back your heart,
Which a feign'd love first got; for injur'd me,
Tho' my just sense of wrongs forbid my stay,
My duty shall be yours.
To the dear pledges of our former love,
My tenderness and care shall be transferr'd,
And they shall cheer, by turns, my Widow'd Nights:
So, take my last farewel; for I despair
To have you whole, and scorn to take you half.

[*Exit.*

VENTIDIUS. I combat Heav'n, which blasts my best designs:
My last attempt must be to win her back;
But Oh, I fear in vain.

[*Exit*

ANTONY. Why was I fram'd with this plain honest heart,
Which knows not to disguise its griefs and weakness,

But bears its workings outward to the world?
I should have kept the mighty anguish in,
And forc'd a smile at *Cleopatra*'s falshood:
Octavia had believ'd it, and had staid;
But I am made a shallow-forded Stream,
Seen to the bottom: all my clearness scorn'd,
And all my faults exposed!—See, where he comes,

Enter Dollabella.

Who has profan'd the Sacred Name of Friend,
And worn it into vileness!
With how secure a brow, and specious form
He guilds the secret Villain! Sure that face
Was meant for honesty; but Heav'n mis-match'd it,
And furnish'd Treason out with Natures pomp,
To make its work more easie.

DOLLABELLA. O, my Friend!

ANTONY. Well, *Dollabella,* you perform'd my message?

DOLLABELLA. I did, unwillingly.

ANTONY. Unwillingly?
Was it so hard for you to bear our parting?
You should have wisht it.

DOLLABELLA. Why?

ANTONY. Because you love me.
And she receiv'd my message, with as true,
With as unfeign'd a sorrow as you brought it?

DOLLABELLA. She loves you, ev'n to madness.

ANTONY. Oh, I know it.
You, Dollabella, do not better know
How much she loves me. And should I
Forsake this Beauty? This all-perfect Creature?

DOLLABELLA. I could not, were she mine.

ANTONY. And yet you first
Perswaded me: How come you alter'd since?

DOLLABELLA. I said at first I was not fit to go;
I could not hear her sighs, and see her tears,
But pity must prevail: and so, perhaps,
It may again with you; for I have promis'd
That she should take her last farewel: and, see,
She comes to claim my word.

Enter Cleopatra.

ANTONY. False *Dollabella!*

DOLLABELLA. What's false, my Lord?

ANTONY. Why, *Dollabella*'s false,
And *Cleopatra*'s false; both false and faithless.

Draw near, you well-join'd wickedness, you Serpents,
Whom I have, in my kindly bosom, warm'd
Till I am stung to death.

DOLLABELLA. My Lord, have I
Deserv'd to be thus us'd?

CLEOPATRA. Can Heav'n prepare
A newer Torment? Can it find a Curse
Beyond our separation?

ANTONY. Yes, if Fate
Be just, much greater: Heav'n should be ingenious
In punishing such crimes. The rowling Stone,
And gnawing Vulture, were slight pains, invented
When *Jove* was young, and no examples known
Of mighty ills; but you have ripen'd sin,
To such a monstrous growth, 'twill pose the Gods
To find an equal Torture. Two, two such,
Oh there's no further name, two such—to me,
To me, who lock'd my Soul within your breasts,
Had no desires, no joys, no life, but you;
When half the Globe was mine, I gave it you
In Dowry with my heart; I had no use,
No fruit of all, but you: a Friend and Mistress
Was what the World could give. Oh, *Cleopatra!*
O *Dollabella!* how could you betray
This tender heart, which with an Infant-fondness
Lay lull'd betwixt your bosoms, and there slept
Secure of injur'd Faith?

DOLLABELLA. If she has wrong'd you,
Heav'n, Hell, and You revenge it.

ANTONY. If she wrong'd me,
Thou wouldst evade thy part of guilt; but swear
Thou lov'st not her.

DOLLABELLA. Not so as I love you.

ANTONY. Not so! Swear, swear, I say, thou dost not love her.

DOLLABELLA. No more than Friendship will allow.

ANTONY. No more?
Friendship allows thee nothing: thou art perjur'd.—
And yet thou didst not swear thou lov'dst her not;
But not so much, no more. Oh trifling Hypocrite,
Who dar'st not own to her, thou dost not love,
Nor own to me thou dost! *Ventidius* heard it;
Octavia saw it.

CLEOPATRA. They are enemies.

ANTONY. *Alexas* is not so: he, he confest it;
He, who, next Hell, best knew it, he avow'd it.
(*To* Dollabella.) Why do I seek a proof beyond your self?

You, whom I sent to bear my last Farewel,
Return'd to plead her stay.
DOLLABELLA. What shall I answer?
If to have lov'd be guilt, then I have sinn'd;
But if to have repented of that love
Can wash away my crime, I have repented.
Yet, if I have offended past forgiveness,
Let not her suffer: she is innocent.
CLEOPATRA. Ah, what will not a Woman do who loves!
What means will she refuse, to keep that heart,
Where all her joys are plac'd! 'Twas I encourag'd,
'Twas I blew up the fire that scorch'd his Soul,
To make you jealous; and by that regain you.
But all in vain; I could not counterfeit:
In spight of all the damms, my love broke o'er,
And drown'd my heart again: Fate took th' occasion;
And thus one minutes feigning has destroy'd
My whole life's truth.
ANTONY. Thin Cobweb Arts of Falshood;
Seen, and broke through at first.
DOLLABELLA. Forgive your Mistress.
CLEOPATRA. Forgive your Friend.
ANTONY. You have convinc'd your selves.
You plead each others Cause: What Witness have you,
That you but meant to raise my jealousie?
CLEOPATRA. Our selves, and Heav'n.
ANTONY. Guilt witnesses for guilt. Hence, Love and Friendship;
You have no longer place in humane breasts,
These two have driv'n you out: avoid my sight;
I would not kill the Man whom I have lov'd;
And cannot hurt the Woman; but avoid me,
I do not know how long I can be tame;
For, if I stay one minute more, to think
How I am wrong'd, my Justice and Revenge
Will cry so loud within me, that my pity
Will not be heard for either.
DOLLABELLA. Heav'n has but
Our sorrow for our sins; and then delights
To pardon erring Man: sweet Mercy seems
Its darling Attribute, which limits Justice;
As if there were degrees in Infinite,
And Infinite would rather want perfection
Than punish to extent.
ANTONY. I can forgive
A Foe; but not a Mistress, and a Friend:
Treason is there in its most horrid shape,

Where trust is greatest: and the Soul resign'd
Is stabb'd by its own Guards: I'll hear no more;
Hence from my sight for ever.

CLEOPATRA. How? for ever!
I cannot go one moment from your sight,
And must I go for ever?
My joys, my only joys are center'd here:
What place have I to go to? my own Kingdom?
That I have lost for you. Or to the *Romans?*
They hate me for your sake. Or must I wander
The wide World o'er, a helpless, banish'd Woman,
Banish'd for love of you; banish'd from you?
I, there's the Banishment! Oh hear me; hear me,
With strictest Justice: For I beg no favour:
And if I have offended you, then kill me,
But do not banish me.

ANTONY. I must not hear you.
I have a Fool within me takes your part;
But Honour stops my ears.

CLEOPATRA. For pity hear me!
Wou'd you cast off a Slave who follow'd you,
Who crouch'd beneath your Spurn?—He has no pity!
See, if he gives one tear to my departure;
One look, one kind farewel. Oh Iron heart!
Let all the Gods look down, and judge betwixt us,
If he did ever love!

ANTONY. No more.—*Alexas!*

DOLLABELLA. A perjur'd Villain!

ANTONY. *to Cleopatra.* Your *Alexas;* yours.

CLEOPATRA. O 'twas his plot: his ruinous design
T' ingage you in my love by jealousie.
Hear him; confront him with me; let him speak.

ANTONY. I have; I have.

CLEOPATRA. And if he clear me not—

ANTONY. Your Creature! one, who hangs upon your smiles!
Watches your eye, to say or to unsay
Whate'er you please! I am not to be mov'd.

CLEOPATRA. Then must we part? Farewel, my cruel Lord,
Th' appearance is against me; and I go
Unjustifi'd, for ever from your sight.
How I have lov'd, you know; how yet I love,
My only comfort is, I know my self:
I love you more, ev'n now you are unkind,
Than when you lov'd me most; so well, so truly,
I'll never strive against it; but die pleas'd,
To think you once were mine.

ANTONY. Good heav'n, they weep at parting.
Must I weep too? that calls 'em innocent.
I must not weep; and yet I must, to think
That I must not forgive.—
Live; but live wretched, 'tis but just you shou'd,
Who made me so: Live from each others sight:
Let me not hear you meet: Set all the Earth,
And all the Seas, betwixt your sunder'd Loves:
View nothing common but the Sun and Skys:
Now, all take several ways;
And each your own sad fate with mine deplore;
That you were false, and I could trust no more.

[*Exeunt severally.*

ACT V. SCENE I.

Enter Cleopatra, Charmion, *and* Iras.

CHARMION. Be juster, Heav'n: such virtue punish'd thus,
Will make us think that Chance rules all above,
And shuffles, with a random hand, the Lots
Which Man is forc'd to draw.
CLEOPATRA. I cou'd tear out these eyes, that gain'd his heart,
And had not pow'r to keep it. O the curse
Of doting on, ev'n when I find it Dotage!
Bear witness, Gods, you heard him bid me go;
You, whom he mock'd with imprecating Vows° curses
Of promis'd Faith.—I'll die, I will not bear it.
You may hold me—

[*She pulls out her Dagger, and they hold her.*

But I can keep my breath; I can die inward,
And choak this Love.

Enter Alexas.

IRAS. Help, O *Alexas*, help!
The Queen grows desperate, her Soul struggles in her,
With all the Agonies of Love and Rage,
And strives to force its passage.
CLEOPATRA. Let me go.
Art thou there, Traitor!—O,
O, for a little breath, to vent my rage!
Give, give me way, and let me loose upon him.
ALEXAS. Yes, I deserve it, for my ill-tim'd truth.
Was it for me to prop
The Ruins of a falling Majesty?

To place my self beneath the mighty flaw,
Thus to be crush'd, and pounded into Atomes,
By its o'erwhelming weight? 'Tis too presuming
For Subjects, to preserve that wilful pow'r
Which courts its own destruction.
CLEOPATRA. I wou'd reason
More calmly with you. Did not you o'er-rule,
And force my plain, direct, and open love
Into these crooked paths of jealousie?
Now, what's th' event? *Octavia* is remov'd;
But *Cleopatra*'s banish'd. Thou, thou, Villain,
Hast push'd my Boat, to open Sea; to prove,
At my sad cost, if thou canst steer it back.
It cannot be; I'm lost too far; I'm ruin'd:
Hence, thou Impostor, Traitor, Monster, Devil—
I can no more: thou, and my griefs, have sunk
Me down so low, that I want voice to curse thee.
ALEXAS. Suppose some shipwrack'd Seaman near the shore,
Dropping and faint, with climbing up the Cliff,
If, from above, some charitable hand
Pull him to safety, hazarding himself
To draw the others weight; wou'd he look back
And curse him for his pains? The case is yours;
But one step more, and you have gain'd the heighth.
CLEOPATRA. Sunk, never more to rise.
ALEXAS. *Octavia*'s gone, and *Dollabella* banish'd.
Belive me, Madam, *Antony* is yours.
His heart was never lost; but started off
To Jealousie, Love's last retreat and covert:
Where it lies hid in Shades, watchful in silence,
And list'ning for the sound that calls it back.
Some other, any man, ('tis so advanc'd)
May perfect this unfinish'd work, which I
(Unhappy only to my self) have left
So easie to his hand.
CLEOPATRA. Look well thou do't; else—
ALEXAS. Else, what your silence threatens.—*Antony*
Is mounted up the *Pharos*;[17] from whose Turret,
He stands surveying our *Ægyptian* Gallies,
Engag'd with *Cæsar*'s Fleet: Now Death or Conquest.
If the first happen, Fate acquits my promise:
If we o'ercome, the Conqueror is yours.

17. The lighthouse of Alexandria.

[*A distant Shout within.*

CHARMION. Have comfort, Madam: Did you mark that Shout?

[*Second Shout nearer.*

IRAS. Hark; they redouble it.
ALEXAS. 'Tis from the Port.
The loudness shows it near: good news, kind Heavens.
CLEOPATRA. *Osiris* make it so.

Enter *Serapion.*

SERAPION. Where, where's the Queen?
ALEXAS. How frightfully the holy Coward stares!
As if not yet recover'd of the assault,
When all his Gods, and, what's more dear to him,
His Offerings were at stake.
SERAPION. O horror, horror!
Ægypt has been; our latest hour has come:
The Queen of Nations from her ancient seat,
Is sunk for ever in the dark Abyss:
Time has unrowl'd her Glories to the last,
And now clos'd up the Volume.
CLEOPATRA. Be more plain:
Say, whence thou com'st, (though fate is in thy face,
Which from thy haggard eyes looks wildly out,
And threatens ere thou speak'st.)
SERAPION. I came from *Pharos;*
From viewing (spare me and imagine it)
Our Land's last hope, your Navy—
CLEOPATRA. Vanquish'd?
SERAPION. No.
They fought not.
CLEOPATRA. Then they fled.
SERAPION. Nor that. I saw,
With *Antony,* your well-appointed Fleet
Row out; and thrice he wav'd his hand on high,
And thrice with cheerful cries they shouted back:
'Twas then, false Fortune, like a fawning Strumpet,
About to leave the Bankrupt Prodigal,
With a dissembled smile wou'd kiss at parting,
And flatter to the last; the well-tim'd Oars,
Now dipt from every bank, now smoothly run
To meet the Foe; and soon indeed they met,
But not as Foes. In few, we saw their Caps
On either side thrown up; the *Ægyptian* Gallies
(Receiv'd like Friends) past through, and fell behind
The *Roman* rear: and now, they all come forward,
And ride within the Port.

CLEOPATRA. Enough, *Serapion:*
I've heard my doom. This needed not, you Gods:
When I lost *Antony,* your work was done;
'Tis but superfluous malice. Where's my Lord?
How bears he this last blow?
SERAPION. His fury cannot be express'd by words:
Thrice he attempted headlong to have faln
Full on his foes, and aim'd at *Cæsar*'s Galley:
With-held, he raves on you; cries, He's betray'd.
Should he now find you—
ALEXAS. Shun him, seek your safety,
Till you can clear your innocence.
CLEOPATRA. I'll stay.
ALEXAS. You must not, haste you to your Monument,
While I make speed to *Cæsar.*
CLEOPATRA. *Caesar!* No,
I have no business with him.
ALEXAS. I can work him
To spare your life, and let this madman perish.
CLEOPATRA. Base fawning Wretch! wouldst thou betray him too?
Hence from my sight, I will not hear a Traytor;
'Twas thy design brought all this ruine on us.
Serapion, thou art honest; counsel me:
But haste, each moment's precious.
SERAPION. Retire; you must not yet see *Antony.*
He who began this mischief,
'Tis just he tempt the danger: let him clear you;
And, since he offer'd you his servile tongue,
To gain a poor precarious life from *Cæsar,*
Let him expose that fawning eloquence,
And speak to *Antony.*
ALEXAS. O Heavens! I dare not,
I meet my certain death.
CLEOPATRA. Slave, thou deserv'st it.
Not that I fear my Lord, will I avoid him;
I know him noble: when he banish'd me,
And thought me false, he scorn'd to take my life;
But I'll be justifi'd, and then die with him.
ALEXAS. O pity me, and let me follow you.
CLEOPATRA. To death, if thou stir hence. Speak, if thou canst,
Now for thy life, which basely thou wou'dst save;
While mine I prize at this. Come, good *Serapion.*

[*Exeunt* Cleopatra, Serapion, Charmion, Iras.

ALEXAS. O that I less cou'd fear to lose this being,
Which, like a Snow-ball, in my coward hand,
The more 'tis grasp'd, the faster melts away.

Poor Reason! what a wretched aid art thou!
For still, in spight of thee,
These two long Lovers, Soul and Body, dread
Their final separation. Let me think:
What can I say, to save myself from death?
No matter what becomes of *Cleopatra.*

ANTONY. *within.* Which way? where?

VENTIDIUS. *within.* This leads to the Monument.

ALEXAS. Ah me! I hear him; yet I'm unprepar'd:
My gift of lying's gone;
And this Court-Devil, which I so oft have rais'd,
Forsakes me at my need. I dare not stay;
Yet cannot far go hence.

[*Exit.*

Enter Antony *and* Ventidius.

ANTONY. O happy *Cæsar!* Thou hast men to lead:
Think not 'tis thou hast conquer'd *Antony;*
But *Rome* has conquered *Ægypt.* I'm betray'd.

VENTIDIUS. Curse on this treach'rous Train!
Their Soil and Heav'n infect 'em all with baseness:
And their young Souls come tainted to the World
With the first breath they draw.

ANTONY. Th' original Villain sure no God created;
He was a Bastard of the Sun, by *Nile,*
Ap'd into Man; with all his Mother's Mud
Crusted about his Soul.

VENTIDIUS. The Nation is
One Universal Traitor; and their Queen
The very Spirit and Extract of 'em all.

ANTONY. Is there yet left
A possibility of aid from Valor?
Is there one God unsworn to my Destruction?
The least unmortgag'd hope? for, if there be,
Methinks I cannot fall beneath the Fate
Of such a Boy as *Cæsar.*
The World's one half is yet in *Antony;*
And, from each limb of it, that's hew'd away,
The Soul comes back to me.

VENTIDIUS. There yet remain
Three Legions in the Town. The last assault
Lopt off the rest: if death be your design,
(As I must wish it now) these are sufficient
To make a heap about us of dead Foes,
An honest Pile for burial.

ANTONY. They're enough.
We'll not divide our Stars; but, side by side

Fight emulous: and with malicious eyes
Survey each other's acts: so every death
Thou giv'st, I'll take on me, as a just debt,
And pay thee back a Soul.

VENTIDIUS. Now you shall see I love you. Not a word
Of chiding more. By my few hours of life,
I am so pleas'd with this brave *Roman* Fate,
That I wou'd not be *Cæsar,* to out-live you.
When we put off this flesh, and mount together,
I shall be shown to all th' Ethereal crowd;
Lo, this is he who dy'd with Antony.

ANTONY. Who knows, but we may pierce through all their Troops,
And reach my Veterans yet? 'Tis worth the tempting,
To o'erleap this Gulph of Fate,
And leave our wond'ring Destinies behind.

Enter Alexas, *trembling.*

VENTIDIUS. See, see, that Villain;
See *Cleopatra* stampt upon that face,
With all her cunning, all her arts of falshood!
How she looks out through those dissembling eyes!
How he sets his count'nance for deceit;
And promises a lye, before he speaks!
Let me dispatch him first.

(Drawing.)

ALEXAS. O spare me, spare me.

ANTONY. Hold; he's not worth your killing. On thy life,
(Which thou mayst keep, because I scorn to take it)
No syllable to justifie thy Queen;
Save thy base tongue its office.

ALEXAS. Sir, she's gone,
Where she shall never be molested more
By Love, or you.

ANTONY. Fled to her *Dollabella!*
Die, Traitor, I revoke my promise, die.

(Going to kill him.)

ALEXAS. O hold, she is not fled.

ANTONY. She is: my eyes
Are open to her falshood; my whole life
Has been a golden dream, of Love and Friendship
But, now I wake, I'm like a Merchant, rows'd
From soft repose, to see his Vessel sinking,
And all his Wealth cast o'er. Ingrateful Woman!
Who follow'd me, but as the Swallow Summer,
Hatching her young ones in my kindly Beams,

Singing her flatt'ries to my morning wake;
But, now my Winter comes, she spreads her wings,
And seeks the spring of *Cæsar.*
ALEXAS. Think not so:
Her Fortunes have, in all things, mixt with yours.
Had she betray'd her Naval force to *Rome,*
How easily might she have gone to *Cæsar,*
Secure by such a bribe!
VENTIDIUS. She sent it first,
To be more welcome after.
ANTONY. 'Tis too plain;
Else wou'd she have appear'd, to clear her self.
ALEXAS. Too fatally she has; she could not bear
To be accus'd by you; but shut her self
Within her Monument: look'd down, and sigh'd;
While, from her unchang'd face, the silent tears
Dropt, as they had not leave, but stole their parting.
Some undistinguish'd words she inly murmur'd;
At last, she rais'd her eyes; and, with such looks
As dying *Lucrece* cast,—
ANTONY. My heart forebodes.—
VENTIDIUS. All for the best: go on.
ALEXAS. She snatch'd her Ponyard,
And, ere we cou'd prevent the fatal blow,
Plung'd it within her breast: then turn'd to me,
Go, bear my Lord (said she) *my last Farewel;*
And ask him if he yet suspect my Faith.
More she was saying, but death rush'd betwixt.
She half pronounc'd your Name with her last breath,
And bury'd half within her.
VENTIDIUS. Heav'n be prais'd.
ANTONY. Then art thou innocent, my poor dear Love?
And art thou dead?
O those two words! their sound shou'd be divided:
Hadst thou been false, and dy'd; or hadst thou liv'd,
And hadst been true—But Innocence and Death!
This shows not well above. Then what am I,
The Murderer of this Truth, This innocence!
Thoughts cannot form themselves in words so horrid
As can express my guilt!
VENTIDIUS. Is't come to this? The Gods have been too gracious:
And thus you thank 'em for't!
ANTONY. *to Alexas.* Why stay'st thou here?
Is it for thee to spy upon my Soul,
And see its inward mourning? Get thee hence;
Thou art not worthy to behold, what now
Becomes a *Roman* Emperor to perform.

ALEXAS. *aside.* He loves her still:
His grief betrays it. Good! the joy to find
She's yet alive, compleats the reconcilement.
I've sav'd my self, and her. But, Oh! the *Romans!*
Fate comes too fast upon my Wit,
Hunts me too hard, and meets me at each double.[18]

[*Exit.*

VENTIDIUS. Wou'd she had dy'd a little sooner, tho,
Before *Octavia* went; you might have treated:
Now 'twill look tame, and would not be receiv'd.
Come, rouse your self, and lets die warm together.
ANTONY. I will not fight: there's no more work for War.
The bus'ness of my angry hours is done.
VENTIDIUS. *Cæsar* is at your Gates.
ANTONY. Why, let him enter;
He's welcom now.
VENTIDIUS. What Lethargy has crept into your Soul?
ANTONY. 'Tis but a scorn of life, and just desire
To free myself from bondage.
VENTIDIUS. Do it bravely.
ANTONY. I will; but not by fighting. O, *Ventidius!*
What shou'd I fight for now? My Queen is dead.
I was but great for her; my Pow'r, my Empire,
Were but my Merchandise to buy her love;
And conquer'd Kings, my Factors. Now she's dead,
Let *Cæsar* take the World,—
An Empty Circle, since the Jewel's gone
Which made it worth my strife: my being's nauseous;
For all the bribes of life are gone away.
VENTIDIUS. Wou'd you be taken?
ANTONY. Yes, I wou'd be taken;
But, as a *Roman* ought, dead, my *Ventidius:*
For I'll convey my Soul from *Cæsar*'s reach,
And lay down life my self. 'Tis time the World
Shou'd have a Lord, and know whom to obey.
We two have kept its homage in suspense,
And bent the Globe, on whose each side we trod,
Till it was dinted inwards: Let him walk
Alone upon't: I'm weary of my part.
My Torch is out; and the World stands before me
Like a black Desart at th' approach of night:
I'll lay me down, and stray no farther on.
VENTIDIUS. I could be griev'd,
But that I'll not out-live you: choose your death;

18. Each attempt to reverse direction.

For, I have seen him in such various shapes,
I care not which I take: I'm only troubled
The life I bear, is worn to such a rag,
'Tis scarce worth giving. I cou'd wish indeed
We threw it from us with a better grace;
That, like two Lyons taken in the Toils,
We might at last thrust out our paws, and wound
The Hunters that inclose us.

ANTONY. I have thought on't.
Ventidius, you must live.

VENTIDIUS. I must not, Sir.

ANTONY. Wilt thou not live, to speak some good of me?
To stand by my fair Fame, and guard th' approaches
From the ill Tongues of Men?

VENTIDIUS. Who shall guard mine,
For living after you?

ANTONY. Say, I command it.

VENTIDIUS. If we die well, our deaths will speak themselves,
And need no living witness.

ANTONY. Thou hast lov'd me,
And fain I wou'd reward thee: I must die;
Kill me, and take the merit of my death,
To make thee Friends with *Cæsar.*

VENTIDIUS. Thank your kindness.
You said I lov'd you; and in recompence,
You bid me turn a Traitor: did I think
You wou'd have us'd me thus? that I shou'd die
With a hard thought of you?

ANTONY. Forgive me, *Roman.*
Since I have heard of *Cleopatra*'s death,
My reason bears no rule upon my tongue,
But lets my thoughts break all at random out:
I've thought better; do not deny me twice.

VENTIDIUS. By Heav'n I will not.
Let it not be t' out-live you.

ANTONY. Kill me first,
And then die thou: for 'tis but just thou serve
Thy Friend, before thy self.

VENTIDIUS. Give me your hand.
We soon shall meet again. Now, Farewel, Emperor. *(Embrace.)*
Methinks that word's too cold to be my last:
Since Death sweeps all distinctions, Farewel, Friend.
That's all.—
I will not make a busi'ness of a trifle;
And yet I cannot look on you, and kill you;
Pray turn your face.

ANTONY. I do: strike home, be sure.
VENTIDIUS. Home, as my sword will reach.

(Kills himself.)

ANTONY. O, thou mistak'st;
That wound was not of thine: give it me back:
Thou robb'st me of my death.
VENTIDIUS. I do indeed;
But, think 'tis the first time I e'er deceiv'd you;
If that may plead my pardon. And you, Gods,
Forgive me, if you will; for I die perjur'd,
Rather than kill my Friend.

(Dies.)

ANTONY. Farewel. Ever my Leader, ev'n in death!
My Queen and thou have got the start of me,
And I'm the lag of Honour.—Gone so soon?
Is death no more? He us'd him carelesly,
With a familiar kindness: ere he knock'd,
Ran to the door, and took him in his arms,
As who shou'd say, *Y'are welcome at all hours,*
A Friend need give no warning. Books had spoil'd him;
For all the Learn'd are Cowards by profession.
'Tis not worth
My further thought; for death, for aught I know,
Is but to think no more. Here's to be satisfi'd.

(Falls on his Sword.)

I've mist my heart. O unperforming hand!
Thou never cou'dst have err'd in a worse time.
My Fortune jades me to the last; and death,
Like a great Man, takes state, and makes me wait
For my admittance.—

(Trampling within.)

Some perhaps from *Cæsar:*
If he shou'd find me living, and suspect
That I plaid booty[19] with my life! I'll mend
My work, ere they can reach me.

(Rises upon his knees.)
Enter Cleopatra, Charmion, and Iras.

CLEOPATRA. Where is my Lord? where is he?
CHARMION. There he lies,
And dead *Ventidius* by him.

19. To play badly intentionally.

CLEOPATRA. My fears were Prophets; I am come too late.
O that accurs'd *Alexas!*

(Runs to him.)

ANTONY. Art thou living?
Or am I dead before I knew? and thou
The first kind Ghost that meets me?

CLEOPATRA. Help me seat him.
Send quickly, send for help.

(They place him in a Chair.)

ANTONY. I am answer'd.
We live both. Sit thee down, my *Cleopatra:*
I'll make the most I can of life, to stay
A moment more with thee.

CLEOPATRA. How is it with you?

ANTONY. 'Tis as with a man
Removing in a hurry; all pack'd up,
But one dear Jewel that his haste forgot;
And he, for that, returns upon the spur:
So I come back, for thee.

CLEOPATRA. Too long, you Heav'ns, you have been cruel to me;
Now show your mended Faith, and give me back
His fleeting life.

ANTONY. It will not be, my Love.
I keep my soul by force.
Say but thou art not false.

CLEOPATRA. 'Tis now too late
To say I'm true: I'll prove it, and die with you.
Unknown to me, *Alexas* feign'd my death:
Which, when I knew, I hasted, to prevent
This fatal consequence. My Fleet betray'd
Both you and me.

ANTONY. And *Dollabella*—

CLEOPATRA. Scarce
Esteem'd before he lov'd; but hated now.

ANTONY. Enough: my life's not long enough for more.
Thou say'st, thou wilt come after: I believe thee;
For I can now believe whate'er thou sayst,
That we may part more kindly.

CLEOPATRA. I will come:
Doubt not, my life, I'll come, and quickly too:
Cæsar shall triumph o'er no part of thee.

ANTONY. But grieve not, while thou stay'st,
My last disastrous times:
Think we have had a clear and glorious day;

And Heav'n did kindly to delay the storm
Just till our close of ev'ning. Ten years love,
And not a moment lost, but all improv'd
To th' utmost joys: What Ages have we liv'd!
And now to die each others; and, so dying,
While hand in hand we walk in Groves below,
Whole Troops of Lovers Ghosts shall flock about us,
And all the Train be ours.

CLEOPATRA. Your words are like the Notes of dying Swans,
Too sweet to last. Were there so many hours
For your unkindness, and not one for love?

ANTONY. No, not a minute.—This one kiss—more worth
Than all I leave to *Cæsar.*

(Dies.)

CLEOPATRA. O, tell me so again,
And take ten thousand kisses, for that word.
My Lord, my Lord: speak, if you yet have being;
Sigh to me, if you cannot speak; or cast
One look: Do anything that shows you live.

IRAS. He's gone too far, to hear you;
And this you see, a lump of sensless Clay,
The leavings of a Soul.

CHARMION. Remember, Madam,
He charg'd you not to grieve.

CLEOPATRA. And I'll obey him.
I have not lov'd a *Roman* not to know
What should become his Wife; his Wife, my *Charmion;*
For 'tis to that high Title I aspire,
And now I'll not die less. Let dull *Octavia*
Survive, to mourn him dead: My nobler Fate
Shall knit our Spousals with a tie too strong
For *Roman* Laws to break.

IRAS. Will you then die?

CLEOPATRA. Why shou'dst thou make that question?

IRAS. *Cæsar* is merciful.

CLEOPATRA. Let him be so
To those that want his mercy: My poor Lord
Made no such Cov'nant with him, to spare me
When he was dead. Yield me to *Cæsar's* pride?
What, to be led in triumph through the Streets,
A spectacle to base *Plebeian* eyes;
While some dejected Friend of *Antony's*,
Close in a corner, shakes his head, and mutters
A secret curse on her who ruin'd him!
I'll none of that.

CHARMION. Whatever you resolve,
I'll follow ev'n to death.
IRAS. I only fear'd
For you; but more shou'd fear to live without you.
CLEOPATRA. Why, now 'tis as it should be. Quick, my Friends,
Dispatch; ere this, the Town's in *Cæsar*'s hands:
My Lord looks down concern'd, and fears my stay,
Lest I shou'd be surpris'd;
Keep him not waiting for his love too long.
You, *Charmion,* bring my Crown and richest Jewels,
With 'em, the Wreath of Victory I made
(Vain Augury!) for him, who now lies dead.
You, *Iras,* bring the cure of all our ills.
IRAS. The Aspics, Madam?
CLEOPATRA. Must I bid you twice?

[*Exeunt* Charmion *and* Iras.

'Tis sweet to die, when they wou'd force life on me,
To rush into the dark aboad of death,
And seize him first; if he be like my Love,
He is not frightful sure.
We're now alone, in secresie and silence;
And is not this like Lovers? I may kiss
These pale, cold lips; *Octavia* does not see me;
And, Oh! 'tis better far to have him thus,
Than see him in her arms.—Oh, welcome, welcome.

Enter Charmion, Iras.

CHARMION. What must be done?
CLEOPATRA. Short Ceremony, Friends;
But yet it must be decent. First, this Laurel
Shall crown my Hero's Head: he fell not basely,
Nor left his Shield behind him. Only thou
Cou'dst triumph o'er thy self; and thou alone
Wert worthy so to triumph.
CHARMION. To what end
These Ensigns° of your Pomp and Royalty? symbols
CLEOPATRA. Dull, that thou art! why 'tis to meet my Love;
As when I saw him first, on *Cydnos* bank,
All sparkling, like a Goddess; so adorn'd,
I'll find him once again: my second Spousals
Shall match my first, in Glory. Haste, haste, both,
And dress the Bride of *Antony.*
CHARMION. 'Tis done.
CLEOPATRA. Now seat me by my Lord. I claim this place;
For I must conquer *Cæsar* too, like him,

And win my share o'th' World. Hail, you dear Relicks
Of my Immortal Love!
O let no Impious hand remove you hence;
But rest for ever here. Let *Ægypt* give
His death that peace, which it deny'd his life.
Reach me the Casket.

IRAS. Underneath the fruit the Aspick lies.

CLEOPATRA. *putting aside the leaves.* Welcom, thou kind Deceiver!
Thou best of Thieves; who, with an easie key,
Dost open life, and, unperceiv'd by us,
Ev'n steal us from our selves: discharging so
Death's dreadful office, better than himself,
Touching our limbs so gently into slumber,
That Death stands by, deceiv'd by his own Image,
And thinks himself but Sleep.

SERAPION. *within.* The Queen, where is she?
The Town is yielded, *Cæsar*'s at the Gates.

CLEOPATRA. He comes too late t' invade the Rights of Death.
Haste, bare my Arm, and rouze the Serpent's fury.

[*Holds out her Arm, and draws it back.*

Coward Flesh—
Wou'dst thou conspire with *Cæsar,* to betray me,
As thou wert none of mine? I'll force thee to't,
And not be sent by him,
But bring, my self my Soul to *Antony.*

[*Turns aside, and then shows her Arm bloody.*

Take hence; the work is done.

SERAPION. *within.* Break ope the door,
And guard the Traitor well.

CHARMION. The next is ours.

IRAS. Now, *Charmion,* to be worthy
Of our great Queen and Mistress.

[*They apply the Aspicks.*

CLEOPATRA. Already, Death, I feel thee in my Veins;
I go with such a will to find my Lord,
That we shall quickly meet.
A heavy numness creeps through every limb,
And now 'tis at my head: My eye-lids fall,
And my dear Love is vanish'd in a mist.
Where shall I find him, where? O turn me to him,
And lay me on his breast.—*Cæsar,* thy worst;
Now part us, if thou canst.

(Dies.)

[Iras *sinks down at her feet, and dies;*
Charmion *stands behind her Chair,*
as dressing her head.

Enter Serapion, *two Priests,* Alexas *bound,* Ægyptians.

TWO PRIESTS. Behold, *Serapion,* what havock Death has made!
SERAPION. 'Twas what I fear'd. *Charmion,* is this well done?
CHARMION. Yes, 'tis well done, and like a Queen, the last
Of her great race: I follow her.

(Sinks down; Dies.)

ALEXAS. 'Tis true,
She has done well: Much better thus to die,
Than live to make a Holy-day in *Rome.*
SERAPION. See, how the Lovers sit in State together,
As they were giving Laws to half Mankind.
Th' impression of a smile left in her face,
Shows she dy'd pleas'd with him for whom she liv'd,
And went to charm him in another World.
Cæsar's just entring: grief has now no leisure.
Secure that Villain, as our pledge of safety
To grace th' Imperial Triumph. Sleep, blest Pair,
Secure from humane chance, long Ages out,
While all the Storms of Fate fly o'er your Tomb;
And Fame, to late Posterity, shall tell,
No Lovers liv'd so great, or dy'd so well.

[*Exeunt.*

EPILOGUE.

POETS, *like Disputants, when Reasons fail,*
Have one sure Refuge left; and that's to rail.
Fop, Coxcomb, Fool, *are thunder'd through the Pit;*
And this is all their Equipage of Wit.
We wonder how the Devil this diff'rence grows,
Betwixt our Fools in Verse, and yours in Prose:
For, 'Faith, the quarrel rightly understood,
'Tis Civil War *with their own Flesh and Blood.*
The thread-bare Author hates the gawdy Coat;
And swears at the Guilt Coach, but swears a-foot:
For 'tis observ'd of every Scribling Man,
He grows a Fop as fast as e'er he can;
Prunes up, and asks his Oracle the Glass,
If Pink or Purple best become his face.
For our poor Wretch, he neither rails nor prays; }

Nor likes your Wit just as you like his Plays; }
He has not yet so much of Mr. Bays.[20] }
He does his best; and if he cannot please,
Wou'd quietly sue out his Writ of Ease.[21]
Yet, if he might his own Grand Jury call,
By the Fair Sex he begs to stand or fall.
Let Cæsar's Pow'r the Mens ambition move,
But grace You him who lost the World for Love.
Yet if some antiquated Lady say,
The last Age is not Copy'd in his Play;
Heav'n help the Man who for that face must drudge,
Which only has the wrinkles of a Judge.
Let not the Young and Beauteous join with those;
For shou'd you raise such numerous Hosts of Foes,
Young Wits and Sparks he to his aid must call;
'Tis more than one Man's work to please you all.

FINIS

20. The character in which Buckingham and Howard satirized Dryden and heroic drama in *The Rehearsal.*

21. An application for discharge from employment or obligation.

The Plain Dealer

William Wycherley was born in Shropshire in 1641, the eldest of six children. His father was a Royalist who became steward to the Marquess of Winchester. Wycherley was educated by his father until at the age of fifteen he was sent to France (at the time, a more hospitable environment for Royalists) and became part of the salon of Julie-Lucine d'Angennes, Madame de Montausier. In France he converted to Catholicism. He returned to England in 1659 shortly before the restoration of the Stuart monarchy, was admitted to the Inner Temple to study law, and then went briefly to Queen's College, Oxford, where he reconverted to the Anglican Church. After Oxford Wycherley embarked on a career as a man who served in the military and about town. He served in Ireland in the Earl of Arran's regiment in 1662, may have served in the diplomatic mission to Spain of Sir Richard Fanshawe in 1664, on his own testimony served at sea in the second Dutch War in 1665 (although in what unit and capacity is unknown), and in 1672 joined the regiment of the Duke of Buckingham, whom he served as equerry and in which he rose to the rank of captain. In London he became the lover of the Duchess of Cleveland, formerly the mistress of Charles II and others. Wycherley wrote four plays: *Love in a Wood* (1671), *The Gentleman Dancing Master* (1672), *The Country Wife* (1675), and *The Plain Dealer* (1676). But in 1677 he became ill and was sent by Charles II to recuperate abroad. When he returned, Charles II made him tutor to one of his illegitimate sons, the Duke of Richmond, at the enormous sum of £1500 a year. Wycherley then unwisely married the Countess of Drogheda, a passionate, jealous, and unstable woman, and in doing so forfeited the favor of the king. The countess was already in debt, and the will of her previous husband was contested by his family. When she died in 1685, Wycherley found himself in still more legal difficulties and was for a time committed to the Fleet Prison for large debts. Wycherley reconverted to Catholicism and in 1686 James II had him released from prison, made him a present of £500, and awarded him a pension of

The copy text is a facsimile of the 1677 quarto (London: The Scolar Press Limited, 1971). Also consulted is Peter Holland's *The Plays of William Wycherley* (Cambridge: Cambridge University Press, 1981), 357–485.

£200. The abdication of James II in 1688 meant the loss of his pension, and Wycherley retreated to his father's estate. His father paid his debts, but aware of his son's profligacy, when he left William the estate did so only as a life tenancy, so Wycherley could not ruin it. With his memory impaired by illness, Wycherley spent most of his time in the countryside; as an old man he asked the young Alexander Pope to help him revise his poems for publication. Eleven days before his death in 1715 he was bullied into marrying a cousin's (Thomas Shrimpton's) mistress (Elizabeth Jackson); Shrimpton, after Wycherley's death, married her himself, and after more lawsuits gained his estate.

The Plain Dealer's two sources are Shakespeare's *Twelfth Night* (c. 1601) and Molière's *Le Misanthrope* (1666), but the play, while borrowing both plot devices and motifs, is nevertheless utterly different from either of its predecessors. Wycherley was sometimes called Manly by his friends, but it is a two-edged compliment and Wycherley deftly uses that fact in the play: on the one hand, Manly is quite right in his savage indignation at the corruption and hypocrisy of Restoration London and its courts in particular; on the other, he is not an impartial, virtuous satirist who stands aloof from the vices that surround him. Aware of the faults of his society and his acquaintances, he is deliberately blind to his own weaknesses. The virtue of Fidelia and the good sense of Freeman and Eliza mitigate Wycherley's portrayal of a vicious society, but Manly's retreat from it at the end of the play indicates that satire can reveal but not mend vice. Alongside the satire is a very funny set of fools, incidents, and mistaken identifications that show why the Earl of Rochester paired Wycherley with Thomas Shadwell as the only writers of true comedy in England in the 1670s.

William Wycherley, *The Plain Dealer. A Comedy.*

PROLOGUE,

SPOKEN BY THE PLAIN DEALER.

I the PLAIN-DEALER *am to Act to Day:*
And my rough Part begins before the Play.
First, you who Scrible, yet hate all that Write,
And keep each other Company in Spite,
As Rivals in your common Mistress, Fame,
And, with faint Praises, one another Damn;
'Tis a good Play (we know) you can't forgive,
But grudge your selves, the pleasure you receive:
Our Scribler therefore bluntly bid me say,
He wou'd not have the Wits pleas'd here to Day.
Next, you, the fine, loud Gentlemen, o'th' Pit,
Who Damn all Playes; yet, if y'ave any Wit,
'Tis but what here you spunge, and daily get;
Poets, like Friends to whom you are in Debt,
You hate: and so Rooks° *laugh, to see undone* cheats

Those Pushing Gamesters whom they live upon[.]
Well, you are Sparks; and still will be i'th' fashion:
Rail then, at Playes, to hide your Obligation.
Now, you shrewd Judges, who the Boxes sway,
Leading the Ladies hearts, and sense astray,
And, for their sakes, see all, and hear no Play;
Correct your Cravats, Foretops, Lock behind;
The Dress and Breeding of the Play ne'r mind:
Plain-dealing *is, you'll say, quite out of fashion;*
You'll hate it here, as in a Dedication.
And your fair Neighbours, in a Limning Poet,[1]
No more than in a Painter will allow it.
Pictures too like, the Ladies will not please:
They must be drawn too here, like Goddesses.
You, as at Lely's[2] *too, would Truncheon° wield,* — staff of authority
And look like Heroes, in a painted Field;
But the coarse Dauber° of the coming Scenes, — clumsy painter
To follow Life, and Nature only means;
Displays you, as you are: makes his fine Woman
A mercenary Jilt, and true to no Man;
His Men of Wit, and Pleasure of the Age,
Are as dull Rogues, as ever cumber'd Stage:
He draws a Friend, only to Custom just;
And makes him naturally break his trust.
I, only, Act a Part like none of you;
And yet, you'll say, it is a Fool's Part too:
An honest Man; who, like you, never winks
At faults; but, unlike you, speaks what he thinks:
The onely Fool who ne'r found Patron yet;
For Truth is now a fault, as well as Wit.
And where else, but on Stages, do we see
Truth pleasing; or rewarded Honesty?
Which our bold Poet does this day in me.
If not to th'Honest, be to th' Prosp'rous kind:
Some Friends at Court let the PLAIN-DEALER *find.*

1. A poet who draws portraits.
2. Peter Lely (1618–80), fashionable portrait painter.

THE PERSONS.[3]

MANLY	Of an honest, surly, nice[4] humour, suppos'd first, in the time of the *Dutch* war, to have procur'd the Command of a Ship, out of Honour, not Interest; and choosing a Sea-life, only to avoid the World.
FREEMAN	*Manly*'s Lieutenant, a Gentleman well Educated, but of a broken Fortune, a complyer with the Age.
VERNISH	*Manly*'s Bosome, and onely Friend.
NOVEL	A pert railing Coxcomb, and an Admirer of Novelties, makes Love to *Olivia.*
MAJOR OLDFOX	An old impertinent Fop, given to Scribling, makes Love to the *Widow Blackacre.*
LORD PLAUSIBLE	A Ceremonious Supple, Commending Coxcomb,[5] in love with *Olivia.*
JERRY-BLACKACRE	A true raw Squire, under Age, and his Mothers Government, bred to the Law.
OLIVIA	*Manly*'s Mistress.
FIDELIA	In love with *Manly,* and follow'd him to Sea in Man's Cloaths.
ELIZA	Cousin to *Olivia.*
LETTICE	*Olivia*'s Woman.
THE WIDOW BLACKACRE	A petulant, litigious Widow, alwayes in Law, and Mother to Squire *Jerry.*

LAWYERS, KNIGHTS OF THE POST,[6] BAYLIFFS, AN ALDERMAN, A BOOKSELLERS PRENTICE, A FOOTBOY, SAILORS, WAITERS, AND ATTENDANTS.

3. Some of the names are charactonyms and indicate the nature of the character: "Vernish" is pronounced "varnish"; "Oldfox" comes from "fox," meaning sword; "Blackacre" was used in law cases to indicate a hypothetical piece of land.

4. In the context of the description of Freeman in the subsequent lines, "nice" here means someone who does not comply with the age, but instead passes judgment upon it, making rigid distinctions. Or as the sailor says in the first scene, a "finical" fellow.

5. A conceited, foolish person.

6. Men who waited by the posts upon which sheriffs posted proclamations and who committed perjury and other legal offense for hire.

THE SCENE
LONDON.

ACT. I.

SCENE I.

Enter Captain Manly, *surlily; and my* Lord Plausible, *following him: and two* Sailors *behind.*

MANLY. Tell not me (my good Lord *Plausible*) of your *Decorums,* supercilious Forms, and slavish Ceremonies; your little Tricks, which you the Spaniels of the World, do daily over and over, for and to one another; not out of love or duty, but your servile fear.

L. PLAUSIBLE. Nay, i'faith, i'faith, you are too passionate, and I must humbly beg your pardon and leave to tell you, they are the Arts, and Rules, the prudent of the World walk by.

MANLY. Let 'em. But I'll have no Leading-strings, I can walk alone; I hate a Harness, and will not tug on in a Faction, kissing my Leader behind, that another Slave may do the like to me.

L. PLAUSIBLE. What, will you be singular then, like no Body? follow[,] Love, and esteem no Body?

MANLY. Rather then be general, like you; follow every Body, Court and kiss every Body; though, perhaps at the same time, you hate every Body.

L. PLAUSIBLE. Why, seriously with your pardon, my dear Friend—

MANLY. With your pardon, my no Friend, I will not, as you do, whisper my hatred, or my scorn, call a man Fool or Knave, by signs, or mouths over his shoulder, whil'st you have him in your arms: for such as you, like common Whores and Pickpockets, are onely dangerous to those you embrace.

L. PLAUSIBLE. Such as I! Heav'ns defend me—upon my Honour—

MANLY. Upon your Title, my Lord, if you'd have me believe you.

L. PLAUSIBLE. Well then, as I am a Person of Honour, I never attempted to abuse, or lessen any person, in my life.

MANLY. What, you were afraid?

L. PLAUSIBLE. No; but seriously, I hate to do a rude thing: no, faith, I speak well of all Mankind.

MANLY. I thought so; but know that speaking well of all Mankind, is the worst kind of Detraction; for it takes away the Reputation of the few good men in the World, by making all alike: now I speak ill of most men, because they deserve it; I that can do a rude thing, rather than an unjust thing.

L. PLAUSIBLE. Well, tell not me, my dear Friend, what people deserve, I ne'r mind that; I, like an Author in a Dedication, never speak well of a man for his sake, but my own; I will not disparage any man, to disparage my self; for to speak ill of people behind their backs, is not like a Person of Honour; and, truly to speak ill of 'em to their faces, is not like a complaisant° person: But if I did say, or do an ill thing to any Body, it shou'd be sure to be behind their backs, out of pure good manners. agreeable

MANLY. Very well; but I, that am an unmannerly Sea-fellow, if I ever speak well of people, (which is very seldom indeed) it shou'd be sure to be behind their backs; and if I wou'd say, or do ill to any, it shou'd be to their faces: I wou'd justle a proud, strutting, over-looking Coxcomb, at the head of his Sycophants, rather than put out my tongue at him, when he were past me; wou'd frown in the arrogant, big, dull face of an overgrown Knave of business, rather than vent my spleen against him, when his back were turn'd; would give fauning Slaves the Lye, whil'st they embrace or commend me; Cowards, whil'st they brag; call a Rascal by no other title, though his Father had left him a Duke's; laugh at Fools aloud, before their Mistresses: And must desire people to leave me, when their visits grow at last as troublesom, as they were at first impertinent.

L. PLAUSIBLE. I wou'd not have my visits troublesom.

MANLY. The onely way to be sure not to have 'em troublesom, is to make 'em when people are not at home; for your visits, like other good turns, are most obliging, when made, or done to a man, in his absence. A pox why shou'd any one, because he has nothing to do go and disturb another mans business?

L. PLAUSIBLE. I beg your pardon, my dear Friend. What, you have business?

MANLY. If you have any, I wou'd not detain your Lordship.

L. PLAUSIBLE. Detain me, dear Sir! I can never have enough of your company.

MANLY. I'm afraid I shou'd be tiresom: I know not what you think.

L. PLAUSIBLE. Well, dear Sir, I see you wou'd have me gone.

MANLY. But I see you won't.

[*Aside.*

L. PLAUSIBLE. Your most faithful—

MANLY. God be w'ye, my Lord.

L. PLAUSIBLE. Your most humble—

MANLY. Farewel.

L. PLAUSIBLE. And eternally—

MANLY. And eternally Ceremony—then the Devil take thee eternally.

[*Aside.*

L. PLAUSIBLE. You shall use no Ceremony, by my life.

MANLY. I do not intend it.

L. PLAUSIBLE. Why do you stir then?

MANLY. Only to see you out of doors, that I may shut 'em, against more welcomes.

L. PLAUSIBLE. Nay, faith that shan't pass upon your most faithful, humble Servant.

MANLY. Nor this any more upon me.

[*Aside.*

L. PLAUSIBLE. Well, you are too strong for me.

MANLY. I'de sooner be visited by the Plague; for that only wou'd keep a man from visits, and his doors shut.

[*Aside.*
[*Exit thrusting out* Lord Plausible.
Manent Sailors.

1 SAILOR. Here's a finical Fellow *Jack!* What a brave fair weather Captain of a Ship he wou'd make!

2 SAILOR. He a Captain of a Ship! it must be when she's in the Dock then; for he looks like one of those that get the King's Commissions for Hulls to sell a Kings Ship, when a brave Fellow has fought her almost to a Long-boat.

1 SAILOR. On my conscience then, *Jack,* that's the reason our Bully *Tar.*[7] sunk our Ship: not only that the *Dutch* might not have her, but that the Courtiers, who laugh at wooden Legs, might not make her Prize.

2 SAILOR. A pox of his sinking, *Tom,* we have made a base, broken, short Voyage of it.

1 SAILOR. Ay, your brisk dealers in Honour, always make quick returns with their Ship to the Dock, and their Men to the Hospitals; 'tis, let me see, just a Month since we set out of the River, and the Wind was almost as cross to us, as the *Dutch.*

2 SAILOR. Well, I forgive him sinking my own poor Truck,° if he wou'd but have given me time and leave to have sav'd black *Kate* of *Wapping*'s[8] small Venture.

cargo

1 SAILOR. Faith I forgive him, since, as the Purser told me, he sunk the value of five or six thousand pound of his own, with which he was to settle himself somewhere in the *Indies,* for our merry Lieutenant was to succeed him in his Commission for the Ship back, for he was resolved never to return again for *England.*

2 SAILOR. So it seemed, by his Fighting.

1 SAILOR. No; but he was a weary of this side of the World here, they say.

7. As the period indicates, "Tar." is an abbreviation of tarpaulin, waterproofed cloth, and metaphorically a seaman.

8. Rough district frequented by sailors and their suppliers in east London on the north bank of the Thames.

2 SAILOR. Ay, or else he wou'd not have bid so fair for a passage into t'other.

1 SAILOR. *Jack,* thou think'st thy self in the Forecastle,[9] thou'rt so waggish; but I tell you then, he had a mind to go live and bask himself on the sunny side of the Globe.

2 SAILOR. What, out of any discontent? for he's alwayes as dogged, as an old Tarpaulin when hindred of a Voyage by a young Pantaloon captain.[10]

1 SAILOR. 'Tis true, I never saw him pleas'd but in the Fight; and then he look'd like one of us, coming from the Pay-table, with a new lining to our Hats under our Arms[.]

2 SAILOR. A pox he's like the Bay of *Biscay,* rough and angry, let the Wind blow where 'twill.

1 SAILOR. Nay, there's no more dealing with him, than with the Land in a Storm, No-Near—

2 SAILOR. 'Tis a hurry-durry° Blade; dost thou remember after we had tug'd hard the old leaky Long-boat, to save his Life, when I welcom'd him ashore, he gave me a box on the ear, and call'd me fawning Water-dog? rough

Enter Manly, *and* Freeman.

1 SAILOR. Hold thy peace, *Jack,* and stand by, the foul weather's coming.

MANLY. You Rascals, Dogs, how cou'd this tame thing get through you?

1 SAILOR. Faith, to tell your Honour the truth, we were at Hob° in the Hall, and whil'st my Brother and I were quarrelling about a Cast, he slunk by us. pitching coins

2 SAILOR. He's a sneaking Fellow I warrant for't.

MANLY. Have more care for the future, you Slaves; go, and with drawn Cutlaces, stand at the Stair foot, and keep all that ask for me from coming up; suppose you were guarding the Scuttle° to the Powder room: let none enter here, at your and their peril. hatch

1 SAILOR. No, for the danger wou'd be the same; you wou'd blow them and us up, if we shou'd.

2 SAILOR. Must no one come to you, Sir?

MANLY. No man, Sir.

1 SAILOR. No man, Sir; but a Woman then, an't like your Honour—

MANLY. No Woman neither, you impertinent Dog. Wou'd you be Pimping? A Sea Pimp is the strangest Monster she has.

2 SAILOR. Indeed, an't like your Honour, 'twill be hard for us to deny a Woman any thing, since we are so newly come on shore.

1 SAILOR. We'll let no old Woman come up, though it were our Trusting Landlady at *Wapping.*

9. Forward part of a ship with the sailors' living quarters.

10. A gentleman sailor, as opposed to a professional seaman.

MANLY. Wou'd you be witty, you Brandy Casks you? you become a jest as ill, as you do a Horse. Be gone, you Dogs, I hear a noise on the Stairs.

[*Exeunt* Sailors.

FREEMAN. Faith, I am sorry you wou'd let the Fop go, I intended to have had some sport with him.

MANLY. Sport with him! A pox then why did you not stay? you shou'd have enjoy'd your Coxcomb, and had him to your self for me.

FREEMAN. No, I shou'd not have car'd for him without you neither; for the pleasure which Fops afford, is like that of Drinking, only good when 'tis shar'd; and a Fool, like a Bottle, which wou'd make you merry in company, will make you dull alone. But how the Devil cou'd you turn a man of his Quality down Stairs? You use a Lord with very little Ceremony, it seems.

MANLY. A Lord! What, thou art one of those who esteem men onely by the marks and value Fortune has set upon 'em, and never consider intrinsick worth; but counterfeit Honour will not be current with me, I weigh the man, not his title; 'tis not the King's stamp can make the Metal better, or heavier: your Lord is a Leaden shilling, which you bend every way; and debases the stamp he bears, instead of being rais'd by't: Here again, you Slaves?

Enter Sailors.

1 SAILOR. Only to receive farther instructions, an't like your Honour: What if a man shou'd bring you money, shou'd we turn him back?

MANLY. All men, I say; must I be pester'd with you too? you Dogs, away.

2 SAILOR. Nay, I know one man your Honour wou'd not have us hinder coming to you, I'm sure.

MANLY. Who's that? speak quickly, Slaves.

2 SAILOR. Why, a man that shou'd bring you a Challenge; For though you refuse Money, Im sure you love Fighting too well to refuse that.

MANLY. Rogue, Rascal, Dog.

[*Kicks the* Sailors *out.*

FREEMAN. Nay, let the poor Rogues have their Forecastle jests; they cannot help 'em in a Fight, scarce when a Ship's sinking.

MANLY. Dam their untimely jests; a Servant's jest is more sauciness than his counsel.

FREEMAN. But what, will you see no Body? not your Friends?

MANLY. Friends—I have but one, and he, I hear, is not in Town; nay, can have but one Friend, for a true heart admits but of one friendship, as of one love; but in having that Friend, I have a thousand, for he has the courage of men in despair, yet the diffidency and caution of Cowards; the secrecie of the Revengeful, and the constancy of Martyrs: one fit to advise, to keep a secret: to fight and dye for his Friend. Such I think him; for I have trusted him with my Mistress in my absence: and the trust of Beauty, is sure the greatest we can shew.

FREEMAN. Well, but all your good thoughts are not for him alone? (I hope:) pray, what d'ye think of me, for a Friend?

MANLY. Of thee! Why, thou art a *Latitudinarian*[11] in Friendship, that is, no Friend; thou dost side with all Mankind, but wilt suffer for none. Thou art indeed like your *Lord Plausible,* the Pink of Courtesie, therefore hast no Friendship; for Ceremony, and great Professing, renders Friendship as much suspected, as it does Religion.

FREEMAN. And no Professing, no Ceremony at all in Friendship, were as unnatural and as undecent as in Religion; and there is hardly such a thing as an honest Hypocrite, who professes himself to be worse than he is, unless it be your self; for though I cou'd never get you to say you were my Friend, I know you'll prove so.

MANLY. I must confess, I am so much your Friend, I wou'd not deceive you, therefore must tell you (not only because my heart is taken up) but according to your rules of Friendship, I cannot be your Friend.

FREEMAN. Why pray?

MANLY. Because he that is (you'll say) a true Friend to a man, is a Friend to all his Friends; but you must pardon me, I cannot wish well to Pimps, Flatterers, Detractors, and Cowards, stiff nodding Knaves, and supple pliant kissing Fools: now, all these I have seen you use, like the dearest Friends in the World.

FREEMAN. Hah, hah, hah—What, you observ'd me, I warrant, in the Galleries at *Whitehall,*[12] doing the business of the place! Pshaw Court Professions, like Court Promises, go for nothing, man. But, faith, cou'd you think I was a Friend to all those I hugg'd, kiss'd, flatter'd, bow'd to? Hah, ha—

MANLY. You told 'em so, and swore it too; I heard you.

FREEMAN. Ay, but, when their backs were turn'd, did not I tell you they were Rogues, Villains, Rascals, whom I despis'd and hated?

MANLY. Very fine! But what reason had I to believe you spoke your heart to me, since you profess'd deceiving so many?

11. Latitudiarians were so called because they allowed latitude for different beliefs. In the late seventeenth century some Christians argued that anyone who accepted the Apostle's Creed should be regarded as a Christian, and even that it was possible that virtuous pagans could be saved.

12. The royal palace in Westminster.

FREEMAN. Why, don't you know, good Captain, that telling truth is a quality as prejudicial, to a man that wou'd thrive in the World, as square Play to a Cheat, or true Love to a Whore! Wou'd you have a man speak truth to his ruine? You are severer than the Law, which requires no man to swear against himself; you wou'd have me speak truth against my self, I warrant, and tell my promising Friend, the Courtier, he has a bad memory?

MANLY. Yes.

FREEMAN. And so make him remember to forget my business; and I shou'd tell the great Lawyer too, that he takes oftner Fees to hold his tongue, than to speak!

MANLY. No doubt on't.

FREEMAN. Ay, and have him hang, or ruine me, when he shou'd come to be a Judge, and I before him. And you wou'd have me tell the new Officer, who bought his Employment lately, that he is a Coward?

MANLY. Ay.

FREEMAN. And so get my self cashiered, not him, he having the better Friends, though I the better Sword. And I shou'd tell the Scribler of Honour, that Heraldry were a prettier and fitter Study, for so fine a Gentleman, than Poetry!

MANLY. Certainly.

FREEMAN. And so find my self maul'd in his next hir'd Lampoon. And you wou'd have me tell the holy Lady too, she lies with her Chaplain.

MANLY. No doubt on't.

FREEMAN. And so draw the Clergy upon my back, and want a good Table to Dine at sometimes. And by the same reason too, I shou'd tell you, that the World thinks you a Mad-man, a Brutal and have you cut my throat, or worse, hate me! What other good success of all my *Plain-dealing* cou'd I have, than what I've mentioned?

MANLY. Why, first your promising Courtier wou'd keep his word, out of fear of more reproaches; or at least wou'd give you no more vain hopes: your Lawyer wou'd serve you more faithfully; for he, having no Honor but his Interest, is truest still to him he knows suspects him: The new Officer wou'd provoke thee to make him a Coward, and so be cashier'd, that thou, or some other honest Fellow, who had more courage than money, might get his place: the Noble Sonnetteer wou'd trouble thee no more with his Madrigals: the praying Lady wou'd leave off railing at Wenching before thee, and not turn away her Chambermaid, for her own known frailty with thee: and I, instead of hating thee, sheu'd love thee, for thy *Plain-dealing;* and in lieu of being mortifi'd, am proud that the World and I think not well of one another.

FREEMAN. Well, Doctors differ. You are for *Plain-dealing,* I find; but against your particular Notions, I have the practice of the whole World. Observe but any Morning what people do when they get together on the *Exchange,*[13] in *Westminster-hall,*[14] or the Galleries in *Whitehall.*

MANLY. I must confess, there they seem to rehearse Bays's grand Dance:[15] here you see a *Bishop* bowing low to a gaudy *Atheist;* a Judge, to a Door-keeper; a great Lord, to a Fishmonger, or a Scrivener with a Jack-chain[16] about his neck; a Lawyer, to a Serjeant at Arms; a velvet *Physician* to a threadbare *Chymist:* and a supple Gentleman Usher, to a surly Beef-eater; and so tread round in a preposterous huddle of Ceremony to each other, whil'st they can hardly hold their solemn false countenances.

FREEMAN. Well, they understand the World.

MANLY. Which I do not, I confess.

FREEMAN. But, Sir, pray believe the Friendship I promise you, real, whatsoever I have profest to others: try me, at least.

MANLY. Why, what wou'd you do for me?

FREEMAN. I wou'd fight for you.

MANLY. That you wou'd do for your own Honour: but what else?

FREEMAN. I wou'd lend you money, if I had it.

MANLY. To borrow more of me another time. That were but putting your money to Interest, a Usurer wou'd be as good a Friend. But what other piece of Friendship?

FREEMAN. I wou'd speak well of you to your Enemies.

MANLY. To encourage others to be your Friends, by a shew of gratitude: but what else?

FREEMAN. Nay, I wou'd not hear you ill spoken of behind your back, by my Friend.

MANLY. Nay, then thou'rt a Friend indeed; but it were unreasonable to expect it from thee, as the World goes now: when new Friends, like new Mistresses, are got by disparaging old ones.

Enter Fidelia.[17]

But here comes another, will say as much at least; dost thou not love me devilishly too, my little Voluntier, as well as he, or any man can?

FIDELIA. Better than any man can love you, my dear Captain.

13. Probably the Royal Exchange in London, where bankers and merchants transacted business, rather than the New Exchange, a location for numerous shops, since the issue here is the manipulation of power.

14. Location of law courts and shops.

15. In Buckingham and Howard's *The Rehearsal,* act 5, scene 1.

16. A notary's chain of office.

17. Fidelia is dressed in men's clothing as a disguise. One reason for the popularity of such "breeches" parts is that they displayed a woman's figure to advantage compared to a dress.

MANLY. Look you there, I told you so.

FIDELIA. As well as you do Truth, or Honour, Sir; as well.

MANLY. Nay, good young Gentleman, enough, for shame; thou hast been a Page, by thy Flattering and Lying, to one of those praying Ladies, who love Flattery so well, they are jealous of it, and wert turn'd away for saying the same things to the old Housekeeper for Sweetmeats, as you did to your Lady; for thou flatterest every thing, and every Body alike.

FIDELIA. You, dear Sir, shou'd not suspect the truth of what I say of you, though to you; Fame, the old Lyar, is believ'd, when she speaks Wonders of you; you cannot be flatter'd, Sir, your Merit is unspeakable.

MANLY. Hold, hold, Sir, or I shall suspect worse of you, that you have been a Cushion-bearer to some State Hypocrite, and turn'd away by the Chaplains, for out flattering their Probation Sermons for a Benefice.[18]

FIDELIA. Suspect me for any thing, Sir, but the want of Love, Faith, and Duty to you, the bravest, worthiest of Mankind; believe me, I cou'd dye for you, Sir.

MANLY. Nay, there you lye, Sir; did not I see thee more afraid in the Fight, than the Chaplain of the Ship, or the Purser that bought his place?

FIDELIA. Can he be said to be afraid, that ventures to Sea with you?

MANLY. Fie, fie, no more, I shall hate thy Flattery worse than thy Cowardice, nay, than thy Bragging.

FIDELIA. Well, I own then I was afraid, mightily afraid; yet for you I wou'd be afraid again, an hundred times afraid: dying is ceasing to be afraid; and that I cou'd do sure for you, and you'll believe me one day.

[*Weeps.*

FREEMAN. Poor Youth! believe his eyes, if not his tongue: he seems to speak truth with them.

MANLY. What, does he cry? A pox on't, a Maudlin Flatterer is as nauseously troublesom, as a Maudlin Drunkard; no more, you little Milksop, do not cry, I'll never make thee afraid again; for of all men, if I had occasion, thou shou'dst not be my Second; and, when I go to Sea again, thou shalt venture thy life no more with me.

FIDELIA. Why, will you leave me behind then? (If you wou'd preserve my life, I'm sure you shou'd not.)

Aside.

MANLY. Leave thee behind! Ay, ay, thou art a hopeful Youth for the shore only; here thou wilt live to be cherish'd by Fortune, and the

18. A sermon given as an audition for a clerical appointment.

great ones; for thou may'st easily come to out-flatter a dull Poet, out-lye a Coffee-house or Gazet-writer, out-swear a Knight of the Post, out-watch a Pimp, out-fawn a Rook, out-promise a Lover, out-rail a Wit, and out-brag a Sea-captain: All this thou canst do, because thou'rt a Coward, a thing I hate, therefore thou'lt do better with the World than with me; and these are the good courses you must take in the World. There's good advice, at least, at parting; go, and be happy with't.

FIDELIA. Parting, Sir! O let me not hear that dismal word.

MANLY. If my words frighten thee, begone the sooner; for, to be plain with thee, Cowardice and I cannot dwell together.

FIDELIA. And Cruelty and Courage never dwelt together sure, Sir. Do not turn me off to shame and misery; for I am helpless and friendless.

MANLY. Friendless! there are half a score Friends for thee then. [*Offers her Gold.*] I leave my self no more: they'll help thee a little. Be gone, go, I must be cruel to thee (if thou call'st it so) out of pity.

FIDELIA. If you wou'd be cruelly pitiful, Sir, let it be with your Sword, not Gold.

[*Exit.*
Enter first Sailor.

1 SAILOR. We have, with much ado, turn'd away two Gentlemen, who told us forty times over, their names were Mr. *Novel,* and Major *Oldfox.*

MANLY. Well, to your Post again.

[*Exit* Sailor.

But how come those Puppies coupled always together?

FREEMAN. O, the Coxcombs keep each other company, to shew each other, as *Novel* calls it; or, as *Oldfox* sayes, like two Knives, to whet one another.

MANLY. And set other peoples teeth an edge.

Enter second Sailor.

2 SAILOR. Here is a Woman, an't like your Honour, scolds and bustles with us, to come in, as much as a Seamans Widow at the *Navy-Office:* her name is Mrs *Blackacre.*

MANLY. That Fiend too!

FREEMAN. The Widow *Blackacre,* is it not? that Litigious She-Pettyfogger,[19] who is at Law and difference with all the World; but I wish I cou'd make her agree with me in the Church: they say she has Fifteen hundred pounds a Year Jointure,[20] and the care of her Son, that is, the destruction of his Estate.

19. From the French *petit vogue* (of small repute), a lawyer ready to take almost any case.
20. A yearly income agreed to in the marriage settlement; in this case, a very healthy sum of money.

MANLY. Her Lawyers, Attornies and Solicitors have Fifteen hundred pound a Year, whilst she is contented to be poor, to make other people so; For she is as vexatious as her Father was, the great Attorney, nay, as a dozen *Norfolk* Attornies,[21] and as implacable an Adversary as a Wife suing for Alimony, or a Parson for his Tithes; and she loves an *Easter* Term,[22] or any Term, not as other Countrey Ladies do, to come up to be fine, Cuckold their Husbands, and take their pleasure; for she has no pleasure, but in vexing others, and is usually cloath'd and dagled° like a Baud in disguise, pursu'd through Alleys by Serjeants. When she is in Town, she lodges in one of the Inns of Chancery,[23] where she breeds her Son, and is her self his Tutoress in Law-French; and for her Countrey abode, tho' she has no Estate there, she chooses *Norfolk*. But, bid her come in, with a pox to her, she is *Olivia*'s Kinswoman, and may make me amends for her visit, by some discourse of that dear Woman.

bespattered

[*Exit* Sailor.

Enter Widow Blackacre, *with a Mantle, and a green Bag,*[24] *and several Papers in the other hand:* Jerry Blackacre *her Son, in a Gown, laden with green Bags, following her.*

WIDOW. I never had so much to do with a Judges Door keeper, as with yours; but—

MANLY. But the incomparable *Olivia,* how does she since I went?

WIDOW. Since you went, my Suit—

MANLY. *Olivia,* I say, is she well?

WIDOW. My Suit, if you had not return'd—

MANLY. Dam your Suit, how does your Cousin *Olivia?*

WIDOW. My Suit, I say, had been quite lost; but now—

MANLY. But now, where is *Olivia?* in Town? For—

WIDOW. For to morrow we are to have a Hearing.

MANLY. Wou'd you would let me have a Hearing to day.

WIDOW. But why won't you hear me?

MANLY. I am no Judge, and you talk of nothing but Suits; but, pray tell me, when did you see *Olivia?*

WIDOW. I am no Visiter, but a Woman of Business; or, if I ever visit, 'tis only the *Chancery-lane*[25] Ladies, Ladies towards the Law; and not any of your lazy, good-for-nothing Flirts, who cannot

21. Norfolk was an area noted for its litigiousness. As early as 1455 the House of Commons petitioned Henry VI to limit the number of lawyers in the area to six.

22. One of the four terms of the courts; at this time the dates were moveable, but it took place in the spring.

23. Buildings where attorneys were trained, and which provided both lodgings and offices for solicitors.

24. The traditional color for the bag that held the briefing papers of lawyers.

25. Street near the Inns of Court.

read Law- French, tho' a Gallant writ it. But, as I was telling you, my Suit—

MANLY. Dam these impertinent, vexatious people of Business, of all Sexes; they are still troubling the World with the tedious recitals of their Law-suits: and one can no more stop their mouths, than a Wit's, when he talks of himself; or an Intelligencer's, when he talks of other people.

WIDOW. And a pox of all vexatious, impertinent Lovers; they are still perplexing the World with the tedious Narrations of their Love-suits, and Discourses of their Mistresses: You are as troublesom to a poor Widow of Business, as a young Coxcombly Rithming Lover.

MANLY. And thou art as troublesom to me, as a Rook to a losing Gamester, or a young putter of Cases to his Mistress and Sempstress, who has Love in her head for another.

WIDOW. Nay, since you talk of putting of Cases, and will not hear me speak, hear our *Jerry* a little; let him put our Case to you, for the Tryal's to-morrow; and since you are my chief Witness, I wou'd have your memory refresh'd and your judgment inform'd, that you may not give your evidence improperly. Speak out, Child.

JERRY. Yes, forsooth. Hemh! Hemh! *John-a-Stiles*—

MANLY. You may talk, young Lawyer, but I shall no more mind you, than a hungry Judge does a Cause, after the Clock has struck One.

FREEMAN. Nay, you'll find him as peevish too.

WIDOW. No matter. *Jerry,* go on. Do you observe it then, Sir, for I think I have seen you in a Gown once. Lord, I cou'd hear our *Jerry* put Cases all day long! Mark him, Sir.

JERRY. *John-a-Stiles*—no—There are first, *Fitz, Pere,* and *Ayle,*—No, no, *Ayle, Pere,* and *Fitz; Ayle* is seized in Fee of *Blackacre; John-a-Stiles* disseises° *Ayle; Ayle* makes Claim, and the Disseisor dyes; then the *Ayle*—no, the *Fitz.*[26] disposses

WIDOW. No, the *Pere,* Sirrah.

JERRY. O, the *Pere:* ay, the *Pere,* Sir, and the *Fitz*—no the *Ayle;* no, the *Pere* and the *Fitz,* Sir, and—

MANLY. Dam *Pere, Mere,* and *Fitz,* Sir.

WIDOW. No, you are out, Child; hear me, Captain then; There are *Ayle, Pere* and *Fitz, Ayle* is seised in Fee of *Blackacre;* and being so seised, *John-a-Stiles* disseises the *Ayle, Ayle* makes Claim, and the Disseisor dyes; and then the *Pere* re-enters, the *Pere* Sirrah, the *Pere*—[*To* Jerry.] And the *Fitz* enters upon the *Pere,* and the

26. John-a-Stiles is a legal convention, like John Doe. Fitz, Pere, Ayle, and Mere are law-French for son, father, grandfather, and mother.

Ayle brings his Writ of Disseisin, in the *Post;* and the *Pere* brings his writ of disseisin, in the *Pere,* and[—]

MANLY. Canst thou hear this stuff, *Freeman?* I cou'd as soon suffer a whole noise of Flatterers at a great man's Levy in a morning; but thou hast servile complacency enough to listen to a Quibling Statesman, in disgrace, nay, and be before hand with him, in laughing at his dull No-jest; but I—

[*Offering to go out.*

WIDOW. Nay, Sir, hold. Where's the *sub-pœna, Jerry?* I must serve you, Sir. You are requir'd, by this, to give your testimony.—

MANLY. I'll be forsworn, to be reveng'd on thee.

[*Exit* Manly, *throwing away the* Subpœna.

WIDOW. Get you gone, for a Lawless companion. Come, *Jerry,* I had almost forgot we were to meet at the Masters[27] at three: let us mind our business still, Child.

JERRY. I, forsooth, e'en so let's.

FREEMAN. Nay, Madam, now I wou'd beg you to hear me a little, a little of my business.

WIDOW. I have business of my own calls me away, Sir.

FREEMAN. My business wou'd prove yours too, dear Madam.

WIDOW. Yours would be some sweet business, I warrant: What, 'tis no *Westminster-Hall* business? Wou'd you have my advice?

FREEMAN. No, faith, 'tis a little *Westminster-Abby* business: I wou'd have your consent.

WIDOW. O fie, fie, Sir; to me such discourse, before my dear Minor there!

JERRY. Ay, ay, Mother, he wou'd be taking Livery and Seisin of your Jointure, by digging the Turf; but I'll watch your waters, Bully, ifac.°[28] Come away, Mother. — in faith

[*Exit* Jerry *haling away his Mother.*
Manet Freeman: *Enter to him* Fidelia.

FIDELIA. Dear Sir, you have pity; beget but some in our Captain for me.

FREEMAN. Where is he?

FIDELIA. Within; swearing, as much as he did in the great storm, and cursing you, and sometimes sinks into calms and sighs, and talks of his *Olivia.*

27. The master of chancery, an officer of the court that had jurisdiction over trusts and estates.

28. Livery and seisin was the transfer of a freehold estate by the delivery of a symbolic piece of turf, and the jointure is the widow's contractual right to her husband's estate as secured usually at the time of marriage; the state of a person's health was determined by examining a person's urine (waters), and Jerry is saying he will examine Freeman's actions closely.

FREEMAN. He wou'd never trust me to see her: is she handsom?

FIDELIA. No, if you'll take my word; but I am not a proper Judge.

FREEMAN. What is she?

FIDELIA. A Gentlewoman, I suppose, but of as mean a Fortune as Beauty; but her Relations wou'd not suffer her to go with him to the *Indies:* and his aversion to this side of the World, together with the late opportunity of commanding the Convoy, wou'd not let him stay here longer, tho' to enjoy her.

FREEMAN. He loves her mightily then.

FIDELIA. Yes, so well, that the remainder of his Fortune (I hear about five or six thousand pounds) he has left her, in case he had dy'ed by the way, or before she cou'd prevail with her Friends to follow him, which he expected she shou'd do; and has left behind him his great bosom Friend to be her Convoy to him.

FREEMAN. What Charms has she for him, if she be not handsom?

FIDELIA. He fancies her, I suppose, the onely Woman of Truth and Sincerity in the World.

FREEMAN. No common Beauty, I confess.

FIDELIA. Or else sure he wou'd not have trusted her with so great a share of his Fortune, in his absence; I suppose (since his late loss) all he has.

FREEMAN. Why, has he left it in her own custody?

FIDELIA. I am told so.

FREEMAN. Then he has shew'd Love to her indeed, in leaving her, like an old Husband that dyes as soon as he has made his Wife a good Jointure; but I'll go in to him, and speak for you, and know more from him of his *Olivia.*

[*Exit.*
Manet Fidelia, *sola.*

FIDELIA. His *Olivia* indeed, his happy *Olivia,*
Yet she was left behind, when I was with him;
But she was ne'r out of his mind or heart.
She has told him she lov'd him; I have shew'd it,
And durst not tell him so, till I had done,
Under this habit, such convincing Acts
Of loving Friendship for him, that through it
He first might find out both my Sex and Love;
And, when I'd had him from his fair *Olivia,*
And this bright World of artful Beauties here,
Might then have hop'd, he wou'd have look'd on me,
Amongst the sooty *Indians;* and I cou'd
To choose, there live his Wife, where Wives are forc'd
To live no longer, when their Husbands dye:
Nay, what's yet worse, to share 'em whil'st they live
With many Rival Wives. But here he comes,

And I must yet keep out of his sight, not
To lose it for ever.

[*Exit.*

Enter Manly *and* Freeman.

FREEMAN. But pray what strange Charms has she that cou'd make you love?

MANLY. Strange Charms indeed! She has Beauty enough to call in question her Wit or Virtue, and her Form wou'd make a starved Hermit a Ravisher; yet her Virtue and Conduct, wou'd preserve her from the subtil Lust of a pamper'd Prelate. She is so perfect a Beauty, that Art cou'd not better it, nor Affectation deform it; yet all this is nothing. Her tongue as well as face, ne'r knew artifice; nor ever did her words or looks contradict her heart: She is all truth, and hates the lying, masking, daubing World, as I do; for which I love her, and for which I think she dislikes not me: for she has often shut out of her conversation for mine, the gaudy fluttering Parrots of the Town, Apes and Echoes of men only, and refus'd their common-place pert chat, flattery, and submissions, to be entertain'd with my sullen bluntness, and honest love. And, last of all, swore to me, since her Parents wou'd not suffer her to go with me, she wou'd stay behind for no other man; but follow me, without their leave, if not to be obtain'd. Which Oath—

FREEMAN. Did you think she wou'd keep?

MANLY. Yes; for she is not (I tell you) like other Women, but can keep her promise, tho' she has sworn to keep it; but, that she might the better keep it, I left her the value of five or six thousand pound: for Womens wants are generally the most importunate Solicitors to Love, or Marriage.

FREEMAN. And Money summons Lovers, more than Beauty, and augments but their importunity, and their number; so makes it the harder for a Woman to deny 'em. For my part, I am for the *French* Maxim, if you would have your Female Subjects Loyal, keep 'em poor: but, in short, that your Mistress may not marry, you have given her a Portion.° dowry

MANLY. She had given me her heart first, and I am satisfi'd with the security; I can never doubt her truth and constancy.

FREEMAN. It seems you do, since you are fain to bribe it with Money. But how come you to be so diffident of the Man that sayes he loves you, and not doubt the Woman that sayes it?

MANLY. I shou'd (I confess) doubt the Love of any other Woman but her, as I do the friendship of any other Man but him I have trusted; but I have such proofs of their faith, as cannot deceive me.

FREEMAN. Cannot!

MANLY. Not but I know, that generally, no Man can be a great Enemy, but under the name of Friend; and if you are a Cuckold, it is your Friend only that makes you so; for your Enemy is not admitted to your house: if you are cheated in your Fortune, 'tis your Friend that does it; for your Enemy is not made your Trustee: if your Honour, or Good Name be injur'd, 'tis your Friend that does it still, because your Enemy is not believ'd against you. Therefore I rather choose to go where honest, downright Barbarity is profest; where men devour one another like generous hungry Lyons and Tygers, not like Crocodiles;[29] where they think the Devil white, of our complexion, and I am already so far an *Indian:* but, if your weak faith doubts this miracle of a Woman, come along with me, and believe, and thou wilt find her so handsom, that thou, who art so much my Friend, wilt have a mind to lie with her, and so will not fail to discover what her faith and thine is to me.

When we're in Love, the great Adversity,
Our Friends and Mistresses at once we try.

Finis Actus Primi.

ACT. II.

SCENE I.

Olivia's *Lodging.*
Enter Olivia, Eliza, Lettice.

OLIVIA. Ah, Cousin, what a World 'tis we live in! I am so weary of it.

ELIZA. Truly, Cousin, I can find no fault with it, but that we cannot always live in't; for I can never be weary of it.

OLIVIA. O hideous! you cannot be in earnest sure, when you say you like the filthy World.

ELIZA. You cannot be in earnest sure, when you say you dislike it.

OLIVIA. You are a very censorious Creature, I find.

ELIZA. I must confess I think we Women as often discover where we love, by railing; as men when they lye, by their swearing; and the World is but a constant Keeping Gallant, whom we fail not to quarrel with, when anything crosses us yet cannot part with't for our hearts.

LETTICE. A Gallant indeed, Madam, whom Ladies first make jealous, and then quarrel with it for being so, for if, by her indiscretion, a Lady be talk'd of for a Man, she cryes presently, *'Tis a censorious world;* if, by her vanity the Intrigue be found out, *'Tis a prying, malicious World;* if, by her over-fondness the Gallant

29. A crocodile lies largely concealed in the water and hunts by stealth.

proves unconstant, *'Tis a false World;* and if, by her nigardliness the Chambermaid tells, *'Tis a perfidious world:* but that, I'm sure, your Ladyship cannot say of the world yet, as bad as 'tis.

OLIVIA. But I may say, *'Tis a very impertinent world.* Hold your peace. And, Cousin, if the World be a Gallant, 'tis such an one as is my aversion. Pray name it no more.

ELIZA. But is it possible the World, which has such variety of Charms for other Women, can have none for you? Let's see—first, what d'ye think of Dressing and fine Cloaths?

OLIVIA. Dressing! Fie, fie, 'tis my aversion. But, come hither, you Dowdy, methinks you might have open'd this Toure[30] better: O hideous! I cannot suffer it! d'ye see how't sits?

ELIZA. Well enough, Cousin, if Dressing be your aversion.

OLIVIA. 'Tis so: and for variety of rich Cloaths, they are more my aversion.

LETTICE. Ay, 'tis because your Ladyship wears 'em too long; for indeed a Gown, like a Gallant, grows one's aversion, by having too much of it.

OLIVIA. Insatiable Creature! I'll be sworn I have had this not above three dayes, Cousin, and within this month have made some six more.

ELIZA. Then your aversion to 'em is not altogether so great.

OLIVIA. Alas! 'tis for my Woman only I wear 'em, Cousin.

LETTICE. If it be for me only, Madam, pray do not wear 'em.

ELIZA. But what d'ye think of Visits—Balls—

OLIVIA. O, I detest 'em.

ELIZA. Of Playes?

OLIVIA. I abominate 'em; filthy, obscene, hideous things?

ELIZA. What say you to *Masquerading* in the Winter, and *Hide-park*[31] in the Summer?

OLIVIA. Insipid pleasures I taste not.

ELIZA. Nay, if you are for more solid pleasures, what think you of a rich, young Husband?

OLIVIA. O horrid! Marriage! what a pleasure you have found out! I nauseate it of all things.

LETTICE. But what does your Ladyship think then of a liberal, handsom, young Lover?

OLIVIA. A handsom, young Fellow, you Impudent! be gone, out of my sight; name a handsome young Fellow to me! Foh, a hideous handsom young Fellow I abominate!

[*Spits.*

30. Decorative fringe of curls on the forehead.
31. Large park in London, originally a royal preserve but opened to the public in 1637.

ELIZA. Indeed! But let's see—will nothing please you? what d'ye think of the Court?

OLIVIA. How? the Court! the Court, Cousin! my aversion, my aversion, my aversion of all aversions.

ELIZA. How? the court! where—

OLIVIA. Where Sincerity is a quality as much out of fashion, and as unprosperous, as Bashfulness; I cou'd not laugh at a Quibble, tho' it were a fat Privy Counsellor's;[32] nor praise a Lord's ill Verses, tho' I were my self the Subject; nor an old Lady's young looks, though I were her Woman; nor sit to a vain young *Simile-maker,* tho' he flatter'd me: in short, I cou'd not glote upon a man when he comes into a Room, and laugh at him when he goes out; I cannot rail at the absent, to flatter the standers by, I—

ELIZA. Well, but Railing now is so common, that 'tis no more Malice, but the fashion; and the absent think they are no more the worse for being rail'd at, than the present think they're the better for being flatter'd: and for the Court—

OLIVIA. Nay, do not defend the Court; for you'll make me rail at it, like a trusting Citizen's Widow.

ELIZA. Or like a *Holborn* Lady,[33] who cou'd not get in to the last Ball, or was out of countenance in the Drawing-room the last Sunday of her appearance there; for none rail at the Court, but those who cannot get into it, or else who are ridiculous when they are there: and I shall suspect you were laugh'd at when you were last there, or wou'd be a Maid of Honour.

OLIVIA. I a Maid of Honour! To be a Maid of Honour were yet of all things my aversion.

ELIZA. In what sense am I to understand you? But, in fine, by the word Aversion, I'm sure you dissemble; for I never knew Woman yet that us'd it, who did not. Come, our tongues belie our hearts, more than our Pocket-glasses do our faces; but methinks we ought to leave off dissembling, since 'tis grown of no use to us; for all wise observers understand us now adayes, as they do Dreams, Almanacks, and *Dutch Gazets,*[34] by the contrary: And a Man no more believes a Woman, when she sayes she has an Aversion for him, than when she sayes she'll Cry out.

OLIVIA. O filthy, hideous! Peace, Cousin, or your discourse will be my Aversion; and you may believe me.

ELIZA. Yes; for if any thing be a Womans Aversion, 'tis *Plain-dealing* from another Woman: and perhaps that's your quarrel to the World; for that will talk, as your Woman sayes.

32. The Privy (private) Council were the monarch's closest advisers.

33. A district close to the City of London, and therefore unfashionable.

34. At the time in which the play is set, the English were at war with the Dutch; the assumption is that the enemy's newspapers must be unreliable.

OLIVIA. Talk not of me sure; for what Men do I converse with? what Visits do I admit?

Enter Boy.

BOY. Here's the Gentleman to wait upon you, Madam.

OLIVIA. On me! you little, unthinking Fop, d'ye know what you say?

BOY. Yes, Madam, 'tis the Gentleman that comes every day to you, who—

OLIVIA. Hold your peace, you heedless little Animal, and get you gone. This Countrey Boy, Cousin, takes my Dancing-master, Taylor, or the spruce Milliner, for Visiters.

[*Exit* Boy.

LETTICE. No, Madam; 'tis Mr. *Novel,* I'm sure, by his talking so loud: I know his voice too, Madam.

OLIVIA. You know nothing, you Buffle-headed,° stupid Creature you; you wou'd make my Cousin believe I receive Visits: But if it be Mr.—what did you call him?

dull

LETTICE. Mr. *Novel,* Madam; he that—

OLIVIA. Hold your peace, I'll hear no more of him; but if it be your Mr.—(I can't think of his name again) I suppose he has follow'd my Cousin hither.

ELIZA. No, Cousin, I will not rob you of the Honour of the Visit: 'tis to you, Cousin, for I know him not.

OLIVIA. Nor did I ever hear of him before, upon my Honour, Cousin; besides, ha'nt I told you, that Visits, and the business of Visits, Flattery and Detraction, are my Aversion? D'ye think then I wou'd admit such a Coxcomb as he is? who, rather than not rail, will rail at the dead, whom none speak ill of; rather than not flatter, will flatter the Poets of the Age, whom none will flatter; who affects Novelty as much as the Fashion, and is as fantastical as changeable, and as well known as the Fashion; who likes nothing, but what is new; nay, wou'd choose to have his Friend, or his Title a new one. In fine, he is my Aversion.

ELIZA. I find you do know him, Cousin; at least, have heard of him.

OLIVIA. Yes, now I remember, I have heard of him.

ELIZA. Well; but, since he is such a Coxcomb, for Heav'ns sake, let him not come up: tell him, Mrs. *Lettice,* your Lady is not within.

OLIVIA. No, *Lettice,* tell him, my Cousin is here, and that he may come up; for, notwithstanding I detest the sight of him, you may like his conversation; and tho' I wou'd use him scurvily, I will not be rude to you, in my own Lodging; since he has follow'd you hither, let him come up, I say.

ELIZA. Very fine! Pray let him go to the Devil, I say, for me: I know him not, nor desire it. Send him away, Mrs. *Lettice.*

OLIVIA. Upon my word, she sha'nt: I must disobey your commands, to comply with your desires. Call him up, *Lettice.*

ELIZA. Nay, I'll swear she shall not stir on that errand.

[*Holds* Lettice.

OLIVIA. Well then, I'll call him myself for you, since you will have it so. Mr. *Novel,* [*Calls out at the door*] Sir. Sir.

Enter Novel.

NOVEL. Madam, I beg your pardon, perhaps you were busie: I did not think you had company with you.

ELIZA. Yet he comes to me, Cousin!

[*Aside*

OLIVIA.—Chairs there.

[*They sit.*

NOVEL. Well, but Madam, d'ye know whence I come now?

OLIVIA. From some melancholy place I warrant, Sir, since they have lost your good company.

ELIZA. So.

NOVEL. From a place, where they have treated me, at dinner, with so much civility and kindness, a pox on 'em, that I cou'd hardly get away to you, dear Madam.

OLIVIA. You have a way with you so new, and obliging, Sir.

ELIZA. You hate Flattery, Cousin!

[*Apart to* Olivia.

NOVEL. Nay faith, Madam, d'ye think my way new? Then you are obliging, Madam. I must confess, I hate imitation, to do any thing like other people: all that know me, do me the Honour to say, I am an Original Faith; but as I was saying, Madam, I have been treated to day, with all the ceremony and kindness imaginable, at my Lady Autums; but the nauseous old Woman at the upper end of her Table—

OLIVIA. Revives the old *Grecian* custom, of serving in a Deaths head with their Banquets.

NOVEL. Hah, ha! fine, just ifaith; nay, and new: 'tis like eating with the Ghost in the *Libertine;*[35] she wou'd frighten a Man from her dinner, with her hollow invitations, and spoil one's stomach—

OLIVIA. To Meat, or Women. I detest her hollow cherry cheeks; she looks like an old Coach new painted: affecting an unseemly smugness, whil'st she is ready to drop in pieces.

ELIZA. You hate Detraction I see, Cousin!

[*Apart to* Olivia.

35. Thomas Shadwell's version of the Don Juan story (1675).

NOVEL. But the silly old Fury, whil'st she affects to look like a Woman of this Age, talks—

OLIVIA. Like one of the last; and as passionately as an old Courtier, who has out-liv'd his Office.

NOVEL. Yes, Madam; but pray let me give you her character. Then, she never counts her age by the years, but—

OLIVIA. By the Masques she has liv'd to see.

NOVEL. Nay then, Madam, I see you think a little harmless railing too great a pleasure for any but your self, and therefore I've done.

OLIVIA. Nay, faith, you shall tell me who you had there at dinner.

NOVEL. If you would hear me, Madam.

OLIVIA. Most patiently: speak, Sir.

NOVEL. Then, we had her daughter—

OLIVIA. Ay, her daughter; the very disgrace to good cloaths, which she alwayes wears, but to heighten her deformity, not mend it; for she is still most splendidly, gallantly, ugly, and looks like an ill piece of daubing in a rich Frame.

NOVEL. So! But have you done with her, Madam? And can you spare her to me a little now?

OLIVIA. Ay, ay, Sir.

NOVEL. Then, she is like—

OLIVIA. She is, you'd say, like a City Bride; the greater Fortune, but not the greater Beauty, for her dress.

NOVEL. Well: yet have you done, Madam? Then she—

OLIVIA. Then she bestows as unfortunately on her face all the graces in fashion, as the languishing eye, the hanging or pouting lip; but as the Fool is never more provoking than when he aims at Wit, the ill-favor'd of our Sex are never more nauseous than when they wou'd be Beauties, adding to their natural deformity, the artificial ugliness of affectation.

ELIZA. So, Cousin, I find one may have a collection of all ones acquaintances Pictures as well at your house as at Mr. *Lely*'s; only the difference is, there we find 'em much handsomer than they are, and like; here, much uglier, and like: and you are the first of the profession of Picture-drawing I ever knew without flattery.

OLIVIA. I draw after the Life; do no Body wrong, Cousin.

ELIZA. No, you hate flattery and detraction!

OLIVIA. But, Mr. *Novel,* who had you besides at dinner?

NOVEL. Nay, the Devil take me if I tell you, unless you will allow me the priviledge of railing in my turn; but, now I think on't, the Women ought to be your Province, as the Men are mine: and you must know, we had him whom—

OLIVIA. Him, whom—

NOVEL. What, Invading me already? And giving the character, before you know the Man?

ELIZA. No, that is not fair, tho' it be usual.

OLIVIA. I beg your pardon, Mr. *Novel;* pray, go on.

NOVEL. Then, I say, we had that familiar Coxcomb, who is at home wheresoe're he comes.

OLIVIA. Ay, that Fool—

NOVEL. Nay then, Madam, your Servant: I'm gone. Taking a Fool out of ones mouth, is worse than taking the Bread out of ones mouth.

OLIVIA. I've done, your pardon, Mr. *Novel,* pray proceed.

NOVEL. I say, the Rogue, that he may be the only Wit in company, will let no Body else talk, and—

OLIVIA. Ay, those Fops who love to talk all themselves are of all things my Aversion.

NOVEL. Then you'll let me speak, Madam, sure. The Rogue, I say, will force his Jest upon you; and I hate a Jest that's forc'd upon a Man, as much as a Glass.

ELIZA. Why, I hope, Sir, he does not expect a Man of your temperance in jesting shou'd do him reason?° — justice

NOVEL. What, interruption from this side too! I must then—

[*Offers to rise.* Olivia *holds him.*

OLIVIA. No, Sir—You must know, Cousin, that Fop he means, tho' he talks only to be commended, will not give you leave to do't.

NOVEL. But, Madam—

OLIVIA. He a Wit! hang him, he's only an Adopter of straggling Jests, and fatherless Lampoons; by the credit of which, he eats at good Tables, and so, like the barren Beggar-woman, lives by borrow'd Children.

NOVEL. Madam—

OLIVIA. And never was Author of any thing but his News: but that is still all his own.

NOVEL. Madam, pray—

OLIVIA. An eternal Babler; and makes no more use of his ears, than a Man that sits at a Play by his mistress, or in Fop-corner: he's, in fine, a base detracting Fellow, and is my Aversion. But who else, pr'ythee, Mr. *Novel,* was there with you? Nay, you sha'nt stir.

NOVEL. I beg your pardon, Madam, I cannot stay in any place, where I'm not allow'd a little Christian liberty of railing.

OLIVIA. Nay, pr'ythee Mr. *Novel,* stay; and tho' you shou'd rail at me, I wou'd hear you with patience: pr'ythee, who else was there with you?

NOVEL. Your Servant, Madam.

OLIVIA. Nay, pr'ythee tell us, Mr. *Novel,* pr'ythee do.

NOVEL. We had no Body else.

OLIVIA. Nay, faith I know you had. Come, my Lord *Plausible* was there too, who is Cousin, a—

ELIZA. You need not tell me what he is, Cousin; for I know him to be a civil, good-natur'd, harmless Gentleman, that speaks well of all the World, and is alwayes in good humour; and—

OLIVIA. Hold, Cousin, hold, I hate Detraction; but I must tell you, Cousin, his civility, is cowardice; his good nature, want of wit; and he has neither courage, or sense to rail: And for his being alwayes in humor, 'tis because he is never dissatisfi'd with himself. In fine, he is my Aversion; and I never admit his Visits beyond my Hall.

NOVEL. No, he visit you! Dam him, cringing, grinning Rogue; if I shou'd see him coming up to you, I wou'd make bold to kick him down again. Ha!—

Enter my Lord Plausible.

My dear Lord, your most humble Servant.

[*Rises and salutes* Plausible, *and kisses him.*

ELIZA. So! I find kissing and railing succeed each other with the angry Men, as well as with the angry Women; and their quarrels are like Love-quarrels, since absence is the only cause of them; for, as soon as the Man appears again, they are over.

[*Aside.*

L. PLAUSIBLE. Your most faithful, humble Servant, generous Mr. *Novel;* and, Madam, I am your eternal Slave, and kiss your fair hands; which I had done sooner, according to your commands, but—

OLIVIA. No excuses, my Lord.

ELIZA. What, you sent for him then, Cousin?

[*Apart.*

NOVEL. Ha! invited!

[*Aside.*

OLIVIA. I know you must divide your self; for your good company is too general a good, to be ingross'd by any particular Friend.

L. PLAUSIBLE. O Lord, Madam, my company! your most obliged, faithful, humble Servant; but I cou'd have brought you good company indeed, for I parted at your door with two of the worthiest, bravest Men—

OLIVIA. Who were they, my Lord?

NOVEL. Who do you call the worthiest, bravest men, pray?

L. PLAUSIBLE. O the wisest, bravest Gentlemen! Men of such Honour, and Virtue! of such good qualities! ah—

ELIZA. This is a Coxcomb, that speaks ill of all people a different way, and Libels every body with dull praise, and commonly in the wrong place, so makes his Panegyricks abusive Lampoons.

[*Aside.*

OLIVIA. But pray let me know who they were?

L. PLAUSIBLE. Ah! such patterns of Heroick Virtue! such—

NOVEL. Well, but who the Devil were they?

L. PLAUSIBLE. The honour of our Nation, the glory of our Age, ah! I cou'd dwell a Twelvemonth on their praise; which indeed I might spare by telling their names: *Sir John Current* and *Sir Richard Court-Title.*

NOVEL. *Court-Title!* Hah, ha.

OLIVIA. And *Sir John Current!* Why will you keep such a Wretch company, my Lord?

L. PLAUSIBLE. Oh, Madam, seriously you are a little too severe; for he is a Man of unquestion'd reputation in every thing.

OLIVIA. Yes, because he endeavours only with the Women, to pass for a Man of Courage; and with the Bullies, for a Wit; with the Wits, for a Man of Business; and with the Men of Business, for a Favourite at Court; and at Court, for good City security.[36]

NOVEL. And, for *Sir Richard,* he—

L. PLAUSIBLE. He loves your choice, pick'd company; persons that—

OLIVIA. He loves a Lord indeed; but—

NOVEL. Pray, dear Madam, let me have but a bold stroke or two at his Picture. He loves a Lord, as you say, tho'—

OLIVIA. Tho' he borrow'd his Money, and ne'r paid him again.

NOVEL. And wou'd bespeak a place three days before at the back-end of a Lords Coach, to *Hide-Park.*

L. PLAUSIBLE. Nay, i'faith, i'faith, you are both too severe.

OLIVIA. Then, to shew yet more his passion for quality, he makes Love to that fulsom Coach-load of Honour, my *Lady Goodly;* for he is always at her Lodging.

L. PLAUSIBLE. Because it is the Conventickle-Gallant,[37] the Meeting-house of all the fair Ladies, and glorious Superfine Beauties of the Town.

NOVEL. Very fine Ladies! there's first—

OLIVIA. Her Honour, as fat as an Hostess.

L. PLAUSIBLE. She is something plump indeed, a goodly, comly, graceful person.

NOVEL. Then there's my *Lady Frances,* what d'ye call'er? as ugly—

OLIVIA. As a Citizens lawfully begotten daughter.

L. PLAUSIBLE. She has wit in abundance; and the handsomest heel, elbow, and tip of an ear, you ever saw.

NOVEL. Heel, and elbow! hah, ha! And there's my *Lady Betty* you know—

36. The City of London was both the financial center of England and associated with Puritan conservatism.

37. A conventicle was a religious meeting of five or more Dissenters from the Church of England. Conventicles were made illegal in 1664, and the implication here is that the "beauties" at Lady Goodly's house are not true "quality" just as Dissenters lacked true religion.

OLIVIA. As sluttish and slatternly, as an *Irish* Woman bred in *France.*[38]

L. PLAUSIBLE. Ah, all she has hangs with a loose Air indeed, and becoming negligence.

ELIZA. You see all faults with Lovers eyes, I find, my Lord.

L. PLAUSIBLE. Ah, Madam, your most obliged, faithful, humble Servant to command! But you can say nothing sure against the Superfine Mistress—

OLIVIA. I know who you mean. She is as censorious and detracting a Jade, as a superannuated Sinner.

L. PLAUSIBLE. She has a smart way of Railery, 'tis confest.

OLIVIA. And then, for Mrs. *Grideline.*[39]

L. PLAUSIBLE. She I'm sure is—

OLIVIA. One that never spoke ill of any body, 'tis confest; for she is as silent in conversation as a Countrey Lover, and no better company than a Clock, or a Weather-glass;° for if she sounds, 'tis but once an hour, to put you in mind of the time of day, or to tell you 'twill be cold or hot, rain or snow.

barometer

L. PLAUSIBLE. Ah, poor creature! she's extremely good and modest.

NOVEL. And for Mrs. *Bridlechin,* she's—

OLIVIA. As proud, as a Churchman's Wife.

L. PLAUSIBLE. She's a Woman of great spirit and honour, and will not make her self cheap, 'tis true.

NOVEL. Then Mrs. *Hoyden,* that calls all people by their Sirnames, and is—

OLIVIA. As familiar a Duck—

NOVEL. As an Actress in the Tyring° room. There I was once beforehand with you, Madam.

dressing

L. PLAUSIBLE. Mrs. *Hoyden!* a poor, affable, good-natur'd Soul! But the Divine Mrs. *Trifle* comes thither too: sure her beauty, virtue and conduct, you can say nothing too.

OLIVIA. No!

NOVEL. No!—pray let me speak, Madam.

OLIVIA. First, can any one be call'd beautiful that squints?

L. PLAUSIBLE. Her eyes languish a little, I own.

NOVEL. Languish! hah, ha.

OLIVIA. Languish! Then, for her conduct, she was seen at the *Countrey Wife,*[40] after the first day. There's for you, my Lord.

L. PLAUSIBLE. But, Madam, she was not seen to use her Fan all the Play long, turn aside her head, or by a conscious blush, discover more guilt than modesty.

38. Irish Catholics had to be educated in France since it was illegal for them to be educated as Catholics in Ireland. The English regarded the Irish as slovenly and the French as lacking in cleanliness.

39. French *gris-de-lin,* flax gray.

40. Wycherley's play of 1675. In the china scene (act 4, scene 3), Horner cuckolds Sir Jasper offstage while Horner is showing his "china."

OLIVIA. Very fine! then you think a Woman modest, that sees the hideous *Country Wife* without blushing, or publishing her detestation of it? D'ye hear him, Cousin?

ELIZA. Yes; and am, I must confess, something of his opinion, and think, that as an over-conscious Fool at a Play, by endeavouring to shew the Author's want of Wit, exposes his own to more censure: so may a Lady call her own modesty in question, by publickly cavilling with the Poets; for all those grimaces of honour, and artificial modesty, disparage a Woman's real Virtue, as much as the use of white and red does the natural complexion; and you must use very, very little, if you wou'd have it thought your own.

OLIVIA. Then you wou'd have a Woman of Honour with passive looks, ears, and tongue, undergo all the hideous obscenity she hears at nasty Plays.

ELIZA. Truly, I think a Woman betrays her want of modesty, by shewing it publickly in a Play-house, as much as a Man does his want of courage by a quarrel there; for the truly modest and stout say least, and are least exceptious, especially in publick.

OLIVIA. O hideous! Cousin, this cannot be your opinion; but you are one of those who have the confidence to pardon the filthy Play.

ELIZA. Why, what is there of ill in't, say you?

OLIVIA. O fie, fie, fie, wou'd you put me to the blush anew? call all the blood into my face again? But, to satisfie you then, first, the clandestine obscenity in the very name of *Horner.*

ELIZA. Truly, 'tis so hidden, I cannot find it out, I confess.

OLIVIA. O horrid! does it not give you the rank conception, or image of a Goat, a Town-bull, or a Satyr? nay, what is yet a filthier image than all the rest, that of an Eunuch?

ELIZA. What then? I can think of a Goat, a Bull, or Satyr, without any hurt.

OLIVIA. I, but Cousin, one cannot stop there.

ELIZA. I can, Cousin.

OLIVIA. O no; for when you have those filthy creatures in your head once, the next thing you think, is what they do; as their defiling of honest Mens Beds and Couches, Rapes upon sleeping and waking Countrey Virgins, under Hedges, and on Haycocks:[41] nay, farther—

ELIZA. Nay, no farther, Cousin, we have enough of your Coment on the Play, which will make me more asham'd than the Play it self.

OLIVIA. O, believe me, 'tis a filthy Play, and you may take my word for a filthy Play, as soon as anothers; But the filthiest thing in that Play, or any other Play, is—

ELIZA. Pray keep it to your self, if it be so.

41. A cone-shaped stack of hay left in a field to dry.

OLIVIA. No, faith, you shall know it, I'm resolv'd to make you out of love with the Play: I say, the lewdest, filthiest thing, is his *China;* nay, I will never forgive the beastly Author his *China:* he has quite taken away the reputation of poor *China* it self, and sully'd the most innocent and pretty Furniture of a Ladies Chamber; insomuch, that I was fain to break all my defil'd Vessels. You see I have none left; nor you, I hope.

ELIZA. You'll pardon me, I cannot think the worse of my *China* for that of the Play-house.

OLIVIA. Why, you will not keep any now sure! 'tis now as unfit an ornament for a Ladies Chamber, as the Pictures that come from *Italy,* and other hot Countries, as appears by their nudities, which I alwayes cover, or scratch out, wheresoe're I find 'em. But *China!* out upon't, filthy *China,* nasty, debauch'd *China!*

ELIZA. All this will not put me out of conceit with *China,* nor the Play, which is Acted to day, or another of the same beastly Author's, as you call him, which I'll go see.

OLIVIA. You will not sure! nay, you sha'not venture your reputation by going, and mine by leaving me alone with two Men here: nay, you'll disoblige me for ever, if—

[*Pulls her back.*

ELIZA. I stay!—your Servant.

[*Exit* Eliza.

OLIVIA. Well—but my Lord, tho' you justifie every body, you cannot in earnest uphold so beastly a Writer, whose Ink is so smutty, as one may say.

L. PLAUSIBLE. Faith, I dare swear the poor Man did not think to disoblige the Ladies, by any amorous, soft, passionate, luscious saying in his Play.

OLIVIA. Foy, my Lord; But what think you, Mr. *Novel,* of the Play? tho' I know you are a Friend to all that are new.

NOVEL. Faith, Madam, I must confess, the new Plays wou'd not be the worse for my advice, but I cou'd never get the silly Rogues, the Poets, to mind what I say; but I'll tell you what counsel I gave the surly Fool you speak of.

OLIVIA. What was't?

NOVEL. Faith, to put his Play into Rithme; for Rithme, you know, often makes mystical Nonsense pass with the Criticks for Wit, and a double meaning saying with the Ladies, for soft, tender, and moving passion. But, now I talk of passion, I saw your old Lover this morning—Captain—

[*Whispers.*
Enter Captain Manly, Freeman, *and* Fidelia *standing behind.*

OLIVIA. Whom?—nay, you need not whisper.

MANLY. We are luckily got hither unobserved:—How! in a close conversation with these supple Rascals, the Out-casts of Sempstresses shops?

FREEMAN. Faith, pardon her, Captain, that, since she cou'd no longer be entertain'd with your manly bluntness, and honest love, she takes up with the pert chat and commonplace flattery of these fluttering Parrots of the Town, Apes and Echoes of Men only.

MANLY. Do not you, Sir, play the Echo too, mock me, dally with my own words, and shew your self as impertinent as they are.

FREEMAN. Nay, Captain—

FIDELIA. Nay, Lieutenant, do not excuse her, methinks she looks very kindly upon 'em both, and seems to be pleas'd with what that Fool there sayes to her.

MANLY. You lye, Sir, and hold your peace, that I may not be provok'd to give you a worse reply.

OLIVIA. *Manly* return'd, d'ye say! And is he safe?

NOVEL. My Lord saw him too. Heark you, my Lord.

[*Whispers to* Plausible.

MANLY. She yet seems concern'd for my safety, and perhaps they are admitted now here but for their news of me: for Intelligence indeed is the common Passport of nauseous Fools, when they go their round of good Tables and Houses.

[*Aside.*

OLIVIA. I heard of his fighting only, without particulars, and confess I alwayes lov'd his Brutal courage, because it made me hope it might rid me of his more Brutal love.

MANLY. What's that?

[*Apart.*

OLIVIA. But is he at last return'd, d'ye say, unhurt?

NOVEL. Ay faith, without doing his business; for the Rogue has been these two years pretending to a wooden Leg, which he wou'd take from Fortune, as kindly, as the Staff of a Marshal of *France,* and rather read his name in a *Gazet*—

OLIVIA. Than in the Entail of a good Estate.

MANLY. So!—

[*Aside.*

NOVEL. I have an Ambition, I must confess, of losing my heart, before such a fair Enemy as your self, Madam; but that silly Rogues shou'd be ambitious of losing their Arms, and—

OLIVIA. Looking like a pair of Compasses.

NOVEL. But he has no use of his Arms, but to set 'em on Kimbow,[42]

42. Akimbo, i.e., with his hands on his hips and his elbows pointing outward.

for he never pulls off his Hat, at least not to me, I'm sure; for you must know, Madam, he has a fanatical hatred to good company: he can't abide me.

L. PLAUSIBLE. O, be not so severe to him, as to say he hates good company; for I assure you he has a great respect, esteem and kindness for me.

MANLY. That kind, civil Rogue has spoken yet ten thousand times worse of me, than t'other.

OLIVIA. Well, if he be return'd, Mr. *Novel,* then shall I be pester'd again with his boistrous Sea-love; have my Alcove smell like a Cabin, my Chamber perfum'd with his Tarpaulin Brandenburgh,° and hear vollies of Brandy sighs, enough to make a Fog in ones Room. Foh! I hate a Lover that smells like *Thames-street!*[43]

morning gown

MANLY. I can bear no longer, and need hear no more.

[*Aside,*

But, since you have these two Pulvillio Boxes, these Essence-Bottles,[44] this pair of Musk-Cats here, I hope I may venture to come yet nearer you.

OLIVIA. Overheard us then?

NOVEL. I hope he heard me not.

[*Aside.*

L. PLAUSIBLE. Most noble and heroick Captain, your most oblig'd, faithful, humble Servant.

NOVEL. Dear Tar, thy humble Servant.

MANLY. Away—Madam

OLIVIA. Nay, I think I have fitted you for listning.

[*Thrust* Novel *and* Plausible *on each side.*

MANLY. You have fitted me, for believing you cou'd not be fickle, tho' you were young; cou'd not dissemble Love, tho' 'twas your interest; nor be vain, tho' you were handsom; nor break your promise, tho' to a parting Lover; nor abuse your best Friend, tho' you had Wit: but I take not your contempt of me worse, than your esteem, or civility for these things here, tho' you know 'em.

NOVEL. Things!

L. PLAUSIBLE. Let the Captain Railly a little.

MANLY. Yes, things: canst thou be angry, thou thing?

[*Coming up to* Novel.

NOVEL. No, since my Lord sayes you speak in Raillery; for, tho' your Sea-raillery be something rough, yet I confess, we use one another too as bad every day at *Lockets,*[45] and never quarrel for the matter.

43. Street on the river front.
44. Containers for perfumes and masking scents.
45. Tavern/eating house in Charing Cross.

L. PLAUSIBLE. Nay, noble Captain, be not angry with him. A word with you, I beseech you.—

[*Whispers to* Manly.

OLIVIA. Well, we Women, like the rest of the Cheats of the World, when our Cullies or Creditors have found us out, and will, or can trust no longer; pay Debts and satisfie Obligations, with a quarrel, the kindest Present a Man can make to his Mistress, when he can make no more Presents: for oftentimes in Love, as at Cards, we are forc'd to play foul, only to give over the game; and use our Lovers, like the Cards, when we can get no more by 'em, throw 'em up in a pet, upon the first dispute.

[*Aside.*

MANLY. My Lord, all that you have made me know by your whispering, which I knew not before, is, that you have a stinking breath: there's a secret, for your secret.

L. PLAUSIBLE. Pshaw! pshaw!

MANLY. But, Madam, tell me, pray, what was't about this spark, cou'd take you? was it the merit of his fashionable impudence, the briskness of his noise, the wit of his laugh, his judgment, or fancy in his garniture? or was it a well-trim'd Glove, or the scent of it that charm'd you?

NOVEL. Very well, Sir, 'gad these Sea-Captains make nothing of dressing: but let me tell you, Sir, a man by his dress, as much as by any thing, shews his wit and judgment, nay, and his courage too.

FREEMAN. How his courage, Mr. *Novel?*

NOVEL. Why, for example, by red Breeches, tuck'd up Hair or Peruke, a greasie broad Belt, and now adayes a short Sword.

MANLY. Thy courage will appear more by thy Belt than thy Sword, I dare swear. Then, Madam, for this gentle piece of courtesie, this Man of tame honour, what cou'd you find in him? was it his languishing affected tone? his mannerly look? his second-hand flattery, the refuse of the Play house tiring-rooms? or his slavish obsequiousness, in watching at the door of your Box at the Playhouse, for your hand to your Chair? or his janty° way of playing with your Fan? or was it the Gunpowder spot on his hand, or the Jewel in his ear, that purchas'd your heart?

° gentile

OLIVIA. Good jealous Captain, no more of your—

L. PLAUSIBLE. No, let him go on, Madam, for perhaps he may make you laugh: and I wou'd contribute to your pleasure any way.

MANLY. Gentle Rogue!

OLIVIA. No, noble Captain, you cannot sure think any thing cou'd take me more than that heroick Title of yours, Captain; for you know we Women love honour inordinately.

NOVEL. Hah, ha, faith she is with thee, Bully, for thy Raillery.

MANLY. Faith so shall I be with you, no Bully, for your grinning.

[*Aside to* Novel.

OLIVIA. Then, that noble Lyon-like meen of yours, that Soldier-like weather-beaten complexion, and that manly roughness of your voice; how can they otherwise than charm us Women, who hate Effeminacy!

NOVEL. Hah, ha! faith I can't hold from laughing.

MANLY. Nor shall I from kicking anon.

[*Aside to* Novel.

OLIVIA. And then, that Captain-like carelessness in your dress, but especially your Scarf; 'twas just such another, only a little higher ty'd, made me in love with my Taylor, as he past by my Window the last Training day;[46] for we Women adore a Martial Man, and you have nothing wanting to make you more one, or more agreeable, but a wooden Leg.

L. PLAUSIBLE. Nay, i'faith there your Ladyship was a Wag, and it was fine, just, and well Railly'd.

NOVEL. Ay, ay, Madam, with you Ladies too, Martial Men must needs be very killing.

MANLY. Peace, you *Bartholomew-Fair Buffoons;*[47] and be not you vain that these laugh on your side, for they will laugh at their own dull jests: but no more of 'em, for I will only suffer now this Lady to be witty and merry.

OLIVIA. You wou'd not have your Panegyrick interrupted. I go on then to your humor. Is there anything more agreeable, than the pretty sullenness of that? than the greatness of your courage? which most of all appears in your spirit of contradiction, for you dare give all Mankind the Lye; and your Opinion is your onely Mistress, for you renounce that too, when it becomes another Mans.

NOVEL. Hah, ha! I cannot hold, I must laugh at thee Tar, faith!

L. PLAUSIBLE. And i'faith, dear Captain, I beg your pardon, and leave to laugh at you too tho' I protest I mean you no hurt; but, when a Lady Raillies, a stander by must be complaisant, and do her reason in laughing: Hah, ha.

MANLY. Why, you impudent, pitiful Wretches, you presume sure upon your Effeminacy to urge me; for you are in all things so like Women, that you may think it in me a kind of Cowardice to beat you.

OLIVIA. No Hectoring,[48] good Captain.

46. A legally appointed day for the training of the City militia or reserve forces.

47. Cloth fair in Smithfield noted for a wide variety of (vulgar) entertainments including puppet shows, prize fights, and freaks.

48. To intimidate by threats, although the word may also mean to brag or bluster.

MANLY. Or, perhaps, you think this Ladies presence secures you; but have a care, she has talk'd her self out of all the respect I had for her; and by using me ill before you, has given me a priviledge of using you so before her: but if you wou'd preserve your respect to her, and not be beaten before her, go, be gone immediately.

NOVEL. Be gone! what?

L. PLAUSIBLE. Nay, worthy, noble, generous Captain.

MANLY. Be gone, I say.

NOVEL. Be gone again! to us be gone!

MANLY. No chattering, Baboons, instantly be gone. Or—

[Manly *Puts 'em out of the Room:* Novel *struts.* Plausible *cringes.*

NOVEL. Well, Madam, we'll go make the Cards ready in your Bedchamber; sure you will not stay long with him.

[*Exeunt* Plausible *and* Novel.

OLIVIA. Turn hither your rage, good Captain Swagger-huff, and be saucy with your Mistress, like a true Captain; but be civil to your Rivals and Betters, and do not threaten any thing but me here; no, not so much as my Windows, nor do not think your self in the Lodgings of one of your Suburb Mistresses beyond the *Tower.*[49]

MANLY. Do not give me cause to think so, for those less infamous Women part with their Lovers, just as you did from me, with unforc'd vows of constancy, and floods of willing tears; but the same winds bear away their Lovers, and their vows: And for their grief, if the credulous unexpected Fools return, they find new Comforters, fresh Cullies, such as I found here. The mercenary love of those Women too suffer shipwrack, with their Gallants fortunes; now you have heard *Chance* has us'd me scurvily, therefore you do too. Well, persevere in your ingratitude, falshood, and disdain; have constancy in something, and I promise you to be as just to your real scorn, as I was to your feign'd love: And henceforward will despise, contemn, hate, loathe, and detest you, most faithfully.

Enter Lettice.

OLIVIA. Get the Hombre Cards[50] ready in the next Room *Lettice,* and.—

[*Whispers to* Lettice.

FREEMAN. Bravely resolv'd, Captain.

FIDELIA. And you'll be sure to keep your word, I hope, Sir.

49. Someone living east of the Tower of London and therefore neither of the City nor the Town.
50. Or ombre, a three-handed card game.

MANLY. I hope so too.

FIDELIA. Do you but hope it, Sir? if you are not as good as your word, 'twill be the first time you ever brag'd sure.

MANLY. She has restor'd my reason with my heart.

FREEMAN. But, now you talk of restoring Captain, there are other things which, next to one's heart, one wou'd not part with; I mean your Jewels and Money, which it seems she has, Sir.

MANLY. What's that to you, Sir?

FREEMAN. Pardon me, whatsoever is yours, I have a share in't, I'm sure which I will not lose for asking, tho' you may be too generous, or too angry now to do't yourself.

FIDELIA. Nay, then I'll make bold to make my claim too.

[*Both going towards* Olivia.

MANLY. Hold, you impertinent, officious Fops—How have I been deceiv'd!

[*Aside.*

FREEMAN. Madam, there are certain Appurtenances to a Lover's heart, call'd Jewels, which alwayes go along with it.

FIDELIA. And which, with Lovers, have no value in themselves, but from the heart they come with; our Captain's, Madam, it seems you scorn to keep, and much more will those worthless things without it, I am confident.

OLIVIA. A Gentleman, so well made as you are, may be confident—us easie Women cou'd not deny you any thing you ask, if 'twere for your self; but, since 'tis for another, I beg your leave to give him my Answer. (An agreeable young fellow this!—And wou'd not be my Aversion!) [*Aside.*] Captain, your young Friend here has a very persuading Face, I confess; yet you might have ask'd me your self, for those Trifles you left with me, which (heark you a little, for I dare trust you with the secret: you are a Man of so much Honour I'm sure;) I say then, not expecting your return, or hoping ever to see you again, I have deliver'd your Jewels to—

[*Aside to* Manly.

MANLY. Whom?

OLIVIA. My Husband.

MANLY. Your husband!

OLIVIA. Ay, my Husband; for, since you cou'd leave me, I am lately, and privately marry'd to one, who is a Man so much Honour and Experience in the World, that I dare not ask him for your Jewels again, to restore 'em to you; lest he shou'd conclude you never wou'd have parted with 'em to me, on any other score, but the exchange of my Honour: which rather than you'd let me lose, you'd lose I'm sure your self, those Trifles of yours.

MANLY. Triumphant Impudence! but marry'd too!

OLIVIA. O, speak not so loud, my Servants know it not: I am marry'd; there's no resisting one's Destiny, or Love, you know.

MANLY. Why, did you love him too?

OLIVIA. Most passionately; nay, love him now, tho' I have marry'd him, and he me: which mutual love, I hope you are too good, too generous a Man to disturb, by any future claim, or visits to me. 'Tis true, he is now absent in the Countrey, but returns shortly; therefore I beg of you, for your own ease and quiet, and my Honour, you will never see me more.

MANLY. I wish I never had seen you.

OLIVIA. But if you shou'd ever have anything to say to me hereafter, let that young Gentleman there, be your Messenger.

MANLY. You wou'd be kinder to him: I find he shou'd be welcome.

OLIVIA. Alas! his Youth wou'd keep my Husband from suspicions, and his visits from scandal; for we Women may have pity for such as he, but no love: And I already think you do not well to spirit him away to Sea, and the Sea is already but too rich with the spoils of the shore.

MANLY. True perfect Woman!—If I cou'd say any thing more injurious to her now, I wou'd; for I could out-rail a bilk'd Whore, or a kick'd Coward: but, now I think on't, that were rather to discover my love, than hatred; and I must not talk, for something I must do.

[*Aside.*

OLIVIA. I think I have given him enough of me now, never to be troubled with him again.—

[*Aside.*
Enter Lettice.

Well, *Lettice,* are the Cards and all ready within? I come then[.] Captain, I beg your pardon: you will not make one at Hombre?

MANLY. No, Madam, but I'll wish you a little good luck before you go.

OLIVIA. No, if you wou'd have me thrive, Curse me: for that you'll do heartily, I suppose.

MANLY. Then, if you will have it so, May all the Curses light upon you, Women ought to fear, and you deserve; first may the Curse of loving Play attend your sordid Covetousness, and Fortune cheat you, by trusting to her, as you have cheated me; the Curse of Pride, or a good Reputation, fall on your Lust; the Curse of Affectation on your Beauty; the Curse of your Husbands com pany on your Pleasures; and the Curse of your Gallant's disappointments in his absence; and the Curse of scorn, Jealousie, or despair, on your love; and then the Curse of loving on!

OLIVIA. And, to requite all your Curses, I will only return you your last; May the Curse of loving me still, fall upon your proud hard heart, that cou'd be so cruel to me in these horrid Curses: but heaven forgive you.

[*Exit* Olivia.

MANLY. Hell, and the Devil, reward thee.

FREEMAN. Well, you see now, Mistresses, like Friends, are lost, by letting 'em handle your Money; and most Women are such kind of Witches, who can have no power over a Man, unless you give 'em Money; but when once they have got any from you, they never leave you, till they have all: therefore I never give a Woman a farthing.

MANLY. Well, there is yet this comfort by losing one's Money with one's Mistress, a Man is out of danger of getting another; of being made prize again by love; who, like a Pyrat, takes you by spreading false Colours: but when once you have run your Ship aground, the treacherous Picaroon loofs,° so by your ruine you saveyour self from slavery at least.

luffs

Enter Boy.

BOY. Mrs. *Lettice,* here's Madam *Blackacre* come to wait upon her Honour.

MANLY. D'ye hear that? let us be gone, before she comes; for henceforth I'll avoid the whole damn'd Sex for ever, and Woman as a sinking Ship.

[*Exeunt* Manly *and* Fidelia.

FREEMAN. And I'll stay, to revenge on her your quarrel to the Sex; for out of love to her Jointure, and hatred to business, I wou'd marry her, to make an end of her thousand Suits, and my thousand engagements, to the comfort of two unfortunate sort of people; my Plaintiffs, and her Defendants; my Creditors, and her Adversaries.

Enter Widow Blackacre, *led in by Major* Oldfox, *and* Jerry Blackacre *following, laden with green Bags.*

WIDOW. 'Tis an arrant Sea-Ruffian, but I am glad I met with him at last, to serve him again, Major, for the last service was not good in Law. *Boy, Duck, Jerry,* where is my Paper of *Memorandums?* give me Child: so. Where is my cousin *Olivia,* now, my kind Relation?

FREEMAN. Here is one that wou'd be your kind Relation, Madam.

WIDOW. What mean you, Sir?

FREEMAN. Why, faith (to be short) to marry you, Widow.

WIDOW. Is not this the wild rude person we saw at Captain *Manly's?*

JERRY. Ay, forsooth, an't please.

WIDOW. What wou'd you? what are you? Marry me!

FREEMAN. Ay faith, for I am a younger Brother, and you are a Widow.

WIDOW. You are an impertinent person, and go about your business.

FREEMAN. I have none, but to marry thee, Widow.

WIDOW. But I have other business, I'd have you to know.

FREEMAN. But you have no business anights, Widow; and I'll make you pleasanter business than any you have: for anights, I assure you, I am a Man of great business; for the business—

WIDOW. Go, I'm sure you're an idle Fellow.

FREEMAN. Try me but, Widow, and employ me as you find my abilities, and industry.

OLDFOX. Pray be civil to the Lady, Mr.—she's a person of quality, a person that is no person—

FREEMAN. Yes, but she's a person that is a Widow: be you mannerly to her, because you are to pretend only to be her Squire, to arm her to her Lawyers Chambers; but I will be impudent and bawdy, for she must love and marry me.

WIDOW. Marry come up, you saucy familiar *Jack!* You think with us Widows, 'tis no more than up, and ride. Gad forgive me, now adayes, every idle, young, hectoring, roaring Companion, with a pair of turn'd red breeches,[51] and a broad Back, thinks to carry away any Widow, of the best degree; but I'd have you to know, Sir, all Widows are not got, like places at Court, by Impudence and Importunity only.

OLDFOX. No, no, soft, soft, you are a young Man, and not fit—

FREEMAN. For a Widow? Yes sure, old Man, the fitter.

OLDFOX. Go to, go to, if others had not laid in their claims before you—

FREEMAN. Not you, I hope.

OLDFOX. Why not I, Sir? Sure I am a much more proportionable match for her, than you, Sir; I, who am an elder Brother, of a comfortable Fortune, and of equal Years with her.

WIDOW. How's that? You unmannerly person? I'd have you to know, I was born but in *Ann' undec' Caroli prim'*.[52]

OLDFOX. Your pardon, Lady, your pardon; be not offended with your very Servant.—But I say, Sir, you are a beggarly younger Brother, twenty Years younger than her; without any Land or Stock, but your great stock of Impudence: therefore what pretension can you have to her?

FREEMAN. You have made it for me; first, because I am a younger Brother.

WIDOW. Why, is that a sufficient Plea to a Relict?° How appears it, Sir? by what foolish custom?

widow

FREEMAN. By custom, time out of mind only. Then, Sir, because I

51. To stretch the life of material, clothes would be unstitched, the inner side turned out, and resewn; the widow is commenting on Freeman's relative poverty.

52. In the eleventh year of (the reign) of Charles I, or 1635–36. Since the play is supposedly taking place during the second Dutch War of 1665–67, the widow is claiming to be about thirty.

have nothing to keep me after her death, I am the likelier to take care of her life. And, for my being twenty Years younger than her, and having a sufficient stock of Impudence, I leave it to her whether they will be valid exceptions to me, in her Widow's Law or Equity.

OLDFOX. Well, she has been so long in *Chancery,* that I'll stand to her Equity and Decree between us. Come, Lady, pray snap up this young Snap° at first, or we shall be troubled with him; give him a City Widow's Answer: (that is, with all the ill-breeding imaginable.) [*Aside to the Widow.*] Come, Madam.

swindler

WIDOW. Well then, to make an end of this foolish Wooing, for nothing interrupts business more; first, for you, Major—

OLDFOX. You declare in my favour then?

FREEMAN. What, direct the Court! (Come, young Lawyer, thou sha't be a Counsel for me.)

[*To* Jerry.

JERRY. Gad, I shall betray your Cause then, as well as an older Lawyer; never stir[.]

WIDOW. First, I say, for you Major, my walking Hospital of an ancient Foundation, thou Bag of Mummy, that wou'dst fall asunder, if 'twere not for thy Cere-cloaths[53]—

OLDFOX. How, Lady?

FREEMAN. Hah, ha—

JERRY. Hey, brave° Mother! use all Suitors thus, for my sake.

excellent

WIDOW. Thou wither'd, hobling, distorted Cripple; nay, thou art a Cripple all over; wou'dst thou make me the Staff of thy Age, the Crutch of thy Decrepidness? Me—

FREEMAN. Well said Widow! faith, thou wou'dst make a Man love thee now, without dissembling.

WIDOW. Thou senseless, impertinent, quibling, driveling, feeble, paralytic, impotent, fumbling, frigid Nicompoop.

JERRY. Hey, brave Mother, for calling of names, ifac!

WIDOW. Wou'dst thou make a Caudlemaker, a Nurse of me? Can't you be Bed-rid, without a Bed-fellow? Won't your Swan-skins Furrs, Flannels, and the scorch'd Trencher keep you warm there? Wou'd you have me your Scotch-warming Pan, with a Pox to you?[54] Me!—

OLDFOX. O Heav'ns!

FREEMAN. I told you I shou'd be thought the fitter Man, Major.

JERRY. Ay, you old Fobus,° and you wou'd have been my Guardian, wou'd you? to have taken care of my Estate, that half of 't shou'd never come to me, by letting long Leases at Pepper-corn Rents?°

fool

a nominal or token rent

53. Sheets wound around a corpse.

54. Swanskin furrs are an expensive kind of flannel; a scorched trencher is a heated platter used as a bed warmer; a Scotch warming pan is a woman.

WIDOW. If I wou'd have marry'd an old Man, 'tis well known I might have marry'd an Earl; nay, what's more, a Judge, and been cover'd the Winter-nights with the Lamb-skins,[55] which I prefer to the Ermins of Nobles:[56] And dost thou think I wou'd wrong my poor Minor there, for you?

FREEMAN. Your Minor is a chopping° Minor, God bless him. strapping

[*Strokes* Jerry *on the head.*

OLDFOX. Your Minor may be a Major of Horse or Foot, for his bigness; and, it seems, you will have the cheating of your Minor to your self.

WIDOW. Pray, Sir, bear Witness; Cheat my Minor! I'll bring my Action of the case for the slander.

FREEMAN. Nay, I wou'd bear false Witness for thee now, Widow, since you have done me justice, and have thought me the fitter Man for you.

WIDOW. Fair, and softly Sir, 'tis my Minor's Case, more than my own: And I must do him Justice now on you.

FREEMAN. How?

OLDFOX. So then.

WIDOW. You are first, (I warrant) some Renegado from the Inns of Court, and the Law; and thou'lt come to suffer for't by the Law: that is, be hang'd.

JERRY. Not about your neck, forsooth, I hope.

FREEMAN. But, Madam—

OLDFOX. Hear the Court.

WIDOW. Thou art some debauch'd, drunken, leud, hectoring, gaming Companion, and want'st some Widow's old Gold to nick° gamble upon; but, I thank you, Sir, that's for my Lawyers.

FREEMAN. Faith, we shou'd ne'r quarrel about that; for Guineys[57] wou'd serve my turn: but, Widow—

WIDOW. Thou art a foul-mouth'd Boaster of thy Lust, a mere Bragadochio of thy Strength for Wine and Women, and wilt belie thy self more than thou dost Women, and art every way a base deceiver of Women: And wou'd deceive me too, wou'd you?

FREEMAN. Nay faith, Widow, this is Judging without seeing the Evidence.

WIDOW. I say, you are a worn-out Whoremaster, at five and twenty both in Body and Fortune: And cannot be trusted by the common Wenches of the Town, lest you shou'd not pay 'em; nor by the Wives of the Town, lest you shou'd pay 'em: so you want Women, and wou'd have me your Baud to procure 'em for you.

55. Used in judges' robes.
56. Ermine was heraldic fur representative of nobility.
57. Guineas were first minted in 1662.

FREEMAN. Faith, if you had any good Acquaintance, Widow, 'twou'd be civilly done of thee; for I am just come from Sea.

WIDOW. I mean, you wou'd have me keep you, that you might turn Keeper; for poor Widows are only us'd like Bauds by you; you go to Church with us, but to get other Women to lie with. In fine, you are a cheating, chousing° Spendthrift: And, having sold your own Annuity, wou'd waste my Jointure.

swindling

JERRY. And make havock of our Estate personal, and all our gilt Plate; I shou'd soon be picking up all our mortgag'd Apostle-Spoons,[58] Bowls and Beakers, out of most of the Ale-houses betwixt *Hercules Pillars* and the *Boatswain* in *Wapping:*[59] nay, and you'd be scouring[60] amongst my Trees, and make 'em knock down one another, like routed reeling Watchmen at midnight. Wou'd you so, Bully?

FREEMAN. Nay, pr'ythee, Widow, hear me.

WIDOW. No, Sir, I'd have you to know, thou pitiful, paltry, lath-back'd Fellow, if I wou'd have marry'd a young Man, 'tis well known, I cou'd have had any young heir in *Norfolk;* nay, the hopefull'st young Man this day at the *Kings-Bench Bar;*[61] I that am a Relict and Executrix of known plentiful Assits and Parts, who understand my self and the Law: And wou'd you have me under Covert Baron again? No, Sir, no Covert Baron for me.[62]

FREEMAN. But, dear Widow, hear me. I value you only, not your Jointure.

WIDOW. Nay, Sir, hold there; I know your love to a Widow, is covetousness of her Jointure: And a Widow, a little stricken in Years, with a good Jointure, is like an old Mansion-house in a good Purchase, never valu'd; but take one, take t'other: And perhaps, when you are in possession, you'd neglect it, let it drop to the ground, for want of necessary repairs, or expenses upon't.

FREEMAN. No, Widow, one wou'd be sure to keep all tight, when one is to forfeit one's Lease by dilapidation.

WIDOW. Fie, fie, I neglect my Business with this foolish discourse of love. *Jerry,* Child, let me see the List of the Jury: I'm sure my Cousin *Olivia* has some Relations amongst 'em. But where is she?

58. A set of thirteen spoons with representations of the apostles and Jesus, usually made of silver, and, by the late seventeenth century, treated as heirlooms.

59. Hercules Pillars, a tavern, was near the Inns of Court, while Wapping was east of the Tower of London. Freeman, with experience at the Inns of Court and as a naval officer, is familiar with both neighborhoods.

60. Scowrers were drunken vandals who roamed London at night; Jerry is saying Freeman would cut down and sell the trees on his estate, a serious diminution of his inheritance.

61. The highest of the three courts at Westminster Hall (the other two were Common Pleas and Exchequer).

62. Law-French for a married woman, under her husband's protection, and therefore unable to maintain actions at law.

FREEMAN. Nay, Widow, but hear me one word only.

WIDOW. Nay, Sir, no more, pray; I will no more hearken to your foolish Love motions, than to offers of Arbitration.

[*Exeunt* Widow Blackacre *and* Jerry.

FREEMAN. Well, I'll follow thee yet; for he that has a pretension at Court, or to a Widow, must never give over for a little ill usage.

OLDFOX. Therefore, I'll get her by Assiduity, Patience, and Long-sufferings, which you will not undergo; for you idle young Fellows leave off Love when it comes to be Business; and Industry gets more Women, than Love.

FREEMAN. Ay, Industry, the Fool's and old Man's merit; but I'll be industrious too, and make a business on't, and get her by Law, Wrangling, and Contests, and not by Sufferings: And, because you are no dangerous Rival, I'll give thee counsel, Major.

If you Litigious Widow e'r wou'd gain,
Sigh not to her; but by the Law complain:
To her, as to a Baud, Defendant Sue
With Statutes, and make Justice Pimp for you.

[Exeunt.
Finis Actus Secundi.

ACT. III.

SCENE I.

Westminster-Hall
Enter Manly *and* Freeman, *two Sailors behind.*

MANLY. I Hate this place, worse than a Man that has inherited a *Chancery* Suit:[63] I wish I were well out on't again.

FREEMAN. Why, you need not be afraid of this place: for a Man without Money, needs no more fear a croud of Lawyers, than a croud of Pickpockets.

MANLY. This, the Reverend° of the Law wou'd have thought the Palace or Residence of Justice; but, if it be, she lives here with the State of a *Turkish* Emperor, rarely seen; and besieg'd, rather than defended by her numerous black Guard° here.

reverent

i.e., lawyers

FREEMAN. Methinks, 'tis like one of their own Halls, in *Christmas* time, whither, from all parts, Fools bring their Money, to try, by the Dice, (not the worst Judges) whether it shall be their own, or no.[64] but, after a tedious fretting and wrangling, they drop away all their Money, on both sides; and finding neither the better, at

63. Chancery dealt with cases of land law, contracts, and trusts; some such cases could drag on for more than a generation.

64. Gambling was permitted in the Inns of Court between Christmas and Twelfth Night.

last, go emptily and lovingly away together to the Tavern, joining their Curses against the young Lawyers Box,[65] that sweeps all, like the old ones.

MANLY. Spoken, like a Revelling *Christmas* Lawyer.

FREEMAN. Yes, I was one, I confess; but was fain to leave the Law, out of Conscience, and fall to making false Musters;[66] rather choose to Cheat the King, than his Subjects; Plunder, rather than take Fees.

MANLY. Well, a Plague, and a Purse Famine, light on the Law; and that Female limb of it, who drag'd me hither to day: but pr'ythee go see if, in that croud of dagled Gowns there, thou canst find her.

Pointing to a croud of Lawyers at *the end of the Stage.*
[*Exit* Freeman
Manet Manly.

How hard it is to be a Hypocrite!
At least to me, who am but newly so.
I thought it once a kind of Knavery,
Nay, Cowardice, to hide ones faults; but now
The common frailty, Love, becomes my shame.
He must not know I love th' ungrateful still,
Lest he contemn me, more than she: for I,
It seems, can undergo a Womans scorn,
But not a Mans—

Enter to him Fidelia.

FIDELIA. Sir, good Sir, generous Captain.

MANLY. Pr'ythee, kind Impertinence, leave me. Why shou'dst thou follow me, flatter my Generosity now, since thou know'st I have no Money left? if I had it, I'd give it thee, to buy my quiet.

FIDELIA. I never follow'd yet, Sir, Reward or Fame, but you alone; nor do I now beg any thing but leave to share your miseries: You shou'd not be a Niggard of 'em, since, methinks, you have enough to spare. Let me follow you now, because you hate me, as you have often said.

MANLY. I ever hated a Coward's company, I must confess.

FIDELIA. Let me follow you, till I am none then; for you, I'm sure, will through such Worlds of dangers, that, I shall be inur'd to 'em; nay, I shall be afraid of your anger more than danger, and so turn valiant out of fear. Dear Captain, do not cast me off, till you have try'd me once more: do not, do not go to Sea again without me.

65. The "box" contains the house's cut of the bets made. Lawyers, like a casino, ultimately take all the money.

66. The names of people not actually serving but whose pay was collected nevertheless.

MANLY. Thou to Sea! to Court, thou Fool; remember the advice I gave thee: thou art a handsom Spaniel, and canst faun naturally; go, busk about,[67] and run thy self into the next great Man's Lobby: first faun upon the Slaves without, and then run into the Ladies Bed-chamber; thou may'st be admitted, at last, to tumble her Bed: go, seek, I say, and lose me; for I am not able to keep thee: I have not Bread for my self.

FIDELIA. Therefore I will not go, because then I may help and serve you.

MANLY. Thou!

FIDELIA. I warrant you, Sir; for, at worst, I cou'd beg or steal for you.

MANLY. Nay, more bragging! dost thou not know there's venturing your life, in stealing? Go, pr'ythee, away: thou art as hard to shake off, as that flattering effeminating mischief, Love.

FIDELIA. Love did you name? Why, you are not so miserable as to be yet in Love, sure!

MANLY. No, no, pr'ythee away, be gone, or—I had almost discover'd my Love and Shame; well, if I had? that thing cou'd not think the worse of me:—or if he did?—no—yes, he shall know it—he shall—but then I must never leave him, for they are such secrets, that make Parasites and Pimps Lords of their Masters; for any slavery or tyranny is easier than Love's.

[*Aside.*

Come hither. Since thou art so forward to serve me, hast thou but resolution enough to endure the torture of a secret? for such, to some, is insupportable.

FIDELIA. I wou'd keep it as safe, as if your dear, precious life depended on't.

MANLY. Dam your dearness. It concerns more than my life, my honour.

FIDELIA. Doubt it not, Sir.

MANLY. And do not discover it, by too much fear of discovering it; but have a great care you let not *Freeman* find it out.

FIDELIA. I warrant you, Sir. I am already all joy, with the hopes of your commands; and shall be all wings, in the execution of 'em: speak quickly, Sir.

MANLY. You said you wou'd beg for me.

FIDELIA. I did, Sir.

MANLY. Then you shall beg for me.

FIDELIA. With all my heart, Sir.

MANLY. That is, Pimp for me.

FIDELIA. How, Sir?

MANLY. D'ye start! thinkest thou, thou cou'dst do me any other

67. 1) array, ornament oneself; 2) make ready, prepare.

service? Come, no dissembling honour: I know you can do it handsomly, thou wert made for't: You have lost your time with me at Sea, you must recover it.

FIDELIA. Do not, Sir, beget your self more Reasons for your Aversion to me, and make my obedience to you a fault: I am the unfittest in the World, to do you such a service.

MANLY. Your cunning arguing against it, shews but how fit you are for it. No more dissembling: here, (I say) you must go use it for me, to *Olivia.*

FIDELIA. To her, Sir?

MANLY. Go flatter, lie, kneel, promise, any thing to get her for me: I cannot live, unless I have her. Didst thou not say thou wou'dst do any thing, to save my life? And she said you had a persuading face.

FIDELIA. But, did you not say, Sir, your honour was dearer to you, than your life? And wou'd you have me contribute to the loss of that, and carry love from you, to the most infamous, most false, and—

MANLY. And most beautiful!—

[*Sighs aside.*

FIDELIA. Most ungrateful Woman, that ever liv'd; for sure she must be so, that could desert you so soon, use you so basely, and so lately too: do not, do not forget it, Sir, and think—

MANLY. No, I will not forget it, but think of revenge: I will lie with her, out of revenge. Go, be gone, and prevail for me, or never see me more.

FIDELIA. You scorn'd her last night.

MANLY. I know not what I did last night; I dissembled last night.

FIDELIA. Heavens!

MANLY. Be gone, I say, and bring me love or compliance back, or hopes at least, or I'll never see thy face again: by—

FIDELIA. O do not swear, Sir, first hear me.

MANLY. I am impatient, away, you'll find me here till twelve.

[*Turns away.*

FIDELIA. Sir—

MANLY. Not one word, no insinuating Argument more, or soothing persuasion; you'll have need of all your Rhetorick with her: go, strive to alter her, not me; be gone.

[*Exit* Manly *at the end of the Stage.*
Manet Fidelia.

Shou'd I discover to him now my Sex,
And lay before him his strange cruelty,
'Twould but incense it more.—No, 'tis not time.
For his Love, must I then betray my own?

Were ever Love or Chance, till now, severe?
Or shifting Woman pos'd with such a task?
Forc'd to beg that which kills her, if obtain'd;
And give away her Lover not to lose him!

[*Exit* Fidelia.
Enter Widow Blackacre *in the middle of half a dozen Lawyers, whisper'd to by a Fellow in black,* Jerry Blackacre *following the croud.*

WIDOW. Offer me a Reference, you saucy Companion you! d'ye know who you speak to? Art thou a Solicitor in *Chancery,* and offer a Reference? A pretty fellow! Mr. Serjeant *Ploddon,* here's a Fellow has the impudence to offer me a Reference![68]

SERJEANT PLODDON. Who's that has the impudence to offer a Reference within these Walls?

WIDOW. Nay, for a Splitter of Causes to do't!

SERJEANT PLODDON. No, Madam, to a Lady learned in the Law, as you are, the offer of a Reference were to impose upon you.

WIDOW. No, no, never fear me for a Reference, Mr. Serjeant. But, come, have you not forgot your Brief? are you sure you shan't make the mistake of—Hark you—[*Whispers.*] Go then, go to your Court of *Common-pleas,* and say one thing over and over again: You do it so naturally, you'll never be suspected for protracting time.

SERJEANT PLODDON. Come, I know the course of the Court, and your business.

[*Exit. Serjeant* Ploddon.

WIDOW. Let's see, *Jerry,* where are my Minutes? Come, Mr. *Quaint,* pray go talk a great deal for me in *Chancery;* let your words be easie, and your Sense hard, my Cause requires it: Branch it bravely, and deck my Cause with flowers, that the Snake may lie hidden. Go, go, and be sure you remember the Decree of my Lord Chancellor, *Tricesimo quart'* of the Queen.[69]

QUAINT. I will, as I see cause, extenuate or examplifie Matter of Fact; baffle Truth, with Impudence; answer Exceptions with Questions, tho' never so impertinent; for Reasons, give 'em Words; for Law and Equity, Tropes and Figures: And so relax and enervate the sinews of their Argument, with the oyl of my Eloquence. But when my Lungs can reason no longer, and not being able to say anything more for our Cause, say everything of our Adversary; whose Reputation, though never so clear and evident in the eye of the World, yet with sharp Invectives—

WIDOW. (Alias *Belin'gsgate.*)[70]

68. Cases could be referred to a master of chancery, where the action would be decided in arbitration, rather than in open court; thus the widow would lose the pleasure of a trial.

69. The thirty-fourth year of the reign of Queen Elizabeth.

70. Billingsgate, the London fish market, and the standard for personal abuse.

QUAINT. With poinant and sowre Invectives, I say, I will deface, wipe out, and obliterate his fair Reputation, even as a Record with the juice of Lemons; and tell such a Story, (for the truth on't is, all that we can do for our Client in *Chancery*, is telling a Story) a fine Story, a long Story, such a Story[—]

WIDOW. Go, save thy breath for the Cause; talk at the Bar, Mr. *Quaint*. You are so copiously fluent, you can weary any ones ears, sooner than your own tongue. Go, weary our Adversaries Counsel, and the Court: Go, thou art a fine-spoken person: Adad, I shall make thy Wife jealous of me: if you can but court the Court into a Decree for us. Go, get you gone, and remember—

[*Whispers.*] [*Exit* Quaint.]

Come, Mr. *Blunder*, pray baul soundly for me, at the *Kings-Bench;* bluster, sputter, question, cavil; but be sure your Argument be intricate enough, to confound the Court: And then you do my business. Talk what you will, but be sure your tongue never stand still; for your own noise will secure your Sense from Censure: 'tis like coughing or heming when one has got the Belly-ake, which stifles the unmannerly noise. Go, dear Rogue, and succeed; and I'll invite thee, ere it be long, to more souz'd° Venison.

pickled

BLUNDER. I'll warrant you, after your Verdict, your Judgment shall not be Arrested, upon if's and and's.

WIDOW. Come, Mr. *Petulant*, let me give you some new instructions, for our Cause in the *Exchequer.* Are the Barons° sate?

judges

PETULANT. Yes, no; may be they are, may be they are not: what know I? what care I?

WIDOW. Hey day! I wish you wou'd but snap up the Counsel on t'other side anon, at the Bar as much; and have a little more patience with me, that I might instruct you a little better.

PETULANT. You instruct me! what is my Brief for, Mistress?

WIDOW. Ay, but you seldom read your Brief, but at the Bar, if you do it then.

PETULANT. Perhaps I do, perhaps I don't, and perhaps 'tis time enough: pray hold your self contented, Mistress.

WIDOW. Nay, if you go there too, I will not be contented, Sir, tho' you, I see, will lose my Cause for want of speaking, I wo'not: You shall hear me, and shall be instructed. Let's see your Brief.

PETULANT. Send your Solicitor to me, instructed by a Woman! I'd have you to know, I do not wear a Bar-gown—

WIDOW. By a Woman! And I'd have you to know, I am no common Woman; but a Woman conversant in the Laws of the Land, as well as your self, tho' I have no Bar-gown.

PETULANT. Go to, go to, Mistress, you are impertinent, and there's your Brief for you: instruct me!

[*Flings her Breviate at her.*

WIDOW. Impertinent to me, you saucy *Jack* you! you return my Breviate, but where's my Fee? You'll be sure to keep that, and scan that so well, that if there chance to be but a brass Half-crown in't, one's sure to hear on't again: wou'd you wou'd but look on your Breviate half so narrowly. But pray give me my Fee too, as well as my Brief.

PETULANT. Mistress, that's without Precedent. When did a Counsel ever return his Fee, pray? And you are impertinent, and ignorant, to demand it.

WIDOW. Impertinent again, and ignorant to me! Gadsbodikins, you puny Upstart in the Law, to use me so, you Green Bag Carrier, you Murderer of unfortunate Causes, the Clerks Ink is scarce off of your fingers, you that newly come from Lamblacking the Judges shooes, and are not fit to wipe mine; you call me impertinent and ignorant! I wou'd give thee a Cuff on the ear, sitting the Courts,[71] if I were ignorant. Marry gep, if it had not been for me, thou hadst been yet but a hearing Counsel at the Bar.

[*Exit* Petulant.
Enter Mr. Buttongown, *crossing the stage in haste.*

Mr. *Buttongown,* Mr. *Buttongown,* whither so fast? what, won't you stay till we are heard?

BUTTONGOWN. I cannot, Mrs. *Blackacre,* I must be at the Council, my Lord's Cause stays there for me.

WIDOW. And mine suffers here.

BUTTONGOWN. I cannot help it.

WIDOW. I'm undone.

BUTTONGOWN. What's that to me?

WIDOW. Consider the five pound Fee, if not my Cause: that was something to you.

BUTTONGOWN. Away, away, pray be not so troublesom, Mistress, I must be gone.

WIDOW. Nay, but consider a little, I am your old Client, my Lord but a new one; or, let him be what he will, he will hardly be a better Client to you, than my self: I hope you believe I shall be in Law as long as I live? therefore am no despicable Client. Well, but go to your Lord, I know you expect he shou'd make you a Judge one day; but I hope his promise to you will prove a true Lord's promise: But, that he might be sure to fail you, I wish you had his Bond for't.

BUTTONGOWN. But what will you yet be thus impertinent, Mistress?

WIDOW. Nay, I beseech you, Sir, stay; if it be but to tell me my Lord's case: come, in short.

71. An assault committed while the courts were in session was punishable with up to life imprisonment, so the widow restrains her urge to box the ears of Petulant.

BUTTONGOWN. Nay, then—

[*Exit* Buttongown.

WIDOW. Well, *Jerry,* observe Child, and lay it up for hereafter: These are those Lawyers who, by being in all Causes, are in none; therefore if you would have 'em for you, let your Adversary fee 'em; for he may chance to depend upon 'em: and so, in being against thee, they'll be for thee.

JERRY. Ay, Mother, they put me in mind of the unconscionable Woers of Widows, who undertake briskly their Matrimonial business for their money; but when they have got it once, let who's will drudge for them; therefore have a care of 'em, forsooth; there's Advice for your Advice.

WIDOW. Well said, Boy, come, Mr. *Splitcause,* pray go see when my Cause in *Chancery* comes on; and go speak with Mr. *Quillit* in the *Kings-Bench* and Mr. *Quirk* in the *Common-Pleas,* and see how our matters go there.

Enter Major Oldfox.

OLDFOX. Lady, a good and propitious morning to you; and may all your Causes go as well, as if I my self were Judge of 'em.

WIDOW. Sir, excuse me, I am busie, and cannot answer Complements in *Westminster-hall.* Go, Mr. *Splitcause,* and come to me again, to that Booksellers, there I'll stay for you, that you may be sure to find me.

OLDFOX. No, Sir, come to the other Booksellers, I'll attend your Ladiship thither.

[*Exit* Splitcause.

WIDOW. Why to the other?

OLDFOX. Because he is my Bookseller, Lady.

WIDOW. What, to sell you Lozenges for your Catarrh?[72] or Medicines for your Corns? what else can a Major deal with a Bookseller for?

OLDFOX. Lady, he Prints for me.

WIDOW. Why, are you an Author?

OLDFOX. Of some few Essayes; deign you, Lady, to peruse 'em. (She is a Woman of parts, and I must win her by shewing mine.)

[*Aside.*]
The Bookseller's Boy [*comes forward*].

BOOKSELLER'S BOY. Will you see *Culpepper,* Mistress? *Aristotle's Problems? The Compleat Midwife?*[73]

72. A mucus discharge from the lungs, a cough.

73. Nicholas Culpeper was the author of medical handbooks. *Aristotle's Problems* (1595) was not by Aristotle but was sufficiently popular to have editions in 1666 and 1670. *The Compleat Midwifes Practice* was published in 1656.

WIDOW. No; let's see *Dalton, Hughs, Shepherd, Wingate.*[74]

BOOKSELLER'S BOY. We have no Law-books.

WIDOW. No? you are a pretty Bookseller then.

OLDFOX. Come, have you e're a one of my Essayes left?

BOOKSELLER'S BOY. Yes, Sir, we have enough, and shall alwayes have 'em.

OLDFOX. How so?

BOOKSELLER'S BOY. Why, they are good, steady, lasting Ware.

OLDFOX. Nay, I hope they will live; let's see. Be pleas'd, Madam, to peruse the poor endeavors of my Pen; for I have a Pen, tho' I say it, that—

[*Gives her a Book.*

JERRY. Pray let me see *St. George for Christendom,* or, *The Seven Champions of England.*[75]

WIDOW. No, no, give him *The Young Clerk's Guide.* What, we shall have you read your self into a humor of Rambling and Fighting, and studying Military Discipline, and wearing red Breeches?

OLDFOX. Nay, if you talk of Military Discipline, shew him my Treatise of *The Art Military.*

WIDOW. Hold, I wou'd as willingly he shou'd read a *Play.*

JERRY. O pray, forsooth Mother, let me have a *Play.*

WIDOW. No, Sirrah, there are young Students of the Law enough spoil'd already, by *Playes;* they wou'd make you in love with your Landress, or what's worse, some Queen of the Stage, that was a Landress; and so turn Keeper before you are of age.

[*Several crossing the Stage.*]

But stay, *Jerry,* is not that Mr. *what-d'y'call-him,* that goes there: he that offer'd to sell me a Suit in *Chancery* for five hundred pound, for a hundred down, and only paying the Clerks Fees?

JERRY. Ay, forsooth, 'tis he.

WIDOW. Then stay here, and have a care of the Bags, whil'st I follow him: have a care of the Bags, I say.

JERRY. And do you have a care, forsooth, of the Statute against *Champartee,* I say.[76]

[*Exit* Widow Blackacre.
Enter Freeman *to them.*

FREEMAN. So, there's a limb of my Widow, which was wont to be inseparable from her: she can't be far.

[*Aside.*]

74. Michael Dalton, William Hughes, William Sheppard, and Edmund Wingate were all authors on legal subjects, whose works were either written or reprinted in the 1660s and 1670s.

75. Probably Richard Johnson's *The Most Famous History of the Seven Champions of Christendom* (1596).

76. An illegal agreement to pay the costs of a case in return for a share of the award.

How now, my pretty Son-in-law that shall be, where's my Widow?

JERRY. My Mother, but not your Widow, will be forthcoming presently.

FREEMAN. Your Servant, Major. what, are you buying Furniture for a little sleeping Closet, which you miscall a Study? For you do only by your Books, as by your Wenches, bind 'em up neatly, and make 'em fine, for other people to use 'em: And your Bookseller is properly your Upholster, for he furnishes your Room, rather than your Head.

OLDFOX. Well, well, good Sea-Lieutenant, study you your Compass, that's more than your head can deal with. (I will go find out the Widow, to keep her out of his sight, or he'll board her, whil'st I am treating a Peace.)

[*Aside.*]
[*Exit* Oldfox.
Manent Freeman, Jerry.

JERRY. Nay pr'ythee, Friend, now, let me have but *The Seven Champions,* you shall trust me no longer than till my Mothers Mr. *Splitcause* comes; for I hope he'll lend me wherewithal to pay for't.

FREEMAN. Lend thee! here, I'll pay him. Do you want Money, Squire? I'm sorry a Man of your Estate shou'd want Money.

JERRY. Nay, my Mother will ne'r let me be at Age: And till then, she sayes—

FREEMAN. At Age! Why, you are at Age already, to have spent an Estate, Man; there are younger than you, have kept their Women these three Years, have had half a dozen Claps, and lost as many thousand pounds at Play.

JERRY. Ay, they are happy Sparks! nay, I know some of my School-Fellows, who, when we were at School, were two Years younger than me; but now, I know not how, are grown Men before me, and go where they will, and look to themselves: but my Curmudgeonly Mother wo'nt allow me wherewithal to be a Man of my self with.

FREEMAN. Why there 'tis, I knew your Mother was in fault: Ask but your School-Fellows what they did, to be Men of themselves.

JERRY. Why, I know they went to Law with their Mothers; for they say, there's no good to be done upon a Widow Mother, till one goes to Law with her: but mine is as plaguy a Lawyer, as any's of our Inn. Then wou'd she marry too, and cut down my Trees: Now I shou'd hate, Man, to have my Father's Wife kiss'd, and slap'd, and t'other thing too, (you know what I mean) by another Man; and our Trees are the purest, tall, even, shady twigs, by my fa—

FREEMAN. Come, Squire, let your Mother and your Trees fall as she pleases rather than wear this Gown, and carry green Bags all thy life; and be pointed at for a Tony:° But you shall be able to deal with her yet the common way; thou shalt make false Love to

fool

some Lawyer's daughter, whose Father, upon the hopes of thy marrying her, shall lend thee Money, and Law, to preserve thy Estate and Trees; and thy Mother is so ugly, no Body will have her, if she cannot cut down thy Trees.

JERRY. Nay, if I had but any Body to stand by me, I am as stomachful° as another[.] brave

FREEMAN. That will I, I'll not see any hopeful young Gentleman abus'd.

BOOKSELLER'S BOY. By any but your self.

[*Aside.*

JERRY. The truth on't is, mine's as arrant a Widow-Mother, to her poor Child, as any's in *England.* She wo'nt so much as let one have six-pence in one's Pocket, to see a Motion,° or the Dancing of the Ropes,° or— puppet show; tight rope

FREEMAN. Come, you sha'nt want Money, there's Gold for you.

JERRY. O-Lurd, Sir, two Guineys! d'ye lend me this? is there no trick in't? Well, Sir, I'll give you my Bond, for security.

FREEMAN. No, no, thou hast given me thy face for security: Any Body wou'd swear, thou dost not look like a Cheat. You shall have what you will of me; and if your Mother will not be kinder to you, come to me, who will.

JERRY. By my fa—he's a curious fine Gentleman!—

[*Aside.*

But, will you stand by one?

FREEMAN. If you can be resolute.

JERRY. Can be resolv'd! Gad, if she gives me but a cross word, I'll leave her to night, and come to you. But, now I have got Money, I'll go to *Jack of All Trades,* at t'other end of the *Hall,* and buy the neatest purest things—

FREEMAN. And I'll follow the great Boy, and my blow at his Mother: steal way the Calf, and the Cow will follow you.

[*Exit* Jerry, *follow'd by* Freeman.
Enter, on the other side, Manly, *Widow* Blackacre, *and* Oldfox.

MANLY. Damn your Cause; can't you lose it without me? which you are like enough to do, if it be as you say, an honest one: I will suffer no longer for't.

WIDOW. Nay, Captain, I tell you, you are my prime Witness; and the Cause is just now coming on, Mr. *Splitcause* tells me. Lord, methinks you shou'd take a pleasure in walking here, as half you see now do; for they have no business here, I assure you.

MANLY. Yes, but I'll assure you then, their business is to persecute me; but d'ye think I'll stay any longer, to have a Rogue, because he knows my name, pluck me aside, and whisper a Newsbook°-secret to me, with a stinking breath? A second come piping an- newspaper gry from the Court, and sputter in my face his tedious complaints against it? A third Law-Coxcomb, because he saw me once at a Reader's dinner,[77] come and put me a long Law-Case, to make a discovery of his indefatigable dulness, and my weari'd patience? A fourth, a most barbarous civil Rogue, who will keep a Man half an hour in the croud with a bow'd body, and a hat off, acting the reform'd sign of the *Salutation* Tavern,[78] to hear his bountiful professions of service and friendship; whil'st he cares not if I were damn'd, and I am wishing him hang'd out of my way? I'd as soon run the Gantlet, as walk t'other turn.

Enter to them Jerry Blackacre *without his Bags; but laden with Trinkets, which he endeavors to hide from his Mother: and follow'd at a distance by* Freeman.

WIDOW. O, are you come, Sir? But where have you been, you Ass? And how came you thus laden?

JERRY. Look here, forsooth Mother, now here's a Duck, here's a Boar-cat,° and here's an Owl. tomcat

[*Making a noise with Cat-calls and other such like Instruments.*

WIDOW. Yes, there is an Owl, Sir.

OLDFOX. He's an ungracious Bird, indeed.

WIDOW. But go, thou Trangame,° and carry back those Trangames, which thou hast stol'n or purloin'd; for no Body wou'd trust a Minor in *Westminster-hall* sure. trinket

JERRY. Hold yourself contented, forsooth, I have these Commodities by a fair Bargain and Sale; and there stands my Witness, and Creditor.

WIDOW. How's that! What, Sir, d'ye think to get the Mother, by giving the Child a Rattle? But where are my Bags, my Writings, you Rascal?

JERRY. O Law! where are they, indeed!

[*Aside.*

WIDOW. How, Sirrah? speak, come—

MANLY. You can tell her, *Freeman,* I suppose.

[*Apart to him.*

FREEMAN. 'Tis true, I made one of your Salt-water Sharks steal 'em, whil'st he was eagerly choosing his Commodities, as he calls 'em, in order to my design upon his Mother.

[*Apart to him.*

77. An end of term dinner given by one of the lecturers at the Inns of Court.

78. "The sign which originally showed the Annuciation by the Angel Gabriel to Mary was changed to two men bowing" (Holland).

WIDOW. Wo'nt you speak? Where were you, I say, you Son of a — an unfortunate Woman? O, major, I'm undone; they are all that concern my Estate, my Jointure, my Husband's Deed of Gift, my Evidences for all my Suits now depending! What will become of them?

FREEMAN. I'm glad to hear this.

[*Aside.*

They'll be all safe, I warrant you, Madam.

WIDOW. O where? where? Come, you Villain, along with me, and shew me where.

[*Exeunt* Widow, Jerry, Oldfox.
Manent Manly, Freeman.

MANLY. Thou hast taken the right way to get a Widow, by making her great Boy Rebel; for, when nothing will make a Widow marry, she'll do't to cross her Children. But canst thou in earnest marry this Harpy, this Volume of shrivel'd blur'd Parchments and Law, this Attornies Desk?

FREEMAN. Ay, ay, I'll marry, and live honestly: that is, give my Creditors, not her, due Benevolence, pay my Debts.

MANLY. Thy Creditors, you see, are not so barbarous, as to put thee in Prison; and wilt thou commit thyself to a noisom Dungeon for thy life? which is the only satisfaction thou canst give thy Creditors, by this match.

FREEMAN. Why, is not she rich?

MANLY. Ay, but he that marries a Widow, for her Money, will find himself as much mistaken, as the Widow, that marries a young Fellow for due Benevolence, as you call it.

FREEMAN. Why, d'ye think I sha'nt deserve Wages? I'll drudge faithfully.

MANLY. I tell thee again, he that is the Slave in the Mine, has the least propriety in the Ore: You may dig, and dig; but if thou wou'dst have her Money, rather get to be her Trustee, than her Husband; for a true Widow will make over her Estate to any Body, and cheat her self, rather than be cheated by her Children, or a second Husband.

Enter to them Jerry, *running in a fright.*

JERRY. O Law! I'm undone, I'm undone, my Mother will kill me: You said you'd stand by one.

FREEMAN. So I will, my brave Squire, I warrant thee.

JERRY. Ay, but I dare not stay till she comes; for she's as furious, now she has lost her Writings, as a Bitch when she has lost her Puppies.

MANLY. The comparison's handsom!

JERRY. O, she's here!

Enter Widow Blackacre, *and* Oldfox.

FREEMAN. [*To the* Sailor.] Take him, *Jack,* and make haste with him, to your Master's Lodging; and be sure you keep him up, till I come.

[*Exeunt* Jerry *and* Sailor.

WIDOW. O my dear Writings! Where's this Heathen Rogue, my Minor?

FREEMAN. Gone to drown, or hang himself.

WIDOW. No, I know him too well, he'll ne'r be *Felo de se* that way; but he may go and choose a Guardian of his own head, and so be *Felo de ses biens:*[79] for he has not yet chosen one.

FREEMAN. Say you so? And he sha'nt want one.

[*Aside.*

WIDOW. But, now I think on't, 'tis you, Sir, have put this Cheat upon me; for there is a saying, *Take hold of a Maid by her Smock, and a Widow by her Writings, and they cannot get from you:* But I'll play fast and loose with you yet, if there be Law; and my Minor and Writings are not forthcoming, I'll bring my Action of Detinue or Trover.[80] But first, I'll try to find out this Guardianless, graceless Villain. Will you jog, Major?

MANLY. If you have lost your Evidence, I hope your Causes cannot go on, and I may be gone?

WIDOW. O no, stay but a making Water while, (as one may say) and I'll be with you again.

[*Exeunt* Widow, *and* Major Oldfox.
Manent Manly, Freeman.

FREEMAN. Well, sure I am the first Man that ever began a Love Intrigue, in *Westminster-hall.*

MANLY. No, sure; for the Love to a Widow generally begins here: And as the Widow's Cause goes against the Heir or Executors, the Jointure Rivals commence their Suit to the Widow.

FREEMAN. Well, but how, pray, have you passed your time here, since I was forc'd to leave you alone? You have had a great deal of patience.

MANLY. Is this a place to be alone, or have patience in? But I have had patience indeed; for I have drawn upon me, since I came, but three Quarrels, and two Law-suits.

FREEMAN. Nay, faith, you are too curst to be let loose in the World; you shou'd be ty'd up again, in your Sea-kennel, call'd a Ship. But how cou'd you quarrel here?

79. *Felo de se* is murder of himself, and *Felo de ses biens* is a conglomeration of Latin and French meaning murderer of his own goods.

80. An action to recover wrongfully taken personal property.

MANLY. How could I refrain? A Lawyer talk'd peremptorily and saucily to me, and as good as gave me the Lye.

FREEMAN. They do it so often to one another at the Bar, that they make no Bones on't elsewhere.

MANLY. However, I gave him a Cuff on the Ear; whereupon he jogs two Men, whose Backs were turn'd to us, (for they were reading at a Booksellers) to Witness I struck him sitting the Courts; which office they so readily promis'd, that I call'd 'em Rascals and Knights of the Post: one of 'em presently calls two other absent Witnesses, who were coming towards us at a distance; whil'st the other, with a Whisper, desires to know my name, that he might have satisfaction by way of Challenge, as t'other by way of Writ; but if it were not rather to direct his Brother's Writ, than his own Challenge: there you see is one of my Quarrels, and two of my Law-suits.

FREEMAN. So:—and the other two?

MANLY. For advising a Poet to leave off Writing, and turn Lawyer, because he is dull, and impudent, and sayes or writes nothing now, but by Precedent.

FREEMAN. And the third Quarrel?

MANLY. For giving more sincere Advice, to a handsom, well-drest, young Fellow (who ask'd it too) not to marry a Wench, that he lov'd, and I had lay'n with.

FREEMAN. Nay, if you will be giving your sincere advice to Lovers, and Poets, you will not fail of Quarrels.

MANLY. Or, if I stay in this place; for I see more Quarrels crouding upon me: let's be gone, and avoid 'em.

Enter Novel, *at a distance, coming towards them.*

A Plague on him, that Sneer is ominous to us; he is coming upon us, and we shall not be rid of him.

NOVEL. Dear Bully, don't look so grum upon me; you told me just now, you had forgiven me a little harmless Raillery upon wooden legs last night.

MANLY. Yes, yes, pray be gone, I am talking of business.

NOVEL. Can't I hear it? I love thee, and will be faithful, and alwayes—

MANLY. Impertinent! 'Tis Business that concerns *Freeman* only.

NOVEL. Well, I love *Freeman* too, and would not divulge his secret: pr'ythee speak, pr'ythee, I must—

MANLY. Pr'ythee let me be rid of thee, I must be rid of thee.

NOVEL. Faith, thou canst hardly, I love thee so. Come, I must know the business.

MANLY. So, I have it now.

[*Aside.*]

Why, if you needs will know it, he has a quarrel, and his Adversary bids him bring two Friends with him: now, I am one, and we are thinking who we shall have for a third.

Several crossing the Stage.

NOVEL. A Pox, there goes a Fellow owes me a Hundred pound, and goes out of Town to morrow: I'll speak with him, and come to you presently.

[*Exit* Novel.

MANLY. No, but you wo'not.
FREEMAN. You are dexterously rid of him.

Enter Oldfox.

MANLY. To what purpose, since here comes another, as impertinent? I know, by his grin, he is bound hither.
OLDFOX. Your Servant, worthy, noble Captain: Well, I have left the Widow, because she carry'd me from your company; for, faith Captain, I must needs tell thee, thou art the only Officer in *England,* who was not an *Edg-hill* Officer,[81] that I care for.
MANLY. I'm sorry for't.
OLDFOX. Why, wou'dst thou have me love them?
MANLY. Any body, rather than me.
OLDFOX. What, you are modest I see! therefore too, I love thee.
MANLY. No, I am not modest, but love to brag my self, and can't patiently hear you fight over the last Civil War; therefore go look out the Fellow I saw just now here, that walks with his Stockings and his Sword out at heels, and let him tell you the History of that scar on his cheek, to give you occasion to shew yours, got in the field at *Bloomsbury,*[82] not that of *Edg-hill:* go to him, poor Fellow, he is fasting, and has not yet the happiness this morning to stink of Brandy and Tobacco; go, give him some to hear you, I am busie.
OLDFOX. Well, ygad, I love thee now, Boy, for thy surliness: thou art no tame Captain, I see, that will suffer—
MANLY. An old Fox.
OLDFOX. All that sha'nt make me angry: I consider that thou art peevish, and fretting at some ill success at Law. Pr'ythee, tell me what ill luck you have met with here.
MANLY. You.
OLDFOX. Do I look like the Picture of ill Luck? Gadsnouns, I love thee more and more; and shall I tell thee what made me love thee first?

81. The first major battle of the English Civil War (1642).
82. A fashionable neighborhood in central London where a garden square was laid out in 1660.

MANLY. Do: that I may be rid of that damn'd quality, and thee.

OLDFOX. 'Twas thy wearing that broad Sword there.

MANLY. Here, *Freeman,* let's change: I'll never wear it more.

OLDFOX. How! you wo'not sure. Pr'ythee don't look like one of our Holyday Captains now adayes, with a Bodkin by your side, your Martinet Rogues.

MANLY. (O, then there's hopes.)

[*Aside.*]

What, d'ye find fault with martinet?[83] let me tell you, Sir, 'tis the best exercise in the World; the most ready, most easie, most graceful exercise that ever was us'd, and the most—

OLDFOX. Nay, nay, Sir, no more, Sir, your Servant, if you praise Martinet once, I have done with you, Sir. Martinet! Martinet!

[*Exit.* Oldfox.

FREEMAN. Nay, you have made him leave you as willingly, as ever he did an Enemy; for he was truly for the King and Parliament: for the Parliament, in their List; and for the King, in cheating 'em of their Pay, and never hurting the King's party in the Field.[84]

Enter a Lawyer towards them.

MANLY. A Pox! this way; here's a Lawyer I know threatning us with another greeting.

LAWYER. Sir, Sir, your very Servant; I was afraid you had forgotten me.

MANLY. I was not afraid you had forgotten me.

LAWYER. No, Sir, we Lawyers have pretty good memories.

MANLY. You ought to have, by your Wits.

LAWYER. O, you are a merry Gentleman, Sir; I remember you were merry, when I was last in your company.

MANLY. I was never merry in thy company, Mr. Lawyer, sure.

LAWYER. Why, I'm sure you jok'd upon me, and shamm'd me all night long.

MANLY. Shamm'd! pr'ythee what barbarous Law-term is that?

LAWYER. Shamming! Why, don't you know that? 'tis all our way of Wit Sir.

MANLY. I am glad I do not know it then: Shamming! What does he mean by't, *Freeman?*

FREEMAN. Shamming, is telling you an insipid, dull Lye with a dull Face, which the slie Wag the Author only laughs at himself; and making himself believe 'tis a good Jest, puts the Sham only upon himself.

83. An infantry drill introduced by a French general, Jean Martinet, in the 1660s.

84. Oldfox was an officer in the parliamentary forces but did not pay his men or do any damage to the king's forces in battle.

MANLY. So, your Lawyers Jest, I find, like his Practice, has more Knavery than Wit in't. I shou'd make the worst Shammer in *England;* I must always deal ingeniuously, as I will with you, Mr. Lawyer, and advise you to be seen rather with Attornies and Solicitors, than such Fellows as I am; they will credit your practice more.

LAWYER. No, Sir, your company's an honour to me.

MANLY. No, faith; go this way, there goes an Attorney, leave me for him: let it never be said, a Lawyers Civility did him hurt.

LAWYER. No, worthy honour'd Sir, I'll not leave you for any Attorney sure.

MANLY. Unless he had a Fee in his hand.

LAWYER. Have you any business here, Sir? try me: I'd serve you sooner than any Attorney breathing.

MANLY. Business!—So, I have thought of a sure way.

[*Aside.*]

Yes, faith, I have a little business.

LAWYER. Have you so, Sir? in what Court, Sir? what is't, Sir? tell me but how I may serve you, and I'll do't, Sir; and take it for as great an honour—

MANLY. Faith, 'tis for a poor Orphan of a Sea-Officer of mine, that has no Money; but if it could be follow'd *in Forma Pauperis;*[85] and when the Legacy's recover'd—

LAWYER. *Forma Pauperis,* Sir!

MANLY. Ay, Sir.

Several crossing the Stage.

LAWYER. Mr. *Bumblecase,* Mr. *Bumblecase,* a word with you; Sir, I beg your pardon at present, I have a little business—

MANLY. Which is not *in Forma Pauperis.*

[*Exit* Lawyer.

FREEMAN. So, you have now found a way to be rid of people without quarrelling.

Enter Alderman.

MANLY. But here's a City Rogue will stick as hard upon us, as if I ow'd him Money.

ALDERMAN. Captain, noble Sir, I am yours heartily d'ye see: Why shou'd you avoid your old Friends?

MANLY. And why shou'd you follow me? I owe you nothing.

ALDERMAN. Out of my hearty respects to you; for there is not a Man in *England*[—]

85. As the name suggests, a legal process where the pauper paid no fees or costs.

MANLY. Thou wou'dst save from hanging, with the expense of a shilling only.

ALDERMAN. Nay, nay, but Captain, you are like enough to tell me—

MANLY. Truth, which you wo'nt care to hear; therefore you had better go talk with some body else.

ALDERMAN. No, I know no body can inform me better, of some young Wit, or Spendthrift, that has a good dip'd° Seat and Estate in *Middlesex, Hertfordshire, Essex,* or *Kent,* any of these wou'd serve my turn: now, if you knew of such a one, and wou'd but help—

mortgaged

MANLY. You to finish his ruine.

ALDERMAN. Ifaith, you shou'd have a snip—

MANLY. Of your Nose; you thirty in the hundred Rascal, wou'd you make me your Squire Setter, your Baud for Mannors?[86]

[*Takes him by the Nose.*

ALDERMAN. Oh!

FREEMAN. Hold, or here will be your third Law-Suit.

ALDERMAN. Gads precious, you hectoring person you, are you wild? I meant you no hurt, Sir; I begin to think (as things go) Land security best, and have, for a convenient Mortgage, some ten, fifteen, or twenty thousand pound by me.

MANLY. Then go lay it out upon an Hospital, and take a Mortgage of Heaven, according to your City custom; for you think, by laying out a little Money, to hook in that too hereafter; do, I say, and keep the Poor you've made, by taking forfeitures, that Heaven may not take yours.

ALDERMAN. No, to keep the Cripples you make this War; this War spoils our Trade.

MANLY. Dam your Trade, 'tis the better for't.

ALDERMAN. What, will you speak against our Trade?

MANLY. And dare you speak against the War, our Trade?

ALDERMAN. Well, he may be a Convoy of ships I am concerned in.

[*Aside.*]

Come, Captain, I will have a fair correspondency with you, say what you will.

MANLY. Then pr'ythee be gone.

ALDERMAN. No, faith; pr'ythee, Captain, let's go drink a Dish of Lac'd Coffee, and talk of the Times: Come, I'll treat you; nay, you shall go, for I have no business here.

MANLY. But I have.

86. "thirty in the hundred" = 30% interest on loans, an illegal rate; "Squire Setter" = a bird dog pointing out good targets (used in underworld slang); "Baud for Mannors" = someone acquiring manors for others.

ALDERMAN. To pick up a Man to give thee a Dinner. Come, I'll do thy business for thee.

MANLY. Faith, now I think on't, so you may, as well as any Man; for 'tis to pick up a Man, to be bound with me, to one who expects City security, for—

ALDERMAN. Nay, then your Servant, Captain; business must be done.

MANLY. Ay, if it can; but hark you, Alderman, without you—

ALDERMAN. Business, Sir, I say, must be done; and there's an Officer of the Treasury I have an Affair with—

[*Several cross the stage.*]
[*Exit Alderman.*

MANLY. You see now what the mighty friendship of the World is; what all Ceremony, Embraces, and plentiful Professions come to: You are no more to believe a professing Friend, than a threatning Enemy; and as no Man hurts you, that tells you he'll do you a mischief, no man, you see, is your Servant, who sayes he is so. Why, the Devil, then shou'd a Man be troubled with the flattery of Knaves, if he be not a Fool, or Cully; or with the fondness of Fools, if he be not a Knave, or Cheat?

FREEMAN. Only for his pleasure; for there is some in laughing at Fools, and disappointing Knaves.

MANLY. That's a pleasure, I think, wou'd cost you too dear, as well as marrying your Widow to disappoint her; but, for my part, I have no pleasure by 'em, but in despising 'em, wheresoe'r I meet 'em; and then, the pleasure of hoping so to be rid of 'em. But now my comfort is, I am not worth a shilling in the World, which all the World shall know; and then I'm sure I shall have none of 'em come near me.

FREEMAN. A very pretty comfort, which I think you pay too dear for: But is the twenty pound gone since the morning?

MANLY. To my Boats Crew: Wou'd you have the poor, honest, brave Fellows want?

FREEMAN. Rather than you, or I.

MANLY. Why, art thou without Money? thou who art a Friend to every Body?

FREEMAN. I ventur'd my last stake upon the Squire, to nick him of his Mother; and cannot help you to a dinner, unless you will go dine with my Lord—

MANLY. No, no, the Ordinary° is too dear for me, where flattery must pay for my dinner: I am no Herald, or Poet. (eating house)

FREEMAN. We'll go then to the Bishops—

MANLY. There you must flatter the old Philosophy:[87] I cannot renounce my reason for a dinner.

87. Aristotelian and Scholastic learning (as opposed to the empiricism championed in the seventeenth century starting with Francis Bacon and embodied in the Royal Society).

FREEMAN. Why, then let's go to your Aldermans.

MANLY. Hang him, Rogue! that were not to dine; for he makes you drunk with Lees° of Sack before dinner, to take away your stomach: and there you must call Usury and Extortion, Gods blessings, or the honest turning of the Penny; hear him brag of the leather Breeches in which he trotted first to Town; and make a greater noise with his Money in his Parlor, than his Casheers do in his Counting house, without hopes of borrowing a shilling.

dregs

FREEMAN. Ay, a pox on't, 'tis like dining with the great Gamesters; and, when they fall to their common Dessert, see the heaps of Gold drawn on all hands, without going to twelve.[88] Let us go to my Lady *Goodly's.*

MANLY. There, to flatter her looks, you must mistake her Grandchildren for her own; praise her Cook, that she may rail at him: and feed her Dogs, not your self.

FREEMAN. What d'ye think of eating with your Lawyer then?

MANLY. Eat with him! Dam him; to hear him employ his barbarous eloquence in a Reading upon the two and thirty good Bits in a shoulder of Veal; and be forc'd your self to praise the cold Bribe pye that stinks; and drink Law-French Wine, as rough and harsh, as his Law-French. A pox on him, I'd rather dine in the Temple Rounds, or Walks, with the Knights without Noses,[89] or the Knights of the Post; who are honester Fellows, and better company. But let us home, and try our Fortune; for I'll stay no longer here, for your damn'd Widow.

FREEMAN. Well, let us go home then; for I must go for my damn'd Widow, and look after my new damn'd Charge; three or four hundred Year ago, a Man might have din'd in this Hall[.]

MANLY. *But now, the Lawyer only here is fed:*
And, Bully-like, by Quarrels gets his bread.

[Exeunt.

ACT. IV.

SCENE I.

Manly's *Lodging.*
Enter Manly, *and Fidelia.*

MANLY. Well, there's success in thy face; hast thou prevailed? say.

FIDELIA. As I could wish, Sir.

MANLY. So, I told thee what thou wert fit for, and thou wou'dst not

88. Meaning unclear. At ordinaries a meal would be served at twelve and then the tables would be cleared for gambling.

89. The statues of knights whose noses have been knocked off over time.

believe me. Come, thank me for bringing thee acquainted with thy Genius. Well, thou hast mollifi'd her heart for me?

FIDELIA. No, Sir, not so; but what's better.

MANLY. How? what's better?

FIDELIA. I shall harden your heart against her.

MANLY. Have a care, Sir, my heart is too much in earnest to be fool'd with, and my desire at heighth, and needs no delayes to incite it; what, you are too good a Pimp already, and know how to endear pleasure, by withholding it? but leave off your Pages, Baudy-house tricks, Sir, and tell me, will she be kind?

FIDELIA. Kinder than you cou'd wish, Sir.

MANLY. So, then: well, pr'ythee, what said she?

FIDELIA. She said—

MANLY. What? thou'rt so tedious; speak comfort to me: what?

FIDELIA. That, of all things, you were her aversion.

MANLY. How?

FIDELIA. That she wou'd sooner take a Bedfellow out of an Hospital, and Diseases, into her Arms, than you.

MANLY. What?

FIDELIA. That she wou'd rather trust her Honour with a dissolute, debauch'd Hector,° nay worse, with a finical baffled Coward, all over loathsom with affectation of the fine Gentleman[.] bully

MANLY. What's all this you say?

FIDELIA. Nay, that my offers of your Love to her, were more offensive, than when Parents wooe their Virgin Daughters, to the enjoyment of Riches onely; and that you were, in all circumstances, as nauseous to her, as a Husband on compulsion.

MANLY. Hold; I understand you not.

FIDELIA. So, 'twill work I see.

[*Aside.*

MANLY. Did you not tell me—

FIDELIA. She call'd you ten thousand Ruffians.

MANLY. Hold, I say.

FIDELIA. Brutes—

MANLY. Hold.

FIDELIA. Sea-Monsters—

MANLY. Damn your intelligence: hear me a little now.

FIDELIA. Nay, surly Coward she call'd you too.

MANLY. Won't you hold yet? Hold, or—

FIDELIA. Nay, Sir, pardon me; I cou'd not but tell you she had the baseness, the injustice, to call you Coward, Sir, Coward, Coward, Sir.

MANLY. Not yet?—

FIDELIA. I've done. Coward, Sir.

MANLY. Did not you say she was kinder than I cou'd wish her?

FIDELIA. Yes, Sir.

MANLY. How then?—O—I understand you now. At first, she appear'd in rage, and disdain, the truest sign of a coming Woman; but, at last, you prevail'd, it seems: did you not?

FIDELIA. Yes, Sir.

MANLY. So then, let's know that only: come; pr'ythee, without delays: I'll kiss thee for that News before hand.

FIDELIA. So; the Kiss, I'm sure, is welcom to me, whatsoe're the News will be to you.

[*Aside.*

MANLY. Come, speak, my dear Voluntier.

FIDELIA. How welcome were that kind word too, if it were not for another Womans sake!

[*Aside.*

MANLY. What, won't you speak? You prevail'd for me, at last, you say?

FIDELIA. No, Sir.

MANLY. No more of your fooling, Sir; it will not agree with my impatience, or temper.

FIDELIA. Then, not to fool you, Sir, I spoke to her for you, but prevail'd for my self; she wou'd not hear me when I spoke in your behalf; but bid me say what I wou'd in my own, tho' she gave me no occasion, she was so coming: and so was kinder, Sir, than you cou'd wish; which I was only afraid to let you know, without some warning.

MANLY. How's this? Young man, you are of a lying age; but I must hear you out, and if—

FIDELIA. I wou'd not abuse you, and cannot wrong her by any report of her, she is so wicked.

MANLY. How, wicked! had she the impudence, at the second sight of you only—

FIDELIA. Impudence, Sir! Oh, she has impudence enough to put a Court out of countenance, and debauch a Stews.° brothel

MANLY. Why, what said she?

FIDELIA. Her tongue, I confess, was silent; but her speaking Eyes gloted such things, more immodest, and lascivious, than Ravishers can act, or Women under a confinement think.

MANLY. I know there are those whose Eyes reflect more Obscenity, than the Glasses in Alcoves; but there are others too who use a little Art with their looks, to make 'em seem more beautiful, not more loving; which vain young Fellows, like you, are apt to interpret in their own favor, and to the Lady's wrong.

FIDELIA. Seldom, Sir; pray, have you a care of gloting Eyes; for he that loves to gaze upon 'em, will find, at last, a thousand Fools and Cuckolds in 'em, instead of *Cupids*.

MANLY. Very well, Sir: but, what, you had only eye-kindness from *Olivia?*

FIDELIA. I tell you again, Sir, no Woman sticks there: Eye-promises of Love they only keep; nay, they are Contracts which make you sure of 'em. In short, Sir, she, seeing me, with shame and amazement dumb, unactive, and resistless, threw her twisting arms about my neck, and smother'd me with a thousand tasteless Kisses: believe me, Sir, they were so to me.

MANLY. Why did you not avoid 'em then?

FIDELIA. I fenced with her eager Arms, as you did with the grapples of the Enemy's Fireship;[90] and nothing but cutting 'em off, cou'd have freed me.

MANLY. Damn'd, damn'd Woman, that cou'd be so false and infamous! And damn'd, damn'd heart of mine, that cannot yet be false, though so infamous! What easie, tame, suffering, trampled things does that little God of talking Cowards make of us! but[—]

FIDELIA. So! it works I find as I expected.

[*Aside.*

MANLY. But she was false to me before, she told me so her self, and yet I cou'd not quite believe it; but she was, so that her second falseness is a favor to me, not an injury, in revenging me upon the Man that wrong'd me first of her Love. Her Love!—a Whores, a Witches Love!—But, what, did she not kiss well, Sir? I'm sure I thought her Lips—but I must not think of 'em more—but yet they are such I cou'd still kiss,—grow to and then tear off with my teeth, grind 'em into mammocks,° and spit 'em into her Cuckolds face.

shreds

FIDELIA. Poor man, how uneasie he is! I have hardly the heart to give so much pain, tho' withal I give him a cure; and to myself new life.

[*Aside.*

MANLY. But what, her Kisses sure cou'd not but warm you into desire at last, or a compliance with hers at least?

FIDELIA. Nay, more, I confess—

MANLY. What more? speak.

FIDELIA. All you cou'd fear had pass'd between us, if I cou'd have been made to wrong you, Sir, in that nature.

MANLY. Cou'd have been made! you lie, you did.

FIDELIA. Indeed, Sir, 'twas impossible for me; besides, we were interrupted by a visit; but, I confess, she would not let me stir, till I promis'd to return to her again, within this hour, as soon as it

90. Fireships were old ships set on fire and grappled onto an enemy ship to set it on fire as well.

shou'd be dark; by which time, she wou'd dispose of her visit, and her servants, and her self, for my reception: which I was fain to promise to get from her.

MANLY. Ha!

FIDELIA. But if ever I go near her again, may you, Sir, think me as false to you, as she is; hate, and renounce me; as you ought to do her, and I hope will do now.

MANLY. Well, but now I think on't, you shall keep your word with your Lady. What, a young Fellow, and fail the first, nay, so tempting an assignation!

FIDELIA. How, Sir?

MANLY. I say you shall go to her when 'tis dark, and shall not disappoint her.

FIDELIA. I, Sir! I shou'd disappoint her more by going; for—

MANLY. How so?

FIDELIA. Her impudence and injustice to you, will make me disappoint her Love; loath her.

MANLY. Come, you have my leave; and if you disgust her, I'll go with you, and act Love, whil'st you shall talk it only.

FIDELIA. You, Sir! nay, then I'll never go near her. You act Love, Sir! You must but act it indeed, after all I have said to you. Think of your Honour, Sir, Love—

MANLY. Well, call it Revenge, and that is Honourable: I'll be reveng'd on her; and thou shalt be my second.

FIDELIA. Not in a base action, Sir, when you are your own Enemy: O go not near her, Sir, for Heav'ns sake, for your own, think not of it.

MANLY. How concern'd you are! I thought I shou'd catch you. What, you are my Rival at last, and are in Love with her your self; and have spoken ill of her, out of your Love to her, not me; and therefore wou'd not have me go to her!

FIDELIA. Heav'n witness for me, 'tis because I love you only, I wou'd not have you go to her.

MANLY. Come, come, the more I think on't, the more I'm satisfi'd you do love her: those kisses, young Man, I knew were irresistible; tis certain.

FIDELIA. There is nothing certain in the World, Sir, but my Truth and your Courage.

MANLY. Your Servant, Sir. Besides false and ungrateful, as she has been to me; and tho' I may believe her hatred to me, great as you report it; yet I cannot think you are so soon, and at that rate, belov'd by her, though you may endeavor it.

FIDELIA. Nay, if that be all, and you doubt it still, Sir, I will conduct you to her; and, unseen, your Ears shall judge of her falseness, and my Truth to you: if that will satisfie you.

MANLY. Yes, there is some satisfaction in being quite out of doubt:

because 'tis that alone with-holds us from the pleasure of Revenge.

FIDELIA. Revenge! What Revenge can you have, Sir? Disdain is best reveng'd by scorn; and faithless Love, by loving another, and making her happy with the others losings: Which, if I might advise—

Enter Freeman.

MANLY. Not a word more.

FREEMAN. What are you talking of Love yet, Captain? I thought you had done with't.

MANLY. Why, what did you hear me say?

FREEMAN. Something imperfectly of Love, I think.

MANLY. I was only wond'ring why Fools, Rascals, and desertless Wretches, shou'd still have the better of men of Merit with all Women, as much as with their own common Mistress, Fortune!

FREEMAN. Because most Women, like Fortune, are blind, seem to do all things in jest, and take pleasure in extravagant actions; their love deserves neither thanks, nor blame, for they cannot help it: 'tis all sympathy; therefore, the noisie, the finical, the talkative, the cowardly and effeminate, have the better of the brave, the reasonable, and Man of Honour; for they have no more reason in their love, or kindness, than Fortune herself.

MANLY. Yes, they have their reason. First, Honour in a Man they fear too much to love; and Sence in a Lover, upbraids their want of it; and they hate anything that disturbs their admiration of themselves; but they are of that vain number, who had rather shew their false generosity, in giving away profusely to worthless Flatterers, than in paying just Debts: And, in short, all Women, like Fortune, (as you say) and Rewards, are lost, by too much meriting.

FIDELIA. All Women, Sir! sure there are some, who have no other quarrel to a Lovers merit, but that it begets their despair of him.

MANLY. Thou art young enough to be credulous; but we—

Enter 1. Sailor.

1. SAILOR. Here are now below, the scolding, daggled Gentlewoman, and that Major Old—old—Fop, I think you call him.

FREEMAN. *Oldfox:* pr'ythee bid 'em come up, with your leave, Captain, for now I can talk with her upon the square; if I shall not disturb you.

MANLY. No; for I'll be gone. Come, Voluntier.

FREEMAN. Nay, pray stay; the Scene between us will not be so tedious to you, as you think: besides, you shall see, how I rigg'd my Squire out, with the remains of my shipwrack'd Wardrobe; he is under your *Sea Valet de Chambre's*° hands, and by this time dest, and will be worth your seeing. Stay, and I'll fetch my Fool.

valet

MANLY. No; you know I cannot easily laugh: besides, my Voluntier and I have business abroad.

[*Exeunt* Manly, Fidelia *on one side,* Freeman *on t'other.*
Enter Major Oldfox, *and Widow* Blackacre.

WIDOW. What, no body here! Did not the Fellow say he was within?

OLDFOX. Yes, Lady; and he may be perhaps a little busie at present; but, if you think the time long till he comes, [*Unfolding Papers*] I'll read you here some of the fruits of my leisure, the overflowing of my fancy and Pen. (To value me right, she must know my parts.) [*Aside.*] Come—

WIDOW. No, no; I have reading work enough of my own, in my Bag, I thank you.

OLDFOX. I, Law, Madam; but here is a Poem, in blank Verse, which I think a handsom Declaration of one's Passion.

WIDOW. O! if you talk of Declarations, I'll shew you one of the prettiest pen'd things, which I mended too my self you must know[.]

OLDFOX. Nay, Lady, if you have us'd your self so much to the reading harsh Law, that you hate smooth Poetry; here is a Character for you, of—

WIDOW. A Character! Nay, then I'll shew you my Bill in Chancery here, that gives you such a Character of my Adversary, makes him as black—

OLDFOX. Pshaw; away, away, Lady. But if you think the Character too long, here is an Epigram not above 20 Lines, upon a cruel Lady; who Decreed her Servant shou'd hang himself, to demonstrate his Passion.

WIDOW. Decreed! if you talk of Decreeing, I have such a Decree here, drawn by the finest Clerk—

OLDFOX. O Lady, Lady, all interruption, and no sence between us, as if we were Lawyers at the Bar! But I had forgot, *Apollo* and *Littleton*[91] never lodge in a head together. If you hate Verses, I'll give you a cast of my Politics in Prose: 'tis a Letter to a Friend in the Countrey; which is now the way of all such sober, solid persons as my self, when they have a mind to publish their disgust to the Times; tho' perhaps, between you and I, they have no Friend in the Countrey. And sure a Politic, serious person may as well have a feign'd Friend in the Countrey to write to, as an idle Poet a feign'd Mistress to write to. And so here is my Letter to a Friend, or no Friend, in the Countrey, concerning the late conjuncture of Affairs, in relation to Coffee-houses: or the Coffee-man's Case.[92]

91. Sir Thomas de Littleton, fifteenth-century authority on land tenure.

92. Coffee houses were ordered closed by royal proclamation in January of 1676 in an effort to stop sedition. The proclamation was never enforced.

WIDOW. Nay, if your Letter have a Case in't, 'tis something; but first I'll read you a Letter of mine, to a Friend in the Countrey, call'd a Letter of Attorney.[93]

Enter to them Freeman, *and* Jerry Blackacre, *in an old gaudy Suit, and Red Breeches of* Freeman's.

OLDFOX. What, Interruption still? O the plague of Interruption! worse to an Author, than the plague of Critics.

[*Aside.*

WIDOW. What's this I see, *Jerry Blackacre,* my Minor, in Red Breeches! What, hast thou left the modest seemly Garb of Gown and Cap, for this? And have I lost all my good Inns of Chancery breeding upon thee then? And thou wilt go a breeding thy self, from our Inn of *Chancery* and *Westminster-hall,* at Coffee-houses and Ordinaries, Play-houses, Tennis-courts, and Baudy-houses.

JERRY. Ay, ay, what then? perhaps I will; but what's that to you? here's my Guardian and Tutor now forsooth, that I am out of your Hucksters hands.

WIDOW. How? thou hast not chosen him for thy Guardian yet?

JERRY. No, but he has chosen me for his Charge, and that's all one; and I'll do any thing he'll have me, and go all the World over with him; to Ordinaries, and Baudy-houses, or any where else.

WIDOW. To Ordinaries and Baudy-houses! have a care, Minor, thou wilt enfeeble there thy Estate, and Body: do not go to Ordinaries and Baudy-houses, good *Jerry.*

JERRY. Why, how come you to know any ill by Baudy-houses? You never had any hurt by 'em, had you, forsooth? Pray hold your self contented; if I do go where Money and Wenches are to be had, you may thank your self; for you us'd me so unnaturally, you wou'd never let me have a Penny to go abroad with; nor so much as come near the Garret, where your Maidens lay; nay, you wou'd not so much as let me play at Hotcockles[94] with 'em, nor have any Recreation with 'em, tho' one shou'd have kist you behind, you were so unnatural a Mother, so you were.

FREEMAN. Ay, a very unnatural Mother, faith, Squire.

WIDOW. But, *Jerry,* consider thou art yet but a Minor; however, if thou wilt go home with me again, and be a good Child, thou shalt see—

FREEMAN. Madam, I must have a better care of my Heir under age, than so; I wou'd sooner trust him alone with a stale Waiting-woman[95] and a Parson, than with his Widow Mother and her Lover or Lawyer.

93. Power of attorney, allowing one person to legally act for another.

94. A game where a blindfolded player guesses who struck him, with obvious double entendre.

95. A decoy to lure Jerry into marriage.

WIDOW. Why, thou Villain, part Mother and Minor! Rob me of my Child and my Writings! but thou shalt find there's Law; and as in the Case of Ravishment, of Guard—*Westminster* the Second.[96]

OLDFOX. Young Gentleman, Squire, pray be rul'd by your Mother, and your Friends.

JERRY. Yes, I'll be rul'd by my Friends, therefore not by my Mother, so I won't: I'll choose him for my Guardian till I am of age; nay, may be for as long as I live.

WIDOW. Wilt thou so, thou Wretch? And when thou'rt of age, thou wilt Sign, Seal, and Deliver too, wilt thou?

JERRY. Yes marry will I, if you go there too.

WIDOW. O do not squeeze Wax, Son; rather go to Ordinaries, and Baudy-houses, than squeeze Wax:[97] If thou dost that, farewell the goodly Mannor of *Blackacre,* with all its Woods, Underwoods, and Appurtenances whatever! Oh, oh!

[*Weeps.*

FREEMAN. Come, Madam, in short, you see I am resolv'd to have a share in the Estate, yours or your Sons; if I cannot get you, I'll keep him, who is less coy, you find; but, if you wou'd have your Son again, you must take me too. Peace, or War? Love, or Law? You see my Hostage is in my hand: I'm in possession.

WIDOW. Nay, if one of us must be ruin'd, e'en let it be him. By my Body, a good one! Did you ever know yet a Widow marry or not marry for the sake of her Child? I'd have you to know, Sir, I shall be hard enough for you both yet, without marrying you: if *Jerry* won't be rul'd by me, what say you, Booby, will you be rul'd? speak.

JERRY. Let one alone, can't you?

WIDOW. Wilt thou choose him for Guardian, whom I refuse for Husband?

JERRY. Ay, to choose, I thank you.

WIDOW. And are all my hopes frustrated? Shall I never hear thee put Cases again to *John* the Butler, or our Vicar? Never see thee amble the Circuit with the Judges; and hear thee, in our Town-Hall, louder than the Cryer?

JERRY. No; for I have taken my leave of Lawyering, and Pettifogging.

WIDOW. Pettifogging! thou profane Villain, hast thou so? Pettifogging!—then you shall take your leave of me, and your Estate too; thou shalt be an Alien to me and it forever. Pettifogging!

JERRY. O, but if you go there too, Mother, we have the Deeds, and Settlements, I thank you: Wou'd you cheat me of my estate, ifac?

96. Statute from 1285 providing remedies against the abduction of a minor.

97. The widow means that Jerry should not press his seal upon the hot wax of a bill of sale.

WIDOW. No, no, I will not cheat your little brother *Bob;* for thou wert not born in Wedlock.

FREEMAN. How's that?

JERRY. How? what Quirk has she got in her head now?

WIDOW. I say thou canst not, shalt not inherit the *Blackacres* Estate.

JERRY. Why? Why, forsooth? What d'ye mean, if you go there too?

WIDOW. Thou art but my base° Child; and, according to the Law, canst not inherit it: nay, thou art not so much as Bastard eigne.°

(base: illegitimate; Bastard eigne: the elder bastard)

JERRY. What, what? Am I then the Son of a Whore, Mother?

WIDOW. The Law says—

FREEMAN. Madam, we know what the Law says; but have a care what you say: do not let your Passion, to ruine your Son, ruine your Reputation.

WIDOW. Hang Reputation, Sir, am not I a Widow? Have no Husband, nor intend to have any? Nor wou'd you, I suppose, now have me for a Wife. So, I think now I'm reveng'd on my Son and you, without marrying, as I told you.

FREEMAN. But, consider, Madam.

JERRY. What, have you no shame left in you, Mother?

WIDOW. Wonder not at it, Major, 'tis often the poor prest Widows case, to give up her Honour to save her Jointure; and seem to be a light Woman, rather than marry: as some young men, they say, pretend to have the filthy Disease,° and lose their credit with most Women, to avoid the importunities of some.

(filthy Disease: venereal disease)

[*Aside to* Oldfox.

FREEMAN. But one word with you, Madam.

WIDOW. No, no, sir. Come, Major, let us make haste, now to the Prerogative Court.[98]

OLDFOX. But, Lady, if what you say be true, will you stigmatise your Reputation on Record? And, if it be not true, how will you prove it?

WIDOW. Pshaw! I can prove any thing; and for my Reputation, know, Major, a wise Woman will no more value her Reputation in disinheriting a Rebellious Son, of a good Estate; than she wou'd in getting him, to inherit an Estate.

[*Exeunt* Widow *and* Oldfox.

FREEMAN. Madam—We must not let her go so, Squire.

JERRY. Nay, the Devil can't stop her tho' if she has a mind to't. But come, Bully Guardian, we'll go and advise with three Attornies, two Proctors, two Sollicitors, and a shrewd man of *White Friers,*[99] neither Attorney, Proctor, or Sollicitor, but as pure a Pimp

98. The archbishop's court responsible for wills.

99. A section in the East End of London, it included Alsatia, a sanctuary for criminals and therefore associated with crafty criminals.

to the Law as any of 'em; and sure all they will be hard enough for her: for I fear, Bully Guardian, you are too good a Joker, to have any Law in your head.

FREEMAN. Thou'rt in the right on't, Squire; I understand no Law: especially that against Bastards, since I'm sure the Custom is against that Law; and more people get Estates by being so, than lose 'em.

[*Exeunt.*

The Scene changes to Olivia's *Lodging.*

[SCENE II.]

Enter Lord Plausible *and Boy with a candle.*

L. PLAUSIBLE. Little Gentleman, your most obedient, faithful, humble Servant: where, I beseech you, is that Divine person your Noble Lady?

BOY. Gone out, my Lord; but commanded me to give you this Letter.

[*Gives him a Letter.*
Enter to him Novel.

L. PLAUSIBLE. Which he must not observe.

[*Aside.*] *Puts it up.*

NOVEL. Hey, Boy, where is thy Lady?

BOY. Gone out, Sir; but I must beg a word with you.

[*Gives him a letter, and Exit.*

NOVEL. For me? So.

[*Puts up the letter.*

Servant, Servant, my Lord; you see the Lady knew of your coming, for she is gone out.

L. PLAUSIBLE. Sir, I humbly beseech you not to censure the Lady's good breeding: she has reason to use more liberty with me, than with any other man.

NOVEL. How, Vicount, how?

L. PLAUSIBLE. Nay, I humbly beseech you, be not in choler; where there is most love, there may be most freedom.

NOVEL. Nay, then 'tis time to come to an eclercisment[100] with you, and to tell you, you must think no more of this Lady's love.

L. PLAUSIBLE. Why, under correction, dear Sir?

NOVEL. There are Reasons, Reasons, Vicount.

L. PLAUSIBLE. What, I beseech you, Noble Sir?

100. Clarification; understanding.

NOVEL. Pr'ythee, pr'ythee, be not impertinent, my Lord; some of you Lords are such conceited, well-assur'd, impertinent Rogues[.]

L. PLAUSIBLE. And you noble Wits are so full of shamming, and droling, one knows not where to have you, seriously.

NOVEL. Well, you shall find me in Bed, with this Lady, one of these dayes.

L. PLAUSIBLE. Nay, I beseech you, spare the Lady's Honour; for her's and mine will be all one shortly.

NOVEL. Pr'ythee, my Lord, be not an Ass: Dost thou think to get her from me? I have had such encouragements—

L. PLAUSIBLE. I have not been thought unworthy of 'em.

NOVEL. What, not like mine! Come to an eclercisement, as I said.

L. PLAUSIBLE. Why, seriously then, she has told me, Vicountess sounded prettily.

NOVEL. And me, that *Novel* was a name she wou'd sooner change her's for, than for any Title in *England.*

L. PLAUSIBLE. She has commended the softness, and respectfulness of my behaviour.

NOVEL. She has prais'd the briskness of my Railery, of all things, Man.

L. PLAUSIBLE. The sleepiness of my Eyes she lik'd.

NOVEL. Sleepiness! dulness, dulness. But the fierceness of mine she ador'd.

L. PLAUSIBLE. The brightness of my hair she lik'd.

NOVEL. The brightness! no, the greasiness, I warrant. But the blackness, and lustre of mine, she admires.

L. PLAUSIBLE. The gentleness of my smile.

NOVEL. The subtilty of my leer.

L. PLAUSIBLE. The clearness of my complexion.

NOVEL. The redness of my lips.

L. PLAUSIBLE. The whiteness of my teeth.

NOVEL. My jaunty way of picking them.

L. PLAUSIBLE. The sweetness of my breath.

NOVEL. Hah ha!—Nay then she abus'd you, 'tis plain; for you know what *Manly* said: the sweetness of your Pulvillio she might mean; but for your breath! ha, ha, ha. Your breath is such, Man, that nothing but Tobacco can perfume: and your Complexion nothing cou'd mend, but the Small Pox.

L. PLAUSIBLE. Well, Sir, you may please to be merry; but, to put you out of all doubt, Sir, she has receiv'd some Jewels from me, of value.

NOVEL. And Presents from me; besides what I presented her jantily, by way of 'Ombre, of three or four hundred pound value, which I'm sure are the earnest Pence for our Love bargain.

L. PLAUSIBLE. Nay then, Sir, with your favor, and to make an end of all your hopes, look you there, Sir, she has writ to me.—

[*Deliver to each other their Letters.*

NOVEL. How! how! Well, well, and so she has to me: look you there.—

L. PLAUSIBLE. What's here!

NOVEL. How's this?

Reads out.

My dear Lord,

You'll excuse me, for breaking my word with you, since 'twas to oblige, not offend you; for I am only gone abroad but to disappoint Novel, *and meet you in the Drawing-room; where I expect you, with as much impatience, as when I us'd to suffer* Novel's *Visits, the most impertinent Fop, that ever affected the name of a Wit, therefore not capable, I hope, to give you jealousie; for, for your sake alone, you saw, I renounc'd an old Lover, and will do all the World. Burn the Letter, but lay up the kindness of it in your heart, with your*

OLIVIA

Very fine! but pray let's see mine.

L. PLAUSIBLE. I understand it not; but sure she cannot think so of me.

Reads the other Letter.

NOVEL. *Humh! ha!—meet—for your sake—umh—quitted an old Lover—World—Burn—in your heart, with your*

OLIVIA

Just the same, the names only alter'd.

L. PLAUSIBLE. Surely there must be some mistake; or some body has abus'd her, and us.

NOVEL. Yes, you are abus'd, no doubt on't, my Lord; but I'll to *White-hall,* and see.

L. PLAUSIBLE. And I, where I shall find you are abus'd.

NOVEL. Where, if it be so, for our comfort, we cannot fail of meeting with Fellow-sufferers enough; for, as *Freeman* said of another, she stands in the Drawing-room, like the Glass, ready for all Comers, to set their Gallantry by her: and, like the Glass too, lets no man go from her, unsatisfi'd with himself.

[*Exeunt ambo.*

Enter Olivia *and* Boy.

OLIVIA. Both here, and just gone?

BOY. Yes, Madam.

OLIVIA. But are you sure neither saw you deliver the other a Letter.

BOY. Yes, yes, Madam, I am very sure.

OLIVIA. Go then to the *Old Exchange,* to *Westminster, Holborn,* and all the other places I told you of; I shall not need you these two hours: Be gone, and take the Candle with you, and be sure you leave word again below, I am gone out, to all that ask.

BOY. Yes, Madam.

[*Exit.*

OLIVIA. And my new Lover will not ask, I'm sure; he has his Lesson, and cannot miss me here, tho' in the dark: which I have purposely design'd, as a remedy against my blushing Gallant's modesty; for young Lovers, like game Cocks,° are made bolder, by being kept without light.

° fighting roosters

Enter her husband Vernish, *as from a Journey.*

VERNISH. Where is she? Darkness everywhere?

[*Softly.*

OLIVIA. What! come before your time? my Soul! my Life! your haste has augmented your kindness; and let me thank you for it thus, and thus—[*Embracing and kissing him*] And tho' (my Soul) the little time since you left me, has seem'd an Age to my impatience, sure it is yet but seven—

VERNISH. How! who's that you expected after seven?

OLIVIA. Ha! my Husband return'd! and have I been throwing away so many kind Kisses on my Husband, and wrong'd my Lover already?

VERNISH. Speak, I say, who was't you expected after seven?

OLIVIA. What shall I say?—oh—

[*Aside.*

Why, 'tis but seven days, is it, dearest, since you went out of Town? and I expected you not so soon.

VERNISH. No, sure, 'tis but five days since I left you.

OLIVIA. Pardon my impatience, dearest, I thought 'em seven at least.

VERNISH. Nay then—

OLIVIA. But, my life, you shall never stay half so long from me again; you shan't, indeed, by this kiss, you shan't.

VERNISH. No, no; but why alone in the dark?

OLIVIA. Blame not my melancholy in your absence—But, my Soul, since you went, I have strange News to tell you: *Manly* is return'd.

VERNISH. Manly return'd! Fortune forbid!

OLIVIA. Met with the *Dutch* in the Channel, fought, sunk his ship, and all he carri'd with him: he was here with me yesterday.

VERNISH. And did you own our Marriage to him?

OLIVIA. I told him I was marry'd, to put an end to his love, and my trouble; but to whom, is yet a secret kept from him, and all the World: And I have us'd him so scurvily, his great spirit will ne'r return, to reason it farther with me; I have sent him to Sea again, I warrant.

VERNISH. 'Twas bravely done. And sure he will now hate the shore more than ever, after so great a disappointment. Be you sure only to keep a while our great secret, till he be gone: in the mean time, I'll lead the easie honest Fool by the Nose, as I us'd to do;

and whil'st he stays, rail with him at thee; and, when he's gone, laugh with thee at him. But have you his Cabinet of Jewels safe? Part not with a Seed Pearl[101] to him, to keep him from starving.

OLIVIA. Nor from hanging.

VERNISH. He cannot recover 'em; and, I think, will scorn to beg 'em again.

OLIVIA. But, my life, have you taken the thousand Guineys he left in my name, out of the Goldsmiths hands?

VERNISH. Ay, ay, they are remov'd to another Goldsmiths.

OLIVIA. Ay, but, my Soul, you had best have a care he find not where the money is; for his present wants (as I'm inform'd) are such, as will make him inquisitive enough.

VERNISH. You say true, and he knows the man too: but I'll remove it to morrow.

OLIVIA. To morrow! O do not stay till to morrow: go to night, immediately.

VERNISH. Now I think on't, you advise well, and I will go presently.

OLIVIA. Presently! instantly: I will not let you stay a jot.

VERNISH. I will then, tho' I return not home till twelve.

OLIVIA. Nay, tho' not till morning, with all my heart: go, dearest; I am impatient till you are gone—

[*Thrusts him out.*]

So, I have at once now brought about those two grateful businesses, which all prudent Women do together, secur'd money and pleasure; and now all interruptions of the last are remov'd. Go Husband, and come up Friend; just the Bucket's in the well, the absence of one brings the other;[102] but I hope, like them too, they will not meet in the way, justle, and clash together.

Enter Fidelia, *and* Manly *treading softly, and staying behind at some distance.*

So, are you come? (but not the Husband-bucket, I hope, again.) Who's there? my dearest?

[*Softly.*

FIDELIA. My life—

OLIVIA. Right, right: where are thy lips? here, take the dumb, and best Welcomes, Kisses and Embraces; 'tis not a time for idle words. In a Duel of Love, as in others, Parlying shews basely. Come, we are alone; and now the Word is only Satisfaction, and defend not thy self.

MANLY. How's this? Wuh, she makes Love like a Devil in a Play; and

101. A small pearl of limited value.

102. Wells were sometimes constructed with counterbalancing buckets; as one bucket was drawn up, the other bucket sank down.

in this darkness, which conceals her Angels face; if I were apt to be afraid, I shou'd think her a devil.

[*Aside.*

OLIVIA. What, you traverse ground, young Gentleman!

[Fidelia *avoiding her.*

FIDELIA. I take breath only.

MANLY. Good Heav'ns! how was I deceiv'd!

[*Aside.*

OLIVIA. Nay, you are a Coward; what are you afraid of the fierceness of my Love?

FIDELIA. Yes, Madam, lest its violence might presage its change; and I must needs be afraid you wou'd leave me quickly, who cou'd desert so brave a Gentleman as *Manly.*

OLIVIA. O! name not his Name; for in a time of stol'n joys, as this is, the filthy name of Husband were not a more alaying sound.

MANLY. There's some comfort yet.

[*Aside.*

FIDELIA. But did you not love him?

OLIVIA. Never. How cou'd you think it?

FIDELIA. Because he thought it, who is a Man of that sense, nice discerning, and diffidency, that I shou'd think it hard to deceive him.

OLIVIA. No; he that distrusts most the World, trusts most to himself, and is but the more easily deceiv'd, because he thinks he can't be deceiv'd; his cunning is like the Coward's Sword, by which he is oftner worsted, than defended.

FIDELIA. Yet, sure, you us'd no common Art, to deceive him.

OLIVIA. I knew he lov'd his own singular moroseness so well, as to dote upon any Copy of it; wherefore I feign'd an hatred to the World too, that he might love me in earnest: but, if it had been hard to deceive him, I'm sure 'twere much harder to love him. A dogged, ill-manner'd—

FIDELIA. D'ye hear, Sir? pray hear her.

[*Aside to* Manly.

OLIVIA. Surly, untractable, snarling Brute! he! a Masty° Dog were as fit a thing to make a Gallant of. (mastiff)

MANLY. Ay, a Goat, or Monkey, were fitter for thee.

[*Aside.*

FIDELIA. I must confess, for my part, (tho' my Rival) I cannot but say, he has a Manly handsomness in's face and meen.

OLIVIA. So has a Saracen in the sign.° (sign on an inn)

FIDELIA. Is proper, and well made,

OLIVIA. As a Drayman.° driver of a cart

FIDELIA. Has Wit,

OLIVIA. He rails at all Mankind.

FIDELIA. And undoubted Corage,

OLIVIA. Like the Hangman's, can murder a Man when his hands are ty'd. He has Cruelty indeed; which is no more Corage, than his Railing is Wit.

MANLY. Thus Women, and Men like Women, are too hard for us, when they think we do not hear 'em; and Reputation, like other Mistresses, is never true to a Man in his absence.

[*Aside.*

FIDELIA. He is—

OLIVIA. Pr'ythee, no more of him; I thought I had satisfi'd you enough before, that he could never be a Rival for you to apprehend; and you need not be more assur'd of my aversion to him, but by the last testimony of my love to you: which I am ready to give you. Come, my Soul, this way—

[*Pulls* Fidelia.

FIDELIA. But, Madam, what cou'd make you dissemble Love to him, when 'twas so hard a thing for you, and flatter his Love to you?

OLIVIA. That which makes all the World flatter and dissemble, 'twas his Money: I had a real passion for that. Yet I lov'd not that so well, as for it to take him; for as soon as I had his Money I hastened his departure: like a Wife, who, when she has made the most of a dying Husband's breath, pulls away the Pillow.

MANLY. Damn'd Money! it's Master's potent Rival still; and, like a saucy Pimp, corrupts, it self, the Mistress it procures for us.

OLIVIA. But I did not think with you, my life, to pass my time in talking. Come hither, come; yet stay, till I have lock'd a door in the other Room, that may chance to let us in some interruption; which reciting Poets, or losing Gamesters, fear not more than I at this time do.

[*Exit* Olivia.

FIDELIA. Well, I hope you are now satisfi'd, Sir, and will be gone, to think of your Revenge?

MANLY. No, I am not satisfi'd, and must stay to be Reveng'd.

FIDELIA. How, Sir? You'll use no violence to her, I hope, and forfeit your own life, to take away hers? that were no Revenge.

MANLY. No, no, you need not fear: my Revenge shall only be upon her honour, not her life.

FIDELIA. How, Sir? her honour? O Heav'ns! Consider, Sir, she has no honour. D'ye call that Revenge? Can you think of such a thing? But reflect, Sir, how she hates and loaths you.

MANLY. Yes, so much she hates me, that it wou'd be a Revenge sufficient, to make her accessary to my pleasure, and then let her know it.

FIDELIA. No, Sir, no; to be Reveng'd on her now, were to disappoint her. Pray, Sir, let us begone.

[*Pulls* Manly.

MANLY. Hold off. What, you are my Rival then; and therefore you shall stay, and keep the door for me, whil'st I go in for you: but, when I'm gone, if you dare to stir off from this very Board, or breathe the least murmuring Accent, I'll cut her Throat first, and if you love her, you will not venture her life; nay, then I'll cut your Throat too; and I know you love your own life at least.

FIDELIA. But, Sir, good Sir.

MANLY. Not a word more, lest I begin my Revenge on her, by killing you.

FIDELIA. But are you sure 'tis Revenge, that makes you do this? how can it be?

MANLY. Whist.° be still

FIDELIA. 'Tis a strange Revenge indeed.

MANLY. If you make me stay, I shall keep my word, and begin with you: no more.

[*Exit* Manly, *at the same door* Olivia *went.*
Manet Fidelia.

FIDELIA. O Heav'ns! is there not punishment enough
In loving well, if you will have't a Crime;
But you must add fresh Torments daily to't,
And punish us like peevish Rivals still,
Because we fain wou'd find a Heaven here?
But did there never any love like me,
That untry'd Tortures you must find me out?
Others, at worst, you force to kill themselves;
But I must be Self-murd'ress of my love,
Yet will not grant me pow'r to end my life,
My cruel life; for when a Lover's hopes
Are dead and gone, life is unmerciful.

[*Sits down and weeps.*
Enter Manly *to her.*

MANLY. I have thought better on't, I must not discover myself now, I am without Witnesses; for if I barely shou'd publish it, she wou'd deny it with as much impudence, as she wou'd act it again with this young Fellow here. Where are you?

FIDELIA. Here—oh—now I suppose we may be gone.

MANLY. I will, but not you; you must stay, and act the second part of a Lover: that is, talk kindness to her.

FIDELIA. Not I, Sir.

MANLY. No disputing, Sir, you must: 'tis necessary to my design, of coming again to morrow night.

FIDELIA. What, can you come again then hither?

MANLY. Yes, and you must make the appointment, and an Apology for your leaving her so soon; for I have said not a word to her, but have kept your counsel, as I expect you shou'd do mine: do this faithfully, and I promise you here, you shall run my Fortune still, and we will never part as long as we live; but if you do not do it, expect not to live.

FIDELIA. 'Tis hard, Sir; but such a consideration will make it easier: you won't forget your promise, Sir?

MANLY. No, by Heav'ns. But I hear her coming.

[*Exit.*

Enter Olivia *to* Fidelia.

OLIVIA. Where is my life? run from me already! you do not love me, dearest; nay, you are angry with me; for you wou'd not so much as speak a kind word to me within: What was the reason?

FIDELIA. I was transported too much.

OLIVIA. That's kind; but come, my Soul, what make you here? let us go in again; we may be surpriz'd in this Room, 'tis so near the stairs.

FIDELIA. No, we shall hear the better here, if any body shou'd come up.

OLIVIA. Nay, I assure you, we shall be secure enough within: Come, Come—

FIDELIA. I am sick, and troubled with a sudden diziness; cannot stir yet.

OLIVIA. Come, I have spirits within.

FIDELIA. O!—don't you hear a noise, Madam?

OLIVIA. No, no, there is none: Come, come.

[*Pulls her.*

FIDELIA. Indeed there is; and I love you so much, I must have a care of your Honour, if you wo'not, and go; but to come to you to morrow night, if you please.

OLIVIA. With all my Soul; but you must not go yet: come, pr'ythee.

FIDELIA. Oh!—I am now sicker, and am afraid of one of my Fits.

OLIVIA. What Fits?

FIDELIA. Of the Falling-sickness:° and I lie generally an hour in a trance; therefore pray consider your honour, for the sake of my love, and let me go, that I may return to you often.

epilepsy

OLIVIA. But will you be sure then to come to morrow night?

FIDELIA. Yes.

OLIVIA. Swear.

FIDELIA. By our past kindness.

OLIVIA. Well, go your wayes then, if you will, you naughty Creature you.

[*Exit* Fidelia.]

These young Lovers, with their fears and modesty, make themselves as bad as old ones to us; and I apprehend their bashfulness more than their tatling.

Fidelia *returns.*

FIDELIA. O, Madam, we're undone! there was a Gentleman upon the stairs, coming up, with a Candle; which made me retire. Look you, here he comes!

Enter Vernish, *and his Man with a Light.*

OLIVIA. How! my Husband! Oh, undone indeed! This way.

[*Exit.*

VERNISH. Ha! You shall not scape me so, Sir.

[*Stops* Fidelia.

FIDELIA. O Heav'ns! more fears, plagues and torments yet in store!

[*Aside.*

VERNISH. Come, Sir, I guess what your business was here; but this must be your business now. Draw.

[*Draws.*

FIDELIA. Sir—
VERNISH. No Expostulations: I shall not care to hear of't. Draw.
FIDELIA. Good Sir.
VERNISH. How, you Rascal! not Courage to draw, yet durst do me the greatest injury in the World? Thy Cowardice shall not save thy life.

[*Offers to run at* Fidelia.

FIDELIA. O hold, Sir, and send but your Servant down, and I'll satisfie you, Sir, I cou'd not injure you, as you imagine.
VERNISH. Leave the light, and be gone.

[*Exit* Servant.]

Now quickly, Sir, what you've to say, or—
FIDELIA. I am a Woman, Sir, a very unfortunate Woman.
VERNISH. How! A very handsom Woman I'm sure then: here are Witnesses of't too, I confess—

[*Pulls off her Peruke, and feels her breasts.*]

Well, I'm glad to find the Tables turn'd, my Wife is in more danger of Cuckolding, than I was.

[*Aside.*]

FIDELIA. Now, Sir, I hope you are so much a Man of Honour, as to let me go, now I have satisfi'd you, Sir.

VERNISH. When you have satisfi'd me, Madam, I will.

FIDELIA. I hope, Sir, you are too much a Gentleman, to urge those secrets from a Woman, which concern her Honour: You may guess my misfortune to be Love, by my disguise; but a pair of Breeches cou'd not wrong you, Sir.

VERNISH. I may believe Love has chang'd your outside, which cou'd not wrong me; but why did my Wife run away?

FIDELIA. I know not, Sir; perhaps because she wou'd not be forc'd to discover me to you, or to guide me from your suspitions, that you might not discover me your self: which ungentleman-like curiosity I hope you will cease to have, and let me go.

VERNISH. Well, Madam, if I must not know who you are, 'twill suffice for me only to know certainly what you are: which you must not deny me. Come, there is a Bed within, the proper Rack for Lovers; and if you are a Woman, there you can keep no secrets, you'll tell me there all unask'd. Come.

[*Pulls her.*

FIDELIA. Oh! what d'ye mean? Help, oh—

VERNISH. I'll show you; but 'tis in vain to cry out: no one dares help you, for I am Lord here.

FIDELIA. Tyrant here; but if you are Master of this House, which I have taken for a Sanctuary, do not violate it your self.

VERNISH. No, I'll preserve you here, and nothing shall hurt you, and will be as true to you, as your disguise; but you must trust me then. Come, come.

FIDELIA. Oh, oh! rather than you should drag me to a deed so horrid, and so shameful, I'll die here a thousand deaths: but you do not look like a Ravisher, Sir.

VERNISH. Nor you like one wou'd put me to't, but if you will—

FIDELIA. Oh! oh! help! help—

Enter Servant.

VERNISH. You saucy Rascal, how durst you come in, when you heard a Woman squeak? that shou'd have been your Cue to shut the door.

SERVANT. I come, Sir, to let you know, the Alderman coming home immediately after you were at his house, has sent his Casheer with the money, according to your Note.

VERNISH. Dam his money! money never came to any sure unseasonably, till now. Bid him stay.

SERVANT. He sayes, he cannot a moment.

VERNISH. Receive it you then.

SERVANT. He sayes, he must have your Receit for it: he is in haste, for I hear him coming up, Sir.

VERNISH. Dam him. Help me in here then with this dishonorer of my Family.

FIDELIA. Oh! oh!

SERVANT. You say she is a Woman, Sir.

VERNISH. No matter, Sir: must you prate?

FIDELIA. Oh Heav'ns! is there—

[*They thrust her in, and lock the door.*

VERNISH. Stay there, my Prisoner; you have a short Reprieve.

I'll fetch the Gold, and that she can't resist;
For with a full hand 'tis we ravish best.

[Exeunt.

Finis Actus quarti.

ACT. V.

SCENE I.

Eliza's *Lodging.*
Enter Olivia, *and* Eliza.

OLIVIA. Ah, Cousin, nothing troubles me, but that I have given the malicious World its Revenge, and Reason now to talk as freely of me, as I us'd to do of it.

ELIZA. Faith, then, let not that trouble you; for, to be plain, Cousin, the world cannot talk worse of you, than it did before.

OLIVIA. How, cousin? I'd have you to know, before this faux pas, this trip of mine, the World cou'd not talk of me.

ELIZA. Only, that you mind other peoples actions so much, that you take no care of your own, but to hide 'em; that, like a Thief, because you know yourself most guilty, you impeach your Fellow Criminals first, to clear your self.

OLIVIA. O wicked world!

ELIZA. That you pretend an aversion to all Mankind, in publick, only that their Wives and Mistresses may not be jealous, and hinder you of their conversation in private.

OLIVIA. Base World!

ELIZA. That, abroad, you fasten quarrels upon innocent men, for talking of you, only to bring 'em to ask you pardon at home, and to become dear Friends with 'em, who were hardly your acquaintance before.

OLIVIA. Abominable World!

ELIZA. That you condemn the obscenity of modern Plays, only that you may not be censur'd for never missing the most obscene of the old ones.

OLIVIA. Damn'd World!

ELIZA. That you deface the nudities of Pictures, and little Statues, only because they are not real.

OLIVIA. O fie, fie, fie; hideous, hideous, Cousin! the obscenity of their Censures makes me blush.

ELIZA. The truth of 'em, the naughty World wou'd say now.

Enter Lettice *hastily.*

LETTICE. O! Madam, here is that Gentleman coming up, who now you say is my Master.

OLIVIA. O! Cousin, whither shall I run? protect me, or—

[Olivia *runs away, and stands at a distance*
Enter Vernish.

VERNISH. Nay, nay, come—

OLIVIA. O, Sir, forgive me.

VERNISH. Yes, yes, I can forgive you being alone in the dark with a Woman in Mans cloaths; but have a care of a Man in Womans cloaths.

OLIVIA. What does he mean? he dissembles, only to get me into his power: Or has my dear Friend made him believe he was a Woman? My Husband may be deceiv'd by him, but I'm sure I was not.

[*Aside.*

VERNISH. Come, come, you need not have lay'n out of your House for this; but perhaps you were afraid, when I was warm with suspitions, you must have discover'd who she was: And pr'ythee, may I not know it?

OLIVIA. She was—(I hope he has been deceiv'd: and since my Lover has play'd the Card, I must not renounce)

[*Aside.*

VERNISH. Come, what's the matter with thee? If I must not know who she is, I'm satisfi'd without. Come hither.

OLIVIA. Sure you do know her; she has told you her self, I suppose.

VERNISH. No, I might have known her better, but that I was interrupted, by the Goldsmith you know, and was forc'd to lock her into your Chamber, to keep her from his sight; but, when I re turn'd, I found she was got away, by tying the Window-curtains to the Balcony, by which she slid down into the street: for, you must know, I jested with her, and made her believe I'd ravish her; which she apprehended, it seems, in earnest.

OLIVIA. Then she got from you?

VERNISH. Yes.

OLIVIA. And is quite gone?

VERNISH. Yes.

OLIVIA. I'm glad on't—otherwise you had ravish'd her Sir? but how dar'st you go so far, as to make her believe you wou'd ravish her?

let me understand that, Sir. What! there's guilt in your face, you blush too: nay, then you did ravish her, you did, you base Fellow. What, ravish a Woman in the first Month of our Marriage! 'Tis a double injury to me, thou base ungrateful Man; wrong my Bed already, Villain! I cou'd tear out those false Eyes, barbarous unworthy Wretch.

ELIZA. So, so!—

VERNISH. Pr'ythee hear, my Dear.

OLIVIA. I will never hear you, my plague, my torment!

VERNISH. I swear—pr'ythee hear me.

OLIVIA. I have heard already too many of your false Oaths and Vows, especially your last in the Church. O wicked Man! And wretched Woman that I was! I wish I had then sunk down into a Grave, rather than to have given you my hand, to be led to your loathsom Bed. Oh-oh-

[*Seems to weep.*

VERNISH. So, very fine! just a Marriage quarrel! which, tho' it generally begins by the Wives fault, yet, in the conclusion, it becomes the Husbands; and whosoever offends at first, he only is sure to ask pardon at last. My Dear—

OLIVIA. My Devil—

VERNISH. Come, pr'ythee be appeas'd, and go home; I have bespoken our Supper betimes: for I cou'd not eat, till I found you. Go, I'll give you all kind of satisfactions; and one, which uses to be a reconciling one, Two hundred of those Guineys I receiv'd last Night, to do what you will with.

OLIVIA. What, wou'd you pay me for being your Baud?

VERNISH. Nay, pr'ythee no more; go, and I'll thoroughly satisfie you, when I come home; and then, too, we will have a fit of laughter, at *Manly,* whom I am going to find at the *Cock* in *Bow-street,*[103] where, I hear, he din'd. Go, dearest, go home.

ELIZA. A very pretty turn, indeed, this!

[*Aside.*

VERNISH. Now, Cousin, since by my Wife I have that honour, and priviledge of calling you so, I have something to beg of you too; which is, not to take notice of our Marriage, to any whatever, yet awhile, for some reasons very important to me: and next, that you will do my Wife the honour to go home with her, and me the favour, to use that power you have with her, in our reconcilement.

ELIZA. That, I dare promise, Sir, will be no hard matter. Your Servant.

[*Exit* Vernish].

103. Tavern noted for upper-class debauchery. On June 1, 1663, Lord Buckhurst, Sir Charles Sedley, and Sir Thomas Ogle got drunk and exposed themselves to passersby from the balcony.

Well, Cousin, this I confess was reasonable hypocrisie; you were the better for't.

OLIVIA. What hypocrisie?

ELIZA. Why, this last deceit of your Husband was lawful, since in your own defence.

OLIVIA. What deceit? I'd have you to know, I never deceiv'd my Husband.

ELIZA. You do not understand me, sure; I say, this was an honest come-off, and a good one: but 'twas a sign your Gallant had had enough of your conversation, since he cou'd so dextrously cheat your Husband, in passing for a Woman?

OLIVIA. What d'ye mean, once more, with my Gallant, and passing for a Woman?

ELIZA. What do you mean? You see your Husband took him for a Woman.

OLIVIA. Whom?

ELIZA. Hey-day! Why, the Man he found you with, for whom last Night you were so much afraid; and who you told me—

OLIVIA. Lord, you rave sure!

ELIZA. Why, did you not tell me last night—

OLIVIA. I know not what I might tell you last night, in a fright.

ELIZA. Ay, what was that fright for? for a Woman? besides, were you not afraid to see your Husband just now? I warrant, only for having been found with a Woman! nay, did you not just now too own your false step, or trip, as you call'd it? which was with a Woman too! Fie, this fooling is so insipid, 'tis offensive.

OLIVIA. And fooling with my Honour will be more offensive. Did you not hear my Husband say, he found me with a Woman, in Mans cloaths? And d'ye think he does not know a Man from a Woman?

ELIZA. Not so well, I'm sure, as you do; therefore I'd rather take your word.

OLIVIA. What, you grow scurrilous, and are I find more censorious, than the World! I must have a care of you, I see.

ELIZA. No, you need not fear yet, I'll keep your secret.

OLIVIA. My secret! I'd have you to know, I have no need of Confidants, tho' you value your self upon being a good one.

ELIZA. O admirable confidence! You show more in denying your wickedness, than other people in glorying in't.

OLIVIA. Confidence, to me! to me such language! nay, then I'll never see your face again. (I'll quarrel with her, that people may never believe I was in her power; but take for malice all the truth she may speak against me. [*Aside.*] *Lettice,* where are you? Let us be gone from this censorious, ill woman.

ELIZA. Nay, thou shalt stay a little, to damn thy self quite.

[*Aside.*]

One word first, pray Madam; can you swear that whom your Husband found you with—

OLIVIA. Swear! ay, that whosoever 'twas that stole up, unknown, into my Room, when 'twas dark, I know not, whether Man or Woman, by Heav'ns, by all that's good; or, may I never more have joyes here, or in the other World: nay, may I eternally—

ELIZA. Be damn'd. So, so, you are damn'd enough already, by your Oaths; and I enough confirm'd: and now you may please to be gone. Yet take this advice with you, in this Plain-dealing Age, to leave off forswearing your self; for when people hardly think the better of a Woman for her real modesty, why shou'd you put that great constraint upon your self to feign it?

OLIVIA. O hideous! hideous advice! Let us go out of the hearing of it: She will spoil us, *Lettice*.

[*Exeunt* Olivia *and* Lettice *at one door,* Eliza *at t' other.*

The Scene changes to the Cock *in* Bow-street.

[SCENE 2.]

A Table, and Bottles,
Manly *and* Fidelia.

MANLY. How! sav'd her Honour, by making her Husband believe you were a Woman! 'twas well, but hard enough to do sure.

FIDELIA. We were interrupted, before he cou'd contradict me.

MANLY. But can't you tell me, d'ye say, what kind of man he was?

FIDELIA. I was so frightned, I confess, I can give no other account of him, but that he was pretty tall, round fac'd, and one I'm sure I ne'r had seen before.

MANLY. But she, you say, made you swear to return to night?

FIDELIA. But I have since sworn, never to go near her again; for the Husband wou'd murder me, or worse, if he caught me again.

MANLY. No, I'll go with you, and defend you to night, and then I'll swear too, never to go near her again.

FIDELIA. Nay, indeed Sir; I will not go, to be accessary to your death too: besides, what shou'd you go again, Sir, for?

MANLY. No disputing, or advice, Sir; you have reason to know I am unalterable. Go, therefore, presently, and write her a Note to enquire if her assignation with you holds; and if not to be at her own house, where else? and be importunate to gain admittance to her to night: let your Messenger, ere he deliver your Letter, enquire first, if her Husband be gone out. Go, 'tis now almost six of the clock; I expect you back here before seven, with leave to see her then. Go, do this dext'rously, and expect the performance of my last nights promise, never to part with you.

FIDELIA. Ay, Sir: but will you be sure to remember that?

MANLY. Did I ever break my word? go, no more replies, or doubts.

[*Exit* Fidelia.
Enter Freeman, *to* Manly.

Where hast thou been?

FREEMAN. In the next Room, with my Lord *Plausible* and *Novel.*

MANLY. Ay, we came hither, because 'twas a private house; but with thee indeed no house can be private, for thou hast that pretty quality of the familiar Fops of the Town, who, in an eating house, alwayes keep company with all people in't, but those they came with.

FREEMAN. I went into their Room, but to keep them, and my own Fool the Squire, out of your room; but you shall be peevish now, because you have no Money: but why the Devil won't you write to those we were speaking of? since your modesty, or your spirit, will not suffer you to speak to 'em, to lend you Money, why won't you try 'em at last, that way?

MANLY. Because I know 'em already, and can bear Want, better than Denials; nay, than Obligations.

FREEMAN. Deny you! they cannot. all of 'em have been your intimate Friends.

MANLY. No, they have been people only I have oblig'd particularly.

FREEMAN. Very well; therefore you ought to go to 'em the rather sure.

MANLY. No, no: those you have oblig'd most, most certainly avoid you, when you can oblige 'em no longer; and they take your Visits like so many Duns:° Friends, like Mistresses, are avoided, for Obligations past. *(debt collectors)*

FREEMAN. Pshaw! but most of 'em are your Relations; Men of great Fortune, and Honour.

MANLY. Yes; but Relations have so much Honour, as to think Poverty taints the blood; and disown their wanting Kindred: believing, I suppose, that as Riches at first makes a Gentleman, the want of 'em degrades him. But damn 'em, now I'm poor, I'll anticipate their contempt, and disown them.

FREEMAN. But you have many a Female acquaintance, whom you have been liberal to, who may have a heart to refund to you a little, if you wou'd ask it: they are not all *Olivia's.*

MANLY. Damn thee! how cou'dst thou think of such a thing? I would as soon rob my Footman of his Wages: Besides, 'twere in vain too; for a Wench is like a Box in an Ordinary, receives all peoples Money easily; but there's no getting, nay shaking any out again: and he that fills it, is sure never to keep the Key.

FREEMAN. Well, but noble Captain, wou'd you make me believe that you, who know half the Town, have so many Friends, and have oblig'd so many, can't borrow fifty or a hundred pound?

MANLY. Why, noble Lieutenant, you who know all the Town, and call all you know Friends, methinks shou'd not wonder at it; since you find Ingratitude too: for how many Lords Families (tho' descended from Blacksmiths, or Tinkers) hast thou call'd Great, and Illustrious? how many ill Tables call[ed] good eating? how many noisie Coxcombs, Wits? how many pert Cocking[104] Cowards stout? how many taudry affected Rogues, well drest? how many Perukes admir'd? and how many ill Verses applauded? and yet canst not borrow a shilling; dost thou expect I, who alwayes spoke truth, shou'd?

FREEMAN. Nay, now you think you have paid me; but hark you, Captain, I have heard of a thing call'd grinning Honour, but never of starving Honour.[105]

MANLY. Well, but it has been the fate of some Brave men: and if they wo'not give me a Ship again, I can go starve any where with a Musket on my shoulder.

FREEMAN. Give you a Ship! why, you will not solicit it.

MANLY. If I have not solicited it by my services, I know no other way.

FREEMAN. Your Servant, Sir; nay then I'm satisfi'd, I must solicit my Widow the closer, and run the desperate fortune of Matrimony on shore.

[*Exit.*
Enter, to Manly, Vernish.

MANLY. How!—Nay, here is a Friend indeed; and he that has him in his arms, can know no wants.

[*Embraces* Vernish.

VERNISH. Dear Sir! and he that is in your arms, is secure from all fears whatever: nay, our Nation is secure by your defeat at Sea, and the *Dutch* that fought against you, have prov'd enemies to themselves only, in bringing you back to us.

MANLY. Fie, fie; this from a Friend? and yet from any other 'twere insufferable: I thought I shou'd never have taken anything ill from you.

VERNISH. A Friends privilege is to speak his mind, tho' it be taken ill.

MANLY. But your tongue need not tell me you think too well of me; I have found it from your heart, which spoke in actions, your unalterable heart: but *Olivia* is false, my Friend, which I suppose is no News to you.

VERNISH. He's in the right on't.

[*Aside.*

104. "Coaching" in some copies of quarto 1; "cocking" means strutting, swaggering, insolent, cocky (Oxford English Dictionary).

105. cf. Shakespeare's *1 Henry IV*, act 5, scene 3, lines 61–62.

MANLY. But cou'dst thou not keep her true to me?

VERNISH. Not for my heart, Sir.

MANLY. But cou'd you not perceive it at all, before I went? cou'd she so deceive us both?

VERNISH. I must confess, the first time I knew it, was three dayes after your departure, when she receiv'd the Money you had left in *Lombard-street,*[106] in her name; and her tears did not hinder her it seems from counting that. You wou'd trust her with all, like a true generous lover!

MANLY. And she, like a mean jilting—

VERNISH. Traytrous—

MANLY. Base—

VERNISH. Damn'd—

MANLY. Covetous—

VERNISH. Mercenary whore.—
I can hardly hold from laughing.

[*Aside.*

MANLY. Ay, a Mercenary Whore indeed; for she made me pay her, before I lay with her.

VERNISH. How!—Why, have you lay'n with her?

MANLY. Ay, ay.

VERNISH. Nay, she deserves you shou'd report it at least, tho' you have not.

MANLY. Report it! by Heav'n, 'tis true.

VERNISH. How! sure not.

MANLY. I do not use to lie, nor you to doubt me.

VERNISH. When?

MANLY. Last night, about seven or eight of the clock.

VERNISH. Ha!—Now I remember, I thought she spake as if she expected some other, rather than me: a confounded Whore indeed!

[*Aside.*

MANLY. But, what, thou wonder'st at it! nay, you seem to be angry too.

VERNISH. I cannot but be enrag'd against her, for her usage of you: damn'd, infamous, common Jade!

MANLY. Nay, her Cuckold, who first Cuckolded me in my Money, shall not laugh all himself; we will do him reason, shan't we?

VERNISH. Ay, ay.

MANLY. But thou dost not, for so great a Friend, take pleasure enough in your Friends Revenge, methinks.

VERNISH. Yes, yes; I'm glad to know it, since you have lay'n with her.

106. Street where goldsmiths, who served as bankers, had their establishments.

MANLY. Thou canst not tell who that Rascal, her Cuckold, is?
VERNISH. No.
MANLY. She wou'd keep it from you, I suppose.
VERNISH. Yes, yes—
MANLY. Thou wou'dst laugh, if thou knewest but all the circumstances of my having her. Come, I'll tell thee.
VERNISH. Dam her; I care not to hear any more of her.
MANLY. Faith, thou shalt. You must know—

Enter Freeman *backwards, endeavouring to keep out* Novel, Lord Plausible, Jerry *and* Oldfox, *who all press in upon him.*

FREEMAN. I tell you, he has a Wench with him, and wou'd be private.
MANLY. Dam'em! a Man can't open a Bottle, in these eating houses, but presently you have these impudent, intruding, buzzing Flies and Insects, in your Glass.—Well, I'll tell thee all anon. In the mean time, pr'ythee go to her, but not from me, and try if you can get her to lend me but a hundred pound of my Money, to supply my present wants; for I suppose there is no recovering any of it by Law.
VERNISH. Not any: think not of it: nor by this way neither.
MANLY. Go, try, at least.
VERNISH. I'll go; but I can satisfie you before hand, 'twill be to no purpose: You'll no more find a refunding Wench—
MANLY. Than a refunding Lawyer; indeed their Fees alike scarce ever return: however, try her, put it to her.
VERNISH. Ay, ay, I'll try her, put it to her home, with a vengeance.

[*Exit* Vernish.
Manent ceteri.

NOVEL. Nay, you shall be our Judge, *Manly.* Come, Major, I'll speak it to your teeth: if people provoke me to say bitter things, to their faces, they must take what follows; tho', like my *Lord Plausible,* I'd rather do't civilly behind their backs.
MANLY. Nay, thou art a dangerous Rogue, I've heard, behind a Mans back.
L. PLAUSIBLE. You wrong him sure, noble Captain; he wou'd do a Man no more harm behind his back, than to his face.
FREEMAN. I am of my Lord's mind.
MANLY. Yes, a Fool, like a Coward, is the more to be fear'd behind a Man's back, more than a Witty Man: for, as a Coward is more bloody than a brave Man, a Fool is more malicious than a Man of Wit.
NOVEL. A Fool, Tar—a Fool! nay, thou art a brave Sea-judge of Wit! a Fool! pr'ythee when did you ever find me want something to say, as you do often?
MANLY. Nay, I confess, thou art alwayes talking, roaring, or making a noise; that I'll say for thee.

NOVEL. Well, and is talking a sign of a Fool?

MANLY. Yes, alwayes talking; especially too if it be loud and fast, is the sign of a Fool.

NOVEL. Pshaw! Talking is like Fencing, the quicker the better; run 'em down, run 'em down; no matter for parrying; push on still, sa, sa, sa: no matter whether you argue in form, push in guard, or no.

MANLY. Or hit, or no; I think thou alwayes talk'st without thinking, *Novel.*

NOVEL. Ay, ay; study'd Play's the worse, to follow the Allegory, as the old Pedant sayes.

OLDFOX. A young Fop!

MANLY. I ever thought the Man of most Wit, had been, like him of most Money, who has no vanity in shewing it everywhere; whil'st the beggarly pusher of his Fortune, has all he has about him still, only to show.

NOVEL. Well, Sir, and makes a pretty show in the World, let me tell you; nay, a better than your close Hunks:° A Pox, give me ready Money in Play; what care I for a Mans reputation? what are we the better for your substantial thrifty Curmudgeon in Wit, Sir? misers

OLDFOX. Thou art a profuse young Rogue indeed.

NOVEL. So much for talking; which I think I have prov'd a mark of Wit; and so is Railing,° Roaring, and making a Noise: for, Railing is Satyr, you know; and Roaring, and making a noise, Humor. abuse

Enter to them, Fidelia, *taking* Manly *aside, and shows him a paper.*

FIDELIA. The hour is betwixt seven and eight exactly: 'tis now half an hour after six.

MANLY. Well, go then to the Piazza, and wait for me; as soon as it is quite dark, I'll be with you: I must stay here yet awhile for my Friend. But is Railing Satyr, *Novel?*

[*Exit* Fidelia.]

FREEMAN. And Roaring, and making a noise, Humor?

NOVEL. What, won't you confess there's Humor in Roaring, and making a noise?

FREEMAN. No.

NOVEL. Nor in cutting Napkins, and Hangings?

MANLY. No, sure.

NOVEL. Dull Fops!

OLDFOX. O Rogue, Rogue, insipid Rogue! Nay, Gentlemen, allow him those things for Wit; for his parts lie only that way.

NOVEL. Peace, old Fool, I wonder not at thee; but that young Fellows shou'd be so dull, as to say, there's no Humor in making a noise, and breaking Windows! I tell you, there's Wit and Humor too, in both: And a Wit is as well known by his Frolick, as by his Simile.

OLDFOX. Pure Rogue! there's your modern Wit for you! Wit, and Humor, in breaking of Windows! There's Mischief, if you will; but no Wit, or Humor.

NOVEL. Pr'ythee, pr'ythee, peace, old Fool. I tell you, where there is Mischief, there's Wit. Don't we esteem the Monky a Wit amongst Beasts, only because he's mischievous? And let me tell you, as good Nature is a sign of a Fool, being Mischievous is a sign of a Wit.

OLDFOX. O Rogue, Rogue! pretend to be a Wit, by doing Mischief and Railing!

NOVEL. Why, thou, old Fool, hast no other pretence to the name of a Wit, but by Railing at new Playes.

OLDFOX. Thou, by Railing at that facetious, noble way of Wit, quibbling.

NOVEL. Thou call'st thy dulness, gravity; and thy dozing, thinking.

OLDFOX. You, Sir, your dulness, spleen: And you talk much, and say nothing.

NOVEL. Thou read'st much, and understand'st nothing, Sir.

OLDFOX. You laugh loud, and break no Jest.

NOVEL. You rail, and no body hangs himself: And thou hast nothing of the Satyr, but in thy face.

OLDFOX. And you have no jest, but your face, Sir.

NOVEL. Thou art an illiterate Pedant.

OLDFOX. Thou art a Fool, with a bad Memory.

MANLY. Come, a Pox on you both, you have done like Wits now; for you Wits, when you quarrel, never give over, till ye prove one another Fools.

NOVEL. And you Fools have never any occasion of laughing at us Wits, but when we quarrel: therefore, let us be Friends, *Oldfox.*

MANLY. They are such Wits as thou art, who make the name of a Wit as scandalous, as that of Bully; and signifie a loud-laughing, talking, incorrigible, Coxcomb; as Bully, a roaring hardned Coward.

FREEMAN. And wou'd have his noise and laughter pass for Wit; as t'other his huffing and blustring, for Courage.

Enter Vernish.

MANLY. Gentlemen, with your leave, here is one I wou'd speak with, and I have nothing to say to you.

Puts 'em out of the Room.
Manent Manly, Vernish.

VERNISH. I told you 'twas in vain, to think of getting Money out of her: she sayes, if a shilling wou'd do't, she wou'd not save you from starving, or hanging, or what you wou'd think worse, begging or flattering; and rails so at you, one wou'd not think you had lay'n with her[.]

MANLY. O, Friend, never trust, for that matter, a Womans railing; for she is no less a dissembler in her hatred, than her love: And as her fondness of her Husband is a sign he's a Cuckold, her railing at another Man is a sign she lies with him.

VERNISH. He's in the right on't: I know not what to trust to.

[*Aside.*

MANLY. But you did not take any notice of it to her, I hope?

VERNISH. So!—Sure he is afraid I shou'd have disprov'd him, by an enquiry of her: all may be well yet.

[*Aside.*

MANLY. What hast thou in thy head, that makes thee seem so unquiet?

VERNISH. Only this base, impudent Womans falseness: I cannot put her out of my head.

MANLY. O, my dear Friend, be not you too sensible of my wrongs, for then I shall feel 'em too, with more pain, and think 'em unsufferable. Dam her, her Money, and that ill-natur'd Whore too, Fortune her self; but if thou wou'dst ease a little my present trouble, pr'ythee go borrow me somewhere else, some Money: I can trouble thee.

VERNISH. You trouble me indeed, most sensibly, when you command me any thing I cannot do: I have lately lost a great deal of Money at Play, more than I can yet pay; so that not only my Money, but my Credit too is gone, and know not where to borrow; but cou'd rob a Church for you. (Yet wou'd rather end your wants, by cutting your throat.)

[*Aside.*

MANLY. Nay, then I doubly feel my poverty, since I'm incapable of supplying thee.

[*Embraces* Vernish.

VERNISH. But, methinks, she that granted you the last favour, (as they call it) shou'd not deny you any thing—

NOVEL. Hey, Tarpaulin, have you done?

[Novel *looks in,*
and retires again.

VERNISH. I understand not that point of kindness, I confess.

MANLY. No, thou dost not understand it, and I have not time to let you know all now, for these Fools, you see, will interrupt us; but anon, at Supper, we'll laugh at leisure together, at *Olivia*'s Cuckold; who took a young Fellow, that goes between his Wife and me, for a Woman.

VERNISH. Ha!

MANLY. Senseless, easie Rascal! 'twas no wonder she chose him for a Husband; but she thought him, I thank her, fitter than me, for that blind, bearing Office.

VERNISH. I cou'd not be deceiv'd in that long Womans hair ty'd up behind; nor those infallible proofs, her pouting, swelling breasts: I have handled too many sure not to know 'em.

[*Aside.*

MANLY. What, you wonder the Fellow cou'd be such a blind Coxcomb!

VERNISH. Yes, yes—

[*Novel looks in again, and retires.*

NOVEL. Nay, pr'ythee come to us, *Manly;* Gad, all the fine things one sayes, in their company, are lost, without thee.

MANLY. Away, Fop; I'm busie yet. You see we cannot talk here at our ease: besides, I must be gone immediately, in order to meeting with *Olivia* again to night.

VERNISH. To night! it cannot be sure—

MANLY. I had an appointment just now from her.

VERNISH. For what time?

MANLY. At half an hour after seven precisely.

VERNISH. Don't you apprehend the Husband?

MANLY. He! snivelling Gull! he a thing to be fear'd! a Husband, the tamest of creatures!

VERNISH. Very fine!

[*Aside.*

MANLY. But, pr'ythee, in the mean time, go try to get me some Money. Tho' thou art too modest to borrow for thy self, thou canst do anything for me I know. Go; for I must be gone to *Olivia:* go, and meet me here, anon.—*Freeman,* where are you!

[*Exit* Manly.
Manet Vernish.

VERNISH. Ay, I'll meet with you, I warrant; but it shall be at Olivia's. Sure it cannot be; she denies it so calmly, and with that honest, modest assurance, it can't be true—and he does not use to lye—but belying a Woman, when she won't be kind, is the onely lye a brave Man will least scruple. But then the Woman in Mans cloaths, whom he calls a Man!—Well, but by her Breasts, I know her to be a Woman:—But then, again, his appointment from her, to meet with him to night! I am distracted more with doubt, than jealousie. Well, I have no way to disabuse or revenge my self, but by going home immediately, putting on a riding Sute, and pretending to my Wife the same business which carry'd me out of Town last, requires me again to go Post to *Oxford* to night;[107] then, if the appointment he boasts of be true, it's sure to hold; and I shall have an opportunity either of clearing her, or revenging my self on both. Perhaps, she is his Wench, of an old date, and I am his Cully, whil'st I think him mine; and he has seem'd to make his Wench rich, only that I might take her off his hands: or if he has but lately lay'n with her, he must needs discover, by her, my treachery to him; which I'm sure he will revenge with my death, and which I must prevent with his, if it were only but for fear of his too just reproaches; for, I must confess, I never had till now any excuse, but that of int'rest, for doing ill to him.

[*Exit* Vernish.
Re-enter Manly *and* Freeman.

MANLY. Come hither, only I say be sure you mistake not the time; You know the house exactly where *Olivia* lodges: 'tis just hard by.

FREEMAN. Yes, yes.

MANLY. Well then, bring 'em all, I say, thither, and all you know that may be then in the house, for the more Witnesses I have of her infamy, the greater will be my revenge: and be sure you come strait up to her Chamber, without more ado. Here, take the Watch: you see 'tis above a quarter past seven; be there in half an hour exactly.

FREEMAN. You need not doubt my diligence or dexterity; I am an old Scowrer, and can naturally beat up a Wench's quarters that won't be civil. Sha'nt we break her Windows too?

MANLY. No, no: be punctual only.

[*Exeunt Ambo.*
Enter Widow Blackacre, *and two Knights of the Post: a Waiter with Wine.*

WIDOW. Sweetheart, are you sure the door was shut close, that none of those Roysters° saw us come in? revellers

WAITER. Yes, Mistress; and you shall have a privater Room above, instantly.

[*Exit Waiter.*

WIDOW. You are safe enough, Gentlemen, for I have been private in this house ere now, upon other occasions, when I was something younger. Come, gentlemen, in short, I leave my business to your care and fidelity: and so, here's to you.

107. The post system allowed a person to travel rapidly with relays of horses for a rider or horses for a carriage. A person travelling the opposite direction would return the horse or horses to the original posting station.

1. KNIGHT. We were ungrateful Rogues, if we shou'd not be honest to you; for we have had a great deal of your Money.

WIDOW. And you have done me many a good job for't: and so, here's to you again.

2. KNIGHT. Why, we have been perjur'd, but six times for you.

1. KNIGHT. Forg'd but four Deeds, with your Husband's last Deed of Gift.

2. KNIGHT. And but three Wills.

1. KNIGHT. And counterfeited Hands and Seals to some six Bonds; I think that's all, Brother.

WIDOW. Ay, that's all, Gentlemen; and so, here's to you again.

2. KNIGHT. Nay, 'twou'd do one's heart good to be forsworn for you: you have a conscience in your wayes, and pay us well.

1. KNIGHT. You are in the right on't, Brother; one wou'd be damn'd for her, with all ones heart.

2. KNIGHT. But there are Rogues, who make us forsworn for 'em; and when we come to be paid, they'll be forsworn too, and not pay us our wages which they promis'd with Oaths sufficient.

1. KNIGHT. Ay, a great Lawyer, that shall be nameless Bilk'd me too.

WIDOW. That was hard, methinks, that a Lawyer shou'd use Gentlemen Witnesses no better.

2. KNIGHT. A Lawyer! d'ye wonder a Lawyer shou'd do't? I was Bilk'd by a Reverend Divine, that preaches twice on Sundayes, and prayes half an hour still before dinner.

WIDOW. How? a Conscientious Divine, and not pay people for damning themselves! Sure then, for all his talking, he does not believe damnation. But come, to our business: pray be sure to imitate exactly the flourish° at the end of this name.

decorative penmanship

[*Pulls out a Deed or two.*

1. KNIGHT. O he's the best in *England* at untangling a flourish, Madam.

WIDOW. And let not the Seal be a jot bigger: observe well the dash too, at the end of this name.

2. KNIGHT. I warrant you, Madam.

WIDOW. Well, these, and many other shifts, poor Widows are put to sometimes; for every body wou'd be riding a Widow, as they say, and breaking into her Jointure: they think marrying a Widow an easie business, like leaping the Hedge, where another has gone over before; a Widow is a meer gap, a gap with them.

Enter to them Major Oldfox, *with two* Waiters.
The Knights of the Post *huddle up the writings.*

What, he here! go then, go, my hearts, you have your instructions.

[*Exeunt Knights of the Post.*

OLDFOX. Come, Madam, to be plain with you, I'll be fob'd off° [imposed upon] no longer. I'll bind her and gag her, but she shall hear me.

[*Aside.*

Look you, Friends, there's the Money I promis'd you; and now do you what you promis'd me: here my Garters, and here's a Gag: You shall be acquainted with my parts, Lady, you shall.

WIDOW. Acquainted with your parts! A Rape! a Rape!—What, will you ravish me?

[*The* Waiters *tye her to the Chair, gag her; and Exeunt.*

OLDFOX. Yes, Lady, I will ravish you: but it shall be through the ear, Lady, the ear onely, with my well-pen'd Acrostics.

Enter to them Freeman, Jerry Blackacre, *three Bayliffs, a Constable, and his Assistants, with the two Knights of the Post.*

What, shall I never read my things undisturb'd again?

JERRY. O Law! my Mother bound hand and foot, and gaping, as if she rose before her time to day!

FREEMAN. What means this, *Oldfox?* But I'll release you from him: you shall be no Mans Prisoner, but mine. Bayliffs, execute your Writ.

[Freeman *untyes her.*

OLDFOX. Nay, then I'll be gone, for fear of being Bayl, and paying her Debts, without being her Husband.

[*Exit* Oldfox.

1. BAYLIFF. We Arrest you, in the King's Name, at the Suit of Mr. *Freeman,* Guardian to *Jeremiah Blackacre* Esq; in an Action of Ten thousand pounds.

WIDOW. How! how! in a Choak-Bayl action![108] What, and the Pen and Ink Gentlemen taken too! Have you confest, you Rogues?

1. KNIGHT. We needed not to confess; for the Bayliffs dog'd us hither to the very door, and overheard all that you and we said.

WIDOW. Undone, undone then! no Man was ever too hard for me, till now. O, *Jerry,* Child, wilt thou vex again the womb that bore thee?

JERRY. Ay, for bearing me before Wedlock, as you say: But I'll teach you call a *Blackacre* Bastard, tho' you were never so much my Mother.

WIDOW. Well, I'm undone: not one trick left? no Law Meush° [loophole] imaginable?

[*Aside.*]

Cruel Sir, a word with you I pray.

108. In this case, an action for large amounts of money where no bail was allowed.

FREEMAN. In vain, Madam; for you have no other way to release your self, but by the Bonds of Matrimony.

WIDOW. How, Sir, how! that were but to sue out an *Habeas Corpus,*[109] for a removal from one Prison to another. Matrimony!

FREEMAN. Well, Bayliffs, away with her.

WIDOW. O stay, Sir, can you be so cruel as to bring me under Covert Baron again? and put it out of my power to sue in my own name. Matrimony, to a Woman, [is] worse than Excommunication, in depriving her of the benefit of the Law: and I wou'd rather be depriv'd of life. But hark you, Sir, I am contented you shou'd hold and enjoy my person by Lease or Patent; but not by the spiritual Patent, call'd a Licence; that is, to have the priviledges of a Husband without the dominion; that is, *Durante beneplacito:*[110] in consideration of which, I will out of my Jointure, secure you an Annuity of Three hundred pounds a Year, and pay your debts; and that's all you younger Brothers desire to marry a Widow for, I'm sure.

FREEMAN. Well, Widow, if—

JERRY. What, I hope, Bully Guardian, you are not making Agreements, without me?

FREEMAN. No, no. First, Widow, you must say no more that he is the Son of a Whore; have a care of that. And then, he must have a setled Exhibition of Forty pounds a Year, and a Nag of Assizes,[111] kept by you, but not upon the Common;[112] and have free ingress, egress, and regress to and from your Maids Garret.

WIDOW. Well, I can grant all that too.

JERRY. Ay, ay, fair words butter no Cabbage; but, Guardian, make her Sign, Sign and Seal: for, otherwise, if you knew her as well as I, you wou'd not trust her word for a farthing.

FREEMAN. I warrant thee, Squire. Well, Widow, since thou art so generous, I will be generous too; and if you'll secure me Four hundred pound a Year, but during your life, and pay my debts, not above a thousand pound; I'll bate you your person, to dispose of as you please.[113]

WIDOW. Have a care, Sir, a Settlement without a Consideration, is void in Law: you must do something for't.

FREEMAN. Pr'ythee then let the Settlement on me be call'd Alimony; and the Consideration our Separation: Come, my Lawyer, with Writings ready drawn, is within, and in haste. Come.

109. An order to produce a prisoner before a judge.

110. A term from the tenure of judges, "during good pleasure"; that is, so long as performance is satisfactory.

111. Horse of good quality according to the legal standard.

112. The horse will not be for common use, but is reserved exclusively for Jerry.

113. Freeman will deduct from the settlement the widow's person; that is, he will not copulate with her.

WIDOW. But, what, no other kind of Consideration, Mr. *Freeman?* Well, a Widow, I see, is a kind of *sine cure,* by custom of which the unconscionable Incumbent enjoyes the profits, without any duty, but does that still elsewhere.

[*Exeunt Omnes.*

The Scene changes to Olivia's *Lodging.*

[SCENE 3.]

Enter Olivia, *with a Candle in her hand.*

OLIVIA. So, I am now prepar'd once more for my timorous young Lover's reception: my Husband is gone; and go thou out too, thou next Interrupter of Love.—[*Puts out the Candle.*] Kind darkness, that frees us Lovers from scandal and bashfulness, from the censure of our Gallants and the World. So, are you there?

Enter to Olivia, Fidelia, *follow'd softly by* Manly.

Come, my dear punctual Lover, there is not such another in the World; thou hast Beauty and Youth to please a Wife; Address and Wit, to amuse and fool a Husband; nay, thou hast all things to be wish'd in a Lover, but your Fits: I hope, my Dear, you won't have one to night; and, that you may not, I'll lock the door, tho' there be no need of it, but to lock out your Fits; for my Husband is just gone out of Town again. Come, where are you?

[*Goes to the door and locks it.*

MANLY. Well, thou hast impudence enough to give me Fits too, and make Revenge it self impotent, hinder me from making thee yet more infamous, if it can be.

[*Aside.*

OLIVIA. Come, come, my Soul, come.

FIDELIA. Presently, my Dear: we have time enough sure.

OLIVIA. How! time enough! True Lovers can no more think they ever have time enough, than love enough. You shall stay with me all night; but that is but a Lover's moment. Come.

FIDELIA. But won't you let me give you and my self the satisfaction of telling you, how I abus'd your Husband last night?

OLIVIA. Not when you can give me, and your self too, the satisfaction of abusing him again, to night. Come.

FIDELIA. Let me but tell you how your Husband—

OLIVIA. O name not his, or *Manly's* more loathsom name, if you love me; I forbid 'em last night: and you know I mention'd my

Husband but once, and he came. No talking pray; 'twas ominous to us. You make me fancy a noise at the door already, but I'm resolv'd not to be interrupted. [*A noise at the door.*] Where are you? Come; for, rather than lose my dear expectation now, tho' my Husband were at the door, and the bloody Ruffian *Manly* here in the room, with all his awful insolence, I wou'd give my self to this dear hand, to be led away, to Heavens of joys, which none but thou canst give. But, what's this noise at the door? So, I told you what talking wou'd come to. [*The noise at the door increases.* Ha!—O Heavens, my Husbands voice!—

[Olivia *Listens at the door.*]

MANLY. *Freeman* is come too soon.

[*Aside.*]

OLIVIA. O 'tis he!—Then here is the happiest minute lost, that ever bashful Boy, or trifling Woman fool'd away! I'm undone! my Husbands reconcilement too was false, as my joy, all delusion: but, come this way, here's a Back door.—

[*Exit, and returns.*

The officious Jade has lock'd us in, instead of locking others out; but let us then escape your way, by the Balcony; and whil'st you pull down the Curtains, I'll fetch, from my Closet, what next will best secure our escape: I have left my Key in the door, and 'twill not suddenly be broke open.

[*Exit.*]
[*A noise as it were, people forcing the door.*

MANLY. Stir not, yet fear nothing.
FIDELIA. Nothing, but your life, Sir.
MANLY. We shall now know this happy Man she calls Husband.

Olivia *Re-enters.*

OLIVIA. Oh, where are you? What, idle with fear? Come, I'll tie the Curtains, if you will hold. Here, take this Cabinet and Purse, for it is thine, if we escape; [Manly *takes from her the Cabinet and Purse*] therefore let us make haste.

[*Exit* Olivia.

MANLY. 'Tis mine indeed now again, and it shall never escape more from me: to you at least.

[*The door broken open, Enter* Vernish *alone, with a dark Lanthorn and a Sword, running at* Manly; *who draws, puts by the thrust, and defends himself, whil'st* Fidelia *runs at* Vernish *behind.*

VERNISH. So, there I'm right, sure—

[*With a low voice.*

MANLY. *Softly.* Sword and Dark Lanthorn, Villain, are some odds; but—

VERNISH. Odds! I'm sure I find more odds than I expected: What, has my insatiable two Seconds at once? but—

[*With a low voice.*
[*Whil'st they fight,* Olivia *re-enters, tying two Curtains together.*

OLIVIA. Where are you now?—What, is he entered then, and are they fighting! O do not kill one that can make no defence. [Manly *throws* Vernish *down, and disarms him.*] How! but I think he has the better on't. here's his Scarf, 'tis he. So, keep him down still: I hope thou hast no hurt, my dearest?

[*Embracing* Manly.
Enter to them Freeman, Lord Plausible, Novel, Jerry Blackacre, *and the* Widow Blackacre, *lighted in by the two Sailors with Torches.*

Ha!—What?—*Manly!* and have I been thus concern'd for him, embracing him? And has he his Jewels again too? What means this? O 'tis too sure, as well as my shame! which I'll go hide for ever.

[*Offers to go out,* Manly *stops her.*

MANLY. No, my dearest, after so much kindness as has past between us, I cannot part with you yet. *Freeman,* let nobody stir out of the Room; for, notwithstanding your lights, we are yet in the dark, till this Gentleman please to turn his face.—

[*Pulls* Vernish *by the sleeve.*]

How! *Vernish!* Art thou the happy Man then? Thou! Thou! Speak, I say; but thy guilty silence tells me all.—Well, I shall not upbraid thee; for my wonder is striking me as dumb, as thy shame has made thee. But what? my little Volunteer hurt, and fainting!

FIDELIA. My wound, Sir, is but a slight one, in my Arm: 'tis only my fear of your danger, Sir, not yet well over.

MANLY. But what's here? more strange things!

[*Observing* Fidelia's *hair unty'd behind, and without a Peruke, which she lost in the scuffle.*

What means this long Womans hair? and face, now all of it appears, too beautiful for a Man; which I still thought Womanish indeed! What, you have not deceiv'd me too, my little Volunteer?

OLIVIA. Me she has I'm sure.

[*Aside.*

MANLY. Speak.

Enter Eliza, *and* Lettice.

ELIZA. What, Cousin, I am brought hither by your Woman, I suppose, to be a witness of the second vindication of your Honour?

OLIVIA. Insulting is not generous: You might spare me, I have you.

ELIZA. Have a care, Cousin, you'll confess anon too much; and I wou'd not have your secrets.

MANLY. Come, your blushes answer me sufficiently, and you have been my Volunteer in love.

[*To* Fidelia.

FIDELIA. I must confess I needed no compulsion to follow you all the world over; which I attempted in this habit, partly out of shame to own my love to you, and fear of a greater shame, your refusal of it: for I knew of your engagement to this Lady, and the constancy of your nature; which nothing cou'd have alter'd, but her self.

MANLY. Dear Madam, I desir'd you to bring me out of confusion, and you have given me more: I know not what to speak to you, or how to look upon you; the sense of my rough, hard, and ill usage of you, (tho' chiefly your own fault) gives me more pain now 'tis over, than you had, when you suffer'd it: and if my heart, the refusal of such a Woman, [*Pointing to* Olivia] were not a Sacrifice to profane your love, and a greater wrong to you than ever yet I did you; I wou'd beg of you to receive it, tho' you us'd it, as she had done; for tho' it deserv'd not from her the treatment she gave it, it does from you.

FIDELIA. Then it has had punishment sufficient from her already, and needs no more from me; and, I must confess, I wou'd not be the onely cause of making you break your last nights Oath to me, of never parting with me: if you do not forget, or repent it.

MANLY. Then, take for ever my heart, and this with it; [*Gives her the Cabinet*] for 'twas given to you before, and my heart was before your due; I only beg leave to dispose of these few—Here, Madam, I never yet left my Wench unpaid.

[*Takes some of the Jewels, and offers them to* Olivia; *she strikes 'em down:* Plausible *and* Novel *take 'em up.*

OLIVIA. So it seems, by giving her the Cabinet.

L. PLAUSIBLE. These Pendents appertain to your most faithful humble Servant.

NOVEL. And this Locket is mine; my earnest for love, which she never paid: therefore my own again.

WIDOW. By what Law, Sir, pray? Cousin *Olivia,* a word: What, do they make a seizure on your Goods and Chattels, *vi & armis?*[114] Make your demand, I say, and bring your Trover, bring your Trover: I'll follow the Law for you.[115]

OLIVIA. And I my revenge.

[*Exit.*

114. With force and weapons; i.e., assault.

115. Trover is a legal action to recover personal property illegally seized by another.

MANLY. *to Vernish.* But 'tis, my Friend, in your consideration most, that I wou'd have return'd part of your Wives portion; for 'twere hard to take all from thee, since thou hast paid so dear for't, in being such a Rascal: yet thy Wife is a Fortune without a Portion; and thou art a man of that extraordinary merit in Vilany, the World and Fortune can never desert thee, tho' I do; therefore be not melancholy. Fare you well, Sir.

[*Exit* Vernish *doggedly.*°] sullenly

Now, Madam, I beg your pardon, [*Turning to* Fidelia] for lessening the Present I made you; but my heart can never be lessen'd: this, I confess, was too small for you before; for you deserve the *Indian* World; and I wou'd now go thither, out of covetousness for your sake only.

FIDELIA. Your heart, Sir, is a Present of that value, I can never make any return to't; [*Pulling* Manly *from the company.*] but I can give you back such a Present as this, which I got by the loss of my Father, a Gentleman of the North, of no mean Extraction, whose onely Child I was, therefore left me in the present possession of Two thousand pounds a Year; which I left, with multitudes of Pretenders, to follow you, Sir; having in several publick places seen you, and observ'd your actions thoroughly, with admiration, when you were too much in love to take notice of mine, which yet was but too visible. The name of my family is *Grey;* my other *Fidelia:* The rest of my Story you shall know, when I have fewer Auditors.

MANLY. Nay, now, Madam, you have taken from me all power of making you any Complement on my part; for I was going to tell you, that for your sake onely, I wou'd quit the unknown pleasure of a retirement; and rather stay in this ill World of ours still, tho odious to me, than give you more frights again at Sea, and make again too great a venture there, in you alone. But if I shou'd tell you now all this, and that your virtue (since greater than I thought any was in the World) had now reconcil'd me to't, my Friend here wou'd say, 'tis your Estate that has made me Friends with the World.

FREEMAN. I must confess I shou'd; for I think most of our quarrels to the World, are just such as we have to a handsom Woman: only because we cannot enjoy her, as we wou'd do.

MANLY. Nay, if thou art a *Plain-dealer* too, give me thy hand; for now I'll say I am thy Friend indeed: And, for your two sakes, tho' I have been so lately deceiv'd in Friends of both Sexes,

I will believe, there are now in the World
Good-natur'd Friends, who are not Prostitutes,
And handsom Women worthy to be Friends:
Yet, for my sake, let no one e're confide
In Tears, or Oaths, in Love, or Friend untry'd.

[*Exeunt* Omnes.

EPILOGUE, SPOKEN BY THE *WIDOW BLACKACRE.*

To you the Judges learned in Stage Laws,
Our Poet now, by me, submits his Cause;
For with young Judges, such as most of you,
The Men by Women best their bus'ness do:
And, truth on't is, if you did not sit here,
To keep for us a Term throughout the Year,
We cou'd not live by'r Tongues; nay, but for you,
Our Chamber-practice wou'd be little too.
And 'tis not only the Stage Practiser
Who, by your meeting, gets her living here;
For, as in Hall of Westminster,
Sleek sempstress vents, amidst the Courts, her Ware:
So, while we Baul, and you in Judgment sit,
The Visor-Mask sells Linen too i'th' Pit.
O many of your Friends, besides us here,
Do live, by putting off their sev'ral Ware.
Here's daily done the great affairs o'th' Nation:
Let Love,and Us then, ne'r have Long-vacation.
But hold; like other Pleaders, I have done
Not my poor Client's bus'ness, but my own.
Spare me a word then, now, for him. First know,
Squires of the Long Robe, he does humbly show,
He has a just Right in abusing you;
Because he is a Brother-Templar *too:*
For, at the Bar, you Railly one another;
And Fool, and Knave, is swallow'd from a Brother:
If not the Poet here, the Templar spare;
And maul him, when you catch him at the Bar.
From you, our common modish Censurers,
Your Favor, not your Judgment, 'tis he fears:
Of all Love begs you then to Rail, find fault; }
For Playes, like Women, by the World are thought, }
(When you speak kindly of 'em) very naught. }

The Beaux' Stratagem

George Farquhar was born in 1677 in Londonderry, the son of a clergyman in a staunchly Protestant town that was besieged by Jacobite forces in 1689. It is a mistake to refer to him as an Irish playwright; during his lifetime, he would have been regarded as one of the "English of Ireland." At seventeen he entered Trinity College, Dublin, as a sizar, a student who received his education in return for menial work at the college. At some point he became friendly with the actor Robert Wilks and left the college to act on the Dublin stage. Unfortunately, during a performance of John Dryden's *The Indian Emperor,* he forgot to exchange his sword for a stage foil, and seriously wounded another actor. He moved to London and wrote the successful *Love and a Bottle* (1698). Playwrights received the gate receipts from the third night of production minus house charges, and, if the play ran longer, from subsequent nights in multiples of three (although this was not always the case). Playwrights also received a payment from a printer for the publication of the play, and, if they were lucky, from a patron to whom the play would be dedicated. But all income from a play was made in its initial presentation unless the author became of sufficient eminence to have his works published by subscription; there was no such thing as copyright. So while Farquhar continued to write plays, to make ends meet he also received a commission in the army under the patronage of the Earl of Orrery, a Boyle and therefore a member of one of the most powerful Protestant families in Ireland, and served primarily as a recruiting officer; this became the subject of the play *The Recruiting Officer* (1706). Farquhar was not unique in this: William Wycherley, John Vanbrugh, and Richard Steele were all military men as well. In 1703 he married a widow with three children. Mary Pernell was ten years his senior and brought little money to the marriage. By 1706, Farquhar was so broke he sold his army commission to pay his debts. *The*

The text is that established by Shirley Strum Kenny's *The Works of George Farquhar*, vol. II (Oxford: Clarendon Press, 1988), 160–243, with some emendation by me, mostly in punctuation. Also consulted was William Archer's edition (New York: Hill and Wang, 1959), 356–456.

Beaux' Stratagem (1707) was his last play, written while ill. He died two months after its premiere.

In 1702 Farquhar published *A Discourse on Comedy,* where he claimed that a comedy is an agreeable tale told for counsel or reproof. In the prologue to *The Beaux' Stratagem* he refers admiringly to Wycherley's harsh satire, but says it is no longer appropriate for a different age. Like his contemporaries William Congreve, John Vanbrugh, and Colley Cibber, Farquhar writes plays that are good humored, at least compared to the savage wit of the earlier generation. Lady Bountiful may be a foolish country woman, but she is essentially benevolent. The threat to expose Foigard, which would lead to his execution, may not seem funny to a modern audience, but to a Protestant from Ireland such as Farquhar, blackmailing an Irish Catholic priest counts as good, clean fun; it is presented so unseriously that Archer subsequently brings in Foigard to guard a thief. And good sense and folly can be found on any social level: Archer does not succeed in seducing Cherry, an innkeeper's daughter, and Squire Sullen with three thousand pounds a year is a drunken sot. The serious subject of an unhappy marriage is resolved with a fantasy of separation at the end of the play, but even the unhappy Mrs. Sullen (played by Anne Oldfield, who was discovered by Farquhar and was one of the great actresses of her age) does not cuckold her husband, although he richly deserves it. In short where Wycherley lashed his age, Farquhar chuckles at it, which may explain the play's extraordinary popularity throughout the eighteenth century and beyond.

The Beaux' Stratagem

PROLOGUE

When strife disturbs or Sloth Corrupts an Age,
Keen Satyr is the Business of the Stage.
When the Plain Dealer *writ, he lash'd those Crimes*
Which then infested most—The Modish Times:
But now when Faction sleeps, and Sloth is fled,
And all our Youth in Active Fields are bred;
When thro' GREAT BRITAIN's *fair extensive Round,*
The Trumps of Fame the Notes of Union *sound;*[1]
When ANNA's[2] *Scepter points the Laws their Course,*
And Her Example gives her Precepts Force:
There scarce is room for Satyr, all our Lays
Must be, or Songs of Triumph, or of Praise:
But as in Grounds best cultivated, Tares° weeds
And Poppies rise among the Golden Ears;[3]
Our Products so, fit for the Field or School,
Must mix with Nature's Favourite Plant—A Fool:

1. The Act of Union between England and Scotland was signed in 1707.
2. ANNA (1675–1714), daughter of James II, was queen 1702–14.
3. The ears are the fruit of a cereal grain such as wheat.

A Weed that has to twenty Summer's ran,
Shoots up in Stalk, and Vegetates to Man.
Simpling[4] *our Author goes from Field to Field,*
And culls such Fools as may Diversion yield.
And, Thanks to Nature, there's no want of those.
For Rain, or Shine, the thriving Coxcomb grows.
Follies, to Night we shew, ne'er lash'd before,
Yet, such as Nature shews you ever Hour;
Nor can the Picture's give a Just Offence,
For Fools are made for Jests to Men of Sense.

DRAMATIS PERSONÆ

MEN.

AIMWELL, ARCHER,	Two Gentlemen of broken Fortunes, the first as Master, and the second as Servant.
COUNT BELLAIR,	A *French* Officer, Prisoner at *Litchfield.*[5]
SULLEN,	A Country Blockhead, brutal to his Wife.
FREEMAN,	A Gentleman from *London.*
FOIGARD,	A Priest, Chaplain to the *French* Officers.
GIBBET,	A High-way-man
HOUNSLOW, BAGSHOT,	His Companions.
BONNIFACE,	Landlord of the Inn.
SCRUB,	Servant to Mr. Sullen.

WOMEN.

LADY BOUNTIFUL,	an old civil Country Gentlewoman, that cures all Distempers, and foolishly fond of her Son *Sullen*[.]
DORINDA,	Lady *Bountiful*'s Daughter.
MRS. SULLEN,	Her Daughter-in-law.
GIPSEY,	Maid to the Ladies.
CHERRY,	The Landlord's Daughter in the Inn.
[FELLOW, SERVANTS.]	

4. Gathering simples (herbal) remedies.
5. Lichfield, a cathedral city in a rural part of central England, north of Birmingham.

SCENE, *Litchfield.*

ACT I

SCENE, an Inn.
Enter Bonniface running.

BONNIFACE. Chamberlain, Maid, *Cherry,* Daughter *Cherry,* all asleep, all dead?

Enter Cherry *running.*

CHERRY. Here, here, Why d'ye baul so, Father? dy'e think we have no Ears?
BONNIFACE. You deserve to have none, you young Minx;—The Company of the Warrington Coach has stood in the Hall this Hour, and no Body to shew them to their Chambers.
CHERRY. And let 'em wait father;[6] there's neither Red-Coat in the Coach, nor Footman behind it.
BONNIFACE. But they threaten to go to another Inn to Night.
CHERRY. That they dare not, for fear the Coachman should overturn[7] them to Morrow—Coming, coming: Here's the London coach arriv'd.

Enter several People with Trunks, Band-boxes,[8] and other Luggage, and cross the Stage.

BONNIFACE. Welcome, Ladies.
CHERRY. Very welcome, Gentlemen—Chamberlain, shew the Lyon and the Rose.[9]

Exit with the Company.
Enter Aimwell *in riding Habit,* Archer *as Footman carrying a Portmantle.*[10]

BONNIFACE. This way, this way, Gentlemen.
AIMWELL. Set down the things, go to the Stable, and see my Horses well rubb'd.
ARCHER. I shall, Sir.
AIMWELL. You're my Landlord, I suppose?
BONNIFACE. Yes, Sir, I'm old *Will. Bonniface,* pretty well known upon this Road, as the saying is.
AIMWELL. O Mr. *Bonniface,* your Servant.

6. Kenny has "farther," but most editors amend to "father."
7. Coaches were unstable and overturned fairly easily, which made driving at night especially hazardous.
8. A lightweight box used for holding hats or other apparel.
9. The rooms at inns typically had names.
10. A case for carrying clothes while travelling.

BONNIFACE. O Sir—What will your Honour please to drink, as the saying is?

AIMWELL. I have heard your Town of *Litchfield* much fam'd for Ale, I think I'll taste that.

BONNIFACE. Sir, I have now in my Cellar Ten Tun of the best Ale in *Staffordshire;* 'tis smooth as Oil, sweet as Milk, clear as Amber, and strong as Brandy; and will be just Fourteen Year old the Fifth Day of next March old Stile.[11]

AIMWELL. You're very exact, I find, in the Age of your Ale.

BONNIFACE. As punctual, Sir, as I am in the Age of my Children: I'll shew you such Ale—Here, Tapster, broach Number 1706,[12] as the saying is;—Sir, you shall taste my *Anno Domini;*[13]—I have liv'd in *Litchfield* Man and Boy above Eight and fifty Years, and I believe have not consum'd Eight and Fifty Ounces of Meat.

AIMWELL. At a Meal, you mean, if one may guess your Sense by your Bulk.

BONNIFACE. Not in my Life, Sir, I have fed purely upon Ale; I have eat my Ale, drank my Ale, and I always sleep upon Ale.

Enter Tapster with a Bottle and Glass.

Now, Sir, you shall see *(Filling it out.)* your Worship's Health; ha! delicious, delicious,—fancy it *Burgundy,* only fancy it, and 'tis worth Ten Shillings a Quart.[14]

AIMWELL. *(Drinks.)* 'Tis confounded strong.

BONNIFACE. Strong! It must be so, or how should we be strong that drink it?

AIMWELL. And have you liv'd so long upon this Ale, Landlord?

BONNIFACE. Eight and fifty Years, upon my Credit, Sir; but it kill'd my Wife, poor Woman, as the saying is.

AIMWELL. How came that to pass?

BONNIFACE. I don't know how, Sir; she would not let the Ale take its natural Course, Sir, she was for qualifying° [modifying] it every now and the with a Dram, as the saying is; and an honest Gentleman that came this way from *Ireland,* made her a Present of a dozen Bottles of Usquebaugh° [whiskey]—But the poor Woman was never well after: But howe're, I was obliged to the Gentleman, you know.

AIMWELL. Why, was it the Usquebaugh that kill'd her?

BONNIFACE. My *Lady Bountiful* said so,—She, good Lady, did what could be done, she cured her of Three Tympanies,° [tumors] but the Fourth carry'd her off; but she's happy, and I'm contented, as the saying is.

11. Until 1752 the English calendar was eleven days behind the calendar of Western Europe.

12. Bonniface is apparently not calling for his fourteen-year-old ale.

13. Latin for "year of our Lord."

14. Ten shillings is half a pound, a significant sum of money, since a servant might be paid as little as two to three pounds a year.

AIMWELL. Who's that *Lady Bountiful,* you mention'd?

BONNIFACE. Ods my Life, Sir, we'll drink her Health. *(Drinks.)* My Lady *Bountiful* is one of the best of Women: Her last Husband Sir *Charles Bountiful* left her worth a Thousand Pound a Year; and I believe she lays out one half on't in charitable Uses for the Good of her Neighbours; she cures Rheumatisms, Ruptures, and broken Shins in Men, Green Sickness, Obstructions, and Fits of the Mother in Women;—The Kings-Evil, Chin-Cough, and Chilblains in Children;[15] in short, she has cured more People in and about *Litchfield* within Ten Years than the Doctors have kill'd in Twenty; and that's a bold Word.

AIMWELL. Has the Lady been any other way useful in her Generation?

BONNIFACE. Yes, Sir, She has a Daughter, by Sir *Charles,* the finest Woman in all our Country, and the greatest Fortune. She has a Son too by her first Husband Squire *Sullen,* who married a fine Lady from *London* t'other Day; if you please, Sir, we'll drink his Health?

AIMWELL. What sort of a Man is he?

BONNIFACE. Why, Sir, the Man's well enough; says little, thinks less, and does—nothing at all, Faith: But he's a Man of great Estate, and values no Body.

AIMWELL. A Sportsman, I suppose.

BONNIFACE. Yes, Sir, he's a Man of Pleasure, he plays at Whisk,[16] and smoaks his Pipe Eight and forty Hours together sometimes.

AIMWELL. And marry'd, you say?

BONNIFACE. Ay, and to a curious Woman, Sir—But he's a—He wants it, here, Sir. *(Pointing to his Forehead.)*

AIMWELL. He has it there, you mean.

BONNIFACE. That's none of my Business, he's my Landlord, and so a Man, you know, wou'd not,—But—I cod, he's no better than—Sir, my humble Service to you. *(Drinks.)* Tho' I value not a Farthing what he can do to me; I pay him his Rent at Quarter day,[17] I have a good running Trade, I have but one Daughter, and I can give her—But no matter for that.

AIMWELL. You're very happy, Mr. *Bonniface,* pray what other Company have you in Town?

BONNIFACE. A power of fine Ladies, and then we have the *French* Officers.[18]

15. "Ruptures" = hernias; "Green Sickness" = anemia; "Fits of the Mother" = a variety of symptoms including uterine diseases and fainting; "Kings-Evil" = scrofula, a skin disease so called because the touch of the ruler was supposed to cure it; "Chin-Cough" = whooping cough; "Chilblains" = skin ulcers caused by cold.

16. Whist, a card game that has some resemblance to bridge.

17. The four days of the year when rent was paid: Lady Day (Feast of the Annunciation), Midsummer Day, Michaelmas, and Christmas.

18. England was currently involved in the War of the Spanish Succession. Captured officers were

AIMWELL. O that's right, you have a good many of those Gentlemen: Pray how do you like their Company?

BONNIFACE. So well, as the saying is, that I cou'd wish we had as many more of 'em, they're full of Money, and pay double for every thing they have; they know, Sir, that we pay'd good round Taxes for the taking of 'em, and so they are willing to reimburse us a little; one of 'em lodges in my House.

Enter Archer.

ARCHER. Landlord, there are some *French* gentlemen below that ask for you.

BONNIFACE. I'll wait on 'em;—Does your master stay long in Town, as the saying is? (*To* Archer.)

ARCHER. I can't tell, as the Saying is.

BONNIFACE. Come from *London?*

ARCHER. No.

BONNIFACE. Going to *London,* may hap?

ARCHER. No.

BONNIFACE. An odd Fellow this. [*Aside.*] I beg your Worship's Pardon, I'll wait on you in half a Minute.

[*Exit.*

AIMWELL. The Coast's clear, I see—Now, my dear *Archer,* welcome to *Litchfield.*

ARCHER. I thank thee, my dear Brother in Iniquity.

AIMWELL. Iniquity! prithee leave Canting,° you need not change your Stile with your Dress. [affectedly pious speech]

ARCHER. Don't mistake me, *Aimwell,* for 'tis still my Maxim, that there is no Scandal like Rags, nor any Crime so shameful as Poverty.

AIMWELL. The World confesses it every Day in its Practice, tho' Men won't own it for their Opinion: Who did that worthy Lord, my Brother, single out of the Side-box[19] to sup with him t'other Night?

ARCHER. *Jack Handycraft,* a handsom, well dress'd, mannerly, sharping Rogue, who keeps the best Company in Town.

AIMWELL. Right, and pray who marry'd my Lady *Manslaughter* t'other Day, the great Fortune?

ARCHER. Why, *Nick Marrabone,*[20] a profess'd Pick-pocket, and a good Bowler; but he makes a handsom Figure, and rides in his Coach, that he formerly used to ride behind.

---

quartered at various locations in England where, having given their word not to escape, were allowed freedom in the area. Their pay and remittances from home were forwarded to them.

19. The most expensive seats at a theater.

20. Marylebone, gambling and sporting district of London.

AIMWELL. But did you observe poor *Jack Generous* in the Park last Week?

ARCHER. Yes, with his Autumnal Perriwig, shading his melancholy Face, his coat older than any thing but its Fashion, with one Hand idle in his Pocket, and with the other picking his useless Teeth; and tho' the Mall[21] was crowded with Company, yet was poor *Jack* as single and solitary as a Lyon in a Desart.

AIMWELL. And as much avoided, for no Crime upon Earth but the want of Money.

ARCHER. And that's enough; Men must not be poor, Idleness is the Root of all Evil; the World's wide enough, let 'em bustle; Fortune has taken the weak under her Protection, but Men of Sense are left to their Industry.

AIMWELL. Upon which Topick we proceed, and I think luckily hitherto: Wou'd not any Man swear now that I am a Man of Quality, and you my Servant, when if our instrinsick Value were known—

ARCHER. Come, come, we are the Men of intrinsick Value, who can strike our Fortunes out of our selves, whose worth is independent of Accidents in Life, or Revolutions in Government; we have Heads to get Money, and Hearts to spend it.

AIMWELL. As to our Hearts, I grant'ye, they are as willing Tits as any within Twenty Degrees; but I can have no great opinion of our Heads from the Service they have done us hitherto, unless it be that they brought us from *London* hither to *Litchfield,* made me a Lord, and you my Servant.

ARCHER. That's more than you cou'd expect already. But what Money have we left?

AIMWELL. But Two hundred Pound.

ARCHER. And our Horses, Cloaths, Rings, *&c.* why we have very good Fortunes now for moderate People; and let me tell you besides, that this Two hundred Pound, with the experience that we are now Masters of, is a better Estate than the Ten thousand we have spent.[22]—Our friends indeed began to suspect that our Pockets were low; but we came off with flying Colours, shew'd no signs of want either in Word or Deed.

AIMWELL. Ay, and our going to *Brussels* was a good Pretence enough for our sudden disappearing; and I warrant you, our Friends imagine that we are gone a volunteering.—

ARCHER. Why, Faith, if this Prospect fails, it must e'en come to that, I am for venturing one of the Hundreds if you will, upon this Knight-Errantry; but in case it should fail, we'll reserve the t'oth-

21. The Mall in St. James's Park (presumably the park indicated in Aimwell's previous speech).

22. As emended by William Archer. Kenny has "and let me tell you, besides Thousand, that this Two hundred Pound, with the experience that we are now Masters of, is a better Estate than the Ten we have spent.—"

er to carry us to some Counterscarp,[23] where we may die as we liv'd in a Blaze.

AIMWELL. With all my Heart; and we have liv'd justly, *Archer,* we can't say that we have spent our Fortunes, but that we have enjoy'd 'em.

ARCHER. Right, so much Pleasure for so much Money, we have had our Penyworths, and had I Millions, I wou'd go to the same Market again. O *London, London!* well, we have had our share, and let us be thankful; Past Pleasures, for ought I know are best, such as we are sure of, those to come may disappoint us.

AIMWELL. It has oftern griev'd the Heart of me, to see how some inhumane Wretches murther their kind Fortunes; those that by sacrificing all to one Appetite, shall starve all the rest.—You shall have some that live only in their Palates, and in their sense of tasting shall drown the other Four: Others are only Epicures in Appearances, such who shall starve their Nights to make a Figure a Days, and famish their own to feed the Eyes of others: A contrary Sort confine their Pleasures to the dark, and contract their spacious Acres to the Circuit of a Muff-string.[24]

ARCHER. Right, but they find the *Indies* in that Spot where they consume 'em, and I think your kind Keepers have much the best on't; for they indulge the most Senses by one Expence, there's the Seeing, Hearing, and Feeling amply gratify'd; and some Philosophers will tell you, that from such a Commerce there arises a sixth Sense that gives infinitely more Pleasure than the other five put together.

AIMWELL. And to pass to the other Extremity, of all Keepers, I think those the worst that keep their Money.

ARCHER. Those are the most miserable Wights in being, they destroy the Rights of Nature, and disappoint the Blessings of Providence: Give me a Man that keeps his Five Senses keen and bright as his Sword, that has 'em always drawn out in their just order and strength, with Reason as Commander at the Head of 'em, that detaches 'em by turns upon whatever Party of Pleasure agreeably offers, and commands 'em to retreat upon the least Appearance of Disadvantage or Danger:—For my part I can stick to my Bottle, while my Wine, my Company, and my Reason holds good; I can be charm'd with *Sappho's*[25] singing without falling in Love with her Face; I love Hunting, but wou'd not, like *Acteon,*[26] be eaten up by my own Dogs; I love a fine House, but let another keep it, and just so I love a fine Woman.

23. The outer face of a ditch in a fortification.
24. A muff is a covering for the hands; the muff-string went around the neck.
25. Greek poet and a conventional name for a woman in pastoral romances.
26. Acteon saw Artemis bathing; she turned him into a stag and he was killed by his own dogs.

AIMWELL. In that last particular you have the better of me.

ARCHER. Ay, you're such an amorous Puppy, that I'm afraid you'll spoil our Sport; you can't counterfeit the Passion without feeling it.

AIMWELL. Tho' the whining part be out of doors in Town, 'tis still in force with the Country Ladies;—And let me tell you *Frank,* the Fool in that Passion shall outdoe the Knave at any time.

ARCHER. Well, I won't dispute it now, you Command for the Day, and so I submit;—At *Nottingham* you know I am to be master.

AIMWELL. And at *Lincoln* I again.

ARCHER. Then at *Norwich* I mount, which, I think, shall be our last Stage, for if we fail there, we'll imbark for *Holland,* bid adieu to *Venus,* and welcome *Mars.*[27]

AIMWELL. A Match! (*Enter* Boniface.) Mum.

BONNIFACE. What will your Worship please to have for Supper?

AIMWELL. What have you got?

BONNIFACE. Sir, we have a delicate piece of Beef in the Pot, and a Pig at the Fire.

AIMWELL. Good Supper-meat, I must confess,—I can't eat Beef, Landlord.

ARCHER. And I hate Pig.

AIMWELL. Hold your prating, Sirrah, Do you know who you are?

BONNIFACE. Please to bespeak something else, I have every thing in the House.

AIMWELL. Have you any Veal?

BONNIFACE. Veal! Sir, we had a delicate Loin of Veal on *Wednesday* last.

AIMWELL. Have you got any Fish or Wildfowl?

BONNIFACE. As for Fish, truly Sir, we are an inland Town, and indifferently provided with Fish, that's the Truth ont, and then for Wildfowl,—we have a delicate Couple of Rabbets.

AIMWELL. Get me the Rabbets fricasy'd.° stewed

BONNIFACE. Fricasy'd! Lard, Sir, they'll eat much better smother'd with Onions.

ARCHER. Pshaw! damn your Onions.

AIMWELL. Again, Sirrah!—Well, Landlord, what you please; but hold, I have a small Charge of Money, and your House is so full of Strangers, that I believe it may be safer in your Custody than mine; for when this Fellow of mine gets drunk, he minds nothing.—Here, Sirrah, reach me the strong Box.

ARCHER. Yes, Sir,—This will give us a Reputation. *(Aside.)*

(Brings the Box.)

AIMWELL. Here, Landlord, the Locks are sealed down both for

27. Venus is the goddess of love and Mars is the god of war.

your Security and mine; it holds somewhat above Two hundred pound; if you doubt it, I'll count them to you after Supper; but be sure you lay it where I may have it at a Minute's warning; for my Affairs are a little dubious at present, perhaps I maybe gone in half an Hour, perhaps I may be your Guest till the best part of that be spent; and pray order your Ostler[28] to keep my Horses always saddled; but one thing above the rest I must beg, that you would let this Fellow have none of your *Anno Domini,* as you call it;—For he's the most insufferable Sot—Here, Sirrah, light me to my Chamber.

Exit lighted by Archer.

BONNIFACE. *Cherry,* Daughter *Cherry?*

Enter Cherry.

CHERRY. D'ye call, Father.

BONNIFACE. Ay, Child, you must lay by this Box for the Gentleman, 'tis full of Money.

CHERRY. Money! all that Money! why, sure Father the Gentleman comes to be chosen Parliament-man. Who is he?

BONNIFACE. I don't know what to make of him, he talks of keeping his Horses ready sadled, and of going perhaps at a minute's warning, or of staying perhaps till the best part of this be spent.

CHERRY. Ay, ten to one, Father, he's a High-way-man.

BONNIFACE. A High-way-man! upon my Life, Girl, you have hit it, and this Box is some new purchased Booty.—Now cou'd we find him out, the money were ours.

CHERRY. He don't belong to our Gang?

BONNIFACE. What Horses have they?

CHERRY. The Master rides upon a Black.

BONNIFACE. A Black! ten to one the Man upon the black Mare; and since he dont belong to our Fraternity, we may betray him with a safe Conscience; I don't think it lawful to harbour any Rogues but my own.—Look'ye, Child, as the saying is, we must go cunningly to work, Proofs we must have, the Gentleman's Servant loves Drink, I'll ply him that way, and ten to one loves a Wench; you must work him t'other way.

CHERRY. Father, wou'd you have me give my Secret for his?

BONNIFACE. Consider, Child, there's Two hundred Pound to boot. *(Ringing without.)* Coming, coming.—Child, mind your Business.

[*Exit* Bonniface.

CHERRY. What a Rogue is my Father! my Father! I deny it.—My Mother was a good, generous, free-hearted Woman, and I can't

28. Hostler, the person who takes care of horses at an inn.

tell how far her good Nature might have extended for the good of her Children. This Landlord of mine, for I think I can call him no more, would betray his Guest, and debauch his Daughter into the bargain,—By a Footman too!

Enter Archer.

ARCHER. What Footman, pray, Mistress, is so happy as to be the Subject of your Contemplation?
CHERRY. Whoever he is, Friend, he'll be but little the better for't.
ARCHER. I hope so, for I'm sure you did not think of me.
CHERRY. Suppose I had?
ARCHER. Why then you're but even with me; for the Minute I came in, I was considering in what manner I should make love to you.
CHERRY. Love to me, Friend!
ARCHER. Yes, Child.
CHERRY. Child! Manners; if you kept a little more distance, Friend, it would become you much better.
ARCHER. Distance! good night, Sauce-box. *(Going.)*
CHERRY. A pretty Fellow! A like his Pride, [*Aside.*]—Sir; pray, Sir; you see, Sir, (Archer *returns.*) I have the Credit to be intrusted with your Master's Fortune here, which sets me a Degree above his Footman; I hope, Sir, you an't affronted.
ARCHER. Let me look you full in the Face, and I'll tell you whether you can affront me or no.—'Sdeath, Child, you have a pair of delicate Eyes, and you don't know what to do with 'em.
CHERRY. Why, Sir, don't I see every body?
ARCHER. Ay, but if some Women had 'em, they wou' kill every body.—Prithee, instruct me, I wou'd fain make Love to you, but I don't know what to say.
CHERRY. Why, did you never make Love to any body before?
ARCHER. Never to a Person of your Figure, I can assure you, Madam, my Addresses have been always confin'd to People within my own Sphere, I never aspir'd so high before.

[*Sings.*]

But you look so bright,
And are dress'd so tight,
That a Man wou'd swear you're Right,
As Arm was e'er laid over.
Such an Air
You freely wear
To ensnare
As makes each Guest a Lover.

Since then, my Dear, I'm your Guest,
Prithee give me of the Best
Of what is ready Drest:
Since then, my Dear, &c.

CHERRY. What can I think of this Man? *(Aside.)* Will you give me that Song, Sir?

ARCHER. Ay, my Dear, take it while 'tis warm. *(Kisses her.)* Death and fire! her Lips are Honey-combs.

CHERRY. And I wish there had been Bees too, to have stung you for your Impudence.

ARCHER. There's a swarm of *Cupids,* my little *Venus,* that has done the Business much better.

CHERRY. This Fellow is misbegotten as well as I. *(Aside.)* What's your Name, Sir?

ARCHER. Name! I gad, I have forgot it. *(Aside.)* Oh! *Martin.*

CHERRY. Where were you born?

ARCHER. In St. *Martin*'s Parish.

CHERRY. What was your Father?

ARCHER. St. *Martin*'s Parish.

CHERRY. Then, Friend, good night.

ARCHER. I hope not.

CHERRY. You may depend upon't.

ARCHER. Upon what?

CHERRY. That you're very impudent.

ARCHER. That you're very handsome.

CHERRY. That you're a Footman.

ARCHER. That you're an Angel.

CHERRY. I shall be rude.

ARCHER. So shall I.

CHERRY. Let go my Hand.

ARCHER. Give me a Kiss. *(Kisses her.)*

Call without. Cherry, Cherry.

CHERRY. I'mm—My Father calls; you plaguy Devil, how durst you stop my Breath so?—Offer to follow me one step, if you dare.

[*Exit.*]

ARCHER. A fair Challenge by this Light; this is a pretty fair opening of an Adventure; but we are Knight-Errants, and so Fortune be our Guide.

Exit.

The End of the First Act.

ACT II. [SCENE I.]

SCENE, *A Gallery in* Lady Bountiful*'s House.*
Mrs. Sullen *and* Dorinda *meeting.*

DORINDA. Morrow, my dear Sister; are you for Church this morning?

MRS. SULLEN. Any where to Pray; for Heaven alone can help me: But, I think, *Dorinda,* there's no Form of Prayer in the Liturgy against bad Husbands.

DORINDA. But there's a Form of Law in *Doctors-Commons;*[29] and I swear, Sister *Sullen,* rather than see you thus continually discontented, I would advise you to apply to that: For besides the part that I bear in your vexatious Broils, as being Sister to the Husband, and Friend to the Wife; your Examples give me such an Impression of Matrimony, that I shall be apt to condemn my Person to a long Vacation all its Life.—But supposing, Madam, that you brought it to a Case of Separation, what can you urge against your Husband? My Brother is, first, the most constant Man alive.

MRS. SULLEN. The most constant Husband, I grant'ye.

DORINDA. He never sleeps from you.

MRS. SULLEN. No, he always sleeps with me.

DORINDA. He allows you a Maintenance suitable to your Quality.

MRS. SULLEN. A Maintenance! Do you take me, Madam, for an hospital Child, that I must sit down and bless my Benefactors for Meat, Drinks and Clothes? As I take it, Madam, I brought your Brother Ten thousand Pounds, out of which, I might expect some pretty things, call'd Pleasures.

DORINDA. You share in all the Pleasures the Country affords.

MRS. SULLEN. Country Pleasures! Racks and Torments! dost think, Child, that my Limbs were made for leaping of Ditches,[30] and clambring over Stiles; or that my Parents wisely foreseeing my future Happiness in Country-pleasures, had early instructed me in the rural Accomplishments of drinking fat° Ale, playing at Whisk, and smoaking Tobacco with my Husband; or of spreading of Plaisters, brewing of Diet-drinks, and stilling Rosemary-Water,[31] with the good old Gentlewoman, my Mother-in-Law?

° strong

DORINDA. I'm sorry, Madam, that it is not more in our power to divert you; I cou'd wish indeed that our Entertainments were a little more polite, or your Taste a little less refin'd: But, pray,

29. The civil law society that pleaded cases of divorce and separation in the ecclesiastical courts.

30. Possibly meant here is the Irish sense of "ditch": that is, the hedge/fence/mound that marks the boundary of a field or property. A "drain" in Ireland is what the English call a ditch.

31. Plaisters are either a paste used for health or cosmetic purposes or a bandage, while diet-drinks and rosemary-water are medicinal drinks.

Madam, how came the Poets and Philosophers that labour'd so much in hunting after Pleasure, to place it at last in a Country Life?

MRS. SULLEN. Because they wanted Money, Child, to find out the Pleasures of the Town: Did you ever see a Poet or Philosopher worth Ten thousand Pounds; if you can shew me such a Man, I'll lay you Fifty Pound you'll find him somewhere within the weekly Bills.[32]—Not that I disapprove rural Pleasures, as the Poets have painted them; in their Landschape every *Phillis* has her *Coridon,*[33] every murmuring Stream, and every flowry Mead gives fresh Alarms to Love.—Besides, you'll find that their Couples were never marry'd:—But yonder I see my *Coridon,* and a sweet Swain it is, Heaven knows.—Come, *Dorinda,* don't be angry, he's my Husband, and your Brother; and between both is he not a sad Brute?

DORINDA. I have nothing to say to your part of him, you're the best Judge.

MRS. SULLEN. O Sister, Sister! if ever you marry, be ware of a sullen, silent Sot, one that's always musing, but never thinks:—There's some Diversion in a talking Blockhead; and since a Woman must wear Chains, I wou'd have the Pleasure of hearing 'em rattle a little.—Now you shall see, but take this by the way;—He came home this Morning at his usual Hour of Four, waken'd me out of a sweet Dream of something else, by tumbling over the Tea-table, which he broke all to pieces, after his Man and he had rowl'd about the Room, like sick Passengers in a Storm, he comes flounce into Bed, dead as a Salmon into a Fishmonger's Basket; his Feet cold as Ice, his Breath hot as a Furnace, and his Hands and his Face as greasy as his Flanel Night-cap.—Oh Matrimony!—He tosses up the Clothes with a barbarous swing over his Shoulders, disorders the whole Oeconomy of my Bed, leaves me half naked, and my whole Night's Comfort is the tuneable Serenade of that wakeful Nightingale, his Nose.—O the Pleasure of counting the melancholly Clock by a snoring Husband!—But now, Sister, you shall see how handsomely, being a well-bred Man, he will beg my Pardon.

Enter Sullen.

SULLEN. My Head akes consumedly.

MRS. SULLEN. Will you be pleased, my Dear, to drink Tea with us this Morning? it may do your Head good.

SULLEN. No.

32. London parishes published weekly bills of mortality; Mrs. Sullen is saying any wealthy person would prefer to live in London.

33. Conventional names for lovers in pastorals.

DORINDA. Coffee, Brother?[34]

SULLEN. Pshaw.

MRS. SULLEN. Will you please dress, and go to Church with me, the Air may help you.

SULLEN. *Scrub.*

Enter Scrub.

SCRUB. Sir.

SULLEN. What Day o'th Week is this?

SCRUB. *Sunday,* an't please your Worship.

SULLEN. *Sunday!* bring me a Dram, and, d'ye hear, set out the Venison-Pasty, and a Tankard of strong Beer upon the Hall-Table, I'll go to breakfast. *(Going.)*

DORINDA. Stay, stay, Brother, you shan't get off so; you were very naught last Night, and must make your Wife Reparation; come, come, Brother, won't you ask Pardon?

SULLEN. For what?

DORINDA. For being drunk last Night.

SULLEN. I can afford it, can't I?

MRS. SULLEN. But I can't, Sir.

SULLEN. Then you may let it alone.

MRS. SULLEN. But I must tell you, Sir, that this is not to be born.

SULLEN. I'm glad on't.

MRS. SULLEN. What is the Reason, Sir, that you use me thus inhumanely?

SULLEN. *Scrub?*

SCRUB. Sir.

SULLEN. Get things ready to shave my Head.

Exeunt.

MRS. SULLEN. Have a care of coming near his Temples, *Scrub,* for fear you meet something there that may turn the Edge of your Razor.—Inveterate Stupidity! did you ever know so hard, so obstinate a Spleen as his? O Sister, Sister! I shall never ha' Good of the Beast till I get him to Town; *London,* dear *London* is the place for managing and breaking a Husband.

DORINDA. And has not a Husband the same Opportunities there for humbling a Wife?

MRS. SULLEN. No, no, Child, 'tis a standing Maxim in conjugal Discipline, that when a Man wou'd enslave his Wife, he hurries her into the Country; and when a Lady would be arbitrary with her Husband, she wheedles her Booby up to Town.—A Man dare not play the Tyrant in *London,* because there are so many Examples to encourage the Subject to rebel. O *Dorinda, Dorinda!* a

34. "Coffee? Brother." in Kenny.

fine Woman may do any thing in *London*. O'my Conscience, she may raise an Army of Forty thousand Men.

DORINDA. I fancy, Sister, you have a mind to be trying your Power that way here in *Litchfield;* you have drawn the *French* count to your Colours already.

MRS. SULLEN. The *French* are a People that can't live without their Gallantries.

DORINDA. And some *English* that I know, Sister, are not averse to such Amusements.

MRS. SULLEN. Well, Sister, since the Truth must out, it may do as well now as hereafter; I think one way to rouse my Lethargick sotish Husband, is to give him a Rival; Security begets Negligence in all People, and Men must be alarm'd to make 'em alert in their Duty: Women are like Pictures, of no Value in the Hands of a Fool, till he hears Men of Sense bid high for the Purchase.

DORINDA. This might do, Sister, if my Brother's Understanding were to be convinc'd into a Passion for you; but I fancy there's a natural Aversion of his side; and I fancy, Sister, that you don't come much behind him, if you dealt fairly.

MRS. SULLEN. I own it, we are united Contradictions, Fire and Water. But I cou'd be contented, with a great many other Wives, to humour the censorious Mob, and give the World an Appearance of living well with my Husband, cou'd I bring him but to dissemble a little Kindness to keep me in Countenance.

DORINDA. But how do you know, Sister, but that instead of rousing your Husband by this Artifice to a counterfeit Kindness, he should awake in a real Fury?

MRS. SULLEN. Let him:—If I can't entice him to the one, I wou'd provoke him to the other.

DORINDA. But how must[35] I behave my self between ye[?]

MRS. SULLEN. You must assist me.

DORINDA. What, against my own Brother!

MRS. SULLEN. He's but half a Brother, and I'm your entire Friend: If I go a step beyond the Bounds of Honour, leave me; till then I expect you should go along with me in every thing, while I trust my Honour in your Hands, you may trust your Brother's in mine.—The *Count* is to dine here to Day.

DORINDA. 'Tis a strange thing, Sister, that I can't like that Man.

MRS. SULLEN. You like nothing, your time is not come; Love and Death have their Fatalities, and strike home one time or other:—You'll pay for all one Day, I warrant'ye.—But come, my Lady's Tea is ready, and 'tis almost Church-time.

Exeunt.

35. "much" in Kenny.

[ACT II. SCENE II.]

SCENE, *The Inn*
Enter Aimwell *dress'd, and* Archer.

AIMWELL. And was she the Daughter of the House?

ARCHER. The Landlord is so blind as to think so; but I dare swear she has better Blood in her Veins.

AIMWELL. Why dost think so?

ARCHER. Because the Baggage has a pert *Je ne S[ais] quoi,*[36] she reads Plays, keeps a Monkey, and is troubled with Vapours.

AIMWELL. By which Discoveries I guess that you know more of her.

ARCHER. Not yet, Faith, the Lady gives herself Airs, forsooth, nothing under a Gentleman.

AIMWELL. Let me take her in hand.

ARCHER. Say one Word more o'that, and I'll declare my self, spoil your Sport there, and every where else; look'ye, *Aimwell,* every Man in his own Sphere.

AIMWELL. Right; and therefore you must pimp for your Master.

ARCHER. In the usual Forms, good Sir, after I have serv'd my self.—But to our Business:—You are so well dress'd, *Tom,* and make so handsome a Figure, that I fancy you may do Execution in a Country Church; the exteriour part strikes first, and you're in the right to make that Impression favourable.

AIMWELL. There's something in that which may turn to Advantage: The Appearance of a Stranger in a. Country Church draws as many Gazers as a blazing Star; no sooner he comes into the Cathedral, but a Train of Whispers runs buzzing round the Congregation in a moment;—Who is he? whence comes he? do you know him?—Then I, Sir, tips me the Verger with half a Crown; he pockets the Simony,[37] and Inducts me into the best Pue in the Church, I pull out my Snuff-box, turn my self round, bow to the Bishop, or the Dean, if he be the commanding Officer; single out a Beauty, rivet both my Eyes to hers, set my Nose a bleeding by the Strength of Imagination, and shew the whole Church my concern by my endeavouring to hide it; after the Sermon, the whole Town gives me to her for a Lover, and, by perswading the Lady that I am dying for her, the Tables are turn'd, and she in good earnest falls in Love with me?

ARCHER. There's nothing in this, *Tom,* without a Precedent; but instead of riveting your Eyes to a Beauty, try to fix 'em upon a Fortune, that's our Business at present.

36. *Je ne sais quoi*—I don't know what.

37. The verger is a church officer who, among other duties, serves as usher at a church. Simony is the sin of buying or selling church offices or the sacraments.

AIMWELL. Pshaw, no Woman can be a Beauty without a Fortune.—Let me alone, for a Mark'sman.

ARCHER. *Tom.*

AIMWELL. Ay.

ARCHER. When were you at Church before, pray?

AIMWELL. Um—I was there at the Coronation.[38]

ARCHER. And how can you expect a Blessing by going to Church now?

AIMWELL. Blessing! nay, *Frank,* I ask but for a Wife.

Exit.

ARCHER. Truly the Man is not very unreasonable in his Demands.

Exit at the opposite Door.
Enter Bonniface *and* Cherry.

BONNIFACE. Well Daughter, as the saying is, have you brought *Martin* to confess?

CHERRY. Pray, Father, don't put me upon getting any thing out of a Man; I'm but young you know, Father, and I don't understand Wheedling.

BONNIFACE. Young! why you Jade, as the saying is, can any Woman wheedle that is not young, you'r Mother was useless at five and twenty; not wheedle! would you make your Mother a Whore and me a Cuckold, as the saying is? I tell you his Silence confesses it, and his Master spends his Money so freely, and is so much a Gentleman every manner of way that he must be a Highwayman.

Enter Gibbet *in a Cloak.*

GIBBET. Landlord, Landlord, is the Coast clear?

BONNIFACE. O, Mr. *Gibbet,* what's the News?

GIBBET. No matter, ask no Questions, all fair and honourable, here, my dear *Cherry, (Gives her a Bag.)* Two hundred Sterling Pounds, as good as any that ever hang'd or sav'd a Rogue; lay 'em by with the rest, and here—Three wedding or mourning Rings, 'tis much the same you know—Here, two Silver-hilted Swords; I took those from Fellows that never shew any part of their Swords but the Hilts: Here is a Diamond Necklace which the Lady hid in the privatest place in the Coach, but I found it out: This Gold Watch I took from a Pawn-broker's Wife; it was left in her Hands by a Person of Quality, there's the Arms upon the Case.

CHERRY. But who had you the Money from?

GIBBET. Ah! poor Woman! I pitied her;—From a poor Lady just elop'd from her Husband, she had made up her Cargo, and was

38. The coronation of Queen Anne in 1702, five years earlier.

bound for *Ireland,* as hard as she cou'd drive; she told me of her Husband's barbarous Usage, and so I left her half a Crown: But I had almost forgot, my dear *Cherry,* I have a Present for you.

CHERRY. What is't?

GIBBET. A pot of Cereuse,[39] my Child, that I took out of Lady's under Pocket.

CHERRY. What, Mr. *Gibbet,* do you think that I paint?

GIBBET. Why, you Jade, your Betters do; I'm sure the Lady that I took it from had a Coronet upon her Handkerchief.—Here, take my Cloak, and go, secure the Premisses.

CHERRY. I will secure 'em.

Exit.

BONNIFACE. But, heark'ye, where's *Hounslow* and *Bagshot?*

GIBBET. They'll be here to Night.

BONNIFACE. D'ye know of any other Gentlemen o'the Pad on this Road?

GIBBET. No.

BONNIFACE. I fancy that I have two that lodge in the House just now.

GIBBET. The Devil! how d'ye smoak 'em?

BONNIFACE. Why, the one is gone to Church.

GIBBET. That's suspitious, I must confess.

BONNIFACE. And the other is now in his Master's Chamber; he pretends to be Servant to the other, we'll call him out, and pump him a little.

GIBBET. With all my Heart.

BONNIFACE. Mr. *Martin,* Mr. *Martin?*

Enter Archer *combing a Perrywig, and singing.*

GIBBET. The Roads are consumed deep; I'm as dirty as old *Brentford* at Christmas.[40]—A good pretty Fellow that; who's Servant are you, Friend?

ARCHER. My Master's.

GIBBET. Really?

ARCHER. Really.

GIBBET. That's much.—The Fellow has been at the Bar, by his Evasions:—But, pray, Sir, what is your Master's Name?

ARCHER. *Tall, all, dall; (Sings and combs the Perrywig.)* This is the most obstinate Curl—

GIBBET. I ask you his Name?

ARCHER. Name, Sir,—*Tall, all dal*—I never ask'd him his Name in my Life. *Tall, all, dall.*

39. Red makeup, or blush.

40. A proverb, possibly because the main road from London to the southwest of England went though Brentford, which, in the winter, would have made it a sea of mud.

BONNIFACE. What think you now?

GIBBET. Plain, plain, he talks now as if he were before a Judge: But, pray, Friend, which way does your Master travel?

ARCHER. A Horseback.

GIBBET. Very well again, an old Offender, right;—But, I mean does he go upwards or downwards?

ARCHER. Downwards, I fear, Sir: *Tall, all.*

GIBBET. I'm afraid my Fate will be a contrary way.[41]

BONNIFACE. Ha, ha, ha! Mr. *Martin* you're very arch.—This Gentleman is only travelling towards *Chester,* and wou'd be glad of your Company, that's all.—Come, Captain, you'll stay to Night, I suppose; I'll shew you a Chamber—Come, Captain.

GIBBET. Farewel, Friend—

Exeunt.

ARCHER. Captain, your Servant.—Captain! a pretty Fellow; s'death, I wonder that the Officers of the Army don't conspire to beat all Scoundrels in Red but their own.

Enter Cherry.

CHERRY. Gone! and *Martin* here! I hope he did not listen; I wou'd have the Merit of the discovery all my own, because I wou'd oblige him to love me. *(Aside.)* Mr. *Martin,* who was that Man with my Father?

ARCHER. Some Recruiting Serjeant, or whip'd out Trooper, I suppose.

CHERRY. All's safe, I find. [*Aside.*]

ARCHER. Come, my Dear, have you con'd over the Catechise I taught you last Night?

CHERRY. Come, question me.

ARCHER. What is Love?

CHERRY. Love is I know not what, it comes I know not how, and goes I know not when.

ARCHER. Very well, an apt Scholar. *(Chucks her under the Chin.)* Where does Love enter?

CHERRY. Into the Eyes.

ARCHER. And where go out?

CHERRY. I won't tell'ye.

ARCHER. What are Objects of that Passion?

CHERRY. Youth, Beauty, and clean Linen.

ARCHER. The Reason?

CHERRY. The two first are fashionable in Nature, and the third at Court.

41. i.e., he will travel upwards when he is hanged.

ARCHER. That's my Dear: What are the Signs and Tokens of that Passion?

CHERRY. A stealing Look, a stammering Tongue, Words improbable, Designs impossible, and Actions impracticable.

ARCHER. That's my good child, kiss me.—What must a Lover do to obtain his Mistress?

CHERRY. He must adore the Person that disdains him, he must bribe the Chambermaid that betrays him, and court the Footman that laughs at him;—He must, he must—

ARCHER. Nay, Child, I must whip you, if you don't mind your Lesson; he must treat his—

CHERRY. O, ay, he must treat his Enemies with Respect, his Friends with indifference, and all the World with Contempt; he must suffer much, and fear more; he must desire much, and hope little; in short, he must embrace his Ruine, and throw himself away.

ARCHER. Had ever Man so hopeful a Pupil as mine? come, my Dear, why is Love call'd a Riddle?

CHERRY. Because, being blind, he leads those that see, and tho' a Child, he governs a Man.

ARCHER. Mighty well.—And why is Love pictur'd blind?

CHERRY. Because the Painters, out of their weakness or privilege of their Art chose to hide those Eyes they cou'd not draw.

ARCHER. That's my dear little Scholar, kiss me again.—And why shou'd Love, that's a Child, govern a Man?

CHERRY. Because that a Child is the end of Love.

ARCHER. And so ends Love's Catechism.—And now, my Dear, we'll go in, and make my Master's Bed.

CHERRY. Hold, hold, Mr. *Martin,*—You have taken a great deal of Pains to instruct me, and what d'ye think I have learn't by it?

ARCHER. What?

CHERRY. That your Discourse and your Habit are Contradictions, and it wou'd be nonsense in me to believe you a Footman any longer.

ARCHER. 'Oons, what a Witch it is!

CHERRY. Depend upon this, Sir, nothing in this Garb shall ever tempt me; for tho' I was born to Servitude, I hate it.—Own your Condition, swear you love me, and then—

ARCHER. And then we shall go make my master's bed.

CHERRY. Yes.

ARCHER. You must know then, that I am born a Gentleman, my Education was liberal; but I went to *London* a younger Brother, fell into the Hands of Sharpers, who stript me of my Money, my Friends disown'd me, and now my Necessity brings me to what you see.

CHERRY. Then take my Hand—promise to marry me before you sleep, and I'll make you Master of two thousand Pound.

ARCHER. How!

CHERRY. Two thousand Pound that I have this Minute in my own Custody; so throw off your Livery this Instant, and I'll go find a Parson.

ARCHER. What said you? A Parson!

CHERRY. What! Do you scruple?

ARCHER. Scruple! no, no, but—two thousand Pound you say?

CHERRY. And better.

ARCHER. S'death, what shall I do—but hearke, Child, what need you make me Master of your self and Money, when you may have the same Pleasure out of me, and still keep your Fortune in your Hands?

CHERRY. Then you won't marry me?

ARCHER. I wou'd marry you, but—

CHERRY. O sweet, Sir, I'm your humble Servant, you're fairly caught, wou'd you perswade me that any Gentleman who cou'd bear the Scandal of wearing a Livery, wou'd refuse two thousand Pound let the Condition be what it wou'd—no, no, Sir,—but I hope you'll Pardon the Freedom I have taken, since it was only to inform my self of the Respect that I ought to pay to you. *(Going.)*

ARCHER. Fairly bit, by *Jupiter*—hold, hold, and have you actually two thousand Pound.

CHERRY. Sir, I have my Secrets as well as you—when you please to be more open, I shall be more free, and be assur'd that I have Discoveries that will match yours, be what they will—in the mean while be satisfy'd that no Discovery I make shall ever hurt you, but beware of my Father.—

[*Exit.*]

ARCHER. So—we're like to have as many Adventures in our Inn, as *Don Quixote* had in his—let me see,—two thousand Pound! If the Wench wou'd promise to dye when the Money were spent, I gad, one wou'd marry her, but the Fortune may go off in a Year or two, and the Wife may live—Lord knows how long? then an Innkeeper's Daughter; ay that's the Devil—there my Pride brings me off.

For whatsoe'er the Sages charge on Pride
The Angels fall, and twenty Faults beside,
On Earth I'm sure, 'mong us of mortal Calling,
Pride saves Man oft, and Woman too from falling.

Exit.

End of the Second Act

ACT III. [SCENE I.]

SCENE, Lady Bountiful's *House*
Enter Mrs. Sullen, Dorinda.

MRS. SULLEN. Ha, ha, ha, my dear Sister, let me embrace thee, now we are Friends indeed! for I shall have a Secret of yours, as a Pledge for mine—now you'll be good for something, I shall have you conversable in the Subjects of the Sex.

DORINDA. But do you think that I am so weak as to fall in Love with a Fellow at first sight?

MRS. SULLEN. Pshaw! now you spoil all, why shou'd not we be as free in our Friendships as the Men? I warrant you the Gentleman has got to his Confident already, has avow'd his Passion, toasted your Health, call'd you ten thousand Angels, has run over your Lips, Eyes, Neck, Shape, Air, and every thing, in a Description that warms their Mirth to a second Enjoyment.

DORINDA. Your Hand, Sister, I an't well.

MRS. SULLEN. So,—she's breeding already—come Child up with it—hem a little—so—now tell me, don't you like the Gentleman that we saw at Church just now?

DORINDA. The Man's well enough.

MRS. SULLEN. Well enough! is he not a Demigod, a *Narcissus,*[42] a Star, the Man i'the Moon?

DORINDA. O Sister, I'm extreamly ill.

MRS. SULLEN. Shall I send to your Mother, Child, for a little of her Cephalic[43] Plaister to put to the Soals of your Feet, or shall I send to the Gentleman for something for you?—Come, unlace your Steas, unbosome your self—the Man is perfectly a pretty Fellow, I saw him when he first came into Church.

DORINDA. I saw him too, Sister, and with an Air that shone, methought like Rays about his Person.

MRS. SULLEN. Well said, up with it.

DORINDA. No forward Coquett Behaviour, no Airs to set him off, no study'd Looks nor artful Posture,—but Nature did it all—.

MRS. SULLEN. Better and better—one Touch more—come—

DORINDA. But then his Looks—did you observe his Eyes?

MRS. SULLEN. Yes, yes, I did—his Eyes, well, what of his Eyes?

DORINDA. Sprightly, but not wandring; they seem'd to view, but never gaz'd on any thing but me—and then his Looks so humble were, and yet so noble, that they aim'd to tell me that he cou'd with Pride dye at my Feet, tho' he scorn'd Slavery any where else.

MRS. SULLEN. The Physick works purely—How d'ye find your self now, my Dear?

42. Narcissus was so beautiful he fell in love with his own reflection.
43. From the Greek word for head.

DORINDA. Hem! Much better, my Dear—O here comes our Mercury![44]

Enter Scrub.

Well, *Scrub,* what News of the Gentleman?

SCRUB. Madam, I have brought you a Packet of News.

DORINDA. Open it quickly, come.

SCRUB. In the first place, I enquir'd who the Gentleman was? they told me he was a Stranger. Secondly, I ask'd what the gentleman was, they answer'd and said, that they never saw him before. Thirdly, I enquir'd what Countryman he was, they reply'd 'twas more than they knew. Fourthly, I demanded whence he came, their Answer was, they cou'd not tell. And fifthly, I ask'd whither he went, and they reply'd they knew nothing of the matter,—and this is all I cou'd learn.

MRS. SULLEN. But what do the People say, Can't they guess?

SCRUB. Why some think he's a Spy, some guess he's a Mountebank, some say one thing, some another; but for my own part, I believe he's a Jesuit.[45]

DORINDA. A Jesuit! why a Jesuit?

SCRUB. Because he keeps his Horses always ready sadled, and his Footman talks *French.*

MRS. SULLEN. His Footman!

SCRUB. Ay, he and the Count's Footmen were Gabbering *French* like two intreaguing Ducks in a Mill-Pond, and I believe they talk'd of me, for they laugh'd consumedly.

DORINDA. What sort of Livery has the Footman?

SCRUB. Livery! Lord, Madam, I took him for a Captain, he's so bedizen'd with Lace, and then he has Tops to his Shoes, up to his mid Leg, a silver headed Cane dangling at his Nuckles,—he carries his Hands in his Pockets just so—*(Walks in the* French *Air.)* and has a fine long Perriwig ty'd up in a Bag—Lord, Madam, he's clear another sort of a Man than I.

MRS. SULLEN. That may easily be—but what shall we do now, Sister?

DORINDA. I have it—This Fellow has a world of Simplicity, and some Cunning, the first hides the latter by abundance—*Scrub.*

SCRUB. Madam.

DORINDA. We have a great mind to know who this Gentleman is, only for our Satisfaction.

SCRUB. Yes, Madam, it would be a Satisfaction, no doubt

DORINDA. You must go and get acquainted with his Footman, and invite him hither to drink a Bottle of your Ale, because you're Butler to Day.

44. Mercury is the messenger of the gods.

45. Jesuits were an arm of the Counter-Reformation; they were proverbial for deceit and assumed to be working to subvert the Crown.

SCRUB. Yes, Madam, I am Butler every Sunday.

MRS. SULLEN. O brave, Sister, O my Conscience, you understand the Mathematicks already—'tis the best Plot in the World, your Mother, you know, will be gone to Church, my Spouse will be got to the Ale-house with his Scoundrels, and the House will be our own—so we drop in by Accident, and ask the Fellow some Questions our selves. In the Countrey you know any Stranger is Company, and we're glad to take up with the Butler in a Country Dance, and happy if he'll do us the Favour.

SCRUB. Oh! Madam, you wrong me, I never refus'd your Ladyship the Favour in my Life.

Enter Gipsey.

GIPSEY. Ladies, Dinner's upon Table.

DORINDA. Scrub, We'll excuse your waiting—Go where we order'd you.

SCRUB. I shall.

[ACT III. SCENE II.]

SCENE *changes to the Inn.*
Enter Aimwell *and* Archer.

ARCHER. Well, *Tom,* I find you're a Marksman.

AIMWELL. A Marksman! who so blind cou'd be, as not discern a Swan among the Ravens?

ARCHER. Well, but heark'ee, *Aimwell.*

AIMWELL. *Aimwell!* call me *Oroondates, Cesario, Amadis,*[46] all that Romance can in a Lover paint, and then I'll answer. O *Archer,* I read her thousands in her Looks, she look'd like *Ceres* in her harvest,[47] Corn, Wine and Oil, Milk and Honey, Gardens, Groves and Purling Streams play 'd on her plenteous Face.

ARCHER. Her Face! her Pocket, you mean; the Corn, Wine and Oil lies there. In short, she has ten thousand Pound, that's the *English* on't.

AIMWELL. Her Eyes—

ARCHER. Are Demi-Cannons to be sure, so I won't stand their Battery. *(Going.)*

AIMWELL. Pray, excuse me, my Passion must have vent.

ARCHER. Passion! what a plague, d'ee think these Romantick Airs will do our Business? Were my Temper as extravagant as yours, my Adventures have some thing more Romantick by half.

AIMWELL. Your Adventures!

46. Conventional names for heroes in romances.

47. Ceres is goddess of the harvest.

ARCHER. Yes, *The Nymph that with her twice ten hundred Pounds*
With brazen Engine hot, and Quoif° clear starch'd maid's cap
Can fire the Guest in warming of the Bed—
There's a Touch of Sublime *Milton* for you, and the Subject but an Inn-keeper's Daughter; I can play with a Girl as an Angler do's with his Fish; he keeps it at the end of his Line, runs it up the Stream, and down the Stream, till at last, he brings it to hand, tickles the Trout, and so whips it into his Basket.

Enter *Bonniface.*

BONNIFACE. Mr. *Martin,* as the saying is—yonder's an honest Fellow below, my *Lady Bountiful*'s Butler, who begs the Honour that you wou'd go Home with him and see his Cellar.

ARCHER. Do my *Baisemains*[48] to the Gentleman, and tell him I will do my self the Honour to wait on him immediately.

Exit Bonniface.

AIMWELL. What do I hear? soft *Orpheus* Play, and fair *Toftida*[49] sing?

ARCHER. Pshaw! damn your Raptures, I tell you here's a Pump going to be put into the Vessel, and the Ship will get into Harbour, my Life on't. You say there's another Lady very handsome there.

AIMWELL. Yes, faith.

ARCHER. I'am in love with her already.

AIMWELL. Can't you give me a Bill upon *Cherry* in the mean time.

ARCHER. No, no, Friend, all her Corn, Wine and Oil is ingross'd to my Market.—And once more I warn you to keep your Anchorage clear of mine, for if you fall foul of me, by this Light you shall go to the Bottom.—What! make Prize of my little Frigat, which I am upon the Cruise for you.

[*Exit.*
Enter Bonniface.

AIMWELL. Well, well, I won't—Landlord, have you any tolerable Company in the House, I don't care for dining alone.

BONNIFACE. Yes, Sir, there's a Captain below; as the saying is, that arriv'd about an Hour ago.

AIMWELL. Gentlemen of his Coat are welcome every where; will you make him a Complement from me, and tell him I should be glad of his Company.

BONNIFACE. Who shall I tell him, Sir, wou'd.—

AIMWELL. Ha! that Stroak was well thrown in [*Aside.*]—I'm only a Traveller like himself, and wou'd be glad of his Company, that's all.

48. Literally "handkissings" with the sense of "give my respects."

49. Katherine Tofts, English soprano, who sang in London 1703–9; at her peak she was paid £500 a year.

BONNIFACE. I obey your Commands, as the saying is.

Exit.
Enter Archer.

ARCHER. S'Death! I had forgot, what Title will you give your self?

AIMWELL. My Brother's to be sure, he wou'd never give me any thing else, so I'll make bold with his Honour this bout—you know the rest of your Cue.

ARCHER. Ay, ay. [*Exit.*]

Enter Gibbet.

GIBBET. Sir, I'm yours.

AIMWELL. 'Tis more than I deserve, Sir, for I don't know you.

GIBBET. I don't wonder at that, Sir, for you never saw me before, I hope. *(Aside.)*

AIMWELL. And pray, Sir, how came I by the Honour of seeing you now?

GIBBET. Sir, I scorn to intrude upon any Gentleman—but my Landlord—

AIMWELL. O, Sir, I ask your Pardon, you're the Captain he told me of.

GIBBET. At your Service, Sir.

AIMWELL. What Regiment, may I be so bold?

GIBBET. A marching Regiment, Sir, an old Corps.

AIMWELL. Very old, if your Coat be Regimental, *(Aside.)* You have serv'd abroad, Sir?

GIBBET. Yes, Sir, in the Plantations, 'twas my Lot to be sent into the worst Service, I wou'd have quitted it indeed, but a Man of Honour, you know—Besides 'twas for the good of my Country that I shou'd be abroad—Any thing for the good of one's Country—I'm a *Roman* for that.

AIMWELL. One of the first, I'll lay my Life *(Aside.)* You found the *West Indies* very hot, Sir?

GIBBET. Ay, Sir, too hot for me.

AIMWELL. Pray, Sir, han't I seen your Face at *Will*'s Coffee-house?

GIBBET. Yes, Sir, and at *White*'s too.[50]

AIMWELL. And where's your Company now, Captain?

GIBBET. They an't come yet.

AIMWELL. Why, d'ye expect 'em here?

GIBBET. They'll be here to Night, Sir.

AIMWELL. Which way do they march?

GIBBET. Across the Country—the Devil's in't, if I han't said enough to encourage him to declare—but I'm afraid he's not right, I must tack about. [*Aside.*]

50. Will's Coffee-house in the Restoration was where the wits gathered, Dryden in particular. By the time of this play, it was in decline. White's chocolate-house, and then coffee-house, was frequented by the fashionable world.

AIMWELL. Is your Company to quarter at *Litchfield?*

GIBBET. In this House, Sir.

AIMWELL. What! all?

GIBBET. My Company's but thin, ha, ha, ha, we are but three, ha, ha, ha.

AIMWELL. You're merry, Sir?

GIBBET. Ay, Sir, you must excuse me, Sir, I understand the World, especially the Art of Travelling; I don't care, Sir, for answering Questions directly upon the Road—for I generally ride with a Charge about me.[51]

AIMWELL. Three or four, I believe. *(Aside.)*

GIBBET. I am credibly inform'd that there are Highway-men upon this Quarter, not, Sir, that I cou'd suspect a Gentleman of your Figure—But truly, Sir, I have got such a way of Evasion upon the Road, that I don't care for speaking Truth to any Man.

AIMWELL. Your Caution may be necessary—Then I presume you're no Captain?

GIBBET. Not I, Sir, Captain is a good travelling Name, and so I take it; it stops a great many foolish Inquiries that are generally made about Gentlemen that travel, it gives a Man an Air of something, and makes the Drawers° obedient—And thus far I am a Captain, and no farther.

tapsters

AIMWELL. And pray, Sir, what is your true Profession?

GIBBET. O, Sir, you must excuse me—upon my word, Sir, I don't think it safe to tell you.

AIMWELL. Ha, ha, ha, upon my word, I commend you.

Enter *Bonniface.*

Well, Mr. *Bonniface,* what's the News?

BONNIFACE. There's another Gentleman below, as the saying is, that hearing you were but two, wou'd be glad to make the third Man if you wou'd give him leave.

AIMWELL. What is he?

BONNIFACE. A Clergyman, as the saying is.

AIMWELL. A Clergyman! is he really a Clergyman? or is it only his travelling Name, as my Friend the Captain has it.

BONNIFACE. O, Sir, he's a Priest and Chaplain to the *French* Officers in Town.

AIMWELL. Is he a *French*-man?

BONNIFACE. Yes, Sir, born at *Brussels.*

GIBBET. A *French*-man and a Priest! I won't be seen in his Company, Sir; I have a Value for my Reputation, Sir.

AIMWELL. Nay, but Captain, since we are by our selves—Can he speak *English,* Landlord[?]

51. By "charge" Gibbet means a sum of money, while Aimwell means a loaded weapon.

BONNIFACE. Very well, Sir, you may know him, as the saying is, to be a Foreigner by his Accent, and that's all.

AIMWELL. Then he has been in *England* before?

BONNIFACE. Never, Sir, but he's Master of Languages, as the saying is, he talks *Latin,* it do's me good to hear him talk *Latin.*

AIMWELL. Then you understand *Latin,* Mr. *Bonniface?*

BONNIFACE. Not I, Sir, as the saying is, but he talks it so very fast that I'm sure it must be good.

AIMWELL. Pray desire him to walk up.

BONNIFACE. Here he is, as the saying is.

Enter Foigard.

FOIGARD. Save you, Gentlemen's, both.

AIMWELL. A *French*-man! Sir, your most humble Servant.

FOIGARD. Och, dear Joy, I am your most faithful Shervant, and yours alsho.

GIBBET. Doctor, you talk very good *English,* but you have a mighty Twang of the Foreigner.

FOIGARD. My *English* is very vel for the vords, but we Foreigners you know cannot bring our Tongues about the Pronunciation so soon.

AIMWELL. A Foreigner! a down-right Teague,[52] by this Light. *(Aside.)* Were you born in *France,* doctor[?]

FOIGARD. I was educated in *France,* but I was borned at *Brussels,* I am a Subject of the King of *Spain,* Joy.

GIBBET. What king of *Spain,* Sir, speak.

FOIGARD. Upon my Shoul Joy, I cannot tell you as yet.

AIMWELL. Nay, Captain, that was too hard upon the Doctor, he's a Stranger.

FOIGARD. O let him alone, dear Joy, I am of a Nation that is not easily put out of Countenance.

AIMWELL. Come, Gentlemen, I'll end the Dispute.—Here, Landlord, is Dinner ready?

BONNIFACE. Upon the Table, as the saying is.

AIMWELL. Gentlemen—pray—that Door—

FOIGARD. No, no fait, the Captain must lead.

AIMWELL. No, Doctor, the Church is our Guide.

GIBBET. Ay, ay, so it is.—

Exit foremost, they follow.

52. Derogatory term for an Irish Catholic, from the Irish name Tadhg.

[ACT III. SCENE III.]

SCENE *Changes to a Gallery in* Lady Bountiful's *House.*
Enter Archer *and* Scrub *singing, and hugging one another,* Scrub *with a Tankard in his Hand,* Gipsey *listning at a distance.*

SCRUB. *Tall, all, dall*—Come, my dear Boy—Let's have that Song once more.

ARCHER. No, no, we shall disturb the Family;—But will you be sure to keep the Secrets?

SCRUB. Pho! upon my Honour, as I'm a Gentleman.

ARCHER. 'Tis enough—You must know then, that my Master is the Lord Viscount *Aimwell;* he fought a Duel t'other day in *London,* wounded his Man so dangerously, that he thinks fit to withdraw till he hears whether the Gentleman's Wounds be mortal or not: He never was in this part of *England* before, so he chose to retire to this Place, that's all.

GIPSEY. And that's enough for me.

Exit.

SCRUB. And where were you when your Master fought?

ARCHER. We never know of our Masters Quarrels.

SCRUB. No! if our Masters in the Country here receive a Challenge, the first thing they do is to tell their Wives; the Wife tells the Servants, the Servants alarm the Tenants, and in half an Hour you shall have the whole County up in Arms.

ARCHER. To hinder two Men from doing what they have no mind for:—But if you should chance to talk, now of my Business?

SCRUB. Talk! ay, Sir, had I not learn't the knack of holding my Tongue, I had never liv'd so long in a great Family.

ARCHER. Ay, ay, to be sure, there are Secrets in all Families.

SCRUB. Secrets, ay;—But I'll say no more.—Come, sit down, we'll make an end of our Tankard: Here—

ARCHER. With all my Heart; who knows but you and I may come to be better acquainted, eh—Here's your Ladies Healths; you have three, I think, and to be sure there must be Secrets among 'em.

SCRUB. Secrets! Ay, Friend, I wish I had a Friend—

ARCHER. Am not I you Friend? come, you and I will be sworn Brothers.

SCRUB. Shall we?

ARCHER. From this Minute.—Give me a kiss—And now Brother *Scrub*—

SCRUB. And, now, Brother *Martin,* I will tell you a Secret that will make your Hair stand an end:—You must know, that I am consumedly in Love.

ARCHER. That's a terrible Secret, that's the Truth on't.

SCRUB. That Jade, *Gipsey,* that was with us just now in the Cellar, is the arrantest Whore that ever wore a Petticoat; and I'm dying for love of her.

ARCHER. Ha, ha, ha—Are you in love with her Person, or her Vertue, Brother *Scrub?*

SCRUB. I should like Vertue best, because it is more durable than Beauty; for Vertue holds good with some Women long, and many a Day after they have lost it.

ARCHER. In the Country, I grant ye, where no Woman's Vertue is lost, till a Bastard be found.

SCRUB. Ay, cou'd I bring her to a Bastard, I shou'd have her all to my self; but I dare not put it upon that Lay, for fear of being sent for a Soldier.—Pray, Brother, how do you Gentlemen in *London* like that same Pressing Act?[53]

ARCHER. Very ill, Brother *Scrub;*—'Tis the worst that ever was made for us: Formerly I remember the good Days, when we cou'd dun our Masters for our Wages, and if they refused to pay us, we cou'd have a Warrant to carry 'em before a Justice; but now if we talk of eating, they have a Warrant for us, and carry us before three Justices.

SCRUB. And to be sure we go, if we talk of eating; for the Justices won't give their own Servants a bad Example. Now this is my Misfortune—I dare not speak in the House, while that Jade *Gipsey* dings about like a Fury—Once I had the better end of the Staff.

ARCHER. And how comes the Change now?

SCRUB. Why, the Mother of all this Mischief is a Priest.

ARCHER. A Priest!

SCRUB. Ay, a damn'd Son of a Whore of *Babylon,* that came over hither to say Grace to the *French* Officers, and eat up our Provisions—There's not a Day goes over his Head without Dinner or Supper in this House.

ARCHER. How came he so familiar in the Family?

SCRUB. Because he speaks *English* as if he had liv'd here all his Life; and tells Lies as if he had been a Traveller from his Cradle.

ARCHER. And this Priest, I'm afraid has converted the Affections of your *Gipsey.*

SCRUB. Converted! ay, and perverted, my dear Friend:—For I'm afraid he has made her a Whore and a Papist.—But this is not all; there's the *French* Count and *Mrs. Sullen,* they're in the Confederacy, and for some private Ends of their own to be sure.

ARCHER. A very hopeful Family,[54] yours, brother *Scrub;* I suppose the Maiden Lady has her Lover too.

53. The Impressment Act of 1703 allowed men with no settled income to be forced into military service.

54. The "family" means the entire household here, including the servants, such as Scrub and Gipsey.

SCRUB. Not that I know;—She's the best on 'em, that's the Truth on't: But they take care to prevent my Curiosity, by giving me so much Business, that I'm a perfect Slave.—What d'ye think is my Place in this Family?

ARCHER. Butler, I suppose.

SCRUB. Ah, Lord help you—I'll tell you—Of a *Monday,* I drive the Coach; of a *Tuesday,* I drive the Plough; on *Wednesday,* I follow the Hounds; a *Thursday,* I dun the Tenants; on *Fryday,* I go to Market; on *Saturday,* I draw Warrants;[55] and a *Sunday,* I draw Beer.

ARCHER. Ha, ha, ha! if variety be a Pleasure in Life, you have enough on't, my dear Brother—But what Ladies are those?

SCRUB. Ours, ours; that upon the right Hand is *Mrs. Sullen,* and the other Mrs.[56] *Dorinda.*—Don't mind 'em, sit still, Man—

Enter Mrs. Sullen *and* Dorinda.

MRS. SULLEN. I have heard my Brother talk of my Lord *Aimwell,* but they say that his Brother is the finer Gentleman.

DORINDA. That's impossible, Sister.

MRS. SULLEN. He's vastly rich, but very close, they say.

DORINDA. No matter for that; if I can creep into his Heart, I'll open his Breast, I warrant him: I have heard say, that People may be guess'd at by the Behaviour of their Servants; I cou'd wish we might talk to that Fellow.

MRS. SULLEN. So do I; for, I think he's a very pretty Fellow: Come this way, I'll throw out a Lure for him presently.

They walk a turn to the opposite side of the Stage, Mrs. Sullen *drops her Glove,* Archer *runs, takes it up, and gives it to her.*

ARCHER. Corn, Wine, and Oil, indeed—But, I think, the Wife has the greatest plenty of Flesh and Blood; she should be my Choice [*Aside.*]—Ah, a, say you so—Madam—Your Ladyship's Glove.

MRS. SULLEN. O, Sir, I thank you—what a handsom Bow the Fellow has?

DORINDA. Bow! why I have known several Footmen come down from *London* set up here for Dancing-Masters, and carry off the best Fortune in the Country.

ARCHER. That Project, for ought I know, had been better than ours, *(Aside.)* Brother *Scrub*—Why don't you introduce me.

SCRUB. Ladies, this is the strange Gentleman's Servant that you see at Church to Day; I understood he came from *London,* and so I invited him to the Cellar, that he might show me the newest Flourish in whetting my Knives.

55. Warrants presumably drawn for the arrest of those in debt to the estate.
56. A title of respect that does not indicate marital status.

DORINDA. And I hope you have made much of him?

ARCHER. O yes, Madam, but the Strength of your Ladyship's Liquor is a little too potent for the Constitution of your humble Servant.

MRS. SULLEN. What, then you don't usually drink Ale?

ARCHER. No, Madam, my constant Drink is Tea, or a little Wine and Water; 'tis prescrib'd me by the Physician for a Remedy against the Spleen.

SCRUB. O la, O la!—a Footman have the Spleen.—

MRS. SULLEN. I thought that Distemper had been only proper to People of Quality.

ARCHER. Madam, like all other Fashions it wears out, and so descends to their Servants; tho' in a great many of us, I believe it proceeds from some melancholly Particles in the Blood, occasion'd by the Stagnation of Wages.

DORINDA. How affectedly the Fellow talks—How long, pray, have you serv'd your present Master?

ARCHER. Not long; my Life has been mostly spent in the Service of the Ladies.

MRS. SULLEN. And pray, which Service do you like best?

ARCHER. Madam, the Ladies pay best; the Honour of serving them is sufficient Wages; there is a Charm in their looks that delivers a Pleasure with their Commands, and gives our Duty the Wings of Inclination.

MRS. SULLEN. That Flight was above the pitch of a Livery; and, Sir, wou'd not you be satisfied to serve a Lady again?

ARCHER. As a Groom of the Chambers, Madam, but not as a Footman.

MRS. SULLEN. I suppose you serv'd as Footman before.

ARCHER. For that Reason I wou'd not serve in that Post again; for my Memory is too weak for the load of Messages that the Ladies lay upon their Servants in *London;* my Lady *Howd'ye,* the last Mistress I serv'd call'd me up one Morning, and told me, *Martin,* go to my Lady *Allnight* with my humble Service; tell her I was to wait on her Ladyship yesterday, and left word with Mrs. *Rebecca,* that the Preliminaries of the Affair she knows of, are stopt till we know the concurrence of the Person that I know of, for which there are Circumstances wanting which we shall accommodate at the old Place; but that in the mean time there is a Person about her Ladyship, that from several Hints and Surmises, was accessary at a certain time to the disappointments that naturally attend things, that to her knowledge are of more Importance

MRS. SULLEN. / DORINDA. } Ha, ha, ha! where are you going, Sir?

ARCHER. Why, I han't half done.—The whole Howd'ye was about half an Hour long; so I hapned to misplace two Syllables, and was turn'd off, and render'd incapable—

DORINDA. The pleasantest Fellow, Sister, I ever saw.—But, Friend, if your Master be marry'd,—I presume you still serve a Lady.

ARCHER. No, Madam, I take care never to come into a marry'd Family; the Commands of the Master and Mistress are always so contrary, that 'tis impossible to please both.

DORINDA. There's a main point gain'd.—My Lord is not marry'd, I find. *(Aside.)*

MRS. SULLEN. But, I wonder, Friend, that in so many good Services, you had not a better Provision made for you.

ARCHER. I don't know how, Madam.—I had a Lieutenancy offer'd me three or four Times; but that is not Bread, Madam—I live much better as I do.

SCRUB. Madam, he sings rarely.—I was thought to do pretty well here in the Country till he came; but alack a day, I'm nothing to my Brother *Martin.*

DORINDA. Does he? Pray, Sir, will you oblige us with a Song?

ARCHER. Are you for Passion, or Humour?

SCRUB. O la! he has the purest Ballad about a Trifle—

MRS. SULLEN. A Trifle! pray, Sir, let's have it.

ARCHER. I'm asham'd to offer you a Trifle, Madam: But since you command me—*(Sings to the Tune of Sir* Simon *the King.)*

SONG OF A TRIFLE

A trifling Song you shall hear,
Begun with a Trifle and ended:
All Trifling People draw near,
And I shall be nobly attended.

Were it not for a Trifle, a few,
That lately have come into Play;
The Men would want something to do,
And the Women want something to say.

What makes Men trifle in Dressing?
Because the Ladies (they know)
Admire, by often Possessing,
That eminent Trifle a Beau.

When the Lover his Moments has trifled,
The Trifle of Trifles to gain:
No sooner the Virgin is Rifled,
But a Trifle shall part 'em again.

What mortal Man wou'd be able,
At White's half an Hour to Sit?
Or who cou'd bear a Tea-Table,
Without talking of Trifles for Wit?

The Court is from Trifles secure,
Gold Keys are no Trifles, we see:

White Rods[57] *are no Trifles, I'm sure,*
Whatever their Bearer may be.

But if you will go to the Place,
Where Trifles abundantly breed,
The Levee[58] *will show you his Grace*
Makes Promises Trifles indeed.

A Coach with six Footmen behind,
I count neither Trifle nor Sin:
But, ye Gods! how oft do we find,
A scandalous Trifle within?

A Flask of Champaign, People think it
A Trifle, or something as bad:
But if you'll contrive how to drink it,
You'll find it no Trifle egad.

A Parson's a Trifle at Sea,
A Widow's a Trifle in Sorrow:
A Peace is a Trifle to-day,
Who knows what may happen to-morrow.

A Black Coat a Trifle may cloak,
Or to hide it, the Red may endeavour:
But if once the Army is broke,
We shall have more Trifles than ever.

The Stage is a Trifle, they say,
The Reason, pray carry along,
Because at ev'ry new Play,
The House they will Trifles so throng.

But with People's Malice to Trifle,
And to set us all on a Foot:
The Author of this is a Trifle,
And his Song is a Trifle to boot.

MRS. SULLEN. Very well, Sir, we're oblig'd to you.—Something for a pair of Gloves. *(Offering him Money.)*

ARCHER. I humbly beg leave to be excused: My Master, Madam, pays me; nor dare I take Money from any other Hand without injuring his Honour, and disobeying his Commands.

Exit.

DORINDA. This is surprising: Did you ever see so pretty a well bred Fellow?

MRS. SULLEN. The Devil take him for wearing that Livery.

57. Symbol of office.

58. A reception held by a distinguished person upon rising from bed.

DORINDA. I fancy, Sister, he may be some Gentleman, a Friend of my Lords, that his Lordship has pitch'd upon for his Courage, Fidelity, and Discretion to bear him Company in this Dress, and who, ten to one was his Second too.

MRS. SULLEN. It is so, it must be so, and it shall be so:—For I like him.

DORINDA. What! better than the *Count?*

MRS. SULLEN. The *Count* happen'd to be the most agreeable Man upon the Place; and so I chose him to serve me in my Design upon my Husband.—But I shou'd like this Fellow better in a Design upon my self.

DORINDA. But now, Sister, for an Interview with this Lord, and this Gentleman; how shall we bring that about?

MRS. SULLEN. Patience! you Country Ladies give no Quarter, if once you be enter'd.[59]—Wou'd you prevent their Desires, and give the Fellows no wishing time.—Look'ye, *Dorinda,* if my Lord *Aimwell* loves you or deserves you, he'll find a way to see you, and there we must leave it.—My Business comes now upon the Tapis°—Have you prepar'd your Brother? under consideration

DORINDA. Yes, yes.

MRS. SULLEN. And how did he relish it?

DORINDA. He said little, mumbled something to himself, promis'd to be guided by me: But here he comes—

Enter Sullen.

SULLEN. What singing was that I heard just now?

MRS. SULLEN. The singing in you[r] Head, my Dear, you complain'd of it all Day.

SULLEN. You're impertinent.

MRS. SULLEN. I was ever so, since I became one Flesh with you.

SULLEN. One Flesh! rather two Carcasses join'd unnaturally together.

MRS. SULLEN. Or rather a living Soul coupled to a dead Body.

DORINDA. So, this is fine Encouragement for me.

SULLEN. Yes, my Wife shews what you must do.

MRS. SULLEN. And my Husband shews you w[hat] you must suffer.

SULLEN. S'death, why can't you be silent?

MRS. SULLEN. S'death why can't you talk?

SULLEN. Do you talk to any purpose?

MRS. SULLEN. Do you think to any purpose?

SULLEN. Sister, heark'ye *(Whispers.)* I shan't be home till it be late.

Exit.

MRS. SULLEN. What did he whisper to ye?

59. Term from hunting; a dog is "entered" to its appropriate prey.

DORINDA. That he wou'd go round the back way, come into the Closet, and listen as I directed him.—But let me beg once more, dear Sister, to drop this Project; for, as I told you before, instead of awaking him to Kindness, you may provoke him to a Rage; and then who knows how far his Brutality may carry him?

MRS. SULLEN. I'm provided to receive him, I warrant you: But here comes the *Count*, vanish.

Exit Dorinda.
Enter Count Bellair.

Don't you wonder, *Monsieur le Count*, that I was not at Church this Afternoon?

COUNT. I more wonder, Madam, that you go dere at all, or how you dare to lift those Eyes to Heaven that are guilty of so much killing.

MRS. SULLEN. If Heaven, Sir, has given to my Eyes with the Power of killing, the Virtue of making a Cure, I hope the one may atone for the other.

COUNT. O largely, Madam; wou'd your Ladyship be as ready to apply the Remedy as to give the Wound?—Consider, Madam, I am doubly a Prisoner; first to the Arms of your General, then to your more conquering Eyes; my first Chains are easy, there a Ransom may redeem me, but from your Fetters I never shall get free.

MRS. SULLEN. Alass, Sir, why shou'd you complain to me of your Capitivity, who am in Chains my self? you know, Sir, that I am bound, nay, must be tied up in that particular that might give you ease: I am like you, a Prisoner of War—Of War indeed:—I have given my Parole of Honour; wou'd you break yours to gain your Liberty?

COUNT. Most certainly I wou'd, were I a Prisoner among the *Turks;* dis is your Case; you're a Slave, Madam, Slave to the worst of *Turks,* a Husband.

MRS. SULLEN. There lies my Foible, I confess; no Fortifications, no Courage, Conduct, nor Vigilancy can pretend to defend a Place, where the Cruelty of the Governour forces the Garrison to Mutiny.

COUNT. And where de Besieger is resolv'd to die before de Place—Here will I fix; *(Kneels.)* With Tears, Vows, and Prayers assault your Heart, and never rise till you surrender; or if I must storm—Love and St. *Michael*—And so I begin the Attack—

MRS. SULLEN. Stand off—Sure he hears me not—And I cou'd almost wish me—did not.—The Fellow makes love very prettily. *(Aside.)* But, Sir, why shou'd you put such a Value upon my Person, when you see it despis'd by one that knows it so much better.

COUNT. He knows it not, tho' he possesses it; if he but knew the Value of the Jewel he is Master of, he wou'd always wear it next his Heart, and sleep with it in his Arms.

MRS. SULLEN. But since he throws me unregarded from him.

COUNT. And one that knows your Value well, comes by, and takes you up, is it not Justice. *(Goes to lay hold on her.)*

Enter Sullen *with his Sword drawn.*

SULLEN. Hold, Villain, hold.

MRS. SULLEN. *(Presenting a Pistol.)* Do you hold.

SULLEN. What! Murther your Husband, to defend your Bully.

MRS. SULLEN. Bully! for shame, Mr. *Sullen;* Bullies wear long Swords, the Gentleman has none, he's a Prisoner you know—I was aware of your Outrage, and prepar'd this to receive your Violence, and, if Occasion were, to preserve my self against the Force of this other Gentleman.

COUNT. O Madam, your Eyes be bettre Fire Arms than your Pistol, they nevre miss.

SULLEN. What! court my Wife to my Face!

MRS. SULLEN. Pray, Mr. *Sullen,* put up, suspend your Fury for a Minute.

SULLEN. To give you time to invent an Excuse.

MRS. SULLEN. I need none.

SULLEN. No, for I heard every Sillable of your Discourse.

COUNT. Ay! and begar, I tink de Dialogue was vera pretty.

MRS. SULLEN. Then I suppose, Sir, you heard something of your own Barbarity.

SULLEN. Barbarity! oons what does the Woman call Barbarity? do I ever meddle with you?

MRS. SULLEN. No.

SULLEN. As for you, Sir, I shall take another time.

COUNT. Ah, begar, and so must I.

SULLEN. Look'e, Madam, don't think that my Anger proceeds from any Concern I have for your Honour, but for my own, and if you can contrive any way of being a Whore without making me a Cuckold, do it and welcome.

MRS. SULLEN. Sir, I thank you kindly, you wou'd allow me the Sin but rob me of the Pleasure—No, no, I'm resolv'd never to venture upon the Crime without the Satisfaction of seeing you punish'd for it.

SULLEN. Then will you grant me this, my Dear? let any Body else do you the Favour but that *French*-man, for I mortally hate his whole Generation.

Exit.

COUNT. Ah, Sir, that be ungrateful, for begar, I love some of your's, Madam.—*(Approaching her.)*

MRS. SULLEN. No, Sir.—

COUNT. No, Sir,—Garzoon, Madam, I am not your Husband.

MRS. SULLEN. 'Tis time to undeceive you, Sir,—I believ'd your Addresses to me were no more than an Amusement, and I hope you will think the same of my Complaisance, and to convince you that you ought, you must know, that I brought you hither only to make you instrumental in setting me right with my Husband, for he was planted to listen by my Appointment.

COUNT. By your Appointment?

MRS. SULLEN. Certainly.

COUNT. And so, Madam, while I was telling twenty Stories to part you from your Husband, begar, I was bringing you together all the while.

MRS. SULLEN. I ask your Pardon, Sir, but I hope this will give you a Taste of the Vertue of the *English* Ladies.

COUNT. Begar, Madam, your Vertue be vera Great, but Garzoon your Honeste be vera little.

Enter Dorinda.

MRS. SULLEN. Nay, now you're angry, Sir.

COUNT. Angry! fair *Dorinda* (*Sings* Dorinda *The Opera Tune, and addresses to* Dorinda.) Madam, when your Ladyship want a Fool, send for me, fair *Dorinda, Revenge, &c.*[60]

Exit.

MRS. SULLEN. There goes the True Humour of his Nation, Resentment with good Manners, and the height of Anger in a Song,—Well Sister, you must be the Judge, for you have heard the Trial.

DORINDA. And I bring in my Brother Guilty.

MRS. SULLEN. But I must bear the Punishment,—'Tis hard Sister.

DORINDA. I own it—but you must have Patience.

MRS. SULLEN. Patience! the Cant of Custom—Providence sends no Evil without a Remedy—shou'd I lie groaning under a Yoke I can shake off, I were accessary to my Ruin, and my Patience were no better than self-Murder.

DORINDA. But how can you shake off the Yoke—Your Divisions don't come within the Reach of Law for a Divorce.

MRS. SULLEN. Law! what Law can search into the remote Abyss of Nature, what Evidence can prove the unaccountable, Disaffections of Wedlock—can a Jury sum up the endless Aversions that are rooted in our Souls, or can a Bench give Judgment upon Antipathies.

DORINDA. They never pretended Sister, they never meddle but in case of Uncleaness.

60. From the popular opera *Il trionfo di camilla* (1696) by Giovanni Bononcini, with libretto by Nicola Francesco Haym.

MRS. SULLEN. Uncleanness! O Sister, casual Violation is a transient Injury, and may possibly be repair'd, but can radical Hatreds be ever reconcil'd—No, no, Sister, Nature is the first Lawgiver, and when she has set Tempers opposite, not all the golden Links of Wedlock, nor Iron Manacles of Law can keep 'um fast.

Wedlock we own ordain'd by Heaven's Decree,
But such as Heaven ordain'd it first to be,
Concurring Tempers in the Man and Wife
As mutual Helps to draw the Load of Life.
View all the Works of Providence above,
The Stars with Harmony and Concord move;
View all the Works of Providence below, }
The Fire the Water, Earth, and Air, we know }
All in one Plant agree to make it grow. }
Must Man the chiefest Work of Art Divine,
Be doom'd in endless Discord to repine.
No, we shou'd injure Heaven by that surmise
Omnipotence is just, were Man but wise.

End of the Third Act.

ACT IV. [SCENE I.]

SCENE *continues.*
Enter Mrs. Sullen.

MRS. SULLEN. Were I born an humble *Turk,* where Women have no Soul nor Property there I must sit contented—But in *England,* a Country whose Women are it's Glory, must Women be abus'd, where Women rule, must Women be enslav'd? nay, cheated into Slavery, mock'd by a Promise of comfortable Society into a Wilderness of Solitude—I dare not keep the Thought about me—O, here comes something to divert me—

Enter a Country Woman.

WOMAN. I come an't please your Ladyship, you're my *Lady Bountiful,* an't ye?

MRS. SULLEN. Well, good Woman go on.

WOMAN. I come seventeen long Mail[61] to have a Cure for my Husband's sore Leg.

MRS. SULLEN. Your Husband! what Woman, cure your Husband!

WOMAN. Ay, poor Man, for his Sore Leg won't let him stir from Home.

61. "Mail" for "mile" (as with "graips" for "gripes"—pain in the bowels—below) is Farquhar's attempt to use a phonetic rendering of the rural accent. He also attempts to provide a phonetic rendering of Foigard's speech.

MRS. SULLEN. There, I confess, you have given me a Reason. Well good Woman, I'll tell you what you must do—You must lay your Husband Leg upon a Table, and with a Choping-knife, you must lay it open as broad as you can, then you must take out the Bone, and beat the Flesh soundly with a rowling-pin, then take Salt, Pepper, Cloves, Mace and Ginger, some sweet Herbs, and season it very well, then rowl it up like Brawn, and put it into the Over for two Hours.

WOMAN. Heavens reward your Ladyship—I have two little Babies too that are piteous bad with the Graips, an't please ye.

MRS. SULLEN. Put a little Pepper and Salt in their Bellies, good Woman.

Enter Lady Bountiful.

I beg your Ladyship's Pardon for taking your Business out of your Hands, I have been a tampering here a little with one of your Patients.

LADY BOUNTIFUL. Come, good Woman, don't mind this mad Creature, I am the Person that you want, I suppose—What wou'd you have, Woman?

MRS. SULLEN. She wants something for her Husband's sore Leg.

LADY BOUNTIFUL. What's the matter with his Leg, Goody?

WOMAN. It come first as one might say with a sort of Dizziness in his Foot, then he had a kind of Laziness in his Joints, and then his Leg broke out, and then it swell'd, and then it clos'd again, and then it broke out again, and then it fester'd, and then it grew better, and then it grew worse again.

MRS. SULLEN. Ha, ha, ha.

LADY BOUNTIFUL. How can you be merry with the Misfortunes of other People?

MRS. SULLEN. Because my own make me sad, Madam.

LADY BOUNTIFUL. The worst Reason in the World, Daughter, your own Misfortunes shou'd teach you to pitty others.

MRS. SULLEN. But the Woman's Misfortunes and mine are nothing alike, her Husband is sick, and mine, alas, is in Health.

LADY BOUNTIFUL. What! wou'd you wish your Husband sick?

MRS. SULLEN. Not of a sore Leg, of all things.

LADY BOUNTIFUL. Well, good Woman, go to the Pantrey, get your Belly-full of Victuals, then I'll give you a Receipt° of Diet-drink for your Husband—But d'ye hear Goody, you must not let your Husband move too much. recipe

WOMAN. No, no, Madam, the poor Man's inclinable enough to lye still.

Exit.

LADY BOUNTIFUL. Well, Daughter *Sullen,* tho' you laugh, I have done Miracles about the Country here with my Receipts.

MRS. SULLEN. Miracles, indeed, if they have cur'd any Body, but, I believe, Madam, the Patient's Faith goes farther toward the Miracle than your Prescription.

LADY BOUNTIFUL. Fancy helps in some Cases, but there's your Husband who has as little Fancy as any Body, I brought him from Death's-door.

MRS. SULLEN. I suppose, Madam, you made him drink plentifully of Asse's Milk.

Enter Dorinda, *runs to* Mrs. Sullen.

DORINDA. News, dear Sister, news, news[!]

Enter Archer *running.*

ARCHER. Where, where is my *Lady Bountiful*—Pray which is the old Lady of you three?

LADY BOUNTIFUL. I am.

ARCHER. O, Madam, the Fame of your Ladyship's Charity, Goodness, Benevolence, Skill and Ability have drawn me hither to implore your Ladyship's Help in behalf of my unfortunate Master, who is this Moment breathing his last.

LADY BOUNTIFUL. Your Master! where is he?

ARCHER. At your Gate, Madam, drawn by the Appearance of your handsome House to view it nearer, and walking up the Avenue within five Paces of the Court-Yard, he was taken ill of a sudden with a sort of I know not what, but down he fell, and there he lies.

LADY BOUNTIFUL. Here, *Scrub, Gipsey,* all run, get my easie Chair down Stairs, put the Gentleman in it, and bring him in quickly, quickly.

ARCHER. Heaven will reward your Ladyship for this charitable Act.

LADY BOUNTIFUL. Is your Master us'd to these Fits?

ARCHER. O yes, Madam, frequently—I have known him have five or six of a Night.

LADY BOUNTIFUL. What's his Name?

ARCHER. Lord, Madam, he's a dying, a Minute's Care or Neglect may save or destroy his Life.

LADY BOUNTIFUL. Ah, poor Gentleman! come Friend, show me the way, I'll see him brought in myself.

Exit with Archer.

DORINDA. O Sister my Heart flutters about strangely, I can hardly forbear running to his Assistance.

MRS. SULLEN. And I'll lay my Life, he deserves your Assistance more than he wants it; did not I tell you that my Lord wou'd find a way to come at you. Love's his Distemper, and you must be the Physitian; put on all your Charms, summon all your Fire into your Eyes, plant the whole Artillery of your Looks against his Breast, and down with him.

DORINDA. O Sister, I'm but a young Gunner, I shall be afraid to shoot, for fear the Piece shou'd recoil and hurt my self.

MRS. SULLEN. Never fear, you shall see me shoot before you, if you will.

DORINDA. No, no, dear Sister, you have miss'd your Mark so unfortunately, that I shan't care for being instructed by you.

Enter Aimwell *in a Chair, carry'd by* Archer *and* Scrub, Lady Bountiful, Gipsey. Aimwell *counterfeiting a Swoon.*

LADY BOUNTIFUL. Here, here, let's see the Hartshorn-drops—*Gipsey* a Glass of fair° Water, his Fit's very strong—Bless me, how his Hands are clinch'd. pure

ARCHER. For shame, Ladies, what d'ye do? why don't you help us—Pray, Madam, (*To* Dorinda.) Take his Hand and open it if you can, whilst I hold his Head. (Dorinda *takes his Hand.*)

DORINDA. Poor, Gentleman,—Oh—he has got my Hand within his, and squeezes it unmercifully—

LADY BOUNTIFUL. 'Tis the Violence of his Convulsion, Child.

ARCHER. O, Madam, he's perfectly possess'd in these Cases—he'll bite you if you don't have a care.

DORINDA. Oh, my Hand, my Hand.

LADY BOUNTIFUL. What's the matter with the foolish Girl? I have got his Hand open, you see, with a great deal of Ease.

ARCHER. Ay, but, Madam, your Daughter's Hand is somewhat warmer than your Ladyship's, and the Heat of it draws the Force of the Spirits that way.

MRS. SULLEN. I find, Friend, you're very learned in these sort of Fits.

ARCHER. 'Tis no wonder, Madam, for I'm often troubled with them my self, I find my self extreamly ill at this Minute. (*Looking hard at* Mrs. Sullen.)

MRS. SULLEN. I fancy I could find a way to cure you. *(Aside.)*

LADY BOUNTIFUL. His Fit holds him very long.

ARCHER. Longer than usual, Madam,—Pray, young Lady, open his Breast, and give him Air.

LADY BOUNTIFUL. Where did his Illness take him first, pray?

ARCHER. To Day at Church, Madam.

LADY BOUNTIFUL. In what manner was he taken?

ARCHER. Very strangely, my Lady. He was of a sudden touch'd with something in his Eyes, which at the first he only felt, but cou'd not tell whether 'twas Pain or Pleasure.

LADY BOUNTIFUL. Wind, nothing but Wind.

ARCHER. By soft Degrees it grew and mounted to his Brain, there his Fancy caught it; there form'd it so beautiful, and dress'd it up in such gay pleasing Colours, that his transported Appetite seiz'd the fair Idea, and straight convey'd it to his Heart. That hospitable Seat of Life sent all its sanguine Spirits forth to meet, and open'd all its sluicy Gates to take the Stranger in.

LADY BOUNTIFUL. Your Master shou'd never go without a Bottle to smell to—Oh!—He recovers—The Lavender Water—Some Feathers to burn under his Nose—*Hungary*-water to rub his Temples—O, he comes to himself. Hem a little, Sir, hem—*Gipsey,* bring the Cordial-water. (Aimwell *seems to awake in amaze.*)

DORINDA. How d'ye, Sir?

AIMWELL. Where am I? *(Rising.)*

Sure I have pass'd the Gulph of silent Death,
And now I land on the Elisian *Shore—*
Behold the Goddess of those happy Plains
Fair Proserpine*—Let me adore thy bright Divinity. (Kneels to* Dorinda, *and kisses her Hand.)*

MRS. SULLEN. So, so, so, I knew where the Fit wou'd end.

AIMWELL. *Euridice* perhaps—*How cou'd thy* Orpheus *keep his word,*
And not look back upon thee;
No Treasure but thy self cou'd sure have brib'd him
To look one Minute off thee.

LADY BOUNTIFUL. Delirious, poor Gentleman.

ARCHER. Very Delirious, Madam, very Delirious.

AIMWELL. *Martin*'s Voice, I think.

ARCHER. Yes, my Lord—How do's your Lordship?

LADY BOUNTIFUL. Lord! did you mind that, Girls.

AIMWELL. Where am I?

ARCHER. In very good Hands, Sir,—You were taken just now with one of your old Fits under the Trees just by this good Lady's House, her Ladyship had you taken in, and has miraculously brought you to your self, as you see—

AIMWELL. I am so confounded with Shame, Madam, that I can now only beg Pardon—And refer my Acknowledgments for your Ladyship's Care, till an Opportunity offers of making some Amends—I dare to be no longer troublesome—*Martin,* give two Guineas to the Servants. *(Going.)*

DORINDA. Sir, you may catch cold by going so soon into the Air, you don't look, Sir, as if you were perfectly recover'd.

Here Archer *talks to* Lady Bountiful *in dumb shew.*

AIMWELL. That I shall never be, Madam, my present Illness is so rooted, that I must expect to carry it to my Grave.

MRS. SULLEN. Don't despair, Sir, I have known several in your Distemper shake it off, with a Fortnight's Physick.

LADY BOUNTIFUL. Come, Sir, your Servant has been telling me that you're apt to relapse if you go into Air—Your good Manners shan't get the better of ours—You shall sit down again, Sir—Come, Sir, we don't mind Ceremonies in the Country—Here, Sir, my Service t'ye—You shall taste my Water; 'tis a Cordial I can assure you, and of my own making—drink it off, Sir, (Aimwell *drinks.*) And how d'ye find your self now, Sir?

AIMWELL. Somewhat better—Tho' very faint still.

LADY BOUNTIFUL. Ay, ay, People are always faint after these Fits—Come Girls, you shall show the Gentleman the House, 'tis but an old Family Building, Sir, but you had better walk about and cool by Degrees than venture immediately into the Air—You'll find some tolerable Pictures—*Dorinda,* show the Gentleman the way. I must go to the poor Woman below.

Exit.

DORINDA. This way, Sir.

AIMWELL. Ladies shall I beg leave for my Servant to wait on you, for he understands Pictures very well.

MRS. SULLEN. Sir, we understand Originals, as well as he do's Pictures, so he may come along.

Exeunt Dorinda, Mrs. Sullen, Aimwell, Archer, Aimwell *leads* Dorinda.

Enter Foigard *and* Scrub *meeting.*

FOIGARD. Save you, Master *Scrub.*

SCRUB. Sir, I won't be sav'd your way—I hate a Priest, I abhor the *French,* and I defie the Devil—Sir, I'm a bold *Briton,* and will spill the last drop of my Blood to keep out Popery and Slavery.

FOIGARD. Master *Scrub,* you wou'd put me down in Politicks, and so I wou'd be speaking with Mrs. *Shipsey.*

SCRUB. Good Mr. Priest, you can't speak with her, she's sick, Sir she's gone abroad, Sir she's—dead two Months ago, Sir.

Enter Gipsey.

GIPSEY. How now, Impudence; how dare you talk so saucily to the Doctor? Pray, Sir, dont take it ill; for the Common-people of *England* are not so civil to Strangers, as—

SCRUB. You lie, you lie—'Tis the Common People that are civilest to Strangers.

GIPSEY. Sirrah, I have a good mind to—Get you out, I say.

SCRUB. I won't.

GIPSEY. You won't, Sauce-box—Pray, Doctor, what is the Captain's Name that came to your Inn last Night?

SCRUB. The Captain! Ah, the Devil, there she hampers me again;—The Captain has me on one side, and the Priest on t'other.—So between the Gown and Sword, I have a fine time on't.—But, *Cedunt Arma togae.*[62] *(Going.)*

GIPSEY. What, Sirrah, won't you march?

SCRUB. No, my Dear, I won't march—But I'll walk—And I'll make bold to listen a little too.

Goes behind the side-Scene,[63] *and listens.*

62. Cicero's *De officiis,* book 1, section 22: "Let arms yield to the gown."

63. Moveable scenery at the side of the stage.

GIPSEY. Indeed, Doctor, the Count has been barbarously treated, that's the Truth on't.

FOIGARD. Ah, Mrs. *Gipsey,* upon my shoul, now, *Gra,*° his Complainings wou'd mollifie the Marrow in your Bones, and move the Bowels of your Commiseration; he veeps, and he dances, and he fistles, and he swears, and he laughs, and he stamps, and he sings: In Conclusion, Joy, he's afflicted, *a la Francois,* and a Stranger wou'd not know whider to cry, or to laugh with him, dear

GIPSEY. What wou'd you have me do, Doctor?

FOIGARD. Noting, Joy, but only hide the Count in *Mrs. Sullen*'s Closet when it is dark.

GIPSEY. Nothing! Is that nothing? it wou'd be both a Sin and a shame, Doctor.

FOIGARD. Here are twenty *Lewidores,*[64] Joy, for your shame; and I will give you an Absolution for the Shin.

GIPSEY. But won't that Money look like a Bribe?

FOIGARD. Dat is according as you shall tauk it.—If you receive the Money beforehand, 'twill be a *Logicè*[65] a Bribe; but if you stay till afterwards, 'twill be, only a Gratification.

GIPSEY. Well, Doctor, I'll take it *Logicè.*—But what must I do with my Conscience, Sir?

FOIGARD. Leave dat wid me, Joy; I am your Priest, *Gra;* and your Conscience is under my Hands.

GIPSEY. But shou'd I put the Count into the Closet—

FOIGARD. Vel, is dere any Shin for a Man's being in a Closhet; one may go to Prayers in a Closhet.

GIPSEY. But if the Lady shou'd come into her Chamber, and go to Bed?

FOIGARD. Vel, and is dere any Shin in going to Bed, Joy?

GIPSEY. Ay, but if the Parties shou'd meet, Doctor?

FOIGARD. Vel den—The Parties must be responsible.—Do you be after putting the Count into the Closet; and leave the Shins wid themselves.—I will come with the Count to instruct you in your Chamber.

GIPSEY. Well, Doctor, your Religion is so pure—Methinks I'm so easie after an Absolution, and can sin afresh with so much security, that I'm resolv'd to die a Martyr to't.—Here's the Key of the Garden-door, in the back way, when 'tis late,—I'll be ready to receive you, but don't so much as whisper, only take hold of my Hand, I'll lead you, and do you lead the Count, and follow me.

Exeunt.

Enter Scrub.

64. Louis d'or, French gold coin.

65. In context it is clear Foigard means "logically" but the phrase is neither grammatical Latin nor French.

SCRUB. What Witchcraft now have these two Imps of the Devil been a hatching here? There's twenty *Lewidores,* I heard that, and saw the Purse: But I must give room to my Betters.

Enter Aimwell *leading* Dorinda, *and making Love in dumb Show*—Mrs. Sullen *and* Archer.

MRS. SULLEN. Pray, Sir, [*To* Archer.] how d'ye like that Piece?

ARCHER. O, 'tis *Leda*—You find, Madam, how *Jupiter* comes disguis'd to make Love[66]—

MRS. SULLEN. But what think you there of *Alexander*'s Battles?

ARCHER. We want only a *Le Brun,* Madam, to draw greater Battles, and a greater General of our own.—The *Danube,* Madam, wou'd make a greater Figure in a Picture than the *Granicus;* and we have our *Ramelies* to match their *Arbela.*[67]

MRS. SULLEN. Pray, Sir, what Head is that in the Corner there?

ARCHER. O, Madam, 'tis poor *Ovid* in his Exile.

MRS. SULLEN. What was he banish'd for?

ARCHER. His ambitious Love, Madam. *(Bowing.)* His Misfortune touches me.

MRS. SULLEN. Was he successful in his Amours?

ARCHER. There he has left us in the dark.—He was too much a Gentleman to tell.

MRS. SULLEN. If he were secret, I pity him.

ARCHER. And if he were successful, I envy him.

MRS. SULLEN. How d'ye like that *Venus* over the Chimney?

ARCHER. *Venus!* I protest, Madam, I took it for your Picture; but now I look again, 'tis not handsome enough.

MRS. SULLEN. Oh, what a Charm is Flattery! if you wou'd see my Picture, there it is, over that Cabinet;—How d'ye like it?

ARCHER. I must admire any thing, Madam, that has the least Resemblance of you—But, methinks, Madam—*(He looks at the Picture and* Mrs. Sullen, *three or four times, by turns.)* Pray, Madam, who drew it?

MRS. SULLEN. A famous Hand, Sir.

Here Aimwell *and* Dorinda *go off.*

ARCHER. A famous hand, Madam—Your Eyes, indeed, are featur'd there; but where's the sparkling Moisture shining fluid, in which they swim? The Picture indeed has your Dimples; but where's the Swarm of killing *Cupids* that shou'd ambush there? the Lips too are figur'd out; but where's the Carnation Dew, the pouting Ripeness, that tempts the Taste in the Original?

66. Jupiter (Zeus) comes to Leda in the form of a swan.

67. Charles Le Brun was a seventeenth-century French painter; in the 1660s he composed a series of paintings on Alexander that implicitly flattered Louis XIV. The general mentioned here is John Churchill, Duke of Marlborough, successful English commander at Ramillies and other battles of the War of the Spanish Succession.

MRS. SULLEN. Had it been my Lot to have match'd with such a Man!

[*Aside.*]

ARCHER. Your Breasts too, presumptuous Man! what! paint Heaven! *Apropo*[*s*], Madam, in the very next Picture is *Salmoneus* that was struck dead with Lightning, for offering to imitate *Jove*'s Thunder; I hope you serv'd the Painter so, Madam?
MRS. SULLEN. Had my Eyes the power of Thunder, they shou'd employ their Lightning better.
ARCHER. There's the finest Bed in that Room, Madam, I suppose 'tis your Ladyship's Bed-Chamber.
MRS. SULLEN. And what then, Sir?
ARCHER. I think the Quilt is the richest that I ever saw:—I can't at this Distance, Madam, distinguish the Figures of the Embroidery; will you give me leave, Madam—
MRS. SULLEN. The Devil take his Impudence.—Sure if I gave him an opportunity, he durst not offer it.—I have a great mind to try.—*(Going.) (Returns.)* S'death what am I doing?—And alone too! Sister, Sister?

Runs out.

ARCHER. I'll follow her close—
For where a French-man *durst attempt to storm,*
A Briton *sure may well the Work perform. (Going.)*

Enter Scrub.

SCRUB. *Martin,* Brother *Martin.*
ARCHER. O, Brother *Scrub,* I beg your Pardon, I was not a-going; here's a Guinea, my Master order'd you.
SCRUB. A Guinea, hi, hi, hi, a Guinea! eh—by this light it is a Guinea; but I suppose you expect One and twenty Shillings in change.
ARCHER. Not at all; I have another for *Gipsey.*
SCRUB. A Guinea for her! Faggot and Fire for the Witch.—Sir, give me that Guinea, and I'll discover a Plot.
ARCHER. A Plot!
SCRUB. Ay, Sir, a Plot, a horrid Plot.—First, it must be a Plot because there's a Woman in't; secondly, it must be a Plot because there's a Priest in't; thirdly, it must be a Plot because there's *French* gold in't; and fourthly, it must be a Plot, because I don't know what to make on't.
ARCHER. Nor any body else, I'm afraid, brother *Scrub.*
SCRUB. Truly I'm afraid so too; for where there's a Priest and a Woman, there's always a Mystery, and a Riddle.—This I know, that here has been the Doctor with a Temptation in one Hand, and an Absolution in the other; and *Gipsey* has sold her self to the Devil; I saw the Price paid down, my Eyes shall take their Oath on't.
ARCHER. And is all this bustle about *Gipsey?*

SCRUB. That's not all; I cou'd hear but a Word here and there; but I remember they mention'd a Count, a Closet, a back Door, and a Key.

ARCHER. The Count! did you hear nothing of Mrs. *Sullen?*

SCRUB. I did hear some word that sounded that way; but whether it was *Sullen* or *Dorinda,* I cou'd not distinguish.

ARCHER. You have told this matter to no Body, Brother?

SCRUB. Told! No, Sir, I thank you for that; I'm resolv'd never to speak one word *pro* nor *con,* till we have a Peace.

ARCHER. You're i'th right, Brother *Scrub;* here's a Treaty a foot between the Count and the Lady.—The Priest and the Chamber-maid are the Plenipotentiaries.—It shall go hard but I find a way to be included in the Treaty.—Where's the Doctor now?

SCRUB. He and *Gipsey* are this moment devouring my Lady's Marmalade in the Closet.

AIMWELL. *(From without.) Martin, Martin.*

ARCHER. I come, Sir, I come.

SCRUB. But you forgot the other Guinea, Brother *Martin.*

ARCHER. Here, I give it with all my Heart.

SCRUB. And I take it with all my Soul.

Exit Archer.

I'cod I'll spoil your Plotting, Mrs. *Gipsey;* and if you shou'd set the Captain upon me, these two Guineas will buy me off.

Exit.

Enter Mrs. Sullen *and* Dorinda *meeting.*

MRS. SULLEN. Well, Sister.

DORINDA. And well, Sister.

MRS. SULLEN. What's become, of my Lord?

DORINDA. What's become of his Servant?

MRS. SULLEN. Servant! he's a prettier Fellow, and a finer Gentleman by fifty Degrees than his Master.

DORINDA. O'my Conscience, I fancy you cou'd beg that Fellow at the Gallows-foot.[68]

MRS. SULLEN. O'my Conscience, I cou'd, provided I cou'd put a Friend of yours in his Room.

DORINDA. You desir'd me, Sister to leave you, when you transgress'd the Bounds of Honour.

MRS. SULLEN. Thou dear censorious Country-Girl—What dost mean? you can't think of the Man without the Bedfellow, I find.

DORINDA. I don't find any thing unnatural in that thought, while the Mind is conversant with Flesh and Blood, it must conform to the Humours of the Company.

68. Condemned criminals were sometimes spared when a woman agreed to marry the criminal.

MRS. SULLEN. How a little Love and good Company improves a Woman; why, Child, you begin to live—you never spoke before.

DORINDA. Because I was never spoke to.—My Lord has told me that I have more Wit and Beauty than any of my Sex; and truly I begin to think the Man is sincere.

MRS. SULLEN. You're in the right, *Dorinda,* Pride is the Life of the Woman, and Flattery is our daily Bread; and she's a Fool that won't believe a Man there, as much as she that believes him in any thing else—But I'll lay you a Guinea, that I had finer things said to me than you had.

DORINDA. Done—What did your Fellow say to'ye?

MRS. SULLEN. My Fellow took the Picture of *Venus* for mine.

DORINDA. But my Lover took me for *Venus* her self.

MRS. SULLEN. Common Cant! Had my Spark call'd me a *Venus* directly, I shou'd have believ'd him a Footman in good earnest.

DORINDA. But my Lover was upon his Knees to me.

MRS. SULLEN. And mine was upon his Tiptoes to me.

DORINDA. Mine vow'd to die for me,

MRS. SULLEN. Mine swore to die with me.

DORINDA. Mine spoke the softest moving things.

MRS. SULLEN. Mine had his moving things too.

DORINDA. Mine kiss'd my Hand Ten Thousand times.

MRS. SULLEN. Mine has all that Pleasure to come.

DORINDA. Mine offer'd Marriage.

MRS. SULLEN. O lard! D'ye call that a moving thing?

DORINDA. The sharpest Arrow in his Quiver, my dear Sister,—Why, my Ten thousand Pounds may lie brooding here these seven Years, and hatch nothing at last but some ill natur'd Clown like yours:—Whereas, If I marry my Lord *Aimwell,* there will be Title, Place and Precedence, the Park, the Play, and the drawing-Room, Splendor, Equipage, Noise and Flambeaux—Hey, my Lady *Aimwell*'s Servants there—Lights, Lights, to the Stairs—My Lady *Aimwell*'s Coach put forward—Stand by, make room for her Ladyship—Are not these things moving?—What! melancholly of sudden?

MRS. SULLEN. Happy, happy Sister! your Angel has been watchful for your Happiness, whilst mine has slept regardless of his Charge.—Long smiling Years of circling Joys for you but not onc Hour for me! *(Weeps.)*

DORINDA. Come, my Dear, we'll talk of something else.

MRS. SULLEN. O *Dorinda,* I own my self a Woman, full of my Sex, a gentle, generous Soul,—easie and yielding to soft Desires; a spacious Heart, where Love and all his Train might lodge. And must the fair Apartment of my Breast be made a Stable for a Brute to lie in?

DORINDA. Meaning your Husband, I suppose.

MRS. SULLEN. Husband! no,—Even Husband is too soft a Name for him.—But, come, I expect my Brother here to Night or to Morrow; he was abroad when my Father marry'd me; perhaps he'll find a way to make me easy.

DORINDA. Will you promise not to make your self easy in the mean time with my Lord's Friend?

MRS. SULLEN. You mistake me, Sister—It happens with us, as among the Men, the greatest Talkers are the greatest Cowards; and there's a Reason for it; those Spirits evaporate in prattle, which might do more Mischief if they took another Course;—Tho' to confess the Truth, I do love that Fellow;—And if I met him drest as he shou'd be, and I undrest as I shou'd be—Look'ye, Sister, I have no supernatural Gifts;—I can't swear I cou'd resist the Temptation,—tho' I can safely promise to avoid it; and that's as much as the best of us can do.

Exeunt Mrs. Sullen *and* Dorinda.

[ACT IV. SCENE II.]

[SCENE *changes to the Inn.*]
Enter Aimwell *and* Archer *laughing.*

ARCHER. And the awkward Kindness of the good motherly old Gentlewoman—

AIMWELL. And the coming Easiness of the young one—S'death, 'tis a pity to deceive her.

ARCHER. Nay, if you adhere to those Principles, stop where you are.

AIMWELL. I can't stop; for I love her to distraction.

ARCHER. S'death, if you love her a hair's breadth beyond discretion, you must go no farther.

AIMWELL. Well, well, any thing to deliver us from sauntering away our idle Evenings at White's, Tom's, or Will's, and be stinted to bear looking at our old Acquaintance, the Cards; because our impotent[69] Pockets can't afford us a Guinea for the mercenary Drabs.

ARCHER. Or be oblig'd to some Purse-proud Coxcomb for a scandalous Bottle, where we must not pretend to our share of the Discourse, because we can't pay our Club° o'th Reckoning;— dam it, I had rather spunge upon *Morris,* and sup upon a Dish of *Bohea* scor'd behind the Door.[70]

share

AIMWELL. And there expose our want of Sense by talking Criticisms, as we shou'd our want of Money by railing at the Government.

69. "importent" in Kenny.

70. Bohea is tea which the proprietor, Morris's Coffee House, would provide on credit ("scored behind the door") to be paid at some future time.

ARCHER. Or be oblig'd to sneak in the side-Box, and between both Houses steal two Acts of a Play, and because we han't Money to see the other three, we come away discontented, and damn the whole five.—[71]

AIMWELL. And Ten thousand such rascally Tricks,—had we outliv'd our Fortunes among our Acquaintance.—But now—

ARCHER. Ay, now is the time to prevent all this.—Strike while the Iron is hot.—This Priest is the luckiest part of our Adventure;—He shall marry you, and pimp for me.

AIMWELL. But I shou'd not like a Woman that can be so fond of a *Frenchman.*

ARCHER. Alas, Sir, Necessity has no Law; the Lady may be in Distress; perhaps she has a confounded Husband, and her Revenge may carry her farther than her Love.—I gad, I have so good an Opinion of her, and of my self, that I begin to fancy strange things; and we must say this for the Honour of our Women, and indeed of our selves, that they do stick to their Men, as they do to their *Magna Charta.*—If the Plot lies as I suspect,—I must put on the Gentleman.—But here comes the Doctor.—I shall be ready.

Exit.
Enter Foigard.

FOIGARD. Sauve you, noble Friend.

AIMWELL. O Sir, your Servant; pray Doctor, may I crave your Name?

FOIGARD. Fat Naam is upon me? My Naam is *Foigard,* Joy.

AIMWELL. *Foigard,* a very good name for a Clergyman: Pray, Doctor *Foigard,* were you ever in *Ireland?*

FOIGARD. *Ireland!* No Joy.—Fat sort of Plaace is dat saam *Ireland?* dey say de People are catcht dere when dey are young.

AIMWELL. And some of 'em when they're old;—as for Example. *(Takes* Foigard *by the Shoulder.)* Sir, I arrest you as a Traytor against the Government; you're a Subject of *England,* and this Morning shew'd me a Commission, by which you serv'd as Chaplain in the *French* Army: This is Death by our Law, and your Reverence must hang for't.[72]

FOIGARD. Upon my Shoul, Noble Friend, dis is strange News you tell me, Fader *Foigard* a Subject of *England,* de Son of a *Burgomaster* of *Brussels* a subject of *England!* Ubooboo—

71. Playgoers were not charged to enter the theater. Admission was collected after the first or second acts, so some members of the audience would stroll into the playhouse and not stay, not necessarily because they could not afford it.

72. As an Irishman Foigard is a subject of England, but Catholics were barred from serving in the British armed forces; some Irish Catholics served in Irish regiments in the French and Spanish armies. Moreover, as a priest Foigard faces draconian penal laws if found in Ireland.

AIMWELL. The Son of a Bogtrotter in *Ireland;* Sir, your Tongue will condemn you before any Bench in the Kingdom.

FOIGARD. And is my Tongue all your Evidensh, Joy?

AIMWELL. That's enough.

FOIGARD. No, no, Joy, for I vill never speak *English* no more.

AIMWELL. Sir, I have other Evidence—Here, *Martin,* you know this Fellow.

Enter Archer

ARCHER. *(In a Brogue.)* Saave you, my dear Cussen, how do's your Health?

FOIGARD. Ah! upon my Shoul dere is my Countryman, and his Brogue will hang mine. *(Aside.) Mynheer, Ick wet neat watt hey zacht, Ick universton ewe neat, sacramant.*[73]

AIMWELL. Altering your Language won't do, Sir, this Fellow knows your Person, and will swear to your Face.

FOIGARD. Faace! fey, is dear a Brogue upon my Faash, too?

ARCHER. Upon my Soulvation dere ish Joy—But Cussen *Mack-shane* vil you not put a remembrance upon me?

FOIGARD. *Mack-shane!* by St. *Paatrick,* dat is Naame, shure enough. *(Aside.)*

AIMWELL. I fancy *Archer,* you have it.

FOIGARD. The Devil hang you, Joy—By fat Acquaintance are you my Cussen?

ARCHER. O, de Devil hang your shelf, Joy, you know we were little Boys togeder upon de School, and your foster Moder's son was marry'd upon my Nurse's Chister, Joy, and so we are *Irish* Cussens.

FOIGARD. De Devil taak the Relation! vel, Joy, and fat School was it?

ARCHER. I tinks it vas—Aay—'Twas *Tipperary.*

FOIGARD. No, no, Joy, it was *Kilkenny.*

AIMWELL. That's enough for us—Self-confession—Come, Sir, we must deliver you into the Hands of the next Magistrate.

ARCHER. He sends you to Gaol, you're try'd next Assizes, and away you go swing into Purgatory.

FOIGARD. And is it so wid you, Cussen?

ARCHER. It vil be sho wid you Cussen, if you don't immediately confess the Secret between you and Mrs. Gipsey—Look'e, Sir, the Gallows or the Secret, take your Choice.

FOIGARD. The Gallows! upon my Shoul I hate that saam Gallow, for it is a Diseash dat is fatal to our Family—Vel den, dere is nothing, Shentlemens, but *Mrs. Shullen* wou'd spaak wid the *Count* in her Chamber at Midnight, and dere is no Haarm, Joy, for I am to conduct the *Count* to de Plash, my shelf.

73. Pidgin Flemish for, apparently, "I don't know what you say, I don't understand you, on the sacrament."

ARCHER. As I guess'd—Have you communicated the matter to the *Count?*

FOIGARD. I have not sheen him since.

ARCHER. Right agen; why then, Doctor,—you shall conduct me to the Lady instead of the *Count.*

FOIGARD. Fat my Cussen to the Lady! Upon my Shoul, gra, dat is too much upon the Brogue.

ARCHER. Come, come, Doctor, consider we have got a Rope about your Neck, and if you offer to squeek, we'll stop your Wind-pipe, most certainly, we shall have another Job for you in a Day or two, I hope.

AIMWELL. Here's Company coming this way, let's into my Chamber, and there concert our Affair farther.

ARCHER. Come, my dear Cussen, come along.

Exeunt.

Enter Bonniface, Hounslow, *and* Bagshot *at one Door,* Gibbet *at the opposite.*

GIBBET. Well, Gentlemen, 'tis a fine Night for our Enterprize.

HOUNSLOW. Dark as Hell.

BAGSHOT. And blows like the Devil; our Landlord here has show'd us the Window where we must break in, and tells us the Plate stands in the Wainscot Cupboard in the Parlour.

BONNIFACE. Ay, ay, Mr. *Bagshot,* as the saying is, Knives and Forks, and Cups, and Canns, and Tumblers, and Tankards—There's one Tankard, as the saying is, that's near upon as big as me, it was a Present to the Squire from his Godmother, and smells of Nutmeg and Toast like an *East India* Ship.

HOUNSLOW. Then you say we must divide at the Stair-head.

BONNIFACE. Yes, Mr. *Hounslow,* as the saying is—At one end of that Gallery lies my *Lady Bountiful* and her Daughter, and at the other *Mrs. Sullen*—As for the Squire—

GIBBET. He's safe enough, I have fairly enter'd him, and he's more than half seas over already—But such a Parcel of Scoundrels are got about him now, that, I gad I was asham'd to be seen in their Company.

BONNIFACE. 'Tis now Twelve, as the saying is—Gentlemen, you must set out at Onc.

GIBBET. *Hounslow,* do you and *Bagshot* see our Arms fix'd, and I'll come to you presently.

HOUNSLOW and BAGSHOT. We will.

Exeunt.

GIBBET. Well, my dear *Bonny,* you assure me that *Scrub* is a Coward.

BONNIFACE. A Chicken, as the saying is—You'll have no Creature to deal with but the Ladies.

GIBBET. And I can assure you, Friend, there's a great deal of Address and good Manners in robbing a Lady, I am the most a Gentleman that way that ever travell'd the Road—But, my dear *Bonny,* this Prize will be a Galleon, a *Vigo* business[74]—I warrant you we shall bring off three or four thousand Pound.

BONNIFACE. In Plate, Jewels and Money, as the saying is, you may.

GIBBET. Why then, *Tyburn,*[75] I defie thee, I'll get up to Town, sell off my Horse and Arms, buy my self some pretty Employment in the Household, and be as snug, and as honest as any Courtier of 'um all.

BONNIFACE. And what think you then of my Daughter *Cherry* for a Wife?

GIBBET. Look'ee, my dear *Bonny*—Cherry *is the Goddess I adore,* as the Song goes; but it is a Maxim that Man and Wife shou'd never have it in their Power to hang one another, for if they should, the Lord have Mercy upon them both.

Exeunt.

End of the Fourth Act.

ACT V. [SCENE I.]

SCENE continues. *Knocking without.*
Enter Bonniface.

BONNIFACE. Coming, coming—A Coach and six foaming Horses at this time o'Night! Some great Man, as the saying is, for he scorns to travel with other People.

Enter Sir Charles Freeman.

SIR CHARLES. What, Fellow! a Publick-house, and a Bed when other People Sleep.

BONNIFACE. Sir, I an't a Bed, as the saying is.

SIR CHARLES. Is Mr. *Sullen*'s Family a Bed, think'e?

BONNIFACE. All but the Squire himself, Sir, as the saying is, he's in the House.

SIR CHARLES. What Company has he?

BONNIFACE. Why, Sir, there's the Constable, Mr. *Gage* the Exciseman,° the Hunchback'd-barber, and two or three other Gentlemen. tax collector

SIR CHARLES. I find my Sister's Letters gave me the true Picture of her Spouse.

Enter Sullen, *Drunk.*

74. Two Spanish treasure ships were captured in Vigo Harbor in Spain in 1702.
75. The location where criminals were hanged.

BONNIFACE. Sir, here's the Squire.

SULLEN. The Puppies left me asleep—Sir.

SIR CHARLES. Well, Sir.

SULLEN. Sir, I'm an unfortunate Man—I have three thousand Pound a Year, and I can't get a Man to drink a Cup of Ale with me.

SIR CHARLES. That's very hard.

SULLEN. Ay, Sir—And unless you have pitty upon me, and smoke one Pipe with me, I must e'en go home to my Wife, and I had rather go to the Devil by half.

SIR CHARLES. But, I presume, Sir, you won't see your Wife to Night, she'll be gone to Bed—you don't use to lye with your Wife in that Pickle?

SULLEN. What! not lye with my Wife! why, Sir, do you take me for an Atheist or a Rake.

SIR CHARLES. If you hate her, Sir, I think you had better lye from her.

SULLEN. I think so too, Friend—But I'm a Justice of Peace, and must do nothing against the Law.

SIR CHARLES. Law! As I take it, Mr. Justice, no Body observes Law for Law's Sake, only for the good of those for whom it was made.

SULLEN. But if the Law orders me to send you to Gaol, you must ly there, my Friend.

SIR CHARLES. Not unless I commit a Crime to deserve it.

SULLEN. A Crime! Oons an't I marry'd?

SIR CHARLES. Nay, Sir, if you call Marriage a Crime, you must disown it for a Law.

SULLEN. Eh!—I must be acquainted with you, Sir—But, Sir, I shou'd be very glad to know the Truth of this Matter.

SIR CHARLES. Truth, Sir, is a profound Sea, and few there be that dare wade deep enough to find the bottom on't. Besides, Sir, I'm afraid the Line of your Understanding mayn't be long enough.

SULLEN. Looke, Sir, I have nothing to say to your Sea of Truth, but if a good Parcel of Land can intitle a Man to a little Truth, I have as much as any He in the Country.

BONNIFACE. I never heard your Worship, as the saying is, talk so much before.

SULLEN. Because I never met with a Man that I lik'd before—

BONNIFACE. Pray, Sir, as the saying is, let me ask you one Question, are not Man and Wife one Flesh?

SIR CHARLES. You and your Wife, Mr. Guts, may be one Flesh, because you are nothing else—but rational Creatures have minds that must be united.

SULLEN. Minds.

SIR CHARLES. Ay, Minds, Sir, don't you think that the Mind takes place of the Body?

SULLEN. In some People.

SIR CHARLES. Then the Interest of the Master must be consulted before that of his Servant.

SULLEN. Sir, you shall dine with me to Morrow.—Oons, I always thought that we were naturally one.

SIR CHARLES. Sir, I know that my two Hands are naturally one, because they love one another, kiss one another, help one another in all Actions of Life, but I cou'd not say so much, if they were always at Cuffs.

SULLEN. Then 'tis plain that we are two.

SIR CHARLES. Why don't you part with her, Sir?

SULLEN. Will you take her, Sir?

SIR CHARLES. With all my Heart.

SULLEN. You shall have her to Morrow Morning, and a Venison-pasty into the Bargain.

SIR CHARLES. You'll let me have her Fortune too?

SULLEN. Fortune! why, Sir, I have no Quarrel at her Fortune—I hate only the Woman, Sir, and none but the Woman shall go.

SIR CHARLES. But her Fortune, Sir—

SULLEN. Can you play at Whist, Sir?

SIR CHARLES. No, truly, Sir.

SULLEN. Not at All-fours.

SIR CHARLES. Neither!

SULLEN. Oons! where was this Man bred. *(Aside.)* Burn me, Sir, I can't go home, 'tis but two a Clock.

SIR CHARLES. For half an Hour, Sir, if you please—But you must consider 'tis late.

SULLEN. Late! that's the Reason I can't go to Bed—Come, Sir.—

Exeunt.

Enter Cherry, *runs across the Stage and knocks at* Aimwell's *Chamber-door.*

Enter Aimwell *in his Night-cap and Gown.*

AIMWELL. What's the matter, you tremble, Child, you're frighted.

CHERRY. No wonder, Sir—But in short, Sir, this very Minute a Gang of Rogues are gone to rob my *Lady Bountiful*'s House.

AIMWELL. How!

CHERRY. I dogg'd 'em to the very Door, and left 'em breaking in.

AIMWELL. Have you alarm'd any Body else with the News.

CHERRY. No, no, Sir, I wanted to have discover'd the whole Plot, and twenty other things to your Man *Martin;* but I have search'd the whole House and can't find him; where is he?

AIMWELL. No matter, Child, will you guide me immediately to the House?

CHERRY. With all my Heart, Sir, my *Lady Bountiful* is my Godmother; and I love Mrs. *Dorinda* so well.—

AIMWELL. *Dorinda!* The Name inspires me, the Glory and the Danger shall be all my own.—Come, my Life, let me but get my Sword.

Exeunt.

[ACT V. SCENE II.]

SCENE, *Changes to a Bed-chamber in* Lady Bountiful*'s House. Enter* Mrs. Sullen, Dorinda, *undress'd, a Table and Lights.*

DORINDA. 'Tis very late, Sister, no News of your Spouse yet?

MRS. SULLEN. No, I'm condemn'd to be alone till towards four, and then perhaps I may be executed with his Company.

DORINDA. Well, my Dear, I'll leave you to your rest; you'll go directly to Bed, I suppose.

MRS. SULLEN. I don't know what to do? hey-hoe.

DORINDA. That's a desiring Sigh, Sister.

MRS. SULLEN. This is a languishing Hour, Sister.

DORINDA. And might prove a Critical Minute, if the pretty Fellow were here.

MRS. SULLEN. Here! what, in my Bed-chamber, at two a Clock o'th' Morning, I undress'd, the Family asleep, my hated Husband abroad, and my lovely Fellow at my Feet—O gad, Sister!

DORINDA. Thoughts are free, Sister, and them I allow you—So, my Dear, good Night.

[*Exit.*]

MRS. SULLEN. A good Rest to my dear *Dorinda*—Thoughts are free! are they so? why then suppose him here, dress'd like a youthful, gay, and burning Bridegroom, *(Here Archer steals out of the closet.)* with Tongue enchanting, Eyes bewitching, Knees imploring. *(Turns a little o' one side, and sees* Archer *in the Posture she describes.)* Ah! *(Shreeks, and runs to the other Side of the Stage.)* Have my Thoughts rais'd a Spirit?—What are you, Sir, a Man or a Devil?

ARCHER. A Man, a Man, Madam. *(Rising.)*

MRS. SULLEN. How shall I be sure of it?

ARCHER. Madam, I'll give you Demonstration this Minute. *(Takes her Hand.)*

MRS. SULLEN. What, Sir! do you intend to be rude?

ARCHER. Yes, Madam, if you please.

MRS. SULLEN. In the Name of Wonder, Whence came ye?

ARCHER. From the Skies, Madam—I'm *Jupiter* in Love, and you shall be my *Alcmena.*[76]

MRS. SULLEN. How came you in?

ARCHER. I flew in at the Window, Madam your Cozen *Cupid* lent me his Wings, and your Sister *Venus* open'd the Casement.

MRS. SULLEN. I'm struck dumb with Admiration.° amazement

ARCHER. And I with wonder. *(Looks passionately at her.)*

76. Zeus, disguised as Alcmena's husband, Amphitryon, slept with Alcmena; the resulting child was Hercules.

MRS. SULLEN. What will become of me?

ARCHER. How beautiful she looks—The teeming Jolly Spring Smiles in her blooming Face, and when she was conceiv'd, her Mother smelt to Roses, look'd on Lilies—

Lillies unfold their white, their fragrant Charms,
When the warm Sun thus Darts into their Arms. (Runs to her.)

MRS. SULLEN. Ah! *(Shreeks.)*

ARCHER. Oons, Madam, what d'ye mean? you'll raise the House.

MRS. SULLEN. Sir, I'll wake the Dead before I'll bear this—What! approach me with the Freedom of a Keeper; I'm glad on't, your Impudence has cur'd me.

ARCHER. If this be Impudence *(Kneels.)* I leave to your partial self; no panting Pilgrim after a tedious, painful Voyage, e'er bow'd before his Saint with more Devotion.

MRS. SULLEN. Now, now, I'm ruin'd if he kneels! *(Aside.)* rise, thou prostrate Ingineer, not all thy undermining Skill shall reach my Heart.[77]—Rise, and know, I am a Woman without my Sex, I can love to all the Tenderness of Wishes, Sighs and Tears—But go no farther—Still to convince you that I'm more than Woman, I can speak my Frailty, confess my Weakness even for you—But—

ARCHER. For me! *(Going to lay bold on her.)*

MRS. SULLEN. Hold, Sir, build not upon that—For my most mortal hatred follows if you disobey what I command you now—leave me this Minute—If he denies, I'm lost. *(Aside.)*

ARCHER. Then you'll promise—

MRS. SULLEN. Any thing another time.

ARCHER. When shall I come?

MRS. SULLEN. To Morrow when you will,

ARCHER. Your Lips must seal the Promise.

MRS. SULLEN. Pshaw!

ARCHER. They must, they must *(Kisses her.)* Raptures and Paradice! and why not now, my Angel? the Time, the Place, Silence and Secresy, all conspire—And now the conscious Stars have pre-ordain'd this Moment for my Happiness. *(Takes her in his Arms.)*

MRS. SULLEN. You will not, cannot sure.

ARCHER. If the Sun rides fast, and disappoints not Mortals of to Morrow's Dawn, this Night shall crown my Joys.

MRS. SULLEN. My Sex's Pride assist me.

ARCHER. My Sex's Strength help me.

MRS. SULLEN. You shall kill me first.

ARCHER. I'll dye with you. *(Carrying her off.)*

MRS. SULLEN. Thieves, Thieves, Murther—

Enter Scrub, *in his Breeches, and one Shoe.*

SCRUB. Thieves, Thieves, Murther, Popery.

77. Military engineers attempt to undermine the enemies' fortifications.

ARCHER. Ha! the very timorous Stag will kill in rutting time. (*Draws and offers to Stab* Scrub)

SCRUB. *(Kneeling.)* O Pray, Sir, spare all I have and take my Life.

MRS. SULLEN. *(Holding* Archer*'s Hand.)* What do's the Fellow mean?

SCRUB. O, Madam, down upon your Knees, your Marrow-bones—He's one of 'um.

MRS. SULLEN. Of whom?

SCRUB. One of the Rogues—I beg your Pardon, Sir, one of the honest Gentlemen that just now are broke into the House.

ARCHER. How!

MRS. SULLEN. I hope, you did not come to rob me?

ARCHER. Indeed I did, Madam, but I wou'd have taken nothing but what you might ha' spar'd, but your crying Thieves has wak'd this dreaming Fool, and so he takes 'em for granted.

SCRUB. Granted! 'tis granted, Sir take all we have.

MRS. SULLEN. The Fellow looks as if he were broke out of *Bedlam.*

SCRUB. Oons, Madam, they're broke in to the House with Fire and Sword, I saw them, heard them, they'll be here this Minute.

ARCHER. What, Thieves!

SCRUB. Under Favour, Sir, I think so.

MRS. SULLEN. What shall we do, Sir?

ARCHER. Madam, I wish your Ladyship a good Night.

MRS. SULLEN. Will you leave me?

ARCHER. Leave you! Lord, Madam, did not you command me to be gone just now upon pain of your immortal Hatred.

MRS. SULLEN. Nay, but pray, Sir—*(Takes hold of him.)*

ARCHER. Ha, ha, ha, now comes my turn to be ravish'd.—You see now, Madam, you must use Men one way or other; but take this by the way, good Madam, that none but a Fool will give you the benefit of his Courage, unless you'll take his Love along with it.—How are they arm'd, Friend?

SCRUB. With Sword and Pistol, Sir.

ARCHER. Hush—I see a dark Lanthorn coming thro' the Gallery.—Madam, be assur'd I will protect you, or lose my Life.

MRS. SULLEN. Your Life! No, Sir, they can rob me of nothing that I value half so much; therefore, now, Sir, let me intreat you to be gone.

ARCHER. No, Madam, I'll consult my own Safety for the sake of yours, I'll work by Stratagem: Have you Courage enough to stand the appearance of 'em?

MRS. SULLEN. Yes, yes, since I have scap'd your Hands, I can face any thing.

ARCHER. Come hither, Brother *Scrub;* don't you know me?

SCRUB. Eh! my dear Brother, let me kiss thee. (*Kisses* Archer.)

ARCHER. This way—Here (Archer *and* Scrub *hide behind the Bed.*)

Enter Gibbet *with a dark Lanthorn in one Hand and a Pistol in t'other.*

GIBBET. Ay, ay, this is the Chamber, and the Lady alone.

MRS. SULLEN. Who are you, Sir? what wou'd you have? d'ye come to rob me?

GIBBET. Rob you! alack a day, Madam, I'm only a younger Brother, Madam; and so, Madam, if you make a Noise, I'll shoot you through the Head; but don't be afraid, Madam. *(Laying his Lanthorn and Pistol upon the Table.)* These Rings, Madam, don't be concern'd, Madam, I have a profound Respect for you, Madam; your Keys, Madam, don't be frighted, Madam, I'm the most of a Gentleman *(Searching her Pockets.)* This Necklace, Madam, I never was rude to a Lady;—I have a Veneration—for this Necklace—

Here Archer *having come round and seiz'd the Pistol, takes* Gibbet *by the Collar, trips up his Heels, and claps the Pistol to his Breast.*

ARCHER. Hold, profane Villain, and take the Reward of thy Sacrilege.

GIBBET. Oh! Pray, Sir, don't kill me; I an't prepar'd.

ARCHER. How many are there of 'em, *Scrub?*

SCRUB. Five and Forty, Sir.

ARCHER. Then I must kill the Villain, to have him out of the way.

GIBBET. Hold, hold, Sir, we are but three, upon my Honour.

ARCHER. *Scrub,* will you undertake to secure him?

SCRUB. Not I, Sir, kill him, kill him.

ARCHER. Run to *Gipsey's* Chamber, there you'll find the Doctor; bring him hither presently.

Exit Scrub *running.*

Come, Rogue, if you have a short Prayer, say it.

GIBBET. Sir, I have no Prayer at all; the Government has provided a Chaplain to say Prayers for us on these Occasions.

MRS. SULLEN. Pray, Sir, don't kill him;—You fright me as much as him.

ARCHER. The Dog shall die, Madam, for being the Occasion of my disappointment.—Sirrah, this Moment is your last.

GIBBET. Sir, I'll give you Two hundred Pound to spare my Life.

ARCHER. Have you no more Rascal?

GIBBET. Yes, Sir, I can command Four hundred; but I must reserve Two of 'em to save my Life at the Sessions.

Enter Scrub *and* Foigard.

ARCHER. Here, Doctor, I suppose *Scrub* and you between you may manage him.—Lay hold of him, Doctor. (Foigard *lays hold of* Gibbet.)

GIBBET. What! turn'd over to the Priest already.—Look'ye, Doctor, you come before your time; I'ant condemn'd yet, I thank'ye.

FOIGARD. Come, my dear Joy, I vill secure your Body and your shoul too; I vill make you a good *Catholick,* and give you an Absolution.

GIBBET. Absolution! can you procure me a Pardon, Doctor?

FOIGARD. No, Joy.—

GIBBET. Then you and your Absolution may go to the Devil.

ARCHER. Convey him into the Cellar, there bind him:—Take the Pistol, and, if he offers to resist, shoot him thro' the Head,—and come back to us with all the speed you can.

SCRUB. Ay, ay, come, Doctor, do you hold him fast, and I'll guard him.

MRS. SULLEN. But how came the Doctor?

ARCHER. In short, Madam—*(Shreeking without.)* S'death! the Rogues are at work with the other Ladies.—I'm vex'd I parted with the Pistol; but must fly to their Assistance.—Will you stay here, Madam, or venture your self with me?

MRS. SULLEN. Oh, with you, dear Sir, with you.

Takes him by the arm and Exeunt.

[ACT V. SCENE III.]

SCENE, *Changes to another Apartment in the same House.*
Enter Bagshot *dragging in* Lady Bountiful, *and* Hounslow *halling in* Dorinda; *the Rogues with Swords drawn.*

HOUNSLOW. Come, come, your Jewels, Mistriss.

BAGSHOT. Your Keys, your Keys, old Gentlewoman.

Enter Aimwell *and* Cherry.

AIMWELL. Turn this way, Villains; I durst engage an Army in such a Cause. *(He engages 'em both.)*

DORINDA. O, Madam, had I but a Sword to help the brave Man?

LADY BOUNTIFUL. There's three or four hanging up in the Hall; but they won't draw. I'll go fetch one however.

Exit.
Enter Archer and *Mrs. Sullen.*

ARCHER. Hold, hold, my Lord, every Man his Bird, pray.

They engage Man to Man, the Rogues are thrown and disarm'd

CHERRY. What! the Rogues taken! then they'll impeach my Father; I must give him timely Notice.

Runs out.

ARCHER. Shall we kill the Rogues?

AIMWELL. No, no we'll bind them.

ARCHER. Ay, ay; here, Madam, lend me your Garter? *(To* Mrs. Sullen *who stands by him.)*

MRS. SULLEN. The Devil's in this Fellow; he fights, loves, and banters, all in a Breath.—Here's a Cord that the Rogues brought with 'em, I suppose.

ARCHER. Right, right, the Rogue's Destiny, a Rope to hang himself.—Come, my Lord,—This is but a scandalous sort of an Office, *(Binding the Rogues together.)* If our Adventures shou'd end in this sort of Hangman-work; but I hope there is something in prospect that—

Enter Scrub.

Well, *Scrub,* have you secur'd your *Tartar?*[78]

SCRUB. Yes, Sir, I left the Priest and him disputing about Religion.

AIMWELL. And pray carry these Gentlemen to reap the Benefit of the Controversy.

Delivers the prisoners to Scrub, *who leads them out.*

MRS. SULLEN. Pray, Sister, how came my Lord here?

DORINDA. And pray, how came the Gentleman here?

MRS. SULLEN. I'll tell you the great piece of Villainy *(They talk in dumb show.)*

AIMWELL. I fancy, *Archer,* you have been more successful in your Adventures than the House-breakers.

ARCHER. No matter for my Adventure, yours is the principal.—Press her this Minute to marry you,—now while she's hurry'd between the Palpitation of her Fear, and the Joy of her Deliverance, now while the Tide of her Spirits are at High-flood—Throw your self at her Feet; speak some *Romantick* Nonsense or other;—Address her like *Alexander* in the height of his Victory, confound her Senses, bear down her Reason, and away with her—The Priest is now in the Cellar, and dares not refuse to do the work.

Enter Lady Bountiful.

AIMWELL. But how shall I get off without being observ'd?

ARCHER. You a Lover! and not find a way to get off—Let me see.

AIMWELL. You bleed, *Archer.*

ARCHER. S'death, I'm glad on't; this Wound will do the Business—I'll amuse the old Lady and Mrs. *Sullen* about dressing my Wound, while you carry off *Dorinda.*

LADY BOUNTIFUL. Gentlemen, cou'd we understand how you wou'd be gratified for the Services—

78. The Tartars were Mongolian (or Turkish) tribesmen who pillaged central Europe in the Middle Ages, and hence metaphorically any brigands.

ARCHER. Come, come, my Lady, this is no time for Complements; I'm wounded, Madam.

LADY BOUNTIFUL. / MRS. SULLEN. How! wounded!

DORINDA. I hope, Sir, you have receiv'd no Hurt?

AIMWELL. None but what you may cure.—*(Makes love in dumb show.)*

LADY BOUNTIFUL. Let me see your Arm, Sir.—I must have some Powder-sugar to stop the Blood—O me! an ugly Gash upon my Word, Sir, you must go into Bed.

ARCHER. Ay, my Lady a Bed wou'd do very well.—Madam, (*To* Mrs. Sullen.) Will you do me the Favour to conduct me to a Chamber.

LADY BOUNTIFUL. Do, do, Daughter—while I get the Lint and the Probe and the Plaister ready.

Runs out one way, Aimwell *carries off* Dorinda *another.*

ARCHER. Come, Madam, why don't you obey your Mother's Commands.

MRS. SULLEN. How can you, after what is past, have the Confidence to ask me?

ARCHER. And if you go to that, how can you, after what is past, have the Confidence to deny me?—Was not this Blood shed in your Defence, and my Life expos'd for your Protection.—Look'ye, Madam, I'm none of your *Romantick* Fools, that fight Gyants and Monsters for nothing; my Valour is down right *Swiss;* I'm a Soldier of Fortune and must be paid.[79]

MRS. SULLEN. 'Tis ungenerous in you, Sir, to upbraid me with your Services.

ARCHER. 'Tis ungenerous in you, Madam, not to reward 'em.

MRS. SULLEN. How! at the Expence of my Honour.

ARCHER. Honour! Can Honour consist with Ingratitude? If you wou'd deal like a Woman of Honour, do like a Man of Honour, d'ye think I wou'd deny you in such a Case?

Enter a Servant.

SERVANT. Madam, my Lady order'd me to tell you that your Brother is below at the gate?

MRS. SULLEN. My brother? Heavens be prais'd. Sir, he shall thank you for your Services, he has it in his Power.

ARCHER. Who is your Brother, Madam?

MRS. SULLEN. *Sir Charles Freeman.*—You'll excuse me, Sir; I must go and receive him.

[*Exit.*]

79. Swiss soldiers were highly prized mercenaries.

ARCHER. *Sir Charles Freeman!* S'death and Hell!—My old Acquaintance. Now unless *Aimwell* has made good use of his time, all our fair Machine goes souse into the Sea like the *Edistone.*[80]

[ACT V. SCENE IV.]

SCENE, *Changes to the Gallery in the same House.*
Enter Aimwell *and* Dorinda.

DORINDA. Well, well, my Lord, you have conquer'd; your late generous Action will I hope, plead for my easie yielding, tho' I must own your Lordship had a Friend in the Fort before.
AIMWELL. The sweets of *Hybla*[81] dwell upon her Tongue.—

Enter Foigard *with a Book.*

Here, Doctor—
FOIGARD. Are you prepar'd boat?
DORINDA. I'm ready: But first, my Lord one Word;—I have a frightful Example of a hasty Marriage in my own Family; when I reflect upon't, it shocks me. Pray, my Lord, consider a little—
AIMWELL. Consider? Do you doubt my Honour or my Love?
DORINDA. Neither: I do believe you equally Just as Brave.—And were your whole Sex drawn out for me to chuse, I shou'd not cast a look upon the Multitude if you were absent.—But my Lord, I'm a Woman; Colours, Concealments may hide a thousand Faults in me;—Therefore know me better first; I hardly dare affirm I know my self in any thing except my Love.
AIMWELL. Such Goodness who cou'd injure; I find my self unequal to the Task of Villain; she has gain'd my Soul, and made it honest like her own;—I cannot hurt her. *(Aside.)* Doctor retire.

Exit Foigard.

Madam, behold your Lover and your Proselite, and judge of my Passion by my Conversion.—I'm all a Lie, nor dare I give a Fiction to your Arms; I'm all Counterfeit, except my Passion.
DORINDA. Forbid it Heaven! a Counterfeit!
AIMWELL. I am no Lord, but a poor needy Man, come with a mean, a scandalous Design to prey upon your Fortune:—But the Beauties of your Mind and Person have so won me from my self, that like a trusty Servant, I prefer the Interest of my Mistress to my own.
DORINDA. Sure I have had the Dream of some poor Mariner, a sleepy image of a welcome Port, and wake involv'd in Storms. Pray, Sir, who are you?

80. A lighthouse destroyed by a great storm in 1703.
81. A mountain in Sicily, famous for its honey.

AIMWELL. Brother to the Man whose Title I usurp'd, but Stranger to his Honour or Fortune.

DORINDA. Matchless Honesty—Once I was proud, Sir, of your Wealth and Title, but now am prouder that you want it: Now I can shew my Love was justly levell'd, and had no Aim but Love. Doctor, come in.

Enter Foigard *at one Door,* Gipsey *at another, who whispers* Dorinda.

Your pardon, Sir, we shannot want you now, Sir? you must excuse me,—I'll wait on you presently.

Exit with Gipsey.

FOIGARD. Upon my Shoul, now, dis is foolish.

Exit.

AIMWELL. Gone! and bid the Priest depart.—It has an ominous Look.

Enter Archer.

ARCHER. Courage, *Tom*—Shall I wish you Joy?

AIMWELL. No.

ARCHER. Oons, Man, what ha' you been doing?

AIMWELL. O, *Archer,* my Honesty, I fear has ruin'd me.

ARCHER. How!

AIMWELL. I have discover'd my self.

ARCHER. Discover'd! and without my Consent? what! have I embark'd my small Remains in the same bottom with yours, and you dispose of all without my Partnership?

AIMWELL. O, *Archer,* I own my Fault.

ARCHER. After Conviction—'Tis then too late for Pardon.—You may remember, Mr. *Aimwell,* that you propos'd this Folly—As you begun, so end it.—Henceforth I'll hunt my Fortune single.—So farewel.

AIMWELL. Stay, my dear *Archer,* but a Minute.

ARCHER. Stay! what to be despis'd, expos'd and laugh'd at—No, I wou'd sooner change Conditions with the worst of the Rogues we just now bound, than bear one scornful Smile from the proud Knight that once I treated as my equal.

AIMWELL. What Knight?

ARCHER. *Sir Charles Freeman,* Brother to the Lady that I had almost—But no matter for that, 'tis a cursed Night's Work, and so I leave you to make your best on't. *(Going.)*

AIMWELL. *Freeman!*—One Word, *Archer.* Still I have Hopes; methought she receiv'd my Confession with Pleasure.

ARCHER. S'death! who doubts it?

AIMWELL. She consented after to the Match; and still I dare believe she will be just.

ARCHER. To her self, I warrant her, as you shou'd have been.
AIMWELL. By all my Hopes, she comes, and smiling comes.

Enter Dorinda *mighty gay.*

DORINDA. Come, my dear Lord,—I fly with Impatience to your arms.—The Minutes of my Absence was a tedious Year. Where's this tedious Priest?

Enter Foigard.

ARCHER. Oons, a brave Girl.
DORINDA. I suppose, my Lord, this Gentleman is privy to our Affairs?
ARCHER. Yes, yes, Madam, I'm to be your Father.
DORINDA. Come, Priest, do your Office.
ARCHER. Make hast, make hast, couple 'em any way. *(Takes* Aimwell's *Hand.)* Come, Madam, I'm to give you—
DORINDA. My Mind's alter'd, I won't.
ARCHER. Eh—
AIMWELL. I'm confounded.
FOIGARD. Upon my Shoul, and sho is my shelf.
ARCHER. What's the matter now, Madam?
DORINDA. Look'ye, Sir, one generous Action deserves another—This Gentleman's Honour oblig'd him to hide nothing from me; my Justice engages me to conceal nothing from him: In short, Sir, you are the Person that you thought you counterfeited; you are the true Lord Viscount *Aimwell;* and I wish your Lordship Joy. Now, Priest, you may be gone; if my Lord is pleas'd now with the Match, let his Lordship marry me in the face of the World.
AIMWELL. *Archer,* What do's she mean?
DORINDA. Here's a Witness for my Truth.

Enter Sir Charles *and* Mrs. Sullen.

SIR CHARLES. My dear Lord *Aimwell,* I wish you Joy.
AIMWELL. Of what?
SIR CHARLES. Of your Honour and Estate: Your Brother died the Day before I left *London;* and all your Friends have writ after you to *Brussels;* among the rest I did my self the Honour.
ARCHER. Hark'ye, Sir Knight, don't you banter now?
SIR CHARLES. 'Tis Truth, upon my Honour.
AIMWELL. Thanks to the pregnant Stars that form'd this Accident.
ARCHER. Thanks to the Womb of Time that brought it forth; away with it.
AIMWELL. Thanks to my Guardian Angel that led me to the Prize—

(Taking Dorinda's *Hand.)*

ARCHER. And double Thanks to the noble *Sir Charles Freeman.* My Lord, I wish you Joy. My Lady I wish you Joy.—I gad, *Sir Charles,* you're the honestest Fellow living.—S'death, I'm grown strangely airy upon this matter—My lord, how d'ye—a word, my Lord; don't you remember something of a previous Agreement, that entitles me to the Moyety of this Lady's Fortune, which, I think will amount to Five thousand Pound.

AIMWELL. Not a Penny, *Archer;* You wou'd ha' cut my Throat just now, because I wou'd not deceive this Lady.

ARCHER. Ay, and I'll cut you Throat again, if you shou'd deceive her now.

AIMWELL. That's what I expected; and to end the Dispute, the Lady's Fortune is Ten thousand Pounds; we'll divide Stakes; take the Ten thousand Pound, or the Lady.

DORINDA. How! is your Lordship so indifferent.

ARCHER. No, no, no, Madam, his Lordship knows very well, that I'll take the Money; I leave you to his Lordship, and so we're both provided for.

Enter Count Bellair.

COUNT. *Mesdames, & M[e]ssieurs,* I am your Servant trice humble; I hear you be rob, here.

AIMWELL. The Ladies have been in some danger, Sir.

COUNT. And Begar, our Inn be rob too.

AIMWELL. Our Inn? by whom?

COUNT. By the Landlord, begar—Garzoon he has rob himself and run away.

ARCHER. Rob'd himself!

COUNT. Ay, begar, and me too of a hundre Pound.

ARCHER. A hundred Pound.

COUNT. Yes, that I ow'd him.

AIMWELL. Our Money's, gone, *Frank.*

ARCHER. Rot the Money, my Wench is gone—*Scavez vous quelque chose de Mademoiselle* Cherry?[82]

Enter a Fellow *with a strong Box and a Letter.*

FELLOW. Is there one *Martin* here?

ARCHER. Ay, Ay, who wants him?

FELLOW. I have a Box here and Letter for him.

ARCHER. *(Taking the Box.)* Ha, ha, ha, what's here? *Legedermain!* by this Light, my Lord, our Money again; but this unfolds the Riddle. *(Opening the Letter, reads.)* Hum, hum, hum—O, 'tis for the Publick good, and must be communicated to the Company.

Mr. Martin

My Father being afraid of an Impeachment by the Rogues that are taken to Night is gone off, but if you can

82. Faulty French for "Have you seen anything of Miss Cherry?"

procure him a Pardon he will make great Discoveries that may be useful to the Country; cou'd I have met you instead of your Master to Night, I wou'd have deliver'd my self into your Hands with a Sum that much exceeds that in your strong Box, which I have sent you, with an Assurance to my dear Martin, *that I shall ever be his most faithful Friend till Death.*

CHERRY BONNIFACE

there's a *Billet-doux* for you—As for the Father I think he ought to be encourag'd, and for the Daughter,—Pray, my Lord, persuade your Bride to take her into Service instead of *Gipsey.*

AIMWELL. I can assure you, Madam, your Deliverance was owing to her Discovery.

DORINDA. Your Command, my Lord, will do without the Obligation. I'll take care of her.

SIR CHARLES. This good Company meets opportunely in favour of a Design I have in behalf of my unfortunate Sister, I intend to part her from her Husband—Gentleman will you assist me?

ARCHER. Assist you? S'Death who wou'd not.

COUNT. Assist! Garzoon, we all assest.

Enter Sullen.

SULLEN. What's all this?—They tell me Spouse that you had like to have been rob'd.

MRS. SULLEN. Truly, Spouse, I was pretty near it—Had not these two Gentlemen interpos'd.

SULLEN. How came these Gentlemen here?

MRS. SULLEN. That's his way of returning Thanks you must know.

COUNT. Garzoon, the Question be *a-propo*[*s*] for all dat.

SIR CHARLES. You promis'd last Night, Sir, that you wou'd deliver your Lady to me this Morning.

SULLEN. Humph.

ARCHER. Humph. What do you mean by humph—Sir, you shall deliver her—In short, Sir, we have sav'd you and your Family, and if you are not civil we'll unbind the Rogues, join with 'um, and set fire to your House—What do's the Man mean? Not part with his Wife!

COUNT. Ay, Garzoon de Man no understan Common Justice.

MRS. SULLEN. Hold, Gentlemen, all things here must move by consent. Compulsion wou'd Spoil us, let my Dear and I talk the matter over, and you shall judge it between us.

SULLEN. Let me know first, who are to be our Judges—Pray, sir, who are you?

SIR CHARLES. I am *Sir Charles Freeman,* to come to take away your Wife.

SULLEN. And you, good Sir?

AIMWELL. *Charles Viscount Aimwell,* come to take away your Sister.

SULLEN. And you pray, Sir?

ARCHER. *Francis Archer,* Esq; come—

SULLEN. To take away my Mother, I hope—Gentlemen, you're heartily welcome, I never met with three more obliging People since I was born—And now, my Dear, if you please, you shall have the first word.

ARCHER. And the last for five Pound.

MRS. SULLEN. Spouse.

SULLEN. Ribb.

MRS. SULLEN. How long have you been marry'd?

SULLEN. By the Almanak, fourteen Months—But by my Account fourteen years.

MRS. SULLEN. 'Tis thereabout by my reckoning.

COUNT. Garzoon, their Account will agree.

MRS. SULLEN. Pray, Spouse, what did you marry for?

SULLEN. To get an Heir to my Estate.

SIR CHARLES. And have you succeeded?

SULLEN. No.

ARCHER. The Condition fails of his side—Pray, Madam, what did you marry for?

MRS. SULLEN. To support the Weakness of my Sex by the Strength of his, and to enjoy the Pleasures of an agreeable Society.

SIR CHARLES. Are your Expectations answer'd?

MRS. SULLEN. No.

COUNT. A clear Case, a clear Case.

SIR CHARLES. What are the Bars to your mutual Contentment?

MRS. SULLEN. In the first Place I can't drink Ale with him.

SULLEN. Nor can I drink Tea with her.

MRS. SULLEN. I can't hunt with you.

SULLEN. Nor can I dance with you.

MRS. SULLEN. I hate Cocking and Racing.

SULLEN. I abhor Ombre° and Piquet.° — fashionable card games

MRS. SULLEN. Your Silence is intollerable.

SULLEN. Your Prating is worse.

MRS. SULLEN. Have we not been a perpetual Offence to each other—A gnawing Vulture at the Heart?

SULLEN. A frightful Goblin to the Sight.

MRS. SULLEN. A Porcupine to the Feeling.

SULLEN. Perpetual Wormwood to the Taste.

MRS. SULLEN. Is there on Earth a thing we cou'd agree in?

SULLEN. Yes—To part.

MRS. SULLEN. With all my Heart,

SULLEN. Your Hand.

MRS. SULLEN. Here.

SULLEN. These Hands join'd us, these shall part us—away—

MRS. SULLEN. North.

SULLEN. South

MRS. SULLEN. East.

SULLEN. West—far as the Poles asunder.

COUNT. Begar the Ceremony be vera pretty.

SIR CHARLES. Now, Mr. *Sullen,* there wants only my Sister's Fortune to make us easie.

SULLEN. Sir *Charles,* you love your Sister, and I love her Fortune; every one to his Fancy.

ARCHER. Then you won't refund?

SULLEN. Not a Stiver.° *small Dutch coin*

COUNT. What is the Portion?

SIR CHARLES. Ten thousand Pound, Sir.

COUNT. Garzoon, I'll pay it, and she shall go home wid me.

ARCHER. Ha, ha, ha, *French* all over—Do you know, Sir, what ten thousand Pound *English* is?

COUNT. No, begar, not *justement.*° *exactly*

ARCHER. Why, Sir, 'tis a hundred thousand Livres.

COUNT. A hundred tousand *Livres*—A Garzoon, me canno' do't, your Beauties and their Fortunes are both too much for me.

ARCHER. Then I will—This Nights Adventure has prov'd strangely lucky to us all—For Captain *Gibbet* in his Walk had made bold, Mr. *Sullen,* with your Study and Escritore, and had taken out all the Writings of your Estate, all the Articles of Marriage with your Lady, Bills, Bonds, Leases, Receipts to an infinite Value, I took 'em from him, I deliver them to *Sir Charles. (Gives him a Parcel of Papers and Parchments.)*

SULLEN. How, my Writings! my Head akes consumedly—Well, Gentlemen, you shall have her Fortune, but I can't talk. If you have a mind, Sir *Charles,* to be merry, and celebrate my Sister's Wedding, and my Divorce, you may command my House—but my Head akes consumedly—*Scrub,* bring me a Dram.

ARCHER. Madam, (*To* Mrs. Sullen.) there's a Country Dance to the Trifle I sung to Day; your Hand, and we'll lead it up.

Here a Dance.

ARCHER. 'Twould be hard to guess which of these Parties is the better pleas'd, the Couple Join'd, or the Couple Parted? the one rejoycing in hopes of an untasted Happiness, and the other in their Deliverance from an experienc'd Misery.

Both happy in their several States we find.
Those parted by consent, and those conjoin'd.
Consent, if mutual, saves the Lawyer's Fee.
Consent is Law enough to set you free.

FINIS

The London Merchant

In the Restoration and eighteenth century, it became not uncommon for the gentry, and even the aristocracy, to write plays. But George Lillo is something of a throwback to the playwrights of the late sixteenth and early seventeenth centuries in that he is not from the upper classes and little is known about him. He was born in either 1691 or 1693 in London. He was a Dissenter (not a member of the Church of England) and a prosperous jeweller. He died in 1739 and was buried in London.

Lillo was also an unusually influential playwright, at a time when serious English drama was in decline. His play *The Fatal Curiousity* (1736) was produced by Henry Fielding, who claimed the work entitled Lillo to be called the foremost tragic playwright of his age. And *The London Merchant* (1731) was admired by and a source for the great German writers Lessing and Goethe. Even in the nineteenth century, Pip in Charles Dickens' *Great Expectations* sees a production of the play.

Aristotle wrote that a tragedy was an imitation of a significant action by characters somewhat above the middle station. In practice, tragedy had concerned itself with the upper classes and the affairs of states. Hamlet is not just a son who has lost a father, but a prince of Denmark whose actions have consequences for the kingdom. Since the characters were elevated, so too was the language. English tragedy was written in blank verse, or for a brief period between 1662 and 1680, in heroic couplets.

Lillo writes a tragedy that centers on the City of London, the world where merchants and artisans powered the economic engine that would make Great Britain the most powerful country in the world. His source is a mid-seventeenth-century ballad; Lillo had several thousand copies printed up and circulated just before production of the play and this may have contributed to the play's success. Suitably, the play is written in prose because the characters are not elevated, at least in the social or political sense.

The text is that established by James L. Steffensen in *The Dramatic Works of George Lillo* (Oxford: Clarendon Press, 1993), 151–209.

Along with the play's innovations in subject and language, the character of Millwood is strikingly original. Through three acts she is a conventional female seductress and villain. In the fourth act, we discover that she is also a victim and her actions are revenge on a society that has abused her. In the final act, her speeches mirror those of Satan in John Milton's *Paradise Lost* and she achieves a tragic stature beyond the pathos of the "she tragedies" that are mentioned in the prologue.

A play of ideas, *The London Merchant* examines economic theory, ethics, and even the death penalty. Yet in its time, according to Lessing, it reduced audiences to tears. Engagement with the emotions was itself seen to be morally instructive, and Lillo combines pathos with didacticism. But he also established that tragedy could be found among the rising middle classes, and the realist playwrights of the twentieth century owe him a debt, whether they are aware of it or not.

The London Merchant: or, The History of George Barnwell.

Learn to be wise from others Harm,
And you shall do full well.
Old Ballad of the Lady's Fall

TO

Sir John Eyles, *Bar.*[1]

Member of Parliament for, and Alderman Of The City of *London* and Sub-Governor of the *South-Sea* Company.[2]

SIR,

If Tragick Poetry be, as Mr. *Dryden* has some where said, the most excellent and most useful Kind of Writing, the more extensively useful the Moral of any Tragedy is, the more excellent that Piece must be of its Kind.

I hope I shall not be thought to insinuate that this, to which I have presumed to prefix your name, is such; that depends on its Fitness to answer the End of Tragedy, the exciting of the Passions, in order to the correcting such of them as are Criminal, either in their Nature, or through their Excess. Whether the following Scenes do this in any tolerable Degree, is, with the Deference, that becomes one who wou'd not be thought vain, submitted to your candid and impartial Judgment.

1. Baronet, a hereditary knighthood. Eyles was a director of the South Sea Company, the East India Company, and the Bank of England. He was appointed sheriff of London in 1720 and made lord mayor of the City in 1726.

2. The South Sea Company was founded in 1711. The company was assigned the national debt from the War of the Spanish Succession in return for a monopoly on trade with South America. In a frenzy of speculation in 1720, the stock rose from around £100 a share to nearly £1,000 a share in less than a year, and crashed spectacularly. Sir Robert Walpole's rise to power in 1722 and control of the English government for over two decades was partially a consequence of his competence in dealing with the economic wreckage left by the bursting of the bubble.

What I wou'd infer is this, I think, evident Truth; that Tragedy is so far from losing its Dignity, by being accommodated to the Circumstances of the Generality of Mankind, that it is more truly august in Proportion to the Extent of its Influence, and the Numbers that are properly affected by it. As it is more truly great to be the Instrument of Good to many, who stand in need of our Assistance, than to a very small Part of that Number.

If Princes, *&c.* were alone liable to Misfortunes, arising from Vice, or Weakness in themselves, or others, there wou'd be good Reason for confining the Characters in Tragedy to those of superior Rank; but, since the contrary is evident, nothing can be more reasonable than to proportion the Remedy to the Disease.

I am far from denying that Tragedies, founded on any instructive and extraordinary Events in History, or a well-invented Fable, where the Persons introduced are of the highest Rank, are without their Use, even to the Bulk of the Audience. The strong Contrast between a *Tamerlane* and a *Bajazet,*[3] may have its Weight with an unsteady People, and contribute to the fixing of them in the Interest of a Prince of the Character of the former, when, thro' their own Levity, or the Arts of designing Men, they are render'd factious and uneasy, tho' they have the highest Reason to be satisfied. The Sentiments and Example of a *Cato,* may inspire his Spectators with a just Sense of the Value of Liberty, when they see that honest Patriot[4] prefer Death to an Obligation from a Tyrant, who wou'd sacrifice the Constitution of his Country, and the Liberties of Mankind, to his Ambition or Revenge.[5] I have attempted, indeed, to enlarge the Province of the graver Kind of Poetry, and should be glad to see it carried on by some abler Hand. Plays, founded on moral Tales in private Life, may be of admirable Use, by carrying Conviction to the Mind, with such irresistible Force, as to engage all the Faculties and Powers of the Soul in the Cause of Virtue, by stifling Vice in its first Principles. They who imagine this to be too much to be attributed to Tragedy, must be Strangers to the Energy of that noble species of Poetry. Shakespear, who has given such amazing Proofs of his Genius, in that as well as in Comedy, in his *Hamlet,* has the following Lines,

Had he the Motive and the Cause for Passion
That I have; he wou'd drown the Stage with Tears
And cleave the general Ear with horrid Speech;
Make mad the Guilty, and appale the Free,
Confound the Ignorant, and amaze indeed
The very Faculty of Eyes and Ears.

And farther, in the same Speech,

I've heard that guilty Creatures at a Play,
Have, by the very cunning of the Scene,
Been so struck to the Soul, that presently
They have proclaim'd their Malefactions.

3. In Nicholas Rowe's *Tamerlane* (1701).

4. In the early eighteenth century, a "Patriot" was not just a lover of his country, but one associated with the Whig Party, which favored new wealth, trade, and parliamentary ascendancy over the monarchy.

5. In Joseph Addison's *Cato* (1713), Caesar is the tyrant who destroys Roman liberty, while Cato commits suicide rather than surrender to Caesar.

Prodigious! yet strictly just. But I shan't take up your valuable Time with my Remarks; only give me Leave just to observe, that he seems so firmly perswaded of the Power of a well-wrote Piece to produce the Effect here ascribed to it, as to make *Hamlet* venture his Soul on the Event, and rather trust that, than a Messenger from the other World, tho' it assumed, as he expresses it, his *noble Father's Form,* and assured him, that it was his *Spirit. I'll have,* says *Hamlet, Grounds more relative.*

> ——*The Play's the Thing,*
> *Wherein I'll catch the Conscience of the King.*

Such Plays are the best Answers to them who deny the Lawfulness of the Stage.[6]

Considering the Novelty of this Attempt, I thought it would be expected from me to say something in its Excuse; and I was unwilling to lose the Opportunity of saying something of the Usefulness of Tragedy in general, and what may be reasonably expected from the farther Improvement of this excellent Kind of Poetry.

Sir, I hope you will not think I have said too much of an Art, a mean Specimen of which I am ambitious enough to recommend to your Favour and Protection. A Mind, conscious of superior Worth, as much despises Flattery, as it is above it. Had I found in my self an Inclination to so contemptible a Vice, I should not have chose Sir JOHN EYLES for my Patron. And indeed the best writ Panegyrick, tho' strictly true, must place you in a Light, much inferior to that in which you have long been fix'd, by the Love and Esteem of your Fellow Citizens; whose Choice of you for one of their Representatives in Parliament, has sufficiently declared their Sense of your Merit. Nor hath the Knowledge of your Worth been confined to the City. The Proprietors in the *South-Sea* Company, in which are included Numbers of Persons, as considerable for their Rank, Fortune, and Understanding, as any in the Kingdom, gave the greatest Proof of their Confidence, in your Capacity and Probity, when they chose you Sub-Governor of their Company, at a Time when their Affairs were in the utmost Confusion, and their Properties in the greatest Danger. Neither is the Court insensible of your Importance. I shall not therefore attempt a Character so well known, nor pretend to add any Thing to a Reputation so well established. Whatever others may think of a Dedication, wherein there is so much said of other Things, and so little of the Person to whom it is address'd, I have Reason to believe that you will the more easily pardon it on that very Account.

I am, SIR,

Your most obedient

humble servant,

GEORGE *LILLO.*

6. There was a lengthy history of attacks on the stage, such as the Puritan lawyer William Prynne's *Histriomastix* (1632) and the nonjuring minister Jeremy Collier's *A Short View of the Prophanity and Immorality of the English Stage* (1698).

PROLOGUE.

Spoke by Mr. CIBBER, Jun.[7]

The Tragick Muse, sublime, delights to show
Princes distrest, and Scenes of Royal Woe;
In awful Pomp, Majestick, to relate
The Fall of Nations, or some Heroe's Fate:
That Scepter'd Chiefs may by Example know
The strange Vicissitude of Things below:
What Dangers on Security attend;
How Pride and Cruelty in Ruin end:
Hence Providence Supream to know; and own
Humanity adds Glory to a Throne.
    In ev'ry former Age, and Foreign Tongue,
With Native Grandure thus the Goddess sung.
Upon our Stage indeed, with wish'd Success,
You've sometimes seen her in a humbler Dress;
Great only in Distress. When she complains
In Southern's, Rowe's, *or* Otway's *moving Strains,*[8]
The Brilliant Drops, that fall from each bright Eye,
The absent Pomp, with brighter Jems, supply.
Forgive us then, if we attempt to show,
In artless Strains, a Tale of private Woe.
A London *Prentice ruin'd is our Theme,*
Drawn from the fam'd old Song, that bears his Name.
We hope your Taste is not so high to scorn
A moral Tale, esteem'd ere you were born;
Which for a Century of rolling Years,
Has fill'd a thousand-thousand Eyes with Tears.
If thoughtless Youth to warn, and shame the Age
From Vice destructive, well becomes the Stage;
If this Example Innocence insure,
Prevent our Guilt, or by Reflection cure;
If Millwood's dreadful Crimes, and sad Despair,
Commend the Virtue of the Good and Fair;
Tho' Art be wanting, and our Numbers° fail, versification
Indulge the Attempt in Justice to the Tale.

7. Theophilus Cibber (1703–58) was the son of Colley Cibber, playwright, manager, and actor at Drury Lane. Theophilus, a notorious rake, played Barnwell.

8. Thomas Southerne (1660–1746), Nicholas Rowe (1674–1718), and Thomas Otway (1652–85) were all gifted playwrights successful in a number of genres. Among their successes were tragedies involving women who were objects of sympathy, such as Southerne's *The Fatal Marriage* (1694), Rowe's *The Fair Penitent* (1703), and Otway's *The Orphan* (1680).

DRAMATIS PERSONÆ.

MEN.

THOROWGOOD
BARNWELL, *Uncle to* George
GEORGE BARNWELL
TRUEMAN
BLUNT

WOMEN.

MARIA
MILLWOOD
LUCY

Officers with their Attendants, Keeper, and Footmen.

SCENE, London, *and an adjacent Village.*

ACT I.

SCENE I.

A Room in Thorowgood's *House.*
Thorowgood *and* Trueman.

TRUEMAN. Sir, the Packet[9] from *Genoa* is arriv'd. [Gives Letters.

THOROWGOOD. Heav'n be praised, the Storm that threaten'd our Royal Mistress, pure Religion, Liberty and Laws, is for a Time diverted; the haughty and revengeful *Spaniard,* disappointed of the Loan on which he depended from *Genoa,* must now attend the slow return of Wealth from his new World, to supply his empty Coffers, ere he can execute his purpos'd Invasion of our happy Island; by which means Time is gain'd to make such Preparations on our Part, as may, Heav'n concurring, prevent his Malice, or turn the meditated Mischief on himself.

TRUEMAN. He must be insensible indeed, who is not affected when the Safety of his Country is concern'd.—Sir, may I know by what means—if I am too bold—

THOROWGOOD. Your Curiosity is laudable; and I gratify it with the greater Pleasure, because from thence you may learn, how honest Merchants, as such, may sometimes contribute to the Safety

9. Fast ships that carried letters.

of their Country, as they do at all times to its Happiness; that if hereafter you should be tempted to any Action that has the Appearance of Vice or Meanness in it, upon reflecting on the Dignity of our Profession, you may with honest Scorn reject whatever is unworthy of it.

TRUEMAN. Shou'd *Barnwell*, or I, who have the Benefit of your Example, by our ill Conduct bring any Imputation on that honourable Name, we must be left without excuse.

THOROWGOOD. You complement, young Man.—

[Trueman *bows respectfully.*

Nay, I'm not offended. As the Name of Merchant never degrades the Gentleman, so by no means does it exclude him; only take heed not to purchase the Character of Complaisant° (obliging) at the Expence of your Sincerity.—But to answer your Question,—The Bank of *Genoa* had agreed, at excessive Interest and on good Security, to advance the King of *Spain* a Sum of Money sufficient to equip his vast Armado,—of which our peerless *Elizabeth* (more than in Name the Mother of her People) being well informed, sent *Walsingham,*[10] her wise and faithful Secretary, to consult the Merchants of this loyal City, who all agreed to direct their several Agents to influence, if possible, the *Genoese* to break their Contract with the *Spanish* Court. 'Tis done, the State and Bank of *Genoa,* having maturely weigh'd and rightly judged of their true Interest, prefer the Friendship of the Merchants of *London,* to that of a Monarch, who proudly stiles himself King of both *Indies.*[11]

TRUEMAN. Happy Success of prudent Councils! What an Expence of Blood and Treasure is here saved?—Excellent Queen! O how unlike to former Princes, who made the Danger of foreign Enemies a Pretence to oppress their Subjects, by Taxes great and grievous to be born.

THOROWGOOD. Not so our gracious Queen, whose richest Exchequer is her Peoples Love, as their Happiness her greatest Glory.

TRUEMAN. On these Terms to defend us, is to make our Protection a Benefit worthy her who confers it, and well worth our Acceptance. —Sir, have you any Commands for me at this Time?

THOROWGOOD. Only to look carefully over the Files to see whether there are any Tradesmens Bills unpaid; if there are, send and discharge 'em. We must not let Artificers° (craftsmen) lose their Time, so useful to the Publick and their Families, in unnecessary Attendance.

10. Sir Francis Walsingham (1532–90) was an adviser to Elizabeth I; among other roles, he directed a network of spies that reported on Spanish attempts to attack England.

11. The East Indies included India, South Asia, and Southeast Asia, as well as the major archipelagos. The West Indies were not only the islands of the Caribbean, but much of South and Central America.

SCENE II.

Thorowgood *and* Maria.

THOROWGOOD. Well, *Maria,* have you given Orders for the Entertainment? I would have it in some measure worthy the Guests. Let there be plenty, and of the best; that the Courtiers may at least commend our Hospitality.

MARIA. Sir, I have endeavoured not to wrong your well-known Generosity by an ill-tim'd Parsimony.

THOROWGOOD. Nay, 'twas a needless Caution, I have no cause to doubt your Prudence.

MARIA. Sir, I find my self unfit for Conversation at present, I should but increase the Number of the Company, without adding to their Satisfaction.

THOROWGOOD. Nay, my Child, this Melancholy must not be indulged.

MARIA. Company will but increase it. I wish you would dispense with my Absence; Solitude best suits my present Temper.

THOROWGOOD. You are not insensible that it is chiefly on your Account these noble Lords do me the Honour so frequently to grace my Board; shou'd you be absent, the Disappointment may make them repent their Condescension, and think their Labour lost.

MARIA. He that shall think his Time or Honour lost in visiting you, can set no real Value on your Daughter's Company, whose only Merit is that she is yours. The Man of Quality,[12] who chuses to converse with a Gentleman and Merchant of your Worth and Character, may confer Honour by so doing, but he loses none.

THOROWGOOD. Come, come, *Maria,* I need not tell you that a young Gentleman may prefer your Conversation to mine, yet intend me no Disrespect at all; for tho' he may lose no Honour in my Company, 'tis very natural for him to expect more Pleasure in yours. I remember the Time, when the Company of the greatest and wisest Man in the Kingdom would have been insipid and tiresome to me, if it had deprived me of an Opportunity of enjoying your Mother's.

MARIA. Your's no doubt was as agreeable to her; for generous Minds know no Pleasure in Society but where 'tis mutual.

THOROWGOOD. Thou know'st I have no Heir, no Child but thee; the Fruits of many Years successful Industry must all be thine; now it would give me Pleasure great as my Love, to see on whom you would bestow it. I am daily solicited by Men of the greatest Rank

12. A gentleman or a member of the aristocracy, someone with a coat of arms whose income comes primarily from land. Typically members of the City ("cits" or "citizens") were not members of the gentry.

and Merit for leave to address you, but I have hitherto declin'd it, in hopes that by Observation I shou'd learn which way your Inclination tends; for as I know Love to be essential to Happiness in the Marriage State, I had rather my Approbation should confirm your Choice, than direct it.

MARIA. What can I say? How shall I answer, as I ought, this Tenderness, so uncommon, even in the best of Parents: But you are without Example; yet had you been less indulgent, I had been wretched. That I look on the Croud of Courtiers, that visit here, with equal Esteem, but equal Indifference, you have observed, and I must needs confess; yet had you asserted your Authority, and insisted on a Parent's Right to be obey'd, I had submitted, and to my Duty sacrificed my Peace.

THOROWGOOD. From your perfect Obedience in every other Instance, I fear'd as much; and therefore wou'd leave you without a Byass in an Affair wherein your Happiness is so immediately concern'd.

MARIA. Whether from a Want of that just Ambition that wou'd become your Daughter, or from some other Cause I know not; but I find high Birth and Titles don't recommend the Man, who owns them, to my Affections.

THOROWGOOD. I wou'd not that they shou'd, unless his Merit recommends him more. A noble Birth and Fortune, tho' they make not a bad Man good, yet they are a real Advantage to a worthy one, and place his Virtues in the fairest Light.

MARIA. I cannot answer for my Inclinations, but they shall ever be submitted to your Wisdom and Authority; and, as you will not compel me to marry where I cannot love, so Love shall never make me act contrary to my Duty. Sir, have I your Permission to retire?

THOROWGOOD. I'll see you to your Chamber.

SCENE III.

A Room in Millwood's *House.*
Millwood *at her Tollet.* Lucy *waiting.*

MILLWOOD. How do I look to Day, *Lucy?*

LUCY. O, killingly, Madam!—A little more Red, and you'll be irresistible!—But why this more than ordinary Care of your Dress and Complexion? What new Conquest are you aiming at?

MILLWOOD. A Conquest wou'd be new indeed!

LUCY. Not to you, who make 'em every Day,—but to me.—Well! 'tis what I'm never to expect,—unfortunate as I am:—But your Wit and Beauty—

MILLWOOD. First made me a Wretch, and still continue me so.—Men, however generous or sincere to one another, are all selfish Hypocrites in their Affairs with us. We are no otherwise esteemed or regarded by them, but as we contribute to their Satisfaction.

LUCY. You are certainly, Madam, on the wrong Side in this Argument: Is not the Expence all theirs? And I am sure it is our own Fault if we hav'n't our Share of the Pleasure.

MILLWOOD. We are but Slaves to Men.

LUCY. Nay, 'tis they that are Slaves most certainly; for we lay them under Contribution.

MILLWOOD. Slaves have no Property; no, not even in themselves.— All is the Victors.

LUCY. You are strangely arbitrary in your Principles, Madam.

MILLWOOD. I would have my Conquests compleat, like those of the *Spaniards* in the New World; who first plunder'd the Natives of all the Wealth they had, and then condemn'd the Wretches to the Mines for Life, to work for more.

LUCY. Well, I shall never approve of your Scheme of Government: I should think it much more politick, as well as just, to find my Subjects an easier Employment.

MILLWOOD. It's a general Maxim among the knowing Part of Mankind, that a Woman without Virtue, like a Man without Honour or Honesty, is capable of any Action, tho' never so vile: And yet what Pains will they not take, what Arts not use, to seduce us from our Innocence, and make us contemptible and wicked, even in their own Opinions? Then is it not just, the Villains, to their Cost, should find us so?—But Guilt makes them suspicious, and keeps them on their Guard; therefore we can take Advantage only of the young and innocent Part of the Sex, who having never injured Women, apprehend no Injury from them.

LUCY. Ay, they must be young indeed.

MILLWOOD. Such a one, I think, I have found.—As I've passed thro' the City, I have often observ'd him receiving and paying considerable Sums of Money; from thence I conclude he is employ'd in Affairs of Consequence.

LUCY. Is he handsome?

MILLWOOD. Ay, ay, the Stripling is well made, and has a good Face.

LUCY. About—

MILLWOOD. Eighteen—

LUCY. Innocent, Handsome, and about Eighteen.—You'll be vastly happy.—Why, if you manage well, you may keep him to your self these two or three Years.

MILLWOOD. If I manage well, I shall have done with him much sooner. Having long had a Design on him, and meeting him Yesterday, I made a full Stop, and gazing wishfully on his Face, ask'd him his Name: He blush'd, and bowing very low, answer'd, *George Barnwell.* I beg'd his Pardon for the Freedom I had taken, and told him, that he was the Person I had long wish'd to see, and to whom I had an Affair of Importance to communicate, at a proper Time and Place. He named a Tavern; I talk'd of Honour and Reputation, and invited him to my House: He swallow'd the Bait, promis'd to come, and this is the Time I expect him. [*Knocking at the Door.*] Some Body knocks,—d'ye hear; I am at Home to no Body to Day but him.—

[Exit Lucy.]

SCENE IV.

MILLWOOD.

Less Affairs must give Way to those of more Consequence; and I am strangely mistaken if this does not prove of great Importance to me and him too, before I have done with him.—Now, after what Manner shall I receive him? Let me consider—what manner of Person am I to receive?—He is young, innocent, and bashful; therefore I must take Care not to put him out of Countenance, at first.—But then, if I have any Skill in Phisiognomy,[13] he is amorous, and, with a little Assistance, will soon get the better of his Modesty.—I'll e'en trust to Nature, who does Wonders in these Matters.—If to seem what one is not, in order to be the better liked for what one really is; if to speak one thing, and mean the direct contrary, be Art in a woman, I know nothing of Nature.

SCENE V.

[*To her.*] Barnwell *bowing very low.* Lucy *at a Distance.*

MILLWOOD. Sir! the Suprize and Joy!—
BARNWELL. Madam.—
MILLWOOD. This is such a Favour,— [*Advancing.*
BARNWELL. Pardon me, Madam,—
MILLWOOD. So unhop'd for,— [*Still advances.*

[Barnwell *salutes her, and retires in Confusion.*]

To see you here.—Excuse the Confusion.—
BARNWELL. I fear I am too bold.—
MILLWOOD. Alas, Sir! I may justly apprehend you think me so.—Please, Sir, to sit.—I am as much at a Loss how to receive this Honour as I ought, as I am surpriz'd at your Goodness in confering it.

13. The ability to judge a person's nature from their face.

BARNWELL. I thought you had expected me—I promis'd to come.

MILLWOOD. That is the more surprizing; few Men are such religious Observers of their Word.

BARNWELL. All, who are honest, are.

MILLWOOD. To one another:—But we simple Women are seldom thought of Consequence enough to gain a Place in your Remembrance.

[*Laying her Hand on his, as by Accident.*

BARNWELL. Her Disorder is so great, she don't perceive she has laid her Hand on mine.—Heaven! how she trembles!—What can this mean! [*Aside.*

MILLWOOD. The Interest I have in all that relates to you, (the Reason of which you shall know hereafter) excites my Curiosity; and, were I sure you would pardon my Presumption, I should desire to know your real Sentiments on a very particular Subject.

BARNWELL. Madam, you may command my poor Thoughts on any Subject;—I have none that I would conceal.

MILLWOOD. You'll think me bold.

BARNWELL. No, indeed.

MILLWOOD. What then are your Thoughts of Love?

BARNWELL. If you mean the Love of Women, I have not thought of it all.—My Youth and Circumstances make such Thoughts improper in me yet: But if you mean the general Love we owe to Mankind, I think no one has more of it in his Temper than my self. —I don't know that Person in the World whose Happiness I don't wish, and wou'd n't promote, were it in my Power.—In an especial manner I love my Uncle, and my Master, but, above all, my Friend.

MILLWOOD. You have a Friend then, whom you love?

BARNWELL. As he does me, sincerely.

MILLWOOD. He is, no doubt, often bless'd with your Company and Conversation.—

BARNWELL. We live in one House, and both serve the same worthy Merchant.

MILLWOOD. Happy, happy Youth!—who e'er thou art, I envy thee, and so must all, who see and know this Youth.—What have I lost, by being form'd a Woman!—I hate my Sex, my self.—Had I been a Man, I might, perhaps, have been as happy in your Friendship, as he who now enjoys it:—But as it is,—Oh!—

BARNWELL. I never observ'd Women before, or this is sure the most beautiful of her Sex. [*Aside.*] You seem disorder'd, Madam! May I know the Cause?

MILLWOOD. Do not ask me,—I can never speak it, whatever is the Cause;—I wish for Things impossible:—I wou'd be a Servant, bound to the same Master, to live in one House with you.

BARNWELL. How strange, and yet how kind, her Words and Actions are!—And the Effect they have on me is as strange.—I feel Desires I never knew before;—I must be gone, while I have Power to go. [*Aside.*] Madam, I humbly take my Leave.—

MILLWOOD. You will not sure leave me so soon!

BARNWELL. Indeed I must.

MILLWOOD. You cannot be so cruel!—I have prepar'd a poor Supper, at which I promis'd my self your Company.

BARNWELL. I am sorry I must refuse the Honour that you design'd me;—But my Duty to my Master calls me hence.—I never yet neglected his Service: He is so gentle, and so good a Master, that, should I wrong him, tho' he might forgive me, I never should forgive my self.

MILLWOOD. Am I refus'd, by the first Man, the second Favour I ever stoop'd to ask?—Go then thou proud hard-hearted Youth.—But know, you are the only Man that cou'd be found, who would let me sue twice for greater Favours.

BARNWELL. What shall I do!—How shall I go or stay!

MILLWOOD. Yet do not,—do not leave me.—I wish my Sex's Pride wou'd meet your Scorn:—But when I look upon you,—When I behold those Eyes,—Oh! spare my Tongue, and let my Blushes (this Flood of Tears to that will force its Way), declare what Woman's Modesty should hide.

BARNWELL. Oh, Heavens! she loves me, worthless as I am; her Looks, her Words, her flowing Tears confess it:—And can I leave her then?—Oh, never,—never.—Madam, dry up those Tears.—You shall command me always;—I will stay here for ever, if you'd have me.

LUCY. So! she has wheedled him out of his Virtue of Obedience already, and will strip him of all the rest, one after another, 'till she has left him as few as her Ladyship, or my self. *Aside.*

MILLWOOD. Now you are kind, indeed; but I mean not to detain you always: I would have you shake off all slavish Obedience to your Master;—but you may serve him still.

LUCY. Serve him still!—Aye, or he'll have no Opportunity of fingering his Cash, and then he'll not serve your End, I'll be sworn. [*Aside.*

SCENE VI.

[*To them.*] Blunt.

BLUNT. Madam, Supper's on the Table.

MILLWOOD. Come, Sir, you'll excuse all Defects.—My Thoughts were too much employ'd on my Guest to observe the Entertainment.

SCENE VII.

Lucy *and* Blunt.

BLUNT. What, is all this Preparation, this elegant Supper, Variety of Wines, and Musick, for the Entertainment of that young Fellow!

LUCY. So it seems.

BLUNT. What, is our Mistress turn'd Fool at last! She's in Love with him, I suppose.

LUCY. I suppose not,—but she designs to make him in Love with her, if she can.

BLUNT. What will she get by that? He seems under Age, and can't be suppos'd to have much Money.

LUCY. But his Master has; and that's the same thing, as she'll manage it.

BLUNT. I don't like this fooling with a handsome young Fellow; while she's endeavouring to ensnare him, she may be caught her self.

LUCY. Nay, were she like me, that would certainly be the Consequence;—for, I confess, there is something in Youth and Innocence that moves me mightily.

BLUNT. Yes, so does the Smoothness and Plumpness of a Patridge move a mighty Desire in the Hawk to be the Destruction of it.

LUCY. Why, Birds are their Prey, as Men are ours; though, as you observ'd, we are sometimes caught our selves:—But that I dare say will never be the Case with our Mistress.

BLUNT. I wish it may prove so; for you know we all depend upon her: Should she trifle away her Time with a young Fellow, that there's nothing to be got by, we must all starve.

LUCY. There's no Danger of that, for I am sure she has no View in this Affair, but Interest.

BLUNT. Well, and what Hopes are there of Success in that?

LUCY. The most promising that can be.—'Tis true, the Youth has his Scruples; but she'll soon teach him to answer them, by stifling his Conscience.—O, the Lad is in a hopeful Way, depend upon't.

SCENE VIII.

Scene draws and discovers Barnwell *and* Millwood
at Supper. An Entertainment of Musick and Singing.
After which they come forward.

BARNWELL. What can I answer!—All that I know is, that you are fair, and I am miserable.

MILLWOOD. We are both so, and yet the Fault is in our selves.

BARNWELL. To ease our present Anguish, by plunging into Guilt, is to buy a Moment's Pleasure with an Age of Pain.

MILLWOOD. I should have thought the Joys of Love as lasting as they are great: If ours prove otherwise, 'tis your Inconstancy must make them so.

BARNWELL. The Law of Heaven will not be revers'd; and that requires us to govern our Passions.

MILLWOOD. To give us Sense of Beauty and Desires, and yet forbid us to taste and be happy, is Cruelty to Nature.—Have we Passions only to torment us!

BARNWELL. To hear you talk,—tho' in the Cause of Vice,—to gaze upon your Beauty,—press your Hand,—and see your Snow-white Bosom heave and fall,—enflames my Wishes;—my Pulse beats high,—my Senses all are in a Hurry, and I am on the Rack of wild Desire;—yet for a Moment's guilty Pleasure, shall I lose my Innocence, my Peace of Mind, and Hopes of solid Happiness?

MILLWOOD. Chimeras all,—

—Come on with me and prove,
No Joy's like Woman kind, nor Heav'n like Love.

BARNWELL. I wou'd not,—yet must on.—

Reluctant thus, the Merchant quits his Ease,
And trusts to Rocks, and Sands, and stormy Seas;
In Hopes some unknown golden Coast to find, }
Commits himself, tho' doubtful, to the Wind, }
Longs much for Joys to come,—yet mourns those left behind. }

The End of the First Act.

ACT II.

SCENE I.

A Room in Thorowgood's *House.*

BARNWELL.

How strange are all Things round me? Like some Thief, who treads forbidden Ground, and fain wou'd lurk unseen, fearful I enter each Apartment of this well known House. To guilty Love, as if that was too little, already have I added Breach of Trust.—A Thief!—Can I know my self that wretched Thing, and look my honest Friend and injured Master in the Face? Tho' Hypocrisy may a while conceal my Guilt, at length it will be known, and publick Shame and Ruin must ensue. In the mean time, what must be my Life? ever to speak a Language foreign to my Heart; hourly to add to the Number of my Crimes in order to conceal 'em.—Sure such was the Condition of the grand Apostate, when first he lost his Purity; like me disconsolate he wander'd, and, while yet in Heaven, bore all his future Hell about him.

SCENE II.

Barnwell *and* Trueman.

TRUEMAN. *Barnwell!* O how I rejoice to see you safe! so will our Master and his gentle Daughter, who during your Absence often inquir'd after you.

BARNWELL. Wou'd he were gone, his officious Love will pry into the Secrets of my Soul. [*Aside.*

TRUEMAN. Unless you knew the Pain the whole Family has felt on your Account, you can't conceive how much you are belov'd; but why thus cold and silent? when my Heart is full of Joy for your Return, why do you turn away? why thus avoid me? what have I done? how am I alter'd since you saw me last? Or rather what have you done? and why are you thus changed? for I am still the same.

BARNWELL. What have I done, indeed? [*Aside.*

TRUEMAN. Not speak nor look upon me!—

BARNWELL. By my Face he will discover all I wou'd conceal; methinks already I begin to hate him. [*Aside.*

TRUEMAN. I cannot bear this Usage from a Friend, one whom till now I ever found so loving, whom yet I love, tho' this Unkindness strikes at the Root of Friendship, and might destroy it in any Breast but mine.

BARNWELL. I am not well; [*Turning to him.*] Sleep has been a Stranger to these Eyes since you beheld them last.

TRUEMAN. Heavy they look indeed, and swoln with Tears;—now they o'erflow;—rightly did my sympathizing Heart forbode last Night when thou wast absent, something fatal to our Peace.

BARNWELL. Your Friendship ingages you too far. My Troubles, whate'er they are, are mine alone, you have no Interest in them, nor ought your Concern for me give you a Moment's Pain.

TRUEMAN. You speak as if you knew of Friendship nothing but the Name. Before I saw your Grief I felt it. Since we parted last I have slept no more than you, but pensive in my Chamber sat alone, and spent the tedious Night in Wishes for your Safety and Return; e'en now, tho' ignorant of the Cause, your Sorrow wounds me to the Heart.

BARNWELL. 'Twill not be always thus: Friendship and all Engagements cease, as Circumstances and Occasions vary; and, since you once may hate me, perhaps it might be better for us both that now you lov'd me less.

TRUEMAN. Sure I but dream! Without a Cause would *Barnwell* use me thus?—ungenerous and ungrateful Youth, farewell,—I shall endeavour to follow your Advice,—[*Going.*] Yet stay, perhaps I am too rash, and angry when the Cause demands Compassion. Some unforeseen Calamity may have befaln him too great to bear.

BARNWELL. What Part am I reduc'd to act;—'tis vile and base to move his Temper thus, the best of Friends and Men.

TRUEMAN. I am to blame, prithee forgive me *Barnwell.*—Try to compose your ruffled Mind, and let me know the Cause that thus transports you from your Self; my friendly Counsel may restore your Peace.

BARNWELL. All that is possible for Man to do for Man, your generous Friendship may effect; but here even that's in vain.

TRUEMAN. Something dreadful is labouring in your Breast, O give it vent and let me share your Grief; 'twill ease your Pain shou'd it admit no cure, and make it lighter by the Part I bear.

BARNWELL. Vain Supposition! my Woes increase by being observ'd, shou'd the Cause be known, they wou'd exceed all Bounds.

TRUEMAN. So well I know thy honest Heart, Guilt cannot harbour there.

BARNWELL. O Torture insupportable! [*Aside.*

TRUEMAN. Then why am I excluded, have I a Thought I would conceal from you?

BARNWELL. If still you urge me on this hated Subject, I'lll never enter more beneath this Roof, nor see your Face again.

TRUEMAN. 'Tis strange,—but I have done, say but you hate me not.

BARNWELL. Hate you!—I am not that Monster yet.

TRUEMAN. Shall our Friendship still continue?

BARNWELL. It's a Blessing I never was worthy of, yet now must stand on Terms; and but upon Conditions can confirm it.

TRUEMAN. What are they?

BARNWELL. Never hereafter, tho' you shou'd wonder at my Conduct, desire to know more than I am willing to reveal.

TRUEMAN. 'Tis hard, but upon any Conditions I must be your Friend.

BARNWELL. Then, as much as one lost to himself can be another's, I am yours. [*Embracing.*

TRUEMAN. Be ever so, and may Heav'n restore your Peace.

BARNWELL. Will Yesterday return?—We have heard the glorious Sun, that till then incessant roll'd, once stopp'd his rapid Course, and once went back: The Dead have risen: and parched Rocks pour'd forth a liquid Stream to quench a Peoples Thirst: The Sea divided, and form'd Walls of Water; while a whole Nation pass'd in safety thro' its sandy Bosom: Hungry Lions have refus'd their Prey: And Men unhurt have walk'd amidst consuming Flames; but never yet did Time once past, return.

TRUEMAN. Tho' the continued Chain of Time has never once been broke, nor ever will, but uninterrupted must keep on its Course, till lost in eternity it ends there where it first begun; yet as Heav'n can repair whatever Evils Time can bring upon us, we ought never to despair.—But Business requires our Attendance;

Business the Youth's best Preservative from ill, as Idleness his worst of Snares. Will you go with me?

BARNWELL. I'll take a little Time to reflect on what has past, and follow you.

SCENE III.

BARNWELL.

I might have trusted *Trueman* and ingaged him to apply to my Uncle to repair the Wrong I have done my Master; but what of *Millwood?* must I expose her too? ungenerous and base! then Heav'n requires it not.—But Heaven requires that I forsake her. What! never see her more! Does Heaven require that,—I hope I may see her, and Heav'n not be offended. Presumptuous Hope,—dearly already have I prov'd my Frailty; should I once more tempt Heav'n, I may be left to fall never to rise again.—Yet shall I leave her, for ever leave her, and not let her know the Cause? She who loves me with such a boundless Passion;—can Cruelty be Duty? I judge of what she then must feel, by what I now indure.—The love of Life and fear of Shame, oppos'd by Inclination strong as Death or Shame, like Wind and Tide in raging Conflict met, when neither can prevail, keep me in doubt.—How then can I determine?

SCENE IV.

Thorowgood *and* Barnwell

THOROWGOOD. Without a Cause assign'd, or Notice given, to absent your self last Night was a Fault, young Man, and I came to chide you for it, but hope I am prevented; that modest Blush, the Confusion so visible in your Face, speak Grief and Shame: When we have offended Heaven, it requires no more; and shall Man, who needs himself to be forgiven, be harder to appease: If my Pardon or Love be of moment to your Peace, look up secure of both.

BARNWELL. This Goodness has o'er come me. [*Aside.*] O Sir! you know not the Nature and Extent of my Offence; and I shou'd abuse your mistaken Bounty to receive 'em. Tho' I had rather die than speak my Shame; tho' Racks could not have forced the guilty Secret from my Breast, your Kindness has.

THOROWGOOD. Enough, enough, whate'er it be, this Concern shews you're convinc'd, and I am satisfied. How painful is the Sense of Guilt to an ingenuous Mind;—some youthful Folly, which it were prudent not to enquire into.—When we consider the frail Condition of Humanity, it may raise our Pity, not our Wonder, that Youth should go astray; when Reason, weak at the best when oppos'd to Inclination, scarce form'd, and wholly unassisted by Experience, faintly contends, or willingly becomes the Slave of Sense. The State of Youth is much to be deplored; and the more so because they see it not; being then to danger most expos'd, when they are least prepar'd for their Defence. [*Aside.*

BARNWELL. It will be known, and you recall your Pardon and abhor me.

THOROWGOOD. I never will. Yet be upon your Guard in this gay thoughtless Season of your Life; now when the Sense of Pleasure's quick, and Passion high, the voluptuous Appetites raging and fierce demand the strongest Curb; take heed of a Relapse: When Vice becomes habitual, the very Power of leaving it is lost.

BARNWELL. Hear me on my Knees confess.

THOROWGOOD. I will not hear a Syllable more upon this Subject; it were not Mercy, but Cruelty, to hear what must give you such Torment to reveal.

BARNWELL. This Generosity amazes and distracts me.

THOROWGOOD. This Remorse makes thee dearer to me than if thou hadst never offended; whatever is your Fault, of this I'm certain, 'twas harder for you to offend than me to pardon.

SCENE V.

BARNWELL.

Villain, Villain, Villain! basely to wrong so excellent a Man: Shou'd I again return to Folly—detested Thought;—but what of *Millwood* then?—Why, I renounce her;—I give her up; —the Struggle's over, and Virtue has prevail'd. Reason may convince, but Gratitude compels. This unlook'd for Generosity has sav'd me from Destruction. [*Going.*

SCENE VI

[*To him.*] *A Footman.*

FOOTMAN. Sir, two Ladies, from your Uncle in the Country, desire to see you.

BARNWELL. Who shou'd they be? [*Aside.*] Tell them I'll wait upon 'em.

SCENE VII.

BARNWELL.

Methinks I dread to see 'em.—Now every Thing alarms me.—Guilt what a coward hast thou made me?

SCENE VIII.

Another Room in Thorowgood's *House.*
Millwood *and* Lucy, *and to them a* Footman.

FOOTMAN. Ladies, he'll wait upon you immediately.
MILLWOOD. 'Tis very well.—I thank you.

SCENE IX.

Barnwell, Millwood, *and* Lucy.

BARNWELL. Confusion! *Millwood.*
MILLWOOD. That angry Look tells me that here I'm an unwelcome Guest; I fear'd as much,—the Unhappy are so every where.
BARNWELL. Will nothing but my utter Ruin content you?
MILLWOOD. Unkind and cruel! lost my self, your Happiness is now my only Care.
BARNWELL. How did you gain Admission?
MILLWOOD. Saying we were desir'd by your Uncle to visit and deliver a Message to you, we were receiv'd by the Family without suspicion, and with much respect directed here.
BARNWELL. Why did you come at all?
MILLWOOD. I never shall trouble you more, I'm come to take my Leave for ever. Such is the Malice of my Fate. I go hopeless, despairing ever to return. This Hour is all I have left me. One short Hour is all I have to bestow on Love and you, for whom I thought the longest Life too short.
BARNWELL. Then we are met to part for ever?
MILLWOOD. It must be so;—yet think not that Time or Absence ever shall put a Period to my Grief, or make me love you less; tho' I must leave you, yet condemn me not.
BARNWELL. Condemn you? No, I approve your Resolution, and rejoice to hear it; 'tis just,—'tis necessary,—I have well weigh'd, and found it so.
LUCY. I'm afraid the young Man has more Sense than she thought he had. [*Aside.*
BARNWELL. Before you came I had determin'd never to see you more.
MILLWOOD. Confusion! [*Aside.*
LUCY. Ay! we are all out; this is a Turn so unexpected, that I shall

make nothing of my Part, they must e'en play the Scene betwixt themselves. [*Aside.*

MILLWOOD. 'Twas some relief to think, tho' absent, you would love me still; but to find, tho' Fortune had been indulgent, that you, more cruel and inconstant, had resolv'd to cast me off.—This, as I never cou'd expect, I have not learnt to bear.

BARNWELL. I am sorry to hear you blame in me a Resolution that so well becomes us both.

MILLWOOD. I have Reason for what I do, but you have none.

BARNWELL. Can we want a Reason for parting, who have so many to wish we never had met?

MILLWOOD. Look on me, *Barnwell,* am I deform'd or old, that Satiety so soon succeeds Enjoyment? nay, look again, am I not she whom Yesterday you thought the fairest and the kindest of her Sex? whose Hand, trembling with Extacy, you prest and moulded thus, while on my Eyes you gazed with such delight, as if Desire increas'd by being fed.

BARNWELL. No more; let me repent my former Follies, if possible, without remembring what they were.

MILLWOOD. Why?

BARNWELL. Such is my Frailty that 'tis dangerous.

MILLWOOD. Where is the Danger, since we are to part?

BARNWELL. The Thought of that already is too painful.

MILLWOOD. If it be painful to part, then I may hope at least you do not hate me?

BARNWELL. No,—no,—I never said I did,—O my heart!—

MILLWOOD. Perhaps you pity me?

BARNWELL. I do,—I do,—indeed, I do.

MILLWOOD. You'll think upon me?

BARNWELL. Doubt it not while I can think at all.

MILLWOOD. You may judge an Embrace at parting too great a Favour, —though it would be the last? [*He draws back.*] A Look shall then suffice,—farewell,—for ever.

SCENE X.

BARNWELL.

If to resolve to suffer be to conquer,—I have conquer'd.
—Painful Victory!

SCENE XI.

Barnwell, Millwood *and* Lucy.

MILLWOOD. One thing I had forgot,—I never must return to my own House again. This I thought proper to let you know, lest your Mind should change, and you shou'd seek in vain to find me there. Forgive me this second Intrusion; I only came to give you this Caution, and that perhaps was needless.

BARNWELL. I hope it was, yet it is kind, and I must thank you for it.

MILLWOOD. My Friend, your Arm. [*To* Lucy.] Now I am gone for ever. [*Going.*

BARNWELL. One thing more;—sure there's no danger in my knowing where you go? If you think otherwise?—

MILLWOOD. Alas! [*Weeping.*

LUCY. We are right I find, that's my Cue. [*Aside.*
Ah; dear Sir, she's going she knows not whether; but go she must.

BARNWELL. Humanity obliges me to wish you well; why will you thus expose your self to needless Troubles?

LUCY. Nay, there's no help for it: She must quit the Town immediately, and the Kingdom as soon as possible; it was no small Matter you may be sure, that could make her resolve to leave you.

MILLWOOD. No more, my Friend; since he for whose dear Sake alone I suffer, and am content to suffer, is kind and pities me. Whereeer I wander through Wilds[14] and Desarts, benighted and forlorn, that Thought shall give me comfort.

BARNWELL. For my Sake! O tell me how; which way am I so curs'd as to bring such Ruin on thee?

MILLWOOD. No matter,—I am contented with my Lot.

BARNWELL. Leave me not in this Incertainty.

MILLWOOD. I have said too much.

BARNWELL. How, how am I the Cause of your Undoing?

MILLWOOD. 'Twill but increase your Troubles.

BARNWELL. My Troubles can't be greater than they are.

LUCY. Well, well, Sir, if she won't satisfy you, I will.

BARNWELL. I am bound to you beyond Expression.

MILLWOOD. Remember, Sir, that I desir'd you not to hear it.

BARNWELL. Begin, and ease my racking Expectation.

LUCY. Why you must know, my Lady here was an only Child; but her Parents dying while she was young, left her and her Fortune (no inconsiderable one, I assure you) to the Care of a Gentleman, who has a good Estate of his own.

MILLWOOD. Ay, ay, the barbarous Man is rich enough;—but what are Riches when compared to Love?

LUCY. For a while he perform'd the Office of a faithful Guardian, settled her in a House, hir'd her Servants;—but you have seen in what manner she liv'd, so I need say no more of that.

MILLWOOD. How I shall live hereafter, Heaven knows.

LUCY. All Things went on as one cou'd wish, till, some Time ago, his Wife dying, he fell violently in love with his Charge, and wou'd

14. "Wiles" in Steffensen.

fain have marry'd her: Now the Man is neither old nor ugly, but a good personable sort of a Man, but I don't know how it was, she cou'd never endure him; in short, her ill Usage so provok'd him, that he brought in an Account of his Executorship, wherein he makes her Debtor to him.—

MILLWOOD. A Trifle in it self, but more than enough to ruin me, whom, by this unjust Account, he had stripp'd of all before.

LUCY. Now she having neither Money, nor Friend, except me, who am as unfortunate as her self, he compell'd her to pass his Account, and give Bond for the Sum he demanded; but still provided handsomely for her, and continued his Courtship, till, being inform'd by his Spies (truly I suspect some in her own Family°) that you were entertain'd at her House, and stay'd with her all Night, he came this Morning raving, and storming like a Madman; talks no more of Marriage, so there's no Hopes of making up Matters that Way, but vows her Ruin, unless she'll allow him the same Favour that he supposes she granted you.

° household

BARNWELL. Must she be ruin'd, or find her Refuge in another's Arms?

MILLWOOD. He gave me but an Hour to resolve in, that's happily spent with you;—and now I go.—

BARNWELL. To be expos'd to all the Rigours of the various Seasons, the Summer's parching Heat, and Winter's Cold; unhous'd to wander Friendless thro' the unhospitable World, in Misery and Want; attended with Fear and Danger, and pursu'd by Malice and Revenge; woud'st thou endure all this for me, and can I do nothing,—nothing to prevent it?

LUCY. 'Tis really a Pity, there can be no Way found out.

BARNWELL. O where are all my Resolutions now; like early Vapours, or the Morning Dew, chas'd by the Sun's warm Beams they're vanish'd and lost, as tho' they had never been.

LUCY. Now I advis'd her, Sir, to comply with the Gentleman; that wou'd not only put an End no to her Troubles, but make her Fortune at once.

BARNWELL. Tormenting Fiend, away.—I had rather perish, nay, see her perish, than have her sav'd by him; I will my self prevent her Ruin, tho' with my own. A Moment's Patience,—I'll return immediately.

SCENE XII.

Millwood *and* Lucy.

LUCY. 'Twas well you came, or, by what I can perceive, you had lost him.

MILLWOOD. That, I must confess, was a Danger I did not foresee; I was only afraid he should have come without Money. You know a House of Entertainment, like mine, is not kept without Expence.

LUCY. That's very true; but then you shou'd be reasonable in your Demands; 'tis pity to discourage a young Man.

MILLWOOD. Leave that to me.

SCENE XIII.

Barnwell *with a Bag of Money,* Millwood *and* Lucy.

BARNWELL. What am I about to do!—Now you, who boast your Reason all-sufficient, suppose your selves in my Condition, and determine for me; whether it's right to let her suffer for my Faults, or, by this small Addition to my Guilt, prevent the ill Effects of what is past.

LUCY. These young Sinners think every Thing in the Ways of Wickedness so strange,—but I cou'd tell him that this is nothing but what's very common; for one Vice as naturally begets another, as a Father a Son:—But he'll find out that himself, if he lives long enough. [*Aside.*

BARNWELL. Here take this, and with it purchase your Deliverance; return to your House, and live in Peace and Safety.

MILLWOOD. So I may hope to see you there again.

BARNWELL. Answer me not,—but fly,—lest,[15] in the Agonies of my Remorse, I take again what is not mine to give, and abandon thee to Want and Misery.

MILLWOOD. Say but you'll come.—

BARNWELL. You are my Fate, my Heaven, or my Hell; only leave me now, dispose of me hereafter as you please.

SCENE XIV.

BARNWELL.

What have I done?—Were my Resolutions founded on Reason, and sincerely made,—why then has Heaven suffer'd me to fall? I sought not the Occasion; and, if my Heart deceives me not, Compassion and Generosity were my Motives.—Is virtue inconsistent with it self, or are Vice and Virtue only empty Names? Or do they depend on Accidents, beyond our Power to produce, or to prevent,—wherein we have no Part, and yet must be determin'd by the Event?—But why should I attempt to reason? All is Confusion, Horror, and Remorse;—I find I am lost,

15. "least" in Steffensen.

cast down from all my late erected Hopes, and plung'd again in Guilt, yet scarce know how or why—

Such undistinguish'd Horrors make my Brain,
Like Hell, the Seat of Darkness, and of Pain.

The End of the Second Act.

ACT III.

SCENE I.

A Room in Thorowgood's *House.*
Thorowgood *and* Trueman.

THOROWGOOD. Methinks I wou'd not have you only learn the Method of Merchandize, and practise it hereafter, merely as a Means of getting Wealth.—'Twill be well worth your Pains to study it as a Science.—See how it is founded in Reason, and the Nature of Things.—How it promotes Humanity, as it has opened and yet keeps up an Intercourse between Nations, far remote from one another in Situation, Customs and Religion; promoting Arts, Industry, Peace and Plenty; by mutual Benefits diffusing mutual Love from Pole to Pole.

TRUEMAN. Something of this I have consider'd, and hope, by your Assistance, to extend my Thoughts much farther.—I have observ'd those Countries, where Trade is promoted and encouraged, do not make Discoveries to destroy, but to improve Mankind,—by Love and Friendship, to tame the fierce, and polish the most savage,—to teach them the Advantages of honest Traffick,—by taking from them, with their own Consent, their useless Superfluities, and giving them, in Return, what, from their Ignorance in manual Arts, their Situation, or some other Accident, they stand in need of.

THOROWGOOD. 'Tis justly observ'd:—The populous East, luxuriant, abounds with glittering Gems, bright Pearls, aromatick Spices, and Health-restoring Drugs: The late found Western World's rich Earth glows with unnumber'd Veins of Gold and Silver Ore.—On every Climate, and on every Country, Heaven has bestowed some good peculiar to it self.—It is the industrious Merchant's Business to collect the various Blessings of each Soil and Climate, and, with the Product of the whole, to enrich his native Country.—Well! I have examin'd your Accounts: They are not only just, as I have always found them, but regularly kept, and fairly enter'd.—I commend your Diligence. Method in Business is the surest Guide. He, who neglects it, frequently stumbles, and always wanders perplex'd, uncertain, and in Danger. Are

Barnwell's Accounts ready for my Inspection? he does not use to be the last on these Occasions.

TRUEMAN. Upon receiving your Orders he retir'd, I thought, in some Confusion.—If you please, I'll go and hasten him.—I hope he has n't been guilty of any Neglect.

THOROWGOOD. I'm now going to the *Exchange*;[16] let him know, at my Return, I expect to find him ready.

SCENE II.

MARIA *with a Book sits and reads.*

How forcible is Truth? The weakest Mind, inspir'd with Love of that,—fix'd and collected in it self,—with Indifference beholds—the united Force of Earth and Hell opposing: Such Souls are rais'd above the Sense of Pain, or so supported, that they regard it not. The Martyr cheaply purchases his Heaven.—Small are his sufferings, great is his Reward;—not so the Wretch, who combats Love with Duty; when the Mind, weaken'd and dissolved by the soft Passion, feeble and hopeless opposes its own Desires.—What is an Hour, a Day, a Year of Pain, to a whole Life of Tortures, such as these?

SCENE III.

Trueman *and* Maria.

TRUEMAN. O, Barnwell!—O, my Friend, how art thou fallen?

MARIA. Ha! *Barnwell!* What of him? Speak, say, what of *Barnwell.*

TRUEMAN. 'Tis not to be conceal'd.—I've News to tell of him that will afflict your generous Father, your self, and all who knew him.

MARIA. Defend us Heaven!

TRUEMAN. I cannot speak it.—See there. [*Gives a Letter,* Maria *reads.*

MARIA. Trueman,

I Know my Absence will surprize my honour'd Master, and your self; and the more, when you shall understand that the Reason of my withdrawing, is my having embezzled part of the Cash with which I was entrusted. After this, 'tis needless to inform you that I intend never to return again: Though this might have been known by examining my Accounts; yet, to prevent that unnecessary Trouble, and to cut off all fruitless Expectations of my Return, I have left this from the lost

George Barnwell.

16. The Royal Exchange was both a shopping center and a place where merchants went to discuss business matters.

TRUEMAN. Lost indeed! Yet how he shou'd be guilty of what he there charges himself withal, raises my Wonder equal to my Grief.—Never had Youth a higher Sense of Virtue—Justly he thought, and as he thought he practised; never was Life more regular than his; an Understanding uncommon at his Years; an open, generous manliness of Temper; his Manners easy, unaffected and engaging.

MARIA. This and much more you might have said with Truth.—He was the delight of every Eye, and Joy of every Heart that knew him.

TRUEMAN. Since such he was, and was my Friend, can I support his Loss?—See the fairest and happiest Maid this wealthy City boasts, kindly condescends to weep for thy unhappy Fate, poor ruin'd *Barnwell!*

MARIA. *Trueman,* do you think a Soul so delicate as his, so sensible of Shame, can e'er submit to live a Slave to Vice?

TRUEMAN. Never, never. So well I know him, I'm sure this Act of his, so contrary to his Nature, must have been caused by some unavoidable Necessity.

MARIA. Is there no Means yet to preserve him?

TRUEMAN. O, that there were.—But few Men recover Reputation lost.—A Merchant never.—Nor wou'd he, I fear, though I shou'd find him, ever be brought to look his injur'd Master in the Face.

MARIA. I fear as much,—and therefore wou'd never have my Father know it.

TRUEMAN. That's impossible.

MARIA. What's the Sum?

TRUEMAN. 'Tis considerable.—I've mark'd it here, to show it, with the Letter, to your Father, at his Return.

MARIA. If I shou'd supply the Money, cou'd you so dispose of that, and the Account, as to conceal this unhappy Mismanagement from my Father?

TRUEMAN. Nothing more easy:—But can you intend it? Will you save a helpless Wretch from Ruin? Oh! 'twere an Act worthy such exalted Virtue as *Maria*'s.—Sure Heaven, in Mercy to my Friend, inspired the generous Thought.

MARIA. Doubt not but I wou'd purchase so great a Happiness at a much dearer Price.—But how shall he be found?

TRUEMAN. Trust to my Diligence for that.—In the mean time, I'll conceal his Absence from your Father, or find such Excuses for it, that the real Cause shall never be suspected.

MARIA. In attempting to save from Shame, one whom we hope may yet return to Virtue, to Heaven and you, the only Witnesses of this Action, I appeal, whether I do any thing misbecoming my Sex and Character.

TRUEMAN. Earth must approve the Deed, and Heaven, I doubt not, will reward it.

MARIA. If Heaven succeed it, I am well rewarded. A Virgin's Fame is sullied by Suspicion's slightest Breath; and therefore as this must be a Secret from my Father, and the World, for *Barnwell*'s sake, for mine let it be so to him.

SCENE IV.

Millwood's *House.*
Lucy *and* Blunt.

LUCY. Well! what do you think of *Millwood*'s Conduct now!

BLUNT. I own it is surprizing:—I don't know which to admire most, her feign'd, or his real Passion; tho' I have sometimes been afraid that her Avarice wou'd discover her:—But his Youth and want of Experience make it the easier to impose on him.

LUCY. No, it is his Love. To do him Justice, notwithstanding his Youth, he don't want Understanding; but you Men are much easier imposed on, in these Affairs, than your Vanity will allow you to believe.—Let me see the wisest of you all, as much in Love with me, as *Barnwell* is with *Millwood,* and I'll engage to make as great a Fool of him.

BLUNT. And all Circumstances consider'd, to make as much Money of him too.

LUCY. I can't answer for that. Her Artifice in making him rob his Master at first, and the various Stratagems, by which she has obliged him to continue in that Course, astonish even me, who know her so well.—

BLUNT. But then you are to consider that the Money was his Master's.

LUCY. There was the Difficulty of it.—Had it been his own, it had been nothing.—Were the World his, she might have it for a Smile: —But those golden Days are done;—he's ruin'd, and *Millwood*'s Hopes of farther Profits there are at an End.

BLUNT. That's no more than we all expected.

LUCY. Being call'd, by his Master, to make up his Accounts, he was forc'd to quit his House and Service, and wisely flies to *Millwood* for Relief and Entertainment.

BLUNT. I have not heard of this before! How did she receive him?

LUCY. As you wou'd expect.—She wonder'd what he meant, was astonish'd at his Impudence,—and, with an Air of Modesty peculiar to her self, swore so heartily, that she never saw him before,—that she put me out of Countenance.

BLUNT. That's much indeed! But how did *Barnwell* behave?

LUCY. He griev'd, and, at length, enrag'd at this barbarous Treatment, was preparing to be gone; when, making toward the Door, show'd a Sum of Money, which he had brought from his Master's,—the last he's ever like to have from thence.

BLUNT. But then *Millwood?*

LUCY. Aye, she, with her usual Address, return'd to her old Arts of lying, swearing, and dissembling.—Hung on his Neck, and wept, and swore 'twas meant in Jest; till the amorous Youth, melted into Tears, threw the Money into her Lap, and swore he had rather die, than think her false.

BLUNT. Strange Infatuation!

LUCY. But what follow'd was stranger still. As Doubts and Fears, follow'd by Reconcilement, ever increase Love, where the Passion is sincere: so in him it caus'd so wild a Transport of excessive Fondness, such Joy, such Grief, such Pleasure, and such Anguish, that Nature in him seem'd sinking with the Weight, and the charm'd Soul dispos'd to quit his Breast for hers.—just then, when every Passion with lawless Anarchy prevail'd,—and Reason was in the raging Tempest lost;—the cruel, artful *Millwood* prevail'd upon the wretched Youth to promise—what I tremble but to think on.

BLUNT. I am amaz'd! what can it be?

LUCY. You will be more so, to hear it is to attempt the Life of his nearest Relation, and best Benefactor.—

BLUNT. His Uncle, whom we have often heard him speak of as a Gentleman of a large Estate and fair Character in the Country, where he lives.

LUCY. The same.—She was no sooner possess'd of the last dear Purchase of his Ruin, but her Avarice, insatiate as the Grave, demands this horrid Sacrifice,—*Barnwell*'s near Relation; and unsuspected Virtue must give too easy Means to seize the good Man's Treasure; whose Blood must seal the dreadful Secret, and prevent the Terrors of her guilty Fears.

BLUNT. Is it possible she cou'd perswade him to do an Act like that! He is, by Nature, honest, grateful, compassionate, and generous: And though his Love, and her artful Perswasions, have wrought him to practise what he most abhors; yet we all can witness for him, with what Reluctance he has still comply'd! So many Tears he shed o'er each Offence, as might, if possible, sanctify Theft, and make a Merit of a Crime.

LUCY. 'Tis true, at the naming the Murder of his Uncle, he started into Rage; and, breaking from her Arms, where she till then had held him with well dissembled Love and false Endearments, call'd her cruel Monster, Devil, and told her she was born for his Destruction.—She thought it not for her Purpose to meet his Rage with Rage, but affected a most passionate Fit of Grief;—rail'd at her Fate, and curs'd her wayward Stars,—that still her Wants shou'd force her to press him to act such Deeds, as she must needs abhor as well as he; but told him Necessity had no Law, and Love no Bounds; that therefore he never truly lov'd, but meant in her Necessity, to forsake her;—then kneel'd and swore, that since, by his Refusal, he had given her Cause to doubt his Love, she never wou'd see him more; unless, to prove it true, he robb'd his Uncle to supply her Wants, and murder'd him, to keep it from Discovery.

BLUNT. I am astonish'd! What said he?

LUCY. Speechless he stood; but in his Face you might have read, that various Passions tore his very Soul. Oft he, in Anguish, threw his Eyes towards Heaven, and then as often bent their Beams on her; then wept and groan'd, and beat his troubled Breast; at length, with Horror, not to be express'd, he cry'd, Thou cursed Fair! have I not given dreadful Proofs of Love! What drew me from my youthful Innocence, to stain my then unspotted Soul, but Love? What caus'd me to rob my worthy gentle Master, but cursed Love? What makes me now a Fugitive from his Service, loath'd by my self, and scorn'd by all the World, but Love? What fills my Eyes with Tears, my Soul with Torture, never felt on this side Death before? Why Love, Love, Love. And why, above all, do I resolve (for, tearing his Hair, he cry'd I do resolve) to kill my Uncle?

BLUNT. Was she not mov'd? It makes me weep to hear the sad Relation.

LUCY. Yes, with Joy, that she had gain'd her Point.—She gave him no Time to cool, but urg'd him to attempt it instantly. He's now gone; if he performs it, and escapes, there's more Money for her; if not, he'll ne'er return, and then she's fairly rid of him.

BLUNT. 'Tis time the World was rid of such a Monster.—

LUCY. If we don't do our Endeavours to prevent this Murder, we are as bad as she.

BLUNT. I'm afraid it is too late.

LUCY. Perhaps not.—Her Barbarity to *Barnwell* makes me hate her. —We've run too great a Length with her already.—I did not think her or my self so wicked, as I find, upon Reflection, we are.

BLUNT. 'Tis true, we have all been too much so.—But there is something so horrid in Murder,—that all other Crimes seem nothing when compared to that.—I wou'd not be involv'd in the Guilt of that for all the World.

LUCY. Nor I, Heaven knows;—therefore, let us clear our selves, by doing all that is in our Power to prevent it. I have just thought of a Way, that, to me, seems probable.—Will you join with me to detect this curs'd Design?

BLUNT. With all my Heart. He who knows of a Murder intended to be committed, and does not discover it, in the Eye of the Law, and Reason, is a Murderer.

LUCY. Let us lose no Time;—I'll acquaint you with the Particulars as we go.

SCENE V.

A Walk at some Distance from a Country Seat.

BARNWELL.

A dismal Gloom obscures the Face of Day; either the Sun has slip'd behind a Cloud, or journeys down the West of Heaven, with more than common Speed, to avoid the Sight of what I'm doom'd to act. Since I set forth on this accursed Design, where'er I tread, methinks, the solid Earth trembles beneath my Feet.—Yonder limpid Stream, whose hoary Fall has made a natural Cascade, as I pass'd by, in doleful Accents seem'd to murmur, Murder. The Earth, the Air, and Water, seem concern'd; but that's not strange, the World is punish'd, and Nature feels the Shock, when Providence permits a good Man's Fall!—Just Heaven! Then what shou'd I be! for him that was my Father's only Brother, and since his Death has been to me a Father, who took me up an Infant, and an Orphan; rear'd me with tenderest Care, and still indulged me with most paternal Fondness;—yet here I stand avow'd his destin'd Murderer.—I stiffen with Horror at my own Impiety;—'tis yet unperform'd.—What if I quit my bloody Purpose, and fly the Place! [*Going, then stops.*]—But whether, O whether, shall I fly?—My Master's once friendly Doors are ever shut against me; and without Money *Millwood* will never see me more, and Life is not to be endured without her:—She's got such firm Possession of my Heart, and governs there with such despotick Sway;—Aye, there's the Cause of all my Sin and Sorrow:—'Tis more than love; 'tis the Fever of the Soul, and Madness of Desire.—In vain does Nature, Reason, Conscience, all oppose it; the impetuous Passion bears down all before it, and drives me on to Lust, to Theft, and Murder. —Oh Conscience! feeble Guide to Virtue, who only shows us when we go astray, but wants the Power to stop us in our Course. —Ha! in yonder shady Walk I see my Uncle.—He's alone.—Now for my Disguise.—[*Plucks out a Vizor.*[17]] This is his Hour of private Meditation. Thus daily he prepares his Soul for Heaven,—whilst I—But what have I to do with Heaven!—Ha! No Struggles, Conscience.—

Hence! Hence Remorse, and ev'ry Thought that's good;
The Storm that Lust begun, must end in Blood.

[*Puts on the Vizor, and draws a Pistol.*

17. Mask covering half the face.

SCENE VI.

A close° *Walk in a Wood.* secluded

UNCLE.

If I was superstitious, I shou'd fear some Danger lurk'd unseen, or Death were nigh:—A heavy Melancholy clouds my Spirits; my Imagination is fill'd with gashly° Forms of dreary Graves, and Bodies chang'd by Death,—when the pale lengthen'd Visage attacks each weeping Eye,—and fills the musing Soul, at once, with Grief and Horror, Pity and Aversion.—I will indulge the Thought. The wise Man prepares himself for Death, by making it familiar to his Mind.—When strong Reflections hold the Mirror near,—and the Living in the Dead behold their future selves, how does each inordinate Passion and Desire cease or sicken at the View?—The Mind scarce moves;—The Blood, curdling, and chill'd, creeps slowly thro' the Veins: fix'd, still, and motionless we stand, so like the solemn Object of our Thoughts, we are almost at present —what we must be hereafter; 'till Curiosity awakes the Soul, and sets it on Inquiry.—

hideous

SCENE VII.

Uncle, George Barnwell *at a Distance.*

UNCLE. O Death, thou strange mysterious Power,—seen every Day, yet never understood—but by the incommunicative Dead, what art thou?—The extensive Mind of Man, that with a Thought circles the Earth's vast Globe,—sinks to the Centre, or ascends above the Stars; that Worlds exotick finds, or thinks it finds,—thy thick Clouds attempts to pass in vain, lost and bewilder'd in the horrid Gloom,—defeated she returns more doubtful than before; of nothing certain, but of Labour lost.

[*During this Speech,* Barnwell *sometimes presents the Pistol, and draws it back again.*

BARNWELL. Oh, 'tis impossible!

[*Throwing down the Pistol. Uncle starts and attempts to draw his Sword.*

UNCLE. A man so near me, arm'd and masqu'd!

BARNWELL. Nay, then there's no Retreat.

[*Plucks a Poniard*° *from his Bosom, and stabs him.* dagger

UNCLE. Oh! I am slain! All gracious Heaven regard the Prayer of thy dying Servant. Bless, with thy choicest Blessings, my dearest Nephew; forgive my Murderer, and take my fleeting Soul to endless Mercy.

[Barnwell *throws off his Mask, runs to him, and, kneeling by him, raises and chafes him.*

BARNWELL. Expiring Saint! Oh, murder'd, martyr'd Uncle! Lift up your dying Eyes, and view your Nephew in your Murderer.—O do not look so tenderly upon me.—Let Indignation lighten from your Eyes, and blast me ere you die.—By Heaven, he weeps in Pity of my Woes.—Tears,—Tears, for Blood.—The Murder'd, in the Agonies of Death, weeps for his Murderer.—O, speak your pious Purpose,—pronounce my Pardon then,—and take me with you.—He wou'd, but cannot.—O why, with such fond Affection do you press my murdering Hand!—What! will you kiss me! [*Kisses him.*

UNCLE. [*Groans and dies.*]

BARNWELL. Life, that hover'd on his Lips but till he had sealed my Pardon, in that Kiss expired. He's gone for ever,—and oh! I follow.—[*Swoons away upon his Uncle's dead Body.*] Do I still live to press the suffering Bosom of the Earth?—Do I still breath, and taint with my infectious Breath the wholesome Air!—Let Heaven, from its high Throne, in Justice or in Mercy, now look down on that dear murder'd Saint, and me the Murderer.—And, if his Vengeance spares,—let Pity strike and end my wretched Being.—Murder the worst of Crimes, and Parricide the worst of Murders, and this the worst of Parricides. *Cain,* who stands on Record from the Birth of Time, and must to its last final Period, as accurs'd, slew a Brother, favour'd above him.—Detested *Nero,* by another's Hand, dispatch'd a Mother, that he fear'd and hated.—But I, with my own Hand, have murder'd a Brother, Mother, Father, and a Friend; most loving and belov'd.—This execrable Act of mine's without a Parallel.—O may it ever stand alone,—the last of Murders, as it is the worst.—

The rich Man thus, in Torment and Despair,
Prefer'd his vain, but charitable Prayer.
The Fool, his own Soul lost, wou'd fain be wise
For others Good; but Heaven his Suit denies.
By Laws and Means well known we stand or fall,
And one eternal Rule remains for all.

The End of the Third Act.

ACT IV.

SCENE I.

A Room in Thorowgood*'s House.*

MARIA.

How falsly do they judge who censure or applaud, as we're afflicted or rewarded here. I know I am unhappy, yet cannot charge my self with any Crime, more than the common Frailties of our Kind, that shou'd provoke just Heaven to mark me out for Sufferings so uncommon and severe. Falsly to accuse our selves, Heaven must abhor; then it is just and right that Innocence should suffer; for Heaven must be just in all its Ways.—Perhaps by that they are kept from moral Evils, much worse than penal, or more improv'd in Virtue; Or may not the lesser ills that they sustain, be the Means of greater Good to others? Might all the joyless Days and sleepless Nights that I have past, but purchase Peace for thee—

Thou dear, dear Cause of all my Grief and Pain,
Small were the Loss, and infinite the Gain:
Tho' to the Grave in secret Love I pine,
So Life, and Fame, and Happiness were thine.

SCENE II.

Trueman *and* Maria.

MARIA. What News of *Barnwell?*

TRUEMAN. None.—I have sought him with the greatest Diligence, but all in vain.

MARIA. Doth my Father yet suspect the Cause of his Absence?

TRUEMAN. All appear'd so just and fair to him, it is not possible he ever shou'd; but his Absence will no longer be conceal'd. Your Father's wise; and though he seems to hearken to the friendly Excuses I wou'd make for *Barnwell;* yet, I am afraid, he regards 'em only as such, without suffering them to influence his Judgment.

MARIA. How does the unhappy Youth defeat all our Designs to serve him! yet I can never repent what we have done. Shou'd he return, 'twill make his Reconciliation with my Father easier, and preserve him from future Reproach from a malicious unforgiving World.

SCENE III.

[*To them.*] Thorowgood *and* Lucy.

THOROWGOOD. This Woman here has given me a sad, (and bating° some Circumstances) too probable Account of *Barnwell's* Defection.

subtracting

LUCY. I am sorry, Sir, that my frank Confession of my former unhappy Course of Life shou'd cause you to suspect my Truth on this Occasion.

THOROWGOOD. It is not that; your Confession has in it all the Appearance of Truth. [*To them.*] Among many other Particulars, she informs me that *Barnwell* has been influenc'd to break his Trust, and wrong me, at several Times, of considerable Sums of Money; now, as I know this to be false, I wou'd fain doubt the whole of her Relation,—too dreadful—to be willingly believ'd.

MARIA. Sir, your Pardon; I find my self on a sudden so indispos'd, that I must retire.—Providence opposes all Attempts to save him.—Poor ruin'd *Barnwell!*—Wretched lost *Maria!*—[*Aside.*

SCENE IV.

Thorowgood, Trueman *and* Lucy.

THOROWGOOD. How am I distress'd on every Side? Pity for that unhappy Youth, fear for the Life of a much valued Friend—and then my Child—the only Joy and Hope of my declining Life.—Her Melancholy increases hourly, and gives me painful Apprehensions of her Loss.—O *Trueman!* this Person informs me, that your Friend, at the Instigation of an impious Woman, is gone to rob and murder his venerable Uncle.

TRUEMAN. O execrable Deed! I am blasted with the Horror of the Thought!

LUCY. This Delay may ruin all.

THOROWGOOD. What to do or think I know not; that he ever wrong'd me, I know is false,—the rest may be so too, there's all my Hope.

TRUEMAN. Trust not to that, rather suppose all true than lose a Moment's Time; even now the horrid Deed may be a doing;—dreadful Imagination!—or it may be done, and we are vainly debating on the Means to prevent what is already past.

THOROWGOOD. This Earnestness convinces me that he knows more than he has yet discover'd. What ho! without there! who waits?

SCENE V.

[*To them.*] *A Servant.*

THOROWGOOD. Order the Groom to saddle the swiftest Horse, and prepare himself to set out with Speed.—An affair of Life and Death demands his Diligence.

SCENE VI.

Thorowgood, Trueman *and* Lucy.

THOROWGOOD. For you, whose Behaviour on this Occasion I have no Time to commend as it deserves, I must ingage your farther Assistance.—Return and observe this *Millwood* till I come. I have your Directions, and will follow you as soon as possible.

SCENE VII.

Thorowgood *and* Trueman.

THOROWGOOD. *Trueman,* you I am sure wou'd not be idle on this Occasion.

SCENE VIII.

TRUEMAN.

He only who is a Friend can judge of my Distress.

SCENE IX.

Millwood*'s House.*

MILLWOOD.

I wish I knew the Event of his Design;—the Attempt without Success would ruin him.—Well! what have I to apprehend from that? I fear too much. The Mischief being only intended, his Friends, in pity of his Youth, turn all their Rage on me. I should have thought of that before.—Suppose the Deed done—then, and then only I shall be secure; or what if he returns without attempting it at all?

SCENE X.

Millwood, *and* Barnwell *bloody.*

MILLWOOD. But he is here, and I have done him wrong; his bloody Hands show he has done the Deed, but show he wants the Prudence to conceal it.

BARNWELL. Where shall I hide me? whether shall I fly to avoid the swift unerring Hand of Justice?

MILLWOOD. Dismiss those Fears; tho' Thousands had pursu'd you to the Door, yet being enter'd here you are safe as Innocence; I have such a Cavern, by Art so cunningly contriv'd, that the piercing Eyes of Jealousy and Revenge may search in vain, nor find the Entrance to the safe Retreat; there will I hide you if any Danger's near.

BARNWELL. O hide me from my self if it be possible; for while I bear my Conscience in my Bosom, tho' I were hid, where Man's Eye never saw, nor Light e'er dawn'd, 'twere all in vain. For oh! that inmate,—that impartial Judge, will try, convict, and sentence me for Murder; and execute me with never ending Torments. Behold these Hands all crimson'd o'er with my dear Uncle's Blood! Here's a Sight to make a Statue start with Horror, or turn a living Man into a Statue.

MILLWOOD. Ridiculous! Then it seems you are afraid of your own Shadow; or what's less than a Shadow, your Conscience.

BARNWELL. Tho' to Man unknown I did the accursed Act, what can we hide from Heav'ns all-seeing Eye?

MILLWOOD. No more of this Stuff;—what advantage have you made of his Death? or what advantage may yet be made of it?—did you secure the Keys of his Treasure,—those no doubt were about him? —what Gold, what Jewels, or what else of Value have you brought me?

BARNWELL. Think you I added Sacrilege to Murder? Oh! had you seen him as his Life flowed from him in a Crimson Flood, and heard him praying for me by the double Name of Nephew and of Murderer; alas, alas! he knew not then that his Nephew was his Murderer; how wou'd you have wish'd as I did, tho' you had a thousand Years of Life to come, to have given them all to have lengthen'd his one Hour. But being dead, I fled the Sight of what my Hands had done, nor cou'd I to have gain'd the Empire of the World, have violated by Theft his sacred Corps.

MILLWOOD. Whining, preposterous, canting Villain, to murder your Uncle, rob him of Life, Natures first, last, dear Prerogative, after which there's no Injury; then fear to take what he no longer wanted, and bring to me your Penury and Guilt. Do you think I'll hazard my Reputation, nay my Life, to entertain you?

BARNWELL. Oh!—*Millwood!*—this from thee;—but I have done,—if you hate me, if you wish me dead, then are you happy,—for Oh! 'tis sure my Grief will quickly end me.

MILLWOOD. In his Madness he will discover all, and involve me in his Ruin;—we are on a Precipice from whence there's no Retreat for both,—then to preserve my self.—[*Pauses.*] There is no other way,—'tis dreadful,—but Reflection comes too late when

Danger's pressing,—and there's no room for Choice.—It must be done.

[*Aside, rings a Bell.*

SCENE XI.

[*To them.*] *A* Servant.

MILLWOOD. Fetch me an Officer and seize this Villain, he has confess'd himself a Murderer; shou'd I let him escape, I justly might be thought as bad as he.

SCENE XII.

Millwood *and* Barnwell.

BARNWELL. O *Millwood!* sure thou dost not, cannot mean it. Stop the Messenger, upon my Knees I beg you, call him back. 'Tis fit I die indeed, but not by you. I will this Instant deliver my self into the Hands of Justice, indeed I will, for Death is all I wish. But thy Ingratitude so tears my wounded Soul, 'tis worse ten thousand times than Death with Torture.

MILLWOOD. Call it what you will, I am willing to live, and live secure; which nothing but your Death can warrant.

BARNWELL. If there be a Pitch of Wickedness that seats the Author beyond the reach of Vengeance, you must be secure. But what remains for me, but a dismal Dungeon, hard-galling Fetters, an awful Tryal, and ignominious Death, justly to fall unpitied and abhorr'd?—After Death to be suspended between Heaven and Earth, a dreadful Spectacle, the warning and horror of a gaping Croud. This I cou'd bear, nay wish not to avoid, had it come from any Hand but thine.—

SCENE XIII.

Millwood, Barnwell, Blunt, *Officer and Attendants.*

MILLWOOD. Heaven defend me! Conceal a Murderer! here, Sir, take this Youth into your Custody, I accuse him of Murder; and will appear to make good my Charge. [*They seize him.*

BARNWELL. To whom, of what, or how shall I complain; I'll not accuse her, the Hand of Heav'n is in it, and this the Punishment of Lust and Parricide; yet Heav'n that justly cuts me off, still suffers her to live, perhaps to punish others; tremendous Mercy! so Fiends are curs'd with Immortality, to be the Executioners of Heaven.—

Be warn'd ye Youths, who see my sad Despair,
Avoid lewd Women, False as they are Fair;
By Reason guided, honest Joys pursue;
The Fair, to Honour and to Virtue true,
Just to her self, will ne'er be false to you.
By my Example learn to shun my Fate,
(How wretched is the Man who's wise too late?)
Ere Innocence, and Fame, and Life be lost,—
Here purchase Wisdom, cheaply, at my Cost.

SCENE XIV.

Millwood *and* Blunt.

MILLWOOD. Where's *Lucy,* why is she absent at such a Time?

BLUNT. Wou'd I had been so too. *Lucy* will soon be here, and, I hope, to thy Confusion, thou Devil!

MILLWOOD. Insolent! This to me?

BLUNT. The worst that we know of the Devil is, that he first seduces to Sin, and then betrays to Punishment.

SCENE XV.

MILLWOOD.

They disapprove of my Conduct then,—and mean to take this Opportunity to set up for themselves.—My Ruin is resolv'd, —I see my Danger, but scorn it and them.—I was not born to fall by such weak Instruments.— [*Going.*

SCENE XVI.

Thorowgood *and* Millwood.

THOROWGOOD. Where is this Scandal of her own Sex, and Curse of ours?

MILLWOOD. What means this Insolence? Who do you seek?

THOROWGOOD. *Millwood.*

MILLWOOD. Well, you have found her then.—I am *Millwood.*—

THOROWGOOD. Then you are the most impious Wretch that e'er the Sun beheld.

MILLWOOD. From your Appearance I shou'd have expected Wisdom and Moderation, but your Manners bely your Aspect.—What is your Business here? I know you not.

THOROWGOOD. Hereafter you may know me better; I am *Barnwell*'s Master.

MILLWOOD. Then you are Master to a Villain; which, I think, is not much to your Credit.

THOROWGOOD. Had he been as much above thy Arts, as my Credit is superior to thy Malice, I need not blush to own him.

MILLWOOD. My Arts;—I don't understand you, Sir! If he has done amiss, what's that to me? Was he my Servant, or yours?—You shou'd have taught him better.

THOROWGOOD. Why shou'd I wonder to find such uncommon Impudence in one arriv'd to such a Height of Wickedness.—When Innocence is banish'd, Modesty soon follows. Know, Sorceress, I'm not ignorant of any of your Arts, by which you first deceiv'd the unwary Youth: I know how, Step by Step, you've led him on, (reluctant and unwilling) from Crime to Crime, to this last horrid Act, which you contriv'd, and, by your curs'd Wiles, even forced him to commit.

MILLWOOD. Ha! *Lucy* has got the Advantage, and accused me first; unless I can turn the Accusation, and fix it upon her and *Blunt,* I am lost. [*Aside.*

THOROWGOOD. Had I known your cruel Design sooner, it had been prevented. To see you punish'd as the Law directs, is all that now remains.—Poor Satisfaction,—for he, innocent as he is, compared to you, must suffer too. But Heaven, who knows our Frame, and graciously distinguishes between Frailty and Presumption, will make a Difference, tho' Man cannot, who sees not the Heart, but only judges by the outward Action.—

MILLWOOD. I find, Sir, we are both unhappy in our Servants. I was surpriz'd at such ill Treatment, without Cause, from a Gentleman of your Appearance, and therefore too hastily return'd it; for which I ask your Pardon. I now perceive you have been so far impos'd on, as to think me engaged in a former Correspondence with your Servant, and, some way or other, accessary to his Undoing.

THOROWGOOD. I charge you as the Cause, the sole Cause of all his Guilt, and all his Suffering, of all he now endures, and must endure, till a violent and shameful Death shall put a dreadful Period to his Life and Miseries together.

MILLWOOD. 'Tis very strange; but who's secure from Scandal and Detraction?—So far from contributing to his Ruin, I never spoke to him till since that fatal Accident, which I lament as much as you.: 'Tis true, I have a Servant, on whose Account he has of late frequented my House; if she has abus'd my good Opinion of her, am I to blame? Has n't *Barnwell* done the same by you?

THOROWGOOD. I hear you; pray go on.

MILLWOOD. I have been inform'd he had a violent Passion for her, and she for him; but till now I always thought it innocent; I know her poor, and given to expensive Pleasures. Now who can tell but she may have influenced the amorous Youth to commit this Murder, to supply her Extravagancies;—it must be so. I now recollect a thousand Circumstances that confirm it: I'll have her and a Man Servant, that I suspect as an Accomplice, secured immediately. I hope, Sir, you will lay aside your ill-grounded Suspicions of me, and join to punish the real Contrivers of this bloody Deed. [*Offers to go.*

THOROWGOOD. Madam, you pass not this Way: I see your Design, but shall protect them from your Malice.

MILLWOOD. I hope you will not use your Influence, and the Credit of your Name, to skreen such guilty Wretches. Consider, Sir! the Wickedness of perswading a thoughtless Youth to such a Crime.

THOROWGOOD. I do,—and of betraying him when it was done.

MILLWOOD. That which you call betraying him, may convince you of my Innocence. She who loves him, tho' she contriv'd the Murder, would never have deliver'd him into the Hands of Justice, as I (struck with the Horror of his Crimes) have done.—

THOROWGOOD. How shou'd an unexperienc'd Youth escape her Snares; the powerful Magick of her Wit and Form might betray the wisest to simple Dotage, and fire the Blood that Age had froze long since. Even I, that with just Prejudice came prepared, had, by her artful Story, been deceiv'd, but that my strong Conviction of her Guilt makes even a Doubt impossible. Those whom subtilly you wou'd accuse, you know are your Accusers; and what proves unanswerably their Innocence, and your Guilt: they accus'd you before the Deed was done, and did all that was in their Power to have prevented it.

MILLWOOD. Sir, you are very hard to be convinc'd; but I have such a Proof, which, when produced, will silence all Objections.

SCENE XVII.

Thorowgood, Lucy, Trueman, Blunt, Officers, *&c.*

LUCY. Gentlemen, pray, place your selves, some on one Side of that Door, and some on the other; watch her Entrance, and act as your Prudence shall direct you.—This Way—[*to* Thorowgood] and note her Behaviour; I have observ'd her, she's driven to the last Extremity, and is forming some desperate Resolution.—I guess at her Design.—

SCENE XVIII.

[*To them.*] Millwood *with a Pistol,* Trueman *secures her.*

TRUEMAN. Here thy Power of doing Mischief ends; deceitful, cruel, bloody Woman!

MILLWOOD. Fool, Hypocrite, Villain,—Man! Thou can'st not call me that.

TRUEMAN. To call thee Woman, were to wrong the Sex, thou Devil!

MILLWOOD. That imaginary Being is an Emblem of thy cursed Sex collected. A Mirrour, wherein each particular Man may see his own Likeness, and that of all Mankind.

THOROWGOOD. Think not by aggravating the Faults of others to extenuate thy own, of which the Abuse of such uncommon Perfections of Mind and Body is not the least.

MILLWOOD. If such I had, well may I curse your barbarous Sex, who robb'd me of 'em, ere I knew their Worth, then left me, too late, to count their Value by their Loss. Another and another Spoiler came, and all my Gain was Poverty and Reproach. My Soul disdain'd, and yet disdains Dependance and Contempt. Riches, no Matter by what Means obtain'd, I saw secur'd the worst of Men from both; I found it therefore necessary to be rich; and, to that End, I summon'd all my Arts. You call 'em wicked, be it so, they were such as my Conversation with your Sex had fumish'd me withal.

THOROWGOOD. Sure none but the worst of Men convers'd with thee.

MILLWOOD. Men of all Degrees and all Professions I have known, yet found no Difference, but in their several Capacities; all were alike wicked to the utmost of their Power. In Pride, Contention, Avarice, Cruelty, and Revenge, the Reverend Priesthood were my unerring Guides. From Suburb-Magistrates, who live by ruin'd Reputations,[18] as the unhospitable Natives of *Cornwall* do by Ship-wrecks, I learn'd, that to charge my innocent Neighbours with my Crimes, was to merit their Protection; for to skreen the Guilty, is the less scandalous, when many are suspected, and Detraction, like Darkness and Death, blackens all Objects, and levels all Distinction. Such are your venal Magistrates, who favour none but such as, by their Office, they are sworn to punish: With them, not to be guilty, is the worst of Crimes; and large Fees privately paid, is every needful Virtue.

THOROWGOOD. Your Practice has sufficiently discover'd your Contempt of Laws, both human and divine; no wonder then that you shou'd hate the Officers of both.

MILLWOOD. I know you and I hate you all; I expect no Mercy, and I ask for none; I follow'd my Inclinations, and that the best of you does every Day. All Actions are alike natural and indifferent to Man and Beast, who devour, or are devour'd, as they meet with others weaker or stronger than themselves.

THOROWGOOD. What Pity it is, a Mind so comprehensive, daring and inquisitive, shou'd be a Stranger to Religion's sweet and powerful Charms.

18. Magistrates outside the City of London were paid by fees and had no regular salary.

MILLWOOD. I am not Fool enough to be an Atheist, tho' I have known enough of Mens Hypocrisy to make a thousand simple Women so. Whatever Religion is in it self, as practis'd by Mankind, it has caus'd the Evils you say it was design'd to cure. War, Plague, and Famine, has not destroy'd so many of the human Race, as this pretended Piety has done; and with such barbarous Cruelty, as if the only Way to honour Heaven, were to turn the present World into Hell.

THOROWGOOD. Truth is Truth, tho' from an Enemy, and spoke in Malice. You bloody, blind, and superstitious Bigots, how will you answer this?

MILLWOOD. What are your Laws, of which, you make your Boast, but the Fool's Wisdom, and the Coward's Valour; the Instrument and Skreen of all your Villanies, by which you punish in others what you act your selves, or wou'd have acted, had you been in their Circumstances. The Judge who condemns the poor Man for being a Thief, had been a Thief himself had he been poor. Thus you go on deceiving, and being deceiv'd, harrassing, plaguing, and destroying one another; but Women are your universal Prey.

Women, by whom you are, the Source of Joy,
With cruel Arts you labour to destroy:
A thousand Ways our Ruin you pursue,
Yet blame in us those Arts, first taught by you.
O—may, from hence, each violated Maid.
By flatt'ring, faithless, barb'rous Man betray'd;
When robb'd of Innocence, and Virgin Fame,
From your Destruction raise a nobler Name;
To right their Sex's Wrongs devote their Mind,
And future Millwoods *prove to plague Mankind.*

The End of the Fourth Act.

ACT V.

SCENE I.

A Room in a Prison.
Thorowgood, Blunt *and* Lucy.

THOROWGOOD. I have recommended to *Barnwell* a Reverend Divine, whose Judgment and Integrity I am well acquainted with; nor has *Millwood* been neglected, but she, unhappy Woman, still obstinate, refuses his Assistance.

LUCY. This pious Charity to the Afflicted well becomes your Character; yet pardon me, Sir, if I wonder you were not at their Trial.

THOROWGOOD. I knew it was impossible to save him, and I and

my Family bear so great a Part in his Distress, that to have been present wou'd have aggravated our Sorrows without relieving his.

BLUNT. It was mournful indeed. *Barnwell's* Youth and modest Deportment, as he past, drew Tears from every Eye: When placed at the Bar, and arraigned before the Reverend Judges, with many Tears and interrupting Sobs he confess'd and aggravated his Offences, without accusing, or once reflecting on *Millwood,* the shameless Author of his Ruin; who dauntless and unconcern'd stood by his Side, viewing with visible Pride and Contempt the vast Assembly, who all with sympathizing Sorrow wept for the wretched Youth. *Millwood,* when called upon to answer, loudly insisted upon her Innocence, and made an artful and a bold Defence; but finding all in vain, the impartial Jury and the learned Bench concurring to find her guilty, how did she curse her self, poor *Barnwell,* us, her Judges, all mankind; But what cou'd that avail? She was condemn'd, and is this Day to suffer with him.

THOROWGOOD. The Time draws on, I am going to visit *Barnwell,* as you are *Millwood.*

LUCY. We have not wrong'd her, yet I dread this Interview. She's proud, impatient, wrathful, and unforgiving. To be the branded Instruments of Vengeance, to suffer in her Shame, and sympathize with her in all she suffers, is the Tribute we must pay for our former ill spent Lives, and long confederacy with her in Wickedness.

THOROWGOOD. Happy for you it ended when it did. What you have done against *Millwood* I know proceeded from a just Abhorrence of her Crimes, free from Interest, Malice, or Revenge. Proselytes to Virtue shou'd be encourag'd. Pursue your proposed Reformation, and know me hereafter for your Friend.

LUCY. This is a Blessing as unhop'd for as unmerited, but Heaven that snatched us from impending Ruin, sure intends you as its Instrument to secure us from Apostacy.

THOROWGOOD. With Gratitude to impute your Deliverance to Heaven is just. Many, less virtuously dispos'd than *Barnwell* was, have never fallen in the Manner he has done,—may not such owe their Safety rather to Providence than to themselves? With Pity and Compassion let us judge him. Great were his Faults, but strong was the Temptation. Let his Ruin learn us Diffidence, Humanity and Circumspection;—for we,—who wonder at his Fate,—perhaps, had we, like him, been tryed,—like him, we had fallen too.

SCENE II.

A Dungeon, A Table and Lamp.
Thorowgood *at a Distance,* Barnwell *reading.*

THOROWGOOD. There see the bitter Fruits of Passion's detested Reign, and sensual Appetite indulg'd. Severe Reflections, Penitence and Tears.

BARNWELL. My honoured injured Master, whose Goodness has covered me a thousand times with Shame, forgive this last unwilling Disrespect,—indeed I saw you not.

THOROWGOOD. 'Tis well, I hope you were better imploy'd in viewing of your self;—your Journey's long, your Time for preparation almost spent,—I sent a Reverend Divine to teach you to improve it, and shou'd be glad to hear of his Success.

BARNWELL. The Word of Truth, which he recommended for my constant Companion in this my sad Retirement, has at length remov'd the Doubts I labour'd under. From thence I've learn'd the infinite Extent of heavenly Mercy; that my Offences, tho' great, are not unpardonable; and that 'tis not my Interest only, but my Duty to believe and to rejoice in that Hope,—So shall Heaven receive the Glory, and future Penitents the Profit of my Example.

THOROWGOOD. Proceed.

BARNWELL. 'Tis wonderful,—that Words shou'd charm Despair, speak Peace and Pardon to a Murderer's Conscience;—but Truth and Mercy flow in every Sentence, attended with Force and Energy divine. How shall I describe my present State of Mind? I hope in doubt,—and trembling I rejoice.—I feel my Grief increase, even as my Fears give way.—Joy and Gratitude now supply more Tears, than the Horror and Anguish of Despair before.

THOROWGOOD. These are the genuine Signs of true Repentance, the only Preparatory, the certain Way to everlasting Peace.—O the Joy it gives to see a Soul form'd and prepar'd for Heaven!—For this the faithful Minister devotes himself to Meditation, Abstinence and Prayer, shunning the vain Delights of sensual Joys, and daily dies that others may live for ever.—For this he turns the sacred Volumes o'er, and spends his Life in painful Search of Truth.—The Love of Riches and the Lust of Power, he looks on with just Contempt and Detestation; who only counts for Wealth the Souls he wins; and whose highest Ambition is to serve Mankind. If the Reward of all his Pains be to preserve one Soul from wandering, or turn one from the Error of his Ways, how does he then rejoice, and own his little Labours over paid!

BARNWELL. What do I owe for all your generous Kindness? but tho' I cannot, Heaven can and will reward you.

THOROWGOOD. To see thee thus, is Joy too great for Words. Farewell, —Heaven strengthen thee.—Farewell.

BARNWELL. O! Sir, there's something I cou'd say, if my sad swelling Heart would give me leave.

THOROWGOOD. Give it vent a while, and try.

BARNWELL. I had a Friend,—'tis true I am unworthy, yet methinks your generous Example might perswade;—cou'd I not see him once before I go from whence there's no return?

THOROWGOOD. He's coming,—and as much thy Friend as ever;—but I'll not anticipate his Sorrow,—too soon he'll see the sad Effect of his contagious Ruin. This Torrent of Domestick Misery bears too hard upon me,—I must retire to indulge a Weakness I find impossible to over-come. [*Aside.*]—Much lov'd—and much lamented Youth—Farewell—Heaven strengthen thee—Eternally Farewell.

BARNWELL. The best of Masters and of Men—Farewell—while I live let me not want your Prayers.

THOROWGOOD. Thou shalt not;—thy Peace being made with Heaven, Death's already vanquish'd;—bear a little longer the Pains that attend this transitory Life, and cease from Pain for ever. [*Exit.*

SCENE III.

BARNWELL.

Perhaps I shall. I find a Power within that bears my Soul above the Fears of Death, and, spight of conscious Shame and Guilt, gives me a Taste of Pleasure more than Mortal.

SCENE IV.

[*To him.*] Trueman *and Keeper.*

KEEPER. Sir, there's the Prisoner.

SCENE V.

Barnwell *and* Trueman.

BARNWELL. *Trueman,*—My Friend, whom I so wisht to see, yet now he's here I dare not look upon him. [*Weeps.*

TRUEMAN. O *Barnwell! Barnwell!*

BARNWELL. Mercy! Mercy! gracious Heaven! for Death, but not for this, was I prepared.

TRUEMAN. What have I suffer'd since I saw you last!—what Pain has Absence given me?—But oh! to see thee thus!

BARNWELL. I know it is dreadful! I feel the Anguish of thy generous Soul,—but I was born to murder all who love me. [*Both weep.*

TRUEMAN. I came not to reproach you;—I thought to bring you Comfort,—but I'm deceiv'd, for I have none to give;—I came to share thy Sorrow, but cannot bear my own.

BARNWELL. My Sense of Guilt indeed you cannot know,—'tis what the Good and Innocent, like you, ne'er conceive;—but other Griefs at present I have none, but what I feel for you.—In your Sorrow I read you love me still,—but yet methinks 'tis strange—when I consider what I am.

TRUEMAN. No more of that,—I can remember nothing but thy Virtues,—thy honest, tender Friendship, our former happy State and present Misery.—O had you trusted me when first the Fair Seducer tempted you, all might have been prevented.

BARNWELL. Alas, thou know'st not what a Wretch I've been! Breach of Friendship was my first and least Offence.—So far was I lost to Goodness,—so devoted to the Author of my Ruin,—that had she insisted on my murdering thee,—I think,—I shou'd have done it.

TRUEMAN. Prithee aggravate thy Faults no more.

BARNWELL. I think I shou'd!—thus Good and Generous as you are, I shou'd have murder'd you!

TRUEMAN. We have not yet embrac'd, and may be interrupted. Come to my Arms!

BARNWELL. Never, never will I taste such Joys on Earth; never will I so sooth my just Remorse. Are those honest Arms, and faithful Bosom, fit to embrace and to support a Murderer?—These Iron Fetters only shall clasp, and flinty Pavement bear me,—[*Throwing himself on the Ground.*] even these too good for such a bloody Monster.

TRUEMAN. Shall Fortune sever those whom Friendship join'd!—Thy Miseries cannot lay thee so low, but Love will find thee.—Here will we offer to stern Calamity,—this Place the Altar, and our selves the Sacrifice.—Our mutual Groans shall eccho to each other thro' the dreary Vault.—Our Sighs shall number the Moments as they pass,—and mingling Tears communicate such Anguish, as Words were never made to express.

BARNWELL. Then be it so.—[*Rising.*] Since you propose an Intercourse of Woe, pour all your Griefs into my Breast,—and in exchange take mine. [*Embracing.*] Where's now the Anguish that you promis'd?—You've taken mine, and make me no Return.—Sure Peace and Comfort dwell within these Arms, and Sorrow can't approach me while I'm here! This too is the Work of Heaven, who, having before spoke Peace and Pardon to me, now sends thee to confirm it.—O take, take some of the Joy that overflows my Breast!

TRUEMAN. I do, I do. Almighty Power, how have you made us capable to bear, at once, the Extreams of Pleasure and of Pain?

SCENE VI.

[*To them.*] Keeper.

KEEPER. Sir.
TRUEMAN. I come.

SCENE VII.

Barnwell *and* Trueman.

BARNWELL. Must you leave me!—Death would soon have parted us for ever.

TRUEMAN. O, my *Barnwell,* there's yet another Task behind:—Again your Heart must bleed for others Woes.

BARNWELL. To meet and part with you, I thought was all I had to do on Earth! What is there more for me to do or suffer?

TRUEMAN. I dread to tell thee, yet it must be known.—*Maria.*

BARNWELL. Our Master's fair and virtuous Daughter!

TRUEMAN. The same.

BARNWELL. No Misfortune, I hope, has reach'd that lovely Maid! Preserve her, Heaven, from every Ill, to show Mankind that Goodness is your Care.

TRUEMAN. Thy, thy Misfortunes, my unhappy Friend, have reach'd her. Whatever you and I have felt, and more, if more be possible, she feels for you.

BARNWELL. *(aside).* I know he doth abhor a Lie, and would not trifle with his dying Friend.—This is, indeed, the bitterness of Death!

TRUEMAN. You must remember, for we all observ'd it, for some Time past, a heavy Melancholy weigh'd her down.—Disconsolate she seem'd, and pin'd and languish'd from a Cause unknown;—till hearing of your dreadful Fate,—the long stifled Flame blaz'd out.—She wept, she wrung her Hands, and tore her Hair, and, in the Transport of her Grief, discover'd her own lost State, whilst she lamented yours.

BARNWELL. Will all the Pain I feel restore thy Ease, lovely unhappy Maid? [*Weeping.*] Why did n't you let me die and never know it?

TRUEMAN. It was impossible;—she makes no Secret of her Passion for you, and is determin'd to see you ere you die;—she waits for me to introduce her.—

SCENE VIII.

BARNWELL.

Vain busy Thoughts be still!—What avails it to think on what I might have been,—I now am,—what I've made my self.

SCENE IX.

[*To him.*] Trueman *and* Maria.

TRUEMAN. Madam, reluctant I lead you to this dismal Scene: This is the Seat of Misery and Guilt.—Here awful Justice reserves her publick Victims.—This is the Entrance to shameful Death.—

MARIA. To this sad Place, then no improper Guest, the abandon'd lost *Maria* brings Despair,—and see the Subject and the Cause of all this World of Woe.—Silent and motionless he stands, as if his Soul had quitted her Abode,—and the lifeless Form alone was left behind;—yet that so perfect, that Beauty and Death,—ever at Enmity,—now seem united there.

BARNWELL. I groan, but murmur not.—Just Heaven, I am your own; do with me what you please.

MARIA. Why are your streaming Eyes still fix'd below?—as tho' thoud'st give the greedy Earth thy Sorrows, and rob me of my Due. —Were Happiness within your Power, you should bestow it where you pleas'd;—but in your Misery I must and will partake.

BARNWELL. Oh! say not so, but fly, abhor, and leave me to my Fate. —Consider what you are:—How vast your Fortune, and how bright your Fame:—Have Pity on your Youth, your Beauty, and unequalled Virtue,—for which so many noble Peers have sigh'd in vain. Bless with your Charms some honourable Lord.—Adorn with your Beauty, and, by your Example, improve the *English* Court, that justly claims such Merit; so shall I quickly be to you—as though I had never been.—

MARIA. When I forget you, I must be so indeed.—Reason, Choice, Virtue, all forbid it.—Let Women, like *Millwood,* if there be more such Women, smile in Prosperity, and in Adversity forsake.—Be it the Pride of Virtue to repair, or to partake, the Ruin such have made.

TRUEMAN. Lovely, ill-fated Maid!—Was there ever such generous Distress before?—How must this peirce his grateful Heart, and aggravate his Woes?

BARNWELL. Ere I knew Guilt or Shame, when Fortune smil'd, and when my youthful Hopes were at the highest; if then to have rais'd my Thoughts to you, had been Presumption in me, never to have been pardon'd,—think how much beneath your self you condescend to regard me now.

MARIA. Let her blush, who, professing Love, invades the Freedom of your Sex's Choice, and meanly sues in Hopes of a Return.—Your inevitable Fate hath render'd hope impossible as vain. Then, why shou'd I fear to avow a Passion so just and so disinterested?

TRUEMAN. If any shou'd take Occasion, from *Millwood*'s Crimes, to libel the best and fairest Part of the Creation, here let them see their Error.—The most distant Hopes of such a tender Passion, from so bright a Maid, might add to the Happiness of the most happy, and make the greatest proud.—Yet here 'tis lavish'd in vain:—Tho' by the rich Present, the generous Donor is undone,—he, on whom it is bestow'd, receives no Benefit.

BARNWELL. So the Aromatick Spices of the East, which all the Living covet and esteem, are, with unavailing Kindness, wasted on the Dead.

MARIA. Yes, fruitless is my Love, and unavailing all my Sighs and Tears.—Can they save thee from approaching Death?—from such a Death?—O terrible Idea!—What is her Misery and Distress, who sees the first last Object of her Love, for whom alone she'd live,—for whom she'd die a thousand, thousand Deaths, if it were possible,—expiring in her Arms? Yet she is happy, when compar'd to me.—Were Millions of Worlds mine, I'd gladly give them in exchange for her Condition.—The most consummate Woe is light to mine. The last of Curses to other miserable Maids, is all I ask—for my Relief, and that's deny'd me.

TRUEMAN. Time and Reflection cure all Ills.

MARIA. All but this;—his dreadful Catastrophe Virtue her self abhors.—To give a Holiday to suburb Slaves, and passing entertain the savage Herd, who, elbowing each other for a Sight, pursue and press upon him like his Fate.—A Mind with Piety and Resolution arm'd, may smile on Death.—But publick Ignominy,—everlasting Shame,—Shame, the Death of Souls,—to die a thousand Times, and yet survive even Death it self, in never dying Infamy—is this to be endured?—Can I, who live in him, and must, each Hour of my devoted Life, feel all these Woes renew'd,—can I endure this!—

TRUEMAN. Grief has impair'd her Spirits; she pants, as in the Agonies of Death.—

BARNWELL. Preserve her, Heaven, and restore her Peace,—nor let her Death be added to my Crime,—[*Bell tolls.*] I am summon'd to my Fate.

SCENE X.

[*To them.*] Keeper and Officers.

KEEPER. The Officers attend you, Sir.—Mrs. *Millwood* is already summon'd.

BARNWELL. Tell 'em, I'm ready.—And now, my Friend, farewell, [*Embracing.*] Support and comfort the best you can this Mourning Fair.—No more.—Forget not to pray for me,—[*Turning to* Maria.] Would you, bright Excellence, permit me the Honour of a chaste Embrace,—the last Happiness this World cou'd give were mine. [*She inclines toward him; they embrace.*] Exalted

Goodness!—O turn your Eyes from Earth, and me, to Heaven,—where Virtue, like yours, is ever heard.—Pray for the Peace of my departing Soul.—Early my Race of Wickedness began, and soon has reach'd the Summet:—Ere Nature has finish'd her Work, and stamp'd me Man,—just at the Time that others begin to stray,—my Course is finish'd. tho' short my Span of Life, and few my Days, yet count my Crimes for Years, and I have liv'd whole Ages.—Thus Justice, in Compassion to Mankind, cuts off a Wretch like me, by one such Example to secure Thousands from future Ruin. Justice and Mercy are in Heaven the same: Its utmost Severity is Mercy to the whole, —thereby to cure Man's Folly and Presumption, which else wou'd render even infinite Mercy vain and ineffectual.

If any Youth, like you,—in future Times,
Shall mourn my Fate,—tho' he abhor my Crimes;
Or tender Maid, like you,—my Tale shall hear,
And to my Sorrows give a pitying Tear:
To each such melting Eye, and throbbing Heart,
Would gracious Heaven this Benefit impart,
Never to know my Guilt,—nor feel my Pain, }
Then must you own, you ought not to complain; }
Since you nor weep,—nor shall I die in vain. }

SCENE XI.

The Place of Execution. The Gallows and Ladders at the farther End of the Stage. A Crowd of Spectators, Blunt *and* Lucy.

LUCY. Heavens! What a Throng!

BLUNT. How terrible is Death when thus prepar'd!

LUCY. Support them, Heaven; thou only can support them; all other Help is vain.

OFFICER WITHIN. Make Way there; make Way, and give the Prisoners Room.

LUCY. They are here: observe them well. How humble and composed young *Barnwell* seems! but *Millwood* looks wild, ruffled with Passion, confounded and amazed.

Enter Barnwell, Millwood, *Officers and Executioner.*

BARNWELL. See, *Millwood,* see, our Journey's at an End. Life, like a Tale that's told, is past away; that short but dark and unknown Passage, Death, is all the Space 'tween us and endless Joys, or Woes eternal.

MILLWOOD. Is this the End of all my flattering Hopes? Were Youth and Beauty given me for a Curse, and Wisdom only to insure my Ruin? They were, they were. Heaven, thou hast done thy worst. Or if thou hast in Store some untried Plague, somewhat that's worse than Shame, Despair and Death, unpitied Death, confirm'd Despair and Soul confounding Shame; something that Men and Angels can't describe, and only Fiends, who bear it, can conceive; now, pour it now on this devoted° Head, that I may feel the worst thou canst inflict and bid Defiance to thy utmost Power.

doomed

BARNWELL. Yet ere we pass the dreadful Gulph of Death, yet ere you're plunged in everlasting Woe, O bend your stubborn Knees and harder Heart, humbly to deprecate the Wrath divine. Who knows but Heaven, in your dying Moments, may bestow that Grace and Mercy which your Life despised.

MILLWOOD. Why name you Mercy to a Wretch like me? Mercy's beyond my Hope; almost beyond my Wish. I can't repent, nor ask to be forgiven.

BARNWELL. O think what 'tis to be for ever, ever miserable; nor with vain Pride oppose a Power, that's able to destroy you.

MILLWOOD. That will destroy me: I feel it will. A Deluge of Wrath is pouring on my Soul. Chains, Darkness, Wheels, Racks, sharp stinging Scorpions, molten Lead and Seas of Sulphur, are light to what I feel.

BARNWELL. O! add not to your vast Account Despair: A Sin more injurious to Heaven, than all you've yet committed.

MILLWOOD. O! I have sinn'd beyond the Reach of Mercy.

BARNWELL. O say not so: 'tis Blasphemy to think it. As yon bright Roof° is higher than the Earth, so and much more does Heaven's Goodness pass our Apprehension. O what created Being shall presume to circumscribe Mercy, that knows no Bounds?

the sky

MILLWOOD. This yields no Hope. Tho' Mercy may be boundless yet 'tis free: And I was doom'd before the World began to endless Pains and thou to Joys eternal.

BARNWELL. O! gracious Heaven! extend thy Pity to her: Let thy rich Mercy flow in plenteous Streams to chase her Fears and heal her wounded Soul.

MILLWOOD. It will not be. Your Prayers are lost in Air, or else returned perhaps with double Blessing to your Bosom, but me they help not.

BARNWELL. Yet hear me, *Millwood!*

MILLWOOD. Away, I will not hear thee: I tell thee, Youth, I am by Heaven devoted a dreadful Instance of its Power to punish. [Barnwell *seems to pray.*] If thou wilt pray, pray for thyself not me. How doth his fervent Soul mount with his Words, and both ascend to Heaven! That Heaven, whose Gates are shut with adamantine Bars against my Prayers, had I the Will to pray—I cannot bear it—Sure 'tis the worst of Torments to behold others enjoy that Bliss that we must never taste.

OFFICER. The utmost Limit of your Time's expired.
MILLWOOD. Incompassed with Horror, whither must I go? I wou'd not live—nor die—That I cou'd cease to be!—or ne'er had been!
BARNWELL. Since Peace and Comfort are denied her here, may she find Mercy where she least expects it, and this be all her Hell.—From our Example may all be taught to fly the first Approach of Vice; but if o'ertaken

By strong Temptation, Weakness, or Surprize,
Lament their Guilt and by Repentance rise;
Th'impenitent alone die unforgiven;
To sin's like Man, and to forgive like Heaven.

SCENE XII.

Trueman, Blunt, *and* Lucy.

LUCY. Heart-breaking Sight.—O wretched, wretched *Millwood!*
TRUEMAN. How is she disposed to meet her Fate?
BLUNT. Who can describe unalterable Woe?
LUCY. She goes to Death encompassed with Horror, loathing Life, and yet afraid to die; no Tongue can tell her Anguish and Despair.
TRUEMAN. Heaven be better to her than her Fears; may she prove a Warning to others, a Monument of Mercy in her self.
LUCY. O Sorrow, insupportable! break, break my Heart.
TRUEMAN. In vain

With bleeding Hearts, and weeping Eyes we show
A humane gen'rous Sense of others Woe;
Unless we mark what drew their Ruin on,
And by avoiding that—prevent our own.

FINIS.

EPILOGUE.

Written by COLLEY CIBBER,[19] Esq,
and spoke by Mrs. CIBBER.[20]

Since Fate has robb'd me of the hapless Youth,
For whom my Heart had hoarded up its Truth;
By all the Laws of Love and Honour, now,
I'm free again to chuse,—and one of you.

19. Colley Cibber (1671–1757), along with his theatrical career, was also poet laureate (a source of much amusement to superior poets, in particular Alexander Pope) from 1730 to his death.
20. Jane Johnson, Theophilus Cibber's first wife, who died in 1734, played the role of Maria.

But soft,—With Caution first I'll round me peep;
Maids in my Case, shou'd look, before they leap:
Here's Choice enough, of various Sorts and Hue, }
The Cit, the Wit, the Rake cock'd up in Cue, }
The fair spruce Mercer, and the tawney Jew. }

Suppose I search the sober Gallery;—No,
There's none but Prentices,—and Cuckolds all a Row;
And these, I doubt, are those that make 'em so.

[Pointing to the Boxes.

'Tis very well, enjoy the Jest:—But you, }
Fine powder'd Sparks;—nay, I'm told 'tis true, }
Your happy Spouses—can make Cuckolds too. }
'Twixt you and them, the Diff'rence this perhaps,
The Cit's asham'd whene'er his Duck he traps;
But you, when Madam's tripping, let her fall,
Cock up your Hats, and take no Shame at all.

What, if some favour'd Poet I cou'd meet?
Whose Love wou'd lay his Lawrels at my Feet.
No,—Painted Passion real Love abhors,—
His Flame wou'd prove the Suit of Creditors.

Not to detain you then with longer Pause, }
In short, my Heart to this Conclusion draws, }
I yield it to the Hand, that's loudest in Applause. }

The Beggar's Opera

John Gay was born in Barnstaple in 1685. The town, in Devon, had been important in the woolen trade since the Middle Ages. Both of his parents were dead by the time he was ten. Gay was educated at the local grammar school and in 1703 apprenticed to a silk merchant in London. Gay returned to Barnstaple after three years and received further education from the Dissenting minister John Hamner. He then returned to London and served as secretary to his friend the playwright Aaron Hill, as well as writing for Hill's paper *The English Apollo*. By 1713 he was a member of the Scriblerians, a glittering circle of Tory satirists that included Jonathan Swift and Alexander Pope. Gay's first big literary success came in 1714; *The Shepherd's Week* burlesqued the conventions of pastoral poetry. He followed this with a play, *The What D'Ye Call It,* which had a very successful run of twenty-one performances at Drury Lane in 1715. Another play, *Three Hours After Marriage,* written with Pope and Dr. John Arbuthnot, ran for seven nights in 1717. *Poems on Several Occasions* was published by subscription in 1720; the large profits on it were lost in the bursting of the South Sea Bubble. Gay was made commissioner of the state lottery at a salary of £150 a year in 1723, so his position was not economically insecure. However, Gay's fortunes became positively robust when *The Beggar's Opera* ran for an unprecedented sixty-two nights in 1728. It continued to be performed at least once every year on the London stage for the rest of the eighteenth century. The play's immense success inspired an explosion of theatrical activity in London. Lavinia Fenton as Polly was a sensation and went on to become Duchess of Bolton. Even Sir Robert Walpole, the play's chief object of satire, applauded the scene of conflict between Peachum and Lockit, which playfully commented on conflict in the cabinet between Walpole and Lord Townshend over foreign policy. But, at least in terms of the theater, Gay pushed his luck too far with his next effort, *Polly,* and Walpole had it banned because of its political satire. Published by subscription in 1729, it

The copy text is a reproduction of the Third Edition, a 1729 quarto, which was printed with the words and music to the opera (New York: Argonaut Books, 1961).

earned Gay at least £1,200. He lived with the Duke and Duchess of Queensbury until his death in 1732 and was buried in Westminster Abbey. Pope's epitaph describes him as "Unblam'd through life, lamented in thy end."

The idea for *The Beggar's Opera,* that of a "Newgate pastoral" came from Swift; Gay portrays the loves and lives of the lower classes of London. He also, however, is elaborating an idea from Farquhar's *The Beaux' Stratagem,* that it is difficult to tell the gentlemen of the town from the gentlemen of the highway. Another topic of satire is politics; Peachum is both the notorious fence and thief-taker Jonathan Wild (executed in 1725) and Walpole, detested (ineffectually) by Tories as an unscrupulous manipulator of parliamentary procedure and the royal family. The contemporary vogue for Italian opera is mocked as well, which leads to the final level of satire: Gay's good-humored indictment of an audience whose ethical, political, and aesthetic failures allow both political and artistic corruption to flourish. Gay's brilliant innovation was to combine new lyrics to well-known tunes in this ballad-opera. The audience's traditional associations with the ballad "Greensleeves" and Gay's lyrics about inequality before the law, for instance, marry a plaintive tune to social commentary and create a theatrical version of Horatian satire, urbane and amiable.

The Beggar's Opera.

DRAMATIS PERSONAE.[1]

MEN.

PEACHUM.
LOCKIT.
MACHEATH.
FILCH.

JEMMY TWITCHER.	MACHEATH'S GANG.
CROOK-FINGER'D JACK.	
WAT DREARY.	
ROBIN OF BAGSHOT.	
NIMMING NED.	
HARRY PADINGTON.	
MAT OF THE MINT.	
BEN BUDGE.	

BEGGAR.
PLAYER.
CONSTABLES, DRAWER, TURNKEY. &C.

1. The names are charactonyms. To "peach" is to inform; "Macheath" means "son of the heath" and the heaths around London were where highwaymen plied their trade; a twitcher and a diver are both pickpockets; "Nimming" is stealing; Bagshot is a heath to the west of London. The Southwark Mint, until an act in 1723 during the reign of George I, was a sanctuary south of the Thames where officers of the law could not arrest criminals (in 1728 it remained dangerous); "Trapes" and "Slammekin" indicate slovenliness; "Trull" and "Doxy" are synonyms for prostitute.

WOMEN.

MRS. PEACHUM.	
POLLY PEACHUM.	
LUCY LOCKIT.	
DIANA TRAPES.	
MRS. COAXER.	WOMEN OF THE TOWN.
DOLLY TRULL.	
MRS. VIXEN.	
BETTY DOXY.	
JENNY DIVER.	
MRS. SLAMMEKIN.	
SUKEY TAWDRY.	
MOLLY BRAZEN.	

INTRODUCTION.

BEGGAR, PLAYER

Beggar.

If Poverty be a Title to Poetry, I am sure no-body can dispute mine. I own myself of the Company of Beggars; and I make one at their weekly festivals at St. *Giles*'s.[2] I have a small yearly Salary for my Catches,[3] and am welcome to a Dinner there whenever I please, which is more than most Poets can say.

PLAYER. As we live by the Muses, 'tis but gratitude in us to encourage poetical merit where-ever we find it. The Muses, contrary to all other ladies, pay no distinction to dress, and never partially mistake the pertness of embroidery for wit, nor the modesty of want for dulness. Be the author who he will, we push his Play as far as it will go. So (though you are in want) I wish you success heartily.

BEGGAR. This piece I own was originally writ for the celebrating the marriage of *James Chanter* and *Moll Lay,* two most excellent ballad-singers. I have introduc'd the Similes that are in all your celebrated *Operas:* The *Swallow,* the *Moth,* the *Bee,* the *Ship,* the *Flower,* &c. Besides, I have a prison Scene, which the ladies always reckon charmingly pathetick. As to the parts, I have observ'd such a nice impartiality to our two ladies, that it is impossible for either of them to take offence. I hope I may be forgiven, that I have not made my *Opera* throughout unnatural, like those in vogue; for I have no Recitative:[4] excepting this, as I have consented to have neither Prologue nor Epilogue, it must be allow'd an Opera in all its forms. The piece indeed hath been heretofore frequently represented by ourselves in our great room at St. *Giles*'s, so that I cannot too often

2. A poor parish near Holborn.

3. Songs sung as a round, frequently generating comical juxtapositions of words.

4. Recitative is the practice of singing the dialogue in an opera.

acknowledge your charity in bringing it now on the Stage.

PLAYER. But I see 'tis time for us to withdraw; the Actors are preparing to begin. Play away the Overture. [*Exeunt.*

THE
BEGGAR'S OPERA

ACT I SCENE I

SCENE, Peachum's *House.*
Peachum *sitting at a Table with a large Book of Accounts before him.*

AIR I. An old Woman cloathed in gray.

Through all the employments of life
Each neighbour abuses his brother;
Whore and Rogue they call Husband and Wife:
All professions be-rogue one another.
The Priest calls the Lawyer a cheat,
The Lawyer be-knaves the Divine;
And the Statesman, because he's so great,
Thinks his trade as honest as mine.

A Lawyer is an honest employment, so is mine. Like me too he acts in a double capacity, both against Rogues and for 'em; for 'tis but fitting that we should protect and encourage Cheats, since we live by 'em.

SCENE II.

PEACHUM, FILCH.

FILCH. Sir, black *Moll* hath sent word her tryal comes on in the afternoon, and she hopes you will order matters so as to bring her off.

PEACHUM. Why, she may plead her belly at worst;[5] to my knowledge she hath taken care of that security. But as the wench is very active and industrious, you may satisfy her that I'll soften the Evidence.

FILCH. *Tom Gagg,* Sir, is found guilty.

PEACHUM. A lazy dog! When I took him the time before, I told him what he would come to if he did not mend his hand. This is death without reprieve. I may venture to book him. [*writes.*] For *Tom Gagg,* forty pounds. Let *Betty Sly* know that I'll save her from Transportation,[6] for I can get more by her staying in *England.*

5. Pregnant women were not executed.
6. To the penal colonies.

FILCH. *Betty* hath brought more goods into our Lock to-year than any five of the gang; and in truth, 'tis a pity to lose so good a Customer.

PEACHUM. If none of the gang take her off, she may, in the common course of business, live a twelve-month longer. I love to let women scape. A good sportsman always lets the Hen-Partridges fly, because the breed of the game depends upon them. Besides, here the Law allows us no reward; there is nothing to be got by the death of women—except our wives.

FILCH. Without dispute, she is a fine woman! 'Twas to her I was oblig'd for my education, and (to say a bold word) she hath train'd up more young fellows to the business than the Gaming-table.

PEACHUM. Truly, *Filch*, thy observation is right. We and the Surgeons are more beholden to women than all the professions besides.

AIR II. The bonny gray-ey'd morn, *&c.*

Filch. *'Tis woman that seduces all mankind,*
By her we first were taught the wheedling arts:
Her very eyes can cheat; when most she's kind,
She tricks us of our money with our hearts.
For her, like Wolves by night we roam for prey,
And practise ev'ry fraud to bribe her charms;
For suits of love, like law, are won by pay,
And Beauty must be fee'd into our arms.

PEACHUM. But make haste to *Newgate*,[7] boy, and let my Friends know what I intend; for I love to make them easy one way or other.

FILCH. When a gentleman is long kept in suspence, penitence may break his spirit ever after. Besides, certainty gives a man a good air upon his tryal, and makes him risque another without fear or scruple. But I'll away, for 'tis a Pleasure to be the messenger of comfort to friends in affliction.

SCENE III.

PEACHUM.

But 'tis now high time to look about me for a decent Execution against next Sessions. I hate a lazy rogue, by whom one can get nothing 'till he is hang'd. A Register of the Gang. [*reading.*] Crook-finger'd *Jack*. A year and a half in the service: Let me see how much the stock owes to his industry; one, two, three, four, five Gold Watches, and seven silver ones. A mighty clean-handed fellow! sixteen Snuff-boxes, five of them of true gold. Six Dozen

7. Prison inside the City of London, used for a variety of prisoners.

of Handkerchiefs, four silver-hilted Swords, half a dozen of Shirts, three Tye-Perriwigs, and a piece of Broad Cloth. Considering these are only the fruits of his leisure hours, I don't know a prettier fellow, for no man alive hath a more engaging presence of mind upon the road. *Wat Dreary,* alias *Brown Will,* an irregular dog, who hath an underhand way of disposing of his goods. I'll try him only for a Sessions or two longer upon his good behaviour. *Harry Padington,* a poor petty-larceny rascal, without the least genius; that fellow, though he were to live these six months, will never come to the gallows with any credit. Slippery *Sam;* he goes off the next Sessions, for the villain hath the impudence to have views of following his trade as a Taylor, which he calls an honest employment. *Mat* of the *Mint;* listed not above a month ago, a promising sturdy fellow, and diligent in his way; somewhat too bold and hasty, and may raise good contributions on the publick, if he does not cut himself short by murder. *Tom Tipple,* a guzzling soaking sot, who is always too drunk to stand himself, or to make others stand. A cart is absolutely necessary for him. *Robin* of *Bagshot,* alias *Gorgon,* alias *Bluff Bob,* alias *Carbuncle,* alias *Bob Booty.*[8]

SCENE IV.

PEACHUM, Mrs. PEACHUM.

MRS. PEACHUM. What of *Bob Booty,* husband? I hope nothing bad hath betided him. You know, my dear, he's a favourite customer of mine. 'Twas he made me a present of this ring.

PEACHUM. I have set his name down in the black-list, that's all, my dear; he spends his life among women, and as soon as his money is gone, one or other of the ladies will hang him for the reward, and there's forty pound lost to us for-ever.

MRS. PEACHUM. You know, my dear, I never meddle in matters of Death; I always leave those affairs to you. Women indeed are bitter bad judges in these cases, for they are so partial to the brave that they think every man handsome who is going to the Camp or the Gallows.

AIR III. Cold and raw, *&c.*

If any wench Venus's girdle wear,
Though she be never so ugly,
Lilies and roses will quickly appear,
And her face look wond'rous smuggly.
Beneath the left ear so fit but a cord,

8. Nicknames for Sir Robert Walpole, the Whig prime minister of England, 1721–42, a gifted politician who used patronage and political dexterity with unprecedented skill.

(A rope so charming a Zone is!)
The youth in his cart hath the air of a lord,
And we cry, There dies an Adonis!

But really, husband, you should not be too hard-hearted, for you never had a finer, braver set of men than at present. We have not had a murder among them all, these seven months. And truly, my dear, that is a great blessing.

PEACHUM. What a dickens is the woman always a whimpring about murder for? No gentleman is ever look'd upon the worse for killing a man in his own defense; and if business cannot be carried on without it, what would you have a gentleman do?

MRS. PEACHUM. If I am in the wrong, my dear, you must excuse me, for no-body can help the frailty of an over-scrupulous Conscience.

PEACHUM. Murder is as fashionable a Crime as a man can be guilty of. How many fine gentlemen have we in *Newgate* every year, purely upon that article? If they have wherewithal to perswade the Jury to bring it in manslaughter, what are they the worse for it? So, my dear, have done upon this subject. Was captain *Macheath* here this morning, for the bank-notes he left with you last week?

MRS. PEACHUM. Yes, my dear; and though the Bank hath stopt payment, he was so cheerful and so agreeable! Sure there is not a finer gentleman upon the road than the Captain! If he comes from *Bagshot* at any reasonable hour he hath promis'd to make one this evening with *Polly,* and me, and *Bob Booty* at a party of Quadrille. Pray, my dear, is the Captain rich?

PEACHUM. The Captain keeps too good company ever to grow rich. *Marybone* and the *Chocolate-houses* are his undoing.[9] The man that proposes to get money by play should have the education of a fine gentleman, and be train'd up to it from his youth.

MRS. PEACHUM. Really, I am sorry upon *Polly*'s account the Captain hath not more discretion. What business hath he to keep company with lords and gentlemen? he should leave them to prey upon one another.

PEACHUM. Upon *Polly*'s account! What, a plague, does the woman mean?—Upon *Polly*'s account!

MRS. PEACHUM. Captain *Macheath* is very fond of the girl.

PEACHUM. And what then?

MRS. PEACHUM. If I have any skill in the ways of women, I am sure *Polly* thinks him a very pretty man.

PEACHUM. And what then? You would not be so mad as to have the wench marry him! Gamesters and highwaymen are generally very good to their whores, but they are very devils to their wives.

9. Marylebone was a sporting and gambling district, and the chocolate houses were also places of gambling.

MRS. PEACHUM. But if Polly should be in love, how should we help her, or how can she help herself? Poor girl, I am in the utmost concern about her.

AIR IV. Why is your faithful slave disdain'd?

If love the virgin's heart invade,
How, like a Moth, the simple maid
Still plays about the flame!
If soon she be not made a wife,
Her honour's sing'd, and then for life
She's—what I dare not name.

PEACHUM. Look ye, wife. A handsome wench in our way of business is as profitable as at the bar of a *Temple* coffee-house, who looks upon it as her livelihood to grant every Liberty but one. You see I would indulge the girl as far as prudently we can. In anything, but marriage! after that, my dear, how shall we be safe? are we not then in her husband's Power? for a husband hath the absolute power over all a wife's secrets but her own. If the girl had the discretion of a court lady, who can have a dozen young fellows at her ear without complying with one, I should not matter it; but *Polly* is tinder, and a spark will at once set her on a flame. Married! If the wench does not know her own profit, sure she knows her own pleasure better than to make herself a property! My daughter to me should be, like a court lady to a minister of state, a key to the whole gang. Married! If the affair is not already done, I'll terrify her from it, by the example of our neighbours.

MRS. PEACHUM. May-hap, my dear, you may injure the girl. She loves to imitate the fine ladies, and she may only allow the Captain liberties in the view of interest.

PEACHUM. But 'tis your duty, my dear, to warn the girl against her ruin, and to instruct her how to make the most of her beauty. I'll go to her this moment, and sift her. In the mean time, wife, rip out the coronets and marks of these dozen of cambric handkerchiefs, for I can dispose of them this afternoon to a chap in the city.

SCENE V.

MRS. PEACHUM.

Never was a man more out of the way in an argument than my husband! Why must our *Polly,* forsooth, differ from her sex, and love only her husband? And why must *Polly*'s marriage, contrary to all observation, make her the less followed by other men? All men are thieves in love, and like a woman the better for being another's property.

AIR V.—Of all the simple things we do, *&c.*

A Maid is like the golden oar,° ore
Which hath guineas intrinsical in't,
Whose worth is never known, before
It is try'd and imprest in the mint.
A Wife's like a guinea in gold,
Stampt with the name of her spouse;
Now here, now there; is bought, or is sold;
And is current in every house.

SCENE VI.

MRS. PEACHUM, FILCH.

MRS. PEACHUM. Come hither, *Filch.* I am as fond of this child, as though my mind misgave me he were my own. He hath as fine a hand at picking a pocket as a woman, and is as nimble-finger'd as a juggler. If an unlucky session does not cut the rope of thy life, I pronounce, boy, thou wilt be a great man in history. Where was your post last night, my boy?

FILCH. I ply'd at the Opera, madam; and considering 'twas neither dark nor rainy, so that there was no great hurry in getting chairs and coaches, made a tolerable hand on't. These seven handkerchiefs, madam.

MRS. PEACHUM. Colour'd ones, I see. They are of sure sale from our ware-house at *Redriff*[10] among the sea-men.

FILCH. And this snuff-box.

MRS. PEACHUM. Set in gold! A pretty encouragement this to a young beginner.

FILCH. I had a fair tug at charming gold watch. Pox take the Taylors for making the fobs so deep and narrow! It stuck by the way, and I was forc'd to make my escape under a coach. Really, madam, I fear I shall be cut off in the flower of my youth, so that every now and then (since I was pumpt[11]) I have thoughts of taking up and going to Sea.

MRS. PEACHUM. You should go to *Hockley in the hole,*[12] and to *Marybone,* child, to learn valour. These are the schools that have bred so many brave men. I thought, boy, by this time thou hadst lost fear as well as shame. Poor lad! how little does he know yet of the *Old-Baily!*[13] For the first fact° I'll ensure thee from being hang'd; and going to Sea, *Filch,* will come time enough upon crime

10. Dockside district in London.
11. Punishment by being repeatedly ducked under a pump.
12. London neighborhood where not only bear and bull baiting took place, but also boxing and fencing matches.
13. Criminal court next to Newgate Prison.

a sentence of transportation. But now, since you have nothing better to do, ev'n go to your book, and learn your catechism; for really a man makes but an ill figure in the Ordinary's paper, who cannot give a satisfactory answer to his questions.[14] But, hark you, my lad. Don't tell me a lye; for you know that I hate a Lyar. Do you know of any thing that hath past between captain *Macheath* and our *Polly?*

FILCH. I beg you, Madam, don't ask me; for I must either tell a lye to you or to Miss *Polly;* for I promis'd her I would not tell.

MRS. PEACHUM. But when the honour of our family is concern'd——

FILCH. I shall lead a sad life with Miss *Polly,* if she ever comes to know that I told you. Besides, I would not willingly forfeit my own honour by betraying any body.

MRS. PEACHUM. Yonder comes my husband and *Polly.* Come, *Filch,* you shall go with me into my own room, and tell me the whole story. I'll give thee a glass of a most delicious Cordial that I keep for my own drinking.

SCENE VII.

PEACHUM, POLLY.

POLLY. I know as well as any of the fine ladies how to make the most of my self and of my man too. A woman knows how to be mercenary, though she hath never been in a court or at an assembly. We have it in our natures, papa. If I allow captain *Macheath* some trifling liberties, I have this watch and other visible marks of his favour to show for it. A girl who cannot grant some things, and refuse what is most material, will make but a poor hand of her beauty, and soon be thrown upon the common.

AIR VI. What shall I do to show how much I love her?

Virgins are like the fair flower in its lustre,
Which in the garden enamels the ground;
Near it the Bees in play flutter and cluster,
And gaudy Butterflies frolick around.
But, when once pluck'd, 'tis no longer alluring,
To Covent-Garden[15] *'tis sent, (as yet sweet,)*
There fades, and shrinks, and grows past all enduring,
Rots, stinks, and dies, and is trod under feet.

PEACHUM. You know, *Polly,* I am not against your toying and trifling with a customer in the way of business, or to get out a secret, or so. But if I find out that you have play'd the fool and are married, you jade you, I'll cut your throat, hussy. Now you know my mind.

14. The report of the prison chaplain, sometimes published after the execution of a criminal.
15. Theater district, market for flowers and vegetables, and a haunt of prostitutes.

SCENE VIII.

PEACHUM, POLLY, MRS. PEACHUM.

AIR VII. Oh *London* is a fine Town.
Mrs. PEACHUM, [*in a very great passion.*]

Our Polly *is a sad slut! nor heeds what we have taught her.*
I wonder any man alive will ever rear a daughter!
For she must have both hoods and gowns, and hoops to swell her pride,
With scarfs and stays, and gloves and lace; and she will have men beside;
And when she's drest with care and cost, all-tempting, fine and gay,
As Men should serve a Cowcumber, she flings herself away.

You baggage! you hussy! you inconsiderate jade! had you been hang'd, it would not have vex'd me, for that might have been your misfortune; but to do such a mad thing by choice! The wench is married, husband.

PEACHUM. Married! The Captain is a bold man, and will risque any thing for money; to be sure he believes her a fortune. Do you think your mother and I should have liv'd comfortably so long together, if ever we had been married? Baggage!

MRS. PEACHUM. I knew she was always a proud slut; and now the wench hath play'd the fool and married, because forsooth she would do like the Gentry. Can you support the expence of a husband, hussy, in gaming, drinking and whoring? have you money enough to carry on the daily quarrels of man and wife about who shall squander most? There are not many husbands and wives, who can bear the charges of plaguing one another in a handsome way. If you must be married, could you introduce no-body into our family but a highwayman? Why, thou foolish jade, thou wilt be as ill us'd, and as much neglected, as if thou hadst married a Lord!

PEACHUM. Let not your anger, my dear, break through the rules of decency, for the Captain looks upon himself in the military capacity, as a gentleman by his profession. Besides what he hath already, I know he is in a fair way of getting, or of dying; and both these ways, let me tell you, are most excellent chances for a wife. Tell me hussy, are you ruin'd or no?

MRS. PEACHUM. With *Polly*'s fortune, she might very well have gone off to a person of distinction. Yes, that you might, you pouting slut!

PEACHUM. What, is the wench dumb? Speak, or I'll make you plead by squeezing out an answer from you. Are really bound wife to him, or are you only upon liking? [*Pinches her.*

POLLY. Oh! [*Screaming.*

MRS. PEACHUM. How the mother is to be pitied who has handsome daughters! Lock, bolts, bars, and lectures of morality are nothing to them: they break through them all. They have as much pleasure in cheating a father and mother, as in cheating at cards.

PEACHUM. Why, *Polly,* I shall soon know if you are married, by *Macheath*'s keeping from our house.

AIR VIII. Grim King of the Ghosts, *&c.*

POLLY.
Can Love be controul'd by advice?
Will Cupid *our mothers obey?*
Though my heart were as frozen as Ice,
At his flame 'twould have melted away.
When he kist me so closely he prest,
'Twas so sweet that I must have comply'd:
So I thought it both safest and best
To marry, for fear you should chide.

MRS. PEACHUM. Then all the hopes of our family are gone for ever and ever!

PEACHUM. And *Macheath* may hang his father and mother-in-law, in hope to get into their daughter's fortune.

POLLY. I did not marry him (as 'tis the fashion) cooly and deliberately for honour or money. But, I love him.

MRS. PEACHUM. Love him! worse and worse! I thought the girl had been better bred. Oh husband, husband! her folly makes me mad! my head swims! I'm distracted! I can't support myself—Oh! [*Faints.*

PEACHUM. See, wench, to what a condition you have reduced your poor mother! a glass of cordial, this instant. How the poor woman takes it to heart! [Polly *goes out, and returns with it.* Ah, hussy, this is now the only comfort your mother has left!

POLLY. Give her another glass, Sir; my Mama drinks double the quantity whenever she is out of order. This, you see, fetches her.

MRS. PEACHUM. The girl shows such a readiness, and so much concern, that I could almost find in my heart to forgive her.

AIR IX. O *Jenny,* O *Jenny,* where hast thou been.

O Polly, *you might have toy'd and kist.*
By keeping men off, you keep them on.
POLLY. *But he so teaz'd me,*
And he so pleas'd me,
What I did, you must have done.

MRS. PEACHUM. Not with a highway-man.—You sorry slut!

PEACHUM. A word with you, wife. 'Tis no new thing for a wench to take a man without consent of Parents. You know 'tis the frailty of woman, my dear.

MRS. PEACHUM. Yes, indeed, the sex is frail. But the first time a woman is frail, she should be somewhat nice° choosy methinks, for then or never is the time to make her fortune. After that, she hath nothing to do but to guard herself from being found out, and she may do what she pleases.

PEACHUM. Make your self a little easy; I have a thought shall soon set all matters again to rights. Why so melancholy, *Polly?* since what is done cannot be undone, we must all endeavour to make the best of it.

MRS. PEACHUM. Well, *Polly;* as far as one woman can forgive another, I forgive thee.———Your Father is too fond of you, hussy.

POLLY. Then all my sorrows are at an end.

MRS. PEACHUM. A mighty likely speech in troth, for a wench who is just married!

AIR X. *Thomas,* I cannot, *&c.*

POLLY.
I, like a ship in storms, was tost;
Yet afraid to put in to Land;
For seiz'd in the port the vessel's lost,
Whose treasure is contreband.
The waves are laid,
My duty's paid.
O joy beyond expression!
Thus, safe a-shore,
I ask no more,
My all is in my possession.

PEACHUM. I hear customers in t'other room; go, talk with 'em, *Polly;* but come to us again, as soon as they are gone—But, heark ye, child, if 'tis the gentleman who was here yesterday about the repeating watch; say, you believe we can't get intelligence of it, till to-morrow. For I lent it to *Suky Straddle,* to make a figure with it to-night at a tavern in *Drury-Lane.*[16] If t'other gentleman calls for the silver-hilted sword; you know beetle-brow'd *Jemmy* hath it on, and he doth not come from *Tunbridge*[17] 'till *Tuesday* night; so that it cannot be had till then.

SCENE IX

PEACHUM, MRS. PEACHUM.

PEACHUM. Dear wife, be a little pacified. Don't let your passion run away with your senses. *Polly,* I grant you, hath done a rash thing.

MRS. PEACHUM. If she had had only an intrigue with the fellow,

16. Also the location of a theater, and also a haunt of prostitutes.

17. Fashionable spa forty miles from London. With both the watch and the sword, Peachum receives them as a fence, loans them to thieves and prostitutes, and receives money from their owners for their return.

why the very best families have excus'd and huddled up a frailty of that sort. 'Tis Marriage, husband, that makes it a blemish.

PEACHUM. But money, wife, is the true fuller's earth for reputations, there is not a spot or a stain but what it can take out. A rich rogue now-a-days is fit company for any gentleman; and the world, my dear, hath not such a contempt for roguery as you imagine. I tell you, wife, I can make this match turn to our advantage.

MRS. PEACHUM. I am very sensible, husband, that captain *Macheath* is worth money, but I am in doubt whether he hath not two or three wives already, and then if he should dye in a Session or two, *Polly*'s dower would come into dispute.

PEACHUM. That, indeed, is a point which ought to be consider'd.

AIR XI. A Soldier and a Sailor.

A Fox may steal your hens, sir,
A whore your health and pence, sir,
Your daughter rob your chest, sir,
Your wife may steal your rest, sir.
A thief your goods and plate.
But this is all but picking,
With rest, pence, chest and chicken;
It ever was decreed, sir,
If Lawyer's hand is fee'd, sir,
He steals your whole estate.

The Lawyers are bitter enemies to those in our way. They don't care that any body should get a clandestine livelihood but themselves.

SCENE X.

Mrs. *PEACHUM, PEACHUM, POLLY.*

POLLY. 'Twas only Nimming *Ned.* He brought in a damask window-curtain, a hoop-petticoat, a pair of silver candlesticks, a perriwig, and one silk stocking, from the fire that happen'd last night.

PEACHUM. There is not a fellow that is cleverer in his way, and saves more goods out of the fire than *Ned.* But now, *Polly,* to your affair; for matters must not be left as they are. You are married then, it seems?

POLLY. Yes, Sir.

PEACHUM. And how do you propose to live, child?

POLLY. Like other women, Sir, upon the industry of my husband.

MRS. PEACHUM. What, is the wench turn'd fool? A highway-man's wife, like a soldier's, hath as little of his pay, as of his company.

PEACHUM. And had not you the common views of a gentlewoman in your marriage, *Polly?*

POLLY. I don't know what you mean, Sir.
PEACHUM. Of a jointure, and of being a widow.
POLLY. But I love him, Sir: how then could I have thoughts of parting with him?
PEACHUM. Parting with him! Why, that is the whole scheme and intention of all Marriage-articles. The comfortable estate of widow-hood, is the only hope that keeps up a wife's spirits. Where is the woman who would scruple to be a wife, if she had it in her power to be a widow whenever she pleas'd? If you have any views of this sort, *Polly,* I shall think the match not so very unreasonable.
POLLY. How I dread to hear your advice! Yet I must beg you to explain yourself.
PEACHUM. Secure what he hath got, have him peach'd the next Sessions, and then at once you are made a rich widow.
POLLY. What, murder the man I love! The blood runs cold at my heart with the very thought of it.
PEACHUM. Fye, *Polly!* what hath murder to do in the affair? Since the thing sooner or later must happen, I dare say, the Captain himself would like that we should get the reward for his death sooner than a stranger. Why, *Polly,* the Captain knows, that as 'tis his employment to rob, so 'tis ours to take Robbers; every man in his business. So there is no malice in the case.
MRS. PEACHUM. Ay, husband, now you have nick'd the matter.[18] To have him peach'd is the only thing could ever make me forgive her.

AIR XII. Now ponder well, ye parents dear.

POLLY. *Oh, ponder well! be not severe;*
So save a wretched wife!
For on the rope that hangs my dear
Depends poor Polly's *life.*

MRS. PEACHUM. But your duty to your parents, hussy, obliges you to hang him. What would many a wife give for such an opportunity!
POLLY. What is a jointure, what is widow-hood to me? I know my heart. I cannot survive him.

AIR XIII. Le printemps rappelle aux armes.[19]

The Turtle thus with plaintive crying,
Her lover dying,
The Turtle thus with plaintive crying

18. Hit the mark.
19. Spring calls to arms.

Laments her Dove.
Down she drops quite spent with sighing
Pair'd in death, as pair'd in love.

Thus, Sir, it will happen to your poor *Polly.*

MRS. PEACHUM. What, is the fool in love in earnest then? I hate thee for being particular: Why, wench, thou art a shame to thy very Sex.

POLLY. But hear me, mother.—If you ever lov'd—

MRS. PEACHUM. Those cursed Play-books she reads have been her ruin. One word more, hussy, and I shall knock your Brains out, if you have any.

PEACHUM. Keep out of the way, *Polly,* for fear of mischief, and consider what is propos'd to you.

MRS. PEACHUM. Away, hussy. Hang your husband, and be dutiful.

SCENE XI.

MRS. PEACHUM, PEACHUM.
[Polly *listning.*

MRS. PEACHUM. The thing, husband, must and shall be done. For the sake of intelligence we must take other measures, and have him peach'd the next Session without her consent. If she will not know her duty, we know ours.

PEACHUM. But really, my dear, it grieves one's heart to take off a great man. When I consider his personal bravery, his fine strategem, how much we have already got by him, and how much more we may get, methinks I can't find in my heart to have a hand in his death. I wish you could have made *Polly* undertake it.

MRS. PEACHUM. But in a case of necessity—our own lives are in danger.

PEACHUM. Then, indeed, we must comply with the customs of the world, and make gratitude give way to interest.—He shall be taken off.

MRS. PEACHUM. I'll undertake to manage *Polly.*

PEACHUM. And I'll prepare matters for the *Old-Baily.*

SCENE XII.

POLLY.

Now I'm a wretch, indeed.—Methinks I see him already in the cart, sweeter and more lovely than the nosegay in his hand!—I hear the crowd extolling his resolution and intrepidity!—What vollies of sighs are sent from the windows of *Holborn,* that so comely a youth should be brought to disgrace!—I see him at the tree!° The whole Circle are in tears!—even Butchers weep!— gallows

Jack Ketch himself hesitates to perform his duty, and would be glad to lose his fee, by a reprieve. What then will become of *Polly!* —As yet I may inform him of their design, and aid him in his escape. It shall be so.—But then he flies, absents himself, and I bar my self from his dear conversation! that too will distract me. —If he keep out of the way, my Papa and Mama may in time relent, and we may be happy.—If he stays, he is hang'd, and then he is lost for ever!—He intended to lye conceal'd in my room, 'till the dusk of the evening: If they are abroad I'll this instant let him out, lest some accident should prevent him. [*Exit, and returns.*

SCENE XIII.

POLLY, MACHEATH

AIR XIV. *Pretty Parrot, say, &c.*

MACHEATH.
Pretty Polly, say,
When I was away,
Did your fancy never stray
To some newer lover?

POLLY.
Without Disguise,
Heaving sighs,
Doting eyes,
My constant heart discover,
Fondly let me loll!

MACHEATH. *O pretty, pretty* Poll.

POLLY. And are you as fond as ever, my dear?

MACHEATH. Suspect my honour, my courage, suspect any thing but my love.—May my pistols miss fire, and my mare slip her shoulder while I am pursu'd, if I ever forsake thee!

POLLY. Nay, my dear, I have no reason to doubt you, for I find in the Romance you lent me, none of the great Heroes were ever false in love.

AIR XV. Pray, fair one, be kind.

MACHEATH.
My heart was so free,
It rov'd like the Bee,
'Till Polly *my passion requited;*
I sipt each flower,
I chang'd ev'ry hour,
But here ev'ry flower is united.

POLLY. Were you sentenc'd to Transportation, sure, my dear, you could not leave me behind you—could you?

MACHEATH. Is there any power, any force that could tear me from thee? You might sooner tear a pension out of the hands of a Courtier, a fee from a Lawyer, a pretty woman from a looking-glass, or any woman from *Quadrille.*—But to tear me from thee is impossible!

AIR XVI.—Over the Hills and far away.

Were I laid on Greenland's *coast,*
And in my arms embrac'd my lass;
Warm amidst eternal frost,
Too soon the half year's night would pass.
POLLY. *Were I sold on* Indian *soil,*
Soon as the burning day was clos'd,
I could mock the sultry toil,
When on my charmer's breast repos'd.
MACHEATH. *And I would love you all the day,*
POLLY. *Every night would kiss and play,*
MACHEATH *If with me you'd fondly stray*
POLLY. *Over the hills and far away.*

POLLY. Yes, I would go with thee. But oh!—how shall I speak it? I must be torn from thee. We must part.
MACHEATH. How! Part!
POLLY. We must, we must.—My Papa and Mama are set against thy life. They now, even now are in search after thee. They are preparing evidence against thee. Thy life depends upon a moment.

AIR XVII. Gin thou wert mine awn thing.

O what pain it is to part!
Can I leave thee, can I leave thee?
O what pain it is to part!
Can thy Polly *ever leave thee?*
But lest death my love should thwart,
And bring thee from my bleeding heart!
Fly hence, and let me leave thee.

One kiss and then—one kiss—begone—farewell.
MACHEATH. My hand, my heart, my dear, is so riveted to thine, that I cannot unloose my hold.
POLLY. But my Papa may intercept thee, and then I should lose the very glimmering of hope. A few weeks, perhaps, may reconcile us all. Shall thy *Polly* hear from thee?
MACHEATH. Must I then go?
POLLY. And will not absence change your love?
MACHEATH. If you doubt it, let me stay—and be hang'd.
POLLY. O how I fear! how I tremble!—Go—but when safety will give you leave, you will be sure to see me again; for 'till then *Polly* is wretched.

AIR XVIII. O the broom, *&c.*

MACHEATH. *The Miser thus a shilling sees,*
Which he's oblig'd to pay,
With sighs resigns it by degrees,
And fears 'tis gone for aye.

POLLY. *The Boy thus, when his Sparrow's flown,*
The bird in silence eyes;
But soon as out of sight 'tis gone,
Whines, whimpers, sobs and cries.

ACT II. SCENE I.

A Tavern near Newgate.
Jemmy Twitcher, *Crook-finger'd* Jack, Wat Dreary, Robin *of* Bagshop, Nimming Ned, Henry Padington, Matt *of the* Mint, Ben Budge, *and the rest of the Gang, at the Table, with Wine, Brandy and Tobacco.*

BEN. But pr'ythee, *Matt,* what is become of thy brother *Tom?* I have not seen him since my return from transportation.

MATT. Poor brother *Tom* had an accident this time twelvemonth, and so clever a made fellow he was, that I could not save him from those fleaing rascals the Surgeons; and now, poor man, he is among the Otamys° at *Surgeon's-Hall.* skeletons

BEN. So it seems, his time was come.

JEMMY. But the present time is ours, and no body alive hath more. Why are the laws levell'd at us? are we more dishonest than the rest of mankind? what we win, gentlemen, is our own by the law of arms, and the right of conquest.

CROOK-FINGER'D JACK. Where shall we find such another set of practical philosophers, who to a man are above the fear of Death?

WAT. Sound men, and true!

ROBIN. Of try'd courage, and indefatigable industry!

NED. Who is there here that would not dye for his friend?

HARRY. Who is there here that would betray him for his interest?

MATT. Show me a gang of Courtiers that can say as much.

BEN. We are for a just partition of the world, for every man hath a right to enjoy life.

MATT. We retrench the superfluities of mankind. The world is avaritious, and I hate avarice. A covetous fellow, like a Jack-daw, steals what he was never made to enjoy, for the sake of hiding it. These are the robbers of mankind, for money was made for the free-hearted and generous, and where is the injury of taking from another, what he hath not the heart to make use of?

JEMMY. Our several stations for the day are fixt. Good luck attend us all. Fill the glasses.

AIR XIX. Fill ev'ry Glass, *&c.*

MATT. *Fill ev'ry glass, for wine inspires us,*
And fires us
With courage, love and joy.
Women and wine should life employ.
Is there ought else on earth desirous?
CHORUS. *Fill ev'ry Glass, &c.*

SCENE II.

To them enter MACHEATH.

MACHEATH. Gentlemen, well met. My heart hath been with you this hour; but an unexpected affair hath detain'd me. No ceremony, I beg you.

MATT. We were just breaking up to go upon duty. Am I to have the honour of taking the air with you, Sir, this evening upon the Heath? I drink a dram now and then with the Stage-coachmen in the way of friendship and intelligence; and I know that about this time there will be passengers upon the western road, who are worth speaking with.

MACHEATH. I was to have been of that party—but—

MATT. But what, Sir?

MACHEATH. Is there any man who suspects my courage?

MATT. We have all been witnesses of it.

MACHEATH. My honour and truth to the gang?

MATT. I'll be answerable for it.

MACHEATH. In the division of our booty, have I ever shown the least marks of avarice or injustice?

MATT. By these questions something seems to have ruffled you. Are any of us suspected?

MACHEATH. I have a fixt confidence, gentlemen, in you all, as men of honour, and as such I value and respect you. *Peachum* is a man that is useful to us.

MATT. Is he about to play us any foul play? I'll shoot him through the head.

MACHEATH. I beg you, gentlemen, act with conduct and discretion. A pistol is your last resort.

MATT. He knows nothing of this meeting.

MACHEATH. Business cannot go on without him. He is a man who knows the world, and is a necessary agent to us. We have had a slight difference, and 'till it is accomodated I shall be oblig'd to keep out of his way. Any private dispute of mine shall be of no ill consequence to my friends. You must continue to act under his direction, for the moment we break loose from him, our gang is ruin'd.

MATT. As a bawd to a whore, I grant you, he is to us of great convenience.

MACHEATH. Make him believe I have quitted the gang, which I can never do but with life. At our private quarters I will continue to meet you. A week or so will probably reconcile us.

MATT. Your instructions shall be observ'd. 'Tis now high time for us to repair to our several duties; so 'till the evening at our quarters in *Moor-fields* we bid you farewell.

MACHEATH. I shall wish my self with you. Success attend you.

[*Sits down melancholy at the Table.*

AIR XX. March in *Rinaldo,*[20] with Drums and Trumpets.

MATT. *Let us take the road.*
Hark! I hear the sound of coaches!
The hour of attack approaches,
To your arms, brave boys, and load.

See the ball I hold!
Let the Chymists toil like asses,
Our fire their fire surpasses,
And turns all our lead to gold.

[The Gang, rang'd in the front of the Stage, load their pistols, and stick them under their girdles;° then go off singing the first part in Chorus. belts

SCENE III.

MACHEATH, DRAWER.

MACHEATH. What a fool is a fond wench! *Polly* is most confoundedly bit.—I love the sex. And a man who loves money, might as well be contented with one guinea, as I with one woman. The town perhaps hath been as much oblig'd to me, for recruiting it with free-hearted ladies, as to any recruiting Officer in the army. If it were not for us and the other gentlemen of the sword, *Drury-Lane* would be uninhabited.

AIR XXI. Would you have a young Virgin, *&c.*

If the heart of a man is deprest with cares,
The mist is dispell'd when a woman appears;
Like the notes of a fiddle, she sweetly, sweetly
Raises the spirits, and charms our ears.
Roses and lillies her cheeks disclose,
But her ripe lips are more sweet than those.
Press her,

20. 1711 opera by Handel.

Caress her,
With blisses,
Her kisses
Dissolve us in pleasure, and soft repose.

I must have women. There is nothing unbends the mind like them. Money is not so strong a cordial for the Time.—Drawer.—[*Enter Drawer.*] Is the Porter gone for all the ladies, according to my directions?

DRAWER. I expect him back every minute. But you know, Sir, you sent him as far as *Hockley in the Hole,* for three of the ladies, for one in *VinegarYard,* and for the rest of them somewhere about *Lewkner's Lane.*[21] Sure some of them are below, for I hear the barr bell. As they come I will show them up.—Coming, coming.

SCENE IV.

Macheath, *Mrs.* Coaxer, Dolly Trull, *Mrs.* Vixen, Betty Doxy, Jenny Diver, *Mrs.* Slammekin, Suky Tawdry, *and* Molly Brazen.

MACHEATH. Dear Mrs. *Coaxer,* you are welcome. You look charmingly to-day. I hope you don't want the repairs of quality, and lay on paint.—*Dolly Trull!* kiss me, you slut; are you as amorous as ever, hussy? You are always so taken up with stealing hearts, that you don't allow your self time to steal anything else. —Ah *Dolly,* thou wilt ever be a Coquette!—Mrs. *Vixen,* I'm yours, I always lov'd a woman of wit and spirit; they make charming mistresses, but plaguy wives.—*Betty Doxy!* Come hither, hussy. Do you drink as hard as ever? You had better stick to good wholesome beer; for in troth, *Betty,* strong-waters will in time ruin your constitution. You should leave those to your betters. —What! and my pretty *Jenny Diver* too! As prim and demure as ever! There is not any Prude, though ever so high bred, hath a more sanctify'd look, with a more mischievous heart. Ah! thou art a dear artful hypocrite.—Mrs. *Slammekin!* as careless and genteel as ever! all you fine ladies, who know your own beauty, affect an undress.—But see, here's *Suky Tawdry* come to contradict what I was saying. Every thing she gets one way she lays out upon her back. Why, *Suky,* you must keep at least a Dozen Tally-men.[22] *Molly Brazen!* [*She kisses him.*] That's well done. I love a free-hearted wench. Thou hast a most agreeable assurance, girl, and art as willing as a Turtle.°—But hark! I hear musick. The Harper is at the door. *If musick be the food of Love, play on.*[23] E're you

° turtledove

21. Vinegar Hill, near St. Giles' Church, and Lewkner Lane, near Drury Lane.
22. Merchants who sell goods on credit and by installment.
23. From the opening speech in Shakespeare's *Twelfth Night.*

seat your selves, ladies, what think you of a dance? Come in. [*Enter Harper.*] Play the *French* Tune, that Mrs. *Slammekin* was so fond of.

[*A Dance* a la ronde *in the* French *manner; near the end of it this Song and Chorus.*

AIR XXII. Cotillon.

Youth's the season made for joys,
Love is then our duty;
She alone who that employs,
Well deserves her beauty.
Let's be gay,
While we may,
Beauty's a flower despis'd in decay.
Youth's the season, &c.

Let us drink and sport to-day,
Ours is not to-morrow.
Love with youth flies swift away,
Age is nought but sorrow.
Dance and sing,
Time's on the wing,
Life never knows the return of spring.
CHORUS. *Let us drink,* &c.

MACHEATH. Now, pray ladies, take your places. Here Fellow, [*Pays the Harper.*] Bid the Drawer bring us more wine. [*Exit Harper.*] If any of the ladies chuse gin, I hope they will be so free to call for it.

JENNY. You look as if you meant me. Wine is strong enough for me. Indeed, Sir, I never drink strong-waters, but when I have the Cholic.

MACHEATH. Just the excuse of the fine ladies! Why, a lady of quality is never without the Cholic. I hope, Mrs. *Coaxer,* you have had good success of late in your visits among the Mercers.

COAXER. We have so many interlopers—Yet with industry, one may still have a little picking. I carried a silver-flower'd lutestring and a piece of black padesoy to Mr. *Peachum*'s Lock but last week.[24]

VIXEN. There's *Molly Brazen* hath the ogle of a Rattle-snake. She rivetted a Linnen-draper's Eye so fast upon her, that he was nick'd of three pieces of cambric before he could look off.

BRAZEN. Oh dear madam!—But sure nothing can come up to your handling of laces! And then you have such a sweet deluding tongue! To cheat a man is nothing; but the woman must have fine parts indeed who cheats a woman!

24. Lutestring and padesoy are both silk fabrics.

VIXEN. Lace, madam, lyes in a small compass, and is of easy conveyance. But you are apt, madam, to think too well of your friends.

COAXER. If any woman hath more art than another, to be sure, 'tis *Jenny Diver.* Though her fellow be never so agreeable, she can pick his pocket as cooly, as if money were her only pleasure. Now that is a command of the passions uncommon in a woman!

JENNY. I never go to the tavern with a man, but in the view of business. I have other hours, and other sort of men for my pleasure. But had I your address, madam—

MACHEATH. Have done with your compliments, ladies; and drink about: You are not so fond of me, *Jenny,* as you use to be.

JENNY. 'Tis not convenient, Sir, to show my fondness among so many rivals. 'Tis your own choice, and not the warmth of my inclination, that will determine you.

AIR XXIII. All in a misty morning.

Before the barn-door crowing,
The Cock by Hens attended,
His eyes around him throwing,
Stands for a while suspended.
Then one he singles from the crew,
And cheers the happy Hen;
With how do you do, and how do you do,
And how do you do again.

MACHEATH. Ah *Jenny!* thou art a dear slut.

TRULL. Pray, madam, were you ever in keeping?

TAWDRY. I hope, madam, I ha'nt been so long upon the town, but I have met with some good fortune as well as my neighbors.

TRULL. Pardon me, madam, I meant no harm by the question; 'twas only in the way of conversation.

TAWDRY. Indeed, madam, if I had not been a fool, I might have liv'd very handsomely with my last friend. But upon his missing five guineas, he turn'd me off. Now I never suspected he had counted them.

SLAMMEKIN. Who do you look upon, madam, as your best sort of keepers?

TRULL. That, madam, is thereafter as they be.

SLAMMEKIN. I, madam, was once kept by a *Jew;* and bating their religion, to women they are a good sort of people.

TAWDRY. Now for my part, I own I like an old fellow: for we always make them pay for what they can't do.

VIXEN. A spruce Prentice, let me tell you, ladies, is no ill thing, they bleed freely. I have sent at least two or three dozen of them in my time to the Plantations.

JENNY. But to be sure, Sir, with so much good fortune as you have had upon the road, you must be grown immensely rich.

MACHEATH. The road, indeed, hath done me justice, but the gaming-table hath been my Ruin.

AIR XXIV. When once I lay with another man's wife.

JENNY. *The Gamesters and Lawyers are jugglers alike,*
If they meddle your all is in danger:
Like Gypsies, if once they can finger a souse,
Your pockets they pick, and they pilfer your house
And give your estate to a stranger.

A man of courage should never put any thing to the risque, but his life. These are the tools of a man of honour. Cards and Dice are fit only for cowardly cheats, who prey upon their friends.

[*She takes up his Pistol.* Tawdry *takes up the other.*

TAWDRY. This, Sir, is fitter for your hand. Besides your loss of money, 'tis a loss to the ladies. Gaming takes you off from women. How fond could I be of you! but before company, 'tis ill bred.
MACHEATH. Wanton hussies!
JENNY. I must and will have a kiss to give my wine a zest.

[*They take him about the neck, and make signs to* Peachum *and Constables, who rush in upon him.*

SCENE V.

To them PEACHUM *and Constables.*

PEACHUM. I seize you, Sir, as my prisoner.
MACHEATH. Was this well done, *Jenny?*—Women are decoy Ducks; who can trust them! Beasts, Jades, Jilts, Harpies, Furies, Whores!
PEACHUM. Your case, Mr. *Macheath,* is not particular. The greatest Heroes have been ruin'd by women. But, to do them justice, I must own they are a pretty sort of creatures, if we could trust them. You must now, Sir, take your leave of the ladies, and if they have a mind to make you a visit, they will be sure to find you at home. This gentleman, ladies, lodges in *Newgate.* Constables, wait upon the Captain to his lodgings.

AIR XXV. When first I laid siege to my *Chloris.*

MACHEATH. *At the Tree I shall suffer with pleasure,*
At the Tree I shall suffer with pleasure,
Let me go where I will,
In all kinds of ill,
I shall find no such furies as these are.

PEACHUM. Ladies, I'll take care the reckoning shall be discharg'd.

[*Exit* Macheath, *guarded with* Peachum *and Constables.*

SCENE VI.

The Women remain.

VIXEN. Look ye, Mrs. *Jenny,* though Mr. *Peachum* may have made a private bargain with you and *Suky Tawdry* for betraying the Captain, as we were all assisting, we ought all to share alike.

COAXER. I think Mr. *Peachum,* after so long an acquaintance, might have trusted me as well as *Jenny Diver.*

SLAMMEKIN. I am sure at least three men of his hanging, and in a year's time too, (if he did me justice) should be set down to my account.

TRULL. Mrs. *Slammekin,* that is not fair. For you know one of them was taken in bed with me.

JENNY. As far as a bowl of punch or a treat, I believe Mrs. *Suky* will join with me.—As for any thing else, ladies, you cannot in conscience expect it.

SLAMMEKIN. Dear madam—

TRULL. I would not for the world—

SLAMMEKIN. 'Tis impossible for me—

TRULL. As I hope to be sav'd, madam—

SLAMMEKIN. Nay then, I must stay here all night—

TRULL. Since you command me. [*Exeunt with great Ceremony.*

SCENE VII. *NEWGATE.*

LOCKIT, Turnkeys, MACHEATH, Constables.

LOCKIT. Noble Captain, you are welcome. You have not been a lodger of mine this year and half. You know the Custom, Sir. Garnish, Captain, garnish.[25] Hand me down those fetters there.

MACHEATH. Those, Mr. *Lockit,* seem to be the heaviest of the whole set. With your leave, I should like the further pair better.

LOCKIT. Look ye, Captain, we know what is fittest for our prisoners. When a gentlemen uses me with civility, I always do the best I can to please him—Hand them down I say—We have them of all prices, from one guinea to ten, and 'tis fitting every gentleman should please himself.

MACHEATH. I understand you, Sir. [*Gives Money.*] The fees here are so many, and so exorbitant, that few fortunes can bear the expence of getting off handsomly, or of dying like a gentleman.

LOCKIT. Those, I see, will fit the Captain better.—Take down the further pair. Do but examine them, Sir——Never was better work.

25. New prisoners paid a tax that provided some (limited) amenities for all prisoners. Moreover, almost anything could be bought in jail, although at a high premium.

—How genteely they are made!—They will fit as easy as a glove, and the nicest man in *England* might not be asham'd to wear them. [*He puts on the chains.*] If I had the best gentleman in the land in my custody I could not equip him more handsomly. And so, Sir— I now leave you to your private meditations.

SCENE VIII.

MACHEATH.

AIR XXVI. Courtiers, Courtiers, think it no harm.

Man may escape from rope and gun;
Nay, some have out-liv'd the Doctor's pill:
Who takes a woman must be undone,
That Basilisk is sure to kill.
The Fly that sips treacle is lost in the sweets,
So he that tastes woman, woman, woman,
He that tastes woman, ruin meets.

To what a woful plight have I brought my self! Here must I (all day long, 'till I am hang'd) be confin'd to hear the reproaches of a wench who lays her ruin at my door.—I am in the custody of her father, and to be sure if he knows of the matter, I shall have a fine time on't betwixt this and my execution.—But I promis'd the wench marriage.—What signifies a promise to a woman? does not man in marriage itself promise a hundred things that he never means to perform? Do all we can, women will believe us; for they look upon a promise as an excuse for following their own inclinations.— But here comes *Lucy,* and I cannot get from her—wou'd I were deaf!

SCENE IX.

MACHEATH, LUCY.

LUCY. You base man you,—how can you look me in the face after what hath past between us?—See here, perfidious wretch, how I am forc'd to bear about the load of Infamy you have laid upon me —O *Macheath!* thou hast robb'd me of my quiet—to see thee tortur'd would give me pleasure.

AIR XXVII. A lovely Lass to a Friar came.

Thus when a good huswife sees a Rat
In her trap in the morning taken,
With pleasure her heart goes pit a pat,
In revenge for her loss of bacon.
Then she throws him
To the Dog or Cat
To be worried, crush'd and shaken.

MACHEATH. Have you no bowels, no tenderness, my dear *Lucy,* to see a husband in these circumstances?

LUCY. A husband!

MACHEATH. In ev'ry Respect but the form, and that, my dear, may be said over us at any time.—Friends should not insist upon ceremonies. From a man of honour, his word is as good as his bond.

LUCY. 'Tis the pleasure of all you fine men to insult the women you have ruin'd.

AIR XXVIII. Twas when the Sea was roaring.

How cruel are the traytors,
Who lye and swear in jest,
To cheat unguarded creatures,
Of virtue, fame, and rest!
Whoever steals a shilling,
Thro' shame the guilt conceals:
In love the perjur'd villain
With boasts the theft reveals.

MACHEATH. The very first opportunity, my dear, (have but patience) you shall be my wife in whatever manner you please.

LUCY. Insinuating monster! And so you think I know nothing of the affair of Miss *Polly Peachum.*—I could tear thy eyes out!

MACHEATH. Sure *Lucy,* you can't be such a fool as to be jealous of *Polly!*

LUCY. Are you not married to her, you brute, you.

MACHEATH. Married! Very good. The wench gives it out only to vex thee, and to ruin me in thy good opinion. 'Tis true, I go the house; I chat with the girl, I kiss her, I say a thousand things to her (as all gentlemen do) that mean nothing, to divert myself; and now the silly jade hath set it about that I am married to her, to let me know what she would be at. Indeed, my dear *Lucy,* these violent passions may be of ill consequence to a woman in your condition.

LUCY. Come, come, Captain, for all your assurance, you know that Miss *Polly* hath put it out of your power to do me the justice you promis'd me.

MACHEATH. A jealous woman believes ev'ry thing her passion suggests. To convince you of my sincerity, if we can find the Ordinary,° I shall have no scruples of making you my wife; and I know the consequences of having two at a time.

chaplain

LUCY. That you are only to be hang'd, and so get rid of them both.

MACHEATH. I am ready, my dear *Lucy,* to give you satisfaction—if you think there is any in marriage.—What can a man of honour say more?

LUCY. So then, it seems, you are not married to Miss *Polly.*

MACHEATH. You know, *Lucy,* the girl is prodigiously conceited.

No man can say a civil thing to her, but (like other fine ladies) her vanity makes her think he's her own for ever and ever.

AIR XXIX. The Sun had loos'd his weary teams.

The first time at the looking-glass
The mother sets her daughter,
The Image strikes the smiling lass
With self-love ever after.
Each time she looks, she, fonder grown,
Thinks ev'ry charm grows stronger:
But alas, vain maid, all eyes but your own
Can see you are not younger.

When women consider their own beauties, they are all alike unreasonable in their demands; for they expect their lovers should like them as long as they like themselves.

LUCY. Yonder is my father—perhaps this way we may light upon the Ordinary, who shall try if you will be as good as your word. —For I long to be made an honest woman.

SCENE X.

PEACHUM, LOCKIT with an Account-Book.

LOCKIT. In this last affair, brother *Peachum,* we are agreed. You have consented to go halves in *Macheath.*

PEACHUM. We shall never fall out about an execution.—But as to that article, pray how stands our last year's account?

LOCKIT. If you will run your eye over it, you'll find 'tis fair and clearly stated.

PEACHUM. This long Arrear of the Government is very hard upon us! Can it be expected that we should hang our acquaintance for nothing, when our betters will hardly save theirs without being paid for it. Unless the people in employment pay better, I promise them for the future, I shall let other rogues live besides their own.

LOCKIT. Perhaps, brother, they are afraid these matters may be carried too far. We are treated by them with contempt, as if our profession were not reputable.

PEACHUM. In one respect indeed, our employment may be reckon'd dishonest, because, like great Statesmen, we encourage those who betray their friends.

LOCKIT. Such language, brother, any where else, might turn to your prejudice. Learn to be more guarded, I beg you.

AIR XXX. How happy are we, *&c.*

When you censure the age,
Be cautious and sage,

Lest the Courtiers offended should be:
If you mention vice or bribe,
'Tis so pat to all the tribe;
Each cries—That was levell'd at me.

PEACHUM. Here's poor *Ned Clincher*'s name, I see. Sure, brother *Lockit,* there was a little unfair proceeding in *Ned*'s Case: for he told me in the condemn'd hold, that for value receiv'd, you had promis'd him a Session or two longer without molestation.

LOCKIT. Mr. *Peachum,*—this is the first time my honour was ever call'd in question.

PEACHUM. Business is at an end—if once we act dishonourably.

LOCKIT. Who accuses me?

PEACHUM. You are warm, brother.

LOCKIT. He that attacks my honour, attacks my livelyhood.—And this usage—Sir—is not to be born.

PEACHUM. Since you provoke me to speak—I must tell you too, that Mrs. *Coaxer* charges you with defrauding her of her information-money, for the apprehending of curl-pated *Hugh.* Indeed, indeed, brother, we must punctually pay our Spies, or we shall have no Information.

LOCKIT. Is this language to me, Sirrah—who have sav'd you from the gallows, Sirrah! [*Collaring each other.*

PEACHUM. If I am hang'd, it shall be for ridding the world of an arrant rascal.

LOCKIT. This hand shall do the office of the halter you deserve, and throttle you—you Dog!—

PEACHUM. Brother, brother,—we are both in the wrong—we shall be both losers in this dispute—for you know we have it in our power to hang each other. You should not be so passionate.

LOCKIT. Nor you so provoking.

PEACHUM. 'Tis our mutual interest; 'tis for the interest of the world we should agree. If I said any thing, brother, to the prejudice of your character, I ask pardon.

LOCKIT. Brother *Peachum*—I can forgive as well as resent.—Give me your hand. Suspicion does not become a friend.

PEACHUM. I only meant to give you occasion to justify yourself: But I must now step home, for I expect the gentleman about this Snuff-box, that *Filch* nimm'd two nights ago in the Park. I appointed him at this hour.

SCENE XI.

LOCKIT, LUCY.

LOCKIT. Whence come you, hussy?

LUCY. My tears might answer that question.

LOCKIT. You have then been whimpering and fondling, like a Spaniel, over the fellow that hath abus'd you.

LUCY. One can't help love; one can't cure it. 'Tis not in my power to obey you, and hate him.

LOCKIT. Learn to bear your husband's death like a reasonable woman. 'Tis not the fashion, now-a-days, so much as to affect sorrow upon these occasions. No woman would ever marry, if she had not the chance of mortality for a release. Act like a woman of spirit, hussy, and thank your father for what he is doing.

AIR XXXI. Of a noble Race was *Shenkin.*

LUCY.[26]

Is then his fate decreed, Sir?
Such a man can I think of quitting?
When first we met, so moves me yet,
O see how my heart is splitting!

LOCKIT. Look ye, *Lucy*—there is no saving him.—So, I think, you must ev'n do like other widows—buy your self weeds,° and be cheerful. black mourning clothes

AIR XXXII.

You'll think, e'er many days ensue,
This sentence not severe;
I hang your husband, child, 'tis true,
But with him hang your care.
Twang dang dillo dee.

Like a good wife, go moan over your dying husband. That, child, is your duty—consider, girl, you can't have the man and the money too—so make yourself as easy as you can by getting all you can from him.

SCENE XII.

LUCY, MACHEATH.

LUCY. Though the Ordinary was out of the way to day, I hope, my dear, you will, upon the first opportunity, quiet my scruples—Oh Sir!—my father's hard heart is not to be soften'd, and I am in the utmost despair.

MACHEATH. But if I could raise a small sum—would not twenty Guineas, think you, move him?—Of all the arguments in the way of business, the perquisite is the most prevailing.—Your father's perquisites for the escape of prisoners must amount to a

26. "Polly" in text.

considerable sum in the year. Money well tim'd, and properly apply'd, will do any thing.

AIR XXXIII. *London* Ladies.

If you at an Office solicit your due,
And would not have matters neglected;
You must quicken the Clerk with the perquisite too,
To do what his duty directed.
Or would you the frowns of a lady prevent,
She too has this palpable failing,
The perquisite softens her into consent;
That reason with all is prevailing.

LUCY. What love or money can do shall be done: for all my comfort depends upon your safety.

SCENE XIII.

LUCY, MACHEATH, POLLY.

POLLY. Where is my dear husband?—Was a rope ever intended for this neck!—O let me throw my arms about it, and throttle thee with love!—Why dost thou turn away from me?—'Tis thy *Polly* —'tis thy wife.
MACHEATH. Was there ever such an unfortunate rascal as I am!
LUCY. Was there ever such another villain!
POLLY. O *Macheath!* was it for this we parted? Taken! Imprison'd! Try'd! Hang'd!—cruel reflection! I'll stay with thee 'till death— no force shall tear thy dear wife from thee now.—What means my love?—Not one kind word! not one kind look! think what thy *Polly* suffers to see thee in this condition.

AIR XXXIV. All in the Downs, *&c.*

Thus when the Swallow, seeking prey,
Within the sash° is closely pent, window
His comfort with bemoaning lay,° song
Without sits pining for th' event.
Her chatt'ring lovers all around her skim;
She heeds them not (poor bird) her soul's with him.

MACHEATH. I must disown her. [*Aside.*] The wench is distracted.
LUCY. Am I then bilk'd of my virtue? Can I have no reparation? Sure men were born to lye, and women to believe them! O Villain! Villain!
POLLY. Am I not thy wife?—Thy neglect of me, thy aversion to me too severely proves it.—Look on me.—Tell me, am I not thy wife?
LUCY. Perfidious wretch!
POLLY. Barbarous husband!

LUCY. Hadst thou been hang'd five months ago, I had been happy.

POLLY. And I too—If you had been kind to me 'till death, it would not have vex'd me—And that's no very unreasonable request, (though from a wife) to a man who hath not above seven or eight days to live.

LUCY. Art thou then married to another? Hast thou two wives, monster?

MACHEATH. If women's tongues can cease for an answer—hear me.

LUCY. I won't.—Flesh and blood can't bear my usage.

POLLY. Shall I not claim my own? Justice bids me speak.

AIR XXXV. Have you heard of a frolicsome ditty.

MACHEATH. *How happy could I be with either,*
Were t'other dear charmer away!
But while you thus teaze me together,
To neither a word will I say;
But tol de rol, &c.

POLLY. Sure, my dear, there ought to be some preference shown to a wife! At least she may claim the appearance of it. He must be distracted with his misfortunes, or he could not use me thus!

LUCY. O Villain, Villain! thou hast deceiv'd me—I could even inform against thee with pleasure. Not a Prude wishes more heartily to have facts against her intimate acquaintance, than I now wish to have facts against thee. I would have her satisfaction, and they should all out.

AIR XXXVI. Irish Trot.

POLLY. *I'm bubbled.*
LUCY. *————————I'm bubbled.*
POLLY. *O how I am troubled!*
LUCY. *Bambouzled, and bit!*
POLLY. *————————————————My distresses are doubled.*
LUCY. *When you come to the Tree, should the Hangman refuse,*
These fingers, with pleasure, could fasten the noose.
POLLY. *I'm bubbled, &c.*

MACHEATH. Be pacified, my dear *Lucy*—This is all a fetch of *Polly*'s to make me desperate with you in case I get off. If I am hang'd, she would fain have the credit of being thought my widow —Really, *Polly*, this is no time for a Dispute of this sort; for whenever you are talking of marriage, I am thinking of hanging.

POLLY. And hast thou the heart to persist in disowning me?

MACHEATH. And hast thou the heart to persist in persuading me that I am married? Why, *Polly*, dost thou seek to aggravate my misfortunes?

LUCY. Really, Miss *Peachum,* you but expose yourself. Besides, 'tis barbarous in you to worry a gentleman in his circumstances.

AIR XXXVII.

POLLY *Cease your funning;*
Force or cunning
Never shall my heart trapan.° deceive
All these sallies
Are but malice
To seduce my constant man.
'Tis most certain,
By their flirting
Women oft have envy shown:
Pleas'd, to ruin
Others wooing;
Never happy in their own!

POLLY. Decency, madam, methinks might teach you to behave yourself with some reserve with the husband, while his wife is present.

MACHEATH. But seriously, *Polly,* this is carrying the joke a little too far.

LUCY. If you are determin'd, madam, to raise a disturbance in the prison, I shall be oblig'd to send for the Turnkey to shew you the door. I am sorry, madam, you force me to be so ill-bred.

POLLY. Give me leave to tell you, madam; these forward Airs don't become you in the least, madam. And my duty, madam, obliges me to stay with my husband, madam.

AIR XXXVIII. Good-morrow, Gossip *Joan.*

LUCY. *Why how now, madam* Flirt?
If you thus must chatter,
And are for flinging dirt,
Let's try who best can spatter;
Madam Flirt!

POLLY. *Why how now, saucy Jade;*
Sure the wench is tipsy!
How can you see me made [To him.
The scoff of such a Gipsy?
Saucy Jade! [To her.

SCENE XIV.

LUCY, MACHEATH, POLLY, PEACHUM.

PEACHUM. Where's my wench? Ah, hussy! hussy!—Come you home, you slut; and when your fellow is hang'd, hang yourself, to make your family some amends.

POLLY. Dear, dear father, do not tear me from him—I must speak; I have more to say to him—Oh! twist thy fetters about me, that he may not haul me from thee!

PEACHUM. Sure all women are alike! If ever they commit the folly, they are sure to commit another by exposing themselves—Away—Not a word more—You are my prisoner now, hussy.

AIR XXXIX. Irish Howl.

POLLY.
No power on earth can e'er divide
The knot that sacred love hath ty'd.
When parents draw against our mind,
The true-love's knot they faster bind.
Oh, oh ray, oh Amborah—oh, oh, &c.

[Holding *Macheath, Peachum* pulling her.

SCENE XV.

LUCY, MACHEATH.

MACHEATH. I am naturally compassionate, wife; so I could not use the wench as she deserv'd; which made you at first suspect there was something in what she said.

LUCY. Indeed, my dear, I was strangely puzzled.

MACHEATH. If that had been the case, her father would never have brought me into this circumstance—No, *Lucy,*—I had rather dye than be false to thee.

LUCY. How happy am I, if you say this from your heart! For I love thee so, that I could sooner bear to see thee hang'd than in the arms of another.

MACHEATH. But couldst thou bear to see me hang'd?

LUCY. O *Macheath,* I can never live to see that day.

MACHEATH. You see, *Lucy,* in the account of Love you are in my debt; and you must now be convinc'd, that I rather chuse to die than be another's.—Make me, if possible, love thee more, and let me owe my life to thee—If you refuse to assist me, *Peachum* and your father will immediately put me beyond all means of escape.

LUCY. My father, I know, hath been drinking hard with the Prisoners: and I fancy he is now taking his nap in his own room—If I can procure the keys, shall I go off with thee, my dear?

MACHEATH. If we are together, 'twill be impossible to lye conceal'd. As soon as the search begins to be a little cool, I will send to thee—'Till then my heart is thy prisoner.

LUCY. Come then, my dear husband—owe thy life to me—and though you love me not—be grateful—But that *Polly* runs in my head strangely.

MACHEATH. A moment of time may make us unhappy for-ever.

AIR XL. The Lass of *Patie*'s Mill.

LUCY.
I like the Fox shall grieve,
Whose mate hath left her side,
Whom Hounds, from morn to eve,
Chase o'er the country wide.
Where can my lover hide?
Where cheat the wary pack?
If Love be not his guide,
He never will come back!

ACT III. SCENE I.

SCENE *Newgate.*
LOCKIT, LUCY.

LOCKIT. To be sure, wench, you must have been aiding and abetting to help him to this escape.

LUCY. Sir, here hath been *Peachum* and his daughter *Polly,* and to be sure they know the Ways of *Newgate* as well as if they had been born and bred in the place all their lives. Why must all your suspicion light upon me?

LOCKIT. *Lucy, Lucy,* I will have none of these shuffling answers.

LUCY. Well then—If I know anything of him I wish I may be burnt!

LOCKIT. Keep your temper, *Lucy,* or I shall pronounce you guilty.

LUCY. Keep yours, Sir,—I do wish I may be burnt. I do—And what can I say more to convince you?

LOCKIT. Did he tip handsomely?—How much did he come down with? Come, hussy, don't cheat your father; and I shall not be angry with you—Perhaps, you have made a better bargain with him than I could have done—How much, my good girl?

LUCY. You know, Sir, I am fond of him, and would have given money to have kept him with me.

LOCKIT. Ah *Lucy!* thy education might have put thee more upon thy guard; for a girl in the bar of an Ale-house is always besieg'd.

LUCY. Dear Sir, mention not my education—for 'twas to that I owe my ruin.

AIR XLI. If Love's a sweet Passion, &c.

When young at the bar you first taught me to score,

And bid me be free of my lips, and no more;
I was kiss'd by the Parson, the Squire, and the Sot:
When the guest was departed, the kiss was forgot.
But his kiss was so sweet, and so closely he prest,
That I languish'd and pin'd 'till I granted the rest.

If you can forgive me, Sir, I will make a fair confession, for to be sure he hath been a most barbarous villain to me.

LOCKIT. And so you have let him escape, hussy—have you?

LUCY. When a woman loves; a kind look, a tender word can persuade her to any thing—and I could ask no other bribe.

LOCKIT. Thou wilt always be a vulgar slut, *Lucy*—If you would not be look'd upon as a fool, you should never do any thing but upon the foot of interest. Those that act otherwise are their own bubbles.

LUCY. But Love, Sir, is a misfortune that may happen to the most discreet woman, and in love we are all fools alike.—Notwithstanding all he swore, I am now fully convinc'd that *Polly Peachum* is actually his wife.—Did I let him escape, (fool that I was!) to go to her?—*Polly* will wheedle her self into his money, and then *Peachum* will hang him, and cheat us both.

LOCKIT. And so I am to be ruin'd, because, forsooth, you must be in love!—a very pretty excuse!

LUCY. I could murder that impudent happy strumpet:—I gave him his life, and that creature enjoys the sweets of it.—Ungrateful *Macheath!*

AIR XLII. *South-Sea* Ballad.

My love is all madness and folly,
Alone I lye,
Toss, tumble, and cry,
What a happy creature is Polly!
Was e'er such a wretch as I!
With rage I redden like scarlet,
That my dear inconstant Varlet,
Stark blind to my charms,
Is lost in the arms
Of that Jilt, that inveigling Harlot!
Stark blind to my charms,
Is lost in the arms
Of that Jilt, that inveigling Harlot!
This, this my resentment alarms.

LOCKIT. And so, after all this mischief, I must stay here to be entertain'd with your catterwauling, mistress Puss!—Out of my sight, wanton Strumpet! you shall fast and mortify yourself into reason, with now and then a little handsome discipline to bring you to your Senses.—Go.

SCENE II.

LOCKIT.

Peachum then intends to outwit me in this affair; but I'll be even with him.—The dog is leaky in his liquor, so I'll ply him that way, get the secret from him, and turn this affair to my own advantage.—Lions, Wolves, and Vulturs don't live together in herds, droves or flocks.—Of all animals of prey, man is the only sociable one. Every one of us preys upon his neighbor, and yet we herd together.—*Peachum* is my companion, my friend—According to the custom of the world, indeed, he may quote thousands of Precedents for cheating me—And shall I not make use of the privilege of friendship to make him a return?

AIR XLIII. *Packington*'s Pound.

Thus Gamesters united in friendship are found,
Though they know that their industry all is a cheat;
They flock to their prey at the Dice-box's sound,
And join to promote one another's deceit.
But if by mishap
They fail of a chap,
To keep in their hands, they each other entrap.
Like Pikes, lank with hunger, who miss of their ends,
They bite their companions, and prey on their friends.

Now, *Peachum,* you and I, like honest Tradesmen, are to have a fair tryal which of us two can over-reach the other.—*Lucy.*—[*Enter* Lucy.] Are there any of *Peachum*'s people now in the house?

LUCY. *Filch,* Sir, is drinking a quartern° of Strong-waters in the next room with black *Moll.* gill

LOCKIT. Bid him come to me.

SCENE III.

LOCKIT, FILCH.

LOCKIT. Why, Boy, thou lookest as if thou wert half starv'd, like a shotten Herring.[27]

FILCH. One had need have the constitution of a horse to go thorough with the business.—Since the favourite Child-getter was disabled by a mis-hap, I have pick'd up a little money by helping the ladies to a pregnancy against their being call'd down to sentence.—But if a man cannot get an honest livelihood any easier way, I am sure, 'tis what I can't undertake for another Session.

27. A herring that has spawned.

LOCKIT. Truly, if that great man should tip off, 'twould be an irreparable loss. The vigor and prowess of a Knight-errant never sav'd half the ladies in distress that he hath done.—But, boy, can'st thou tell me where thy master is to be found?

FILCH. At his Lock,[28] Sir, at the *Crooked Billet.*

LOCKIT. Very well.—I have nothing more with you. [*Exit* Filch.] I'll go to him there, for I have many important affairs to settle with him; and in the way of those transactions, I'll artfully get into his secret.—So that *Macheath* shall not remain a day longer out of my clutches.

SCENE IV. *A GAMING-HOUSE.*

MACHEATH in a fine tarnish'd Coat, BEN BUDGE,
MATT OF THE MINT.

MACHEATH. I am sorry, gentlemen, the road was so barren of money. When my friends are in difficulties, I am always glad that my fortune can be serviceable to them. [*Gives them money.*] You see, gentlemen, I am not a meer Court friend, who professes every thing and will do nothing.

AIR XLIV. Lillibullero.

The modes of the Court so common are grown,
That a true friend can hardly be met;
Friendship for interest is but a loan,
Which they let out for what they can get.
'Tis true, you find
Some friends so kind,
Who will give you good counsel themselves to defend.
In sorrowful ditty,
They promise, they pity,
But shift you for money, from friend to friend.

But we, gentlemen, have still honour enough to break through the corruptions of the world.—And while I can serve you, you may command me.

BEN. It grieves my heart that so generous a man should be involv'd in such difficulties, as oblige him to live with such ill company, and herd with gamesters.

MATT. See the partiality of mankind!—One man may steal a horse, better than another look over a hedge.—Of all mechanics, of all servile handycrafts-men, a gamester is the vilest. But yet, as many of the Quality are of the profession, he is admitted amongst the politest company. I wonder we are not more respected.

28. "A Cant word, signifying, a Warehouse where stolen goods are deposited" (Gay's note).

MACHEATH. There will be deep play to-night at *Mary-bone,* and consequently money may be pick'd up upon the road. Meet me there, and I'll give you the hint who is worth setting.° attempting

MATT. The fellow with a brown coat with a narrow gold binding, I am told, is never without money.

MACHEATH. What do you mean, *Matt?*—Sure you will not think of meddling with him!—He's a good honest kind of a fellow, and one of us.

BEN. To be sure, Sir, we will put our selves under your direction.

MACHEATH. Have an eye upon the money-lenders.—A *Rouleau,*° roll or two, would prove a pretty sort of an expedition. I hate extortion.

MATT. Those *Rouleaus* are very pretty things.—I hate your Bank bills—there is such a hazard in putting them off.

MACHEATH. There is a certain man of distinction, who in his time hath nick'd me out of a great deal of the ready.° He is in my cash,[29] cash *Ben;*—I'll point him out to you this evening, and you shall draw upon him for the debt.—The company are met; I hear the Dice-box in the other room. So, gentlemen, your servant. You'll meet me at *Marybone.*

SCENE V. PEACHUM'S *LOCK.*

A Table with Wine, Brandy, Pipes and Tobacco.

LOCKIT. The Coronation account, brother *Peachum,* is of so intricate a nature, that I believe it will never be settled.[30]

PEACHUM. It consists indeed of a great variety of articles.—It was worth to our people, in fees of different kinds, above ten instalments.[31]—This is part of the account, brother, that lies open before us.

LOCKIT. A lady's tail° of rich Brocade—that, I see, is train dispos'd of.

PEACHUM. To Mrs. *Diana Trapes,* the Tally-Woman, and she will make a good hand on't in shoes and slippers, to trick out young ladies, upon their going into keeping.—

LOCKIT. But I don't see any article of the Jewels.

PEACHUM. Those are so well known, that they must be sent abroad —you'll find them enter'd upon the article of Exportation.—As for the Snuff-boxes, Watches, Swords, *&c.*—I thought it best to enter them under their several heads.

LOCKIT. Seven and twenty women's pockets compleat; with the several things therein contain'd; all seal'd, number'd, and enter'd.

29. Owes me money.

30. George II was crowned in 1728; Peachum is presumably referring to the large takings for pick-pockets from the crowds at the event.

31. The installment of a lord mayor, which would have smaller crowds.

PEACHUM. But, brother, it is impossible for us now to enter upon this affair.—We should have the whole day before us.—Besides, the account of the last half year's Plate is in a book by it self, which lies at the other Office.

LOCKIT. Bring us then more liquor.—To-day shall be for pleasure—to-morrow for business.—Ah brother, those daughters of ours are two slippery hussies—keep a watchful eye upon *Polly,* and *Macheath* in a day or two shall be our own again.

AIR XLV. Down in the North Country.

LOCKIT.

What Gudgeons are we men!
Ev'ry woman's easy prey.
Though we have felt the Hook, agen
We bite, and they betray.

The bird that hath been trapt,
When he hears his calling mate,
To her he flies, again he's clapt
Within the wiry Grate.

PEACHUM. But what signifies catching the Bird, if your daughter *Lucy* will set open the door of the Cage?

LOCKIT. If men were answerable for the follies and frailties of their wives and daughters, no friends could keep a good correspondence together for two days.—This is unkind of you, brother; for among good friends, what they say or do goes for nothing.

Enter a Servant.

SERVANT. Sir, here's Mrs. *Diana Trapes* wants to speak with you.

PEACHUM. Shall we admit her, brother *Lockit?*

LOCKIT. By all means—she's a good customer, and a fine-spoken woman—and a woman who drinks and talks so freely will enliven the conversation.

PEACHUM. Desire her to walk in. [*Exit Servant.*

SCENE VI.

PEACHUM, LOCKIT, Mrs. *TRAPES.*

PEACHUM. Dear Mrs. *Dye,* your servant—one may know by your kiss, that your Ginn is excellent.

TRAPES. I was always very curious° in my liquors. particular

LOCKIT. There is no perfum'd breath like it—I have been long acquainted with the flavour of those lips—han't I, Mrs. *Dye?*

TRAPES. Fill it up.—I take as large draughts of liquor, as I did of love.—I hate a Flincher in either.

AIR XLVI. A Shepherd kept Sheep, *&c.*

In the days of my youth I could bill like a Dove, fa, la la, &c.
Like a Sparrow at all times was ready for love, fa, la la, &c.
The life of all mortals in kissing should pass,
Lip to lip while we're young—then the lip to the glass, fa, la la, &c.

But now, Mr. *Peachum,* to our business.—If you have blacks of any kind, brought in of late; Mantoes—Velvet Scarfs—Petticoats —Let it be what it will—I am your chap—for all my ladies are very fond of mourning.

PEACHUM. Why, look ye, Mrs. *Dye*—you deal so hard with us, that we can afford to give the gentlemen, who venture their lives for the goods, little or nothing.

TRAPES. The hard times oblige me to go very near in my dealing.—To be sure, of late years I have been a great sufferer by the Parliament. —Three thousand pounds would hardly make me amends.—The Act for destroying the Mint[32] was a severe cut upon our business—'till then, if a customer stept out of the way—we knew where to have her —no doubt you know Mrs. *Coaxer*—there's a wench now ('till today) with a good suit of cloaths of mine upon her back, and I could never set eyes upon her for three Months together.—Since the Act too against imprisonment for small sums,[33] my loss there too hath been very considerable, and it must be so, when a lady can borrow a handsome petticoat, or a clean gown, and I not have the least hank upon her! And, o' my conscience, now-a-days most ladies take a delight in cheating, when they can do it with safety.

PEACHUM. Madam, you had a handsome gold watch of us t'other day for seven Guineas.—Considering we must have our profit—to a gentleman upon the road, a gold watch will be scarce worth the taking.

TRAPES. Consider, Mr. *Peachum,* that watch was remarkable, and not of very safe sale.—If you have any black Velvet Scarfs—they are a handsome winter wear; and take with most gentlemen who deal with my customers.—'Tis I that put the ladies upon a good foot. 'Tis not youth or beauty that fixes their price. The gentlemen always pay according to their dress, from half a crown to two guineas; and yet those hussies make nothing of bilking of me.—Then too, allowing for accidents.—I have eleven fine customers now down under the Surgeon's hands,—what with fees and other expenses, there are great goings-out, and no comings-in, and not a farthing to pay for at least a month's cloathing.—We run great risques—great risques indeed.

PEACHUM. As I remember, you said something just now of Mrs. *Coaxer.*

32. The act eliminating the status of the Mint as a sanctuary.
33. The Insolvent Debtors Relief Acts of 1728 (there were two).

TRAPES. Yes, Sir.—To be sure I stript her of a suit of my own cloaths about two hours ago; and have left her as she should be, in her shift, with a lover of hers at my house. She call'd him up stairs, as he was going to *Marybone* in a hackney-coach.—And I hope, for her own sake and mine, she will perswade the Captain to redeem her, for the Captain is very generous to the ladies.

LOCKIT. What Captain?

TRAPES. He thought I did not know him.—An intimate acquaintance of yours, Mr. *Peachum*—Only Captain *Macheath*—as fine as a Lord.

PEACHUM. To-morrow, Mrs. *Dye*, you shall set your own price upon any of the goods you like—we have at least half a dozen Velvet Scarfs, and all at your service. Will you give me leave to make you a present of the suit of night-cloaths for your own wearing?—But are you sure it is Captain *Macheath?*

TRAPES. Though he thinks I have forgot him; no body knows him better. I have taken a great deal of the Captain's money in my time at second-hand, for he always lov'd to have his ladies well drest.

PEACHUM. Mr. *Lockit* and I have a little business with the Captain; —you understand me—and we will satisfie you for Mrs. *Coaxer*'s debt.

LOCKIT. Depend upon it—we will deal like men of honour.

TRAPES. I don't enquire after your affairs—so whatever happens, I wash my hands on't—It hath always been my Maxim, that one friend should assist another.—But if you please—I'll take one of the Scarfs home with me, 'tis always good to have something in hand.

SCENE VII. *NEWGATE.*

LUCY.

Jealousy, rage, love and fear are at once tearing me to pieces, How am I weather-beaten and shatter'd with distresses!

AIR XLVII. One evening having lost my way.

I'm like a skiff on the Ocean tost,
Now high, now low, with each billow born,
With her rudder broke, and her anchor lost,
Deserted and all forlorn.
While thus I lye rolling and tossing all night,
That Polly *lyes sporting on seas of delight!*
Revenge, revenge, revenge,
Shall appease my restless sprite.

I have the Rats-bane ready.—I run no risque; for I can lay her death upon the Ginn, and so many dye of that naturally that I shall never be call'd in question.—But say I were to be hang'd—I never could be hang'd for any thing that would give me greater comfort, than the poysoning that slut.

Enter FILCH.

FILCH. Madam, here's Miss *Polly* come to wait upon you.
LUCY. Show her in.

SCENE VIII.

LUCY, POLLY.

LUCY. Dear madam, your servant.—I hope you will pardon my passion, when I was so happy to see you last.—I was so over-run with the spleen, that I was perfectly out of my self. And really when one hath the spleen, every thing is to be excus'd by a friend.

AIR XLVIII. Now *Roger,* I'll tell thee, because thou'rt my son.

When a wife's in her pout,
(As she's sometimes, no doubt)
The good husband as meek as a lamb,
Her vapours to still,
First grants her her will,
And the quieting draught is a dram.
Poor Man! And the quieting draught is a dram.

—I wish all our quarrels might have so comfortable a reconciliation.
POLLY. I have no excuse for my own behaviour, madam, but my misfortunes.—And really, madam, I suffer too upon your account.
LUCY. But, Miss *Polly*—in the way of friendship, will you give me leave to propose a glass of Cordial to you?
POLLY. Strong-waters are apt to give me the head-ache—I hope, Madam, you will excuse me.
LUCY. Not the greatest lady in the land could have better in her closet, for her own private drinking.—You seem mighty low in spirits, my dear.
POLLY. I am sorry, madam, my health will not allow me to accept of your offer.—I should not have left you in the rude manner I did when we met last, madam, had not my Papa haul'd me away so unexpectedly—I was indeed somewhat provok'd, and perhaps might use some expressions that were disrespectful.—But really, madam, the Captain treated me with so much contempt and cruelty, that I deserv'd your pity, rather than your resentment.
LUCY. But since his escape, no doubt all matters are made up

again.—Ah *Polly! Polly!* 'tis I am the unhappy wife; and he loves you as if you were only his mistress.

POLLY. Sure, madam, you cannot think me so happy as to be the object of your jealousy.—A man is always afraid of a woman who loves him too well—so that I must expect to be neglected and avoided.

LUCY. Then our cases, my dear *Polly,* are exactly alike. Both of us indeed have been too fond.

AIR XLIX. *O Bessy Bell,* &c.

POLLY. *A curse attends that woman's love,*
Who always would be pleasing.
LUCY. *The pertness of the billing Dove,*
Like tickling, is but teasing.
POLLY. *What then in love can woman do?*
LUCY. *If we grow fond they shun us.*
POLLY. *And when we fly them, they pursue:*
LUCY. *But leave us when they've won us.*

LUCY. Love is so very whimsical in both sexes, that it is impossible to be lasting.—But my heart is particular, and contradicts my own observation.

POLLY. But really, mistress *Lucy,* by his last behaviour, I think I ought to envy you.—When I was forc'd from him, he did not shew the least tenderness.—But perhaps, he hath a heart not capable of it.

AIR L.—Would Fate to me *Belinda* give.

Among the men, Coquets we find,
Who court by turns all woman-kind;
And we grant all their hearts desir'd,
When they are flatter'd, and admir'd.

The Coquets of both sexes are self-lovers, and that is a love no other whatever can dispossess. I hear, my dear *Lucy,* our husband is one of those.

LUCY. Away with these melancholy reflections,—indeed, my dear *Polly,* we are both of us a cup too low.—Let me prevail upon you, to accept of my offer.

AIR LI. Come, sweet lass.

Come, sweet lass,
Let's banish sorrow
'Till to-morrow;
Come, sweet lass,
Let's take a chirping° glass. cheering
Wine can clear
The vapours of despair;

And make us light as air;
Then drink, and banish care.

I can't bear, child, to see you in such low Spirits.—And I must persuade you to what I know will do you good.—I shall now soon be even with the hypocritical Strumpet. [*Aside.*

SCENE IX.

POLLY.

All this wheedling of *Lucy* cannot be for nothing.—At this time too! when I know she hates me!—The dissembling of a woman is always the fore-runner of mischief.—By pouring Strong-waters down my throat, she thinks to pump some secrets out of me—I'll be upon my guard, and won't taste a drop of her liquor, I'm resolv'd.

SCENE X.

LUCY, *with Strong-waters.* POLLY.

LUCY. Come, Miss *Polly.*

POLLY. Indeed, child, you have given yourself trouble to no purpose. —You must, my dear, excuse me.

LUCY. Really, Miss *Polly,* you are as squeamishly affected about taking a cup of Strong-waters, as a lady before company. I vow, *Polly,* I shall take it monstrously ill if you refuse me.—Brandy and Men (though women love them ever so well) are always taken by us with some reluctance—unless 'tis in private.

POLLY. I protest, madam, it goes against me.—What do I see! *Macheath* again in custody!—Now every glimmering of happiness is lost.

[*Drops the glass of liquor on the ground.*

LUCY. Since things are thus, I'm glad the wench hath escap'd: for by this event, 'tis plain, she was not happy enough to deserve to be poison'd.

SCENE XI.

LOCKIT, MACHEATH, PEACHUM, LUCY, POLLY.

LOCKIT. Set your heart to rest, Captain.—You have neither the chance of Love or Money for another escape—for you are order'd to be call'd down upon your Tryal immediately.

PEACHUM. Away, hussies!—This is not a time for a man to be hamper'd with his wives.—You see, the gentleman is in chains already.

LUCY. O husband, husband, my heart long'd to see thee; but to see thee thus distracts me.

POLLY. Will not my dear husband look upon his *Polly?* Why hadst thou not flown to me for protection? with me thou hadst been safe.

AIR LII. The last time I went o'er the Moor.

POLLY. *Hither, dear husband, turn your eyes.*
LUCY. *Bestow one glance to cheer me.*
POLLY. *Think with that look, thy* Polly *dyes.*
LUCY. *O shun me not,—but hear me.*
POLLY. *'Tis* Polly *sues.*
LUCY. ———————*'Tis* Lucy *speaks.*
POLLY. *Is thus true love requited?*
LUCY. *My heart is bursting.*
POLLY. ——————————————*Mine too breaks.*
LUCY. *Must I,*
POLLY. ———————*Must I be slighted?*

MACHEATH. What would you have me say, ladies?—You see, this affair will soon be at an end, without my disobliging either of you.

PEACHUM. But the settling this point, Captain, might prevent a Law-suit between your two widows.

AIR LIII. *Tom Tinker*'s my true love, *&c.*

MACHEATH.
Which way shall I turn me—how can I decide?
Wives, the day of our death, are as fond as a bride.
One wife is too much for most husbands to hear,
But two at a time there's no mortal can bear.
This way, and that way, and which way I will,
What would comfort the one, t'other wife would take ill.

POLLY. But if his own misfortunes have made him insensible to mine—a Father sure will be more compassionate—Dear, dear Sir, sink the material evidence, and bring him off at his Tryal—*Polly,* upon her knees begs it of you.

AIR LIV. I am a poor Shepherd undone.

When my Hero in court appears,
And stands arraign'd for his life,
Then think of poor Polly*'s tears;*
For Ah! poor Polly*'s his wife.*
Like the Sailor he holds up his hand,
Distrest on the dashing wave.
To die a dry death at land,
Is as bad as a watry grave.
And alas, poor Polly!

Alack, and well-a-day!
Before I was in love,
Oh! every Month was May.

LUCY. If *Peachum*'s heart is harden'd; sure you, Sir, will have more compassion on a daughter.—I know the evidence is in your power.—How then can you be a tyrant to me? [*Kneeling.*

AIR LV. *Ianthe* the lovely, *&c.*

When he holds up his hand arraign'd for his life,
O think of your daughter, and think I'm his wife!
What are cannons, or bombs, or clashing of swords?
For death is more certain by witnesses words.
Then nail up their lips; that dread thunder allay;
And each month of my life will hereafter by May.

LOCKIT. *Macheath*'s time is come, *Lucy.*—We know our own affairs, therefore let us have no more whimpering or whining.

AIR LVI. A Cobler there was, *&c.*

Our selves, like the Great, to secure a retreat,
When matters require it, must give up our gang:
And good reason why,
Or, instead of the fry,
Ev'n Peachum *and I,*
Like poor petty rascals, might hang, hang;
Like poor petty rascals, might hang.

PEACHUM. Set your heart at rest, *Polly.*—Your husband is to dye to-day.—Therefore, if you are not already provided, 'tis high time to look about for another. There's comfort for you, you slut.

LOCKIT. We are ready, Sir, to conduct you to the *Old Baily.*

AIR LVII. Bonny *Dundee.*

MACHEATH. *The charge is prepar'd; the Lawyers are met;*
The Judges all rang'd (a terrible show!)
I go, undismay'd.—For death is a debt,
A debt on demand.—So, take what I owe.
Then farewell, my love—dear charmers, adieu.
Contented I die—'tis the better for you.
Here ends all disputes the rest of our lives,
For this way at once I please all my wives.

Now, Gentlemen, I am ready to attend you.

SCENE XII.

LUCY, POLLY, FILCH.

POLLY. Follow them, *Filch,* to the Court. And when the Tryal is over, bring me a particular account of his behaviour, and of every thing that happen'd.—You'll find me here with Miss *Lucy.* [*Exit* Filch.] But why is all this Musick?

LUCY. The prisoners, whose Tryals are put off till next Session, are diverting themselves.

POLLY. Sure there is nothing so charming as Musick! I'm fond of it to distraction—But alas!—now, all mirth seems an insult upon my affliction.—Let us retire, my dear *Lucy,* and indulge our sorrows.—The noisy crew, you see, are coming upon us. [*Exeunt.*

A Dance of Prisoners in chains, &c.

SCENE XIII. *THE CONDEMN'D HOLD*

MACHEATH, *in a melancholy posture.*

AIR LVIII. Happy Groves.

O cruel, cruel, cruel case!
Must I suffer this disgrace?

AIR LIX. Of all the girls that are so smart.

Of all the friends in time of grief,
When threatning Death looks grimmer,
Not one so sure can bring relief,
As this best friend a brimmer. [Drinks.

AIR LX. *Britons* strike home.

Since I must swing,—I scorn, I scorn, to wince or whine. [Rises.

AIR LXI. Chevy Chase.

But now again my spirits sink;
I'll raise them high with wine. [Drinks a glass of wine.

AIR LXII. To old Sir *Simon* the King.

But valour the stronger grows,
The stronger liquor we're drinking.
And how can we feel our woes,
When we've lost the trouble of thinking? [Drinks.

AIR LXIII. Joy to great *Cæsar.*

If thus—A man can die
Much bolder with brandy. [Pours out a bumper of brandy.

AIR LXIV. There was an old woman, *&c.*

So I drink off this bumper—And now I can stand the test,
And my Comrades shall see, that I die as brave as the best. [Drinks.

AIR LXV. Did you ever hear of a gallant sailor.

But can I leave my pretty hussies,
Without one tear, or tender sigh?

AIR LXVI. Why are mine eyes still flowing.

Their eyes, their lips, their busses
Recall my love—Ah must I die!

AIR LXVII. Green sleeves.

Since laws were made for ev'ry degree,
To curb vice in others, as well as me,
I wonder we han't better company,
Upon Tyburn *tree!*
But gold from law can take out the sting;
And if rich men like us were to swing,
'Twould thin the land, such numbers to string
Upon Tyburn *tree!*

JAILOR. Some friends of yours, Captain, desire to be admitted— I leave you together.

SCENE XIV.

MACHEATH, BEN BUDGE, MATT of the MINT.

MACHEATH. For my having broke Prison, you see, gentlemen, I am order'd immediate execution.—The Sheriffs officers, I believe, are now at the door.—That *Jemmy Twitcher* should peach me, I own surpriz'd me!—'Tis a plain proof that the world is all alike, and that even our Gang can no more trust one another than other people. Therefore, I beg you, gentlemen, look well to your selves, for in all probability you may live some months longer.

MATT. We are heartily sorry, Captain, for your misfortune.—But 'tis what we must all come to.

MACHEATH. *Peachum* and *Lockit*, you know, are infamous Scoundrels. Their lives are as much in your power, as yours are in theirs—Remember your dying friend!—'Tis my last request.— Bring those villains to the Gallows before you, and I am satisfied.

MATT. We'll do it.

JAILOR. Miss *Polly* and Miss *Lucy* intreat a word with you.

MACHEATH. Gentlemen, adieu.

SCENE XV.

LUCY, MACHEATH, POLLY.

MACHEATH. My dear *Lucy*—My dear *Polly*—Whatsoever hath past between us is now at an end—If you are fond of marrying again, the best advice I can give you, is to ship yourselves to the *West-Indies,* where you'll have a fair chance of getting a husband a-piece; or by good luck, two or three, as you like best.

POLLY. How can I support this sight!

LUCY. There is nothing moves one so much as a great man in distress.

AIR LXVII. All you that must take a leap, *&c.*

LUCY. *Would I might be hang'd!*
POLLY. *————————————And I would so too!*
LUCY. *To be hang'd with you.*
POLLY. *———————————My dear, with you.*
MACHEATH. *O leave me to thought! I fear! I doubt!*
I tremble! I droop!—See, my courage is out.

[Turns up the empty bottle.

POLLY. *No token of love?*
MACHEATH. *—————————See, my courage is out.*

[Turns up the empty pot.

LUCY. *No token of love?*
POLLY. *—————————Adieu.*
LUCY. *————————————Farewell.*
MACHEATH. *But hark! I hear the toll of the bell.*
CHORUS. *Tol de rol lol,* &c.

JAILOR. Four women more, Captain, with a child a-peice! See, here they come. [*Enter women and children.*

MACHEATH. What—four wives more!—This is too much.—Here—tell the Sheriffs officers I am ready. [*Exit* Macheath *guarded.*

SCENE XVI.

To them, Enter PLAYER and BEGGAR.

PLAYER. But, honest friend, I hope you don't intend that *Macheath* shall be really executed.

BEGGAR. Most certainly, Sir.—To make the piece perfect, I was for doing strict poetical Justice.—*Macheath* is to be hang'd; and for the other personages of the Drama, the Audience must have suppos'd they were all hang'd or transported.

PLAYER. Why then, friend, this is a down-right deep Tragedy. The catastrophe is manifestly wrong, for an Opera must end happily.

BEGGAR. Your objection, Sir, is very just; and is easily remov'd. For you must allow, that in this kind of Drama, 'tis no matter how absurdly things are brought about—So—you rabble there—run and cry a Reprieve—let the prisoner be brought back to his wives in triumph.

PLAYER. All this we must do, to comply with the taste of the town.

BEGGAR. Through the whole piece you may observe such a similitude of manners in high and low life, that it is difficult to determine whether (in the fashionable vices) the fine gentlemen imitate the gentlemen of the road, or the gentlemen of the road the fine gentlemen.—Had the Play remain'd, as I at first intended, it would have carried a most excellent moral. 'Twould have shown that the lower sort of people have their vices in a degree as well as the rich: And that they are punish'd for them.

SCENE XVII.

To them MACHEATH *with Rabble,* &c.

MACHEATH. So, it seems, I am not left to my choice, but must have a wife at last.—Look ye, my dears, we will have no controversie now. Let us give this day to mirth, and I am sure she who thinks her self my wife will testifie her joy by a dance.

ALL. Come, a Dance—a Dance.

MACHEATH. Ladies, I hope you will give me leave to present a Partner to each of you. And (if I may without offence) for this time, I take *Polly* for mine.—And for life, you slut,—for we were really marry'd.—As for the rest.—But at present keep your own secret.

A DANCE.

Air LXIX. Lumps of Pudding, *&c.*

Thus I stand like the Turk, with his Doxies around;
From all Sides their Glances his Passion confound;
For Black, Brown, and Fair, his Inconstancy burns,
And the different beauties subdue him by turns:
Each calls forth her charms, to provoke his desires:
Though willing to all; with but one he retires.
But think of this maxim, and put off your sorrow,
The wretch of to-day, may be happy to-morrow.

CHORUS: *But think of this maxim,* &c.

FINIS.

PART 4

Drama

OF THE NINETEENTH AND EARLY TWENTIETH CENTURIES

THE NINETEENTH-CENTURY English language stage was dominated by stars and spectacle; innovation and originality was to be found in places like Germany and the Scandinavian countries, or in the emergent form of the novel, and this despite the large numbers of theater companies, particularly in the United States. Companies were built around theatrical roles: the leading lady, the leading man, the ingenue, the soubrette, the heavy (villain), etc. Star actors travelled to both sides of the Atlantic and drew fanatical audiences to see them perform the classics. Genres such as melodrama and the drawing room comedy met the expectations of the audience but did not challenge contemporary social mores. In fact, the tyranny of audience expectations militated against experimentation; James O'Neill, the father of Eugene O'Neill, a talented actor, became so identified with the role of the Count of Monte Cristo that he had difficulty getting audiences to see him as anything else. However, the influence of dramatic realism as pioneered by Henrik Ibsen and August Strindberg eventually led to a revival of serious English-language theater in the United

States, England, and Ireland. Joseph A. Herne's *Margaret Fleming* (1890) is conventionally regarded as the beginning of realism in American drama. Bernard Shaw combined realism with philosophical analysis in his plays, and the Abbey Theatre in Ireland dramatized rural life in a language naturally poetic.

The Shaughraun

Dion Boucicault was the most successful English language playwright of the nineteenth century, a comic actor admired on three continents, a significant contributor in the development of copyright for plays, and a theatrical innovator in special effects such as stage illusions and fireproof scenery. This fame makes it odd that doubt surrounds significant events in his life, starting with his parentage. His father, Samuel Boursiquot, a Dublin wine merchant of Huguenot descent, was twenty-six years older than his mother, Anne. Anne Darley was from a literary family; her brother George was a poet and her brother Charles was the first professor of English at Cork. Boucicault was born in December of 1820 (the exact date is disputed), by which time his mother may have already begun her affair with Dionysius Lardner, who may have been Dion's father. By 1821, Lardner was living with the family, and when he became professor of natural philosophy and astronomy at University College London, the family moved there. Boucicault, an indifferent student, was briefly Lardner's apprentice in civil engineering, but by eighteen he was acting under a pseudonym in provincial theaters. He began writing plays before he reached London, but his first big hit was the still stageable *London Assurance* in 1841. Boucicault churned out original plays, as well as translations/adaptations of French plays. In France, he met and married a French widow with property, Anne Guiot, in 1845. Within three years she was dead (of what is unknown) and Boucicault was back working in London. For Charles Kean he created the great double role of *The Corsican Brothers* (1852) and promptly fell out with him when he became involved with Kean's nineteen-year-old ward Agnes Robertson. Boucicault had six

Andrew Parkin's edition of *Selected Plays of Dion Boucicault* indicates a first production of November 14, 1874 (Washington: The Catholic University of America Press, 1987), 258. My copy text is from "Dicks' Standard Plays" reprint ed from the University of Toronto Libraries; this text has the cast and numerous stage directions that detail the blocking of the actors (such as "*Crosses to her, behind* R."). I have retained the costume descriptions and stage directions to indicate how detailed a nineteenth-century play text was. I have also standardized spellings such as "Ballyragget," for instance, which also is printed as "Ballyraggett."

children with Agnes, although he claimed, when he ran off to Australia with the twenty-one-year-old actress Louise Thorndyke in 1885, that he and Agnes had never been married. Moving to New York in 1853, Boucicault wrote a number of plays for Agnes, who became a major star. With others, Boucicault was instrumental in having copyright laws modeled on the French laws passed in the United States; this meant he collected royalties most of the time when his plays were performed, instead of receiving a single fee up-front. Boucicault developed one of his cleverest schemes with *The Poor of New York* in 1857; with minor changes for local color, the play could easily become *The Poor of Philadelphia, The Poor of London, The Poor of Liverpool,* etc. He had another huge hit with *The Colleen Bawn* (1860) and created the comic role of Myles na Coppaleen; in London, Queen Victoria saw the play three times. He proceeded to lose his fortune on an ill-fated attempt to open his own theater complex. He went on to make a new one, especially with his Irish plays *Arrah-na-pogue* (1865) and *The Shaughraun* (1874). But by the 1880s, theatrical tastes had changed, Boucicault could no longer play the athletic comical parts that had been his forte, and he died in New York in 1890, already a name in eclipse.

Boucicault is the master of combining comedy, melodrama, and spectacle in the form of a "well-made play." Each act ends at a moment of high dramatic tension, "the curtain-closer." While these plays frequently are on topical and controversial subjects, the play is constructed so that no audience need be offended. A good example of this is Agnes's starring role in *The Octoroon* (1859), a play about slavery successful in both the North and the South on the eve of the Civil War. A Northern audience saw the play as an indictment of the horrors of slavery. A Southern audience saw the portrayal of an essentially benign system perverted by a Yankee villain. Since the play's outcomes are determined by audience expectations rather than some inner causality, Boucicault had no problem writing two different endings. In the American version, the title character must die tragically, since miscegenation is not a possibility. In the English version, she runs off with the young hero. Equally in *The Shaughraun,* both the Fenian and the English officer are noble figures and end happily, while the Irish informers suffer their richly deserved fates. Nevertheless, at a time when anti-Catholicism was common in the United States, the Irish priest is a benevolent figure, and Irish aspirations are treated sympathetically.

The Shaughraun

AN ORIGINAL DRAMA, IN THREE ACTS,
ILLUSTRATIVE OF IRISH LIFE AND CHARACTER.
BY DION BOUCICAULT, ESQ.

DRAMATIS PERSONNÆ

First Performed at Wallack's Theatre, New York, 1875.

CAPTAIN MOLINEUX (a young English Officer, commanding a detachment at Ballyragget.[1])

ROBERT FFOLLIOTT (a young Irish Gentleman—under sentence as a Fenian[2]—in love with Arte O'Neale)

FATHER DOLAN (the Parish Priest of Suil-a-beg, his tutor and guardian)

CORRY KINCHELA (a Squireen[3])

HARVEY DUFF (a Police Agent in disguise of a peasant, under the name of Keach)

CONN (the Shaughraun,[4] the soul of every fair, the life of every funeral, the first fiddle at all weddings and patterns[5]

SERGEANT JONES (of the 41st)

SULLIVAN, REILLY, MANGAN } peasants

DOYLE }

DONOVAN }

ARTE O'NEAL (in love with Robert)

CLAIRE FFOLLIOTT (a Sligo Lady)

MRS. O'KELLY (Conn's Mother)

MOYA (Father Dolan's Niece, in love with Conn),

BRIDGET MADIGAN (a Keener[6])

1. Ballyragget is a town in County Kilkenny on the river Nore. But Boucicault is selecting names of places because they sound unmistakably Irish; thus, Suil-a-beg is apparently in County Sligo, while Conn poaches on Keim-an-eigh (in County Cork) and in the Maumturk Mountains in Connemara in west County Galway.

2. The Fenians were founded as a fraternal society in 1858 in New York by John O'Mahony and were dedicated to Irish independence. With the Irish Republican Brotherhood, they had risen unsuccessfully against the English government in Ireland in 1867.

3. Literally "a little squire" and hence one who wishes to be above his station and who apes the English.

4. From Irish *seachran,* to wander or roam, and hence a vagabond. Boucicault played Conn; he was fifty-four at the time.

5. A fair on the feast day of a saint.

6. A mourner who wails in lamentation for the dead.

NANCY MALONE (a Keener)

Peasants, Soldiers, Constabulary.

CAPTAIN MOLINEUX.—Full suit of regimentals—infantry officer's tunic—crimson sash—shako[7] and sword.

ROBERT FFOLLIOTT.—Dark blue pilot coat and trousers—black glazed sailor's hat—long gray ulster.[8]

FATHER DOLAN.—Plain black clerical frock (no collar)—black knee breeches and gaiters[9]—cassock, broad-brimmed wide-awake hat,[10] and cane.

CORRY KINCHELA.—*1st Dress:* Green cut-away coat—light breeches and waistcoat—Napoleon boots.

2ND DRESS: Scarlet hunting-coat—white waistcoat and breeches, and top-boots—white hat, and hunting whip. *3rd Dress:* Frieze overcoat,[11] and broad-brimmed wide-awake hat.

HARVEY DUFF.—Ragged gray frieze overcoat—Irish billycock hat[12]—red waistcoat—brown breeches—patched gray stockings —ankle-jacks[13]—no neckerchief—check shirt-collar, open, and throat visible.

CONN.—*1st Dress:* Old patched scarlet hunting-coat—brown cord breeches—old yellow top boots—check shirt, and old black velvet hunting-cap. *2nd Dress:* Gray coat, and large broad-brimmed hat.

SULLIVAN, REILLY, MANGAN, AND DOYLE.—A mixed costume, combining the Irish peasant and the smuggler, in various garbs of poverty and ferocity. Ragged pea jackets—Guernsey shirts°— loose breeches, with old fisherman's boots over-hairy caps and sou'westers. sweaters

DONOVAN and Farming Peasantry in various garbs.

ARTE O'NEAL.—Neat dress of the present period.

CLAIRE FFOLLIOTT.—*1st Dress:* Fashionable walking-dress. *2nd Dress:* Dark green riding-dress, gilt buttons—black Spanish hat and feathers, gold loop in front.

MRS. O'KELLY.—Black petticoat—brown bedgown—close

white cap, fitted to the head, without ribbon or border—spotted handkerchief crossed down her neck—blue stockings—shoes and buckles.

MOYA.—Coloured bodice—smart short petticoat—apron—hair decorated with blue ribbon.

BRIDGET MADIGAN.—Cloak with hood—dark and well-worn

7. Cylindical military hat with a visor and plume.
8. An overcoat with a cape and sleeves.
9. A covering extending from the instep to the lower part of the leg.
10. Black hat with rounded crown and upturned side brims.
11. Coat of heavy coarse wool.
12. Bowler.
13. Lace-up boots reaching up around the ankles.

drapery beneath it—haybands[14] round the ankles, and highlow boots.

NANCY MALONE.—Irish field peasant—same style in different colours.

IRISH GIRLS. To correspond in dress with Mrs. O'Kelly.

STAGE DIRECTIONS.

EXITS AND ENTRANCES.—R. means *Right;* L. *Left;* D. F. *Door in Flat;* R. D. *Right Door;* L. D. *Left Door;* S. E. *Second Entrance;* U. E. *Upper Entrance;*
M. D. *Middle Door;* L. U. E. *Left Up Entrance;* R. U. E. *Right Upper Entrance;*
L. S. E. *Left Second Entrance;* P. S. *Prompt Side;* O. P. *Opposite Prompt.*

RELATIVE POSITIONS. R. means *Right;* L. *Left;* C. *Centre;* R. C. *Right of Centre;*
L. C. *Left of Centre.*
R. RC. C. LC.[15] L.

The Reader is supposed to be on the Stage facing the Audience.[16]

SCENE I.—*Suil-a-beg. The Cottage of Arte O'Neal,—The Stage is a Yard in the rear of the Cottage.—The Dairy window is seen facing audience, R.—Door* 3 E. L., *in return of Cottage.—The ruins of Suil-a-more Castle cover a bold headland in the half distance.—The Atlantic bounds the picture.—Sunset.—Music.*

CLAIRE FFOLLIOTT *at work at a churn,* R. C.

CLAIRE. Phoo! How my arms ache! *(Sings.)*

Where are you going, my pretty maid?
I'm going a-milking, sir, she said.[17]

Enter MRS. O'KELLY (*house,* L.)

MRS. O'KELLY. Sure, miss, this is too hard work entirely for the likes of you!

CLAIRE. Go on, now, Mrs. O'Kelly, and mind your own business. Do you think I'm not equal to making the butter come?

14. Rope made of twisted hay.
15. LC.] "LO." in copy text.
16. That is, the stage directions are from the viewpoint of the actors.
17. Traditional folk song which includes the lyrics,
"What is your fortune, my pretty maid?"
"My face is my fortune, Sir," she said.

MRS. O'KELLY. It's yourself can make the butter come. You have only got to look at the milk and the butter will rise. But, oh, miss! who's this coming up the cliff? It can't be a vision!

(*Looks*, R.)

CLAIRE. 'Tis one of the officers from Ballyragget.
MRS. O'KELLY. Run in quick, before he sees you, and I'll take the churn.
CLAIRE. Not I!—I'll stop where I am. If he was the Lord Lieutenant himself I'd not stir or take a tuck out of my gown. Go tell the mistress.
MRS. O'KELLY. And is this the way you will receive the quality?

[*Exit house*, L.

CLAIRE. *(Sings, working.)*

Then what is your fortune, my pretty maid?

He is stopping to reconnoitre. *(Sings again.)*

What is your fortune, my pretty maid?

Here he comes. *(Continues to sing.)*

My face is my fortune, sir, she said.

There's no lie in that, any way; and a mighty small income I've got.

Enter MOLINEUX, 3 E. R., *looking about.*

MOLINEUX. My good girl.
CLAIRE. Sir to you. *(Aside.)* He takes me for the dairymaid.
MOLINEUX. Is this place called Swillabeg?
CLAIRE. No; it is called Shoolabeg.
MOLINEUX. Beg pardon; your Irish names are so unpronounceable. You see, I'm an Englishman.
CLAIRE. I remarked your misfortune. Poor creature, you couldn't help it.
MOLINEUX. I do not regard it as a misfortune.
CLAIRE. Got accustomed to it, I suppose. Were you born so?
MOLINEUX. Is your mistress at home?
CLAIRE. My mistress. Oh, 'tis Miss O'Neal you mane!
MOLINEUX. Delicious brogue—quite delicious! Will you take her my card?
CLAIRE. I'm afeared the butter will spoil if I lave it now.
MOLINEUX. What is your pretty name?
CLAIRE. Claire! What's your's?
MOLINEUX. Molineux—Captain Molineux. Now, Claire, I'll give you a crown if you will carry my name to your mistress.

"Sir," she said, "Sir," she said,
"My face is my fortune, Sir," she said.
"Then I can't marry you, my pretty maid."
"Nobody asked you, Sir," she said.

CLAIRE. Will you take my place at the churn while I go?
MOLINEUX. How do you work the infernal thing?

(*Crosses to her, behind* R.)

CLAIRE. Take hould beside me, and I'll show you. *(He takes handle of churn beside her, they work together.)* There, that's it! Beautiful! You were intended for a dairymaid!
MOLINEUX. I know a dairymaid that was intended for me.
CLAIRE. That speech only wanted a taste of the brogue to be worthy of an Irishman.
MOLINEUX. *(Kissing her.)* Now I'm perfect.
CLAIRE. *(Starting away.)* What are you doing?
MOLINEUX. Tasting the brogue. Stop, my dear; you forget the crown I promised you. Here it is. *(He hands her the money.)* Don't hide your blushes, they become you.
CLAIRE. Never fear, I'll be even wid your honour yet. Don't let—*(up to porch)*—the butther spoil while I'm gone. *(Going, and looking at card.)* What's your name again—Mulligrubs?
MOLINEUX. No; Molineux.
CLAIRE. I ax your pardon. You see I'm Irish, and the English names are so unpronounceable.

[*Exit* L, house.

MOLINEUX. *(Churning gravely.)* She's as fresh and fragrant as one of her own pats of butter. If the mistress be as sweet as the maid, I shall not regret being stationed in this wilderness. Deuced hard work this milk pump! There is a strange refinement about that Irish girl. When I say strange, I am no judge, for I've never done the agricultural shows. I have never graduated in dairymaids, but this one must be the cream of the dairy. Confound this piston-rod; I feel like a Chinese toy![18]

Enter ARTE O'NEAL (*house* 2 E. L.), *followed by* CLAIRE.

ARTE. What can he want? (*Advancing* L.) What is he doing?
CLAIRE. I have not the slightest idea.

(Crosses to R., *behind.)*

ARTE. Captain Molineux.
MOLINEUX. *(Confused.)* Oh, a thousand pardons! I was just a—amusing myself. I am—a—very fond of machinery, and so—*(Bows.)* Miss O'Neal I presume?
ARTE. *(Introducing Claire.)* My cousin, Miss Claire Ffolliott.
MOLINEUX. Miss Ffolliott! Really I took her for a—*(Aside.)* Oh, lord! what have I done?
ARTE. *(Aside.)* Claire has been at some mischief here.

18. A Chinese toy was a figure of a man with a rounded, ballasted bottom; when pushed over, it immediately bobbed back up.

CLAIRE. *(At churn, and aside to Molineux.)* Don't hide your blushes, they become you.

MOLINEUX. *(Aside.)* Spare me!

ARTE. I hope you come to tell me how I can be of some service to you.

MOLINEUX. I have just arrived with a detachment of our regiment at Ballyragget. The government received information that a schooner carrying a distinguished Fenian hero was hovering about the coast, intending to land her passengers in this neighbourhood. So a gunboat has been sent round to these waters, and we are under orders to cooperate with her. Deuced bore, not to say ridiculous—there is no foundation for the scare—but we find ourselves quartered here without any resources.

ARTE. But I regret I cannot extend to you the hospitalities of Suil-a-beg. An unmarried girl is unable to play the hostess.

CLAIRE. Even two unmarried girls couldn't play the hostess.

MOLINEUX. But you own the finest shooting in the west of Ireland. The mountains are full of grouse, and the streams about here are full of salmon!

CLAIRE. The captain would beg leave to sport over your domain—shall I spare you the humiliation of confessing that you are not mistress in your own house, much less lady of the manor. (*Up* C.) Do you see that ruin yonder! Oh—'tis the admiration of the traveller, and the study of painters who come from far and near to copy it. It was the home of my forefathers when they kept open house for the friend—the poor—or the stranger. The mortgagee has put up a gate now, so visitors pay sixpence a head to admire the place, and their guide points across to this cabin where the remains of the ould family, two lonely girls, live. God knows how —you ask leave to kill game on Suil-a-more and Keim-an-eigh. (*Crosses to the dairy window,* 2 E. R.) Do you see that salmon? It was snared last night in the pool a-Bricken by Conn, the Shaughraun. He killed those grouse at daylight on the side of Maumturk.[19] That's our daily food, and we owe it to a poacher. (*Down* R.

MOLINEUX. You have to suffer bitterly indeed for ages of family imprudence, and the Irish extravagance of your ancestors.

ARTE. Yes, sir, the extravagance of their love for their country, and the imprudence of their fidelity to their faith!

MOLINEUX. But surely you cannot be without some relatives!

CLAIRE. I have a brother—the heir to the estate.

MOLINEUX. Is he abroad?

CLAIRE. Yes, he is a convict working out his sentence in Australia![20]

MOLINEUX. Oh, I beg pardon. I did not know. *(To Arte.)* Have you any relatives?

19. Maumturk] Maurnturk.

20. While transportation to Australia for criminals largely ended in 1853, sixty-three Irish Fenians were shipped to Australia in 1867, arriving in 1868.

ARTE. (L.) Yes, I am the affianced wife of her brother!

MOLINEUX. *(Confused.)* Really, ladies, I have to offer a thousand apologies.

ARTE. I do not accept one—it carries insult to the man I love.

MOLINEUX. At least you will allow me to regret having roused such distressing memories?

CLAIRE. Do you think they ever sleep?

MOLINEUX. No!—naturally—of course not—I meant *(Aside.)* I am astray on an Irish bog here, and every step I take gets me deeper in the mire. (*Crosses to* L.)

CLAIRE. *(Aside.)* How confused he is. That's a good fellow, although he is an Englishman.

ARTE. I am very sorry we have not the power to grant you a privilege, which, you see, we do not enjoy.

KINCHELA. *(Outside.)* Holloo! Is there nobody at home? (*Music* 2.)

ARTE. Here comes a gentleman who can oblige you.

KINCHELA. *(Outside.)* Holloo! one of you! Don't you hear me? Bridget come—come and hould my pony.

MOLINEUX. Who is this stentorian gentleman?

CLAIRE. Mr. Corry Kinchela; one who has trimmed his fortunes with prudence, and his conscience with economy.

Enter CORRY KINCHELA, 3 E. R.

KINCHELA. Where the devil is everybody? Oh, there you are! (*Down to* L. C.) I had to stable my own Horse! Oh, my service to you, sir!—I believe I've the honour of addressing Captain Molineux. I'm just back from Dublin, and thought I'd stop on my road to tell you the court has decreed the sale of this estate, undher foreclosure, and in two months you'll have to turn out.

ARTE. In two months, then, even this poor shelter will be taken from us.

(*Crosses slowly to* R. *of Claire, and down both,* R.)

KINCHELA. I'm afeard the rightful owner will want to see the worth of his money! But never fear, two handsome girls like yourselves will not be long wanting a shelter—or—a welcome. Eh, captain? oh! ho! It will be pick and choose for them anywhere, I'm thinking.

MOLINEUX. *(Aside.)* This fellow is awfully offensive to me.

KINCHELA. I've been away for the last few weeks, so I've not been able to pay my respects to you officers, and invite you all to sport over this property. You are right welcome, captain. My name is Kinchela—Mr. Corry Kinchela—of Ballyragget House, where I'll be proud to see my tablecloth under your chin. I don't know why one of these girls didn't introduce me.

MOLINEUX. They paid me the compliment of presuming that I had no desire to form your acquaintance.

(*Crosses to* C.)

KINCHELA. What! do you know, sir, that you are talking to a person of position and character?

MOLINEUX. I don't care a straw for your position, and I don't like your character. *(Back turned to Kinchela.)*

KINCHELA. Do you mean to insult me, sir?

MOLINEUX. I am incapable of it.

KINCHELA. Ah!

MOLINEUX. In the presence of ladies; but I believe I should be entitled to do so, for you insulted them in mine. *(Turning to Claire.)* I ask your pardon for the liberty I took with you when I presented myself.

CLAIRE. *(Offering her hand.)* The liberty you took with him when he presented himself clears the account.

KINCHELA. We'll meet again, sir.

MOLINEUX. I hope not; Good evening.

(To Arte, shaking hands.)

ARTE. I would delay you, captain; but you have a long way across the mountain, and the darkness is falling; the road is treacherous.

[*Molineux goes up to Claire, shakes hands with her again, and exits,* R. 3 E.

KINCHELA. The devil guide him to pass the night in a bog-hole up to his neck. Listen hither, you, too. *(Crosses to Claire.)* Sure, I don't want to be too hard upon you. To be sure the sale of this place will never cover my mortgage on it; it will come to me every acre of it. *(Turns to Arte.)* Bedad, the law ought to throw your own sweet self in as a makeweight to square my account. *(She turns away up* C, *he turns to Claire.)* See now, there's your brother, Robert Ffolliott, going to rot over there in Australia, and here in a few weeks you both will be without a roof over your heads. Now, isn't it a cruel thing entirely to let this go on when, if that girl would only say the word, I'd make her Mrs. Kinchela. *(Claire gets to porch.)* And I've got a hoult of the ear of our county member;[21] shure he'll get Robert the run of the country—as free as a fish in a pond he'll be over there. And, stop now—*(To Arte)*—You shall send him a £1,000 that I'll give you on your wedding day.

ARTE. I'd rather starve with Robert Ffolliott in a jail than own the county of Sligo if I'd to carry you as a mortgage on it. (*Crosses to* L.)

KINCHELA. *(Down to her).* Do you think the boy cares what becomes of you, or who owns you? Not a ha'porth! How many letters have you had from him for the last past year!

ARTE. *(Up by Claire).* Alas! not one.

KINCHELA. Not one! *(Aside).* I know that, for I've got them all safe under lock and key. *(Crosses to* R., *then up to them, aloud.)* See that

21. Both Ireland and Australia were part of the United Kingdom; thus the member of Parliament whom Kinchela has the ear of can intercede for Robert in Australia.

now; not one thought, not a sign from him, and here I am, every day in the week, like a dog at your door. It is too hard on me entirely. I've some sacret schaming[22] behind my back to ruin me entirely in your heart—

Enter FATHER DOLAN, *from house,* L.

I know that it is the same that's sending over to Robert Ffolliott the money, without which he'd starve outright beyant there. I'd like to find out who it is. (*Crosses to* R.)

FATHER DOLAN. *(At porch,)* I am the man, Mr. Kinchela!

KINCHELA. (*Down* R.) Father Dolan, may I ask, sir, on what grounds you dare to impache me in the good opinion of these girls?

FATHER DOLAN. Certainly. *(Turns to Arte).* Miss O'Neal—Claire, my dear—will you leave me awhile—(*music,* 3)—alone with Mr. Kinchela; he wants to know the truth about himself.

CLAIRE. And you can't insult him in the presence of ladies. Come, Arte.

[*Arte crosses to door, turns, curtseys to Kinchela, and exit. Claire follows, with a look at him.*

FATHER DOLAN. The father of young Ffolliott bequeathed to you and to me the care of his infant son—Heaven forgive me if I grew so fond of my darling charge, I kept no watch over you, my partner, in the trust. Year after year you dipped° the estate with your sham improvements skimmed and false accounts; you reduced the rents to impoverish the income, so it might not suffice to pay the interest on the mortgages.

KINCHELA. Go on, sir; this is mighty fine—go on. I wish I had a witness by, I'd make you pay for this. (*Crosses to* L.) Is there anything more?

FATHER DOLAN. (R.) There is; you hope to buy the lad's inheritance for an old song when it is sold. Thus you fulfil the trust confided to you by your benefactor, his poor father, whose hand you held when he expired in my arms—thus you have kept the oath to the dead!

KINCHELA. (L.) Would not every acre of it have escheated° to the transferred Crown, as the estate of a convicted felon, only I saved it for young Ffolliott by getting his family to make it over before the sentence was pronounced upon him?

FATHER DOLAN. Yes; to make it over to you in trust for these two girls, his sister and his betrothed.

KINCHELA. To be sure, wasn't you by, and helped to persuade him? More betoken,° you were a witness to the deed. significantly

FATHER DOLAN. I was. I helped you to defraud the orphan boy, and since then have been a witness how you have robbed these helpless women. Oh! beware, Kinchela! When these lands were torn

22. Boucicault uses a quasi-phonetic spelling to indicate a (stage) Irish pronunciation. This pronunciation is restricted to the lower-class characters. Here, schaming = scheming.

from Owen Roe O'Neal[23] in the old times, he laid his curse on the spoilers, for Suil-a-more was the dowry of his bride, Grace Ffolliott. Since then many a strange family have tried to hold possession of the place; but every year one of them would die—the land seemed to swallow them up one by one. Till the O'Neals and Ffolliotts returned none other thrived upon it.

KINCHELA. Sure that's the raison I want Arte O'Neal for my wife. Won't that kape the ould blood to the fore? Ah, ah, sir! why wouldn't you put in the good word for me to the girl? Do I ask betther than to give back all I have to the family? Sure there's nothing, sir, done that can't be mended that way.

FATHER DOLAN. I'd rather rade the service over her grave, and hear the sods falling on her coffin, than spake the holy words to make her your wife. Corry Kinchela, I know it was by your means and to serve this end, my darling boy—her lover—was denounced and convicted.

KINCHELA. 'Tis false!

FATHER DOLAN. It is true! But the truth is locked in my soul, and Heaven keeps the key. *(Up to porch).*

KINCHELA. *(Aside.)* Some false-hearted cur has confessed again me. *(Aloud.)* Very well, sir. (*Crosses to* R.) Then out of that house these girls shall turn, homeless and beggars.

FATHER DOLAN. Not homeless, while I have a roof over me—not beggars, I thank God, who gives me the crust to share with them.

[*Exit into house,* L.

KINCHELA. How could he know I had any hand in bringing young Ffolliot to the dock? Who can have turned tail on me? (*To* C.)

Enter HARVEY DUFF, 3 E. R.

HARVEY DUFF. Whisht, sir!

KINCHELA. Who's there?—Harvey Duff?

HARVEY DUFF. (R. C.) I saw your coppaleen° beyant under the hedge, and I knew yourself was in it. I've great news entirely for you—news enough to burst a budget°—

pony

small pouch

KINCHELA. You are always finding a mare's nest.[24]

HARVEY DUFF. I've found one now wid a divil's egg in it.

KINCHELA. Well, out with it.

HARVEY DUFF. There was a fire last night on Rathgarron Head. You know what that means?

23. Eoghan Ruadh O'Néill (1590–1649) left Ireland in 1607 during "The Flight of the Earls," after a failed attempt to end English rule in Ulster ended in 1603. He became an officer of an Irish regiment in the Spanish army and commanded troops in Ireland fighting for an independent Irish nation from 1642 until his death. As with place-names, Boucicault is using O'Néill's name because of its evocative quality rather than for any specific historical event.

24. To find something that appears remarkable but turns out to be commonplace.

KINCHELA. A signal to some smuggler at sea that the coast is clear, and to run in and land his cargo.

HARVEY DUFF. Divil a keg was landed from that ship, barrin' only one man that was put ashore—not a boy was on the strand to meet the boat, nor a car, nor a skip to hurry off the things—only one thing, and that was Conn, the Shaughraun—'twas himself that lighted the signal—'twas him that stud up to his middle in the salt say to carry the man ashore. I seen it all as I lay on the flat of my stomach on the edge of the cliff, and looked down on the pair o' them below.

KINCHELA. Well, what's all this to me?

HARVEY DUFF. Wait, sure. I'm hatching the egg for you. "Who's that," ses I to myself, "that Conn would carry in his two arms as tindher as a mother would hould a child?—who's that," ses I, "that he's capering all around for all the world like a dog that's just onloosed?—who's that he's houlding by the two hands of him, as if 'twas Moya Dolan herself he'd got before him instead of a ragged sailor boy?"

KINCHELA. Well, did you find out who it was?

HARVEY DUFF. Maybe I didn't get snug behind the bushes beside the pathway up the cliff. They passed close to me, talking low; but I heard his voice, and saw the man as plain as I see you now.

KINCHELA. (C. L.) Saw whom?

HARVEY DUFF. (C.) Robert Ffolliott. 'Twas himself I tell you.

KINCHELA. Are you sure?

HARVEY DUFF. Am I sure? Do you think I can mistake the face that turned upon me in the coort when they sentenced him on my evidence, or the voice that said "if there's justice in Heaven, you and I will meet again on this side of the grave?—then," ses he, "have your soul ready," and the look he fixed upen me shrivelled up my soul inside like a boiled cockle that ye might pick out with a pin. Am I sure? I wish I was as sure of Heaven. (*To* R.)

KINCHELA. He has escaped from the penal settlement—ay, that's it — and where would he go to straight but here, into the trap baited with the girl he loves?

(Up to cottage, down L.*, and over to* R.*, Harvey Duff following him.)*

HARVEY DUFF. There'll be a price offered for him, sir—and your honour will put it in my way to airn an honest penny. Wouldn't they hang him this time? Egorra! I'd be peaceable if he was only out of the way for good.

KINCHELA. Listen to me—D'ye know what took me to Dublin? I heard that the Queen had resolved to release the Fenian prisoners under sentence.

HARVEY DUFF. Murther alive—I'm a corpse.

KINCHELA. I saw the secretary—he mistook my fear for hope—"It is thrue," ses he, "I'm expecting every day to get the despatch, I wish you joy."

HARVEY DUFF. Bejabers I'd have liked to seen your face when you got that polthogue° in the gob. blow

KINCHELA. Robert Ffolliott returned! a free man, he will throw his estates into Chancery.[25] *(To* R. *corner.)*

HARVEY DUFF. Where will he throw me!

KINCHELA. He's a fugitive convict still, can't we deal with him?

HARVEY DUFF. If his own people around here get to know he's among them, why a live coal in a keg of gunpowdher would not give an "idaya"° of the county Sligo. idea

KINCHELA. I know it—High and low they love him as they hate me — bad cess° to them. (*Crosses* L.) luck

HARVEY DUFF. Oh, nivir fear—he'll keep in the dark for his own sake. *(Music.)*

KINCHELA. Keep a watch on the Shaughraun—find out where the pair o' em lie in hiding.—Bring me the news to Ballyragget house—meanwhile, I'll think what's best to be done—Be off, quick! [*Exit Harvey Duff* 3. E. R.] Robert Ffolliott here—tare an' ages[26]—I'm ruined, horse and foot—I'll have all Connaught and the Coort of Chancery on me back. Harvey Duff is right—'tis life or death with me and him—Well, it shall be life with you, Arte O'Neal—and death to him that parts us.

[*Exit* 3. E. R.

SCENE II.—*The Devil's Jowl.—A cleft in the rocks on the sea-coast.*

Enter ROBERT FFOLLIOTT, L.

ROBERT. It must be past the hour when Conn promised to return.—How often he and I have climbed these rocks together in search of the seabirds' eggs—and waded for cockles in the strand below—Dear faithful truant to ramble with you—how many a lecture from my dear old tutor, Father Dolan, who told me I ought to be ashamed of my love for the Shaughraun. Ah! my heart was not so much to blame after all.

MOLINEUX. (*Outside,* R.) Holloa!

ROBERT. That's not his voice.

MOLINEUX. *(Still outside.)* Holloa!

ROBERT. Why it's a man in the uniform of an officer—he has seen me. *(Calls.)* Take care, sir—don't take that path—turn to the right —round that boulder—that's the road—Egad, another step and he would have gone over the cliff.—He is some stranger who has lost his way.

MOLINEUX. *(Entering.)* What an infernal country!—First I was nearly smothered in a bog, and then, thanks to you my good fellow, I

25. Robert will seek to reclaim his estates through the court concerned with estates and equity.

26. A mild oath derived from "Christ's tears and agues."

escaped breaking my neck—Do you know the way to Ballyragget! How far is it to the barracks?

ROBERT. Two miles.

MOLINEUX. Irish miles, of course.

ROBERT. I shall be happy to show you the road but regret I cannot be your guide. The safest for a stranger is by the cliff to Suil-a-beg.

MOLINEUX. But I have just come from there.

ROBERT. From Suil-a-beg?

MOLINEUX. I shall not regret to revisit the place—charming spot—I've just passed there the sweetest hour of my life.

ROBERT. You saw the lady of the house I presume?

MOLINEUX. Pardon me, sir, I mistook your yachting costume—perhaps you are acquainted with Miss Ffolliott.

ROBERT. Yes; but we have not met for some time. I thought you referred to Arte—I mean Miss O'Neal.

MOLINEUX. Oh! she is charming, of course; but Miss Ffolliott is an angel. She has so occupied my thoughts that I have lost my way—in fact, instead of going straight home, I have been revolving in an orbit[27] round that house by a kind of centrifugal attraction, of which she is the centre.

ROBERT. But surely you admired Miss O'Neal?

MOLINEUX. Oh, she is well enough, bright little thing but besides Claire Ffolliott—

ROBERT. I prefer the beauty of Miss O'Neal.

MOLINEUX. I don't admire your taste.

ROBERT. Well, let us drink to each of them.

MOLINEUX. With pleasure, if you can supply the opportunity. *(Robert pulls out his flask, and fills cup.)* Ah! I see you are provided. Allow me to present myself—Captain Molineux, of the 49th. Here's to Miss Claire Ffolliott.

ROBERT. Here's to Miss Arte O'Neal.

(They drink.)

MOLINEUX. I beg your pardon—I did not catch your name.

ROBERT. I did not mention it. *(A pause.)*

MOLINEUX. This liquor is American whisky, I perceive.

ROBERT. Do you find anything wrong about it?

MOLINEUX. Nothing whatever. *(He offers his cup to be filled again.)* But it reminds me of a duty I have to perform. We have orders to capture a dangerous person who will be, or has been, landed on this coast lately, and as these rocks are just the kind of place where he might find refuge—

ROBERT. Not at all unlikely.—I'll keep a look-out for him.

MOLINEUX. I propose to revisit this spot again to-night with a file of men. Here's your health.

27. orbit] obit.

ROBERT. Sir, accept my regards. Here's good luck to you.

MOLINEUX. Good night. *(Music 5.—A whistle heard outside.)* What's that?

ROBERT. 'Tis a ring at the bell. A friend of mine is waiting for me on the cliff above. *(Aside.)* 'Tis Conn!

MOLINEUX. Oh, I beg pardon! Farewell.

[*Going,* R.

ROBERT. Stop. You might not fare well if you ascend that path alone.

MOLINEUX. Why not?

ROBERT. Because my friend's at the top of it, and if he saw you coming out alone—*(aside)*—he would think I had been caught, and egad! the Shaughraun might poach the Captain!

MOLINEUX. Well, if he met me, what then?

ROBERT. (*Crosses* to R.) You see the poor fellow is mad on one point—he can't bear the sight of one colour, and that is red. His mother was frightened by a mad bull, and the minute Conn sees a bit of scarlet, such, for example, as your coat there, the bull breaks out in him, and he might toss you over the cliff; so, by your leave—

MOLINEUX. This is the most extraordinary country I was ever in.

[*Exeunt, arm-in-arm,* L. H. 1 E.

SCENE III.—*Exterior of Father Dolan's Cottage.—Night.—Lighted window.*

Enter MOYA *with pail, which she puts down,* R.

MOYA. There! now I've spancelled° the cow and fed the pig, my uncle will be ready for his tay. Not a sign of Conn for the past three nights. What's come to him? hobbled

Enter Mrs. O'KELLY, L.

MRS. O'KELLY. Is that yourself, Moya? I've come to see if that vagabond of mine has been round this way.

MOYA. Why would he be here—hasn't he a home of his own.

MRS. O'KELLY. The shebeen° is his home when he's not in gaol.° His father died o' drink, and Conn will go the same way. informal tavern jail

MOYA. I thought your husband was drowned at sea?

MRS. O'KELLY. And, bless him, so he was.

MOYA. *(Aside.)* Well, that's a quare way of dying o' drink.

MRS. O'KELLY. The best of men he was, when he was sober—a betther never dhrawed the breath o' life.

MOYA. But you say he never was sober.

MRS. O'KELLY. Nivir! An' Conn takes afther him!

MOYA. Mother.

MRS. O'KELLY. Well.

MOYA. I'm afeard I'll take afther Conn.

MRS. O'KELLY. Heaven forbid, and purtect you agin him. You are a good, dacent girl, an' desarve the best of husbands.

MOYA. Them's the only ones that gets the worst. More betoken yourself, Mrs. O'Kelly.

MRS. O'KELLY. Conn nivir did an honest day's work in his life—but dhrinkin', an' fishin', an' shootin', an' sportin', and love-makin'.

MOYA. Sure, that's how the quality pass their lives.

MRS. O'KELLY. That's it. A poor man that spoorts the sowl of a gentleman is called a blackguard.

CONN (*Entering* L.)

CONN. There's somebody talking about me.

MOYA. *(Running to him.)* Conn!

CONN. My darlin', was the mother makin' little of me? Don't believe a word that comes out o' her! She's jealous—a devil a haperth less.[28] She's choking wid it this very minute, just bekase she sees my arms about ye. She's as proud of me as an ould hen that's got a duck for a chicken. Hould your whist now!° Wipe your mouth, an' give me a kiss! (*Crosses to* C.)

keep silent

MRS. O'KELLY. *(Embracing him.)* Oh, Conn, what have you been afther? The polis were in my cabin to-day about ye. They say you stole Squire Foley's horse.

CONN. Stole his horse! Sure the baste is safe and sound in his paddock this minute.

MRS. O'KELLY. But he says you stole it for the day to go huntin'.

CONN. Well, here's a purty thing, for a horse to run away with a man's characther like this! Oh, wurra! may I never die in sin, but this was the way of it. I was standing by ould Foley's gate, when I heard the cry of the hounds comin' across the tail end of the bog, and there they wor, my dear, spread out like the tail of a paycock, an' the finest dog fox you'd ever seen saling ahead of them up the boreen,° and right across the churchyard. It was enough to raise the inhabitants. Well, as I looked, who should come up and put his head over the gate beside me but the Squire's brown mare, small blame to her. Divil a thing I said to her, nor she to me, for the hounds had lost their scent, we knew by their yelp and whine as they hunted among the grave-stones, when, whish! the fox went by us. I leapt on the gate, an' gave a shriek of a view holloo to the whip; in a minute the pack caught the scent again, an' the whole field came roarin' past. The mare lost her head, an' tore at the gate. "Stop," ses I, "ye devil!" and I slipped the taste of a rope over her head an' into her mouth. Now mind the cunnin' of the baste, she was quiet in a minute. "Come home now," ses I, "asy!" and I threw my leg across her. Be gabers! no sooner was I on her bare back than whoo! holy rocket! she was

grassy lane

28. Half-penny worth.

over the gate, an' tearin' like mad afther the hounds. "Yoicks!" ses I; "come back the thief of the world, where are you takin' me to?" as she went through the huntin' field an' laid me besides the masther of the hounds, Squire Foley himself. He turned the colour of his leather breeches. "Mother of Moses!" ses he, "is that Conn the Shaughraun on my brown mare?" "Bad luck to me!" ses I "It's no one else!" "You sthole my horse," says the Squire. "That's a lie!" ses I, "for it was your horse sthole me!"

MOYA. An' what did he say to that?

CONN. I couldn't sthop to hear, for just then we took a stone wall and a double ditch together, and he stopped behind to keep an engagement he had in the ditch.

MRS. O'KELLY. You'll get a month in jail for this.

CONN. Well, it was worth it.

MRS. O'KELLY. An' what brings you here? Don't you know Father Dolan has forbidden you the house?

CONN. The Lord bless him! I know it well, but I've brought something wid me to-night that will get me absolution. I've left it —(*putting her* L.)—wid the ladies at Suil-a-beg, but they will bring it up here to share wid his riverence.

MRS. O'KELLY. What is it at all?

CONN. Go down, mother, an' see, an' when you see it, kape your tongue betune your teeth, if one of your sex can.

MRS. O'KELLY. Well, but you're a quare mortil.

[*Exit* L.

MOYA. Oh, Conn! I'm afeared my uncle won't see you. (*Father Dolan inside calls* "Moya.") There! he's calling me. *(Going* R. *taking pail.)*

CONN. Go in an' tell him I'm sthravagin[29] outside till he's soft. Now put on your sweetest lip, darlin'.

MOYA. Never fear! sure he does be always telling me my heart is too near my mouth.

CONN. Ah! I hope nobody will ever measure the distance but me, my jewel. *(Music.)*

MOYA. Ah! Conn, do you see those flowers? I picked 'em by the way-side as I came along, and I put them in my breast. They are dead already; the life and fragrance have gone out of them; killed by the heat of my heart. So it may be with you, if I picked you and put you there. *(Pause.)* Won't the life go out of your love? hadn't I better lave you where you are?

CONN. For another girl to make a posy of me. Ah,—*(taking pail)* my darling Moya! sure if I was one of those flowers, and you were to pass me by like that, I do believe that I'd pluck myself and walk afther you on my own stalk. [*Exeunt,* R.

29. To loiter about opportunistically.

SCENE IV.—*A Room in Father Dolan's House. Fireplace* L. *Window at back door,* R. *Lamp on table,* L. C. FATHER DOLAN *reading, sits arm chair,* L.

FATHER DOLAN. What keeps Moya so long outside? Moya!—

Enter MOYA *with tea things, door* R.; *they are on a tray, and she has a kettle in her hand.*

MOYA. Yes, uncle, here's your tay, I was waiting for the kettle to boil.

(Puts things on table, gives Father Dolan a cup of tea. then to fire with kettle.)

FATHER DOLAN. I thought I heard voices outside!

MOYA. It was only the pig!

FATHER DOLAN. And I heard somebody singing.

MOYA. It was the kettle, uncle.

FATHER DOLAN. Go tell that pig not to come here till he's cured, and if I hear any strange kettles singing round here my kettle will boil over.

MOYA. Sure uncle! I never knew that happen but you put your fire out. *(At fire kneeling.)*

FATHER DOLAN. See, now, Moya, that ragamuffin Conn will be your ruin. What makes you so fond of the rogue?

MOYA. All the batins I got for him when I was a child an' the hard words you gave me since.

FATHER DOLAN. Has he one good quality undher heaven? If he has I'll forgive him.

MOYA. He loves me.

FATHER DOLAN. Love! Oh, that word covers more sin than charity. I think I hear it raining, Moya. *(she gets* R. *of table)* and I would not keep a dog out in such a night.

MOYA. Oh! *(Laughs behind his back.)*

FATHER DOLAN. You may let him stand out of the wet (*Moya beckons on Conn, who enters,* 3 E. R.) but don't let him open his month. Gi' me a cup of tay, Moya; I hope it will be stronger than the last.

MOYA. Oh! what will I do? He wants his tay stronger, and I've no more tay in the house.

(A pause. Conn pours whisky into teapot. She gives cup of tea.)

FATHER DOLAN. Well, haven't you a word to say for yourself?

CONN. Divil a one, your riverence!

FATHER DOLAN. You are going to ruin?

CONN. I am, bad luck to me!

FATHER DOLAN. And you want to take a dacent girl along with you. *(Still reading.)*

CONN. I'm a vagabone entirely.

FATHER DOLAN. What sort of a life do you lead? What is your occupation? Stealing salmon out of the river of a night!

(Puts down book and takes up cup of tea.)

CONN. No, sir; I'm not so bad as that, but I'll confess to a couple of throut. Sure the salmon is out of sayson.

(He pulls two trout out of his bag, L. *of him, and gives them to Moya, who takes them.)*

FATHER DOLAN. And don't you go poaching the grouse on the hill-side.
CONN. I do! divil a lie in it.

(Pulls out four grouse.)

FATHER DOLAN. D'ye know where all this leads to?
CONN. Well, along with the grouse I'll go to pot.

(Moya laughs and removes the game and fish. She receives trout on tray from which she has taken the tea-things. She stands on his L. *for the trout and* R. *for the game. Moya returns and busies herself at dresser.)*

FATHER DOLAN. Bless me, Moya!—Moya! this tay is very strong, and has a curious taste.
CONN. Maybe the wather is to blame in regard of being smoked.
FATHER DOLAN. And it smells of whisky.
CONN. It's not the tay you smell, sir, it's me.
FATHER DOLAN. That reminds me. *(Rising, puts down tea and takes up book.)* Didn't you give me a promise last Aister—a blessed promise, made on your two knees—that you would lave off drhink?
CONN. I did, barrin' one thimbleful a day, just to take the cruelty out o' the wather.
FATHER DOLAN. One thimbleful. I allowed that concession, no more.
CONN. God bless ye, ye did; an' I kep' my word.
FATHER DOLAN. Kept your word! how dare you say that! Didn't I find you ten days after stretched out drunk as a fiddler at Tim O'Maley's wake!
CONN. Ye did, bad luck to me!
FATHER DOLAN. And you took only one thimbleful?
CONN. Divil a drhop more—see this. Ah, will ye listen to me, sir? I'll tell you how it was. When they asked me to the wake, I wint—oh, I wouldn't decave you, I wint. There was the Mulcaheys, and the Malones, and the—
FATHER DOLAN. (*Still corner of table,* L.) I don't want to hear about that. Come to the drink—
CONN. Av coorse—egorra! I came to that soon enough. Well, sir, when afther blessing the keeners, and the rest o' 'em, I couldn't despise a drink out of respect for the corpse—long life to it! "But, boys," ses I, "I'm on a puniance," ses I. "Is there a thimble in the house," ses I, "for a divil a dhrop more than the full an it will pass my lips this blessed day."
FATHER DOLAN. Ah!
CONN. Well, as the divil's luck would have it, there was only one thimble in the place, and that was a tailor's thimble, an' they couldn't get it

full.[30] *(Father Dolan, to conceal his laughter, goes up, puts his book in recess, then comes down).* Egorra! but they got me full first.

FATHER DOLAN. *(At table.)* Ah, Conn, I'm afeared liquor is not the worst of your doings. We lost sight of you lately for more than[31] six months. In what jail did you pass that time?

CONN. I was on my thravels?

FATHER DOLAN. Where?

CONN. Round the world. See, sir. Afther masther was tuck an' they sint him away the heart seemed to go out o' me entirely. I stand by the say—look over it, an' see the ships sailin' away to where he may be, till the longing grew too big for my body—an' one night I jumped into the coast-guard boat, stuck up the sail, and wint to say.

FATHER DOLAN. (L.) Bless the boy, you didn't think you could get to Australia in a skiff.

(*Rises and stands back to fire. Moya gradually down,* R.)

CONN. I didn't think at all—I wint. All night I tossed about, an' the next day and that night, till at daylight I came across a big ship. "Sthop," ses I,—"take me aboard—I'm out of my coorse." They whipped me on deck, an' took me before the Captain. "Where do you come from?" ses he. "Suil-a-beg," ses I. "I'll be obleeged to you to lave me anywhere handy by there." "You'll have to go to Melbourne first," ses he. "Is that anywhere in the County Sligo?" "Why, ye omadhann,"° ses he, "you won't see home for six months." Then I set up a wierasth-ru.° "Poor devil," ses the Captain; "I'm sorry for you, but you must cross the ocean. What sort of work can ye do best?" "I can play the fiddle," ses I. "Take him forrad, and be good to him," ses he. An' so they did. That's how I got my passage to Australia.

idiot

lament

FATHER DOLAN. You rogue, you boarded that ship on purpose.

(Goes down stage.)

MOYA. (*Coming down,* L. C.) Ay, to get nearer to the young masther. And did you find him, Conn? *(Goes to him.)*

CONN. I did. And oh, sir, when *he* laid eyes on me, he put his two arums around my neck, an' sobbed an' clung to me like when we were children together. "What brings you here?" ses he. "To bring you back wid me," ses I. "That's impossible," ses he; "I am watched." "So is the salmon in the Glenamoy," ses I; "but I get 'em. So is the grouse on Keim-an-Eigh; but I poach 'em. And now I've come to poach you," ses I. An' I did it. (*Music, 7.*)

Enter ROBERT FFOLLIOTT *with* CLAIRE *and* ARTE, D. R. Claire *down,* R.

FATHER DOLAN. Is this the truth you are telling me? You found him?

(After an irrepressible gesture, and an inarticulate attempt to bless Conn.)

30. A tailor's thimble is open at both ends.
31. than] the.

CONN. Safe, and in fine condition.

(Seizes Moya, and stops her mouth as she is about to utter a cry on seeing Robert.)

FATHER DOLAN. Escaped and free! Tell me—
CONN. Oh, egorra! he must speak for himself now.
ROBERT. (R.) Father Dolan!

(Throws off disguise, and embraces him.)

FATHER DOLAN. Robert, my darling boy! Oh, blessed day! Do I hold you to my heart again?

(He embraces him).

CONN. *(Aside to Moya.)* There's nobody looking. *(Kisses her).*
MOYA. Conn, behave.
ARTE. He has been hiding[32] on the sea shore among the rocks a whole day and two nights.
CLAIRE. All alone, with sea-weed for his bed. *(Goes up to fire).*
MOYA. Oh, if I'd only known that!
CONN. An' nothin' to eat but a piece of tobacco an' a cockle.
ARTE. And he wouldn't stop at Suil-a-beg to taste a morsel; he would come over here to see you.
FATHER DOLAN. Come near the fire. Moya, hurry now, and put food on the table. Sit ye down; let me see you all around me once again. *(Moya brings in food.)* And to think I cannot offer you a glass of wine, nor warm your welcome with a glass of liquor! I have not got a bottle in the house. *(Conn pulls out his bottle, and puts it on the table.)*

The rogue—. *(They form a group round the fire.)*

ROBERT. We may thank poor Conn, who contrived my escape. I made my way across to America.
CLAIRE. But how did you escape, Conn?
CONN. Oh, asy enough; they turned me out.
ARTE. Turned you out!
CONN. As if I wor a stray cat. "Very well," says I, "Bally-mulligan is my parish. I'm a pauper; send me, or gi' me board wages where I am." "No," ses they, "we've Irish enough here already." "Then send me back to Sligo," ses I, an' they did.
CLAIRE. They might take you for a cat, for you seem always to fall upon your legs.
FATHER DOLAN. I can't get over my surprise to see my blessed child there sitting by my side. Now, we'll all drink his health.

(*Music.* 8. *Gives glass to Claire,* &c.)

CONN. Which thimble am I to drink out of?

32. hiding] riding.

FATHER DOLAN. The tailor's, you reprobate, are you ready? Now, then—*(The face of Harvey Duff appears at the window).* Here's his health, and long life to him. May Heaven keep watch over—

ROBERT. *(His glass in hand* L., *with* R. *slowly pointing to the window.)* Look!—look there.

(Harvey Duff disappears; they turn).

CLAIRE. What was it?

ARTE. How pale you are!

ROBERT. The face—I saw the face—there at the window—the same I saw when I was in the dock!

CLAIRE. Ah, Robert, you dream!

ROBERT. The police spy—Harvey Duff—the man that denounced me. 'Twas his white face pressed against the glass yonder, glaring at me. [*Exit Conn,* R. 3 E.] Can it be a vision?

(Father Dolan, up to window.)

ARTE. It was. You are weak, dear; eat—recover your strength.

(Robert sits L. *of table—Arte at his feet.)*

MOYA. It wasn't a face, but an empty stomach.

ROBERT. It gave my heart a turn. You must be right. It was a weakness—the disorder of my brain—it must be so.

FATHER DOLAN. The night is very dark. *(Closes curtains—Conn re-enters.)* Well?

CONN. Nothing.

FATHER DOLAN. I thought so. Come, now refresh yourself.

(Sits on bench, with his back to the audience).

CONN. *(Aside.)* Moya, there was somebody there!

MOYA. How d'ye know!—did ye see him?

CONN. No; but I left Tatthers outside.

MOYA. Your dog. Why didn't he bark?

CONN. He couldn't. I found this in his mouth.

MOYA. What's that?

CONN. The sate of a man's breeches.

[*Exit,* 3 E. R.

ROBERT. *(Eating.)* My visit here must be a short one. The vessel that landed me is now standing off and on the coast, awaiting my signal to send in a boat ashore to take me away again.

ARTE. I am afraid your arrival was expected by the authorities. They are on the watch.

ROBERT. I know they are. I've had a chat with them on the subject, and a very nice fellow the authority seemed to be, and a great admirer of my rebel sister there.

CLAIRE. Captain Molineux. *(Crosses to fireplace.)*

ROBERT. He and I met this morning at the Coot's Nest.

CLAIRE. How dare the fellow talk about me?

ROBERT. Look at her!—she is all ablaze!—her face is the colour of his coat!

CLAIRE. I never saw the creature but once.

ROBERT. Then you made good use of your time. I never saw a man in such a condition; he's not a man—he's a trophy. (*Music,* 9.)

CLAIRE. Robert, you are worse than he is.

FATHER DOLAN. I could listen to him all night.

ARTE. So could I.

(The window is dashed open, Conn leaps in.)

CONN. Sir—quick—away with yeez—hide!—the red-coats are on us!

ARTE. Oh, Robert, fly!

MOYA. (R. 3 E.) This way—by the kitchen—through the garden.

CONN. No; the back dure is watched by a couple of them. Is it locked?

MOYA. Fast!

CONN. Give me your coat and hat, I'll make a dash out. Tatthers will attend to one, I'll stretch the other, and the rest will give me chase, thinking it is yourself, and then you can slip off unbeknonst.

(*Three knocks,* D. F.)

FATHER DOLAN. It is too late!

MOYA. Hide yourself in the old clock-case in the kitchen. There's just enough room in it for him.

ARTE. Quick, Robert, quick! Oh, save yourself if you can!

(*Crosses to* 3 E. R. *Exit with Robert,* D. R.)

CLAIRE. Oh, I wish I was a man, I wouldn't give him up without a fight!

(*Crosses to* R. *Exit* 3 E. R.)

CONN. Egorra, the blood of the old stock is in her. *(Standing by* D. F., *with uplifted chair.)* I'm ready, sir. (*Two knocks,* D. F.)

FATHER DOLAN. Conn, put that down, and open the door.

(Conn opens door. SERGEANT *and two* SOLDIERS *enter; they stand at door. Sergeant draws window-curtain, and discovers two Soldiers outside, and then exits, saluting* CAPTAIN MOLINEUX *as he enters.*

MOLINEUX. I deeply regret to disturb your household at such an hour, but my duty is imperative.

Enter CLAIRE *and* ARTE, 3 E. R.

A convict escaped from penal servitude has landed on this coast, and I am charged with his capture. Miss Ffolliott, I am sorry to be obliged to perform so painful a duty in your presence, and in yours, Miss O'Neal.[33]

33. O'Neal] O'Neale.

CLAIRE. Especially, sir, when the man you seek is my brother!
ARTE. And my affianced husband!
MOLINEUX. Believe me, I would exchange places with him, if I could. (L. C.)

Enter a SERGEANT, D. F.

SERGEANT. *(Saluting.)* Please, sir, there's a mad dog, sir, a-sitting at the back door, and he has bit four of our men awful.
CONN. Tatthers was obliged to perform his painful duty.
CLAIRE. Call off the dog, Conn. Moya, open the back door. (*Crosses to back of table, and gets* L.)

[*Exit Conn, with Moya,* 3 E. R.

MOLINEUX. Your assurance gives me hope that we have been misled. (*To* R. C.)
ARTE. The house is very small, sir. Here is a bedroom; let your men search it. (*To opening,* L.)

Enter MOYA, CONN, *and two* SOLDIERS, 3 E. R. *The two Soldiers remain at door,* 3 E. R.

MOYA. *(To the two Soldiers.)* I suppose you've seen there never a human being in my kitchen barrin' the cat? My bedroom is up-stairs —maybe you'd like to search that.

(*Down* R.)

MOLINEUX. I shall be obliged, sir, to visit every room—sound every piece of furniture, from the roof to the cellar; but the indignity of the proceeding is more offensive to my feelings than it can be to yours. I will accept your simple assurance that the person we are in search of is not in your house. Give me that, and I will withdraw my men.
CLAIRE. *(Offering her hand to Molineux.)* Thank you!

(*Goes up* C.)

ARTE. *(Aside, to Father Dolan, and* R. *of him.)* Save him, sir! oh, save him!
FATHER DOLAN. *(Aside.)* Oh, God, help me in this great temptation.
ARTE. *(Aside, and* L. *of him.)* You will not betray him. Speak—say he is not here!
MOLINEUX. I await your reply.
CONN. (*Aside,* R.) I wish he would take my word.
FATHER DOLAN. The lad—the person you seek—my poor boy! Oh, sir, for mercy's sake, don't ask me. He has been here, but—
MOLINEUX. He is gone—he went before we arrived?
ARTE. Yes—yes! *(Crosses to Claire.)*
CONN. Yes, sir: he wint away before he came here at all.
MOLINEUX. Have I your word as a priest, sir, that Robert Ffolliott is not under this roof?

(Crosses to him.)
(Father Dolan, after a passionate struggle with himself, turns from Molineux, and buries his face in his hands.)
ROBERT *enters,* 3 E. R.

ROBERT. No, sir. Robert Ffolliott is here!

(Arte, with a suppressed cry, throws herself into Claire's arms.)

MOLINEUX. I am very sorry for it. *(Goes slowly up to L. of Sergeant — Robert crosses, and embraces Father Dolan.)* Secure your prisoner!

(Claire crosses behind to fireplace—Arte moves a little to the R.—Moya drops on stool that she has placed.)
(The Sergeant advances, C. Robert meets him, is handcuffed—Sergeant retires two or three paces—Father Dolan totters across, and falls on his knees—Robert raises him, and puts him in chair, R. *of table—The Sergeant touches Robert on shoulder, then moves to door—Robert is passing out, when Arte throws her arms around his neck.)*

FATHER DOLAN. What have I done?—what have I done? *(Sinking into chair.)*
CONN. Be asy, father. Sure, he'd rather have the iron on his hand, than you the sin upon your sowll.

(Tableau.—Slow Act Drop.)

ACT II.

SCENE I.—*Room in Ballyragget House.—Music.*

Enter KINCHELA *and* HARVEY DUFF, L.
Music.

KINCHELA. (R.) Come in. How pale you are! Did he resist?
HARVEY DUFF. (L.) Give me a glass of sperrets!
KINCHELA. Recover yourself. Is he wounded?
HARVEY DUFF. Divil a scratch, but I am.
KINCHELA. Where?
HARVEY DUFF. Nivir mind.
KINCHELA. You are faint; come and sit down.
HARVEY DUFF. No, I'm easier on my feet.
KINCHELA. How did it happen?
HARVEY DUFF. While I was peeping through the key-hole of the kitchen dure.
KINCHELA. I mean how was he taken?
HARVEY DUFF. I did not stop to see, for when he got sight of my face agin the windy, his own turned as white as your shirt. I believe he knew me.
KINCHELA. Impossible! that black wig disguises you completely. You

have shaved off your great red whiskers. Your own mother wouldn't know you.

HARVEY DUFF. No, she wouldn't; the last time I went home she pelted me wid the poker. But if the people round here suspected I was Harvey Duff, they would tear me to rags; there wouldn't survive of me a piece as big as the one I left in the mouth of that divil of a dog!

KINCHELA. Don't be afraid, my good fellow. I'll take care of you.

(Gets glass and bottle from flat., R. *Harvey D. drinks, and returns glass to him before he speaks.)*

HARVEY DUFF. And it is yourself you'll be taking care of at the same time. There a pair of us, Misther Kinchela, mind me, now. We are harnessed to the same pole, and as I'm drhuv you must travel.

KINCHELA. What do you mean?

HARVEY DUFF. I mane that I have been your parthner in this game to chate young Ffolliott out of his liberty first, then out of his estate, and now out of his wife! Where's my share?

KINCHELA. Your share! Share of what?

(Puts away bottle and glass).

HARVEY DUFF. Oh, not the wife. Take her and welcome; but where's my share of the money?

KINCHELA. Were you not handsomely paid at the time for doing your duty? (*Crosses to* L).

HARVEY DUFF. My jooty! Was it my jooty to come down here among the people disguised as a Fenian delegate, and pass myself off for a head centre,[34] so that I could swear them in an' denounce 'em? Who gave me the office to trap young Ffolliott? Who was it picked out Andy Donovan, an' sent him in irons across the say, laving his young wife to die in a madhouse?

KINCHELA. Hush! not so loud. (*Crosses to* E.)

HARVEY DUFF. Do you remember the curse of Bridget Madigan, when her only boy was found guilty on my evidence? Take your share of that, an' give me some of what I have airned.

KINCHELA. You want a share of my fortune?

HARVEY DUFF. A share of our fortune!

KINCHELA. (R.) Every penny I possess is invested in this estate. If Robert Ffolliott returns home a free man I could not hould more of it than would stick to my brogues when I was kicked out. Listen to this letter that I found here to-night waiting for me. It is from London. *(Reads.)* "On Her Majesty's service. The Home Office. In reply to your inquiries concerning Robert Ffolliott, undergoing penal ser-

34. The structure of the Fenians was compartmentalized into cells so that a member knew only the other members of his own section. Harvey recruits new members so he can betray them for the reward.

vitude, I am directed by his lordship to inform you that Her Majesty has been pleased to extend a full pardon to the Fenian prisoners."

HARVEY DUFF. Pardoned! I'm a corpse!

KINCHELA. *(Reads.)* "But as Robert Ffolliott has effected his escape, the pardon will not extend to him unless he should reconstitute himself a prisoner."

HARVEY DUFF. Oh, lor'! that is exactly what he has done. He has gave himself up.

KINCHELA. Was he not captured?

HARVEY DUFF. No bad luck to it. Our schame to catch him has only qualified him for a pardon.

KINCHELA. What! has an infernal fate played such a trick upon me?

HARVEY DUFF. The divil will have his joke.

KINCHELA. His freedom and return here is your death warrant and my ruin. (*To* R.)

HARVEY DUFF. I'll take the next ship to furrin parts. (*To* L.)

KINCHELA. Stay! the news is only known to ourselves.

HARVEY DUFF. In a couple of days it will be all over Ireland, and they will let him out! Tare alive! what'll I do? Where will I go? I'll swear an information against meself, and get sent to jail for purtection.

KINCHELA. Listen, I've a plan. Can I rely upon your help?

HARVEY DUFF. I'll do anything short of murder, but I'll get somebody to do that for me. What's to be done?

KINCHELA. *(Close to Harvey Duff.)* I'll visit him in prison, and offer him the means to escape. Now what more likely than he should be killed while making the attempt?

HARVEY DUFF. Oh! whew! the soldiers will not dhraw a trigger on him barrin' a magistrate is by to give the ordher.

KINCHELA. But the police will. You will go at once to the police- barracks at Sligo, pick your men, tell 'em you apprehend an attempt at rescue. The late attack on the police-van at Manchester, and the explosion at Clerkenwell prison in London will warrant extreme measures.[35]

HARVEY DUFF. The police won't fire if he doesn't defend himself.

KINCHELA. But he will!

HARVEY DUFF. Where will he get the arms?

KINCHELA. I will provide them for him!

HARVEY DUFF. Corry Kinchela, the divil must be proud of you!

KINCHELA. We must get some of our own people to help, and if the police hesitate, sure it's the duty of every loyal subject to kill a fugitive convict. What men could we depend on at a pinch?

HARVEY DUFF. There's Sullivan an' Doyle.

35. At Clerkenwell Prison on December 13, 1867, in the rescue of a Fenian prisoner, twelve people were killed and more than fifty wounded. In Manchester on September 18, 1867, two Fenians were rescued and Sergeant Charles Brett was killed during the rescue. Subsequently three Fenians (the "Manchester Martyrs") were executed after a dubious trial.

KINCHELA. Which Doyle?
HARVEY DUFF. Jim Doyle.
KINCHELA. Jim Doyle!
HARVEY DUFF. Yes, the man with the big carbuncle on the end of his[36] nose. Then there's Reilly.
KINCHELA. Reilly? He's transported.
HARVEY DUFF. No, no; he's not.
KINCHELA. Oh, but he will, and you'll be hanged.
HARVEY DUFF. And so will you—an' Mangan, an' all their smuggling crew.
KINCHELA. Where can you find them?
HARVEY DUFF. At the Coot's Nest. They expect a lugger in at every tide.
KINCHELA. Have them ready and sober to-night. Come to me for instructions at midday. *(Going—stops).* Ah! that will do—he will fall into that trap—*(rubs his hands)*—it can't fail.

[*Exit,* R.

HARVEY DUFF. *(Speaking after Kinch's exit.)* Harvey Duff, take a friend's advice—get out of this place as quick as you can. Take your little pickin's and your passage across the salt say; find some place where a rogue can live peaceably—have some show and a chance of making an honourable living.

[*Exit* L.—*Scene changes. Music.*

SCENE II.—*Parlour at Father Dolan's—(as before.)*
Father Dolan at fireside. Claire looking out of window; window curtains open. Curtains of opening closed.

FATHER DOLAN. There, my darling, do not sob so bitterly. Sure that will do no good, and only spoil your blue eyes.
ARTE. What's the good of my eyes if I can't see him. Let me cry. God help me! what else can I do? Oh, if I could only see him—speak to him—one minute! Do you think they would let me in?
FATHER DOLAN. I have sent a letter to the Captain. Moya has carried it to the barracks.
ARTE. If Claire had gone instead of Moya had she pleaded for us, he would not refuse her.
CLAIRE. But I could not go.
ARTE. Why not?
CLAIRE. I could not ask that Englishman a favour.
FATHER DOLAN. You speak unkindly and unjustly. He acted with a gentle forbearance, and a respect for my character and our sorrow, I cannot forget.

36. his] her.

CLAIRE. Nor can I?

FATHER DOLAN. It made a deep impression on my heart.

CLAIRE. Yes; a bitter curse on the day I ever laid eyes on him. (*Coming down* R.)

ARTE. *(Rising, and down to to her behind table.)* Oh, Claire, you wrong him! Surely I have no cause to regard him as a friend; but you did not see the tears in his eyes when I appealed to his mercy—

CLAIRE. Didn't I?

FATHER DOLAN. *(Still seated.)* Poor fellow, he suffered for what he was obliged to do. You should not hate the man.

CLAIRE. *(Up.)* I don't! And that's what ails me!

ARTE. Are you mad?

CLAIRE. *(Down)* I am! I've tried to hate him, and I can't! Do you think I was blind to all you saw? I tried to shut my eyes; but I only shut him in. I could not shut him out! I hate his country and his people. *(Crosses to* L. *Arte to table.)*

FATHER DOLAN. You were never there.

CLAIRE. (L.) Never! and I wish they had never been here, particularly this fellow, who has the impudence to upset all my principles with his chalky smile and bloodless courtesy. I can't stand the ineffable resignation with which he makes a fool of himself and me. (*Father Dolan goes to fire, and* MOYA *enters,* D. F. R.) *(Eagerly.)* Well, have you seen him? Can't you speak?

MOYA. I will when I get my breath. Yes, I saw him, and, oh! how good and—

CLAIRE. (L.) Stop that! we know all about that! Where is his answer?—quick!

MOYA. (R.) He's bringing it himself!

CLAIRE. Oh! *(Turns away.)* We don't want him here. *(To window.)*

ARTE. (C.) Did you see the young master?

MOYA. No, miss; nobody was let in to see him.

FATHER DOLAN. What kept you so long then?

MOYA. Conn come back wid me *(Arte gets in front of table),* and knowing you did not want him round here, I was thrying to get away from him—that's what kept me; but he was at my heels all the way and Tatthers at his heels. A nice sthreel[37] we made along the road.

FATHER DOLAN. Where is he?

MOYA. They are both outside.

FATHER DOLAN. The pair of vagabonds? Why does he not go home?

MOYA. (*Going up* R.) He says the ould woman is no consolation.

CONN. *(Sings outside.)*

"If I were dead an' in my grave,
No other tombstone would I have

37. A group sauntering aimlessly.

But I'd dig a grave both wide and deep,
With a jug of punch at my head and feet.
"Ri tooral loo."

FATHER DOLAN. Is the fellow so insensible to our sorrow that he sets it to the tune of a jug of punch?

CLAIRE. Don't blame poor Conn. The boy is so full of sport that I believe he would sing at his own funeral. *(At desk.)*

MOYA. Long life to ye, miss, for the good word.

CONN. *(Entering,* 3 E. R., *and speaking to his dog.)* Lie down now, an' behave.

FATHER DOLAN. Where have you been all night?

CONN. Where would I be but undher his prison windy, keeping up his heart wid the songs and the divarshin!

ARTE. Diversion. *(Father Dolan, down to Arte.)*

CONN. Sure I had all the soldiers dancing to my fiddle, and I put Tatthers through all his thricks. I had 'em all in fits of laffin' when I made him dance to my tunes. That's the way the masther knew I was waiting on him. He guessed what I was at, for when I struck up "Where's the slave?" he answered inside with "My lodging is on the cowld ground"; then when I made Tatthers dance to "Tell me the sorrow in my heart"—till I thought they'd have died wid the fun—he sung back "The girl I left behind me," mainin' yourself, Miss Arte, an' I purtended that the tears runnin' down my nose was with the laffin'.

(Moya puts stool by Conn. Wipes his eyes with apron.)

FATHER DOLAN. I did you great wrong. I ask your pardon.

ARTE. What is to be done?

CONN. I've only to whisper five words on the cross-roads and I'd go bail I'd have him out of that before night.

FATHER DOLAN. Yes; you would raise the country to attack the barracks, and rescue him. I will not give countenance to violence.

(Crosses to L. *with Arte.)*

CLAIRE. 'Tis the shortest way out!

ARTE. Oh, any way but that!

MOYA. *(Aside to Conn, taking up stool.)* Come into my kitchen. Have you had nothin' to ate since yesterday?

CONN. Yes, my heart, I've that in my mouth all the night.

[*Exit, with Moya,* 3 E. R.

CLAIRE. *(Who is watching at window.)* Here he comes.

(A knock. After Molineux passes[38] *window, Claire crosses, and sits by fire, back to audience.)*

38. passes] pass.

FATHER DOLAN. There's a knock at the door.
ARTE. 'Tis he!
CLAIRE. I know that.
FATHER DOLAN. Why did you not let him in? *(Crosses to door.)*
CLAIRE. *(Aside.)* Because I was trying to keep him out.

(Father Dolan opens door. Molineux enters D. F. R. Arte to front of table.)

MOLINEUX. Good day, sir. I ventured to intrude in person to bring you this order, necessary to obtain admission to see Mr. Ffolliott, and that I might entreat you to bear me no ill-will for the painful duty I had to perform last night. *(Hands a paper to Arte.)*
CLAIRE. Oh, no, sir; you had to deprive us of a limb, and I suppose you performed the operation professionally well. Do you come for your fee in the form of our gratitude?
FATHER DOLAN. Forgive her, sir! Claire, this is too bad!
MOLINEUX. *(Awkward.)* Oh, no—not at all! Pray don't mention it—I assure you.
ARTE. This paper is signed by Mr. Kinchela—are we indebted to him for the favour?
MOLINEUX. The prisoner is now in the custody of the civil power, and Mr. Kinchela is the magistrate of the district.
FATHER DOLAN. *(Taking his hat from desk.)* Come, Arte. Come, Claire.
ARTE. *(To Molineux.)* We are grateful—*(giving hands)*—very grateful for your kindness in our affliction. *(Aside to Molineux, and pointing to Claire.)* Don't mind her.

[*Father Dolan takes Molineux's hand, and then exit with Arte,* D. F. R.

MOLINEUX. *(Aside.)* Don't mind her; I wish I did not. *(Aloud.)* May I be permitted to accompany you to—

(Advances to upper corner R. of table, and puts down cap.)

CLAIRE. *(Still seated.)* To the prison? Do you wish to make the people about here believe I am in custody. A fine figure I'd make hanging on the arm of the policeman who arrested my brother!
MOLINEUX. You cannot make me feel more acutely than I do the misery of my condition. I did not sleep a wink last night.
CLAIRE. And how many winks do you suppose I got?
MOLINEUX. I tried to act with as much tenderness as the nature of my duty would permit.
CLAIRE. That's the worst part of it.
MOLINEUX. Do you reproach me with my gentleness?
CLAIRE. I do! You have not even left us the luxury of complaint.
MOLINEUX. Really, I don't understand you.
CLAIRE. No wonder. I don't understand myself! *(Rising, and at fire.)*
MOLINEUX. Well, if you don't understand yourself, you shall understand me, Miss Ffolliott. You oblige me to take refuge from your cruelty, and place myself under the protection of your generosity. You extort

from me a confession that I feel is premature, for our acquaintance has been short.

CLAIRE. And not sweet.

MOLINEUX. I ask your pity for my position last night, when I found myself obliged to arrest the brother of the woman I love.

CLAIRE. *(At* L. *of table.)* Captain Molineux, do you mean to insult me? Oh, sir, you know I am a friendless girl, alone in this house—my brother in a jail! I have no protection!

MOLINEUX. Miss Ffolliott—Claire!

Enter CONN, *followed by* MOYA, 3 E. R.

CONN. Did you call, miss?

CLAIRE. *(After a pause.)* No. (*Turns to* L.)

CONN. I thought I heard a screech. *(Music.)*

CLAIRE. Go away; I don't want you.

MOYA. *(Aside to Conn.)* Don't you see what's the matther?

CONN. No.

MOYA. You're an omadhann. Come out of that, an' I'll tell you.

[*Exit with Conn,* 3 E. R. *Claire crosses to* R, *then to bench, sits face to audience, handkerchief to face.*

CLAIRE. There! what will those pair think of us? Do you see what you have exposed me to? Is it not enough to play the character of executioner of my brother, but you must add to your part this scene of outrage on me! *(Sits down, and weeps passionately.)*

MOLINEUX. Forgive me. I ask it most humbly. If I said I would give my heart's blood to the last to spare you one of those tears, you might feel the avowal was an offence. What can I say? Miss Ffolliott, for mercy sake don't cry so bitterly!—forget what I've done! *(Front of table.)*

CLAIRE. I—I can't!

MOLINEUX. On my knees, I implore your pardon. I'll go away. I'll never see you again. *(Claire suddenly and mechanically arrests his movement by catching his arm. Molineux kisses her hand.)* Heaven bless you—farewell!

CLAIRE. *(Without moving her hands from face.)* Don't go.

MOLINEUX. *(Advances a little.)* Did I hear right? You bid me stay?

CLAIRE. Am I mad? *(Rises, and goes to fireplace.)*

MOLINEUX. Miss Ffolliott, I am here.

CLAIRE. I forgive you on one condition.

MOLINEUX. I accept it, whatever it may be.

CLAIRE. Save my brother.

MOLINEUX. I'll do my best. Anything else?

CLAIRE. Never speak of love to me again.

MOLINEUX. *(Close to her.)* Never, never! On my honour I will never breathe a—

CLAIRE. Until he is free.
MOLINEUX. And then may I—may I—

(He stands beside her at fireplace; her head bent down, he steals his arm around her.)

CLAIRE. Not a word until then.
MOLINEUX. Not a word!

(Claire leans her head on his shoulder. Slow close in, as he kisses her.)

SCENE III.—*Room in the Barracks.*

Enter the SERGEANT, followed by KINCHELA, L.

KINCHELA. I am Mr. Kinchela, the magistrate. I wish to see the prisoner; he must be removed to police quarters.
SERGEANT. We shall be glad to get rid of him.—It is the police business. Our men don't half like it. [*Exit,* R.)
KINCHELA. Now I'll know at once by his greeting whether those girls have been speakin' about me. (*Goes to* L.)

Enter ROBERT, *followed by* SERGEANT, R., *who crosses to L.*

ROBERT. Kinchela, my dear friend, I knew you would not fail me.
KINCHELA. *(Aside.)* 'Tis all right. *(Turns coldly, and with stiff manner.)* Pardon me, Mr. Ffolliott, you forget your position and mine—I bear Her Majesty's commission as justice of the peace, and whatever friendship once united us it ceased when you became a rebel.
ROBERT. Do I hear aright? Your letters to me breathed the most devoted—
KINCHELA. *(To Sergeant.)* You can leave us. *(Sergeant goes out* L. *—he suddenly changes his manner.)* My dear young master, forgive me, in the presence of that fellow I was obliged to play the magistrate.
ROBERT. (R.) Egad! you took my breath away.
KINCHELA. (L.) Didn't I do it well—my devotion to you and the precious charge you left in my care exposes me to suspicion. I am watched, and to preserve my character for loyalty I am obliged to put on airs—Oh! I'm your mortal enemy, mind that.
ROBERT. You!
KINCHELA. Every man, woman, an' child in the county Sligo believes it, and hate me. I've played my part so well that your sister an' Miss O'Neal took offence at my performance.
ROBERT. No—ha! ha!
KINCHELA. Yes! ho! ho! they actually believe I am what I am obliged to appear, and they hate me cordially. I'm the biggest blackguard—
ROBERT. You! my best friend!
KINCHELA. Oh, I don't mind it! The truth is, I'm afeard if I had betrayed my game to them—you know the weakness of the sex—they could not have kept my secret.

ROBERT. But surely Father Dolan?

KINCHELA. He is just as bad.

ROBERT. Forgive them.

KINCHELA. I do.

ROBERT. The time will come when they will repent their usage of you.

KINCHELA. Ay, by my soul it will.

ROBERT. They have no friend, no protector but you; for now my chains will be more firmly riveted than ever.

KINCHELA. Whisht! you must escape.

ROBERT. It is impossible! How? When?

KINCHELA. To-night! To-morrow, when you are removed to Sligo jail, it might not be so aisy; but to-night I can help you.

ROBERT. To regain my freedom?

KINCHELA. Is that ship that landed you within reach?

ROBERT. Every night at eight o'clock she runs in shore, and lies-to off the coast; a bonfire lighted on Rathgarron Head is to be the signal for her to send off her skiff under the ruine of St. Bridget's Abbey to take me on board.

KINCHELA. That signal will be fired to night, and you shall be there to meet the boat.

ROBERT. Do you, indeed, mean this, Kinchela? Will you risk this for my sake?

KINCHELA. I will lay down my life if you want it. *(They embrace.)*

ROBERT. What am I to do?

KINCHELA. Give me your promise that you will not breathe a word to mortal about the place I am going to propose; neither to your sister, nor to Miss O'Neal, nor, above all, to Father Dolan.

ROBERT. Must I play a part to deceive them? (*Crosses to* L.)

KINCHELA. My life and liberty are staked in the attempt as well as yours.

ROBERT. I give you the promise.

KINCHELA. To-night your quarters will be changed to the old Gate Tower. Wait till dark, then use this chisel to pick out the stones that form the back of the fireplace in your room. The wall there is only one course thick. *(He gives Robert chisel.)*

ROBERT. You are sure?

KINCHELA. Conn, the Shaughraun, was shut up in that cell last spring, and he picked his way out through the wall with a two-pronged fork. He was creeping out of the hole he had made when they caught him. The wall has been rebuilt, but the place has not served as a prison since.

ROBERT. Where shall I find myself when I am outside?

KINCHELA. In a yard enclosed by four low walls. There's a door in one of them that's bolted on the inside. Open that, and you are free.

ROBERT. Are there no sentinels posted there?

KINCHELA. No; but if there is, there's a double-barrelled pistol that will clear your road. *(Hands pistol. Robert examines it.) (Aside.)* I'll put Duff outside that door; there'll be an end to him.

ROBERT. *(Returning the pistol.)* Take it back. I will not buy my liberty at the price of any man's life. I will take my chance; but, stay, the signal on Rathgarron Head! Who will light the bonfire? *(Conn playing outside.)* Hark!—'tis Conn! Do you hear? Poor fellow! he is playing "I'm under your window, darling." Ah! I can employ him. How will he do it?—how will I send him word?

KINCHELA. You won't betray me?

ROBERT. No, no. *(Writes in his book—repeats as he writes.)* "Be at Rathgarron Head to-night, beside the tar barrel." What signal can I give him that he will be able to hear or see across the bay?

KINCHELA. *(Dictating.)* "When you hear two gunshots on St. Bridget's Abbey, light the fire."

ROBERT. *(Writes.)* "When you hear two gunshots—" For that purpose I accept it.

KINCHELA. *(Gives Robert the pistol.—Aside.)* No matter for what purpose. He will use it to serve mine. If they hang him for murdering Harvey Duff, I'll be afther killing two birds wid one stone.

ROBERT. Beg the sentry to come here.

KINCHELA. What are you going to do?

ROBERT. You will see. *(Taking out coins.)*

KINCHELA. Here is the Sergeant.

(*He enters* L.)

ROBERT. *(Folding money in the paper.)* Will you give these few pence to the fiddler outside, and beg the fellow to move on?

(Hands paper to Sergeant.)

SERGEANT. The men encourage him about the place. *(Going.)* There's Father Dolan and Miss O'Neal outside; they have got a pass to see you.

ROBERT. Show them in.

[*Exit Sergeant,* L.

KINCHELA. Now, watch their manner towards me; but you won't mind a word they say against me.

ROBERT (L.) Not I. I know you better. *(Fiddle outside.)* Hush! 'tis Conn. He has got the letter. Listen—"I'll be faithful and true!" Ay, as the ragged dog at your heels is faithful and true to you, so you have been to me, my dear, devoted, loving playfellow—my wild companion!

Enter ARTE *and* FATHER DOLAN, L.

ARTE. Robert! *(Embracing him.)* Mr. Kinchela!

FATHER DOLAN. I am surprised to find you here, sir!

KINCHELA. *(Aside to Robert.)* D'ye hear?

ROBERT. *(Aside to Kinchela.)* All right!

ARTE. You do not know that man.

KINCHELA. Oh, yes he does. I've made a clane breast of it.

ROBERT. Yes, he has told me all.

KINCHELA. How I brought all of you to ruin, and betrayed my trust—(*Crossing to* L.)—and grew rich and fat on my plundher. I defy you to make me out a bigger blackguard than I've painted myself, so my sarvice to you!

[*Exit* L.

FATHER DOLAN. (L.) When St. Patrick made a clean sweep of all the venomous reptiles in Ireland, some of the vermin must have found refuge in the bodies of such men as that.

ROBERT. This is the first uncharitable word I ever heard you utter.

FATHER DOLAN. Heaven forgive me for it, and him! You're right, my vocation is to pray for sinners, not revile them.

ARTE. And mine to comfort you, and not to bring our complaints to add to your misfortune.

ROBERT. (*Crossing to* C.) Hold up your hearts; mine is full of hope.

FATHER DOLAN. Hope; where do you find it?

ROBERT. In her eyes! You might as well ask me where I find love. I was in prison when I stood liberated on American soil. The chains were on my soul when I stretched it longing across the ocean towards my home; but now I am in prison, this narrow cell is Ireland. I breathe my native air, and am free!

FATHER DOLAN. They will send you back again.

ARTE (R.) Ah, sure! the future belongs to heaven, the present is our own.

FATHER DOLAN. I believe I was wrong to come here at all. I feel like a mourning band on a white hat! *(Music.)*

SERGEANT (*Entering* L.)

SERGEANT. Sorry to disturb you, sir, but we are ordered to shift your quarters. You will occupy the room in the Old Gate Tower. The guard is waiting, sir, when you are ready. [*Exit,* R.

ROBERT. I am prepared to accompany you.

ARTE. Must we leave you?

ROBERT. For the present, but we shall soon meet again. Now will you indulge a strange humour of mine? You know the ruins of St. Bridget's Abbey, where we have so often sat together?

ARTE. Can I ever forget it! We go there often; the place is full of you.

ROBERT. Go there to-night at nine o'clock.

ARTE. I'll offer up a prayer at the old shrine.

ROBERT. Ay, with all my heart, for I may want it.

FATHER DOLAN. What do you mean? There's some mischief going on; I know it by his eye. He used to wear the same look when he was going to give me the slip and be off from his Latin grammar to play truant with Conn the Shaughraun.

ROBERT. Ask me nothing, for I can answer you only one word—hope!

FATHER DOLAN. 'Tis the finest word in the Irish language.

ARTE. There's a finer—faith. *(Embraces Robert.)*

FATHER DOLAN. And love is the mother of those heavenly twins. I declare my heart is lifted up between you, as if your young ones were its wings. *(Backs up stage a little.)*

ROBERT. Good night, and not for the last time.

SERGEANT *enters,* R.

ARTE. Goodnight!

FATHER DOLAN. I leave my heart with you. God bless
you! (R. *hand to Robert*)

ROBERT. Remember, to-night at the Abbey.

ARTE. *(Aside.)* At nine o'clock.

ROBERT. I shall be there. *(She utters an exclamation.)* Hush! [*Exit Father Dolan with Arte,* L.] You gave the money to the fiddler?

SERGEANT. Yes, sir!

ROBERT. (*Aside, crosses to* R.) Ah, I forgot! Conn can't read. What will he do to decipher my note?—bah! I must trust to his cunning to get at the contents. Now, sergeant, lead me to my new cell in the Gate Tower.

[*Exeunt,* R.

SCENE IV.—*Mrs. O'Kelly's Cabin.—Exterior.—Evening.*

CONN. (*Entering with a paper in his hand,* R.) There's writing upon it. Himself has sent me a letther. Well, this is the first I ever got, and well to be sure, *(Looks at it—turns it over.)* I'd know more about it if there was nothing in it; but it's the writin' bothers me.

MRS. O'KELLY. (*Entering,* D. F. R.) Is that yourself, Conn?

CONN. *(Aside.)* I wish it was somebody else that had book larnin'.

MRS. O'KELLY. What have you there?

CONN. It's a letther the masther is afther writin' to me.

MRS. O'KELLY. What's in it?

CONN. Tuppence was in it for postage. *(Aside.)* That's all I made out of it.

MRS. O'KELLY. I mane what does he say in it?

CONN. Rade it!

MRS. O'KELLY. You know I can't.

CONN. Oh, ye ignorant ould woman!

MRS. O'KELLY. I know I am; but I took care to send you to school, Conn, though the sixpence a week it cost me was pinched out of my stomach and off my back.

CONN. The Lord be praised that ye had it to spare, anyway.

MRS. O'KELLY. Go on, now—it's makin' fun of yer ould mother ye are. Tell me what the young masther says.

CONN. In the letther?

MRS. O'KELLY. Yes!

CONN. *(Aside.)* Murther, what'll I do? *(Aloud.)* Now, mind, it's a sacret. *(Reads.)* "Collee costhum garanga caravat selibubu luckli rastuck pig."

MRS. O'KELLY. What's that—it's not English!

CONN. No; it's in writin'—now kape that to yourself.

CLAIRE. (*Entering* R.) Conn, there is some project on foot to-night to rescue my brother—don't deny it—he has almost confessed as much to Father Dolan. Tell me the truth!

CONN. I would not decaive you Well, I promised not to say a word about it; but there it is; rade it for yourself.

CLAIRE. *(Looks at note.)* Yes; 'tis his hand.

CONN. I knew it in a minute.

CLAIRE. It is in pencil!

CONN. *(To Mrs. O'Kelly.)* I told you it wasn't in English.

CLAIRE *(Reads.)* "Be at Rathgarron Head to-night beside the tar- barrel. When you hear two gunshots in St. Bridget's Abbey, light the fire."

CONN. Yon wouldn't believe me when I read that to you ten minutes ago. The signal fire that's to tell the ship out at sea beyant there to send a boat ashore to take him off.

MRS. O'KELLY. Oh, blessed day! Is it to escape from gaol he'd be thrying?

CLAIRE. He has told my cousin to be in the ruins to-night.

CONN. There's going to be a scrimmage, an' I'm not in it. I'm to be sent away like this. It's too hard on me intirely. Oh, if I could find somebody to take my place and fire the signal! I'd bring him out of gaol this night if I had to tear a hole in the wall wid my five fingers!

CLAIRE. I'll take your place!

CONN. You will!

MRS. O'KELLY. (*Crosses to* C.) Oh, Miss Claire, don't go; there'll be gunshots and bagginets!° This is one of Conn's divilments, and ye'll be all murthered! Oh, weir asthru! what'll I do? — bayonets

CONN. Will ye hould your whisht?

MRS. O'KELLY. No, I won't! I'll go an' inform agin ye before ye get into throuble, and then, maybe, they'll let you off aisy.

CLAIRE. (*Crosses to* L.) Here comes the Captain. For Heaven's sake, pacify her! She will betray us.

CONN. Well, come inside, mother, darlin'! There! I'll stop wid ye. Will that aise your mind? You onsensible ould woman!

MRS. O'KELLY. (R.) Conn, don't lave me alone in the world. Sure, I've nobody left but yourself, an' if ye're taken from me, I'll be a widdy.

CONN. Then both of us will be two widdy together. Don't ye hear Miss Claire is going to take my place?

MRS. O'KELLY. (*Crosses to* C.) Heaven bless an' purtect every hair of your head, miss! And will ye, indeed, spend one night by the mother's fireside?

CONN. And I'll play all the tunes you love best on my fiddle till I warm the cockles of your ould heart! *(Sings.)*

"Oh, then, Conn, my son, was a fine young man,
An' to every one cuish° he had one shin; — thigh
Till he wint to the wars of a bloody day,

When a big cannon-ball whipped his two shins away,
An' my rickety a—"

[*Exeunt.*
Enter ARTE *and* MOLINEUX, L.

ARTE. I have invited the Captain to pass the evening at Suil-a-beg, but he will not be parsuaded.

MOLINEUX. I may not desert my post till the police arrive from Sligo to relieve me of my charge.

ARTE. But your soldiers are there?

MOLINEUX. Soldiers will not move without orders, besides, my men have such a distaste for this business, that I believe, if left to defend their prisoner against an attempt to rescue him, they would disgrace themselves.

ARTE. *(Aside to Claire.)* Get him away; an attempt will be made to-night. (*Crosses to* R.)

CLAIRE. *(Aside.)* Leave us!

ARTE. Well, good day, Captain. Come Claire. [*Exit* R.

CLAIRE. *(After a pause.)* It is a lovely evening. (*Going* R.)

MOLINEUX. You are not going home.

CLAIRE. Not yet. I shall take a stroll along the shore to Rathgarron Head!

MOLINEUX. Alone?

CLAIRE. I suppose so!

MOLINEUX. Is it far?

CLAIRE. No!

MOLINEUX. Not far—ahem! would you allow me to go part of the road beside you? *(Music.)*

CLAIRE. Pray do not neglect your duty on my account, besides I want to consult my feelings in solitude uninfluenced by your presence.

MOLINEUX. That sweet confession gives me hope and courage.

CLAIRE. Good night! leave me, light a meditative cigar, and go back to your duty. *(He takes out cigar-case.)* Leave me to wander by the light of the rising moon, and sit down on the rocks beside the sea.

(He takes match—she lights one and keeps the box.)

MOLINEUX. How good you are!—an angel!

CLAIRE. Of light. There, good night!

MOLINEUX. Good night! *(She goes off very slowly* R. *He moves away — turns.)* Oh, if I had some excuse to follow her a little way. *(He brushes the light away from the end of his cigar, and calls.)* Miss Ffolliott, pardon me, but my cigar is out, and you have my matches —ha! ha! sorry to trouble you, oh, don't come back, I beg.

(*Follows her out* R.)

CONN. *(Leaping out of window and fastening shutters.)* I've locked the dure an' barred the shutters!

MRS. O'KELLY. *(Inside.)* Conn, let me out!

CONN. Behave now, or I'll tell the neighbours you've been drinking. Good night, mother! (*Runs out* R.)

SCENE V.—*The interior of prison, large window* R. *old fireplace* R. C., *small window* C., door L. *Through window* R. *is seen exterior and court-yard—night.*

ROBERT. (*Discovered listening,* D. L.) They are relieving guard. *(Drum.)* I shall not receive another visit for the night. Now to work —that must be the wall Kinchela spoke of. I see some new brick-work there, but where shall I land? Is there much of a drop into the yard below? (*Looks out of window* R.) The wall hides the interior—can I reach[39] this window?

(*Climbs to window* L. *as Conn is seen at window* R.)

CONN. Divil a sowl about this side of the tower. There's a light in his cell. I wondher is he alone? No matter. Where's my iron pick? Now to make a hole in the wall. *(Disappears.)*

ROBERT. The yard seems to be on a level of this chamber. Where's my chisel? *(Begins to work.)* The mortar is as soft as butter. This was done by government contract. It's an ill wind that blows nobody any— What's that? It sounds like somebody at work on the wall. Can it be a rat? *(Listens.)* No, it stops now. *(He works.)* There it goes again. *(He stops.)* Now it stops. It echoes me as if there was some one on the other side. Oh, Lord! my heart sinks at the thought. I'll satisfy myself.

(*He goes to window,* L.)

CONN. (*Appearing at window,* R.) There's a rat in the chimbley! Gorra! maybe I'm all wrong, and himself is not in it at all.

(*Looks in at window as Robert, having climbed, looks out* L.)

ROBERT. I can't see round the corner, but there seems to be no one there.

CONN. Divil a sowl in it. I wish I could see crooked. Here goes again. (*Disappears* L.)

ROBERT. The noise has ceased—it was a rat *(Works.)* This brick is loose enough to pull out; but if that goes, the rest seem shaky. They will fall together. *(A mass of brickwork falls, and discovers Conn.)* Conn!

CONN. Whisht! Who the devil would it be? Asy, for the love of Heaven, now! Come asy! I've left Tatthers in the guard-room with the men. Stop till I break another coorse of bricks for ye.

(The scene moves—pivots on a point at the back. The Prison moves off and show the exterior of Tower with Conn clinging to the walls, and Robert creeping through the orifice. The walls of the Yard appear to occupy three-fourths of stage.)

39. can I reach] can reach.

Enter KINCHELA, HARVEY DUFF, *and four* CONSTABULARY, 3 E. R. *Conn and Robert disappear into the Yard.*

KINCHELA. Whisht! there's a noise in the yard! This door is boulted on the inside; but there's a pile of rubbish shot against the back wall that we can see[40] over. *(To Harvey Duff.)* Harvey Duff, you will stand there; the rest come wid me.

(Kinchela and four Constabulary go up, R, and disappear behind wall. Harvey Duff, holding a short carbine ready, stands R. of door with his back to wall.)

HARVEY DUFF.[41] Now, my fine fellow—now, Mr. Robert Ffolliott, you said we must meet once again on this side o' the grave, and so we will—ho! ha! *(Conn's head appears over the wall.)* I don't think you'll like this meetin' more than the last. *(Conn, after signing to Robert, gets sitting on the wall, with his legs dangling just above Harvey Duff's head.)* You tould me to have my sowl ready. I wondher if yours is in good condition. Whisht! I hear the boults moving. He is coming! He is—Conn—

(Conn drops on Harvey Duff's shoulders, who falls forward with a cry—Conn over him. Door opens. ROBERT *appears.)*

CONN. Run, sir, run! I've got him safe!

(Robert leaps over Harvey Duff's body, and runs off, R. At the same moment Constabulary mount the back wall—leap into Yard. The Sergeant, with a light, appears at the breach in the wall of the Prison.)

SERGEANT. Where is he?
CONN. I've got him—here he is, nivir fear! Hould him fast.

(The CONSTABULARY *enter by the door in the wall, and seize Harvey Duff, who is lying on his face.)*

CONN. Don't let him go! Hould him down!

(Runs off as Constabulary raise Harvey Duff.)

KINCHELA. (*Coming round corner,* R.) Where is he? Harvey Duff! Bungling fools, he has escaped!

(Harvey Duff gesticulates faintly, and falls back.)

SCENE VI.—*The Coot's Nest.—Night.*

ROBERT. (*Entering,* R.) Escaped once more, and free! My disguise is secreted here in some nook of the rocks—in Conn's cupboard, as he calls it—but I cannot find it in the darkness. I hope the poor fel-

40. see] sea.
41. *Harvey Duff*] *Harvey C.*

low has got clear away. I would not have him hurt for my sake. *(A whistle.)* Ah! there he is! *(He whistles.)* Thank you, kind Providence, for protecting him. Here he comes—leaping from crag to crag like a goat.

CONN. (*Entering,* R.) Hurroo! tare an' ages, Masther, jewel, but we did that well! But it goes agin my conscience that I did not crack the skull of that thief when I had him fair and asy under my foot. I'll never get absolution for that!

ROBERT. We must not remain in this place—it is the first they will search. I must make my way to St. Bridget's Abbey at once; there Arte is waiting for me. Where is my great coat, my hat, and beard?

CONN. I have the bundle snug inside. But sure, the Captain knows you in that skin. Didn't he meet you here? It will be no cover for you now. Whisht!

ROBERT. What! Do you hear anything?

CONN. No; but Tatthers does. I left the baste to watch on the cliff above. There agin; d'ye hear him? He's givin' tongue; lie close. I'll go see what it is. [*Exit* L.

ROBERT. Yonder is the schooner, creeping in with the tide. I can reach the ruins by the seashore; the rocks will conceal me. Then one brief moment with my darling girl—

Re-enter CONN, *with the coat, hat, and beard.*

CONN. Speak low; they are close by.

ROBERT. The constabulary?

CONN. Yes; and wid them those smugglin' thieves, Mangan, Sullivan, and Reilly; they are guidin' the polis—the mongrel curs go do that! They know every hole in these rocks.

ROBERT. But the signal—who will set the match to the tar barrel on Rathgarron Head?

CONN. Nivir fear, sir. Miss Claire is there by this time, and waitin' beside it, lookin' an' listenin' for the two gunshots your honour will fire in the ruins beyant.

ROBERT. Where is my pistol? *(Feeling in his pocket.)* I cannot find it—gone! No; it cannot be lost. By Heaven! it must have fallen from my pocket as I climbed the wall! *(Putting on disguise.)*

CONN. Murther alive! what will we do now?

ROBERT. I must swim out to the schooner.

CONN. It is a mile, an' agin the tide. Stop! will ye lave it to me, and I'll go bail I'll find a way of getting them two shots for me? Ah, do, sir! Only this once give me my head an' let me go.

ROBERT. What do you propose to do?

CONN. Don't you recollect once when the Ballyragget hounds couldn't find a fox, after dhrawing every cover in the country, damn a hair of one could they smell, an' the whole field lookin' blazes. You were masther of the hunt. "What will we do at all?" says you. "You shall have a fox," ses I, and I whipt in a red herring[42] into the tail o' me coat and away I wint across the fields.

ROBERT. Ha! ha! I remember it well.

CONN. You, he! an' a devil a one on the whole field but yourself knew that there was a two-legged fox to the fore. Now, I'll give them vagabones another taste of the red herring. I will cut in and cross your scent. I'll lade them off, nivir fear, and be jabers I'll show them the finest run of the huntin' sayson.

ROBERT. How, Conn, how?

CONN. Asy—look where they are coming down the cliff; slip out this way, quick, before they catch sight of us; when we get round the corner we must divide up; you go by the shore below, I'll take the cliff above. [*Exit Robert,* R.] Begorra, it isn't the first time I've played the fox! [*Exit,* R.

SCENE VII.—*Rathgarron Head.*

Enter CLAIRE *and* MOLINEUX, L.

CLAIRE (R.) Here we are at Rathgarron Head—are you not tired?

MOLINEUX. I don't know. If you asked if I was dying I should say I could not tell. I feel as if it was all a dream, in which I am not myself.

CLAIRE. Who are you, then?

MOLINEUX. Somebody much happier than I can ever be. I wish I could describe to you the change that has taken place in me since we met.

CLAIRE. Oh, I can understand it, for I feel the very—

(Stops suddenly.)

MOLINEUX. Eh! what do you feel?

CLAIRE. Do you see those ruins on yonder headland? That is St. Bridget's Abbey! A lovely ruin! How effective is that picture, with the moon shining on it!

MOLINEUX. Splendid, no doubt; but when I'm beside you I cannot admire ruins or moonshine. The most effective picture is on this headland, and I cannot detach my eyes from the loveliness that is before me.

CLAIRE. *(Aside.)* I cannot stand this. I never played so contemptible a part.

MOLINEUX. What is the matter?

CLAIRE. Go home—go away! Why did you come here?

MOLINEUX. My dear Miss Ffolliott, I hope I have not been intruding on you. If I have, I pray you forgive me. I will retrace my steps. *(Going.)*

CLAIRE. No, stop!

42. Figuratively, a deception by introducing an irrelevant issue, but here used in its literal sense; hunting dogs would chase the scent of a dried (red) herring rather than a game trail.

MOLINEUX. *(Returning.)* Yes.

CLAIRE. I encouraged you to follow me.

MOLINEUX. I fear I pressed myself upon you.

CLAIRE. *(Aside.)* Oh! why is he so willingly deceived! His gentleness and truth make me ashamed of the part I play. (*Moves to* R.)

MOLINEUX. I have said or done something to offend you. Tell me what it is. It will afford me much pleasure to plead for pardon for what I haven't done.

CLAIRE. Yon want to know what ails me?

MOLINEUX. Yes.

CLAIRE. Do you see that tar barrel? (R.)

MOLINEUX. Good gracious! what has a tar-barrel got to do with my offence?

CLAIRE. Nothing; but it has everything to do with mine.

MOLINEUX. *(Aside, after a pause.)* I wonder whether there's madness in the family?

CLAIRE. Do you see that tar-barrel?

MOLINEUX. I see something like a tar-barrel in that pile of brushwood.

CLAIRE. Will you oblige me with a match?

MOLINEUX. Certainly. *(Aside.)* There's no doubt about it. So lovely, and yet so afflicted! I feel even more tenderly towards her than I did!

CLAIRE. If I were to ask you to light that bonfire, would you do it?

MOLINEUX. With pleasure. *(Aside.)* It is the moon that affects her. I wish I had an umbrella.

CLAIRE. Captain Molineux, my brother has escaped from the prison, guarded by your soldiers. He is now in yonder ruins. This pile of fuel, when lighted, will be the signal for the schooner you see yonder to send a boat ashore to take off the fugitive. I have been a decoy to entice you away from your duty, so that I might deprive your men of the orders they await to pursue my brother, who has broken gaol. Now do you understand my conduct?

MOLINEUX. Miss Ffolliott!

CLAIRE. Now do you understand why every tender word you have spoken has tortured me like poison? Why every throb in your honest heart has been a knife in mine?

MOLINEUX. I thought you were mad. I fear 'tis I have been so.

CLAIRE. You can redeem your professional honour; you can repair the past. I have no means here of lighting that beacon. If the signal is not fired, my brother will be recaptured; but the blood that revolts in my heart against what I am doing is the same that beats in his. He would disdain to owe his liberty to my duplicity and to your infatuation. There's your road. Good night!

[*Claire goes out hastily.—Music.*

MOLINEUX. So I have been her dupe! No—she was not laughing at me! *(Looks off.)* She is not laughing at me, as one who—see where she has thrown herself on the ground. I hear her sobs. I cannot leave her alone, and in this wild place; and yet what can I do to—poor thing!—I—I don't know how to act. There again—oh, what a moan that was! I cannot let her lie there!

[*Hastily exit,* R.

SCENE VIII.—*The Ruins of St Bridget's Abbey.*—ARTE *discovered kneeling before the broken shrine,* L.—MOYA *is looking towards* R *down the cliff.*

MOYA. There is not a sound to be heard barrin' the sheam of the waves as they lick the shore below.

ARTE. I was afraid to come here alone. Even with you beside me I tremble.

MOYA. There's something moving in the strand below. Look, miss, it is a goat! (*Arte crosses to* R.) There it is, creeping under the shadow of the rocks.

ARTE. I see nothing!

MOYA. Whisht! I'll give him the offis.

(She sings.)

Enter H. DUFF, REILLY, SULLIVAN, *and* DOYLE. *They carry carbines.* L. 2 E.

HARVEY DUFF. There they are—there's a pair of them—'tis Moya with her. The constabulary are giving him chase, but here is where he will run to airth—here's the trap, and there's the bait.

ARTE. There! there he is! and see those men pursue him! Fly, Robert, fly!

MOYA. They will catch him, miss.

ARTE. No; he gains upon them—he has turned the point. He will scale the cliff on this side.

(Crosses to L. *as if to meet him.)*

HARVEY DUFF. *(Seizing Moya.)* Reilly, take hould of her—quick.

(Reilly seizes Arte—drags her to front of shrine.)

ARTE. Who are you, who dare to lay hands on me? Do you know who I am?

HARVEY DUFF. Yes, I do, well enough, You are the sweetheart of the man we want to catch.

ARTE. *(Crying.)* Robert! Robert! beware!

HARVEY DUFF. Stop her screeching—she'll scare him off (*Sullivan crosses to* R. C.)

MOYA. Help! murther! thieves! fire!

HARVEY DUFF. Hould your yelp, or I'll choke you—och—gorra—she's bitin' me!

MOYA *(Cries.)* Don't come here—don't come.

(Stifles her cries with the handkerchief he tears from her head.)

KINCHELA. (*Looking over the parapet,* R.) We have lost his track.

HARVEY DUFF. Aye, but we have found it—here he comes—stand close now, an head him off. *(Kinchela disappears,* R. *The figure of Robert Ffolliott is seen emerging from one side of the*[43] *ruin,* L. *He advances, Sullivan and Doyle both start out. He looks from side to side.)* Stand and surrender! *(He rushes up the ruins to the window at the back.)* Fire, Sullivan—give it to him. Why don't you fire? *(Sullivan fires—the shot takes effect—he falls, and rolls down to a lower platform.)* Ha! ha! that stopped him—he's got it. (*He raises himself, and faintly tries to escape by a breach in the wall,* L.) Give it to them again! *(Doyle fires—He falls, and tumbling from one platform to another, rolls on his face on the stage—Reilly releasing Arte at second shot, gets* L. *of her.)*

KINCHELA. (*Appearing* R.) What are you about? Those two shots are the signal, and see the fire is lighted on Rathgarron Head.

HARVEY DUFF. 'Tis lighted too late!

(*Throws Moya up,* R. C.)

KINCHELA. No; for there comes the boat from the schooner, and see that man in the water swimming towards her? 'Tis Robert Ffolliott escaped!

HARVEY DUFF. Oho! if that's Robert Ffolliott, I'd like to know who's this?

CONN. *(Raising himself slowly, and allowing his hat and beardto fall back, and facing Harvey Duff with smile on hisblood-stained face).* The Shaughraun!

(He falls back. Moya, who has been released by Harvey Duff in his astonishment, utters a faint cry, and throws herself upon the body. A ray of moon-light striking through the ruined window, falls on the figure of the Saint on the Shrine, whose extended arms seem to invoke protection over the prostrate group).

ACT III.

SCENE I.—*Mrs. O'Kelly's Cottage.—Music.*

Enter FATHER DOLAN *and* CLAIRE, L.

FATHER DOLAN. Be patient, Claire!

CLAIRE. Patient! My cousin has disappeared—no trace of Arte can be found—Moya has also been spirited away—perhaps murdered, as they murdered Conn!

FATHER DOLAN. *(Knocking at door).* Mrs. O'Kelly, 'tis I—Father Dolan.

Enter MRS. O'KELLY, D. F. R

MRS. O'KELLY. (C.) Blessings on your path; it always leads to the poor and to the sore-hearted!

43. the] he.

FATHER DOLAN. (R.) This is a sad business! Did you hear why they killed your poor boy?

MRS. O'KELLY. *(Sobbing).* Because he'd got a fine shute of clothes on him; they shot at the man that wasn't in it, and they killed my poor boy!

CLAIRE (L). Did they bring him home insensible?

MRS. O'KELLY. No, miss—they brought him home on a shutter, an' there now he lies wid Tatthers beside him. The cratur' won't let a hand go near the body.

CLAIRE. Poor fellow! he met his death while aiding my brother to escape.

Enter MOLINEUX, L.

You see what your men have done!

MRS. O'KELLY. It was the polis, not the sodgers, murthered him. Don't blame the Captain, miss; God bless him, he was in my cabin before daylight—he never spoke a word, but he put five goolden pounds in my hand *(Crosses to him.);* and, thanks to himself, my Conn will have the finest wake this day! wid Nancy Malone and Biddy Madigan for keeners—There'll be ating and dhrinking, and six of the O'Kellys to carry him out as grand as a mimber o' parliament—Och hone!°—my darlin' boy, it will be a grand day for you, but your poor ould mother will be left alone in her cabin buried alive while yourself is going to glory—och—o—o hone! alas

[*Exit,* L., *crying.*

MOLINEUX. In the name of Bedlam does she propose to give a dance and a supper party in honour of the melancholy occasion!

CLAIRE. They are only going to wake poor Conn!

FATHER DOLAN. And your five pounds will be spent in whisky, and cakes, and consolation, and fiddlers, and grief, and meat and drink for the poor.

MOLINEUX. What a compound! You Irish do mix up your—

CLAIRE. *(Interrupting him.)* Never mind what we mix—have you discovered any traces of Arte and Moya? Have you done anything?

MOLINEUX. I've been thinking.

CLAIRE. Thinking! what's the good of thinking? My cousin Arte has been stolen—where is she? The country is full of police and soldiers, and yet two girls have been carried off under your noses—perhaps murdered, for all you know or care—and there you stand like a goose, thinking!

MOLINEUX. Pray don't be so impetuous. You Irish—

CLAIRE. I won't be called "You Irish."

MOLINEUX. I beg your pardon; you do make me so nervous.

CLAIRE. Oh, do I! My impetuosity didn't make you nervous last night, did it? No matter; go on—a penny for your thoughts.

MOLINEUX. If Miss O'Neal and Moya were present in the ruins when Conn was shot, they must have been witnesses of the deed. Since then they have disappeared. It struck me that those who killed the boy must have some reason for removing all evidences of the transaction.

FATHER DOLAN. He is right.

CLAIRE. Well?

MOLINEUX. I questioned the constabulary, and find they had no hand in it. The deed was done by a posse of fellows assembled to assist in the pursuit by a police agent named Harvey Duff!

FATHER DOLAN and CLAIRE. Harvey Duff!

MOLINEUX. You know him?

CLAIRE. He has thought it out while we have been blundering. Blinded by our tears, we could not see; deafened by our complaints, we could not hear. *(Seizes both his hands.)* Forgive me!

MOLINEUX. There she goes again! I've done nothing to deserve all this.

CLAIRE. Nothing! You have unearthed the fox, you have drawn the badger; now the rogue is in sight our course is clear. (*Crosses to* R.)

MOLINEUX. It is? I confess I don't see it!

FATHER DOLAN. These two girls were the only witnesses of the deed!

CLAIRE. And that is why they have been carried off?

FATHER DOLAN. No one else was present to prove how Conn was killed.

CONN. (*Looking out of the window,* F. L.) Yes; I was there!

ALL. Conn alive!

CONN. Whisht! No; I'm dead!

FATHER DOLAN. Why, you provoking vagabond—*(Up to him)*—is this the way you play upon our feelings? Are you hurt?

CONN. I've a crack over the lug, an' a scratch across the small o' me back. Sure, miss, if I hadn't dhrawed them to shoot, you'd have never had the signal.

MOLINEUX. Brave fellow! how did you escape?

CONN. I'll tell you, sir; but—whoo! gorra!—dead men tell no tales, an' here I am takin' away the characther of the corporation. When the masther got out of jail, there was Kinchela an' his gang waitin' outside to murdther us. We ga' them the slip; and while the masther got off, I led them away afther me to St. Bridget's. Then, afther I got them two shots out of them, I rouled down an' lay as quiet as a sack of pitaties.

CLAIRE. Arte and Moya were in the ruins?

(Goes to him.)

CONN. They were standing by and thrying to screech blue murther. "Stop their mouths," said a voice that I knew was Kinchela's. Sullivan and Reilly whipt them up and put them on a car that was waitin' outside. After that, sorra a thing I remember till I found myself laid out on a shutter, wid candles all around me, an' whisky bottles, an' cakes, an' sugar, an' lemon, an' tobacco, an' bacon, an' snuff, an' the devil in all! I thought I was in heaven.

FATHER DOLAN. And that's his idea of heaven! And you let your poor ould mother believe you dead?—you did not relieve her sorrow?

CONN. Would you have me spile a wake afther invitin' all the neighbours?

MOLINEUX. Will you allow me on this occasion to say, "You Irish—"

CLAIRE. Yes, and you need not say any more.

CONN. Then I remembered the polis would be wanting me for the share I had in helping tha masther to break jail. Ah, sir, don't let on to the mother—she'd never hould her whisht; an' I want to be dead, if you please, to folly up the blackguards that have hoult of Moya and Miss O'Neal.

MOLINEUX. Do you know the place where these ruffians resort?

CONN. I'm conceited I do.

FATHER DOLAN. I'll answer for him; he knows every disreputable den in the country.

CONN. What would you do now, if I didn't?

CLAIRE. Here comes your mother with the mourners.

CONN. Hoo! she'll find some of the whisky gone. *(Disappears.)*

CLAIRE. Now what's to be done?

MOLINEUX. I will proceed at once to Ballyragget House, and see Mr. Kinchela. I will confront him with this evidence.

CLAIRE. You don't know him.

MOLINEUX. I think I do; but he does not know me.

CLAIRE. You will fight him.

MOLINEUX. Oh, no. I looked in his eye; there's no fight there; men who bully women have the courage of the cur—there's no pluck in them. I shall take a guard and arrest him for aiding your brother to escape, that he might murder him safely during his flight.

CLAIRE. Who can prove it.

Enter ROBERT, L.

ROBERT. I can!

CLAIRE. Robert!

(Crosses to him—embrace.)

FATHER DOLAN. (R.) Good gracious, what brings you back?

ROBERT. The news I heard on board the schooner. A pardon has been granted to the Fenian prisoners.

CLAIRE. A pardon!

MOLINEUX. I congratulate you, sir. (*Shakes hands with Robert. Robert and Claire crosses to* R. C.) Oh, by Jove! Excuse my swearing, but a light breaks in upon me—Kinchela knew of this pardon. I'll go to Ballyragget House at once.

ROBERT. I have just come from there. I went to tax him with his villainy. He has fled.

MOLINEUX. I thought there was no fight in him.

CLAIRE. But Arte is in his power.

ROBERT. Arte in his power! what do you mean?

CLAIRE. He loves her—he has carried her off.

ROBERT. My wife and her fortune. Ha! he played for a high game.

MOLINEUX. And on finding he could not win, he stole half the stakes.

FATHER DOLAN. This man is in league with a desperate crew, half ruffians, half smugglers. Their dens, known only to themselves, are in the bogs and caves of the sea-shore.

ROBERT. I'll unearth him wherever he is. *(Music.)* I'll hunt him with every honest lad of the county Sligo in the pack, and kill him like a rat. (*Crosses to* R.)

MOLINEUX. I'll send over to Sligo, and get a warrant to arrest this fellow. I like to have the law on my side. If we are to have a hunt, let us have a license. Where shall I find you?

FATHER DOLAN. At my house.

CLAIRE. *(To Robert, who offers his arm to her.)* No, give your arm to Father Dolan.

FATHER DOLAN. Free, and at home! Heaven be praised!

ROBERT. Not free till Arte is so.

[*Exit with Father Dolan,* R.

CLAIRE. *(After watching them off, turns, and advances rapidly to Molineux.)* What's your Christian name, or have you English such things amongst you?

MOLINEUX. Yes, my Christian name is Harry!

CLAIRE. Harry!

[*Kissing him. She runs off, R. He assumes a military position and marches off, R., whistling "The British Grenadiers."*[44]

VOICES. (*Outside,* L.) Oh! Ohone! Oh, houldup. Don't give way.

Enter MRS. O'KELLY, NANCY MALONE, BIDDY MADIGAN, *and* PEASANTS, L.
DOYLE and WOMEN, *six or seven* MEN, *one* WOMAN. *They exeunt at once,* D. F.

MRS. O'KELLY. You are kindly welcome. The dark cloud is over the house, but—

NANCY. We come to share the sorrow that's in it this hour.

BIDDY. It will be a fine berrin', Mrs. O'Kelly. There will be a grand waste of victuals.

MRS. O'KELLY. Step inside, ma'am.

(They all enter the cabin. A woman enters L., and exits cottage.) Then Reilly, followed by Sullivan.—Music. The voices of the Keeners are heard inside singing an Irish lament. During this, other Peasants and Girls enter in couples, and go into cabin.—Scene changes.)

44. Traditional British marching song:
"Some talk of Alexander, and some of Hercules,
Of Hector and Lysander, and such great names as these.
But of all the world's great heroes, there's none that can compare.
With a tow, row, row, row, row, row, to the British Grenadiers."

SCENE II.—*Mrs. O'Kelly's Cabin (Interior.) Door in F. R., Fireplace* R. CONN *is lying on a shutter, L., supported by an old table, a three-legged stool, and a keg, Table* R., *covered with food and drinking cups, plates of snuff, jugs of punch, lighted candles in bottles, &c.—Tableau of an Irish Wake. A group of women around Conn,* L. C. MRS. O'KELLY *seated* R.C. MRS. MALONE and REILLY *near her, seated* R. SULLIVAN, DOYLE, *and Peasantry (male and female) at table,* R. *The women (seated) are rocking to and fro during the wail.*

CHORUS.—*"The Oolaghaun."*[45]

Male voices—

Och, Oolaghaun!—och, Oolaghaun!
Make his bed both wide and deep!
Och, Oolaghaun! och, Oolaghaun!
He's only gone to sleep!

Female voices—

Why did ye die?—oh, why did ye die?
And lave us all alone to cry?

Together—

Why did ye die?—why did ye die?
Laving us to sigh, och hone!
Why did ye die?—why did ye die?
Oolaghaun!—oh, Oolaghaun!

(During the following rhapsody the music of the wail and the chorus subdued recurs as if to animate the Keeners).

BIDDY. Oh, oh, oho! *(Rocking herself).* Oh, oo, Oolaghaun! The widdy had a son—an only son—wail for the widdy!

Chorus. (All)—
Why did ye die?—why did ye die?

BIDDY. I see her when she was a fair young girl—a fine girl, wid a child at her breast.

Chorus—
Laving us to sigh! Och, hone!

BIDDY. Then I see a proud woman wid a boy by her side. He was as bould as a bull-calf that runs beside of the cow.

Chorus—
Why did ye die?—why did ye die?

BIDDY. For the girl grew ould as the child grew big, and the woman grew wake as the boy grew strong. *(Rising, and flinging back her hair).* The boy grew strong, for she fed him wid her heart's blood. Ah, hogoola! Where is he now? Cowld in his bed! Why did ye die? *(Sits.)*

45. "Oolaghaun" may be a phonetic rendering of the Irish word *uileacán* = alas.

Chorus—
Laving us to sigh! Och, hone!

(*All the women on the* L. *join crowd up stage,* R. C.)

BIDDY. None was like him—none could compare, and—Good luck to ye, gi' me a dhrop of something to put the sperret in one, for the fire's getting low. *(Sullivan hands her his jug of punch.)*
MRS. O'KELLY. Oh, oh! its mighty consolin' to hear this. Mrs. Malone, you are not ating.
NANCY. No, ma'am, I'm drinkin'. I dhrink now and agin by way of variety. Biddy is not up to herself.
REILLY. Oh! wait till she'll rise on the top of a noggin.
BIDDY. *(After drinking places the jug beside her,* L, *and rises on low stool.)* He was brave! he was brave! he was open-handed! he had the heart of a lion, and the legs of a fox.

(Conn takes the jug, empties it quietly, and, unobserved by all, replaces it on stool.)

BIDDY. His voice was softer than the cuckoo of an evening, and sweeter than the blackbird afther a summer shower. Ye colleens, ye will nivir hear the voice of Conn again. *(Sits and blows her nose.)*
CONN. *(Aside.)* It's a mighty pleasant thing to die like this, once in a way, and hear all the good things said about ye afther you're dead and gone, when they can do you no good.
BIDDY. His name will be the pride of the O'Kellys for evermore.
CONN. *(Aside.)* I was a big blackguard when I was alive.
BIDDY. Noble and beautiful!
CONN. *(Aside.)* Ah! go on out o' that!
BIDDY. *(Taking up her jug.)* Oh, he was sweet and sthrong—Who the devil's been at my jug of punch? *(Goes up to crowd.)*
MRS. O'KELLY. *(Sobbing and rising.)* Nobody is dhrinkin'—yez all despise the occasion—if yez lave behind ye liquor enough to swim a fly—oh, hoo! There's a hole in your mug, Mr. Donovan, I'd be glad to see it in the bottle—oh, hoo!

(*Knock without,* R. D.)

SULLIVAN. What's that?

(The door is opened.)
Enter MOLINEUX.—*They all rise.*

MOLINEUX. I don't come to disturb this—a—melancholy—a—entertainment—I mean a—this festive solemnity—
MRS. O'KELLY. *(Wiping own chair for him with her apron.)* Heaven bless you for coming to admire the last of him. Here he is—ain't he beautiful? *(Leads him up.)*
MOLINEUX. *(Aside.)* The vagabond is winking at me. I've great mind to kick the keg from under him and send him reeling on the floor.

(*Sullivan offers him snuff,* R.)

MRS. O'KELLY. How often have I put him to bed as a child, and sung him to sleep! Now he will be put to bed with a shovel, and oh! the song was nivir sung that will awaken him.

MOLINEUX. If any words could put life into him, I came here to speak them. *(Music.)* Robert Ffolliott has been pardoned and has returned home a free man.

ALL. Hurroo! hurroo!

MOLINEUX. But his home is desolate, for the girl he loves has been stolen away. The man who robbed him of his liberty first, then his estate, has now stolen his betrothed.

ALL. Who is it?

MOLINEUX. Mr. Corry Kinchela. The ruffians who shot that brave fellow who lies there were led by Kinchela's agent, Harvey Duff.

ALL. Harvey Duff!

(Biddy seizes axe from L.*—Mrs. O'Kelly crosses to fire for poker.—Donovan gets scythe and kneels* R, *sharpening it with stone.—Tableaux.)*

(Molineux first encounters the edge of axe—stepping back, confronts Mrs. O'Kelly with the poker—which she flourishes savagely—and, crossing in front, eyes with his glass° Donovan sharpening scythe.) monocle

BIDDY. Harvey Duff sent my only boy across the say?

DONOVAN. I've a long reckoning agin him; but I've kept it warm in my heart.

MRS. O'KELLY. An' I've a short one, and there it lies!

(Pointing to Conn.)

ALL. Where is he?

MOLINEUX. Kinchela and his men are hiding in some den, where they hold Miss O'Neal and Moya prisoners.

ALL. Moya Dolan?

MOLINEUX. The niece of your minister!—the sweet-heart of poor Conn! My men shall aid you in the search; but you are familiar with every hole and corner in the county—you must direct it. Robert Ffolliott awaits you all at Suil-a-beg to lead the hunt—that is, after you have paid your melancholy respects to the Shaughraun.

MRS. O'KELLY. No; you could not plaze him betther than to go now. Bring back the news that you have revenged his murder, an' he'll go under the sod wid a light heart.

ALL. Hurroo! To Suil-a-beg!—To Suil-a-beg!

[*Exeunt rapidly, All,* R. D. *but Reilly and Sullivan. Molineux gives Conn a pinch of snuff—he sneezes.—Reilly and Sullivan turn and watch him off; then rush down* C.

REILLY. (R. C.) Sullivan, you must warn Kinchela. Quick! There's not an hour to lose.

SULLIVAN. (L. C.) Where shall I find him?

(Conn rises and listens.)

REILLY. At the Coot's Nest! The lugger came in last night. Tell him to get aboord—take the two women wid him, for he'll have to run for his life.

SULLIVAN. Ay, and, bedad, for ours too! If he's caught we're in for it.

(Conn creeps to door, and locks it very quietly.)

REILLY. I feel the rope around my neck. (*Going* R.)

SULLIVAN. The other end is chokin' me. (*Going* L.)

(As they turn to go they face Conn, they stagger back astonished.)

BOTH. Murdher, alive!

CONN. That's what I am. Murdher, alive! that will live to see you both hanged for it. *(Advances.)* I'll be at your wake, and begorra I'll give you both a fine characther. *(Sullivan and Reilly rush to the door.)* Asy, boys, asy! The dure is fast an' here's the key. You're in a fine thrap, ho! ho! You made a mistake last night. *(Sullivan whispers Reilly.)* Take it asy now.

(They rush to the tables R., *and each seizes a knife.)*

REILLY. (R.) Did ye forget ma bouchal° that ye're dead? boy

SULLIVAN. (*Advancing slowly,* L.) Sure, if we made a mistake last night we can repair it now!

CONN. Oh—tare an' ages—what'll I do?

(*Retreats behind table,* R.)

REILLY. We'll just lay you out agin comfortable where you wor. Devil a sowl will be the wiser.

CONN. Help! help!

(Reilly advances and receives the contents of a mug; then Sullivan, who gets the plate of snuff in his eyes. Conn jumps over the table, and makes for the window at back.)

REILLY. Screeching won't save ye! They are miles away by this time.

CONN. *(Rushing to window, and dashing the shutters open.)* Help!

(Reilly and Sullivan drag Conn back by the hair of his head, and throw him down.)

SULLIVAN. Shut the windy! I'll quiet him!

MOLINEUX *appears at window.*

MOLINEUX. *(Presenting revolver.)* Drop those knives! *(A pause.)* Do you hear what I said—drop those knives! *(They let their knives fall.)* Now open the door!

CONN. There's the key! *(Hands it to Reilly. Reilly doggedly unlocks the door.* MOLINEUX *appears at door and enters.)* Help me up! *(To Sullivan.)* The hangman will do as much for you, one day.

(Sullivan helps Conn to rise.)

MOLINEUX. (R. C.) Now! *(Reilly makes a start as if he would escape.)* If you put your head outside the cabin, I'll put a bullet in it! (*Reilly retires down stage,* R.) What men are these?

CONN. (L. C.) Two of Kinchela's chickens. They know the road we want to thraval.

MOLINEUX. Take that! *(Hands Conn the revolver.)* Do you know how to use it?

CONN. I'll thry! *(Turns to Sullivan.)* What part of the world would you[46] like to be sent to? *(Pointing weapon at him.)*

MOLINEUX. *(Drawing his sword and turning to Reilly.)* Attention, my friend! Now put your hands in your pockets! *(Repeats.—Reilly obeys him.)* Now take me direct to where your employer, Mr. Kinchela, has imprisoned Miss O'Neal; and if, on the road, you take your hands out of your pockets, and attempt to move beyond the reach of my sword, upon my honour, as an officer and a gentleman, I shall cut you down! Forward!

[*Exeunt, D. F. R.*

CONN. Attintion! Put your hand in my pocket. *(Sullivan obeys him.)* Now take me straight to where Moya Dolan is shut up; an' if ye stir a peg out o' that on the road, by the piper that played before Julius Caesar, I'll save the country six feet of rope. *(As they go out scene changes.)*

SCENE III.—*Hogan's Shanty. (Lights half down.)*

Enter ARTE *and* MOYA, L.

ARTE. 'Tis getting dark. Will they keep us another night in this fearful place?

MOYA. I don't care what becomes of me. I wish they would kill me, as they killed CONN—I've nothin' to live for!

ARTE. I have! I'll live to bring Kinchela to the dock, where he brought my Robert. I'll live to tear the mask from his face!

(*Crosses to* L.)

MOYA. I'd like to put my ten commandments on the face of Harvey Duff[47]—the murdherin' villain, if I should only live to see him go up a ladder, and spoil a market.[48]

Enter KINCHELA, D. F. L.

46. would you] you.

47. i.e., write (scratch) with her fingers on the face of Harvey, as the finger of God wrote the Ten Commandments on stone.

48. Executions were sometimes public spectacles done in what would be the main square of a provincial town where markets would normally be held.

KINCHELA. *(Crossing to Arte.)* You look pale; but I see you kape a proud lip still, Miss O'Neal. You despise me now, but afther another month or two, never fear, we'll get on finely together.

ARTE. Do you dream you can keep up here for a month? Why, before a week has passed there's not a sod in the county (*crosses to* C.) Sligo but will be turned up to search for us, and then we'll see who'll look the paler, you or I.

KINCHELA. Before midnight you will be safe on board a lugger that lies snug beside this shanty, and before daylight you and I will be on our way to a delightful retirement, where you and I will pass our honeymoon together.

MOYA. And what's to become of me?

(Music.)

Enter HARVEY DUFF, *with* MANGAN *and* DOYLE, R.

HARVEY DUFF. I'll take care of you! The wind is fair, and the tide will serve in an hour. Come, ladies, all on board is the word, if you plaze.

(Mangan and Doyle seize Arte and Moya.)

ARTE. Kinchela, I implore you not to add this cowardly act to your list of crimes! Release me and this girl, and, on my honour, I will bear no witness against you, nor against any concerned in last night's work.

KINCHELA. It is too late.

ARTE. *(Struggling with Doyle.)* Kinchela, if you have any respect—any love for me, will you see me outraged thus?

HARVEY DUFF. *(Aside to Kinchela.)* Ffolliott has returned.

KINCHELA. Ha! (*Crosses to* R.) Away with them!

MOYA. *(To Mangan.)* Lave your hould, I'll go asy!

(*Drops her cloak while struggling with Mangan, she releases herself and boxes his ears. Arte is taken off first by Doyle* R.)

HARVEY DUFF. (L.) Robert Ffolliott is pardoned, and he's huntin' the bogs this minute, with half the County Sligo at his back.

KINCHELA. Never fear, they can't discover this place till we are gone. No one ever knew of it but our own fellows.

HARVEY DUFF. And Conn, the Shaughraun.

KINCHELA. He is wiped out.

HARVEY DUFF. We are safe.

KINCHELA. Go, keep watch on the cliff (*crosses to* L.) while I get these girls aboard.

HARVEY DUFF. I'll be onaisy in my mind till we are clear o' this. [*Exit,* R.

KINCHELA. Robert Ffolliott pardoned, afther all the throuble I took to get him convicted? And this is the way a loyal man is thrated! I am betrayed. No matther; if[49] he can recover his estate, he can't recover

49. if] it.

his wife. She is mine—mine! She hates me now, but I concait she'll get over that. [*Exit*, R.

Enter CONN *and* SULLIVAN, D. F. L.

CONN. Not a sowl in it—you deceive me!

SULLIVAN. No, they are here! *(Points to the cloak.)* What's that?

CONN. Moya's cloak! *(He picks it up. Releases Sullivan, who creeps off while Conn examines cloak.)* 'Tis hers—she's here! Oh, he's slipped out of my pocket—he's off—gone to rouse up the whole pack! What'll I do? Where can I hide until the masther an' the Captain come up? They can't be far behind. If I could get behind one of them big hogsheads, or inside one o' them. Whisht! there was a cry. 'Twas Miss O'Neal's voice. I am only one agin twenty, but I'll make it lively for them while it lasts! [*Exit* R.

SCENE IV.—*Shed looking out upon a Rocky Cave) The topmasts of a ship are seen over the edge of the precipice. Bales, kegs, hogsheads, naval gear lie about* R. *and* L.—*Music.—Break of day.*

Enter HARVEY DUFF *rapidly*, 1 E. R. *He looks round, and he is very pale.*

HARVEY DUFF. Kinchela, hurry—quick!

Enter KINCHELA, L.

KINCHELA. What's the matter?

HARVEY DUFF. I was watching on the cliff above, where I could hear the shouts of the people in the glen as they hunted every hole in the rocks. I could see Robert Ffolliott and Miss Claire hounding them on; when I turned my eyes down here, and on this vary place where we are standing I saw—

KINCHELA. Who?

HARVEY DUFF. Conn, the Shaughraun!

KINCHELA. You are mad with fright. *(Up the rock.)*

HARVEY DUFF. So would you be, if you saw a dead man as plain as I saw him. *(Distant cries and shouts.)* D'ye hear them?—they are coming close to us!

KINCHELA. Go back to your post on the cliff, and keep watch while I get these women on board. We have no time to lose. Mangan! Doyle!

HARVEY DUFF. *(Who has been looking round.)* I'll be on my oath I saw him here! [*Exit*, R.

Enter MOYA *and* MANGAN, 1 E. L.

MOYA. Where do you want me to go?

KINCHELA. On board that ship below there.

MOYA. Do you think I'm a fly, or a seagull?

(*Down to corner*, L.)

KINCHELA. You see this ladder?—by that road you can gain the ledge below. There we'll find a basket—we'll send you down like a bucket in a well.
MOYA. If I don't choose to go down?
KINCHELA. Then you'll be carried, my beauty!
MOYA. Standoff!
KINCHELA. Tie her hands. Mangan, go get me a taste of rope!

[*He seizes her. Mangan exits,* 2. E. L.

MOYA. Help! help! Is there nivir a man within reach of my voice?
KINCHELA. Mangan, bring the rope, curse you!
MOYA. Help! murdher! fire!

(A shot is fired from the hogshead, R. *Kinchela throws up his hands—staggers, falls,* L. C. *Moya utters a cry, and falls on her knees,* R., *and covering her face with her hands. The hogshead rises a little—advances to Moya, and covers her like an extinguisher. The legs of* CONN *have been seen under the barrel as it moves. Enter* MANGAN, 2 E. L., *with the rope.* DOYLE *with* ARTE, 1 E. L. SULLIVAN, 2 E. L. *Sullivan kneels over Kinchela.)*

MANGAN. Who fired that shot?
DOYLE. She has killed him, and escaped!
ARTE. Brave girl! she has avenged me.
SULLIVAN. He's not dead. See, he moves! There's life in him still. *(Shouts outside.)*
DOYLE. They are coming!—away wid ye to the lugger. Quick!

(The men look off, R.)

SULLIVAN. Must we lave him here?

(Crosses to corner, R.)

DOYLE. We can't carry him down the ladder.

(During the foregoing Arte creeps to the back.)

SULLIVAN. Everyone for himself; the devil take the hindmost. *(Going up to rock piece.)*
ARTE. *(Who has lifted the end of the ladder.)* Stop where you are! *(Throws the ladder over.)* I have been your prisoner; now you are mine!

(Shouts outside nearer.) (The men look bewildered from side to side, and then rush off, 1 E. L. *Conn pops his head out from, the top of the hogshead, and looks out.)*

CONN. Is that you, miss?
ARTE. Conn, where's Moya?
CONN. She's inside. *(Shouts.)*

(Conn disappears, raises the hogshead. They emerge from it.)

HARVEY DUFF. *(Outside.)* Kinchela, away wid you—quick!
CONN. Stand aside. Here comes the flower of the flock. *(Shouts.)*

(*They retire—Arte to* L., *behind shed; Conn and Moya to* R.)

HARVEY DUFF *rushes on from* 1 E. R., *very pale.*

HARVEY DUFF. The crowd are upon us; we are betrayed! What's the matter, man? Up, I tell you! Are you mad or drunk? Stop, then; I'm off. *(Runs up to the back.)* The ladder gone!—gone! *(Runs to* KINCHELA.*)* Spake, man! What will we do?—what does it mean?

ARTE *appears,* L, MOYA, R, *from behind hogshead.*

MOYA. It means that the wind has changed and the tide doesn't serve.
ARTE. It means that you are on your way to a delightful retirement, where you and he will pass your honeymoon together.
HARVEY DUFF. (*Conn advances to his side,* R.) The murdher's out.
CONN. And you are in for it. *(Shouts outside.)* D'ye hear them cries —the hounds are on your track, Harvey Duff!
HARVEY DUFF. (L.) What will I do? What will I do?
CONN. Say your prayers, if ever you knew any—for your time is come. Look! There they come—down the cliff side. Ha! they've caught sight of you.

(Shouts.—Harvey Duff rushes up to the edge of the precipice, looks over, wrings his hands in terror.)

CONN. D'ye see that wild ould woman, wid the knife? that's Bridget Madigan, whose son's life you swore away.
HARVEY DUFF. Save me!—you can—they will tear me into rags. *(To Arte, on his knees.)*
CONN. D'ye know Andy Donovan? that's him with the scythe! You sent his brother across the say! *(Shouts outside.)* Egorra, he knows you! Look at him!
HARVEY DUFF. *(On his knees, to Conn.)* Spare me! pity me!
CONN. Ay, as you spared me! as you spared them at whose side you knelt before the altar!—as you pitied them whose salt you ate, but whose blood you dhrank! There's death coming down upon you from above!—there's death waiting for you below! Now, informer, take your choice!

(Shouts.—Harvey Duff, bewildered with fright, and running alternately to the edge of the cliff and back to look at the approaching crowd, staggers like a drunken man, uttering inarticulate cries of fear.)

(The crowd, headed by BIDDY MADIGAN, NANCY MALONE, *rush in at* 1st *and* 2nd E. R. *Uttering a scream of terror, Harvey Duff leaps over the cliff. The crowd pursue him to the edge and lean over.)*

Enter ROBERT FFOLLIOTT, CLAIRE, FATHER DOLAN, *and* CONSTABULARY, R.—*Enter* MOLINEUX, *followed by* SERGEANT *and* SIX SOLDIERS, *with* MANGAN, SULLIVAN, *and* DOYLE *in custody,* 2 E. L.

ROBERT (L. *Embracing Arte.*) Arte!
CLAIRE. Has the villain escaped?
MOLINEUX. I've bagged a few; but I've missed the principal offender.
CONN. I didn't—there's my bird.
FATHER DOLAN. Is he dead?

(Molineux approaches Kinchela, and examines him).

MOLINEUX. I fear not; the bullet has entered here, but it has struck something in his breast. *(Draws out a pocket-book).* This pocket-book has saved his life!

(He hands it to Father Dolan, who opens it, draws out letter, and reads).

KINCHELA. *(Reviving and rising).* Where am I?
MOLINEUX. You are in custody.
KINCHELA. What for?
MOLINEUX. For an attempt to assassinate this gentleman.
KINCHELA. He was a felon, escaping from justice!
FATHER DOLAN. (R. C.) He was a free man, and you knew it, as this letter proves!

(The crowd utter a cry of rage, and advance towards Kinchela. Father Dolan stands between them and him. Kinchela flies for protection to the constabulary, R.)

KINCHELA. Save me—protect me!
FATHER DOLAN. *(Facing the crowd.)* Stand back!—do you hear me. Must I speak twice?

(The crowd retire, and lower their weapons.)

MOLINEUX. Take him away! *(Crosses to Claire.)*
KINCHELA. Yes, take me away, quick—don't you hear? or them divils won't give you the chance.

[*Exit with constabulary,* R. 2 E.

MRS. O'KELLY. (*Outside,* R. 1 E.) Where's my boy? Where is he?
CONN. Och, murdher—here's the ould mother! Hide me!

Enter MRS. O'KELLY.

MRS. O'KELLY. Where is he—where is my vagabone? *(Father Dolan. brings him forward by the ear.)* Oh, Conn, ye thief o' the world—my boy—my darlin'!

(Falls on his neck.)

CONN. Whisht, mother, don't cry. See this—I'll never be kilt again.

MOYA. (R. C.) Sure, if he hadn't have been murdhered, he couldn't have saved us.

MRS. O'KELLY. And after letting me throw all the money away over the wake!

(Goes up with Conn and Moya.)

MOLINEUX. Turn the ceremony into a wedding. I really don't see you Irish make much distinction.

CLAIRE. (R.) I believe that in England the wedding often turns out the more melancholy occasion of the two.

MOLINEUX. (R. C.) Will you try?

ROBERT. He has earned you, Claire. I give my consent.

ARTE. But what is to become of Conn. Father Dolan will never give his consent.

FATHER DOLAN. *(To Conn.)* Come here. Will you reform?

CONN. I don't know what that is, but I will!

FATHER DOLAN. Will you mend your ways, and your coat? No; you can't! How do I know but that you will go poaching of a night?

CONN. Moya will go bail I won't.

FATHER DOLAN. And the drink?

MOYA. I will take care there is no hole in the thimble.

FATHER DOLAN. I won't trust either of you—you have deceived me so often. Can you find anyone to answer for you?

CONN. Oh, murdher! What'll I do? Divil a friend I have in the world, barrin Tatthers! *(Moya whispers in his ear.)* Oh! they won't!

MOYA. Thry!

CONN. *(To the audience.)* She says you will go bail for me.

MOYA. I didn't!

CONN. You did!

MOYA. I didn't!

CONN. You are the only friend I have. Long life t'ye!—Many a time have you looked over my faults—will you be blind to them now, and hould out your hands once more to a poor Shaughraun?

OMNES. Hurroo! Hurroo! *(Till curtain.)*

Disposition of the Characters at the Fall of the Curtain.

PEASANTS. SOLDIERS

BIDDY.

MANGAN.

REILLY.

SULLIVAN.

DOYLE.

SEARGEANT.

CLAIRE. MOL. MRS. O'K. MOYA. CONN. FATHER D. ROBERT. ARTE.

R. L.

The Playboy of the Western World

John Millington Synge was born in 1871 in Rathfarnham, Ireland (a short distance south of Dublin) to an affluent family of the Anglo-Irish Protestant Ascendancy, the youngest of eight children. Landowners whose income primarily came from their tenants, and descended from fervent defenders of the Church of Ireland, the Synges had as much as any to lose from Irish independence, yet Synge grew up to be a nationalist in his politics, and, after reading Darwin in his teens, an atheist. His drama, however, enraged nationalists, and his marriage proposals to the religious Cherrie Matheson were turned down because of his religious views. Synge intended to be a musician and composer, and studied at the Royal Irish Academy of Music, in Europe, and at Trinity College, Dublin, but ultimately developed literary ambitions. In 1896 he met William Butler Yeats in Paris. Yeats suggested he live on the Aran Islands. Synge spent five summers there starting in 1898 learning the Irish language and studying folklore and, ultimately, writing *The Aran Islands,* which was published by Jack Yeats in 1907. He subsequently claimed that the language of his plays was shaped by the Hiberno-English of the islanders, but other playwrights, such as T. C. Murray, while admiring the poetical nature of his dialogue, denied that it was an accurate representation of how people in the west of Ireland spoke.

Synge began submitting plays to the Irish National Theatre Society in 1900, but his first plays accepted were the comedy *The Shadow of the Glen* (first performed in 1903) and the tragedy *Riders to the Sea* (first performed in 1904). The nationalist journalist Arthur Griffith attacked the former because of its sympathetic portrayal of an adulterous Irish wife, and the latter was criticized by the Irish nationalist Patrick Pearse (subsequently executed by the British because of the 1916 Easter Rising) for its fatalistic paganism. Synge's nationalism was of a different variety not merely from that of Griffith and Pearse but from that of Yeats. In his view the Irish language was probably not

My copy text is from *The Complete Plays of John M. Synge* (New York: Random House, 1935), 1–80.

going to survive, the influence of the Roman Catholic Church was unhelpful, and Ireland needed to strike out a new identity for itself. It is therefore unsurprising that *The Playboy of the Western World* (1907) was greeted with a week of riots. There were many objections to the play—the use of the word "shifts," the portrayal of the Irish as ignorant and prone to violence, and even the idea of a national theater in the English language—but the plot of the play alone would have enraged many. The news that Christy has killed his father makes him a hero, until they see him attempt to do so in their village, and the villagers recoil from the act. The villagers are both drawn to violence and too cowardly to face either the necessity for it or the consequences of it. The absent priest who Shawn defers to is a symbol of both colonial and religious oppression, yet Pegeen will marry Shawn and presumably give birth to scrawny, sickly children who also will be unable to escape the narrow life of rural Ireland. Christy, son of Mahon, can redeem only himself. The play angered the Irish and Irish Americans for years, creating controversy in the Irish Players' tour in the United States in 1911, including a suppression of the play in Philadelphia. Underrated in his own lifetime, Synge died of Hodgkin's disease in 1909.

Synge saw in Irish-English a naturally poetic language that would allow his drama to escape the confinement of realism. And the Abbey Theatre was the right venue for his work. Because the stage of the Abbey was so small, it perforce eschewed spectacle in favor of an emphasis on the language of the plays. The acting style of the company was also ideally suited for Synge; very little "business" occurred during any actor's speech. Instead the other actors would efface themselves so that the utterance itself had primacy in production; two characters exchanging a glance while another character is speaking is an enormous reaction within the Abbey style. Eugene O'Neill is one of many playwrights influenced by Synge's work, and the Irish Players' tour had a role in inspiring the Little Theater Movement in the United States.

The Playboy of the Western World

A Comedy in Three Acts

By J. M. Synge

PREFACE

In writing THE PLAYBOY OF THE WESTERN WORLD, as in my other plays, I have used one or two words only that I have not heard among the country people of Ireland, or spoken in my own nursery before I could read the newspapers. A certain number of the phrases I employ I have heard also from herds and fishermen along the coast from Kerry to Mayo, or from beggar-women and ballad singers nearer Dublin; and I am glad to acknowledge how much I owe to the folk imagination of these fine people. Anyone who has lived in real intimacy with the Irish peasantry will know that the wildest sayings and ideas in this play are tame indeed, compared with the fancies one may hear in any little hillside cabin in Geesala, or Carraroe, or Dingle Bay.[1] All art is a collaboration;

1. All locations in the west of Ireland where many people would have been native speakers of Irish: Geesala is a village in County Mayo, Carraroe is in Connemara in County Galway, and Dingle Bay is in County Kerry.

and there is little doubt that in the happy ages of literature, striking and beautiful phrases were as ready to the story-teller's or the playwright's hand, as the rich cloaks and dresses of his time. It is probable that when the Elizabethan dramatist took his ink-horn and sat down to his work he used many phrases that he had just heard, as he sat at dinner, from his mother or his children. In Ireland, those of us who know the people have the same privilege. When I was writing "The Shadow of the Glen," some years ago, I got more aid than any learning could have given me from a chink in the floor of the old Wicklow house where I was staying, that let me hear what was being said by the servant girls in the kitchen. This matter, I think, is of importance, for in countries where the imagination of the people, and the language they use, is rich and living, it is possible for a writer to be rich and copious in his words, and at the same time to give the reality, which is the root of all poetry, in a comprehensive and natural form. In the modern literature of towns, however, richness is found only in sonnets, or prose poems, or in one or two elaborate books that are far away from the profound and common interests of life. One has, on one side, Mallarme and Huysmans producing this literature; and on the other, Ibsen and Zola dealing with the reality of life in joyless and pallid words.[2] On the stage one must have reality, and one must have joy; and that is why the intellectual modern drama has failed, and people have grown sick of the false joy of the musical comedy, that has been given them in place of the rich joy found only in what is superb and wild in reality. In a good play every speech should be as fully flavoured as a nut or apple, and such speeches cannot be written by anyone who works among people who have shut their lips on poetry. In Ireland, for a few years more, we have a popular imagination that is fiery and magnificent, and tender; so that those of us who wish to write start with a chance that is not given to writers in places where the springtime of the local life has been forgotten, and the harvest is a memory only, and the straw has been turned into bricks.

J. M. S.
January 21st, 1907.

PERSONS

CHRISTOPHER MAHON.

OLD MAHON, his father, a squatter.

MICHAEL JAMES FLAHERTY (called MICHAEL JAMES), a publican.

MARGARET FLAHERTY (called PEGEEN MIKE), his daughter.

WIDOW QUIN, a woman of about thirty.

SHAWN KEOUGH, her cousin, a young farmer.

PHILLY CULLEN AND JIMMY FARRELL, small farmers.

SARA TANSEY, SUSAN BRADY, AND HONOR BLAKE, village girls.

A BELLMAN.

SOME PEASANTS.

2. Stéphane Mallarmé (1842–98), French symbolist poet; Joris-Karl Huysmans (1848–1907), French novelist who began as a naturalist writer but embraced "decadence" and aestheticism; Émile Zola (1840–1902), French playwright and novelist who epitomized literary naturalism; Henrik Ibsen (1828–1906), Norwegian dramatist who rejected the romanticism of his early works for uncompromising realism.

The action takes place near a village, on a wild coast of Mayo. The first Act passes on an evening of autumn, the other two Acts on the following day.

ACT I.

SCENE: [*Country public-house or shebeen, very rough and untidy. There is a sort of counter on the right with shelves, holding many bottles and jugs, just seen above it. Empty barrels stand near the counter. At back, a little to left of counter, there is a door into the open air, then, more to the left, there is a settle with shelves above it, with more jugs, and a table beneath a window. At the left there is a large open fire-place, with turf fire, and a small door into inner room. Pegeen, a wild looking but fine girl, of about twenty, is writing at table. She is dressed in the usual peasant dress.*]

PEGEEN—[*slowly as she writes.*]—Six yards of stuff for to make a yellow gown. A pair of lace boots with lengthy heels on them and brassy eyes. A hat is suited for a wedding-day. A fine tooth comb. To be sent with three barrels of porter in Jimmy Farrell's creel cart[3] on the evening of the coming Fair to Mister Michael James Flaherty. With the best compliments of this season. Margaret Flaherty.

SHAWN KEOGH—[*a fat and fair young man comes in as she signs, looks round awkwardly, when he sees she is alone.*]—Where's himself?

PEGEEN—[*without looking at him.*]—He's coming. *(She directs the letter.)* To Mister Sheamus Mulroy, Wine and Spirit Dealer, Castlebar.[4]

SHAWN—[*uneasily.*]—I didn't see him on the road.

PEGEEN. How would you see him *(licks stamp and puts it on letter)* and it dark night this half hour gone by?

SHAWN—[*turning towards the door again.*]—I stood a while outside wondering would I have a right to pass on or to walk in and see you, Pegeen Mike *(comes to fire),* and I could hear the cows breathing, and sighing in the stillness of the air, and not a step moving any place from this gate to the bridge.

PEGEEN—[*putting letter in envelope.*]—It's above at the cross-roads he is, meeting Philly Cullen; and a couple more are going along with him to Kate Cassidy's wake.

SHAWN—[*looking at her blankly.*]—And he's going that length in the dark night?

PEGEEN—[*impatiently.*] He is surely, and leaving me lonesome on the scruff of the hill. *(She gets up and puts envelope on dresser, then winds clock.)* Isn't it long the nights are now, Shawn Keogh, to be leaving a poor girl with her own self counting the hours to the dawn of day?

3. Cart carrying a wicker basket.
4. The largest town in County Mayo.

SHAWN—[*with awkward humour.*]—If it is, when we're wedded in a short while you'll have no call to complain, for I've little will to be walking off to wakes or weddings in the darkness of the night.

PEGEEN—[*with rather scornful good humour.*]—You're making mighty certain, Shaneen, that I'll wed you now.

SHAWN. Aren't we after making a good bargain, the way we're only waiting these days on Father Reilly's dispensation[5] from the bishops, or the Court of Rome.

PEGEEN—[*looking at him teasingly, washing up at dresser.*]—It's a wonder Shaneen, the Holy Father'd be taking notice of the likes of you; for if I was him I wouldn't bother with this place where you'll meet none but Red Linahan, has a squint in his eye, and Patcheen is lame in his heel, or the mad Mulrannies were driven from California and they lost in their wits. We're a queer lot these times to go troubling the Holy Father on his sacred seat.

SHAWN—[*scandalized.*] If we are, we're as good this place as another, maybe, and as good these times as we were for ever.

PEGEEN—[*with scorn.*]—As good, is it? Where now will you meet the like of Daneen Sullivan knocked the eye from a peeler,[6] or Marcus Quin, God rest him, got six months for maiming ewes,[7] and he a great warrant to tell stories of holy Ireland till he'd have the old women shedding down tears about their feet. Where will you find the like of them, I'm saying?

SHAWN—[*timidly.*] If you don't it's a good job, maybe; for *(with peculiar emphasis on the words)* Father Reilly has small conceit to have that kind walking around and talking to the girls.

PEGEEN—[*impatiently, throwing water from basin out of the door.*] — Stop tormenting me with Father Reilly *(imitating his voice)* when I'm asking only what way I'll pass these twelve hours of dark, and not take my death with the fear. [*Looking out of door.*]

SHAWN—[*timidly.*] Would I fetch you the widow Quin, maybe?

PEGEEN. Is it the like of that murderer? You'll not, surely.

SHAWN—[*going to her, soothingly.*]—Then I'm thinking himself will stop along with you when he sees you taking on, for it'll be a long night-time with great darkness, and I'm after feeling a kind of fellow above in the furzy ditch,° groaning wicked like a maddening dog, the way it's good cause you have, maybe, to be fearing now. bank

PEGEEN—[*turning on him sharply.*]—What's that? Is it a man you seen?

SHAWN—[*retreating.*] I couldn't see him at all; but I heard him groaning

5. Permission for a marriage to occur when ecclesiastical law would normally not permit it (such as the marriage of cousins)

6. British slang for a police officer, derived from Sir Robert Peel, a reformer of British law enforcement.

7. Damaging the landlord's livestock was a traditional form of agrarian protest in Ireland.

out, and breaking his heart. It should have been a young man from his words speaking.

PEGEEN—[*going after him.*]—And you never went near to see was he hurted or what ailed him at all?

SHAWN. I did not, Pegeen Mike. It was a dark, lonesome place to be hearing the like of him.

PEGEEN. Well, you're a daring fellow, and if they find his corpse stretched above in the dews of dawn, what'll you say then to the peelers, or the Justice of the Peace?

SHAWN—[*thunderstruck.*] I wasn't thinking of that. For the love of God, Pegeen Mike, don't let on I was speaking of him. Don't tell your father and the men is coming above; for if they heard that story, they'd have great blabbing this night at the wake.

PEGEEN. I'll maybe tell them, and I'll maybe not.

SHAWN. They are coming at the door, Will you whisht, I'm saying?

PEGEEN. Whisht yourself.

[*She goes behind counter. Michael James, fat jovial publican,° comes in followed by Philly Cullen, who is thin and mistrusting, and Jimmy Farrell, who is fat and amorous, about forty-five.*] pub owner

MEN—[*together.*]—God bless you. The blessing of God on this place.

PEGEEN. God bless you kindly.

MICHAEL—[*to men who go to the counter.*]—Sit down now, and take your rest. *(Crosses to Shawn at the fire.)* And how is it you are, Shawn Keogh? Are you coming over the sands to Kate Cassidy's wake?

SHAWN. I am not, Michael James. I'm going home the short cut to my bed.

PEGEEN—[*speaking across the counter.*]—He's right too, and have you no shame, Michael James, to be quitting off for the whole night, and leaving myself lonesome in the shop?

MICHAEL—[*good-humouredly.*] Isn't it the same whether I go for the whole night or a part only? and I'm thinking it's a queer daughter you are if you'd have me crossing backward through the Stooks of the Dead Women,[8] with a drop taken.

PEGEEN. If I am a queer daughter, it's a queer father'd be leaving me lonesome these twelve hours of dark, and I piling the turf with the dogs barking, and the calves mooing, and my own teeth rattling with the fear.

JIMMY—[*flatteringly.*]—What is there to hurt you, and you a fine, hardy girl would knock the head of any two men in the place?

PEGEEN—[*working herself up.*]—Isn't there the harvest boys with their tongues red for drink, and the ten tinkers is camped in the east glen, and the thousand militia—bad cess° to them!—walking idle through luck

8. Unidentified, but from context a rock formation shaped like hay stacks.

the land.[9] There's lots surely to hurt me, and I won't stop alone in it, let himself do what he will.

MICHAEL. If you're that afeard, let Shawn Keogh stop along with you. It's the will of God, I'm thinking, himself should be seeing to you now. [*They all turn on Shawn.*]

SHAWN—[*in horrified confusion.*]—I would and welcome, Michael James, but I'm afeard of Father Reilly; and what at all would the Holy Father and the Cardinals of Rome be saying if they heard I did the like of that?

MICHAEL—[*with contempt.*]—God help you! Can't you sit in by the hearth with the light lit and herself beyond in the room? You'll do that surely, for I've heard tell there's a queer fellow above, going mad or getting his death, maybe, in the gripe° of the ditch, so she'd be safer this night with a person here. hollow

SHAWN—[*with plaintive despair.*]—I'm afeard of Father Reilly, I'm saying. Let you not be tempting me, and we near married itself.

PHILLY—[*with cold contempt.*]—Lock him in the west room. He'll stay then and have no sin to be telling to the priest.

MICHAEL—[*to Shawn, getting between him and the door.*]—Go up now.

SHAWN—[*at the top of his voice.*]—Don't stop me, Michael James. Let me out of the door, I'm saying, for the love of the Almighty God. Let me out *(trying to dodge past him)*. Let me out of it, and may God grant you His indulgence in the hour of need.

MICHAEL—[*loudly.*] Stop your noising, and sit down by the hearth. [*Gives him a push and goes to counter laughing.*]

SHAWN—[*turning back, wringing his hands.*]—Oh, Father Reilly and the saints of God, where will I hide myself to-day? Oh, St. Joseph and St. Patrick and St. Brigid, and St. James, have mercy on me now!

[*Shawn turns round, sees door clear, and makes a rush for it.*]

MICHAEL—[*catching him by the coattail.*]—You'd be going, is it?

SHAWN—[*screaming.*] Leave me go, Michael James, leave me go, you old Pagan, leave me go, or I'll get the curse of the priests on you, and of the scarlet-coated bishops of the courts of Rome. [*With a sudden movement he pulls himself out of his coat, and disappears out of the door, leaving his coat in Michael's hands.*]

MICHAEL—[*turning round, and holding up coat.*]—Well, there's the coat of a Christian man. Oh, there's sainted glory this day in the lonesome west; and by the will of God I've got you a decent man, Pegeen, you'll have no call to be spying after if you've a score of young girls, maybe, weeding in your fields.

PEGEEN [*taking up the defence of her property.*]—What right have you

9. Pegeen expresses fear of migrant harvest workers returning from Scotland and England, "tinkers," a perjorative term for Irish gypsies, and English garrison soldiers, respectively.

to be making game of a poor fellow for minding the priest, when it's your own the fault is, not paying a penny pot-boy to stand along with me and give me courage in the doing of my work? [*She snaps the coat away from him, and goes behind counter with it.*]

MICHAEL—[*taken aback.*]—Where would I get a pot-boy? Would you have me send the bell-man screaming in the streets of Castlebar?

SHAWN—[*opening the door a chink and putting in his head, in a small voice.*]—Michael James!

MICHAEL—[*imitating him.*]—What ails you?

SHAWN. The queer dying fellow's beyond looking over the ditch. He's come up, I'm thinking, stealing your hens. *(Looks over his shoulder.)* God help me, he's following me now *(he runs into room),* and if he's heard what I said, he'll be having my life, and I going home lonesome in the darkness of the night. [*For a perceptible moment they watch the door with curiosity. Some one coughs outside. Then Christy Mahon, a slight young man, comes in very tired and frightened and dirty.*]

CHRISTY—[*in a small voice.*]—God save all here!

MEN. God save you kindly.

CHRISTY—[*going to the counter.*]—I'd trouble you for a glass of porter, woman of the house. [*He puts down coin.*]

PEGEEN—[*serving him.*]—You're one of the tinkers, young fellow, is beyond camped in the glen?

CHRISTY. I am not; but I'm destroyed walking.

MICHAEL—[*patronizingly.*] Let you come up then to the fire. You're looking famished with the cold.

CHRISTY. God reward you. *(He takes up his glass and goes a little way across to the left, then stops and looks about him.)* Is it often the police do be coming into this place, master of the house?

MICHAEL. If you'd come in better hours, you'd have seen "Licensed for the sale of Beer and Spirits, to be consumed on the premises," written in white letters above the door, and what would the polis want spying on me, and not a decent house within four miles, the way every living Christian is a bona fide,[10] saving one widow alone?

CHRISTY—[*with relief.*]—It's a safe house, so. [*He goes over to the fire, sighing and moaning. Then he sits down, putting his glass beside him and begins gnawing a turnip, too miserable to feel the others staring at him with curiosity.*]

MICHAEL—[*going after him.*]—Is it yourself fearing the polis? You're wanting, maybe?

CHRISTY. There's many wanting.

MICHAEL. Many surely, with the broken harvest and the ended wars.[11]

10. In Ireland a person travelling more than three miles could be served after legal hours.

11. Both the Land Wars of the second half of the nineteenth century in Ireland, where (Catholic) Irish tenant farmers pressured (Protestant) landlords to sell their lands, and the Boer War in South Africa from 1899–1902.

(He picks up some stockings, etc., that are near the fire, and carries them away furtively.) It should be larceny, I'm thinking?

CHRISTY—[*dolefully.*] I had it in my mind it was a different word and a bigger.

PEGEEN. There's a queer lad. Were you never slapped in school, young fellow, that you don't know the name of your deed?

CHRISTY—[*bashfully.*] I'm slow at learning, a middling scholar only.

MICHAEL. If you're a dunce itself, you'd have a right to know that larceny's robbing and stealing. Is it for the like of that you're wanting?

CHRISTY—[*with a flash of family pride.*]—And I the son of a strong farmer *(with a sudden qualm),* God rest his soul, could have bought up the whole of your old house a while since, from the butt of his tailpocket, and not have missed the weight of it gone.

MICHAEL—[*impressed.*] If it's not stealing, it's maybe something big.

CHRISTY—[*flattered.*] Aye; it's maybe something big.

JIMMY. He's a wicked-looking young fellow. Maybe he followed after a young woman on a lonesome night.

CHRISTY—[*shocked.*] Oh, the saints forbid, mister; I was all times a decent lad.

PHILLY—[*turning on Jimmy.*]—You're a silly man, Jimmy Farrell. He said his father was a farmer a while since, and there's himself now in a poor state. Maybe the land was grabbed from him, and he did what any decent man would do.

MICHAEL—[*to Christy, mysteriously.*]—Was it bailiffs?

CHRISTY. The divil a one.

MICHAEL. Agents?

CHRISTY. The divil a one.

MICHAEL. Landlords?

CHRISTY—[*peevishly.*] Ah, not at all, I'm saying. You'd see the like of them stories on any little paper of a Munster town. But I'm not calling to mind any person, gentle, simple, judge or jury, did the like of me. [*They all draw nearer with delighted curiosity.*]

PHILLY. Well, that lad's a puzzle-the-world.

JIMMY. He'd beat Dan Davies' circus, or the holy missioners making sermons on the villainy of man. Try him again, Philly.

PHILLY. Did you strike golden guineas out of solder, young fellow, or shilling coins itself?

CHRISTY. I did not, mister, not sixpence nor a farthing coin.

JIMMY. Did you marry three wives maybe? I'm told there's a sprinkling have done that among the holy Luthers of the preaching north.[12]

CHRISTY—[*shyly.*]—I never married with one, let alone with a couple or three.

PHILLY. Maybe he went fighting for the Boers, the like of the man beyond, was judged to be hanged, quartered and drawn. Were you off

12. i.e., among the Protestants of Ulster.

east, young fellow, fighting bloody wars for Kruger[13] and the freedom of the Boers?

CHRISTY. I never left my own parish till Tuesday was a week.

PEGEEN—[*coming from counter.*]—He's done nothing, so. *(To Christy.)* If you didn't commit murder or a bad, nasty thing, or false coining, or robbery, or butchery, or the like of them, there isn't anything that would be worth your troubling for to run from now. You did nothing at all.

CHRISTY—[*his feelings hurt.*]—That's an unkindly thing to be saying to a poor orphaned traveller, has a prison behind him, and hanging before, and hell's gap gaping below.

PEGEEN [*with a sign to the men to be quiet.*]—You're only saying it. You did nothing at all. A soft lad the like of you wouldn't slit the windpipe of a screeching sow.

CHRISTY—[*offended.*] You're not speaking the truth.

PEGEEN—[*in mock rage.*]—Not speaking the truth, is it? Would you have me knock the head of you with the butt of the broom?

CHRISTY—[*twisting round on her with a sharp cry of horror.*]—Don't strike me. I killed my poor father, Tuesday was a week, for doing the like of that.

PEGEEN [*with blank amazement.*]—Is it killed your father?

CHRISTY—[*subsiding.*] With the help of God I did surely, and that the Holy Immaculate Mother may intercede for his soul.

PHILLY—[*retreating with Jimmy.*]—There's a daring fellow.

JIMMY. Oh, glory be to God!

MICHAEL—[*with great respect.*]—That was a hanging crime, mister honey. You should have had good reason for doing the like of that.

CHRISTY—[*in a very reasonable tone.*]—He was a dirty man, God forgive him, and he getting old and crusty, the way I couldn't put up with him at all.

PEGEEN. And you shot him dead?

CHRISTY—[*shaking his head.*]—I never used weapons. I've no license, and I'm a law-fearing man.

MICHAEL. It was with a hilted knife maybe? I'm told, in the big world it's bloody knives they use.

CHRISTY—[*loudly, scandalized.*]—Do you take me for a slaughter-boy?

PEGEEN. You never hanged him, the way Jimmy Farrell hanged his dog from the license, and had it screeching and wriggling three hours at the butt of a string, and himself swearing it was a dead dog, and the peelers swearing it had life?[14]

CHRISTY. I did not then. I just riz the loy° and let fall the edge of it on the ridge of his skull, and he went down at my feet like an empty sack, and never let a grunt or groan from him at all. spade

13. Stephen Kruger (1825–1904) was the leader of the Boer rebellion against the United Kingdom; some Irishmen served in the Boer forces.

14. Rather than pay a license fee for a dog, Jimmy has killed it.

MICHAEL—[*making a sign to Pegeen to fill Christy's glass.*]—And what way weren't you hanged, mister? Did you bury him then?

CHRISTY—[*considering.*] Aye. I buried him then. Wasn't I digging spuds in the field?

MICHAEL. And the peelers never followed after you the eleven days that you're out?

CHRISTY—[*shaking his head.*]—Never a one of them, and I walking forward facing hog, dog, or divil on the highway of the road.

PHILLY—[*nodding wisely.*]—It's only with a common week-day kind of a murderer them lads would be trusting their carcase, and that man should be a great terror when his temper's roused.

MICHAEL. He should then. *(To Christy.)* And where was it, mister honey, that you did the deed?

CHRISTY—[*looking at him with suspicion.*]—Oh, a distant place, master of the house, a windy corner of high, distant hills.

PHILLY—[*nodding with approval.*]—He's a close man, and he's right, surely.

PEGEEN. That'd be a lad with the sense of Solomon to have for a pot-boy, Michael James, if it's the truth you're seeking one at all.

PHILLY. The peelers is fearing him, and if you'd that lad in the house there isn't one of them would come smelling around if the dogs itself were lapping poteen° from the dungpit of the yard. moonshine

JIMMY. Bravery's a treasure in a lonesome place, and a lad would kill his father, I'm thinking, would face a foxy divil with a pitchpike on the flags of hell.

PEGEEN. It's the truth they're saying, and if I'd that lad in the house, I wouldn't be fearing the loosed kharki cut-throats,[15] or the walking dead.

CHRISTY—[*swelling with surprise and triumph.*]—Well, glory be to God!

MICHAEL—[*with deference.*]—Would you think well to stop here and be pot-boy, mister honey, if we gave you good wages, and didn't destroy you with the weight of work?

SHAWN—[*coming forward uneasily.*]—That'd be a queer kind to bring into a decent quiet household with the like of Pegeen Mike.

PEGEEN—[*very sharply.*]—Will you whisht? Who's speaking to you?

SHAWN—[*retreating.*] A bloody-handed murderer the like of

PEGEEN—[*snapping at him.*]—Whisht I am saying; we'll take no fooling from your like at all. *(To Christy with a honeyed voice.)* And you, young fellow, you'd have a right to stop, I'm thinking, for we'd do our all and utmost to content your needs.

CHRISTY—[*overcome with wonder.*]—And I'd be safe in this place from the searching law?

MICHAEL. You would, surely. If they're not fearing you, itself, the peelers

15. Discharged British soldiers.

in this place is decent droughty° poor fellows, wouldn't touch a cur dog and not give warning in the dead of night. thirsty

PEGEEN—[*very kindly and persuasively.*]—Let you stop a short while anyhow. Aren't you destroyed walking with your feet in bleeding blisters, and your whole skin needing washing like a Wicklow sheep.

CHRISTY—[*looking round with satisfaction.*] It's a nice room, and if it's not humbugging me you are, I'm thinking that I'll surely stay.

JIMMY—[*jumps up.*]—Now, by the grace of God, herself will be safe this night, with a man killed his father holding danger from the door, and let you come on, Michael James, or they'll have the best stuff drunk at the wake.

MICHAEL—[*going to the door with men.*] And begging your pardon, mister, what name will we call you, for we'd like to know?

CHRISTY. Christopher Mahon.

MICHAEL. Well, God bless you, Christy, and a good rest till we meet again when the sun'll be rising to the noon of day.

CHRISTY. God bless you all.

MEN. God bless you. [*They go out except Shawn, who lingers at door.*]

SHAWN—[*to Pegeen.*]—Are you wanting me to stop along with you and keep you from harm?

PEGEEN—[*gruffly.*] Didn't you say you were fearing Father Reilly?

SHAWN. There'd be no harm staying now, I'm thinking, and himself in it too.

PEGEEN. You wouldn't stay when there was need for you, and let you step off nimble this time when there's none.

SHAWN. Didn't I say it was Father Reilly . . .

PEGEEN. Go on, then, to Father Reilly *(in a jeering tone),* and let him put you in the holy brotherhoods, and leave that lad to me.

SHAWN. If I meet the Widow Quin . . .

PEGEEN. Go on, I'm saying, and don't be waking this place with your noise. *(She hustles him out and bolts the door.)* That lad would wear the spirits from the saints of peace. *(Bustles about, then takes off her apron and pins it up in the window as a blind. Christy watching her timidly. Then she comes to him and speaks with bland good-humour.)* Let you stretch out now by the fire, young fellow. You should be destroyed travelling.

CHRISTY—[*shyly again, drawing off his boots.*) I'm tired, surely, walking wild eleven days, and waking fearful in the night. [*He holds up one of his feet, feeling his blisters, and looking at them with compassion.*]

PEGEEN—[*standing beside him, watching him with delight.*]—You should have had great people in your family, I'm thinking, with the little, small feet you have, and you with a kind of a quality name, the like of what you'd find on the great powers and potentates of France and Spain.

CHRISTY—[*with pride.*]—We were great surely, with wide and windy acres of rich Munster land.

PEGEEN. Wasn't I telling you, and you a fine, handsome young fellow with a noble brow?

CHRISTY—[*with a flash of delighted surprise.*] Is it me?

PEGEEN. Aye. Did you never hear that from the young girls where you come from in the west or south?

CHRISTY—[*with venom.*]—I did not then. Oh, they're bloody liars in the naked parish where I grew a man.

PEGEEN. If they are itself, you've heard it these days, I'm thinking, and you walking the world telling out your story to young girls or old.

CHRISTY. I've told my story no place till this night, Pegeen Mike, and it's foolish I was here, maybe, to be talking free, but you're decent people, I'm thinking, and yourself a kindly woman, the way I wasn't fearing you at all.

PEGEEN—[*filling a sack with straw.*]—You've said the like of that, maybe, in every cot and cabin where you've met a young girl on your way.

CHRISTY—[*going over to her, gradually raising his voice.*]—I've said it nowhere till this night, I'm telling you, for I've seen none the like of you the eleven long days I am walking the world, looking over a low ditch or a high ditch on my north or my south, into stony scattered fields, or scribes° of bog, where you'd see young, limber girls, and fine prancing women making laughter with the men. strips

PEGEEN. If you weren't destroyed travelling, you'd have as much talk and streeleen,° I'm thinking, as Owen Roe O'Sullivan or the poets of the Dingle Bay,[16] and I've heard all times it's the poets are your like, fine fiery fellows with great rages when their temper's roused. flattery

CHRISTY—[*drawing a little nearer to her.*]—You've a power of rings, God bless you, and would there be any offence if I was asking are you single now?

PEGEEN. What would I want wedding so young?

CHRISTY—[*with relief.*]—We're alike, so.

PEGEEN—[*she puts sack on settle and beats it up.*]—I never killed my father. I'd be afeard to do that, except I was the like of yourself with blind rages tearing me within, for I'm thinking you should have had great tussling when the end was come.

CHRISTY—[*expanding with delight at the first confidential talk he has ever had with a woman.*]—We had not then. It was a hard woman was come over the hill, and if he was always a crusty kind when he'd a hard woman setting him on, not the divil himself or his four fathers could put up with him at all.

PEGEEN—[*with curiosity.*]—And isn't it a great wonder that one wasn't fearing you?

CHRISTY—[*very confidentially.*]—Up to the day I killed my father, there wasn't a person in Ireland knew the kind I was, and I there drinking,

16. Eoghan Rua Ó Súilleabháin 1748–82), a great Irish-language poet particularly associated with Munster; Dingle was also traditionally a center for Irish-language poetry.

waking, eating, sleeping, a quiet, simple poor fellow with no man giving me heed.

PEGEEN—[*getting a quilt out of the cupboard and putting it on the sack.*]—It was the girls were giving you heed maybe, and I'm thinking it's most conceit you'd have to be gaming with their like.

CHRISTY—[*shaking his head, with simplicity.*] Not the girls itself, and I won't tell you a lie. There wasn't anyone heeding me in that place saving only the dumb beasts of the field. [*He sits down at fire.*]

PEGEEN—[*with disappointment.*]—And I thinking you should have been living the like of a king of Norway or the Eastern world.

[*She comes and sits beside him after placing bread and mug of milk on the table.*]

CHRISTY—[*laughing piteously.*]—The like of a king, is it? And I after toiling, moiling, digging, dodging from the dawn till dusk with never a sight of joy or sport saving only when I'd be abroad in the dark night poaching rabbits on hills, for I was a divil to poach, God forgive me, *(very naively)* and I near got six months for going with a dung fork and stabbing a fish.

PEGEEN. And it's that you'd call sport, is it, to be abroad in the darkness with yourself alone?

CHRISTY. I did, God help me, and there I'd be as happy as the sunshine of St. Martin's Day,[17] watching the light passing the north or the patches of fog, till I'd hear a rabbit starting to screech and I'd go running in the furze. Then when I'd my full share I'd come walking down where you'd see the ducks and geese stretched sleeping on the highway of the road, and before I'd pass the dunghill, I'd hear himself snoring out, a loud lonesome snore he'd be making all times, the while he was sleeping, and he a man'd be raging all times, the while he was waking, like a gaudy officer you'd hear cursing and damning and swearing oaths.

PEGEEN. Providence and Mercy, spare us all!

CHRISTY. It's that you'd say surely if you seen him and he after drinking for weeks, rising up in the red dawn, or before it maybe, and going out into the yard as naked as an ash tree in the moon of May, and shying clods against the visage of the stars till he'd put the fear of death into the banbhs° and the screeching sows. piglets

PEGEEN. I'd be well-night afeard of that lad myself, I'm thinking. And there was no one in it but the two of you alone?

CHRISTY. The divil a one, though he'd sons and daughters walking all great states and territories of the world, and not a one of them, to this day, but would say their seven curses on him, and they rousing up to let a cough or sneeze, maybe, in the deadness of the night.

PEGEEN [*nodding her head.*]—Well, you should have been a queer lot. I never cursed my father the like of that, though I'm twenty and more years of age.

17. November 11.

CHRISTY. Then you'd have cursed mine, I'm telling you, and he a man never gave peace to any, saving when he'd get two months or three, or be locked in the asylums for battering peelers or assaulting men *(with depression)* the way it was a bitter life he led me till I did up a Tuesday and halve his skull.

PEGEEN—[*putting her hand on his shoulder.*]—Well, you'll have peace in this place, Christy Mahon, and none to trouble you, and it's near time a fine lad like you should have your good share of the earth.

CHRISTY. It's time surely, and I a seemly fellow with great strength in me and bravery of . . . [*Someone knocks.*]

CHRISTY—[*clinging to Pegeen.*]—Oh, glory! it's late for knocking, and this last while I'm in terror of the peelers, and the walking dead. [*Knocking again.*]

PEGEEN. Who's there?

VOICE—[*outside.*] Me.

PEGEEN. Who's me?

VOICE. The Widow Quin.

PEGEEN [*jumping up and giving him the bread and milk.*]—Go on now with your supper, and let on to be sleepy, for if she found you were such a warrant to talk, she'd be stringing gabble till the dawn of day. *(He takes bread and sits shyly with his back to the door.)*

PEGEEN [*opening door, with temper.*]—What ails you, or what is it you're wanting at this hour of the night?

WIDOW QUIN—[*coming in a step and peering at Christy.*]—I'm after meeting Shawn Keogh and Father Reilly below, who told me of your curiosity man, and they fearing by this time he was maybe roaring, romping on your hands with drink.

PEGEEN [*pointing to Christy.*]—Look now is he roaring, and he stretched away drowsy with his supper and his mug of milk. Walk down and tell that to Father Reilly and to Shaneen Keogh.

WIDOW QUIN—[*coming forward.*]—I'll not see them again, for I've their word to lead that lad forward for to lodge with me.

PEGEEN—[*in blank amazement.*]—This night, is it?

WIDOW QUIN—[*going over.*]—This night. "It isn't fitting," says the priesteen, "to have his likeness lodging with an orphaned girl." *(To Christy.)* God save you, mister!

CHRISTY—[*shyly.*]—God save you kindly.

WIDOW QUIN—[*looking at him with half-amazed curiosity.*]—Well, aren't you a little smiling fellow? It should have been great and bitter torments did rouse your spirits to a deed of blood.

CHRISTY—[*doubtfully.*] It should, maybe.

WIDOW QUIN. It's more than "maybe" I'm saying, and it'd soften my heart to see you sitting so simple with your cup and cake, and you fitter to be saying your catechism than slaying your da.

PEGEEN—[*at counter, washing glasses.*]—There's talking when any'd see he's fit to be holding his head high with the wonders of the world.

Walk on from this, for I'll not have him tormented and he destroyed travelling since Tuesday was a week.

WIDOW QUIN—[*peaceably.*] We'll be walking surely when his supper's done, and you'll find we're great company, young fellow, when it's of the like of you and me you'd hear the penny poets singing in an August Fair.

CHRISTY—[*innocently.*] Did you kill your father?

PEGEEN—[*contemptuously.*] She did not. She hit himself with a worn pick, and the rusted poison did corrode his blood the way he never overed it, and died after. That was a sneaky kind of murder did win small glory with the boys itself. [*She crosses to Christy's left.*]

WIDOW QUIN—[*with good-humour.*]—If it didn't, maybe all knows a widow woman has buried her children and destroyed her man is a wiser comrade for a young lad than a girl, the like of you, who'd go helter-skeltering after any man would let you a wink upon the road.

PEGEEN—[*breaking out into wild rage.*]—And you'll say that, Widow Quin, and you gasping with the rage you had racing the hill beyond to look on his face.

WIDOW QUIN—[*laughing derisively.*]—Me, is it? Well, Father Reilly has cuteness° to divide you now. *(She pulls Christy up.)* There's great temptation in a man did slay his da, and we'd best be going, young fellow; so rise up and come with me. cleverness

PEGEEN—[*seizing his arm.*]—He'll not stir. He's pot-boy in this place, and I'll not have him stolen off and kidnabbed while himself's abroad.

WIDOW QUIN. It'd be a crazy pot-boy'd lodge him in the shebeen where he works by day, so you'd have a right to come on, young fellow, till you see my little houseen, a perch[18] off on the rising hill.

PEGEEN. Wait till morning, Christy Mahon. Wait till you lay eyes on her leaky thatch is growing more pasture for her buck goat than her square of fields, and she without a tramp itself to keep in order her place at all.

WIDOW QUIN. When you see me contriving in my little gardens, Christy Mahon, you'll swear the Lord God formed me to be living lone, and that there isn't my match in Mayo for thatching, or mowing, or shearing a sheep.

PEGEEN—[*with noisy scorn.*]—It's true the Lord God formed you to contrive indeed. Doesn't the world know you reared a black lamb at your own breast, so that the Lord Bishop of Connaught felt the elements of a Christian, and he eating it after in a kidney stew? Doesn't the world know you've been seen shaving the foxy skipper from France for a threepenny bit and a sop of grass° tobacco would wring the liver from a mountain goat you'd meet leaping the hills? uncured

WIDOW QUIN—[*with amusement.*]—Do you hear her now, young fel-

18. Literally twenty-one feet in Ireland, here and later in the play used metaphorically for a short distance.

low? Do you hear the way she'll be rating at your own self when a week is by?

PEGEEN—[*to Christy.*]—Don't heed her. Tell her to go into her pigsty and not plague us here.

WIDOW QUIN. I'm going; but he'll come with me.

PEGEEN—[*shaking him.*]—Are you dumb, young fellow?

CHRISTY—[*timidly, to Widow Quin.*]—God increase you; but I'm pot-boy in this place, and it's here I'd liefer stay.

PEGEEN—[*triumphantly.*] Now you have heard him, and go on from this.

WIDOW QUIN—[*looking round the room.*]—It's lonesome this hour crossing the hill, and if he won't come along with me, I'd have a right maybe to stop this night with yourselves. Let me stretch out on the settle, Pegeen Mike; and himself can lie by the hearth.

PEGEEN—[*short and fiercely.*]—Faith, I won't. Quit off or I will send you now.

WIDOW QUIN—[*gathering her shawl up.*]—Well, it's a terror to be aged a score. *(To Christy.)* God bless you now, young fellow, and let you be wary, or there's right torment will await you here if you go romancing with her like, and she waiting only, as they bade me say, on a sheepskin parchment to be wed with Shawn Keogh of Killakeen.

CHRISTY—[*going to Pegeen as she bolts the door.*]—What's that she's after saying?

PEGEEN. Lies and blather, you've no call to mind. Well, isn't Shawn Keogh an impudent fellow to send up spying on me? Wait till I lay hands on him. Let him wait, I'm saying.

CHRISTY. And you're not wedding him at all?

PEGEEN. I wouldn't wed him if a bishop came walking for to join us here.

CHRISTY. That God in glory may be thanked for that.

PEGEEN. There's your bed now. I've put a quilt upon you I'm after quilting a while since with my own two hands, and you'd best stretch out now for your sleep, and may God give you a good rest till I call you in the morning when the cocks will crow.

CHRISTY—[*as she goes to inner room.*]—May God and Mary and St. Patrick bless you and reward you, for your kindly talk. [*She shuts the door behind her. He settles his bed slowly, feeling the quilt with immense satisfaction.*]—Well, it's a clean bed and soft with it, and it's great luck and company I've won me in the end of time—two fine women fighting for the likes of me—till I'm thinking this night wasn't I a foolish fellow not to kill my father in the years gone by.

CURTAIN

ACT II.

SCENE, [*as before. Brilliant morning light. Christy, looking bright and cheerful, is cleaning a girl's boots.*]

CHRISTY—[*to himself, counting jugs on dresser.*]—Half a hundred beyond. Ten there. A score that's above. Eighty jugs. Six cups and a broken one. Two plates. A power of glasses. Bottles, a school-master'd be hard set to count, and enough in them, I'm thinking, to drunken all the wealth and wisdom of the County Clare. *(He puts down the boot carefully.)* There's her boots now, nice and decent for her evening use, and isn't it grand brushes she has? *(He puts them down and goes by degrees to the looking-glass.)* Well, this'd be a fine place to be my whole life talking out with swearing Christians, in place of my old dogs and cat, and I stalking around, smoking my pipe and drinking my fill, and never a day's work but drawing a cork an odd time, or wiping a glass, or rinsing out a shiny tumbler for a decent man. *(He takes the looking-glass from the wall and puts it on the back of a chair; then sits down in front of it and begins washing his face.)* Didn't I know rightly I was handsome, though it was the divil's own mirror we had beyond, would twist a squint across an angel's brow; and I'll be growing fine from this day, the way I'll have a soft lovely skin on me and won't be the like of the clumsy young fellows do be ploughing all times in the earth and dung. *(He starts.)* Is she coming again? *(He looks out.)* Stranger girls. God help me, where'll I hide myself away and my long neck naked to the world? *(He looks out.)* I'd best go to the room maybe till I'm dressed again. [*He gathers up his coat and the looking-glass, and runs into the inner room. The door is pushed open, and Susan Brady looks in, and knocks on door.*]

SUSAN. There's nobody in it. [*Knocks again.*]

NELLY—[*pushing her in and following her, with Honor Blake and Sara Tansey.*] It'd be early for them both to be out walking the hill.

SUSAN. I'm thinking Shawn Keogh was making game of us and there's no such man in it at all.

HONOR—[*pointing to straw and quilt.*]—Look at that. He's been sleeping there in the night. Well, it'll be a hard case if he's gone off now, the way we'll never set our eyes on a man killed his father, and we after rising early and destroying ourselves running fast on the hill.

NELLY. Are you thinking them's his boots?

SARA—[*taking them up.*]—If they are, there should be his father's track on them. Did you never read in the papers the way murdered men do bleed and drip?

SUSAN. Is that blood there, Sara Tansey?

SARA—[*smelling it.*]—That's bog water, I'm thinking, but it's his own they are surely, for I never seen the like of them for whity mud, and red mud, and turf on them, and the fine sands of the sea. That man's been walking, I'm telling you. [*She goes down right, putting on one of his boots.*]

SUSAN—[*going to window.*]—Maybe he's stolen off to Belmullet with the boots of Michael James, and you'd have a right so to follow after him, Sara Tansey, and you the one yoked the ass cart and drove ten miles to set your eyes on the man bit the yellow° lady's nostril on the northern shore. [*She looks out.*] English

SARA—[*running to window with one boot on.*]—Don't be talking, and we fooled to-day. *(Putting on other boot.)* There's a pair do fit me well, and I'll be keeping them for walking to the priest, when you'd be ashamed this place, going up winter and summer with nothing worth while to confess at all.

HONOR—[*who has been listening at the door.*]—Whisht! there's some-one inside the room. *(She pushes door a chink open.)* It's a man. [*Sara kicks off boots and puts them where they were. They all stand in a line looking through chink.*]

SARA. I'll call him. Mister! Mister! *(He puts in his head.)* Is Pegeen within?

CHRISTY—[*coming in as meek as a mouse, with the looking-glass held behind his back.*]—She's above on the cnuceen,° seeking the nanny goats, the way she'd have a sup of goat's milk for to colour my tea. small hill

SARA. And asking your pardon, is it you's the man killed his father?

CHRISTY—[*sidling toward the nail where the glass was hanging.*] —I am, God help me!

SARA—[*taking eggs she has brought.*]—Then my thousand welcomes to you, and I've run up with a brace of duck's eggs for your food today. Pegeen's ducks is no use, but these are the real rich sort. Hold out your hand and you'll see it's no lie I'm telling you.

CHRISTY—[*coming forward shyly, and holding out his left hand.*]—They're a great and weighty size.

SUSAN. And I run up with a pat of butter, for it'd be a poor thing to have you eating your spuds dry, and you after running a great way since you did destroy your da.

CHRISTY. Thank you kindly.

HONOR. And I brought you a little cut of cake, for you should have a thin stomach on you, and you that length walking the world.

NELLY. And I brought you a little laying pullet—boiled and all she is—was crushed at the fall of night by the curate's car. Feel the fat of that breast, Mister.

CHRISTY. It's bursting, surely. [*He feels it with the back of his hand, in which he holds the presents.*]

SARA. Will you pinch it? Is your right hand too sacred for to use at all? *(She slips round behind him.)* It's a glass he has. Well, I never seen to this day a man with a looking-glass held to his back. Them that kills their fathers is a vain lot surely. [*Girls giggle.*]

CHRISTY—[*smiling innocently and piling presents on glass.*]—I'm very thankful to you all to-day . . .

WIDOW QUIN—[*coming in quickly, at door.*]—Sara Tansey, Susan Brady, Honor Blake! What in glory has you here at this hour of day?

GIRLS—[*giggling.*] That's the man killed his father.

WIDOW QUIN—[*coming to them.*]—I know well it's the man; and I'm after putting him down in the sports below for racing, leaping, pitching, and the Lord knows what.

SARA—[*exuberantly.*] That's right, Widow Quin. I'll bet my dowry that he'll lick the world.

WIDOW QUIN. If you will, you'd have a right to have him fresh and nourished in place of nursing a feast. *(Taking presents.)* Are you fasting or fed, young fellow?

CHRISTY. Fasting, if you please.

WIDOW QUIN—[*loudly.*] Well, you're the lot. Stir up now and give him his breakfast. *(To Christy.)* Come here to me *(she puts him on bench beside her while the girls make tea and get his breakfast)* and let you tell us your story before Pegeen will come, in place of grinning your ears off like the moon of May.

CHRISTY—[*beginning to be pleased.*]—It's a long story; you'd be destroyed listening.

WIDOW QUIN. Don't be letting on to be shy, a fine, gamey, treacherous lad the like of you. Was it in your house beyond you cracked his skull?

CHRISTY—[*shy but flattered.*]—It was not. We were digging spuds in his cold, sloping, stony, divil's patch of a field.

WIDOW QUIN. And you went asking money of him, or making talk of getting a wife would drive him from his farm?

CHRISTY. I did not, then; but there I was, digging and digging, and "You squinting idiot," says he, "let you walk down now and tell the priest you'll wed the Widow Casey in a score of days."

WIDOW QUIN. And what kind was she?

CHRISTY—[*with horror.*]—A walking terror from beyond the hills, and she two score and five years, and two hundredweights and five pounds[19] in the weighing scales, with a limping leg on her, and a blinded eye, and she a woman of noted misbehaviour with the old and young.

GIRLS—[*clustering round him, serving him.*]—Glory be.

WIDOW QUIN. And what did he want driving you to wed with her?

[*She takes a bit of the chicken.*]

CHRISTY—[*eating with growing satisfaction.*] He was letting on I was wanting a protector from the harshness of the world, and he without a thought the whole while but how he'd have her hut to live in and her gold to drink.

WIDOW QUIN. There's maybe worse than a dry hearth and a widow woman and your glass at night. So you hit him then?

19. In the imperial system, a hundredweight is 112 pounds, so the Widow Casey weighs 229 pounds.

CHRISTY—[*getting almost excited.*]—I did not. "I won't wed her," says I, "when all know she did suckle me for six weeks when I came into the world, and she a hag this day with a tongue on her has the crows and seabirds scattered, the way they wouldn't cast a shadow on her garden with the dread of her curse."

WIDOW QUIN—[*teasingly.*] That one should be right company.

SARA—[*eagerly.*] Don't mind her. Did you kill him then?

CHRISTY. "She's too good for the like of you," says he, "and go on now or I'll flatten you out like a crawling beast has passed under a dray." "You will not if I can help it," says I. "Go on," says he, "or I'll have the divil making garters of your limbs tonight." "You will not if I can help it," says I. [*He sits up, brandishing his mug.*]

SARA. You were right surely.

CHRISTY—[*impressively.*] With that the sun came out between the cloud and the hill, and it shining green in my face. "God have mercy on your soul," says he, lifting a scythe; "or on your own," says I, raising the loy.

SUSAN. That's a grand story.

HONOR. He tells it lovely.

CHRISTY—[*flattered and confident, waving bone.*]—He gave a drive with the scythe, and I gave a lep to the east. Then I turned around with my back to the north, and I hit a blow on the ridge of his skull, laid him stretched out, and he split to the knob of his gullet.

[*He raises the chicken bone to his Adam's apple.*]

GIRLS—[*together.*] Well, you're a marvel! Oh, God bless you! You're the lad surely!

SUSAN. I'm thinking the Lord God sent him this road to make a second husband to the Widow Quin, and she with a great yearning to be wedded, though all dread her here. Lift him on her knee, Sara Tansey.

WIDOW QUIN. Don't tease him.

SARA—[*going over to dresser and counter very quickly, and getting two glasses and porter.*]—You're heroes surely, and let you drink a supeen with your arms linked like the outlandish lovers in the sailor's song. *(She links their arms and gives them the glasses.)* There now. Drink a health to the wonders of the western world, the pirates, preachers, poteen-makers, with the jobbing° jockies, parching peelers, and the juries fill their stomachs selling judgments of the English law. [*Brandishing the bottle.*]

°cheating

WIDOW QUIN. That's a right toast, Sara Tansey. Now Christy.

[*They drink with their arms linked, he drinking with his left hand, she with her right. As they are drinking, Pegeen Mike comes in with a milk can and stands aghast. They all spring away from Christy. He goes down left. Widow Quin remains seated.*]

PEGEEN—[*angrily, to Sara.*]—What is it you're wanting?
SARA—[*twisting her apron.*]—An ounce of tobacco.
PEGEEN. Have you tuppence?
SARA. I've forgotten my purse.
PEGEEN. Then you'd best be getting it and not fooling us here. *(To the Widow Quin, with more elaborate scorn.)* And what is it you're wanting, Widow Quin?
WIDOW QUIN—[*insolently.*] A penn'orth of starch.
PEGEEN—[*breaking out.*]—And you without a white shift or a shirt in your whole family since the drying of the flood. I've no starch for the like of you, and let you walk on now to Killamuck.
WIDOW QUIN—[*turning to Christy, as she goes out with the girls.*] —Well, you're mighty huffy this day, Pegeen Mike, and, you young fellow, let you not forget the sports and racing when the noon is by.

[*They go out.*]

PEGEEN—[*imperiously.*] Fling out that rubbish and put them cups away. *(Christy tidies away in great haste).* Shove in the bench by the wall. *(He does so.)* And hang that glass on the nail. What disturbed it at all?
CHRISTY—[*very meekly.*]—I was making myself decent only, and this a fine country for young lovely girls.
PEGEEN—[*sharply.*] Whisht your talking of girls. [*Goes to counter right.*]
CHRISTY. Wouldn't any wish to be decent in a place . . .
PEGEEN. Whisht I'm saying.
CHRISTY—[*looks at her face for a moment with great misgivings, then as a last effort, takes up a loy, and goes towards her, with feigned assurance*].—It was with a loy the like of that I killed my father.
PEGEEN—[*still sharply.*]—You've told me that story six times since the dawn of day.
CHRISTY—[*reproachfully.*] It's a queer thing you wouldn't care to be hearing it and them girls after walking four miles to be listening to me now.
PEGEEN—[*turning round astonished.*]—Four miles.
CHRISTY—[*apologetically.*] Didn't himself say there were only four bona fides living in the place?
PEGEEN. It's bona fides by the road they are, but that lot came over the river lepping the stones. It's not three perches when you go like that, and I was down this morning looking on the papers the post-boy does have in his bag. *(With meaning and emphasis.)* For there was great news this day, Christopher Mahon. [*She goes into room left.*]
CHRISTY—[*suspiciously.*] Is it news of my murder?
PEGEEN—[*inside.*] Murder, indeed.
CHRISTY—[*loudly.*] A murdered da?
PEGEEN [*coming in again and crossing right.*]—There was not, but a story filled half a page of the hanging of a man. Ah, that should be a fearful end, young fellow, and it worst of all for a man who destroyed his da, for the like of him would get small mercies, and when it's

dead he is, they'd put him in a narrow grave, with cheap sacking wrapping him round, and pour down quicklime on his head, the way you'd see a woman pouring any frish-frash from a cup.

CHRISTY—[*very miserably.*]—Oh, God help me. Are you thinking I'm safe? You were saying at the fall of night, I was shut of jeopardy and I here with yourselves.

PEGEEN—[*severely.*] You'll be shut of jeopardy no place if you go talking with a pack of wild girls the like of them do be walking abroad with the peelers, talking whispers at the fall of night.

CHRISTY—[*with terror.*]—And you're thinking they'd tell?

PEGEEN—[*with mock sympathy.*]—Who knows, God help you.

CHRISTY—[*loudly.*] What joy would they have to bring hanging to the likes of me?

PEGEEN. It's queer joys they have, and who knows the thing they'd do, if it'd make the green stones cry itself to think of you swaying and swiggling at the butt of a rope, and you with a fine, stout neck, God bless you! the way you'd be a half an hour, in great anguish, getting your death.

CHRISTY—[*getting his boots and putting them on.*]—If there's that terror of them, it'd be best, maybe, I went on wandering like Esau or Cain and Abel on the sides of Neifin or the Erris plain.[20]

PEGEEN [*beginning to play with him.*]—It would, maybe, for I've heard the Circuit Judges this place is a heartless crew.

CHRISTY—[*bitterly.*] It's more than Judges this place is a heartless crew. *(Looking up at her.)* And isn't it a poor thing to be starting again and I a lonesome fellow will be looking out on women and girls the way the needy fallen spirits do be looking on the Lord?

PEGEEN. What call have you to be that lonesome when there's poor girls walking Mayo in their thousands now?

CHRISTY—[*grimly.*] It's well you know what call I have. It's well you know it's a lonesome thing to be passing small towns with the lights shining sideways when the night is down, or going in strange places with a dog nosing before you and a dog nosing behind, or drawn to the cities where you'd hear a voice kissing and talking deep love in every shadow of the ditch, and you passing on with an empty, hungry stomach failing from your heart.

PEGEEN. I'm thinking you're an odd man, Christy Mahon. The oddest walking fellow I ever set my eyes on to this hour to-day.

CHRISTY. What would any be but odd men and they living lonesome in the world?

PEGEEN. I'm not odd, and I'm my whole life with my father only

CHRISTY—[*with infinite admiration.*]—How would a lovely handsome woman the like of you be lonesome when all men should be thronging around to hear the sweetness of your voice, and the little infant

20. Neifin is a mountain in County Mayo and Erris plain is in northwestern Mayo.

children should be pestering your steps I'm thinking, and you walking the roads.

PEGEEN. I'm hard set to know what way a coaxing fellow the like of yourself should be lonesome either.

CHRISTY. Coaxing?

PEGEEN. Would you have me think a man never talked with the girls would have the words you've spoken to-day? It's only letting on you are to be lonesome, the way you'd get around me now.

CHRISTY. I wish to God I was letting on; but I was lonesome all times, and born lonesome, I'm thinking, as the moon of dawn. [*Going to door.*]

PEGEEN—[*puzzled by his talk.*]—Well, it's a story I'm not understanding at all why you'd be worse than another, Christy Mahon, and you a fine lad with the great savagery to destroy your da.

CHRISTY. It's little I'm understanding myself, saving only that my heart's scalded this day, and I going off stretching out the earth between us, the way I'll not be waking near you another dawn of the year till the two of us do arise to hope or judgment with the saints of God, and now I'd best be going with my wattle° in my hand, for hanging is a poor thing *(turning to go),* and it's little welcome only is left me in this house to-day. — stick

PEGEEN [*sharply.*] Christy! *(He turns round.)* Come here to me. *(He goes towards her.)* Lay down that switch and throw some sods on the fire. You're pot-boy in this place, and I'll not have you mitch off° from us now. — steal away

CHRISTY. You were saying I'd be hanged if I stay.

PEGEEN—[*quite kindly at last.*]—I'm after going down and reading the fearful crimes of Ireland for two weeks or three, and there wasn't a word of your murder. *(Getting up and going over to the counter.)* They've likely not found the body. You're safe so with ourselves.

CHRISTY—[*astonished, slowly.*]—It's making game of me you were *(following her with fearful joy),* and I can stay so, working at your side, and I not lonesome from this mortal day.

PEGEEN. What's to hinder you from staying, except the widow woman or the young girls would inveigle you off?

CHRISTY—[*with rapture.*]—And I'll have your words from this day filling my ears, and that look is come upon you meeting my two eyes, and I watching you loafing around in the warm sun, or rinsing your ankles when the night is come.

PEGEEN—[*kindly, but a little embarrassed.*] I'm thinking you'll be a loyal young lad to have working around, and if you vexed me a while since with your leaguing with the girls, I wouldn't give a thraneen° for a lad hadn't a mighty spirit in him and a gamey heart. [*Shawn Keogh runs in carrying a cleeve° on his back, followed by the Widow Quin.*] — trifle; straw basket

SHAWN—[*to Pegeen.*]—I was passing below, and I seen your mountainy sheep eating cabbages in Jimmy's field. Run up or they'll be bursting surely.

PEGEEN. Oh, God mend them! [*She puts a shawl over her head and runs out.*]

CHRISTY—[*looking from one to the other. Still in high spirits.*] —I'd best go to her aid maybe. I'm handy with ewes.

WIDOW QUIN—[*closing the door.*]—She can do that much, and there is Shaneen has long speeches for to tell you now. [*She sits down with an amused smile.*]

SHAWN—[*taking something from his pocket and offering it to Christy.*]—Do you see that, mister?

CHRISTY—[*looking at it.*]—The half of a ticket to the Western States!° The United States

SHAWN—[*trembling with anxiety.*]—I'll give it to you and my new hat *(pulling it out of hamper);* and my breeches with the double seat *(pulling it off);* and my new coat is woven from the blackest shearings for three miles around *(giving him the coat);* I'll give you the whole of them, and my blessing, and the blessing of Father Reilly itself, maybe, if you'll quit from this and leave us in the peace we had till last night at the fall of dark.

CHRISTY—[*with a new arrogance.*]—And for what is it you're wanting to get shut of me?

SHAWN—[*looking to the Widow for help.*]—I'm a poor scholar with middling faculties to coin a lie, so I'll tell you the truth, Christy Mahon. I'm wedding with Pegeen beyond, and I don't think well of having a clever fearless man the like of you dwelling in her house.

CHRISTY—[*almost pugnaciously.*]—And you'd be using bribery for to banish me?

SHAWN—[*in an imploring voice.*]—Let you not take it badly, mister honey, isn't beyond the best place for you where you'll have golden chains and shiny coats and you riding upon hunters with the ladies of the land. [*He makes an eager sign to the Widow Quin to come to help him.*]

WIDOW QUIN—[*coming over.*]—It's true for him, and you'd best quit off and not have that poor girl setting her mind on you, for there's Shaneen thinks she wouldn't suit you though all is saying that she'll wed you now. [*Christy beams with delight.*]

SHAWN—[*in terrified earnest.*]—She wouldn't suit you, and she with the divil's own temper the way you'd be strangling one another in a score of days. *(He makes the movement of strangling with his hands.)* It's the like of me only that she's fit for, a quiet simple fellow wouldn't raise a hand upon her if she scratched itself.

WIDOW QUIN—[*putting Shawn's hat on Christy.*]—Fit them clothes on you anyhow, young fellow, and he'd maybe loan them to you for the sports. *(Pushing him towards inner door.)* Fit them on and you can give your answer when you have them tried.

CHRISTY—[*beaming, delighted with the clothes.*]—I will then. I'd like herself to see me in them tweeds and hat. [*He goes into room and shuts the door.*]

SHAWN—[*in great anxiety.*]—He'd like herself to see them. He'll not leave us, Widow Quin. He's a score of divils in him the way it's well nigh certain he will wed Pegeen.

WIDOW QUIN—[*jeeringly.*] It's true all girls are fond of courage and do hate the like of you.

SHAWN—[*walking about in desperation.*]—Oh, Widow Quin, what'll I be doing now? I'd inform again him, but he'd burst from Kilmainham[21] and he'd be sure and certain to destroy me. If I wasn't so God-fearing, I'd near have courage to come behind him and run a pike into his side. Oh, it's a hard case to be an orphan and not to have your father that you're used to, and you'd easy kill and make yourself a hero in the sight of all. *(Coming up to her.)* Oh, Widow Quin, will you find me some contrivance when I've promised you a ewe?

WIDOW QUIN. A ewe's a small thing, but what would you give me if I did wed him and did save you so?

SHAWN—[*with astonishment.*] You?

WIDOW QUIN. Aye. Would you give me the red cow you have and the mountainy ram, and the right of way across your rye path, and a load of dung at Michaelmas,[22] and turbary[23] upon the western hill?

SHAWN—[*radiant with hope.*]—I would surely, and I'd give you the wedding-ring I have, and the loan of a new suit, the way you'd have him decent on the wedding-day. I'd give you two kids for your dinner, and a gallon of poteen, and I'd call the piper on the long car to your wedding from Crossmolina or from Ballina. I'd give you . . .

WIDOW QUIN. That'll do so, and let you whisht, for he's coming now again. [*Christy comes in very natty in the new clothes. Widow Quin goes to him admiringly.*]

WIDOW QUIN. If you seen yourself now, I'm thinking you'd be too proud to speak to us at all, and it'd be a pity surely to have your like sailing from Mayo to the Western World.

CHRISTY—[*as proud as a peacock.*]—I'm not going. If this is a poor place itself, I'll make myself contented to be lodging here.

[*Widow Quin makes a sign to Shawn to leave them.*]

SHAWN. Well, I'm going measuring the race-course while the tide is low, so I'll leave you the garments and my blessing for the sports to-day. God bless you! [*He wriggles out.*]

WIDOW QUIN—[*admiring Christy.*]—Well, you're mighty spruce, young fellow. Sit down now while you're quiet till you talk with me.

CHRISTY—[*swaggering.*] I'm going abroad on the hillside for to seek Pegeen.

WIDOW QUIN. You'll have time and plenty for to seek Pegeen, and you heard me saying at the fall of night the two of us should be great company.

21. Jail near Dublin.
22. September 29, one of the four "quarter days" when rents were paid.
23. The right to cut peat.

CHRISTY. From this out I'll have no want of company when all sorts is bringing me their food and clothing *(he swaggers to the door, tightening his belt),* the way they'd set their eyes upon a gallant orphan cleft his father with one blow to the breeches belt. *(He opens door, then staggers back.)* Saints of glory! Holy angels from the throne of light!

WIDOW QUIN—[*going over.*]—What ails you?

CHRISTY. It's the walking spirit of my murdered da!

WIDOW QUIN—[*looking out.*]—Is it that tramper?

CHRISTY—[*wildly.*] Where'll I hide my poor body from that ghost of hell? [*The door is pushed open, and old Mahon appears on threshold. Christy darts in behind door.*]

WIDOW QUIN—[*in great amusement.*]—God save you, my poor man.

MAHON—[*gruffly.*] Did you see a young lad passing this way in the early morning or the fall of night?

WIDOW QUIN. You're a queer kind to walk in not saluting at all.

MAHON. Did you see the young lad?

WIDOW QUIN—[*stiffly.*] What kind was he?

MAHON. An ugly young streeler° with a murderous gob on him, and a little switch in his hand. I met a tramper seen him coming this way at the fall of night. idler

WIDOW QUIN. There's harvest hundreds do be passing these days for the Sligo boat. For what is it you're wanting him, my poor man?

MAHON. I want to destroy him for breaking the head on me with the clout of a loy. *(He takes off a big hat, and shows his head in a mass of bandages and plaster, with some pride.)* It was he did that, and amn't I a great wonder to think I've traced him ten days with that rent in my crown?

WIDOW QUIN—[*taking his head in both hands and examining it with extreme delight.*]—That was a great blow. And who hit you? A robber maybe?

MAHON. It was my own son hit me, and he the divil a robber, or anything else, but a dirty, stuttering lout.

WIDOW—[*letting go his skull and wiping her hands in her apron.*] —You'd best be wary of a mortified scalp, I think they call it, lepping around with that wound in the splendour of the sun. It was a bad blow surely, and you should have vexed him fearful to make him strike that gash in his da.

MAHON. Is it me?

WIDOW QUIN—[*amusing herself.*]—Aye. And isn't it a great shame when the old and hardened do torment the young?

MAHON—[*raging.*] Torment him is it? And I after holding out with the patience of a martyred saint till there's nothing but destruction on, and I'm driven out in my old age with none to aid me.

WIDOW QUIN—[*greatly amused.*]—It's a sacred wonder the way that wickedness will spoil a man.

MAHON. My wickedness, is it? Amn't I after saying it is himself has me destroyed, and he a liar on walls, a talker of folly, a man you'd see stretched the half of the day in the brown ferns with his belly to the sun.

WIDOW QUIN. Not working at all?

MAHON. The divil a work, or if he did itself, you'd see him raising up a haystack like the stalk of a rush, or driving our last cow till he broke her leg at the hip, and when he wasn't at that he'd be fooling over little birds he had—finches and felts[24]—or making mugs at his own self in the bit of glass we had hung on the wall.

WIDOW QUIN—[*looking at Christy.*]—What way was he so foolish? It was running wild after the girls may be?

MAHON—[*with a shout of derision.*]—Running wild, is it? If he seen a red petticoat coming swinging over the hill, he'd be off to hide in the sticks, and you'd see him shooting out his sheep's eyes between the little twigs and the leaves, and his two ears rising like a hare looking out through a gap. Girls, indeed!

WIDOW QUIN. It was drink maybe?

MAHON. And he a poor fellow would get drunk on the smell of a pint. He'd a queer rotten stomach, I'm telling you, and when I gave him three pulls from my pipe a while since, he was taken with contortions till I had to send him in the ass cart to the females nurse.

WIDOW QUIN—[*clasping her hands.*]—Well, I never till this day heard tell of a man the like of that!

MAHON. I'd take a mighty oath you didn't surely, and wasn't he the laughing joke of every female woman where four baronies meet, the way the girls would stop their weeding if they seen him coming the road to let a roar at him, and call him the looney of Mahon's.

WIDOW QUIN. I'd give the world and all to see the like of him. What kind was he?

MAHON. A small low fellow.

WIDOW QUIN. And dark?

MAHON. Dark and dirty.

WIDOW QUIN—[*considering.*] I'm thinking I seen him.

MAHON—[*eagerly.*] An ugly young blackguard.

WIDOW QUIN. A hideous, fearful villain, and the spit of you.

MAHON. What way is he fled?

WIDOW QUIN. Gone over the hills to catch a coasting steamer to the north or south.

MAHON. Could I pull up on him now?

WIDOW QUIN. If you'll cross the sands below where the tide is out, you'll be in it as soon as himself, for he had to go round ten miles by the top of the bay. *(She points to the door).* Strike down by the head beyond and then follow on the roadway to the north and east. [*Mahon goes abruptly.*]

WIDOW QUIN—[*shouting after him.*]—Let you give him a good ven-

24. "Felt" is used in Scotland and Ireland for any of several kinds of thrushes.

geance when you come up with him, but don't put yourself in the power of the law, for it'd be a poor thing to see a judge in his black cap reading out his sentence on a civil warrior the like of you. [*She swings the door to and looks at Christy, who is cowering in terror, for a moment, then she bursts into a laugh.*]

WIDOW QUIN. Well, you're the walking Playboy of the Western World, and that's the poor man you had divided to his breeches belt.

CHRISTY—[*looking out: then, to her.*]—What'll Pegeen say when she hears that story? What'll she be saying to me now?

WIDOW QUIN. She'll knock the head of you, I'm thinking, and drive you from the door. God help her to be taking you for a wonder, and you a little schemer making up the story you destroyed your da.

CHRISTY—[*turning to the door, nearly speechless with rage, half to himself.*]—To be letting on he was dead, and coming back to his life, and following after me like an old weazel tracing a rat, and coming in here laying desolation between my own self and the fine women of Ireland, and he a kind of carcase that you'd fling upon the sea . . .

WIDOW QUIN—[*more soberly.*]—There's talking for a man's one only son.

CHRISTY—[*breaking out.*]—His one son, is it? May I meet him with one tooth and it aching, and one eye to be seeing seven and seventy divils in the twists of the road, and one old timber leg on him to limp into the scalding grave. *(Looking out.)* There he is now crossing the strands, and that the Lord God would send a high wave to wash him from the world.

WIDOW QUIN—[*scandalised.*] Have you no shame? *(putting her hand on his shoulder and turning him round.)* What ails you? Near crying, is it?

CHRISTY—[*in despair and grief.*]—Amn't I after seeing the love-light of the star of knowledge shining from her brow, and hearing words would put you thinking on the holy Brigid speaking to the infant saints, and now she'll be turning again, and speaking hard words to me, like an old woman with a spavindy[25] ass she'd have, urging on a hill.

WIDOW QUIN. There's poetry talk for a girl you'd see itching and scratching, and she with a stale stink of poteen on her from selling in the shop.

CHRISTY—[*impatiently.*] It's her like is fitted to be handling merchandise in the heavens above, and what'll I be doing now, I ask you, and I a kind of wonder was jilted by the heavens when a day was by. [*There is a distant noise of girls' voices. Widow Quin looks from window and comes to him, hurriedly.*]

WIDOW QUIN. You'll be doing like myself, I'm thinking, when I did destroy my man, for I'm above many's the day, odd times in great spir-

25. Spavin is a form of arthritis that attacks the hocks of livestock.

its, abroad in the sunshine, darning a stocking or stitching a shift; and odd times again looking out on the schooners, hookers, trawlers is sailing the sea, and I thinking on the gallant hairy fellows are drifting beyond, and myself long years living alone.

CHRISTY—[*interested.*] You're like me, so.

WIDOW QUIN. I am your like, and it's for that I'm taking a fancy to you, and I with my little houseen above where there'd be myself to tend you, and none to ask were you a murderer or what at all.

CHRISTY. And what would I be doing if I left Pegeen?

WIDOW QUIN. I've nice jobs you could be doing, gathering shells to make a whitewash for our hut within, building up a little goose-house, or stretching a new skin on an old curragh[26] I have, and if my hut is far from all sides, it's there you'll meet the wisest old men, I tell you, at the corner of my wheel, and it's there yourself and me will have great times whispering and hugging. . . .

VOICES—[*outside, calling far away.*]—Christy! Christy Mahon! Christy!

CHRISTY. Is it Pegeen Mike?

WIDOW QUIN. It's the young girls, I'm thinking, coming to bring you to the sports below, and what is it you'll have me to tell them now?

CHRISTY. Aid me for to win Pegeen. It's herself only that I'm seeking now. *(Widow Quin gets up and goes to window.)* Aid me for to win her, and I'll be asking God to stretch a hand to you in the hour of death, and lead you short cuts through the Meadows of Ease, and up the floor of Heaven to the Footstool of the Virgin's Son.

WIDOW QUIN. There's praying.

VOICES—[*nearer.*] Christy! Christy Mahon!

CHRISTY—[*with agitation.*]—They're coming. Will you swear to aid and save me for the love of Christ?

WIDOW QUIN—[*looks at him for a moment.*]—If I aid you, will you swear to give me a right of way I want, and a mountainy ram, and a load of dung at Michaelmas, the time that you'll be master here?

CHRISTY. I will, by the elements and stars of night.

WIDOW QUIN. Then we'll not say a word of the old fellow, the way Pegeen won't know your story till the end of time.

CHRISTY. And if he chances to return again?

WIDOW QUIN. We'll swear he's a maniac and not your da. I could take an oath I seen him raving on the sands to-day. [*Girls run in.*]

SUSAN. Come on to the sports below. Pegeen says you're to come.

SARA. The lepping's beginning, and we've a jockey's suit to fit upon you for the mule race on the sands below.

HONOR. Come on, will you?

CHRISTY. I will then if Pegeen's beyond.

SARA. She's in the boreen[27] making game of Shaneen Keogh.

26. Small boat made from skins or tarred canvas stretched over a frame.

27. Green lane.

CHRISTY. Then I'll be going to her now. [*He runs out followed by the girls.*]

WIDOW QUIN. Well, if the worst comes in the end of all, it'll be great game to see there's none to pity him but a widow woman, the like of me, has buried her children and destroyed her man. [*She goes out.*]

CURTAIN

ACT III.

SCENE, [*as before. Later in the day. Jimmy comes in, slightly drunk.*]

JIMMY—[*calls.*] Pegeen! *(Crosses to inner door.)* Pegeen Mike! *(Comes back again into the room.)* Pegeen! *(Philly comes in the same state.)* *(To Philly.)* Did you see herself?

PHILLY. I did not; but I sent Shawn Keogh with the ass cart for to bear him home. *(Trying cupboards which are locked.)* Well, isn't he a nasty man to get into such staggers at a morning wake? and isn't herself the divil's daughter for locking, and she so fussy after that young gaffer, you might take your death with drought and none to heed you?

JIMMY. It's little wonder she'd be fussy, and he after bringing bankrupt ruin on the roulette man, and the trick-o'-the-loop man, and breaking the nose of the cockshot-man, and winning all in the sports below, racing, lepping, dancing, and the Lord knows what! He's right luck, I'm telling you.

PHILLY. If he has, he'll be rightly hobbled yet, and he not able to say ten words without making a brag of the way he killed his father, and the great blow he hit with the loy.

JIMMY. A man can't hang by his own informing, and his father should be rotten by now. [*Old Mahon passes window slowly.*]

PHILLY. Supposing a man's digging spuds in that field with a long spade, and supposing he flings up the two halves of that skull, what'll be said then in the papers and the courts of law?

JIMMY. They'd say it was an old Dane, maybe, was drowned in the flood. *(Old Mahon comes in and sits down near door listening.)* Did you never hear tell of the skulls they have in the city of Dublin, ranged out like blue jugs in a cabin of Connaught?

PHILLY. And you believe that?

JIMMY—[*pugnaciously.*] Didn't a lad see them and he after coming from harvesting in the Liverpool boat? "They have them there," says he, "making a show of the great people there was one time walking the world. White skulls and black skulls and yellow skulls, and some with full teeth, and some haven't only but one."

PHILLY. It was no lie, maybe, for when I was a young lad there was a graveyard beyond the house with the remnants of a man who had thighs as long as your arm. He was a horrid man, I'm telling you, and there was many a fine Sunday I'd put him together for fun, and he with shiny bones, you wouldn't meet the like of these days in the cities of the world.

MAHON—[*getting up.*]—You wouldn't is it? Lay your eyes on that skull, and tell me where and when there was another the like of it, is splintered only from the blow of a loy.

PHILLY. Glory be to God! And who hit you at all?

MAHON—[*triumphantly.*] It was my own son hit me. Would you believe that?

JIMMY. Well, there's wonders hidden in the heart of man!

PHILLY—[*suspiciously.*] And what way was it done?

MAHON—[*wandering about the room.*]—I'm after walking hundreds and long scores of miles, winning clean beds and the fill of my belly four times in the day, and I doing nothing but telling stories of that naked truth. *(He comes to them a little aggressively.)* Give me a supeen and I'll tell you now. [*Widow Quin comes in and stands aghast behind him. He is facing Jimmy and Philly, who are on the left.*]

JIMMY. Ask herself beyond. She's the stuff hidden in her shawl.

WIDOW QUIN—[*coming to Mahon quickly.*]—you here, is it? You didn't go far at all?

MAHON. I seen the coasting steamer passing, and I got a drought upon me and a cramping leg, so I said, "The divil go along with him," and turned again. *(Looking under her shawl.)* And let you give me a supeen, for I'm destroyed travelling since Tuesday was a week.

WIDOW QUIN—[*getting a glass, in a cajoling tone.*]—Sit down then by the fire and take your ease for a space. You've a right to be destroyed indeed, with your walking, and fighting, and facing the sun *(giving him poteen from a stone jar she has brought in.)* There now is a drink for you, and may it be to your happiness and length of life.

MAHON—[*taking glass greedily and sitting down by fire.*]—God increase you!

WIDOW QUIN—[*taking men to the right stealthily.*]—Do you know what? That man's raving from his wound to-day, for I met him a while since telling a rambling tale of a tinker had him destroyed. Then he heard of Christy's deed, and he up and says it was his son had cracked his skull. O isn't madness a fright, for he'll go killing someone yet, and he thinking it's the man has struck him so?

JIMMY—[*entirely convinced.*] It's a fright, surely. I knew a party was kicked in the head by a red mare, and he went killing horses a great while, till he eat the insides of a clock and died after.

PHILLY—[*with suspicion.*]—Did he see Christy?

WIDOW QUIN. He didn't. *(With a warning gesture.)* Let you not be putting him in mind of him, or you'll be likely summoned if there's murder done. *(Looking round at Mahon.)* Whisht! He's listening. Wait now till you hear me taking him easy and unravelling all. *(She goes to Mahon.)* And what way are you feeling, mister? Are you in contentment now?

MAHON—[*slightly emotional from his drink.*]—I'm poorly only, for it's a hard story the way I'm left to-day, when it was I did tend him from his hour of birth, and he a dunce never reached his second book, the way he'd come from school, many's the day, with his legs lamed under him, and he blackened with his beatings like a tinker's ass. It's a hard story, I'm saying, the way some do have their next and nighest raising up a hand of murder on them, and some is lonesome getting their death with lamentation in the dead of night.

WIDOW QUIN—[*not knowing what to say.*]—To hear you talking so quiet, who'd know you were the same fellow we seen pass to-day?

MAHON. I'm the same surely. The wrack and ruin of three score years; and it's a terror to live that length, I tell you, and to have your sons going to the dogs against you, and you wore out scolding them, and skelping° them, and God knows what. beating

PHILLY—[*to Jimmy.*]—He's not raving. *(To Widow Quin.)* Will you ask him what kind was his son?

WIDOW QUIN—[*to Mahon, with a peculiar look.*]—Was your son that hit you a lad of one year and a score maybe, a great hand at racing and lepping and licking the world?

MAHON—[*turning on her with a roar of rage.*]—Didn't you hear me say he was the fool of men, the way from this out he'll know the orphan's lot with old and young making game of him and they swearing, raging, kicking at him like a mangy cur. [*A great burst of cheering outside, someway off.*]

MAHON—[*putting his hands to his ears.*]—What in the name of God do they want roaring below?

WIDOW QUIN—[*with the shade of a smile.*]—They're cheering a young lad, the champion Playboy of the Western World.

[*More cheering.*]

MAHON—[*going to window.*] It'd split my heart to hear them, and I with pulses in my brain-pan for a week gone by. Is it racing they are?

JIMMY—[*looking from door.*]—It is then. They are mounting him for the mule race will be run upon the sands. That's the playboy on the winkered° mule. blinkered

MAHON [*puzzled.*] That lad, is it? If you said it was a fool he was, I'd have laid a mighty oath he was the likeness of my wandering son *(uneasily, putting his hand to his head.)* Faith, I'm thinking I'll go walking for to view the race.

WIDOW QUIN—[*stopping him, sharply*]—You will not. You'd best take the road to Belmullet, and not be dilly-dallying in this place where there isn't a spot you could sleep.

PHILLY—[*coming forward.*]—Don't mind her. Mount there on the bench and you'll have a view of the whole. They're hurrying before the tide will rise, and it'd be near over if you went down the pathway through the crags below.

MAHON [*mounts on bench, Widow Quin beside him.*]—That's a right view again the edge of the sea. They're coming now from the point. He's leading. Who is he at all?

WIDOW QUIN. He's the champion of the world, I tell you, and there isn't a hap'orth[28] isn't falling lucky to his hands to-day.

PHILLY—[*looking out, interested in the race.*]—Look at that. They're pressing him now.

JIMMY. He'll win it yet.

PHILLY. Take your time, Jimmy Farrell. It's too soon to say.

WIDOW QUIN—[*shouting.*] Watch him taking the gate. There's riding.

JIMMY—[*cheering.*] More power to the young lad!

MAHON. He's passing the third.

JIMMY. He'll lick them yet!

WIDOW QUIN. He'd lick them if he was running races with a score itself.

MAHON. Look at the mule he has, kicking the stars.

WIDOW QUIN. There was a lep! *(catching hold of Mahon in her excitement.)* He's fallen! He's mounted again! Faith, he's passing them all!

JIMMY. Look at him skelping her!

PHILLY. And the mountain girls hooshing° him on! cheering

JIMMY. It's the last turn! The post's cleared for them now!

MAHON. Look at the narrow place. He'll be into the bogs! *(With a yell.)* Good rider! He's through it again!

JIMMY. He's neck and neck!

MAHON. Good boy to him! Flames, but he's in! [*Great cheering, in which all join.*]

MAHON [*with hesitation.*] What's that? They're raising him up. They're coming this way. *(With a roar of rage and astonishment.)* It's Christy! by the stars of God! I'd know his way of spitting and he astride the moon. [*He jumps down and makes for the door, but Widow Quin catches him and pulls him back.*]

WIDOW QUIN. Stay quiet, will you. That's not your son. *(To Jimmy.)* Stop him, or you'll get a month for the abetting of manslaughter and be fined as well.

JIMMY. I'll hold him.

MAHON [*struggling.*] Let me out! Let me out, the lot of you! till I have my vengeance on his head to-day.

WIDOW QUIN—[*shaking him, vehemently.*]—That's not your son. That's a man is going to make a marriage with the daughter of this house, a place with fine trade, with a license, and with poteen too.

MAHON—[*amazed.*] That man marrying a decent and a moneyed girl! Is it mad yous are? Is it in a crazy-house for females that I'm landed now?

WIDOW QUIN. It's mad yourself is with the blow upon your head. That lad is the wonder of the Western World.

28. A small amount; i.e., every little thing is going Christy's way.

MAHON. I seen it's my son.

WIDOW QUIN. You seen that you're mad. *(Cheering outside.)* Do you hear them cheering him in the zig-zags of the road? Aren't you after saying that your son's a fool, and how would they be cheering a true idiot born?

MAHON—[*getting distressed.*]—It's maybe out of reason that that man's himself. *(Cheering again.)* There's none surely will go cheering him. Oh, I'm raving with a madness that would fright the world! *(He sits down with his hand to his head.)* There was one time I seen ten scarlet divils letting on they'd cork my spirit in a gallon can; and one time I seen rats as big as badgers sucking the life blood from the butt of my lug;° but I never till this day confused that dribbling idiot with a likely man. I'm destroyed surely. ear

WIDOW QUIN. And who'd wonder when it's your brain-pan that is gaping now?

MAHON. Then the blight of the sacred drought upon myself and him, for I never went mad to this day, and I not three weeks with the Limerick girls drinking myself silly, and parlatic° from the dusk to dawn. *(To Widow Quin, suddenly.)* Is my visage astray? paralytic

WIDOW QUIN. It is then. You're a sniggering maniac, a child could see.

MAHON—[*getting up more cheerfully.*]—Then I'd best be going to the union[29] beyond, and there'll be a welcome before me, I tell you *(with great pride),* and I a terrible and fearful case, the way that there I was one time, screeching in a straightened waistcoat, with seven doctors writing out my sayings in a printed book. Would you believe that?

WIDOW QUIN. If you're a wonder itself, you'd best be hasty, for them lads caught a maniac one time and pelted the poor creature till he ran out, raving and foaming, and was drowned in the sea.

MAHON—[*with philosophy.*]—It's true mankind is the divil when your head's astray. Let me out now and I'll slip down the boreen, and not see them so.

WIDOW QUIN—[*showing him out.*]—That's it. Run to the right, and not a one will see. [*He runs off.*]

PHILLY—[*wisely.*] You're at some gaming, Widow Quin; but I'll walk after him and give him his dinner and a time to rest, and I'll see then if he's raving or as sane as you.

WIDOW QUIN—[*annoyed.*] If you go near that lad, let you be wary of your head, I'm saying. Didn't you hear him telling he was crazed at times?

PHILLY. I heard him telling a power; and I'm thinking we'll have right sport, before night will fall. [*He goes out.*]

JIMMY. Well, Philly's a conceited and foolish man. How could that madman have his senses and his brain-pan slit? I'll go after them and see

29. Union work houses originally provided lodging and food to laborers in exchange for harsh labor, but over the nineteenth century came to provide shelter for the elderly, ill, and mad.

him turn on Philly now. [*He goes; Widow Quin hides poteen behind counter. Then hubbub outside.*]

VOICES. There you are! Good jumper! Grand lepper! Darlint boy! He's the racer! Bear him on, will you! [*Christy comes in, in Jockey's dress, with Pegeen Mike, Sara, and other girls, and men.*]

PEGEEN—[*to crowd.*]—Go on now and don't destroy him and he drenching with sweat. Go along, I'm saying, and have your tug-of-warring till he's dried his skin.

CROWD. Here's his prizes! A bagpipes! A fiddle was played by a poet in the years gone by! A flat and three-thorned blackthorn[30] would lick the scholars out of Dublin town!

CHRISTY—[*taking prizes from the men.*]—Thank you kindly, the lot of you. But you'd say it was little only I did this day if you'd seen me a while since striking my one single blow.

TOWN CRIER—[*outside, ringing a bell.*]—Take notice, last event of this day! Tug-of-warring on the green below! Come on, the lot of you! Great achievements for all Mayo men!

PEGEEN. Go on, and leave him for to rest and dry. Go on, I tell you, for he'll do no more. *(She hustles crowd out; Widow Quin following them.)*

MEN—[*going.*]—Come on then. Good luck for the while!

PEGEEN—[*radiantly, wiping his face with her shawl.*]—Well, you're the lad, and you'll have great times from this out when you could win that wealth of prizes, and you sweating in the heat of noon!

CHRISTY—[*looking at her with delight.*]—I'll have great times if I win the crowning prize I'm seeking now, and that's your promise that you'll wed me in a fortnight, when our banns is called.

PEGEEN—[*backing away from him.*]—You've right daring to go ask me that, when all knows you'll be starting to some girl in your own townland, when your father's rotten in four months, or five.

CHRISTY—[*indignantly.*] Starting from you, is it? *(He follows her.)* I will not, then, and when the airs is warming in four months, or five, it's then yourself and me should be pacing Neifin in the dews of night, the times sweet smells do be rising, and you'd see a little shiny new moon, maybe, sinking on the hills.

PEGEEN [*looking at him playfully.*]—And it's that kind of a poacher's love you'd make, Christy Mahon, on the sides of Neifin, when the night is down?

CHRISTY. It's little you'll think if my love's a poacher's, or an earl's itself, when you'll feel my two hands stretched around you, and I squeezing kisses on your puckered lips, till I'd feel a kind of pity for the Lord God is all ages sitting lonesome in his golden chair.

PEGEEN. That'll be right fun, Christy Mahon, and any girl would walk

30. A sturdy stick that could be used either for walking support or as a weapon.

her heart out before she'd meet a young man was your like for eloquence, or talk, at all.

CHRISTY—[*encouraged.*] Let you wait, to hear me talking, till we're astray in Erris, when Good Friday's by, drinking a sup from a well, and making mighty kisses with our wetted mouths, or gaming in a gap or sunshine, with yourself stretched back unto your necklace, in the flowers of the earth.

PEGEEN—[*in a lower voice, moved by his tone.*]—I'd be nice so, is it?

CHRISTY—[*with rapture.*]—If the mitred bishops seen you that time, they'd be the like of the holy prophets, I'm thinking, do be straining the bars of Paradise to lay eyes on the Lady Helen of Troy, and she abroad, pacing back and forward, with a nosegay in her golden shawl.

PEGEEN—[*with real tenderness.*]—And what is it I have, Christy Mahon, to make me fitting entertainment for the like of you, that has such poet's talking, and such bravery of heart?

CHRISTY—[*in a low voice.*]—Isn't there the light of seven heavens in your heart alone, the way you'll be an angel's lamp to me from this out, and I abroad in the darkness, spearing salmons in the Owen, or the Carrowmore?

PEGEEN. If I was your wife, I'd be along with you those nights, Christy Mahon, the way you'd see I was a great hand at coaxing bailiffs, or coining funny nick-names for the stars of night.

CHRISTY. You, is it? Taking your death in the hailstones, or in the fogs of dawn.

PEGEEN. Yourself and me would shelter easy in a narrow bush, *(with a qualm of dread)* but we're only talking, maybe, for this would be a poor, thatched place to hold a fine lad is the like of you.

CHRISTY—[*putting his arm round her.*]—If I wasn't a good Christian, it's on my naked knees I'd be saying my prayers and paters° to every jackstraw you have roofing your head, and every stony pebble is paving the laneway to your door. Our Fathers

PEGEEN—[*radiantly.*] If that's the truth, I'll be burning candles from this out to the miracles of God that have brought you from the south today, and I, with my gowns bought ready, the way that I can wed you, and not wait at all.

CHRISTY. It's miracles, and that's the truth. Me there toiling a long while, and walking a long while, not knowing at all I was drawing all times nearer to this holy day.

PEGEEN. And myself, a girl, was tempted often to go sailing the seas till I'd marry a Jew-man, with ten kegs of gold, and I not knowing at all there was the like of you drawing nearer, like the stars of God.

CHRISTY. And to think I'm long years hearing women talking that talk, to all bloody fools, and this the first time I've heard the like of your voice talking sweetly for my own delight.

PEGEEN. And to think it's me is talking sweetly, Christy Mahon, and I the fright of seven townlands for my biting tongue. Well, the heart's a wonder; and, I'm thinking, there won't be our like in Mayo, for gallant lovers, from this hour, to-day. *(Drunken singing is heard outside.)* There's my father coming from the wake, and when he's had his sleep we'll tell him, for he's peaceful then. [*They separate.*]

MICHAEL—[*singing outside*]—

The jailor and the turnkey
They quickly ran us down,
And brought us back as prisoners
more to Cavan town. [*He comes in supported by Shawn.*]
There we lay bewailing
All in a prison bound. . . . [*He sees Christy. Goes and shakes him drunkenly by the hand, while Pegeen and Shawn talk on the left.*]

MICHAEL—[*to Christy.*]—The blessing of God and the holy angels on your head, young fellow. I hear tell you're after winning all in the sports below; and wasn't it a shame I didn't bear you along with me to Kate Cassidy's wake, a fine, stout lad, the like of you, for you'd never see the match of it for flows of drink, the way when we sunk her bones at noonday in her narrow grave, there were five men, aye, and six men, stretched out retching speechless on the holy stones.

CHRISTY—[*uneasily, watching Pegeen.*]—Is that the truth?

MICHAEL. It is then, and aren't you a louty schemer to go burying your poor father unbeknownst when you'd a right to throw him on the crupper of a Kerry mule and drive him westwards, like holy Joseph in the days gone by, the way we could have given him a decent burial, and not have him rotting beyond, and not a Christian drinking a smart drop to the glory of his soul?

CHRISTY—[*gruffly.*] It's well enough he's lying, for the likes of him.

MICHAEL—[*slapping him on the back.*]—Well, aren't you a hardened slayer? It'll be a poor thing for the household man where you go sniffing for a female wife; and (pointing to Shawn) look beyond at that shy and decent Christian I have chosen for my daughter's hand, and I after getting the gilded dispensation this day for to wed them now.

CHRISTY. And you'll be wedding them this day, is it?

MICHAEL—[*drawing himself up.*]—Aye. Are you thinking, if I'm drunk itself, I'd leave my daughter living single with a little frisky rascal is the like of you?

PEGEEN—[*breaking away from Shawn.*]—Is it the truth the dispensation's come?

MICHAEL—[*triumphantly.*] Father Reilly's after reading it in gallous° Latin, and "It's come in the nick of time," says he; "so I'll wed them in a hurry, dreading that young gaffer who'd capsize the stars." splendid

PEGEEN—[*fiercely.*] He's missed his nick of time, for it's that lad, Christy Mahon, that I'm wedding now.

MICHAEL—[*loudly with horror.*]—You'd be making him a son to me, and he wet and crusted with his father's blood?

PEGEEN. Aye. Wouldn't it be a bitter thing for a girl to go marrying the like of Shaneen, and he a middling kind of a scarecrow, with no savagery or fine words in him at all?

MICHAEL—[*gasping and sinking on a chair.*]—Oh, aren't you a heathen daughter to go shaking the fat of my heart, and I swamped and drownded with the weight of drink? Would you have them turning on me the way that I'd be roaring to the dawn of day with the wind upon my heart? Have you not a word to aid me, Shaneen? Are you not jealous at all?

SHAWN[31]—[*In great misery.*]—I'd be afeard to be jealous of a man did slay his da.

PEGEEN. Well, it'd be a poor thing to go marrying your like. I'm seeing there's a world of peril for an orphan girl, and isn't it a great blessing I didn't wed you, before himself came walking from the west or south?

SHAWN. It's a queer story you'd go picking a dirty tramp up from the highways of the world.

PEGEEN—[*playfully.*] And you think you're a likely beau to go straying along with, the shiny Sundays of the opening year, when it's sooner on a bullock's liver you'd put a poor girl thinking than on the lily or the rose?

SHAWN. And have you no mind of my weight of passion, and the holy dispensation, and the drift of heifers I am giving, and the golden ring?

PEGEEN. I'm thinking you're too fine for the like of me, Shawn Keogh of Killakeen, and let you go off till you'd find a radiant lady with droves of bullocks on the plains of Meath, and herself bedizened in the diamond jewelleries of Pharaoh's ma. That'd be your match, Shaneen. So God save you now! [*She retreats behind Christy.*]

SHAWN. Won't you hear me telling you . . . ?

CHRISTY—[*with ferocity.*]—Take yourself from this, young fellow, or I'll maybe add a murder to my deeds to-day.

MICHAEL—[*springing up with a shriek.*]—Murder is it? Is it mad yous are? Would you go making murder in this place, and it piled with poteen for our drink to-night? Go on to the foreshore if it's fighting you want, where the rising tide will wash all traces from the memory of man. [*Pushing Shawn towards Christy.*]

SHAWN—[*shaking himself free, and getting behind Michael.*] —I'll not fight him, Michael James. I'd liefer live a bachelor, simmering in passions to the end of time, than face a lepping savage the like of him has descended from the Lord knows where. Strike him yourself, Michael James, or you'll lose my drift of heifers and my blue bull from Sneem.

MICHAEL. Is it me fight him, when it's father-slaying he's bred to now? (*Pushing Shawn.*) Go on you fool and fight him now.

31. Standardized from "Shaneen" in the text—the one time in the speech prefixes "Shaneen" is used.

SHAWN—[*coming forward a little.*]—Will I strike him with my hand?

MICHAEL. Take the loy is on your western side.

SHAWN. I'd be afeard of the gallows if I struck him with that.

CHRISTY—[*taking up the loy.*]—Then I'll make you face the gallows or quit off from this. [*Shawn flies out of the door.*]

CHRISTY. Well, fine weather be after him, *(going to Michael, coaxingly)* and I'm thinking you wouldn't wish to have that quaking blackguard in your house at all. Let you give us your blessing and hear her swear her faith to me, for I'm mounted on the spring-tide of the stars of luck, the way it'll be good for any to have me in the house.

PEGEEN [*at the other side of Michael.*]—Bless us now, for I swear to God I'll wed him, and I'll not renege.

MICHAEL—[*standing up in the centre, holding on to both of them.*] —It's the will of God, I'm thinking, that all should win an easy or a cruel end, and it's the will of God that all should rear up lengthy families for the nurture of the earth. What's a single man, I ask you, eating a bit in one house and drinking a sup in another, and he with no place of his own, like an old braying jackass strayed upon the rocks? *(To Christy.)* It's many would be in dread to bring your like into their house for to end them, maybe, with a sudden end; but I'm a decent man of Ireland, and I liefer face the grave untimely and I seeing a score of grandsons growing up little gallant swearers by the name of God, than go peopling my bedside with puny weeds the like of what you'd breed, I'm thinking, out of Shaneen Keogh. *(He joins their hands.)* A daring fellow is the jewel of the world, and a man did split his father's middle with a single clout, should have the bravery of ten, so may God and Mary and St. Patrick bless you, and increase you from this mortal day.

CHRISTY AND PEGEEN. Amen, O Lord!

[*Hubbub outside.*]

[*Old Mahon rushes in, followed by all the crowd, and Widow Quin. He makes a rush at Christy, knocks him down, and begins to beat him.*]

PEGEEN—[*dragging back his arm.*]—Stop that, will you. Who are you at all?

MAHON. His father, God forgive me!

PEGEEN—[*drawing back.*]—Is it rose from the dead?

MAHON. Do you think I look so easy quenched with the tap of a loy? [*Beats Christy again.*]

PEGEEN—[*glaring at Christy.*]—And it's lies you told, letting on you had him slitted, and you nothing at all.

CHRISTY—[*clutching Mahon's stick.*]—He's not my father. He's a raving maniac would scare the world. *(Pointing to Widow Quin.)* Herself knows it is true.

CROWD. You're fooling Pegeen! The Widow Quin seen him this day, and you likely knew! You're a liar!

CHRISTY—[*dumbfounded.*] It's himself was a liar, lying stretched out with an open head on him, letting on he was dead.

MAHON. Weren't you off racing the hills before I got my breath with the start I had seeing you turn on me at all?

PEGEEN. And to think of the coaxing glory we had given him, and he after doing nothing but hitting a soft blow and chasing northward in a sweat of fear. Quit off from this.

CHRISTY—[*piteously.*] You've seen my doings this day, and let you save me from the old man; for why would you be in such a scorch of haste to spur me to destruction now?

PEGEEN. It's there your treachery is spurring me, till I'm hard set to think you're the one I'm after lacing in my heart-strings half-an-hour gone by. *(To Mahon.)* Take him on from this, for I think bad the world should see me raging for a Munster liar, and the fool of men.

MAHON. Rise up now to retribution, and come on with me.

CROWD—[*jeeringly.*] There's the playboy! There's the lad thought he'd rule the roost in Mayo. Slate° him now, mister. beat

CHRISTY—[*getting up in shy terror.*]—What is it drives you to torment me here, when I'd asked the thunders of the might of God to blast me if I ever did hurt to any saving only that one single blow.

MAHON—[*loudly.*] If you didn't, you're a poor good-for-nothing, and isn't it by the like of you the sins of the whole world are committed?

CHRISTY—[*raising his hands.*]—In the name of the Almighty God. . . .

MAHON. Leave troubling the Lord God. Would you have him sending down droughts, and fevers, and the old hen and the cholera morbus?[32]

CHRISTY—[*to Widow Quin.*]—Will you come between us and protect me now?

WIDOW QUIN. I've tried a lot, God help me, and my share is done.

CHRISTY—[*looking round in desperation.*]—And I must go back into my torment is it, or run off like a vagabond straying through the Unions with the dusts of August making mudstains in the gullet of my throat, or the winds of March blowing on me till I'd take an oath I felt them making whistles of my ribs within?

SARA. Ask Pegeen to aid you. Her like does often change.

CHRISTY. I will not then, for there's torment in the splendour of her like, and she a girl any moon of midnight would take pride to meet, facing southwards on the heaths of Keel.[33] But what did I want crawling forward to scorch my understanding at her flaming brow?

PEGEEN—[*to Mahon, vehemently, fearing she will break into tears.*]—Take him on from this or I'll set the young lads to destroy him here.

MAHON—[*going to him, shaking his stick.*]—Come on now if you wouldn't have the company to see you skelped.

32. "the old hen" is influenza; cholera is an infection of the small intestine that can be fatal because of dehydration.

33. Achill Island, off the coast of Mayo.

PEGEEN—[*half laughing, through her tears.*]—That's it, now the world will see him pandied,° and he an ugly liar was playing off the hero, and the fright of men. paddled

CHRISTY—[*to Mahon, very sharply.*]—Leave me go!

CROWD. That's it. Now Christy. If them two set fighting, it will lick the world.

MAHON—[*making a grab at Christy.*]—Come here to me.

CHRISTY—[*more threateningly.*]—Leave me go, I'm saying.

MAHON. I will maybe, when your legs is limping, and your back is blue.

CROWD. Keep it up, the two of you. I'll back the old one. Now the playboy.

CHRISTY—[*in low and intense voice.*]—Shut your yelling, for if you're after making a mighty man of me this day by the power of a lie, you're setting me now to think if it's a poor thing to be lonesome, it's worse maybe to go mixing with the fools of earth.

[*Mahon makes a movement towards him.*]

CHRISTY—[*almost shouting.*]—Keep off . . . lest I do show a blow unto the lot of you would set the guardian angels winking in the clouds above. [*He swings round with a sudden rapid movement and picks up a loy.*]

CROWD—[*half frightened, half amused.*]—He's going mad! Mind yourselves! Run from the idiot!

CHRISTY. If I am an idiot, I'm after hearing my voice this day saying words would raise the topknot on a poet in a merchant's town. I've won your racing, and your lepping, and . . .

MAHON. Shut your gullet and come on with me.

CHRISTY. I'm going, but I'll stretch you first. [*He runs at old Mahon with the loy, chases him out of the door, followed by crowd and Widow Quin. There is a great noise outside, then a yell, and dead silence for a moment. Christy comes in, half dazed, and goes to fire.*]

WIDOW QUIN—[*coming in, hurriedly, and going to him.*]—They're turning again you. Come on, or you'll be hanged, indeed.

CHRISTY. I'm thinking, from this out, Pegeen'll be giving me praises the same as in the hours gone by.

WIDOW QUIN—[*impatiently.*] Come by the back-door. I'd think bad to have you stifled on the gallows tree.

CHRISTY—[*indignantly.*] I will not, then. What good'd be my life-time, if I left Pegeen?

WIDOW QUIN. Come on, and you'll be no worse than you were last night; and you with a double murder this time to be telling to the girls.

CHRISTY. I'll not leave Pegeen Mike.

WIDOW QUIN—[*impatiently.*] Isn't there the match of her in every parish public, from Binghamstown unto the plain of Meath? Come on, I tell you, and I'll find you finer sweethearts at each waning moon.

CHRISTY. It's Pegeen I'm seeking only, and what'd I care if you brought me a drift of chosen females, standing in their shifts itself, maybe, from this place to the Eastern World?

SARA—[*runs in, pulling off one of her petticoats.*]—They're going to hang him. *(Holding out petticoat and shawl.)* Fit these upon him, and let him run off to the east.

WIDOW QUIN. He's raving now; but we'll fit them on him, and I'll take him, in the ferry, to the Achill boat.

CHRISTY—[*struggling feebly.*]—Leave me go, will you? when I'm thinking of my luck to-day, for she will wed me surely, and I a proven hero in the end of all. [*They try to fasten petticoat round him.*]

WIDOW QUIN. Take his left hand, and we'll pull him now. Come on, young fellow.

CHRISTY—[*suddenly starting up.*]—You'll be taking me from her? You're jealous, is it, of her wedding me? Go on from this.

[*He snatches up a stool, and threatens them with it.*]

WIDOW QUIN—[*going.*]—It's in the mad-house they should put him, not in jail, at all. We'll go by the back-door, to call the doctor, and we'll save him so. [*She goes out, with Sara, through inner room. Men crowd in the doorway. Christy sits down again by the fire.*]

MICHAEL—[*in a terrified whisper.*]—Is the old lad killed surely?

PHILLY. I'm after feeling the last gasps quitting his heart. [*They peer in at Christy.*]

MICHAEL—[*with a rope.*]—Look at the way he is. Twist a hangman's knot on it, and slip it over his head, while he's not minding at all.

PHILLY. Let you take it, Shaneen. You're the soberest of all that's here.

SHAWN. Is it me to go near him, and he the wickedest and worst with me? Let you take it, Pegeen Mike.

PEGEEN. Come on, so. [*She goes forward with the others, and they drop the double hitch over his head.*]

CHRISTY. What ails you?

SHAWN—[*triumphantly, as they pull the rope tight on his arms.*] —Come on to the peelers, till they stretch you now.

CHRISTY. Me!

MICHAEL. If we took pity on you, the Lord God would, maybe, bring us ruin from the law to-day, so you'd best come easy, for hanging is an easy and a speedy end.

CHRISTY. I'll not stir. *(To Pegeen.)* And what is it you'll say to me, and I after doing it this time in the face of all?

PEGEEN. I'll say, a strange man is a marvel, with his mighty talk; but what's a squabble in your back-yard, and the blow of a loy, have taught me that there's a great gap between a gallous story and a dirty deed. *(To Men.)* Take him on from this, or the lot of us will be likely put on trial for his deed to-day.

CHRISTY—[*with horror in his voice.*]—And it's yourself will send me off, to have a horny-fingered hangman hitching his bloody slip-knots at the butt of my ear.

MEN—[*pulling rope.*]—Come on, will you? [*He is pulled down on the floor.*]

CHRISTY—[*twisting his legs round the table.*]—Cut the rope, Pegeen, and I'll quit the lot of you, and live from this out, like the madmen of Keel, eating muck and green weeds, on the faces of the cliffs.

PEGEEN. And leave us to hang, is it, for a saucy liar, the like of you? *(To men.)* Take him on, out from this.

SHAWN. Pull a twist on his neck, and squeeze him so.

PHILLY. Twist yourself. Sure he cannot hurt you, if you keep your distance from his teeth alone.

SHAWN. I'm afeard of him. *(To Pegeen.)* Lift a lighted sod, will you, and scorch his leg.

PEGEEN—[*blowing the fire, with a bellows.*] Leave go now, young fellow, or I'll scorch your shins.

CHRISTY. You're blowing for to torture me *(His voice rising and growing stronger.)* That's your kind, is it? Then let the lot of you be wary, for, if I've to face the gallows, I'll have a gay march down, I tell you, and shed the blood of some of you before I die.

SHAWN—[*in terror.*]—Keep a good hold, Philly. Be wary, for the love of God. For I'm thinking he would liefest wreak his pains on me.

CHRISTY—[*almost gaily.*]—If I do lay my hands on you, it's the way you'll be at the fall of night, hanging as a scarecrow for the fowls of hell. Ah, you'll have a gallous jaunt I'm saying, coaching out through Limbo with my father's ghost.

SHAWN—[*to Pegeen.*]—Make haste, will you? Oh, isn't he a holy terror, and isn't it true for Father Reilly, that all drink's a curse that has the lot of you so shaky and uncertain now?

CHRISTY. If I can wring a neck among you, I'll have a royal judgment looking on the trembling jury in the courts of law. And won't there be crying out in Mayo the day I'm stretched upon the rope with ladies in their silks and satins snivelling in their lacy kerchiefs, and they rhyming songs and ballads on the terror of my fate? [*He squirms round on the floor and bites Shawn's leg.*]

SHAWN—[*shrieking.*] My leg's bit on me. He's the like of a mad dog, I'm thinking, the way that I will surely die.

CHRISTY—[*delighted with himself.*]—You will then, the way you can shake out hell's flags of welcome for my coming in two weeks or three, for I'm thinking Satan hasn't many have killed their da in Kerry, and in Mayo too. [*Old Mahon comes in behind on all fours and looks on unnoticed.*]

MEN—[*to Pegeen.*]—Bring the sod, will you?

PEGEEN [*coming over.*]—God help him so. *(Burns his leg.)*

CHRISTY—[*kicking and screaming.*] O, glory be to God!

[*He kicks loose from the table, and they all drag him towards the door.*]

JIMMY—[*seeing old Mahon.*]—Will you look what's come in? [*They all drop Christy and run left.*]

CHRISTY—[*scrambling on his knees face to face with old Mahon.*] —Are you coming to be killed a third time, or what ails you now?

MAHON. For what is it they have you tied?

CHRISTY. They're taking me to the peelers to have me hanged for slaying you.

MICHAEL—[*apologetically.*] It is the will of God that all should guard their little cabins from the treachery of law, and what would my daughter be doing if I was ruined or was hanged itself?

MAHON—[*grimly, loosening Christy.*]—It's little I care if you put a bag on her back, and went picking cockles till the hour of death; but my son and myself will be going our own way, and we'll have great times from this out telling stories of the villainy of Mayo, and the fools is here. *(To Christy, who is freed.)* Come on now.

CHRISTY. Go with you, is it? I will then, like a gallant captain with his heathen slave. Go on now and I'll see you from this day stewing my oatmeal and washing my spuds, for I'm master of all fights from now. *(Pushing Mahon.)* Go on, I'm saying.

MAHON. Is it me?

CHRISTY. Not a word out of you. Go on from this.

MAHON [*walking out and looking back at Christy over his shoulder.*] — Glory be to God! *(With a broad smile.)* I am crazy again! [*Goes.*]

CHRISTY. Ten thousand blessings upon all that's here, for you've turned me a likely gaffer° in the end of all, the way I'll go romancing through a romping lifetime from this hour to the dawning of the judgment day. [*He goes out.*] master

MICHAEL. By the will of God, we'll have peace now for our drinks. Will you draw the porter, Pegeen?

SHAWN—[*going up to her.*]—It's a miracle Father Reilly can wed us in the end of all, and we'll have none to trouble us when his vicious bite is healed.

PEGEEN—[*hitting him a box on the ear.*]—Quit my sight. *(Putting her shawl over her head and breaking out into wild lamentations.)* Oh my grief, I've lost him surely. I've lost the only Playboy of the Western World.

CURTAIN

St. Joan

George Bernard Shaw was born in Dublin in 1856 to yet another unconventional Irish Protestant family. Bernard Shaw hated school, and the most important early formative influence on him was the charismatic musician George Vandaleur Lee, who lived with his family in Dublin for some time. When Lee went to London, Bernard Shaw's mother followed him with her daughter. Bernard Shaw spent the years from fifteen to twenty as a clerk before following his mother to London. Once there, subsidized by his family, he read voraciously, wrote novels, and eventually became a newspaper music critic in 1888. Bernard Shaw also became a committed Socialist and was a member of the Fabian Society founded in 1884. Throughout his life Bernard Shaw found himself in opposition to social conventions: he was a vegetarian at a time when people were vegetarians in English-speaking countries only by necessity. He opposed British involvement in World War I and persisted despite public scorn. He argued for the reform of English spelling and punctuation. In 1898 he married an Irish heiress, Charlotte Payne-Townsend; on friendly terms throughout their long marriage, they may never have consummated the marriage, although Bernard Shaw had affairs with married women. In 1891 he published *The Quintessence of Ibsenism,* which not only praised the intellectual, realist drama of the Norwegian playwright, but attacked the melodrama and light comedy that had dominated the English speaking stage in the nineteenth century. In 1895 he was one of the founders of the London School of Economics.

Bernard Shaw got off to a rocky start as a playwright; his play *Mrs. Warren's Profession* (1893) was banned because of its subject, prostitution. His first genuine hit was *The Devil's Disciple* (1897), a play about the American Revolution, staged successfully in New York. From then on, while his plays were frequently the subject of controversy, they were also frequently successful, and he was regarded as one of the world's most important dramatists. He wrote more than sixty plays, becoming

Copy text is (by agreement with The Society of Authors) the Penguin edition under the supervision of Dan H. Lawrence (London: Penguin Books, 2003). Also consulted is the Bretano's New York edition of 1924. This does not include a *Dramatis Personae.*

a wealthy man in the process. In 1925 he received the Nobel Prize for literature and in 1938 an Oscar for his work on the film version of *Pygmalion*.

Bernard Shaw rejected the clear demarcation between good and evil characteristic of nineteenth-century melodrama. He both plays with and reacts against the conventions of the well-made play, such as the curtain closer (ending each act at a moment of high dramatic tension). Not only are his characters the product of their environment, but those who judge them do so because of their own social conditioning, economic status, and biological imperatives. The plays also dramatize the conflicts generated by changes in ideas and technology. Unlike the serious drama of Henrik Ibsen, however, Bernard Shaw's plays incorporate significant themes with dazzling humor.

In *St. Joan* (1924) he reexamines the life of the title character, who is called by her saints to drive the English out of France. As a realist, Bernard Shaw had no use for miraculous events: Joan being sent to the Dauphin coincides with the hens beginning to lay and this is humorously presented as a miracle. Joan drives the English from Orleans with the help of French troops inspired by her absolute confidence and ability to seize the initiative and with a lucky shift of the wind. She is, however, too revolutionary (and demanding and impetuous) for her French allies, and, to her aristocratic and clerical enemies, a threat to the established order as both an early nationalist and a proto-Protestant. By standing for the individual consciousness as opposed to received opinion, whether in the conduct of war or religion, she is a martyr to her ideals and executed because her time is not ready for them.

Saint Joan

DRAMATIS PERSONAE (in order of appearance)

ROBERT DE BAUDRICOURT
STEWARD
JOAN
BERTRAND DE POULENGEY
ARCHBISHOP OF RHEIMS
MONSEIGNEUR DE LA TRÉMOUILLE
PAGE (French)
GILLES DE RAIS (Bluebeard)
CAPTAIN LA HIRE
DAUPHIN (subsequently Charles VII)
DUCHESS LA TRÉMOUILLE
DUNOIS (The Bastard)
SENTRY
NOBLEMAN (Richard de Beauchamp, earl of Warwick)
CHAPLAIN (John de Stogumber)
PAGE (English)
BISHOPE OF BEAUVAIS (Cauchon)
BROTHER JOHN LEMAÎTRE (Inquisitor)
CANON JOHN D'ESTIVET (Promoter°) prosecutor
CANON DE COURCELLES
BROTHER MARTIN LADVENU
EXECUTIONER

noblemen, men at arms, canons, assessors,
Dominican monks, scribes

SCENE I

A fine spring morning on the river Meuse, between Lorraine and Champagne, in the year 1429 A.D., in the castle of Vaucouleurs.[1]

Captain Robert de Baudricourt, a military squire, handsome and physically energetic, but with no will of his own, is disguising that defect in his usual fashion by storming terribly at his steward, a trodden worm, scanty of flesh, scanty of hair, who might be any age from 18 to 55, being the sort of man whom age cannot wither because he has never bloomed.

The two are in a sunny stone chamber on the first floor of the castle. At a plain strong oak table, seated in chair to match, the captain presents his left profile. The steward stands facing him at the other side of

1. About 190 miles northeast of Paris.

the table, if so deprecatory a stance as his can be called standing. The mullioned thirteenth-century window[2] *is open behind him. Near it in the corner is a turret with a narrow arched doorway leading to a winding stair which descends to the courtyard. There is a stout fourlegged stool under the table, and a wooden chest under the window.*

ROBERT. No eggs! No eggs!! Thousand thunders, man, what do you mean by no eggs?

STEWARD. Sir: it is not my fault. It is the act of God.

ROBERT. Blasphemy. You tell me there are no eggs; and you blame your Maker for it.

STEWARD. Sir: what can I do? I cannot lay eggs.

ROBERT [*sarcastic*] Ha! You jest about it.

STEWARD. No, sir, God knows. We all have to go without eggs just as you have, sir. The hens will not lay.

ROBERT. Indeed! [*Rising*] Now listen to me, you.

STEWARD [*humbly*] Yes, sir.

ROBERT. What am I?

STEWARD. What are you, sir?

ROBERT [*coming at him*] Yes: what am I? Am I Robert, squire of Baudricourt and captain of this castle of Vaucouleurs; or am I a cowboy?

STEWARD. Oh, sir, you know you are a greater man here than the king himself.

ROBERT. Precisely. And now, do you know what you are?

STEWARD. I am nobody, sir, except that I have the honor to be your steward.

ROBERT [*driving him to the wall, adjective by adjective*] You have not only the honor of being my steward, but the privilege of being the worst, most incompetent, drivelling snivelling jibbering jabbering idiot of a steward in France. [*He strides back to the table*].

STEWARD [*cowering on the chest*] Yes, sir: to a great man like you I must seem like that.

ROBERT [*turning*] My fault, I suppose. Eh?

STEWARD [*coming to him deprecatingly*] Oh, sir: you always give my most innocent words such a turn!

ROBERT. I will give your neck a turn if you dare tell me when I ask you how many eggs there are that you cannot lay any.

STEWARD [*protesting*] Oh sir, oh sir—

ROBERT. No: not oh sir, oh sir, but no sir, no sir. My three Barbary hens and the black are the best layers in Champagne. And you come and tell me that there are no eggs! Who stole them? Tell me that, before I kick you out through the castle gate for a liar and a seller of my goods to thieves. The milk was short yesterday, too: do not forget that.

2. A window divided by vertical units which support the arch or lintel.

STEWARD [*desperate*] I know, sir. I know only too well. There is no milk: there are no eggs: tomorrow there will be nothing.

ROBERT. Nothing! You will steal the lot: eh?

STEWARD. No, sir: nobody will steal anything. But there is a spell on us: we are bewitched.

ROBERT. That story is not good enough for me. Robert de Baudricourt burns witches and hangs thieves. Go. Bring me four dozen eggs and two gallons of milk here in this room before noon, or Heaven have mercy on your bones! I will teach you to make a fool of me. [*He resumes his seat with an air of finality*].

STEWARD. Sir: I tell you there are no eggs. There will be none—not if you were to kill me for it—as long as The Maid is at the door.

ROBERT. The Maid! What maid? What are you talking about?

STEWARD. The girl from Lorraine, sir. From Domrémy.[3]

ROBERT [*rising in fearful wrath*] Thirty thousand thunders! Fifty thousand devils! Do you mean to say that that girl, who had the impudence to ask to see me two days ago, and whom I told you to send back to her father with my orders that he was to give her a good hiding, is here still?

STEWARD. I have told her to go, sir. She wont.

ROBERT. I did not tell you to tell her to go: I told you to throw her out. You have fifty men-at-arms and a dozen lumps of able-bodied servants to carry out my orders. Are they afraid of her?

STEWARD. She is so positive, sir.

ROBERT [*seizing him by the scruff of the neck*] Positive! Now see here. I am going to throw you downstairs.

STEWARD. No, sir. Please.

ROBERT. Well, stop me by being positive. It's quite easy: any slut of a girl can do it.

STEWARD [*hanging limp in his hands*] Sir, sir: you cannot get rid of her by throwing me out. [*Robert has to let him drop. He squats on his knees on the floor, contemplating his master resignedly*]. You see, sir, you are much more positive than I am. But so is she.

ROBERT. I am stronger than you are, you fool.

STEWARD. No, sir: it isnt that: it's your strong character, sir. She is weaker than we are: she is only a slip of a girl; but we cannot make her go.

ROBERT. You parcel of curs: you are afraid of her.

STEWARD [*rising cautiously*] No sir: we are afraid of you; but she puts courage into us. She really doesnt seem to be afraid of anything. Perhaps you could frighten her, sir.

ROBERT [*grimly*] Perhaps. Where is she now?

STEWARD. Down in the courtyard, sir, talking to the soldiers as usual. She is always talking to the soldiers except when she is praying.

3. Now Domrémy-la-Pucelle, after Joan's nickname "The Maid," in Lorraine in northeastern France.

ROBERT. Praying! Ha! You believe she prays, you idiot. I know the sort of girl that is always talking to soldiers. She shall talk to me a bit. [*He goes to the window and shouts fiercely through it*] Hallo, you there!

A GIRL'S VOICE [*bright, strong, and rough*] Is it me, sir?

ROBERT. Yes, you.

THE VOICE. Be you captain?

ROBERT. Yes, damn your impudence, I be captain. Come up here. [*To the soldiers in the yard*] Shew her the way, you. And shove her along quick. [*He leaves the window, and returns to his place at the table, where he sits magisterially*].

STEWARD [*whispering*] She wants to go and be a soldier herself. She wants you to give her soldier's clothes. Armor, sir! And a sword! Actually! [*He steals behind Robert*].

Joan appears in the turret doorway. She is an ablebodied country girl of 17 or 18, respectably dressed in red, with an uncommon face; eyes very wide apart and bulging as they often do in very imaginative people, a long well-shaped nose with wide nostrils, a short upper lip, resolute but full-lipped mouth, and handsome fighting chin. She comes eagerly to the table, delighted at having penetrated to Baudricourt's presence at last, and full of hope as to the results. His scowl does not check or frighten her in the least. Her voice is normally a hearty coaxing voice, very confident, very appealing, very hard to resist.

JOAN [*bobbing a curtsey*] Good morning, captain squire. Captain: you are to give me a horse and armor and some soldiers, and send me to the Dauphin.[4] Those are your orders from my Lord.

ROBERT [*outraged*] Orders from your lord! And who the devil may your lord be? Go back to him, and tell him that I am neither duke nor peer at his orders: I am squire of Baudricourt; and I take no orders except from the king.

JOAN [*reassuringly*] Yes, squire: that is all right. My Lord is the King of Heaven.

ROBERT. Why, the girl's mad. [*To the steward*] Why didn't you tell me so, you blockhead?

STEWARD. Sir: do not anger her: give her what she wants.

JOAN [*impatient, but friendly*] They all say I am mad until I talk to them, squire. But you see that it is the will of God that you are to do what He has put into my mind.

ROBERT. It is the will of God that I shall send you back to your father with orders to put you under lock and key and thrash the madness out of you. What have you to say to that?

JOAN. You think you will, squire; but you will find it all coming quite different. You said you would not see me; but here I am.

4. The heir to the throne of France.

STEWARD [*appealing*] Yes, sir. You see, sir.
ROBERT. Hold your tongue, you.
STEWARD [*abjectly*] Yes, sir.
ROBERT [*to Joan, with a sour loss of confidence*] So you are presuming on my seeing you, are you?
JOAN [*sweetly*] Yes, squire.
ROBERT [*feeling that he has lost ground, brings down his two fists squarely on the table, and inflates his chest imposingly to cure the unwelcome and only too familiar sensation*] Now listen to me. I am going to assert myself.
JOAN [*busily*] Please do, squire. The horse will cost sixteen francs. It is a good deal of money: but I can save it on the armor. I can find a soldier's armor that will fit me well enough: I am very hardy; and I do not need beautiful armor made to my measure like you wear. I shall not want many soldiers: the Dauphin will give me all I need to raise the siege of Orleans.[5]
ROBERT [*flabbergasted*] To raise the siege of Orleans!
JOAN [*simply*] Yes, squire: that is what God is sending me to do. Three men will be enough for you to send with me if they are good men and gentle to me. They have promised to come with me. Polly and Jack and—
ROBERT. Polly!! You impudent baggage, do you dare call squire Bertrand de Poulengey Polly to my face?
JOAN. His friends call him so, squire: I did not know he had any other name. Jack—
ROBERT. That is Monsieur John of Metz, I suppose?
JOAN. Yes, squire. Jack will come willingly: he is a very kind gentleman, and gives me money to give to the poor. I think John Godsave will come, and Dick the Archer, and their servants John of Honecourt and Julian. There will be no trouble for you, squire: I have arranged it all: you have only to give the order.
ROBERT [*contemplating her in a stupor of amazement*] Well, I am damned!
JOAN [*with unruffled sweetness*] No, squire: God is very merciful; and the blessed saints Catherine[6] and Margaret,[7] who speak to me every day [*he gapes*], will intercede for you. You will go to paradise; and your name will be remembered for ever as my first helper.
ROBERT [*to the steward, still much bothered, but changing his tone as he pursues a new clue*] Is this true about Monsieur de Poulengey?
STEWARD [*eagerly*] Yes, sir, and about Monsieur de Metz too. They both want to go with her.

5. Important city on the Loire River about 80 miles southwest of Paris.

6. Probably Catherine of Alexandria, a possibly mythical martyr who argued successfully with philosophers and converted soldiers; she was beheaded, and from her neck flowed milk and honey.

7. Another virgin martyr, also possibly mythical and also beheaded.

ROBERT [*thoughtful*] Mf! [*He goes to the window, and shouts into the courtyard*] Hallo! You there: send Monsieur de Poulengey to me, will you? [*He turns to Joan*] Get out; and wait in the yard.

JOAN [*smiling brightly at him*] Right, squire. [*She goes out*].

ROBERT [*to the steward*] Go with her, you, you dithering imbecile. Stay within call; and keep your eye on her. I shall have her up here again.

STEWARD. Do so in God's name, sir. Think of those hens, the best layers in Champagne; and—

ROBERT. Think of my boot; and take your backside out of reach of it.

The steward retreats hastily and finds himself confronted in the doorway by Bertrand de Poulengey, a lymphatic° French gentleman-at-arms, aged 36 or thereabout, employed in the department of the provost-marshal, dreamily absent-minded, seldom speaking unless spoken to, and then slow and obstinate in reply; altogether in contrast to the self-assertive, loud-mouthed, superficially energetic, fundamentally will-less Robert. The steward makes way for him, and vanishes. sluggish

Poulengey salutes, and stands awaiting orders.

ROBERT [*genially*] It isnt service, Polly. A friendly talk. Sit down. [*He hooks the stool from under the table with his instep*].

Poulengey, relaxing, comes into the room: places the stool between the table and the window: and sits down ruminatively. Robert, half sitting on the end of the table, begins the friendly talk.

ROBERT. Now listen to me, Polly. I must talk to you like a father.

Poulengey looks up at him gravely for a moment, but says nothing.

ROBERT. It's about this girl you are interested in. Now, I have seen her. I have talked to her. First, she's mad. That doesnt matter. Second, she's not a farm wench. She's a bourgeoise. That matters a good deal. I know her class exactly. Her father came here last year to represent his village in a lawsuit: he is one of their notables. A farmer. Not a gentleman farmer: he makes money by it, and lives by it. Still, not a laborer. Not a mechanic. He might have a cousin a lawyer, or in the Church. People of this sort may be of no account socially; but they can give a lot of bother to the authorities. That is to say, to me. Now no doubt it seems to you a very simple thing to take this girl away, humbugging her into the belief that you are taking her to the Dauphin. But if you get her into trouble, you may get me into no end of a mess, as I am her father's lord, and responsible for her protection. So friends or no friends, Polly, hands off her.

POULENGEY [*with deliberate impressiveness*] I should as soon think of the Blessed Virgin herself in that way, as of this girl.

ROBERT [*coming off the table*] But she says you and Jack and Dick have offered to go with her. What for? You are not going to tell me that you take her crazy notion of going to the Dauphin seriously, are you?

POULENGEY [*slowly*] There is something about her. They are pretty foulmouthed and foulminded down there in the guardroom, some of them. But there hasn't been a word that has anything to do with her being a woman. They have stopped swearing before her. There is something. Something. It may be worth trying.

ROBERT. Oh, come, Polly! pull yourself together. Common-sense was never your strong point; but this is a little too much. [*He retreats disgustedly*].

POULENGEY [*unmoved*] What is the good of commonsense? If we had any commonsense we should join the Duke of Burgundy and the English king. They hold half the country, right down to the Loire. They have Paris. They have this castle: you know very well that we had to surrender it to the Duke of Bedford, and that you are only holding it on parole. The Dauphin is in Chinon,[8] like a rat in a corner, except that he wont fight. We dont even know that he is the Dauphin: his mother says he isnt; and she ought to know. Think of that! the queen denying the legitimacy of her own son!

ROBERT. Well, she married her daughter to the English king. Can you blame the woman?

POULENGEY. I blame nobody. But thanks to her, the Dauphin is down and out; and we may as well face it. The English will take Orleans: the Bastard will not be able to stop them.

ROBERT. He beat the English the year before last at Montargis. I was with him.

POULENGEY. No matter: his men are cowed now; and he cant work miracles. And I tell you that nothing can save our side now but a miracle.

ROBERT. Miracles are all right, Polly. The only difficulty about them is that they dont happen nowadays.

POULENGEY. I used to think so. I am not so sure now. [*Rising, and moving ruminatively towards the window*] At all events this is not a time to leave any stone unturned. There is something about the girl.

ROBERT. Oh! You think the girl can work miracles, do you?

POULENGEY. I think the girl herself is a bit of a miracle. Anyhow, she is the last card left in our hand. Better play her than throw up the game. [*He wanders to the turret*].

ROBERT [*wavering*] You really think that?

POULENGEY [*turning*] Is there anything else left for us to think?

ROBERT [*going to him*] Look here, Polly. If you were in my place would you let a girl like that do you out of sixteen francs for a horse?

POULENGEY. I will pay for the horse.

ROBERT. You will!

POULENGEY. Yes: I will back my opinion.

ROBERT. You will really gamble on a forlorn hope to the tune of sixteen francs?

8. On the banks of the Vienne River, southwest of Orleans.

POULENGEY. It is not a gamble.

ROBERT. What else is it?

POULENGEY. It is a certainty. Her words and her ardent faith in God have put fire into me.

ROBERT [*giving him up*] Whew! You are as mad as she is.

POULENGEY [*obstinately*] We want a few mad people now. See where the sane ones have landed us!

ROBERT [*his irresoluteness now openly swamping his affected decisiveness*] I shall feel like a precious fool. Still, if you feel sure—?

POULENGEY. I feel sure enough to take her to Chinon—unless you stop me.

ROBERT. This is not fair. You are putting the responsibility on me.

POULENGEY. It is on you whichever way you decide.

ROBERT. Yes: thats just it. Which way am I to decide? You dont see how awkward this is for me. [*Snatching at a dilatory step with an unconscious hope that Joan will make up his mind for him*] Do you think I ought to have another talk to her?

POULENGEY [*rising*] Yes. [*He goes to the window and calls*] Joan!

JOAN'S VOICE. Will he let us go, Polly?

POULENGEY. Come up. Come in. [*Turning to Robert*] Shall I leave you with her?

ROBERT. No: stay here; and back me up.

Poulengey sits down on the chest. Robert goes back to his magisterial chair, but remains standing to inflate himself more imposingly. Joan comes in, full of good news.

JOAN. Jack will go halves for the horse.

ROBERT. Well!! [*He sits, deflated*].

POULENGEY [*gravely*] Sit down, Joan.

JOAN [*checked a little, and looking to Robert*] May I?

ROBERT. Do what you are told.

Joan curtsies and sits down on the stool between them. Robert outfaces his perplexity with his most peremptory air.

ROBERT. What is your name?

JOAN [*chattily*] They always call me Jenny in Lorraine. Here in France I am Joan. The soldiers call me The Maid.

ROBERT. What is your surname?

JOAN. Surname? What is that? My father sometimes calls himself d'Arc; but I know nothing about it. You met my father. He—

ROBERT. Yes, yes; I remember. You come from Domrémy in Lorraine, I think.

JOAN. Yes; but what does it matter? we all speak French.

ROBERT. Dont ask questions: answer them. How old are you?

JOAN. Seventeen: so they tell me. It might be nineteen. I dont remember.

ROBERT. What did you mean when you said that St Catherine and St Margaret talked to you every day?

JOAN. They do.

ROBERT. What are they like?

JOAN [*suddenly obstinate*] I will tell you nothing about that: they have not given me leave.

ROBERT. But you actually see them; and they talk to you just as I am talking to you?

JOAN. No: it is quite different. I cannot tell you: you must not talk to me about my voices.

ROBERT. How do you mean? voices?

JOAN. I hear voices telling me what to do. They come from God.

ROBERT. They come from your imagination.

JOAN. Of course. That is how the messages of God come to us.

POULENGEY. Checkmate.

ROBERT. No fear! [*To Joan*] So God says you are to raise the siege of Orleans?

JOAN. And to crown the Dauphin in Rheims Cathedral.[9]

ROBERT [*gasping*] Crown the D—! Gosh!

JOAN. And to make the English leave France.

ROBERT [*sarcastic*] Anything else?

JOAN [*charming*] Not just at present, thank you, squire.

ROBERT. I suppose you think raising a siege is as easy as chasing a cow out of a meadow. You think soldiering is anybody's job?

JOAN. I do not think it can be very difficult if God is on your side, and you are willing to put your life in His hand. But many soldiers are very simple.

ROBERT [*grimly*] Simple! Did you ever see English soldiers fighting?

JOAN. They are only men. God made them just like us; but He gave them their own country and their own language; and it is not His will that they should come into our country and try to speak our language.

ROBERT. Who has been putting such nonsense into your head? Dont you know that soldiers are subject to their feudal lord, and that it is nothing to them or to you whether he is the duke of Burgundy or the king of England or the king of France? What has their language to do with it?

JOAN. I do not understand that a bit. We are all subject to the King of Heaven; and He gave us our countries and our languages, and meant us to keep to them. If it were not so it would be murder to kill an Englishman in battle; and you, squire, would be in great danger of hell fire. You must not think about your duty to your feudal lord, but about your duty to God.

POULENGEY. It's no use, Robert: she can choke you like that every time.

ROBERT. Can she, by Saint Denis![10] We shall see. [*To Joan*] We are not

9. Also "Reims," city in northeastern France and the traditional location for French coronations.

10. Or St. Dionysius of Paris, patron saint of France. A number of saints' lives coalesce in his name, but the first story is of a missionary who was sent to Gaul

talking about God: we are talking about practical affairs. I ask you again, girl, have you ever seen English soldiers fighting? Have you ever seen them plundering, burning, turning the countryside into a desert? Have you heard no tales of their Black Prince[11] who was blacker than the devil himself, or of the English king's father?

JOAN. You must not be afraid, Robert—

ROBERT. Damn you, I am not afraid. And who gave you leave to call me Robert?

JOAN. You were called so in church in the name of our Lord. All the other names are your father's or your brother's or anybody's.

ROBERT. Tcha!

JOAN. Listen to me, squire. At Domrémy we had to fly to the next village to escape from the English soldiers. Three of them were left behind, wounded. I came to know these three poor goddams quite well. They had not half my strength.

ROBERT. Do you know why they are called goddams?

JOAN. No. Everyone calls them goddams.

ROBERT. It is because they are always calling on their God to condemn their souls to perdition. That is what goddam means in their language. How do you like it?

JOAN. God will be merciful to them; and they will act like His good children when they go back to the country He made for them, and made them for. I have heard the tales of the Black Prince. The moment he touched the soil of our country the devil entered into him, and made him a black fiend. But at home, in the place made for him by God, he was good. It is always so. If I went into England against the will of God to conquer England, and tried to live there and speak its language, the devil would enter into me; and when I was old I should shudder to remember the wickedness I did.

ROBERT. Perhaps. But the more devil you were the better you might fight. That is why the goddams will take Orleans. And you cannot stop them, nor ten thousand like you.

JOAN. One thousand like me can stop them. Ten like me can stop them with God on our side. [*She rises impetuously, and goes at him, unable to sit quiet any longer*]. You do not understand, squire. Our soldiers are always beaten because they are fighting only to save their skins; and the shortest way to save your skin is to run away. Our knights are thinking only of the money they will make in ransoms: it is not kill or be killed with them, but pay or be paid. But I will teach them all to fight that the will of God may be done in France; and then they will drive the poor goddams before them like sheep. You and Polly

around AD 250, and was beheaded in Paris at Montmartre (Martyrs' Hill). He is said to have carried his head to his place of burial.

11. Edward, Prince of Wales, defeated the French at Crécy (1346) and Poitiers (1356).

will live to see the day when there will not be an English soldier on the soil of France; and there will be but one king there: not the feudal English king, but God's French one.

ROBERT [*to Poulengey*] This may be all rot, Polly; but the troops might swallow it, though nothing that we can say seems able to put any fight into them. Even the Dauphin might swallow it. And if she can put fight into him, she can put it into anybody.

POULENGEY. I can see no harm in trying. Can you? And there is something about the girl—

ROBERT [*turning to Joan*] Now listen you to me; and [*desperately*] dont cut in before I have time to think.

JOAN [*plumping down on the stool again, like an obedient schoolgirl*] Yes, squire.

ROBERT. Your orders are, that you are to go to Chinon under the escort of this gentleman and three of his friends.

JOAN [*radiant, clasping her hands*] Oh, squire! Your head is all circled with light, like a saint's.

POULENGEY. How is she to get into the royal presence?

ROBERT [*who has looked up for his halo rather apprehensively*] I dont know: how did she get into my presence? If the Dauphin can keep her out he is a better man than I take him for. [*Rising*] I will send her to Chinon; and she can say I sent her. Then let come what may: I can do no more.

JOAN. And the dress? I may have a soldier's dress, maynt I, squire?

ROBERT. Have what you please. I wash my hands of it.

JOAN [*wildly excited by her success*] Come, Polly. [*She dashes out*].

ROBERT [*shaking Poulengey's hand*] Goodbye, old man, I am taking a big chance. Few other men would have done it. But as you say, there is something about her.

POULENGEY. Yes: there is something about her. Goodbye. [*He goes out*].

Robert, still very doubtful whether he has not been made a fool of by a crazy female, and a social inferior to boot, scratches his head and slowly comes back from the door.

The steward runs in with a basket.

STEWARD. Sir, sir—

ROBERT. What now?

STEWARD. The hens are laying like mad, sir. Five dozen eggs!

ROBERT [*stiffens convulsively: crosses himself: and forms with his pale lips the words*] Christ in heaven! [*Aloud but breathless*] She did come from God.

SCENE II

Chinon, in Touraine. An end of the throne room in the castle, curtained off to make an antechamber. The Archbishop of Rheims, close on 50, a full-fed prelate with nothing of the ecclesiastic about him except his imposing bearing, and the Lord Chamberlain, Monseigneur de la Trémouille, a monstrous arrogant wineskin of a man, are waiting for the Dauphin. There is a door in the wall to the right of the two men. It is late in the afternoon on the 8th of March, 1429. The Archbishop stands with dignity whilst the Chamberlain, on his left, fumes about in the worst of tempers.

LA TRÉMOUILLE. What the devil does the Dauphin mean by keeping us waiting like this? I dont know how you have the patience to stand there like a stone idol.

THE ARCHBISHOP. You see, I am an archbishop; and an archbishop is a sort of idol. At any rate he has to learn to keep still and suffer fools patiently. Besides, my dear Lord Chamberlain, it is the Dauphin's royal privilege to keep you waiting, is it not?

LA TRÉMOUILLE. Dauphin be damned! saving your reverence. Do you know how much money he owes me?

THE ARCHBISHOP. Much more than he owes me, I have no doubt, because you are a much richer man. But I take it he owes you all you could afford to lend him. That is what he owes me.

LA TRÉMOUILLE. Twenty-seven thousand: that was his last haul. A cool twenty-seven thousand!

THE ARCHBISHOP. What becomes of it all? He never has a suit of clothes that I would throw to a curate.

LA TRÉMOUILLE. He dines on a chicken or a scrap of mutton. He borrows my last penny; and there is nothing to shew for it. [*A page appears in the doorway*]. At last!

THE PAGE. No, my lord: it is not His Majesty. Monsieur de Rais is approaching.

LA TRÉMOUILLE. Young Bluebeard! Why announce him?

THE PAGE. Captain La Hire is with him. Something has happened, I think.

Gilles de Rais, a young man of 25, very smart and self-possessed, and sporting the extravagance of a little curled beard dyed blue at a clean-shaven court, comes in. He is determined to make himself agreeable, but lacks natural joyousness, and is not really pleasant. In fact when he defies the Church some eleven years later he is accused of trying to extract pleasure from horrible cruelties, and hanged. So far, however, there is no shadow of the gallows on him. He advances gaily to the Archbishop. The page withdraws.

BLUEBEARD. Your faithful lamb, Archbishop. Good day, my lord. Do you know what has happened to La Hire?

LA TRÉMOUILLE. He has sworn himself into a fit, perhaps.

BLUEBEARD. No: just the opposite. Foul Mouthed Frank, the only man in Touraine who could beat him at swearing, was told by a soldier that he shouldnt use such language when he was at the point of death.

THE ARCHBISHOP. Nor at any other point. But was Foul Mouthed Frank on the point of death?

BLUEBEARD. Yes: he has just fallen into a well and been drowned. La Hire is frightened out of his wits.

Captain La Hire comes in: a war dog with no court manners and pronounced camp ones.

BLUEBEARD. I have just been telling the Chamberlain and the Archbishop. The Archbishop says you are a lost man.

LA HIRE [*striding past Bluebeard, and planting himself between the Archbishop and La Trémouille*] This is nothing to joke about. It is worse than we thought. It was not a soldier, but an angel dressed as a soldier.

THE ARCHBISHOP
THE CHAMBERLAIN
BLUEBEARD [*exclaiming all together*] An angel!

LA HIRE. Yes, an angel. She has made her way from Champagne with half a dozen men through the thick of everything: Burgundians, Goddams, deserters, robbers, and Lord knows who; and they never met a soul except the country folk. I know one of them: de Poulengey. He says she's an angel. If ever I utter an oath again may my soul be blasted to eternal damnation!

THE ARCHBISHOP. A very pious beginning, Captain.

Bluebeard and La Trémouille laugh at him. The page returns.

THE PAGE. His Majesty.

They stand perfunctorily at court attention. The Dauphin, aged 26, really King Charles the Seventh since the death of his father, but as yet uncrowned, comes in through the curtains with a paper in his hands. He is a poor creature physically; and the current fashion of shaving closely, and hiding every scrap of hair under the headcovering or headdress, both by women and men, makes the worst of his appearance. He has little narrow eyes, near together, a long pendulous nose that droops over his thick short upper lip, and the expression of a young dog accustomed to be kicked, yet incorrigible and irrepressible. But he is neither vulgar nor stupid; and he has a cheeky humor which enables him to hold his own in conversation. Just at present he is excited, like a child with a new toy. He comes to the Archbishop's left hand. Bluebeard and La Hire retire towards the curtains.

CHARLES. Oh, Archbishop, do you know what Robert de Baudricourt is sending me from Vaucouleurs?

THE ARCHBISHOP [*contemptuously*] I am not interested in the newest toys.

CHARLES [*indignantly*] It isnt a toy. [*Sulkily*] However, I can get on very well without your interest.

THE ARCHBISHOP. Your Highness is taking offence very unnecessarily.

CHARLES. Thank you. You are always ready with a lecture, arnt you?

LA TRÉMOUILLE [*roughly*] Enough grumbling. What have you got there?

CHARLES. What is that to you?

LA TRÉMOUILLE. It is my business to know what is passing between you and the garrison at Vaucouleurs. [*He snatches the paper from the Dauphin's hand, and begins reading it with some difficulty, following the words with his finger and spelling them out syllable by syllable*].

CHARLES [*mortified*] You all think you can treat me as you please because I owe you money, and because I am no good at fighting. But I have the blood royal in my veins.

THE ARCHBISHOP. Even that has been questioned, your Highness. One hardly recognizes in you the grandson of Charles the Wise.

CHARLES. I want to hear no more of my grandfather. He was so wise that he used up the whole family stock of wisdom for five generations, and left me the poor fool I am, bullied and insulted by all of you.

THE ARCHBISHOP. Control yourself, sir. These outbursts of petulance are not seemly.

CHARLES. Another lecture! Thank you. What a pity it is that though you are an archbishop saints and angels dont come to see you!

THE ARCHBISHOP. What do you mean?

CHARLES. Aha! Ask that bully there [*pointing to La Trémouille*].

LA TRÉMOUILLE [*furious*] Hold your tongue. Do you hear?

CHARLES. Oh, I hear. You neednt shout. The whole castle can hear. Why dont you go and shout at the English, and beat them for me?

LA TRÉMOUILLE [*raising his fist*] You young—

CHARLES [*running behind the Archbishop*] Dont you raise your hand to me. It's high treason.

LA HIRE. Steady, Duke! Steady!

THE ARCHBISHOP [*resolutely*] Come, come! this will not do. My Lord Chamberlain: please! please! we must keep some sort of order. [*To the Dauphin*] And you, sir: if you cannot rule your kingdom, at least try to rule yourself.

CHARLES. Another lecture! Thank you.

LA TRÉMOUILLE [*over the paper to the Archbishop handing*] Here: read the accursed thing for me. He has sent the blood boiling into my head: I cant distinguish the letters.

CHARLES [*coming back and peering round La Trémouille's left shoulder*] I will read it for you if you like. I can read, you know.

LA TRÉMOUILLE [*with intense contempt, not at all stung by the taunt*] Yes: reading is about all you are fit for. Can you make it out, Archbishop?

THE ARCHBISHOP. I should have expected more common-sense from De Baudricourt. He is sending some cracked country lass here—

CHARLES [*interrupting*] No: he is sending a saint: an angel. And she is coming to me: to me, the king, and not to you, Archbishop, holy as you are. She knows the blood royal if you dont. [*He struts up to the curtains between Bluebeard and La Hire*].

THE ARCHBISHOP. You cannot be allowed to see this crazy wench.

CHARLES [*turning*] But I am the king; and I will.

LA TRÉMOUILLE [*brutally*] Then she cannot be allowed to see you. Now!

CHARLES. I tell you I will. I am going to put my foot down—

BLUEBEARD [*laughing at him*] Naughty! What would your wise grandfather say?

CHARLES. That just shews your ignorance, Bluebeard. My grandfather had a saint who used to float in the air when she was praying, and told him everything he wanted to know. My poor father had two saints, Marie de Maillé and the Gasque of Avignon.[12] It is in our family; and I dont care what you say: I will have my saint too.

THE ARCHBISHOP. This creature is not a saint. She is not even a respectable woman. She does not wear women's clothes. She is dressed like a soldier, and rides round the country with soldiers. Do you suppose such a person can be admitted to your Highness's court?

LA HIRE. Stop. [*Going to the Archbishop*] Did you say a girl in armor, like a soldier?

THE ARCHBISHOP. So De Baudricourt describes her.

LA HIRE. But by all the devils in hell—Oh, God forgive me, what am I saying?—by Our Lady and all the saints, this must be the angel that struck Foul Mouthed Frank dead for swearing.

CHARLES [*triumphant*] You see! A miracle!

LA HIRE. She may strike the lot of us dead if we cross her. For Heaven's sake, Archbishop, be careful what you are doing.

THE ARCHBISHOP [*severely*] Rubbish! Nobody has been struck dead. A drunken blackguard who has been rebuked a hundred times for swearing has fallen into a well, and been drowned. A mere coincidence.

LA HIRE. I do not know what a coincidence is. I do know that the man is dead, and that she told him he was going to die.

THE ARCHBISHOP. We are all going to die, Captain.

LA HIRE [*crossing himself*] I hope not. [*He backs out of the conversation*].

BLUEBEARD. We can easily find out whether she is an angel or not. Let

12. Marie de Maille (more properly Jeanne Marie de Maille) was actually a contemporary of St. Joan. She was a baroness who lost everything after her husband died. With what she could scrape together she tended the sick poor. The Gasque of Avignon is the nickname of Marie d'Avignon, a French seer who prophesied that the French Crown would be saved by a woman warrior. She was known as "the Gasque" because she was either originally from Monaco (a Monagasque), or was descended from a Monagasque family.

us arrange when she comes that I shall be the Dauphin, and see whether she will find me out.

CHARLES. Yes: I agree to that. If she cannot find the blood royal I will have nothing to do with her.

THE ARCHBISHOP. It is for the Church to make saints: let De Baudricourt mind his own business, and not dare usurp the function of his priest. I say the girl shall not be admitted.

BLUEBEARD. But, Archbishop—

THE ARCHBISHOP [*sternly*] I speak in the Church's name. [*To the Dauphin*] Do you dare say she shall?

CHARLES [*intimidated but sulky*] Oh, if you make it an excommunication matter, I have nothing more to say, of course. But you havnt read the end of the letter. De Baudricourt says she will raise the siege of Orleans, and beat the English for us.

LA TRÉMOUILLE. Rot!

CHARLES. Well, will you save Orleans for us, with all your bullying?

LA TRÉMOUILLE [*savagely*] Do not throw that in my face again: do you hear? I have done more fighting than you ever did or ever will. But I cannot be everywhere.

THE DAUPHIN. Well, thats something.

BLUEBEARD [*coming between the Archbishop and Charles*] You have Jack Dunois at the head of your troops in Orleans: the brave Dunois, the handsome Dunois, the wonderful invincible Dunois, the darling of all the ladies, the beautiful bastard. Is it likely that the country lass can do what he cannot do?

CHARLES. Why doesnt he raise the siege, then?

LA HIRE. The wind is against him.

BLUEBEARD. How can the wind hurt him at Orleans? It is not in the Channel.

LA HIRE. It is on the river Loire; and the English hold the bridgehead. He must ship his men across the river and upstream, if he is to take them in the rear. Well, he cannot, because there is a devil of a wind blowing the other way. He is tired of paying the priests to pray for a west wind. What he needs is a miracle. You tell me that what the girl did to Foul Mouthed Frank was no miracle. No matter: it finished Frank. If she changes the wind for Dunois, that may not be a miracle either; but it may finish the English. What harm is there in trying?

THE ARCHBISHOP [*who has read the end of the letter and become more thoughtful*] It is true that De Baudricourt seems extraordinarily impressed.

LA HIRE. De Baudricourt is a blazing ass; but he is a soldier; and if he thinks she can beat the English, all the rest of the army will think so too.

LA TRÉMOUILLE [*to the Archbishop, who is hesitating*] Oh, let them have their way. Dunois' men will give up the town in spite of him if somebody does not put some fresh spunk into them.

THE ARCHBISHOP. The Church must examine the girl before anything decisive is done about her. However, since his Highness desires it, let her attend the Court.

LA HIRE. I will find her and tell her. [*He goes out*].

CHARLES. Come with me, Bluebeard; and let us arrange so that she will not know who I am. You will pretend to be me. [*He goes out through the curtains*].

BLUEBEARD. Pretend to be that thing! Holy Michael! [*He follows the Dauphin*].

LA TRÉMOUILLE. I wonder will she pick him out!

THE ARCHBISHOP. Of course she will.

LA TRÉMOUILLE. Why? How is she to know?

THE ARCHBISHOP. She will know what everybody in Chinon knows: that the Dauphin is the meanest-looking and worst-dressed figure in the Court, and that the man with the blue beard is Gilles de Rais.

LA TRÉMOUILLE. I never thought of that.

THE ARCHBISHOP. You are not so accustomed to miracles as I am. It is part of my profession.

LA TRÉMOUILLE [*fueled° and a little scandalized*] heated
But that would not be a miracle at all.

THE ARCHBISHOP [*calmly*] Why not?

LA TRÉMOUILLE. Well, come! what is a miracle?

THE ARCHBISHOP. A miracle, my friend, is an event which creates faith. That is the purpose and nature of miracles. They may seem very wonderful to the people who witness them, and very simple to those who perform them. That does not matter: if they confirm or create faith they are true miracles.

LA TRÉMOUILLE. Even when they are frauds, do you mean?

THE ARCHBISHOP. Frauds deceive. An event which creates faith does not deceive: therefore it is not a fraud, but a miracle.

LA TRÉMOUILLE [*scratching his neck in his perplexity*] Well, I suppose as you are an archbishop you must be right. It seems a bit fishy to me. But I am no churchman, and dont understand these matters.

THE ARCHBISHOP. You are not a churchman; but you are a diplomatist and a soldier. Could you make our citizens pay war taxes, or our soldiers sacrifice their lives, if they knew what is really happening instead of what seems to them to be happening?

LA TRÉMOUILLE. No, by Saint Denis: the fat would be in the fire before sundown.

THE ARCHBISHOP. Would it not be quite easy to tell them the truth?

LA TRÉMOUILLE. Man alive, they wouldnt believe it.

THE ARCHBISHOP. Just so. Well, the Church has to rule men for the good of their souls as you have to rule them for the good of their bodies. To do that, the Church must do as you do: nourish their faith by poetry.

LA TRÉMOUILLE. Poetry! I should call it humbug.

THE ARCHBISHOP. You would be wrong, my friend. Parables are not lies because they describe events that have never happened. Miracles are not frauds because they are often—I do not say always—very simple and innocent contrivances by which the priest fortifies the faith of his flock. When this girl picks out the Dauphin among his courtiers, it will not be a miracle for me, because I shall know how it has been done, and my faith will not be increased. But as for the others, if they feel the thrill of the supernatural, and forget their sinful clay in a sudden sense of the glory of God, it will be a miracle and a blessed one. And you will find that the girl herself will be more affected than anyone else. She will forget how she really picked him out. So, perhaps, will you.

LA TRÉMOUILLE. Well, I wish I were clever enough to know how much of you is God's archbishop and how much the most artful fox in *Touraine*. Come on, or we shall be late for the fun; and I want to see it, miracle or no miracle.

THE ARCHBISHOP [*detaining him a moment*] Do not think that I am a lover of crooked ways. There is a new spirit rising in men: we are at the dawning of a wider epoch. If I were a simple monk, and had not to rule men, I should seek peace for my spirit with Aristotle and Pythagoras rather than with the saints and their miracles.

LA TRÉMOUILLE. And who the deuce was Pythagoras?

THE ARCHBISHOP. A sage who held that the earth is round, and that it moves round the sun.

LA TRÉMOUILLE. What an utter fool! Couldnt he use his eyes?

They go out together through the curtains, which are presently withdrawn, revealing the full depth of the throne room with the Court assembled. On the right are two Chairs of State on a dais. Bluebeard is standing theatrically on the dais, playing the king, and, like the courtiers, enjoying the joke rather obviously. There is a curtained arch in the wall behind the dais; but the main door, guarded by men-at-arms, is at the other side of the room; and a clear path across is kept and lined by the courtiers. Charles is in this path in the middle of the room. La Hire is on his right. The Archbishop, on his left, has taken his place by the dais: La Trémouille at the other side of it. The Duchess de la Trémouille, pretending to be the Queen, sits in the Consort's chair, with a group of ladies in waiting close by, behind the Archbishop.

The chatter of the courtiers makes such a noise that nobody notices the appearance of the page at the door.

THE PAGE. The Duke of—[*Nobody listens*]. The Duke of—[*The chatter continues. Indignant at his failure to command a hearing, he snatches the halberd of the nearest man-at-arms, and thumps the floor with it. The chatter ceases; and everybody looks at him in silence*]. Attention! [*He restores the halberd to the man-at-arms*]. The Duke of Vendôme presents Joan the Maid to his Majesty.

CHARLES [*putting his finger on his lip*] Ssh! [*He hides behind the nearest courtier, peering out to see what happens*].

BLUEBEARD [*majestically*] Let her approach the throne.

Joan, dressed as a soldier, with her hair bobbed and hanging thickly round her face, is led in by a bashful and speechless nobleman, from whom she detaches herself to stop and look around eagerly for the Dauphin.

THE DUCHESS [*to the nearest lady in waiting*] My dear! Her hair! *All the ladies explode in uncontrollable laughter.*

BLUEBEARD [*trying not to laugh, and waving his hand in deprecation of their merriment*] Ssh—ssh! Ladies! Ladies!!

JOAN [*not at all embarrassed*] I wear it like this because I am a soldier. Where be Dauphin?

A titter runs through the Court as she walks to the dais.

BLUEBEARD [*condescendingly*] You are in the presence of the Dauphin.

Joan looks at him sceptically for a moment, scanning him hard up and down to make sure. Dead silence, all watching her. Fun dawns in her face.

JOAN. Coom, Bluebeard! Thou canst not fool me. Where be Dauphin?

A roar of laughter breaks out as Gilles, with a gesture of surrender, joins in the laugh, and jumps down from the dais beside La Trémouille. Joan, also on the broad grin, turns back, searching along the row of courtiers, and presently makes a dive, and drags out Charles by the arm.

JOAN [*releasing him and bobbing him a little curtsey*] Gentle little Dauphin, I am sent to you to drive the English away from Orleans and from France, and to crown you king in the cathedral at Rheims, where all true kings of France are crowned.

CHARLES [*triumphant, to the Court*] You see, all of you: she knew the blood royal. Who dare say now that I am not my father's son? [*To Joan*] But if you want me to be crowned at Rheims you must talk to the Archbishop, not to me. There he is [*he is standing behind her*]!

JOAN [*turning quickly, overwhelmed with emotion*] Oh, my lord! [*She falls on both knees before him, with bowed head, not daring to look up*] My lord: I am only a poor country girl; and you are filled with the blessedness and glory of God Himself; but you will touch me with your hands, and give me your blessing, wont you?

BLUEBEARD [*whispering to La Trémouille*] The old fox blushes.

LA TRÉMOUILLE. Another miracle!

THE ARCHBISHOP [*touched, putting his hand on her head*] Child: you are in love with religion.

JOAN [*startled: looking up at him*] Am I? I never thought of that. Is there any harm in it?

THE ARCHBISHOP. There is no harm in it, my child. But there is danger.

JOAN [*rising, with a sunflush of reckless happiness irradiating her face*]

There is always danger, except in heaven. Oh, my lord, you have given me such strength, such courage. It must be a most wonderful thing to be Archbishop.

The Court smiles broadly: even titters a little.

THE ARCHBISHOP [*drawing himself up sensitively*] Gentlemen: your levity is rebuked by this maid's faith. I am, God help me, all unworthy; but your mirth is a deadly sin.

Their faces fall. Dead silence.

BLUEBEARD. My lord: we were laughing at her, not at you.

THE ARCHBISHOP. What? Not at my unworthiness but at her faith! Gilles de Rais: this maid prophesied that the blasphemer should be drowned in his sin—

JOAN [*distressed*] No!

THE ARCHBISHOP [*silencing her by a gesture*] I prophesy now that you will be hanged in yours if you do not learn when to laugh and when to pray.

BLUEBEARD. My lord: I stand rebuked. I am sorry: I can say no more. But if you prophesy that I shall be hanged, I shall never be able to resist temptation, because I shall always be telling myself that I may as well be hanged for a sheep as a lamb.

The courtiers take heart at this. There is more tittering.

JOAN [*scandalized*] You are an idle fellow, Bluebeard; and you have great impudence to answer the Archbishop.

LA HIRE [*with a huge chuckle*] Well said, lass! Well said!

JOAN [*impatiently to the Archbishop*] Oh, my lord, will you send all these silly folks away so that I may speak to the Dauphin alone?

LA HIRE [*goodhumoredly*] I can take a hint. [*He salutes; turns on his heel; and goes out*].

THE ARCHBISHOP. Come, gentlemen. The Maid comes with God's blessing, and must be obeyed.

The courtiers withdraw, some through the arch, others at the opposite side. The Archbishop marches across to the door, followed by the Duchess and La Trémouille. As the Archbishop passes Joan, she falls on her knees, and kisses the hem of his robe fervently. He shakes his head in instinctive remonstrance; gathers the robe from her; and goes out. She is left kneeling directly in the Duchess's way.

THE DUCHESS [*coldly*] Will you allow me to pass, please?

JOAN [*hastily rising, and standing back*] Beg pardon, maam, I am sure.

The Duchess passes on. Joan stares after her; then whispers to the Dauphin.

JOAN. Be that Queen?

CHARLES. No. She thinks she is.

JOAN [*again staring after the Duchess*] Oo-oo-ooh! [*Her awestruck amaze-*

ment at the figure cut by the magnificently dressed lady is not wholly complimentary].

LA TRÉMOUILLE [*very surly*] I'll trouble your Highness not to gibe at my wife. [*He goes out. The others have already gone*].

JOAN [*to the Dauphin*] Who be old Gruff-and-Grum?

CHARLES. He is the Duke de la Trémouille.

JOAN. What be his job?

CHARLES. He pretends to command the army. And whenever I find a friend I can care for, he kills him.

JOAN. Why dost let him?

CHARLES [*petulantly moving to the throne side of the room to escape from her magnetic field*] How can I prevent him? He bullies me. They all bully me.

JOAN. Art afraid?

CHARLES. Yes: I am afraid. It's no use preaching to me about it. It's all very well for these big men with their armor that is too heavy for me, and their swords that I can hardly lift, and their muscle and their shouting and their bad tempers. They like fighting: most of them are making fools of themselves all the time they are not fighting; but I am quiet and sensible; and I dont want to kill people: I only want to be left alone to enjoy myself in my own way. I never asked to be a king: it was pushed on me. So if you are going to say "Son of St Louis: gird on the sword of your ancestors, and lead us to victory" you may spare your breath to cool your porridge; for I cannot do it. I am not built that way; and there is an end of it.

JOAN [*trenchant and masterful*] Blethers! We are all like that to begin with. I shall put courage into thee.

CHARLES. But I dont want to have courage put into me. I want to sleep in a comfortable bed, and not live in continual terror of being killed or wounded. Put courage into the others, and let them have their bellyful of fighting; but let me alone.

JOAN. It's no use, Charlie: thou must face what God puts on thee. If thou fail to make thyself king, thoult be a beggar: what else art fit for? Come! Let me see thee sitting on the throne. I have looked forward to that.

CHARLES. What is the good of sitting on the throne when the other fellows give all the orders? However! [*he sits enthroned, a piteous figure*] here is the king for you! Look your fill at the poor devil.

JOAN. Thourt not king yet, lad: thourt but Dauphin. Be not led away by them around thee. Dressing up dont fill empty noddle. I know the people: the real people that make thy bread for thee; and I tell thee they count no man king of France until the holy oil has been poured on his hair, and himself consecrated and crowned in Rheims Cathedral. And thou needs new clothes, Charlie. Why does not Queen look after thee properly?

CHARLES. We're too poor. She wants all the money we can spare to put on her own back. Besides, I like to see her beautifully dressed; and I dont care what I wear myself: I should look ugly anyhow.

JOAN. There is some good in thee, Charlie; but it is not yet a king's good.

CHARLES. We shall see. I am not such a fool as I look. I have my eyes open; and I can tell you that one good treaty is worth ten good fights. These fighting fellows lose all on the treaties that they gain on the fights. If we can only have a treaty, the English are sure to have the worst of it, because they are better at fighting than at thinking.

JOAN. If the English win, it is they that will make the treaty: and then God help poor France! Thou must fight, Charlie, whether thou will or no. I will go first to hearten thee. We must take our courage in both hands: aye, and pray for it with both hands too.

CHARLES [*descending from his throne and again crossing the room to escape from her dominating urgency*] Oh do stop talking about God and praying. I cant bear people who are always praying. Isnt it bad enough to have to do it at the proper times?

JOAN [*pitying him*] Thou poor child, thou hast never prayed in thy life. I must teach thee from the beginning.

CHARLES. I am not a child: I am a grown man and a father; and I will not be taught any more.

JOAN. Aye, you have a little son. He that will be Louis the Eleventh when you die. Would you not fight for him?

CHARLES. No: a horrid boy. He hates me. He hates everybody, selfish little beast! I dont want to be bothered with children. I dont want to be a father; and I dont want to be a son: especially a son of St Louis. I dont want to be any of these fine things you all have your heads full of: I want to be just what I am. Why cant you mind your own business, and let me mind mine?

JOAN [*again contemptuous*] Minding your own business is like minding your own body: it's the shortest way to make yourself sick. What is my business? Helping mother at home. What is thine? Petting lapdogs and sucking sugar-sticks. I call that muck. I tell thee it is God's business we are here to do: not our own. I have a message to thee from God; and thou must listen to it, though thy heart break with the terror of it.

CHARLES. I dont want a message; but can you tell me any secrets? Can you do any cures? Can you turn lead into gold, or anything of that sort?

JOAN. I can turn thee into a king, in Rheims Cathedral; and that is a miracle that will take some doing, it seems.

CHARLES. If we go to Rheims, and have a coronation, Anne will want new dresses. We cant afford them. I am all right as I am.

JOAN. As you are! And what is that? Less than my father's poorest shepherd. Thourt not lawful owner of thy own land of France till thou be consecrated.

CHARLES. But I shall not be lawful owner of my own land anyhow. Will the consecration pay off my mortgages? I have pledged my last acre to the Archbishop and that fat bully. I owe money even to Bluebeard.

JOAN [*earnestly*] Charlie: I come from the land, and have gotten my strength working on the land; and I tell thee that the land is thine to rule righteously and keep God's peace in, and not to pledge at the pawnshop as a drunken woman pledges her children's clothes. And I come from God to tell thee to kneel in the cathedral and solemnly give thy kingdom to Him for ever and ever, and become the greatest king in the world as His steward and His bailiff, His soldier and His servant. The very clay of France will become holy: her soldiers will be the soldiers of God: the rebel dukes will be rebels against God: the English will fall on their knees and beg thee let them return to their lawful homes in peace. Wilt be a poor little Judas, and betray me and Him that sent me?

CHARLES [*tempted at last*] Oh, if I only dare!

JOAN. I shall dare, dare, and dare again, in God's name! Art for or against me?

CHARLES [*excited*] I'll risk it, I warn you I shant be able to keep it up; but I'll risk it. You shall see. [*Running to the main door and shouting*] Hallo! Come back, everybody. [*To Joan, as he runs back to the arch opposite*] Mind you stand by and dont let me be bullied. [*Through the arch*] Come along, will you: the whole Court. [*He sits down in the royal chair as they all hurry in to their former places, chattering and wondering*] Now I'm in for it; but no matter: here goes! [*To the page*] Call for silence, you little beast, will you?

THE PAGE [*snatching a halberd as before and thumping with it repeatedly*] Silence for His Majesty the King. The King speaks. [*Peremptorily*] Will you be silent there? [*Silence*].

CHARLES [*rising*] I have given the command of the army to The Maid. The Maid is to do as she likes with it. [*He descends from the dais*].

General amazement. La Hire, delighted, slaps his steel thigh-piece with his gauntlet.

LA TRÉMOUILLE [*turning threateningly towards Charles*] What is this? *I* command the army.

Joan quickly puts her hand on Charles's shoulder as he instinctively recoils. Charles, with a grotesque effort culminating in an extravagant gesture, snaps his fingers in the Chamberlain's face.

JOAN. Thourt answered, old Gruff-and-Grum. [*Suddenly flashing out her sword as she divines that her moment has come*] Who is for God and His Maid? Who is for Orleans with me?

LA HIRE [*carried away, drawing also*] For God and His Maid! To Orleans!

ALL THE KNIGHTS [*following his lead with enthusiasm*] To Orleans!

Joan, radiant, falls on her knees in thanksgiving to God. They all kneel, except the Archbishop, who gives his benediction with a sigh, and La Trémouille, who collapses, cursing.

SCENE III

Orleans, 29 April, 1429. Dunois, aged 26, is pacing up and down a patch of ground on the south bank of the silver Loire, commanding a long view of the river in both directions. He has had his lance stuck up with a pennon,[13] which streams in a strong east wind. His shield with its bend sinister lies beside it. He has his commander's baton in his hand. He is well built, carrying his armor easily. His broad brow and pointed chin give him an equilaterally triangular face, already marked by active service and responsibility, with the expression of a good-natured and capable man who has no affectations and no foolish illusions. His page is sitting on the ground, elbows on knees, cheeks on fists, idly watching the water. It is evening; and both man and boy are affected by the loveliness of the Loire.

DUNOIS [*halting for a moment to glance up at the streaming pennon and shake his head wearily before he resumes his pacing*] West wind, west wind, west wind. Strumpet: steadfast when you should be wanton, wanton when you should be steadfast. West wind on the silver Loire: what rhymes to Loire? [*He looks again at the pennon, and shakes his fist at it*] Change, curse you, change, English harlot of a wind, change. West, west, I tell you. [*With a growl he resumes his march in silence, but soon begins again*] West wind, wanton wind, wilful wind, womanish wind, false wind from over the water, will you never blow again?

THE PAGE [*bounding to his feet*] See! There! There she goes!

DUNOIS [*startled from his reverie: eagerly*] Where? Who? The Maid?

THE PAGE. No: the kingfisher. Like blue lightning. She went into that bush.

DUNOIS [*furiously disappointed*] Is that all? You infernal young idiot: I have a mind to pitch you into the river.

THE PAGE [*not afraid, knowing his man*] It looked frightfully jolly, that flash of blue. Look! There goes the other!

DUNOIS [*running eagerly to the river brim*] Where? Where?

THE PAGE [*pointing*] Passing the reeds.

DUNOIS [*delighted*] I see.

They follow the flight till the bird takes cover.

THE PAGE. You blew me up because you were not in time to see them yesterday.

DUNOIS. You knew I was expecting The Maid when you set up your yelping. I will give you something to yelp for next time.

THE PAGE. Arnt they lovely? I wish I could catch them.

DUNOIS. Let me catch you trying to trap them, and I will put you in the

13. A sometimes triangular banner on a lance indicating the personal ensign of a bachelor knight.

iron cage for a month to teach you what a cage feels like. You are an abominable boy. *The page laughs, and squats down as before.*

DUNOIS [*pacing*] Blue bird, blue bird, since I am friend to thee, change thou the wind for me. No: it does not rhyme. He who has sinned for thee: thats better. No sense in it, though. [*He finds himself close to the page*] You abominable boy! [*He turns away from him*] Mary in the blue snood, kingfisher color: will you grudge me a west wind?

A SENTRY'S VOICE WESTWARD. Halt! Who goes there?

JOAN'S VOICE. The Maid.

DUNOIS. Let her pass. Hither, Maid! To me!

Joan, in splendid armor, rushes in in a blazing rage. The wind drops; and the pennon flaps idly down the lance; but Dunois is too much occupied with Joan to notice it.

JOAN [*bluntly*] Be you Bastard of Orleans?

DUNOIS [*cool and stern, pointing to his shield*] You see the bend sinister. Are you Joan the Maid?

JOAN. Sure.

DUNOIS. Where are your troops?

JOAN. Miles behind. They have cheated me. They have brought me to the wrong side of the river.

DUNOIS. I told them to.

JOAN. Why did you? The English are on the other side!

DUNOIS. The English are on both sides.

JOAN. But Orleans is on the other side. We must fight the English there. How can we cross the river?

DUNOIS [*grimly*] There is a bridge.

JOAN. In God's name, then, let us cross the bridge, and fall on them.

DUNOIS. It seems simple; but it cannot be done.

JOAN. Who says so?

DUNOIS. I say so; and older and wiser heads than mine are of the same opinion.

JOAN [*roundly*] Then your[14] older and wiser heads are fatheads: they have made a fool of you; and now they want to make a fool of me too, bringing me to the wrong side of the river. Do you not know that I bring you better help than ever came to any general or any town?

DUNOIS [*smiling patiently*] Your own?

JOAN. No: the help and counsel of the King of Heaven. Which is the way to the bridge?

DUNOIS. You are impatient, Maid.

JOAN. Is this a time for patience? Our enemy is at our gates; and here we stand doing nothing. Oh, why are you not fighting? Listen to me: I will deliver you from fear. I—

DUNOIS [*laughing heartily, and waving her off*] No, no, my girl: if you

14. "your" is in Bretano; "you" is in the Penguin. Dunois is only 26, so the former makes more sense.

delivered me from fear I should be a good knight for a story book, but a very bad commander of the army. Come! let me begin to make a soldier of you. [*He takes her to the water's edge*]. Do you see those two forts at this end of the bridge? the big ones?

JOAN. Yes. Are they ours or the goddams'?

DUNOIS. Be quiet, and listen to me. If I were in either of those forts with only ten men I could hold it against an army. The English have more than ten times ten goddams in those forts to hold them against us.

JOAN. They cannot hold them against God. God did not give them the land under those forts: they stole it from Him. He gave it to us. I will take those forts.

DUNOIS. Single-handed?

JOAN. Our men will take them. I will lead them.

DUNOIS. Not a man will follow you.

JOAN. I will not look back to see whether anyone is following me.

DUNOIS [*recognizing her mettle, and clapping her heartily on the shoulder*] Good. You have the makings of a soldier in you. You are in love with war.

JOAN [*startled*] Oh! And the Archbishop said I was in love with religion.

DUNOIS. I, God forgive me, am a little in love with war myself, the ugly devil! I am like a man with two wives. Do you want to be like a woman with two husbands?

JOAN [*matter-of-fact*] I will never take a husband. A man in Toul took an action against me for breach of promise; but I never promised him. I am a soldier: I do not want to be thought of as a woman. I will not dress as a woman. I do not care for the things women care for. They dream of lovers, and of money. I dream of leading a charge, and of placing the big guns. You soldiers do not know how to use the big guns: you think you can win battles with a great noise and smoke.

DUNOIS [*with a shrug*] True. Half the time the artillery is more trouble than it is worth.

JOAN. Aye, lad; but you cannot fight stone walls with horses: you must have guns, and much bigger guns too.

DUNOIS [*grinning at her familiarity, and echoing it*] Aye, lass; but a good heart and a stout ladder will get over the stoniest wall.

JOAN. I will be first up the ladder when we reach the fort, Bastard. I dare you to follow me.

DUNOIS. You must not dare a staff officer, Joan: only company officers are allowed to indulge in displays of personal courage. Besides, you must know that I welcome you as a saint, not as a soldier. I have daredevils enough at my call, if they could help me.

JOAN. I am not a daredevil: I am a servant of God. My sword is sacred: I found it behind the altar in the church of St Catherine, where God hid it for me; and I may not strike a blow with it. My heart is full of courage, not of anger. I will lead; and your men will follow: that is all I can do. But I must do it: you shall not stop me.

DUNOIS. All in good time. Our men cannot take those forts by a sally across the bridge. They must come by water, and take the English in the rear on this side.

JOAN [*her military sense asserting itself*] Then make rafts and put big guns on them; and let your men cross to us.

DUNOIS. The rafts are ready; and the men are embarked. But they must wait for God.

JOAN. What do you mean? God is waiting for them.

DUNOIS. Let Him send us a wind then. My boats are downstream: they cannot come up against both wind and current. We must wait until God changes the wind. Come: let me take you to the church.

JOAN. No. I love church; but the English will not yield to prayers: they understand nothing but hard knocks and slashes. I will not go to church until we have beaten them.

DUNOIS. You must: I have business for you there.

JOAN. What business?

DUNOIS. To pray for a west wind. I have prayed; and I have given two silver candlesticks; but my prayers are not answered. Yours may be: you are young and innocent.

JOAN. Oh yes: you are right. I will pray: I will tell St Catherine: she will make God give me a west wind. Quick: shew me the way to the church.

THE PAGE [*sneezes violently*] At-cha!!!

JOAN. God bless you, child! Coom, Bastard.

They go out. The page rises to follow. He picks up the shield, and is taking the spear as well when he notices the pennon, which is now streaming eastward.

THE PAGE [*dropping the shield and calling excitedly after them*] Seigneur! Seigneur! Mademoiselle!

DUNOIS [*running back*] What is it? The kingfisher? [*He looks eagerly for it up the river*].

JOAN [*joining them*] Oh, a kingfisher! Where?

THE PAGE. No: the wind, the wind, the wind [*pointing to the pennon*]: that is what made me sneeze.

DUNOIS [*looking at the pennon*] The wind has changed. [*He crosses himself*] God has spoken. [*Kneeling and handing his baton to Joan*] You command the king's army. I am your soldier.

THE PAGE [*looking down the river*] The boats have put off. They are ripping upstream like anything.

DUNOIS [*rising*] Now for the forts. You dared me to follow. Dare you lead?

JOAN [*bursting into tears and flinging her arms round Dunois, kissing him on both cheeks*] Dunois, dear comrade in arms, help me. My eyes are blinded with tears. Set my foot on the ladder, and say 'Up, Joan.'

DUNOIS [*dragging her out*] Never mind the tears: make for the flash of the guns.

JOAN [*in a blaze of courage*] Ah!

DUNOIS [*dragging her along with him*] For God and Saint Dennis!

THE PAGE [*shrilly*] The Maid! The Maid! God and The Maid! Hurray-ay-ay! [*He snatches up the shield and lance, and capers out after them, mad with excitement*].

SCENE IV

A tent in the English camp. A bullnecked English chaplain of 50 is sitting on a stool at a table, hard at work writing. At the other side of the table an imposing nobleman, aged 46, is seated in a handsome chair turning over the leaves of an illuminated Book of Hours. The nobleman is enjoying himself: the chaplain is struggling with suppressed wrath. There is an unoccupied leather stool on the nobleman's left. The table is on his right.

THE NOBLEMAN. Now this is what I call workmanship. There is nothing on earth more exquisite than a bonny book, with well-placed columns of rich black writing in beautiful borders, and illuminated pictures cunningly inset. But nowadays, instead of looking at books, people read them. A book might as well be one of those orders for bacon and bran that you are scribbling.

THE CHAPLAIN. I must say, my lord, you take our situation very coolly. Very coolly indeed.

THE NOBLEMAN [*supercilious*] What is the matter?

THE CHAPLAIN. The matter, my lord, is that we English have been defeated.

THE NOBLEMAN. That happens, you know. It is only in history books and ballads that the enemy is always defeated.

THE CHAPLAIN. But we are being defeated over and over again. First, Orleans—

THE NOBLEMAN [*poohpoohing*] Oh, Orleans!

THE CHAPLAIN. I know what you are going to say, my lord: that was a clear case of witchcraft and sorcery. But we are still being defeated. Jargeau, Meung, Beaugency, just like Orleans. And now we have been butchered at Patay, and Sir John Talbot taken prisoner. [*He throws down his pen, almost in tears*] I feel it, my lord: I feel it very deeply. I cannot bear to see my countrymen defeated by a parcel of foreigners.

THE NOBLEMAN. Oh! you are an Englishman, are you?

THE CHAPLAIN. Certainly not, my lord: I am a gentleman. Still, like your lordship, I was born in England; and it makes a difference.

THE NOBLEMAN. You are attached to the soil, eh?

THE CHAPLAIN. It pleases your lordship to be satirical at my expense: your greatness privileges you to be so with impunity. But your lordship knows very well that I am not attached to the soil in a vulgar manner, like a serf. Still, I have a feeling about it; [*with growing agitation*] and I am not ashamed of it; and [*rising wildly*] by God, if this goes on any longer I will fling my cassock to the devil, and take arms myself, and strangle the accursed witch with my own hands.

THE NOBLEMAN [*laughing at him goodnaturedly*] So you shall, chaplain: so you shall, if we can do nothing better. But not yet, not quite yet.

The Chaplain resumes his seat very sulkily.

THE NOBLEMAN [*airily*] I should not care very much about the witch—you see, I have made my pilgrimage to the Holy Land; and the Heavenly Powers, for their own credit, can hardly allow me to be worsted by a village sorceress—but the Bastard of Orleans is a harder nut to crack; and as he has been to the Holy Land too, honors are easy between us as far as that goes.

THE CHAPLAIN. He is only a Frenchman, my lord.

THE NOBLEMAN. A Frenchman! Where did you pick up that expression? Are these Burgundians and Bretons and Picards and Gascons beginning to call themselves Frenchmen, just as our fellows are beginning to call themselves Englishmen? They actually talk of France and England as their countries. Theirs, if you please! What is to become of me and you if that way of thinking comes into fashion?

THE CHAPLAIN. Why, my lord? Can it hurt us?

THE NOBLEMAN. Men cannot serve two masters. If this cant of serving their country once takes hold of them, goodbye to the authority of their feudal lords, and goodbye to the authority of the Church. That is, goodbye to you and me.

THE CHAPLAIN. I hope I am a faithful servant of the Church; and there are only six cousins between me and the barony of Stogumber, which was created by the Conqueror. But is that any reason why I should stand by and see Englishmen beaten by a French bastard and a witch from Lousy Champagne?

THE NOBLEMAN. Easy, man, easy: we shall burn the witch and beat the bastard all in good time. Indeed I am waiting at present for the Bishop of Beauvais, to arrange the burning with him. He has been turned out of his diocese by her faction.

THE CHAPLAIN. You have first to catch her, my lord.

THE NOBLEMAN. Or buy her. I will offer a king's ransom.

THE CHAPLAIN. A king's ransom! For that slut!

THE NOBLEMAN. One has to leave a margin. Some of Charles's people will sell her to the Burgundians; the Burgundians will sell her to us; and there will probably be three or four middlemen who will expect their little commissions.

THE CHAPLAIN. Monstrous. It is all those scoundrels of Jews: they get in every time money changes hands. I would not leave a Jew alive in Christendom if I had my way.

THE NOBLEMAN. Why not? The Jews generally give value. They make you pay; but they deliver the goods. In my experience the men who want something for nothing are invariably Christians.

A page appears.

THE PAGE. The Right Reverend the Bishop of Beauvais: Monseigneur Cauchon.

Cauchon, aged about 60, comes in. The page withdraws. The two Englishmen rise.

THE NOBLEMAN [*with effusive courtesy*] My dear Bishop, how good of you to come! Allow me to introduce myself: Richard de Beauchamp, Earl of Warwick, at your service.

CAUCHON. Your lordship's fame is well known to me.

WARWICK. This reverend cleric is Master John de Stogumber.

THE CHAPLAIN [*glibly*] John Bowyer Spenser Neville de Stogumber, at your service, my lord: Bachelor of Theology, and Keeper of the Private Seal to His Eminence the Cardinal of Winchester.

WARWICK [*to Cauchon*] You call him the Cardinal of England, I believe. Our king's uncle.[15]

CAUCHON. Messire John de Stogumber: I am always the very good friend of His Eminence. [*He extends his hand to the chaplain who kisses his ring*].

WARWICK. Do me the honor to be seated. [*He gives Cauchon his chair, placing it at the head of the table*].

Cauchon accepts the place of honor with a grave inclination. Warwick fetches the leather stool carelessly, and sits in his former place. The chaplain goes back to his chair Though Warwick has taken second place in calculated deference to the Bishop, he assumes the lead in opening the proceedings as a matter of course. He is still cordial and expansive; but there is a new note in his voice which means that he is coming to business.

WARWICK. Well, my Lord Bishop, you find us in one of our unlucky moments. Charles is to be crowned at Rheims, practically by the young woman from Lorraine; and—I must not deceive you, nor flatter your hopes—we cannot prevent it. I suppose it will make a great difference to Charles's position.

CAUCHON. Undoubtedly. It is a masterstroke of The Maid's.

THE CHAPLAIN [*again agitated*] We were not fairly beaten, my lord. No Englishman is ever fairly beaten.

Cauchon raises his eyebrow slightly, then quickly composes his face.

WARWICK. Our friend here takes the view that the young woman is a sorceress. It would, I presume, be the duty of your reverend lord ship to denounce her to the Inquisition, and have her burnt for that offence.

CAUCHON. If she were captured in my diocese: yes.

15. Henry Beaufort, cardinal of Winchester, was an immensely wealthy illegitimate son of John of Gaunt; he was an important figure in English politics despite his French birth.

WARWICK [*feeling that they are getting on capitally*] Just so. Now I suppose there can be no reasonable doubt that she is a sorceress.

THE CHAPLAIN. Not the least. An arrant witch.

WARWICK [*gently reproving their interruption*] We are asking for the Bishop's opinion, Messire John.

CAUCHON. We shall have to consider not merely our own opinions here, but the opinions—the prejudices, if you like—of a French court.

WARWICK [*correcting*] A Catholic court, my lord.

CAUCHON. Catholic courts are composed of mortal men, like other courts, however sacred their function and inspiration may be. And if the men are Frenchmen, as the modern fashion calls them, I am afraid the bare fact that an English army has been defeated by a French one will not convince them that there is any sorcery in the matter.

THE CHAPLAIN. What! Not when the famous Sir Talbot himself has been defeated and actually taken prisoner by a drab from the ditches of Lorraine!

CAUCHON. Sir John Talbot, we all know, is a fierce and formidable soldier, Messire; but I have yet to learn that he is an able general. And though it pleases you to say that he has been defeated by this girl, some of us may be disposed to give a little of the credit to Dunois.

THE CHAPLAIN [*contemptuously*] The Bastard of Orleans!

CAUCHON. Let me remind—

WARWICK [*interposing*] I know what you are going to say, my lord. Dunois defeated me at Montargis.

CAUCHON [*bowing*] I take that as evidence that the Seigneur Dunois is a very able commander indeed.

WARWICK. Your lordship is the flower of courtesy. I admit, on our side, that Talbot is a mere fighting animal, and that it probably served him right to be taken at Patay.

THE CHAPLAIN [*chafing*] My lord: at Orleans this woman had her throat pierced by an English arrow, and was seen to cry like a child from the pain of it. It was a death wound; yet she fought all day; and when our men had repulsed all her attacks like true Englishmen, she walked alone to the wall of our fort with a white banner in her hand; and our men were paralyzed, and could neither shoot nor strike whilst the French fell on them and drove them on to the bridge, which immediately burst into flames and crumbled under them, letting them down into the river, where they were drowned in heaps. Was this your bastard's generalship? or were those flames the flames of hell, conjured up by witchcraft?

WARWICK. You will forgive Messire John's vehemence, my lord; but he has put our case. Dunois is a great captain, we admit; but why could he do nothing until the witch came?

CAUCHON. I do not say that there were no supernatural powers on her side. But the names on that white banner were not the names of Satan and Beelzebub, but the blessed names of our Lord and His holy mother. And your commander who was drowned—Clahz-da I think you call him—

WARWICK. Glasdale. Sir William Glasdale.

CAUCHON. Glass-dell, thank you. He was no saint; and many of our people think that he was drowned for his blasphemies against The Maid.

WARWICK [*beginning to look very dubious*] Well, what are we to infer from all this, my lord? Has The Maid converted you?

CAUCHON. If she had, my lord, I should have known better than to have trusted myself here within your grasp.

WARWICK [*blandly deprecating*] Oh! oh! My lord!

CAUCHON. If the devil is making use of this girl—and I believe he is—

WARWICK [*reassured*] Ah! You hear, Messire John? I knew your lordship would not fail us. Pardon my interruption. Proceed.

CAUCHON. If it be so, the devil has longer views than you give him credit for.

WARWICK. Indeed? In what way? Listen to this, Messire John.

CAUCHON. If the devil wanted to damn a country girl, do you think so easy a task would cost him the winning of half a dozen battles? No, my lord: any trumpery imp could do that much if the girl could be damned at all. The Prince of Darkness does not condescend to such cheap drudgery. When he strikes, he strikes at the Catholic Church, whose realm is the whole spiritual world. When he damns, he damns the souls of the entire human race. Against that dreadful design The Church stands ever on guard. And it is as one of the instruments of that design that I see this girl. She is inspired, but diabolically inspired.

THE CHAPLAIN. I told you she was a witch.

CAUCHON [*fiercely*] She is not a witch. She is a heretic.

THE CHAPLAIN. What difference does that make?

CAUCHON. You, a priest, ask me that! You English are strangely blunt in the mind. All these things that you call witchcraft are capable of a natural explanation. The woman's miracles would not impose on a rabbit: she does not claim them as miracles herself. What do her victories prove but that she has a better head on her shoulders than your swearing Glass-dells and mad bull Talbots, and that the courage of faith, even though it be a false faith, will always outstay the courage of wrath?

THE CHAPLAIN [*hardly able to believe his ears*] Does your lordship compare Sir John Talbot, three times Governor of Ireland, to a mad bull?!!!

WARWICK. It would not be seemly for you to do so, Messire John, as you are still six removes from a barony. But as I am an earl, and Talbot is only a knight, I may make bold to accept the comparison. [*To the Bishop*] My lord: I wipe the slate as far as the witchcraft goes. None the less, we must burn the woman.

CAUCHON. I cannot burn her. The Church cannot take life. And my first duty is to seek this girl's salvation.

WARWICK. No doubt. But you do burn people occasionally.

CAUCHON. No. When The Church cuts off an obstinate heretic as a dead branch from the tree of life, the heretic is handed over to the secular arm. The Church has no part in what the secular arm may see fit to do.

WARWICK. Precisely. And I shall be the secular arm in this case. Well, my lord, hand over your dead branch; and I will see that the fire is ready for it. If you will answer for The Church's part, I will answer for the secular part.

CAUCHON [*with smouldering anger*] I can answer for nothing. You great lords are too prone to treat The Church as a mere political convenience.

WARWICK [*smiling and propitiatory*] Not in England, I assure you.

CAUCHON. In England more than anywhere else. No, my lord: the soul of this village girl is of equal value with yours or your king's before the throne of God; and my first duty is to save it. I will not suffer your lordship to smile at me as if I were repeating a meaningless form of words, and it were well understood between us that I should betray the girl to you. I am no mere political bishop: my faith is to me what your honor is to you; and if there be a loophole through which this baptized child of God can creep to her salvation, I shall guide her to it.

THE CHAPLAIN [*rising in a fury*] You are a traitor.

CAUCHON [*springing up*] You lie, priest. [*Trembling with rage*] If you dare do what this woman has done—set your country above the holy Catholic Church—you shall go to the fire with her.

THE CHAPLAIN. My lord: I—I went too far. I—[*he sits down with a submissive gesture*].

WARWICK [*who has risen apprehensively*] My lord: I apologize to you for the word used by Messire John de Stogumber. It does not mean in England what it does in France. In your language traitor means betrayer: one who is perfidious, treacherous, unfaithful, disloyal. In our country it means simply one who is not wholly devoted to our English interests.

CAUCHON. I am sorry: I did not understand. [*He subsides into his chair with dignity*].

WARWICK [*resuming his seat, much relieved*] I must apologize on my own account if I have seemed to take the burning of this poor girl too lightly. When one has seen whole countrysides burnt over and over again as mere items in military routine, one has to grow a very thick skin. Otherwise one might go mad: at all events, I should. May I venture to assume that your lordship also, having to see so many heretics burned from time to time, is compelled to take—shall I say a professional view of what would otherwise be a very horrible incident?

CAUCHON. Yes: it is a painful duty: even, as you say, a horrible one. But in comparison with the horror of heresy it is less than nothing. I am not thinking of this girl's body, which will suffer for a few moments only, and which must in any event die in some more or less painful manner, but of her soul, which may suffer to all eternity.

WARWICK. Just so; and God grant that her soul may be saved! But the practical problem would seem to be how to save her soul without saving her body. For we must face it, my lord: if this cult of The Maid goes on, our cause is lost.

THE CHAPLAIN [*his voice broken like that of a man who has been crying*] May I speak, my lord?

WARWICK. Really, Messire John, I had rather you did not, unless you can keep your temper.

THE CHAPLAIN. It is only this. I speak under correction; but The Maid is full of deceit: she pretends to be devout. Her prayers and confessions are endless. How can she be accused of heresy when she neglects no observance of a faithful daughter of The Church?

CAUCHON [*flaming up*] A faithful daughter of The Church! The Pope himself at his proudest dare not presume as this woman presumes. She acts as if she herself were The Church. She brings the message of God to Charles; and The Church must stand aside. She will crown him in the cathedral of Rheims: she, not The Church! She sends letters to the king of England giving him God's command through her to return to his island on pain of God's vengeance, which she will execute. Let me tell you that the writing of such letters was the practice of the accursed Mahomet, the anti-Christ. Has she ever in all her utterances said one word of The Church? Never. It is always God and herself.

WARWICK. What can you expect? A beggar on horseback! Her head is turned.

CAUCHON. Who has turned it? The devil. And for a mighty purpose. He is spreading this heresy everywhere. The man Hus, burnt only thirteen years ago at Constance, infected all Bohemia with it.[16] A man named WcLeef, himself an anointed priest, spread the pestilence in England; and to your shame you let him die in his bed.[17] We have such people here in France too: I know the breed. It is cancerous, if it be not cut out, stamped out, burnt out, it will not stop until it has brought the whole body of human society into sin and corruption, into waste and ruin. By it an Arab camel driver drove Christ and His Church out of Jerusalem, and ravaged his way west like a wild beast until at last there stood only the Pyrenees and God's mercy between France and damnation. Yet what did the camel driver do at the beginning more than this shepherd girl is doing? He had his voices

16. John Hus was a Czech religious reformer executed in 1415.
17. John Wycliffe (1320–84), English Bible translator.

from the angel Gabriel: she has her voices from St Catherine and St Margaret and the Blessed Michael. He declared himself the messenger of God, and wrote in God's name to the kings of the earth. Her letters to them are going forth daily. It is not the Mother of God now to whom we must look for intercession, but to Joan the Maid. What will the world be like when The Church's accumulated wisdom and knowledge and experience, its councils of learned, venerable pious men, are thrust into the kennel by every ignorant laborer or dairymaid whom the devil can puff up with the monstrous self-conceit of being directly inspired from heaven? It will be a world of blood, of fury, of devastation, of each man striving for his own hand: in the end a world wrecked back into barbarism. For now you have only Mahomet and his dupes, and the Maid and her dupes; but what will it be when every girl thinks herself a Joan and every man a Mahomet? I shudder to the very marrow of my bones when I think of it. I have fought it all my life; and I will fight it to the end. Let all this woman's sins be forgiven her except only this sin; for it is the sin against the Holy Ghost; and if she does not recant in the dust before the world, and submit herself to the last inch of her soul to her Church, to the fire she shall go if she once falls into my hand.

WARWICK [*unimpressed*] You feel strongly about it, naturally.

CAUCHON. Do not you?

WARWICK. I am a soldier, not a churchman. As a pilgrim I saw something of the Mahometans. They were not so ill-bred as I had been led to believe. In some respects their conduct compared favorably with ours.

CAUCHON [*displeased*] I have noticed this before. Men go to the East to convert the infidels. And the infidels pervert them. The Crusader comes back more than half a Saracen. Not to mention that all Englishmen are born heretics.

THE CHAPLAIN. Englishmen heretics!!! [*Appealing to Warwick*] My lord: must we endure this? His lordship is beside himself. How can what an Englishman believes be heresy? It is a contradiction in terms.

CAUCHON. I absolve you, Messire de Stogumber, on the ground of invincible ignorance. The thick air of your country does not breed theologians.

WARWICK. You would not say so if you heard us quarrelling about religion, my lord! I am sorry you think I must be either a heretic or a blockhead because, as a travelled man, I know that the followers of Mahomet profess great respect for our Lord, and are more ready to forgive St Peter for being a fisherman than your lordship is to forgive Mahomet for being a camel driver. But at least we can proceed in this matter without bigotry.

CAUCHON. When men call the zeal of the Christian Church bigotry I know what to think.

WARWICK. They are only east and west views of the same thing.

CAUCHON [*bitterly ironical*] Only east and west! Only!!

WARWICK. Oh, my Lord Bishop, I am not gainsaying you. You will carry The Church with you, but you have to carry the nobles also. To my mind there is a stronger case against The Maid than the one you have so forcibly put. Frankly, I am not afraid of this girl becoming another Mahomet, and superseding The Church by a great heresy. I think you exaggerate that risk. But have you noticed that in these letters of hers, she proposes to all the kings of Europe, as she has already pressed on Charles, a transaction which would wreck the whole social structure of Christendom?

CAUCHON. Wreck The Church. I tell you so.

WARWICK [*whose patience is wearing out*] My lord: pray get The Church out of your head for a moment; and remember that there are temporal institutions in the world as well as spiritual ones. I and my peers represent the feudal aristocracy as you represent The Church. We are the temporal power. Well, do you not see how this girl's idea strikes at us?

CAUCHON. How does her idea strike you, except as it strikes at all of us, through The Church?

WARWICK. Her idea is that the kings should give their realms to God, and then reign as God's bailiffs.

CAUCHON [*not interested*] Quite sound theologically, my lord. But the king will hardly care, provided he reign. It is an abstract idea: a mere form of words.

WARWICK. By no means. It is a cunning device to supersede the aristocracy, and make the king sole and absolute autocrat. Instead of the king being merely the first among his peers, he becomes their master. That we cannot suffer: we call no man master. Nominally we hold our lands and dignities from the king, because there must be a keystone to the arch of human society; but we hold our lands in our own hands, and defend them with our own swords and those of our own tenants. Now by The Maid's doctrine the king will take our lands—our lands!—and make them a present to God; and God will then vest them wholly in the king.

CAUCHON. Need you fear that? You are the makers of kings after all. York or Lancaster in England, Lancaster or Valois in France: they reign according to your pleasure.[18]

WARWICK. Yes; but only as long as the people follow their feudal lords, and know the king only as a travelling show, owning nothing but the highway that belongs to everybody. If the people's thoughts and hearts were turned to the king, and their lords became only the king's servants in their eyes, the king could break us across his knee one by one; and then what should we be but liveried courtiers in his halls?

18. York and Lancaster were the two English families fighting for the crown of England in the War of the Roses; Lancaster and Valois are the English and French families contesting the rule of France.

CAUCHON. Still you need not fear, my lord. Some men are born kings; and some are born statesmen. The two are seldom the same. Where would the king find counsellors to plan and carry out such a policy for him?

WARWICK [*with a not too friendly smile*] Perhaps in the Church, my lord.

Cauchon, with an equally sour smile, shrugs his shoulders, and does not contradict him.

WARWICK. Strike down the barons; and the cardinals will have it all their own way.

CAUCHON [*conciliatory, dropping his polemical tone*] My lord: we shall not defeat The Maid if we strive against one another. I know well that there is a Will to Power in the world. I know that while it lasts there will be a struggle between the Emperor and the Pope, between the dukes and the political cardinals, between the barons and the kings. The devil divides us and governs. I see you are no friend to The Church: you are an earl first and last, as I am a churchman first and last. But can we not sink our differences in the face of a common enemy? I see now that what is in your mind is not that this girl has never once mentioned The Church, and thinks only of God and herself, but that she has never once mentioned the peerage, and thinks only of the king and herself.

WARWICK. Quite so. These two ideas of hers are the same idea at bottom. It goes deep, my lord. It is the protest of the individual soul against the interference of priest or peer between the private man and his God. I should call it Protestantism if I had to find a name for it.

CAUCHON [*looking hard at him*] You understand it wonderfully well, my lord. Scratch an Englishman, and find a Protestant.

WARWICK [*playing the pink*[19] *of courtesy*] I think you are not entirely void of sympathy with The Maid's secular heresy, my lord. I leave you to find a name for it.

CAUCHON. You mistake me, my lord. I have no sympathy with her political presumptions. But as a priest I have gained a knowledge of the minds of the common people; and there you will find yet another most dangerous idea. I can express it only by such phrases as France for the French, England for the English, Italy for the Italians, Spain for the Spanish, and so forth. It is sometimes so narrow and bitter in country folk that it surprises me that this country girl can rise above the idea of her village for its villagers. But she can. She does. When she threatens to drive the English from the soil of France she is undoubtedly thinking of the whole extent of country in which French is spoken. To her the French-speaking people are what the Holy Scriptures describe as a nation. Call this side of her

19. The highest type.

heresy Nationalism if you will: I can find you no better name for it. I can only tell you that it is essentially anti-Catholic and anti-Christian; for the Catholic Church knows only one realm, and that is the realm of Christ's kingdom. Divide that kingdom into nations, and you dethrone Christ. Dethrone Christ, and who will stand between our throats and the sword? The world will perish in a welter of war.

WARWICK. Well, if you will burn the Protestant, I will burn the Nationalist, though perhaps I shall not carry Messire John with me there. England for the English will appeal to him.

THE CHAPLAIN. Certainly England for the English goes without saying: it is the simple law of nature. But this woman denies to England her legitimate conquests, given her by God because of her peculiar fitness to rule over less civilized races for their own good. I do not understand what your lordships mean by Protestant and Nationalist: you are too learned and subtle for a poor clerk like myself. But I know as a matter of plain commonsense that the woman is a rebel; and that is enough for me. She rebels against Nature by wearing man's clothes, and fighting. She rebels against The Church by usurping the divine authority of the Pope. She rebels against God by her damnable league with Satan and his evil spirits against our army. And all these rebellions are only excuses for her great rebellion against England. That is not to be endured. Let her perish. Let her burn. Let her not infect the whole flock. It is expedient that one woman die for the people.

WARWICK [*rising*] My lord: we seem to be agreed.

CAUCHON [*rising also, but in protest*] I will not imperil my soul. I will uphold the justice of the Church. I will strive to the utmost for this woman's salvation.

WARWICK. I am sorry for the poor girl. I hate these severities. I will spare her if I can.

THE CHAPLAIN [*implacably*] I would burn her with my own hands.

CAUCHON [*blessing him*] Sancta simplicitas°! holy simplicity

SCENE V

The ambulatory in the cathedral of Rheims, near the doors of the vestry. A pillar bears one of the stations of the cross. The organ is playing the people out of the nave after the coronation. Joan is kneeling in prayer before the station. She is beautifully dressed, but still in male attire. The organ ceases as Dunois, also splendidly arrayed, comes into the ambulatory from the vestry.

DUNOIS. Come, Joan! you have had enough praying. After that fit of crying you will catch a chill if you stay here any longer. It is all over: the cathedral is empty; and the streets are full. They are calling for The Maid. We have told them you are staying here alone to pray; but they want to see you again.

JOAN. No: let the king have all the glory.

DUNOIS. He only spoils the show, poor devil. No, Joan: you have crowned him; and you must go through with it. *Joan shakes her head reluctantly.*

DUNOIS [*raising her*] Come come! it will be over in a couple of hours. It's better than the bridge at Orleans: eh?

JOAN. Oh, dear Dunois, how I wish it were the bridge at Orleans again! We lived at that bridge.

DUNOIS. Yes, faith, and died too: some of us.

JOAN. Isnt it strange, Jack? I am such a coward: I am frightened beyond words before a battle; but it is so dull afterwards when there is no danger: oh, so dull! dull! dull!

DUNOIS. You must learn to be abstemious in war, just as you are in your food and drink, my little saint.

JOAN. Dear Jack: I think you like me as a soldier likes his comrade.

DUNOIS. You need it, poor innocent child of God. You have not many friends at court.

JOAN. Why do all these courtiers and knights and churchmen hate me? What have I done to them? I have asked nothing for myself except that my village shall not be taxed; for we cannot afford war taxes. I have brought them luck and victory: I have set them right when they were doing all sorts of stupid things: I have crowned Charles and made him a real king; and all the honors he is handing out have gone to them. Then why do they not love me?

DUNOIS [*rallying her*] Sim-ple-ton! Do you expect stupid people to love you for shewing them up? Do blundering old military dug-outs[20] love the successful young captains who supersede them? Do ambitious politicians love the climbers who take the front seats from them? Do archbishops enjoy being played off their own altars, even by saints? Why, I should be jealous of you myself if I were ambitious enough.

JOAN. You are the pick of the basket here, Jack: the only friend I have among all these nobles. I'll wager your mother was from the country. I will go back to the farm when I have taken Paris.

DUNOIS. I am not so sure that they will let you take Paris.

JOAN [*startled*] What!

DUNOIS. I should have taken it myself before this if they had all been sound about it. Some of them would rather Paris took you, I think. So take care.

JOAN. Jack: the world is too wicked for me. If the goddams and the Burgundians do not make an end of me, the French will. Only for my voices I should lose all heart. That is why I had to steal away to pray here alone after the coronation. I'll tell you something, Jack. It is in the bells I hear my voices. Not today, when they all rang: that was

20. A rough shelter in the ground; here metaphorically an old soldier unwilling to leave his established position.

nothing but jangling. But here in this corner, where the bells come down from heaven, and the echoes linger, or in the fields, where they come from a distance through the quiet of the countryside, my voices are in them. [*The cathedral clock chimes the quarter*] Hark! [*She becomes rapt*] Do you hear? 'Dear-child-of-God': just what you said. At the half-hour they will say 'Be-brave-go-on'. At the three-quarters they will say 'I-am-thy-Help'. But it is at the hour, when the great bell goes after 'God-will-save-France': it is then that St Margaret and St Catherine and sometimes even the blessed Michael[21] will say things that I cannot tell beforehand. Then, oh then—

DUNOIS [*interrupting her kindly but, not sympathetically*] Then, Joan, we shall hear whatever we fancy in the booming of the bell. You make me uneasy when you talk about your voices: I should think you were a bit cracked if I hadnt noticed that you give me very sensible reasons for what you do, though I hear you telling others you are only obeying Madame Saint Catherine.

JOAN [*crossly*] Well, I have to find reasons for you, because you do not believe in my voices. But the voices come first; and I find the reasons after: whatever you may choose to believe.

DUNOIS. Are you angry, Joan?

JOAN. Yes. [*Smiling*] No: not with you. I wish you were one of the village babies.

DUNOIS. Why?

JOAN. I could nurse you for awhile.

DUNOIS. You are a bit of a woman after all.

JOAN. No: not a bit: I am a soldier and nothing else. Soldiers always nurse children when they get a chance.

DUNOIS. That is true. [*He laughs*].

King Charles, with Bluebeard on his left and La Hire on his right, comes from the vestry, where he has been disrobing. Joan shrinks away behind the pillar. Dunois is left between Charles and La Hire.

DUNOIS. Well, your Majesty is an anointed king at last. How do you like it?

CHARLES. I would not go through it again to be emperor of the sun and moon. The weight of those robes! I thought I should have dropped when they loaded that crown on to me. And the famous holy oil they talked so much about was rancid: phew! The Archbishop must be nearly dead: his robes must have weighed a ton: they are stripping him still in the vestry.

DUNOIS [*drily*] Your majesty should wear armor oftener. That would accustom you to heavy dressing.

CHARLES. Yes: the old jibe! Well, I am not going to wear armor: fighting is not my job. Where is The Maid?

JOAN [*coming forward between Charles and Bluebeard, and falling on her*

21. The archangel Michael is captain of the host of heaven.

knee] Sire: I have made you king: my work is done. I am going back to my father's farm.

CHARLES [*surprised, but relieved*] Oh, are you? Well, that will be very nice.

Joan rises, deeply discouraged.

CHARLES [*continuing heedlessly*] A healthy life, you know.

DUNOIS. But a dull one.

BLUEBEARD. You will find the petticoats tripping you up after leaving them off for so long.

LA HIRE. You will miss the fighting. It's a bad habit, but a grand one, and the hardest of all to break yourself of.

CHARLES [*anxiously*] Still, we dont want you to stay if you would really rather go home.

JOAN [*bitterly*] I know well that none of you will be sorry to see me go. [*She turns her shoulder to Charles and walks past him to the more congenial neighborhood of Dunois and La Hire*].

LA HIRE. Well, I shall be able to swear when I want to. But I shall miss you at times.

JOAN. La Hire: in spite of all your sins and swears we shall meet in heaven; for I love you as I love Pitou, my old sheep dog. Pitou could kill a wolf. You will kill the English wolves until they go back to their country and become good dogs of God, will you not?

LA HIRE. You and I together: yes.

JOAN. No: I shall last only a year from the beginning.

ALL THE OTHERS. What!

JOAN. I know it somehow.

DUNOIS. Nonsense!

JOAN. Jack: do you think you will be able to drive them out?

DUNOIS [*with quiet conviction*] Yes: I shall drive them out. They beat us because we thought battles were tournaments and ransom markets. We played the fool while the goddams took war seriously. But I have learnt my lesson, and taken their measure. They have no roots here. I have beaten them before; and I shall beat them again.

JOAN. You will not be cruel to them, Jack?

DUNOIS. The goddams will not yield to tender handling. We did not begin it.

JOAN [*suddenly*] Jack: before I go home, let us take Paris.

CHARLES [*terrified*] Oh no no. We shall lose everything we have gained. Oh dont let us have any more fighting. We can make a very good treaty with the Duke of Burgundy.

JOAN. Treaty! [*She stamps with impatience*].

CHARLES. Well, why not, now that I am crowned and anointed? Oh, that oil!

The Archbishop comes from the vestry, and joins the group between Charles and Bluebeard.

CHARLES. Archbishop: The Maid wants to start fighting again.

THE ARCHBISHOP. Have we ceased fighting, then? Are we at peace?

CHARLES. No: I suppose not; but let us be content with what we have done. Let us make a treaty. Our luck is too good to last; and now is our chance to stop before it turns.

JOAN. Luck! God has fought for us; and you call it luck! And you would stop while there are still Englishmen on this holy earth of dear France!

THE ARCHBISHOP [*sternly*] Maid: the king addressed himself to me, not to you. You forget yourself. You very often forget yourself.

JOAN [*unabashed, and rather roughly*] Then speak, you; and tell him that it is not God's will that he should take his hand from the plough.

THE ARCHBISHOP. If I am not so glib with the name of God as you are, it is because I interpret His will with the authority of the Church and of my sacred office. When you first came you respected it, and would not have dared to speak as you are now speaking. You came clothed with the virtue of humility; and because God blessed your enterprises accordingly, you have stained yourself with the sin of pride. The old Greek tragedy is rising among us. It is the chastisement of hubris.

CHARLES. Yes: she thinks she knows better than everyone else.

JOAN [*distressed, but naïvely incapable of seeing the effect she is producing*] But I do know better than any of you seem to. And I am not proud: I never speak unless I know I am right.

BLUEBEARD [*exclaiming* {Ha ha!
CHARLES *together*] {Just so.

THE ARCHBISHOP. How do you know you are right?

JOAN. I always know. My voices—

CHARLES. Oh, your voices, your voices. Why dont the voices come to me? I am king, not you.

JOAN. They do come to you; but you do not hear them. You have not sat in the field in the evening listening for them. When the angelus[22] rings you cross yourself and have done with it; but if you prayed from your heart, and listened to the thrilling of the bells in the air after they stop ringing, you would hear the voices as well as I do. [*Turning brusquely from him*] But what voices do you need to tell you what the blacksmith can tell you: that you must strike while the iron is hot? I tell you we must make a dash at Compiègne[23] and relieve it as we relieved Orleans. Then Paris will open its gates; or if not, we will break through them. What is your crown worth without your capital?

LA HIRE. That is what I say too. We shall go through them like a red hot shot through a pound of butter. What do you say, Bastard?

22. A bell tolled in the morning, at noon, and in the evening to signal the start of a devotion in memory of the Annunciation.

23. City on the Oise River in northern France.

DUNOIS. If our cannon balls were all as hot as your head, and we had enough of them, we should conquer the earth, no doubt. Pluck and impetuosity are good servants in war, but bad masters: they have delivered us into the hands of the English every time we have trusted to them. We never know when we are beaten: that is our great fault.

JOAN. You never know when you are victorious: that is a worse fault. I shall have to make you carry looking-glasses in battle to convince you that the English have not cut off all your noses. You would have been besieged in Orleans still, you and your councils of war, if I had not made you attack. You should always attack; and if you only hold on long enough the enemy will stop first. You dont know how to begin a battle; and you dont know how to use your cannons. And I do.

She squats down on the flags with crossed ankles, pouting.

DUNOIS. I know what you think of us, General Joan.

JOAN. Never mind that, Jack. Tell them what you think of me.

DUNOIS. I think that God was on your side; for I have not forgotten how the wind changed, and how our hearts changed when you came; and by my faith I shall never deny that it was in your sign that we conquered. But I tell you as a soldier that God is no man's daily drudge, and no maid's either. If you are worthy of it He will sometimes snatch you out of the jaws of death and set you on your feet again; but that is all: once on your feet you must fight with all your might and all your craft. For He has to be fair to your enemy too: dont forget that. Well, He set us on our feet through you at Orleans; and the glory of it has carried us through a few good battles here to the coronation. But if we presume on it further, and trust to God to do the work we should do ourselves, we shall be defeated; and serve us right!

JOAN. But—

DUNOIS. Sh! I have not finished. Do not think, any of you, that these victories of ours were won without generalship. King Charles: you have said no word in your proclamations of my part in this campaign; and I make no complaint of that; for the people will run after The Maid and her miracles and not after the Bastard's hard work finding troops for her and feeding them. But I know exactly how much God did for us through The Maid, and how much He left me to do by my own wits; and I tell you that your little hour of miracles is over, and that from this time on he who plays the war game best will win—if the luck is on his side.

JOAN. Ah! if, if, if, if! If ifs and ans were pots and pans there'd be no need of tinkers. [*Rising impetuously*] I tell you, Bastard, your art of war is no use, because your knights are no good for real fighting. War is only a game to them, like tennis and all their other games: they make rules as to what is fair and what is not fair, and heap armor on themselves and on their poor horses to keep out the arrows; and when they fall they cant get up, and have to wait for their squires to come and lift them to arrange about the ransom with the man that has poked them off their horse. Cant you see that all the like of that is gone by and done with? What use is armor against gunpowder? And if it was, do you think men that are fighting for France and for God will stop to bargain about ransoms, as half your knights live by doing? No: they will fight to win; and they will give up their lives out of their own hand into the hand of God when they go into battle, as I do. Common folks understand this. They cannot afford armor and cannot pay ransoms; but they followed me half naked into the moat and up the ladder and over the wall. With them it is my life or thine, and God defend the right! You may shake your head, Jack; and Bluebeard may twirl his billygoat's beard and cock his nose at me; but remember the day your knights and captains refused to follow me to attack the English at Orleans! You locked the gates to keep me in; and it was the townsfolk and the common people that followed me, and forced the gate, and shewed you the way to fight in earnest.

BLUEBEARD [*offended*] Not content with being Pope Joan, you must be Caesar and Alexander as well.

THE ARCHBISHOP. Pride will have a fall, Joan.

JOAN. Oh, never mind whether it is pride or not: is it true? is it commonsense?

LA HIRE. It is true. Half of us are afraid of having our handsome noses broken; and the other half are out for paying off their mortgages. Let her have her way, Dunois: she does not know everything; but she has got hold of the right end of the stick. Fighting is not what it was; and those who know least about it often make the best job of it.

DUNOIS. I know all that. I do not fight in the old way: I have learnt the lesson of Agincourt,[24] of Poitiers and Crecy. I know how many lives any move of mine will cost; and if the move is worth the cost I make it and pay the cost. But Joan never counts the cost at all: she goes ahead and trusts to God: she thinks she has God in her pocket. Up to now she has had the numbers on her side; and she has won. But I know Joan; and I see that some day she will go ahead when she has only ten men to do the work of a hundred. And then she will find that God is on the side of the big battalions. She will be taken by the enemy. And the lucky man that makes the capture will receive sixteen thousand pounds from the Earl of Ouareek.

JOAN [*flattered*] Sixteen thousand pounds! Eh, laddie, have they offered that for me? There cannot be so much money in the world.

DUNOIS. There is, in England. And now tell me, all of you, which of you will lift a finger to save Joan once the English have got her? I speak first, for the army. The day after she has been dragged from her horse by a goddam or a Burgundian, and he is not struck dead: the day after she is locked in a dungeon, and the bars and bolts do not fly open

24. Agincourt was Henry V's victory over the French in 1415.

at the touch of St Peter's angel: the day when the enemy finds out that she is as vulnerable as I am and not a bit more invincible, she will not be worth the life of a single soldier to us; and I will not risk that life, much as I cherish her as a companion-in-arms.

JOAN. I dont blame you, Jack: you are right. I am not worth one soldier's life if God lets me be beaten; but France may think me worth my ransom after what God has done for her through me.

CHARLES. I tell you I have no money; and this coronation, which is all your fault, has cost me the last farthing I can borrow.

JOAN. The Church is richer than you. I put my trust in the Church.

THE ARCHBISHOP. Woman: they will drag you through the streets, and burn you as a witch.

JOAN [*running to him*] Oh, my lord, do not say that. It is impossible. I a witch!

THE ARCHBISHOP. Peter Cauchon knows his business. The University of Paris has burnt a woman for saying that what you have done was well done, and according to God.

JOAN [*bewildered*] But why? What sense is there in it? What I have done is according to God. They could not burn a woman for speaking the truth.

THE ARCHBISHOP. They did.

JOAN. But you know that she was speaking the truth. You would not let them burn me.

THE ARCHBISHOP. How could I prevent them?

JOAN. You would speak in the name of the Church. You are a great prince of the Church. I would go anywhere with your blessing to protect me.

THE ARCHBISHOP. I have no blessing for you while you are proud and disobedient.

JOAN. Oh, why will you go on saying things like that? I am not proud and disobedient. I am a poor girl, and so ignorant that I do not know A from B. How could I be proud? And how can you say that I am disobedient when I always obey my voices, because they come from God.

THE ARCHBISHOP. The voice of God on earth is the voice of the Church Militant; and all the voices that come to you are the echoes of your own wilfulness.

JOAN. It is not true.

THE ARCHBISHOP [*flushing angrily*] You tell the Archbishop in his cathedral that he lies; and yet you say you are not proud and disobedient.

JOAN. I never said you lied. It was you that as good as said my voices lied. When have they ever lied? If you will not believe in them: even if they are only the echoes of my own commonsense, are they not always right? and are not your earthly counsels always wrong?

THE ARCHBISHOP [*indignantly*] It is waste of time admonishing you.

CHARLES. It always comes back to the same thing. She is right; and everyone else is wrong.

THE ARCHBISHOP. Take this as your last warning. If you perish through setting your private judgment above the instructions of your spiritual directors, the Church disowns you, and leaves you to whatever fate your presumption may bring upon you. The Bastard has told you that if you persist in setting up your military conceit above the counsels of your commanders—

DUNOIS [*interposing*] To put it quite exactly, if you attempt to relieve the garrison in Compiègne without the same superiority in numbers you had at Orleans—

THE ARCHBISHOP. The army will disown you, and will not rescue you. And His Majesty the King has told you that the throne has not the means of ransoming you.

CHARLES. Not a penny.

THE ARCHBISHOP. You stand alone: absolutely alone, trusting to your own conceit, your own ignorance, your own headstrong presumption, your own impiety in hiding all these sins under the cloak of a trust in God. When you pass through these doors into the sunlight, the crowd will cheer you. They will bring you their little children and their invalids to heal: they will kiss your hands and feet, and do what they can, poor simple souls, to turn your head, and madden you with the self-confidence that is leading you to your destruction. But you will be none the less alone: they cannot save you. We and we only can stand between you and the stake at which our enemies have burnt that wretched woman in Paris.

JOAN [*her eyes skyward*] I have better friends and better counsel than yours.

THE ARCHBISHOP. I see that I am speaking in vain to a hardened heart. You reject our protection, and are determined to turn us all against you. In future, then, fend for yourself; and if you fail, God have mercy on your soul.

DUNOIS. That is the truth, Joan. Heed it.

JOAN. Where would you all have been now if I had heeded that sort of truth? There is no help, no counsel, in any of you. Yes: I am alone on earth: I have always been alone. My father told my brothers to drown me if I would not stay to mind his sheep while France was bleeding to death: France might perish if only our lambs were safe. I thought France would have friends at the court of the king of France; and I find only wolves fighting for pieces of her poor torn body. I thought God would have friends everywhere, because He is the friend of everyone; and in my innocence I believed that you who now cast me out would be like strong towers to keep harm from me. But I am wiser now; and nobody is any the worse for being wiser. Do not think you can frighten me by telling me that I am alone. France is alone; and God is alone; and what is my loneliness before the loneliness of my country and my God? I see now that the loneliness of God is His strength: what would He be if He listened to your jealous little counsels? Well, my loneliness shall be my strength too; it is better to be alone with God; His friendship will not fail me, nor His counsel, nor His love. In His strength I will dare, and dare, and dare, until I die. I will go out now to the common people, and let the love in their eyes comfort me for the hate in yours. You will all be glad to see me burnt; but if I go through the fire I shall go through it to their hearts for ever and ever. And so, God be with me!

She goes from them. They stare after her in glum silence for a moment. Then Gilles de Rais twirls his beard.

BLUEBEARD. You know, the woman is quite impossible. I dont dislike her, really; but what are you to do with such a character?

DUNOIS. As God is my judge, if she fell into the Loire I would jump in in full armor to fish her out. But if she plays the fool at Compiègne, and gets caught, I must leave her to her doom.

LA HIRE. Then you had better chain me up; for I could follow her to hell when the spirit rises in her like that.

THE ARCHBISHOP. She disturbs my judgment too: there is a dangerous power in her outbursts. But the pit is open at her feet; and for good or evil we cannot turn her from it.

CHARLES. If only she would keep quiet, or go home! *They follow her dispiritedly.*

SCENE VI

Rouen,[25] *30 May 1431. A great stone hall in the castle, arranged for a trial-at-law, but not a trial-by-jury, the court being the Bishop's court with the Inquisition participating: hence there are two raised chairs side by side for the Bishop and the Inquisitor as judges. Rows of chairs radiating from them at an obtuse angle are for the canons, the doctors of law and theology, and the Dominican monks, who act as assessors. In the angle is a table for the scribes, with stools. There is also a heavy rough wooden stool for the prisoner. All these are at the inner end of the hall. The further end is open to the courtyard through a row of arches. The court is shielded from the weather by screens and curtains.*

Looking down the great hall from the middle of the inner end, the judicial chairs and scribes' table are to the right. The prisoner's stool is to the left. There are arched doors right and left. It is a fine sunshiny May morning.

Warwick comes in through the arched doorway on the judges' side, followed by his page.

25. A city on the Seine in northern France.

THE PAGE [*pertly*] I suppose your lordship is aware that we have no business here. This is an ecclesiastical court; and we are only the secular arm.

WARWICK. I am aware of that fact. Will it please your impudence to find the Bishop of Beauvais for me, and give him a hint that he can have a word with me here before the trial, if he wishes?

THE PAGE [*going*] Yes, my lord.

WARWICK. And mind you behave yourself. Do not address him as Pious Peter.

THE PAGE. No, my lord. I shall be kind to him, because, when The Maid is brought in, Pious Peter will have to pick a peck of pickled pepper.

Cauchon enters through the same door with a Dominican monk and a canon, the latter carrying a brief.

THE PAGE. The Right Reverend his lordship the Bishop of Beauvais. And two other reverend gentlemen.

WARWICK. Get out; and see that we are not interrupted.

THE PAGE. Right, my lord [*he vanishes airily*].

CAUCHON. I wish your lordship good-morrow.

WARWICK. Good-morrow to your lordship. Have I had the pleasure of meeting your friends before? I think not.

CAUCHON [*introducing the monk, who is on his right*] This, my lord, is Brother John Lemaître, of the order of St Dominic. He is acting as deputy for the Chief Inquisitor into the evil of heresy in France. Brother John: the Earl of Warwick.

WARWICK. Your Reverence is most welcome. We have no Inquisitor in England, unfortunately; though we miss him greatly, especially on occasions like the present.

The Inquisitor smiles patiently, and bows. He is a mild elderly gentleman, but has evident reserves of authority and firmness.

CAUCHON [*introducing the Canon, who is on his left*] This gentleman is Canon John D'Estivet, of the Chapter of Bayeaux. He is acting as Promoter.

WARWICK. Promoter?

CAUCHON. Prosecutor, you would call him in civil law.

WARWICK. Ah! prosecutor. Quite, quite. I am very glad to make your acquaintance, Canon D'Estivet.

D'Estivet bows. [He is on the young side of middle age, well mannered, but vulpine° beneath his veneer]. foxlike

WARWICK. May I ask what stage the proceedings have reached? It is now more than nine months since The Maid was captured at Compiègne by the Burgundians. It is fully four months since I bought her from the Burgundians for a very handsome sum, solely that she might be brought to justice. It is very nearly three months since I delivered her up to you, my Lord Bishop, as a person suspected of heresy. May I suggest that you are taking a rather unconscionable time to make up your minds about a very plain case? Is this trial never going to end?

THE INQUISITOR [*smiling*] It has not yet begun, my lord.

WARWICK. Not yet begun! Why, you have been at it eleven weeks!

CAUCHON. We have not been idle, my lord. We have held fifteen examinations of The Maid: six public and nine private.

THE INQUISITOR [*always patiently smiling*] You see, my lord, I have been present at only two of these examinations. They were proceedings of the Bishop's court solely, and not of the Holy Office. I have only just decided to associate myself—that is, to associate the Holy Inquisition—with the Bishop's court. I did not at first think that this was a case of heresy at all. I regarded it as a political case, and The Maid as a prisoner of war. But having now been present at two of the examinations, I must admit that this seems to be one of the gravest cases of heresy within my experience. Therefore everything is now in order, and we proceed to trial this morning. [*He moves towards the judicial chairs*].

CAUCHON. This moment, if your lordship's convenience allows.

WARWICK [*graciously*] Well, that is good news, gentlemen. I will not attempt to conceal from you that our patience was becoming strained.

CAUCHON. So I gathered from the threats of your soldiers to drown those of our people who favor The Maid.

WARWICK. Dear me! At all events their intentions were friendly to you, my lord.

CAUCHON [*sternly*] I hope not. I am determined that the woman shall have a fair hearing. The justice of the Church is not a mockery, my lord.

THE INQUISITOR [*returning*] Never has there been a fairer examination within my experience, my lord. The Maid needs no lawyers to take her part: she will be tried by her most faithful friends, all ardently desirous to save her soul from perdition.

D'ESTIVET. Sir: I am the Promotor; and it has been my painful duty to present the case against the girl; but believe me, I would throw up my case today and hasten to her defence if I did not know that men far my superiors in learning and piety, in eloquence and persuasiveness, have been sent to reason with her, to explain to her the danger she is running, and the ease with which she may avoid it. [*Suddenly bursting into forensic eloquence, to the disgust of Cauchon and the Inquisitor, who have listened to him so far with patronizing approval*] Men have dared to say that we are acting from hate; but God is our witness that they lie. Have we tortured her? No. Have we ceased to exhort her; to implore her to have pity on herself; to come to the bosom of her Church as an erring but beloved child? Have we—

CAUCHON [*interrupting drily*] Take care, Canon. All that you say is true; but if you make his lordship believe it I will not answer for your life, and hardly for my own.

WARWICK [*deprecating, but by no means denying*] Oh, my lord, you are very hard on us poor English. But we certainly do not share your pious desire to save The Maid: in fact I tell you now plainly that her death is a political necessity which I regret but cannot help. If the Church lets her go—

CAUCHON [*with fierce and menacing pride*] If the Church lets her go, woe to the man, were he the Emperor himself, who dares lay a finger on her! The Church is not subject to political necessity, my lord.

THE INQUISITOR [*interposing smoothly*] You need have no anxiety about the result, my lord. You have an invincible ally in the matter: one who is far more determined than you that she shall burn.

WARWICK. And who is this very convenient partisan, may I ask?

THE INQUISITOR. The Maid herself. Unless you put a gag in her mouth you cannot prevent her from convicting herself ten times over every time she opens it.

D'ESTIVET. That is perfectly true, my lord. My hair bristles on my head when I hear so young a creature utter such blasphemies.

WARWICK. Well, by all means do your best for her if you are quite sure it will be of no avail. [*Looking hard at Cauchon*] I should be sorry to have to act without the blessing of the Church.

CAUCHON [*with a mixture of cynical admiration and contempt*] And yet they say Englishmen are hypocrites! You play for your side, my lord, even at the peril of your soul. I cannot but admire such devotion; but I dare not go so far myself. I fear damnation.

WARWICK. If we feared anything we could never govern England, my lord. Shall I send your people in to you?

CAUCHON. Yes: it will be very good of your lordship to withdraw and allow the court to assemble.

Warwick turns on his heel, and goes out through the courtyard. Cauchon takes one of the judicial seats; and D'Estivet sits at the scribes' table, studying his brief.

CAUCHON [*casually, as he makes himself comfortable*] What scoundrels these English nobles are!

THE INQUISITOR [*taking the other judicial chair on Cauchon's left*] All secular power makes men scoundrels. They are not trained for the work; and they have not the Apostolic Succession. Our own nobles are just as bad.

The Bishop's assessors hurry into the hall, headed by Chaplain de Stogumber and Canon de Courcelles, a young priest of 30. The scribes sit at the table, leaving a chair vacant opposite D'Estivet. Some of the assessors take their seats: others stand chatting, waiting for the proceedings to begin formally. De Stogumber, aggrieved and obstinate, will not take his seat: neither will the Canon, who stands on his right.

CAUCHON. Good morning, Master de Stogumber. [*To the Inquisitor*] Chaplain to the Cardinal of England.

THE CHAPLAIN [*correcting him*] Of Winchester, my lord. I have to make a protest, my lord.

CAUCHON. You make a great many.

THE CHAPLAIN. I am not without support, my lord. Here is Master de Courcelles, Canon of Paris, who associates himself with me in my protest.

CAUCHON. Well, what is the matter?

THE CHAPLAIN [*sulkily*] Speak you, Master de Courcelles, since I do not seem to enjoy his lordship's confidence. [*He sits down in dudgeon next to Cauchon, on his right*].

COURCELLES. My lord; we have been at great pains to draw up an indictment of The Maid on sixty-four counts. We are now told that they have been reduced, without consulting us.

THE INQUISITOR. Master de Courcelles: I am the culprit. I am overwhelmed with admiration for the zeal displayed in your sixty-four counts; but in accusing a heretic, as in other things, enough is enough. Also you must remember that all the members of the court are not so subtle and profound as you, and that some of your very great learning might appear to them to be very great nonsense. Therefore I have thought it well to have your sixty-four articles cut down to twelve—

COURCELLES [*thunderstruck*] Twelve!!!

THE INQUISITOR. Twelve will, believe me, be quite enough for your purpose.

THE CHAPLAIN. But some of the most important points have been reduced almost to nothing. For instance, The Maid has actually declared that the blessed saints Margaret and Catherine, and the holy Archangel Michael, spoke to her in French. That is a vital point.

THE INQUISITOR. You think, doubtless, that they should have spoken in Latin?

CAUCHON. No: he thinks they should have spoken in English.

THE CHAPLAIN. Naturally, my lord.

THE INQUISITOR. Well, as we are all here agreed, I think, that these voices of The Maid are the voices of evil spirits tempting her to her damnation, it would not be very courteous to you, Master de Stogumber, or to the King of England, to assume that English is the devil's native language. So let it pass. The matter is not wholly omitted from the twelve articles. Pray take your places, gentlemen; and let us proceed to business.

All who have not taken their seats, do so.

THE CHAPLAIN. Well, I protest. That is all.

COURCELLES. I think it hard that all our work should go for nothing. It is only another example of the diabolical influence which this woman exercises over the court. [*He takes his chair, which is on the Chaplain's right*].

CAUCHON. Do you suggest that I am under diabolical influence?

COURCELLES. I suggest nothing, my lord. But it seems to me that there is a conspiracy here to hush up the fact that The Maid stole the Bishop of Senlis's horse.

CAUCHON [*keeping his temper with difficulty*] This is not a police court. Are we to waste our time on such rubbish?

COURCELLES [*rising, shocked*] My lord: do you call the Bishop's horse rubbish?

THE INQUISITOR [*blandly*] Master de Courcelles: The Maid alleges that she paid handsomely for the Bishop's horse, and that if he did not get the money the fault was not hers. As that may be true, the point is one on which The Maid may well be acquitted.

COURCELLES. Yes, if it were an ordinary horse. But the Bishop's horse! how can she be acquitted for that? [*He sits down again, bewildered and discouraged*].

THE INQUISITOR. I submit to you, with great respect, that if we persist in trying The Maid on trumpery issues on which we may have to declare her innocent, she may escape us on the great main issue of heresy, on which she seems so far to insist on her own guilt. I will ask you, therefore, to say nothing, when The Maid is brought before us, of these stealings of horses, and dancings round fairy trees with the village children, and prayings at haunted wells, and a dozen other things which you were diligently inquiring into until my arrival. There is not a village girl in France against whom you could not prove such things: they all dance round haunted trees, and pray at magic wells. Some of them would steal the Pope's horse if they got the chance. Heresy, gentlemen, heresy is the charge we have to try. The detection and suppression of heresy is my peculiar business: I am here as an inquisitor, not as an ordinary magistrate. Stick to the heresy, gentlemen; and leave the other matters alone.

CAUCHON. I may say that we have sent to the girl's village to make inquiries about her, and there is practically nothing serious against her.

THE CHAPLAIN	[*rising and*	{Nothing serious, my lord—
COURCELLES	*clamoring together*]	{What! the fairy tree not—

CAUCHON [*out of patience*] Be silent, gentlemen; or speak one at a time.

Courcelles collapses into his chair, intimidated.

THE CHAPLAIN [*sulkily resuming his seat*] That is what The Maid said to us last Friday.

CAUCHON. I wish you had followed her counsel, sir. When I say nothing serious, I mean nothing that men of sufficiently large mind to conduct an inquiry like this would consider serious. I agree with my colleague the Inquisitor that it is on the count of heresy that we must proceed.

LADVENU [*a young but ascetically fine-drawn Dominican who is sitting next Courcelles, on his right*] But is there any great harm in the girl's heresy? Is it not merely her simplicity? Many saints have said as much as Joan.

THE INQUISITOR [*dropping his blandness and speaking very gravely*] Brother Martin: if you had seen what I have seen of heresy, you would not think it a light thing even in its most apparently harmless and even lovable and pious origins. Heresy begins with people who are to all appearance better than their neighbors. A gentle and pious girl, or a young man who has obeyed the command of our Lord by giving all his riches to the poor, and putting on the garb of poverty, the life of austerity, and the rule of humility and charity, may be the founder of a heresy that will wreck both Church and Empire if not ruthlessly stamped out in time. The records of the Holy Inquisition are full of histories we dare not give to the world, because they are beyond the belief of honest men and innocent women; yet they all began with saintly simpletons. I have seen this again and again. Mark what I say: the woman who quarrels with her clothes, and puts on the dress of a man, is like the man who throws off his fur gown and dresses like John the Baptist: they are followed, as surely as the night follows the day, by bands of wild women and men who refuse to wear any clothes at all. When maids will neither marry nor take regular vows, and men reject marriage and exalt their lusts into divine inspirations, then, as surely as the summer follows the spring, they begin with polygamy, and end by incest. Heresy at first seems innocent and even laudable; but it ends in such a monstrous horror of unnatural wickedness that the most tender-hearted among you, if you saw it at work as I have seen it, would clamor against the mercy of the Church in dealing with it. For two hundred years the Holy Office has striven with these diabolical madnesses; and it knows that they begin always by vain and ignorant persons setting up their own judgment against the Church, and taking it upon themselves to be the interpreters of God's will. You must not fall into the common error of mistaking these simpletons for liars and hypocrites. They believe honestly and sincerely that their diabolical inspiration is divine. Therefore you must be on your guard against your natural compassion. You are all, I hope, merciful men: how else could you have devoted your lives to the service of our gentle Savior? You are going to see before you a young girl, pious and chaste; for I must tell you, gentlemen, that the things said of her by our English friends are supported by no evidence, whilst there is abundant testimony that her excesses have been excesses of religion and charity and not of worldliness and wantonness. This girl is not one of those whose hard features are the sign of hard hearts, and whose brazen looks and lewd demeanor condemn them before they are accused. The devilish pride that has led her into her present peril has left no mark on her countenance. Strange as it may seem to you, it has even left no mark on her character outside those special matters in which she is proud; so that you will see a diabolical pride and a natural humility seated side by side in the selfsame soul. Therefore be on your guard. God forbid that I should tell you to harden your hearts; for her punishment if we condemn her will be so cruel that we should forfeit our own hope of divine mercy were there one grain of malice against her in our hearts. But if you hate cruelty—and if any man here does not hate it I command him on his soul's salvation to quit this holy court—I say, if you hate cruelty, remember that nothing is so cruel in its consequences as the toleration of heresy. Remember also that no court of law can be so cruel as the common people are to those whom they suspect of heresy. The heretic in the hands of the Holy Office is safe from violence, is assured of a fair trial, and cannot suffer death, even when guilty, if repentance follows sin. Innumerable lives of heretics have been saved because the Holy Office has taken them out of the hands of the people, and because the people have yielded them up, knowing that the Holy Office would deal with them. Before the Holy Inquisition existed, and even now when its officers are not within reach, the unfortunate wretch suspected of heresy, perhaps quite ignorantly and unjustly, is stoned, torn in pieces, drowned, burned in his house with all his innocent children, without a trial, unshriven, unburied save as a dog is buried: all of them deeds hateful to God and most cruel to man. Gentlemen: I am compassionate by nature as well as by my profession; and though the work I have to do may seem cruel to those who do not know how much more cruel it would be to leave it undone, I would go to the stake myself sooner than do it if I did not know its righteousness, its necessity, its essential mercy. I ask you to address yourself to this trial in that conviction. Anger is a bad counsellor: cast out anger. Pity is sometimes worse: cast out pity. But do not cast out mercy. Remember only that justice comes first. Have you anything to say, my lord, before we proceed to trial?

CAUCHON. You have spoken for me, and spoken better than I could. I do not see how any sane man could disagree with a word that has fallen from you. But this I will add. The crude heresies of which you have told us are horrible; but their horror is like that of the black death: they rage for a while and then die out, because sound and sensible men will not under any incitement be reconciled to nakedness and incest and polygamy and the like. But we are confronted today throughout Europe with a heresy that is spreading among men not weak in mind nor diseased in brain: nay, the stronger the mind, the more obstinate the heretic. It is neither discredited by fantastic extremes nor corrupted by the common lusts of the flesh; but it, too, sets up the private judgment of the single erring mortal against the considered wisdom and experience of the Church. The mighty structure of Catholic Christendom will never be shaken by naked madmen or by the sins of Moab and Ammon.[26] But it may be betrayed from within, and brought to barbarous ruin and desolation, by this arch heresy which the English Commander calls Protestantism.

THE ASSESSORS [*whispering*] Protestantism! What was that? What does the Bishop mean? Is it a new heresy? The English Commander, he said. Did you ever hear of Protestantism? etc., etc.

CAUCHON [*continuing*] And that reminds me. What provision has the Earl of Warwick made for the defence of the secular arm should The Maid prove obdurate, and the people be moved to pity her?

THE CHAPLAIN. Have no fear on that score, my lord. The noble earl has eight hundred men-at-arms at the gates. She will not slip through our English fingers even if the whole city be on her side.

CAUCHON [*revolted*] Will you not add, God grant that she repent and purge her sin?

THE CHAPLAIN. That does not seem to me to be consistent; but of course I agree with your lordship.

CAUCHON [*giving him up with a shrug of contempt*] The court sits.

THE INQUISITOR. Let the accused be brought in.

LADVENU [*calling*] The accused. Let her be brought in.

Joan, chained by the ankles, is brought in through the arched door behind the prisoner's stool by a guard of English soldiers. With them is the Executioner and his assistants. They lead her to the prisoner's stool, and place themselves behind it after taking off her chain. She wears a page's black suit. Her long imprisonment and the strain of the examinations which have preceded the trial have left their mark on her; but her vitality still holds; she confronts the court unabashed, without a trace of the awe which their formal solemnity seems to require for the complete success of its impressiveness.

THE INQUISITOR [*kindly*] Sit down, Joan. [*She sits on the prisoner's stool*]. You look very pale today. Are you not well?

JOAN. Thank you kindly: I am well enough. But the Bishop sent me some carp; and it made me ill.

CAUCHON. I am sorry. I told them to see that it was fresh.

JOAN. You meant to be good to me, I know; but it is a fish that does not agree with me. The English thought you were trying to poison me—

CAUCHON

[*Together*] {What!

THE CHAPLAIN

{No, my lord.

26. The women of Moab seduced the men of Israel to lust and idolatry (Numbers 25:1–3); David's son Ammon raped his sister Tamar (2 Samuel 13).

JOAN [*continuing*] They are determined that I shall be burnt as a witch; and they sent their doctor to cure me; but he was forbidden to bleed me because the silly people believe that a witch's witchery leaves her if she is bled; so he only called me filthy names. Why do you leave me in the hands of the English? I should be in the hands of the Church. And why must I be chained by the feet to a log of wood? Are you afraid I will fly away?

D'ESTIVET [*harshly*] Woman: it is not for you to question the court: it is for us to question you.

COURCELLES. When you were left unchained, did you not try to escape by jumping from a tower sixty feet high? If you cannot fly like a witch, how is it that you are still alive?

JOAN. I suppose because the tower was not so high then. It has grown higher every day since you began asking me questions about it.

D'ESTIVET. Why did you jump from the tower?

JOAN. How do you know that I jumped?

D'ESTIVET. You were found lying in the moat. Why did you leave the tower?

JOAN. Why would anybody leave a prison if they could get out?

D'ESTIVET. You tried to escape?

JOAN. Of course I did; and not for the first time either. If you leave the door of the cage open the bird will fly out.

D'ESTIVET [*rising*] That is a confession of heresy. I call the attention of the court to it.

JOAN. Heresy, he calls it! Am I a heretic because I try to escape from prison?

D'ESTIVET. Assuredly, if you are in the hands of the Church, and you wilfully take yourself out of its hands, you are deserting the Church; and that is heresy.

JOAN. It is great nonsense. Nobody could be such a fool as to think that.

D'ESTIVET. You hear, my lord, how I am reviled in the execution of my duty by this woman. [*He sits down indignantly*].

CAUCHON. I have warned you before, Joan, that you are doing yourself no good by these pert answers.

JOAN. But you will not talk sense to me. I am reasonable if you will be reasonable.

THE INQUISITOR [*interposing*] This is not yet in order. You forget, Master Promoter, that the proceedings have not been formally opened. The time for questions is after she has sworn on the Gospels to tell us the whole truth.

JOAN. You say this to me every time. I have said again and again that I will tell you all that concerns this trial. But I cannot tell you the whole truth: God does not allow the whole truth to be told. You do not understand it when I tell it. It is an old saying that he who tells too much truth is sure to be hanged. I am weary of this argument: we have been over it nine times already. I have sworn as much as I will swear; and I will swear no more.

COURCELLES. My lord: she should be put to the torture.

THE INQUISITOR. You hear, Joan? That is what happens to the obdurate. Think before you answer. Has she been shewn the instruments?

THE EXECUTIONER. They are ready, my lord. She has seen them.

JOAN. If you tear me limb from limb until you separate my soul from my body you will get nothing out of me beyond what I have told you. What more is there to tell that you could understand? Besides, I cannot bear to be hurt; and if you hurt me I will say anything you like to stop the pain. But I will take it all back afterwards; so what is the use of it?

LADVENU. There is much in that. We should proceed mercifully.

COURCELLES. But the torture is customary.

THE INQUISITOR. It must not be applied wantonly. If the accused will confess voluntarily, then its use cannot be justified.

COURCELLES. But this is unusual and irregular. She refuses to take the oath.

LADVENU [*disgusted*] Do you want to torture the girl for the mere pleasure of it?

COURCELLES [*bewildered*] But it is not a pleasure. It is the law. It is customary. It is always done.

THE INQUISITOR. That is not so, Master, except when the inquiries are carried on by people who do not know their legal business.

COURCELLES. But the woman is a heretic. I assure you it is always done.

CAUCHON [*decisively*] It will not be done today if it is not necessary. Let there be an end of this. I will not have it said that we proceeded on forced confessions. We have sent our best preachers and doctors to this woman to exhort and implore her to save her soul and body from the fire: we shall not now send the executioner to thrust her into it.

COURCELLES. Your lordship is merciful, of course. But it is a great responsibility to depart from the usual practice.

JOAN. Thou are a rare noodle, Master. Do what was done last time is thy rule, eh?

COURCELLES [*rising*] Thou wanton: dost thou dare call me noodle?

THE INQUISITOR. Patience, Master, patience: I fear you will soon be only too terribly avenged.

COURCELLES [*mutters*] Noodle indeed! [*He sits down, much discontented*].

THE INQUISITOR. Meanwhile, let us not be moved by the rough side of a shepherd lass's tongue.

JOAN. Nay: I am no shepherd lass, though I have helped with the sheep like anyone else. I will do a lady's work in the house—spin or weave—against any woman in Rouen.

THE INQUISITOR. This is not a time for vanity, Joan. You stand in great peril.

JOAN. I know it: have I not been punished for my vanity? If I had not worn my cloth of gold surcoat in battle like a fool, that Burgundian soldier would never have pulled me backwards off my horse; and I should not have been here.

THE CHAPLAIN. If you are so clever at woman's work why do you not stay at home and do it?

JOAN. There are plenty of other women to do it; but there is nobody to do my work.

CAUCHON. Come! we are wasting time on trifles. Joan: I am going to put a most solemn question to you. Take care how you answer; for your life and salvation are at stake on it. Will you for all you have said and done, be it good or bad, accept the judgment of God's Church on earth? More especially as to the acts and words that are imputed to you in this trial by the Promoter here, will you submit your case to the inspired interpretation of the Church Militant?

JOAN. I am a faithful child of the Church. I will obey the Church—

CAUCHON [*hopefully leaning forward*] You will?

JOAN.—provided it does not command anything impossible.

Cauchon sinks back in his chair with a heavy sigh. The Inquisitor purses his lips and frowns. Ladvenu shakes his head pitifully.

D'ESTIVET. She imputes to the Church the error and folly of commanding the impossible.

JOAN. If you command me to declare that all that I have done and said, and all the visions and revelations I have had, were not from God, then that is impossible: I will not declare it for anything in the world. What God made me do I will never go back on; and what He has commanded or shall command I will not fail to do in spite of any man alive. That is what I mean by impossible. And in case the Church should bid me do anything contrary to the command I have from God, I will not consent to it, no matter what it may be.

THE ASSESSORS [*shocked and indignant*] Oh! The Church contrary to God! What do you say now? Flat heresy. This is beyond everything, etc., etc.

D'ESTIVET [*throwing down his brief*] My lord: do you need anything more than this?

CAUCHON. Woman: you have said enough to burn ten heretics. Will you not be warned? Will you not understand?

THE INQUISITOR. If the Church Militant tells you that your revelations and visions are sent by the devil to tempt you to your damnation, will you not believe that the Church is wiser than you?

JOAN. I believe that God is wiser than I; and it is His commands that I will do. All the things that you call my crimes have come to me by the command of God. I say that I have done them by the order of God: it is impossible for me to say anything else. If any Churchman says the contrary I shall not mind him: I shall mind God alone, whose command I always follow.

LADVENU [*pleading with her urgently*] You do not know what you are saying, child. Do you want to kill yourself? Listen. Do you not believe that you are subject to the Church of God on earth?

JOAN. Yes. When have I ever denied it?

LADVENU. Good. That means, does it not, that you are subject to our Lord the Pope, to the cardinals, the archbishops, and the bishops for whom his lordship stands here today?

JOAN. God must be served first.

D'ESTIVET. Then your voices command you not to submit yourself to the Church Militant?

JOAN. My voices do not tell me to disobey the Church; but God must be served first.

CAUCHON. And you, and not the Church, are to be the judge?

JOAN. What other judgment can I judge by but my own?

THE ASSESSORS [*scandalized*] Oh! [*They cannot find words*].

CAUCHON. Out of your own mouth you have condemned yourself. We have striven for your salvation to the verge of sinning ourselves: we have opened the door to you again and again; and you have shut it in our faces and in the face of God. Dare you pretend, after what you have said, that you are in a state of grace?

JOAN. If I am not, may God bring me to it: if I am, may God keep me in it!

LADVENU. That is a very good reply, my lord.

COURCELLES. Were you in a state of grace when you stole the Bishop's horse?

CAUCHON [*rising in a fury*] Oh, devil take the Bishop's horse and you too! We are here to try a case of heresy; and no sooner do we come to the root of the matter than we are thrown back by idiots who understand nothing but horses. [*Trembling with rage, he forces himself to sit down*].

THE INQUISITOR. Gentlemen, gentlemen: in clinging to these small issues you are The Maid's best advocates. I am not surprised that his lordship has lost patience with you. What does the Promoter say? Does he press these trumpery matters?

D'ESTIVET. I am bound by my office to press everything; but when the woman confesses a heresy that must bring upon her the doom of excommunication, of what consequence is it that she has been guilty also of offences which expose her to minor penances? I share the impatience of his lordship as to these minor charges. Only, with great respect, I must emphasize the gravity of two very horrible and blasphemous crimes which she does not deny. First, she has intercourse with evil spirits, and is therefore a sorceress. Second, she wears men's clothes, which is indecent, unnatural, and abominable; and in spite of our most earnest remonstrances and entreaties, she will not change them even to receive the sacrament.

JOAN. Is the blessed St Catherine an evil spirit? Is St Margaret? Is Michael the Archangel?

COURCELLES. How do you know that the spirit which appears to you is an archangel? Does he not appear to you as a naked man?

JOAN. Do you think God cannot afford clothes for him?

The assessors cannot help smiling, especially as the joke is against Courcelles.

LADVENU. Well answered, Joan.

THE INQUISITOR. It is, in effect, well answered. But no evil spirit would be so simple as to appear to a young girl in a guise that would scandalize her when he meant her to take him for a messenger from the Most High. Joan: the Church instructs you that these apparitions are demons seeking your soul's perdition. Do you accept the instruction of the Church?

JOAN. I accept the messenger of God. How could any faithful believer in the Church refuse him?

CAUCHON. Wretched woman: again I ask you, do you know what you are saying?

THE INQUISITOR. You wrestle in vain with the devil for her soul, my lord: she will not be saved. Now as to this matter of the man's dress. For the last time, will you put off that impudent attire, and dress as becomes your sex?

JOAN. I will not.

D'ESTIVET [*pouncing*] The sin of disobedience, my lord.

JOAN [*distressed*] But my voices tell me I must dress as a soldier.

LADVENU. Joan, Joan: does not that prove to you that the voices are the voices of evil spirits? Can you suggest to us one good reason why an angel of God should give you such shameless advice?

JOAN. Why, yes: what can be plainer commonsense? I was a soldier living among soldiers. I am a prisoner guarded by soldiers. If I were to dress as a woman they would think of me as a woman; and then what would become of me? If I dress as a soldier they think of me as a soldier, and I can live with them as I do at home with my brothers. That is why St Catherine tells me I must not dress as a woman until she gives me leave.

COURCELLES. When will she give you leave?

JOAN. When you take me out of the hands of the English soldiers. I have told you that I should be in the hands of the Church, and not left night and day with four soldiers of the Earl of Warwick. Do you want me to live with them in petticoats?

LADVENU. My lord: what she says is, God knows, very wrong and shocking; but there is a grain of worldly sense in it such as might impose on a simple village maiden.

JOAN. If we were as simple in the village as you are in your courts and palaces, there would soon be no wheat to make bread for you.

CAUCHON. That is the thanks you get for trying to save her, Brother Martin.

LADVENU. Joan: we are all trying to save you. His lordship is trying to save you. The Inquisitor could not be more just to you if you were his own daughter. But you are blinded by a terrible pride and self-sufficiency.

JOAN. Why do you say that? I have said nothing wrong. I cannot understand.

THE INQUISITOR. The blessed St Athanasius has laid it down in his creed that those who cannot understand are damned.[27] It is not enough to be simple. It is not enough even to be what simple people call good. The simplicity of a darkened mind is no better than the simplicity of a beast.

JOAN. There is great wisdom in the simplicity of a beast, let me tell you; and sometimes great foolishness in the wisdom of scholars.

LADVENU. We know that, Joan: we are not so foolish as you think us. Try to resist the temptation to make pert replies to us. Do you see that man who stands behind you [*he indicates the Executioner]?*

JOAN [*turning and looking at the man*] Your torturer? But the Bishop said I was not to be tortured.

LADVENU. You are not to be tortured because you have confessed everything that is necessary to your condemnation. That man is not only the torturer: he is also the Executioner. Executioner: let The Maid hear your answers to my questions. Are you prepared for the burning of a heretic this day?

THE EXECUTIONER. Yes, Master.

LADVENU. Is the stake ready?

THE EXECUTIONER. It is. In the market-place. The English have built it too high for me to get near her and make the death easier. It will be a cruel death.

JOAN [*horrified*] But you are not going to burn me now?

THE INQUISITOR. You realize it at last.

LADVENU. There are eight hundred English soldiers waiting to take you to the market-place the moment the sentence of excommunication has passed the lips of your judges. You are within a few short moments of that doom.

JOAN [*looking round desperately for rescue*] Oh God!

LADVENU. Do not despair, Joan. The Church is merciful. You can save yourself.

JOAN [*hopefully*] Yes, my voices promised me I should not be burnt. St Catherine bade me be bold.

CAUCHON. Woman: are you quite mad? Do you not yet see that your voices have deceived you?

JOAN. Oh no: that is impossible.

CAUCHON. Impossible! They have led you straight to your excommunication, and to the stake which is there waiting for you.

LADVENU [*pressing the point hard*] Have they kept a single promise to

27. *Quicumque Vult* (Whosoever wishes) asserts Trinitarian doctrine and that all who do not keep the Catholic faith whole and undefiled are damned.

you since you were taken at Compiègne? The devil has betrayed you. The Church holds out its arms to you.

JOAN [*despairing*] Oh, it is true: it is true: my voices have deceived me. I have been mocked by devils: my faith is broken. I have dared and dared; but only a fool will walk into a fire: God, who gave me my commonsense, cannot will me to do that.

LADVENU. Now God be praised that He has saved you at the eleventh hour! [*He hurries to the vacant seat at the scribes' table, and snatches a sheet of paper, on which he sets to work writing eagerly*].

CAUCHON. Amen!

JOAN. What must I do?

CAUCHON. You must sign a solemn recantation of your heresy.

JOAN. Sign? That means to write my name. I cannot write.

CAUCHON. You have signed many letters before.

JOAN. Yes; but someone held my hand and guided the pen. I can make my mark.

THE CHAPLAIN [*who has been listening with growing alarm and indignation]* My lord: do you mean that you are going to allow this woman to escape us?

THE INQUISITOR. The law must take its course, Master de Stogumber. And you know the law.

THE CHAPLAIN [*rising, purple with fury*] I know that there is no faith in a Frenchman. [*Tumult, which he shouts down*]. I know what my lord the Cardinal of Winchester will say when he hears of this. I know what the Earl of Warwick will do when he learns that you intend to betray him. There are eight hundred men at the gate who will see that this abominable witch is burnt in spite of your teeth.

THE ASSESSORS [*meanwhile*] What is this? What did he say? He accuses us of treachery! This is past bearing. No faith in a Frenchman! Did you hear that? This is an intolerable fellow. Who is he? Is this what English Churchmen are like? He must be mad or drunk, etc., etc.

THE INQUISITOR [*rising*] Silence, pray! Gentlemen: pray silence! Master Chaplain: bethink you a moment of your holy office: of what you are, and where you are. I direct you to sit down.

THE CHAPLAIN [*folding his arms doggedly, his face working convulsively*] I will NOT sit down.

CAUCHON. Master Inquisitor: this man has called me a traitor to my face before now.

THE CHAPLAIN. So you are a traitor. You are all traitors. You have been doing nothing but begging this damnable witch on your knees to recant all through this trial.

THE INQUISITOR [*placidly resuming his seat*] If you will not sit, you must stand: that is all.

THE CHAPLAIN. I will NOT stand [*he flings himself back into his chair*].

LADVENU [*rising with the paper in his hand*] My lord: here is the form of recantation for The Maid to sign.

CAUCHON. Read it to her.

JOAN. Do not trouble. I will sign it.

THE INQUISITOR. Woman: you must know what you are putting your hand to. Read it to her, Brother Martin. And let all be silent.

LADVENU [*reading quietly*] 'I, Joan, commonly called The Maid, a miserable sinner, do confess that I have most grievously sinned in the following articles. I have pretended to have revelations from God and the angels and the blessed saints, and perversely rejected the Church's warnings that these were temptations by demons. I have blasphemed abominably by wearing an immodest dress, contrary to the Holy Scripture and the canons of the Church. Also I have clipped my hair in the style of a man, and, against all the duties which have made my sex specially acceptable in heaven, have taken up the sword, even to the shedding of human blood, inciting men to slay each other, invoking evil spirits to delude them, and stubbornly and most blasphemously imputing these sins to Almighty God. I confess to the sin of sedition, to the sin of idolatry, to the sin of disobedience, to the sin of pride, and to the sin of heresy. All of which sins I now renounce and abjure and depart from, humbly thanking you Doctors and Masters who have brought me back to the truth and into the grace of our Lord. And I will never return to my errors, but will remain in communion with our Holy Church and in obedience to our Holy Father the Pope of Rome. All this I swear by God Almighty and the Holy Gospels, in witness whereto I sign my name to this recantation.'

THE INQUISITOR. You understand this, Joan?

JOAN [*listless*] It is plain enough, sir.

THE INQUISITOR. And is it true?

JOAN. It may be true. If it were not true, the fire would not be ready for me in the market-place.

LADVENU [*taking up his pen and a book, and going to her quickly lest she should compromise herself again*] Come, child: let me guide your hand. Take the pen. [*She does so; and they begin to write, using the book as a desk*] J.E.H.A.N.E. So. Now make your mark by yourself.

JOAN [*makes her mark, and gives him back the pen, tormented by the rebellion of her soul against her mind and body*] There!

LADVENU [*replacing the pen on the table, and handing the recantation to Cauchon with a reverence*] Praise be to God, my brothers, the lamb has returned to the flock; and the shepherd rejoices in her more than in ninety and nine just persons. [*He returns to his seat*].

THE INQUISITOR [*taking the paper from Cauchon*] We declare thee by this act set free from the danger of excommunication in which thou stoodest. [*He throws the paper down to the table*].

JOAN. I thank you.

THE INQUISITOR. But because thou has sinned most presumptuously against God and the Holy Church, and that thou mayst repent thy errors in solitary contemplation, and be shielded from all temptation to return to them, we, for the good of thy soul, and for a penance that may wipe out thy sins and bring thee finally unspotted to the throne of grace, do condemn thee to eat the bread of sorrow and drink the water of affliction to the end of thy earthly days in perpetual imprisonment.

JOAN [*rising in consternation and terrible anger*] Perpetual imprisonment! Am I not then to be set free?

LADVENU [*mildly shocked*] Set free, child, after such wickedness as yours! What are you dreaming of?

JOAN. Give me that writing. [*She rushes to the table; snatches up the paper; and tears it into fragments*] Light your fire: do you think I dread it as much as the life of a rat in a hole? My voices were right.

LADVENU. Joan! Joan!

JOAN. Yes: they told me you were fools [*the word gives great offence],* and that I was not to listen to your fine words nor trust to your charity. You promised me my life; but you lied [*indignant exclamations*]. You think that life is nothing but not being stone dead. It is not the bread and water I fear: I can live on bread: when have I asked for more? It is no hardship to drink water if the water be clean. Bread has no sorrow for me, and water no affliction. But to shut me from the light of the sky and the sight of the fields and flowers; to chain my feet so that I can never again ride with the soldiers nor climb the hills; to make me breathe foul damp darkness, and keep from me everything that brings me back to the love of God when your wickedness and foolishness tempt me to hate Him: all this is worse than the furnace in the Bible that was heated seven times.[28] I could do without my warhorse; I could drag about in a skirt; I could let the banners and the trumpets and the knights and soldiers pass me and leave me behind as they leave the other women, if only I could still hear the wind in the trees, the larks in the sunshine, the young lambs crying through the healthy frost, and the blessed blessed church bells that send my angel voices floating to me on the wind. But without these things I cannot live; and by your wanting to take them away from me, or from any human creature, I know that your counsel is of the devil, and that mine is of God.

THE ASSESSORS [*in great commotion*] Blasphemy! blasphemy! She is possessed. She said our counsel was of the devil. And hers of God. Monstrous! The devil is in our midst, etc., etc.

D'ESTIVET [*shouting above the din*] She is a relapsed heretic, obstinate, incorrigible, and altogether unworthy of the mercy we have shewn her. I call for her excommunication.

THE CHAPLAIN [*to the Executioner*] Light your fire, man. To the stake with her.

The Executioner and his assistants hurry out through the courtyard.

28. In Dan 3:19–30, Nebuchadnezzar casts Shadrach, Meshach, and Abednego into the furnace, where they are saved by God.

LADVENU. You wicked girl: if your counsel were of God would He not deliver you?

JOAN. His ways are not your ways. He wills that I go through the fire to His bosom; for I am His child, and you are not fit that I should live among you. That is my last word to you.

The soldiers seize her.

CAUCHON [*rising*] Not yet.

They wait. There is a dead silence. Cauchon turns to the Inquisitor with an inquiring look. The Inquisitor nods affirmatively. They rise solemnly, and intone the sentence antiphonally.

CAUCHON. We decree that thou art a relapsed heretic.

THE INQUISITOR. Cast out from the unity of the Church.

CAUCHON. Sundered from her body.

THE INQUISITOR. Infected with the leprosy of heresy.

CAUCHON. A member of Satan.

THE INQUISITOR. We declare that thou must be excommunicate.

CAUCHON. And now we do cast thee out, segregate thee, and abandon thee to the secular power.

THE INQUISITOR. Admonishing the same secular power that it moderate its judgment of thee in respect of death and division of the limbs. [*He resumes his seat*].

CAUCHON. And if any true sign of penitence appear in thee, to permit our Brother Martin to administer to thee the sacrament of penance.

THE CHAPLAIN. Into the fire with the witch [*he rushes at her, and helps the soldiers to push her out*].

Joan is taken away through the courtyard. The assessors rise in disorder, and follow the soldiers, except Ladvenu, who has hidden his face in his hands.

CAUCHON [*rising again in the act of sitting down*] No, no: this is irregular. The representative of the secular arm should be here to receive her from us.

THE INQUISITOR [*also on his feet again*] That man is an incorrigible fool.

CAUCHON. Brother Martin: see that everything is done in order.

LADVENU. My place is at her side, my Lord. You must exercise your own authority. [*He hurries out*].

CAUCHON. These English are impossible: they will thrust her straight into the fire. Look!

He points to the courtyard, in which the glow and flicker of fire can now be seen reddening the May daylight. Only the Bishop and the Inquisitor are left in the court.

CAUCHON [*turning to go*] We must stop that.

THE INQUISITOR [*calmly*] Yes; but not too fast, my lord.

CAUCHON [*halting*] But there is not a moment to lose.

THE INQUISITOR. We have proceeded in perfect order. If the English choose to put themselves in the wrong, it is not our business to put them in the right. A flaw in the procedure may be useful later on: one never knows. And the sooner it is over, the better for that poor girl.

CAUCHON [*relaxing*] That is true. But I suppose we must see this dreadful thing through.

THE INQUISITOR. One gets used to it. Habit is everything. I am accustomed to the fire: it is soon over. But it is a terrible thing to see a young and innocent creature crushed between these mighty forces, the Church and the Law.

CAUCHON. You call her innocent!

THE INQUISITOR. Oh, quite innocent. What does she know of the Church and the Law? She did not understand a word we were saying. It is the ignorant who suffer. Come, or we shall be late for the end.

CAUCHON [*going with him*] I shall not be sorry if we are: I am not so accustomed as you.

They are going out when Warwick comes in, meeting them.

WARWICK. Oh, I am intruding. I thought it was all over.

[*He makes a feint of retiring*].

CAUCHON. Do not go, my lord. It is all over.

THE INQUISITOR. The execution is not in our hands, my lord; but it is desirable that we should witness the end. So by your leave—[*He bows, and goes out through the courtyard*].

CAUCHON. There is some doubt whether your people have observed the forms of law, my lord.

WARWICK. I am told that there is some doubt whether your authority runs in this city, my lord. It is not in your diocese. However, if you will answer for that I will swear for the rest.

CAUCHON. It is to God that we both must answer. Good morning, my lord.

WARWICK. My lord: good morning.

They look at one another for a moment with unconcealed hostility. Then Cauchon follows the Inquisitor out. Warwick looks round. Finding himself alone, he calls for attendance.

WARWICK. Hallo: some attendance here! [*Silence*]. Hallo, there! [*Silence*]. Hallo! Brian, you young blackguard, where are you? [*Silence*]. Guard! [*Silence*]. They have all gone to see the burning: even that child.

The silence is broken by someone frantically howling and sobbing.

WARWICK. What in the devil's name—?

The Chaplain staggers in from the courtyard like a demented creature, his face streaming with tears, making the piteous sounds that Warwick has heard. He stumbles to the prisoner's stool, and throws himself upon it with heartrending sobs.

WARWICK [*going to him and patting him on the shoulder*] What is it, Master John? What is the matter?

THE CHAPLAIN [*clutching at his hand*] My lord, my lord: for Christ's sake pray for my wretched guilty soul.

WARWICK [*soothing him*] Yes, yes: of course I will. Calmly, gently—

THE CHAPLAIN [*blubbering miserably*] I am not a bad man, my lord.

WARWICK. No, no: not at all.

THE CHAPLAIN. I meant no harm. I did not know what it would be like.

WARWICK [*hardening*] Oh! You saw it, then?

THE CHAPLAIN. I did not know what I was doing. I am a hotheaded fool; and I shall be damned to all eternity for it.

WARWICK. Nonsense! Very distressing, no doubt; but it was not your doing.

THE CHAPLAIN [*lamentably*] I let them do it. If I had known, I would have torn her from their hands. You don't know: you havnt seen: it is so easy to talk when you dont know. You madden yourself with words: you damn yourself because it feels grand to throw oil on the flaming hell of your own temper. But when it is brought home to you; when you see the thing you have done; when it is blinding your eyes, stifling your nostrils, tearing your heart, then—then—[*Falling on his knees*] O God, take away this sight from me! O Christ, deliver me from this fire that is consuming me! She cried to Thee in the midst of it: Jesus! Jesus! Jesus! She is in Thy bosom; and I am in hell for evermore.

WARWICK [*summarily hauling him to his feet*] Come come, man! you must pull yourself together. We shall have the whole town talking of this. [*He throws him not too gently into a chair at the table*] If you have not the nerve to see these things, why do you not do as I do, and stay away?

THE CHAPLAIN [*bewildered and submissive*] She asked for a cross. A soldier gave her two sticks tied together. Thank God he was an Englishman! I might have done it; but I did not: I am a coward, a mad dog, a fool. But he was an Englishman too.

WARWICK. The fool! they will burn him too if the priests get hold of him.

THE CHAPLAIN [*shaken with a convulsion*] Some of the people laughed at her. They would have laughed at Christ. They were French people, my lord: I know they were French.

WARWICK. Hush! someone is coming. Control yourself.

Ladvenu comes back through the courtyard to Warwick's right hand, carrying a bishop's cross which he has taken from a church. He is very grave and composed.

WARWICK. I am informed that it is all over, Brother Martin.

LADVENU [*enigmatically*] We do not know, my lord. It may have only just begun.

WARWICK. What does that mean, exactly?

LADVENU. I took this cross from the church for her that she might see it to the last: she had only two sticks that she put into her bosom. When the fire crept round us, and she saw that if I held the cross before her I should be burnt myself, she warned me to get down and save myself. My lord: a girl who could think of another's danger in such a moment was not inspired by the devil. When I had to snatch the cross from her sight, she looked up to heaven. And I do not believe that the heavens were empty. I firmly believe that her Savior appeared to her then in His tenderest glory. She called to Him and died. This is not the end for her, but the beginning.

WARWICK. I am afraid it will have a bad effect on the people.

LADVENU. It had, my lord, on some of them. I heard laughter. Forgive me for saying that I hope and believe it was English laughter.

THE CHAPLAIN [*rising frantically*] No: it was not. There was only one Englishman there that disgraced his country; and that was the mad dog, de Stogumber. [*He rushes wildly out, shrieking*] Let them torture him. Let them burn him. I will go pray among her ashes. I am no better than Judas: I will hang myself.

WARWICK. Quick, Brother Martin: follow him: he will do himself some mischief. After him, quick.

Ladvenu hurries out, Warwick urging him. The Executioner comes in by the door behind the judges' chairs; and Warwick, returning, finds himself face to face with him.

WARWICK. Well, fellow: who are you?

THE EXECUTIONER [*with dignity*] I am not addressed as fellow, my lord. I am the Master Executioner of Rouen: it is a highly skilled mystery. I am come to tell your lordship that your orders have been obeyed.

WARWICK. I crave your pardon, Master Executioner; and I will see that you lose nothing by having no relics to sell. I have your word, have I, that nothing remains, not a bone, not a nail, not a hair?

THE EXECUTIONER. Her heart would not burn, my lord; but everything that was left is at the bottom of the river. You have heard the last of her.

WARWICK [*with a wry smile, thinking of what Ladvenu said*] The last of her? Hm! I wonder!

EPILOGUE

A restless fitfully windy night in June 1456, full of summer lightning after many days of heat. King Charles the Seventh of France, formerly Joan's Dauphin, now Charles the Victorious, aged 51, is in bed in one of his royal chateaux. The bed, raised on a dais of two steps, is towards the side of the room so as to avoid blocking a tall lancet window in the middle. Its canopy bears the royal arms in embroidery. Except for the canopy and the huge down pillows there is nothing to distinguish it from a broad settee with bed-clothes and a valance. Thus its occupant is in full view from the foot.

Charles is not asleep: he is reading in bed, or rather looking at the pictures in Fouquet's Boccaccio[29] *with his knees doubled up to make a reading-desk. Beside the bed on his left is a little table with a picture of the Virgin, lighted by candles of painted wax. The walls are hung from ceiling to floor with painted curtains which stir at times in the draughts. At first glance the prevailing yellow and red in these hanging pictures is somewhat flamelike when the folds breathe in the wind.*

The door is on Charles's left, but in front of him close to the corner farthest from him. A large watchman's rattle, handsomely designed and gaily painted, is in the bed under his hand.

Charles turns a leaf. A distant clock strikes the half-hour softly. Charles shuts the book with a clap; throws it aside; snatches up the rattle; and whirls it energetically, making a deafening clatter. Ladvenu enters, 25 years older, strange and stark in bearing, and still carrying the cross from Rouen. Charles evidently does not expect him; for he springs out of bed on the farther side from the door.

CHARLES. Who are you? Where is my gentleman of the bedchamber? What do you want?

LADVENU [*solemnly*] I bring you glad tidings of great joy. Rejoice, O king; for the taint is removed from your blood, and the stain from your crown. Justice, long delayed, is at last triumphant.

CHARLES. What are you talking about? Who are you?

LADVENU. I am brother Martin.

CHARLES. And who, saving your reverence, may Brother Martin be?

LADVENU. I held this cross when The Maid perished in the fire. Twenty-five years have passed since then: nearly ten thousand days. And on every one of those days I have prayed to God to justify His daughter on earth as she is justified in heaven.

CHARLES [*reassured, sitting down on the foot of the bed*] Oh, I remember now. I have heard of you. You have a bee in your bonnet about The Maid. Have you been at the inquiry?

LADVENU. I have given my testimony.

CHARLES. Is it over?

LADVENU. It is over.

CHARLES. Satisfactorily?

LADVENU. The ways of God are very strange.

CHARLES. How so?

LADVENU. At the trial which sent a saint to the stake as a heretic and a sorceress, the truth was told; the law was upheld; mercy was shewn beyond all custom; no wrong was done but the final and dreadful wrong of the lying sentence and the pitiless fire. At this inquiry from which I have just come, there was shameless perjury, courtly cor-

29. Jean Fouquet (1420–81) illustrated Giovanni Boccaccio's *On the Fates of Famous Men* (written 1355–60).

ruption, calumny of the dead who did their duty according to their lights, cowardly evasion of the issue, testimony made of idle tales that could not impose on a ploughboy. Yet out of this insult to justice, this defamation of the Church, this orgy of lying and foolishness, the truth is set in the noonday sun on the hilltop; the white robe of innocence is cleansed from the smirch of the burning faggots; the holy life is sanctified; the true heart that lived through the flame consecrated; a great lie is silenced for ever; and a great wrong is set right before all men.

CHARLES. My friend: provided they can no longer say that I was crowned by a witch and a heretic, I shall not fuss about how the trick has been done. Joan would not have fussed about it if it came all right in the end: she was not that sort: I knew her. Is her rehabilitation complete? I made it pretty clear that there was to be no nonsense about it.

LADVENU. It is solemnly declared that her judges were full of corruption, cozenage,[30] fraud, and malice. Four falsehoods.

CHARLES. Never mind the falsehoods: her judges are dead.

LADVENU. The sentence on her is broken, annulled, annihilated, set aside as non-existent, without value or effect.

CHARLES. Good. Nobody can challenge my consecration now, can they?

LADVENU. Not Charlemagne nor King David himself was more sacredly crowned.

CHARLES [*rising*] Excellent. Think of what that means to me!

LADVENU. I think of what it means to her!

CHARLES. You cannot. None of us ever knew what anything meant to her. She was like nobody else; and she must take care of herself wherever she is; for I cannot take care of her; and neither can you, whatever you may think: you are not big enough. But I will tell you this about her. If you could bring her back to life, they would burn her again within six months, for all their present adoration of her. And you would hold up the cross, too, just the same. So [*crossing himself*] let her rest; and let you and I mind our own business, and not meddle with hers.

LADVENU. God forbid that I should have no share in her, nor she in me! [*He turns and strides out as he came, saying*] Henceforth my path will not lie through palaces, nor my conversation be with kings.

CHARLES [*following him towards the door, and shouting after him*] Much good may it do you, holy man! [*He returns to the middle of the chamber, where he halts, and says quizzically to himself*] That was a funny chap. How did he get in? Where are my people? [*He goes impatiently to the bed, and swings the rattle. A rush of wind through the open door sets the walls swaying agitatedly. The candles go out. He calls in the darkness*] Hallo! Someone come and shut the windows: everything is being blown all over the place. [*A flash of summer lightning shews*

30. To deceive through artful coaxing and deception.

up the lancet window. A figure is seen in silhouette against it] Who is there? Who is that? Help! Murder! [*Thunder. He jumps into bed, and hides under the clothes*].

JOAN'S VOICE. Easy, Charlie, easy. What art making all that noise for? No one can hear thee. Thourt asleep. [*She is dimly seen in a pallid greenish light by the bedside*].

CHARLES [*peeping out*] Joan! Are you a ghost, Joan?

JOAN. Hardly even that, lad. Can a poor burnt-up lass have a ghost? I am but a dream that thourt dreaming. [*The light increases: they become plainly visible as he sits up*] Thou looks older, lad.

CHARLES. I am older. Am I really asleep?

JOAN. Fallen asleep over thy silly book.

CHARLES. That's funny.

JOAN. Not so funny as that I am dead, is it?

CHARLES. Are you really dead?

JOAN. As dead as anybody ever is, laddie. I am out of the body.

CHARLES. Just fancy! Did it hurt much?

JOAN. Did what hurt much?

CHARLES. Being burnt.

JOAN. Oh, that! I cannot remember very well. I think it did at first; but then it all got mixed up; and I was not in my right mind until I was free of the body. But do not thou go handling fire and thinking it will not hurt thee. How hast been ever since?

CHARLES. Oh, not so bad. Do you know, I actually lead my army out and win battles? Down into the moat up to my waist in mud and blood. Up the ladders with the stones and hot pitch raining down. Like you.

JOAN. No! Did I make a man of thee after all, Charlie?

CHARLES. I am Charles the Victorious now. I had to be brave because you were. Agnes put a little pluck into me too.

JOAN. Agnes! Who was Agnes?

CHARLES. Agnes Sorel.[31] A woman I fell in love with. I dream of her often. I never dreamed of you before.

JOAN. Is she dead, like me?

CHARLES. Yes. But she was not like you. She was very beautiful.

JOAN [*laughing heartily*] Ha ha! I was no beauty: I was always a rough one: a regular soldier. I might almost as well have been a man. Pity I wasnt: I should not have bothered you all so much then. But my head was in the skies; and the glory of God was upon me; and, man or woman, I should have bothered you as long as your noses were in the mud. Now tell me what has happened since you wise men knew no better than to make a heap of cinders of me?

CHARLES. Your mother and brothers have sued the courts to have your

31. The daughter of a soldier, Sorel (1422–50) was Charles's mistress and mother of three of his children.

case tried over again. And the courts have declared that your judges were full of corruption and cozenage, fraud and malice.

JOAN. Not they. They were as honest a lot of poor fools as ever burned their betters.

CHARLES. The sentence on you is broken, annihilated, annulled: null, non-existent, without value or effect.

JOAN. I was burned, all the same. Can they unburn me?

CHARLES. If they could, they would think twice before they did it. But they have decreed that a beautiful cross be placed where the stake stood, for your perpetual memory and for your salvation.

JOAN. It is the memory and the salvation that sanctify the cross, not the cross that sanctifies the memory and the salvation. [*She turns away, forgetting him*] I shall outlast that cross. I shall be remembered when men will have forgotten where Rouen stood.

CHARLES. There you go with your self-conceit, the same as ever! I think you might say a word of thanks to me for having had justice done at last.

CAUCHON [*appearing at the window between them*] Liar!

CHARLES. Thank you.

JOAN. Why, if it isnt Peter Cauchon! How are you, Peter? What luck have you had since you burned me?

CAUCHON. None. I arraign the justice of Man. It is not the justice of God.

JOAN. Still dreaming of justice, Peter? See what justice came to with me! But what has happened to thee? Art dead or alive?

CAUCHON. Dead. Dishonoured. They pursued me beyond the grave. They excommunicated my dead body: they dug it up and flung it into the common sewer.

JOAN. Your dead body did not feel the spade and the sewer as my live body felt the fire.

CAUCHON. But this thing that they have done against me hurts justice; destroys faith; saps the foundation of the Church. The solid earth sways like the treacherous sea beneath the feet of men and spirits alike when the innocent are slain in the name of law, and their wrongs are undone by slandering the pure of heart.

JOAN. Well, well, Peter, I hope men will be the better for remembering me; and they would not remember me so well if you had not burned me.

CAUCHON. They will be the worse for remembering me: they will see in me evil triumphing over good, falsehood over truth, cruelty over mercy, hell over heaven. Their courage will rise as they think of you, only to faint as they think of me. Yet God is my witness I was just: I was merciful: I was faithful to my light: I could do no other than I did.

CHARLES [*scrambling out of the sheets and enthroning himself on the side of the bed*] Yes: it is always you good men that do the big mischiefs.

Look at me! I am not Charles the Good, nor Charles the Wise, nor Charles the Bold. Joan's worshippers may even call me Charles the Coward because I did not pull her out of the fire. But I have done less harm than any of you. You people with your heads in the sky spend all your time trying to turn the world upside down; but I take the world as it is, and say that top-side-up is right-side-up; and I keep my nose pretty close to the ground. And I ask you, what king of France has done better, or been a better fellow in his little way?

JOAN. Art really king of France, Charlie? Be the English gone?

DUNOIS [*coming through the tapestry on Joan's left, the candles relighting themselves at the same moment, and illuminating his armor and surcoat cheerfully*] I have kept my word: the English are gone.

JOAN. Praised be God! now is fair France a province in heaven. Tell me all about the fighting, Jack. Was it thou that led them? Wert thou God's captain to thy death?

DUNOIS. I am not dead. My body is very comfortably asleep in my bed at Chateaudun; but my spirit is called here by yours.

JOAN. And you fought them my way, Jack: eh? Not the old way, chaffering for ransoms; but The Maid's way: staking life against death, with the heart high and humble and void of malice, and nothing counting under God but France free and French. Was it my way, Jack?

DUNOIS. Faith, it was any way that would win. But the way that won was always your way. I give you best, lassie. I wrote a fine letter to set you right at the new trial. Perhaps I should never have let the priests burn you; but I was busy fighting; and it was the Church's business, not mine. There was no use in both of us being burned, was there?

CAUCHON. Ay! put the blame on the priests. But I, who am beyond praise and blame, tell you that the world is saved neither by its priests nor its soldiers, but by God and His Saints. The Church Militant sent this woman to the fire; but even as she burned, the flames whitened into the radiance of the Church Triumphant.

The clock strikes the third quarter. A rough male voice is heard trolling an improvised tune.

Rum tum trumpledum,
Bacon fat and rumpledum,
Old Saint mumpledum,
Pull his tail and stumpledum
O my Ma—ry Ann!

A ruffianly English soldier comes through the curtains and marches between Dunois and Joan.

DUNOIS. What villainous troubador taught you that doggrel?

THE SOLDIER. No troubadour. We made it up ourselves as we marched. We were not gentlefolks and troubadours. Music straight out of the heart of the people, as you might say. Rum tum trumpledum, Bacon fat and rumpledum, Old Saint mumpledum, Pull his tail and stumpledum: that dont mean anything, you know; but it keeps you marching. Your servant, ladies and gentlemen. Who asked for a saint?

JOAN. Be you a saint?

THE SOLDIER. Yes, lady, straight from hell.

DUNOIS. A saint, and from hell!

THE SOLDIER. Yes, noble captain: I have a day off. Every year, you know. Thats my allowance for my one good action.

CAUCHON. Wretch! In all the years of your life did you do only one good action?

THE SOLDIER. I never thought about it: it came natural like. But they scored it up for me.

CHARLES. What was it?

THE SOLDIER. Why, the silliest thing you ever heard of. I—

JOAN [*interrupting him by strolling across to the bed, where she sits beside Charles*] He tied two sticks together, and gave them to a poor lass that was going to be burned.

THE SOLDIER. Right. Who told you that?

JOAN. Never mind. Would you know her if you saw her again?

THE SOLDIER. Not I. There are so many girls! and they all expect you to remember them as if there was only one in the world. This one must have been a prime sort; for I have a day off every year for her; and so, until twelve o'clock punctually, I am a saint, at your service, noble lords and lovely ladies.

CHARLES. And after twelve?

THE SOLDIER. After twelve, back to the only place fit for the likes of me.

JOAN [*rising*] Back there! You! that gave the lass the cross!

THE SOLDIER [*excusing his unsoldierly conduct*] Well, she asked for it; and they were going to burn her. She had as good a right to a cross as they had; and they had dozens of them. It was her funeral, not theirs. Where was the harm in it?

JOAN. Man: I am not reproaching you. But I cannot bear to think of you in torment.

THE SOLDIER [*cheerfully*] No great torment, lady. You see I was used to worse.

CHARLES. What! worse than hell?

THE SOLDIER. Fifteen years' service in the French wars. Hell was a treat after that.

Joan throws up her arms, and takes refuge from despair of humanity before the picture of the Virgin.

THE SOLDIER [*continuing*]—Suits me somehow. The day off was dull at first, like a wet Sunday. I dont mind it so much now. They tell me I can have as many as I like as soon as I want them.

CHARLES. What is hell like?

THE SOLDIER. You wont find it so bad, sir. Jolly. Like as if you were always drunk without the trouble and expense of drinking. Tip top company too: emperors and popes and kings and all sorts. They chip me about giving that young judy the cross; but I dont care: I stand up to them proper, and tell them that if she hadnt a better right to it than they, she'd be where they are. That dumbfounds them, that does. All they can do is gnash their teeth, hell fashion; and I just laugh, and go off singing the old chanty: Rum turn trample—Hullo! Who's that knocking at the door?

They listen. A long gentle knocking is heard.

CHARLES. Come in.

The door opens; and an old priest, white-haired, bent, with a silly but benevolent smile, comes in and trots over to Joan.

THE NEWCOMER. Excuse me, gentle lords and ladies. Do not let me disturb you. Only a poor old harmless English rector. Formerly chaplain to the cardinal: to my lord of Winchester. John de Stogumber, at your service. [*He looks at them inquiringly*] Did you say anything? I am a little deaf, unfortunately. Also a little—well, not always in my right mind, perhaps; but still, it is a small village with a few simple people. I suffice: I suffice: they love me there; and I am able to do a little good. I am well connected, you see; and they indulge me.

JOAN. Poor old John! What brought thee to this state?

DE STOGUMBER. I tell my folks they must be very careful. I say to them, "If you only saw what you think about you would think quite differently about it. It would give you a great shock. Oh, a great shock." And they all say "Yes, Parson: we all know you are a kind man, and would not harm a fly." That is a great comfort to me. For I am not cruel by nature, you know.

THE SOLDIER. Who said you were?

DE STOGUMBER. Well, you see, I did a very cruel thing once because I did not know what cruelty was like. I had not seen it, you know. That is the great thing: you must see it. And then you are redeemed and saved.

CAUCHON. Were not the sufferings of our Lord Christ enough for you?

DE STOGUMBER. No. Oh no: not at all. I had seen them in pictures, and read of them in books, and been greatly moved by them, as I thought. But it was no use: it was not our Lord that redeemed me, but a young woman whom I saw actually burned to death. It was dreadful: oh, most dreadful. But it saved me. I have been a different man ever since, though a little astray in my wits sometimes.

CAUCHON. Must then a Christ perish in torment in every age to save those that have no imagination?

JOAN. Well, if I saved all those he would have been cruel to if he had not been cruel to me, I was not burnt for nothing, was I?

DE STOGUMBER. Oh no; it was not you. My sight is bad: I cannot distinguish your features: but you are not she: oh no: she was burned to a cinder: dead and gone, dead and gone.

THE EXECUTIONER [*stepping from behind the bed curtains on Charles's right, the bed being between them*] She is more alive than you, old man. Her heart would not burn; and it would not drown. I was a master at my craft: better than the master of Paris, better than the master of Toulouse; but I could not kill The Maid. She is up and alive everywhere.

THE EARL OF WARWICK [*sallying from the bed curtains on the other side, and coming to Joan's left hand*] Madam: my congratulations on your rehabilitation. I feel that I owe you an apology.

JOAN. Oh, please dont mention it.

WARWICK [*pleasantly*] The burning was purely political. There was no personal feeling against you, I assure you.

JOAN. I bear no malice, my lord.

WARWICK. Just so. Very kind of you to meet me in that way: a touch of true breeding. But I must insist on apologizing very amply. The truth is, these political necessities sometimes turn out to be political mistakes; and this one was a veritable howler; for your spirit conquered us, madam, in spite of our faggots. History will remember me for your sake, though the incidents of the connection were perhaps a little unfortunate.

JOAN. Ay, perhaps just a little, you funny man.

WARWICK. Still, when they make you a saint, you will owe your halo to me, just as this lucky monarch owes his crown to you.

JOAN [*turning from him*] I shall owe nothing to any man: I owe everything to the spirit of God that was within me. But fancy me a saint! What would St Catherine and St Margaret say if the farm girl was cocked up beside them!

A clerical-looking gentleman in black frockcoat and trousers, and tall hat, in the fashion of the year 1920, suddenly appears before them in the corner on their right. They all stare at him. Then they burst into uncontrollable laughter.

THE GENTLEMAN. Why this mirth, gentlemen?

WARWICK. I congratulate you on having invented a most extraordinarily comic dress.

THE GENTLEMAN. I do not understand. You are all in fancy dress: I am properly dressed.

DUNOIS. All dress is fancy dress, is it not, except our natural skins?

THE GENTLEMAN. Pardon me: I am here on serious business, and cannot engage in frivolous discussions. [*He takes out a paper, and assumes a dry official manner*]. I am sent to announce to you that Joan of Arc, formerly known as The Maid, having been the subject of an inquiry instituted by the Bishop of Orleans—

JOAN [*interrupting*] Ah! They remember me still in Orleans.

THE GENTLEMAN [*emphatically, to mark his indignation at the interruption*]—by the Bishop of Orleans into the claim of the said Joan of Arc to be canonized as a saint—

JOAN [*again interrupting*] But I never made any such claim.

THE GENTLEMAN [*as before*]—the Church has examined the claim exhaustively in the usual course, and, having admitted the said Joan successively to the ranks of Venerable and Blessed,—

JOAN [*chuckling*] Me venerable!

THE GENTLEMAN.—has finally declared her to have been endowed with heroic virtues and favored with private revelations, and calls the said Venerable and Blessed Joan to the communion of the Church Triumphant as Saint Joan.

JOAN [*rapt*] Saint Joan!

THE GENTLEMAN. On every thirtieth day of May, being the anniversary of the death of the said most blessed daughter of God, there shall in every Catholic church to the end of time be celebrated a special office in commemoration of her; and it shall be lawful to dedicate a special chapel to her, and to place her image on its altar in every such church. And it shall be lawful and laudable for the faithful to kneel and address their prayers through her to the Mercy Seat.

JOAN. Oh no. It is for the saint to kneel. [*She falls on her knees, still rapt*].

THE GENTLEMAN [*putting up his paper, and retiring beside the Executioner*] In Basilica Vaticana, the sixteenth day of May, nineteen hundred and twenty.

DUNOIS [*raising Joan*] Half an hour to burn you, dear Saint, and four centuries to find out the truth about you!

DE STOGUMBER. Sir: I was chaplain to the Cardinal of Winchester once. They always would call him the Cardinal of England. It would be a great comfort to me and to my master to see a fair statue to The Maid in Winchester Cathedral. Will they put one there, do you think?

THE GENTLEMAN. As the building is temporarily in the hands of the Anglican heresy, I cannot answer for that.

A vision of the statue in Winchester Cathedral is seen through the window.

DE STOGUMBER. Oh look! look! that is Winchester.

JOAN. Is that meant to be me? I was stiffer on my feet.

The vision fades.

THE GENTLEMAN. I have been requested by the temporal authorities of France to mention that the multiplication of public statues to The Maid threatens to become an obstruction to traffic. I do so as a matter of courtesy to the said authorities, but must point out on behalf of the Church that The Maid's horse is no greater obstruction to traffic than any other horse.

JOAN. Eh! I am glad they have not forgotten my horse.

A vision of the statue before Rheims Cathedral appears.

JOAN. Is that funny little thing me too?

CHARLES. That is Rheims Cathedral where you had me crowned. It must be you.

JOAN. Who has broken my sword? My sword was never broken. It is the sword of France.

DUNOIS. Never mind. Swords can be mended. Your soul is unbroken; and you are the soul of France.

The vision fades. The Archbishop and the Inquisitor are now seen on the right and left of Cauchon.

JOAN. My sword shall conquer yet: the sword that never struck a blow. Though men destroyed my body, yet in my soul I have seen God.

CAUCHON [*kneeling to her*] The girls in the field praise thee; for thou hast raised their eyes; and they see that there is nothing between them and heaven.

DUNOIS [*kneeling to her*] The dying soldiers praise thee, because thou art a shield of glory between them and the judgment.

THE ARCHBISHOP [*kneeling to her*] The princes of the Church praise thee, because thou hast redeemed the faith their worldlinesses have dragged through the mire.

WARWICK [*kneeling to her*] The cunning counsellors praise thee, because thou hast cut the knots in which they have tied their own souls.

DE STOGUMBER [*kneeling to her*] The foolish old men on their deathbeds praise thee, because their sins against thee are turned into blessings.

THE INQUISITOR [*kneeling to her*] The judges in the blindness and bondage of the law praise thee, because thou hast vindicated the vision and the freedom of the living soul.

THE SOLDIER [*kneeling to her*] The wicked out of hell praise thee, because thou hast shewn them that the fire that is not quenched is a holy fire.

THE EXECUTIONER [*kneeling to her*] The tormentors and executioners praise thee, because thou hast shewn that their hands are guiltless of the death of the soul.

CHARLES [*kneeling to her*] The unpretending praise thee, because thou hast taken upon thyself the heroic burdens that are too heavy for them.

JOAN. Woe unto me when all men praise me! I bid you remember that I am a saint, and that saints can work miracles. And now tell me: shall I rise from the dead, and come back to you a living woman?

A sudden darkness blots out the walls of the room as they all spring to their feet in consternation. Only the figures and the bed remain visible.

JOAN. What! Must I burn again? Are none of you ready to receive me?

CAUCHON. The heretic is always better dead. And mortal eyes cannot distinguish the saint from the heretic. Spare them. [*He goes out as he came*].

DUNOIS. Forgive us, Joan: we are not yet good enough for you. I shall go back to my bed. [*He also goes*].

WARWICK. We sincerely regret our little mistake; but political necessities, though occasionally erroneous, are still imperative; so if you will be good enough to excuse me—[*He steals discreetly away*].

THE ARCHBISHOP. Your return would not make me the man you once thought me. The utmost I can say is that though I dare not bless you, I hope I may one day enter into your blessedness. Meanwhile, however—[*He goes*].

THE INQUISITOR. I who am of the dead, testified that day that you were innocent. But I do not see how The Inquisition could possibly be dispensed with under existing circumstances. Therefore—[*He goes*].

DE STOGUMBER. Oh, do not come back: you must not come back. I must die in peace. Give us peace in our time, O Lord! [*He goes*].

THE GENTLEMAN. The possibility of your resurrection was not contemplated in the recent proceedings for your canonization. I must return to Rome for fresh instructions. [*He bows formally, and withdraws*].

THE EXECUTIONER. As a master in my profession I have to consider its interests. And, after all, my first duty is to my wife and children. I must have time to think over this. [*He goes*].

CHARLES. Poor old Joan! They have all run away from you except this blackguard who has to go back to hell at twelve o'clock. And what can I do but follow Jack Dunois' example, and go back to bed too? [*He does so*].

JOAN [*sadly*] Goodnight, Charlie.

CHARLES [*mumbling in his pillows*] Goo ni. [*He sleeps. The darkness envelops the bed*].

JOAN [*to the soldier*] And you, my one faithful? What comfort have you for Saint Joan?

THE SOLDIER. Well, what do they all amount to, these kings and captains and bishops and lawyers and such like? They just leave you in the ditch to bleed to death; and the next thing is, you meet them down there, for all the airs they give themselves. What I say is, you have as good a right to your notions as they have to theirs, and perhaps better. [*Settling himself for a lecture on the subject*] You see, it's like this. If—[*the first stroke of midnight is heard softly from a distant bell*]. Excuse me: a pressing appointment—[*He goes on tiptoe*].

The last remaining rays of light gather into a white radiance descending on Joan. The hour continues to strike.

JOAN. O God that madest this beautiful earth, when will it be ready to receive Thy saints? How long, O Lord, how long?

THE END

Drama in English: From the Middle Ages to the Early Twentieth Century was designed and typeset in Minion Pro by Kachergis Book Design of Pittsboro, North Carolina. It was printed on 50-pound House Natural Smooth, and bound by Sheridan Books of Chelsea, Michigan.